The Harper Book of American Quotations

Staff

Executive Editor	Raymond V. Hand, Jr.
Senior Editor	Margaret E. Huffman
Indexer	Cynthia Crippen, AEIOU, Inc.
Researchers	Sally Bunch
	Hayden Carruth
	David A. Graff
	Donald H. Graff
	Ernest S. Hildebrand, Jr.
	Frank B. Latham
	Mary Varchaver
	David H. Scott
Keyboarder	Antje L. Munroe
Proofreaders	Daniel Blum
	Bernie Borok
	Robert A. Brainerd
	Diana Puglisi, Literary House, Inc.

The Harper Book of
AMERICAN
QUOTATIONS

Gorton Carruth and Eugene Ehrlich

A Hudson Group Book

1817

Harper & Row, Publishers, New York
Cambridge, Philadelphia, San Francisco
London, Mexico City, São Paulo, Singapore, Sydney

FIRST EDITION

Library of Congress Cataloging-in-Publication Data

Carruth, Gorton.
   The Harper book of American quotations.

   "A Hudson Group book."
   Includes index.
   1. Quotations, American.   I. Ehrlich, Eugene H.   II. Title.
PN6084.A5C37   1988   081   88-45018
ISBN 0-06-015975-8

88 89 90 91 92 CC/RRD 10 9 8 7 6 5 4 3 2 1

Contents

* Special categories highlighted in the text.

CONTENTS

* Special categories highlighted in the text.

American Documents

Preface

The Harper Book of American Quotations is the first major collection of American quotations to appear in twenty years. Readers' needs were paramount in establishing the organization and design of the volume. Under 264 subject categories, arranged alphabetically and numbered consecutively, are more than eight thousand familiar and not-so-familiar quotations by and about Americans. In making our selections, we did not restrict ourselves to aphoristic expression. What we sought instead were quotations that said something revealing about the lives and manners of our people, the operations and goals of our institutions, and the interplay between those institutions and the lives of people.

The quotations are organized by subject categories covering a comprehensive range of interests, from *101. Government* to *187. Politics,* from *159. Motion Pictures* to *220. Sports,* from *13. American Indians* and *34. Black Americans* to *50. Civil Rights* and *258. Women's Rights,* from *14. American Revolution* to *243. Vietnam War.* Readers wishing to locate any quotation in the book will be much helped by its exceptionally detailed index.

Though some of the more than fourteen hundred men and women quoted are not household names, most are widely known for their contributions to various fields of learning as well as to politics, government, sports, art, and science. Well known or not, these men and women represent many occupations, many shades of opinion, and every part of our country. As might be expected, a great number of the people whose words are collected here have played a part in making American history, from the distant past, when North America was a sparsely settled outpost of European culture, to the present, when the United States plays so prominent a role in the world's cultural, political, and economic affairs. What brings together in this book so varied a group of people is the fact that they all had memorable things to say about themselves, about others, or about our lives and our country.

The Harper Book of American Quotations provides a generous selection of ideas and opinions from America's past but by no means overlooks contemporary thought. For example, the coverage includes such current topics as *229. Television & Radio, 228. Technology,* and *217. Space Exploration.* Two subject categories, *246. George Washington* and *137. Abraham Lincoln,* are devoted entirely to what Americans and foreign observers have said about these great presidents. In addition, a half dozen fascinating subject categories readers may want to turn to again and again have been highlighted to make them especially easy to find: *33. Berraisms, 37.*

Boston Toast, 41. Campaign Slogans, 78. Epitaphs, 99. Goldwynisms, and *133. Last Words.*
There are also separate categories for all fifty American states as well as for all regions and several
of our major cities.

Organization of quotations by discrete subject categories affords readers a kind of intellectual drama not found in quotation dictionaries organized by authors' names. Readers thus
can see, within a single page or two, contrasting points of view on a subject. For example, in
262. Writers, the quotations include both high praise and savage attacks on Walt Whitman's
poetry:

> Mr. Whitman's muse is at once indecent and ugly, lascivious and
> gawky, lubricious and coarse.
>
> LAFCADIO HEARN

> I found it [*Leaves of Grass*] the most extraordinary piece of wit
> and wisdom that America has yet contributed. . . . I greet you
> [Whitman] at the beginning of a great career.
>
> RALPH WALDO EMERSON

As one might expect, a category sure to present conflicting opinions is *243. Vietnam War.*
In more than fifty comments on this unpopular war, this category points up the lack of unanimity
observable in many aspects of American life, a characteristic borne out by many hundreds of other
quotations. Readers of this book occupy front-row seats in the theater of American wit and
wisdom.

A feature of *The Harper Book of American Quotations* not found in other collections is
the inclusion of key American documents, usually given in their entirety. These documents, like
the special categories of quotations mentioned above, have been highlighted so readers can find
them easily. The documents begin with the history-making Mayflower Compact of November
11, 1620, and end with the "I have a dream" speech of Martin Luther King, Jr., of August 28,
1963. Among the other documents are the full texts of the Declaration of Independence, the
Preamble to the U.S. Constitution, and the Bill of Rights.

A great number of the quotations are infused with recognizable aspects of the American
spirit and character:

> **Bluntness**: "New York is a sucked orange." (Ralph Waldo Emer-
> son)

> **Practicality**: "Always do right—this will gratify some and
> astonish the rest." (Mark Twain)

> **Candor**: "Mom and Pop were just a couple of kids when they
> got married. He was eighteen, she was sixteen, and I was
> three." (Billie Holiday)

Derisiveness: "Studying literature at Harvard is like learning about women at the Mayo Clinic." (attributed to Roy Blount, Jr.)

Harshness: "She runs the gamut of emotions from A to B." (Dorothy Parker)

Overall, most of the quotations are characterized by aptness and eloquence, for it is these attributes that preserve words for posterity:

> Our chiefs are killed. . . . The old men are all dead. . . . The little children are freezing to death. My people, some of them have run away to the hills and have no blankets, no food. No one knows where they are, perhaps freezing to death. I want to have time to look for my children and see how many of them I can find. Hear me, my chiefs. My heart is sick and sad. From where the sun now stands I will fight no more forever.
>
> CHIEF JOSEPH, TO THE NEZ PERCÉ TRIBE AFTER SURRENDERING TO U.S. FORCES, OCTOBER, 1877.

When readers turn to the book for the first time, they may want to have a quick introduction to the American character. In this case, they can turn to category *15. Americans,* which offers more than fifty quotations. The first is from Henry Adams: "The American mind exasperated the European as a buzz-saw might exasperate a pine forest." The last is from Woodrow Wilson: "A man who thinks of himself as belonging to a particular national group in America has not yet become an American."

But comments made about Americans by Americans do not tell the entire story. There may be much to learn by seeing what foreign nationals have said about us. In subject category *16. America Seen from Abroad,* the quotations range from perceptive criticism: "The Americans are a queer people; they can't rest" (Stephen Leacock), to altogether too much bile: "I am willing to love all mankind, *except an American*" (Samuel Johnson). There are sixty-one lively comments on the subject, which should whet the reader's appetite for browsing through the whole book.

In compiling this book, we tried to keep in mind what readers want most in a collection of quotations. First of all, there is the need to refresh one's memory of the familiar. What was it Patrick Henry said about liberty, freedom, and death: "Is life so dear or peace so sweet as to be purchased at the price of chains and slavery? Forbid it, Almighty God—I know not what course others may take; but as for me, give me liberty, or give me death!" And what did Franklin Roosevelt say about fear: "Let me assert my firm belief that the only thing we have to fear is fear itself—nameless, unreasoning, unjustified terror which paralyzes needed efforts to convert retreat into advance." And could Yogi Berra really have phrased his wisdom in the words many of us recall: "It ain't over till it's over"?

We believe also that readers want to be sure that people reputed to have said something quotable actually did say it. It is commonly believed, for example, that George Washington advised the country against "entangling alliances," but it actually was Thomas Jefferson, in his first inaugural address, who said, "Peace, commerce, and honest friendship with all nations, entangling alliances with none." Washington used other words, "permanent alliances," in his Farewell Address, and that full quotation can be found near Jefferson's in category *68. Diplomacy.*

Again, readers want to know when and under what circumstances an apt phrase, sentence, or thought was expressed. For example, there is Notre Dame coach Knute Rockne's familiar locker-room exhortation, "Win this one for the Gipper." Subject category *220. Sports* makes it clear: "The Gipper" was the nickname of one of Rockne's players, George Gipp, an all-American fullback who died on December 4, 1920. Before a big game in the following season, 1921, the coach called for extraordinary team effort by invoking the memory of the team's fallen gridiron hero.

Finally, many people want to know where they can read further about a quotation. Sometimes a witty phrase or insightful observation takes on even deeper meaning when read in the context of an entire speech or essay. Sorting out the hidden meanings of all familiar quotations is beyond the scope of this collection, but, by consulting the carefully researched sources given here, readers can find them out for themselves.

We suppose that nearly every standard quotation in *The Harper Book of American Quotations* is familiar to some people. Most of the quotations, however, are certainly not familiar to everyone, especially to a new generation of readers who are unlikely to be as steeped in the history and literature of America as they might wish. Even so, as editors, we could not believe our assignment properly completed if we remained content with a selection of only familiar, so-called standard quotations. With the help of others, including prominent editors and writers on American subjects, we read some hundreds of books to find apt quotations that would supplement quotations in earlier collections. We believe that the more than one thousand fresh quotations we added to our collection help make *The Harper Book of American Quotations* the exceptionally informative and colorful collection of old and new that we planned.

In addition to achieving a proper balance between familiar and unfamiliar quotations, we tried to reach a degree of accuracy not commonly found in other quotation dictionaries. Wherever possible, we checked original sources in the effort to make sure that the quotations were accurately rendered. In addition, we took particular care to make the attribution for each quotation as complete and correct as we could make it.

By returning to original sources, we often were able to provide a larger context for the quotations we selected than is usually found in other collections. As a result, our quotations often are more complete and helpful. By supplying words that precede or that follow a familiar quotation, we were able to clarify meaning or enlarge significance. For example, General Sherman is often quoted as having said that war is war, and sometimes that war is hell. We give his words as: "If the people raise a howl against my barbarity and cruelty, I will answer that war is war, and not popularity-seeking. If they want peace, they and their relatives must stop the war." This fuller quotation surely gives readers greater insight into the meaning of Sherman's words.

The Harper Book of American Quotations took more than five years to complete. In that time we amassed thousands more quotations than there was room for in the present volume. Collecting so many candidate quotations gave us an unanticipated advantage, the luxury of winnowing our vast files to select the best among many fine quotations. What constitutes the best is, of course, open to discussion. More quotations were discussed, discarded, and sometimes reinstated than we care to remember. But we believe the extra labor was worthwhile. The collection we offer represents both the diversity and the unity of the American people, past and present, in words that are forceful and to the point. While it is unlikely that many people will read this book from beginning to end, as we have several times, anyone doing so will gain a fresh understanding of the panorama of events, ideas, and contradictions that shaped America and Americans.

To make *The Harper Book of American Quotations* as easy as possible for readers to use, we adopted a three-tiered organizational system: (1) quotations were grouped within broadly defined subject categories that appear in alphabetical order; (2) within these subject categories the quotations were listed alphabetically by author; and (3) an exceptionally complete index was developed as an integral part of the book.

By turning to the *subject categories,* readers can find subjects of immediate interest. Titles of the subject categories were chosen for ease of recall, for example, *18. Anger, 51. Civil War, 89. Florida, 179. Pain,* and *249. Wealth.* Once readers are familiar with the titles of the subject categories, they can use the running heads at the tops of pages to find any category quickly and easily. The categories are also listed in the table of contents and the index, but readers will probably find it easier to use the running heads to find quotations on any of the 264 subjects in the book.

Within each subject category, as has been stated, the *quotations* are listed in alphabetical order by author, so that for a quotation by John Adams, readers will look toward the beginning of a category, and for one by Mark Twain, toward the end. When there are several quotations by the same author, as frequently is the case, the quotations by that author are given chronologically.

In the *index,* a quotation appears (1) under the name of its author, (2) under the topic of the quotation, and (3) under one or more familiar or key words. Thus, "Don't give up the ship" can be located in the index by author, Oliver Hazard Perry; by topics, **Duty** and **Patriotism**; and by familiar words, Don't and Ship. This quotation can also be located under its subject category, 162. Navy.

Readers should be aware that many index entries are highly specific. For example, Build appears also in the forms Builder, Building, and Built. These entries are close to one another, but forms of a key word sometimes are separated by other entry words, as is the case for Buried and Bury. Readers uncertain of the form of a key word they are searching for are advised to look carefully up and down index columns before abandoning their search.

Once a desired index entry is found, it will be seen that the entry is followed by a category number and a quotation number. For example, "youth condemns; maturity condones, 264:31" means that the quotation containing these words is number 31 in category 264.

For readers' convenience, a biographical list of people whose words are quoted in this book is supplied beginning on page 1.

We wish to acknowledge the help given us in compiling *The Harper Book of American Quotations.* The names of those who worked with us almost continuously, without whom we would have had great difficulty in completing the project, are listed opposite the title page. We thank all of them for their hard work and loyalty, but we wish especially to express our debt to Raymond V. Hand, Jr., first of all for his skill in managing many parts of the project and for the contribution he made in judging the quality of quotations that were candidates for inclusion. But a further word must be said about his uncanny research ability. He many times found the unfindable and never flagged when searching for some final bit of information needed to settle a time-consuming dispute.

We want to thank Margaret E. Huffman. She too was an indefatigable researcher, saving us from error countless times by tracking down original sources. She was instrumental also in shaping a massive manuscript into its final form. Without Peggy Huffman's loyalty and hard work over the years, the book would not have appeared on schedule.

Among those who supplied us with quotations or helped shape our project are Daniel Aaron, Annie Dillard, Byron Dobell, John Hollander, Byron Hollinshead, Alfred Kazin, David McCullough, Max Morath, Jean Strouse, and Geoffrey C. Ward. We thank them for their contributions.

At a time some years ago, when the project appeared to be foundering, Carol Cohen, editorial director of trade reference books at Harper & Row, came to our rescue. To her we owe a special debt and special thanks.

We owe our thanks also to Eric Wirth, our production editor at Harper & Row, who made the production of this complex book infinitely easier.

It might interest those who have read to this point that Ralph Waldo Emerson contributed by far the largest number of quotations in this book—616 by our count. This reminds us that the real contributors to our book have been the originators of the eight thousand or so quotations. We hope the words of living authors will not come back to haunt them, and we apologize if we misrepresented or misinterpreted any person's intent or meaning. Our thanks to them all.

Gorton Carruth
Eugene Ehrlich
1988

The Harper Book of American Quotations

Biographical List

Unless otherwise indicated, the people listed below are American.

ABBOTT, GEORGE (1899–   ) Playwright and producer

ABZUG, BELLA (1920–   ) Politician

ACE, JANE (1905–1974) Radio performer

ACHESON, DEAN G. (1893–1971) Secretary of state

ADAMS, ABIGAIL (1744–1818) Wife of John Adams

ADAMS, ANSEL (1902–1984) Photographer

ADAMS, BROOKS (1848–1927) Historian

ADAMS, CHARLES FRANCIS, SR. (1807–1886) Politician and diplomat

ADAMS, CHARLES FRANCIS, JR. (1835–1915) Historian

ADAMS, FRANKLIN P[IERCE] [F.P.A.] (1881–1960) Journalist and humorist

ADAMS, GRACE [KINCKLE] (1900–   ) Historian and sociologist

ADAMS, HENRY [BROOKS] (1838–1918) Historian

ADAMS, JOHN (1735–1826) President (1797–1801)

ADAMS, JOHN QUINCY (1767–1848) President (1825–1829)

ADAMS, MAUDE (1872–1953) Actress

ADAMS, SAMUEL (1722–1803) Revolutionary patriot and statesman

ADDAMS, CHARLES (1912–   ) Cartoonist

ADDAMS, JANE (1860–1935) Social worker and peace advocate

ADE, GEORGE (1866–1944) Playwright and humorist

ADLER, ALFRED (1870–1937) Austrian psychiatrist

ADLER, POLLY (1900–1962) Businesswoman and madam

ADLER, RENATA (1938–   ) Writer and film critic

AGASSIZ, LOUIS (1807–1873) Geologist and zoologist

AGNEW, SPIRO T. (1918–   ) Vice president (1969–1973)

ALCOTT, A[MOS] BRONSON (1799–1888) Philosopher and educator

ALCOTT, LOUISA MAY (1832–1888) Author

ALDRICH, THOMAS BAILEY (1836–1907) Author and editor

ALEXANDER, SHANA (1925–   ) Journalist, author, and lecturer

ALGREN, NELSON (1909–1981) Author

ALI, MUHAMMAD (1942–   ) Boxer

ALLEN, ELIZABETH [CHASE] AKERS (1832–1911) Poet

ALLEN, ETHAN (1738–1789) Revolutionary general

ALLEN, FRED (1894–1956) Radio comedian

ALLEN, FREDERICK LEWIS (1890–1954) Editor and author

ALLEN, GEORGE (1808–1876) Clergyman, educator, and author

ALLEN, HERVEY (1889–1949) Novelist and poet

ALLEN, JAMES LANE (1849–1925) Novelist

ALLEN, WILLIAM (1784–1868) Clergyman, author, and educator

ALLEN, WOODY (1935–   ) Filmmaker and writer

AMES, EDWARD SCRIBNER (1870–1958) Clergyman and educator

AMES, FISHER (1758–1808) Statesman

AMES, NATHANIEL (1708–1764) Physician and almanac-maker

ANDERSON, MARGARET [CAROLYN] (1886–1973) Editor and writer

ANDERSON, MARIAN (1902–   ) Concert singer

ANDERSON, MAXWELL (1888–1959) Playwright

ANDERSON, SHERWOOD (1876–1941) Poet and author

ANDRÉ, JOHN (1751–1780) British officer

ANTHONY, SUSAN B. (1820–1906) Suffragist and reformer

ANTRIM, MINNA [THOMAS] (1856?–?) Author

APPLETON, THOMAS GOLD (1812–1884) Writer

ARBUS, DIANE (1923–1971) Photographer

ARENDT, HANNAH (1906–1975) Political scientist, author, and teacher

ARMSTRONG, LOUIS (1900–1971) Jazz musician

ARMSTRONG, NEIL ALDEN (1930–   ) Astronaut

ARNOLD, BENEDICT (1741–1801) Revolutionary officer and traitor

ARNOLD, MATTHEW (1822–1888) English poet and essayist

ARNOW, HARRIETTE [SIMPSON] (c.1910–1986) Journalist and author

ARTHUR, CHESTER ALAN (1830–1886) President (1881–1885)

ASIMOV, ISAAC (1920–   ) Author

ASTOR, NANCY [LANGHORNE] (1879–1964) Member of British Parliament

ASTOR, [WILLIAM] VINCENT (1891–1959) Businessman

ATHERTON, GERTRUDE (1857–1948) Novelist

ATKINSON, [JUSTIN] BROOKS (1894–1984) Drama critic

AUDEN, W[YSTAN] H[UGH] (1907–1973) Poet

AUDUBON, JOHN JAMES (1785–1851) Naturalist and artist

AUSTIN, MARY (1868–1934) Writer

AXLINE, VIRGINIA MAE (1911–   ) Child psychotherapist and author

BABBITT, IRVING (1865–1933) Educator

BACON, LEONARD (1887–1954) Poet

BAER, GEORGE F. (1842–1914) Lawyer and industrialist

BAEZ, JOAN (1941–   ) Folk singer

BAGBY, GEORGE WILLIAM (1828–1883) Humorist and lecturer

BAILEY, FRANCIS (c.1735–1815) Printer and journalist

BAILEY, PEARL (1918–   ) Singer

BAILEY, PHILIP JAMES (1816–1902) English poet

BAKER, DOROTHY (1907–1968) Novelist and playwright

BAKER, RUSSELL [WAYNE] (1925–   ) Columnist and author

BALBOA, VASCO NUÑEZ DE (1475–1519) Spanish explorer

BALDWIN, JAMES (1924–1987) Author

BALL, LUCILLE (1911–   ) Comedian

BALLARD, W[ILLIS] T[ODHUNTER] (1903–   ) Novelist

BANCROFT, GEORGE (1800–1891) Historian and statesman

BANKHEAD, TALLULAH [BROCKMAN] (1903–1968) Actress

BARKLEY, ALBEN W[ILLIAM] (1877–1956) Vice president (1949–1953)

BARNUM, P[HINEAS] T[AYLOR] (1810–1891) Showman

BARR, AMELIA E[DITH] (1831–1919) Novelist

BARRETT, LAURENCE I[RWIN] (1935–   ) Journalist and author

BARRETT, RONA (1936–   ) Columnist and television interviewer

BARRY, JACK (1939–1984) Television host and producer

BARRYMORE, ETHEL (1879–1959) Actress

BARRYMORE, JOHN (1882–1942) Actor

BARRYMORE, LIONEL (1878–1954) Actor

BARUCH, BERNARD M[ANNES] (1870–1965) Financier and statesman

BATES, KATHARINE LEE (1859–1929) Editor and author

BAUM, VICKI (1888–1960) Novelist

BAXTER, RICHARD (1615–1691) English Puritan writer and scholar

BEARD, CHARLES AUSTIN (1874–1948) Historian and educator

BEARD, JAMES [ANDREWS] (1903–1985) Food consultant and author

BEARD, MARY RITTER (1876–1958) Historian

BEATON, CECIL (1904–1980) English photographer and theatrical designer

BEAUMARCHAIS, PIERRE AUGUSTIN CARON DE (1732–1799) French dramatist

BEAUREGARD, PIERRE GUSTAVE TOUTANT DE (1818–1893) Confederate officer

BECKER, CARL LOTUS (1873–1945) Historian and author

BEE, BERNARD E[LLIOTT] (1824–1861) Army officer

BEECHER, CATHARINE ESTHER (1800–1878) Educator

BEECHER, HENRY WARD (1813–1887) Congregational clergyman and lecturer

BEER, THOMAS (1889–1940) Writer

BEERS, ETHEL LYNN (ELIOT) (1827–1879) Poet

BEHN, APHRA (1640–1689) English playwright and novelist

BEIRNE, FRANCIS F. (1890–?) Author

BELLAMY, EDWARD (1850–1898) Author

BELLOW, SAUL (1915–) Novelist

BELLOWS, GEORGE (1882–1925) Artist

BEMELMANS, LUDWIG (1898–1962) Satirist and illustrator

BENCHLEY, ROBERT (1889–1945) Humorist and author

BENEDICT, RUTH (1887–1948) Anthropologist

BENÉT, STEPHEN VINCENT (1898–1943) Novelist and poet

BENHAM, [WILLIAM] GURNEY (1849–1944) English journalist

BENNETT, ARNOLD (1867–1931) English novelist and dramatist

BENNETT, JAMES GORDON (1795–1872) Newspaper editor

BERENSON, BERNARD (1865–1959) Art critic

BERKELEY, GEORGE (1685–1753) English bishop and author

BERLIN, IRVING (1888–) Songwriter

BERRA, [LAWRENCE PETER] YOGI (1925–) Baseball player and manager

BERRIGAN, DANIEL (1921–) Roman Catholic priest and peace activist

BERRIGAN, PHILIP (1923–) Author and political activist

BETHE, HANS A[LBRECHT] (1906–) Physicist

BEVERIDGE, ALBERT J[EREMIAH] (1862–1927) Politician and historian

BIDDLE, CHARLES [JOHN] (1819–1873) Congressman and lawyer

BIERCE, AMBROSE (1842–1913?) Newspaperman and short-story writer

BILLINGS, JOSH (1818–1885) Humorist, real name Henry Wheeler Shaw

BINNEY, HORACE (1780–1875) Congressman and lawyer

BIRD, CAROLINE (1915–) Author and journalist

BIRMINGHAM, STEPHEN (1931–) Writer

BIRRELL, AUGUSTINE (1850–1933) British politician and man of letters

BISHOP, THOMAS BRIGHAM (1835–1905) Songwriter

BISSET, JACQUELINE (1946–) Actress

BLACK, HUGO LAFAYETTE (1886–1971) Associate Justice of Supreme Court

BLACK, SHIRLEY TEMPLE (1928–) Actress and diplomat

BLAINE, JAMES G[ILLESPIE] (1830–1893) Secretary of state

BLAKE, JAMES W. (1862–1935) Songwriter

BLAND, JAMES A. (1854–1911) Songwriter

BLEASE, COLEMAN LIVINGSTON (1868–1942) Politician

BLOOMER, AMELIA JENKS (1818–1894) Social reformer

BLOUNT, ROY A[LTON], JR. (1941–) Writer and humorist

BOAS, FRANZ (1858–1942) Anthropologist

BOGART, HUMPHREY (1900–1957) Actor

BOKER, GEORGE HENRY (1823–1890) Diplomat and writer

BOLDT, GEORGE H[UGO] (1903–1984) Jurist

BOLTON, CHARLES E[DWARD] (1841–1901) Lecturer and traveler

BOORSTIN, DANIEL J. (1914–) Author and historian

BOOTH, EDWIN (1833–1893) Actor

BOOTH, JOHN WILKES (1838–1865) Actor, assassin of Abraham Lincoln

BORAH, WILLIAM E[DGAR] (1865–1940) Politician

BOSSIDY, JOHN COLLINS (1860–1928) Oculist

BOWERS, CLAUDE G[ERNADE] (1878–1958) Journalist, diplomat, and historian

BRADDOCK, EDWARD (1695–1755) British general

BRADLEY, BILL (1943–   ) Politician and athlete

BRADLEY, OMAR [NELSON] (1893–   ) General

BRADSTREET, ANNE (1612?–1672) Colonial poet

BRAGG, BRAXTON (1817–1876) Confederate army officer

BRAGG, EDWARD S[TUYVESANT] (1827–1912) Army officer and congressman

BRAINARD, JOHN G[ARDINER] C[ALKINS] (1796–1828) Poet

BRAISTED, HARRY (fl. 1898) Songwriter

BRALEY, BERTON (1882–1966) Poet and novelist

BRANDEIS, LOUIS D[EMBITZ] (1856–1941) Associate Justice of Supreme Court

BRANN, WILLIAM COWPER (1855–1898) Journalist

BREMER, FREDRIKA (1801–1865) Novelist

BRENLY, BOB (1954–   ) Baseball player

BRENNAN, WILLIAM J[OSEPH] (1906–   ) Associate Justice of Supreme Court

BRESLIN, JIMMY (1929–   ) Newspaperman and author

BRICE, FANNY (1891–1951) Singer and comedian

BRIDGES, HORACE JAMES (1880–1955) Writer and lecturer

BROCK, LOU (1936–   ) Baseball player

BROCKENBROUGH, JOHN (fl. 1808) President of Bank of Virginia

BRODIE, JOHN [RILEY] (1935–   ) Football player and broadcaster

BROGAN, DENIS WILLIAM (1900–1974) English political scientist

BROKAW, TOM (1940–   ) Television anchorman

BROMFIELD, LOUIS (1896–1956) Novelist

BROOKE, EDWARD W[ILLIAM] (1919–   ) Politician

BROOKE, RUPERT (1887–1915) English poet

BROOKS, LOUISE (1906–1985) Actress

BROOKS, PHILLIPS (1835–1893) Clergyman

BROOKS, VAN WYCK (1886–1963) Author and critic

BROTHERS, JOYCE (1929–   ) Psychologist and author

BROTHERTON, ALICE WILLIAMS (1880s–1930) Writer and lecturer

BROUN, HEYWOOD HALE (1918–   ) Author and broadcaster

BROUN, MRS. HEYWOOD HALE (c.1925–   ) Actress

BROWN, EDMUND G[ERALD] "PAT" (1905–   ) Lawyer and public official

BROWN, JOHN (1800–1859) Abolitionist

BROWNING, ROBERT (1812–1889) English poet

BROWNLOW, LOUIS (1879–1963) Journalist and public administrator

BRYAN, WILLIAM JENNINGS (1860–1925) Statesman

BRYANT, WILLIAM CULLEN (1794–1878) Poet and editor

BRYCE, JAMES (1838–1922) British historian, diplomat, and jurist

BRZEZINSKI, ZBIGNIEW (1928–   ) Political scientist

BUCHANAN, JAMES (1791–1868) President (1857–1861)

BUCK, PEARL S[YDENSTRICKER] (1892–1973) Novelist

BUCKINGHAM, J[AMES] S[ILK] (1786–1855) English author and traveler

BUCKLEY, WILLIAM F., JR. (1925–   ) Author and editor

BUNNER, HENRY CUYLER (1855–1896) Writer

BURBANK, LUTHER (1849–1926) Horticulturist

BURCHARD, SAMUEL D[ICKINSON] (1812–1891) Clergyman

BURGES, TRISTAM (1770–1853) Congressman

BURGESS, [FRANK] GELETT (1866–1951) Humorist and poet

BURGOYNE, JOHN (1722–1792) British general and dramatist

BURKE, EDMUND (1729–1797) British statesman and orator

BURKE, KENNETH (1897–   ) Literary critic

BURR, AARON (1756–1836) Vice president (1801–1805)

BURR, AMELIA JOSEPHINE (1878–1940?) Poet

BURROUGHS, EDGAR RICE (1875–1950) Writer

BURROUGHS, JOHN (1837–1921) Naturalist and writer

BURT, [MAXWELL] STRUTHERS (1882–1954) Writer

BUSH, VANNEVAR (1890–1974) Electrical engineer

BUTLER, BENJAMIN F[RANKLIN] (1818–1893) Army officer and politician

BUTLER, NICHOLAS MURRAY (1862–1947) Educator

BUTLER, SAMUEL (1835–1902) English satirist

BUTLER, WILLIAM ALLEN (1825–1902) Lawyer and author

BYRNES, JAMES F[RANCIS] (1879–1972) Jurist and statesman

CABELL, JAMES BRANCH (1879–1958) Novelist

CADMAN, SAMUEL PARKES (1864–1936) Clergyman and author

CAEN, HERB (1916–   ) Newspaper columnist and author

CAHAN, ABRAHAM (1860–1951) Author and editor

CAINE, LYNN (1925?–   ) Author and lecturer

CALDWELL, ERSKINE (1903–1987) Novelist

CALDWELL, JAMES (1734–1781) Clergyman and patriot

CALHOUN, JOHN C[ALDWELL] (1782–1850) Vice president (1825–1832)

CALLOWAY, CAB[ELL] (1907–   ) Jazz singer and bandleader

CANNON, JOSEPH G[URNEY] (1836–1926) Politician

CAPOTE, TRUMAN (1924–1984) Author

CARABILLO, [VIRGINIA A.] TONI (1926–   ) Writer, editor, and graphic designer

CARDOZO, BENJAMIN [NATHAN] (1870–1938) Associate Justice of Supreme Court

CARLETON, WILL (1845–1912) Poet

CARMAN, [WILLIAM] BLISS (1861–1929) Canadian poet

CARNEGIE, ANDREW (1835–1919) Industrialist

CARNEGIE, DALE (1888–1955) Author

CARNEY, JULIA (1823–1908) Poet

CARRUTH, WILLIAM HERBERT (1859–1924) Educator and author

CARRYL, GUY WETMORE (1873–1904) Author and journalist

CARSON, JOHNNY (1925–   ) Television entertainer

CARSON, RACHEL (1907–1964) Marine biologist and author

CARTER, JIMMY [JAMES EARL, JR.] (1924–   ) President (1977–1981)

CARY, PHOEBE (1824–1871) Poet

CATHER, WILLA (1873–1947) Novelist

CATT, CARRIE CHAPMAN (1859–1947) Women's suffrage leader

CAWEIN, MADISON (1865–1914) Poet

CHAFEE, ZECHARIAH, JR. (1885–1957) Law educator and author

CHANNING, WILLIAM ELLERY (1780–1842) Clergyman and writer

CHANNING, WILLIAM HENRY (1810–1884) Clergyman

CHAPMAN, ARTHUR (1873–1935) Writer and editor

CHAPMAN, JOHN JAY (1862–1933) Author and critic

CHASE, ILKA (1905–1978) Author and actress

CHASE, SALMON P[ORTLAND] (1808–1873) Chief Justice of Supreme Court

CHEEVER, JOHN (1912–1982) Author

CHESNUT, MARY BOYKIN (1823–1886) Confederate diarist

CHESTERTON, G[ILBERT] K[EITH] (1874–1936) English author

CHILD, JULIA [McWILLIAMS] (1912–   ) Cooking consultant and author

CHILD, LYDIA M[ARIA] (1802–1880) Writer and social activist

CHISHOLM, SHIRLEY (1924–   ) Politician

CHOATE, JOSEPH HODGES (1832–1917) Lawyer and diplomat

CHOATE, RUFUS (1799–1859) Congressman and senator

CLAFLIN, TENNESSEE [CELESTE] (1845–1923) Reformer

CLAIBORNE, CRAIG (1920–   ) Editor, writer on cooking

CLARK, ABRAHAM (1726–1794) Congressman, signer of Declaration of Independence

CLARK, [CHARLES] BADGER (1883–1957) Poet

CLARK, McDONALD (1798–1842) Poet

CLARK, MARK (1896–1984) Army officer

CLARKE, JAMES FREEMAN (1810–1888) Clergyman and author

CLAY, HENRY (1777–1852) Statesman

CLEGHORN, SARAH N[ORCLIFFE] (1876–1959) Poet

CLEVELAND, [STEPHEN] GROVER (1837–1908) President (1885–1889, 1893–1897)

COBB, HOWELL (1815–1868) Politician and Confederate general

COBB, IRVIN S[HREWSBURY] (1876–1944) Journalist and author

COBBETT, WILLIAM (1763–1835) English political essayist

COBURN, FOSTER DWIGHT (1846–1924) Public official and author

COCKRAN, [WILLIAM] BOURKE (1854–1923) Politician and orator

COFFMAN, LOTUS DELTA (1875–1938) Educator

COHAN, GEORGE M[ICHAEL] (1878–1942) Playwright, songwriter, and actor

COHEN, FELIX S. (1907–1953) Jurist

COHN, ROY M[ARCUS] (1927–1986) Lawyer

COLBY, FRANK MOORE (1865–1925) Editor

COLERIDGE, SAMUEL TAYLOR (1772–1834) English poet and critic

COLLINS, J[AMES] LAWTON (1882–1963) Army officer

COLTON, CALVIN (1789–1857) Journalist and author

COMMAGER, HENRY STEELE (1902–) Historian

COMMONER, BARRY (1917–) Biologist and educator

COMPTON, KARL TAYLOR (1887–1954) Physicist

CONANT, JAMES BRYANT (1893–) Chemist and educator

CONKLING, ROSCOE (1829–1888) Lawyer and politician

COOK, [FLAVIUS] JOSEPH[US] (1838–1901) Lecturer

COOKE, [ALFRED] ALISTAIR (1908–) Journalist, broadcaster, and author

COOKE, EDMUND VANCE (1866–1932) Writer and lecturer

COOLIDGE, CALVIN (1872–1933) President (1923–1929)

COOLIDGE, SUSAN (1845–1905) Author

COOPER, JAMES FENIMORE (1789–1851) Novelist

COOPER, PETER (1791–1883) Industrialist and philanthropist

COOPER, THOMAS (1759–1839) Scientist and educator

COPLEY, JOHN SINGLETON (1738–1815) Painter

CORNWALLIS, CHARLES (1738–1805) British general and statesman

CORWIN, THOMAS (1794–1865) Politician and public official

COSELL, HOWARD (1918–) Sports journalist

COTTON, JOHN (1584–1652) Congregational clergyman

COUSINS, NORMAN (1912–) Editor and writer

COX, SAMUEL SULLIVAN (1824–1889) Lawyer and politician

CRANE, HART (1899–1932) Poet

CRANE, STEPHEN (1871–1900) Author and journalist

CRAPSEY, ADELAIDE (1878–1914) Poet

CRÈVECOEUR, MICHEL GUILLAUME JEAN DE (1735–1813) Colonial writer

CRIST, JUDITH (1922–) Film and drama critic

CROCKETT, DAVY (1786–1836) Frontiersman and politician

CROKER, RICHARD (1841–1922) Politician

CRONKITE, WALTER (1916–) Radio and television news correspondent

CROSS, WILBUR L[UCIUS] (1862–1948) Educator and politician

CROTHERS, SAMUEL McCHORD (1857–1927) Clergyman and essayist

CULBERTSON, ELY (1891–1955) Authority on contract bridge

CULLEN, COUNTEE (1903–1946) Poet

CUMMINGS, E[DWARD] E[STLIN] (1894–1962) Poet and painter

CUNNINGHAM, IMOGEN (1883–1976) Photographer

CUOMO, MARIO (1932–) Politician

CUPPY, WILL (1884–1949) Humorist and critic

CURTIS, GEORGE WILLIAM (1824–1892) Essayist, editor, and reformer

CUSTER, GEORGE ARMSTRONG (1839–1876) Army officer

DACHÉ, LILLY (1904–   ) Hat designer

DACRE, HARRY (d. 1922) English songwriter

DANA, CHARLES A[NDERSON] (1819–1897) Editor and publisher

DANA, RICHARD HENRY, JR. (1815–1882) Lawyer and writer

DANIELS, JONATHAN [WORTH] (1902–1981) Author and editor

DANIELS, JOSEPHUS (1862–1948) Editor and statesman

DARBY, WILLIAM (1775–1854) Geographer and author

D'ARCY, HUGH ANTOINE (1843–1925) Actor and writer

DARROW, CLARENCE S[EWARD] (1857–1938) Lawyer

DAUGHERTY, HARRY (1860–1941) Lawyer and politician

DAVIS, ADELLE (1904–1974) Nutritionist and author

DAVIS, ANGELA (1944–   ) Political activist and teacher

DAVIS, BETTE (1908–   ) Actress

DAVIS, DAVID (1815–1886) Associate Justice of Supreme Court

DAVIS, DOROTHY SALISBURY (1916–   ) Author

DAVIS, ELMER (1890–1958) Radio commentator and writer

DAVIS, JEFFERSON (1808–1889) Confederate president (1861–1865)

DAVIS, JOHN (1775–1854) English sailor and author

DAVIS, REBECCA HARDING (1831–1910) Novelist

DAWES, CHARLES GATES (1865–1951) Diplomat and financier

DAY, LILLIAN [ABRAMS] (1893–?) Author

DEAN, JOHN [WESLEY] (1938–   ) Presidential aide and journalist

DEARBORN, HENRY (1751–1829) Public official

DEBS, EUGENE V[ICTOR] (1855–1926) Socialist labor leader

DE CASSERES, BENJAMIN (1873–1945) Poet and journalist

DECATUR, STEPHEN (1779–1820) Naval officer

DECTER, MIDGE (1927–   ) Writer and editor

DE FOREST, JOHN W[ILLIAM] (1826–1906) Writer

DE GAULLE, CHARLES (1890–1970) President of France (1959–1969)

DELEON, DANIEL (1852–1914) Socialist leader

DE MILLE, AGNES (1908–   ) Dancer and choreographer

DEMPSEY, JACK (1895–1983) Boxer

DENNY, LUDWELL (1894–1970) Journalist and writer

DENVER, JOHN (1943–   ) Singer and songwriter

DEPEW, CHAUNCEY M[ITCHELL] (1834–1928) Industrialist

DERBY, GEORGE HORATIO (1823–1861) Humorist

DEUTSCH, BABETTE (1895–1982) Poet

DE VOTO, BERNARD A[UGUSTINE] (1897–1955) Author and editor

DE VRIES, PETER (1910–   ) Novelist

DEWEY, GEORGE (1837–1917) Naval officer

DEWEY, JOHN (1859–1952) Philosopher and educator

DICKENS, CHARLES (1812–1870) English novelist

DICKINSON, CHARLES MONROE (1842–1924) Diplomat

DICKINSON, EMILY (1830–1886) Poet

DICKINSON, JOHN (1732–1808) Revolutionary patriot and essayist

DIDION, JOAN (1934–   ) Author and editor

DILLARD, ANNIE (1945–   ) Author

DILLER, PHYLLIS (1917–   ) Comedian and author

DIMAGGIO, JOE (1914–   ) Baseball player

DIRKSEN, EVERETT M[CKINLEY] (1896–1969) Politician

DIX, DOROTHEA LYNDE (1802–1887) Educator and social reformer

DIX, DOROTHY (1861–1951) Journalist

DIXON, FRANK (1866–1925) Clergyman and lecturer

DOLE, CHARLES FLETCHER (1845–1927) Clergyman and author

DOLE, SANFORD B[ALLARD] (1844–1926) Political leader

DONNELLY, IGNATIUS (1831–1901) Politician, author, and editor

DOUGLAS, HELEN GAHAGAN (1900–1980) Member of Congress and author

DOUGLAS, MICHAEL (1944–   ) Film producer, director, and actor

DOUGLAS, STEPHEN A[RNOLD] (1813–1861) Politician

DOUGLAS, WILLIAM O[RVILLE] (1898–1980) Associate Justice of Supreme Court

DOUGLASS, FREDERICK (1817–1895) Abolitionist, reformer, and writer

DOW, DOROTHY [MINERVA] (1899–?) Poet

DOW, LORENZO (1777–1834) Evangelist

DRAKE, JOSEPH RODMAN (1795–1820) Poet

DREISER, THEODORE (1871–1945) Novelist

DRESBACH, GLENN WARD (1889–1906) Poet

DRESSER, PAUL (1857–1906) Songwriter

DRESSLER, MARIE (1869–1934) Actress

DU BOIS, W[ILLIAM] E[DWARD] B[URGHARDT] (1868–1963) Educator and author

DUBOS, RENÉ (1901–1982) Bacteriologist

DULLES, JOHN FOSTER (1888–1959) Secretary of state

DUNBAR, PAUL LAURENCE (1872–1906) Poet and novelist

DUNCAN, ISADORA (1878–1927) Dancer

DUNNE, FINLEY PETER (1867–1936) Humorist

DURANT, WILL[IAM] (1885–1981) Educator and author

DURANTE, JIMMY (1893–1980) Comedian

DUROCHER, LEO (1905–   ) Baseball manager

DURYEA [or DURYEE], WILLIAM RANKIN (1838–?) Clergyman and poet

DWIGHT, TIMOTHY (1752–1817) Clergyman and educator

DYER, MARY (d. 1660) Quaker martyr

DYLAN, BOB (1941–   ) Singer and composer

EARHART, AMELIA (1898–1937) Aviation pioneer

EASTMAN, GEORGE (1854–1932) Inventor and industrialist

EDDY, MARY BAKER (1821–1910) Founder of Christian Science

EDELMAN, MARIAN WRIGHT (1939–   ) Lawyer and public official

EDISON, THOMAS ALVA (1847–1931) Inventor

EDWARDS, INDIA [MOFFETT] (1900?–   ) Political party executive

EDWARDS, JONATHAN (1703–1758) Clergyman and author

EHRLICHMAN, JOHN D[ANIEL] (1925–   ) Presidential advisor and author

EINSTEIN, ALBERT (1879–1955) Physicist

EISENHOWER, DWIGHT D[AVID] (1890–1969) President (1953–1961)

EL BAZ, FAROUK (1938–   ) Geologist and corporate executive

ELIOT, CHARLES WILLIAM (1834–1926) President of Harvard University

ELIOT, T[HOMAS] S[TEARNS] (1888–1965) Poet

ELKINS, STEPHEN BENTON (1841–1911) Industrialist and political leader

ELLIOTT, MAXINE (1868–1940) Actress

ELLIOTT, [ALON]ZO (1891–1964) Composer and lyricist

ELLISON, RALPH W[ALDO] (1914–   ) Writer and lecturer

EMERSON, RALPH WALDO (1803–1882) Essayist and poet

EMMETT, DANIEL DECATUR (1815–1904) Songwriter and minstrel

ENGEL, ALBERT J[OSEPH] (1924–   ) Jurist

ERIKSON, ERIK H[OMBURGER] (1902–   ) Psychoanalyst

ERIKSON, KAI (1931–   ) Sociologist and educator

ERSKINE, JOHN (1879–1951) Educator and writer

ERVIN, SAM J[AMES], JR. (1896–1985) Senator

EVANS, AUGUSTA J[ANE] (1835–1909) Novelist

EVANS, OLIVER (1755–1819) Inventor

EVANS, OLIVER [WENDELL] (1915–   ) Teacher and writer

EVANS, ROWLAND, JR. (1921–   ) Newspaper columnist and author

EVERETT, EDWARD (1794–1865) Clergyman, orator, and statesman

EXLEY, FREDERICK [EARL] (1929–   ) Author

FADIMAN, CLIFTON (1904–   ) Author and editor

FALWELL, JERRY (1933–   ) Evangelist and political activist

FARLEY, JAMES A[LOYSIUS] (1888–1976) Politician and public official

FARRAGUT, DAVID GLASGOW (1801–1870) Naval officer

FARRELL, JAMES T[HOMAS] (1904–1979) Novelist

FARRELL, THOMAS (1892–1967) Army engineer

FAULKNER, WILLIAM (1897–1962) Novelist

FERBER, EDNA (1887–1968) Author

FERLINGHETTI, LAWRENCE (1920?–   ) Poet

FERN, FANNY (1811–1872) Writer, real name Sara Payson Willis

FERRELL, ROBERT H[UGH] (1921–   ) Historian, educator, and author

FIELD, DAVID DUDLEY (1805–1894) Jurist

FIELD, EUGENE (1850–1895) Poet and journalist

FIELDS, W[ILLIAM] C[LAUDE DUKENFIELD] (1880–1946) Comedian and actor

FINLEY, JOHN [HUSTON] (1863–1940) Educator, editor, and author

FISCHER, MARTIN H[ENRY] (1879–1962) Scientist

FISKE, JOHN (1842–1901) Philosopher and historian

FISKE, MINNIE MADDERN (1865–1932) Actress

FITZGERALD, FRANCES (1940–   ) Journalist and author

FITZGERALD, F[RANCIS] SCOTT [KEY] (1896–1940) Author

FITZGERALD, ZELDA SAYRE (1900–1948) Artist and author

FLANDRAU, CHARLES [MACOMB] (1871–1938) Author

FLEXNER, ABRAHAM (1866–1959) Educator and author

FLYNN, ELIZABETH GURLEY (1890–1964) Labor organizer and author

FORBES, ESTHER (1894–1967) Novelist

FORD, GERALD R[UDOLPH] (1913–   ) President (1974–1977)

FORD, HENRY (1863–1947) Founder of Ford Motor Company

FORGY, HOWELL M[AURICE] (1908–   ) Navy chaplain at Pearl Harbor, 1941

FORREST, NATHAN BEDFORD (1821–1877) Confederate general

FORSTER, E[DWARD] M[ORGAN] (1879–1970) English novelist

FOSDICK, HARRY EMERSON (1878–1969) Clergyman and author

FOSS, SAM WALTER (1858–1911) Editor and humorist

FOSTER, GEORGE (1949–   ) Baseball player

FOSTER, STEPHEN COLLINS (1826–1864) Composer

FOWLER, GENE (1890–1960) Playwright and author

FOX, MURIEL (1928–   ) Public relations executive

FRANK, WALDO (1889–1967) Author

FRANKEL, MAX (1930–   ) Journalist and editor

FRANKFURTER, FELIX (1882–1965) Associate Justice of Supreme Court

FRANKLAND, MARK (1934–   ) Foreign correspondent and author

FRANKLIN, BENJAMIN (1706–1790) Revolutionary statesman, philosopher, and inventor

FRÉMONT, JOHN C[HARLES] (1813–1890) Explorer and army officer

FRENEAU, PHILIP (1752–1832) Revolutionary poet

FRIEDAN, BETTY (1921–   ) Writer and women's rights activist

FRIEDMAN, MILTON (1912–   ) Economist

FRIEDMAN, ROSE (c.1915–   ) Writer and economist

FRISCO, JOE (1890–1958) Comedian

FRITZ, JOHN (1822–1913) Authority on iron and steel manufacture

FROHMAN, CHARLES (1860–1915) Theatrical manager

FROMM, ERICH (1900–1980) Psychoanalyst

FROST, ROBERT (1874–1963) Poet

FULBRIGHT, J[AMES] WILLIAM (1905–   ) Politician

FULLER, MARGARET (1810–1850) Author and social reformer

FULLER, R[ICHARD] BUCKMINSTER (1895–1983) Engineer, architect, and designer

GABOR, ZSA ZSA (1923–   ) Actress

GALBRAITH, JOHN KENNETH (1908–   ) Economist

GARAGIOLA, JOE (1926–   ) Baseball player and broadcaster

GARBO, GRETA (1905–   ) Actress

GARDNER, AUGUSTUS P[EABODY] (1865–1918) Politician

GARFIELD, JAMES A[BRAM] (1831–1881) President (1881)

GARLAND, HAMLIN (1860–1940) Author

GARLAND, JUDY (1922–1969) Singer and actress

GARNER, JOHN NANCE (1868–1967) Vice president (1933–1941)

GARRISON, WILLIAM LLOYD (1805–1879) Abolitionist and reformer

GENTHE, ARNOLD (1869–1942) Photographer

GEORGE III (1738–1820) King of England

GEORGE, HENRY (1839–1897) Economist, writer, and lecturer

GEROULD, KATHERINE [FULLERTON] (1879–1944) Writer

GERRY, ELBRIDGE (1837–1927) Vice president (1813–1814)

GERSHWIN, GEORGE (1898–1937) Composer

GIBBONS, JAMES CARDINAL (1834–1921) Roman Catholic prelate

GIBBONS, JAMES SLOAN (1810–1892) Abolitionist

GIBBS, WOLCOTT (1902–1958) Writer and critic

GILCHRIST, MARIE (1893–?) Author

GILDER, RICHARD WATSON (1844–1909) Poet and editor

GILES, HENRY (1809–1882) Author

GILMAN, CHARLOTTE PERKINS (1860–1935) Women's rights advocate

GILPIN, LAURA (1891–1979) Photographer and writer

GLADDEN, WASHINGTON (1836–1918) Clergyman and author

GLADSTONE, WILLIAM E[WART] (1809–1898) British statesman

GLASGOW, ELLEN (1874–1945) Novelist

GLASS, CARTER (1858–1946) Statesman

GOGARTY, OLIVER ST. JOHN (1878–1957) Irish writer and physician

GOLDBERG, ISAAC (1887–1938) Writer and lecturer

GOLDMAN, EMMA (1869–1940) Anarchist leader

GOLDMAN, ERIC [FREDERICK] (1915–   ) Historian and author

GOLDMAN, PETER [LOUIS] (1933–   ) Journalist and author

GOLDWATER, BARRY M[ORRIS] (1909–   ) Politician

GOLDWYN, SAMUEL (1882–1974) Motion picture producer

GOMPERS, SAMUEL (1850–1924) Labor leader

GOODMAN, ROY M[ATZ] (1930–   ) Politician

GOODRICH, SAMUEL (1793–1860) Writer

GRAHAM, KATHARINE (1917–   ) Newspaper publisher

GRAHAM, MARGARET COLLIER (1850–1910) Author

GRAHAM, VIRGINIA (1912–   ) Performer and lecturer

GRANT, ULYSSES S[IMPSON] (1822–1885) President (1869–1877)

GRAU, SHIRLEY ANN (1929–   ) Author

GRAY, FRANCINE DU PLESSIX (1930–   ) Author

GREELEY, HORACE (1811–1872) Newspaperman and political leader

GREENE, ALBERT GORTON (1802–1868) Lawyer and poet

GREENE, NATHANAEL (1742–1786) Revolutionary officer

GREENOUGH, HORATIO (1805–1852) Sculptor

GREGORY, DICK (1932–   ) Comedian and civil rights activist

GREY, EDWARD [VISCOUNT FALLODON] (1862–1933) English statesman

GRIFFITH, D[AVID] W[ARK] (1875–1948) Motion picture producer and director

GRIMKÉ, ANGELINA (1805–1879) Abolitionist and women's rights advocate

GRISWOLD, ALFRED WHITNEY (1906–1963) Historian and educator

GROSE, FRANCIS (1731–1791) English antiquary and publisher

GROVES, LESLIE RICHARD (1896–1970) Army officer

GROW, GALUSHA A[ARON] (1822–1907) Political leader

GUEST, EDGAR A[LBERT] (1881–1959) Journalist and poet

GUINAN, [MARY LOUISE] TEXAS (1884–1933) Nightclub performer

GUITEAU, CHARLES J[ULIUS] (1840?–1882) Assassin of James A. Garfield

GUITERMAN, ARTHUR (1871–1943) Poet

GUNTHER, JOHN (1901–1970) Journalist and author

GUTHRIE, [WILLIAM] TYRONE (1900–1971) English theatrical director

GUTHRIE, WOODY (1912–1967) Folksinger and composer

HAGEN, WALTER (1892–1969) Golfer

HAGUE, FRANK (1876–1956) Mayor of Jersey City, N.J.

HALE, EDWARD EVERETT (1822–1909) Clergyman and author

HALE, NATHAN (1755–1776) Revolutionary patriot

HALL, G[RANVILLE] STANLEY (1846–1924) Psychologist and educator

HALLECK, FITZ-GREENE (1790–1867) Poet

HALSEY, MARGARET (1910–   ) Author

HALSEY, WILLIAM FREDERICK (1882–1959) Naval officer

HAMILL, [WILLIAM] PETE (1935–   ) Journalist and author

HAMILTON, ALEXANDER (1757–1804) Political leader

HAMILTON, GAIL (1833–1896) Writer

HAMILTON, THOMAS (1914–   ) College president

HAMMERSTEIN, OSCAR, II (1895–1960) Lyricist and librettist

HAMMOND, JAMES HENRY (1807–1864) Political leader

HANCOCK, JOHN (1737–1793) Revolutionary patriot and statesman

HAND, LEARNED (1872–1961) Jurist

HANDLIN, OSCAR (1915–   ) Historian and educator

HANNA, MARK [MARCUS ALONZO] (1837–1904) Political leader

HARDIN, GARRETT [JAMES] (1915–   ) Ecologist

HARDING, FLORENCE KLING DE WOLFE (1860–1924) Wife of Warren G. Harding

HARDING, WARREN G[AMALIEL] (1865–1923) President (1921–1923)

HARLAN, JOHN MARSHALL (1833–1911) Associate Justice of Supreme Court

HARRINGTON, MICHAEL (1928–   ) Author

HARRIS, CHARLES K[ASSELL] (1865–1930) Songwriter

HARRIS, JOEL CHANDLER (1848–1908) Author

HARRIS, SYDNEY J[USTIN] (1917–   ) Columnist

HARRISON, BENJAMIN (1833–1901) President (1889–1893)

HARRISON, HENRY [SYDNOR] (1880–1930) Novelist

HARRISON, WILLIAM HENRY (1773–1841) President (1841)

HART, LORENZ (1895–1943) Lyricist

HART, MOSS (1904–1961) Playwright

HARTE, [FRANCIS] BRET[T] (1836–1902) Author

HARTMANN, ROBERT T[ROWBRIDGE] (1917–   ) Journalist and author

HAVEMEYER, HENRY O[SBORNE] (1847–1907) Sugar refiner

HAWTHORNE, NATHANIEL (1804–1864) Author

HAY, JOHN [MILTON] (1838–1905) Statesman and author

HAYES, HELEN (1900–   ) Actress

HAYES, RUTHERFORD B[IRCHARD] (1822–1893) President (1877–1881)

HAYES, [WAYNE WOODROW] WOODY (1913–1987) Football coach

HAYNE, PAUL HAMILTON (1830–1886) Poet

HAYNE, ROBERT YOUNG (1791–1839) Politician

HAYS, ELINOR [RICE] (c.1902–   ) Author

HAYWOOD, WILLIAM D[UDLEY] "BIG BILL" (1869–1928) Labor leader

HEARN, LAFCADIO (1850–1904) Author

HEARST, GEORGE (1820–1891) Mining magnate

HEARST, WILLIAM RANDOLPH (1863–1951) Newspaper publisher

HELLMAN, LILLIAN (1905–1984) Playwright

HELPER, HINTON ROWAN (1829–1909) Writer

HEMINGWAY, ERNEST (1899–1961) Author

HENRY, O. (1862–1910) Short story writer, real name William Sydney Porter

HENRY, PATRICK (1736–1799) Revolutionary leader

HEPBURN, KATHARINE (1909–   ) Actress

HERFORD, OLIVER (1863–1935) Author and illustrator

HERNDON, WILLIAM HENRY (1818–1891) Law partner of Abraham Lincoln

HERSHFIELD, HARRY (1885–1974) Cartoonist and columnist

HEWITT, ABRAM [STEVENS] (1822–1903) Businessman and politician

HEYWARD, DUBOSE (1885–1940) Author

HIGGINSON, THOMAS WENTWORTH (1823–1911) Clergyman, author, and army officer

HILL, JOE (1879–1915) Labor organizer

HILLMAN, SIDNEY (1887–1946) Labor leader

HOAR, GEORGE FRISBIE (1826–1904) Lawyer and politician

HOBSON, LAURA Z[AMETKIN] (1900–1986) Novelist

HOCKING, WILLIAM ERNEST (1873–1966) Philosopher and author

HOFFA, [JAMES RIDDLE] JIMMY (1913–1975?) Union official

HOGAN, FRANK J. (1877–1944) Lawyer

HOLIDAY, BILLIE (1915–1959) Blues singer

HOLLAND, JOSIAH GILBERT (1819–1881) Editor and writer

HOLLANDER, JOHN (1929–   ) Writer

HOLLINGS, ERNEST [FREDERICK] (1922–   ) Politician

HOLME, THOMAS (1624–1695) Mapmaker, colonial legislator

HOLMES, JOHN HAYNES (1879–1964) Unitarian minister and writer

HOLMES, OLIVER WENDELL, SR. (1809–1894) Physician and author

HOLMES, OLIVER WENDELL, JR. (1841–1935) Associate Justice of Supreme Court

HOMANS, GEORGE C[ASPAR] (1910–   ) Sociologist

HOOK, SIDNEY (1902–   ) Philosopher and teacher

HOOVER, HERBERT [CLARK] (1874–1964) President (1929–1933)

HOPKINS, ERNEST MARTIN (1877–1964) Educator

HOPKINS, HARRY LLOYD (1890–1946) Politician and administrator

HOPKINS, JOHNS (1795–1873) Financier and philanthropist

HOPPER, HEDDA (1890–1966) Columnist

HORACK, H. CLAUDE (1877–1958) Law school dean

HORNEY, KAREN (1885–1952) Psychiatrist and author

HOUSTON, SAM (1793–1863) Soldier and politician

HOVEY, RICHARD (1864–1900) Poet

HOWAR, BARBARA [DEARING] (1934–   ) Television correspondent

HOWARD, ANTHONY [MICHELL] (1934–   ) Journalist and editor

HOWARD, JOSEPH KINSEY (1906–1951) Author

HOWE, EDGAR WATSON (1853–1937) Journalist and author

HOWE, JULIA WARD (1819–1910) Author and women's rights leader

HOWE, LOUISE KAPP (1934–1984) Author

HOWE, LOUIS McHENRY (1871–1936) Secretary to Franklin D. Roosevelt

HOWELLS, WILLIAM DEAN (1837–1920) Author and editor

HOYT, CHARLES H[ALE] (1860–1900) Playwright

HUBBARD, ELBERT [GREEN] (1856–1915) Writer, founder of Roycroft Press

HUBBARD, FRANK McKINNEY "KIN" (1868–1930) Humorist

HUGHES, CHARLES EVANS (1862–1948) Chief Justice of Supreme Court

HUGHES, JAMES P[ETER] (1874–1961) Jurist

HUGHES, [JAMES] LANGSTON (1902–1967) Poet

HUGHES, RUPERT (1872–1956) Writer and editor

HULL, ISAAC (1773–1843) Naval officer

HUMPHREY, HUBERT H[ORATIO] (1911–1978) Vice president (1965–1969)

HUNEKER, JAMES GIBBONS (1860–1921) Musician and critic

HUTCHENS, JOHN K[ENNEDY] (1905–   ) Journalist and editor

HUTCHINS, ROBERT M[ANUEL] (1899–1977) Educator

HUXLEY, ALDOUS (1894–1963)   English novelist and critic

HYLAN, JOHN F. (1868–1936)   Lawyer and politician

ICKES, HAROLD L[eCLAIR] (1874–1952)   Lawyer and politician

INGALLS, JOHN JAMES (1833–1900)   Politician and orator

INGERSOLL, ROBERT GREEN (1833–1899)   Lawyer and lecturer

IRVING, WASHINGTON (1783–1859)   Author

IRWIN, JAMES (1930–   )   Astronaut

ISHERWOOD, CHRISTOPHER (1904–1986)   Playwright and writer

JACKSON, ANDREW (1767–1845)   President (1829–1837)

JACKSON, HELEN [FISKE] HUNT (1830–1885)   Novelist

JACKSON, JESSE [LOUIS] (1941–   )   Civil rights leader and politician

JACKSON, MAHALIA (1911–1972)   Gospel singer

JACKSON, REGGIE (1946–   )   Baseball player

JACKSON, ROBERT H[OUGHWOUT] (1892–1954)   Associate Justice of the Supreme Court

JACKSON, SHIRLEY (1919–1965)   Author

JACKSON, THOMAS JONATHAN "STONEWALL" (1824–1863)   Confederate general

JACOB, IAN (1899–   )   British army officer

JACOBS, JANE (1916–   )   Author

JACOBS, JOE (1896–1940)   Boxing manager

JAMES, ALICE [ARCHER SEWALL] (1870–1955)   Poet and author

JAMES, HENRY, SR. (1811–1882)   Philosopher

JAMES, HENRY, JR. (1843–1916)   Novelist

JAMES, WILLIAM (1842–1910)   Philosopher and psychologist

JANEWAY, ELIZABETH [HALL] (1913–   )   Author

JAY, JOHN (1817–1894)   Lawyer and diplomat

JEFFERS, [JOHN] ROBINSON (1887–1962)   Poet

JEFFERSON, JOSEPH (1829–1905)   Actor

JEFFERSON, THOMAS (1743–1826)   President (1801–1809)

JEWETT, SARAH ORNE (1849–1909)   Writer

JOHNSON, ANDREW (1808–1875)   President (1865–1869)

JOHNSON, GERALD WHITE (1890–1980)   Journalist and author

JOHNSON, JAMES WELDON (1871–1938)   Author

JOHNSON, JOHN G[RAVER] (1841–1917)   Lawyer

JOHNSON, [CLAUDIA TAYLOR] LADY BIRD (1912–   )   Wife of Lyndon B. Johnson

JOHNSON, LYNDON BAINES (1908–1973)   President (1963–1969)

JOHNSON, PHILANDER CHASE (1866–1939)   Editor

JOHNSON, RICHARD M[ENTOR] (1781–1850)   Vice president (1837–1841)

JOHNSON, ROBERT UNDERWOOD (1853–1937)   Author

JOHNSON, SAMUEL (1709–1784)   English lexicographer

JOHNSON, WILLIAM (1771–1834)   Associate Justice of Supreme Court

JOHNSTON, ALVA (1888–1950)   Journalist and author

JOHNSTON, MARY (1870–1936)   Novelist

JOLSON, AL (1886–1950)   Singer and actor

JONES, FREDERICK S. (1862–1944)   Educator

JONES, JOHN PAUL (1747–1792)   Naval officer

JONES, [MARY] MOTHER (1830–1930)   Labor leader

JONES, RUFUS MATTHEW (1863–1948)   Quaker teacher and author

JONES, [THOMAS ALBERT DWIGHT] TAD (1887–1957)   Football coach

JONES, WESLEY LIVSEY (1863–1932)   Lawyer and politician

JONG, ERICA (1942–   )   Author

JORDAN, BARBARA C. (1936–   )   Member of Congress and educator

JOSEPH, CHIEF (c.1840–1904)   Nez Percé leader

KAEL, PAULINE (1919–   )   Film critic

KAHN, OTTO [HERMANN] (1867–1934)   Banker

KAMEHAMEHA I (c.1758–1819)   King of Hawaii

KASE, TOSHIKAZU (1903–   )   Japanese diplomat

KATZENBACH, NICHOLAS deB[ELLEVILLE] (1922–   )   Lawyer and public official

KAUFMAN, GEORGE S[IMON] (1889–1961)   Playwright

KEILLOR, GARRISON (1942–   ) Writer and radio performer

KELLER, HELEN (1880–1968) Author and lecturer

KEMBLE, [FRANCES ANNE] FANNY (1809–1893) English actress

KEMPTON, [JAMES] MURRAY (1918–   ) Journalist

KENNAN, GEORGE F[ROST] (1904–   ) Diplomat and historian

KENNEDY, FLORYNCE R. (1916–   ) Lawyer and feminist

KENNEDY, JOHN FITZGERALD (1917–1963) President (1961–1963)

KENNEDY, ROBERT F[RANCIS] (1925–1968) Politician

KENNEDY, ROSE FITZGERALD (1890–   ) Mother of John and Robert Kennedy

KENNEDY, STEPHEN P[ATRICK] (1906–1978) New York City police commissioner

KENNEDY, THOMAS (1887–1963) Union official

KENT, FRANK RICHARDSON (1877–1958) Journalist

KENT, ROCKWELL (1882–1971) Artist and writer

KERNER, OTTO, JR. (1908–1976) Jurist and politician

KERR, CLARK (1911–   ) Educator

KERR, JEAN (1923–   ) Author

KEY, FRANCIS SCOTT (1779–1843) Lawyer and poet

KEYSERLING, HERMANN (1880–1946) German social philosopher

KIERAN, JAMES M[ICHAEL] (1863–1936) Educator and college president

KILGALLEN, DOROTHY (1913–1965) Columnist and radio commentator

KILMER, JOYCE (1886–1918) Poet

KING, BILLIE JEAN (1943–   ) Tennis player

KING, CLARENCE (1842–1901) Geologist and mining engineer

KING, MARTIN LUTHER, JR. (1929–1968) Clergyman and civil rights leader

KING, STODDARD (1889–1933) Humorist and author

KINROSS, LORD (1904–1976) British author and journalist

KIPLING, RUDYARD (1865–1936) English author

KIRKPATRICK, JEANE J[ORDAN] (1926–   ) Diplomat

KISSINGER, HENRY A[LFRED] (1923–   ) Political scientist and public official

KNEBEL, FLETCHER (1911–   ) Journalist and author

KNIGHT, DAVID (1921–   ) Author

KNIGHT, ERIC (1897–1943) Author

KNOTT, JAMES PROCTOR (1830–1911) Lawyer and public official

KNOWLES, JOHN (1926–1979) Physician, administrator, and author

KNOX, HENRY (1750–1806) Revolutionary officer

KOCH, EDWARD (1924–   ) Mayor of New York City

KOSSUTH, LAJOS (1802–1894) Hungarian statesman and patriot

KRUTCH, JOSEPH WOOD (1893–1970) Critic, editor, and author

KUHN, [MARGARET] MAGGIE (1905–   ) Social activist and author

KURALT, CHARLES (1934–   ) Television news correspondent

LAFAYETTE, MARQUIS DE (1757–1834) French soldier and statesman

LA FOLLETTE, ROBERT M[ARION], SR. (1885–1925) Politician

LAFOLLETTE, SUZANNE (c.1882–1983) Editor and author

LAGUARDIA, FIORELLO H[ENRY] (1882–1947) Mayor of New York City

LAMARR, HEDY (1914–   ) Actress

LAMB, ARTHUR J. (1870–1928) Songwriter

LAMPTON, WILLIAM J[AMES] (c.1850–1917) Journalist and author

LANCHESTER, ELSA (1902–1986) English actress

LANDERS, ANN (1918–   ) Columnist

LANDIS, KENESAW MOUNTAIN (1866–1944) Commissioner of Baseball

LANDON, ALF[RED MOSSMAN] (1887–1987) Politician

LANE, RALPH (1530–1603) English colonist, head of Roanoke Island colony

LANGEVIN, PAUL (1872–1946) French physicist

LANIER, SIDNEY (1842–1881) Poet

LARDNER, RING[OLD WILMER] (1885–1933) Author

LAWRENCE, AMOS (1786–1852) Merchant and philanthropist

LAWRENCE, D[AVID] H[ERBERT] (1885–1930) English novelist

LAWRENCE, GERTRUDE (1901–1952) Actress

LAWRENCE, JAMES (1781–1813) Naval officer

LAWSON, JOHN (d. 1711) English traveler in America

LAZARUS, EMMA (1849–1887) Poet and essayist

LEACHMAN, CLORIS (1930–) Actress

LEACOCK, STEPHEN [BUTLER] (1869–1944) Canadian humorist and economist

LE CORBUSIER (1887–1965) French architect

LEE, GERALD STANLEY (1862–1944) Clergyman and writer

LEE, [NELLE] HARPER (1926–) Author

LEE, HENRY "LIGHT-HORSE HARRY" (1756–1818) Revolutionary soldier and statesman

LEE, RICHARD HENRY (1732–1794) Revolutionary statesman

LEE, ROBERT E[DWARD] (1807–1870) Confederate army general

LEEK, SYBIL (1923–1982) Astrologer and author

LEGMAN, GERSHON (1917–) Writer and medical researcher

LE GUIN, URSULA K[ROEBER] (1929–) Author

LEHMAN, HERBERT H[ENRY] (1878–1963) Banker and politician

LENIN, V[LADIMIR] I[LICH] (1870–1924) Russian Communist leader

LENNON, JOHN (1940–1980) Composer and performer

LEOPOLD, ALDO (1886–1948) Conservationist

LERNER, ALAN JAY (1918–1986) Lyricist and librettist

LERNER, GERDA (1920–) Historian and author

LESLIE, [JOHN RANDOLPH] SHANE (1885–1971) Irish journalist and author

LE SUEUR, MERIDEL (1900–) Author

LEVANT, OSCAR (1906–1972) Pianist and composer

LEVENSON, SAM[UEL] (1911–1980) Comedian

LEVY, LEONARD W[ILLIAMS] (1923–) Historian

LEWIS, JOHN L[LEWELLYN] (1880–1969) Labor leader

LEWIS, SAM[UEL M.] (1883–1959) Lyricist

LEWIS, SINCLAIR (1885–1951) Novelist

LEWISOHN, LUDWIG (1883–1955) Novelist and critic

LIBERACE, [WLADZIU VALENTINO] LEE (1920–1987) Pianist

LIFTON, ROBERT JAY (1926–) Psychiatrist and author

LILIENTHAL, DAVID E[LY] (1899–1981) Public administrator

LILIUOKALANI, LYDIA KAMEKEHA (1838–1917) Queen of Hawaii

LINCOLN, ABRAHAM (1809–1865) President (1861–1865)

LINDBERGH, ANNE MORROW (1906–) Author

LINDSAY, JOHN V[LIET] (1921–) Mayor of New York City

LINDSAY, [NICHOLAS] VACHEL (1879–1931) Poet

LINDSEY, ROBERT [HUGHES] (1935–) Journalist and author

LINKLATER, ERIC (1899–1974) English writer

LIPPMANN, WALTER (1889–1974) Journalist and author

LIVINGSTON, ROBERT R. (1746–1813) Statesman

LLOYD, HENRY DEMAREST (1847–1903) Writer

LOCKWOOD, BELVA ANN (1830–1917) Lawyer and women's rights advocate

LODGE, HENRY CABOT, JR. (1902–1985) Politician and diplomat

LOFLAND, JOHN (1798–1849) Poet

LOGAN (1725–1780) Mingo Indian chief

LOMBARDI, VINCE[NT THOMAS] (1913–1970) Football coach

LONDON, [JOHN GRIFFITH] JACK (1876–1916) Author

LONDON, MEYER (1871–1926) Socialist labor leader

LONG, EARL K[EMP] (1895–1960) Politician

LONG, HUEY P[IERCE] (1893–1935) Politician

LONGFELLOW, HENRY WADSWORTH (1807–1882) Poet

LONGWORTH, ALICE ROOSEVELT (1884–1980) Daughter of Theodore Roosevelt

Loos, Anita (1893–1981)   Writer

Lorimer, George Horace (1868–1937)   Editor

Loud, Pat[ricia Russell] (1926–   )   Author

Louis, Joe (1914–1981)   Boxer

Love, Edmund (1912–   )   Military historian

Lovecraft, H[oward] P[hillips] (1890–1937)   Writer

Lowell, Amy (1874–1925)   Poet

Lowell, James Russell (1819–1891)   Poet

Luce, Clare Boothe (1903–1987)   Writer, politician, and diplomat

Luciano, Charles "Lucky" (1897–1962)   Crime boss

Lundeen, Ernest (c.1880–1940)   Lawyer and politician

Lyon, Matthew (1750–1822)   Army officer and congressman

McAllister, [Samuel] Ward (1827–1895)   Lawyer

Macapagal, Diosdado (1910–   )   President of the Philippines

MacArthur, Douglas (1880–1964)   Army general

McAuliffe, Anthony [Clement] (1898–1975)   Army officer

McBride, Mary Margaret (1899–1976)   Journalist and radio broadcaster

McCabe, Charles (1899–1970)   Newspaper publisher

McCarthy, Eugene J[oseph] (1916–   )   Politician and author

McCarthy, Mary [Therese] (1912–   )   Author

McClellan, George B[rinton] (1826–1885)   Army officer

McCullers, Carson (1917–1967)   Author

McGinley, Phyllis (1905–1978)   Author

McGovern, George [Stanley] (1922–   )   Politician

McIver, Charles D[uncan] (1860–1906)   Educator

Mackay, Alexander (1808–1849)   Scottish journalist

Mackay, Charles (1814–1889)   British poet and journalist

McKechnie, Bill (1886–1965)   Baseball manager

McKinley, William (1843–1901)   President (1897–1901)

MacLaine, Shirley (1934–   )   Actress and author

McLaughlin, Mignon (1915?–   )   Writer and editor

McLaurin, A[nselm] J[oseph] (1848–1909)   Politician

MacLeish, Archibald (1892–1982)   Poet and dramatist

McMahon, [James O']Brien (1903–1952)   Lawyer and politician

McPhee, John [Angus] (1931–   )   Author

McPherson, Aimee Semple (1890–1944)   Evangelist

McReynolds, James Clark (1862–1946)   Associate Justice of Supreme Court

MacWhite, Michael (1883–?)   Irish diplomat

McWilliams, Carey (1905–1980)   Editor and author

Macy, John [Albert] (1877–1932)   Author and critic

Madison, James (1751–1836)   President (1809–1817)

Mailer, Norman (1923–   )   Author

Malcolm X [El-Hajj Malik El Shabazz] (1925–1965)   Black Muslim leader

Mann, Horace (1796–1859)   Educator

Mansfield, Katherine (1888–1923)   English writer

Mansfield, [Michael Joseph] Mike (1903–   )   Politician

Mao Tse-tung [or Zedong] (1893–1976)   Chinese leader

Marcy, William L[earned] (1786–1857)   Politician and lawyer

Marion, Frances (1886–1973)   Writer

Markham, [Charles] Edwin (1852–1940)   Poet

Marquand, J[ohn] P[hillips] (1893–1960)   Author

Marquis, Don[ald Robert Perry] (1878–1937)   Columnist and poet

Marryat, Frederick (1792–1848)   British naval officer and author

MARSH, GEORGE PERKINS (1801–1882) Lawyer, diplomat, and philologist

MARSHALL, [SARAH] CATHERINE (1914–   ) Writer

MARSHALL, GEORGE C[ATLETT] (1880–1959) Army general and statesman

MARSHALL, JOHN (1755–1835) Chief Justice of the Supreme Court

MARSHALL, PETER (1902–1949) Clergyman and author

MARSHALL, THOMAS RILEY (1854–1925) Vice president (1913–1921)

MARTIN, [JOHN LEONARD] PEPPER (1904–1965) Baseball player

MARTINEAU, HARRIET (1802–1876) English author

MARX, [JULIUS H.] GROUCHO (1890–1977) Comedian

MARYANNA, SISTER (1910–   ) Poet and writer

MASON, DONALD F[RANCIS] (1913–   ) Navy pilot

MASON, GEORGE (1725–1792) Revolutionary statesman

MASTERS, EDGAR LEE (1869–1950) Poet

MATHER, COTTON (1663–1728) Clergyman and author

MATHER, INCREASE (1639–1723) Clergyman and author

MATTHEWS, [JAMES] BRANDER (1852–1929) Educator and writer

MAUGHAM, W[ILLIAM] SOMERSET (1874–1965) English author

MAULDIN, [WILLIAM HENRY] BILL (1921–   ) Cartoonist

MAYHEW, JONATHAN (1720–1766) Clergyman

MAZO, EARL (1919–   ) Writer and journalist

MEAD, MARGARET (1901–1978) Anthropologist and author

MELLEN, J. GRENVILLE (1888–   ) Public official

MELVILLE, HERMAN (1819–1891) Novelist

MENCKEN, H[ENRY] L[OUIS] (1880–1956) Newspaperman and author

MENNINGER, KARL [AUGUSTUS] (1893–   ) Psychiatrist

MENOTTI, GIAN CARLO (1911–   ) Composer

MERRYMAN, MILDRED PLEW (1893–?) Poet

MEYER, AGNES [ELIZABETH ERNST] (1887–1970) Writer and translator

MICHENER, JAMES A[LBERT] (1907–   ) Novelist

MILBURN, JOHN G[EORGE] (1851–1930) Lawyer

MILLAY, EDNA ST. VINCENT (1892–1950) Poet

MILLER, ALICE DUER (1874–1942) Novelist

MILLER, HENRY (1891–1980) Novelist

MILLER, [CINCINNATUS HEINE] JOAQUIN (1841–1913) Poet

MILLER, MERLE (1919–1986) Journalist and author

MILLETT, [KATHERINE MURRAY] KATE (1934–   ) Feminist and author

MILLS, [DARIUS] OGDEN (1825–1910) Financier and philanthropist

MINOW, NEWTON (1926–   ) Lawyer and public official

MITCHEL, JOHN (1815–1875) Irish patriot and author

MITCHELL, DONALD GRANT (1822–1908) Writer

MITCHELL, MARGARET (1900–1949) Novelist

MITFORD, JESSICA (1917–   ) Author

MITFORD, NANCY (1904–1973) Author

MIZNER, WILSON (1876–1933) Playwright

MODERWELL, HIRAM K. (1888–   ) Author

MONROE, HARRIET (c.1861–1936) Poet and editor

MONROE, JAMES (1758–1831) President (1817–1825)

MONROE, MARILYN (1926–1962) Actress

MOODY, DWIGHT L[YMAN] (1837–1899) Evangelist and educator

MOODY, WILLIAM VAUGHN (1869–1910) Poet and playwright

MOON, WILLIAM LEAST HEAT (1939–   ) Author

MOORE, CLEMENT C[LARKE] (1779–1863) Teacher, scholar, and poet

MOORE, GRACE (1898–1947) Singer and actress

MOORE, MARIANNE [CRAIG] (1887–1972) Poet

MORE, PAUL ELMER (1864–1937) Essayist

MORGAN, HENRY (1915–   ) Radio and television performer

MORGAN, J[OHN] P[IERPONT] (1837–1913) Financier

MORGAN, ROBIN (1941–) Poet and editor

MORISON, SAMUEL ELIOT (1887–1976) Historian

MORLEY, CHRISTOPHER [DARLINGTON] (1890–1957) Author

MORRIS, GEORGE POPE (1802–1864) Poet and journalist

MORROW, DWIGHT W[HITNEY] (1873–1931) Lawyer, banker, and diplomat

MORSE, SAMUEL F[INLEY] B[REESE] (1791–1872) Inventor and artist

MORTON, OLIVER [HAZARD] P[ERRY] (1823–1877) Politician

MOSES, [ANNA MARY ROBERTSON] GRANDMA (1860–1961) Painter

MOSES, ROBERT (1888–1981) Public official

MOULTON, [ELLEN] LOUISE CHANDLER (1835–1908) Poet

MOWAT, ROBERT B[ALMAIN] (1883–1941) British historian

MOYNIHAN, DANIEL PATRICK (1927–) Politician and author

MUIR, JOHN (1838–1914) Naturalist

MULLIGAN, JAMES H[ILARY] (1844–1916) Lawyer and politician

MULLINS, EDGAR YOUNG (1860–1928) Theologian and author

MUNDELEIN, GEORGE WILLIAM CARDINAL (1872–1939) Roman Catholic prelate

MUNDT, KARL EARL (1900–1974) Politician

MURROW, EDWARD R[OSCOE] (1908–1965) News reporter and commentator

MUSSOLINI, BENITO (1883–1945) Italian Fascist premier

MYRDAL, [KARL] GUNNAR (1898–1987) Sociologist and economist

NADER, RALPH (1934–) Consumer advocate

NAMATH, [JOSEPH WILLIAM] JOE (1943–) Football player

NASH, OGDEN (1902–1971) Poet

NATHAN, GEORGE JEAN (1882–1958) Critic, author, and editor

NATHAN, ROBERT (1894–1985) Novelist

NATION, CARRY [AMELIA MOORE] (1846–1911) Temperance agitator

NEFF, PAT [MORRIS] (1871–1952) Public official and college president

NELSON, PAULA (1945–) Author

NEWTON, HUEY P[ERCY] (1942–) Political activist

NIEBUHR, REINHOLD (1892–1971) Theologian, teacher, and author

NIMITZ, CHESTER [WILLIAM] (1885–1966) Naval officer

NIN, ANAÏS (1903–1977) Author

NIXON, PAT[RICIA RYAN] (1912–) Wife of Richard M. Nixon

NIXON, RICHARD M[ILHOUS] (1913–) President (1969–1974)

NIZER, LOUIS (1902–) Lawyer and writer

NOCK, ALBERT JAY (1870–1945) Author and educator

NORRIS, [BENJAMIN] FRANK[LIN] (1870–1902) Novelist

NORRIS, KATHLEEN (1880–1966) Author

NORTON, CHARLES ELIOT (1827–1908) Author, editor, and educator

NORTON, ELEANOR HOLMES (1937–) Lawyer and civil rights activist

NORWORTH, JACK (1879–1959) Actor

NOVAK, ROBERT D[AVID] (1931–) Journalist

NYE, [EDGAR WILSON] BILL (1850–1896) Humorist

OCHS, ADOLPH S[IMON] (1858–1935) Newspaper publisher

O'CONNELL, WILLIAM CARDINAL (1859–1944) Roman Catholic prelate

O'CONNOR, [MARY] FLANNERY (1925–1964) Author

O'HARA, THEODORE (1820–1867) Confederate army officer and poet

OLMSTED, FREDERICK LAW (1822–1903) Landscape architect

OLNEY, RICHARD (1835–1917) Statesman

OLSEN, TILLIE (1912–) Author

ONASSIS, JACQUELINE [BOUVIER KENNEDY] (1929–) Editor

O'NEILL, EUGENE [GLADSTONE] (1888–1953) Playwright

OPPENHEIM, JAMES (1882–1932)   Poet and novelist

OPPENHEIMER, J[ULIUS] ROBERT (1904–1967)   Physicist

OSBORN, FAIRFIELD (1887–1969)   Naturalist and author

O'SULLIVAN, JOHN L[OUIS] (1813–1895)   Editor and diplomat

OTIS, JAMES (1725–1783)   Revolutionary statesman

OWENS, MARY (1808–1877)   Early sweetheart of Abraham Lincoln

PAGE, WILLIAM TYLER (1868–1942)   Clerk of the House of Representatives

PAIGE, [LEROY ROBERT] SATCHEL (1906–1982)   Baseball player

PAINE, ALBERT BIGELOW (1861–1937)   Author and editor

PAINE, THOMAS (1737–1809)   Revolutionary patriot, philosopher, and author

PALEY, GRACE (1922–   )   Author

PARKER, DOROTHY [ROTHSCHILD] (1893–1967)   Author

PARKER, JOHN (1729–1775)   Revolutionary patriot

PARKER, THEODORE (1810–1860)   Clergyman and abolitionist

PARKINSON, RICHARD (1748–1815)   English agricultural writer

PARKMAN, FRANCIS (1823–1893)   Historian

PARTON, JAMES (1822–1891)   Author

PASTERNAK, JOSEPH (1901–   )   Film producer

PATTON, GEORGE S[MITH] (1885–1945)   Army general

PAULDING, JAMES KIRKE (1778–1860)   Author

PAXTON, TOM (1937–   )   Songwriter and singer

PAYNE, JOHN HOWARD (1791–1852)   Actor and playwright

PEATTIE, DONALD CULROSS (1898–1964)   Botanist and author

PEGLER, [JAMES] WESTBROOK (1894–1969)   Journalist

PENN, WILLIAM (1644–1718)   English Quaker, founder of Pennsylvania

PEPPER, CLAUDE [DENSON] (1900–   )   Politician

PERELMAN, S[IDNEY] J[OSEPH] (1904–1979)   Author and humorist

PERKINS, FRANCES (1882–1965)   Public official

PERRIN, NOEL (1927–   )   Educator and author

PERRY, ELEANOR [BAYER] (1915?–1981)   Author and screenwriter

PERRY, GEORGE SESSIONS (1910–1956)   Author

PERRY, OLIVER HAZARD (1785–1819)   Naval officer

PERSHING, JOHN J[OSEPH] (1860–1948)   Army general

PETIGRU, JAMES LOUIS (1789–1863)   Lawyer and politician

PETRY, ANN [LANE] (1912–   )   Author

PHELPS, AUSTIN (1820–1890)   Clergyman and author

PHELPS, WILLIAM LYON (1865–1943)   Educator and literary critic

PHILLIPS, WENDELL (1811–1884)   Abolitionist and reformer

PIATT, DONN (1819–1891)   Journalist

PICKETT, GEORGE EDWARD (1825–1875)   Confederate general

PICKFORD, MARY (1893–1979)   Actress

PIERCE, OVID WILLIAMS (1910–   )   Writer and teacher

PINCKNEY, CHARLES (1757–1824)   Politician

PINKNEY, WILLIAM (1764–1822)   Lawyer and politician

PITKIN, WALTER BOUGHTON (1878–1953)   Writer

PITT, WILLIAM (1708–1788)   English statesman

PITT, WILLIAM, THE YOUNGER (1759–1806)   English statesman

PLATH, SYLVIA (1932–1963)   Poet

PLIMPTON, GEORGE (1927–   )   Author and editor

PLUNKITT, GEORGE WASHINGTON (1842–1924)   Tammany political leader

POE, EDGAR ALLAN (1809–1849)   Author

POLK, JAMES K[NOX] (1795–1849)   President (1845–1849)

POLLOCK, CHANNING (1880–1946)   Novelist and playwright

PORTER, COLE (1893–1964)   Composer and lyricist

PORTER, HORACE (1837–1921)   Army officer and diplomat

PORTER, SYLVIA (1913–   )   Newspaper columnist and author

POTTER, HENRY CODMAN (1835–1908)   Clergyman

POUND, EZRA [LOOMIS] (1885–1972)   Poet

POUND, ROSCOE (1870–1964)   Educator and author

PRENTICE, GEORGE DENNISON (1802–1870)   Journalist

PRENTISS, SEARGENT S[MITH] (1808–1850)   Lawyer and politician

PRESCOTT, WILLIAM (1726–1795)   Revolutionary soldier

PRESTON, KEITH (1884–1927)   Journalist and humorist

PRICE, M[ORGAN] PHILIPS (1885–1973)   Author

PRIEST, IVY BAKER (1905–1975)   Government official

PULITZER, JOSEPH (1847–1911)   Newspaper publisher

PYLE, ERNIE (1900–1945)   Journalist and war correspondent

QUAY, MATTHEW STANLEY (1833–1904)   Politician

QUINCY, JOSIAH (1744–1775)   Lawyer and political leader

QUINN, SALLY (1941–   )   Journalist

RAMEY, ESTELLE R. (1917–   )   Physiologist

RAND, AYN (1905–1982)   Author

RANDALL, JAMES RYDER (1839–1908)   Journalist and songwriter

RANDOLPH, JOHN (1773–1833)   Statesman and orator

RANKIN, JEANNETTE (1880–1973)   Member of Congress

RANSOM, JOHN CROWE (1888–1974)   Poet

RAPER, JOHN W. (1870–1950)   Newspaper columnist

RAVITCH, DIANE (1938–   )   Historian and author

RAYBURN, SAM[UEL TALIAFERRO] (1882–1961)   Lawyer and politician

READ, THOMAS BUCHANAN (1822–1872)   Poet and artist

REAGAN, NANCY [DAVIS] (1923–   )   Wife of Ronald Reagan

REAGAN, RONALD [WILSON] (1911–   )   President (1981–   )

REED, JOHN (1887–1920)   Writer and revolutionary

REED, THOMAS BRACKETT (1839–1902)   Lawyer and politician

REED, WILLIS (1942–   )   Basketball player and coach

REEDY, GEORGE (1917–   )   Author and educator

REESE, LIZETTE WOODWORTH (1856–1935)   Writer

REID, CHRISTIAN (1846–1920)   Writer

REILLY, KEVIN (1937–   )   Computer scientist

REPPLIER, AGNES (1855–1950)   Essayist

RESTON, JAMES (1909–   )   Journalist

REUTHER, WALTER [PHILIP] (1907–1970)   Labor leader

RHODES, CECIL [JOHN] (1853–1902)   British colonial administrator

RICE, GRANTLAND (1880–1954)   Journalist

RICH, ADRIENNE (1929–   )   Poet

RICKEY, [WESLEY] BRANCH (1881–1965)   Baseball executive

RIDGWAY, MATTHEW B[UNKER] (1895–   )   Army general

RIGGS, [ROBERT LARIMORE] BOBBY (1918–   )   Tennis player

RIIS, JACOB [AUGUST] (1849–1914)   Journalist and social reformer

RILEY, JAMES WHITCOMB (1849–1916)   Poet

RINEHART, MARY ROBERTS (1876–1916)   Novelist

RIVERS, JOAN (1937–   )   Comedian

ROBINSON, EDWIN ARLINGTON (1869–1935)   Poet

ROBINSON, JOHN (c.1576–1625)   English clergyman

ROBINSON, JOSEPH T[AYLOR] (1872–1937)   Lawyer and politician

ROCKEFELLER, JOHN D[AVISON] (1839–1937)   Industrialist

ROCKEFELLER, NELSON A[LDRICH] (1908–1979)   Politician

ROCKNE, KNUTE (1888–1931) Football player and coach

ROE, ANNE (1904–) Psychologist and teacher

ROEBLING, JOHN A[UGUSTUS] (1806–1869) Civil engineer

ROEBLING, WASHINGTON A[UGUSTUS] (1837–1926) Civil engineer

ROGERS, WILL[IAM PENN ADAIR] (1879–1935) Humorist and writer

ROLLIN, BETTY (1936–) Television journalist and author

ROOSEVELT, [ANNA] ELEANOR (1884–1962) Lecturer and writer, wife of Franklin D. Roosevelt

ROOSEVELT, FRANKLIN DELANO (1882–1945) President (1933–1945)

ROOSEVELT, THEODORE (1858–1919) President (1901–1909)

ROOT, ELIHU (1845–1937) Lawyer and statesman

ROOT, GEORGE FREDERICK (1820–1895) Composer and teacher

ROSEN, AL[BERT LEONARD] (1924–) Baseball player

ROSS, HAROLD [WALLACE] (1892–1951) Editor

ROSSI, ALICE S[CHAERR] (1922–) Sociologist and educator

ROSSNER, JUDITH (1935–) Novelist

ROSTOW, WALT W[HITMAN] (1916–) Economist and educator

ROURKE, CONSTANCE M. (1885–1941) Author

ROVERE, RICHARD (1915–1979) Writer and editor

ROWAN, CARL T[HOMAS] (1925–) Journalist

ROWLAND, HELEN (1876–?) Author

ROYAL, DARRELL K. (1924–) Football coach and university official

RUBIN, JERRY (1938–) Antiwar activist and writer

RUBINSTEIN, HELENA (1871?–1965) Business executive

RUNYON, [ALFRED] DAMON (1884–1946) Columnist and writer

RUSH, BENJAMIN (c.1745–1813) Physician and political leader

RUSKIN, JOHN (1819–1900) English art critic and author

RUSSELL, ANNA (1911–) Comedian

RUSSELL, BERTRAND (1872–1970) English philosopher and mathematician

SABIN, FLORENCE (1871–1953) Anatomist and teacher

SAGAN, CARL [EDWARD] (1934–) Astronomer and author

ST. JOHNS, ADELA ROGERS (1894–) Journalist and screenwriter

SALA, GEORGE AUGUSTUS (1828–1895) Writer and foreign correspondent

SANDBURG, CARL (1878–1967) Poet and biographer

SANFORD, EDWARD TERRY (1865–1930) Associate Justice of the Supreme Court

SANKEY, IRA DAVID (1840–1908) Evangelist and hymn writer

SANTAYANA, GEORGE (1863–1952) Philosopher and poet

SANTOS, ROBERT (1934–) Business executive

SARMIENTO, DOMINGO FAUSTINO (1811–1888) Argentine political leader

SASSOON, SIEGFRIED (1886–1967) English author

SAUNDERS, FREDERICK (1807–1902) Librarian and author

SAVAS, EMANUEL (1931–) Management educator and author

SAXE, JOHN GODFREY (1816–1887) Poet and editor

SCHELLING, FELIX EMANUEL (1858–1945) Educator and author

SCHLAFLY, PHYLLIS (1924–) Author and antifeminist leader

SCHLESINGER, ARTHUR M., JR. (1917–) Historian

SCHMIDT, BENNO C., JR. (1942–) Lawyer and university president

SCHULBERG, BUDD (1914–) Novelist

SCHULZ, CHARLES M[ONROE] (1922–) Cartoonist

SCHURZ, CARL (1829–1906) Army officer and statesman

SCOLLARD, CLINTON (1860–1932) Poet

SCOTT, EVELYN (1893–1963) Novelist and poet

SCOTT, HAZEL (1920–) Jazz pianist and singer

SCOTT, WINFIELD (1786–1866)   Army general

SCOTT-MAXWELL, FLORIDA [PIER] (1883–?) Psychologist and author

SEARS, EDMUND HAMILTON (1810–1876)   Clergyman and author

SEDGWICK, ELLERY (1872–1960)   Editor

SEEGER, ALAN (1888–1916)   Poet

SEGAL, ERICH (1937–   )   Teacher and writer

SELDES, GILBERT [VIVIAN] (1893–   )   Journalist and critic

SEWARD, WILLIAM H[ENRY] (1801–1872) Statesman

SEYMOUR, CHARLES (1912–1977)   Art historian

SHAW, GEORGE BERNARD (1856–1950)   Irish playwright

SHEEHY, GAIL (1937–   )   Author

SHEPARD, ODELL (1884–1967)   Author

SHEPHERD, JEAN (1929–   )   Author

SHERIDAN, PHILIP H[ENRY] (1831–1888) Army general

SHERMAN, JOHN (1823–1900)   Member of Congress and statesman

SHERMAN, WILLIAM T[ECUMSEH] (1820–1891) Army officer

SHIELDS, REN (1868–1913)   Songwriter

SHULTZ, GEORGE P[RATT] (1920–   )   Cabinet official

SILL, EDWARD ROWLAND (1841–1887)   Poet and essayist

SILLS, BEVERLY (1929–   )   Opera singer and administrator

SILVERMAN, SIME (1873–1933)   Journalist

SINCLAIR, UPTON [BEALL] (1878–1968)   Novelist

SINGER, ISAAC BASHEVIS (1904–   )   Author

SIPLE, PAUL (1908–1968)   Explorer, geographer, and author

SIRICA, JOHN J[OSEPH] (1904–   )   Jurist

SITTING BULL (c.1813–1890)   Sioux leader

SKINNER, CORNELIA OTIS (1901–1979)   Actress and author

SMITH, ADAM (1930–   )   Writer, real name George Goodman

SMITH, ALFRED E[MANUEL] (1873–1944)   Politician

SMITH, BETTY (1896–1972)   Novelist

SMITH, GERRIT (1797–1874)   Politician and reformer

SMITH, HAZEL BRANNON (1914?–   )   Newspaper owner and editor

SMITH, JOSEPH (1805–1844)   Founder of the Mormon Church

SMITH, LANGDON (1858–1908)   War correspondent

SMITH, LILLIAN (1897–1966)   Author

SMITH, LIZ (1923–   )   Newspaper columnist

SMITH, LOGAN PEARSALL (1865–1946)   Essayist

SMITH, SAMUEL FRANCIS (1808–1895)   Clergyman and poet

SMITH, SYDNEY (1771–1845)   English clergyman, essayist

SOULE, JOHN L.B. (1815–1891)   Newspaperman

SOUTHEY, ROBERT (1774–1843)   English poet

SPENCER, HERBERT (1820–1903)   English philosopher

SPOCK, BENJAMIN (1903–   )   Physician and author

SPOFFORD, HARRIET PRESCOTT (1835–1921) Novelist and poet

SPOLIN, VIOLA (1911–   )   Theatrical producer and director

STACY, WALTER PARKER (1884–1951)   Jurist

STAFFORD, WENDELL PHILLIPS (1861–1953) Jurist and poet

STALLINGS, LAURENCE (1894–1968)   Novelist and playwright

STANFORD, SALLY (1903–1982)   Madam, politician, and author

STANTON, CHARLES E. (1859–1933)   Army officer

STANTON, EDWIN M[CMASTERS] (1814–1869) Secretary of war

STANTON, ELIZABETH CADY (1815–1902) Women's rights leader

STANWYCK, BARBARA (1907–   )   Actress

STARK, FREYA (1893–   )   English writer and photographer

STARK, JOHN (1728–1822)   Revolutionary officer

STEDMAN, EDMUND CLARENCE (1833–1908) Poet and anthologist

STEFFENS, [JOSEPH] LINCOLN (1866–1936) Journalist

STEIN, GERTRUDE (1874–1936)   Writer

STEINBECK, JOHN [ERNST] (1902–1968)   Novelist

STEINBERG, SAUL (1914–   )   Painter and cartoonist

STEINEM, GLORIA (1934–) Editor, writer, and feminist

STEINER, GEORGE (1929–) Author and educator

STENGEL, [CHARLES DILLON] CASEY (1890–1975) Baseball player and manager

STEPHENS, ALEXANDER HAMILTON (1812–1883) Confederate vice president (1861–1865)

STERLING, ANDREW B. (1874–?) Songwriter

STEUBEN, FRIEDRICH WILHELM VON (1730–1794) Prussian army officer

STEVENS, THADDEUS (1792–1868) Politician

STEVENS, WALLACE (1879–1955) Poet

STEVENSON, ADLAI E[WING] (1900–1965) Politician and statesman

STEWART, POTTER (1915–1985) Associate Justice of Supreme Court

STIMSON, HENRY L[EWIS] (1867–1950) Statesman

STODDARD, RICHARD HENRY (1825–1903) Poet and critic

STOLBERG, BENJAMIN (1891–1951) Author and journalist

STORY, JOSEPH (1779–1845) Associate Justice of Supreme Court

STOWE, HARRIET BEECHER (1811–1896) Writer and abolitionist

STRAUS, OSCAR SOLOMON (1850–1926) Lawyer and diplomat

STREISAND, BARBRA (1942–) Singer

STRICKLAND, WILLIAM (c.1787–1854) Engraver, architect, and engineer

STRONG, GEORGE A[UGUSTUS] (1832–1912) Author

STRUNK, WILLIAM, JR. (1869–1946) Teacher and editor

STRUNSKY, SIMEON (1879–1948) Editor and essayist

STUART, GILBERT [CHARLES] (1755–1828) Portrait painter

SUGDEN, JOE (1870–1959) Baseball player

SULLIVAN, [ANNE MANSFIELD] ANNIE (1866–1936) Teacher of Helen Keller

SULLIVAN, LOUIS HENRI (1856–1924) Architect

SULZBERGER, ARTHUR HAYS (1891–1968) Newspaper publisher

SUMNER, CHARLES (1811–1874) Public official and orator

SUMNER, WILLIAM GRAHAM (1840–1910) Economist and sociologist

SUNDAY, [WILLIAM ASHLEY] BILLY (1862–1935) Evangelist

SUTTON, HORACE (1919–) Editor and writer

SWANSON, GLORIA (1899–1983) Actress

SZILARD, LEO (1898–1964) Physicist

TAFT, ROBERT A[LPHONSO] (1889–1953) Politician

TAFT, WILLIAM HOWARD (1857–1930) President (1909–1913)

TALMADGE, CONSTANCE (1900–1973) Actress

TANEY, ROGER BROOKE (1777–1864) Chief Justice of Supreme Court

TARKENTON, FRAN[CIS ASBURY] (1940–) Football player and sportscaster

TARKINGTON, [NEWTON] BOOTH (1869–1946) Author

TAYLOR, BAYARD (1825–1878) Author

TAYLOR, BERT LESTON (1866–1921) Journalist

TAYLOR, EDWARD THOMPSON (1793–1871) Clergyman

TAYLOR, MAXWELL D[AVENPORT] (1901–1987) Army general and diplomat

TAYLOR, TOM (1817–1880) English dramatist and editor

TAYLOR, ZACHARY (1784–1850) President (1849–1850)

TEASDALE, SARA (1884–1933) Poet

TELLER, EDWARD (1908–) Physicist

TENNYSON, ALFRED (1809–1892) English poet

THACKERAY, WILLIAM MAKEPEACE (1811–1863) English novelist

THAYER, ERNEST LAWRENCE (1863–1940) Author of "Casey at the Bat"

THEROUX, PAUL (1941–) Author

THOMAS, DYLAN (1914–1953) British poet

THOMAS, FRANKLIN (1878–1954) Sociologist and teacher

THOMAS, NORMAN [MATTOON] (1884–1968) Socialist politician

THOMPSON, DOROTHY (1894–1961) Writer

THOMPSON, HUNTER S[TOCKTON] (1939–) Author and journalist

THOREAU, HENRY DAVID (1817–1862) Naturalist and writer

THURBER, JAMES [GROVER] (1894–1961) Writer and artist

THUROW, LESTER C[ARL] (1938–) Economist and educator

TIBBETS, PAUL W. (1915–) Pilot of the *Enola Gay* mission to Hiroshima

TIMROD, HENRY (1828–1867) Poet

TOBIAS, ANDREW (1947–) Author

TOCQUEVILLE, ALEXIS DE (1805–1859) French writer

TOFFLER, ALVIN (1928–) Author

TOMLIN, LILY (1939–) Actress

TOYNBEE, ARNOLD (1889–1975) English historian

TRACY, SPENCER (1900–1967) Actor

TRILLIN, CALVIN (1935–) Writer

TROLLOPE, ANTHONY (1815–1882) English novelist

TROLLOPE, FRANCES [MILTON] (1780–1863) Novelist

TROTSKY, LEON (1879–1940) Russian Communist leader

TROWBRIDGE, JOHN TOWNSEND (1827–1916) Writer

TRUMAN, BESS [WALLACE] (1885–1982) Wife of Harry S Truman

TRUMAN, HARRY S (1884–1972) President (1945–1953)

TRUMAN, MARTHA ELLEN (1853–1947) Mother of Harry S Truman

TUBMAN, HARRIET (c.1820–1913) Abolitionist

TUCHMAN, BARBARA W[ERTHEIM] (1912–) Historian

TUCKER, BENJAMIN R[ICKETSON] (1854–1939) Author and educator

TUCKER, SOPHIE [ABRUZA] (1884–1966) Entertainer

TUGWELL, REXFORD GUY (1891–) Economist and public official

TURNER, FREDERICK JACKSON (1861–1932) Historian

TWAIN, MARK (1835–1910) Author, real name Samuel Langhorne Clemens

TWEED, WILLIAM MARCY (1823–1878) Tammany politician

TYLER, JOHN, JR. (1819–1896) Confederate leader, son of Pres. John Tyler

UDALL, STEWARD L[EE] (1920–) Public official

UNDERWOOD, OSCAR W[ILDER] (1862–1929) Lawyer and politician

UPDIKE, JOHN [HOYER] (1932–) Author

VAIL, ALFRED (1807–1859) Pioneer in telegraphy

VAN BUREN, ABIGAIL (1918–) Columnist

VAN BUREN, MARTIN (1782–1862) President (1837–1841)

VANDERBILT, AMY (1908–1974) Author on etiquette

VANDERBILT, CORNELIUS (1794–1877) Financier and railroad magnate

VANDERBILT, WILLIAM HENRY (1821–1885) Railroad magnate

VANDERBILT, WILLIAM K[ISSAN] (1849–1920) Railroad magnate

VANDERLIP, FRANK (1864–1937) Bank president

VANDIVER, WILLARD D[UNCAN] (1854–1932) Politician and educator

VAN DOREN, MARK (1894–1972) Author and critic

VAN DYKE, HENRY (1852–1933) Clergyman and author

VAN HORNE, HARRIET (1920–) Columnist

VAN LOON, HENDRIK WILLEM (1882–1944) Writer and historian

VANZETTI, BARTOLOMEO (1888–1927) Anarchist

VEBLEN, THORSTEIN [BUNDE] (1857–1929) Social scientist and author

VEECK, [WILLIAM LOUIS] BILL (1914–1986) Baseball executive

VIDAL, GORE (1925–) Author

VIGUERIE, RICHARD A. (1933–) Political activist and author

VIORST, JUDITH [STAHL] (1931–) Author

VON BRAUN, WERNHER (1912–1977) Rocket engineer

VONNEGUT, KURT (1922–) Author

WALKER, [JAMES JOHN] JIMMY (1881–1946) Mayor of New York City

WALKER, STANLEY (1898–1962) Journalist

WALLACE, GEORGE [CORLEY] (1919–) Politician

WALLACE, HENRY A[GARD] (1888–1965) Agriculturist and politician

WALLACE, LEW[IS] (1827–1905) Army officer and novelist

WALLACE, WILLIAM ROSS (1819–1881) Poet

WALPOLE, HORACE (1717–1797) English author

WALTERS, BARBARA (1931–   ) Television interviewer and reporter

WARD, ARTEMUS (1834–1867) Humorist, real name Charles Farrar Browne

WARD, EDWARD (1667–1731) English poet and satirist

WARD, NATHANIEL (c.1578–1652) Clergyman and author

WARE, EUGENE [FITCH] (1841–1911) Lawyer and poet

WARNER, ANNA BARTLETT (1827–1915) Writer

WARNER, CHARLES DUDLEY (1829–1900) Editor and writer

WARNER, JACK (1892–1978) Film producer

WARREN, EARL (1891–1971) Chief Justice of Supreme Court

WASHBURNE, ELIHU BENJAMIN (1816–1887) Lawyer and politician

WASHINGTON, BOOKER T[ALIAFERRO] (1856–1915) Educator

WASHINGTON, GEORGE (1732–1799) President (1789–1797)

WATT, JAMES [GAIUS] (1938–   ) Lawyer and public official

WAYNE, ANTHONY (1745–1796) Revolutionary officer

WAYNE, JOHN (1907–1979) Actor

WEBB, WALTER PRESCOTT (1888–1963) Author and educator

WEBSTER, DANIEL (1782–1852) Lawyer and statesman

WEBSTER, NOAH (1758–1843) Lexicographer and author

WEEMS, MASON LOCKE (1759–1825) Clergyman and author

WEINBERGER, CASPAR (1917–   ) Public official

WELLES, [GEORGE] ORSON (1915–1985) Film director and actor

WELLS, CAROLYN (1869–1942) Writer and humorist

WELLS, H[ERBERT] G[EORGE] (1866–1946) English author

WELLS, ROLLIN J[OHN] (1848–1923) Poet

WELTY, EUDORA (1909–   ) Author

WENDELL, BARRETT (1855–1921) Educator and author

WESLEY, JOHN (1703–1791) English clergyman and founder of Methodism

WEST, JESSAMYN (1902–1984) Novelist and screenwriter

WEST, MAE (1893–1980) Actress

WESTCOTT, EDWARD NOYES (1848–1898) Banker and novelist

WESTMORELAND, WILLIAM C[HILDS] (1914–   ) Army general

WHALEN, GROVER A. (1886–1962) New York City police commissioner

WHARTON, EDITH [NEWBOLD JONES] (1862–1937) Novelist

WHIPPLE, EDWIN PERCY (1819–1886) Author and lecturer

WHISTLER, JAMES ABBOTT McNEILL (1834–1903) Artist

WHITE, E[LWYN] B[ROOKS] (1899–1985) Author and essayist

WHITE, THEODORE H[AROLD] (1915–1986) Journalist and author

WHITE, WILLIAM ALLEN (1868–1944) Newspaper editor and author

WHITE, WILLIAM LINDSAY (1900–1973) Newspaper editor and author

WHITMAN, WALT[ER] (1819–1892) Poet

WHITNEY, WILLIAM DWIGHT (1827–1894) Teacher and philologist

WHITTIER, JOHN GREENLEAF (1807–1892) Poet

WICKER, [THOMAS GREY] TOM (1926–   ) Journalist and author

WIDDEMER, MARGARET (1893?–1978) Author

WIENER, NORBERT (1894–1964) Mathematician

WIGFALL, LOUIS T[RESEVANT] (1816–1874) Confederate leader

WIGGLESWORTH, MICHAEL (1631–1705) Clergyman and poet

WILCOX, ELLA WHEELER (1850–1919) Journalist and poet

WILDE, OSCAR (1854–1900) Irish poet and dramatist

WILDER, THORNTON [NIVEN] (1897–1975) Novelist and playwright

WILEY, GEORGE A. (1931–1973) Educator and civil rights leader

WILL, GEORGE F. (1941–   ) Political columnist

WILLARD, FRANCES (1839–1898) Educator and temperance leader

WILLIAMS, CHARLES D[AVID] (1860–1923) Protestant Episcopal bishop of Michigan

WILLIAMS, JOHN ALEXANDER (1938–   ) College professor and author

WILLIAMS, ROGER (c.1603–1683) Founder of Rhode Island

WILLIAMS, SAMUEL [WELLS] (1812–1884) Missionary and scholar

WILLIS, NATHANIEL PARKER (1806–1867) Editor and writer

WILLKIE, WENDELL L[EWIS] (1892–1944) Lawyer and business executive

WILLSON, MEREDITH (1902–   ) Composer and lyricist

WILSON, CHARLES ERWIN (1890–1961) Industrialist and public official

WILSON, EDMUND (1895–1972) Author and critic

WILSON, FLIP (1933–   ) Comedian

WILSON, HARRY LEON (1867–1939) Author

WILSON, HENRY (1812–1875) Politician

WILSON, JOSEPH (1779–1857) Carver

WILSON, [THOMAS] WOODROW (1856–1924) President (1913–1921)

WINTHROP, JOHN (1587–1649) First governor of Massachusetts Bay Colony

WISE, JOHN (1652–1725) Clergyman

WISE, STEPHEN [SAMUEL] (1874–1949) Jewish clergyman

WISTER, OWEN (1860–1938) Novelist

WITHERSPOON, JOHN (1723–1794) Clergyman and college president

WOLFE, JAMES (1727–1759) British army officer

WOLFE, THOMAS [CLAYTON] (1900–1938) Novelist

WOLFE, TOM (1931–   ) Author

WOOLLCOTT, ALEXANDER (1887–1943) Journalist and author

WOOLMAN, JOHN (1720–1772) Clergyman and abolitionist

WORK, HENRY CLAY (1832–1884) Songwriter

WORTHINGTON, ROBIN (1932–   ) Writer

WOUK, HERMAN (1915–   ) Novelist

WRIGHT, ANNA (1890–1968) Writer and teacher

WRIGHT, FRANK LLOYD (1869–1959) Architect

WRIGHT, [JAMES CLAUD] JIM [JR.] (1922–   ) Politician

WRIGHT, ORVILLE (1871–1948) Pioneer aviator

WRIGHT, RICHARD (1908–1960) Author

WRIGHT, WILBUR (1867–1912) Pioneer aviator

WYLIE, ELINOR [MORTON] (1885–1928) Poet

WYLIE, PHILIP [GORDON] (1902–1971) Author

WYNN, EARLY (1920–   ) Baseball pitcher

YANKWICH, LÉON R[ENÉ] (1888–1975) Journalist and author

YELLEN, JACK (1892–   ) Songwriter

YOUNG, ANDREW [JACKSON, JR.] (1932–   ) Politician and diplomat

YOUNG, BRIGHAM (1801–1877) Mormon leader

YOUNG, WHITNEY M[OORE], JR. (1921–1971) Educator and civil rights leader

YOUNGMAN, HENNY (1905–   ) Comedian

ZANGWILL, ISRAEL (1864–1926) English playwright and novelist

American Quotations

1. ACTION

1 In this country . . . men seem to live for action as long as they can and sink into apathy when they retire.

> CHARLES FRANCIS ADAMS, diary entry, April 15, 1836.

2 Never do today what you can do as well tomorrow.

> ATTRIBUTED TO AARON BURR, in James Parton, *The Life and Times of Aaron Burr,* 1857.

3 Why should we be cowed by the name of Action? . . . To think is to act.

> RALPH WALDO EMERSON, "Spiritual Laws," *Essays,* First Series, 1841.

4 Act, if you like,—but you do it at your peril. Men's actions are too strong for them. Show me a man who has acted and who has not been the victim and slave of his action.

> RALPH WALDO EMERSON, "Goethe," *Representative Men,* 1850.

5 Well done is better than well said.

> BENJAMIN FRANKLIN, *Poor Richard's Almanack,* 1737.

6 I find the great thing in this world is not so much where we stand, as in what direction we are moving: To reach the port of heaven, we must sail sometimes with the wind and sometimes against it—but we must sail, and not drift, nor lie at anchor.

> OLIVER WENDELL HOLMES, SR., *The Autocrat of the Breakfast-Table,* 1858.

7 As life is action and passion, it is required of a man that he should share the passion and action of his time, at peril of being judged not to have lived.

> OLIVER WENDELL HOLMES, JR., Memorial Day address, 1884.

8 Concern should drive us into action and not into a depression.

> KAREN HORNEY, *Self-Analysis,* 1942.

9 It is not book learning young men need, nor instruction about this and that, but a stiffening of the vertebrae which will cause them to be loyal to a trust to act promptly, concentrate their energies, do a thing—"carry a message to Garcia."

> ELBERT HUBBARD, *A Message to Garcia,* first printed in *The Philistine* magazine, March, 1900. (The message to Gen. Calixto Garcia y Inigues, commander of Cuban forces fighting the Spanish during the Spanish-American War, was carried by Lt. Andrew S. Rowan of the Bureau of Military Intelligence and delivered on May 1, 1898.)

10 Having thus chosen our course, without guile and with pure purpose, let us renew our trust in God, and go forward without fear and with manly hearts.

> ABRAHAM LINCOLN, in a message to Congress, July 4, 1861.

11 Only the insider can make the decisions, not because he is inherently a better man, but because

he is so placed that he can understand and can act.

> WALTER LIPPMANN, "Insiders and Outsiders," the *New Republic* magazine, November 13, 1915.

12 Trust no Future, howe'er pleasant.
Let the dead Past bury its dead!
Act,—act in the living Present!
Heart within, and God o'erhead!

> HENRY WADSWORTH LONGFELLOW, "A Psalm of Life," 1839.

13 Do not delay:
Do not delay; the golden moments fly!

> HENRY WADSWORTH LONGFELLOW, *The Masque of Pandora,* 1875.

14 Every man feels instinctly that all the beautiful sentiments in the world weigh less than a single lovely action.

> JAMES RUSSELL LOWELL, "Rousseau and the Sentimentalists," *Among My Books,* 1870 (first published in the *North American Review,* July, 1867).

15 Risk! Risk anything! Care no more for the opinion of others, for those voices. Do the hardest thing on earth for you. Act for yourself. Face the truth.

> KATHERINE MANSFIELD, *Journal,* October 14, 1922.

16 What the Puritans gave the world was not thought, but action.

> WENDELL PHILLIPS, in a speech entitled "The Pilgrims," December 21, 1855.

17 The country needs and, unless I mistake its temper, the country demands bold, persistent experimentation. It is common sense to take a method and try it; if it fails, admit it frankly and try another. But above all, try something.

> FRANKLIN D. ROOSEVELT, in an address at Oglethorpe University, Atlanta, Georgia, May 22, 1932.

18 It behooves every man to remember that the work of the critic . . . is of altogether secondary importance, and that, in the end, progress is accomplished by the man who does . . . things.

> THEODORE ROOSEVELT, quoted in *The Forum* magazine, 1894.

19 I wish to preach, not the doctrine of ignoble ease, but the doctrine of the strenuous life.

> THEODORE ROOSEVELT, in a speech in Chicago, April 10, 1899.

20 Rhetoric is a poor substitute for action, and we have trusted only to rhetoric. If we are really to be a great nation, we must not merely talk; we must act big.

> THEODORE ROOSEVELT, quoted in the *Metropolitan,* September, 1917.

21 Get action. Seize the moment. Man was never intended to become an oyster.

> THEODORE ROOSEVELT, speaking to his children, quoted in David McCullough, *Mornings on Horseback,* 1981.

22 We know what a person thinks not when he tells us what he thinks, but by his actions.

> ISAAC BASHEVIS SINGER, quoted in the *New York Times Magazine,* November 26, 1978.

23 Caution is the confidential agent of selfishness.

> WOODROW WILSON, in a speech at Chicago, Illinois, February 12, 1909.

2. ADMIRATION

See also AFFECTION

1 Admiration, *n.* Our polite recognition of another's resemblance to ourselves.

> AMBROSE BIERCE, *The Devil's Dictionary,* 1906.

2 The less a man thinks or knows about his virtues, the better we like him.

> RALPH WALDO EMERSON, "Spiritual Laws," *Essays,* First Series, 1841.

3 Each man is a hero and an oracle to somebody, and to that person whatever he says has an enhanced value.

> RALPH WALDO EMERSON, "Quotation and Originality," *Letters and Social Aims,* 1876.

4 Admiration is the Daughter of Ignorance.

> BENJAMIN FRANKLIN, *Poor Richard's Almanack,* 1736.

5 There is much difference between imitating a good man, and counterfeiting him.

> BENJAMIN FRANKLIN, *Poor Richard's Almanack,* 1738.

6 The capacity to admire others is not my most fully developed trait.

> HENRY KISSINGER, *The White House Years,* 1979.

---

3. ADVERSITY

See also AFFLICTION; PAIN; SORROW; TROUBLE

---

1 The best way out of a difficulty is through it.

> Anonymous.

2 Strengthen me by sympathizing with my strength, not my weakness.

> A. BRONSON ALCOTT, "Sympathy," *Table Talk,* 1877.

3 Difficulty, my brethren, is the nurse of greatness—a harsh nurse, who roughly rocks her foster-children into strength and athletic proportion.

> WILLIAM CULLEN BRYANT, in a speech welcoming Louis Kossuth, December 15, 1851.

4 They seemed
Like old companions in adversity.

> WILLIAM CULLEN BRYANT, "A Winter Piece," 1821.

5 Bad times have a scientific value. These are occasions a good learner would not miss.

> RALPH WALDO EMERSON, "Considerations by the Way," *The Conduct of Life,* 1860.

6 Strong men greet war, tempest, hard times. They wish, as Pindar said, "to tread the floors of hell, with necessities as hard as iron."

> RALPH WALDO EMERSON, "The Progress of Culture," *Letters and Social Aims,* 1876.

7 Oh, fear not in a world like this,
And thou shalt know erelong,
Know how sublime a thing it is
To suffer and be strong.

> HENRY WADSWORTH LONGFELLOW, "The Light of Stars," in the *Knickerbocker* magazine, January, 1839.

8 And the night shall be filled with music,
And the cares, that infest the day,
Shall fold their tents, like the Arabs,
And as silently steal away.

> HENRY WADSWORTH LONGFELLOW, "The Day Is Done," 1845.

9 The nearer the dawn the darker the night.

> HENRY WADSWORTH LONGFELLOW, *Tales of a Wayside Inn,* 1863.

10 Let us be of good cheer, however, remembering that the misfortunes hardest to bear are those which never come.

> JAMES RUSSELL LOWELL, "Democracy," an address delivered in Birmingham, England, October 6, 1884, published in *Democracy and Other Addresses,* 1886.

11 When a man is finally boxed and he has no choice, he begins to decorate his box.

> JOHN STEINBECK, *Sweet Thursday,* 1954.

12 Laugh and the world laughs with you,
Weep and you weep alone;
For the sad old earth must borrow its mirth,
But has trouble enough of its own.

> ELLA WHEELER WILCOX, "Solitude," published in the *New York Sun,* February 25, 1883.

---

4. ADVICE

See also WISDOM

---

1 Good night, sleep tight,
Don't let the bedbugs bite.

> Anonymous.

2 Do others or they will do you.

> Popular saying (also given as "Do unto others before they do unto you").

3 Molasses catches more flies than vinegar.

> Popular saying.

4 Don't take any wooden nickels.

> Ibid.

5 Be good. And if you can't be good, be careful.

> Ibid.

6 If you can't be good, be sanitary.

> Attributed to American soldiers in France during World War I.

7 Vain man! Mind your own business! Do no wrong! Do all the good you can! Eat your canvas-back ducks! Drink your Burgundy! Sleep your siesta, when necessary, and trust in God.

> JOHN ADAMS, in a letter to Thomas Jefferson, March 14, 1820.

8 When women are the advisers, the lords of creation don't take the advice till they have persuaded themselves that it is just what they intended to do; then they act upon it, and if it succeeds, they give the weaker vessel half the credit of it; if it fails, they generously give her the whole.

> LOUISA MAY ALCOTT, *Little Women,* 1868.

9 Never play cards with any man named "Doc." Never eat at any place called "Mom's." And never, never, no matter what else you do in your whole life, *never* sleep with anyone whose troubles are worse than your own.

> NELSON ALGREN, quoted in H.E.F. Donahue, *Conversations with Nelson Algren,* 1964.

10 Advice, *n.* The smallest current coin.

> AMBROSE BIERCE, *The Devil's Dictionary,* 1906.

11 I leave this rule for others when I'm dead, Be always sure you're right—then go ahead.

> DAVY CROCKETT, *Autobiography,* 1834.

12 My father advised me that life itself was a crap game: it was one of the two lessons I learned as a child. The other was that overturning a rock was apt to reveal a rattlesnake. As lessons go those two seem to hold up, but not to apply.

> JOAN DIDION, *Play It As It Lays,* 1970.

13 Trust thyself: every heart vibrates to that iron string.

> RALPH WALDO EMERSON, "Self-Reliance," *Essays,* First Series, 1841.

14 Trust men, and they will be true to you; treat them greatly, and they will show themselves great.

> RALPH WALDO EMERSON, "On Prudence," *Essays,* First Series, 1841.

15 Go put your creed into the deed, Nor speak with double tongue.

> RALPH WALDO EMERSON, "Ode," sung in the Town Hall, Concord, Massachusetts, July 4, 1857.

16 Write it on your heart that every day is the best day in the year. No man has learned anything rightly, until he knows that every day is Doomsday.

> RALPH WALDO EMERSON, "Works and Days," *Society and Solitude,* 1870.

17 Never give a sucker an even break.

> W.C. FIELDS, a favorite saying, which he used in the film *Poppy,* 1932. (This line was also used by Edward Albee, the theater manager and grandfather of the playwright.)

18 Among the most disheartening and dangerous of . . . advisors, you will often find those closest to you, your dearest friends, members of your own family, perhaps, loving, anxious, and knowing nothing whatever.

> MINNIE MADDERN FISKE, in a letter to Alexander Woollcott, 1908, quoted in Alexander Woollcott, *Mrs. Fiske,* 1917.

19 Beware of the young Doctor & the old Barber.

> BENJAMIN FRANKLIN, *Poor Richard's Almanack,* 1733.

20 Keep your mouth wet, feet dry.

> Ibid.

21 Teach your child to hold his tongue, he'll learn fast enough to speak.

> BENJAMIN FRANKLIN, *Poor Richard's Almanack,* 1734.

22 Eat to please thyself, but dress to please others.

> BENJAMIN FRANKLIN, *Poor Richard's Almanack,* 1738.

23 If you would keep your Secret from an enemy, tell it not to a friend.

> BENJAMIN FRANKLIN, *Poor Richard's Almanack,* 1741.

24 Let thy discontents be thy Secrets;—if the world knows them 'twill despise *thee* and increase *them.*

> Ibid.

25 Up, Sluggard, and waste not life; in the grave will be sleeping enough.

> Ibid.

26 There's a time to wink as well as to see.

> BENJAMIN FRANKLIN, *Poor Richard's Almanack,* 1747.

27 Be civil to *all;* sociable to *many;* familiar with few; Friend to *one;* Enemy to *none.*

> BENJAMIN FRANKLIN, *Poor Richard's Almanack,* 1756.

28 Work as if you were to live 100 years,
Pray as if you were to die To-morrow.

> BENJAMIN FRANKLIN, *Poor Richard's Almanack,* 1757.

29 Dally not with other Folks Women or Money.

> Ibid.

30 Fools need Advice most, but wise Men only are the better for it.

> BENJAMIN FRANKLIN, *Poor Richard's Almanack,* 1758.

31 Early to Bed, and early to rise,
Makes a Man healthy, wealthy, and wise.

> Ibid.

32 Be studious in your profession, and you will be learned. Be industrious and frugal, and you will be rich. Be sober and temperate, and you will be healthy. Be in general virtuous, and you will be happy. At least, you will, by such conduct, stand the best chance for such consequences.

> BENJAMIN FRANKLIN, in a letter to John Alleyn, August 9, 1768.

33 Use no hurtful deceit; think innocently and justly and, if you speak, speak accordingly.

> BENJAMIN FRANKLIN, *Autobiography,* 1788.

34 Beware of over-great pleasure in being popular or even beloved.

> MARGARET FULLER, in a letter to her brother Arthur, December 20, 1840, quoted in Alice Rossi, *The Feminist Papers,* 1973.

35 Don't hurry, don't worry. You're only here for a short visit. So be sure to stop and smell the flowers.

> WALTER HAGEN, professional golfer, quoted in the *New York Times,* May 22, 1977.

36 A good scare is worth more to a man than good advice.

> EDGAR WATSON HOWE, *Country Town Sayings,* 1911.

37 Take care that you never spell a word wrong. Always before you write a word, consider how it is spelled, and, if you do not remember it, turn to a dictionary. It produces great praise to a lady to spell well.

> THOMAS JEFFERSON, in a letter to his daughter, Martha Jefferson, November 28, 1783.

38 Do not bite at the bait of pleasure, till you know there is no hook beneath it. The art of life is the art of avoiding pain; and he is the best pilot, who steers clearest of the rocks and shoals with which it is beset. . . . Leave the bustle and tumult of society to those who have not talents to occupy themselves without them. Friendship is but another name for an alliance with the follies and the misfortunes of others. Our own share of miseries is sufficient: why enter then as volunteers into those of another?

> THOMAS JEFFERSON, in a letter to Mrs. Maria Cosway, who stole Jefferson's heart while he was in Paris, October 12, 1786.

39 Be a listener only, keep within yourself, and endeavor to establish with yourself the habit of silence, especially on politics. In the fevered state of our country, no good can ever result from any attempt to set one of these fiery zealots to rights, either in fact or principle. They are determined as to the facts they will believe, and the opinions on which they will act. Get by them, therefore, as you would by an angry bull; it is not for a man of sense to dispute the road with such an animal.

> THOMAS JEFFERSON, in a letter to his grandson, Thomas Jefferson Randolph, November 24, 1808.

40 *A Decalogue of Canons for observation in practical life*
　1. Never put off till tomorrow what you can do today.
　2. Never trouble another for what you can do yourself.
　3. Never spend your money before you have it.
　4. Never buy what you do not want, because it is cheap; it will be dear to you.
　5. Pride costs us more than hunger, thirst, and cold.
　6. We never repent of having eaten too little.
　7. Nothing is troublesome that we do willingly.
　8. How much pain have cost us the evils which have never happened.
　9. Take things always by their smooth handle.
　10. When angry, count ten, before you speak; if very angry, an hundred.

> THOMAS JEFFERSON, in a letter to Thomas Jefferson Smith, February 21, 1825. (Jefferson's first canon by the Earl of Chesterfield in a letter in 1749. Benjamin Franklin also included the advice in *Poor Richard's Almanack*.)

41 Cheer up, the worst is yet to come.

> PHILANDER CHASE JOHNSON, "Shooting Stars," in *Everybody's Magazine*, May, 1920.

42 Don't throw a monkey-wrench into the machinery.

> Ibid.

43 Forgive your enemies, but never forget their names.

> Attributed to John F. Kennedy.

44 We must combine the toughness of the serpent and the softness of the dove, a tough mind and a tender heart.

> MARTIN LUTHER KING, JR., *Strength to Love*, 1963.

45 Quarrel not at all. No man resolved to make the most of himself can spare time for personal contention. Still less can he afford to take all the consequences, including the vitiating of his temper and loss of self control. Yield larger things to which you can show no more than equal right; and yield lesser ones, though clearly your own. Better give your path to a dog than be bitten by him in contesting for the right. Even killing the dog would not cure the bite.

> ABRAHAM LINCOLN, in a letter to J.M. Cutts, October 26, 1863.

46 When you have got an elephant by the hind leg, and he is trying to run away, it's best to let him run.

> ABRAHAM LINCOLN, speaking to Charles Anderson Dana during the last day of Lincoln's life, April 14, 1865.

47 Never let your inferiors do you a favor. It will be extremely costly.

> H.L. MENCKEN, "Sententiae," *The Vintage Mencken*, 1955.

48 Keep your eyes open and your mouth shut.

> JOHN STEINBECK, *Sweet Thursday*, 1954.

49 We should be careful and discriminating in all the advice we give. We should be especially careful in giving advice that we would not think of following ourselves. Most of all, we ought to avoid giving counsel which we don't follow when it damages those who take us at our word.

> ADLAI E. STEVENSON, in a lecture at the University of Texas, September 28, 1955.

50 Aim above morality. Be not simply good; be good for something.

> HENRY DAVID THOREAU, *Walden*, 1854.

51 I have lived some thirty years on this planet, and I have yet to hear the first syllable of valuable or even earnest advice from my seniors.

> Ibid.

52 Early to rise and early to bed makes a male healthy and wealthy and dead.

> James Thurber, "The Shrike and the Chipmunks," *Fables for Our Time,* 1940.

53 Keep 35 pounds of air in the tires and have it greased once in a while and have the oil changed every thousand miles.

> Harry S Truman, in a letter to his mother and sister, written from the White House, October 13, 1945, quoted in Robert H. Ferrell, *Off the Record,* 1980.

54 Study men, not historians.

> Harry S Truman, quoted in Robert H. Ferrell, *Off the Record,* 1980.

55 Now, Harry, you behave yourself.

> Attributed to Martha Ellen Truman, a customary farewell to her oldest son.

56 Put all your eggs in one basket—and watch that basket.

> Mark Twain, "Pudd'nhead Wilson's Calendar," *Pudd'nhead Wilson,* 1894.

57 He had only one vanity: he thought he could give advice better than any other person.

> Mark Twain, "The Man That Corrupted Hadleyburg," 1900.

58 Always do right—this will gratify some and astonish the rest.

> Mark Twain, a message to the Young People's Society, Greenpoint Presbyterian Church, Brooklyn, N.Y., February 16, 1901. (This was a favorite quote of Harry S Truman's; Truman had it framed and kept behind his desk in the Oval Office.)

59 People who fight fire with fire usually end up with ashes.

> Abigail Van Buren, in her newspaper column "Dear Abby," March 7, 1974.

60 Associate yourself with men of good quality if you esteem your own reputation; for 'tis better to be alone than in bad company.

> George Washington, "Rules of Civility," 1747, collected in Charles Moore, *George Washington's Rules of Civility and Decent Behavior in Company and Conversation,* 1926.

61 One cool judgment is worth a thousand hasty counsels. The thing to do is to supply light and not heat.

> Woodrow Wilson, in a speech in Pittsburgh, Pennsylvania, January 29, 1916.

62 I would have you a man of sense as well as sensibility. You will find goodness and truth everywhere you go. If you have to choose, choose truth. For that is closest to Earth. Keep close to Earth, my boy: in that lies strength. Simplicity of heart is just as necessary to an architect as for a farmer or a minister if the architect is going to build great buildings.

> Ann Wright, to her son Frank Lloyd Wright, in Frank Lloyd Wright, *An Autobiography,* 1932, revised 1943.

---

5. AFFECTION

See also Friends; Love

---

1 They love him most for the enemies that he has made.

> Gen. Edward S. Bragg, nominating speech for Grover Cleveland at the Democratic National Convention, July, 1884.

2 Th' affection iv th' American people is always aimed thrue an' is invaryably fatal.

> Finley Peter Dunne, *Mr. Dooley's Philosophy,* 1900.

3 What is so pleasant as these jets of affection which make a young world for me again? . . . The moment we indulge our affections, the earth is metamorphosed; there is no winter and no night; all tragedies, all ennuis, vanish,—all duties even.

> Ralph Waldo Emerson, "Friendship," *Essays,* First Series, 1841.

4 The effect of the indulgence of this human affection is a certain cordial exhilaration.

> Ibid.

5 Talk not of wasted affection, affection never
     was wasted;

If it enrich not the heart of another, its
    waters, returning
Back to their springs, like the rain, shall fill
    them full of refreshment;
That which the fountain sends forth returns
    again to the fountain.

> HENRY WADSWORTH LONGFELLOW, *Evangeline*,
> 1847.

---

6. AFFLICTION

See also ADVERSITY; PAIN; SORROW;
TROUBLE

---

1 The delicate and infirm go for sympathy, not to
the well and buoyant, but to those who have suffered like themselves.

> CATHERINE ESTHER BEECHER, "Statistics of
> Female Health," *Woman Suffrage and Women's
> Professions,* 1871.

2 No man ever stated his griefs as lightly as he
might. Allow for exaggeration in the most patient
and sorely ridden hack that ever was driven.

> RALPH WALDO EMERSON, "Spiritual Laws,"
> *Essays,* First Series, 1841.

3 The chamber of flame in which the martyr passes
is more magnificent than the royal apartment from
which majesty looks out on his sufferings.

> RALPH WALDO EMERSON, entry written in 1861,
> *Journals,* 1909–1914.

4 Some maladies are rich and precious and only to
be acquired by the right of inheritance or purchased
with gold.

> NATHANIEL HAWTHORNE, *Mosses from an Old
> Manse,* 1846.

5 There are a good many real miseries in life that
we cannot help smiling at, but they are the smiles
that make wrinkles and not dimples.

> OLIVER WENDELL HOLMES, SR., *The Poet at the
> Breakfast-Table,* 1872.

6 We could never learn to be brave and patient, if
there were only joy in the world.

> HELEN KELLER, quoted in the *Atlantic Monthly,*
> May, 1890.

7 [The Devil] impregnates the air with such malig-
nant salts as, meeting with the salt of our microcosm, shall immediately cast us into that fermenta-
tion and putrefaction which will utterly dissolve all
the vital ties within us.

> COTTON MATHER, *The Wonders of the Invisible
> World,* 1692.

8 If misery loves company, misery has company
enough.

> HENRY DAVID THOREAU, entry dated September
> 1, 1851, in his *Journal,* 1906.

9 Adam and Eve had many advantages, but the
principal one was that they escaped teething.

> MARK TWAIN, "Puddn'head Wilson's Calendar,"
> *Puddn'head Wilson,* 1894.

---

7. AGE

See also YOUTH

---

1 Pull out a gray hair and seven will come to its
funeral.

> Pennsylvania Dutch saying.

2 Don't trust anyone over 30.

> Popular slogan of the 1960s, quoted in Jerry
> Rubin, *Growing (Up) at 37,* 1976.

3 Even in America, the Indian summer of life
should be a little sunny and a little sad, like the
season, and infinite in wealth and depth of tone—
but never hustled.

> HENRY ADAMS, *The Education of Henry Adams,*
> 1907.

4 It is easy to believe that life is long and one's gifts
are vast—easy at the beginning, that is. But
the limits of life grow more evident; it becomes

clear that great work can be done rarely, if at all.

ALFRED ADLER, in the *New Yorker* magazine, February 19, 1972.

5 The surest sign of age is loneliness.

A. BRONSON ALCOTT, *Tablets,* 1868.

6 A man is not old until regrets take the place of dreams.

JOHN BARRYMORE, quoted in Gene Fowler, *Good Night, Sweet Prince,* 1943.

7 To me, old age is always fifteen years older than I am.

BERNARD BARUCH, quoted in the *New York Times,* June 6, 1984.

8 A man in old age is like a sword in a shop window.

HENRY WARD BEECHER, *Life Thoughts,* 1858.

9 I had lost something in youth and made money instead.

STEPHEN VINCENT BENÉT, *James Shore's Daughter,* 1934.

10 The stones and trees, insensible to time,
    Nor age nor wrinkle on their front are seen;
    If Winter come, and greenness then do fade,
    A Spring returns, and they more youthful
        made;
    But man grows old, lies down, remains
        where once he's laid.

ANNE BRADSTREET, *Contemplations,* 1650.

11 Perhaps one has to be very old before one learns how to be amused rather than shocked.

PEARL S. BUCK, *China, Past and Present,* 1972.

12 Come, Captain Age,
    With your great sea-chest full of treasure!
    Under the yellow and wrinkled tarpaulin
    Disclose the carved ivory
    And the sandalwood inlaid with pearl
    Riches of wisdom and years.

SARAH N. CLEGHORN, "Come, Captain Age," *Three Score,* 1936.

13 At twenty a man is full of fight and hope. He wants to reform the world. When he's seventy he still wants to reform the world, but he knows he can't.

CLARENCE DARROW, in an interview, April 18, 1936.

14 In all the world there are no people so piteous and forlorn as those who are forced to eat the bitter bread of dependency in their old age, and find how steep are the stairs of another man's house.

DOROTHY DIX, *Dorothy Dix, Her Book,* 1926.

15 It may be, old age is gentle and fair . . .
    Still I shall tremble at a gray hair.

DOROTHY DOW, "Unbeliever," *Time and Love,* 1942.

16 Many a man that cudden't direct ye to th' drug store on th' corner whin he was thirty will get a respectful hearin' whin age has further impaired his mind.

FINLEY PETER DUNNE, "Old Age," quoted in the *New York Times,* June 8, 1984.

17 I am long on ideas, but short on time. I expect to live to be only about a hundred.

THOMAS ALVA EDISON, quoted in the *Golden Book* magazine, April, 1931.

18 I grow old . . . I grow old . . .
    I shall wear the bottoms of my trousers
        rolled.

T.S. ELIOT, "The Love Song of J. Alfred Prufrock," 1915.

19 Here I am, an old man in a dry month,
    Being read to by a boy, waiting for rain.

T.S. ELIOT, "Gerontion," 1920.

20 Sad spectacle that a man should live and be fed that he may fill a paragraph every year in the newspapers for his wonderful age, as we record the weight and girth of the Big Ox or Mammoth Girl. We do not count a man's years until he has nothing else to count.

RALPH WALDO EMERSON, entry written in 1840, *Journals,* 1909–1914.

21 The man and woman of seventy assume to know all, they have outlived their hope, they renounce aspiration, accept the actual for the necessary, and talk down to the young.

> RALPH WALDO EMERSON, "Circles," *Essays*, First Series, 1841.

22 Nature abhors the old, and old age seems the only disease; all others run into this one.

> Ibid.

23 Spring still makes Spring in the mind,
> When sixty years are told;
Love wakes anew this throbbing heart,
> And we are never old.

> RALPH WALDO EMERSON, "The World-Soul," 1847.

24 In youth, we clothe ourselves with rainbows, and go as brave as the zodiac. In age, we put out another sort of perspiration—gout, fever, rheumatism, caprice, doubt, fretting, avarice.

> RALPH WALDO EMERSON, "Fate," *The Conduct of Life*, 1860.

25 It is time to be old,
> To take in sail.

> RALPH WALDO EMERSON, "Terminus," 1867.

26 The port, well worth the cruise, is near,
> And every wave is charmed.

> Ibid.

27 Nature is full of freaks, and now puts an old head on young shoulders, and then a young heart beating under fourscore winters.

> RALPH WALDO EMERSON,, "Old Age," *Society and Solitude*, 1870.

28 Youth is everywhere in place. Age, like woman, requires fit surroundings.

> Ibid.

29 At 20 years of age the Will reigns; at 30 the Wit; at 40 the Judgment.

> BENJAMIN FRANKLIN, *Poor Richard's Almanack*, 1741.

30 All would live long, but none would be old.

> BENJAMIN FRANKLIN, *Poor Richard's Almanack*, 1749.

31 Old Boys have their Playthings as well as young Ones; the Difference is only in the Price.

> BENJAMIN FRANKLIN, *Poor Richard's Almanack*, 1752.

32 Call him not old whose visionary brain
Holds o'er the past its undivided reign.
For him in vain the envious seasons roll
Who bears eternal summer in his soul.

> OLIVER WENDELL HOLMES, SR., "The Old Player," 1855.

33 A person is always startled when he hears himself seriously called an old man for the first time.

> OLIVER WENDELL HOLMES, SR., *The Autocrat of the Breakfast-Table*, 1858.

34 A man over ninety is a great comfort to all his elderly neighbors: he is a picket-guard at the extreme outpost; and the young folks of sixty and seventy feel that the enemy must get by him before he can come near their camp.

> OLIVER WENDELL HOLMES, SR., *The Guardian Angel*, 1867.

35 I am as old as Egypt to myself.

> OLIVER WENDELL HOLMES, SR., "Wind-Clouds and Star-Drifts," *The Poet at the Breakfast-Table*, 1872.

36 Don't you stay at home of evenings?
> Don't you love a cushioned seat
In a corner, by the fireside, with your slippers
> on your feet?
Don't you wear warm fleecy flannels?
> Don't you muffle up your throat?
Don't you like to have one help you when
> you're putting on your coat?

> OLIVER WENDELL HOLMES, SR., "The Archbishop and Gil Blas," 1879.

37 To be seventy years young is sometimes far more cheerful and hopeful than to be forty years old.

> OLIVER WENDELL HOLMES, SR., in a letter to Julia Ward Howe on her seventieth birthday, May 27, 1889.

38 I used to think that the main-spring was broken by 80, although my father kept on writing. I hope I was wrong for I am keeping on in the same way. I like it and want to produce as long as I can.

> OLIVER WENDELL HOLMES, JR., in a letter to Sir Frederick Pollock, c.1925, quoted in Catherine Drinker Bowen, *Yankee from Olympus*, 1944.

39 The riders in a race do not stop short when they reach the goal. There is a little finishing canter before coming to a standstill. There is time to hear the kind voice of friends and to say to one's self: "The work is done."

> OLIVER WENDELL HOLMES, JR., in a radio broadcast celebrating his 90th birthday, March 8, 1931.

40 As you become older, gradually accustom yourself to neglect.

> EDGAR WATSON HOWE, *Sinner Sermons*, 1926.

41 After a man passes sixty, his mischief is mainly in his head.

> Ibid.

42 Whenever a man's friends begin to compliment him about looking young, he may be sure that they think he is growing old.

> WASHINGTON IRVING, "Bachelors," *Bracebridge Hall*, 1822.

43 The same space of time seems shorter as we grow older . . . in youth we may have an absolutely new experience, subjective or objective, every hour of the day. Apprehension is vivid, retentiveness strong, and our recollections of that time, like those of a time spent in rapid and interesting travel, are of something intricate, multitudinous, and long-drawn out. But as each passing year converts some of this experience into automatic routine which we hardly note at all, the days and the week smooth themselves out in recollection to contentless units, and the years grow hollow and collapse.

> WILLIAM JAMES, *The Principles of Psychology*, 1890.

44 Tranquility is the old man's milk. I go to enjoy it in a few days, and to exchange the roar and tumult of bulls and bears for the prattle of my grandchildren and senile rest.

> THOMAS JEFFERSON, in a letter to Edward Rutledge, June 24, 1797.

45 Good wishes are all an old man has to offer to his country or friends.

> THOMAS JEFFERSON, in a letter to Thomas Law, January 15, 1811.

46 Of all the faculties of the human mind that of memory is the first which suffers decay from age.

> THOMAS JEFFERSON, in a letter to Benjamin H. Latrobe, July 12, 1812.

47 I see no comfort in outliving one's friends, and remaining a mere monument of the times which are past.

> THOMAS JEFFERSON, in a letter to Charles Pinckney, September 3, 1816.

48 Tranquility is the *summum bonum* of old age.

> THOMAS JEFFERSON, in a letter to Mark L. Hill, April 5, 1820.

49 Why can't we build orphanages next to homes for the elderly? If someone's sitting in a rocker, it won't be long before a kid will be in his lap.

> CLORIS LEACHMAN, quoted in *Good Housekeeping* magazine, October, 1973.

50 I stay a little longer, as one stays
To cover up the embers that still burn.

> HENRY WADSWORTH LONGFELLOW, "Three Friends of Mine," in *A Book of Sonnets*, 1874.

51 The course of my long life hath reached at
        last,
In fragile bark o'er a tempestuous sea,
The common harbor, where must rendered
        be
Account of all the actions of the past.

> HENRY WADSWORTH LONGFELLOW, "Old Age," from "Seven Sonnets and a Canzone," 1874.

52 It is too late! Ah, nothing is too late
Till the tired heart shall cease to palpi-
        tate. . . .
Chaucer, at Woodstock with the nightingales,
At sixty wrote the Canterbury Tales;

Goethe at Weimar, toiling to the last,
Completed Faust when eighty years were
    past.
These are indeed exceptions; but they show
How far the gulf-stream of our youth may
    flow
Into the arctic regions of our lives.

    HENRY WADSWORTH LONGFELLOW, "Morituri
    Salutamus," *The Masque of Pandora,* 1875.

53 Whatever poet, orator, or sage
May say of it, old age is still old age.

    Ibid.

54 Age is opportunity no less
Than youth itself, though in another dress,
And as the evening twilight fades away
The sky is filled with stars, invisible by day.

    Ibid.

55 To be seventy years old is like climbing the
Alps. You reach a snow-crowned summit, and see
behind you the deep valley stretching miles and
miles away, and before you other summits higher
and whiter, which you may have strength to climb,
or may not. Then you sit down and meditate and
wonder which it will be.

    HENRY WADSWORTH LONGFELLOW, in a letter to
    George W. Childs, March 13, 1877.

56 As life runs on, the road grows strange
    With faces new,—and near the end
The milestones into headstones change,
    'Neath every one a friend.

    JAMES RUSSELL LOWELL, "Sixty-Eighth
    Birthday," 1887.

57 I promise to keep on living as though I expected
to live forever. Nobody grows old by merely living
a number of years. People grow old only by desert-
ing their ideals. Years may wrinkle the skin, but to
give up interest wrinkles the soul.

    DOUGLAS MACARTHUR, quoted in the *New York
    Times,* June 8, 1984.

58 Of middle age the best that can be said is that
a middle-aged person has likely learned how to have
a little fun in spite of his troubles.

    DON MARQUIS, *The Almost Perfect State,* 1927.

59 The older I grow the more I distrust the familiar doctrine that age brings wisdom.

    H.L. MENCKEN, *Prejudices,* Third Series, 1922.

60 Middle age is when you've met so many people
that every new person you meet reminds you of
someone else.

    OGDEN NASH, *Versus,* 1949.

61 I have a bone to pick with Fate,
Come here and tell me, girlie,
Do you think my mind is maturing late,
Or simply rotted early?

    OGDEN NASH, "Lines on Facing Forty," in *Good
    Intentions,* 1937.

62 How old would you be if you didn't know how
old you was?

    SATCHEL PAIGE, quoted in the *New York Times,*
    June 8, 1984.

63 At sixty, labor ought to be over, at least from
direct necessity. It is painful to see old age working
itself to death, in what are called civilized countries, for its daily bread.

    THOMAS PAINE, *The Rights of Man,* 1791–1792.

64 The young man who has not wept is a savage,
and the old man who will not laugh is a fool.

    GEORGE SANTAYANA, *Dialogues in Limbo,* 1925.

65 Old places and old persons in their turn, when
spirit dwells in them, have an intrinsic vitality of
which youth is incapable; precisely the balance and
wisdom that comes from long perspectives and
broad foundations.

    GEORGE SANTAYANA, *My Host the World,* 1953.

66 Never have I enjoyed youth so thoroughly as I
have in my old age. . . . Nothing is inherently and
invincibly young except spirit. And spirit can enter
a human being perhaps better in the quiet of old age
and dwell there more undisturbed than in the turmoil of adventure.

    Ibid.

67 I'm growing fonder of my staff;
    I'm growing dimmer in the eyes;
    I'm growing fainter in my laugh;

I'm growing deeper in my sighs;
I'm growing careless of my dress;
I'm growing frugal of my gold;
I'm growing wise; I'm growing—yes,—
I'm growing old.

JOHN GODFREY SAXE, "I'm Growing Old."

68 Age puzzles me. I thought it was a quiet time. My seventies were interesting and fairly serene, but my eighties are passionate. I grow more intense as I age.

FLORIDA SCOTT-MAXWELL, *The Measure of My Days,* 1972.

69 There are compensations for growing older. One is the realization that to be sporting isn't at all necessary. It is a great relief to reach this stage of wisdom.

CORNELIA OTIS SKINNER, *Dithers and Jitters,* 1937.

70 We grow with years more fragile in body, but morally stouter, and we can throw off the chill of a bad conscience almost at once.

LOGAN PEARSALL SMITH, *Afterthoughts,* 1931.

71 In youth, everything seems possible; but we reach a point in the middle years when we realize that we are never going to reach all the shining goals we had set for ourselves. And in the end, most of us reconcile ourselves, with what grace we can, to living with our ulcers and arthritis, our sense of partial failure, our less-than-ideal families—and even our politicians!

ADLAI E. STEVENSON, *Call to Greatness,* 1954.

72 The youth gets together his materials to build a bridge to the moon, or, perchance, a palace or temple on the earth, and, at length, the middle-aged man concludes to build a woodshed with them.

HENRY DAVID THOREAU, entry dated July 14, 1852, *Journal,* 1906.

73 How earthy old people become—mouldy as the grave! Their wisdom smacks of the earth. There is no foretaste of immortality in it. They remind me of earthworms and mole crickets.

HENRY DAVID THOREAU, entry dated August 16, 1853, *Journal,* 1906.

74 If within the old man there is not a young man,
—within the sophisticated, one unsophisticated,
—then he is but one of the devil's angels.

HENRY DAVID THOREAU, entry dated October 26, 1853, *Journal,* 1906.

75 A little more tired at close of day,
A little less anxious to have our way;
A little less ready to scold and blame;
A little more care of a brother's name;
And so we are nearing the journey's end,
Where time and eternity meet and blend.

ROLLIN J. WELLS, "Growing Old."

76 There's no such thing as old age, there is only sorrow.

EDITH WHARTON, "A First Word," *A Backward Glance,* 1934.

77 Old age, calm, expanded, broad with the haughty breadth of the universe,
Old age, flowing free with the delicious near-by freedom of death.

WALT WHITMAN, "Song of the Open Road," 1856.

78 Good in all, . . .
The grandeur and exquisiteness of old age,
In the superb vistas of death.

WALT WHITMAN, "Song at Sunset," 1860.

79 I see in you the estuary that enlarges and spreads itself grandly as it pours in the great sea.

WALT WHITMAN, "To Old Age," 1860.

80 Women sit or move to and fro, some young.
The young are beautiful—but the old are more beautiful than the young.

WALT WHITMAN, "Beautiful Women," 1860.

81 Youth, large, lusty, loving—youth full of grace, force, fascination.
Do you know that Old Age may come after you with equal grace, force, fascination?

WALT WHITMAN, "Youth, Day, Old Age and Night," 1881.

82 O Time and Change!—with hair as gray
As was my sire's that winter day,
How strange it seems, with so much gone
Of life and love, to still live on!

JOHN GREENLEAF WHITTIER, "Snow-Bound,"
1866.

---

8. AGRICULTURE

---

1 The American farmer is entitled not only to tariff schedules on his products but to protection from substitutes therefor.

Plank in the Republican National Platform, 1932.

2 Precious soil, . . . by what singular custom of law is it that thou wast made to constitute the riches of the freeholder? What should we American farmers be without the distinct possession of that soil? It feeds, it clothes us, from it we draw even a great exuberancy, our best meat, our richest drink, the very honey of our bees comes from this privileged spot. No wonder we should thus cherish its possession, no wonder that so many Europeans . . . cross the Atlantic to realise that happiness.

MICHEL GUILLAUME JEAN DE CRÈVECOEUR,
Letters from an American Farmer, 1782.

3 The glory of the farmer is that, in the division of labors, it is his part to create. All trade rests at last on his primitive activity.

RALPH WALDO EMERSON, "Farming," *Society and Solitude,* 1870.

4 The first farmer was the first man, and all historic nobility rests on possession and use of land.

Ibid.

5 Drop a grain of California gold into the ground, and there it will lie unchanged until the end of time; . . . drop a grain of our blessed gold [wheat] into the ground and lo! a mystery.

EDWARD EVERETT, in a speech on agriculture given in Boston, October, 1855.

6 There seem to be but three ways for a nation to acquire wealth. The first is by war, as the Romans did, in plundering their conquered neighbors. This is robbery. The second by commerce, which is generally cheating. The third by agriculture, the only honest way, wherein man receives a real increase of the seed thrown into the ground, in a kind of continual miracle, wrought by the hand of God in his favor, as a reward for his innocent life and his virtuous industry.

BENJAMIN FRANKLIN, "Positions to be Examined Concerning National Wealth," April 4, 1769.

7 There is no gilding of setting sun or glamor of poetry to light up the ferocious and endless toil of the farmers' wives.

HAMLIN GARLAND, "Melons and Early Frost,"
Boy Life on the Prairie, 1899.

8 [Romanticizing 19th-century rural life] is a delusion, the mere gilding of a hard task, a halo around a dull and laborious life by the passage of time. Ah, well: there is no harm done in looking back wistfully at this distance—it is safe enough. It is a phase of life passed away. The "check-rowing-automatic-corn-planter and coverer" has taken the place of the girls and boys with aprons and hoes.

HAMLIN GARLAND, "Between Hay an' Grass,"
Boy Life on the Prairie, 1899.

9 Those who labor in the earth are the chosen people of God, if He ever had a chosen people, whose breasts He has made His peculiar deposit for substantial and genuine virtue. It is the focus in which He keeps alive that sacred fire, which otherwise might escape from the face of the earth.

THOMAS JEFFERSON, *Notes on the State of Virginia,* 1784.

10 Whenever there are in any country uncultivated lands and unemployed poor, it is clear that the laws of property have been so far extended as to violate natural right. The earth is given as a common stock for man to labor and live on. . . . The small landowners are the most precious part of a state.

THOMAS JEFFERSON, letter to James Madison,
October 28, 1785.

11 Were we directed from Washington when to sow, and when to reap, we should soon want bread.

THOMAS JEFFERSON, note written in 1821.

12 Bowed by the weight of centuries he leans
Upon his hoe and gazes on the ground,
The emptiness of ages in his face,
And on his back the burden of the world.

> EDWIN MARKHAM, "The Man With the Hoe,"
> 1899.

13 No one hates his job so heartily as a farmer.

> H.L. MENCKEN, "What is Going on in the
> World," the *American Mercury,* November,
> 1933.

14 A farm is an irregular patch of nettles, bounded by short-term notes, containing a fool and his wife who didn't know enough to stay in the city.

> S.J. PERELMAN, *Acres and Pains,* 1947.

15 The common fate of part-time farmers is to be sneered at. Real farmers regard us with the amused tolerance a racing driver might feel for a small child pedaling down the sidewalk, making motor noises in his throat. . . . Visitors from the city . . . see us as people on whom the country is wasted. All those golden afternoons! We *could* be fishing. We could be rambling over the hills with binoculars and bird book, or lying under an apple tree reading, or getting a tan down on the dock.

> NOEL PERRIN, *Second Person Rural,* 1980.

16 The farmer is endeavoring to solve the problem of a livelihood by a formula more complicated than the problem itself. To get his shoestrings he speculates in herds of cattle.

> HENRY DAVID THOREAU, *Walden,* 1854.

17 Mr. Beecher's farm is not a triumph. It would be easier if he worked it on shares with some one; but he cannot find any body who is willing to stand half the expense, and not many that are able. Still, persistence in any cause is bound to succeed. He was a very inferior farmer when he first began, but a prolonged and unflinching assault upon his agricultural difficulties has had its effect at last, and he is now fast rising from affluence to poverty.

> MARK TWAIN, "Rev. Henry Ward Beecher's
> Farm," 1885. (Twain had written of Beecher and
> his farm in a piece entitled "Rev. H.W. Beecher,"
> which ran in the *Buffalo Express* on September
> 25, 1869.)

18 Blessed be agriculture! if one does not have too much of it.

> CHARLES DUDLEY WARNER, *My Summer in a
> Garden,* 1870.

19 I know of no pursuit in which more real and important services can be rendered to any country than by improving its agriculture, its breed of useful animals, and other branches of a husbandman's cares.

> GEORGE WASHINGTON, letter to John Sinclair,
> July 20, 1794.

20 When *tillage* begins, other arts follow. The farmers, therefore, are the founders of human civilization.

> DANIEL WEBSTER, in a speech entitled "Remarks
> on the Agriculture of England," delivered at the
> Boston State House, January 13, 1840.

21 Anything can happen at a county agricultural fair. It is the perfect human occasion, the harvest of the fields and of the emotions. To the fair come the man and his cow, the boy and his girl, the wife and her green tomato pickle, each anticipating victory and the excitement of being separated from his money by familiar devices. It is at a fair that man can be drunk forever on liquor, love, or fights; at a fair that your front pocket can be picked by a trotting horse looking for sugar, and your hind pocket by a thief looking for his fortune.

> E.B. WHITE, "Fall," *One Man's Meat,* 1944.

22 Heap high the farmer's wintry hoard!
   Heap high the golden corn!
No richer gift has Autumn poured
   From out her lavish horn!

> JOHN GREENLEAF WHITTIER, "The Corn-Song,"
> in the poem "The Huskers," *Songs of Labor,*
> 1850.

23 Give fools their gold, and knaves their
      power;
   Let fortune's bubbles rise and fall;
Who sows a field, or trains a flower,
   Or plants a tree, is more than all.

> JOHN GREENLEAF WHITTIER, "A Song of
> Harvest," 1858.

9. ALABAMA

1 Audemus jura nostra defendere. (We dare defend our rights.)

> State motto.

2 Alabama . . . seems to have a bad name even among those who reside in it.

> J.S. Buckingham, in *The Slave States of America*, 1839, quoted in Peter Yapp, *The Traveller's Dictionary of Quotation*, 1983.

3 They [the black conjure women] say that on the memories of the oldest slaves their fathers knew there was one indelible imprint of an awful event—a shower of stars over Alabama. Many an Alabamian to this day reckons dates from "the year the stars fell"—though he and his neighbor frequently disagree as to what year of our Lord may be so designated. All are sure, however, that once upon a time stars fell on Alabama, changing the land's destiny.

> Carl Carmer, *Stars Fell on Alabama*, 1934.

4 Some day I hope an American painter will do justice to the loveliness of the masterpieces of the backwoods architects of Alabama.

> Ibid.

5 Birmingham is not like the rest of the state. It is an industrial monster sprung up in the midst of a slow-moving pastoral. It does not belong. . . . Birmingham is a new city in an old land.

> Ibid.

6 Mobile stays in the heart, loveliest of cities. I have made many journeys down the Black Warrior and I have always found happiness at its mouth. . . . The old city rests apart, remembering the five flags that have flown over her. Spain and France and England and the Old South, grown harmonious through the mellowing of time, are echoes in the streets.

> Ibid.

7 Mobile is a city of intimacies that have stood the test of time.

> Ibid.

8 I came from Alabama with my banjo on my
  knee,
  I'm goin' to Lou'siana, my true love for to
  see.
  It rain'd all night the day I left, the weather
  it was dry;
  The sun so hot I froze to death;
  Susanna, don't you cry.
  Oh! Susanna, oh, don't you cry for me,
  For I'm goin' to Lou'siana with my banjo on
  my knee.

> Stephen Foster, "Oh! Susanna," 1848.

9 I have never once thought of work in connection with the word Mobile. *Not anybody working.* A city surrounded with shells, the empty shells of bygone fiestas. Bunting everywhere, and the friable relics of yesterday's carnival. Gaiety always in retreat, always vanishing, like clouds brushing a mirror. In the center of this glissando, Mobile itself, very prim, very proper, Southern and not Southern, listless but upright, slatternly yet respectable, bright but not wicked. Mozart for the Mandolin. Not Segovia feathering Bach. Not grace and delicacy so much as anemia. Fever coolth, Musk. Fragrant ashes.

> Henry Miller, writing of Mobile in *The Air-Conditioned Nightmare*, 1945.

10 As I have walk'd in Alabama my morning
  walk,
  I have seen where the she-bird the
    mocking-bird sat on her nest in the
    briers hatching her brood.
  I have seen the he-bird also,
  I have paus'd to hear him near at hand
    inflating his throat and joyfully singing.

> Walt Whitman, "Starting from Paumanok," *Leaves of Grass*, 1881.

10. ALASKA

1 North to the future.

State motto.

2 Seward's icebox.

Name applied to Alaska after Sec. of State William H. Seward signed a treaty for its purchase from Russia for $7,200,000, 1867.

3 The 49th star twinkles. The Senate can make it gleam.

Editorial comment on statehood for Alaska, in the *Houston Press,* 1958.

4 Thinking back to my boyhood, Alaska, for all of us . . . was synonymous with the gold and glamour of the Yukon and Klondike: the home of sourdoughs and Eskimos. . . . We thought of it as the cruel Artic region. . . . The change in less than a century heartens as we view the future. The future is bound to be a bright, useful one. You are no longer an Arctic frontier. You constitute a bridge to the continent of Asia and all its people.

Dwight D. Eisenhower, in a speech at Anchorage, Alaska, June 12, 1960.

5 Nature has many tricks wherewith she convinces man of his finity . . . but the most tremendous, the most stupefying of all, is the passive phase of the White Silence. All movement ceases, the sky clears, the heavens are as brass; the slightest whisper seems sacrilege, and man becomes timid, affrighted at the sound of his own voice. Sole speck of life journeying across the ghostly wastes of a dead world, he trembles at his audacity, realizes that his is a maggot's life, nothing more.

Jack London, "The White Silence," the *Overland Monthly,* February, 1899.

6 As for the hardship, it cannot be conveyed by printed page or word of mouth. No man may know who has not undergone. And those who have undergone, out of their knowledge, claim

that in the making of the world God grew tired, and when He came to the last barrowload, "just dumped it anyhow," and that was how Alaska happened to be.

Jack London, "Gold Hunters of the North," collected in *Revolution and Other Essays,* 1910.

7 A handful of people clinging to a subcontinent.

John McPhee, *Coming into the Country,* 1977.

8 Alaska is a foreign country significantly populated with Americans. Its languages extend to English. Its nature is its own.

Ibid.

9 You may read in the booklets that the winters in Alaska aren't so bad because they're dry. But just talk to some of the people who have been through them. At sixty below, your fingers freeze while you're unhitching a dog. You must move with the caution of a man with a bad heart; to breathe hard is to frost your lungs. You dare not perspire; your clothes would freeze on you. To get your feet wet is to lose your feet. To touch a piece of metal is worse than a bad burn.

Ernie Pyle, *Home Country,* 1947.

10 I had always been skeptical about this all-night-daylight business. It was my belief that it would be an inferior brand, pumped up by the Chamber of Commerce, and not really what an honest man would call daylight at all. But, as usual, I was wrong. We had actual daylight all night long. (This was in June.) True, it wasn't so light at midnight as at noon. But you could stand out in the open at midnight, anywhere on the whole mainland of Alaska, and read a newspaper with ease.

Ibid.

11 The Eskimos are a gentle people. I like gentle people, because there are so many in the world who are not gentle. Sometimes in a big city I just sit all day in my room, with my head down, afraid to go out and talk to tough people. I expect Eskimos have spells like that too.

Ibid.

11. AMBITION

1 Could I have obtained a troop of horse or a company of foot, I should infallibly have been a soldier.

> JOHN ADAMS, in a letter to Thomas Cushing, March 13, 1817.

2 My whole life has been a succession of disappointments. I can scarcely recollect a single instance of success to anything that I ever undertook. Yet, with fervent gratitude to God, I confess that my life has been equally marked by great and signal successes which I neither aimed at nor anticipated.

> JOHN QUINCY ADAMS, diary entry, August 9, 1833.

3 I want the voice of honest praise
   To follow me behind,
And to be thought, in future days,
   The friend of humankind;
That after-ages, as they rise,
   Exulting may proclaim,
In choral union to the skies,
   Their blessings on my name.

> JOHN QUINCY ADAMS, "The Wants of Man," 1841.

4 Ambition. *n.* An overmastering desire to be vilified by enemies while living and made ridiculous by friends when dead.

> AMBROSE BIERCE, *The Devil's Dictionary,* 1906.

5 Hitch your wagon to a star. Let us not fag in paltry works which serve our pot and bag alone. Let us not lie and steal. No god will help. We shall find all their teams going the other way; every god will leave us. Work rather for those interests which the divinities honor and promote—justice, love, freedom, knowledge, utility.

> RALPH WALDO EMERSON, "Civilization," *Society and Solitude,* 1870.

6 Ambition has its disappointments to sour us, but never the good fortune to satisfy us.

> BENJAMIN FRANKLIN, "On True Happiness," in *The Pennsylvania Gazette,* November 20, 1735.

7 Heaven is not reached at a single bound;
But we build the ladder by which we rise
From the lowly earth to the vaulted skies,
And we mount to its summit round by round.

> JOSIAH GILBERT HOLLAND, "Gradatim," 1872.

8 Every nation has a prominent citizen who builds a pyramid.

> EDGAR WATSON HOWE, *Sinner Sermons,* 1926.

9 The early tire gits the roofin' tack.

> KIN HUBBARD, *Abe Martin's Broadcast,* 1930.

10 I had rather be shut up in a very modest cottage, with my books, my family and a few old friends, dining on simple bacon, and letting the world roll on as it liked, than to occupy the most splendid post which any human power can give.

> THOMAS JEFFERSON, in a letter to Alexander Donald, February 7, 1788.

11 The little spice of ambition which I had in my younger days has long since evaporated, and I set still less store by a posthumous than a present name.

> THOMAS JEFFERSON, in a letter to James Madison, April, 1795.

12 The trouble with being number one in the world—at anything—is that it takes a certain mentality to attain that position in the first place, and that is something of a driving, perfectionist attitude, so that once you do achieve number one, you don't relax and enjoy it.

> BILLIE JEAN KING, *Billie Jean,* 1982.

13 I see, but cannot reach, the height
   That lies forever in the light,
   And yet forever and forever,
When seeming just within my grasp,
I feel my feeble hands unclasp,
And sink discouraged into night!

> HENRY WADSWORTH LONGFELLOW, "A Village Church," *The Golden Legend,* 1851.

14 Most people would succeed in small things, if they were not troubled with great ambitions.

> HENRY WADSWORTH LONGFELLOW, "Table-Talk," *Drift Wood,* collected in *Prose Works,* 1857.

15 My own thoughts
Are my companions; my designs and labors
And aspirations are my only friends.

HENRY WADSWORTH LONGFELLOW, *The Masque of Pandora,* 1875.

16 Greatly begin! Though thou have time
But for a line, be that sublime—
Not failure, but low aim is crime.

JAMES RUSSELL LOWELL, "For an Autograph," 1868.

17 What men prize most is a privilege, even if it be that of chief mourner at a funeral.

JAMES RUSSELL LOWELL, "Democracy," an address given at Birmingham, England, October 6, 1884, published in *Democracy and Other Addresses,* 1886.

18 A fierce unrest seethes at the core
Of all existing things:
It was the eager wish to soar
That gave the gods their wings.

DON MARQUIS, "Unrest," *Dreams and Dust,* 1915.

19 Go for the moon. If you don't get it, you'll still be heading for a star.

WILLIS REED, quoting one of his high school coaches, in Bill Bradley, *Life on the Run,* 1976.

20 There are two things to aim at in life: first, to get what you want; and, after that, to enjoy it. Only the wisest of mankind achieve the second.

LOGAN PEARSALL SMITH, *Afterthoughts,* 1931.

21 As for the pyramids, there is nothing to wonder at in them so much as the fact that so many men could be found degraded enough to spend their lives constructing a tomb for some ambitious booby, whom it would have been wiser and manlier to have drowned in the Nile, and then given his body to the dogs.

HENRY DAVID THOREAU, *Walden,* 1854.

22 [Inherited wealth is] as certain death to ambition as cocaine is to morality.

WILLIAM K. VANDERBILT, in an interview, 1905.

23 There is always room as the top.

Attributed to Daniel Webster, responding to advice that he not enter the crowded legal profession, c.1801.

24 The common ambition strains for elevations, to become some privileged exclusive.

WALT WHITMAN, *Democratic Vistas,* 1870.

25 We cross the prairie as of old
The Pilgrims crossed the sea,
To make the West, as they the East,
The homestead of the free.

JOHN GREENLEAF WHITTIER, "The Kansas Emigrants," 1854.

12. AMERICA

See also AMERICA SEEN FROM ABROAD

1 Having undertaken for the Glory of God, and Advancement of the Christian Faith, and the Honor of our King and Country, a voyage to plant the first colony in the northern Parts of Virginia; do by these Presents, solemnly and mutually in the Presence of God and one of another, covenant and combine ourselves together into a civil Body Politick, for our better Ordering and Preservation, and Furtherance of the Ends aforesaid; And by Virtue hereof to enact, constitute, and frame, such just and equal laws, Ordinances, Acts, Constitutions and Offices, from time to time, as shall be thought most meet and convenient for the General good of the Colony; unto which we promise all due Submission and Obedience.

The Mayflower Compact, signed by 43 Pilgrims in Provincetown Harbor (now Massachusetts), November 21, 1620.

2 E pluribus unum. (Out of many, one.)

Motto for the Seal of the United States, first appearing on the title page of the *Gentleman's Journal,* January, 1692. Said to have been chosen by the Swiss artist Pierre Eugene du Simitière, one of several who submitted designs for the seal, it was recommended by John Adams, Benjamin

Franklin, and Thomas Jefferson on August 10, 1776, and adopted on June 20, 1782.

3 As for America, it is the ideal fruit of all your youthful hopes and reforms. Everybody is fairly decent, respectable, domestic, bourgeois, middle-class, and tiresome. There is absolutely nothing to revile except that it's a bore.

> HENRY ADAMS, in a letter to Charles Milnes Gaskell, December 17, 1908.

4 American society is a sort of flat, fresh-water pond which absorbs silently, without reaction, anything which is thrown into it.

> HENRY ADAMS, in a letter to Royal Cortissoz, September 20, 1911.

5 I always consider the settlement of America with reverence and wonder, as the opening of a grand scene and design in providence, for the illumination of the ignorant and the emancipation of the slavish part of mankind all over the earth.

> JOHN ADAMS, in his notes for "A Dissertation on the Canon and Feudal Law," 1765.

6 Our country is too big for union, too sordid for patriotism, too democratic for liberty.

> FISHER AMES, in a letter to Thomas Dwight, October 26, 1803.

7 I like it here, just because it is the Great Void where you have to balance without handholds.

> W.H. AUDEN, in a letter to Naomi Mitchison, 1942.

8 In America, we have people who are too rich, people who are too poor, people who are hungry, people who are sick, people who are homeless, people who are imprisoned, people who are bored, people who are strung-out, people who are lonely, people who are exploited, people who lose and can't find their way, people who give up on life. America, we better live as sisters and brothers. Let us take care of our land. We cannot stand up for every other land. Stand up for ourselves.

> PEARL BAILEY, Hurry Up, America, and Spit, 1976.

9 America! America!
God shed His grace on thee

And crown thy good with brotherhood
From sea to shining sea!

> KATHERINE LEE BATES, "America the Beautiful," published in The Congregationalist, July 4, 1895.

10 I have fallen in love with American names,
The sharp names that never get fat,
The snakeskin titles of mining claims,
The plumed war-bonnet of Medicine Hat,
Tucson and Deadwood and Lost Mule
    Flat. . . .
You may bury my body in Sussex grass,
You may bury my tongue at Champmedy.
I shall not be there. I shall rise and pass.
Bury my heart at Wounded Knee.

> STEPHEN VINCENT BENÉT, "American Names," 1927.

11 It is a noble land that God has given us: a land that can feed and clothe the world; a land whose coastlines would enclose half the countries of Europe; a land set like a sentinel between the two imperial oceans of the globe.

> ALBERT J. BEVERIDGE, in a speech in Indianapolis, Indiana, September 16, 1898.

12 My country, 'tis of thee
Sweet land of felony
    Of thee I sing—
Land where my father fried
Young witches and applied
Whips to the Quaker's hide
And made him spring.

> AMBROSE BIERCE, "A Rational Anthem," Black Beetles in Amber, 1892.

13 The twentieth century ideals of America have been the ideals of the Jew for more than twenty centuries.

> LOUIS D. BRANDEIS, "A Call to the Educated Jew," in the Menorah Journal, January, 1915.

14 All I want is the same thing you want. To have a nation with a government that is as good and honest and decent and competent and compassionate and as filled with love as are the American people.

> JIMMY CARTER, in a speech at Sacramento, California, May 20, 1976.

15 We become not a melting pot but a beautiful mosaic. Different people, different beliefs, different yearnings, different hopes, different dreams.

> JIMMY CARTER, in a speech at Pittsburgh, Pennsylvania, October 27, 1976.

16 The Constitution, in all its provisions, looks to an indestructible Union, composed of indestructible States.

> SALMON P. CHASE, in a Supreme Court opinion, *Texas* v. *White,* 1869.

17 Nothing that you say about the whole country is going to be true.

> ALISTAIR COOKE, *Alistair Cooke's America,* 1973.

18 America owes most of its social prejudices to the exaggerated religious opinions of the different sects which were so instrumental in establishing the colonies.

> JAMES FENIMORE COOPER, *The American Democrat,* 1838.

19 The rest of the earth, I am told, is in some places too full, in others half depopulated. Misguided religion, tyranny, and absurd laws everywhere depress and afflict mankind. Here we have in some measure regained the ancient dignity of our species; our laws are simple and just, we are a race of cultivators, our cultivation is unrestrained, and therefore everything is prosperous and flourishing.

> MICHEL GUILLAUME JEAN DE CRÈVECOEUR, *Letters from an American Farmer,* 1782.

20 What then is the American, this new man? He is either an European, or the descendant of an European, hence that strange mixture of blood, which you will find in no other country. I could point out to you a family whose grandfather was an Englishman, whose wife was Dutch, whose son married a French woman, and whose present four sons have now four wives of different nations. *He* is an American, who leaving behind him all his ancient prejudices and manners, receives new ones from the new mode of life he has embraced, the new government he obeys, and the new rank he holds.

> Ibid.

21 Here individuals of all nations are melted into a new race of men, whose labors and posterity will one day cause great changes in the world.

> Ibid.

22 next to of course god america i
love you land of the pilgrims' and so forth
    oh
say can you see by the dawn's early my
country 'tis of centuries come and go
and are no more what of it we should worry
in every language even deafanddumb
thy sons acclaim your glorious name by gorry
by jing by gee by gosh by gum

> E.E. CUMMINGS, "next to of course god america i," *is 5,* 1926.

23 Th' enthusyasm iv this counthry . . . always makes me think iv a bonfire on an ice-floe. It burns bright so long as ye feed it, an' it looks good, but it don't take hold, somehow, on th' ice.

> FINLEY PETER DUNNE, *Mr. Dooley's Philosophy,* 1900.

24 Every generation of Americans has wanted more material wealth, more luxury for the next generation. In my opinion the time has come when we must hope our children and their children ad infinitum will want from life more than material success. They must have enough of that to ensure a roof, clothing, food and some recreation, but, if we are to survive for another two hundred years, we must change our way of life.

> INDIA EDWARDS, *Pulling No Punches,* 1977.

25 Whatever America hopes to bring to pass in the world must first come to pass in the heart of America.

> DWIGHT D. EISENHOWER, in his first inaugural address, January 20, 1953.

26 They proclaimed to all the world the revolutionary doctrine of the divine rights of the common man. That doctrine has ever since been the heart of the American faith.

> DWIGHT D. EISENHOWER, referring to the founding fathers, in a speech at the Columbia University Bicentennial dinner, May 30, 1954.

27 America is woven of many strands; I would recognize them and let it so remain. . . . Our fate is to become one, and yet many—This is not prophecy, but description.

> RALPH ELLISON, *Invisible Man,* 1952.

28 I esteem it a chief felicity of this country that it excels in women.

> RALPH WALDO EMERSON, "Manners," *Essays,* Second Series, 1844.

29 In America the geography is sublime, but the men are not: the inventions are excellent, but the inventors one is sometimes ashamed of.

> RALPH WALDO EMERSON, "Considerations by the Way," *The Conduct of Life,* 1860.

30 The office of America is to liberate, to abolish kingcraft, priestcraft, caste, monopoly, to pull down the gallows, to burn up the bloody statute-book, to take in the immigrant, to open the doors of the sea and the fields of the earth.

> RALPH WALDO EMERSON, entry written in 1867, *Journals,* 1909–1914.

31 America is the country of young men, and too full of work hitherto for leisure and tranquility; yet we have had robust centenarians, and examples of dignity and wisdom.

> RALPH WALDO EMERSON, "Old Age," *Society and Solitude,* 1870.

32 I hate this shallow Americanism which hopes to get rich by credit, to get knowledge by raps on midnight tables, to learn the economy of the mind by phrenology, or skill without study, or mastery without apprenticeship.

> RALPH WALDO EMERSON, "Success," *Society and Solitude,* 1870.

33 America means opportunity, freedom, power.

> RALPH WALDO EMERSON, "Public and Private Education," *Uncollected Lectures,* 1932.

34 We're not a political people. We've just been preaching the issues. We're trying to be the moral conscience of the nation. I don't equate America with Christianity. I don't wrap the cross in a flag.

> JERRY FALWELL, at a news conference in Washington, D.C., January 27, 1981.

35 Who stole America?

> LAWRENCE FERLINGHETTI, *Starting from San Francisco,* 1961.

36 France was a land, England was a people, but America, having about it still that quality of the idea, was harder to utter—it was the graves at Shiloh, and the tired, drawn, nervous faces of its great men, and the country boys dying in the Argonne for a phrase that was empty before their bodies withered. It was a willingness of the heart.

> F. SCOTT FITZGERALD, *The Crack-Up,* 1945.

37 We go forth all to seek America. And in the seeking we create her. In the quality of our search shall be the nature of the America that we created.

> WALDO FRANK, *Our America,* 1919.

38 There is much cant in American moralism and not a little inconsistency.

> J. WILLIAM FULBRIGHT, in a speech in the U.S. Senate, March 25, 1964.

39 Our country has liberty without license, and authority without despotism.

> JAMES CARDINAL GIBBONS, in a speech in Rome, Italy, March 25, 1887.

40 America will tolerate the taking of human life without giving it a second thought. But don't misuse a household pet.

> DICK GREGORY, *The Shadow that Scares Me,* 1968.

41 Thou, O my country, hast thy foolish ways,
Too apt to purr at every stranger's praise.

> OLIVER WENDELL HOLMES, SR., "An After-Dinner Poem," 1843.

42 America is the only place where man is full-grown!

> OLIVER WENDELL HOLMES, SR., *The Professor at the Breakfast-Table,* 1860.

43 One flag, one land, one heart, one hand,
One Nation, evermore!

> OLIVER WENDELL HOLMES, SR., "Voyage of the Good Ship Union," 1862.

44 The only foes that threaten America are the enemies at home, and these are ignorance, superstition and incompetence.

> ELBERT HUBBARD, in *The Philistine* magazine, published from 1895–1915.

45 An American Religion: Work, play, breathe, bathe, study, live, laugh, and love.

> ELBERT HUBBARD, *The Roycroft Dictionary and Book of Epigrams,* 1923.

46 O, yes,
> I say it plain,
> America never was America to me.
> And yet I swear this oath—
> America will be!

> LANGSTON HUGHES, "Let America Be America Again," in *The Poetry of the Negro,* 1949.

47 We are the standard-bearers in the only really authentic revolution, the democratic revolution against tyrannies. Our strength is not to be measured by our military capacity alone, by our industry, or by our technology. We will be remembered, not for the power of our weapons, but for the power of our compassion, our dedication to human welfare.

> HUBERT H. HUMPHREY, *The Cause Is Mankind,* 1964.

48 The union shall be preserved.

> ANDREW JACKSON, in a letter to Martin Van Buren, July 23, 1831.

49 America is American: that is incontestable.

> HENRY JAMES, in a letter to Grace Norton, 1870.

50 One loves America above all things, for her youth, her greenness, her plasticity, innocence, good intentions, friends, everything.

> WILLIAM JAMES, in a letter to Mrs. Henry Whitman, 1899.

51 It is part of the American character to consider nothing as desperate, to surmount every difficulty by resolution and contrivance.

> THOMAS JEFFERSON, in a letter to Martha Jefferson, March 28, 1787.

52 I do believe we shall continue to grow, to multiply and prosper until we exhibit an association powerful, wise, and happy beyond what has yet been seen by men.

> THOMAS JEFFERSON, in a letter to John Adams, January 21, 1812.

53 I pray we are still a young and courageous nation, that we have not grown so old and so fat and so prosperous that all we can think about is to sit back with our arms around our money bags. If we choose to do that I have no doubt that the smoldering fires will burst into flame and consume us— dollars and all.

> LYNDON B. JOHNSON, in a speech in Congress, May 7, 1947.

54 The Great Society is a place where every child can find knowledge to enrich his mind and to enlarge his talents. . . . It is a place where the city of man serves not only the needs of the body and the demands of commerce but the desire for beauty and the hunger for community. . . . It is a place where men are more concerned with the quality of their goals than the quantity of their goods.

> LYNDON B. JOHNSON, in a speech at Ann Arbor, Michigan, May 22, 1964.

55 For this is what America is all about. It is the uncrossed desert and the unclimbed ridge. It is the star that is not reached and the harvest that is sleeping in the unplowed ground.

> LYNDON B. JOHNSON, in his inaugural address, January 20, 1965.

56 A rich harvest in a hungry land is impressive. The sight of healthy children is impressive. These—not mighty arms—are the achievements which the American nation believes to be impressive.

> LYNDON B. JOHNSON, in a speech at Johns Hopkins University, April 7, 1965.

57 I cannot see why, if we have the will to do it, we can't provide for our own happiness, education, health, and environment. . . . We're greedy but not short on the wherewithal to meet our problems.

> LYNDON B. JOHNSON, quoted in Doris Kearns, *Lyndon Johnson and the American Dream,* 1976.

58 Solitude is un-American.

ERICA JONG, *Fear of Flying,* 1973.

59 Our national experience was never shared by any country and will never be shared by any country in the future. Never again will it be given to a national society to develop a vast, unpopulated area in the northern, temperate zone of the world. Think of the potential wealth of this continent, and the way in which people harnessed it to their needs, and also devastated, by their greed, its lakes and forests and sea-boards. All this wealth and space presented possibilities in America which have made the American outlook unique, and therefore inapplicable to any other society.

GEORGE F. KENNAN, in an interview with George Urban, *Encounter,* September, 1976.

60 The United States has to move very fast to even stand still.

JOHN F. KENNEDY, quoted in "Sayings of the Week," the *Observer,* July 21, 1963.

61 Our nation is moving toward two societies, one black, one white—separate and unequal.

OTTO KERNER, JR., in the *Report of the National Advisory Commission on Civil Disorders,* 1968.

62 Many of the ugly pages of American history have been obscured and forgotten. . . . America owes a debt of justice which it has only begun to pay. If it loses the will to finish or slackens in its determination, history will recall its crimes and the country that would be great will lack the most indispensable element of greatness—justice.

MARTIN LUTHER KING, JR., *Where Do We Go from Here: Chaos or Community?* 1967.

63 When I was a boy it was a dream, an incredible place where tolerance was natural and personal freedom unchallenged. Even when I learned later that America, too, had massive problems, I could never forget what an inspiration it had been to the victims of persecution, to my family, and to me during cruel and degrading years.

HENRY KISSINGER, *White House Years,* 1979.

64 America is a tune. It must be sung together.

GERALD STANLEY LEE, *Crowds,* 1913.

65 Intellectually I know that America is no better than any other country; emotionally I know she is better than every other country.

SINCLAIR LEWIS, in an interview in Berlin, Germany, December 29, 1930.

66 We are a people with a faith in each other, and when we lose that faith we are weak, however heavily armed. We are a people with a faith in reason, and the unending pursuit of new knowledge; and when we lose that faith we are insecure, though we be ever so heavily armed. We are a people with a faith in God, and a deep sense of stewardship to our Creator, the Father of us all; and when that is no longer strong within us, we are weak and we are lost, however heavily armed with weapons—with atomic weapons—we may be.

DAVID E. LILIENTHAL, *This I Do Believe,* 1949.

67 All the armies of Europe, Asia and Africa combined, with all the treasure of the earth (our own excepted) in their military chest, with a Bonaparte for a commander, could not, by force, take a drink from the Ohio, or make a track on the Blue Ridge, in a trial of a thousand years.

ABRAHAM LINCOLN, in an address, "The Perpetuation of Our Political Institutions," Springfield, Illinois, January 27, 1837.

68 At what point, then, is the approach of danger to be expected? I answer, if it ever reach us, it must spring up amongst us; it cannot come from abroad. If destruction be our lot, we must ourselves be its author and finisher. As a nation of freemen, we must live through all time, or die by suicide.

Ibid.

69 America, which has the most glorious present still existing in the world today, hardly stops to enjoy it, in her insatiable appetite for the future.

ANNE MORROW LINDBERGH, *Gift from the Sea,* 1955.

70 America is the last abode of romance and other medieval phenomena.

ERIC LINKLATER, *Juan in America,* 1931.

71 We are an uprooted people, newly arrived, and *nouveau riche.* As a nation we have all the vulgarity that goes with that, all the scattering of soul.

> WALTER LIPPMANN, *Drift and Mastery,* 1914.

72 To me Americanism means . . . an imperative duty to be nobler than the rest of the world.

> MEYER LONDON, in a speech to Congress, January 18, 1916.

73 Thou, too, sail on, O Ship of State!
Sail on, O Union, strong and great!
Humanity with all its fears,
With all the hopes of future years,
Is hanging breathless on thy fate!

> HENRY WADSWORTH LONGFELLOW, "The Building of the Ship," 1849.

74 She that lifts up the manhood of the poor,
She of the open soul and open door,
With room about her hearth for all mankind!

> JAMES RUSSELL LOWELL, "Ode Recited at the Harvard Commemoration," July 21, 1865.

75 Her children shall rise up to bless her name,
And wish her harmless length of days,
The mighty mother of a mighty brood,
Blessed in all tongues and dear to every
  blood,
The beautiful, the strong, and, best of all,
  the good.

> JAMES RUSSELL LOWELL, "Ode for the Fourth of July," 1876.

76 Conspicuous waste beyond the imagination of Thorstein Veblen has become the mark of American life. As a nation we find ourselves overbuilt, if not overhoused; overfed, although millions of poor people are undernourished; overtransported in overpowered cars; and also . . . overdefended or overdefensed.

> EUGENE J. MCCARTHY, *America Revisited,* 1978.

77 America is a hurricane, and the only people who do not hear the sound are those fortunate if incredibly stupid and smug White Protestants who live in the center, in the serene eye of the big wind.

> NORMAN MAILER, *Advertisements for Myself,* 1961.

78 This country can seduce God. Yes, it has that seductive power—the power of dollarism.

> MALCOLM X, *Malcolm X Speaks,* 1965.

79 Nowhere in the world is superiority more easily attained, or more eagerly admitted. The chief business of the nation, as a nation, is the setting up of heroes, mainly bogus.

> H.L. MENCKEN, *Prejudices,* Third Series, 1923.

80 I have never been able to look upon America as young and vital, but rather as prematurely old, as a fruit which rotted before it had a chance to ripen.

> HENRY MILLER, *The Air-conditioned Nightmare,* 1945.

81 America is still a government of the naive, for the naive, and by the naive. He who does not know this, nor relish it, has no inkling of the nature of his country.

> CHRISTOPHER MORLEY, *Inward Ho!,* 1923.

82 The forests of America, however slighted by man, must have been a great delight to God, because they were the best He ever planted.

> JOHN MUIR, quoted in John Gunther, *Inside U.S.A.,* 1947.

83 We find it almost as difficult as the communists to believe that anyone could think ill of us, since we are as persuaded as they that our society is so essentially virtuous that only malice could prompt criticism of any of our actions.

> REINHOLD NIEBUHR, *The Irony of American History,* 1962.

84 The springs of American civilization, unlike those of the elder world, lie revealed in the clear light of History. In appearance they are feeble; in reality, copious and full of force. Acting at the sources of life, instruments otherwise weak become mighty for good and evil, and men, lost elsewhere in the crowd, stand forth as agents of Destiny.

> FRANCIS PARKMAN, in his preface to *Pioneers,* 1865.

85 America, my country, is almost a continent and hardly yet a nation.

> EZRA POUND, in an essay written in 1912, included in *Patria Mia,* 1950.

86 America is not just a power: it is a promise. It is not enough for our country to be extraordinary in might; it must be exemplary in meaning. Our honor and our role in the world finally depend on the living proof that we are a just society.

> NELSON A. ROCKEFELLER, *Unity, Freedom and Peace: A Blueprint for Tomorrow,* 1968.

87 If we ever pass out as a great nation, we ought to put on our tombstone "America died of the delusion that she had moral leadership."

> WILL ROGERS, *The Autobiography of Will Rogers,* 1949.

88 We, here in America, hold in our hands the hope of the world, the fate of the coming years; and shame and disgrace will be ours if, in our eyes, the light of high resolve is dimmed, if we trail in the dust the golden hopes of men.

> THEODORE ROOSEVELT, quoted in Nelson A. Rockefeller, *Unity, Freedom and Peace: A Blueprint for Tomorrow,* 1968.

89 America is a young country with an old mentality.

> GEORGE SANTAYANA, *Winds of Doctrine,* 1913.

90 It is veneer, rouge, aestheticism, art museums, new theaters, etc. that make America impotent. The good things are football, kindness, and jazz bands.

> GEORGE SANTAYANA, in a letter to Van Wyck Brooks, May 22, 1927.

91 America is the greatest of opportunities and the worst of influences.

> GEORGE SANTAYANA, *The Last Puritan,* 1935.

92 In America, getting on in the world means getting out of the world we have known before.

> ELLERY SEDGWICK, *The Happy Profession,* 1946.

93 My country, 'tis of thee,
Sweet land of liberty,
  Of thee I sing;
Land where my fathers died;
Land of the pilgrims' pride,
From every mountain side
  Let freedom ring.

> SAMUEL FRANCIS SMITH, "America," printed for the Fourth of July program at the Boston Sabbath School Union, 1831.

94 In the United States there is more space where nobody is than where anybody is. That is what makes America what it is.

> GERTRUDE STEIN, *The Geographical History of America,* 1936.

95 Who is the United States? Not the judiciary; not the President; but the sovereign power of the people, exercised through their representatives in Congress, with the concurrence of the executive.

> THADDEUS STEVENS, in a speech in Congress, December 18, 1865.

96 Throughout its history, America has given hope, comfort and inspiration to freedom's cause in all lands. The reservoir of good will and respect for America was not built up by American arms or intrigue; it was built upon our deep dedication to the cause of human liberty and human welfare.

> ADLAI E. STEVENSON, *Call to Greatness,* 1954.

97 By "America," I suppose we all think of not *just* the real estate or inhabitants of the United States, but also of the idea that we who live here share and cherish in common—the concept of government by the free consent of the governed as the only tolerable system of management of human affairs.

> ADLAI E. STEVENSON, "War, Weakness, and Ourselves," *Look* magazine, November, 1954.

98 America is a land of wonders, in which everything is in constant motion and every change seems an improvement.

> ALEXIS DE TOCQUEVILLE, *Democracy in America,* 1835.

99 The majority . . . believe that a man by following his own interest, rightly understood, will be led to do what is just and good. They hold that every man is born in possession of the right of self-government, and that no one has the right of constraining his fellow creatures to be happy. They have all a lively faith in the perfectibility of man, they judge that the diffusion of knowledge must necessarily be

advantageous, and the consequences of ignorance fatal; they all consider society as a body in a state of improvement, humanity as a changing scene, in which nothing is, or ought to be, permanent; and they admit that what appears to them today to be good, may be superseded by something better to-morrow. I do not give all these opinions as true, but as American opinions.

> Ibid.

100 *October 12, the Discovery.*
> It was wonderful to find America, but it
>   would have been more wonderful to
>   miss it.

MARK TWAIN, "Pudd'nhead Wilson's Calendar," *Pudd'nhead Wilson,* 1894.

101 There isn't a single human characteristic that can be safely labeled as "American!"

MARK TWAIN, "What Paul Bourget Thinks of Us," published in the *North American Review,* January, 1895.

102 In Boston they ask, How much does he know? In New York, How much is he worth? In Philadelphia, Who were his parents?

> Ibid.

103 Don't read your reviews,
    A*M*E*R*I*C*A:
    you are the only land.

JOHN UPDIKE, "Notes to a Poem," *Picked Up Pieces,* 1976.

104 America is a vast conspiracy to make you happy.

JOHN UPDIKE, "How to Love America and Leave It at the Same Time," *Problems,* 1980.

105 Oh, it's home again, and home again,
        America for me!
    I want a ship that's westward bound to
        plough the rolling sea,
    To the blessed Land of Room Enough
        beyond the ocean bars,
    Where the air is full of sunlight and the
        flag is full of stars.

HENRY VAN DYKE, "America for Me," 1909.

106 The preservation of the sacred fire of liberty and the destiny of the republican model of government are justly considered, perhaps, as *deeply,* as *finally* staked on the experiment entrusted to the hands of the American people.

GEORGE WASHINGTON, in his first inaugural address, April 30, 1789.

107 One Country, one Constitution, one Destiny.

DANIEL WEBSTER, in a speech, March 15, 1837.

108 America has proved that it is practicable to elevate the mass of mankind—that portion which in Europe is called the laboring, or lower class—to raise them to self respect, to make them competent to act a part in the great right, and great duty, of self-government; and this she has proved may be done by education and the diffusion of knowledge. She holds out an example, a thousand times more enchanting than ever was presented before, to those nine-tenths of the human race who are born without hereditary fortune or hereditary rank.

DANIEL WEBSTER, "Address Delivered at the Completion of the Bunker Hill Monument," June 17, 1843.

109 These States are the amplest poem.

WALT WHITMAN, "By Blue Ontario's Shore," 1856.

110 O America because you build for mankind I build for you.

> Ibid.

111 I see not America only, not only Liberty's
        nation but other nations preparing,
    I see tremendous entrances and exits, new
        combination, the solidarity of races.

WALT WHITMAN, "Years of the Modern," 1865.

112 Lo, body and soul—this land,
    My own Manhattan with spires, and the
        sparkling and hurrying tides, and the
        ships,
    The varied and ample land, the South and
        the North in the light, Ohio's shores
        and flashing Missouri,
    And ever the far-spreading prairies cover'd
        with grass and corn.

WALT WHITMAN, "When Lilacs Last in the Dooryard Bloom'd," 1865–1866.

113 I hear America singing, the varied carols I hear.

WALT WHITMAN, "I Hear America Singing," 1867.

114 I say, the true nationality of the States, the genuine union, when we come to a mortal crisis, is, and is to be, after all, neither the written law, nor, (as is generally supposed) either self-interest, or common pecuniary or material objects—but the fervid and tremendous Idea, melting everything else with resistless heat, and solving all lesser and definite distinctions in vast, indefinite, spiritual, emotional power.

WALT WHITMAN, *Democratic Vistas,* 1871.

115 I say we had best look our times and lands searchingly in the face, like a physician diagnosing some deep disease. Never was there, perhaps, more hollowness of heart than at present, and here in the United States. Genuine belief seems to have left us. The underlying principles of the States are not honestly believ'd in, (for all this hectic glow, and these melodramatic screamings) nor is humanity itself believ'd in. What penetrating eye does not everywhere see through the mask?

Ibid.

116 Sail, sail thy best, ship of Democracy,
Of value is thy freight, 'tis not the Present only,
The Past is also stored in thee,
Thou holdest not the venture of thyself alone, not of the Western continent alone,
Earth's *résumé* entire floats on thy keel O ship, is steadied by thy spars,
With thee Time voyages in trust, the antecedent nations sink or swim with thee.

WALT WHITMAN, "Thou Mother with Thy Equal Brood," 1872.

117 There exists in the world today a gigantic reservoir of good will toward us, the American people.

WENDELL WILLKIE, *One World,* 1943.

118 America is not a mere body of traders; it is a body of free men. Our greatness is built upon our freedom—is moral, not material. We have a great ardor for gain; but we have a deep passion for the rights of man.

WOODROW WILSON, in a speech in New York City, December 6, 1911.

119 Just what is it that America stands for? If she stands for one thing more than another, it is for the sovereignty of self-governing people.

WOODROW WILSON, in a speech in Pittsburgh, Pennsylvania, January 29, 1916.

120 America is not anything if it consists of each of us. It is something only if it consists of all of us.

Ibid.

121 America cannot be an ostrich with its head in the sand.

WOODROW WILSON, in a speech at Des Moines, Iowa, February 1, 1916.

122 Sometimes people call me an idealist. Well, that is the way I know I am an American. . . . America is the only idealist Nation in the world.

WOODROW WILSON, in a speech in Sioux Falls, South Dakota, September 8, 1919.

123 Ours is become a nation too great to offend the least, too mighty to be unjust to the weakest, too lofty and noble to be ungenerous to the poorest and lowliest.

STEPHEN WISE, in a speech, July 4, 1905.

13. AMERICAN INDIANS

1 The Indians have not been without excuse for their evil deeds. Our own people have given them intoxicating drinks, taught them to swear, violated the rights of womanhood among them, robbed them of their dues, and then insulted them! What more would be necessary to cause one nation to rise against another? What more, I ask. Yet there are many who curse this people, and cry "Exterminate

the fiends." Dare we, as a nation, thus bring a curse upon ourselves and on future generations?

> An unidentified white woman forced to flee from her home during the Sioux uprising of 1862, quoted in Alexander B. Adams, *Sitting Bull,* 1973.

2 An Indian who is as bad as the white men could not live in our nation; he would be put to death, and eat up by the wolves. The white men are bad schoolmasters; they carry false looks, and deal in false actions; they smile in the face of the poor Indian to cheat him; they shake them by the hand to gain their confidence, to make them drunk, to deceive them, and ruin our wives. We told them to let us alone, and keep away from us; but they followed on, and beset our paths, and they coiled themselves among us, like the snake. They poisoned us by their touch.

> BLACK HAWK, in a speech at Prairie du Chien, Wisconsin, August, 1835.

3 This country was a lot better off when the Indians were running it.

> VINE DELORIA, JR., in the *New York Times Magazine,* March 3, 1970.

4 And it is now discovered that nothing can be done without corrupting their Chiefs. This is so inconsistent with the principles of our government that it is high time the legislature should exercise its function and pass all laws for the regulation of the Indians. If they have too much land circumscribe them. Furnish them with the means of agriculture, and you will thereby lay the foundation of their civilization by making them husbandmen. Treat them humanely and liberally but put an end to treating with them, and obtaining their country by corrupting their Chiefs which is the only way by which a treaty can be obtained.

> ANDREW JACKSON, in a letter to John C. Calhoun, August 25, 1820.

5 [The Indian] is neither more defective in ardor, nor more impotent with his female, than the white reduced to the same diet and exercise.

> THOMAS JEFFERSON, *Notes on the State of Virginia,* 1784.

6 The Indians . . . will often carve figures on their pipes not destitute of design and merit. They will crayon out an animal, a plant, or a country, so as to prove the existence of a germ in their minds which only wants cultivation. They astonish you with strokes of the most sublime oratory; such as prove their reason and sentiment strong, their imagination glowing and elevated.

> Ibid.

7 I believe the Indian to be in body and mind equal to the white man.

> THOMAS JEFFERSON, in a letter to François Jean de Beauvoir, Chevalier de Chastellux, June 7, 1785.

8 If you tie a horse to a stake, do you expect he will grow fat? If you pen an Indian up on a small spot of earth, and compel him to stay there, he will not be contented, nor will he grow and prosper. I have asked some of the great white chiefs where they get their authority to say to the Indian that he shall stay in one place, while he sees white men going where they please. They can not tell me.

> CHIEF JOSEPH, in the *North American Review,* April, 1879.

9 I know that my race must change. We can not hold our own with the white men as we are. We only ask an even chance to live as other men live. We ask to be recognized as men. We ask that the same law shall work alike on all men. If the Indian breaks the law, punish him by the law. If the white man breaks the law, punish him also.

> Ibid.

10 When you first came we were very many, and you were few; now you are many, and we are getting very few, and we are poor.

> RED CLOUD, in a speech at the Cooper Union, New York City, July 16, 1870.

11 The only good Indians I ever saw were dead.

> GEN. PHILIP H. SHERIDAN, on being introduced to an Indian chief identified as a "good Indian," at Fort Cobb, Indian Territory, January, 1869. (The incident was reported by Edward Ellis.)

12 What treaty that the whites ever made with us red men have they kept? Not one. When I was a boy the Sioux owned the world. The sun rose and set in their lands. They sent 10,000 horsemen to battle. Where are the warriors to-day? Who slew them? Where are our lands? Who owns them? What white man can say I ever stole his lands or a penny of his money? Yet they say I am a thief. . . . What law have I broken? Is it wrong for me to love my own? Is it wicked in me because my skin is red; because I am a Sioux; because I was born where my fathers lived; because I would die for my people and my country?

> SITTING BULL, quoted in W. Fletcher Johnson, *Life of Sitting Bull,* 1891.

13 The American Indian is of the soil, whether it be the region of forests, plains, pueblos, or mesas. He fits into the landscape, for the hand that fashioned the continent also fashioned the man for his surroundings. He once grew as naturally as the wild sunflowers; he belongs just as the buffalo belonged.

> LUTHER STANDING BEAR, *Land of the Spotted Eagle,* 1933.

14 The white man does not understand the Indian for the reason that he does not understand America. He is too far removed from its formative processes. The roots of the tree of his life have not yet grasped the rock and soil.

> Ibid.

15 The [James Fenimore] Cooper Indians are dead—died with their creator. The kind that are left are of altogether a different breed, and cannot be successfully fought with poetry, and sentiment, and soft soap, and magnanimity.

> MARK TWAIN, in a letter to the *San Francisco Alta California,* May 28, 1867.

16 It is painfully clear that the United States needs its Indians and their culture. A society increasingly homogenized and mechanized—a society headed toward ant-hill conformity and depersonalized living—desperately needs the lessons of a culture that has a deep reverence for nature, and values the simple, the authentic, and the humane.

> STEWART L. UDALL, *American Way* magazine, May, 1971.

14. AMERICAN REVOLUTION

See also ARMY; REVOLUTION

1 Don't tread on me.

> Motto of the first official American flag, raised by Lt. John Paul Jones aboard Commodore Esek Hopkins's flagship *Alfred,* on the Delaware River at Philadelphia, December 3, 1775.

2 The said states hereby severally enter into a firm league of friendship with each other, for their common defence, the security of their Liberties, and their mutual and general welfare.

> Articles of Confederation, November 15, 1777.

3 His Britannic Majesty acknowledges the said United States, viz. New Hampshire, Massachusetts Bay, Rhode Island, and Providence Plantations, Connecticut, New York, New Jersey, Pennsylvania, Delaware, Maryland, Virginia, North Carolina, South Carolina, and Georgia, to be free, sovereign and independent States; that he treats with them as such, and for himself, his heirs and successors, relinquishes all claims to the Government, proprietary and territorial rights of the same, and every path thereof.

> First article of the Treaty of Paris, September 3, 1783.

4 This is the most magnificent movement of all! There is a dignity, a majesty, a sublimity, in this last effort of the patriots that I greatly admire. The people should never rise without doing something to be remembered—something notable and striking. This destruction of the tea is so bold, so daring, so firm, intrepid and inflexible, and it must have so important consequences, and so lasting, that I can't but consider it as an epocha in history!

> JOHN ADAMS, diary entry on the Boston Tea Party, December 17, 1773.

5 The die was now cast; I had passed the Rubicon. Swim or sink, live or die, survive or perish with my country was my unalterable determination.

> JOHN ADAMS, in a conversation with Jonathan Sewell, 1774.

6 You ask what is thought of *Common Sense.* Sensible men think there are some whims, some sophisms, some artful addresses to superstitious notions, some keen attempts upon the passions, in the pamphlet. But all agree, there is a great deal of good sense delivered in clear, simple, concise, and nervous style. His sentiments of the abilities of America and of the difficulty of a reconciliation with Great Britain are generally approved. But his notions and plans of continental government are not much applauded. Indeed, this writer has a better hand in pulling down than building.

> JOHN ADAMS, on Tom Paine, in a letter to Abigail Adams, March 19, 1776, quoted in George F. Scheer and Hugh Rankin, *Rebels and Redcoats,* 1957.

7 There is something very unnatural and odious in a government a thousand leagues off. A whole government of our own choice, managed by persons whom we love, revere, and can confide in, has charms in it for which men will fight.

> JOHN ADAMS, in a letter to Abigail Adams, May 17, 1776.

8 Yesterday the greatest question was decided, which ever was debated in America, and a greater perhaps never was nor will be decided among men. A resolution was passed without one dissenting colony "that these United Colonies are, and of right ought to be, free and independent states."

> JOHN ADAMS, in a letter to Abigail Adams, July 3, 1776.

9 The second day of July, 1776, will be the most memorable epoch in the history of America. I am apt to believe that it will be celebrated by succeeding generations as the great anniversary festival. It ought to be commemorated as the day of deliverance, by solemn acts of devotion to God Almighty. It ought to be solemnized with pomp and parade, with shows, games, sports, guns, bells, bonfires, and illustrations, from one end of this continent to the other, from this time forward forevermore.

> JOHN ADAMS, in his second letter to Abigail Adams, July 3, 1776.

10 I must study politics and war that my sons may have liberty to study mathematics and philosophy.

> JOHN ADAMS, in a letter to Abigail Adams, May 12, 1780.

11 The Revolution was effected before the war commenced. The Revolution was in the minds and hearts of the people; a change in their religious sentiments of their duties and obligations. . . . *This radical change in the principles, opinions, sentiments, and affections of the people, was the real American Revolution.*

> JOHN ADAMS, in a letter to Hezekiah Niles, February 13, 1818.

12 Military power . . . will never awe a sensible American tamely to surrender his liberty.

> SAMUEL ADAMS, 1768, quoted in *The American Heritage Book of the Revolution,* 1958.

13 I wish for a permanent union with the mother country, but only on the terms of liberty and truth. No advantage that can accrue to America from such a union, can compensate for the loss of liberty.

> SAMUEL ADAMS, 1774, quoted in *The American Heritage Book of the Revolution,* 1958.

14 What a glorious morning for America!

> SAMUEL ADAMS, remark, when he first heard shots fired at the Battle of Lexington, April 19, 1775.

15 In the name of the great Jehovah and the Continental Congress.

> ETHAN ALLEN, reply to Capt. William Delaplace, British commander at Fort Ticonderoga, who had asked by whose authority Allen demanded the fort's surrender, May 10, 1775.

16 The heart which is conscious of its own rectitude, cannot attempt to palliate a step which the world may censure as wrong; I have ever acted from a principle of love to my country, since the commencement of the present unhappy contest between Great Britain and the Colonies; the same principle of love to my country actuates my present conduct, however it may appear inconsistent to the world, who very seldom judge right of any man's actions.

> BENEDICT ARNOLD, in a letter to General Washington, written after Arnold had learned his plot to surrender West Point had been discovered and he had fled to safety on the British sloop *Vulture,* September 25, 1780.

17 I was in the State House Yard when the Declaration of Independence was read. There were very few respectable people present.

> Attributed to Charles Biddle, on the first public reading of the Declaration of Independence, at Philadelphia, July 8, 1776.

18 Those who invented this machinery of checks and balances were anxious not so much to develop public opinion as to resist and build up breakwaters against it. No men were less revolutionary in spirit than the heroes of the American Revolution. They made a revolution in the name of Magna Charta and the Bill of Rights: they were penetrated by a sense of the dangers incident to democracy.

> JAMES BRYCE, *The American Commonwealth,* 1888.

19 The fortune of war, General Gates, has made me your prisoner.

> GENERAL JOHN BURGOYNE, surrendering to the Americans at Saratoga, New York, October 16, 1777.

20 An Englishman is the unfittest person on earth to argue another Englishman into slavery.

> EDMUND BURKE, speech on Conciliation with America, March 22, 1775.

21 A great revolution has happened—a revolution made, not by chopping and changing of power in any of the existing states, but by the appearance of a new state, of a new species, in a new part of the globe. It has made as great a change in all the relations and balances, and gravitations of power, as the appearance of a new planet would in the system of the solar world.

> EDMUND BURKE, *Detached Papers,* 1782.

22 Now put Watts into 'em boys! Give 'em Watts!

> Attributed to the Reverend James Caldwell, who is said to have spoken these words to American troops while handing out hymn books by the English writer Isaac Watts, to be used for gun wadding, at the Battle of Springfield, New Jersey, June 23, 1780.

23 While Gen'l Howe with a Large Armament is advancing towards N. York, our Congress resolved to Declare the United Colonies Free and Independent States. A Declaration for this Purpose, I expect, will this day pass Congress. . . . It is gone so far that we must now be a free independent State, or a Conquered Country.

> ABRAHAM CLARK, member of the Continental Congress from New Jersey, in a letter to Elias Dayton, Philadelphia, July 4, 1776.

24 The flame of civil war is now broke out in America, and I have not the least doubt it will rage with a violence equal to what it has ever done in any other country at any time. . . . You must also know, I think that the people have gone too far to retract and that they will adopt the proverb which says, "When the sword of rebellion is drawn, the sheath should be thrown away." And the Americans have it in their power to baffle all that England can do against them.

> JOHN SINGLETON COPLEY, in a letter to his Tory half-brother Henry Pelham, August 6, 1775.

25 The difficulties I have had to struggle with, have not been occasioned by the opposite army. They always keep at a considerable distance, and disappear on our approach. But the constant incursions of Refugees, North Carolinians, and Back-Mountain-men, and the perpetual risings in the different parts of this province . . . keep the whole country in continual alarm.

> GEN. CHARLES CORNWALLIS to Gen. Henry Clinton, January 6, 1781.

26 Our new calamities being shared equally by all, will become lighter; our mutual affection for each other, will in this great transmutation become the strongest link of our new society, will afford us every joy we can receive on a foreign soil, and preserve us in unity, as the gravity and coherency of matter prevents the world from dissolution.

> MICHEL GUILLAUME JEAN DE CRÈVECOEUR, on the Revolution, *Letters from an American Farmer,* 1782.

27 The cause of liberty is a cause of too much dignity, to be sullied by turbulence and tumult. It ought to be maintained in a manner suitable to her nature. Those who engage in it, should breathe a sedate, yet fervent spirit, animating them to actions

of prudence, justice, modesty, bravery, humanity, and magnanimity.

> JOHN DICKINSON, *Letters from a Farmer in Pennsylvania,* 1768.

28 Then join hand in hand, brave Americans all,
By uniting we stand, by dividing we fall.

> JOHN DICKINSON, "A Song for American Freedom," called the Liberty Song, first published in *The Boston Gazette,* July 18, 1768.

29 Our cause is just. Our union is perfect.

> JOHN DICKINSON, "Declaration on the Causes and Necessity of Taking up Arms," 1775.

30 By the rude bridge that arched the flood,
Their flag to April's breeze unfurled,
Here once the embattled farmers stood,
And fired the shot heard round the world.

> RALPH WALDO EMERSON, "Hymn Sung at the Completion of the Concord Monument," July 4, 1837, collected in *Poems,* 1847.

31 Most American heroes of the Revolutionary period are by now two men, the actual man and the romantic image. Some are even three men—the actual man, the image, and the debunked remains.

> ESTHER FORBES, *Paul Revere,* 1942.

32 You are a member of Parliament, and one of that Majority which has doomed my Country to Destruction. You have begun to burn our Towns and murder our People. Look upon your Hands! They are stained with the Blood of your Relations! You and I were long Friends. You are now my Enemy, and I am Yours, B. Franklin

> BENJAMIN FRANKLIN, in a letter (never sent) to his friend William Strahan, a London printer and publisher, written July 5, 1775.

33 We must all hang together or assuredly we shall all hang separately.

> BENJAMIN FRANKLIN, to John Hancock, at the signing of the Declaration of Independence, July 4, 1776.

34 'Tis done! and Britain for her madness sighs—
Take warning, tyrants, and henceforth be wise.

> PHILIP FRENEAU, 1778.

35 The die is now cast, the Colonies must either submit or triumph; I do not wish to come to severer measures, but we must not retreat.

> GEORGE III OF ENGLAND, in a letter to Lord North, September 11, 1774.

36 I am not sorry that the line of conduct seems now chalked out, which the enclosed dispatches thoroughly justify; the New England Governments are in a state of rebellion, blows must decide whether they are to be subject to this country or independent.

> GEORGE III OF ENGLAND, in a letter to Lord North, November 18, 1774.

37 Experience has thoroughly convinced me that the Country gains nothing by granting to Her Dependencies indulgencies, for opening the Door encourages a desire for more which if not complied with causes discontent, and the former benefit is obliterated.

> GEORGE III OF ENGLAND, in a letter to Lord North, November 12, 1778.

38 I can never suppose this country so far lost to all ideas of self-importance as to be willing to grant America independence; if that could ever be adopted I shall despair of this country being ever preserved from a state of inferiority and consequently falling into a very low class among the European States.

> GEORGE III OF ENGLAND, in a letter to Lord North, March 7, 1780.

39 I cannot conclude without mentioning how sensibly I feel the dismemberment of America from this empire, and that I should be miserable indeed if I did not feel that no blame on that account can be laid at my door, and did I not also know that knavery seems to be so much the striking feature of its inhabitants that it may not in the end be an evil that they will become aliens to this kingdom.

> GEORGE III OF ENGLAND, in a letter to the Earl of Shelburne, November 10, 1782.

40 [The American Revolution] was a vindication of liberties inherited and possessed. It was a conservative revolution.

WILLIAM E. GLADSTONE, "Kin Beyond the Sea," published in the *North American Review,* September, 1878.

41 Treason of the blackest dye was yesterday discovered! General Arnold, who commanded at West Point, lost to every sentiment of honor, of public and private obligation, was about to deliver up that important post into the hands of the enemy. Such an event must have given the American cause a deadly wound, if not a fatal stab. Happily, the treason has been timely discovered to prevent the fatal misfortune. The providential train of circumstances which led to it affords the most convincing proof that the liberties of America are the object of divine protection.

> Gen. Nathanael Greene's general orders to the Continental Army after the discovery of Benedict Arnold's treason, September 26, 1780.

42 We fight, get beat, rise, and fight again.

> GEN. NATHANAEL GREENE, in a letter to Chevalier de la Luzerne, French ambassador to the U.S., after the battle of Hobkirk's Hill, South Carolina, April, 1781.

43 I wish to be useful, and every kind of service, necessary to the public good, becomes honorable by being necessary.

> NATHAN HALE, to his friend Capt. William Hull, when the latter objected to Hale's going behind enemy lines to spy on the British, September 10, 1776.

44 There, I guess King George will be able to read that.

> JOHN HANCOCK, referring to the large size of his signature on the Declaration of Independence, July 4, 1776.

45 Tarquin and Caesar had each his Brutus,—Charles the First, his Cromwell, and George the Third—["Treason!" shouted the Speaker] may profit by their example. If this be treason, make the most of it.

> PATRICK HENRY, in a speech in the Virginia House of Burgesses, May 29, 1765.

46 The distinctions between Virginians, Pennsylvanians, New Yorkers, New Englanders, are no more. I am not a Virginian but an American.

> PATRICK HENRY, addressing the First Continental Congress, September 5, 1774.

47 It is natural for man to indulge in the illusions of hope. We are apt to shut our eyes against a painful truth, and listen to the song of that siren till she transforms us into beasts. Is this the part of wise men, engaged in a great and arduous struggle for liberty? . . . For my part, whatever anguish of spirit it may cost, I am willing to know the whole truth; to know the worst, and to provide for it.

> PATRICK HENRY, in a speech in the Virginia Convention, March 23, 1775.

48 We are not weak if we make a proper use of those means which the God of Nature has placed in our power. Three millions of people, armed in the holy cause of liberty, and in such a country as that which we possess, are invincible by any force which our enemy can send against us. Besides, sir, we shall not fight our battles alone. There is a just God who presides over the destinies of nations, and who will raise up friends to fight our battles for us. The battle, sir, is not to the strong alone; it is to the vigilant, the active, the brave.

> Ibid.

49 If we wish to be free; if we mean to preserve inviolate those inestimable privileges for which we have been so long contending; if we mean not basely to abandon the noble struggle in which we have been so long engaged, and which we have pledged ourselves never to abandon until the glorious object of our contest shall be obtained—we must fight! I repeat it, sir, we must fight! An appeal to arms, and to the God of hosts, is all that is left us.

> Ibid.

50 The war is actually begun! The next gale that sweeps from the north will bring to our ears the clash of resounding arms! Our brethren are already in the field!

> Ibid.

Declaration of Independence, July 4, 1776

The Declaration was adopted by the Second Continental Congress on July 4 and signed then only by John Hancock, the presiding officer, and Charles Thomson, the secretary. On August 2 other members signed a parchment copy, though their names were withheld from the public to prevent their arrest and hanging as traitors.

When, in the course of human events, it becomes necessary for one people to dissolve the political bands which have connected them with another, and to assume, among the powers of the earth, the separate and equal station to which the laws of nature and of nature's God entitle them, a decent respect to the opinions of mankind requires that they should declare the causes which impel them to the separation.

We hold these truths to be self-evident, that all men are created equal, that they are endowed by their Creator with certain unalienable rights, that among these are life, liberty, and the pursuit of happiness. That, to secure these rights, governments are instituted among men, deriving their just powers from the consent of the governed. That, whenever any form of government becomes destructive of these ends, it is the right of the people to alter or to abolish it, and to institute new government, laying its foundation on such principles, and organizing its powers in such form, as to them shall seem most likely to effect their safety and happiness.

Prudence, indeed, will dictate that governments long established should not be changed for light and transient causes; and, accordingly, all experience has shown, that mankind are more disposed to suffer, while evils are sufferable, than to right themselves by abolishing the forms to which they are accustomed.

But, when a long train of abuses and usurpations, pursuing invariably the same object, evinces a design to reduce them under absolute despotism, it is their right, it is their duty, to throw off such government, and to provide new guards for their future security. Such has been the patient sufferance of these colonies; and such is now the necessity which constrains them to alter their former systems of government. The history of the present King of Great Britain is a history of repeated injuries and usurpations, all having in direct object the establishment of an absolute tyranny over these states. To prove this, let facts be submitted to a candid world.

He has refused his assent to laws the most wholesome and necessary for the public good.

He has forbidden his governors to pass laws of immediate and pressing importance, unless suspended in their operation till his assent should be obtained; and when so suspended, he has utterly neglected to attend to them.

He has refused to pass other laws for the accommodation of large districts of people, unless those people would relinquish the right of representation in the legislature; a right inestimable to them and formidable to tyrants only.

He has called together legislative bodies at places unusual, uncomfortable, and distant from the depository of their public records, for the sole purpose of fatiguing them into compliance with his measures.

He has dissolved representative houses repeatedly, for opposing, with manly firmness, his invasions on the rights of the people.

He has refused for a long time, after such dissolutions, to cause others to be elected; whereby the legislative powers, incapable of annihilation, have returned to the people at large for their exercise; the state remaining in the meantime exposed to all the dangers of invasion from without, and convulsions within.

He has endeavored to prevent the population of these states; for that purpose obstructing the laws for naturalization of foreigners; refusing to pass others to encourage their migrations hither, and raising the conditions of new appropriations of lands.

He has obstructed the administration of justice, by refusing his assent to laws for establishing judiciary powers.

He has made judges dependent on his will alone, for the tenure of their offices, and the amount and payment of their salaries.

He has erected a multitude of new offices, and sent hither swarms of officers to harass our people, and eat out their substance.

He has kept among us, in times of peace, standing armies, without the consent of our legislatures.

He has affected to render the military independent of and superior to the civil power.

He has combined with others to subject us to a jurisdiction foreign to our constitution, and unacknowledged by our laws; giving his assent to their acts of pretended legislation:

For quartering large bodies of armed troops among us;

For protecting them, by a mock trial, from punishment for any murders which they should commit on the inhabitants of these states;

For cutting off our trade with all parts of the world;

For imposing taxes on us without our consent;

For depriving us, in many cases, of the benefits of trial by jury;

For transporting us beyond seas to be tried for pretended offenses;

For abolishing the free system of English laws in a neighboring province, establishing therein an arbitrary government, and enlarging its boundaries, so as to render it at once an example and fit instrument for introducing the same absolute rule into these colonies;

For taking away our charters, abolishing our most valuable laws, and altering fundamentally the forms of our governments;

For suspending our own legislatures, and declaring themselves invested with power to legislate for us in all cases whatsoever.

He has abdicated government here, by declaring us out of his protection, and waging war against us.

He has plundered our seas, ravaged our coasts, burnt our towns, and destroyed the lives of our people.

He is at this time transporting large armies of foreign mercenaries to complete the works of death, desolation, and tyranny, already begun with circumstances of cruelty and perfidy scarcely paralleled in the most barbarous ages, and totally unworthy the head of a civilized nation.

He has constrained our fellow citizens, taken captive on the high seas, to bear arms against their country, to become the executioners of their friends and brethren, or to fall themselves by their hands.

He has excited domestic insurrections amongst us, and has endeavored to bring on the inhabitants of our frontiers, the merciless Indian savages, whose known rule of warfare is an undistinguished destruction of all ages, sexes, and conditions.

In every stage of these oppressions, we have petitioned for redress, in the most humble terms. Our repeated petitions have been answered only by repeated injury. A prince, whose character is thus marked by every act which may define a tyrant, is unfit to be the ruler of a free people.

Nor have we been wanting in attentions to our British brethren. We have warned them from time to time of attempts by their legislature to extend an unwarrantable jurisdiction over us. We have reminded them of the circumstances of our emigration and settlement here. We have appealed to their native justice and magnanimity, and we have conjured them by the ties of our common kindred, to disavow these usurpations, which would inevitably interrupt our connections and correspondence. They too have been deaf to the voice of justice and of consanguinity. We must, therefore, acquiesce in the necessity, which denounces our separation, and hold them, as we hold the rest of mankind, enemies in war, in peace friends.

We, therefore, the representatives of the United States of America, in General Congress assembled, appealing to the Supreme Judge of the world for the rectitude of our intentions, do, in the name, and by authority of the good people of these colonies, solemnly publish and declare, that these United Colonies are, and of right ought to be free and independent states; that they are absolved from all allegiance to the British Crown, and that all political connection between them and the state of Great Britain is and ought to be totally dissolved; and that, as free and independent states, they have full power to levy war, conclude peace, contract alliances, establish commerce, and to do all other acts and things which independent states may of right do. And for the support of this declaration, with a firm reliance on the protection of Divine Providence, we mutually pledge to each other our lives, our fortunes, and our sacred honor.

51 Is life so dear or peace so sweet as to be purchased at the price of chains and slavery? Forbid it, Almighty God! I know not what course others may take; but as for me, give me liberty, or give me death!

Ibid.

52 The evacuation of Boston was not simply that one flag went down and another flag went up over the Province House and the Old State House; that soldiers in homespun followed down to the wharves other soldiers in red coats. On the 17th day of March, 1776, republicanism under George Washington drove imperialism under Sir William Howe out of Boston, never to come back.

GEORGE FRISBIE HOAR, in a speech in the U.S. Senate, March 18, 1901.

53 This was the object of the Declaration of Independence. Not to find out new principles, or new arguments, never before thought of, not merely to say things which had never been said before; but to place before mankind the common sense of the subject, in terms so plain and firm as to command their assent, and to justify ourselves in the independent stand we are compelled to take.

THOMAS JEFFERSON, in a letter to Henry Lee, May 8, 1825.

54 I have not yet begun to fight.

JOHN PAUL JONES, as his ship the *Bonhomme Richard* was sinking and the British were demanding his surrender, September 23, 1779.

55 After the sacrifices that I have made in this cause, I have the right to ask two favors at your hands: the one is, to serve without pay, at my own expense; and the other, that I be allowed to serve at first as a volunteer in the ranks.

MARQUIS DE LAFAYETTE, in a letter to Congress, July 23, 1777.

56 That these United Colonies are, and of right ought to be, free and independent States; that they are absolved from all allegiance to the British Crown; and that all political connection between them and the State of Great Britain is, and ought to be, totally dissolved.

RICHARD HENRY LEE, resolution introduced before the Continental Congress June 7, 1776, adopted July 2, 1776.

57 The history of modern, civilized America opened with one of those great, really liberating,

really revolutionary wars of which there have been so few compared to the vast number of wars of conquest which, like the present imperialist war, were caused by squabbles among kings, landowners or capitalists over the division of usurped lands or ill-gotten gains. That was the war the American people waged against the British robbers who oppressed America and held her in colonial slavery, in the same way as these "civilized" bloodsuckers are still oppressing and holding in colonial slavery hundreds of millions of people in India, Egypt, and all parts of the world.

> V.I. LENIN, *Pravda,* August 22, 1918.

58 Listen, my children, and you shall hear
Of the midnight ride of Paul Revere,
On the eighteenth of April in Seventy-five.
Hardly a man is now alive
Who remembers that famous day and year.

> HENRY WADWORTH LONGFELLOW, "Paul Revere's Ride," 1861.

59 Make no mistake; the American Revolution was not fought to *obtain* freedom, but to *preserve* the liberties that Americans already had as colonials. Independence was no conscious goal, secretly nurtured in cellar or jungle by bearded conspirators, but a reluctant last resort, to preserve "life, liberty, and the pursuit of happiness."

> SAMUEL ELIOT MORISON, *The Oxford History of the American People,* 1965.

60 If the American Revolution had produced nothing but the Declaration of Independence, it would have been worth while.

> Ibid.

61 From the east to the west blow the trumpet to arms!
Through the land let the sound of it flee;
Let the far and near all unite, with a cheer,
In defense of our Liberty Tree.

> THOMAS PAINE, "The Liberty Tree," July, 1775.

62 Arms, as a last resource, must decide the contest; the appeal was the choice of the king, and the continent hath accepted the challenge.

> THOMAS PAINE, *Common Sense,* January 10, 1776.

63 The Sun never shined in a cause of greater worth. 'Tis not the affair of a City, a County, a Province, or a Kingdom; but of a Continent—of at least one eighth part of the habitable Globe.

> Ibid.

64 Everything that is right or natural pleads for separation. The blood of the slain, the weeping voice of nature cries, *'tis time to part.*

> Ibid.

65 O ye that love mankind! Ye that dare oppose, not only the tyranny, but the tyrant, stand forth! Every spot of the old world is overrun with oppression. Freedom hath been hunted round the globe. Asia and Africa have long expelled her, Europe regards her like a stranger, and England hath given her warning to depart. O! receive the fugitive, and prepare in time an asylum for mankind.

> Ibid.

66 These are the times that try men's souls. The summer soldier and the sunshine patriot will, in this crisis, shrink from the service of his country; but he that stands it NOW, deserves the love and thanks of man and woman.

> THOMAS PAINE, *The American Crisis,* No. 1, published in the *Pennsylvania Journal,* December 19, 1776; issued as a pamphlet, December 23, 1776.

67 It is not a field of a few acres of ground, but a cause, that we are defending, and whether we defeat the enemy in one battle, or by degrees, the consequences will be the same.

> THOMAS PAINE, *The American Crisis,* No. 4, September 12, 1777.

68 We fight not to enslave, but to set a country free, and to make room upon the earth for honest men to live in.

> Ibid.

69 It is the object only of war that makes it honorable. And if there was ever a just war since the world began, it is this in which America is now engaged.

> THOMAS PAINE, *The American Crisis,* No. 5, March 21, 1778.

70 It is now nearly three years since the tyranny of Britain received its first repulse by the arms of America. A period which has given birth to a new world and erected a monument to the folly of the old.

    Ibid.

71 America has surmounted a greater variety and combination of difficulties than, I believe, ever fell to the share of any one people in the same space of time, and has replenished the world with more useful knowledge and sounder maxims of civil government than were ever produced in any age before. Had it not been for America there had been no such thing as freedom left throughout the whole universe. England hath lost hers in a long chain of right reasoning from wrong principles, and it is from this country now she must learn the resolution to redress herself, and the wisdom how.

    Ibid.

72 Stand your ground. Don't fire unless fired upon, but if they mean to have a war let it begin here.

    CAPT. JOHN PARKER, addressing his men at Lexington Green, April 19, 1775.

73 If I were an American, as I am an Englishman, while a foreign troop was landed in my country, I never would lay down my arms—never, never, never!

    WILLIAM PITT, the Younger, in a speech in the House of Commons, November 18, 1777.

74 It is a most accursed, wicked, barbarous, cruel, unnatural, unjust, and diabolical war.

    WILLIAM PITT, the Younger, 1781.

75 Don't one of you fire until you see the whites of their eyes.

    Attributed to Col. William Prescott, and also to Gen. Israel Putnam, at the Battle of Bunker Hill, June 17, 1775.

76 Under God we are determined that wheresoever, whensoever, or howsoever we shall be called to make our exit, we will die free men.

    JOSIAH QUINCY, "Observations on the Boston Port Bill," 1774.

77 A more impudent, false, and atrocious Proclamation was never fabricated by the hands of man.

    AMBROSE SERLE, secretary to Lord Howe, writing about the Declaration of Independence in his journal, c.1776, quoted in George F. Scheer and Hugh Rankin, *Rebels and Redcoats,* 1957.

78 We beat them today or Molly Stark's a widow.

    COL. JOHN STARK, addressing his troops before the battle of Bennington, August 16, 1777.

79 I can answer but for three things, a firm belief in the justice of our Cause, close attention in the prosecution of it, and the strictest integrity.

    GEORGE WASHINGTON, following his appointment as commander-in-chief of the Continental Army, June 19, 1775.

80 Let us therefore animate and encourage each other, and show the whole world that a Freeman, contending for liberty on his own ground, is superior to any slavish mercenary on earth.

    GEORGE WASHINGTON, general orders, Headquarters, New York, July 2, 1776.

81 The time is now near at hand which must probably determine whether Americans are to be freemen or slaves; whether they are to have any property they can call their own; whether their houses and farms are to be pillaged and destroyed, and themselves consigned to a state of wretchedness from which no human efforts will deliver them. The fate of unborn millions will now depend, under God, on the courage and conduct of this army. Our cruel and unrelenting enemy leaves us only the choice of brave resistance, or the most abject submission. We have, therefore, to resolve to conquer or die.

    GEORGE WASHINGTON, address to the Continental Army before the battle of Long Island, August 27, 1776.

82 There is nothing that gives a man consequence, and renders him fit for command, like a support that renders him independent of everybody but the State he serves.

    GEORGE WASHINGTON, in a letter to Congress, September 24, 1776.

83 To place any dependence upon militia, is, assuredly, resting upon a broken staff.

> Ibid.

84 Such is my situation that if I were to wish the bitterest curse to an enemy on this side of the grave, I should put him in my stead with my feelings.

> GEORGE WASHINGTON, in a letter to his cousin, Lund Washington, after the British had driven American forces from Long Island and lower Manhattan, September 30, 1776.

85 If every nerve is not strained to recruit the new army with all possible expedience I think the game is pretty near up.

> GEORGE WASHINGTON, in a letter to his brother, John Augustine Washington, December 18, 1776.

86 I do not mean to exclude altogether the idea of patriotism. I know it exists, and I know it has done much in the present contest. But I will venture to assert, that a great and lasting war can never be supported on this principle alone. It must be aided by a prospect of interest, or some reward.

> GEORGE WASHINGTON, in a letter to John Banister, Valley Forge, April 21, 1778.

87 Nothing short of independence, it appears to me, can possibly do. A peace on other terms would, if I may be allowed the expression, be a peace of war. The injuries we have received from the British nation were so unprovoked, and have been so great and so many, that they can never be forgotten.

> Ibid.

88 An Ardent Desire to spare the further Effusion of Blood, will readily incline me to listen to such terms for the surrender of your Posts of York & Gloucester, as are admissible.

> GEORGE WASHINGTON, reply to Lord Cornwallis's request for a cease-fire, October 17, 1781.

89 I have the Honor to inform Congress, that a Reduction of the British Army under the Command of Lord Cornwallis, is most happily effected. The unremitting Ardor which actuated every Officer and Soldier in the combined Army in this Occasion, has principally led to this Important Event, at an earlier period than my most sanguine Hope had induced me to expect.

> GEORGE WASHINGTON, in his report on the victory at Yorktown, Virginia, October 19, 1781.

90 The victory of that day turns out to be much more considerable than at first expected. . . . Tell the Philadelphia ladies that the heavenly, sweet, pretty redcoats, the accomplished gentlemen of the Guards and Grenadiers have humbled themselves on the plains of Monmouth.

> GEN. ANTHONY WAYNE, referring to the Battle of Monmouth, New Jersey, in a letter to Richard Peters, July 12, 1778.

91 I desired as many as could to join together in fasting and prayer, that God would restore the spirit of love and of a sound mind to the poor deluded rebels in America.

> JOHN WESLEY, *Journal*, August 1, 1777.

---

15. AMERICANS

See also AMERICAN INDIANS; AMERICA SEEN FROM ABROAD; BLACK AMERICANS

---

1 From the old-world point of view, the American had no mind; he had an economic thinking-machine which could work only on a fixed line. The American mind exasperated the European as a buzz-saw might exasperate a pine forest.

> HENRY ADAMS, *The Education of Henry Adams*, 1906.

2 Good Americans, when they die, go to Paris.

> THOMAS APPLETON, quoted in Oliver Wendell Holmes, *The Autocrat of the Breakfast-Table*, 1858.

3 The making of an American begins at that point where he himself rejects all other ties, any other history, and himself adopts the vesture of his adopted land.

> JAMES BALDWIN, *Notes of a Native Son*, 1955.

4 Alien, *n.* An American sovereign in his probationary state.

AMBROSE BIERCE, *The Devil's Dictionary,* 1906.

5 Great has been the Greek, the Latin, the Slav, the Celt, the Teuton, and the Anglo-Saxon, but greater than any of these is the American, in which are blended the virtues of them all.

WILLIAM JENNINGS BRYAN, in a speech, "America's Mission," Washington, D.C. February 22, 1899.

6 We believe we must be the family of America, recognizing that at the heart of the matter we are bound one to another.

MARIO CUOMO, in the keynote address at the Democratic National Convention, July 16, 1984.

7 God will save the good American, and seat him at His right hand on the Golden Throne.

THEODORE DREISER, *Life, Art, and America,* 1917.

8 Here in America we are descended in blood and in spirit from revolutionaries and rebels—men and women who dared to dissent from accepted doctrine. As their heirs, may we never confuse honest dissent with disloyal subversion.

DWIGHT D. EISENHOWER, in a speech at the Columbia University Bicentennial dinner, May 31, 1954.

9 We are a puny and a fickle folk. Avarice, hesitation, and following are our diseases.

RALPH WALDO EMERSON, "The Method of Nature," *Nature; Addresses and Lectures,* 1849.

10 The American is only the continuation of the English genius into new conditions, more or less propitious.

RALPH WALDO EMERSON, *English Traits,* 1856.

11 One day we will cast out the passion for Europe, by the passion for America.

RALPH WALDO EMERSON, "Considerations by the Way," *The Conduct of Life,* 1860.

12 Our American people cannot be taxed with slowness in performance, or in praising their performance.

RALPH WALDO EMERSON, "Success," *Society and Solitude,* 1870.

13 There are no second acts in American lives.

F. SCOTT FITZGERALD, in his notes for *The Last Tycoon,* 1941.

14 Americans see history as a straight line and themselves standing at the cutting edge of it as representatives for all mankind. They believe in the future as if it were a religion; they believe that there is nothing they cannot accomplish, that solutions wait somewhere for all problems, like brides.

FRANCES FITZGERALD, *Fire in the Lake,* 1972.

15 We are a people who do not want to keep much of the past in our heads. It is considered unhealthy in America to remember mistakes, neurotic to think about them, psychotic to dwell on them.

LILLIAN HELLMAN, *Scoundrel Time,* 1976.

16 Every American owns all America.

OLIVER WENDELL HOLMES, SR., *The Professor at the Breakfast-Table,* 1859.

17 Despite the focus in the media on the affluent and the poor, the average man is neither. Despite the concentration on TV commercials on the blond, blue-eyed WASP, the real American prototype is of Italian or Irish or Polish or Greek or Lithuanian or German or Hungarian or Russian or any one of the still amazing number of national origins represented in this country—a "white ethnic," sociologists soberly call him.

LOUISE KAPP HOWE, *The White Majority,* 1970.

18 He said he should be afraid to go to America without understanding English. I told him the Americans were a strange set of fellows that run about all parts of the world without caring to learn the language before hand.

WASHINGTON IRVING, entry dated August 19, 1804, in his *Journals,* 1919.

19 Turning our eyes to other nations, our great desire is to see our brethren of the human race secured in the blessings enjoyed by ourselves, and advancing in knowledge, in freedom, and in social happiness.

ANDREW JACKSON, in his first message to Congress, December 8, 1829.

20 Our flag is red, white and blue, but our nation is a rainbow—red, yellow, brown, black and white—and we're all precious in God's sight. America is not like a blanket—one piece of unbroken cloth, the same color, the same texture, the same size. America is more like a quilt—many patches, many pieces, many colors, many sizes, all woven and held together by a common thread. . . . Even in our fractured state, all of us count and all of us fit somewhere.

JESSE JACKSON, in a speech before the Democratic National Convention, July 16, 1984.

21 It's a complex fate, being an American, and one of the responsibilities it entails is fighting against a superstitious valuation of Europe.

HENRY JAMES, in a letter written in 1872, quoted in Percy Lubbock, *Letters of Henry James*, 1920.

22 My God! how little do my country men know what precious blessings they are in possession of, and which no other people on earth enjoy. I confess I had no idea of it myself. While we shall see multiplied instances of Europeans going to live in America, I will venture to say no man now living will ever see an instance of an American removing to settle in Europe and continuing there.

THOMAS JEFFERSON, in a letter to James Monroe from Paris, France, June 17, 1785.

23 Nothing so challenges the American spirit as tackling the biggest job on earth. . . . Americans are stimulated by the big job—the Panama Canal, Boulder Dam, Grand Coulee, Lower Colorado River developments, the tallest building in the world, the mightiest battleship.

LYNDON B. JOHNSON, in a speech to Congress, April 30, 1941.

24 You can always tell the Irish,
    You can always tell the Dutch
You can always tell a Yankee;
    But you cannot tell him much.

ERIC KNIGHT, "All Yankees Are Liars."

25 I don't think it does any harm just once in a while to acknowledge that the whole country isn't in flames, that there are people in the country besides politicians, entertainers, and criminals.

CHARLES KURALT, quoted in *American Way* magazine, March, 1978.

26 We have been the recipients of the choicest bounties of Heaven. We have been preserved, these many years, in peace and prosperity. We have grown in numbers, wealth, and power as no other nation has ever grown; but we have forgotten God. We have forgotten the gracious hand which preserved us in peace, and multiplied and enriched and strengthened us; and we have vainly imagined, in the deceitfulness of our hearts, that all these blessings were produced by some superior wisdom and virtue of our own.

ABRAHAM LINCOLN, in a proclamation issued on March 30, 1863, for a national day of fasting and prayer to be observed on April 30, 1863.

27 Let us have done with British-Americans and Irish-Americans and German-Americans, and so on, and all be Americans. . . . If a man is going to be an American at all let him be so without any qualifying adjectives; and if he is going to be something else, let him drop the word American from his personal description.

HENRY CABOT LODGE, in an address, December 21, 1888.

28 The American is nomadic in religion, in ideas, in morals.

JAMES RUSSELL LOWELL, *Fireside Travels*, 1864.

29 For some reason or other, the European has rarely been able to see America except in caricature.

JAMES RUSSELL LOWELL, "On a Certain Condescension in Foreigners," 1869.

30 Till after our Civil War it never seemed to enter the head of any foreigner, especially of any Englishman, that an American had what could be called a country, except as a place to eat, sleep, and trade in. Then it seemed to strike them suddenly. "By Jove, you know, fellahs don't fight like that for a shop-till!" No, I rather think not. To Americans America is something

more than a promise and an expectation. It has a past and traditions of its own. A descent from men who sacrificed everything and came hither, not to better their fortunes, but to plant their idea in virgin soil, should be a good pedigree. There was never colony save this that went forth, not to seek gold, but God.

Ibid.

31 We Americans are the peculiar, chosen people—the Israel of our time; we bear the ark of the liberties of the world.

HERMAN MELVILLE, *White-Jacket,* 1850.

32 We are the pioneers of the world; the advance guard sent on through the wilderness of untried things to break a new path in the New World that is ours. In our youth is our strength; in our inexperience, our wisdom.

Ibid.

33 The men the American people admire most extravagantly are the most daring liars; the men they detest most violently are those who try to tell them the truth.

Attributed to H.L. Mencken.

34 With all of our differences, whenever we are confronted with a threat to our security we are not then Republicans or Democrats but Americans; we are not then fifty states but the United States.

RICHARD M. NIXON, *The Challenges We Face,* 1960.

35 The American leader class has really had it in terms of their ability to lead. It's really sickening to have to receive them at the White House as I often do and to hear them whine and whimper and that's one of the reasons why I enjoy very much more receiving labor leaders and people from middle America who still have character and guts and a bit of patriotism.

RICHARD M. NIXON, diary entry, September, 1972, in *The Memoirs of Richard Nixon,* 1978.

36 Our citizenship in the United States is our national character. Our citizenship in any particular state is only our local distinction. By the latter we

are known at home, by the former to the world. Our great title is AMERICANS—our inferior one varies with the place.

THOMAS PAINE, *The American Crisis,* April 19, 1783.

37 Americans are notoriously hard to divide along class lines. With the exception of professors of sociology (who know exactly where in the upper middle class they fit) and a few billionaires—who hope they are upper-class, but have a horrible fear there may be a real aristocracy hiding somewhere in Boston or Philadelphia—most of us have only the vaguest idea what class we belong to.

NOEL PERRIN, *Third Person Rural,* 1983.

38 Americans are getting like a Ford car—they all have the same parts, the same upholstering and make exactly the same noises.

WILL ROGERS, *The Autobiography of Will Rogers,* 1949.

39 We don't know what we want, but we are ready to bite somebody to get it.

Ibid.

40 The saving grace of America lies in the fact that the overwhelming majority of Americans are possessed of two great qualities—a sense of humor and a sense of proportion.

FRANKLIN D. ROOSEVELT, in a speech in Savannah, Georgia, November 18, 1933.

41 From the very beginning our people have markedly combined practical capacity for affairs with power of devotion to an ideal. The lack of either quality would have rendered the possession of the other of small value.

THEODORE ROOSEVELT, in a speech in Philadelphia, Pennsylvania, November 22, 1902.

42 The American people abhor a vacuum.

THEODORE ROOSEVELT, in a speech in Cairo, Illinois, October 3, 1907.

43 There is no room in this country for hyphenated Americans. . . . The one absolutely certain way of bringing this nation to ruin, of preventing all possibility of it continuing to be a nation at all, would

be to permit it to become a tangle of squabbling nationalities.

> THEODORE ROOSEVELT, in a speech, "Americanism," New York City, October 12, 1915.

44 Americans are eminently prophets; they apply morals to public affairs; they are impatient and enthusiastic. Their judgments have highly speculative implications, which they often make explicit; they are men with principles, and fond of stating them. Moreover, they have an intense self-reliance; to exercise private judgment is not only a habit with them but a conscious duty.

> GEORGE SANTAYANA, *Character and Opinion in the United States,* 1920.

45 The American people never carry an umbrella. They prepare to walk in eternal sunshine.

> ALFRED E. SMITH, in a syndicated newspaper article, 1931.

46 In America everybody is, but some are more than others.

> GERTRUDE STEIN, *Everybody's Autobiography,* 1938.

47 Americans have always assumed, subconsciously, that all problems can be solved; that every story has a happy ending; that the application of enough energy and good will can make everything come out right. In view of our history, this assumption is natural enough. As a people, we have never encountered any obstacle that we could not overcome.

> ADLAI E. STEVENSON, *Call to Greatness,* 1954.

48 The Jew is neither a newcomer nor an alien in this country or on this continent; his Americanism is as original and ancient as that of any race or people with the exception of the American Indian and other aborigines. He came in the caravels of Columbus, and he knocked at the gates of New Amsterdam only thirty-five years after the Pilgrim Fathers stepped ashore on Plymouth Rock.

> OSCAR SOLOMON STRAUS, "America and the Spirit of American Judaism," an address given before the American Hebrew Congregation, New York City, January 18, 1911.

49 Old elephants limp off to the hills to die; old Americans go out to the highway and drive themselves to death with huge cars.

> HUNTER S. THOMPSON, *Fear and Loathing in Las Vegas,* 1972.

50 For we cannot tarry here,
  We must march my darlings, we must bear the brunt of danger,
  We the youthful sinewy races, all the rest on us depend, Pioneers! O Pioneers!

> WALT WHITMAN, "Pioneers! O Pioneers!" 1865.

51 Our leading men are not of much account and never have been, but the average of the people is immense, beyond all history. Sometimes I think in all departments, literature and art included, that will be the way our superiority will exhibit itself. We will not have great individuals or great leaders, but a great average bulk, unprecedentedly great.

> WALT WHITMAN, "An Interviewer's Item," October 17, 1879, in *Specimen Days and Collect,* 1882.

52 We have earned the slogan "Yanks, go home!"

> EDMUND WILSON, in his preface to *Europe Without Baedeker,* 1967.

53 Some Americans need hyphens in their names, because only part of them has come over; but when the whole man has come over, heart and thought and all, the hyphen drops of its own weight out of his name.

> WOODROW WILSON, in a speech in Washington, D.C., May 16, 1914.

54 You cannot become thorough Americans if you think of yourselves in groups. America does not consist of groups. A man who thinks of himself as belonging to a particular national group in America has not yet become an American.

> WOODROW WILSON, in an address at Convention Hall, Philadelphia, Pennsylvania, May 10, 1915.

16. AMERICA SEEN FROM ABROAD

See also AMERICA

1 That which in England we call the Middle Classes is in America virtually the nation.

MATTHEW ARNOLD, *A Word About America,* 1882.

2 Until I went to the United States I had never seen a people with institutions which seemed expressly and thoroughly suited to it. I had not properly appreciated the benefits proceeding from this cause.

MATTHEW ARNOLD, *A Word More About America,* 1885.

3 The combination of a hatred of war and militarism with an innocent delight in playing soldiers is one of the apparent contradictions of American life that one has to accept.

DENIS WILLIAM BROGAN, *The American Character,* 1944.

4 A people that has licked a more formidable enemy than Germany or Japan, primitive North America . . . a country whose national motto has been "root, hog, or die."

Ibid.

5 The American race seems to have developed two classes, and only two, the upper-middle, and the lower-middle.

RUPERT BROOKE, *Letters from America,* 1916.

6 America excites an admiration which must be felt on the spot to be understood.

JAMES BRYCE, *The American Commonwealth,* 1888.

7 The American imagination is peculiarly sensitive to the impression of great size. "A big thing" is their habitual phrase of admiration. . . . The sense of immensity, the sense that the same thought and purpose are animating millions of other men in sympathy with himself, lifts a man out of himself, and sends him into transports of eagerness and zeal about things intrinsically small, but great through the volume of human feeling they have attracted.

Ibid.

8 Pessimism is the luxury of a handful; optimism is the private delight, as well as public profession, of nine hundred and ninety-nine out of every thousand, for nowhere does the individual associate himself more constantly and directly with the greatness of his country.

Ibid.

9 Individualism, the love of enterprise, and the pride in personal freedom, have been deemed by Americans not only their choicest, but their peculiar and exclusive possessions.

Ibid.

10 Young men, there is America—which at this day serves for little more than to amuse you with stories of savage men and uncouth manners; yet shall, before you taste of death, show itself equal to the whole of that commerce which now attracts the envy of the world.

EDMUND BURKE, in his second speech "On Conciliation with America," March 22, 1775.

11 America has a new delicacy, a coarse, rank refinement.

G.K. CHESTERTON, *Charles Dickens,* 1906.

12 There is nothing the matter with Americans except their ideals. The real American is all right; it is the ideal American who is all wrong.

G.K. CHESTERTON, in the *New York Times,* February 1, 1931.

13 I might express it somewhat abruptly by saying that most Americans are born drunk, and really require a little wine or beer to sober them. They have a sort of permanent intoxication from within, a sort of invisible champagne. . . . Americans do not need to drink to inspire them to do anything, though they do sometimes, I think, need a little for the deeper and more delicate purpose of teaching them how to do nothing.

G.K. CHESTERTON, in the *New York Times,* June 28, 1931.

14 The possible destiny of the United States of America—as a nation of a hundred millions of freemen—stretching from the Atlantic to the Pacific, living under the laws of Alfred, and speaking the language of Shakespeare and Milton, is an august conception. Why would we not wish to see it realized? America would then be England viewed through a solar microscope; Great Britain in a state of glorious magnification!

SAMUEL TAYLOR COLERIDGE, April 10, 1833, in *Table Talk,* 1836.

15 I believe there is no country, on the face of the earth, where there is less freedom of opinion on any subject in reference to which there is a broad difference of opinion, than in this.

CHARLES DICKENS, on the United States, in a letter to John Forster, February 24, 1842.

16 It would be well, there can be no doubt, for the American people as a whole, if they loved the Real less, and the Ideal somewhat more.

CHARLES DICKENS, *American Notes,* 1842.

17 America is rather like life. You can usually find in it what you look for. . . . It will probably be interesting, and it is sure to be large.

E.M. FORSTER, *Two Cheers for Democracy,* 1951.

18 What distinguishes America is not its greater or lesser goodness, but simply its unrivalled power to do that which is good or bad.

MARK FRANKLAND, in the London *Observer,* November 6, 1977.

19 The most characteristic thing in America, mechanical America, is that it can make poetry out of material things. America's poetry is not in literature, but in architecture.

OLIVER ST. JOHN GOGARTY, *As I Was Going Down Sackville Street,* 1937.

20 Sir, they [the American colonists] are a race of convicts, and ought to be thankful for any thing we allow them short of hanging.

SAMUEL JOHNSON, quoted in James Boswell, *The Life of Samuel Johnson,* 1791.

21 I am willing to love all mankind, *except an American.*

Ibid.

22 America is fundamentally the land of the overrated child.

HERMANN KEYSERLING, *America Set Free,* 1929.

23 When I first arrived in the States a shrewd American said to me: "A European coming to America for the first time, should skip New York and fly directly to Kansas. Start from the Middle. The East will only mislead you."

LORD KINROSS, *The Innocents at Home,* 1959.

24 Let there be no misunderstanding about the matter. I love these [American] People, and if any contemptuous criticism has to be done, I will do it myself. My heart has gone out to them beyond all other peoples; and for the life of me I cannot tell why.

RUDYARD KIPLING, *American Notes,* 1891.

25 Oh, America, the sun sets in you.
Are you the grave of our day?

D.H. LAWRENCE, "The Evening Land," *Birds Beasts, and Flowers,* 1923.

26 Perhaps you have to be born an Englishwoman to realize how much attention American men shower on women and how tremendously considerate all the nice ones among them are of a woman's wishes.

GERTRUDE LAWRENCE, *A Star Danced,* 1945.

27 The Americans are a queer people; they can't rest.

STEPHEN LEACOCK, quoted in Fred J. Ringel *America as Others See It,* 1932.

28 The American sign of civic progress is to tear down the familiar and erect the monstrous.

SHANE LESLIE, *American Wonderland,* 1936.

29 There is no part of the world perhaps, where you have more difficulty in obtaining permission to be alone, and indulge in a reverie, than in America.

The Americans are as gregarious as school-boys and think it an incivility to leave you by yourself.

FREDERICK MARRYAT, *Diary in America with Remarks on Its Institutions,* 1839.

30 When you consider how indifferent Americans are to the quality and cooking of the food they put into their insides, it cannot but strike you as peculiar that they should take such pride in the mechanical appliances they use for its excretion.

W. SOMERSET MAUGHAM, *A Writer's Notebook,* 1949.

31 Things on the whole move much faster in America; people don't *stand for election,* they *run for office.* If a person say he's *sick,* it doesn't mean regurgitating; it means *ill. Mad* means angry, not *insane.* Don't ask for the left-luggage; it's called a check-room. A nice joint means a good pub, not roast meat.

JESSICA MITFORD, *Daughters and Rebels,* 1960.

32 The United States is the greatest single achievement of European civilization.

ROBERT BALMAIN MOWAT, *The United States of America,* 1938.

33 Though I have kind invitations enough to visit America, I could not, even for a couple of months, live in a country so miserable as to possess no castles.

JOHN RUSKIN, *Praeterita,* 1885–1889.

34 Examples to the contrary notwithstanding, the essence of the United States is to be found in its small towns. This cannot be said of any other country.... The American village ... is a small edition of the whole country, in its civil government, its press, its schools, its banks, its town hall, its census, its spirit, and its appearance.

DOMINGO FAUSTINO SARMIENTO, *Travels in the United States in 1847,* translated by Michael A. Rockland, 1970.

35 You have set up in New York harbor a monstrous idol which you call Liberty. The only thing that remains to complete that monument is to put on its pedestal the inscription written by Dante on the gate of Hell: "All hope abandon, ye who enter here."

GEORGE BERNARD SHAW, in a speech to the Academy of Political Science, New York City, April 11, 1933.

36 I have traveled a good deal, but I never saw in any country anything like this 100 percent American.

Ibid.

37 In the four quarters of the globe, who reads an American book? or goes to an American play? or looks at an American picture or statue? What does the world yet owe to American physicians or surgeons? What new substances have their chemists discovered? or what old ones have they analyzed? What new constellations have been discovered by the telescopes of Americans? What have they done in mathematics? Who drinks out of American glasses? or eats from American plates? or wears American coats or gowns? or sleeps in American blankets? Finally, under which of the old tyrannical governments of Europe is every sixth man a slave, whom his fellow-creatures may buy, and sell, and torture?

SYDNEY SMITH, "America," in the *Edinburgh Review,* January-May, 1820.

38 See what it is to have a nation to take its place among civilized states before it has either gentlemen or scholars. They have in the course of twenty years acquired a distinct national character for low, lying knavery.

ROBERT SOUTHEY, in a letter to Walter Savage Landor, 1812.

39 In the first place the genius of this nation is not in the least to be compared with that of the Prussians, Austrians, or French. You say to your soldier, "Do this," and he doeth it. But I am obliged to say, "This is the reason why you ought to do that," and then he does it.

FRIEDRICH WILHELM VON STEUBEN, in a letter to a Prussian officer, quoted in J. Lawton Collins, *War in Peacetime: The History and Lessons of Korea,* 1969.

40 None can care for literature in itself who do not take a special pleasure in the sound of names; and there is no part of the world where nomenclature

is so rich, poetical, humorous, and picturesque as the United States of America. All times, races, and languages have brought their contribution. Pekin is in the same State with Euclid, with Bellefontaine, and with Sandusky. . . . Old, red Manhattan lies, like an Indian arrowhead under a steam factory, below Anglified New York. The names of the States and Territories themselves form a chorus of sweet and most romantic vocables: Delaware, Ohio, Indiana, Florida, Dakota, Iowa, Wyoming, Minnesota, and the Carolinas; there are few poems with a nobler music for the ear: a songful, tuneful land; and if the new Homer shall arise from the Western continent, his verse will be enriched, his pages sing spontaneously, with the names of states and cities that would strike the fancy in a business circular.

ROBERT LOUIS STEVENSON, *Across the Plains,* 1892.

41 If an American were condemned to confine his activity to his own affairs, he would be robbed of one half of his existence.

ALEXIS DE TOCQUEVILLE, *Democracy in America,* 1835–1840.

42 In America, the most democratic of nations, those complaints against property in general, which are so frequent in Europe, are never heard, because in America there are no paupers. As everyone has property of his own to defend, everyone recognizes the principle upon which he holds it.

Ibid.

43 I know of no country in which there is so little independence of mind and real freedom of discussion as in America.

Ibid.

44 The Americans, in their intercourse with strangers, appear impatient of the smallest censure and insatiable of praise.

Ibid.

45 I do not hesitate to avow that although the women of the United States are confined within the narrow circle of domestic life, and their situation is in some respects one of extreme dependence, I have

nowhere seen woman occupying a loftier position; and if I were asked . . . to what the singular prosperity and growing strength of that people ought mainly to be attributed, I should reply: To the superiority of their women.

Ibid.

46 America is a large friendly dog in a small room. Every time it wags its tail it knocks over a chair.

Attributed to Arnold Toynbee.

47 I do not like the Americans of the lower orders. I am not comfortable among them. They tread on my corns and offend me. They make my daily life unpleasant. But I do respect them. I acknowledge their intelligence and personal dignity. I know that they are men and women worthy to be so called.

ANTHONY TROLLOPE, *North America,* 1862.

48 Men and women do not beg in the States;—they do not offend you with tattered rags; they do not complain to heaven of starvation; they do not crouch to the ground for halfpence. If poor, they are not abject in their poverty. They read and write. They walk like human beings made in God's form. They know that they are men and women, owing it to themselves and to the world that they should earn their bread by their labor, but feeling that when earned it is their own. If this be so,—if it be acknowledged that it is so,—should not such knowledge in itself be sufficient testimony of the success of the country and of her institutions?

Ibid.

49 Other nations have been called thin-skinned, but the citizens of the Union have, apparently, no skins at all; they wince if a breeze blows over them, unless it be tempered with adulation.

FRANCES TROLLOPE, *Domestic Manners of the Americans,* 1832.

50 The next Augustan age will dawn on the other side of the Atlantic. There will, perhaps, be a Thucydides at Boston, a Xenophon at New York, and, in time, a Virgil at Mexico, and a Newton at Peru.

HORACE WALPOLE, in a letter, November, 1774.

51 The Inhabitants seem very Religious, showing many outward and visible Signs of an inward and Spiritual Grace: But tho' they wear in their Faces the Innocence of Doves, you will find them in their Dealings, as Subtile as Serpents. Interest is their Faith, Money their God, and Large Possessions the only Heaven they covet.

> EDWARD WARD, *A Trip to New-England,* 1699. (Ward is thought to have based this book on the experiences of others. He probably never visited America.)

52 Every time Europe looks across the Atlantic to see the American eagle, it observes only the rear end of an ostrich.

> H.G. WELLS, *America,* 1907.

53 Of course America had often been discovered before, but it had always been hushed up.

> Attributed to Oscar Wilde.

54 America is one long expectoration.

> OSCAR WILDE, in a newspaper interview, 1882.

55 I am lost in wonder and amazement. It is not a country, but a world. . . . The West I liked best. The people are stronger, fresher, saner than the rest. They are ready to be taught. The surroundings of nature have instilled in them a love of the beautiful, which but needs development and direction. The East I found a feeble reflex of Europe; in fact, I may say that I was in America for a month before I saw an American.

> OSCAR WILDE, quoted in the *St Louis Daily Democrat,* February 26, 1882.

56 The Americans are certainly hero-worshippers, and always take their heroes from the criminal classes.

> OSCAR WILDE, in a letter to Norman Forbes-Robertson, April 19, 1882.

57 The cities of America are inexpressibly tedious. The Bostonians take their learning too sadly: culture with them is an accomplishment rather than an atmosphere; their "Hub," as they call it, is the paradise of prigs. Chicago is a sort of monster-shop, full of bustle and bores. Political life at Washington is like political life in a suburban vestry. Balti-more is amusing for a week, but Philadelphia is dreadfully provincial; and though one can dine in New York, one could not dwell there.

> OSCAR WILDE, "The American Invasion," in the *Court and Society Review,* March, 1887.

58 The youth of America is their oldest tradition. It has been going on now for three hundred years.

> OSCAR WILDE, in *A Woman of No Importance,* 1893.

59 The Americans are in general the dirtiest, most contemptible cowardly dogs that you can conceive. There is no depending on them in action. They fall down dead in their own dirt and desert by battalions, officers and all. Such rascals as those are rather an encumbrance than any real strength to an army.

> GEN. JAMES WOLFE, in a letter of 1758, quoted in Brian Connell, *The Savage Years,* 1959.

60 America is God's Crucible, the great Melting-Pot where all the races of Europe are melting and reforming.

> ISRAEL ZANGWILL, *The Melting Pot,* 1908.

61 No, the real American has not yet arrived. He is only in the Crucible, I tell you—he will be the fusion of all races, perhaps the coming superman.

> Ibid.

---

17. ANCESTRY

1 Blood is a destiny. One's genius descends in the stream from long lines of ancestry.

> A. BRONSON ALCOTT, *Tablets,* 1868.

2 To be a Jew is a destiny.

> VICKI BAUM, *And Life Goes On,* 1932.

3 Genealogy, *n.* An account of one's descent from an ancestor who did not particularly care to trace his own.

> AMBROSE BIERCE, *The Devil's Dictionary,* 1906.

4 The behavior of an individual is determined not by his racial affiliation, but by the character of his ancestry and his cultural environment.

> FRANZ BOAS, *Race and Democratic Society,* 1945.

5 By descent, I am one fourth German, one fourth Irish, one fourth English, and another quarter French. My God! If my ancestors are permitted to look down upon me, they might perhaps upbraid me. But I am also an American!

> JOSEPH G. CANNON, speech in Congress, April, 1917, quoted in Edward Boykin, *The Wit and Wisdom of Congress,* 1961.

6 The son imbibes a portion of the intelligence, refinement and habits of the father, and he shares in his associations. These must be enumerated as the legitimate advantages of birth, and without invading the private arrangements of families and individuals, and establishing a perfect community of education, they are unavoidable.

> JAMES FENIMORE COOPER, *The American Democrat,* 1838.

7 When England grew very corrupt, God brought over a number of pious persons, and planted them in New England, and this land was planted with a noble vine. But how is the gold become dim! How greatly have we forsaken the pious examples of our fathers!

> JONATHAN EDWARDS, *The Great Christian Doctrine of Original Sin Defended,* 1758.

8 Men resemble their contemporaries even more than their progenitors.

> RALPH WALDO EMERSON, "The Uses of Great Men," *Representative Men,* 1850.

9 Every book is a quotation, and every house is a quotation out of all forests and mines and stone-quarries; and every man is a quotation from all his ancestors.

> RALPH WALDO EMERSON, "Plato, or, the Philosopher," *Representative Men,* 1850.

10 How shall a man escape from his ancestors, or draw off from his veins the black drop which he drew from his father's or his mother's life?

> RALPH WALDO EMERSON, *The Conduct of Life,* 1860.

11 There is something frightful in the way in which not only characteristic qualities, but particular manifestations of them, are repeated from generation to generation.

> OLIVER WENDELL HOLMES, SR., *The Guardian Angel,* 1867.

12 This body in which we journey across the isthmus between the two oceans is not a private carriage, but an omnibus.

> Ibid.

13 There is no king who has not had a slave among his ancestors, and no slave who has not had a king among his.

> HELEN KELLER, *The Story of My Life,* 1903.

14 *They* talk about their Pilgrim blood,
  Their birthright high and holy!
A mountain-stream that ends in mud
  Methinks is melancholy.

> JAMES RUSSELL LOWELL, "An Interview with Miles Standish," printed in the *Boston Courier,* December 30, 1845.

15 I cannot say that I am descended from the bastards of Oliver Cromwell, or his courtiers, or from the Puritans who punish their horses for breaking the Sabbath, or from those who persecuted the Quakers and burned the witches.

> Attributed to Matthew Lyon, Irish-born officer in the Green Mountain Boys.

16 It is worthwhile for anyone to have behind him a few generations of honest, hard-working ancestry.

> JOHN P. MARQUAND, *The Late George Apley,* 1937.

17 i have often noticed that
ancestors never boast
of the descendants who boast
of ancestors i would
rather start a family than
finish one blood will tell but often
it tells too much

> DON MARQUIS, "a roach of the taverns," *archy and mehitabel,* 1927.

18 With him for a sire and her for a dam,
What should I be but just what I am?

> EDNA ST. VINCENT MILLAY, *A Few Figs from
> Thistles,* 1920.

19 When we are planning for posterity, we ought
to remember that virtue is not hereditary.

> THOMAS PAINE, *Common Sense,* 1776.

20 My forefathers didn't come over on the *Mayflower,* but they met the boat.

> Attributed to Will Rogers.

21 The stream is brightest at its spring,
And blood is not like wine;
Nor honored less than he who heirs
Is he who founds a line.

> JOHN GREENLEAF WHITTIER, "Amy
> Wentworth," 1862.

18. ANGER

See also INVECTIVE; REVENGE

1 When massa curse, he break no bone.

> American slave saying, quoted in John Davis,
> *Travels of Four Years and a Half in the United
> States of America,* 1802.

2 Never forget what a man had said to you when
he was angry. If he has charged you with any thing,
you had better look it up.

> HENRY WARD BEECHER, *Life Thoughts,* 1858.

3 Anger is an expensive luxury in which only men
of a certain income can indulge.

> GEORGE WILLIAM CURTIS, *Prue and I,* 1856.

4 Never go to bed mad. Stay up and fight.

> PHYLLIS DILLER, *Phyllis Diller's Housekeeping
> Hints,* 1966.

5 A man makes his inferiors his superiors by heat.
. . . Self-control is the rule.

> RALPH WALDO EMERSON, *Letters and Social
> Aims,* 1876.

6 Take this remark from *Richard* poor and lame,
Whate'er's begun in anger ends in shame.

> BENJAMIN FRANKLIN, *Poor Richard's Almanack,*
> 1734.

7 Anger and Folly walk cheek by jole [jowl];
Repentance treads on both their Heels.

> BENJAMIN FRANKLIN, *Poor Richard's Almanack,*
> 1741.

8 A man in a Passion rides a mad Horse.

> BENJAMIN FRANKLIN, *Poor Richard's Almanack,*
> 1749.

9 The end of Passion is the beginning of Repentance.

> Ibid.

10 *Anger* is never without a Reason, but seldom
with a good One.

> BENJAMIN FRANKLIN, *Poor Richard's Almanack,*
> 1753.

11 Like an unchecked cancer, hate corrodes the
personality and eats away its vital unity. Hate destroys a man's sense of values and his objectivity.
It causes him to describe the beautiful as ugly and
the ugly as beautiful, and to confuse the true with
the false and the false with the true.

> MARTIN LUTHER KING, JR., *Strength to Love,*
> 1963.

12 Every stroke our fury strikes is sure to hit ourselves at last.

> WILLIAM PENN, *Some Fruits of Solitude,* 1693.

13 When angry, count to four; when very angry,
swear.

> MARK TWAIN, "Pudd'nhead Wilson's Calendar,"
> *Pudd'nhead Wilson,* 1894.

19. ANIMALS

1 A mule is an animal that has neither pride of
ancestry nor hope of posterity.

> Anonymous.

2 The more I see of men, the more I like dogs.

> Anonymous.

3 How much wood would a woodchuck chuck
If a woodchuck could chuck wood?

> Tongue twister.

4 A dog teaches a boy fidelity, perseverance, and to turn around three times before lying down.

> ROBERT BENCHLEY, quoted in the introduction to *Artemus Ward, His Book,* 1964 edition.

5 The Dodo never had a chance. He seems to have been invented for the sole purpose of becoming extinct and that was all he was good for.

> WILL CUPPY, *How to Become Extinct,* 1941.

6 Everything belonging to the spider is admirable.

> JONATHAN EDWARDS, "The Spider," written about 1714.

7 Dear Children,
We should not ask "What is an animal" but "What sort of a thing do we call an animal?" Well, we call something an animal which has certain characteristics: it takes nourishment, it descends from parents similar to itself, it grows, it moves by itself, it dies if its time has run out. That's why we call the worm, the chicken, the dog, the monkey an animal. What about us humans? Think about it in the above-mentioned way and then decide for yourselves whether it is a natural thing to regard ourselves as animals.

> ALBERT EINSTEIN, in a letter to a fifth grade class in Ohio, whose members were surprised to find human beings classified as animals, January 17, 1953.

8 Who can guess how much industry and providence and affection we have caught from the pantomime of brutes?

> RALPH WALDO EMERSON, *Nature,* 1836.

9 Kings and Bears often worry their Keepers.

> BENJAMIN FRANKLIN, *Poor Richard's Almanack,* 1739.

10 I wish the bald eagle had not been chosen as the representative of our country: he is a bird of bad moral character, . . . generally poor, and often very lousy.

> BENJAMIN FRANKLIN, in a letter to Sarah Bache, January 26, 1784.

11 Cats and monkeys, monkeys and cats—all human life is there.

> HENRY JAMES, *The Madonna of the Future and Other Tales,* 1879.

12 I heard there the nightingale in all its perfection, and I do not hesitate to pronounce that in America it would be deemed a bird of the third rank only, our mockingbird, and fox-colored thrush being unquestionably superior to it.

> THOMAS JEFFERSON, in a letter to Abigail Adams, June 21, 1785.

13 The horse does abominate the camel; the mighty elephant is afraid of a mouse; and they say that the lion, which scorneth to turn his back upon the stoutest animal, will tremble at the crowing of a cock.

> INCREASE MATHER, *An Essay for the Recording of Illustrious Providences,* popularly known as *Remarkable Providences,* 1684.

14 If you don't need them, don't feed them. That goes for cats, rats, mother-in-laws and so forth.

> JAMES MURPHY, rodent control officer, Washington, D.C., quoted in the *New York Times,* August 10, 1985.

15 A door is what a dog is perpetually on the wrong side of.

> OGDEN NASH, "A Dog's Best Friend Is His Illiteracy," *The Private Dining Room,* 1953.

16 The turtle lives 'twixt plated decks
Which practically conceal its sex.
I think it clever of the turtle
In such a fix to be so fertile.

> OGDEN NASH, "The Turtle," *Hard Lines,* 1931.

17 Pigs get a bad press. Pigs are regarded as selfish and greedy—as living garbage pails. Pigs are the villains in George Orwell's *Animal Farm.* Pigs have little mean eyes. There is truth in this account—not that it's entirely the fault of the pigs.

For perhaps five thousand generations pigs have been deliberately bred to be gluttonous. . . . Do the same thing with human beings for five thousand generations, and it would be interesting to see what kind of people resulted.

NOEL PERRIN, *Second Person Rural,* 1980.

18 There is something in the unselfish and self-sacrificing love of a brute, which goes directly to the heart of him who has had frequent occasion to test the paltry friendship and gossamer fidelity of mere Man.

EDGAR ALLAN POE, "The Black Cat," 1843.

19 The wild goose is more cosmopolite than we; he breaks his fast in Canada, takes a luncheon in the Susquehanna, and plumes himself for the night in a Louisiana bayou.

HENRY DAVID THOREAU, entry dated March 21, 1840, in his *Journal,* 1906.

20 If you pick up a starving dog and make him prosperous, he will not bite you. This is the principal difference between a dog and a man.

MARK TWAIN, "Puddn'head Wilson's Calendar," *Pudd'nhead Wilson,* 1894.

21 As a thinker and planner the ant is the equal of any savage race of men; as a self-educated specialist in several arts she is the superior of any savage race of men; and in one or two high mental qualities she is above the reach of any man, savage or civilized.

MARK TWAIN, *What Is Man?* 1906.

22 Or if some time when roaming round,
    A noble wild beast greets you,
With black stripes on a yellow ground,
    Just notice if he eats you.
This simple rule may help you learn
    The Bengal Tiger to discern.

CAROLYN WELLS, "How to Tell Wild Animals," in *Baubles,* 1917.

23 They say a reasonable amount o' fleas is good fer a dog—keeps him from broodin' over bein' a dog, mebbe.

EDWARD NOYES WESTCOTT, in *Daniel Harum,* 1898.

24 I think I could turn and live with animals,
        they are so placid and self-contain'd,
I stand and look at them long and long.
They do not sweat and whine about their
        condition,
They do not lie awake in the dark and weep
        for their sins,
They do not make me sick discussing their
        duty to God,
Not one is dissatisfied, not one is demented
        with the mania of owning things,
Not one kneels to another, nor to his kind
        that lived thousands of years ago,
Not one is respectable or unhappy over the
        whole earth.

WALT WHITMAN, *Song of Myself,* 1855.

20. APPETITE

See also DRINKING; FOOD; WINE & SPIRITS

1 Hunger iz a slut hound on a fresh track.

JOSH BILLINGS, *Josh Billings' Encyclopedia of Wit and Wisdom,* 1874.

2 Taking food and drink is a great enjoyment for healthy people, and those who do not enjoy eating seldom have much capacity for enjoyment or usefulness of any sort.

CHARLES WILLIAM ELIOT, *The Happy Life,* 1896.

3 Let the stoics say what they please, we do not eat for the good of living, but because the meat is savory and the appetite is keen.

RALPH WALDO EMERSON, "Nature," *Essays,* Second Series, 1844.

4 Eat to live, and not live to eat.

BENJAMIN FRANKLIN, *Poor Richard's Almanack,* 1733.

5 I saw few die of Hunger, of Eating, 100000.

BENJAMIN FRANKLIN, *Poor Richard's Almanack,* 1736.

6 A full Belly makes a dull Brain; The Muses starve in a Cook's Shop.

> BENJAMIN FRANKLIN, *Poor Richard Improved,* 1758.

7 Why does it take so much trouble to keep your stomach full and quiet?

> SHIRLEY ANN GRAU, "Margaret," *The Keepers of the House,* 1964.

8 In order to know whether a human being is young or old, offer it food of different kinds at short intervals. If young, it will eat anything at any hour of the day or night. If old, it observes stated periods.

> OLIVER WENDELL HOLMES, SR., *The Professor at the Breakfast-Table,* 1860.

9 Your supper is like the hidalgo's dinner, very little meat, and a great deal of tablecloth.

> HENRY WADSWORTH LONGFELLOW, *The Spanish Student,* 1843.

---

21. ARCHITECTURE

---

1 Architect, *n.* One who drafts a plan of your house, and plans a draft of your money.

> AMBROSE BIERCE, *The Devil's Dictionary,* 1906.

2 The Gothic cathedral is a blossoming in stone subdued by the insatiable demand of harmony in man. The mountain of granite blooms into an eternal flower.

> RALPH WALDO EMERSON, "History," *Essays,* First Series, 1841.

3 The men who have reduced locomotion to its simplest elements, in the trotting wagon and the yacht *America,* are nearer to Athens at this moment than they who would bend the Greek temple to every use.

> HORATIO GREENOUGH, quoted in John A. Kouwenhoven, *Made in America,* 1948.

4 If cities were built by the sound of music, then some edifices would appear to be constructed by

grave, solemn tones; others to have danced forth to light, fantastic airs.

> NATHANIEL HAWTHORNE, entry dated January 4, 1839, in *Passages from the American Notebooks,* 1868.

5 In dim cathedrals, dark with vaulted gloom,
What holy awe invests the saintly tomb!

> OLIVER WENDELL HOLMES, SR., "A Rhymed Lesson," 1846.

6 In the elder days of Art,
  Builders wrought with greatest care
Each minute and unseen part;
  For the Gods see everywhere.

> HENRY WADSWORTH LONGFELLOW, "The Builders," 1849.

7 Ah, to build, to build!
That is the noblest art of all the arts.
Painting and sculpture are but images,
Are merely shadows cast by outward things
On stone or canvas, having in themselves
No separate existence. Architecture,
Existing in itself, and not in seeming
A something it is not, surpasses them
As substance shadow.

> HENRY WADSWORTH LONGFELLOW, "Michael Angelo," 1882.

8 I venture to predict that long after the public has wearied of Frank Lloyd Wright's inverted oatmeal dish and silo with awkward cantilevering, their jaundiced skin and the ingenious spiral ramp leading down past the abstractions which mirror the tortured maladjustments of our time, the Metropolitan will still wear well.

> ROBERT MOSES, on the Guggenheim Museum and the Metropolitan Museum, quoted in the *New York Times,* May 21, 1959.

9 A real building is one on which the eye can light and stay lit.

> EZRA POUND, writing in *The Dial* magazine, 1923.

10 The completed work, when constructed in accordance with my designs, will not only be the greatest bridge in existence, but it will be the great-

est engineering work of the continent, and of the age.

> JOHN A. ROEBLING, in his proposal for the Brooklyn Bridge, 1867, quoted in David McCullough, *The Great Bridge,* 1972.

11 I realized that architecture was made for people who go about on their feet, that that is what architecture is made for.

> GERTRUDE STEIN, "Raoul Dufy," 1946.

12 Form ever follows function.

> LOUIS HENRY SULLIVAN, "The Tall Office Building Artistically Considered," *Lippincott's Magazine,* March, 1896.

13 No house should ever be *on* a hill or *on* anything. It should be *of* the hill. Belonging to it. Hill and house should live together each the happier for the other.

> FRANK LLOYD WRIGHT, *An Autobiography,* 1932.

14 The physician can bury his mistakes, but the architect can only advise his clients to plant vines.

> FRANK LLOYD WRIGHT, in the *New York Times Magazine,* October 4, 1953.

---

22. ARGUMENT

---

1 The world is divided into people who think they are right.

> Anonymous.

2 If you can't lick 'em, join 'em.

> Popular saying.

3 Compromise, *n.* Such an adjustment of conflicting interests as gives each adversary the satisfaction of thinking he has got what he ought not to have, and is deprived of nothing except what was justly his due.

> AMBROSE BIERCE, *The Devil's Dictionary,* 1906.

4 We arg'ed the thing at breakfast, we arg'ed
    the thing at tea,

And the more we arg'ed the question, the
    more we didn't agree.

> WILL CARLETON, "Betsy and I Are Out," 1873.

5 To think is to differ.

> CLARENCE DARROW, during the Scopes trial in Dayton, Tennessee, July 13, 1925.

6 Let me never fall into the vulgar mistake of dreaming that I am persecuted whenever I am contradicted.

> RALPH WALDO EMERSON, entry written in 1838, *Journals,* 1909–1914.

7 One lesson we learn early,—that in spite of seeming different, men are all of one pattern. . . . In fact, the only sin which we never forgive in each other is difference of opinion.

> RALPH WALDO EMERSON, "Clubs," *Society and Solitude,* 1870.

8 An association of men who will not quarrel with one another is a thing which never yet existed, from the greatest confederacy of nations down to a town meeting or a vestry.

> THOMAS JEFFERSON, in a letter to John Taylor, June 1, 1798.

9 In stating prudential rules for our government in society, I must not omit the important one of never entering into dispute or argument with another. I never saw an instance of one of two disputants convincing the other by argument. I have seen many, on their getting warm, becoming rude, and shooting one another. Conviction is the effect of our own dispassionate reasoning, either in solitude, or weighing within ourselves, dispassionately, what we hear from others, standing uncommitted in argument ourselves.

> THOMAS JEFFERSON, in a letter to Thomas Jefferson Randolph, November 24, 1808.

10 Compromise makes a good umbrella but a poor roof.

> JAMES RUSSELL LOWELL, in an address entitled "On Democracy," given in Brimingham, England, October 6, 1884, published in *Democracy and Other Addresses,* 1886.

11 i have noticed
that when
chickens quit
quarrelling over their
food they often
find that there is
enough for all of them
i wonder if
it might not
be the same way with the
human race

> DON MARQUIS, "random thoughts by archy,"
> *archy's life of mehitabel,* 1933.

12 'Tis by our quarrels that we spoil our prayers.

> COTTON MATHER, *The Wonders of the Invisible
> World,* 1693.

13 Con was a thorn to brother Pro—
On Pro we often sicked him:
Whatever Pro would claim to know
Old Con would contradict him!

> CHRISTOPHER MORLEY, "The Twins," in *Hide
> and Seek,* 1920.

14 Men always lose half of what is gained by violence. What is gained by argument, is gained forever.

> WENDELL PHILLIPS, *Speeches, Lectures and
> Letters,* 1863.

15 The best way to win an argument is to begin by being right.

> JILL RUCKELSHAUS, quoted in the *Saturday
> Evening Post,* March 3, 1973.

16 It would be almost unbelievable, if history did not record the tragic fact that men have gone to war and cut each other's throat because they could not agree as to what was to become of them after their throats were cut.

> WALTER PARKER STACY, quoted in Sam J. Ervin,
> Jr., *Humor of a Country Lawyer,* 1983.

17 For some reason, too deep to fathom, men contend more furiously over the road to heaven, which they cannot see, than over their visible walks on earth.

> Ibid.

18 It were not best that we should all think alike; it is difference of opinion that makes horse races.

> MARK TWAIN, "Pudd'nhead Wilson's Calendar,"
> *Pudd'nhead Wilson,* 1894.

19 By a sudden and adroit movement I placed my left eye agin the Secesher's fist.

> ARTEMUS WARD, in *Artemus Ward, His Book,*
> 1862.

20 I am not arguing with you—I am telling you.

> JAMES ABBOTT MCNEILL WHISTLER, *The
> Gentle Art of Making Enemies,* 1890.

21 Invariably, it is this for which I write: the joy, than which there is nothing purer, of an argument firmly made, like a nail straightly driven, its head flush to the plank.

> GEORGE F. WILL, *The Pursuit of Virtue and
> Other Tory Notions,* 1982.

---

23. ARIZONA

---

1 Ditat Deus. [God enriches.]

> State motto.

2 Come to Arizona, where Summer spends the Winter.

> Travel slogan, c.1935 (to which wits sometimes
> added, "and where Hell spends the Summer").

3 Land of extremes. Land of contrasts. Land of surprises. Land of contradictions. A land that is never to be fully understood but always to be loved by sons and daughters sprung from such a diversity of origins, animated by such a diversity of motives and ideals, that generations must pass before they can ever fully understand each other. That is Arizona.

> Federal Writers' Project, *Arizona: The Grand
> Canyon State,* 1956.

4 A very, very wicked soldier died there once, and of course went straight to the hottest corner of

perdition—and the next day he *telegraphed back for his blankets.*

> GEORGE HORATIO DERBY, characterizing Yuma, Ariz., quoted in Mark Twain, *Roughing It,* 1872.

5 Most of those old settlers told it like it was, rough and rocky. They named their towns Rimrock, Rough Rock, Round Rock, and Wide Ruins, Skull Valley, Bitter Springs, Wolf Hole, Tombstone. It's a tough country. The names of Arizona towns tell you all you need to know.

> CHARLES KURALT, *Dateline America,* 1979.

6 I don't know about you, but I am suspicious of Pleasantville, New York. I am sure that Sawmill, Arizona, is more my kind of town. Or Window Rock or Hermits Rest or Turkey Flat or Grasshopper Junction. I could settle down here, just for the pleasure of having folks back home say, "Oh, don't you know what happened to old Charles? Lives now in Jackrabbit, Arizona. Just down the road from Cowlick and Bumble Bee."

> CHARLES KURALT, *Dateline America,* 1979.

7 Across the Colorado River from Needles, the dark and jagged ramparts of Arizona stood up against the sky, and behind them the huge tilted plain rising toward the backbone of the continent again.

> JOHN STEINBECK, *Travels with Charley,* 1962.

24. ARKANSAS

1 Regnat populus. (Let the people rule.)

> State motto.

2 If I die in Arkansaw
Jes' ship my body to my mother-in-law.

> Folk song.

3 Biggest fool I ever saw
Come from state of Arkansaw;
Put his shirt on over his coat,
Button his britches up round his throat.

American folk song, quoted in Howard W. Odum, *Wings on My Feet,* 1929.

4 If I could rest anywhere it would be in Arkansaw where the men are of the real half-horse, half-alligator breed such as grows nowhere else on the face of the universal earth.

> Attributed to Davy Crockett, 1834.

5 Oh, 'twas down in the woods of the
    Arkansaw,
And the night was cloudy and the wind was
    raw,
And he didn't have a bed and he didn't have a
    bite,
And if he hadn't fiddled he'd 'a' traveled all
    night.

> ALBERT BIGELOW PAINE, *The Arkansaw Bear,* 1898.

6 So the duke said these Arkansaw lunkheads couldn't come up to Shakespeare; what they wanted was low comedy—and maybe something rather worse than low comedy, he reckoned. He said he could size their style. So next morning he got some big sheets of wrapping paper and some black paint, and drawed off some handbills. . . . At the bottom was the biggest line of all, which said: LADIES AND CHILDREN NOT ADMITTED. "There," says he, "if that line don't fetch them, I don't know Arkansaw!"

> MARK TWAIN, *The Adventures of Huckleberry Finn,* 1884.

25. ARMY

See also AMERICAN REVOLUTION; FORCE; MILITARISM; NAVY; NUCLEAR AGE; WAR; and individual wars

1 SNAFU—Situation Normal, All Fouled Up.

> Acronym that gained popularity in the U.S. armed forces during World War II, originally with vulgar definition.

2 The difficult we do immediately. The impossible takes a little longer.

> Motto of the United States Army Service Forces in World War II.

3 The infantry, the infantry, with dirt behind the ears,
  The infantry, the infantry, can drink their weight in beers;
  The cavalry, the artillery, and the goddamned engineers
  Can never beat the infantry in a hundred thousand years.

> Soldiers' song.

4 You're in the army now,
  You're not behind the plow;
  You'll never get rich, you son of a bitch,
  You're in the army now.

> Soldiers' song.

5 Done give myself to Uncle Sam,
  Now I ain't worth a good goddam,
  I don't want no mo' camp,
  Lawd, I want to go home.

> Soldiers' song, quoted in Howard W. Odum, *Wings On My Feet*, 1929.

6 It were better to be a soldier's widow than a coward's wife.

> THOMAS BAILEY ALDRICH, *Mercedes*, 1884.

7 Lay him low, lay him low,
  In the clover or the snow!
  What cares he? he cannot know:
    Lay him low!

> GEORGE HENRY BOKER, "Dirge for a Soldier," 1862.

8 The nation which forgets its defenders will be itself forgotten.

> CALVIN COOLIDGE, speech at Northampton, Massachusetts, accepting the Republican vice-presidential nomination, July 27, 1920.

9 For glory lights the soldier's tomb,
  And beauty weeps the brave.

> JOSEPH RODMAN DRAKE, "To the Defenders of New Orleans."

10 Standing armies are sometimes . . . composed of persons who have rendered themselves unfit to live in civil society; who have no other motives of conduct than those which a desire of the present gratification of their passions suggests; who have no property in any country; men who have given up their own liberties, and envy those who enjoy liberty; . . . who, for the addition of one penny a day to their wages, would desert from the Christian cross and fight under the crescent of the Turkish sultan.

> JOHN HANCOCK, in a speech at Boston, March 5, 1774.

11 The soldiers of America have killed more Americans, twenty times over, than they have foreign foes.

> ELBERT HUBBARD, *The Philistine*, published 1895–1915.

12 A soldier is a slave—he does what he is told to do—everything is provided for him—his head is a superfluity. He is only a stick used by men to strike other men.

> ELBERT HUBBARD, *The Roycroft Dictionary and Book of Epigrams*, 1923.

13 I think with the Romans, that the general of today should be a soldier tomorrow if necessary.

> THOMAS JEFFERSON, in a letter to James Madison, January 1, 1797.

14 The Creator has not thought proper to mark those in the forehead who are of stuff to make good generals. We are first, therefore, to seek them blindfold, and then let them learn the trade at the expense of great losses.

> THOMAS JEFFERSON, in a letter to Gen. Theodorus Bailey, February 6, 1813.

15 The American Army is a beautiful little army. Some day, when all the Indians are happily dead or drunk, it ought to make the finest scientific and survey corps that the world has ever seen.

> RUDYARD KIPLING, *American Notes*, 1891.

16 A soldier has a hard life, and but little consideration.

> ROBERT E. LEE, in a letter to his wife, November 5, 1855.

17 Our army would be invincible if it could be properly organized and officered. There never were such men in an army before. They will go anywhere and do anything if properly led. But there is the difficulty—proper commanders—and where can they be obtained?

> ROBERT E. LEE, in a letter to Gen. John B. Hood, May 21, 1863.

18 Ninepunce a day fer killin' folks comes kind o' low fer murder.

> JAMES RUSSELL LOWELL, *The Biglow Papers,* First Series, 1848.

19 The world has turned over many times since I took the oath on the Plain at West Point, and the hopes and dreams have long since vanished. But I still remember the refrain of one of the most popular barrack ballads of that day, which proclaimed, most proudly, that "Old soldiers never die. They just fade away." And like the soldier of the ballad, I now close my military career and just fade away—an old soldier who tried to do his duty as God gave him the light to see that duty.

> GEN. DOUGLAS MACARTHUR, speech to Congress, April 19, 1951.

20 I find in existence a new and heretofore unknown and dangerous concept that the members of the Armed Forces owe their primary allegiance and loyalty to those who temporarily exercise the authority of the executive branch of the government, rather than to the country and its Constitution they are sworn to defend. No proposition could be more dangerous. None could cast greater doubt on the integrity of the Armed Forces.

> GEN. DOUGLAS MACARTHUR, in an address to the Massachusetts legislature, July 25, 1951.

21 A general is just as good or just as bad as the troops under his command make him.

> GEN. DOUGLAS MACARTHUR, on receiving a Congressional resolution of gratitude, August 16, 1962.

22 No man in uniform, be he private or five-star general, may decide for himself whether an order is consonant with his personal views. While the loyalty he owes his superiors is reciprocated with equal force in the loyalty owed him from above, the authority of his superiors is not open to question.

> GEN. MATTHEW B. RIDGWAY, *The Korean War,* 1967.

23 In setting our military goals we need first of all to recognize that most of the world's most basic woes do not lend themselves to purely military solutions.

> Ibid.

24 Physical courage is never in short supply in a fighting army. Moral courage sometimes is.

> Ibid.

25 There is something magnificent, a contagion of enthusiasm, in the sight of a great volunteer army. The North and the South knew the thrill during our own great war. Conscription may form a great and admirable machine, but it differs from the trained army of volunteers as a body differs from a soul. But it costs a country heavy in grief, does a volunteer army; for the flower of the country goes.

> MARY ROBERTS RINEHART, *Kings, Queens and Pawns,* 1915.

26 Air power is our initial line of defense, but no one has proved to my satisfaction that we will have only world wars to be settled only by big bangs. . . . Infantrymen at one time or another become indispensable. Nothing we have discovered or expect to discover will reduce the need for brave men to fight our battles.

> GEN. MAXWELL D. TAYLOR, c.1955, quoted in his obituary in the *New York Times,* April 21, 1987.

27 When we assumed the Soldier, we did not lay aside the Citizen; and we shall most sincerely rejoice with you in that happy hour when the establishment of American Liberty, upon the most firm and solid ground, shall enable us to return to our Private Stations.

> GEORGE WASHINGTON, address to the legislature of New York, June 26, 1775.

28 Let it be your pride, therefore, to show all men everywhere not only what good soldiers you are, but also what good men you are, keeping yourselves

fit and straight in everything, and pure and clean through and through. Let us set for ourselves a standard so high that it will be a glory to live up to it, and then let us live up to it and add a new laurel to the crown of America.

> WOODROW WILSON, message to United States forces, September 4, 1917.

---

26. ART

See also BEAUTY

---

1 I don't know anything about art, but I know what I like.

> Popular saying, quoted in Gelett Burgess, *Are You a Bromide?* 1907.

2 Every artist dips his brush in his own soul, and paints his own nature into his pictures.

> HENRY WARD BEECHER, *Proverbs from Plymouth Pulpit,* 1870.

3 Art strives for form, and hopes for beauty.

> GEORGE BELLOWS, quoted in Stanley Walker, *City Editor,* 1934.

4 Painting, *n.* The art of protecting flat surfaces from the weather and exposing them to the critic.

> AMBROSE BIERCE, *The Devil's Dictionary,* 1906.

5 Religion and art spring from the same root and are close kin. Economics and art are strangers.

> WILLA CATHER, *On Writing,* 1949.

6 Art is the stored honey of the human soul, gathered on wings of misery and travail.

> THEODORE DREISER, *Life, Art and America,* 1917.

7 To my mind the old masters are not art; their value is in their scarcity.

> THOMAS A. EDISON, quoted in *Golden Book* magazine, April, 1931.

8 Every nation, every race, has not only its own creative, but its own critical turn of mind; and is even more oblivious of the shortcomings and limitations of its critical habits than of those of its creative genius.

> T.S. ELIOT, "Tradition and the Individual Talent," *The Sacred Wood,* 1919.

9 No poet, no artist of any art, has his complete meaning alone. His significance, his appreciation is the appreciation of his relation to the dead poets and artists. . . . You must set him, for contrast and comparison, among the dead.

> Ibid.

10 Our arts are happy hits. We are like the musician on the lake, whose melody is sweeter than he knows; or like a traveler, surprised by a mountain echo, whose trivial word returns to him in romantic thunders.

> RALPH WALDO EMERSON, "Art," *Essays,* First Series, 1841.

11 Art is the path of the creator to his work.

> RALPH WALDO EMERSON, "The Poet," *Essays,* Second Series, 1844.

12 Perpetual modernness is the measure of merit in every work of art.

> RALPH WALDO EMERSON, "Plato," *Representative Men,* 1850.

13 "Ah!" said a brave painter to me . . . "if a man has failed, you will find he has dreamed instead of working. There is no way to success in our art but to take off your coat, grind paint, and work like a digger on the railroad, all day and every day."

> RALPH WALDO EMERSON, "Power," *The Conduct of Life,* 1860.

14 The torpid artist seeks inspiration at any cost, by virtue or by vice, by friend or by fiend, by prayer or by wine.

> Ibid.

15 Art is a jealous mistress, and if a man have a genius for painting, poetry, music, architecture, or philosophy, he makes a bad husband and an ill provider, and should be wise in season and not fetter himself with duties which will embitter his days and spoil him for his proper work.

RALPH WALDO EMERSON, "Wealth," *The Conduct of Life,* 1860.

16 From its first to its last works, Art is the spirit's voluntary use and combination of things to serve its end.

RALPH WALDO EMERSON, "Art," *Society and Solitude,* 1870.

17 Every genuine work of art has as much reason for being as the earth and the sun.

Ibid.

18 Artists must be sacrificed to their art. Like bees, they must put their lives into the sting they give.

RALPH WALDO EMERSON, "Inspiration," *Letters and Social Aims,* 1876.

19 Every artist was first an amateur.

RALPH WALDO EMERSON, "The Progress of Culture," *Letters and Social Aims,* 1876.

20 To me nature is everything that man is born to, and art is the difference he makes in it.

JOHN ERSKINE, in *Gentle Reader,* December, 1931.

21 One picture in ten thousand, perhaps, ought to live in the applause of mankind, from generation to generation until the colors fade and blacken out of sight or the canvas rot entirely away.

NATHANIEL HAWTHORNE, *The Marble Faun,* 1860.

22 The temple of art is built of words.

JOSIAH GILBERT HOLLAND, "Art and Life," *Plain Talk on Familiar Subjects,* 1865.

23 The one thing that marks the true artist is a clear perception and a firm, bold hand, in distinction from that imperfect mental vision and uncertain touch which give us the feeble pictures and the lumpy statues of the mere artisans on canvas or in stone.

OLIVER WENDELL HOLMES, SR., *The Professor at the Breakfast-Table,* 1860.

24 The artist needs no religion beyond his work.

ELBERT HUBBARD, in the *Philistine* magazine, published from 1895–1915.

25 Art is not a thing: it is a way.

ELBERT HUBBARD, *One Thousand and One Epigrams,* 1911.

26 Build your art horse-high, pig-tight, and bull-strong.

ELBERT HUBBARD, *The Roycroft Dictionary and Book of Epigrams,* 1923.

27 Scratch an artist and you surprise a child.

JAMES GIBBONS HUNEKER, *The Man and His Music,* 1900.

28 Great art is an instant arrested in eternity.

JAMES GIBBONS HUNEKER, *The Pathos of Distance,* 1913.

29 Art is nothing more than the shadow of humanity.

Attributed to Henry James.

30 In art economy is always beauty.

HENRY JAMES, "The Altar of the Dead," *Prefaces,* 1907–1909.

31 It is art that *makes* life, makes interest, makes importance, for our consideration and application of these things, and I know of no substitute whatever for the force and beauty of its process.

HENRY JAMES, letter to H.G. Wells, July 10, 1915.

32 It seems likely that many of the young who don't wait for others to call them artists, but simply announce that they are, don't have the patience to make art.

PAULINE KAEL, *Kiss Kiss Bang Bang,* 1968.

33 Art must unquestionably have a social value; that is, as a potential means of communication it must be addressed, and in comprehensible terms, to the understanding of mankind.

ROCKWELL KENT, *It's Me O Lord,* 1955.

34 Art is Power.

HENRY WADSWORTH LONGFELLOW, *Hyperion,* 1839.

35 Art is the child of Nature; yes,
Her darling child, in whom we trace

The features of the mother's face,
Her aspect and her attitude.

> HENRY WADSWORTH LONGFELLOW, *Keramos,* 1878.

36 Art is the gift of God, and must be used Unto His glory.

> HENRY WADSWORTH LONGFELLOW, *Michael Angelo,* written from 1872–1882, published posthumously, 1886.

37 Sculpture is more than painting. It is greater to raise the dead to life than to create Phantoms that seem to live.

> Ibid.

38 Art is the desire of a man to express himself, to record the reactions of his personality to the world he lives in.

> AMY LOWELL, *Tendencies in Modern American Poetry,* 1917.

39 The truth is, as everyone knows, that the great artists of the world are never puritans, and seldom ever ordinarily respectable. No virtuous man—that is, virtuous in the YMCA sense—has ever painted a picture worth looking at, or written a symphony worth hearing, or a book worth reading, and it is highly improbable that the thing has ever been done by a virtuous woman.

> H.L. MENCKEN, *Prejudices,* First Series, 1919.

40 And now too late, we see these things are one:
That art is sacrifice and self-control,
And who loves beauty must be stern of soul.

> ALICE DUER MILLER, "An American to France," *Welcome Home,* 1923.

41 I don't advise any one to take it [painting] up as a buisness proprosition, unless they really have talent, and are crippled so as to deprive them of physical labor,
Then with help they might make a living,
But with taxes and income tax there is little money in that kind of art for the ordinary artis
But I will say that I have did remarkable for one of my years, and experience,
As for publicity, that I'm too old to care for now,

> GRANDMA MOSES, "How I Paint and Why," the *New York Times Magazine,* May 11, 1947.

42 If I didn't start painting, I would have raised chickens.

> GRANDMA MOSES, *Grandma Moses, My Life's History,* 1947.

43 Art is a reaching out into the ugliness of the world for vagrant beauty and the imprisoning of it in a tangible dream.

> GEORGE JEAN NATHAN, *The Critic and the Drama,* 1922.

44 Great art is as irrational as great music. It is mad with its own loveliness.

> GEORGE JEAN NATHAN, *The House of Satan,* 1926.

45 Authors and actors and artists and such
Never know nothing and never know much.

> DOROTHY PARKER, "Bohemia," *Sunset Gun,* 1928.

46 Were I called on to define, very briefly, the term *art,* I should call it "the reproduction of what the senses perceive in nature through the veil of the soul."

> EDGAR ALLAN POE, *Marginalia,* 1844.

47 Good art weathers the ages because once in so often a man of intelligence commands the mass to adore it.

> EZRA POUND, *Imaginary Letters,* 1930.

48 Art's long hazard, where no man may choose
Whether he plays to win, or toils to lose.

> EDWIN ARLINGTON ROBINSON, "Caput Mortuum," *Collected Poems,* 1921.

49 An artist is a dreamer consenting to dream of the actual world.

> GEORGE SANTAYANA, *The Life of Reason,* 1905–1906.

50 Nothing is so poor and melancholy as an art that is interested in itself and not in its subject.

> Ibid.

51 Fashion is a potency in art, making it hard to judge between the temporary and the lasting.

> EDMUND CLARENCE STEDMAN, *The Poets of America,* 1885.

52 After a little while I murmured to Picasso that I liked his portrait of Gertrude Stein. Yes, he said, everybody said that she does not look like it but that does not make any difference, she will, he said.

> GERTRUDE STEIN, *The Autobiography of Alice B. Toklas,* 1933.

53 He knows all about art, but he doesn't know what he likes.

> JAMES THURBER, in *The New Yorker,* November 4, 1939.

54 I deplore any action which denies artistic talent an opportunity to express itself because of prejudice against race origin.

> BESS TRUMAN, quoted by Helen Weigel Brown in *Liberty* magazine, June 9, 1945.

55 I am glad the old masters are all dead, and I only wish they had died sooner.

> MARK TWAIN, in a letter to the *San Francisco Alta California,* May 28, 1867.

56 A great artist can paint a great picture on a small canvas.

> CHARLES DUDLEY WARNER, *Washington Irving,* 1881.

57 Listen! There never was an artistic period. There never was an Art-loving nation.

> JAMES ABBOTT McNEILL WHISTLER, "Ten O'Clock," 1888.

58 To say of a picture, as is often said in its praise, that it shows great and earnest labor, is to say that it is incomplete and unfit for view.

> JAMES ABBOTT McNEILL WHISTLER, *The Gentle Art of Making Enemies,* 1890.

59 Art should be independent of all clap-trap—should stand alone, and appeal to the artistic sense of eye and ear, without confounding this with emotions entirely foreign to it, as devotion, pity, love, patriotism, and the like.

> Ibid.

27. AUTHORITY

See also LAW; LIBERTY; MAJORITY RULE; POWER

1 If you happen to want a policeman, there's never one within miles.

> Saying, recorded in Gelett Burgess, *Are You a Bromide?* 1907. (Now usually given as "You can never find a cop when you need one.")

2 The Deity, then, has not given any order or family of men authority over others, and if any men have given it, they only could give it for themselves.

> SAMUEL ADAMS, speech delivered at Philadelphia, August, 1776, collected in *Early American Orations,* 1902.

3 Where the people possess no authority, their rights obtain no respect.

> GEORGE BANCROFT, address published in the *Boston Courier,* October 22, 1834.

4 There is no stopping the world's tendency to throw off imposed restraints, the religious authority that is based on the ignorance of the many, the political authority that is based on the knowledge of the few.

> VAN WYCK BROOKS, *From a Writer's Notebook,* 1957.

5 Men in authority will always think that criticism of their policies is dangerous. They will always equate their policies with patriotism, and find criticism subversive.

> HENRY STEELE COMMAGER, *Freedom and Order,* 1966.

6 Never do anything against conscience, even if the state demands it.

> ALBERT EINSTEIN, quoted by Virgil G. Hinshaw, Jr., in *Albert Einstein: Philosopher-Scientist,* 1949.

7 All authority belongs to the people.

> Attributed to Thomas Jefferson, from a letter to Spencer Roane, June 27, 1821. (Jefferson's words were actually, "The people, to whom all authority belongs, . . .")

8 He who is firmly seated in authority soon learns to think security, and not progress, the highest lesson of statecraft.

> JAMES RUSSELL LOWELL, *Among My Books*, 1870.

9 No man is fit to command another that cannot command himself.

> WILLIAM PENN, *No Cross, No Crown*, 1669.

---

28. AUTUMN

See also NATURE; WEATHER

---

1 November is the most disagreeable month in the whole year.

> LOUISA MAY ALCOTT, *Little Women*, 1868.

2 October is nature's funeral month. Nature glories in death more than in life. The month of departure is more beautiful than the month of coming,— October than May. Every green thing loves to die in bright colors.

> HENRY WARD BEECHER, *Proverbs from Plymouth Pulpit*, 1870.

3 Yet one smile more, departing, distant sun!
   One mellow smile through the soft vapory air,
  Ere, o'er the frozen earth, the loud winds run,
  Or snows are sifted o'er the meadows bare.

> WILLIAM CULLEN BRYANT, "November," in the *United States Literary Gazette*, November 15, 1824.

4 The melancholy days are come, the saddest of the year,
   Of wailing winds, and naked wood, and meadows brown and sere.
   Heaped in the hollows of the grove, the autumn leaves lie dead;
   They rustle to the eddying gust, and to the rabbit's tread;
   The robin and the wren are flown, and from the shrubs the jay,

And from the wood-top calls the crow
   through all the gloomy day.

> WILLIAM CULLEN BRYANT, "The Death of the Flowers," 1825.

5 On my cornice linger the ripe black grapes ungathered;
   Children fill the groves with the echoes of their glee,
   Gathering tawny chestnuts, and shouting when beside them
   Drops the heavy fruit of the tall black-walnut tree.

> WILLIAM CULLEN BRYANT, "The Third of November," 1861.

6 Glorious are the woods in their latest gold and crimson,
   Yet our full-leaved willows are in their freshest green.
   Such a kindly autumn, so mercifully dealing
   With the growths of summer, I never yet have seen.

> Ibid.

7 The sweet calm sunshine of October, now
   Warms the low spot; upon its grassy mold
   The purple oak-leaf falls; the birchen bough
   Drops its bright spoil like arrow-heads of gold.

> WILLIAM CULLEN BRYANT, "October," 1866.

8 The scarlet of the maples can shake me like a cry
   Of bugles going by.
   And my lonely spirit thrills
   To see the frosty asters like a smoke upon the hills.

> BLISS CARMAN, "A Vagabond Song," *Songs from Vagabondia*, 1894.

9 There is something in October sets the gypsy blood astir;
   We must rise and follow her.

> Ibid.

10 A haze on the far horizon,
   The infinite, tender sky,

The ripe, rich tint of the cornfields,
    And the wild geese sailing high,—
And all over upland and lowland
    The charm of the goldenrod,—
Some of us call it Autumn,
    And others call it God.

> WILLIAM HERBERT CARRUTH, "Each in His
> Own Tongue," in *Poems,* 1908.

11 These are the days when skies put on
The old, old sophistries of June,—
A blue and gold mistake.

> EMILY DICKINSON, "Indian Summer," in *Poems,*
> 1890.

12 [Indian summers] are the reconciling days
which come to graduate the autumn into winter,
and to comfort us after the first attacks of the cold.
Soothsayers, prediction as well as memory, they
look over December and January into the crepuscu-
lar light of March and April.

> RALPH WALDO EMERSON, entry written in 1842,
> *Journals,* 1909–1914.

13 My Sorrow, when she's here with me,
    Thinks these dark days of autumn rain
Are beautiful as days can be;
    She loves the bare, the withered tree;
    She walks the sodden pasture lane.

> ROBERT FROST, "My November Guest," in *A
> Boy's Will,* 1913.

14 A solitary maple on a woodside flames in single
scarlet, recalls nothing so much as the daughter of
a noble house dressed for a fancy ball, with the
whole family gathered round to admire her before
she goes.

> HENRY JAMES, *The American Scene,* 1907.

15 It was Autumn, and incessant
    Piped the quails from shocks and sheaves,
And, like living coals, the apples
    Burned among the withering leaves.

> HENRY WADSWORTH LONGFELLOW, "Pegasus in
> Pound," 1846.

16 O, it sets my heart a-clickin' like the tickin'
    of a clock,

When the frost is on the punkin and the
    fodder's in the shock.

> JAMES WHITCOMB RILEY, "When the Frost Is
> on the Punkin," 1883.

17 The tints of autumn—a mighty flower garden
blossoming under the spell of the enchanter, Frost.

> JOHN GREENLEAF WHITTIER, "Pawtucket
> Falls," published in the *Middlesex Standard,*
> Lowell, Massachusetts, August 29, 1844.

18 Along the river's summer walk,
    The withered tufts of asters nod;
And trembles on its arid stalk
    The hoar plume of the golden-rod.
And on the ground a sombre fir,
And azure-studded juniper,
The silver birch its buds of purple shows,
And scarlet berries tell where bloomed the
    sweet wild rose!

> JOHN GREENLEAF WHITTIER, "The Last Walk
> in Autumn," 1857.

29. AVARICE

1 The dog with the bone is always in danger.

> Popular saying.

2 Things are in the saddle,
    And ride mankind.

> RALPH WALDO EMERSON, "Ode, Inscribed to
> W.H. Channing," *Poems,* 1847.

3 Avarice and Happiness never saw each other,
how then shou'd they become acquainted?

> BENJAMIN FRANKLIN, *Poor Richard's Almanack,*
> 1734.

4 If I knew a miser, who gave up every kind of
comfortable living, all the pleasure of doing good
to others, all the esteem of his fellow-citizens, and
the joys of benevolent friendship, for the sake of
accumulating wealth, Poor man, said I, you pay too
much for your whistle.

> BENJAMIN FRANKLIN, *The Whistle,* 1779.

5 Punishment of a miser,—to pay the drafts of his heir in his tomb.

> NATHANIEL HAWTHORNE, entry dated July 10, 1838, *Passages from the American Notebooks,* 1868.

6 each generation wastes a little more
  of the future with greed and lust for riches

> DON MARQUIS, "what the ants are saying," in *the lives and times of archy and mehitabel,* 1950.

7 What most people don't seem to realize is that there is just as much money to be made out of the wreckage of a civilization as from the upbuilding of one.

> MARGARET MITCHELL, *Gone with the Wind,* 1936.

8 All the men in America make money their pursuit.

> RICHARD PARKINSON, *A Tour in America,* 1805.

9 Probably the greatest harm done by vast wealth is the harm that we of moderate means do ourselves when we let the vices of envy and hatred enter deep into our own nature.

> THEODORE ROOSEVELT, in a speech in Providence, Rhode Island, August 23, 1902.

10 In order to make a man or a boy covet a thing, it is only necessary to make the thing difficult to attain.

> MARK TWAIN, *The Adventures of Tom Sawyer,* 1876.

---

30. BASEBALL

See also BERRAISMS; SPORTS

---

1 Records are made to be broken.

> Old baseball saying, quoted in Fred Lieb, *Baseball as I Have Known It,* 1977.

2 Washington, first in war, first in peace, last in the American League.

> Popular saying, referring to the Washington Senators, quoted in Howard Cosell, *Like It Is,* 1974.

3 Say it ain't so, Joe!

> Attributed to a young fan confronting Joe Jackson of the Chicago White Sox, after hearing that Jackson had conspired with gamblers to fix the 1919 World Series, quoted in Fred Lieb, *Baseball as I Have Known It,* 1977.

4 Rooting for the Yankees is like rooting for U.S. Steel.

> Saying, quoted in Bill Veeck, *The Hustler's Handbook,* 1965.

5 Ruthlessly pricking our gonfalon bubble,
  Making a Giant hit into a double—
  Words that are heavy with nothing but
    trouble:
  "Tinker to Evers to Chance."

> FRANKLIN P[IERCE] ADAMS [F.P.A.], in "Baseball's Sad Lexicon," the *New York Mail,* July, 1910. (The Chicago Cubs in those days had a great double-play combination in shortstop Joe Tinker, second baseman Johnny Evers, and first baseman Frank Chance.)

6 When I was 4, I learned that Santa Claus didn't exist. When I was 9, I found out my father didn't know everything. When the Dodgers left I was 20, and things have never been the same.

> MARTY ADLER, Dodgers fan, on the team's move from Brooklyn to Los Angeles in 1957, quoted in *American Way* magazine, October 15, 1986.

7 By the end of the season, I feel like a used car.

> BOB BRENLY, catcher, quoted in *American Way* magazine, May 14, 1985.

8 Your bat is your life. It's your weapon. You don't want to go into battle with anything that feels less than perfect.

> LOU BROCK, quoted in *American Way* magazine, April 29, 1986.

9 I have found most baseball players to be afflicted with tobacco-chewing minds.

> HOWARD COSELL, *Like It Is,* 1974.

10 I'm just a ball player with one ambition, and that is to give all I've got to help my ball club win. I've never played any other way.

> JOE DIMAGGIO, quoted in Joseph Durso, *Casey,* 1967.

11 In me younger days 'twas not considhered ray-spictable f'r to be an athlete. An athlete was always a man that was not sthrong enough f'r wurruk. Fractions dhruv him fr'm school an' th' vagrancy laws dhruv him to baseball.

> FINLEY PETER DUNNE, *Mr. Dooley's Opinions,* 1901.

12 Nice Guys Finish Last.

> LEO DUROCHER, title of his book, 1975.

13 I believe in rules. Sure I do. If there weren't any rules, how could you break them?

> LEO DUROCHER, *Nice Guys Finish Last,* 1975.

14 Give me some scratching, diving, hungry ballplayers who come to kill you.

> Ibid.

15 Ballplayers are a superstitious breed, nobody more than I, and while you are winning you'd murder anybody who tried to change your sweatshirt, let alone your uniform.

> Ibid.

16 Managing a ball club is the most vulnerable job in the world. . . . If you don't win, you're going to be fired. If you do win, you've only put off the day you're going to be fired. And no matter what you do, you're going to be second-guessed. The manager is the only person in the ball park who has to call it right now. Everybody else can call it after it's over.

> Ibid.

17 I don't know why people like the home run so much. A home run is over as soon as it starts. . . . The triple is the most exciting play of the game. A triple is like meeting a woman who excites you, spending the evening talking and getting more excited, then taking her home. It drags on and on. You're never sure how it's going to turn out.

> GEORGE FOSTER, quoted in several newspapers, 1978.

18 The mound is a mountain. You are at the bottom trying to hit uphill. The pitcher is King Kong. The bat should have telephone wires on it, the way it feels. Somebody must have put grease in the resin. Even the spikes are complaining through

your shoes; they can't find the right spot in the batter's box.

> JOE GARAGIOLA, *Baseball Is a Funny Game,* 1960.

19 It's pitching, hitting and defense that wins. Any two can win. All three make you unbeatable.

> Ibid.

20 Baseball is a drama with an endless run and an ever-changing cast.

> Ibid.

21 Baseball gives you every chance to be great. Then it puts every pressure on you to prove that you haven't got what it takes. It never takes away the chance, and it never eases up on the pressure.

> Ibid.

22 Baseball is a game of race, creed, and color. The race is to first base. The creed is the rules of the game. The color? Well, the home team wears white uniforms, and the visiting team wears gray.

> Ibid.

23 The new definition of a heathen is a man who has never played baseball.

> ELBERT HUBBARD, *The Roycroft Dictionary and Book of Epigrams,* 1923.

24 No baseball fan has to explain his mania to any other baseball fan. They are a fraternity. It is less easy, often it is hopeless, to try to explain it to anyone else. You grow technical, and you do not make sense. You grow sentimental, and you are deemed soft in the head. How, the benighted outsider asks you with no little condescension, can you grow sentimental about a cold-blooded professional sport?

> JOHN K. HUTCHENS, "Confessions of a Baseball Fan," the *New York Times Magazine,* July 14, 1946.

25 This team, it all flows from me. I've got to keep it going. I'm the straw that stirs the drink.

> REGGIE JACKSON, at spring training in 1977, quoted in Bob Abel and Michael Valenti, *Sports Quotes,* 1983.

26 Regardless of the verdict of juries, no player that throws a ball game, no player that entertains

proposals or promises to throw a game, no player that sits in a conference with a bunch of crooked players and gamblers where the ways and means of throwing games are discussed, and does not promptly tell his club about it, will ever again play professional baseball.

> Kenesaw Mountain Landis, statement issued in August, 1921, after a Cook County jury found eight members of the Chicago White Sox not guilty of fixing the 1919 World Series, quoted in Joseph Durso, *Casey,* 1967.

27 You can't even celebrate a victory. If you win today, you must start worrying about tomorrow. If you win a pennant, you start worrying about the World Series. As soon as that's over, you start worrying about next season.

> Bill McKechnie, quoted in Frank Graham and Dick Hyman, *Baseball Wit and Wisdom,* 1962.

28 Take me out to the ball game,
Take me out with the crowd.
Buy me some peanuts and cracker-jack—
I don't care if I never get back.

> Jack Norworth, "Take Me Out to the Ball Game," 1908.

29 For it's one, two, three strikes you're out
At the old ball game.

> Ibid.

30 The greatest thrill in the world is to end the game with a home run and watch everybody else walk off the field while you're running the bases on air.

> Al Rosen, quoted in Frank Graham and Dick Hyman, *Baseball Wit and Wisdom,* 1962.

31 Open the window, Aunt Minnie—here it comes.

> Pittsburgh Pirates sportscaster Rosey Rosewell, whenever a Pirate hit a home run in Forbes Field, a small baseball park situated near a residential area.

32 Baseball is an allegorical play about America, a poetic, complex, and subtle play of courage, fear, good luck, mistakes, patience about fate, and sober self-esteem. . . . It is impossible to understand America without a thorough knowledge of baseball.

> Saul Steinberg, quoted in Harold Rosenberg, *Saul Steinberg,* 1978.

33 Maybe God can do something about such a play; man cannot.

> Casey Stengel, on Pittsburgh Pirate Bill Virdon's key eighth-inning hit in the seventh game of the 1960 World Series. (Pittsburgh went on to win 10–9).

34 Don't cut my throat. I may want to do that later myself.

> Casey Stengel, speaking to his barber after his team, the Brooklyn Dodgers of 1935, lost a doubleheader, quoted in Joseph Durso, *Casey,* 1967.

35 I'll never make the mistake of being seventy again.

> Casey Stengel, announcing his retirement as manager of the New York Yankees in 1960, quoted in Norman MacLean, *Casey Stengel: A Biography,* 1976.

36 It just shows you how easy this business is.

> Casey Stengel, remark to the press after his fledgling New York Mets beat his former team, the Yankees, 4–3, on March 23, 1962.

37 I had many years that I was not so successful as a ball player, as it is a game of skill.

> Casey Stengel, quoted in Joseph Durso, *Casey,* 1967.

38 That feller runs splendid but he needs help at the plate, which coming from the country chasing rabbits all winter give him strong legs, although he broke one falling out of a tree, which shows you can't tell, and when a curve ball comes he waves at it and if pitchers don't throw curves you have no pitching staff, so how is a manager going to know whether to tell boys to fall out of trees and break legs so he can run fast even if he can't hit a curve ball?

> Ibid.

39 There was ease in Casey's manner as he
        stepped into his place;
  There was pride in Casey's bearing, and a
        smile on Casey's face.
  And when, responding to the cheers, he
        lightly doffed his hat,
  No stranger in the crowd could doubt 'twas
        Casey at the bat.

> ERNEST LAWRENCE THAYER, "Casey at
> the Bat," *San Francisco Examiner,* June 3,
> 1888.

40 Oh, somewhere in this favored land the sun
        is shining bright;
  The band is playing somewhere, and
        somewhere hearts are light,
  And somewhere men are laughing, and
        somewhere children shout;
  But there is no joy in Mudville—mighty
        Casey has struck out.

> Ibid.

41 Baseball's unique possession, the real source of
our strength, is the fan's memory of the times his
daddy took him to the game to see the great players
of his youth. Whether he remembers it or not, the
excitement of those hours, the step they represented
in his own growth and the part those afternoons—
even *one* afternoon—played in his relationship
with his own father is bound up in his feeling
toward the local ball club and toward the game.
When he takes his own son to the game, as his
father once took him, there is a spanning of the
generations that is warm and rich and—if I may use
the word—lovely.

> BILL VEECK, *The Hustler's Handbook,*
> 1965.

42 Baseball is not the sport of the wealthy, it is the
sport of the wage earner.

> Ibid.

43 I learned early on to leave the ball game in the
ball park on the way home.

> EARLY WYNN, responding to a question about his
> consistency as a pitcher—he had just won his
> 300th game, 1962.

31. BEAUTY

1 Beauty is only skin deep, but ugly goes clear to
the bone.

> Saying, recorded in Arthur Block, *Murphy's Law,*
> 1977.

2 Sometimes I do get to places just when God's
ready to have somebody click the shutter.

> ANSEL ADAMS, quoted in *American Way*
> magazine, October, 1974.

3 What is lovely never dies,
  But passes into other loveliness,
  Star-dust, or sea-foam, flower or winged air.

> THOMAS BAILEY ALDRICH, "A Shadow of the
> Night," in *The Sister's Tragedy, with Other
> Poems, Lyrical and Dramatic,* 1891.

4 One thing about being born without beauty—
you don't look for it.

> Attributed to Imogen Cunningham.

5 Beauty is not caused, It is.

> EMILY DICKINSON, *Further Poems,* 1929.

6 I died for beauty, but was scarce
  Adjusted in the tomb,
  When one who died for truth was slain
  In an adjoining room.
  He questioned softly why I failed?
  "For beauty," I replied.
  "And I for truth,—the two are one;
  We brethren are," he said.
  And so, as kinsmen met at night,
  We talked between the rooms,
  Until the moss had reached our lips,
  And covered up our names.

> EMILY DICKINSON, "I died for Beauty," in
> *Poems,* 1890.

7 Beauty crowds me till I die,
  Beauty, mercy have on me!
  But if I expire to-day
  Let it be in sight of thee!

> EMILY DICKINSON, "Beauty crowds me till I
> die," published in *The Single Hound,* 1914.

8 Beauty, what is that? . . . Beauty neither buys food nor keeps up a home.

> MAXINE ELLIOTT, in a newspaper interview, 1908.

9 Beauty is the mark God sets upon virtue.

> RALPH WALDO EMERSON, "Beauty," *Nature,* 1836.

10 Rhodora! if the sages ask thee why
This charm is wasted on the earth and sky,
Tell them, dear, that if eyes were made for
  seeing,
Then Beauty is its own excuse for being.

> RALPH WALDO EMERSON, "The Rhodora," published in the *Western Messenger,* July, 1839.

11 Though we travel the world over to find the beautiful, we must carry it with us or we find it not.

> RALPH WALDO EMERSON, "Art," *Essays,* First Series, 1841.

12 The beautiful rests on the foundations of the necessary.

> RALPH WALDO EMERSON, "The Poet," *Essays,* Second Series, 1844.

13 We ascribe beauty to that which is simple; which has no superfluous parts; which exactly answers its end; which stands related to all things; which is the mean of many extremes.

> RALPH WALDO EMERSON, "Beauty," *The Conduct of Life,* 1860.

14 The secret of ugliness consists not in irregularity, but in being uninteresting.

> Ibid.

15 Beauty without grace is the hook without the bait. Beauty, without expression, tires.

> Ibid.

16 Beauty rests on necessities. The line of beauty is the line of perfect economy.

> Ibid.

17 Beauty brings its own fancy price, for all that a man hath will he give for his love.

> RALPH WALDO EMERSON, "Social Aims," *Letters and Social Aims,* 1876.

18 Beauty is the virtue of the body, as virtue is the beauty of the soul.

> RALPH WALDO EMERSON, "Michael Angelo," *Natural History of Intellect,* 1893.

19 Nothing in human life, least of all in religion, is ever right until it is beautiful.

> HARRY EMERSON FOSDICK, *As I See Religion,* 1932.

20 I believe long habits of virtue have a sensible effect on the countenance.

> BENJAMIN FRANKLIN, in one of the letters known collectively as the "Busy-Body Papers," the *American Weekly Mercury,* February 18, 1729.

21 Beauty & folly are old companions.

> BENJAMIN FRANKLIN, *Poor Richard's Almanack,* 1734.

22 A Ship under sail and a big-bellied Woman,
Are the handsomest two things that can be
  seen common.

> BENJAMIN FRANKLIN, *Poor Richard's Almanack,* 1735.

23 There is certainly no absolute standard of beauty. That precisely is what makes its pursuit so interesting.

> JOHN KENNETH GALBRAITH, "Some Reflections on Public Architecture and Public Works," the *New York Times Magazine,* October 9, 1960.

24 Beauty is the index of a larger fact than wisdom.

> OLIVER WENDELL HOLMES, SR., *The Professor at the Breakfast-Table,* 1860.

25 Wisdom is the abstract of the past, but beauty is the promise of the future.

> Ibid.

26 I'm tired of all this nonsense about beauty being only skin-deep. That's deep enough. What do you want—an adorable pancreas?

> JEAN KERR, "Mirror, Mirror, on the Wall, I Don't Want to Hear One Word Out of You," in *The Snake Has All the Lines,* 1960.

27 But a celestial brightness—a more ethereal
    beauty—
Shone on her face and encircled her form,
    when, after confession,
Homeward serenely she walked with God's
    benediction upon her.
When she had passed, it seemed like the
    ceasing of exquisite music.

> HENRY WADSWORTH LONGFELLOW, *Evangeline*,
> 1847.

28 Christian endeavor is notoriously hard on female pulchritude.

> H.L. MENCKEN, "The Aesthetic Recoil," *The
> American Mercury*, July, 1931.

29   Euclid alone
Has looked on Beauty bare. Fortunate they
Who, though once only and then but far
    away,
Have heard her massive sandal set on stone.

> EDNA ST. VINCENT MILLAY, "Euclid Alone Has
> Looked on Beauty Bare," *Sonnets*, 1923.

30 Beauty is ever to the lonely mind
A shadow fleeting; she is never plain.
She is a visitor who leaves behind
The gift of grief, the souvenir of pain.

> ROBERT NATHAN, "Beauty is ever to the lonely
> mind," in *Selected Poems of Robert Nathan*,
> 1936.

31 Helen, thy beauty is to me
    Like those Nicaean barks of yore,
That gently, o'er a perfumed sea,
    The weary, way-worn wanderer bore
To his own native shore.

> EDGAR ALLAN POE, "To Helen," 1831.

32   Thy hyacinth hair, thy classic face,
Thy Naiad airs have brought me home
    To the glory that was Greece
And the grandeur that was Rome.

> Ibid.

33 Beauty of whatever kind, in its supreme development, invariably excites the sensitive soul to
tears.

> EDGAR ALLAN POE, "The Rationale of Verse,"
> printed in *The Pioneer*, March, 1843.

34 There are no ugly women, only lazy ones.

> HELENA RUBINSTEIN, *My Life for Beauty*, 1966.

35 Beauty as we feel it is something indescribable:
what it is or what it means can never be said.

> GEORGE SANTAYANA, "Expression," *The Sense of
> Beauty*, 1896.

36 Spirit of Beauty, whose sweet impulses,
Flung like the rose of dawn across the sea,
Alone can flush the exalted consciousness
With shafts of sensible divinity—
Light of the world, essential loveliness.

> ALAN SEEGER, "Ode to Natural Beauty," 1916.

37 Beauty vanishes like a vapor,
Preach the men of musty morals!

> HARRIET PRESCOTT SPOFFORD, "Evanescence,"
> collected in Edmund Clarence Stedman, *An
> American Anthology, 1787–1900*, 1906.

38 Beauty is momentary in the mind—
The fitful tracing of a portal;
But in the flesh it is immortal.

> WALLACE STEVENS, "Peter Quince at the
> Clavier," *Harmonium*, 1923.

39 So much has been said and sung of beautiful
young girls, why doesn't somebody wake up to the
beauty of old women?

> HARRIET BEECHER STOWE, *Uncle Tom's Cabin*,
> 1852.

40 O, beauty are you not enough?
Why am I crying after love?

> SARA TEASDALE, "Spring Night," in *Rivers to the
> Sea*, 1915.

41 Anatomists see no beautiful woman in all their
lives, but only a ghastly sack of bones with Latin
names to them, and a network of nerves and muscles and tissues inflamed by disease.

> MARK TWAIN, letter to the *San Francisco Alta
> California*, May 28, 1867.

42 Beauty is altogether in the eye of the beholder.

> LEW WALLACE, *The Prince of India*, 1893.

43 Art's perfect forms no moral need,
And beauty is its own excuse.

JOHN GREENLEAF WHITTIER, dedication, *Songs of Labor,* 1850. (Whittier noted that he was "indebted to Emerson." The second line echoes a line in Emerson's "The Rhodora." See quotation 10 above.)

44 The Beauty which old Greece or Rome
  Sung, painted, wrought, lies close at home;
    We need but eye and ear
  In all our daily walks to trace
  The outlines of incarnate grace,
    The hymns of gods to hear!

JOHN GREENLEAF WHITTIER, "To— Lines written after a Summer Day's Excursion," 1851.

45 O Beauty, old yet ever new!
  Eternal Voice and Inward Word.

JOHN GREENLEAF WHITTIER, "The Shadow and the Light," 1860.

46 Beauty seen is never lost,
  God's colors all are fast.

JOHN GREENLEAF WHITTIER, "Sunset on the Bearcamp," 1876.

47 Say not of Beauty she is good,
  Or aught but beautiful.

ELINOR WYLIE, "Beauty," *Nets to Catch the Wind,* 1921.

---

32. BELIEF

See also RELIGION

---

1 His mind kept open house.

Anonymous.

2 When I read [in the Bible] that a big fish swallowed Jonah—it does not say whale. . . . I believe it. And I believe in a God who can make a whale and can make a man and make both do what He pleases.

WILLIAM JENNINGS BRYAN, at the Scopes trial, Dayton, Tennessee, July 21, 1925.

3 One miracle is just as easy to believe as another.

Ibid.

4 It is wanting to know the end that makes us believe in God, or witchcraft, believe, at least, in something.

TRUMAN CAPOTE, *Other Voices, Other Rooms,* 1948.

5 There is no force so democratic as the force of an ideal.

CALVIN COOLIDGE, in a speech in New York City, November 27, 1920.

6 Faith is a fine invention
  When gentlemen can see.
  But microscopes are prudent
  In an emergency.

EMILY DICKINSON, "Faith Is a Fine Invention," in *Poems,* Second Series, 1891.

7 We are born believing. A man bears beliefs as a tree bears apples.

RALPH WALDO EMERSON, "Worship," *The Conduct of Life,* 1860.

8 All ages of belief have been great; all of unbelief have been mean.

RALPH WALDO EMERSON, "The Sovereignty of Ethics," *Lectures and Biographical Sketches,* 1883.

9 Every idea is an incitement. It offers itself for belief and, if believed, it is acted on unless some other belief outweighs it, or some failure of energy stifles the movements at its birth.

OLIVER WENDELL HOLMES, JR., in a dissenting Supreme Court opinion, *Gitlow* v. *People of New York,* 1925.

10 Our faith is faith in someone else's faith, and in the greatest matters this is most the case.

WILLIAM JAMES, "The Will to Believe," in the *New World* magazine, June, 1896.

11 What is it men cannot be made to believe!

THOMAS JEFFERSON, in a letter to Richard Henry Lee, April 22, 1786.

12 Credulity is not a crime.

THOMAS PAINE, *The Age of Reason,* 1794–1795.

13 God's miracles are to be found in nature itself; the wind and waves, the wood that becomes a tree—all of these are explained biologically, but behind them is the hand of God. And I believe that is true of creation itself.

> RONALD REAGAN, in *Sincerely, Ronald Reagan*, 1976.

14 Copernicus . . . did not publish his book [on the nature of the solar system] until he was on his deathbed. He knew how dangerous it is to be right when the rest of the world is wrong.

> THOMAS BRACKETT REED, in a speech at Waterville, Maine, July 30, 1885.

15 Skepticism is the chastity of the intellect, and it is shameful to surrender it too soon or to the first comer; there is nobility in preserving it coolly and proudly through a long youth, until at last, in the ripeness of instinct and discretion, it can be safely exchanged for fidelity and happiness.

> GEORGE SANTAYANA, *Skepticism and Animal Faith*, 1923.

16 What do I believe? As an American I believe in generosity, in liberty, in the rights of man. These are social and political faiths that are part of me, as they are, I suppose, part of all of us. Such beliefs are easy to express. But part of me too is my relation to all life, my religion. And this is *not* so easy to talk about. Religious experience is highly intimate and, for me, at least, ready words are not at hand.

> ADLAI E. STEVENSON, speaking at Libertyville, Illinois, May 21, 1954.

17 No one is so thoroughly superstitious as the godless man.

> HARRIET BEECHER STOWE, *Uncle Tom's Cabin*, 1852.

18 My land, the power of training! of influence! of education! It can bring a body up to believe anything.

> MARK TWAIN, *A Connecticut Yankee in King Arthur's Court*, 1889.

19 If the man doesn't believe as we do, we say he is a crank, and that settles it. I mean it does nowadays, because now we can't burn him.

> MARK TWAIN, *Following the Equator*, 1897.

20 In religion and politics people's beliefs and convictions are in almost every case gotten at second-hand, and without examination, from authorities who have not themselves examined the questions at issue but have taken them at second-hand from other non-examiners, whose opinions about them were not worth a brass farthing.

> MARK TWAIN, *Mark Twain's Autobiography*, 1959.

---

33. BERRAISMS

See also BASEBALL

The sayings of baseball great Lawrence P. "Yogi" Berra are the stuff that legends are built of. While it is doubtful that Berra actually said many of the things attributed to him—he has denied ever having said some of them—there is no doubt that they are among the most favored American quotations.

1 Baseball is 90 percent mental. The other half is physical.

> On the game of baseball.

2 You observe a lot by watching.

> On his qualifications to be a coach.

3 That's his style of hittin'. If you can't imitate him, don't copy him.

> On the batting technique of Frank Robinson.

4 It gets late early out there.

> On having trouble with the sun at Yankee Stadium in the fall.

5 Nobody goes there anymore, it's too crowded.

> On a popular restaurant.

6 Wotta house. Nothin' but rooms!

> On his new house in Montclair, New Jersey.

7 I guess the first thing I ought to say is that I thank everybody for making this day necessary.

> Opening remark in his address at the Baseball Hall of Fame induction ceremony, August 7, 1972.

8 It ain't over till it's over.

> On the game of baseball.

---

34. BLACK AMERICANS

See also AMERICANS; CIVIL RIGHTS; EQUALITY; SLAVERY

---

1 No Viet Cong ever called me "Nigger."

> MUHAMMAD ALI, quoted in Norman Mailer, *The Fight,* 1975.

2 Out of the huts of history's shame
I rise
Up from a past that's rooted in pain
I rise
I'm a black ocean, leaping and wide,
Welling and swelling I bear in the tide.

> MAYA ANGELOU, "Still I Rise," in *And Still I Rise,* 1978.

3 If we do not now dare everything, the fulfillment of that prophecy, re-created from the Bible in song by a slave, is upon us: *God gave Noah the rainbow sign, No more water, the fire next time!*

> JAMES BALDWIN, *The Fire Next Time,* 1963.

4 To be black and conscious in America is to be in a constant state of rage.

> JAMES BALDWIN, quoted in Joan Didion, *The White Album,* 1979.

5 Let me state here and now that the black woman in America can justly be described as a "slave of a slave."

> FRANCES M. BEAL, "Double Jeopardy: To Be Black and Female," in Robin Morgan, *Sisterhood Is Powerful,* 1970.

6 The destiny of the colored American . . . is the destiny of America.

> FREDERICK DOUGLASS, in a speech in Boston, February 12, 1862.

7 Where justice is denied, where poverty is enforced, where ignorance prevails, and where any one class is made to feel that society is in an organized conspiracy to oppress, rob, and degrade them, neither persons nor property will be safe.

> FREDERICK DOUGLASS, in an address on the twenty-fourth anniversary of Emancipation in the District of Columbia, Washington, D.C., April, 1886.

8 If a man calls me a nigger, he is calling me something I am not. The nigger exists only in his own mind; therefore his mind is the nigger. I must feel sorry for such a man.

> DICK GREGORY, *The Shadow that Scares Me,* 1968.

9 [Civil Rights:] What black folks are given in the U.S. on the installment plan, as in civil-rights bills. Not to be confused with *human rights,* which are the dignity, stature, humanity, respect, and freedom belonging to all people by right of their birth.

> DICK GREGORY, *Dick Gregory's Political Primer,* 1972.

10 Misery is often the parent of the most affecting touches in poetry. Among the blacks is misery enough, God knows, but no poetry.

> THOMAS JEFFERSON, *Notes on the State of Virginia,* 1784.

11 We have come over a way that with tears
　　has been watered,
We have come, treading our path through
　　the blood of the slaughtered.

> JAMES WELDON JOHNSON, *Lift Every Voice and Sing,* 1900.

12 Being a Negro in America means trying to smile when you want to cry. It means trying to hold on to physical life amid psychological death. It means the pain of watching your children grow up with clouds of inferiority in their mental skies. It means having your legs cut off, and then being condemned for being a cripple. It means seeing your mother and father spiritually murdered by the slings and arrows of daily exploitation, and then being hated for being an orphan.

> MARTIN LUTHER KING, JR., *Where Do We Go from Here: Chaos or Community?,* 1967.

13 To be a Negro in America is to hope against hope.

> Ibid.

14 When we ask Negroes to abide by the law, let us also declare that the white man does not abide by law in the ghettos. Day in and day out he violates welfare laws to deprive the poor of their meager allotments; he flagrantly violates building codes and regulations; his police make a mockery of law; he violates laws on equal employment and education and the provisions for civic services. The slums are the handiwork of a vicious system of the white society; Negroes live in them, but they do not make them, any more than a prisoner makes a prison.

> MARTIN LUTHER KING, JR., *The Trumpet of Conscience,* 1967.

15 It is not good to be a Negro in the land of the free and the home of the brave.

> RUDYARD KIPLING, *From Sea to Sea,* 1889.

16 Black people cannot and will not become integrated into American society on any terms but those of self-determination and autonomy.

> GERDA LERNER, *Black Women in White America,* 1972.

17 In the right to eat the bread, without the leave of anybody else, which his own hand earns, he is my equal and the equal of Judge Douglas, and the equal of every living man.

> ABRAHAM LINCOLN, on the equality of blacks and whites, in the first Lincoln-Douglas debate, Ottawa, Illinois, August 21, 1858.

18 Of those who were slaves at the beginning of the rebellion, full one hundred thousand are now in the United States military service, about one-half of which number actually bear arms in the ranks; thus giving the double advantage of taking so much labor from the insurgent cause and supplying the places which otherwise must be filled with so many white men. So far as tested, it is difficult to say they are not as good soldiers as any.

> ABRAHAM LINCOLN, in his third annual message to Congress, December 8, 1863.

19 Lynching is a murder. For the past four hundred years our people have been lynched physically but now it's done politically. We're lynched politically, we're lynched economically, we're lynched socially, we're lynched in every way that you can imagine.

> MALCOLM X, speaking on the television program "Open Mind," October 15, 1961.

20 I think that what you should realize is that in America there are 20 million black people, all of whom are in prison. You don't have to go to Sing Sing to be in prison. If you're born in America with a black skin, you're born in prison, and the masses of black people in America today are beginning to regard our plight or predicament in this society as one of a prison inmate.

> MALCOLM X, in an interview with Kenneth B. Clark, June, 1963.

21 We want no integration with this wicked race that enslaved us. We want complete separation from this race of devils. But we should not be

expected to leave America and go back to our own homeland empty-handed. After four hundred years of slave labor, we have some *back pay* coming, a bill owed to us that must be collected.

> MALCOLM X, in a speech, December 1, 1963.

22 The common goal of 22 million Afro-Americans is respect as *human beings,* the God-given right to be a *human being.* Our common goal is to obtain the *human rights* that America has been denying us. We can never get civil rights in America until our *human rights* are first restored. We will never be recognized as citizens there until we are first recognized as *humans.*

> MALCOLM X, "Racism: The Cancer that Is Destroying America," *The Egyptian Gazette,* August 25, 1964.

23 Racism is a human problem and a crime that is absolutely so ghastly that a person who is fighting racism is well within his rights to fight against it by any means necessary until it is eliminated.

> MALCOLM X, in a speech, December 12, 1964.

24 One of the things that make a Negro unpleasant to white folks is the fact that he suffers from their injustice. He is thus a standing rebuke to them.

> H.L. MENCKEN, *Minority Report,* 1956.

25 The economic situation of the Negroes in America is pathological.

> GUNNAR MYRDAL, *An American Dilemma,* 1944.

26 If ever America undergoes great revolutions, they will be brought about by the presence of the black race on the soil of the United States; that is to say, they will owe their origin, not to the equality, but to the inequality of condition.

> ALEXIS DE TOCQUEVILLE, *Democracy in America,* 1840.

27 Segregation now, segregation tomorrow, segregation forever!

> GEORGE WALLACE, quoted in Martin Luther King, Jr., *Why We Can't Wait,* 1963.

28 During the next half century or more, my race must continue passing through the severe American crucible. We are to be tested in our patience, our forbearance, our perseverance, our power to endure wrong, to withstand temptations, to economize, to acquire and use skill; our ability to compete, to succeed in commerce, to disregard the superficial for the real, the appearance for the substance, to be great and yet small, learned and yet simple, high and yet the servant of all. This, this is the passport to all that is best in the life of our Republic, and the Negro must possess it, or be debarred.

> BOOKER T. WASHINGTON, in a speech accepting an honorary Master's Degree from Harvard University, June, 1896.

---

35. BOOKS

See also EDUCATION; LITERATURE; POET; POETRY; WRITERS

---

1 A good book is fruitful of other books; it perpetuates its fame from age to age, and makes eras in the lives of its readers.

> A. BRONSON ALCOTT, *Tablets,* 1868.

2 Books are the most mannerly of companions, accessible at all times, in all moods, frankly declaring the author's mind, without offence.

> A. BRONSON ALCOTT, *Concord Days,* 1872.

3 That is a good book which is opened with expectation, and closed with profit.

> A. BRONSON ALCOTT, *Table-Talk,* 1877.

4 One must be a wise reader to quote wisely and well.

> Ibid.

5 Where is human nature so weak as in the bookstore!

> HENRY WARD BEECHER, "Subtleties of Book Buyers," *Star Papers,* 1855.

6 A library is but the soul's burial-ground. It is the land of shadows.

> HENRY WARD BEECHER, *Star Papers,* 1855.

7 The covers of this book are too far apart.

> AMBROSE BIERCE, a one-sentence book review, quoted in C.H. Grattan, *Bitter Bierce,* 1929.

8 There are persons who honestly do not see the use of books in the home, either for information—have they not radio and even television?—or for decoration—is there not the wallpaper?

> PEARL S. BUCK, "In Search of Readers," in Helen Hull, *The Writer's Book,* 1950.

9 Books are the true levellers. They give to all, who will faithfully use them, the society, the spiritual presence, of the best and greatest of our race.

> WILLIAM ELLERY CHANNING, in his lecture "Self-Culture," 1838.

10 It is chiefly through books that we enjoy intercourse with superior minds, and these invaluable means of communication are in the reach of all. In the best books, great men talk to us, give us their most precious thoughts, and pour their souls into ours.

> Ibid.

11 Wouldst thou find my ashes? Look
   In the pages of my book;
   And, as these thy hands doth turn,
   Know here is my funeral urn.

> ADELAIDE CRAPSEY, "The Immortal Residue," *Verse,* 1915.

12 Books tell me so much that they inform me of nothing. Sophistry, the bane of freemen, launches forth in all her deceiving attire! After all, most men reason from passions; and shall such an ignorant individual as I am decide, and say this side is right, that side is wrong? Sentiment and feeling are the only guides I know.

> MICHEL GUILLAUME JEAN DE CRÈVECOEUR, *Letters from an American Farmer,* 1782.

13 He ate and drank the precious words,
   His spirits grew robust;
   He knew no more that he was poor,
   Nor that his frame was dust.
   He danced along the dingy days,
   And this bequest of wings

Was but a book. What liberty
   A loosened spirit brings!

> EMILY DICKINSON, "A Book (1)," *Poems,* 1890.

14 There is no frigate like a book
   To take us lands away,
   Nor any coursers like a page
   Of prancing poetry.

> EMILY DICKINSON, "A Book (2)," *Poems,* Third Series, 1896.

15 Book banning is as old as books.

> WILLIAM O. DOUGLAS, *We the Judges,* 1956.

16 Between the Bible and novels there is a gulf fixed which few novel readers are willing to pass. The consciousness of virtue, the dignified pleasure of having performed one's duty, the serene remembrance of a useful life, the hopes of an interest in the Redeemer, and the promise of a glorious inheritance in the favor of God are never found in novels.

> TIMOTHY DWIGHT, *Travels in New England and New York,* 1823.

17 Don't join the book burners. Don't think you are going to conceal faults by concealing evidence that they ever existed.

> DWIGHT D. EISENHOWER, speech at Dartmouth College, June 14, 1953.

18 Books are the quietest and most constant of friends . . . and the most patient of teachers.

> CHARLES W. ELIOT, *The Happy Life,* 1896.

19 A man is known by the books he reads.

> RALPH WALDO EMERSON, entry written in June, 1830, *Journals,* 1909–1914.

20 Some books leave us free and some books make us free.

> RALPH WALDO EMERSON, entry written December 22, 1839, *Journals,* 1909–1914.

21 Books are the best things, well used; abused, among the worst.

> RALPH WALDO EMERSON, "The American Scholar," *Nature, Addresses, and Lectures,* 1849.

22 Meek young men grow up in libraries, believing it their duty to accept the views which Cicero, which Locke, which Bacon, have given; forgetful

that Cicero, Locke, and Bacon were only young men in libraries when they wrote these books. Hence, instead of Man Thinking, we have the bookworm.

Ibid.

23 The virtue of books is to be readable.

RALPH WALDO EMERSON, "Eloquence," *Society and Solitude,* 1870.

24 'Tis the good reader that makes the good book; in every book he finds passages which seem confidences or asides hidden from all else and unmistakably meant for his ear.

RALPH WALDO EMERSON, "Success," *Society and Solitude,* 1870.

25 There are books ... which take rank in your life with parents and lovers and passionate experiences.

RALPH WALDO EMERSON, "Books," *Society and Solitude,* 1870.

26 I do not hesitate to read good books in translations. What is really best in any book is translatable—any real insight or broad human sentiment.

Ibid.

27 Be sure to read no mean books. Shun the spawn of the press on the gossip of the hour. Do not read what you shall learn, without asking, in the street and the train.

Ibid.

28 The profit of books is according to the sensibility of the reader. The profoundest thought or passion sleeps as in a mine, until an equal mind and heart finds and publishes it.

RALPH WALDO EMERSON, "Quotation and Originality," *Letters and Social Aims,* 1876.

29 We prize books, and they prize them most who are themselves wise.

Ibid.

30 In the highest civilization, the book is still the highest delight. He who has once known its satisfactions is provided with a resource against calamity.

Ibid.

31 If we encountered a man of rare intellect, we should ask him what books he read.

Ibid.

32 Men over forty are no judges of a book written in a new spirit.

RALPH WALDO EMERSON, "The Man of Letters," *Lectures and Biographical Sketches,* 1883.

33 When you reread a classic you do not see more in the book than you did before; you see more in *you* than there was before.

CLIFTON FADIMAN, *Any Number Can Play,* 1957.

34 Books cannot change. A thousand years hence they are what you find them today, speaking the same words, holding forth the same comfort.

EUGENE FIELD, *Love Affairs of a Bibliomaniac,* 1896.

35 Read much, but not many Books.

BENJAMIN FRANKLIN, *Poor Richard's Almanack,* 1738.

36 I may as well confess myself the author of several books against the world in general.

ROBERT FROST, "New Hampshire," *New Hampshire,* 1923.

37 Books won't stay banned. They won't burn. Ideas won't go to jail.

ALFRED WHITNEY GRISWOLD, *Essays on Education,* 1954.

38 Whatever an author puts between the two covers of his book is public property; whatever of himself he does not put there is his private property, as much as if he had never written a word.

GAIL HAMILTON, *Country Living and Country Thinking,* 1862.

39 All that wearies profoundly is to be condemned for reading. The mind profits little by what is termed heavy reading.

LAFCADIO HEARN, "Reading," published in the *New Orleans Item,* April 22, 1881.

40 All good books are alike in that they are truer than if they really happened and after you are finished reading one you will feel that all that happened to you and afterwards it all belongs to you.

ERNEST HEMINGWAY, *Death in the Afternoon,* 1932.

41 The first thing naturally when one enters a scholar's study or library, is to look at his books. One gets a notion very speedily of his tastes and the range of his pursuits by a glance round his bookshelves.

OLIVER WENDELL HOLMES, SR., *The Poet at the Breakfast-Table,* 1872.

42 The foolishest book is a kind of leaky boat on a sea of wisdom; some of the wisdom will get in anyhow.

Ibid.

43 The mortality of all inanimate things is terrible to me, but that of books most of all.

WILLIAM DEAN HOWELLS, letter to Charles Eliot Norton, April 6, 1903.

44 No book is of much importance; the vital thing is, What do you yourself think?

ELBERT HUBBARD, in *The Philistine* magazine, published from 1895–1915.

45 This will never be a civilized country until we expend more money for books than we do for chewing-gum.

Ibid.

46 The only reason for the existence of a novel is that it does attempt to represent life.

HENRY JAMES, "The Art of Fiction," in *Partial Portraits,* 1888.

47 As long as mixed grills and combination salads are popular, anthologies will undoubtedly continue in favor.

ELIZABETH JANEWAY, quoted in Helen Hull, *The Writer's Book,* 1950.

48 I cannot live without books.

THOMAS JEFFERSON, in a letter to John Adams, June 10, 1815.

49 Books constitute capital. A library book lasts as long as a house, for hundreds of years. It is not, then, an article of mere consumption but fairly of capital, and often in the case of professional men, setting out in life, it is their only capital.

THOMAS JEFFERSON, in a letter to James Madison, September, 1821.

50 The pleasant books, that silently among
   Our household treasures take familiar places,
   And are to us as if a living tongue
   Spake from the printed leaves or pictured faces!

HENRY WADSWORTH LONGFELLOW, dedication, *The Seaside and the Fireside,* 1849.

51 The love of learning, the sequestered nooks,
   And all the sweet serenity of books.

HENRY WADSWORTH LONGFELLOW, "Morituri Salutamus," *The Masque of Pandora,* 1875.

52 For books are more than books, they are the life
   The very heart and core of ages past,
   The reason why men lived and worked and died,
   The essence and quintessence of their lives.

AMY LOWELL, "The Boston Athenaeum," *A Dome of Many-Coloured Glass,* 1912.

53 All books are either dreams or swords,
   You can cut, or you can drug, with words.

AMY LOWELL, *Sword Blades and Poppy Seed,* 1914.

54 Books are the bees which carry the quickening pollen from one to another mind.

JAMES RUSSELL LOWELL, "Nationality in Literature," a review of Longfellow's *Kavanagh,* published in the *North American Review,* July, 1849.

55 What a sense of security in an old book which Time has criticized for us!

JAMES RUSSELL LOWELL, "Library of Old Authors," *My Study Windows,* 1871.

56 To produce a mighty book, you must choose a mighty theme. No good and enduring volume can

ever be written on the flea, though many there be that have tried it.

Herman Melville, *Moby-Dick,* 1851.

57 Those whom books will hurt will not be proof against events. Events, not books, should be forbid.

Herman Melville, "The Encantadas," *The Piazza Tales,* 1856.

58 There are some people who read too much: bibliobibuli. I know some who are constantly drunk on books, as other men are drunk on whiskey or religion. They wander through this most diverting and stimulating of worlds in a haze, seeing nothing and hearing nothing.

H.L. Mencken, *Minority Report,* 1956.

59 A book ought to be like a man or a woman, with some individual character in it, though eccentric, yet its own; with some blood in its veins and speculation in its eyes.

John Mitchel, *Jail Journal,* 1854.

60 As sheer casual reading matter, I still find the English dictionary the most interesting book in our language.

Albert Jay Nock, *Memoirs of a Superfluous Man,* 1943.

61 Wear the old coat and buy the new book.

Austin Phelps, *The Theory of Preaching; Lectures on Homiletics,* 1881.

62 The enormous multiplication of books in every branch of knowledge is one of the greatest evils of this age; since it presents one of the most serious obstacles to the acquisition of correct information, by throwing in the reader's way piles of lumber in which he must painfully grope for the scraps of useful matter, peradventure interspersed.

Edgar Allan Poe, *Marginalia,* 1844–1849.

63 Any book which serves to lower the sum of human gaiety is a moral delinquent.

Agnes Repplier, *Books and Men,* 1890.

64 We all know that books burn—yet we have the greater knowledge that books cannot be killed by fire. People die, but books never die. No man and no force can abolish memory.

Franklin D. Roosevelt, in a message to the American Booksellers Association, April 23, 1942.

65 Autobiographies ought to begin with Chapter Two.

Ellery Sedgwick, in the first chapter of his autobiographical book, *The Happy Profession,* 1946.

66 People say that life is the thing, but I prefer reading.

Logan Pearsall Smith, *Afterthoughts,* 1931.

67 The book of moonlight is not written yet.

Wallace Stevens, "The Comedian as the Letter C," *Harmonium,* 1923.

68 The House was quiet and the world was
        calm.
    The reader became the book; and summer
        night
Was like the conscious being of the book.

Wallace Stevens, "The House Was Quiet and the World Was Calm," *Transport to Summer,* 1947.

69 Read the best books first, or you may not have a chance to read them at all.

Henry David Thoreau, *A Week on the Concord and Merrimack Rivers,* 1849.

70 Books . . . in which each thought is of unusual daring; such as an idle man cannot read, and a timid one would not be entertained by, which even make us dangerous to existing institutions—such call I good books.

Ibid.

71 Books must be read as deliberately and reservedly as they are written.

Henry David Thoreau, *Walden,* 1854.

72 How many a man has dated a new era in his life from the reading of a book.

Ibid.

73 Books are the treasured wealth of the world, the fit inheritance of generations and nations.

Ibid.

74 As part of my research for *An Anthology of Author's Atrocity Stories About Publishers,* I conducted a study (employing my usual controls) that showed the average shelf life of a trade book to be somewhere between milk and yogurt.

CALVIN TRILLIN, *Uncivil Liberties,* 1982.

75 No girl was ever ruined by a book.

Attributed to Mayor James J. Walker, of New York City.

76 Books are to be call'd for, and supplied, on the assumption that the process of reading is not a half sleep, but, in the highest sense, an exercise, a gymnast's struggle; that the reader is to do something for himself.

WALT WHITMAN, *Democratic Vistas,* 1870.

77 Camerado, this is no book,
Who touches this touches a man,
(Is it night? are we here together alone?)
It is I you hold and who holds you,
I spring from the pages into your
     arms—decease calls me forth.

WALT WHITMAN, "So Long!" *Leaves of Grass,* 1891–1892.

78 I would never read a book if it were possible for me to talk half an hour with the man who wrote it.

WOODROW WILSON, addressing his students at Princeton University, c.1900.

36. BOSTON

1 If you hear an owl hoot, "To whom," instead of "To who," you can make up your mind he was born and educated in Boston.

Anonymous.

2 I hate the purse proud ostentation of the city of Boston. It is not the pride I like, it is not mine.

. . . A really noble man will not wish to show off before others any thing like superiority. I am an aristocrat, but not one of Boston.

CHARLES FRANCIS ADAMS, *Diary,* September 4, 1824.

3 In the course of my life I have tried Boston socially on all sides: I have summered it and wintered it, tried it drunk and tried it sober; and, drunk or sober, there's nothing in it—save Boston!

CHARLES FRANCIS ADAMS, JR., *Charles Francis Adams, An Autobiography,* 1916.

4 Only Bostonians can understand Bostonians and thoroughly sympathize with the inconsequences of the Boston mind.

HENRY ADAMS, *The Education of Henry Adams,* 1907.

5 No doubt the Bostonian has always been noted for a certain chronic irritability—a sort of Bostonitis—which, in its primitive Puritan form, seemed due to knowing too much of his neighbors, and thinking too much of himself.

Ibid.

6 I have just returned from Boston. It is the only thing to do if you find yourself up there.

FRED ALLEN, letter to Groucho Marx, June 12, 1953.

7 A Boston man is the East wind made flesh.

Attributed to Thomas Gold Appleton.

8 Boston is a state of mind.

Attributed to Thomas Appleton, as well as to Emerson and Twain. (Appleton, a noted nineteenth-century wit, was called one of the Seven Wise Men of Boston.)

9 Boston runs to brains as well as to beans and brown bread. But she is cursed with an army of cranks whom nothing short of a straitjacket or a swamp elm club will ever control.

WILLIAM COWPER BRANN, in his monthly journal *The Iconoclast,* published 1891, 1894–1898.

10 All Puritan vulgarity centers in Boston. The Back Bay conservatives are impoverished by cus-

tom and taboo. They are the lifeless and sterile of this country.

> ISADORA DUNCAN, interview in Boston, 1922.

11 The readers of the *Boston Evening Transcript*
Sway in the wind like a field of ripe corn.

> T.S. ELIOT, "The Boston Evening Transcript," *Prufrock and Other Observations*, 1917.

12 The society of Boston was and is quite uncivilized but refined beyond the point of civilization.

> T.S. ELIOT, writing of Henry James in the *Little Review*, 1918.

13 We say the cows laid out Boston. Well, there are worse surveyors.

> RALPH WALDO EMERSON, "Wealth," *The Conduct of Life*, 1860.

14 The rocky nook with hill-tops three
Looked eastward from the farms,
And twice each day the flowing sea
Took Boston in its arms.

> RALPH WALDO EMERSON, "Boston," 1867.

15 I do not speak with any fondness but the language of coolest history, when I say that Boston commands attention as the town which was appointed in the destiny of nations to lead the civilization of North America.

> RALPH WALDO EMERSON, "Boston," *Natural History of the Intellect*, 1893.

16 There are not ten men in Boston equal to Shakespeare.

> Attributed to William E. Gladstone speaking to an anonymous Bostonian, 1891.

17 Gouge: to squeeze out a man's eye with the thumb, a cruel practice used by the Bostonians in America.

> FRANCIS GROSE, *A Classical Dictionary of the Vulgar Tongue*, 1785.

18 Boston State-house is the hub of the solar system. You couldn't pry that out of a Boston man if you had the tire of all creation straightened out for a crow-bar.

> OLIVER WENDELL HOLMES, SR., *The Autocrat of the Breakfast-Table*, 1858.

19 Full of crooked little streets; but I tell you Boston has opened, and kept open, more turnpikes that lead straight to free thought and free speech and free deeds than any other city of live men or dead men.

> OLIVER WENDELL HOLMES, SR., *The Professor at the Breakfast-Table*, 1860.

20 That's all I claim for Boston—that it is the thinking center of the continent, and therefore of the planet.

> Ibid.

21 I never thought he would come to good, when I heard him attempting to sneer at an unoffending city so respectable as Boston.

> Ibid.

22 The heart of the world beats under the three hills of Boston.

> Ibid.

23 Even Boston provinciality is a precious testimony to the authoritative personality of the city. Cosmopolitanism is a modern vice, and we're antique, we're classic, in the other thing. Yes, I'd rather be a Bostonian, at odds with Boston, than one of the curled darlings of any other community.

> WILLIAM DEAN HOWELLS, *A Modern Instance*, 1882.

24 [The Boston Brahmins are] simmering in their own fat and putting a nice brown on each other.

> HENRY JAMES, SR., to William Dean Howells, quoted in Howells' *Literary Friends and Acquaintances*, 1901.

25 He had never been a very systematic patriot, but it vexed him to see the United States treated as little better than a vulgar smell in his friend's nostril, and he finally spoke up for them quite as if it had been Fourth of July, proclaiming that any American who ran them down ought to be carried home in irons and compelled to live in Boston.

> HENRY JAMES, *The American*, 1877.

26 A solid man of Boston.
A comfortable man, with dividends,
And the first salmon, and the first green
   peas.

> HENRY WADSWORTH LONGFELLOW, "John
> Endicott," in *The New England Tragedies,* 1868.

27 In Boston the onus lies upon every respectable person to prove that he has not written a sonnet, preached a sermon, or delivered a lecture.

> CHARLES MACKAY, *Life and Liberty in America,*
> 1859.

28 [Marriage is] a damnably serious business, particularly around Boston. Remember . . . that you not only marry a wife but also your wife's entire family.

> JOHN P. MARQUAND, *The Late George Apley,*
> 1937.

29 In proportion as Boston furnished the fundamentals for an ideally cultivated life, it is not surprising that Boston should have received her share of gibes and jests from many larger but less fortunate neighbors.

> Ibid.

30 The Bostonians are really, as a race, far inferior in point of anything beyond mere talent to any other set upon the continent of North America. They are decidedly the most servile imitators of the English it is possible to conceive.

> EDGAR ALLAN POE, in a letter to Frederick
> William Thomas, February 14, 1849.

31 Boston looks like a town that has been paid for; Boston has a balance at its bankers.

> GEORGE AUGUSTUS SALA, correspondent for the
> London *Daily Telegraph,* in *My Diary in
> America in the Midst of War,* 1865.

32 Boston is a moral and intellectual nursery always busy applying first principles to trifles.

> Attributed to George Santayana.

33 Boston has carried the practice of hypocrisy to the nth degree of refinement, grace and failure.

> Attributed to Lincoln Steffens.

34 Tomorrow night I appear for the first time before a Boston audience—4000 critics.

> MARK TWAIN, in a letter to Pamela Clemens
> Moffet, November 9, 1869.

35 One feels in Boston, as one feels in no other part of the States, that the intellectual movement has ceased.

> H.G. WELLS, "The Future in America,"
> 1906.

36 Massachusetts has been the wheel within New England, and Boston the wheel within Massachusetts. Boston therefore is often called the "hub of the world," since it has been the source and fountain of the ideas that have reared and made America.

> F.B. ZINCKLE, clergyman and author, *Last
> Winter in the United States,* 1868.

---

37. BOSTON TOAST

Once a few clever lines appear in print, more on the same subject, and in the same style, are bound to appear. At the 1910 Holy Cross College alumni dinner, held at Harvard, an alumnus named John Collins Bossidy offered a toast that concluded:

1 And this is good old Boston,
   The home of the bean and the cod,

Where the Lowells talk to the Cabots,
And the Cabots talk only to God.

In 1924, the versifier and newspaper columnist Franklin P. Adams [F.P.A.] was inspired to write a quatrain of his own when a report appeared that one of the Boston Cabots was seeking an injunction to prevent a man named Kabotschnik from changing his name to Cabot:

2 Then here's to the City of Boston,
   The town of the cries and the groans,

Where the Cabots can't see the
  Kabotschniks
And the Lowells won't speak to the Cohns.

Bergen Evans, in his *Dictionary of Quotations,*
1968, supplies yet another quatrain, writer unknown:

3 Here's to good old Boston,
  The home of the bean and the cod,
  Where the Lowells can't speak to the
  Cabots,

For the Kabots speak Yiddish, by
  God!

Ira Gershwin's lyrics for "Love Is Sweeping the
Country," from *Of Thee I Sing,* 1931, include
the lines:

4 Boston upper zones
  Are changing social habits
  And I hear the Cohns
  Are taking up the Cabots.

---

38. BRAVERY

See also CHARACTER; COWARDICE; FEAR

---

1 Bravery is the capacity to perform properly even
when scared half to death.

GEN. OMAR BRADLEY, quoted in Joe Garagiola,
Baseball Is a Funny Game, 1960.

2 Courage, considered in itself or without reference to its causes, is no virtue, and deserves no
esteem. It is found in the best and the worst, and
is to be judged according to the qualities from
which it springs and with which it is conjoined.

WILLIAM ELLERY CHANNING, *War,* 1835.

3 Courage takes many forms. There is physical
courage, there is moral courage. Then there is a still
higher type of courage—the courage to brave pain,
to live with it, to never let others know of it and
to still find joy in life; to wake up in the morning
with an enthusiasm for the day ahead.

HOWARD COSELL, *Like It Is,* 1974.

4 This will remain the land of the free only so long
as it is the home of the brave.

ELMER DAVIS, *But We Were Born Free,*
1954.

5 To fight aloud is very brave,
  But gallanter, I know,

Who charge within the bosom
The cavalry of woe.

EMILY DICKINSON, "To fight aloud is very
brave," *Poems,* 1890.

6 Courage is the price that life exacts for granting
peace.

Attributed to Amelia Earhart.

7 Heroism feels and never reasons and therefore is
always right.

RALPH WALDO EMERSON, "Heroism," *Essays,*
First Series, 1841.

8 O friend, never strike sail to a fear! Come into
port greatly, or sail with God the seas.

Ibid.

9 Courage charms us, because it indicates that
a man loves an idea better than all things in
the world, that he is thinking neither of his bed,
nor his dinner, nor his money, but will venture
all to put in act the invisible thought of his
mind.

RALPH WALDO EMERSON, entry written in 1859,
Journals, 1909–1914.

10 Great men, great nations, have not been boast-
ers and buffoons, but perceivers of the terror of life,
and have manned themselves to face it.

RALPH WALDO EMERSON, "Fate," *The Conduct
of Life,* 1860.

11 The courage of the tiger is one, and of the horse another.

> RALPH WALDO EMERSON, "Courage," *Society and Solitude,* 1870.

12 Show me a hero and I will write you a tragedy.

> F. SCOTT FITZGERALD, "Notebooks," in *The Crack-Up,* 1945.

13 Grace under pressure.

> ERNEST HEMINGWAY, defining "guts," in the *New Yorker,* November 30, 1929.

14 Courage without conscience is a wild beast.

> ROBERT G. INGERSOLL, speech in New York, May 29, 1882.

15 The next year, the next decade, in all likelihood the next generation, will require more bravery and wisdom on our part than any period in our history. We will be face to face, every day, in every part of our lives and times, with the real issue of our age— the issue of survival.

> JOHN FITZGERALD KENNEDY, speech in Milwaukee, March 11, 1959, quoted in James MacGregor Burns, *John Kennedy, A Political Profile,* 1960.

16 It was involuntary. They sank my boat.

> JOHN FITZGERALD KENNEDY, on being asked how he became a hero, quoted in Arthur M. Schlesinger, Jr., *A Thousand Days,* 1965.

17 They are slaves who fear to speak
For the fallen and the weak.

> JAMES RUSSELL LOWELL, "Stanzas on Freedom," 1843.

18 Familiarity with danger makes a brave man braver, but less daring. Thus with seamen: he who goes the oftenest round Cape Horn goes the most circumspectly.

> HERMAN MELVILLE, *White-Jacket,* 1850.

19 Few men's courage is proof against protracted meditation unrelieved by action.

> HERMAN MELVILLE, *Moby-Dick,* 1851.

20 That man is not truly brave who is afraid either to seem or to be, when it suits him, a coward.

> EDGAR ALLAN POE, *Marginalia,* 1844–1849.

21 We cannot afford to accumulate a deficit in the books of human fortitude.

> FRANKLIN D. ROOSEVELT, acceptance speech at the Democratic National Convention in Philadelphia, June 27, 1936.

22 It takes far less courage to kill yourself than it takes to make yourself wake up one more time. It's harder to stay where you are than to get out.

> JUDITH ROSSNER, *Nine Months in the Life of an Old Maid,* 1969.

23 The enemy say that Americans are good at a long shot, but cannot stand the cold iron. I call upon you instantly to give a lie to the slander. Charge!

> GEN. WINFIELD SCOTT, address to the 11th Infantry Regiment before the U.S. victory over British forces at Chippawa, Canada, July 5, 1814.

24 I would define true courage to be a perfect sensibility of the measure of danger, and a mental willingness to endure it.

> WILLIAM TECUMSEH SHERMAN, *Memoirs,* 1875.

25 If you're scared, just holler and you'll find it ain't so lonesome out there.

> JOE SUGDEN, quoted in Joe Garagiola, *Baseball Is a Funny Game,* 1960.

26 I am less affected by their heroism who stood up for half an hour in the front line at Buena Vista, than by the steady and cheerful valor of the men who inhabit the snowplow for their winter quarters; who have not merely the three-o'-clock-in- the-morning courage, which Bonaparte thought was the rarest, but whose courage does not go to rest so early, who go to sleep only when the storm sleeps or the sinews of their iron steed are frozen.

> HENRY DAVID THOREAU, *Walden,* 1854.

27 Courage is resistance to fear, mastery of fear—not absence of fear. Except a creature be part coward it is not a compliment to say it is brave; it is merely a loose misapplication of the word. Consider the flea!—incomparably the bravest of all the creatures of God, if ignorance of fear were courage. Whether you are asleep or awake he will attack you, caring nothing for the fact that in bulk and strength you are to him as are the massed armies of the earth to a sucking

child; he lives both day and night and all days and nights in the very lap of peril and the immediate presence of death, and yet is no more afraid than is the man who walks the streets of a city that was threatened by an earthquake ten centuries before. When we speak of Clive, Nelson, and Putnam as men who "didn't know what fear was," we ought always to add the flea—and put him at the head of the procession.

> MARK TWAIN, "Pudd'nhead Wilson's Calendar," *Pudd'nhead Wilson,* 1894.

39. BUSINESS

See also DEBT; ECONOMICS; LABOR
MOVEMENT; MONEY; POVERTY; WEALTH

1 When business is good it pays to advertise; when business is bad you've got to advertise.

> Anonymous.

2 Monopolies are odious, contrary to the spirit of free government and the principles of commerce, and ought not to be suffered.

> Maryland Declaration of 1776, condemning grants of monopolies by the British crown.

3 A corporation is just like any natural person, except that it has no pants to kick or soul to damn, and, by God, it ought to have both!

> Attributed to an unidentified Western judge, quoted in Morris L. Ernst and Alexander Lindey *Hold Your Tongue,* 1932.

4 Auctioneer, *n.* The man who proclaims with a hammer that he has picked a pocket with his tongue.

> AMBROSE BIERCE, *The Devil's Dictionary,* 1906.

5 Commerce, *n.* A kind of transaction in which A plunders from B the goods of C, and for compensation B picks the pocket of D of money belonging to E.

> Ibid.

6 Corporation, *n.* An ingenious device for obtaining individual profit without individual responsibility.

> Ibid.

7 Merchant, *n.* One engaged in a commercial pursuit. A commercial pursuit is one in which the thing pursued is a dollar.

> Ibid.

8 Piracy, *n.* Commerce without its folly-swaddles, just as God made it.

> Ibid.

9 Trusts are largely private affairs.

> JAMES G. BLAINE, speech at the opening of the Harrison presidential campaign, Portland, Maine, 1888.

10 In no country does one find so many men of eminent capacity for business, shrewd, forcible, and daring, who are so uninteresting, so intellectually barren, outside the sphere of their business knowledge.

> JAMES BRYCE, *The American Commonwealth,* 1888.

11 No invention of modern times, not even that of negotiable paper, has so changed the face of commerce and delighted lawyers with a variety of new and intricate problems as the creation of incorporated joint stock companies.

> Ibid.

12 He who considers the irresponsible nature of the power which three or four men, or perhaps one man, can exercise through a great corporation, such as a railroad or telegraph company, the injury they can inflict on the public as well as on their competitors, the cynical audacity with which they have often used their wealth to seduce officials and legislators from the path of virtue, will find nothing unreasonable in the desire of the American masses to regulate the management of corporations and narrow the range of their action.

> Ibid.

13 A power has risen up in the government greater than the people themselves, consisting of many and

various and powerful interests . . . held together by the cohesive power of the vast surplus in the banks.

> JOHN C. CALHOUN, in a speech in the U.S. Senate, May 27, 1836.

14 Mr. Morgan buys his partners; I grow my own.

> ANDREW CARNEGIE, quoted in Burton J. Hendrick, *Life of Andrew Carnegie,* 1932.

15 The trusts and combinations—the communism of pelf.

> GROVER CLEVELAND, in a letter to Congressman T.C. Catchings of Mississippi, August, 1894.

16 [Andrew] Carnegie exemplifies to me a truth about American money men that many earnest people fail to grasp—which is that the chase and the kill are as much fun as the prize, which you then proceed to give away.

> ALISTAIR COOKE, *America,* 1973.

17 I recall an advertising tycoon, Bruce Barton, saying in the late 1940s, when we were in a dither about the Russians: "What we ought to do is to send up a flight of a thousand B-29s and drop a million Sears, Roebuck catalogs all over Russia.

> Ibid.

18 Civilization and profits go hand in hand.

> CALVIN COOLIDGE, in a speech in New York City, November 27, 1920.

19 Our government offers no objection to the carrying on of commerce by our citizens with the people of Russia. Our government does not propose, however, to enter into relations with another regime which refuses to recognize the sanctity of international obligations. I do not propose to barter away for the privilege of trade any of the cherished rights of humanity. I do not propose to make merchandise of any American principles.

> CALVIN COOLIDGE, in a message to Congress, December 6, 1923.

20 The business of America is business.

> CALVIN COOLIDGE, in a speech before the Society of American Newspaper Editors, January 17, 1925.

21 Commerce is entitled to a complete and efficient protection in all its legal rights, but the moment it presumes to control a country, or to substitute its fluctuating expedients for the high principles of natural justice that ought to lie at the root of every political system, it should be frowned on, and rebuked.

> JAMES FENIMORE COOPER, *The American Democrat,* 1838.

22 I have always recognized that the object of business is to make money in an honorable manner. I have endeavored to remember that the object of life is to do good.

> PETER COOPER, speaking in 1874.

23 The employer puts his money into . . . business and the workman his life. The one has as much right as the other to regulate that business.

> CLARENCE DARROW, in an article in the *Railroad Trainman,* November, 1909.

24 Humans must breathe, but corporations must make money.

> ALICE EMBREE, quoted in Robin Morgan, *Sisterhood Is Powerful,* 1970.

25 Commerce is of trivial import; love, faith, truth of character, the aspiration of man, these are sacred.

> RALPH WALDO EMERSON, "Circles," *Essays,* First Series, 1841.

26 We rail at trade, but the historian of the world will see that it was the principle of liberty; that it settled America, and destroyed feudalism, and made peace and keeps peace; that it will abolish slavery.

> RALPH WALDO EMERSON, entry written December 31, 1843, *Journals,* 1909–1914.

27 The craft of the merchant is this bringing a thing from where it abounds to where it is costly.

> RALPH WALDO EMERSON, "Wealth," *The Conduct of Life,* 1860.

28 The greatest meliorator of the world is selfish, huckstering trade.

> RALPH WALDO EMERSON, "Works and Days," *Society and Solitude,* 1870.

29 Trade, that pride and darling of our ocean, that educator of nations, that benefactor in spite of itself, ends in shameful defaulting, bubble, and bankruptcy, all over the world.

Ibid.

30 No nation was ever ruined by trade.

Attributed to Benjamin Franklin.

31 *Drive thy Business, let not that drive thee.*

BENJAMIN FRANKLIN, *Poor Richard's Almanack,* 1758.

32 Let all your things have their places; let each part of your business have its time.

BENJAMIN FRANKLIN, *Autobiography,* 1798.

33 History suggests that capitalism is a necessary condition for political freedom. Clearly it is not a sufficient condition.

MILTON FRIEDMAN, *Capitalism and Freedom,* 1962.

34 Men have been swindled by other men on many occasions. The autumn of 1929 was, perhaps, the first occasion when men succeeded on a large scale in swindling themselves.

JOHN KENNETH GALBRAITH, *The Great Crash, 1929,* 1955.

35 Earnest attention should be given to those combinations of capital commonly called Trusts.

BENJAMIN HARRISON, in a message to Congress, December 3, 1889.

36 The mother of all trusts is the customs tariff law.

HENRY O. HAVEMEYER, in testimony before the Industrial Commission, 1899.

37 The notion that a business is clothed with a public interest and has been devoted to the public use is little more than a fiction intended to beautify what is disagreeable to the sufferers.

OLIVER WENDELL HOLMES, JR., in a Supreme Court opinion, *Tyson* v. *Banton,* 1927.

38 Many of the optimists in the world don't own a hundred dollars, and because of their optimism never will.

EDGAR WATSON HOWE, "The Blessing of Business," 1918.

39 I do not dislike your bank [the second National Bank] any more than all banks. But ever since I read the history of the South Sea Bubble I have been afraid of banks.

ANDREW JACKSON, in a conversation with Nicholas Biddle many years after the panic of 1819, recorded in a memorandum of Nicholas Biddle, in the Biddle Papers, Library of Congress.

40 Ministers and merchants love nobody.

THOMAS JEFFERSON, in a letter to John Langdon, September 11, 1785.

41 The selfish spirit of commerce, which knows no country, and feels no passion or principle but that of gain.

THOMAS JEFFERSON, in a letter to Larkin Smith, April 15, 1809.

42 Price-cutting and rebating, collecting information of the trade of competitors, the operation of companies under other names to obviate prejudice or secure an advantage, or for whatever reason, are all legitimate methods of competition. . . . There is no rule of fairness or reasonableness which regulates competition.

JOHN G. JOHNSON AND JOHN G. MILBURN, brief for the Standard Oil Company, filed in the U.S. Circuit Court, St. Louis, Missouri, 1909.

43 A man's success in business today turns upon his power of getting people to believe he has something that they want.

GERALD STANLEY LEE, *Crowds,* 1913.

44 These capitalists generally act harmoniously and in concert, to fleece the people.

ABRAHAM LINCOLN, in a speech in the Illinois Legislature, January, 1837.

45 The simple opposition between the people and big business has disappeared because the people themselves have become so deeply involved in big business.

WALTER LIPPMANN, address to the Academy of Political Science, March 25, 1931, quoted in Ronald Steel, *Walter Lippmann and the American Century,* 1980.

46 Corporations have no souls, but they can love each other.

> HENRY DEMAREST LLOYD, *Wealth Against Commonwealth,* 1894.

47 There is no better ballast for keeping the mind steady on its keel, and saving it from all risk of *crankiness,* than business.

> JAMES RUSSELL LOWELL, "New England Two Centuries Ago," *Among My Books,* 1870.

48 Perhaps the most revolting character that the United States ever produced was the Christian businessman.

> H.L. MENCKEN, *Minority Report,* 1956.

49 Years ago William Jennings Bryan once described big business as "nothing but a collection of organized appetites."

> DANIEL PATRICK MOYNIHAN, in a letter to his constituents titled "Special Report to New York," June, 1986.

50 The Octopus.

> FRANK NORRIS, title of his novel concerning the railroad monopoly in the West, 1901.

51 We believe there are many opportunities for U.S. companies to sell finished goods to Japan, and we would like to see more "Made in America" labels on products sold in our stores.

> TAKEO OZAWA, director of the Japan External Trade Organization, quoted in *American Way* magazine, June, 1973.

52 An indefinable something is to be done, in a way nobody knows how, at a time nobody knows when, that will accomplish nobody knows what. That, as I understand it, is the program against the trusts.

> THOMAS BRACKETT REED, in a letter to Sereno E. Payne, December 2, 1902.

53 A Holding Company is a thing where you hand an accomplice the goods while the policeman searches you.

> WILL ROGERS, March 13, 1935, quoted in Donald Day, *The Autobiography of Will Rogers,* 1949.

54 No business which depends for existence on paying less than living wages to its workers has any right to continue in this country. By business I mean the whole of commerce as well as the whole of industry; by workers I mean all workers—the white-collar class as well as the man in overalls; and by living wages I mean more than a bare subsistence level—I mean the wages of decent living.

> FRANKLIN D. ROOSEVELT, in a statement issued June 16, 1933.

55 Where a trust becomes a monopoly, the state has an immediate right to interfere.

> THEODORE ROOSEVELT, in a message to the New York State Legislature, January 3, 1900.

56 The biggest corporation, like the humblest private citizen, must be held to strict compliance with the will of the people.

> THEODORE ROOSEVELT, in a speech in Cincinnati, Ohio, 1902.

57 The great corporations which we have grown to speak of rather loosely as trusts are the creatures of the state, and the state not only has the right to control them, but it is in duty bound to control them whenever the need of such control is shown.

> THEODORE ROOSEVELT, in a speech at Providence, Rhode Island, August 23, 1902.

58 I hold it to be our duty to see that the wage worker, the small producer, the ordinary consumer, shall get their fair share of the benefit of business prosperity. But it either is or ought to be evident to everyone that business has to prosper before anybody can get any benefit from it.

> THEODORE ROOSEVELT, address to the Ohio Constitutional Convention, February 1, 1912.

59 We demand that big business give people a square deal; in return we must insist that when any one engaged in big business honestly endeavors to do right, he shall himself be given a square deal.

> THEODORE ROOSEVELT, writing on the Taft administration's efforts to dissolve the Steel Trust, *Autobiography,* 1913.

60 Homestead, Braddock, Birmingham, they
    make their steel with men.
Smoke and blood is the mix of steel.

> CARL SANDBURG, "Smoke and Steel," 1920.

61 There is something new under the sun, new and momentous; revolutionary. It is businessmen saying that wages must be kept up, that mass production means we must have mass prosperity.

> LINCOLN STEFFENS, address given in 1928, first published in *Lincoln Steffens Speaking,* 1936, quoted in Justin Kaplan, *Lincoln Steffens: A Biography,* 1974.

62 Well, I've got just as much conscience as any man in business can afford to keep—just a little, you know, to swear by, as 't were.

> HARRIET BEECHER STOWE, *Uncle Tom's Cabin,* 1852.

63 Trade curses everything it handles; and though you trade in messages from Heaven, the whole curse of trade attaches to the business.

> HENRY DAVID THOREAU, *Walden,* 1854.

64 This world is a place of business. What an infinite bustle! . . . There is no sabbath. It would be glorious to see mankind at leisure for once. It is nothing but work, work, work. I cannot easily buy a blank-book to write thoughts in; they are commonly ruled for dollars and cents.

> HENRY DAVID THOREAU, in the essay "Life Without Principle," 1863.

65 October. This is one of the peculiarly dangerous months to speculate in stocks in. The others are July, January, September, April, November, May, March, June, December, August, and February.

> MARK TWAIN, "Pudd'nhead Wilson's Calendar," *Pudd'nhead Wilson,* 1894.

66 Gentlemen: You have undertaken to ruin me. I will not sue you, for law takes too long. I will ruin you.

> Sincerely, Cornelius Vanderbilt

> CORNELIUS VANDERBILT, letter to his associates, Charles Morgan and Cornelius Garrison, who had been scheming to ruin a Vanderbilt transit company and establish one of their own, 1854.

67 The railroads are not run for the benefit of the dear public. That cry is all nonsense. They are built for men who invest their money and expect to get a fair percentage on the same.

> WILLIAM H. VANDERBILT, comment made to reporters, October 8, 1882, and printed in the *Chicago Daily News* on October 9.

68 What is good for the country is good for General Motors, and what's good for General Motors is good for the country.

> CHARLES ERWIN WILSON, industrialist, testifying before the Senate Armed Forces Committee, 1952.

69 We have witnessed in modern business the submergence of the individual within the organization, and yet the increase to an extraordinary degree of the power of the individual, of the individual who happens to control the organization. Most men are individuals no longer so far as their business, its activities, or its moralities are concerned. They are not units but fractions.

> WOODROW WILSON, speech at Chattanooga, Tennessee, August 31, 1910.

70 Business underlies everything in our national life, including our spiritual life. Witness the fact that in the Lord's Prayer, the first petition is for daily bread. No one can worship God or love his neighbor on an empty stomach.

> WOODROW WILSON, speech in New York City, May 23, 1912.

71 Nothing is illegal if a hundred businessmen decide to do it.

> Attributed to Andrew Young.

---

40. CALIFORNIA

See also HOLLYWOOD; SAN FRANCISCO

---

1 Eureka. (I have found it.)

> State motto.

2 Q. How many Californians does it take to change a light bulb?
  A. Six. One to change the bulb and five to share the experience.

> Anonymous.

3 We cultivate and irrigate, but it is God who exaggerates.

> Attributed to an unidentified Californian, speaking of the state's agricultural productivity.

4 California is a great place—if you happen to be an orange.

> Attributed to Fred Allen.

5 California, more than any other part of the Union, is a country by itself, and San Francisco a capital.

> JAMES BRYCE, *The American Commonwealth,* 1888.

6 Whatever starts in California unfortunately has an inclination to spread.

> JIMMY CARTER, remark at a cabinet meeting, March 21, 1977, quoted in Robert Shogan, *Promises to Keep: Carter's First 100 Days,* 1977.

7 The men [of California] are thriftless, proud, and extravagant, and very much given to gaming; and the women have but little education, and a good deal of beauty, and their morality, of course, is none of the best; yet the instances of infidelity are much less frequent than one would at first suppose. . . . The women have but little virtue, but then the jealousy of their husbands is extreme, and their revenge deadly and almost certain. A few inches of cold steel has been the punishment of many an unwary man, who has been guilty, perhaps, of nothing more than indiscretion of manner.

> RICHARD HENRY DANA, JR., *Two Years Before the Mast,* 1840.

8 The attraction and superiority of California are in its days. It has better days, and more of them, than any other country.

> RALPH WALDO EMERSON, entry written in April-May, 1871, *Journals,* 1909–1914.

9 California is the only state in the union where you can fall asleep under a rose bush in full bloom and freeze to death.

> Attributed to W.C. Fields.

10 It's a shame to take this country away from the rattlesnakes.

> Attributed to D.W. Griffith.

11 East is East, and West is San Francisco, according to Californians. Californians are a race of people; they are not merely inhabitants of a State.

> O. HENRY, "A Municipal Report," *Strictly Business,* 1910.

12 Thought is barred in this City of Dreadful Joy and conversation is unknown.

> ALDOUS HUXLEY, on Los Angeles, in *Jesting Pilate,* 1926.

13 California is a tragic country—like Palestine, like every Promised Land.

> CHRISTOPHER ISHERWOOD, *Exhumations,* 1966.

14 These Californian scoundrels are invariably lighthearted; crime cannot overshadow the exhilaration of outdoor life, remorse and gloom are banished like clouds before this perennially sunny climate. They make amusement out of killing you, and regard a successful plundering time as a sort of pleasantry.

> CLARENCE KING, *Mountaineering in the Sierra Nevada,* 1872.

15 California is a queer place—in a way, it has turned its back on the world, and looks into the void Pacific. It is absolutely selfish, very empty, but not false, and at least, not full of false effort.

> D.H. LAWRENCE, in a letter to J.M. Murphy, September 24, 1923.

16 A circus without a tent.

> CAREY MCWILLIAMS, describing Los Angeles, in *Southern California Country,* 1946.

17 The land around San Juan Capistrano is the pocket where the Creator keeps all his treasures. Anything will grow there.

> FRANCES MARION, *Westward the Dream,* 1948.

18 Nineteen suburbs in search of a metropolis.

> H.L. MENCKEN, describing Los Angeles, in *Americana,* 1925.

19 Lonely as God, and white as a winter moon, Mount Shasta starts up sudden and solitary from the heart of the great black forests of Northern California.

Joaquin Miller, *Life Amongst the Modocs,* 1873.

20 It is hereby earnestly proposed that the U.S.A. would be much better off if that big, sprawling, incoherent, shapeless, slobbering civic idiot in the family of American communities, the City of Los Angeles, could be declared incompetent and placed in charge of a guardian like any individual mental defective.

Westbrook Pegler, in the *New York World Telegram,* November 22, 1938.

21 I attended a dinner the other morning given for the Old Settlers of California. No one was allowed to attend unless he had been in the State 2 and one half years.

Will Rogers, *The Illiterate Digest,* 1924.

22 What was the use of my having come from Oakland it was not natural to have come from there yes write about it if I like or anything if I like but not there, there is no there there.

Gertrude Stein, *Everybody's Autobiography,* 1937.

23 If Carmel's founders should return, they could not afford to live there, but it wouldn't go that far.

They would be instantly picked up as suspicious characters and deported over the city line.

John Steinbeck, *Travels with Charley,* 1962.

24 The Mojave is a big desert and a frightening one. It's as though nature tested a man for endurance and constancy to prove whether he was good enough to get to California.

Ibid.

25 I know of no more startling development of the morality of trade and all the modes of getting a living than the rush to California affords. . . . It is only three thousand miles nearer to hell.

Henry David Thoreau, on the California gold rush, entry dated February 1, 1852, in his *Journal,* 1906.

26 All scenery in California requires *distance* to give it its highest charm.

Mark Twain, *Roughing It,* 1872.

27 If you tilt the whole country sideways, Los Angeles is the place where everything loose will fall.

Attributed to Frank Lloyd Wright.

41. CAMPAIGN SLOGANS

See also Elections; Politics

Most presidential campaign slogans have an extremely short shelf life. Nonetheless, many have acquired a special irony, and some retain a substantial degree of their original flavor. Even though passage of time may have robbed some of these slogans of a degree of their original meaning, they are considered sufficiently memorable to enter American folklore.

1 Tippecanoe and Tyler, too.

Whig (Harrison-Tyler) campaign, 1840.

2 Log Cabin and Hard Cider.

Whig (Harrison-Tyler) campaign, 1840.

3 Fifty-four forty or fight.

Democratic (Polk) campaign, 1844.

4 We inscribe in our banner Free Soil, Free Speech, Free Labor, and Free Men.

Free Soil Party (Van Buren) campaign, 1848.

5 We Polked You in '44, We Shall Pierce You in '52.

Democratic (Pierce) campaign, 1852.

6 Free Speech, Free Press, Free Soil, Free Men, Fremont and Victory!

Republican (Frémont) campaign, 1856.

7 Peace at any price; peace and union.

> American (Know-Nothing) Party (Fillmore) campaign, 1856.

8 I know nothing but my Country, my whole Country, and nothing but my Country.

> American (Know-Nothing) Party campaign, 1856.

9 Don't Swap Horses.

> Republican (Lincoln) campaign, 1864.

10 Turn the rascals out!

> Liberal Republican Party (Greeley) campaign, 1872.

11 A Public Office Is a Public Trust.

> Democratic (Cleveland) campaign, 1884.

12 Blaine, Blaine, James G. Blaine,
The Continental liar from the State of
    Maine.

> Political taunt used by the Democrats during the presidential campaign of 1884. (Blaine supporters responded with their own taunt:
> "Ma, Ma, Where's my Pa?
> Gone to the White House, ha, ha, ha."
> Candidate Cleveland acknowledged that he had fathered an illegitimate child.)

13 Grandfather's Hat Fits Ben.

> Republican (Harrison) campaign, 1888. (Benjamin Harrison was the grandson of Pres. William Henry Harrison.)

14 No Crown of Thorns, No Cross of Gold.

> Democratic (Bryan) campaign, 1900.

15 Four more years of the full dinner pail.

> Republican (McKinley) campaign, 1900.

16 McKinley drinks soda water, Bryan drinks rum; McKinley is a gentleman, Bryan is a bum.

> Republican (McKinley) campaign, 1900.

17 Same Old Flag and Victory—Stand Pat.

> Republican (T. Roosevelt) campaign, 1904.

18 Get on the Raft with Taft.

> Republican (W. H. Taft) campaign, 1908.

19 He Kept Us Out of War.

> Democratic (Wilson) campaign, 1916.

20 Back to Normalcy.

> Republican (Harding) campaign, 1920.

21 Cox and Cocktails.

> Democratic (Cox) campaign, 1920.

22 Convict No. 9653 for President.

> Socialist Party (Debs) campaign, 1920.

23 Keep Cool with Coolidge.

> Republican (Coolidge) campaign, 1924.

24 A Chicken in Every Pot.

> Republican (Hoover) campaign, 1928.

25 Life, Liberty, and Landon.

> Republican (Landon) campaign, 1936.

26 Roosevelt for Ex-President.

> Republican (Willkie) campaign, 1940.

27 Let's Re-Re-Re-Elect Roosevelt.

> Democratic (F.D. Roosevelt) campaign, 1944.

28 Had Enough?

> Republican (Dewey) campaign, 1944.

29 I Like Ike.

> Republican (Eisenhower) campaign, 1952.

30 You never had it so good.

> Democratic (Stevenson) campaign, 1952.

31 I Still Like Ike.

> Republican (Eisenhower) campaign, 1956.

32 We Need Adlai Badly.

> Democratic (Stevenson) campaign, 1956.

33 We're Madly for Adlai.

> Democratic (Stevenson) campaign, 1956.

34 All the Way With LBJ.

> Democratic (Johnson) campaign, 1964.

35 In Your Heart You Know He's Right.

> Republican (Goldwater) campaign, 1964.

36 A Choice Not an Echo.

> Republican (Goldwater) campaign, 1964.

37 Nixon's The One.

> Republican (Nixon) campaign, 1968.

38 Nixon: Now More Than Ever.

> Republican (Nixon) campaign, 1972.

39 Grits and Fritz.

> Democratic (Carter-Mondale) campaign, 1976.

---

42. CHANGE

See also PROGRESS; REFORM

---

1 Never swap horses crossing a stream.

> Popular saying, c.1840.

2 If we learn the art of yielding what must be yielded to the changing present we can save the best of the past.

> DEAN ACHESON, in an address to the Law Club of Chicago, January 22, 1937.

3 Controversial proposals, once accepted, soon became hallowed.

> DEAN ACHESON, in a speech at Independence, Missouri, March 31, 1962.

4 We must adjust to changing times and still hold to unchanging principles.

> JIMMY CARTER, quoting his high school teacher Julia Coleman in his inaugural address, January 20, 1977.

5 When great changes occur in history, when great principles are involved, as a rule the majority are wrong. The minority are usually right.

> EUGENE V. DEBS, addressing the jury at his trial for sedition, Cleveland, Ohio, September 12, 1918.

6 People wish to be settled. It is only as far as they are unsettled that there is any hope for them.

> RALPH WALDO EMERSON, entry written in 1840, *Journals,* 1909–1914.

7 To ask for overt renunciation of a cherished doctrine is to expect too much of human nature. Men do not repudiate the doctrines and dogmas to which they have sworn their loyalty. Instead they rationalize, revise, and re-interpret them to meet new needs and new circumstances, all the while protesting that their heresy is the purest orthodoxy.

> J. WILLIAM FULBRIGHT, *Old Myths and New Realities,* 1964.

8 These are the days when men of all social disciplines and all political faiths seek the comfortable and the accepted; when the man of controversy is looked upon as a disturbing influence; when originality is taken to be a mark of instability; and when, in minor modification of the scriptural parable, the bland lead the bland.

> JOHN KENNETH GALBRAITH, *The Affluent Society,* 1976.

9 Familiarity may breed contempt in some areas of human behavior, but in the field of social ideas it is the touchstone of acceptability.

> Ibid.

10 It is an axiom of statesmanship, which the successful founders of tyranny have understood and acted upon, that great changes can best be brought about under old forms.

> HENRY GEORGE, *Progress and Poverty,* 1879.

11 The transformations of this century are not merely a matter of historic events; there is no day on which history will leap from necessity to freedom. There is rather a molecular process, composed of millions and even billions of personal deci-

sions, whereby men and women assert their will to take control of their own destiny.

> MICHAEL HARRINGTON, *Fragments of the Century,* 1973.

12 No nation is free from the terrible burdens of historic evils; no nation is composed of angels, free from human frailty. The relevant question is not— is this people perfect? but—what are they doing about their imperfections? In what direction are they moving—and how fast?

> HUBERT H. HUMPHREY, *Beyond Civil Rights: A New Day of Equality,* 1968.

13 Great innovations should not be forced on slender majorities.

> THOMAS JEFFERSON, in a letter to Thaddeus Kosciusko, May 2, 1808.

14 The dogmas of the quiet past are inadequate to the stormy present. The occasion is piled high with difficulty, and we must rise with the occasion. As our case is new, so we must think anew and act anew.

> ABRAHAM LINCOLN, in his second annual message to Congress, December 1, 1862.

15 Enjoy the Spring of Love and Youth,
    To some good angel leave the rest;
For Time will teach thee soon the truth,
    There are no birds in last year's nest!

> HENRY WADSWORTH LONGFELLOW, "It Is Not Always May," 1841.

16 To say that a thing has never yet been done among men is to erect a barrier stronger than reason, stronger than discussion.

> THOMAS BRACKETT REED, in a speech in the House of Representatives, April 12, 1878.

17 Most new things are not good, and die an early death; but those which push themselves forward and by slow degrees force themselves on the attention of mankind are the unconscious productions of human wisdom, and must have honest consideration, and must not be made the subject of unreasoning prejudice.

> THOMAS BRACKETT REED, in the *North American Review,* December, 1902.

18 Science and technology revolutionize our lives, but memory, tradition and myth frame our response. Expelled from individual consciousness by the rush of change, history finds its revenge by stamping the collective unconscious with habits, values, expectations, dreams. The dialectic between past and future will continue to form our lives.

> ARTHUR M. SCHLESINGER, JR., "The Challenge of Change," in the *New York Times Magazine,* July 27, 1986.

19 All change is a miracle to contemplate; but it is a miracle which is taking place every instant.

> HENRY DAVID THOREAU, *Walden,* 1854.

20 It used to be a good hotel, but that proves nothing—I used to be a good boy, for that matter.

> MARK TWAIN, *The Innocents Abroad,* 1869.

21 Habit is habit, and not to be flung out of the window by any man, but coaxed downstairs a step at a time.

> MARK TWAIN, "Pudd'nhead Wilson's Calendar," *Pudd'nhead Wilson,* 1894.

22 An individual is more apt to change, perhaps, than all the world around him.

> DANIEL WEBSTER, in a speech in the U.S. Senate, March 7, 1850.

23 Let that which stood in front go behind,
Let that which was behind advance to the
    front,
Let bigots, fools, unclean persons, offer new
    propositions,
Let the old propositions be postponed.

> WALT WHITMAN, "Reversals," 1856.

---

43. CHARACTER

See also CONDUCT; GREATNESS;
INDIVIDUALITY; PRINCIPLE; REPUTATION

---

1 There is so much good in the worst of us,
    And so much bad in the best of us,

That it ill behooves any of us
To find fault with the rest of us.

    Anonymous.

2 These are times in which a Genius would wish to live. It is not in the still calm of life, or the repose of a pacific station, that great characters are formed. . . . Great necessities call out great virtues.

    ABIGAIL ADAMS, in a letter to John Quincy Adams, January 19, 1780.

3 Temperament is a fate from whose jurisdiction its victims hardly escape, but do its bidding herein, be it murder or martyrdom.

    A. BRONSON ALCOTT, *Tablets,* 1868.

4 One's outlook is a part of his virtue.

    A. BRONSON ALCOTT, *Concord Days,* 1872.

5 "My lady" . . . had yet to learn that money cannot buy refinement of nature, that rank does not always confer nobility, and that true breeding makes itself felt in spite of external drawbacks.

    LOUISA MAY ALCOTT, *Little Women,* 1868.

6 I'm the foe of moderation, the champion of excess. If I may lift a line from a die-hard whose identity is lost in the shuffle, "I'd rather be strongly wrong than weakly right."

    TALLULAH BANKHEAD, *Tallulah,* 1952.

7 Morality is character and conduct such as is required by the circle or community in which the man's life happens to be placed. It shows how much good men require of us.

    HENRY WARD BEECHER, in *Life Thoughts,* a collection of Beecher extracts compiled by Edna Dean Proctor, 1859.

8 Many men build as cathedrals were built, the part nearest the ground finished; but that part which soars toward heaven, the turrets and the spires, forever incomplete.

    Ibid.

9 Happiness is not the end of life: character is.

    Ibid.

10 The prouder a man is, the more he thinks he deserves; and the more he thinks he deserves, the less he really does deserve.

    HENRY WARD BEECHER, *Royal Truths,* 1866.

11 The cynic is one who never sees a good quality in a man, and never fails to see a bad one. He is the human owl, vigilant in darkness, and blind to light, mousing for vermin, and never seeing noble game.

    HENRY WARD BEECHER, *Proverbs from Plymouth Pulpit,* 1870.

12 Cynic, *n.* A blackguard whose faulty vision sees things as they are, not as they ought to be. Hence the custom among the Scythians of plucking out a cynic's eyes to improve his vision.

    AMBROSE BIERCE, *The Devils' Dictionary,* 1906.

13 Our vocabulary is defective; we give the same name to woman's lack of temptation and man's lack of opportunity.

    AMBROSE BIERCE, *Epigrams,* 1909–1912.

14 Character contributes to beauty. It fortifies a woman as her youth fades. A mode of conduct, a standard of courage, discipline, fortitude and integrity can do a great deal to make a woman beautiful.

    JACQUELINE BISSET, quoted in the *Los Angeles Times,* May 16, 1974.

15 If the misery of others leaves you indifferent and with no feeling of sorrow, then you cannot be called a human being.

    JIMMY CARTER, *Keeping Faith,* 1982.

16 Everybody in America is soft, and hates conflict. The cure for this, both in politics and social life, is the same,—hardihood. Give them raw truth.

    JOHN JAY CHAPMAN, *Practical Agitation,* 1898.

17 My mind is as open as a forty-acre field, but that doesn't mean I'm going to change it.

    EVERETT DIRKSEN, quoted in Neil MacNeil, *Dirksen: Portrait of a Public Man,* 1970.

18 Life is not a static thing. The only people who do not change their minds are incompetents in asylums, who can't, and those in cemeteries.

    Ibid.

19 Character isn't inherited. One builds it daily by the way one thinks and acts, thought by thought, action by action. If one lets fear or hate or anger take possession of the mind, they become self-forged chains.

> HELEN GAHAGAN DOUGLAS, commencement address, Marlboro College, 1975, from *A Full Life,* 1982.

20 Pride ruined the angels.

> RALPH WALDO EMERSON, "The Sphinx," first published in the *Dial,* January, 1841.

21 He who would gather immortal palms must not be hindered by the name of goodness, but must explore if it be goodness. Nothing is at last sacred but the integrity of your own mind.

> RALPH WALDO EMERSON, "Self-Reliance," *Essays,* First Series, 1841.

22 A character is like an acrostic or Alexandrian stanza;—read it forward, backward, or across, it still spells the same thing.

> Ibid.

23 The force of character is cumulative.

> Ibid.

24 Let a man then know his worth, and keep things under his feet. Let him not peep or steal, or skulk up and down with the air of a charity-boy, a bastard, or an interloper in the world which exists for him.

> Ibid.

25 Human character evermore publishes itself. The most fugitive deed and word, the mere air of doing a thing, the intimated purpose, expresses character.

> RALPH WALDO EMERSON, "Spiritual Laws," *Essays,* First Series, 1841.

26 The only reward of virtue is virtue.

> RALPH WALDO EMERSON, "Friendship," *Essays,* First Series, 1841.

27 Self-trust is the essence of heroism.

> RALPH WALDO EMERSON, "Heroism," *Essays,* First Series, 1841.

28 There are geniuses in trade, as well as in war, or the State, or letters; and the reason why this or that man is fortunate is not to be told. It lies in the man: that is all anybody can tell you about it.

> RALPH WALDO EMERSON, "Character," *Essays,* Second Series, 1844.

29 No change of circumstances can repair a defect of character.

> Ibid.

30 Some men appear to feel that they belong to a Pariah caste. They fear to offend, they bend and apologize, and walk through life with a timid step.

> RALPH WALDO EMERSON, "Behavior," *The Conduct of Life,* 1860.

31 A little integrity is better than any career.

> Ibid.

32 The louder he talked of his honor, the faster we counted our spoons.

> RALPH WALDO EMERSON, "Worship," *The Conduct of Life,* 1860.

33 Gross and obscure natures, however decorated, seem impure shambles; but character gives splendor to youth and awe to wrinkled skin and gray hairs.

> RALPH WALDO EMERSON, "Beauty," *The Conduct of Life,* 1860.

34 Character, that sublime health which values one moment as another, and makes us great in all conditions.

> RALPH WALDO EMERSON, "Works and Days," *Society and Solitude,* 1870.

35 Don't *say* things. What you *are* stands over you the while, and thunders so that I cannot hear what you say to the contrary.

> RALPH WALDO EMERSON, "Social Aims," *Letters and Social Aims,* 1876.

36 There is no end to the sufficiency of character. It can afford to wait; it can do without what is called success.

> RALPH WALDO EMERSON, "Character," *Lectures and Biographical Sketches,* 1903–1904.

37 A great character, founded on the living rock of principle, is a dispensation of Providence, designed to have not merely an immediate, but a continuous, progressive, and never-ending agency. It survives the man who possessed it; survives his age—perhaps his country, his language.

> EDWARD EVERETT, in a speech in Beverly, Massachusetts, July 4, 1835.

38 You Can't Cheat an Honest Man.

> W.C. FIELDS, a favorite saying and the title of one of his films, quoted in Robert Lewis Taylor, *W.C. Fields, His Follies and Fortunes,* 1949.

39 He believed in character, he wanted to jump back a whole generation and trust in character again as the eternally valuable element. Everything else wore out.

> F. SCOTT FITZGERALD, "Babylon Revisited," in the collection *Babylon Revisited,* 1960.

40 Three may keep a Secret, if two of them are dead.

> BENJAMIN FRANKLIN, *Poor Richard's Almanack,* 1735.

41 Many Foxes grow grey, but few grow good.

> BENJAMIN FRANKLIN, *Poor Richard's Almanack,* 1749.

42 To be *proud* of *Knowledge,* is to be *blind* with *Light;* to be *proud* of *Virtue,* is to *poison* yourself with the *Antidote.*

> BENJAMIN FRANKLIN, *Poor Richard's Almanack,* 1756.

43 A Ploughman on his Legs is higher than a Gentleman on his Knees.

> BENJAMIN FRANKLIN, *Poor Richard's Almanack,* 1758.

44 Pride breakfasted with Plenty, dined with Poverty, and supped with Infamy.

> Ibid.

45 To look up and not down,
To look forward and not back,
To look out and not in—and
To lend a hand.

> EDWARD EVERETT HALE, *Ten Times One is Ten,* 1870.

46 In times like these in which we live, it will not do to be overscrupulous.

> ALEXANDER HAMILTON, letter to John Jay, May 7, 1800.

47 God give us men! A time like this demands
Strong minds, great hearts, true faith, and
  ready hands.
Men whom the lust of office does not kill;
Men whom the spoils of office cannot buy;
Men who possess opinions and a will;
Men who have honor; men who will not lie.

> JOSIAH GILBERT HOLLAND, "Wanted," 1872.

48 We must have a weak spot or two in a character before we can love it much. People that do not laugh or cry, or take more of anything than is good for them, or use anything but dictionary words, are admirable subjects for biographies. But we don't always care most for those flat-pattern flowers that press best in the herbarium.

> OLIVER WENDELL HOLMES, SR., *The Professor at the Breakfast-Table,* 1860.

49 Build thee more stately mansions, O my soul,
As the swift seasons roll!
Leave thy low-vaulted past!
Let each new temple, nobler than the last,
Shut thee from heaven with a dome more
  vast,
Till thou at length art free,
Leaving thine outgrown shell by life's
  unresting sea!

> OLIVER WENDELL HOLMES, SR., "The Chambered Nautilus," 1858.

50 I try not to be prejudiced, but do not make much headway against it.

> EDGAR WATSON HOWE, *Sinner Sermons,* 1926.

51 God will not look you over for medals, degrees or diplomas, but for scars.

> ELBERT HUBBARD, *One Thousand and One Epigrams,* 1911.

52 There is a healthful hardiness about real dignity, that never dreads contact and communion with others, however humble.

> WASHINGTON IRVING, "The Country Church," *The Sketch Book,* 1819–1820.

53 Wounded vanity knows when it is mortally hurt; and limps off the field, piteous, all disguises thrown away. But pride carries its banner to the last; and fast as it is driven from one field unfurls it in another.

> HELEN HUNT JACKSON, *Ramona*, 1884.

54 If in my high moments, I have done some good, offered some service, shed some light, healed some wounds, rekindled some hope, or stirred someone from apathy and indifference, or in any way along the way helped somebody, then this campaign has not been in vain. . . . If in my low moments, in word, deed or attitude, through some error of temper, taste or tone, I have caused anyone discomfort, created pain or revived someone's fears, that was not my truest self. . . . I am not a perfect servant. I am a public servant doing my best against the odds. As I develop and serve, be patient. God is not finished with me yet.

> JESSE JACKSON, in a speech before the Democratic National Convention, July 16, 1984.

55 Go on deserving applause, and you will be sure to meet with it; and the way to deserve it is to be good, and to be industrious.

> THOMAS JEFFERSON, letter to John Wayles Eppes, July 28, 1787.

56 There is a natural aristocracy among men. The grounds of this are virtue and talents.

> THOMAS JEFFERSON, letter to John Adams, October 28, 1813.

57 Men are disposed to live honestly, if the means of doing so are open to them.

> THOMAS JEFFERSON, letter to M. Barré de Marbois, June 14, 1817.

58 We believed . . . that man was a rational animal, endowed by nature with rights, and with an innate sense of justice. . . . We believed that . . . wisdom and virtue were not hereditary.

> THOMAS JEFFERSON, discussing the views of the majority of delegates to the Constitutional Convention of 1787, in a letter to William Johnson, June 12, 1823.

59 I have a dream that my four little children will one day live in a nation where they will not be judged by the color of their skin, but by the content of their character.

> MARTIN LUTHER KING, JR., speech at the Civil Rights March in Washington, August 28, 1963.

60 I know I have a first-rate mind, but that's no source of pride to me. Intelligent people are a dime a dozen. But I am proud of having character.

> Attributed to Henry Kissinger, in Richard Valeriani, *Travels with Henry,* 1979.

61 Turning the other cheek is a kind of moral jiu-jitsu.

> GERALD STANLEY LEE, *Crowds,* 1913.

62 Character is like a tree and reputation like its shadow. The shadow is what we think of it; the tree is the real thing.

> ABRAHAM LINCOLN, quoted in Anthony Gross, *Lincoln's Own Stories,* 1912.

63 In this world a man must either be anvil or hammer.

> HENRY WADSWORTH LONGFELLOW, "The Story of Brother Bernardus," *Hyperion,* 1839.

64 Lives of great men all remind us
  We can make our lives sublime,
And, departing, leave behind us
  Footprints on the sands of time.

> HENRY WADSWORTH LONGFELLOW, "A Psalm of Life," 1839.

65 We judge ourselves by what we feel capable of doing, while others judge us by what we have already done.

> HENRY WADSWORTH LONGFELLOW, *Kavanagh,* 1849.

66 Not in the clamor of the crowded street,
Not in the shouts and plaudits of the throng,
But in ourselves, our triumph and defeat.

> HENRY WADSWORTH LONGFELLOW, "The Poet," 1876.

67 They are slaves who fear to speak
For the fallen and the weak.

> JAMES RUSSELL LOWELL, "Stanzas on Freedom," 1843.

68 A marciful Providence fashioned us holler
O' purpose thet we might our princerples
swaller.

> JAMES RUSSELL LOWELL, *The Biglow Papers,*
> First Series, 1848.

69 It is by presence of mind in untried emergencies
that the native metal of a man is tested.

> JAMES RUSSELL LOWELL, "Abraham Lincoln,"
> printed in the *North American Review,* January
> 1864.

70 Mishaps are like knives, that either serve us
or cut us, as we grasp them by the blade or the
handle.

> JAMES RUSSELL LOWELL, "Cambridge Thirty
> Years Ago," *Fireside Travels,* 1864.

71 No beggar ever felt him condescend,
No prince presume; for still himself he bare
At manhood's simple level, and where'er
He met a stranger, there he left a friend.

> JAMES RUSSELL LOWELL, "Agassiz," 1874
> (written after the death of Louis Agassiz in
> 1873).

72 The wisest man could ask no more of Fate
Than to be simple, modest, manly, true,
Safe from the Many, honored by the Few;
To count as naught in World, or Church, or
State,
But inwardly in secret to be great.

> JAMES RUSSELL LOWELL, "Jeffries Wyman,"
> 1874.

73 Sincerity is impossible, unless it pervade the
whole being, and the pretence of it saps the very
foundation of character.

> JAMES RUSSELL LOWELL, "Essay on Pope,"
> lecture given in 1855 and published in *Lectures on
> English Poets,* 1897.

74 You must believe in yourself, my son, or no one
else will believe in you. Be self-confident, self-reli-
ant, and even if you don't make it, you will know
you have done your best. Now, go to it.

> MARY HARDY MACARTHUR, advice to her son
> Douglas on the morning of his West Point
> examination, quoted in Douglas MacArthur,
> *Reminiscences,* 1964.

75 Be ashamed to die until you have won some
victory for humanity.

> HORACE MANN, commencement address at
> Antioch College, 1859.

76 Conscience is the inner voice which warns us
that someone may be looking.

> H.L. MENCKEN, "Sententiae," in *The Vintage
> Mencken,* 1955.

77 Character is what you are in the dark.

> Attributed to Dwight L. Moody.

78 Of more worth is one honest man to society, and
in the sight of God, than all the crowned ruffians
that ever lived.

> THOMAS PAINE, *Common Sense,* 1776.

79 Character is much easier kept than recovered.

> THOMAS PAINE, *The American Crisis,* No. 13,
> April 19, 1783.

80 Private character, always dear, always to be respected, seems almost to be canonized by the grave.
When men go hence, their evil deeds should follow
them, and, for me might sleep oblivious in their
tomb. But if the mouldering ashes of the dead are
to be raked up, let it not be for the furtherance of
injustice.

> JOHN RANDOLPH, speaking in Congress, February
> 1, 1805, quoted in Russell Kirk, *John Randolph
> of Roanoke,* 1951.

81 The pessimist . . . is seldom an agitating individual. His creed breeds indifference to others, and he
does not trouble himself to thrust his views upon
the unconvinced.

> AGNES REPPLIER, "Some Aspects of Pessimism,"
> *Books and Men,* 1888.

82 I learned years ago not to doze off or leave my
wallet lying around in the presence of people who
tell me that they are more moral than others.

> CARL T. ROWAN, "In the Name of Morality,"
> the *Washington Star,* October 17, 1980.

83 Fame is what you have taken,
Character's what you give:

When to this truth you waken,
　Then you begin to live!

BAYARD TAYLOR, "Improvisations," 1899.

84 We falsely attribute to men a determined character—putting together all their yesterdays—and averaging them—we presume we know them—Pity the man who has a character to support—it is worse than a large family—he is silent poor indeed. . . . A large soul will meet you as not having known you—taking you for what you are to be, a narrow one for what you have been—for a broad and roaming soul is as uncertain—what it may say or be—as a scraggy hill side or pasture.

HENRY DAVID THOREAU, entry dated April 28, 1841, in his *Journal,* 1906.

85 How often must one feel as he looks back on his past life that he has gained a talent but lost a character. . . . Society does nominally estimate men by their talents—but really feels and knows them by their characters.

HENRY DAVID THOREAU, entry dated March 28, 1842, in his *Journal,* 1906.

86 There are continents and seas in the moral world, to which every man is an isthmus or inlet, yet unexplored by him.

HENRY DAVID THOREAU, *Walden,* 1854.

87 There is no odor so bad as that which arises from goodness tainted. It is human, it is divine, carrion.

Ibid.

88 I know of no more encouraging fact than the unquestionable ability of man to elevate his life by a conscious endeavor.

HENRY DAVID THOREAU, "Where I Lived, and What I Lived For," *Walden,* 1854.

89 Three things ruin a man. Power, money, and women. I never wanted power. I never had any money, and the only woman in my life is up at the house right now.

HARRY S TRUMAN, speaking to a reporter on his 75th birthday, quoted by Mary McGrory in the *New York Post,* December 29, 1972.

90 Being too good is apt to be uninteresting.

HARRY S TRUMAN, a favorite saying of his mother and one he loved to quote, noted in Margaret Truman, *Harry S Truman,* 1972.

91 The best index to a person's character is (a) how he treats people who can't do him any good, and (b) how he treats people who can't fight back.

ABIGAIL VAN BUREN, in her newspaper column, "Dear Abby," May 16, 1974.

92 Few men have virtue to withstand the highest bidder.

GEORGE WASHINGTON, in a letter to Robert Howe, August 17, 1779, quoted in *Maxims of Washington,* 1942.

93 I hope I shall always possess firmness and virtue enough to maintain (what I consider the most enviable of all titles) the character of an "Honest Man."

GEORGE WASHINGTON, in a letter to Alexander Hamilton, August 28, 1788, quoted in *Maxims of Washington,* 1942.

94 Nothing endures but personal qualities.

WALT WHITMAN, "Song of the Broad-Axe," 1856.

95 A strong being is the proof of the race and
　of the ability of the universe,
When he or she appears materials are
　overaw'd.

Ibid.

96 There is something awfully small about someone who cannot admit that anyone else is exceptionally large.

GEORGE F. WILL, *The Pursuit of Virtue and Other Tory Notions,* 1982.

44. CHARITY

1 Private beneficence is totally inadequate to deal with the vast numbers of the city's disinherited.

JANE ADDAMS, *Twenty Years at Hull House,* 1910.

2 Give plenty of what is given to you,
  Listen to pity's call;
Don't think the little you give is great,
  And the much you get is small.

> PHOEBE CARY, "A Legend of the Northland."

3 I feel obliged to withhold my approval of the plan to indulge a benevolent and charitable sentiment through the appropriation of public funds for that purpose. I can find no warrant for such an appropriation in the Constitution.

> GROVER CLEVELAND, vetoing a bill authorizing the distribution of seed to Texas farmers hit by drought, February 16, 1887.

4 Th' dead ar-re always pop'lar. I knowed a society wanst to vote a monyment to a man an' refuse to help his family, all in wan night.

> FINLEY PETER DUNNE, "On Charity," *Mr. Dooley in Peace and War*, 1898.

5 Do not tell me . . . of my obligation to put all poor men in good situations. Are they *my* poor? I tell thee, thou foolish philanthropist, that I grudge the dollar, the dime, the cent I give to such men as do not belong to me and to whom I do not belong.

> RALPH WALDO EMERSON, "Self-Reliance," *Essays*, First Series, 1841.

6 We do not quite forgive a giver. The hand that feeds us is in some danger of being bitten.

> RALPH WALDO EMERSON, "Gifts," *Essays*, Second Series, 1844.

7 Philanthropies and charities have a certain air of quackery.

> RALPH WALDO EMERSON, *Nature, Addresses, and Lectures*, 1849.

8 There is a spirit which, like the father of evil, is constantly "walking to and fro about the earth, seeking whom it may devour": it is the spirit of false philanthropy.

> ROBERT YOUNG HAYNE, speech in the U.S. Senate, January 21, 1830.

9 I believe . . . that the moral sense is as much a part of our constitution as that of feeling, seeing, or hearing . . . [and] that every human mind feels pleasure in doing good to another.

> THOMAS JEFFERSON, in a letter to John Adams, October 14, 1816.

10 I appeal to any white man to say if he ever entered Logan's cabin hungry and he gave him not meat; if ever he came cold and naked and he clothed him not?

> LOGAN, Lingo Indian chief, in a message to Lord Dunmore, governor of Virginia, November 11, 1774, quoted in Thomas Jefferson, *Notes on the State of Virginia*, 1784.

11 The greatest grace of a gift, perhaps, is that is anticipates and admits of no return.

> HENRY WADSWORTH LONGFELLOW, letter to Mrs. James T. Fields, February 28, 1871.

12 That is no true alms which the hand can hold;
He gives nothing but worthless gold
  Who gives from a sense of duty.

> JAMES RUSSELL LOWELL, *The Vision of Sir Launfal*, 1848.

13 Not what we give, but what we share,—
For the gift without the giver is bare;
Who gives himself with his alms feeds three,—
  Himself, his hungering neighbor, and me.

> Ibid.

14 Charity has in it sometimes, perhaps often, a savor of superiority.

> JAMES RUSSELL LOWELL, speech in Westminster Abbey, December 13, 1881.

15 Charity . . . is kind, it is not easily provok'd, it thinks no evil, it believes all things, hopes all things.

> COTTON MATHER, *The Wonders of the Invisible World*, 1693. (Mather drew his inspiration from St. Paul's first epistle to the Corinthians.)

16 A strong argument for the religion of Christ is this—that offences against charity are about the only ones which men on their deathbeds can be made—not to understand—but to feel—as crimes.

> EDGAR ALLAN POE, *Marginalia*, 1844–1849.

17 I am weary seeing our laboring classes so wretchedly housed, fed, and clothed, while thousands of dollars are wasted every year over unsightly statues. If these great men must have outdoor memorials let them be in the form of handsome blocks of buildings for the poor.

ELIZABETH CADY STANTON, diary entry, 1886, in Theodore Stanton and Harriot Stanton Blatch, *Elizabeth Cady Stanton,* 1922.

18 Whatever capital you divert to the support of a shiftless and good-for-nothing person is so much diverted from some other employment, and that means from somebody else.

WILLIAM GRAHAM SUMNER, *The Forgotten Man and Other Essays,* 1919.

19 As for Doing-good, that is one of the professions which are full. . . . I have tried it fairly and, strange as it may seem, am satisfied it does not agree with my constitution.

HENRY DAVID THOREAU, *Walden,* 1854.

20 Behold, I do not give lectures or a little
　　charity,
When I give I give myself.

WALT WHITMAN, "Song of Myself," 1855.

---

45. CHASTITY

See also SEX

---

1 I am as pure as the driven slush.

Attributed to Tallulah Bankhead.

2 It is a duty we cannot shirk to point to the true ideal, to chastity, to a single standard of morals for men and women.

JOSEPHUS DANIELS, in a memorandum to U.S. naval commanders, February 27, 1915.

3 Chastity is the cement of civilization and progress. Without it there is no stability in society.

MARY BAKER EDDY, *Science and Health with Key to the Scriptures,* 1875.

4 The generative energy, which, when we are loose, dissipates and makes us unclean, when we are continent invigorates and inspires us. Chastity is the flowering of man; and what are called Genius, Heroism, Holiness, and the like, are but various fruits which succeed it.

HENRY DAVID THOREAU, *Walden,* 1854.

5 Simplified spelling is all right, but, like chastity, you can carry it too far.

MARK TWAIN, in a speech, "The Alphabet and Simplified Spelling," New York City, December 9, 1907.

6 It is better to be looked over than overlooked.

MAE WEST, quoted in Joseph Weintraub, *The Wit and Wisdom of Mae West,* 1967.

7 I used to be Snow White—but I drifted.

Ibid.

---

46. CHICAGO

---

1 I will.

Motto of Chicago

2 It takes only 18 hours to get to Chicago. But what's the use?

FRANKLIN P[IERCE] ADAMS [F.P.A.], in his newspaper column, "The Conning Tower." (F.P.A. began his career in Chicago but left to work in New York City.)

3 This is a great uninteresting place of 600,000 inhabitants.

MATTHEW ARNOLD, in a letter to his sister, Frances Arnold, January 23, 1884.

4 Of all the places in the world, the one which from its literary societies sends me the most intelligent and thoughtful criticism upon my poetry is Chicago.

ROBERT BROWNING, letter to Chauncey M. Depew, a New York politician and well known orator, c.1886.

5 Perhaps the most typically American place in America.

> JAMES BRYCE, *The American Commonwealth,* 1888.

6 I'm impressed with people from Chicago. Hollywood is hype, New York is talk, Chicago is work.

> Attributed to Michael Douglas, film producer, director, and actor.

7 This is the greatest and most typically American of all cities. New York is bigger and more spectacular and can outmatch it in other superlatives, but it is a "world" city, more European in some respects than American.

> JOHN GUNTHER, *Inside U.S.A.,* 1947.

8 The last copy of the Chicago *Daily News* I picked up had three crime stories on its front page. But by comparison to the gaudy days, this is small-time stuff. Chicago is as full of crooks as a saw with teeth, but the era when they ruled the city is gone forever.

> Ibid.

9 Chicago sounds rough to the maker of verse;
One comfort we have—Cincinnati sounds
    worse.

> OLIVER WENDELL HOLMES, SR., "Welcome to the Chicago Commercial Club," January 14, 1880.

10 I have struck a city,—a real city,—and they call it Chicago. The other places do not count. San Francisco was a pleasure-resort as well as a city, and Salt Lake was a phenomenon. This place is the first American city I have encountered. . . . Having seen it, I urgently desire never to see it again. It is inhabited by savages.

> RUDYARD KIPLING, *American Notes,* 1891.

11 New York is one of the capitals of the world and Los Angeles is a constellation of plastic, San Francisco is a lady, Boston has become Urban Renewal, Philadelphia and Baltimore and Washington wink like dull diamonds in the smog of Eastern Megalopolis, and New Orleans is unremarkable past the French Quarter. Detroit is a one-trade town, Pittsburgh has lost its golden triangle, St. Louis has become the golden arch of the corporation, and nights in Kansas City close early. The oil depletion allowance makes Houston and Dallas naught but checkerboards for this sort of game. But Chicago is a great American city. Perhaps it is the last of the great American cities.

> NORMAN MAILER, *Miami and the Siege of Chicago,* 1968.

12 Sputter, city! Bead with fire
Every ragged roof and spire.

> MILDRED PLEW MERRYMAN, "To Chicago at Night."

13 And yonder where, gigantic, willful, young,
Chicago sitteth at the northwest gates,
With restless violent hands and casual tongue
Molding her mighty fates . . . .

> WILLIAM VAUGHN MOODY, "An Ode in Time of Hesitation," 1901.

14 If one got behind Michigan Avenue, one had the feeling that Chicago had been, and to some extent still was, a whited sepulcher. Insulls and Rockefellers had lived on the whited exterior. Inside were the dead men's bones of the slums.

> M. PHILIPS PRICE, *America After Sixty Years: The Travel Diaries of Two Generations of Englishmen,* 1936.

15 Hog Butcher for the World,
Tool Maker, Stacker of Wheat,
Player with Railroads and the Nation's
    Freight Handler;
Stormy, husky, brawling,
City of the Big Shoulders.

> CARL SANDBURG, opening lines of "Chicago," *Chicago Poems,* 1916.

16 In back of the yards the dreary two-story frame houses were scattered farther apart, and there were great spaces bare—that seemingly had been overlooked by the great sore of a city as it spread itself over the surface of the prairie.

> UPTON SINCLAIR, *The Jungle,* 1906.

17 The line of the buildings stood clear-cut and black against the sky; here and there out of the mass rose the great chimneys, with the river of smoke

streaming away to the end of the world. It was a study in colors now, this smoke; in the sunset light it was black and brown and gray and purple. All the sordid suggestions of the place were gone—in the twilight it was a vision of power.

Ibid.

18 Chicago gave me a snowstorm and this morning I walked for an hour on the crisp surface in a world which must be parks and sheets of water in summer: Greek temples scattered about and skyscrapers in the background, and the lake with blocks of ice making a white horizon. Inside the hotel it is like the Balkans grown prosperous—square, squat females with furs and loud cordial voices telling everybody's business in the lounge.

FREYA STARK, English travel writer and photographer, in a letter, January 9, 1944.

19 First in violence, deepest in dirt, lawless, unlovely, ill-smelling, irreverent, new; an overgrown gawk of a—village, the "tough" among cities, a spectacle for the nation.

LINCOLN STEFFENS, *The Shame of the Cities,* 1904.

20 Chicago likes audacity and is always willing to have anybody try anything once; no matter who you are, where you come from, or what you set out to do, Chicago will give you a chance. The sporting spirit is the spirit of Chicago.

LINCOLN STEFFENS, *The Autobiography of Lincoln Steffens,* 1931.

21 That astonishing Chicago—a city where they are always rubbing the lamp, and fetching up the genii, and contriving and achieving new impossibilities. It is hopeless for the occasional visitor to try to keep up with Chicago—she outgrows his prophecies faster than he can make them. She is always a novelty, for she is never the Chicago you saw when you passed through the last time.

MARK TWAIN, *Life on the Mississippi,* 1883.

22 Satan (impatiently) to Newcomer: The trouble with you Chicago people is, that you think you are the best people down here; whereas you are merely the most numerous.

MARK TWAIN, "Puddn'head Wilson's New Calendar," *Following the Equator,* 1897.

23 Rise, stricken city! From thee throw
The ashen sackcloth of thy woe;
And build, as to Amphion's strain,
To songs of cheer thy walls again!

JOHN GREENLEAF WHITTIER, "Chicago," 1871 (inspired by the great fire that wiped out the city in October of that year).

24 Then lift once more thy towers on high,
And fret with spires the western sky,
To tell that God is yet with us,
And love is still miraculous!

Ibid.

47. CHOICE

1 And say not thou "My country right or
     wrong,"
Nor shed thy blood for an unhallowed cause.

JOHN QUINCY ADAMS, "Congress, Slavery, and an Unjust War," c.1847.

2 "There's no free will," says the philosopher;
     "to hang is most unjust."
"There is no free will," assents the officer;
     "we hang because we must."

AMBROSE BIERCE, *Collected Works,* 1911.

3 If decisions were a choice between alternatives, decisions would come easy. Decision is the selection and formulation of alternatives.

KENNETH BURKE, *Towards a Better Life,* 1932.

4 Mankind likes to think in terms of extreme opposites. It is given to formulating its beliefs in terms of *Either-Ors,* between which it recognizes no intermediate possibilities. When forced to recognize that the extremes cannot be acted upon, it is still inclined to hold that they are all right in theory but that when it comes to practical matters circumstances compel us to compromise.

JOHN DEWEY, *Experience and Education,* 1938.

5 The Will (without any metaphysical refining) is plainly, that by which the mind chooses any thing. The faculty of the Will is that faculty or power or principle of mind by which it is capable of choosing.

> JONATHAN EDWARDS, *The Freedom of the Will*, 1754.

6 To hazard the contradiction—freedom is necessary.

> RALPH WALDO EMERSON, *The Conduct of Life*, 1860.

7 Any color, so long as it's red,
  Is the color that suits me best,
Though I will allow there is much to be said
  For yellow and green and the rest.

> EUGENE FIELD, "Red," in *The Poems of Eugene Field*, 1910.

8 Two roads diverged in a wood, and I—
  I took the one less traveled by,
And that has made all the difference.

> ROBERT FROST, "The Road Not Taken," *Mountain Interval*, 1916.

9 The question of free will is insoluble on strictly psychologic grounds.

> WILLIAM JAMES, *Psychology, Briefer Course*, 1892.

10 It is not a new observation that the people of any country (if, like the Americans, intelligent and well-informed) seldom adopt and steadily persevere for many years in an erroneous opinion respecting their interests.

> JOHN JAY, *The Federalist*, No. 3, 1787–1788.

11 Gentlemen Prefer Blondes.

> ANITA LOOS, book title, 1925.

12 A society which is clamoring for choice, which is filled with many articulate groups, each urging its own brand of salvation, its own variety of economic philosophy, will give each new generation no peace until all have chosen or gone under, unable to bear the conditions of choice.

> MARGARET MEAD, *Coming of Age in Samoa*, 1928.

13 Chief among our gains must be reckoned this possibility of choice, the recognition of many possible ways of life, where other civilizations have recognized only one. Where other civilizations give a satisfactory outlet to only one temperamental type, be he mystic or soldier, businessman or artist, a civilization in which there are many standards offers a possibility of satisfactory adjustment to individuals of many different temperamental types, of diverse gifts and varying interests.

> Ibid.

48. CHRISTMAS

1 Christmas is over. Uncork your ambition!
  Back to the battle! Come on, competition!

> FRANKLIN P. ADAMS [F.P.A], "For the Other 364 Days."

2 Christmas won't be Christmas without any presents.

> LOUISA MAY ALCOTT, *Little Women*, 1868.

3 I have always been subconsciously embarrassed by the "function" of Christmas and New Years. The spirit of "loving kindness," that is presumed to come to a head like a boil once a year, when it has been magnificently concealed up to that moment!

> JOHN BARRYMORE, writing in his diary, December 31, 1925, quoted in Gene Fowler, *Good Night, Sweet Prince*, 1943.

4 O little town of Bethlehem,
  How still we see thee lie!
Above thy deep and dreamless sleep
  The silent stars go by.

> PHILLIPS BROOKS, "O Little Town of Bethlehem," 1868.

5 Most all the time, the whole year round, there
  ain't no flies on me,
But jest 'fore Christmas I'm as good as I kin
  be!

> EUGENE FIELD, "Jest 'fore Christmas," in *Love-Songs of Childhood*, 1894.

6 I heard the bells on Christmas Day
Their old, familiar carols play,
And wild and sweet
The words repeat
Of peace on earth, good-will to men!

HENRY WADSWORTH LONGFELLOW, "Christmas Bells," *Flower-de-Luce,* 1867.

7 'Twas the night before Christmas, when all
through the house
Not a creature was stirring,—not even a
mouse:
The stockings were hung by the chimney with
care,
In hopes that St. Nicholas soon would be
there.

CLEMENT C. MOORE, "A Visit from St. Nicholas," printed anonymously in the *Troy Sentinel,* December 23, 1823.

8 It came upon the midnight clear,
That glorious song of old,
From angels bending near the earth
To touch their harps of gold;
"Peace on the earth, good will to men
From Heaven's all-gracious King"—
The world in solemn stillness lay
To hear the angels sing.

EDMUND HAMILTON SEARS, "Christmas Carol," 1850.

---

49. CITIES

See also BOSTON; CHICAGO; HOLLYWOOD; NEW ORLEANS; NEW YORK CITY; SAN FRANCISCO; WASHINGTON, D.C.

---

1 I think of American cities as enormous agglomerations in whose inmost dark recesses innumerable elevators are constantly ascending and descending, like the angels of the ladder.

ARNOLD BENNETT, *Your United States,* 1912.

2 With eight or nine exceptions . . . American cities differ from one another only herein, that some of them are built more with brick than with wood,
and others more with wood than with brick. In all else they are alike, both great and small.

JAMES BRYCE, *The American Commonwealth,* 1914.

3 Whatever events in progress shall go to disgust men with cities, and infuse into them the passion for country life, and country pleasures, will render a service to the whole face of this continent.

RALPH WALDO EMERSON, "The Young American," *Nature; Addresses and Lectures,* 1849.

4 Cities give us collision. 'Tis said, London and New York take the nonsense out of man.

RALPH WALDO EMERSON, "Culture," *The Conduct of Life,* 1860.

5 The axis of the earth sticks out visibly through the center of each and every town or city.

OLIVER WENDELL HOLMES, SR., *The Autocrat of the Breakfast-Table,* 1858.

6 The mobs of great cities add just so much to the support of pure government as sores do to the strength of the human body.

THOMAS JEFFERSON, *Notes on the State of Virginia,* 1784.

7 The city as a center where, any day in any year, there may be a fresh encounter with a new talent, a keen mind or a gifted specialist—this is essential to the life of a country. To play this role in our lives a city must have a soul—a university, a great art or music school, a cathedral or a great mosque or temple, a great laboratory or scientific center, as well as the libraries and museums and galleries that bring past and present together. A city must be a place where groups of women and men are seeking and developing the highest things they know.

MARGARET MEAD, in *Redbook* magazine, August, 1978.

8 To qualify as a city, any collection of people must have an orchestra, a large library, a system of parks, a transportation system, a university and, yes, a public stadium in which to gather and a professional team to play there. If a town doesn't have these things, it's got no right to call itself a city.

JAMES A. MICHENER, quoting an unidentified New Yorker, in *Sports in America,* 1976.

9 It is our misfortune that all the towns of the Republic are alike, or differ in scarcely anything else than in natural position or wealth.

FREDERICK LAW OLMSTED, *A Journey through Texas,* 1857.

10 There are almost no beautiful cities in America, though there are many beautiful parts of cities, and some sections that are glorious without being beautiful, like downtown Chicago. Cities are too big and too rich for beauty; they have outgrown themselves too many times.

NOEL PERRIN, *Third Person Rural,* 1983.

11 No rural community, no suburban community, can ever possess the distinctive qualities that city dwellers have for centuries given to the world.

AGNES REPPLIER, "Town and Suburb," in *Eight Decades,* 1937.

12 They say New Yorkers never know how filthy their streets are until they get back from a tour through Europe, and I suppose that applies to most of our cities.

LINCOLN STEFFENS, in a letter, c.1889, quoted in Justin Kaplan, *Lincoln Steffens: A Biography,* 1974.

13 I have been through hundreds of towns and cities in every climate and against every kind of scenery, and of course they are all different, and the people have points of difference, but in some ways they are alike. American cities are like badger holes, ringed with trash—all of them—surrounded by piles of wrecked and rusting automobiles, and almost smothered with rubbish.

JOHN STEINBECK, *Travels with Charley,* 1962.

14 The tumultous populace of large cities are ever to be dreaded. Their indiscriminate violence prostrates for the time all public authority, and its consequences are sometimes extensive and terrible.

GEORGE WASHINGTON, in a letter to the Marquis de Lafayette, July 28, 1791.

15 Visitors to Los Angeles, then and now, were put out because the residents of Los Angeles had the inhospitable idea of building a city comfortable to live in, rather than a monument to astonish the eye of jaded travelers.

JESSAMYN WEST, *Hide and Seek,* 1973.

16 A great city is that which has the greatest men and women,
  If it be a few ragged huts it is still the greatest city in the whole world.

WALT WHITMAN, "Song of the Broad-Axe," 1856.

50. CIVIL RIGHTS

See also BLACK AMERICANS; EQUALITY; JUSTICE; STATES' RIGHTS; WOMEN'S RIGHTS

1 Among the natural rights of the colonists are these: first, a right to life; secondly, to liberty; thirdly, to property; together with the right to support and defend them in the best manner they can.

SAMUEL ADAMS, "The Rights of the Colonists," 1772.

2 Political right and public happiness are different words for the same idea. They who wander into metaphysical labyrinths, or have recourse to original contracts, to determine the rights of men, either impose on themselves or mean to delude others. Public utility is the only certain criterion.

SAMUEL ADAMS, in an address, "American Independence," August, 1776.

3 Intellectual and spiritual leaders hailed the cause of civil rights and gave little thought to where the civil disobedience road might end. But defiance of the law, even for the best reasons, opens a tiny hole in the dike and soon a trickle becomes a flood. . . . And while no thinking person denies that social injustice exists; no thinking person can condone any group's, for any reason, taking justice into its own hands. Once this is permitted, democracy dies; for democracy is sustained through one great premise: the premise that civil rights are balanced by civil responsibilities.

SPIRO T. AGNEW, quoted in Robert Marsh, *Agnew, the Unexplained Man,* 1971.

4 Racism is the new Calvinism which asserts that one group has the stigmata of superiority and the other has those of inferiority.

> RUTH BENEDICT, *Race: Science and Politics,* 1940.

5 For racial discrimination to result in the exclusion from jury service of otherwise qualified groups not only violates our Constitution and the laws enacted under it but is at war with our basic concepts of a democratic society and a representative government.

> HUGO BLACK, in a Supreme Court opinion, *Smith* v. *State of Texas,* 1940.

6 They [the makers of the Constitution] conferred, as against the government, the right to be let alone—the most comprehensive of rights and the right most valued by civilized men.

> LOUIS D. BRANDEIS, in a dissenting Supreme Court opinion, *Olmstead* v. *United States,* 1928.

7 Anglo-Saxon civilization has taught the individual to protect his own rights; American civilization will teach him to respect the rights of others.

> WILLIAM JENNINGS BRYAN, in a speech, "America's Mission," Washington, D.C., February 22, 1899.

8 Men speak of natural rights, but I challenge any one to show where in nature any rights existed or were recognized until there was established for their declaration and protection a duly promulgated body of corresponding laws.

> CALVIN COOLIDGE, in his speech accepting the Republican vice presidential nomination, Northampton, Massachusetts, July 27, 1920.

9 No man can put a chain about the ankle of his fellow man without at last finding the other end fastened about his own neck.

> FREDERICK DOUGLASS, in a speech in Washington, D.C., October 22, 1883.

10 The problem of the twentieth century is the problem of the color line.

> W.E.B. DU BOIS, in a speech at the first Pan-African Conference, London, England, January, 1900.

11 Wherever snow falls there is usually civil freedom.

> RALPH WALDO EMERSON, "Civilization," *Society and Solitude,* 1870.

12 We hear about constitutional rights, free speech and the free press. Every time I hear those words I say to myself, "That man is a Red, that man is a Communist." You never heard a real American talk in that manner.

> FRANK HAGUE, in a speech at the fiftieth anniversary dinner of the Jersey City Chamber of Commerce, January 12, 1938.

13 Beyond the limits of his confining skin, no man can own any *thing.* "Property" refers not to things owned but to the rights granted by society; they must periodically be re-examined in the light of social justice.

> GARRETT HARDIN, *Exploring New Ethics for Survival,* 1972.

14 The liberty of the citizen to do as he likes so long as he does not interfere with the liberty of others to do the same, which has been a shibboleth from some well-known writers, is interfered with by school laws, by the Post Office, by every state or municipal institution which takes his money for purposes thought desirable, whether he likes it or not.

> OLIVER WENDELL HOLMES, JR., in a dissenting Supreme Court opinion, *Lochner* v. *New York,* 1905.

15 If there is any principle of the Constitution that more imperatively calls for attachment than any other it is the principle of free thought—not free thought for those who agree with us but freedom for the thought that we hate.

> OLIVER WENDELL HOLMES, JR., in a dissenting Supreme Court opinion, *United States* v. *Schwimmer,* 1929.

16 Order is the first responsibility of government; without it, there can be no justice and no progress. Those who imply that continued rioting and disruption will lead to social progress are very wrong; such behavior leads instead to hardening resistance to progress, and to repression.

HUBERT H. HUMPHREY, *Beyond Civil Rights: A New Day of Equality,* 1968.

17 No official, high or petty, can prescribe what shall be orthodox in politics, nationalism, religion, or other matters of opinion, or force citizens to confess by word or act their faith therein.

ROBERT H. JACKSON, in a Supreme Court opinion, *West Virginia Board of Education* v. *Barnette,* 1943.

18 A bill of rights is what the people are entitled to against every government on earth, general or particular; and what no just government should refuse, or rest on inference.

THOMAS JEFFERSON, in a letter to James Madison, December 20, 1787.

19 If we cannot secure all our rights, let us secure what we can.

THOMAS JEFFERSON, in a letter to James Madison, March 15, 1789.

20 Bear in mind this sacred principle, that though the will of the majority is in all cases to prevail, that will to be rightful must be reasonable; that the minority possess their equal rights, which equal law must protect, and to violate would be oppression.

THOMAS JEFFERSON, in his first inaugural address, March 4, 1801.

21 No man has a natural right to commit aggression on the equal rights of another, and this is all from which the laws ought to restrain him; every man is under the natural duty of contributing to the necessities of the society, and this is all the laws should enforce on him; and no man having a natural right to be the judge between himself and another, it is his natural duty to submit to the umpirage of an impartial third.

THOMAS JEFFERSON, in a letter to Francis W. Gilmer, June 7, 1816.

22 A rioter with a Molotov cocktail in his hands is not fighting for civil rights any more than a Klansman wearing a sheet and a mask.

LYNDON B. JOHNSON, *The Vantage Point: Perspectives of the Presidency, 1963–1969,* 1971.

23 "We, the people." It is a very eloquent beginning. But when that document was completed on the seventeenth of September in 1787 I was not included in that "We, the people." I felt somehow for many years that George Washington and Alexander Hamilton just left me out by mistake. But through the process of amendment, interpretation, and court decision I have finally been included in "We, the people."

BARBARA JORDAN, debating an impeachment motion in Congress after the Watergate scandals, July 25, 1974.

24 Every American ought to have the right to be treated as he would wish to be treated, as one would wish his children to be treated. This is not the case.

JOHN F. KENNEDY, in a television address following the struggle for registration of two black students at the University of Alabama, June 11, 1963.

25 No one has been barred on account of his race from fighting or dying for America—there are no "white" or "colored" signs on the foxholes or graveyards of battle.

JOHN F. KENNEDY, on civil rights, in a message to Congress, June 19, 1963.

26 I have a dream that one day on the red hills of Georgia the sons of former slaves and the sons of former slaveowners will be able to sit down together at the table of brotherhood.

MARTIN LUTHER KING, JR., speaking at the Civil Rights March on Washington, D.C., August 28, 1963.

27 Nonviolent action, the Negro saw, was the way to supplement, not replace, the process of change. It was the way to divest himself of passivity without arraying himself in vindictive force.

MARTIN LUTHER KING, JR., *Why We Can't Wait,* 1964.

28 I am aware that there are many who wince at a distinction between property and persons—who hold both sacrosanct. My views are not so rigid. A life is sacred. Property is intended to serve life, and no matter how much we surround it with rights and

Martin Luther King, Jr.: "I have a dream" speech, August 28, 1963

Delivered at a rally at the Lincoln Memorial, in Washington, D.C., before more than 200,000 people, this speech struck at the conscience of a whole nation. Some find in it a presentiment of Dr. King's death—he was assassinated on April 4, 1968.

Five score years ago, a great American, in whose symbolic shadow we stand, signed the Emancipation Proclamation. This momentous decree came as a great beacon light of hope to millions of Negro slaves who had been seared in the flames of withering injustice. It came as a joyous daybreak to end the long night of captivity.

But one hundred years later, we must face the tragic fact that the Negro is still not free. One hundred years later, the life of the Negro is still sadly crippled by the manacles of segregation and the chains of discrimination. One hundred years later, the Negro lives on a lonely island of poverty in the midst of a vast ocean of material prosperity. One hundred years later, the Negro is still languished in the corners of American society and finds himself an exile in his own land. So we have come here today to dramatize an appalling condition.

In a sense we have come to our nation's Capital to cash a check. When the architects of our republic wrote the magnificent words of the Constitution and the Declaration of Independence, they were signing a promissory note to which every American was to fall heir. This note was a promise that all men would be guaranteed the unalienable rights of life, liberty, and the pursuit of happiness.

It is obvious today that America has defaulted on this promissory note insofar as her citizens of color are concerned. Instead of honoring this sacred obligation, America has given the Negro people a bad check; a check which has come back marked "insufficient funds." But we refuse to believe that the bank of justice is bankrupt. We refuse to believe that there are insufficient funds in the great vaults of opportunity of this nation. So we have come to cash this check—a check that will give us upon demand the riches of freedom and the security of justice.

We have also come to this hallowed spot to remind America of the fierce urgency of *now*. This is no time to engage in the luxury of cooling off or to take the tranquilizing drug of gradualism. *Now* is the time to make real the promises of democracy. *Now* is the time to rise from the dark and desolate valley of segregation to the sunlit path of racial justice. *Now* is the time to open the doors of opportunity to all of God's children. *Now* is the time to lift our nation from the quicksands of racial injustice to the solid rock of brotherhood.

It would be fatal for the nation to overlook the urgency of the moment and to underestimate the determination of the Negro. This sweltering summer of the Negro's legitimate discontent will not pass until there is an invigorating autumn of freedom and equality. Nineteen sixty-three is not an end, but a beginning. Those who hope that the Negro needed to blow off steam and will now be content will have a rude awakening if the nation returns to business as usual. There will be neither rest nor tranquillity in America until the Negro is granted his citizenship rights. The whirlwinds of revolt will continue to shake the foundations of our nation until the bright day of justice emerges.

But there is something that I must say to my people who stand on the warm threshold which leads into the palace of justice. In the process of gaining our rightful place we must not be guilty of wrongful deeds. Let us not seek to satisfy our thirst for freedom by drinking from the cup of bitterness and hatred. We must forever conduct our struggle on the high plane of dignity and discipline. We must not allow our creative protest to degenerate into physical violence. Again and again we must rise to the majestic heights of meeting physical force with soul force.

The marvelous new militancy which has engulfed the Negro community must not lead us to a distrust of all white people, for many of our white brothers, as evidenced by their presence here today, have come to realize that their destiny is tied up with our destiny and their freedom is inextricably bound to our freedom. We cannot walk alone.

And as we walk, we must make the pledge that we shall march ahead. We cannot turn back. There are those who are asking the devotees of civil rights, "When will you be satisfied?"

We can never be satisfied as long as the Negro is the victim of the unspeakable horrors of police brutality.

We can never be satisfied as long as our bodies, heavy with the fatigue of travel, cannot gain lodging in the motels of the highways and the hotels of the cities.

We cannot be satisfied as long as the Negro's basic mobility is from a smaller ghetto to a larger one.

We can never be satisfied as long as a Negro in Mississippi cannot vote and a Negro in New York believes he has nothing for which to vote.

No, no, we are not satisfied, and we will not be satisfied until justice rolls down like waters and righteousness like a mighty stream.

I am not unmindful that some of you have come here out of great trials and tribulations. Some of you have come fresh from narrow jail cells. Some of you have come from areas where your quest for freedom left you battered by the storms of persecution and staggered by the winds of police brutality. You have been the veterans of creative suffering. Continue to work with the faith that unearned suffering is redemptive.

Go back to Mississippi, go back to Alabama, go back to South Carolina, go back to Georgia, go back to Louisiana, go back to the slums and ghettos of our Northern cities, knowing that somehow this situation can and will be changed. Let us not wallow in the valley of despair.

I say to you today, my friends, that in spite of the difficulties and frustrations of the moment I still have a dream. It is a dream deeply rooted in the American dream.

I have a dream that one day this nation will rise up and live out the true meaning of its creed: "We hold these truths to be self-evident; that all men are created equal."

I have a dream that one day on the red hills of Georgia the sons of former slaves and the sons of former slaveowners will be able to sit down together at the table of brotherhood.

I have a dream that one day even the state of Mississippi, a desert state sweltering with the heat of injustice and oppression, will be transformed into an oasis of freedom and justice.

I have a dream that my four little children will one day live in a nation where they will not be judged by the color of their skin but by the content of their character.

I have a dream today.

I have a dream that one day the state of Alabama, whose governor's lips are presently dripping with the words of interposition and nullification, will be transformed into a situation where little black boys and black girls will be able to join hands with little white boys and white girls and walk together as sisters and brothers.

I have a dream today.

I have a dream that one day every valley shall be exalted, every hill and mountain shall be made low, the rough places will be made plain, and the crooked places will be made straight, and the glory of the Lord shall be revealed, and all flesh shall see it together.

This is our hope. This is the faith with which I return to the South. With this faith we will be able to hew out of the mountain of despair a stone of hope. With this faith we will be able to transform the jangling discords of our nation into a beautiful symphony of brotherhood.

With this faith we will be able to work together, to pray together, to struggle together, to go to jail together, to stand up for freedom together, knowing that we will be free one day.

This will be the day when all of God's children will be able to sing with new meaning, "My country 'tis of thee, sweet land of liberty, of thee I sing. Land where my fathers died, land of the Pilgrims' pride, from every mountainside, let freedom ring."

And if America is to be a great nation, this must become true. So let freedom ring from the prodigious hilltops of New Hampshire. Let freedom ring from the mighty mountains of New York. Let freedom ring from the heightening Alleghenies of Pennsylvania!

Let freedom ring from the snowcapped Rockies of Colorado! Let freedom ring from the curvaceous peaks of California! But not only that; let freedom ring from Stone Mountain of Georgia! Let freedom ring from Lookout Mountain of Tennessee!

Let freedom ring from every hill and molehill of Mississippi. From every mountainside, let freedom ring.

When we let freedom ring, when we let it ring from every village and every hamlet, from every state and every city, we will be able to speed up that day when all of God's children, black men and white men, Jews and Gentiles, Protestants and Catholics, will be able to join hands and sing in the words of the old Negro spiritual, "Free at last! Free at last! Thank God Almighty, we are free at last!"

respect, it has no personal being. It is part of the earth man walks on; it is not man.

MARTIN LUTHER KING, JR., *The Trumpet of Conscience,* 1967.

29   A nation riven by factions, in which the minority has no hope of ever becoming a majority, or in which some group knows it is perpetually outcast, will seem oppressive to its members, whatever the legal pretensions.

HENRY KISSINGER, *White House Years,* 1979.

30   The fight must go on. The cause of civil liberty must not be surrendered at the end of one or even one hundred defeats.

ABRAHAM LINCOLN, in a letter to Henry Asbury, November 19, 1858.

31 In a free government the security for civil rights must be the same as for religious rights. It consists in the one case in the multiplicity of interests, and in the other in the multiplicity of sects.

JAMES MADISON, *The Federalist,* 1787–1788. (Also attributed to Alexander Hamilton.)

32 I think that the black man in America wants to be recognized as a human being and it's almost impossible for one who has enslaved another to bring himself to accept the person who used to pull his plow, who used to be an animal, subhuman, who used to be considered as such by him—it's almost impossible for that person in his right mind to accept that person as his equal.

MALCOLM X, speaking on the television program "The Open Mind," October 15, 1961.

33 We are not fighting for integration, nor are we fighting for separation. We are fighting for recognition as human beings.

> MALCOLM X, in a speech in New York City, 1964.

34 I for one believe that if you give people a thorough understanding of what confronts them and the basic causes that produce it, they'll create their own program, and when the people create a program, you get action.

> MALCOLM X, quoted in John Henrik Clarke, *Malcolm X: The Man and His Time*, 1969.

35 Anyone who possesses a natural right may make use of all legitimate means to protect it, and to safeguard it from violation.

> WILLIAM CARDINAL O'CONNELL, in a pastoral letter on workers' rights, November 23, 1912.

36 The moment a mere numerical superiority by either states or voters in this country proceeds to ignore the needs and desires of the minority, and for their own selfish purpose or advancement, hamper or oppress that minority, or debar them in any way from equal privileges and equal rights—that moment will mark the failure of our constitutional system.

> FRANKLIN D. ROOSEVELT, in a radio broadcast, March 2, 1930.

37 Freedom of speech and press . . . does not protect disturbances to the public peace or the attempt to subvert the government. It does not protect publications or teachings which tend to subvert or imperil the government, or to impede or hinder it in the performance of its governmental duties.

> EDWARD TERRY SANFORD, in a Supreme Court decision, *Gitlow* v. *the People of New York*, 1925.

38 Voting for the right is doing nothing for it.

> HENRY DAVID THOREAU, "Civil Disobedience," 1849.

39 You can't hold a man down without staying down with him.

> Attributed to Booker T. Washington.

40 There is nothing much to be "taught" about equality—you either believe it or you don't. But there is much that can be taught about rights and about liberty, including the basic stuff: that a right derives from a responsibleness, and that men become free as they become willing to accept restrictions on their acts. These are elementary concepts, of course, but an awful lot of youngsters seem to emerge from high school and even from college without acquiring them. Until they *are* acquired, the more subtle, intricate, and delicate problems of civil rights and freedom of speech are largely incomprehensible.

> E.B. WHITE, in a letter to Robert M. Hutchins, January 4, 1957.

41 The core of the civil rights problem is the matter of achieving equal opportunity for Negroes in the labor market. For it stands to reason that all our other civil rights depend on that one for fulfillment. We cannot afford better education for our children, better housing or medical care unless we have jobs.

> WHITNEY M. YOUNG, JR., quoted in Nelson A. Rockefeller, *Unity, Freedom and Peace: A Blueprint for Tomorrow*, 1968.

51. CIVIL WAR

See also CONSTITUTION; GOVERNMENT; LINCOLN; MAJORITY RULE; SLAVERY; STATES RIGHTS; WAR

1 We, the people of the State of South Carolina, in Convention assembled, do declare and ordain, and it is hereby declared and ordained, that the ordinance adopted by us in Convention, on the 23rd day of May, in the year of our Lord 1788, whereby the Constitution of the United States of America was ratified, and also all Acts and parts of Acts of the General Assembly of this State ratifying amendments of the said Constitution are hereby repealed; and that the union now subsisting between South Carolina and other States, under the name of the United States of America, is hereby dissolved.

"An Ordinance to Dissolve the Union Between the State of South Carolina and Other States united with her under the compact entitled the Constitution of the United States of America," December 20, 1860.

2 The war against the Confederate States is unconstitutional and repugnant to civilization, and will result in a bloody and shameful overthrow of our Constitution, and while recognizing the obligations of Maryland to the Union, we sympathize with the South in the struggle for their rights; for the sake of humanity we are for peace and reconciliation, and solemnly protest against this war, and will take no part in it.

> Resolution of the Maryland Legislature, May 10, 1861.

3 A rich man's war and a poor man's fight.

> Slogan used during the conscription riots in New York City, July, 1863. (Anyone who was drafted could hire a volunteer to take his place. This loophole favored those who could afford to pay for evading military service.)

4 A reckless and unprincipled tyrant has invaded your soil. Abraham Lincoln, regardless of all moral, legal and constitutional restraints, has thrown his Abolition hosts among you, who are murdering and imprisoning your citizens, confiscating and destroying your property, and committing other acts of violence and outrage too shocking and revolting to humanity to be enumerated.

> P.G.T. Beauregard, proclamation to the people of Virginia, June 1, 1861.

5 See! There is Jackson standing like a stone wall.

> Bernard E. Bee, at the first Battle of Bull Run, July 21, 1861.

6 "All quiet along the Potomac," they said,
   "Except, now and then a stray picket
Is shot as he walks on his beat to and fro
   By a rifleman hid in the thicket."

> Ethel Lynn Beers, "The Picket Guard," printed in *Harper's Weekly*, September 30, 1861.

7 All quiet along the Potomac to-night,
   No sound save the rush of the river,

While soft falls the dew on the face of the
      dead—
   The picket's off duty forever.

> Ibid.

8 Universal suffrage, furloughs and whiskey have ruined us.

> Gen. Braxton Bragg, after the Battle of Shiloh, April 6–7, 1862.

9 It was not merely the superior physical force of the North that prevailed [in the Civil War]; it was the moral forces which rule the world, forces which had long worked against slavery, and were ordained to save North America from the curse of hostile nations established side by side.

> James Bryce, *The American Commonwealth,* 1888.

10 Since Vicksburg they have not a word to say against Grant's habits. He has the disagreeable habit of not retreating before irresistible veterans.

> Mary Boykin Chesnut, diary entry, Richmond, Virginia, January 1, 1864.

11 If it [the Republican Party] accomplishes its object and gives the government to the North, I turn my eyes from the consequences. To the fifteen States of the South, that government will appear an alien government. . . . It will represent to their eye a vast region of States organized upon anti-slavery, flushed by triumph, cheered onward by the voices of the pulpit, tribune, and press; its mission to inaugurate freedom and put down the oligarchy; its constitution the glittering and sounding generalities of natural right which make up the Declaration of Independence. And then and thus is the beginning of the end.

> Rufus Choate, in a letter to the Maine Whig Committee, August 9, 1856. (Choate was calling on the Whigs to help defeat the Republican Party, which, he believed, would bring the country into civil war.)

12 Only two things stand in the way of an amicable settlement of the whole difficulty: the Landing of the Pilgrims and Original Sin.

> Gen. Howell Cobb, on the attempt to negotiate an end to the conflict, 1863.

13 The Red Badge of Courage.

> STEPHEN CRANE, title of his best-known work,
> 1895.

14 For the first time in history, a self-governing
republic is capable of maintaining itself against internal rebellion. What monarchy could have carried through this war as we have carried it? Could
our army have fought for a country owned by any
one man or by any number of men or families?

> RICHARD HENRY DANA, JR., in a speech given at
> Faneuil Hall in Boston after news of Lee's
> surrender, April 10, 1865, quoted in Catherine
> Drinker Bowen, *Yankee from Olympus,* 1944.

15 All we ask is to be let alone.

> Attributed to Jefferson Davis, in his inaugural
> address as President of the Confederate States of
> America, February 18, 1861.

16 I worked night and day for twelve years to prevent the war, but I could not. The North was mad
and blind, would not let us govern ourselves, and
so the war came. Now it must go on until the last
man of this generation falls in his tracks and his
children seize his musket and fight our battles.

> JEFFERSON DAVIS, to James F. Jaquess and James
> R. Gilmore, who had secured Lincoln's unofficial
> approval to explore possible terms of peace with
> Davis, July 17, 1864.

17 Damn the torpedoes—full speed ahead!

> ADM. DAVID FARRAGUT, at the Battle of Mobile
> Bay, August 5, 1864.

18 We are Coming, Father Abraham,
Three Hundred Thousand More.

> JAMES SLOAN GIBBONS, war poem published in
> the *New York Evening Post,* July 16, 1862 (in
> response to Lincoln's call for 300,000 additional
> troops).

19 No terms except an unconditional and immediate surrender can be accepted. I propose to move
immediately upon your words.

> ULYSSES S. GRANT, in a message to Gen. Simon
> B. Buckner at Fort Donelson, February 16, 1862.

20 I purpose to fight it out on this line, if it takes
all summer.

> ULYSSES S. GRANT, dispatch to Washington,
> D.C., before Spotsylvania Court House, May 11,
> 1864.

21 The rebels now have in their ranks their last
man. The little boys and old men are guarding
prisoners and railroad bridges, and forming a good
part of their forces, manning forts and positions,
and any man lost by them cannot be replaced. They
have robbed the cradle and the grave.

> ULYSSES S. GRANT, in a letter issued for
> publication, August 16, 1864.

22 The war is over—the rebels are our countrymen
again.

> ULYSSES S. GRANT, directing Union forces to
> refrain from cheering Gen. Lee's surrender,
> Appomattox Court House, April 9, 1865.

23 Sir, you dare not make war on cotton. No power
on earth dares make war upon it. Cotton is king.

> JAMES HENRY HAMMOND, replying to William
> Seward in the U.S. Senate, March, 1858. (The
> book *Cotton is King, or Slavery in the Light of
> Political Economy,* by David Christy, had been
> published in 1855.)

24 Let the only walls the foe shall scale
Be ramparts of the dead!

> PAUL HAMILTON HAYNE, "Vicksburg."

25 Mine eyes have seen the glory of the coming
of the Lord:
He is trampling out the vintage where the
grapes of wrath are stored:
He hath loosed the fateful lightning of his
terrible swift sword:
His truth is marching on.

> JULIA WARD HOWE, "Battle Hymn of the
> Republic," *Atlantic Monthly,* February, 1862.

26 I can anticipate no greater calamity for the country than a dissolution of the Union. It would be an
accumulation of all the evils we complain of, and
I am willing to sacrifice anything but honor for its
preservation.

> ROBERT E. LEE, in a letter, January 23, 1861.

27 If the Union is dissolved, and the government
disrupted, I shall return to my native state and

share the miseries of my people, and save in defense will draw my sword no more.

> ROBERT E. LEE, in a letter, January 23, 1861.

28 Never mind, General, all this has been *my* fault; it is *I* that have lost this fight, and you must help me out of it in the best way you can.

> ROBERT E. LEE, to Gen. Cadmus M. Wilcox at the close of the Battle of Gettysburg, July 3, 1863.

29 This has been a sad day for us, Colonel, a sad day; but we can't expect always to gain victories.

> ROBERT E. LEE, to Col. A.J. Lyon Fremantle, British Army, at the close of the Battle of Gettysburg, July 3, 1863.

30 I have been up to see the Congress and they do not seem to be able to do anything except to eat peanuts and chew tobacco, while my army is starving.

> ROBERT E. LEE, speaking of the Confederate Congress to his son, Gen. George Washington Custis Lee, March, 1865, recalled by George Taylor Lee in the *South Atlantic Quarterly,* July, 1927.

31 We failed, but in the good providence of God apparent failure often proves a blessing.

> ROBERT E. LEE, in a letter to George W. Jones, March 22, 1869.

32 If we do not make common cause to save the good old ship of the Union on this voyage, nobody will have a chance to pilot her on another voyage.

> ABRAHAM LINCOLN, in a speech in Cleveland, Ohio, February 15, 1861.

33 Plainly, the central idea of secession is the essence of anarchy. A majority held in restraint by constitutional checks and limitations, and always changing easily with deliberate changes of popular opinions and sentiments, is the only true sovereign of a free people.

> ABRAHAM LINCOLN, in his first inaugural address, March 4, 1861.

34 In your hands my dissatisfied fellow-countrymen, and not in mine, is the momentous issue of civil war. The government will not assail you.

> Ibid.

35 My paramount object in this struggle is to save the Union, and is not either to save or to destroy slavery. If I could save the Union without freeing any slave, I would do it; and if I could save it by freeing all the slaves, I would do it; and if I could save it by freeing some and leaving others alone, I would also do that.

> ABRAHAM LINCOLN, in a letter to Horace Greeley, August 22, 1862. (Lincoln had already written but not released the Emancipation Proclamation.)

36 I intend no modification of my oft-expressed personal wish that all men everywhere could be free.

> ABRAHAM LINCOLN, in a letter to Horace Greeley, August 22, 1862.

37 Our strife pertains to ourselves—to the passing generations of men—and it can without convulsion be hushed forever with the passing of one generation.

> ABRAHAM LINCOLN, in his second annual message to Congress, December 1, 1862.

38 Fellow-citizens, *we* cannot escape history. We of this Congress and this Administration will be remembered in spite of ourselves. No personal significance or insignificance can spare one or another of us. The fiery trial through which we pass will light us down, in honor or dishonor, to the latest generation.

> Ibid.

39 I have heard, in such a way as to believe it, of your recently saying that both the army and the government needed a dictator. Of course it was not for this, but in spite of it, that I have given you the command. Only those generals who gain successes can set up dictators. What I ask of you now is military success, and I will risk the dictatorship. . . . Beware of rashness, but with energy and sleepless vigilance go forward and give us victories.

> ABRAHAM LINCOLN, in a letter to Gen. Joseph Hooker, appointing him commander of the Army of the Potomac, January 26, 1863.

40 Tell me the brand of whiskey that Grant drinks. I would like to send a barrel of it to my other generals.

John Brown: last speech, November 2, 1859

With his execution by hanging at Harper's Ferry on December 2, 1859, John Brown became a martyr to the abolitionist cause. This plain yet eloquent address to the court, which was almost immediately distributed by broadside throughout the North, prophesied the bloody conflict that followed. John Brown soon entered American folklore.

I have, may it please the Court, a few words to say.

In the first place, I deny everything but what I have all along admitted, of a design on my part to free the slaves. I intended, certainly, to have made a clean thing of that matter, as I did last winter when I went into Missouri and there took slaves without the snapping of a gun on either side, moved them through the country, and finally leaving them in Canada. I designed to have done the same thing again, on a larger scale. That was all I intended to do. I never did intend murder, or treason, or the destruction of property, or to excite or incite the slaves to rebellion, or to make insurrection.

I have another objection, and that is that it is unjust that I should suffer such a penalty. Had I interfered in the manner which I admit, and which I admit has been fairly proved—for I admire the truthfulness and candor of the greatest portion of the witnesses who have testified in this case—had I so interfered in behalf of the rich, the powerful, the intelligent, the so-called great, or in behalf of any of their friends, either father, mother, brother, sister, wife, or children, or any of that class, and suffered and sacrificed what I have in this interference, it would have been all right; and every man in this court would have deemed it an act worthy of reward rather than punishment.

This court acknowledges, too, as I suppose, the validity of the law of God. I see a book kissed here which I suppose to be the Bible, or at least the New Testament, which teaches me that all things whatsoever I would that men should do to me, I should do even so to them. It teaches me, further, to remember them that are in bonds as bound with them. I endeavored to act up to that instruction. I say I am yet too young to understand that God is any respecter of persons. I believe that to have interfered as I have done—as I have always freely admitted I have done—in behalf of His despised poor is no wrong but right.

Now, if it is deemed necessary that I should forfeit my life for the furtherance of the ends of justice and mingle my blood further with the blood of my children and with the blood of millions in this slave country whose rights are disregarded by wicked, cruel, and unjust enactments—I say, let it be done!

Let me say one word further.

I feel entirely satisfied with the treatment I have received on my trial. Considering all the circumstances, it has been more generous than I expected. But I feel no consciousness of guilt. I have stated from the first what was my intention and what was not. I never had any design against the liberty of any person, nor any disposition to commit treason, or excite slaves to rebel, or make any general insurrection. I never encouraged any man to do so but always discouraged any idea of that kind.

Let me say, also, in regard to the statements made by some of those who were connected with me. I fear it has been stated by some of them that I have induced them to join me. But the contrary is true. I do not say this to injure them but as regretting their weakness. Not one but joined me of his own accord, and the greater part at their own expense. A number of them I never saw and never had a word of conversation with till the day they came to me; and that was for the purpose I have stated.

Now, I am done.

ABRAHAM LINCOLN, responding to comments about Gen. Grant's drinking, printed in the *New York Herald,* November 26, 1863 (probably apocryphal).

41 When Grant once gets possession of a place, he holds on to it as if he had inherited it.

ABRAHAM LINCOLN, to Benjamin F. Butler, June 22, 1864.

42 I pray that our Heavenly Father may assuage the anguish of your bereavement, and leave you only the cherished memory of the loved and lost, and the solemn pride that must be yours to have laid so costly a sacrifice upon the altar of freedom.

ABRAHAM LINCOLN, in a letter to Mrs. Bixby, November 21, 1864. (Lincoln was informed that Mrs. Bixby had lost five sons in battle. Actually, two had been killed.)

43 With malice toward none, with charity for all, with firmness in the right, as God gives us to see the right, let us strive on to finish the work we are in, to bind up the nation's wounds, to care for him who shall have borne the battle, and for his widow and his orphan, to do all which may achieve and cherish a just and lasting peace among ourselves, and with all nations.

ABRAHAM LINCOLN, in his second inaugural address, March 4, 1865.

44 Enough lives have been sacrificed. We must extinguish our resentments if we expect harmony and union.

ABRAHAM LINCOLN, to his Cabinet, April 14, 1865, a few hours before he was shot at Ford's Theater.

45 All quiet along the Potomac.

Attributed to Gen. George B. McClellan, c.1861.

46 Hanging from the beam
        Slowly swaying (such the law),
    Gaunt the shadow on your green,
        Shenandoah!
    The cut is on the crown
        (Lo, John Brown),
    And the stabs shall heal no more.
    Hidden in the cap
        Is the anguish none can draw;
    So your future veils its face,
        Shenandoah!
    But the streaming beard is shown
        (Weird John Brown),
    The meteor of the war.

HERMAN MELVILLE, "The Portent," on the execution of John Brown in 1859.

47 This war was really never contemplated in earnest. I believe if either the North or the South had expected that their differences would result in this obstinate struggle, the cold-blooded Puritan and the cock-hatted Huguenot and Cavalier would have made a compromise.

GEN. GEORGE E. PICKETT, in a letter to La Salle Corbell, his fiancée, June 27, 1862.

48 Up, men, and to your posts! Don't forget today that you are from Old Virginia.

GEN. GEORGE E. PICKETT, to his troops before the ill-fated charge at the Battle of Gettysburg, July 3, 1863.

49 The terrible grumble, and rumble, and roar,
    Telling the battle was on once more,
    And Sheridan twenty miles away.

THOMAS BUCHANAN READ, "Sheridan's Ride," published in *A Summer Story, Sheridan's Ride and Other Poems,* 1865.

50 Say to the seceded states: "Wayward sisters, depart in peace."

> GEN. WINFIELD SCOTT, letter to William Seward, March 3, 1861. (Scott was then general-in-chief of the Army.)

51 It is an irrespressible conflict between opposing and enduring forces.

> WILLIAM H. SEWARD, in his address "The Irrepressible Conflict," October 25, 1858.

52 I begin to regard the death and mangling of a couple thousand men as a small affair, a kind of morning dash—and it may be well that we become so hardened.

> GEN. WILLIAM T. SHERMAN, in a letter to his wife, July, 1864.

53 In revolution men fall and rise. Long before this war is over, much as you hear me praised now, you may hear me cursed and insulted.

> GEN. WILLIAM T. SHERMAN, in a letter to his wife, 1864.

54 If the people raise a great howl against my barbarity and cruelty, I will answer that war is war, and not popularity-seeking. If they want peace, they and their relatives must stop the war.

> GEN. WILLIAM T. SHERMAN, in a letter to Gen. Halleck before Sherman's devastating march through Georgia, September 4, 1864.

55 Until we can repopulate Georgia, it is useless for us to occupy it; but the utter destruction of its roads, houses and people will cripple their military resources. I can make this march, and make Georgia howl.

> GEN. WILLIAM T. SHERMAN, telegram to Gen. Grant from Atlanta, Georgia, September 9, 1864.

56 I give full credit to your statements of the distress that will be occasioned by it and yet shall not revoke my order, because my orders are not designed to meet the humanities of the case.

> GEN. WILLIAM T. SHERMAN, to the mayor of Atlanta, Georgia, after the latter protested Sherman's order to evacuate the city, September 12, 1864.

57 Sleep sweetly in your humble graves,
   Sleep, martyrs of a fallen cause;
Though yet no marble column craves
   The pilgrim here to pause.

> HENRY TIMROD, "Ode Sung at the Occasion of Decorating the Graves of the Confederate Dead, at Magnolia Cemetery, Charleston, S.C., 1867," published in *Poems,* 1873.

58 He is a scientific Goth, resembling Alaric, destroying the country as he goes and delivering the people over to starvation. Nor does he bury his dead, but leaves them to rot on the battlefield.

> JOHN TYLER, discussing Gen. Grant in a letter to Sterling Price, June 7, 1864.

59 Let's have the Union restored as it was, if we can; but if we can't, *I'm in favor of the Union as it wasn't.*

> ARTEMUS WARD, "In Canada," *Artemus Ward: His Travels,* 1865.

60 Secession! Peaceable secession! Sir, your eyes and mine are never destined to see that miracle. The dismemberment of this vast country without convulsion! The breaking up of the fountains of the great deep without ruffling the surface! Who is so foolish—I beg everybody's pardon—as to expect to see any such thing?

> DANIEL WEBSTER, speech in the U.S. Senate, March 7, 1850.

61   I hear the great drums pounding,
   And the small drums steady whirring,
   And every blow of the great convulsive
      drums,
   Strikes me through and through.

> WALT WHITMAN, "Dirge for Two Veterans," 1865.

62 How those old Greeks, indeed, would have seized on him! . . . The gods, the destinies, seem to have concentrated upon him.

> WALT WHITMAN, writing of Gen. Grant, September 28, 1879, in *Specimen Days and Collect,* 1882.

63 This Federal government is dead. The only question is whether we will give it a decent, peaceable, Protestant burial, or whether we shall have an Irish wake at the burial.

> SEN. LOUIS T. WIGFALL of Texas, an active supporter of secession, in a Senate speech, January, 1861.

64 We are constantly thinking of the great war . . . which saved the Union . . . but it was a war that did a great deal more than that. It created in this country what had never existed before—a national consciousness. It was not the salvation of the Union, it was the rebirth of the Union.

> WOODROW WILSON, Memorial Day address, Arlington National Cemetery, May 31, 1915.

65 Marching Through Georgia.

> HENRY CLAY WORK, title of one of his best-known songs, 1865.

---

52. COLORADO

---

1 Nil sine Numine. (Nothing without Providence.)

> State motto.

2 Please do not Shoot the Pianist
He is doing His Best

> Sign seen in a Leadville, Colorado, saloon by Oscar Wilde during his U.S. tour, 1882.

3 I don't know any other American city quite so fascinatingly strange [as Denver]. Not merely because the yellow cabs are painted green or because the fourteenth step on the state capitol bears the proud plaque, ONE MILE ABOVE SEA LEVEL. . . . The remarkable thing about Denver is its ineffable closedness; when it moves, or opens up, it is like a Chippendale molting its veneer. . . . It is probably the most self-sufficient, isolated, self-contained, and complacent city in the world.

> JOHN GUNTHER, *Inside U.S.A.*, 1947.

4 After some hours we reached the level plain, and later the city of Denver. . . . The pulse of that town

was too like the rushing mighty wind in the Rocky Mountain tunnel. It made me tired because complete strangers desired me to do something to mines which were in mountains, and to purchase building blocks upon inaccessible cliffs; and once, a woman urged that I should supply her with strong drinks. I had almost forgotten that such attacks were possible in any land, for the outward and visible signs of public morality in American towns are generally safeguarded. For that I respect this people.

> RUDYARD KIPLING, *American Notes,* 1891.

5 The Grand Canyon is carven deep by the master hand; it is the gulf of silence, widened in the desert; it is all time inscribing the naked rock; it is the book of earth.

> DONALD CULROSS PEATTIE, *The Road of a Naturalist,* 1941.

6 Passing through your wonderful mountains and cañons I realize that this state is going to be more and more the playground for the entire Republic. . . . You will see this the real Switzerland of America.

> THEODORE ROOSEVELT, on a visit to Colorado in 1905.

---

53. CONDUCT

See also BELIEF; CHARACTER; DUTY;
INDIVIDUALITY; PRINCIPLE; REPUTATION

---

1 I expect to pass through this world but once; any good thing, therefore, that I can do, or any kindness that I can show to any fellow creature, let me do it now; let me not defer or neglect it, for I shall not pass this way again.

> Author unknown. (The words sometimes are attributed to Stephen Grellet, 1773–1855, a French-born Quaker clergyman who came to the U.S. in 1795, but they are not found in his writings.)

2 A strong nation, like a strong person, can afford to be gentle, firm, thoughtful, and restrained. It can afford to extend a helping hand to others. It's a

weak nation, like a weak person, that must behave with bluster and boasting and rashness and other signs of insecurity.

> JIMMY CARTER, in a speech in New York City, October 14, 1976.

3 A refined simplicity is the characteristic of all high bred deportment, in every country.

> JAMES FENIMORE COOPER, *The American Democrat,* 1838.

4 Decency—generosity—cooperation—assistance in trouble—devotion to duty; these are the things that are of greater value than surface appearances and customs.

> DWIGHT D. EISENHOWER, in a letter to Mamie Doud Eisenhower, June 11, 1943.

5 There are men whose manners have the same essential splendor as the simple and awful sculpture on the friezes of the Parthenon, and the remains of the earliest Greek art.

> RALPH WALDO EMERSON, "History," *Essays,* First Series, 1841.

6 We are bound hand and foot with our decorums and superstitions. England has achieved respectability at what a cost! America with a valet's eyes admires and copies in vain.

> RALPH WALDO EMERSON, entry written in 1845, *Journals,* 1909–1914.

7 Manners require time, as nothing is more vulgar than haste.

> RALPH WALDO EMERSON, "Behavior," *The Conduct of Life,* 1860.

8 Good manners are made up of petty sacrifices.

> RALPH WALDO EMERSON, *Letters and Social Aims,* 1876.

9 He is not well-bred, that cannot bear Ill-Breeding in others.

> BENJAMIN FRANKLIN, *Poor Richard's Almanack,* 1748.

10 Act uprightly, and despise Calumny; Dirt may stick to a Mud Wall, but not to polish'd Marble.

> BENJAMIN FRANKLIN, *Poor Richard's Almanack,* 1757.

11 Perhaps if we could examine the manners of different nations with impartiality, we should find no people so rude as to be without any rules of politeness; nor any so polite as not to have some remains of rudeness.

> BENJAMIN FRANKLIN, "Remarks Concerning the Savages of North America," 1783.

12 I do not love my neighbor as myself, and apologize to no one. I treat my neighbor as fairly and politely as I hope to be treated, but there is no law in nature or common sense ordering me to go beyond that.

> EDGAR WATSON HOWE, *Success Easier Than Failure,* 1917.

13 Whenever you are to do a thing, though it can never be known but to yourself, ask yourself how you would act were all the world looking at you, and act accordingly.

> THOMAS JEFFERSON, in a letter to Peter Carr, August 19, 1785.

14 The moral sense, or conscience, is as much a part of man as his leg or arm. It is given to all human beings in a stronger or weaker degree, as force of members is given them in a greater or less degree.

> THOMAS JEFFERSON, in a letter to Peter Carr, August 10, 1787.

15 I never did, or countenanced, in public life, a single act inconsistent with the strictest good faith; having never believed there was one code of morality for a public, and another for a private man.

> THOMAS JEFFERSON, in a letter to Don Valentine de Feronda, October 4, 1809.

16 The manners of every nation are the standard of orthodoxy within itself. But these standards being arbitrary, reasonable people in all allow free toleration for the manners, as for the religion, of others.

> THOMAS JEFFERSON, in a letter to Jean Baptiste Say, March 2, 1815.

17 The love of property and a consciousness of right or wrong have conflicting places in our organization, which often make a man's course seem crooked—his conduct a riddle.

ABRAHAM LINCOLN, in a speech at Hartford, Connecticut, March 5, 1860.

18 It is an open question whether any behavior based on fear of eternal punishment can be regarded as ethical or should be regarded as merely cowardly.

MARGARET MEAD, in *Redbook* magazine, February, 1971.

19 I believe in the brotherhood of man, all men, but I don't believe in brotherhood with anybody who doesn't want brotherhood with me. I believe in treating people right, but I'm not going to waste my time trying to treat somebody right who doesn't know how to return that treatment.

MALCOLM X, in a speech in New York City, December 12, 1964.

20 If we ever learn to treat the living with the tenderness with which we instinctively treat the dead, we shall then have a civilization well worth distributing.

THOMAS BRACKETT REED, quoted in Samuel Walker McCall, *The Life of Thomas Brackett Reed,* 1914.

21 It is disturbing to discover in oneself these curious revelations of the validity of the Darwinian theory. If it is true that we have sprung from the ape, there are occasions when my own spring appears not to have been very far.

CORNELIA OTIS SKINNER, *The Ape in Me,* 1959.

22 Absolutely speaking, Do unto others as you would that they should do unto you is by no means a golden rule, but the best of current silver. An honest man would have but little occasion for it. It is golden not to have any rule at all in such a case.

HENRY DAVID THOREAU, "Sunday," *A Week on the Concord and Merrimack Rivers,* 1849.

23 Be good, and you will be lonesome.

MARK TWAIN, from the frontispiece of *Following the Equator,* 1897.

24 Good breeding consists in concealing how much we think of ourselves and how little we think of the other person.

MARK TWAIN, *Mark Twain's Notebook,* 1935.

25 Be courteous to all, but intimate with few, and let those few be well tried before you give them your confidence.

GEORGE WASHINGTON, *Maxims of Washington,* 1942.

26 Every action in company, ought to be with some sign of respect to those present.

Ibid.

---

54. CONGRESS

See also CONSTITUTION; DEMOCRACY; ELECTIONS; GOVERNMENT; POLITICS

---

1 Freedom of speech and debate in Congress shall not be impeached or questioned in any court, or placed out of Congress, and the members of Congress shall be protected in their persons from arrests and imprisonments, during the time of their going to and from, and attendance on Congress, except for treason, felony, or breach of the peace.

Articles of Confederation, November, 1777.

2 We favor an amendment to the Federal Constitution providing for election of United States senators by the direct vote of the people.

Plank in Democratic National Platform, 1900.

3 You can't use tact with a Congressman. A Congressman is a hog. You must take a stick and hit him on the snout.

A member of President Grant's cabinet, c.1875, quoted in Henry Adams, *The Education of Henry Adams,* 1907.

4 A distinguished member since 1948 of the "most exclusive gentlemen's club in the world," Senator Smith reaffirms the growing realization, wisely recognized by her astute constituents, that ability and proven performance, rather than sex, provide the reasonable standards for political selection.

Columbia University, on awarding the Doctor of Law degree to Margaret Chase Smith of Maine, June 1, 1955.

5 Congress is a very *unrepresentative* institution. Not only from an economic class point of view, but from *every* point of view—sex, race, age, vocation. Some people say this is because the political system tends to homogenize everything, that a Congressman by virtue of the fact that he or she represents a half million people has to appeal to all sorts of disparate groups. I don't buy that at all. These men in Congress don't represent a homogeneous point of view. They represent their *own* point of view—by reason of their sex, background and class.

> BELLA ABZUG, quoted in Mel Ziegler, *Bella!* 1972.

6 In Britain the government has to come down in front of Parliament every day to explain its actions, but here the President never answers directly to Congress.

> Ibid.

7 You can't have a Congress that responds to the needs of the workingman when there are practically no people here who represent him.

> BELLA ABZUG, quoted in *Redbook* magazine, April, 1974.

8 The Congress, in short, is not, was not intended to be, and cannot be an Executive.

> DEAN G. ACHESON, *A Democrat Looks at His Party,* 1955.

9 The business of the Congress is tedious beyond expression. . . . Every man in it is a great man, an orator, a critic, a statesman; and therefore every man upon every question must show his oratory, his criticism, and his political abilities.

> JOHN ADAMS, discussing the Continental Congress in a letter to his wife, October 9, 1774.

10 Congress, *n.* A body of men who meet to repeal laws.

> AMBROSE BIERCE, *The Devil's Dictionary,* 1906.

11 Senate, *n.* A body of elderly gentlemen charged with high duties and misdemeanors.

> Ibid.

12 Senator, *n.* The fortunate bidder in an auction of votes.

> Ibid.

13 [Congress] is an institution designed only to react, not to plan or lead.

> JIMMY BRESLIN, *How the Good Guys Finally Won,* 1975.

14 If we in the Senate would stop calling each other "distinguished," we might have ten working days a year.

> SEN. EDWARD W. BROOKE, quoted in the *Reader's Digest,* April, 1972.

15 The weakness of Congress is the strength of the President. . . . The tendency everywhere in America to concentrate power and responsibility in one man is unmistakable. . . . There is no danger that the President should become a despot, that is, should attempt to make his will prevail against the will of the majority. But he may have a great part to play as the leader of the majority and the exponent of its will. He is in some respects better fitted both to represent and to influence public opinion than Congress is.

> JAMES BRYCE, *The American Commonwealth,* 1888.

16 The seniority system keeps a handful of old men . . . in control of the Congress. These old men stand implacably across the paths that could lead us toward a better future. But worse than they, I think, are the majority of members of both Houses who continue to submit to the senility system.

> SHIRLEY CHISHOLM, *Unbought and Unbossed,* 1970.

17 The great object for us to seek here, for the Constitution identifies the vice-presidency with the Senate, is to continue to make this chamber, as it was intended by the fathers, the citadel of liberty.

> CALVIN COOLIDGE, in his inaugural address as vice president, March 4, 1921.

18 Congress cannot properly even discuss a subject that Congress cannot legally control, unless it be to ascertain its own powers.

> JAMES FENIMORE COOPER, *The American Democrat,* 1838.

19 Sure the people are stupid: the human race is stupid. Sure Congress is an inefficient instrument of government. But the people are not stupid enough

to abandon representative government for any other kind, including government by the guy who knows.

> Bernard De Voto, "Sometimes They Vote Right Too," *The Easy Chair,* 1955.

20 It is his jooty to rigorously enforce th' rules iv th' Sinit. There ar-re none. Th' Sinit is ruled be courtesy, like th' longshoreman's union.

> Finley Peter Dunne, "The Vice-President," *Dissertations by Mr. Dooley,* 1906.

21 Some statesmen go to Congress and some go to jail. It is the same thing, after all.

> Eugene Field, *The Tribune Primer,* 1882.

22 We [in the Senate] have the power to do any damn fool thing we want to do, and we seem to do it about every ten minutes.

> Sen. J. William Fulbright, quoted in *Time* magazine, February 4, 1952.

23 It is Congress that voters mistrust, not their own congressmen.

> Peter Goldman, *Newsweek* magazine, November 6, 1978.

24 I look at the Senators and pray for the country.

> Edward Everett Hale, chaplain of the Senate, when asked, "Do you pray for the Senators?" quoted in Van Wyck Brooks, *New England: Indian Summer,* 1940.

25 I do not know much about books; I have not read very much; but I have traveled a good deal and observed men and things and I have made up my mind after all my experience that the members of the Senate are the survivors of the fittest.

> George Hearst, taking his seat in a Senate so filled with business magnates that it was popularly called the "Millionaire's Club," 1886, quoted in Richard Hofstadter, *The American Political Tradition,* 1948.

26 The executive in our government is not the sole, it is scarcely the principal object of my jealousy. The tyranny of the legislature is the most formidable dread at present and will be for many years. That of the executive will come in its turn, but it will be at a remote period.

> Thomas Jefferson, in a letter to James Madison, March 15, 1789.

27 Congress is the great commanding theater of this nation, and the threshold to whatever department of office a man is qualified to enter.

> Thomas Jefferson, in a letter to William Wirt, 1808.

28 That one hundred and fifty lawyers should do business together ought not to be expected.

> Thomas Jefferson, in his *Autobiography,* begun January 6, 1821.

29 It is really more questionable than may at first be thought, whether Bonaparte's dumb legislature, which said nothing and did much, may not be preferable to one which talks much and does nothing.

> Ibid.

30 I asked a man in prison once how he happened to be there and he said he had stolen a pair of shoes. I told him if he had stolen a railroad he would be a United States Senator.

> Mary "Mother" Jones, quoted in Eve Merriam, *Growing Up Female in America,* 1971.

31 What can you expect from that zoo?

> John F. Kennedy, on Congress, quoted in *U.S. News & World Report,* July 22, 1968.

32 We had better seats for *Hello Dolly!*

> Attributed to Robert F. Kennedy, when shown his seat as freshman Senator from New York (a two-seat fifth row was created for Kennedy and Joseph D. Tydings, freshman Senator from Maryland), January 4, 1965.

33 I have passed two hours in the Representatives' hall and Senate chamber today. I could learn nothing of the merits of any of the questions, but I had a preference, such as one feels in seeing two dogs fight, that one should beat.

> Amos Lawrence, in his diary, May, 1836.

34 Being elected to Congress, though I am very grateful to our friends for having done it, has not pleased me as much as I expected.

> Abraham Lincoln, in a letter to Joshua F. Speed, October 22, 1846.

35 If you want to see some real crooks, take a look at our senators and congressmen in America. They call somebody a gangster, a racket guy or a crook

because he's doin' somethin' against the law, when they're the worst kind of thieves, within the law.

> CHARLES "LUCKY" LUCIANO, quoted in Martin A. Gosch and Richard Hammer, *The Last Testament of Lucky Luciano*, 1975.

36 The Senate is the last primitive society in the world. We still worship the elders of the tribe and honor the territorial imperative.

> Attributed to EUGENE J. MCCARTHY.

37 The American, if he has a spark of national feeling, will be humiliated by the very prospect of a foreigner's visit to Congress—these, for the most part, illiterate hacks whose fancy vests are spotted with gravy, and whose speeches, hypocritical, unctuous, and slovenly, are spotted also with the gravy of political patronage.

> MARY MCCARTHY, "America the Beautiful," *Commentary* magazine, September, 1947.

38 Give us clear vision, that we may know where to stand and what to stand for—because unless we stand for something, we shall fall for anything.

> PETER MARSHALL, Senate chaplain, in a Senate prayer, 1947.

39 Congress is so strange. A man gets up to speak and says nothing. Nobody listens—and then everybody disagrees.

> BORIS MARSHALOV, quoted in the *Reader's Digest*, March, 1941.

40 To hear some men talk of the government, you would suppose that Congress was the law of gravitation, and kept the planets in their places.

> WENDELL PHILLIPS, *Speeches, Lectures and Letters*, 1863.

41 There are two periods when Congress does no business: one is before the holidays, and the other after.

> Attributed to GEORGE DENNISON PRENTICE.

42 You have no idea how destitute of talent are more than half of the members of Congress. Nine out of ten of your ordinary acquaintances are fully equal to them.

> SEARGENT SMITH PRENTISS, congressman from Mississippi, in a letter to his sister, February, 1833.

43 One thing our Founding Fathers could not foresee—they were farmers, professional men, businessmen giving of their time and effort to an idea that became a country—was a nation governed by professional politicians who had a vested interest in getting reelected. They probably envisioned a fellow serving a couple of hitches and then looking early forward to getting back to the farm.

> RONALD REAGAN, from an interview quoted in Edmund G. Brown, *Reagan: The Political Chameleon*, 1976.

44 While I stand here a member of this House there is no man on the face of the earth so poor nor any corporation so rich that I will prostitute myself to injustice for the sake of that temporary advantage which comes of maintaining a false position because some dishonest men are clamoring against me. It is the duty of every member of this House to act upon his conscience and his sense of duty. It is his business to stand up for what he believes to be right, careless of what may happen to him in consequence thereof.

> THOMAS BRACKETT REED, in a speech in the House of Representatives, 1884.

45 One of the greatest delusions in the world is the hope that the evils of this world can be cured by legislation. I am happy in the belief that the solution of the great difficulties of life and government is in better hands even than those of this body.

> THOMAS BRACKETT REED, in a speech in the House of Representatives, 1886.

46 A gelatinous existence, the scorn of all vertebrate animals.

> THOMAS BRACKETT REED, describing the House of Representatives, "Two Congresses Contrasted," *North American Review*, August, 1892.

47 The right of the minority is to draw its salaries, and its function is to make a quorum.

> THOMAS BRACKETT REED, quoted in Leon A. Harris, *The Fine Art of Political Wit*, 1964.

48 I do strive to think well of my fellow man, but no amount of striving can give me confidence in the wisdom of a congressional vote.

> AGNES REPPLIER, quoted in Emma Repplier, *Agnes Repplier, A Memoir,* 1957.

49 Talking about stopping War, I will bet any man in the United States 5 thousand even that there ain't a man in this Country that can draw up a bill that the Senate themselves won't go to war over while they are arguing it.

> WILL ROGERS, in his newspaper column, July 22, 1923.

50 I could study all my life and not think up half the amount of funny things they can think of in one Session of Congress. Besides my jokes don't do anybody any harm. You don't have to pay attention to them. But everyone of the jokes those Birds make is a LAW and hurts somebody (generally everybody).

> WILL ROGERS, March 1, 1925, quoted in Donald Day, *The Autobiography of Will Rogers,* 1949.

51 This country has come to feel the same when Congress is in session as we do when the baby gets hold of a hammer. It's just a question of how much damage he can do with it before we can take it away from him.

> WILL ROGERS, July 4, 1930, quoted in Donald Day, *The Autobiography of Will Rogers,* 1949.

52 The U.S. Senate may not be the most refined and deliberative body in existence but they got the most unique rules. Any member can call anybody in the world anything he can think of and they can't answer him, sue him, or fight him. Our constitution protects aliens, drunks and U.S. Senators. There ought to be one day (just one) where there is an open season on Senators.

> WILL ROGERS, in his newspaper column, March 6, 1935.

53 Never blame a legislative body for not doing something. When they do nothing, that don't hurt anybody. When they do something is when they become dangerous.

> WILL ROGERS, quoted in Richard Ketchum, *Will Rogers: His Life and Times,* 1973.

54 You see, ordinarily you have got to work your way up as a humorist, and first get into Congress. Then you work your way up into the Senate and then, if your stuff is funny enough, it goes into the Congressional Record.

> WILL ROGERS, quoted in the *New York Times,* January 28, 1984.

55 You see, they have two of these bodies—Senate and House. That is for the convenience of visitors. If there is nothing funny happening in one, there is sure to be in the other; and in case one body passes a good bill, why, the other can see it in time and kill it.

> Ibid.

56 Though the President is commander-in-chief, Congress is his commander; and, God willing, he shall obey. He and his minions shall learn that this is not a government of kings and satraps, but a government of the people, and that Congress is the people.

> THADDEUS STEVENS, in a speech in the House of Representatives, January 3, 1867.

57 The debates of that great assembly are frequently vague and perplexed and . . . seem to drag their slow length along rather than to advance towards a distinct object. Some such state of things will, I believe, always arise in the public assemblies of democracies.

> ALEXIS DE TOCQUEVILLE, *Democracy in America,* 1835–1840.

58 We do not elect our wisest and best men to represent us. . . . In general, we elect men of the type that subscribes to only one principle—to get reelected.

> TERRY M. TOWNSEND, in an address in New York City, January 30, 1940.

59 It could probably be shown by facts and figures that there is no distinctly native American criminal class except Congress.

> MARK TWAIN, "Pudd'nhead Wilson's New Calendar," *Following the Equator,* 1897.

60 Fleas can be taught nearly anything that a Congressman can.

> MARK TWAIN, *What Is Man?* 1917.

61 I venture to say that if you search the earth all over with a ten horsepower microscope, you won't be able to find such another pack of poppycock gabblers as the present Congress.

> ARTEMUS WARD, *Artemus Ward: His Travels*, 1865.

62 This is a Senate of equals, of men of individual honor and personal character, and of absolute independence. We know no masters, we acknowledge no dictators. This is a hall for mutual consultation and discussion; not an arena for the exhibition of champions.

> DANIEL WEBSTER, in a speech in the U.S. Senate, January 26, 1830.

63 It is said that the titles of most bills in Congress are like the titles of Marx Brothers movies ("Duck Soup," "Animal Crackers"): they do not tell much about the contents.

> GEORGE F. WILL, *Newsweek* magazine, October 3, 1977.

64 I believe if we introduced the Lord's Prayer here, senators would propose a large number of amendments to it.

> SEN. HENRY WILSON of Massachusetts, quoted in Leon A. Harris, *The Fine Art of Political Wit*, 1964.

---

55. CONNECTICUT

---

1 Qui transtulit sustinet. (He who transplanted sustains.)

> State motto.

2 The land of steady habits.

> Anonymous, c.1774, widely used in the 18th century because of Connecticut voters' tendency to return elected officials to office.

3 Dark as the frost-nipped leaves that strew the ground,
  The Indian hunter here his shelter found;
Here cut his bow and shaped his arrow true,
Here built his wigwam and his bark canoe,
Speared the quick salmon leaping up the streams
And slew the deer 'neath moonlight's misty beams.

> JOHN G.C. BRAINARD, "To the Connecticut River," quoted in Lewis Sprague Mills, *The Story of Connecticut*, 1932.

4 I loved those hills, I loved the flowers
  That dashed with gems their sunny swell,
And oft I fondly dreamed for hours,
  By streams within those mountain dells.

> SAMUEL GOODRICH, "Memory of Home," quoted in Lewis Sprague Mills, *The Story of Connecticut*, 1932.

5 'Tis a rough land of earth, and stone and tree,
  Where breathes no castled lord or cabined slave;
Where thought, and tongues, and hands, are bold and free,
  And friends will find a welcome, foes a grave;
And where none kneel, save when to Heaven they pray,
  Nor even then, unless in their own way.

> FITZ-GREENE HALLECK, "Connecticut," quoted in Lewis Sprague Mills, *The Story of Connecticut*, 1932.

6 Connecticut in her blue-laws, laying it down as a principle, that the laws of God should be the law of the land.

> THOMAS JEFFERSON, in a letter to John Adams, January 24, 1814.

7 Here's to the town of New Haven,
  The home of the truth and the light,
    Where God speaks to Jones,
    In the very same tones,
  That he uses with Hadley and Dwight.

> FREDERICK S. JONES, "A Toast on New Haven: Lux et Veritas," in a letter to Rev. Samuel C. Bushnell, January, 1915. (Bushnell had sent Jones the celebrated verse about Boston written by John C. Bossidy.) [See BOSTON TOAST]

8 Taken as a group, they [Connecticut peddlers] were probably no less honest than itinerant salesmen are wont to be, but the point is that they were probably no more so. Aggressive, pervasive, with a foot in every American door, they gave the country at large its first clear notions of the New England character, and there are some parts of the country, one fears, that have not yet revised the opinions then formed. The word "Yankee" came to mean "Connecticut Yankee," and throughout the Old South, long before Abolition days, it came to be pronounced "Damyank."

ODELL SHEPARD, *Connecticut Past and Present,* 1939.

9 I asked him how far we were from Hartford. He said he had never heard of the place; which I took to be a lie, but allowed it to go at that. At the end of an hour we saw a far-away town sleeping in a valley by a winding river; and beyond it on a hill, a vast gray fortress, with towers and turrets, the first I had ever seen out of a picture. "Bridgeport?" said I, pointing. "Camelot," said he.

MARK TWAIN, *A Connecticut Yankee in King Arthur's Court,* 1890.

10 "Qui Transtulit Sustinet," the motto of light,
'Neath the folds of that banner we strike for
the right,
Connecticut's watchword, o'er hill and o'er plain,
The hand that transplanted, that hand will
sustain.

S.S. WELD, lines reprinted in Lewis Sprague Mills, *The Story of Connecticut,* 1932.

---

56. CONQUEST

See also FORCE; MILITARISM; NUCLEAR AGE; VICTORY; WAR

---

1 We assert that no nation can long endure half republic and half empire, and we warn the American people that imperialism abroad will lead quickly and inevitably to despotism at home.

Plank in the Democratic Party national platform, 1900.

2 The great nations, like lions roused from their lairs, are roaring and springing upon the prey, and the little nations, like packs of hungry wolves, are standing by, licking their jaws, and waiting for their share of the spoils.

HENRY WARD BEECHER, *Life Thoughts,* 1858.

3 We are a conquering race. We must obey our blood and occupy new markets and if necessary new lands.

ALBERT J. BEVERIDGE, "Grant, the Practical," address delivered to the Middlesex Club of Massachusetts, Boston, April 27, 1898.

4 Maintaining, as I do, the tenets of a line of precedents from Washington's day, which proscribe entangling alliances with foreign states, I do not favor a policy of acquisition of new and distant territory or the incorporation of remote interests with our own.

GROVER CLEVELAND, message to Congress, December 8, 1885.

5 We shall not make Britain's mistake. Too wise to try to govern the world, we shall merely own it. Nothing can stop us.

LUDWELL DENNY, *America Conquers Britain,* 1930.

6 There are people who eat the earth and eat all the people on it like in the Bible with the locusts. And other people who stand around and watch them eat it.

LILLIAN HELLMAN, *The Little Foxes,* 1939.

7 The race to which we belong is the most arrogant and rapacious, the most exclusive and indomitable in history. It is the conquering and the unconquerable race, through which alone man has taken possession of the physical and moral world. All other races have been its enemies or its victims.

JOHN JAMES INGALLS, in a speech in the U.S. Senate, January 23, 1890.

8 If there be one principle more deeply rooted than any other in the mind of every American, it is that we should have nothing to do with conquest.

THOMAS JEFFERSON, in a letter to William Short, July 28, 1791.

9 I candidly confess that I have ever looked on Cuba as the most interesting addition which could ever be made to our system of States. The control which, with Florida, this island would give us over the Gulf of Mexico, and the countries and isthmus bordering on it, as well as all those whose waters flow into it, would fill up the measure of our political well-being.

> THOMAS JEFFERSON, in a letter to James Monroe, October 24, 1823.

10 The mission of the United States is one of benevolent assimilation.

> WILLIAM MCKINLEY, in a letter to Harrison Gray Otis, December 21, 1898.

11 The thirst for glory is an epidemic which robs a people of their judgment, seduces their vanity, cheats them of their interests, and corrupts their consciences.

> WILLIAM GRAHAM SUMNER, *The Conquest of the United States by Spain,* 1899.

57. THE CONSTITUTION

See also DEMOCRACY; GOVERNMENT; PRESIDENCY; STATES' RIGHTS; VICE PRESIDENCY

1 Whenever the Constitution comes between men and the virtue of the white women of South Carolina, I say—to Hell with the Constitution!

> Attributed to Gov. Coleman L. Blease of South Carolina, 1911.

2 The American Constitution is no exception to the rule that everything which has power to win the obedience and respect of men must have its roots deep in the past, and that the more slowly every institution has grown, so much the more enduring is it likely to prove. There is little in this Constitution that is absolutely new. There is much that is as old as Magna Charta.

> JAMES BRYCE, *The American Commonwealth,* 1888.

3 When the Constitution was first framed I predicted that it would last fifty years. I was mistaken. It will evidently last longer than that. But I was mistaken only in point of time. The crash will come, but not quite so quick as I thought.

> Attributed to Aaron Burr, in James Parton, *The Life and Times of Aaron Burr,* 1857.

4 The Constitution of the United States was made not merely for the generation that then existed, but for posterity—unlimited, undefined, endless, perpetual posterity.

> HENRY CLAY, in a speech in the U.S. Senate, February 6, 1850.

5 He who takes the oath today to preserve, protect, and defend the Constitution of the United States only assumes the solemn obligation which every patriotic citizen—on the farm, in the workshop, in the busy marts of trade, and everywhere—should share with him. The Constitution, which prescribes his oath, my countrymen, is yours; the government you have chosen him to administer for a time is yours.

> GROVER CLEVELAND, in his first inaugural address, March 4, 1885.

6 The Constitution of the United States is a law for rulers and people, equally in war and in peace, and covers with the shield of its protection all classes of men, at all times, and under all circumstances. No doctrine involving more pernicious consequences was ever invented by the wit of man than that any of its provisions can be suspended during any of the great exigencies of government. Such a doctrine leads directly to anarchy or despotism.

> DAVID DAVIS, in a Supreme Court opinion, *ex parte Milligan,* 1866.

7 The Fifth Amendment is an old friend and a good friend. It is one of the great landmarks in man's struggle to be free of tyranny, to be decent and civilized.

> WILLIAM O. DOUGLAS, *An Almanac of Liberty,* 1954.

8 As the British Constitution is the most subtle organism which has proceeded from progressive

history, so the American Constitution is the most wonderful work ever struck off at a given time by the brain and purpose of man.

> WILLIAM GLADSTONE, "Kin Beyond the Sea," the *North American Review,* September, 1878.

9 In the United States, the Constitution is a health chart left by the Founding Fathers which shows whether or not the body politic is in good health. If the national body is found to be in poor health, the Founding Fathers also left a prescription for the restoration of health called the Declaration of Independence.

> DICK GREGORY, in *Dick Gregory's Political Primer,* 1972.

10 Constitutions should consist only of general provisions; the reason is that they must necessarily be permanent, and that they cannot calculate for the possible change of things.

> ALEXANDER HAMILTON, in a speech in the U.S. Senate, June 28, 1788.

11 If the Constitution is to be construed to mean what the majority at any given period in history wish the Constitution to mean, why a written Constitution and deliberate processes of amendment?

> FRANK J. HOGAN, in a speech to the American Bar Association, July 10, 1939.

12 I do not think the United States would come to an end if we [the Supreme Court] lost our power to declare an act of Congress void.

> OLIVER WENDELL HOLMES, JR., in a speech in New York City, February 15, 1913.

13 There is nothing to howl about. There have always been changes in the interpretation laid on the Constitution, and there always will be.

> OLIVER WENDELL HOLMES, JR., responding to reporters' questions about Franklin D. Roosevelt's National Recovery Act, c.1933.

14 We are under a Constitution, but the Constitution is what the judges say it is, and the judiciary is the safeguard of our liberty and of our property under the Constitution.

> CHARLES EVANS HUGHES, in an address at Elmira, New York, May 3, 1907.

15 There are very good articles in it, and very bad. I do not know which preponderate.

> THOMAS JEFFERSON, in a letter to William S. Smith, November 13, 1787.

16 The Constitution . . . is unquestionably the wisest ever yet presented to men.

> THOMAS JEFFERSON, in a letter to David Humphrey, March 18, 1789.

17 In questions of power . . . let no more be heard of confidence in man, but bind him down from mischief by the chains of the Constitution.

> THOMAS JEFFERSON, Kentucky Resolutions, November 10, 1798.

18 Some men look at constitutions with sanctimonious reverence, and deem them like the Ark of the Covenant, too sacred to be touched. They ascribe to the men of the preceding age a wisdom more than human, and suppose what they did to be beyond amendment. I knew that age well; I belonged to it, and labored with it. It deserved well of its country. It was very like the present, but without the experience of the present; and forty years of experience in government is worth a century of book-reading.

> THOMAS JEFFERSON, in a letter to Samuel Kercheval, July 12, 1816.

19 Experience has already shown that the impeachment it [the Constitution] has provided is not even a scarecrow.

> THOMAS JEFFERSON, in a letter to Spencer Roane, September 6, 1819.

20 You seem . . . to consider the judges as the ultimate arbiters of all constitutional questions; a very dangerous doctrine indeed, and one which would place us under the despotism of an oligarchy. Our judges are as honest as other men, and not more so.

> THOMAS JEFFERSON, in a letter to William Jarvis, September 28, 1820.

21 This member of the government was at first considered as the most harmless and helpless of all its organs. But it has proved that the power of declaring what the law is, *ad libitum,* by sapping

Preamble to the Constitution of the United States, June 21, 1788, and the first ten amendments, known as the Bill of Rights, December 15, 1791

Objections to the Constitution had been registered by some states because it contained few explicit guarantees of personal rights and liberties. Therefore, even before the Constitution itself was adopted by the states, the ten amendments were passed by Congress on September 25, 1787, and sent to the states, thus helping to overcome their reluctance to ratify the Constitution.

PREAMBLE

We, the people of the United States, in order to form a more perfect union, establish justice, insure domestic tranquillity, provide for the common defense, promote the general welfare, and secure the blessings of liberty to ourselves and our posterity, do ordain and establish this Constitution for the United States of America.

AMENDMENT I

Congress shall make no law respecting an establishment of religion, or prohibiting the free exercise thereof; or abridging the freedom of speech or of the press; or the right of the people peaceably to assemble, and to petition the government for a redress of grievances.

AMENDMENT II

A well-regulated militia being necessary to the security of a free State, the right of the people to keep and bear arms shall not be infringed.

AMENDMENT III

No soldier shall, in time of peace, be quartered in any house without the consent of the owner, nor in time of war, but in a manner to be prescribed by law.

AMENDMENT IV

The right of the people to be secure in their persons, houses, papers, and effects, against unreasonable searches and seizures, shall not be violated, and no warrants shall issue but upon probable cause, supported by oath or affirmation, and particularly describing the place to be searched, and the persons or things to be seized.

AMENDMENT V

No person shall be held to answer for a capital, or otherwise infamous crime, unless on a presentment or indictment of a grand jury, except in cases arising in the land or naval forces, or in the militia, when in actual service in time of war of public danger; nor shall any person be subject for the same offense to be twice put in jeopardy of life or limb; nor shall be compelled in any criminal case to be a witness against himself, nor be deprived of life, liberty or property, without due process of law; nor shall private property be taken for public use without just compensation.

AMENDMENT VI

In all criminal prosecutions, the accused shall enjoy the right to a speedy and public trial, by an impartial jury of the State and district wherein the crime shall have been committed, which district shall have been previously ascertained by law, and to be informed of the nature and cause of the accusation; to be confronted with the witnesses against him; to have compulsory process for obtaining witnesses in his favor, and to have the assistance of counsel for his defense.

AMENDMENT VII

In suits at common law, where the value in controversy shall exceed twenty dollars, the right of trial by jury shall be preserved, and no fact tried by a jury shall be otherwise re-examined in any court of the United States, than according to the rules of the common law.

AMENDMENT VIII

Excessive bail shall not be required, nor excessive fines imposed, nor cruel and unusual punishments inflicted.

AMENDMENT IX

The enumeration in the Constitution of certain rights shall not be construed to deny or disparage others retained by the people.

AMENDMENT X

The powers not delegated to the United States by the Constitution, nor prohibited by it to the States, are reserved to the States respectively, or to the people.

---

and mining, slyly, and without alarm, the foundations of the Constitution, can do what open force would not dare to attempt.

> THOMAS JEFFERSON, on the Supreme Court, in a letter to Edward Livingston, March 25, 1825.

22 Outside of the Constitution we have no legal authority more than private citizens, and within it we have only so much as that instrument gives us. This broad principle limits all our functions and applies to all subjects.

> ANDREW JOHNSON, in a message to the House of Representatives, March 2, 1867.

23 I cannot be ignorant of the fact that many worthy and patriotic citizens are desirous of having the National Constitution amended. While I make no recommendation of amendments, I fully recognize the rightful authority of the people over the whole subject, to be exercised in either of the modes prescribed in the instrument itself; and I should, under existing circumstances, favor rather than oppose a fair opportunity being afforded the people to act upon it.

> ABRAHAM LINCOLN, in his first inaugural address, March 4, 1861.

24 The particular phraseology of the Constitution of the United States confirms and strengthens the principle, supposed to be essential to all written constitutions, that a law repugnant to the Constitution is void, and that courts, as well

as other departments, are bound by that instrument.

> JOHN MARSHALL, in a Supreme Court opinion, *Marbury v. Madison*, 1803.

25 We admit . . . that the powers of the government are limited. . . . But we think the sound construction of the Constitution must allow to the national legislature that discretion, with respect to the means by which the powers it confers are to be carried into execution, which will enable that body to perform the high duties assigned to it, in the manner most beneficial to the people. Let the end be legitimate, let it be within the scope of the constitution, and all means which are appropriate, which are plainly adapted to that end, which are not prohibited, but consistent with the letter and spirit of the constitution, are constitutional.

> JOHN MARSHALL, in a Supreme Court opinion, *McCulloch v. Maryland*, 1819.

26 I yield slowly and reluctantly to the conviction that our Constitution cannot last. . . . The Union has been preserved thus far by miracles. I fear they cannot continue.

> JOHN MARSHALL, in a letter to Joseph Story, 1832.

27 A constitution is a thing *antecedent* to a government, and a government is only the creature of a constitution. The constitution of a country is not the act of its government, but of the people constituting a government.

> THOMAS PAINE, *The Rights of Man*, 1791–1792.

28 All that is valuable in the Constitution is one thousand years old.

> WENDELL PHILLIPS, in a speech in Boston, February 17, 1861.

29 Our Constitution is an affair of compromise between the States, and this is the master-key which unlocks all its difficulties. If any of the parties to the compact are dissatisfied with their share of influence, it is an affair of amicable discussion, in the mode pointed out by the Constitution itself, but no cause for dissolving the confederacy.

> JOHN RANDOLPH, in a letter to James Lloyd, December 15, 1814.

30 The United States Constitution has proved itself the most marvelously elastic compilation of rules of government ever written.

> FRANKLIN D. ROOSEVELT, in a radio address, March 2, 1930.

31 Our Constitution is so simple and practical that it is possible always to meet extraordinary needs by changes in emphasis and arrangement without loss of essential form. That is why our constitutional system has proved itself the most superbly enduring political mechanism the modern world has produced.

> FRANKLIN D. ROOSEVELT, in his first inaugural address, March 4, 1933.

32 For most Americans the Constitution had become a hazy document, cited like the Bible on ceremonial occasions but forgotten in the daily transactions of life.

> ARTHUR M. SCHLESINGER, JR., *The Imperial Presidency*, 1973.

33 There is a higher law than the Constitution.

> WILLIAM H. SEWARD, opposing compromise on the issue of slavery, in a speech in the U.S. Senate, March 11, 1850.

34 The American Constitution, one of the few modern political documents drawn up by men who were forced by the sternest circumstances to think out what they really had to face, instead of chopping logic in a university classroom.

> GEORGE BERNARD SHAW, in his preface to *Getting Married*, 1908.

35 [The Constitution] was a charter of anarchism. It was not really a Constitution at all. It was not an instrument of government; it was a guarantee to a whole nation that they never could be governed at all. And that is exactly what they wanted. . . . The ordinary man . . . is an anarchist. He wants to do as he likes.

> GEORGE BERNARD SHAW, in an address before the Academy of Political Science, New York City, April 11, 1933.

36 The power vested in the American courts of justice of pronouncing a statute to be unconstitu-

tional forms one of the most powerful barriers that have ever been devised against the tyranny of political assemblies.

> ALEXIS DE TOCQUEVILLE, *Democracy in America,* 1835–1840.

37 Should the states reject this excellent Constitution, the probability is that an opportunity will never again offer to make another in peace—the next will be drawn in blood.

> Attributed to George Washington, on signing the Constitution, September 17, 1787.

38 The basis of our political systems is the right of the people to make and to alter their constitutions of government. But the constitution which at any time exists till changed by an explicit and authentic act of the whole people is sacredly obligatory upon all. The very idea of the power and the right of the people to establish government presupposes the duty of every individual to obey the established government.

> GEORGE WASHINGTON, in his Farewell Address, September 17, 1796.

39 If in the opinion of the people the distribution or modification of the constitutional powers be in any particular wrong, let it be corrected by an amendment in the way which the Constitution designates. But let there be no change by usurpation; for though this in one instance may be the instrument of good, it is the customary weapon by which free governments are destroyed.

> Ibid.

40 We may be tossed upon an ocean where we can see no land—nor, perhaps, the sun or stars. But there is a chart and a compass for us to study, to consult, and to obey. That chart is the Constitution.

> DANIEL WEBSTER, in an address at Springfield, Massachusetts, September 29, 1847.

58. CONTEMPLATION

1 To make a prairie it takes a clover and one
        bee,
   One clover, and a bee,
   And revery.
   The revery alone will do
   If bees are few.

> EMILY DICKINSON, "To Make a Prairie," *Poems, Third Series,* 1896.

2 The revelation of thought takes men out of servitude into freedom.

> RALPH WALDO EMERSON, "Fate," *The Conduct of Life,* 1860.

3 All civil mankind have agreed in leaving one day for contemplation against six for practice.

> RALPH WALDO EMERSON, "The Preacher," *Lectures and Biographical Sketches,* 1883.

4 I am weary of swords and courts and kings. Let us go into the garden and watch the minister's bees.

> MARY JOHNSTON, *To Have and to Hold,* 1900.

5 My own thoughts
   Are my companions.

> HENRY WADSWORTH LONGFELLOW, *The Masque of Pandora,* 1875.

6 The mind can weave itself warmly in the cocoon of its own thoughts, and dwell a hermit anywhere.

> JAMES RUSSELL LOWELL, "On a Certain Condescension in Foreigners," published in the *Atlantic Monthly,* January, 1869.

7 Solitude is as needful to the imagination as society is wholesome for the character.

> JAMES RUSSELL LOWELL, "Dryden," *Among My Books,* 1870.

8 Leisure and the cultivation of human capacities are inextricably interdependent.

> MARGARET MEAD, in *Redbook* magazine, December, 1963.

9 Once upon a midnight dreary, while I
      pondered weak and weary,
Over many a quaint and curious volume of
      forgotten lore.

> EDGAR ALLAN POE, "The Raven," published in
> the *New York Evening Mirror,* January 24,
> 1845.

10 Ice is an interesting subject for contemplation.
They told me that they had some in the ice-houses
at Fresh Pond five years old which was as good as
ever. Why is it that a bucket of water soon becomes
putrid, but frozen remains sweet forever? It is commonly said that this is the difference between the
affections and the intellect.

> HENRY DAVID THOREAU, "The Pond in
> Winter," *Walden,* 1854.

11 From his cradle to his grave a man never does
a single thing which has any first and foremost
object save one—to secure peace of mind, spiritual
comfort, for himself.

> MARK TWAIN, *What Is Man?* 1906.

12 I loafe and invite my soul,
I lean and loafe at my ease observing a spear
      of summer grass.

> WALT WHITMAN, *Song of Myself,* 1855.

13 When I, sitting, heard the astronomer, where
      he lectured with much applause in the
      lectureroom,
How soon unaccountable I became tired and
      sick,
'Till rising and gliding out, I wander'd off by
      myself,
In the mystical moist night-air, and from
      time to time,
Look'd up in perfect silence at the stars.

> WALT WHITMAN, "When I Heard the Learn'd
> Astronomer," 1865.

59. CONVERSATION

See also ARGUMENT; FRIENDS; GOSSIP;
INVECTIVE; LANGUAGE; ORATORY; SPEECH

1 Most of us know how to say nothing; few of us
know when.

> Anonymous.

2 Ninety-two percent of the stuff told you in confidence you couldn't get anybody else to listen to.

> FRANKLIN P. ADAMS [F.P.A.], quoted in Robert
> E. Drennan, *The Algonquin Wits,* 1968.

3 No one means all he says, and yet very few say
all they mean, for words are slippery and thought
is viscous.

> HENRY ADAMS, *The Education of Henry Adams,*
> 1907.

4 Debate is masculine; conversation is feminine.

> A. BRONSON ALCOTT, *Concord Days,* 1872.

5 Many can argue, not many converse.

> Ibid.

6 Bore, *n.* A person who talks when you wish him
to listen.

> AMBROSE BIERCE, *The Devil's Dictionary,*
> 1906.

7 I don't care how much a man talks, if he only
says it in a few words.

> JOSH BILLINGS, "Affurisms," from *Josh Billings:
> His Sayings,* 1865.

8 Silence is a still noise.

> JOSH BILLINGS, *Josh Billings' Encyclopedia of
> Wit and Wisdom,* 1874.

9 Repartee is what you wish you'd said.

> HEYWOOD BROUN, quoted in Robert E. Drennan,
> *The Algonquin Wits,* 1968.

10 If you don't say anything, you won't be called
on to repeat it.

> Attributed to Calvin Coolidge.

11 Two may talk and one may hear, but three cannot take part in a conversation of the most sincere and searching sort. In good company, there is never such discourse between two, across the table, as takes place when you leave them alone.

> RALPH WALDO EMERSON, "Friendship," *Essays,* First Series, 1841.

12 In conversation the game is, to say something new with old words, and you shall observe a man of the people picking his way along, step by step, using every time an old boulder, yet never setting his foot on an old place.

> RALPH WALDO EMERSON, entry written in 1849, *Journals,* 1909–1914.

13 Conversation is an art in which a man has all mankind for his competitors, for it is that which all are practicing every day while they live.

> RALPH WALDO EMERSON, "Considerations by the Way," *The Conduct of Life,* 1860.

14 The music that can deepest reach,
And cure all ill, is cordial speech.

> Ibid.

15 You may talk of all subjects save one, namely, your maladies.

> RALPH WALDO EMERSON, "Behavior," *The Conduct of Life,* 1860.

16 Wise, cultivated, genial conversation is the last flower of civilization. . . . Conversation is our account of ourselves.

> RALPH WALDO EMERSON, "Woman," *Miscellanies,* 1884.

17 When you speak to a man, look on his eyes; when he speaks to thee, look on his mouth.

> BENJAMIN FRANKLIN, *Poor Richard's Almanack,* 1740.

18 One has to grow up with good talk in order to form the habit of it.

> HELEN HAYES, with Lewis Funke, *A Gift of Joy,* 1965.

19 [He] sought to inject a few raisins of conversation into the tasteless dough of existence.

> O. HENRY, "The Complete Life of John Hopkins," published in the *New York Sunday World Magazine,* April 17, 1904.

20 Stop not, unthinking, every friend you meet
To spin your wordy fabric in the street;
While you are emptying your colloquial pack,
The fiend *Lumbago* jumps upon his back.

> OLIVER WENDELL HOLMES, SR., *A Rhymed Lesson,* 1846.

21 Speak clearly, if you speak at all;
Carve every word before you let it fall. . . .
And when you stick on conversation's burrs,
Don't strew your pathway with those
dreadful *urs.*

> Ibid.

22 But little-minded people's thoughts move in such a small circle that five minutes' conversation gives you an arc long enough to determine their whole curve.

> OLIVER WENDELL HOLMES, SR., *The Autocrat of the Breakfast-Table,* 1858.

23 Think twice before you speak and then say it to yourself.

> ELBERT HUBBARD, in *The Philistine,* published from 1895–1915.

24 Conversation's got to have some root in the past, or else you've got to explain every remark you make, an' it wears a person out.

> SARAH ORNE JEWETT, *The Country of the Pointed Firs,* 1896.

25 A single conversation across the table with a wise man is better than ten years' study of books.

> HENRY WADSWORTH LONGFELLOW, a translation of a Chinese proverb, in *Hyperion,* 1839.

26 In general those who nothing have to say
Contrive to spend the longest time in
doing it;
They turn and vary it in every way,
Hashing it, stewing it, mincing it,
ragouting it.

> JAMES RUSSELL LOWELL, "An Oriental Apologue," 1849.

27 No, never say nothin' without you're
    compelled tu,
  An' then don't say nothin' thet you can be
    held tu.

> JAMES RUSSELL LOWELL, *The Biglow Papers,*
> Second Series, 1866.

28 Years ago, I tried to top everybody, but I don't
anymore. I realized it was killing conversation.
When you're always trying for a topper you aren't
really listening. It ruins communication.

> GROUCHO MARX, interview in the *Los Angeles
> Times,* 1967, quoted in Groucho Marx, *The
> Groucho Phile,* 1976.

29 The Americans . . . have invented so wide a
range of pithy and hackneyed phrases that they can
carry on an amusing and animated conversation
without giving a moment's reflection to what they
are saying and so leave their minds free to consider
the more important matters of big business and
fornication.

> W. SOMERSET MAUGHAM, *Cakes and Ale,*
> 1930.

30 A bore is a man who, when you ask him how he
is, tells you.

> BERT LESTON TAYLOR, *The So-Called Human
> Race,* 1922.

31 We are in great haste to construct a magnetic
telegraph from Maine to Texas; but Maine and
Texas, it may be, have nothing important to communicate.

> HENRY DAVID THOREAU, *Walden,* 1854.

32 War talk by men who have been in a war is
always interesting; whereas moon talk by a poet
who has not been on the moon is likely to be dull.

> MARK TWAIN, *Life on the Mississippi,*
> 1883.

33 Lettuce is like conversation: it must be fresh and
crisp, and so sparkling that you scarcely notice the
bitter in it.

> CHARLES DUDLEY WARNER, *My Summer in a
> Garden,* 1870.

60. COWARDICE

See also BRAVERY; CHARACTER; FEAR

1 I'd rather have them say "There he goes" than
"Here he lies."

> Anonymous.

2 Caution, caution, sir! It is nothing but the word
of cowardice.

> JOHN BROWN, quoted by Bruce Catton in *Life*
> magazine, September 12, 1955.

3 There is no calamity which a great nation can
invite which equals that which follows from a supine submission to wrong and injustice, and the
consequent loss of national self-respect and honor,
beneath which are shielded and defended a people's
safety and greatness.

> GROVER CLEVELAND, message to Congress,
> December 17, 1895. (The U.S. had become
> involved in a dispute between Great Britain and
> Venezuela, and war with Britain appeared
> likely.)

4 This Republic was not established by cowards;
and cowards will not preserve it.

> ELMER DAVIS, Phi Beta Kappa oration at
> Harvard University, 1953, published in *But We
> Were Born Free,* 1954.

5 Man is timid and apologetic; he is no longer
upright; he dares not say "I think," "I am," but he
quotes some saint or sage.

> RALPH WALDO EMERSON, "Self-Reliance,"
> *Essays,* First Series, 1841.

6 Cowardice, as distinguished from panic, is almost
always simply a lack of ability to suspend the func-
tioning of the imagination.

> ERNEST HEMINGWAY, introduction to the
> anthology *Men at War,* 1942.

7 An utterly fearless man is a far more dangerous
comrade than a coward.

> HERMAN MELVILLE, *Moby-Dick,* 1851.

8 There are several good protections against temptations, but the surest is cowardice.

> MARK TWAIN, "Pudd'nhead Wilson's New Calendar," *Following the Equator,* 1897.

61. CRIME

See also JUSTICE; LAW; PUNISHMENT

1 Lizzie Borden took an axe
And gave her mother forty whacks.
When she saw what she had done
She gave her father forty-one.

> Anonymous verse, on the murder of Lisbeth "Lizzie" Borden's father and stepmother in Fall River, Massachusetts, August 4, 1892.

2 A murderer is one who is presumed to be innocent until he is proved insane.

> Anonymous.

3 Jesse James had a wife,
She's a mourner all her life;
His children they were brave;
Oh, the dirty little coward
That shot Mr. Howard,
Has laid poor Jesse in his grave.

> Song entitled "Jesse James," by Robert Ford, commemorating the murder of James (who had adopted the name Thomas Howard) on April 3, 1882.

4 The trouble with [Adolf] Eichmann was precisely that so many were like him, and that the many were neither perverted nor sadistic, that they were, and still are, terribly and terrifyingly normal. . . . This new type of criminal . . . commits his crimes under circumstances that make it well-nigh impossible for him to know or to feel that he is doing wrong.

> HANNAH ARENDT, *Eichmann in Jerusalem,* 1963.

5 Early one June morning in 1872 I murdered my father—an act which made a deep impression on me at the time.

> AMBROSE BIERCE, first sentence of the short story, "An Imperfect Conflagration," 1886.

6 Accomplice, *n.* One associated with another in a crime, having guilty knowledge and complicity, as an attorney who defends a criminal, knowing him guilty. This view of the attorney's position in the matter has not hitherto commanded the assent of attorneys, no one having offered them a fee for assenting.

> AMBROSE BIERCE, *The Devil's Dictionary,* 1906.

7 Habeas Corpus, *n.* A writ by which a man may be taken out of jail when confined for the wrong crime.

> Ibid.

8 Crime is contagious. If the government becomes a lawbreaker, it breeds contempt for law.

> LOUIS D. BRANDEIS, in a dissenting opinion, *Olmstead* v. *U.S.,* 1928.

9 Even an attorney of moderate talent can postpone doomsday year after year, for the system of appeals that pervades American jurisprudence amounts to a legalistic wheel of fortune, a game of chance, somewhat fixed in the favor of the criminal, that the participants play interminably. . . . But at intervals the wheel does pause to declare a winner—or, though with increasing rarity, a loser.

> TRUMAN CAPOTE, *In Cold Blood,* 1965.

10 The "flatfoot mentality" insists that any individual or organization that wants to change *anything* in our present system is somehow subversive of "the American way," and should be under continuous surveillance.

> TONI CARABILLO, "The "Flatfoot Mentality,' " *Hollywood NOW News,* August, 1975.

11 In England there was a time when one hundred different offenses were punishable with death, and it made no difference. The English people strangely found out that so fast as they repealed the severe penalties and so fast as they did away with punishing men by death, crime decreased instead of increased; that the smaller the penalty the fewer the crimes. Hanging men in our country jails does not prevent murder. It makes murderers.

CLARENCE DARROW, address to prisoners in the Cook County Jail, 1902.

12 If every man and woman and child in the world had a chance to make a decent, fair, honest living, there would be no jails, and no lawyers and no courts.

Ibid.

13 Everybody is a potential murderer. I've never killed anyone, but I frequently get satisfaction reading the obituary notices.

CLARENCE DARROW, in a newspaper interview in Chicago, April 18, 1937.

14 While there is a lower class I am in it, while there is a criminal element I am of it, and while there is a soul in prison I am not free.

EUGENE DEBS, during his trial on charges of violating the Espionage Act of 1917, June 16, 1918.

15 Commit a crime, and the earth is made of glass. Commit a crime, and it seems as if a coat of snow fell on the ground, such as reveals in the woods the track of every partridge and fox and squirrel and mole.

RALPH WALDO EMERSON, "Compensation," *Essays,* First Series, 1841.

16 Murder, in the murderer, is no such ruinous thought as poets and romancers will have it; it does not unsettle him, or fright him from his ordinary notice of trifles.

RALPH WALDO EMERSON, "Experience," *Essays,* Second Series, 1844.

17 The reason of idleness and crime is the deferring of our hopes. Whilst we are waiting we beguile the time with jokes, with sleep, with eating, and with crimes.

RALPH WALDO EMERSON, "Nominalist and Realist," *Essays,* Second Series, 1844.

18 If a man steal enough, he may be sure that his punishment will practically amount but to the loss of a part of the proceeds of his theft; and if he steal enough to get off with a fortune, he will be greeted by his acquaintances as a viking might have been greeted after a successful cruise.

HENRY GEORGE, *Progress and Poverty,* 1879.

19 There are two kinds of crimes: those committed by people who are caught and convicted, and those committed by people who are not. Which category a particular crime falls into is directly related to the wealth, power, and prestige of the criminal. The former category includes such crimes as purse snatching, mugging, armed robbery, and breaking and entering. The latter category includes war atrocities, embezzlement, most political actions, and budget appropriations.

DICK GREGORY, *Dick Gregory's Political Primer,* 1972.

20 I can tell you this on a stack of Bibles: prisons are archaic, brutal, unregenerative, overcrowded hell holes where the inmates are treated like animals with absolutely not one humane thought given to what they are going to do once they are released. You're an animal in a cage and you're treated like one.

JIMMY HOFFA, *Hoffa: The Real Story,* 1975.

21 It is not only vain, but wicked, in a legislator to frame laws in opposition to the laws of nature, and to arm them with the terrors of death. This is truly creating crimes in order to punish them.

THOMAS JEFFERSON, "Note on the Crimes Bill," 1779.

22 Man was born into barbarism when killing his fellow man was a normal condition of existence. He became endowed with a conscience. And he has now reached the day when violence toward another human being must become as abhorrent as eating another's flesh.

MARTIN LUTHER KING, JR., *Why We Can't Wait,* 1963.

23 The contempt for law and the contempt for the human consequences of lawbreaking go from the bottom to the top of American society.

MARGARET MEAD, quoted in Claire Safran, "Impeachment?" in *Redbook* magazine, April, 1974.

24 When is conduct a crime, and when is a crime not a crime? When Somebody Up There—a monarch, a dictator, a Pope, a legislator—so decrees.

JESSICA MITFORD, *Kind and Unusual Punishment,* 1971.

25 A kleptomaniac is a person who helps himself because he can't help himself.

HENRY MORGAN, quoted in Leo Rosten, *Infinite Riches,* 1978.

26 No people is wholly civilized where a distinction is drawn between stealing an office and stealing a purse.

THEODORE ROOSEVELT, acceptance speech upon his nomination for president on an independent ticket, Chicago, Illinois, June 22, 1912.

27 A crowded police court docket is the surest of all signs that trade is brisk and money plenty.

MARK TWAIN, *Roughing It,* 1872.

28 Apart from insuring our country's survival, there can be no higher national priority than controlling domestic violence. The first duty of government is to protect the citizen from assault. Unless it does this, all the civil rights and civil liberties in the world aren't worth a dime.

RICHARD A. VIGUERIE, *The New Right—We're Ready to Lead,* 1981.

29 There is no refuge from confession but suicide; and suicide is confession.

DANIEL WEBSTER, arguing in a murder trial in Salem, Massachusetts in 1830.

---

62. CULTURE

---

1 No man ever looks at the world with pristine eyes. He sees it edited by a definite set of customs and institutions and ways of thinking.

RUTH BENEDICT, *Patterns of Culture,* 1934.

2 In this era of affluence and of permissiveness, we have, in all but cultured areas, bred a nation of overprivileged youngsters, saturated with vitamins, television and plastic toys. But they are nurtured from infancy on a Dick-and-Jane literary and artistic level; and the cultural drought, as far as entertainment is concerned, sets in when they are between six and eight.

JUDITH CRIST, *The Private Eye, the Cowboy and the Very Naked Girl,* 1968.

3 A political orator wittily compared our party promises to western roads, which opened stately enough, with planted trees on either side, to tempt the traveller, but soon became narrower and narrower, and ended in a squirrel-track, and ran up a tree. So does culture with us; it ends in head-ache.

RALPH WALDO EMERSON, "Experience," *Essays,* Second Series, 1844.

4 'Tis wonderful how soon a piano gets into a log hut on the frontier. You would think they found it under a pine stump.

RALPH WALDO EMERSON, "Civilization," *Society and Solitude,* 1870.

5 Men who sit back and pride themselves on their culture haven't any to speak of.

ELBERT HUBBARD, *The Roycroft Dictionary and Book of Epigrams,* 1923.

6 Culture is only culture when the owner is not aware of its existence. Capture culture, hog-tie it, and clap your brand upon it, and you find the shock has killed the thing you loved. You can brand a steer, but you can not brand deer.

Ibid.

7 All of us confront limits of body, talent, temperament. But that is not all. We are, all of us, also constrained by our time, our place, our civilization. We are bound by the culture we have in common, that culture which distinguishes us from other people in other times and places. Cultural constraints condition and limit our choices, shaping our characters with their imperatives.

JEANE J. KIRKPATRICK, in a commencement address at Georgetown University, May 24, 1981.

8 Though it may not be realized, it is strictly true, that a few first-class poets, philosophs, and authors, have substantially settled and given status to the entire religion, education, law, sociology, &c., of the hitherto civilized world.

WALT WHITMAN, *Democratic Vistas,* 1870.

9 As now taught, accepted, and carried out, are not the processes of culture rapidly creating a class of supercilious infidels, who believe in nothing? Shall a man lose himself in countless masses of adjustments, and be so shaped with reference to this, that,

and the other, that the simply good and healthy and brave parts of him are reduced and clipp'd away, like the bordering of a box in a garden?

Ibid.

63. DEATH

See also LIFE

1 Here today, gone tomorrow.

Anonymous.

2 I in the burying place may see
  Graves shorter there than I;
From death's arrest no age is free,
  Young children too may die.

FROM *The New England Primer*, compiled by Benjamin Harris, c.1683.

3 *Xerxes* the great did die;
And so must you and I.

Ibid.

4 Swing low, sweet chariot—
  Comin' for to carry me home;
I looked over Jordan and what did I see?
  A band of angels comin' after me—
Comin' for to carry me home.

Spiritual, c.1850.

5 Dying is one of the few things that can be done as easily lying down.

Attributed to Woody Allen.

6 Close his eyes; his work is done.
  What to him is friend or foeman,
Rise of moon, or set of sun,
  Hand of man, or kiss of woman?

GEORGE HENRY BOKER, "Dirge for a Soldier," 1862.

7 Why do not you look at this miserable little life, with all its ups and downs, as I do? At the very worst, 'tis but a scratch, a temporary ill, to be soon cured by that dear old doctor, Death.

EDWIN BOOTH, in a letter to William Winter, 1886.

8   The hills
Rock-ribbed and ancient as the sun,—the vales
Stretching in pensive quietness between;
The venerable woods—rivers that move
In majesty, and the complaining brooks
That make the meadows green; and, poured
    round all,
Old Ocean's gray and melancholy waste,—
Are but the solemn decorations all
Of the great tomb of man.

WILLIAM CULLEN BRYANT, "Thanatopsis," published in the *North American Review*, September, 1817.

9   All that tread
The globe are but a handful to the tribes
That slumber in its bosom.

Ibid.

10 So live that when thy summons comes to join
  The innumerable caravan that moves
  To the pale realm of shade, where each shall
    take
  His chamber in the silent halls of death,
  Thou go not like the quarry-slave at night,
  Scourged to his dungeon, but, sustained and
    soothed
  Like one who wraps the drapery of his couch
  About him, and lies down to pleasant
    dreams.

WILLIAM CULLEN BRYANT, "Thanatopsis," lines added when the poem was reissued in *Poems*, 1821.

11 Raise then, the hymn to Death. Deliverer!
  God hath anointed thee to free the oppressed
  And crush the oppressor.

WILLIAM CULLEN BRYANT, "Hymn to Death," 1821.

12 Since every death diminishes us a little, we grieve—not so much for the death as for ourselves.

LYNN CAINE, *Widow*, 1974.

13 One grey curiously cool afternoon a week later Jesus Fever died. It was as if someone had been

tickling his ribs, for he died in a spasm of desperate giggles. "Maybe," as Zoo said, "God done told somethin funny."

TRUMAN CAPOTE, *Other Voices, Other Rooms,* 1948.

14 Because I could not stop for Death,
 He kindly stopped for me;
 The Carriage held but just Ourselves
 And Immortality.

EMILY DICKINSON, "The Chariot," *Poems,* 1890.

15 This quiet Dust was Gentlemen and Ladies,
  And Lads and Girls
 Was Laughter and Ability and Sighing
  And Frocks and Curls.

EMILY DICKINSON, "This Quiet-Dust," published in *The Single Hound,* 1914.

16 This is the hour of lead
 Remembered if outlived
 As freezing persons recollect
 The snow—
 First chill, then stupor, then
 The letting go.

EMILY DICKINSON, "After Great Pain," in *Further Poems,* 1929.

17 The world feels dusty
 When we stop to die;
 We want the dew then,
 Honors taste dry.

EMILY DICKINSON, "The world feels dusty," *Further Poems,* 1929.

18 The bodies of those that made such a noise and tumult when alive, when dead, lie as quietly among the graves of their neighbors as any others.

JONATHAN EDWARDS, *Procrastination,* c.1740.

19 April is the cruellest month, breeding
 Lilacs out of the dead land, mixing
 Memory and desire, stirring
 Dull roots with spring rain.

T.S. ELIOT, *The Waste Land,* 1922.

20 Funeral eloquence
 Rattles the coffin-lid.

RALPH WALDO EMERSON, "Ode Inscribed to W.H. Channing," in *Poems,* 1847.

21 Turn the key and bolt the door,
 Sweet is death forevermore.

RALPH WALDO EMERSON, "The Past," 1867.

22 Down in de cornfield
 Hear dat mournful sound!
 All de darkies am a weeping
 Massa's in de cold, cold ground.

STEPHEN FOSTER, "Massa's in de Cold, Cold Ground," 1852.

23 Gone are the days when my heart was young
  and gay,
 Gone are my friends from the cotton fields
  away,
 Gone from the earth to a better land I know.

STEPHEN FOSTER, "Old Black Joe," 1860.

24 When Death puts out our Flame, the Snuff
  will tell,
 If we are Wax, or Tallow, by the Smell.

BENJAMIN FRANKLIN, *Poor Richard's Almanack,* 1739.

25 9 Men in 10 are suicides.

BENJAMIN FRANKLIN, *Poor Richard's Almanack,* 1749.

26 Death? Why this fuss about death. Use your imagination, try to visualize a world *without* death!

CHARLOTTE PERKINS GILMAN, *The Living of Charlotte Perkins Gilman,* 1935.

27 And isn't it funny, she thought, that it takes two generations to kill off a man? . . . First him, and then his memory.

SHIRLEY ANNE GRAU, "Margaret," *The Keepers of the House,* 1964.

28 And I hear from the outgoing ship in the bay
  The song of the sailors in glee:
 So I think of the luminous footprints that
   bore
   The comfort o'er dark Galilee,
 And wait for the signal to go to the shore,
  To the ship that is waiting for me.

BRET HARTE, "The Two Ships," collected in *The Writings of Bret Harte,* 1896.

29 We sometimes congratulate ourselves at the moment of waking from a troubled dream; it may be so the moment after death.

> NATHANIEL HAWTHORNE, journal entry, October 25, 1835.

30 Of all the events which constitute a person's biography, there is scarcely one—none, certainly, of anything like a similar importance—to which the world so easily reconciles itself as to his death.

> NATHANIEL HAWTHORNE, *The House of the Seven Gables,* 1851.

31 Oh, nobody knows when de Lord is goin ter call, *Roll dem bones.*
It may be in de Winter time, and maybe in de Fall, *Roll dem bones.*
But yer got ter leabe yer baby and yer home an all—*So roll dem bones.*

> DUBOSE HEYWARD, "Gamesters All," in *Carolina Chansons,* 1922.

32 Behold—not him we knew!
This was the prison which his soul looked through.

> OLIVER WENDELL HOLMES, SR., "The Last Look," 1858.

33 There are three wicks you know to the lamp of a man's life: brain, blood, and breath. Press the brain a little, its light goes out, followed by both the others. Stop the heart a minute, and out go all three of the wicks. Choke the air out of the lungs, and presently the fluid ceases to supply the other centers of flame, and all is soon stagnation, cold, and darkness.

> OLIVER WENDELL HOLMES, SR., *The Professor at the Breakfast-Table,* 1860.

34 Fast as the rolling seasons bring
The hour of fate to those we love,
Each pearl that leaves the broken string
Is set in Friendship's crown above.
As narrower grows the earthly chain,
The circle widens in the sky;
These are our treasures that remain,
But those are stars that beam on high.

> OLIVER WENDELL HOLMES, SR., "F.W.C.," 1864.

35 Whom the gods love die young no matter how long they live.

> ELBERT HUBBARD, in *The Philistine* magazine, published from 1895–1915.

36 Who can look down upon the grave even of an enemy, and not feel a compunctious throb, that he should ever have warred with the poor handful of earth that lies mouldering before him.

> WASHINGTON IRVING, *The Sketch-Book,* 1819–1820.

37 Man passes away; his name perishes from record and recollection; his history is as a tale that is told, and his very monument becomes a ruin.

> Ibid.

38 When death comes, he respects neither age nor merit. He sweeps from this earthly existence the sick and the strong, the rich and the poor.

> ANDREW JACKSON, in a letter, December 12, 1824.

39 Oh, write of me, not "Died in bitter pains,"
But "Emigrated to another star!"

> HELEN HUNT JACKSON, "Emigravit," collected in Edmund Clarence Stedman, *An American Anthology,* 1906.

40 Thomas Carlyle is incontestably dead at last, by the acknowledgment of all newspapers. I had, however, the pleasure of an intimate intercourse with him when he was an infinitely deader man than he is now.

> HENRY JAMES, SR., in the *Atlantic Monthly,* May, 1881.

41 The strong lean upon death as on a rock.

> ROBINSON JEFFERS, "Gale in April," 1930.

42 I agree with you entirely in condemning the mania of giving names to objects of any kind after persons still living. Death alone can seal the title of any man to this honor, by putting it out of his power to forfeit it.

> THOMAS JEFFERSON, in a letter to Benjamin Rush, September 23, 1800.

43 There is a fulness of time when men should go, and not occupy too long the ground to which others have a right to advance.

> THOMAS JEFFERSON, in a letter to Benjamin Rush, August 17, 1811.

44 The dead have no rights. They are nothing; and nothing cannot own something.

> THOMAS JEFFERSON, in a letter to Samuel Kercheval, July 12, 1816.

45 I enjoy good health: I am happy in what is around me, yet I assure you I am ripe for leaving all, this year, this day, this hour.

> THOMAS JEFFERSON, in a letter to John Adams, August 1, 1816.

46 It is of some comfort to us both that the term is not very distant at which we are to deposit in the same cerement our sorrows and suffering bodies, and to ascend in essence to an ecstatic meeting with the friends we have loved and lost, and whom we shall still love and never lose again.

> THOMAS JEFFERSON, in a letter to John Adams, November 13, 1818.

47 And God said, Go down, Death, go down;
Go down to Savannah, Georgia,
Down to Yamacraw,
And find Sister Caroline.
She's borne the burden and the heat of the
    day,
She's labored long in my vineyard,
And she's tired—
She's weary—
Go down, Death, and bring her to me.

> JAMES WELDON JOHNSON, "Go Down, Death," published in the *American Mercury* magazine, April, 1927.

48 There is a Reaper whose name is Death,
    And, with his sickle keen,
He reaps the bearded grain at a breath,
    And the flowers that grow between.

> HENRY WADSWORTH LONGFELLOW, "The Reaper and the Flowers," *Voices of the Night,* 1839.

49 Oh, not in cruelty, not in wrath,
    The Reaper came that day;
'Twas an angel visited the green earth,
    And took the flowers away.

> Ibid.

50 And, as she looked around, she saw how
        Death, the consoler,
Laying his hand upon many a heart, had
        healed it forever.

> HENRY WADSWORTH LONGFELLOW, *Evangeline,* 1847.

51 There is no flock, however watched and
        tended,
    But one dead lamb is there!
There is no fireside howsoe'er defended,
    But has one vacant chair.

> HENRY WADSWORTH LONGFELLOW, "Resignation," in *The Seaside and the Fireside,* 1849.

52 There is no Death! What seems so is
        transition;
    This life of mortal breath
Is but a suburb of the life elysian,
    Whose portal we call Death.

> Ibid.

53   Time has laid his hand
Upon my heart, gently, not smiting it,
But as a harper lays his open palm
Upon his harp, to deaden its vibrations.

> HENRY WADSWORTH LONGFELLOW, "The Cloisters," *The Golden Legend,* 1851.

54 The young may die, but the old must!

> Ibid.

55 The grave itself is but a covered bridge
Leading from light to light, through a brief
        darkness!

> HENRY WADSWORTH LONGFELLOW, "A Covered Bridge at Lucerne," *The Golden Legend,* 1851.

56 There is no confessor like unto Death!
Thou canst not see him, but he is near:
Thou needst not whisper above thy breath,
And he will hear.

HENRY WADSWORTH LONGFELLOW, "The Inn at Genoa," *The Golden Legend,* 1851.

57 Death never takes one alone, but two!
Whenever he enters in at a door,
Under roof of gold or roof of thatch,
He always leaves it upon the latch,
And comes again ere the year is o'er
Never one of a household only!

HENRY WADSWORTH LONGFELLOW, "The Farm-House in the Odenwald," *The Golden Legend,* 1851.

58 So Nature deals with us, and takes away
Our playthings one by one, and by the
hand
Leads us to rest so gently, that we go
Scarce knowing if we wish to go or stay,
Being too full of sleep to understand
How far the unknown transcends the
what we know.

HENRY WADSWORTH LONGFELLOW, "Nature," in *The Masque of Pandora and Other Poems,* 1876.

59 We bargain for the graves we lie in.

JAMES RUSSELL LOWELL, *The Vision of Sir Launfal,* 1848.

60 In what eternal, unstirring paralysis, and deadly, hopeless trance, yet lies antique Adam who died sixty round centuries ago?

HERMAN MELVILLE, *Moby-Dick,* 1851.

61 Death, however,
Is a spongy wall,
Is a sticky river,
Is nothing at all.

EDNA ST. VINCENT MILLAY, "Moriturus," in *The Buck in the Snow and Other Poems,* 1928.

62 I shall die, but that is all that I shall do for Death; I am not on his pay-roll. . . . Am I a spy in the land of the living, that I should deliver men to Death?

EDNA ST. VINCENT MILLAY, "Conscientious Objector," written in 1917, published in *Wine from These Grapes,* 1934.

63 At end of Love, at end of Life,
At end of Hope, at end of Strife,
At end of all we cling to so—
The sun is setting—must we go?
At dawn of Love, at dawn of Life,
At dawn of Peace that follows Strife,
At dawn of all we long for so—
The sun is rising—let us go.

LOUISE CHANDLER MOULTON, "At End," *Poems and Sonnets,* 1909.

64 On fame's eternal camping-ground
Their silent tents are spread,
And glory guards, with solemn round,
The bivouac of the dead.

THEODORE O'HARA, "The Bivouac of the Dead," 1847.

65 All victory ends in the defeat of death. That's sure. But does defeat end in the victory of death? That's what I wonder!

EUGENE O'NEILL, *Mourning Becomes Electra,* 1931.

66 Guns aren't lawful;
Nooses give;
Gas smells awful;
You might as well live.

DOROTHY PARKER, "Résumé," *Enough Rope,* 1927.

67 Dying
Is an art, like everything else.
I do it exceptionally well.
I do it so it feels like hell,
I do it so it feels real.
I guess you could say I've a call.

SYLVIA PLATH, "Lady Lazarus," *Ariel,* 1961.

68 Out—out are the lights—out all!
And, over each quivering form,
The curtain, a funeral pall,
Comes down with the rush of a storm,
And the angels, all pallid and wan,
Uprising, unveiling, affirm
That the play is the tragedy, "Man," And its
hero the Conqueror Worm.

EDGAR ALLAN POE, "The Conqueror Worm," published in *Graham's Magazine,* March, 1843.

69 Take thy beak from out my heart, and take
      thy form from off my door!
  Quoth the Raven, "Nevermore."

    EDGAR ALLAN POE, "The Raven," 1845.

70 Thank Heaven! the crisis,
    The danger, is past,
  And the lingering illness
    Is over at last—
  And the fever called "Living"
    Is conquered at last.

    EDGAR ALLAN POE, "For Annie," 1849.

71 It's all a world where bugs and emperors
  Go singularly back to the same dust.

    EDWIN ARLINGTON ROBINSON, "Ben Jonson
    Entertains a Man from Stratford," *The Man
    Against the Sky,* 1916.

72 I shall have more to say when I am dead.

    EDWIN ARLINGTON ROBINSON, "John Brown,"
    in *The Three Taverns,* 1920.

73 When you cease to make a contribution you
begin to die.

    ELEANOR ROOSEVELT, in a letter, February 19,
    1960, quoted in Joseph P. Lash, *Eleanor: The
    Years Alone,* 1972.

74 Pile the bodies high at Austerlitz and
      Waterloo.
  Shovel them under and let me work—
  I am the grass; I cover all.

    CARL SANDBURG, "Grass," *Cornhuskers,*
    1918.

75 For a man who has done his natural duty, death
is as natural and welcome as sleep.

    Attributed to George Santayana.

76 I have a rendezvous with Death
  At some disputed barricade,
  When Spring comes round with rustling
      shade
  And apple blossoms fill the air.

    ALAN SEEGER, "I Have a Rendezvous with
    Death," published in the *North American
    Review,* October, 1916.

77 Death is the mother of beauty; hence from
    her
  Alone shall come fulfillment to our dreams.

    WALLACE STEVENS, "Sunday Morning,"
    Harmonium, 1923.

78 Judge Gary never saw a blast furnace until after
his death.

    BENJAMIN STOLBERG, *The Story of the
    CIO,* 1938. (Elbert H. Gary, 1846–1927, a
    lawyer, was the chairman of United States Steel.)

79 There is no death to such as thou, dear Eva!
neither darkness nor shadow of death; only such a
bright fading as when the morning star fades in the
golden dawn.

    HARRIET BEECHER STOWE, *Uncle Tom's Cabin,*
    1852.

80 The bitterest tears shed over graves are for
words left unsaid and deeds left undone.

    HARRIET BEECHER STOWE, *Little Foxes,* a
    collection of her essays, 1865.

81 Whoever has lived long enough to find out what
life is, knows how deep a debt of gratitude we owe
to Adam, the first great benefactor of our race. He
brought death into the world.

    MARK TWAIN, "Pudd'nhead Wilson's Calendar,"
    Pudd'nhead Wilson, 1894.

82 Each person is born to one possession which
outvalues all the others—his last breath.

    Ibid.

83 The report of my death was an exaggeration.

    MARK TWAIN, in a cable from London to the
    Associated Press, June 2, 1897.

84 Those corpses of young men,
  Those martyrs that hang from the gibbets,
      those hearts pierc'd by the gray lead,
  Cold and motionless as they seem, live
      elsewhere with unslaughter'd vitality.

    WALT WHITMAN, "Europe," written in 1850,
    published in the first edition of *Leaves of Grass,*
    1855.

85 All goes onward and outward, nothing
    collapses,

And to die is different from what any one
    supposed, and luckier.

> WALT WHITMAN, "Song of Myself,"
> 1855.

86 Has any one supposed it lucky to be born?
    I hasten to inform him or her it is just as
        lucky to die, and I know it.

> Ibid.

87 The dull nights go over and the dull days
        also,
    The soreness of lying so much in bed goes
        over,
    The physician after long putting off gives
        silent and terrible look for an answer,
    The children come hurried and weeping, and
        the brothers and sisters are sent for.

> WALT WHITMAN, "To Think of Time,"
> 1855.

88 And I will show that there is no imperfection
        in the present, and can be none in the
        future,
    And I will show that whatever happens to
        anybody it may be turn'd to beautiful
        results,
    And I will show that nothing can happen
        more beautiful than death.

> WALT WHITMAN, "Starting from Paumanok,"
> 1860.

89 Come lovely and soothing death,
    Undulate round the world, serenely arriving,
        arriving,
    In the day, in the night, to all, to each,
    Sooner or later delicate death.

> WALT WHITMAN, "When Lilacs Last in the
> Dooryard Bloom'd," first published in *Sequel to
> Drum-Taps,* 1865–1866.

90 Prais'd be the fathomless universe,
    For life and joy, and for objects and
        knowledge curious,
    And for love, sweet love—but praise! praise!
        praise!
    For the sure-enwinding arms of
        cool-enfolding death.

> Ibid.

91 Joy, shipmate, joy!
    (Pleas'd to my soul at death I cry,)
    Our life is closed, our life begins,
    The long, long anchorage we leave,
    The ship is clear at last, she leaps!
    She swiftly courses from the shore,
    Joy, shipmate, joy.

> WALT WHITMAN, "Joy, Shipmate, Joy,"
> 1871.

92 Death softens all resentments, and the conscious of a common inheritance of frailty and weakness modifies the severity of judgment.

> JOHN GREENLEAF WHITTIER, note, *Ichabod,*
> 1850.

93 Henceforward, listen as we will,
    The voices of that hearth are still;
    Look where we may, the wide earth o'er
        Those lighted faces smile no more. . . .
    We turn the pages that they read,
        Their written words we linger o'er,
    But in the sun they cast no shade,
    No voice is heard, no sign is made,
        No step is on the conscious floor!
    Yet Love will dream, and Faith will trust
        (Since He who knows our need is just)
    That somehow, somewhere, meet we must.

> JOHN GREENLEAF WHITTIER, "Snow-Bound,"
> 1866.

94 I am the Dark Cavalier; I am the Last
        Lover:
    My arms shall welcome you when other arms
        are tired.

> MARGARET WIDDEMER, "The Dark Cavalier,"
> 1958.

95 Death observes no ceremony.

> JOHN WISE, *A Vindication of the Government of
> New England Churches,* 1717.

64. DEBT

See also BUSINESS; ECONOMICS; MONEY;
POVERTY; WEALTH

1 We are opposed to the issuing of interest-bearing bonds of the United States in time of peace.

> Plank in the Democratic Party national platform, 1896.

2 We oppose cancellation of the debts owing to the United States by foreign nations.

> Plank in the Democratic Party national platform, 1932.

3 Public credit means the contracting of debts which a nation never can pay.

> WILLIAM COBBETT, in *Advice to Young Men*, 1829.

4 Well, they hired the money, didn't they?

> CALVIN COOLIDGE, to Myron T. Herrick, U.S. ambassador to France, after Herrick proposed a generous restructuring of the French war debt, 1925.

5 Always pay; for first or last you must pay your entire debt.

> RALPH WALDO EMERSON, "Compensation," *Essays,* First Series, 1841.

6 A man in debt is so far a slave.

> RALPH WALDO EMERSON, "Wealth," *The Conduct of Life,* 1860.

7 Rather go to Bed supperless than rise in Debt.

> BENJAMIN FRANKLIN, *Poor Richard's Almanack,* 1758.

8 The second Vice is Lying, the first is running in Debt.

> Ibid.

9 A national debt, if it is not excessive, will be to us a national blessing.

> ALEXANDER HAMILTON, in a letter to Robert Morris, April 30, 1781.

10 If a national debt is considered a national blessing, then we can get on by borrowing. But as I believe it is a national curse, my vow shall be to pay the national debt.

> ANDREW JACKSON, in a letter dated July 4, 1824.

11 What is to hinder them [government officials] from creating a perpetual debt? The laws of nature, I answer. The earth belongs to the living, not to the dead. The will and the power of man expire with his life, by nature's law. . . . We may consider each generation as a distinct nation, with a right, by the will of its majority, to bind themselves, but none to bind the succeeding generation, more than the inhabitants of another country.

> THOMAS JEFFERSON, in a letter to John W. Eppes, June 24, 1813.

12 I sincerely believe . . . that banking establishments are more dangerous than standing armies, and that the principle of spending money to be paid by posterity, under the name of funding, is but swindling futurity on a large scale.

> THOMAS JEFFERSON, in a letter to John Taylor, May 28, 1816.

13 The debt we may contract doth not deserve our regard if the work be but accomplished. No nation ought to be without a debt. A national debt is a national bond; and when it bears no interest, is in no case a grievance.

> THOMAS PAINE, quoted in Howard Fast, *The Selected Work of Tom Paine,* 1943.

14 Any government, like any family, can for a year spend a little more than it earns. But you and I know that a continuance of that habit means the poorhouse.

> FRANKLIN D. ROOSEVELT, in a radio speech, July 30, 1932.

15 Let us have the courage to stop borrowing to meet continuing deficits. Stop the deficits.

> Ibid.

16 Solvency is entirely a matter of temperament and not of income.

> LOGAN PEARSALL SMITH, *Afterthoughts,* 1931.

17 As a very important source of strength and security, cherish public credit. One method of preserving it is to use it as sparingly as possible.

GEORGE WASHINGTON, in his Farewell Address, September 17, 1796.

65. DELAWARE

1 Liberty and independence.

State motto.

2 Know the mold—and you will understand the people of the state. Hardheaded with money. Courteous, to minimum requirements, with no urban frills. Completely self-sufficient in private living. Fine judges of good food and drink—in the castles of their own homes, which accounts for the indifferent public eating places throughout the state to this day. Honest at heart—but watch yourself carefully in all business transactions, for Delawareans are, of ancient times, close traders. Comfortably cynical in all basic philosophy. And utterly unchangeable, come hell, high water, the Du Pont overlordship, or thermonuclear reaction.

JAMES WARNER BELLAH, "Delaware," *American Panorama: East of the Mississippi,* 1960.

3 Delaware has fought and bucked, hated, reviled, admired and fawned upon, ignored and courted the Du Ponts, but in the end, it has invariably bowed to Du Pont's benevolent paternalism.

Ibid.

4 A state that has three counties when the tide is out, and two when it is in.

JOHN JAMES INGALLS, in a speech in the U.S. Senate, c.1885.

5 Delaware will probably remain what it ever has been, a mere county of England, conquered indeed, and held under by force, but always disposed to counter-revolution.

THOMAS JEFFERSON, in a letter to Barnabas Bidwell, July 5, 1806.

6 Delaware is like a diamond, diminutive, but having within it inherent value.

JOHN LOFLAND, 1847, quoted in Federal Writers' Project, *Delaware: A Guide to the First State,* 1938.

66. DEMOCRACY

See also CONSTITUTION; ELECTIONS; GOVERNMENT; POLITICS

1 When annual elections end, there slavery begins.

JOHN ADAMS, *Thoughts on Government,* 1776.

2 The declaration that our People are hostile to a government made by themselves, for themselves, and conducted by themselves, is an insult.

JOHN ADAMS, to the citizens of Westmoreland County, Virginia, 1798.

3 Democracy has given to conscience absolute liberty.

GEORGE BANCROFT, in an address published in the *Boston Post,* October 6, 1835.

4 Vote, *n.* The instrument and symbol of a freeman's power to make a fool of himself and a wreck of his country.

AMBROSE BIERCE, *The Devil's Dictionary,* 1906.

5 The humblest citizen in all the land, when clad in the armor of a righteous cause, is stronger than all the hosts of error.

WILLIAM JENNINGS BRYAN, in his "Cross of Gold" speech at the Democratic National Convention, Chicago, July 8, 1896.

6 There is a sense in which it is true that the people are wiser than the wisest man. But what is true of their ultimate judgment after the lapse of time sufficient for full discussion, is not equally true of decisions that have to be promptly taken.

JAMES BRYCE, *The American Commonwealth,* 1888.

7 No one not apathetic to the value issues of the day . . . can in good conscience contribute to the ascendancy of ideas he considers destructive of the best in civilization. To do so is to be guilty of supine and unthinking fatalism of the sort that is the surest poison of democracy and the final abnegation of man's autonomy.

> WILLIAM F. BUCKLEY, JR., *God and Man at Yale,* 1951.

8 The Ship of Democracy, which has weathered all storms, may sink through the mutiny of those on board.

> GROVER CLEVELAND, in a letter to Wilson S. Bissell, February 15, 1894.

9 If our democracy is to flourish, it must have criticism; if our government is to function it must have dissent.

> HENRY STEELE COMMAGER, *Freedom, Loyalty, Dissent,* 1954.

10 A monarchy is like a man-of-war—bad shots between wind and water hurt it exceedingly; there is danger of capsizing. But democracy is a raft. You cannot easily overturn it. It is a wet place, but it is a pretty safe one.

> JOSEPH COOK, *Labor,* 1879.

11 The governments of the past could fairly be characterized as devices for maintaining in perpetuity the place and position of certain privileged classes, without any ultimate protection for the rights of the people. The Government of the United States is a device for maintaining in perpetuity the rights of the people, with the ultimate extinction of all privileged classes.

> CALVIN COOLIDGE, in a speech in Philadelphia, September 25, 1924.

12 The tendency of democracies is, in all things, to mediocrity.

> JAMES FENIMORE COOPER, *The American Democrat,* 1838.

13 It is as unjust to require that men of refinement and training should defer in their habits and associations to the notions of those who are their inferiors in these particulars, as it is to insist that

political power should be the accompaniment of birth.

> Ibid.

14 The American doctrinaire is the converse of the American demagogue, and, in his way, is scarcely less injurious to the public. The first deals in poetry, the last in cant.

> Ibid.

15 The principal advantage of a democracy, is a general elevation in the character of the people.

> Ibid.

16 All that democracy means is as equal a participation in rights as is practicable.

> Ibid.

17 It is a besetting vice of democracies to substitute public opinion for law. This is the usual form in which masses of men exhibit their tyranny.

> Ibid.

18 Democracy, I do not conceive that ever God did ordain as a fit government either for church or commonwealth. If the people be governors, who shall be governed? As for monarchy, and aristocracy, they are both of them clearly approved, and directed in Scripture, yet so as referreth the sovereignty to Himself, and setteth theocracy in both, as the best form of government in the commonwealth, as well as in the church.

> JOHN COTTON, *The Bloudy Tenent Washed and Made White in the Bloud of the Lamb,* 1647.

19 Democracy is on trial in the world, on a more colossal scale than every before.

> CHARLES FLETCHER DOLE, *The Spirit of Democracy,* 1906.

20 A vigorous democracy—a democracy in which there are freedom from want, freedom from fear, freedom of religion, and freedom of speech—would never succumb to communism or any other ism.

> HELEN GAHAGAN DOUGLAS, in a speech in Congress on March 26, 1946, in *A Full Life,* 1982.

21 As men and women of character and of faith in the soundness of democratic methods, we must work like dogs to justify that faith.

> DWIGHT D. EISENHOWER, in a letter to Mamie Doud Eisenhower, September 15, 1942.

22 Democracy is morose, and runs to anarchy.

> RALPH WALDO EMERSON, "Nominalist and Realist," *Essays,* Second Series, 1844.

23 Democracy becomes a government of bullies tempered by editors.

> RALPH WALDO EMERSON, entry written in 1847, *Journals,* 1909–1914.

24 In every society some men are born to rule, and some to advise.

> RALPH WALDO EMERSON, "The Young American," *Addresses and Lectures,* 1849.

25 The democrat is a young conservative; the conservative is an old democrat. The aristocrat is the democrat ripe and gone to seed.

> RALPH WALDO EMERSON, "Napoleon," *Representative Men,* 1850.

26 Shall we judge a country by the majority, or by the minority? By the minority, surely.

> RALPH WALDO EMERSON, "Considerations by the Way," *The Conduct of Life,* 1860.

27 The price of democratic survival in a world of aggressive totalitarianism is to give up some of the democratic luxuries of the past.

> J. WILLIAM FULBRIGHT, "American Foreign Policy in the 20th Century Under an 18th-Century Constitution," *Cornell Law Quarterly,* Fall, 1961.

28 We are inclined to confuse freedom and democracy, which we regard as moral principles, with the way in which they are practiced in America—with capitalism, federalism, and the two-party system, which are not moral principles but simply the preferred and accepted practices of the American peoples.

> J. WILLIAM FULBRIGHT, *Old Myths and New Realities,* 1964.

29 To put political power in the hands of men embittered and degraded by poverty is to tie fire-brands to foxes and turn them loose amid the standing corn.

> HENRY GEORGE, *Progress and Poverty,* 1879.

30 The evils we experience flow from the excess of democracy. The people do not want virtue, but are the dupes of pretended patriots.

> ELBRIDGE GERRY, in a speech at the Constitutional Convention, 1787.

31 The voice of the people has been said to be the voice of God; and, however generally this maxim has been quoted and believed, it is not true to fact. The people are turbulent and changing; they seldom judge or determine right.

> ALEXANDER HAMILTON, in a speech at the Constitutional Convention, June 18, 1787.

32 It is of great importance in a republic not only to guard against the oppression of its rulers, but to guard one part of society against the injustice of the other part.

> ALEXANDER HAMILTON, *The Federalist,* 1787–1788.

33 It has been observed that a pure democracy, if it were practicable, would be the most perfect government. Experience has proved that no position is more false than this. The ancient democracies, in which the people themselves deliberated, never possessed one feature of good government. Their very character was tyranny; their figure deformity.

> ALEXANDER HAMILTON, in a speech in Congress, June 21, 1788.

34 Democracy, it must be emphasized, is a practical necessity and not just a philosophic value.

> MICHAEL HARRINGTON, *Toward a Democratic Left,* 1968.

35 In contrast to totalitarianism, democracy can face and live with the truth about itself.

> SIDNEY HOOK, in the *New York Times Magazine,* September 30, 1951.

36 I swear to the Lord
  I still can't see
 Why Democracy means
  Everybody but me.

LANGSTON HUGHES, "The Black Man Speaks," in *Jim Crow's Last Stand,* 1943.

37 The death of democracy is not likely to be an assassination from ambush. It will be a slow extinction from apathy, indifference, and undernourishment.

ROBERT M. HUTCHINS, *Great Books,* 1954.

38 The animosities of sovereigns are temporary and may be allayed; but those which seize the whole body of a people, and of a people, too, who dictate their own measures, produce calamities of long duration.

THOMAS JEFFERSON, in a letter to Charles William Frederick Dumas, May 6, 1786.

39 If any of our countrymen wish for a king, give them Aesop's fable of the frogs who asked a king; if this does not cure them, send them to Europe. They will go back good republicans.

THOMAS JEFFERSON, in a letter to Dr. David Ramsay, August 4, 1787.

40 [The people] are the only sure reliance for the preservation of our liberty.

THOMAS JEFFERSON, in a letter to James Madison, December 20, 1787.

41 Every government degenerates when trusted to the rulers of the people alone. The people themselves therefore are its only safe depositories.

THOMAS JEFFERSON, in a letter to Abbé Arnoud, July 19, 1789.

42 The republican is the only form of government which is not eternally at open or secret war with the rights of mankind.

THOMAS JEFFERSON, in a letter to William Hunter, March 11, 1790.

43 Some honest men fear that a republican government can not be strong, that this government is not strong enough; but would the honest patriot, in the full tide of successful experiment, abandon a government which has so far kept us free and firm, on the theoretic and visionary fear that this government, the world's best hope, may by possibility want energy to preserve itself?

THOMAS JEFFERSON, in his first inaugural address, March 4, 1801.

44 Sometimes it is said that man cannot be trusted with the government of himself. Can he, then, be trusted with the government of others? Or have we found angels in the forms of kings to govern him? Let history answer this question.

Ibid.

45 A republican government is slow to move, yet when once in motion, its momentum becomes irresistible.

THOMAS JEFFERSON, in a letter to Francis C. Gray, March 4, 1815.

46 I am not among those who fear the people. They, and not the rich, are our dependence for continued freedom.

THOMAS JEFFERSON, in a letter to Samuel Kercheval, July 12, 1816.

47 I know no safe depository of the ultimate powers of society but the people themselves; and if we think them not enlightened enough to exercise their control with a wholesome discretion, the remedy is not to take it from them, but to inform their discretion by education.

THOMAS JEFFERSON, in a letter to William C. Jarvis, September 28, 1820.

48 The constitutions of most of our States assert that all power is inherent in the people.

THOMAS JEFFERSON, in a letter to John Cartwright, June 5, 1824.

49 All eyes are opened or opening to the rights of man. The general spread of the light of science has already laid open to every view the palpable truth, that the mass of mankind has not been born with saddles on their backs, nor a favored few booted and spurred, ready to ride them legitimately, by the grace of God.

THOMAS JEFFERSON, in a letter to Roger C. Weightman, June 24, 1826.

50 Humble as I am, plebeian as I may be deemed, permit me in the presence of this brilliant assemblage to enunciate the truth that courts and cabi-

Virginia Declaration of Rights, June 12, 1776

An influential document in the history of the rights of man (it was widely read by revolutionary leaders in France), this declaration directly affected the drafting of the Declaration of Independence and the Bill of Rights. The Virginia Declaration was written chiefly by George Mason.

A Declaration of Rights made by the representatives of the good people of Virginia, assembled in full and free convention: which rights do pertain to them and their posterity, as the basis and foundation of government.

Section 1. That all men are by nature equally free and independent and have certain inherent rights, of which, when they enter into a state of society, they cannot, by any compact, deprive or divest their posterity; namely, the enjoyment of life and liberty, with the means of acquiring and possessing property, and pursuing and obtaining happiness and safety.

Section 2. That all power is vested in, and consequently derived from, the people, that magistrates are their trustees and servants and at all times amenable to them.

Section 3. That government is, or ought to be, instituted for the common benefit, protection, and security of the people, nation, or community; of all the various modes and forms of government, that is best which is capable of producing the greatest degree of happiness and safety and is most effectually secured against the danger of maladministration. And that, when any government shall be found inadequate or contrary to these purposes, a majority of the community has an indubitable, inalienable, and indefeasible right to reform, alter, or abolish it, in such manner as shall be judged most conducive to the public weal.

Section 4. That no man, or set of men, is entitled to exclusive or separate emoluments or privileges from the community, but in consideration of public services; which, not being descendible, neither ought the offices of magistrate, legislator, or judge to be hereditary.

Section 5. That the legislative and executive powers of the state should be separate and distinct from the judiciary; and that the members of the two first may be restrained from oppression, by feeling and participating the burdens of the people, they should, at fixed periods, be reduced to a private station, return into that body from which they were originally taken, and the vacancies be supplied by frequent, certain, and regular elections, in which all, or any part, of the former members, to be again eligible, or ineligible, as the laws shall direct.

Section 6. That elections of members to serve as representatives of the people, in assembly, ought to be free; and that all men, having sufficient evidence of permanent common interest with, and attachment to, the community, have the right of suffrage and cannot be taxed or deprived of their property for public uses without their own consent, or that of their representatives so elected, nor bound by any law to which they have not, in like manner, assembled for the public good.

Section 7. That all power of suspending laws, or the execution of laws, by any authority, without consent of the representatives of the people, is injurious to their rights and ought not to be exercised.

Section 8. That in all capital or criminal prosecutions a man has a right to demand the cause and nature of his accusation, to be confronted with the accusers and witnesses, to call for evidence in his favor, and to a speedy trial by an impartial jury of twelve men of his vicinage, without whose unanimous consent he cannot be found guilty; nor can he be compelled to give evidence against himself; that no man be deprived of his liberty except by the law of the land or the judgment of his peers.

Section 9. That excessive bail ought not to be required, nor excessive fines imposed, nor cruel and unusual punishments inflicted.

Section 10. That general warrants, whereby an officer or messenger may be commanded to search suspected places without evidence of a fact committed, or to seize any person or persons not named, or whose offense is not particularly described and supported by evidence, are grievous and oppressive and ought not to be granted.

Section 11. That in controversies respecting property, and in suits between man and man, the ancient trial by jury is preferable to any other and ought to be held sacred.

Section 12. That the freedom of the press is one of the great bulwarks of liberty and can never be restrained but by despotic governments.

Section 13. That a well-regulated militia, composed of the body of the people, trained to arms, is the proper, natural, and safe defense of a free state; that standing armies, in time of peace, should be avoided as dangerous to liberty; and that in all cases the military should be under strict subordination to, and governed by, the civil power.

Section 14. That the people have a right to uniform government; and, therefore, that no government separate from or independent of the government of Virginia ought to be erected or established within the limits thereof.

Section 15. That no free government, or the blessings of liberty, can be preserved to any people but by a firm adherence to justice, moderation, temperance, frugality, and virtue, and by frequent recurrence to fundamental principles.

Section 16. That religion, or the duty which we owe to our Creator, and the manner of discharging it, can be directed only by reason and conviction, not by force or violence; and therefore all men are equally entitled to the free exercise of religion, according to the dictates of conscience; and that it is the mutual duty of all to practise Christian forbearance, love, and charity toward each other.

---

nets, the President and his advisers, derive their power and their greatness from the people.

> ANDREW JOHNSON, speech on taking the oath of office for the vice presidency, March 4, 1865.

51 Those who bewail the loss of personal liberty have not learned one of the essentials of a democracy. They should know that no one has the personal liberty in a republic to do what the majority has properly declared shall not be done.

> WESLEY LIVSEY JONES, in a speech in the U.S. Senate, February 22, 1919.

52 The deadliest foe of democracy is not autocracy but liberty frenzied.

> OTTO KAHN, in a speech at the University of Wisconsin, January 14, 1918.

53 And so the chauvinists of all times and places go their appointed way: plucking the easy fruits, reaping the little triumphs of the day at the expense of someone else tomorrow, deluging in noise and filth anyone who gets in their way, dancing their reckless dance on the prospects for human progress, drawing the shadow of a great doubt over the validity of democratic institutions. And until peoples

learn to spot the fanning of mass emotions and the sowing of bitterness, suspicion, and intolerance as crimes in themselves—as perhaps the greatest disservice that can be done to the cause of popular government—this sort of thing will continue to occur.

> George F. Kennan, *American Diplomacy, 1900–1950,* 1951.

54 A democracy is peaceloving. It does not like to go to war. It is slow to rise to provocation. When it has once been provoked to the point where it must grasp the sword, it does not easily forgive its adversary for having produced this situation. The fact of the provocation then becomes itself the issue. Democracy fights in anger—it fights for the very reason that it was forced to go to war.

> Ibid.

55 It is surely a curious characteristic of democracy: this amazing ability to shift gears overnight in one's ideological attitudes, depending on whether one considers one's self at war or at peace. Day before yesterday, let us say, the issues at stake between ourselves and another power were not worth the life of a single American boy. Today, nothing else counts at all; our cause is holy; the cost is no consideration; violence must know no limitations short of unconditional surrender.

> Ibid.

56 We, the people, are the boss, and we will get the kind of political leadership, be it good or bad, that we demand and deserve.

> John F. Kennedy, *Profiles in Courage,* 1955.

57 Vietnam presumably taught us that the United States could not serve as the world's policeman; it should also have taught us the dangers of trying to be the world's midwife to democracy when the birth is scheduled to take place under conditions of guerrilla war.

> Jeane J. Kirkpatrick, "Dictatorship and Double Standards," *Commentary* magazine, November, 1979.

58 Although there is no instance of a revolutionary "socialist" or Communist society being democratized, right-wing autocracies do sometimes evolve into democracies—given time, propitious economic, social, and political circumstances, talented leaders, and a strong indigenous demand for representative government.

> Ibid.

59 Although most governments in the world are, as they always have been, autocracies of one kind or another, no idea holds greater sway in the mind of educated Americans than the belief that it is possible to democratize governments, anytime, anywhere, under any circumstances.

> Ibid.

60 On the whole, with scandalous exceptions, Democracy has given the ordinary worker more dignity than he ever had.

> Sinclair Lewis, *It Can't Happen Here,* 1935.

61 Cure the evils of Democracy by the evils of Fascism! Funny therapeutics! I've heard of their curing syphilis by giving the patient malaria, but I've never heard of their curing malaria by giving the patient syphilis.

> Ibid.

62 Democracy, which began by liberating man politically, has developed a dangerous tendency to enslave him through the tyranny of majorities and the deadly power of their opinion.

> Ludwig Lewisohn, *The Modern Drama,* 1915.

63 The ballot is stronger than the bullet.

> Abraham Lincoln, in a speech, May 19, 1856.

64 As I would not be a slave, so I would not be a master. This expresses my idea of democracy. Whatever differs from this, to the extent of the difference, is no democracy.

> Abraham Lincoln, fragment, written about August 1, 1858, quoted in Roy P. Basler, *The Collected Works of Abraham Lincoln,* 1953.

65 A majority held in restraint by constitutional checks and limitations, and always changing easily with deliberate changes of popular opinions and sentiments, is the only true sovereign of a free people.

ABRAHAM LINCOLN, in his first inaugural address, March 4, 1861.

66 It is now for them [the American people] to demonstrate to the world that those who can fairly carry an election can also suppress a rebellion; that ballots are the rightful and peaceful successors of bullets; and that when ballots have fairly and constitutionally decided, there can be no successful appeal back to bullets. . . . Such will be a great lesson of peace: teaching men that what they cannot take by an election, neither can they take it by war.

ABRAHAM LINCOLN, in a message to Congress in special session, July 4, 1861.

67 A democracy which fails to concentrate authority in an emergency inevitably falls into such confusion that the ground is prepared for the rise of a dictator.

WALTER LIPPMANN, in his column in the *New York Herald Tribune,* February 24, 1933.

68 There exists . . . some kind of rule which in a democratic society limits what the voters will stand for in the way of sacrifice for the public good—the public good which is not immediately, obviously, and directly to their own personal advantage.

WALTER LIPPMANN, in his column in the *New York Herald Tribune,* December 29, 1966.

69 Democracy gives every man
   The right to be his own oppressor.

JAMES RUSSELL LOWELL, *The Biglow Papers,* 1867.

70 Puritanism, believing itself quick with the seed of religious liberty, laid, without knowing it, the egg of democracy.

JAMES RUSSELL LOWELL, "New England Two Centuries Ago," *Among My Books,* 1870.

71 In a democracy the people meet and exercise the government in person; in a republic, they assemble and administer it by their representatives and agents. A democracy, consequently, will be confined to a small spot. A republic may be extended over a large region.

JAMES MADISON, *The Federalist,* No. 14, 1787–1788.

72 In a democracy such as ours military policy is dependent on public opinion.

GEORGE C. MARSHALL, in *Yank* magazine, January 28, 1943.

73 The government of the Union, then, is emphatically and truly a government of the people. In form and in substance it emanates from them. Its powers are granted by them, and are to be exercised directly on them and for their benefit.

JOHN MARSHALL, Supreme Court opinion, *McCulloch* v. *Maryland,* 1819.

74 The most popular man under a democracy is not the most democratic man, but the most despotic man. The common folk delight in the exactions of such a man. They like him to boss them. Their natural gait is the goosestep.

H.L. MENCKEN, *Prejudices,* Second Series, 1920.

75 Democracy is the theory that the common people know what they want, and deserve to get it good and hard.

H.L. MENCKEN, "Sententiae," in *The Vintage Mencken,* 1955.

76 Only a country that is rich and safe can afford to be a democracy, for democracy is the most expensive and nefarious kind of government ever heard of on earth.

H.L. MENCKEN, from his notebooks, in *Minority Report,* 1956.

77 Democracies are indeed slow to make war, but once embarked upon a martial venture are equally slow to make peace and reluctant to make a tolerable, rather than a vindictive, peace.

REINHOLD NIEBUHR, *The Structure of Nations and Empires,* 1959.

78 There is what I call the American idea. . . . This idea demands, as the proximate organization thereof, a democracy—that is, a government of all the people, by all the people, for all the people.

THEODORE PARKER, in a speech at Boston, May 29, 1850. (Parker used this phrase in several speeches and is thought to have inspired Abraham Lincoln's use of it in the Gettysburg Address.)

79 Democracy is direct self-government, over all the people, for all the people, by all the people.

> THEODORE PARKER, in a sermon delivered in Boston, Massachusetts, July 4, 1858.

80 One has the right to be wrong in a democracy.

> CLAUDE PEPPER, in the *Congressional Record,* May 27, 1946.

81 Is it, or is it not a fact, that the air of a democracy agrees better with mere talent than with genius?

> EDGAR ALLAN POE, *Marginalia,* 1844–1849.

82 A democratic form of government, a democratic way of life, presupposes free public education over a long period; it presupposes also an education for personal responsibility that too often is neglected.

> ELEANOR ROOSEVELT, "Let Us Have Faith in Democracy," Department of Agriculture *Land Policy Review,* January, 1942.

83 Not only our future economic soundness but the very soundness of our democratic institutions depends on the determination of our government to give employment to idle men. The people of America are in agreement in defending their liberties at any cost, and the first line of that defense lies in the protection of economic security.

> FRANKLIN D. ROOSEVELT, in a Fireside Chat, April 14, 1938.

84 Democracy can thrive only when it enlists the devotion of those whom Lincoln called the common people. Democracy can hold that devotion only when it adequately respects their dignity by so ordering society as to assure to the masses of men and women reasonable security and hope for themselves and for their children.

> FRANKLIN D. ROOSEVELT, in his acceptance speech at the Democratic National Convention in Chicago, Illinois, July 19, 1940.

85 The first requisite of a good citizen in this Republic of ours is that he shall be able and willing to pull his weight.

> THEODORE ROOSEVELT, in a speech in New York City, November 11, 1902.

86 Universal suffrage, to justify itself, must be based on universal service. It is only you and your kind who have the absolutely clear title to the management of the Republic.

> THEODORE ROOSEVELT, in a speech to the soldiers at Camp Upton, November 18, 1917.

87 You are very much afraid of dictators, and you arrived at a state of society in which every ward boss was a dictator, and in which every financier was in his way a dictator, and every man who represented big business was a dictator and they had no responsibility.

> GEORGE BERNARD SHAW, in an address before the Academy of Political Science, New York City, April 11, 1933.

88 I have spoken at . . . election meetings. I have heard all the cheers and heard the candidates talking, and . . . I have seen the profound feeling, and the older I get, the more I feel [campaigning] to be, as part of a government of the country, something entirely intolerable and disgraceful to human nature.

> Ibid.

89 We have nothing to fear in this country from a dictatorship. It cannot live here. We are not organized to carry it on. We have no desire for it.

> ALFRED E. SMITH, in a speech at Harvard University, June 22, 1933.

90 All the ills of democracy can be cured by more democracy.

> ALFRED E. SMITH, in a speech in Albany, New York, June 27, 1933.

91 Democracy appears to me potentially a higher form of political organization than any kind of dictatorship. But if it turns out that in America, which could afford a decent living for everyone, the comfortable majority is willing to condone the misery and abuse of a minority for an indefinite period, the exploitation by the majority becomes as repugnant as exploitation by an oligarchy, and democracy loses half its supposed superiority.

> BENJAMIN SPOCK, *Decent and Indecent,* 1968.

92 I hunted far enough to suspect that the Fathers of the Republic who wrote our Sacred Constitution of the United States not only did not, but did not want to, establish a democratic government.

> LINCOLN STEFFENS, *The Autobiography of Lincoln Steffens,* 1931.

93 The central tenet of statesmanship in a democracy is that unless the people understand it and participate in it, no long-term program can endure.

> ADLAI E. STEVENSON, in a speech at Newark, New Jersey, May 5, 1959.

94 There will never be a free and enlightened State until the State comes to recognize the individual as a higher and independent power, from which all its own power and authority are derived, and treats him accordingly.

> HENRY DAVID THOREAU, "Civil Disobedience," 1849.

95 Any man more right than his neighbors constitutes a majority of one.

> Ibid.

96 The health of a democratic society may be measured by the quality of functions performed by private citizens.

> ALEXIS DE TOCQUEVILLE, *Democracy in America,* 1835–1840.

97 I confess that in America I saw more than America; I sought there the image of democracy itself, with its inclinations, its character, its prejudices, and its passions, in order to learn what we have to fear or to hope from its progress.

> Ibid.

98 Americans acquire the habit of always considering themselves as standing alone, and they are apt to imagine that their whole destiny is in their own hands. Thus not only does democracy make every man forget his ancestors, but it hides his descendants, and separates his contemporaries from him; it throws him back upon himself alone, and threatens in the end to confine him entirely within the solitude of his own heart.

> Ibid.

99 The century on which we are entering can be and must be the century of the common man.

> HENRY A. WALLACE, in an address, May 8, 1942.

100 Universal suffrage could not long exist in a community where there was great inequality of property. The holders of estates would be obliged in such case either in some way to restrain the right of suffrage, or else such right of suffrage would ere long divide the property.

> DANIEL WEBSTER, in a speech in Boston, 1820.

101 The people's government made for the people, made by the people, and answerable to the people.

> DANIEL WEBSTER, in a speech in the U.S. Senate, January 26, 1830.

102 Democracy is the recurrent suspicion that more than half of the people are right more than half of the time.

> E.B. WHITE, *The Wild Flag,* 1946.

103 I speak the pass-word primeval, I give the
        sign of democracy,
    By God! I will accept nothing which all
        cannot have their counterpart of on the
        same terms.

> WALT WHITMAN, "Song of Myself," 1855.

104 Where the populace rise at once against the
        never-ending audacity of elected
        persons.

> WALT WHITMAN, "Song of the Broad-Axe," 1856.

105 I say that democracy can never prove itself beyond cavil until it founds and luxuriantly grows its own forms of art, poems, schools, theology, displacing all that exists, or that has been produced anywhere in the past, under opposite influences.

> WALT WHITMAN, *Democratic Vistas,* 1870.

106 Democracy most of all affiliates with the open air, is sunny and hardy and sane only with Nature—just as much as Art is. Something is required to temper both—to check them, restrain them from excess, morbidity.

WALT WHITMAN, "Nature and Democracy-Morality," *Specimen Days and Collect*, 1882.

107 I believe in Democracy because it releases the energies of every human being.

WOODROW WILSON, in a speech in New York City, September 4, 1912.

108 The beauty of a democracy is that you never can tell when a youngster is born what he is going to do with himself, and that no matter how humbly he is born, no matter where he is born, no matter what circumstances hamper him at the outset, he has got a chance to master the minds and lead the imaginations of the whole country.

WOODROW WILSON, in a speech to the Chamber of Commerce in Columbus, Ohio, December 10, 1915.

109 I am all kinds of a democrat, so far as I can discover—but the root of the whole business is this, that I believe in the patriotism and energy and initiative of the average man.

WOODROW WILSON, in a speech in Philadelphia, June 29, 1916.

67. DESTINY

See also FATE

1 Destiny is not a matter of chance, it is a matter of choice; it is not a thing to be waited for, it is a thing to be achieved.

WILLIAM JENNINGS BRYAN, in a speech in Washington, D.C., February 22, 1899.

2 Alas! that one is born in blight,
Victim of perpetual slight, . . .
And another is born
To make the sun forgotten.

RALPH WALDO EMERSON, "Destiny," in *Poems*, 1847.

3 The world is mathematical, and has no casualty, in all its vast and flowing curve. Success has no more eccentricity than the gingham and muslin we weave in our mills.

RALPH WALDO EMERSON, "Power," *The Conduct of Life*, 1860.

4 There is no chance, and no anarchy, in the universe. All is system and gradation. Every god is there sitting in his sphere.

RALPH WALDO EMERSON, "Illusions," *The Conduct of Life*, 1860.

5 The thirst for adventure is the vent which Destiny offers; a war, a crusade, a gold mine, a new country, speak to the imagination and offer swing and play to the confined powers.

RALPH WALDO EMERSON, "Boston," *Natural History of Intellect*, 1893.

6 This nation, this generation, in this hour has man's first chance to build a Great Society, a place where the meaning of man's life matches the marvels of man's labor.

LYNDON B. JOHNSON, in his acceptance speech at the Democratic Party National Convention, August, 1964.

7 Every man meets his Waterloo at last.

WENDELL PHILLIPS, in a speech on November 1, 1859.

8 There is a mysterious cycle in human events. To some generations much is given. Of others much is expected. This generation of Americans has a rendezvous with destiny.

FRANKLIN D. ROOSEVELT, in his acceptance speech at the Democratic Party National Convention, June, 1936.

9 The longest day must have its close—the gloomiest night will wear on to a morning. An eternal, inexorable lapse of moments is ever hurrying the day of the evil to an eternal night, and the night of the just to an eternal day.

HARRIET BEECHER STOWE, *Uncle Tom's Cabin*, 1852.

10 This day we fashion Destiny, our web of Fate we spin.

JOHN GREENLEAF WHITTIER, "The Crisis," 1848.

68. DIPLOMACY

See also GOVERNMENT; STATESMANSHIP

1 Dollar Diplomacy.

> Term applied to the policy initiated by Sec. of State Philander C. Knox, in which diplomatic efforts were exerted to increase U.S. foreign investment, and such investment was likewise used as an element of diplomacy, c.1910.

2 The Democratic party favors the League of Nations as the surest . . . means of maintaining the peace of the world.

> Plank in the Democratic Party national platform, 1920.

3 The Republican party maintains the traditional American policy of noninterference in the political affairs of other nations. This government has definitely refused membership in the League of Nations and to assume any obligations under the covenant of the League.

> Plank in the Republican Party national platform, 1928.

4 I take it as clear, that, where an important purpose of diplomacy is to further enduring good relations between states, the methods—the modes of conduct—by which relations between states are carried on must be designed to inspire trust and confidence. To achieve this result, the conduct of diplomacy should conform to the same moral and ethical principles which inspire trust and confidence when followed by and between individuals.

> DEAN G. ACHESON, in a speech at Amherst College, December 9, 1964, quoted in Eugene McCarthy, *The Limits of Power,* 1967.

5 Consul, *n.* In American politics, a person who having failed to secure an office from the people is given one by the Administration on condition that he leave the country.

> AMBROSE BIERCE, *The Devil's Dictionary,* 1906.

6 Diplomacy, *n.* The patriotic art of lying for one's country.

> Ibid.

7 There is no room for the quick-draw artist in the diplomatic arena; the stakes are always too high and the penalties too dear.

> EDMUND G. BROWN, in *Reagan: The Political Chameleon,* 1976.

8 For the mass public, it is easier to understand problems if they are reduced to black/white dichotomies. It is easier to understand policies if they are attached to individuals who are simplistically labeled as hawks or doves. Yet in today's world any attempt to reduce its complexities to a single set of ideological propositions, to a single personality, or to a single issue is in itself a distortion. Such a distortion also raises the danger that public emotions could become so strong as to make the management of a genuinely complex foreign policy well-nigh impossible.

> ZBIGNIEW BRZEZINSKI, *Power and Principle,* 1983.

9 The Soviet Union can choose either confrontation or cooperation. The United States is adequately prepared to meet either choice. We would prefer cooperation.

> JIMMY CARTER, in a commencement address at the United States Naval Academy, Annapolis, June 7, 1978.

10 Only when a menaced country has the wholehearted support of its people and the will to resist to the limit of its resources should we consider an appeal for help.

> J. LAWTON COLLINS, *War in Peacetime: The History and Lessons of Korea,* 1969.

11 The League [of Nations] exists as a foreign agency. We hope it will be helpful. But the United States sees no reason to limit its own freedom and independence of action by joining it.

> CALVIN COOLIDGE, in a message to Congress, December 6, 1923.

12 American diplomacy is easy on the brain but hell on the feet.

> CHARLES G. DAWES, in a speech in Washington, June 2, 1931.

13 You'll never run it without an iron fist. There isn't any other way. You've got to find a guy who won't be too much of a burglar. Let him steal a little and share the rest with the people. That makes sense to me.

> EVERETT M. DIRKSEN, speaking of U.S. policy in Latin America, in Neil MacNeil, *Dirksen: Portrait of a Public Man,* 1970.

14 Limited policies inevitably are defensive policies, and defensive policies inevitably are losing policies.

> JOHN FOSTER DULLES, *War or Peace,* 1950.

15 There is no nook or cranny in all the world into which Communist influence does not penetrate.

> Ibid.

16 We look on the world as a whole. We cannot be weak anywhere without creating danger everywhere.

> JOHN FOSTER DULLES, quoted in Andrew H. Berding, *Dulles on Diplomacy,* 1965.

17 I think that a young State, like a young Virgin, should modestly stay at home, and wait the Application of Suitors for an Alliance with her; and not run about offering her Amity to all the World; and hazarding their Refusal. . . . Our Virgin is a jolly one; and tho at present not very rich, will in time be a great Fortune, and where she has a favorable Predisposition, it seems to me well worth cultivating.

> BENJAMIN FRANKLIN, in a letter to Charles W.F. Dumas, September 22, 1778.

18 We are handicapped by policies based on old myths rather than current realities.

> J. WILLIAM FULBRIGHT, in a speech in the U.S. Senate, March 27, 1964.

19 There are few ironclad rules of diplomacy but to one there is no exception. When an official reports that talks were useful, it can safely be concluded that nothing was accomplished.

> JOHN KENNETH GALBRAITH, "The American Ambassador," *Foreign Service Journal,* June, 1969.

20 Diplomacy is to do and say
The nastiest thing in the nicest way.

> Attributed to Isaac Goldberg.

21 Once upon a time our traditional goal in war—and can anyone doubt that we are at war?—was victory. Once upon a time we were proud of our strength, our military power. Now we seem ashamed of it. Once upon a time the rest of the world looked to us for leadership. Now they look to us for a quick handout and a fence-straddling international posture.

> BARRY M. GOLDWATER, *Why Not Victory?* 1962.

22 The open door.

> JOHN HAY, characterizing the trade policy he had just negotiated with China, January 2, 1900.

23 [Henry Kissinger] believes all power begins in the White House. It is his firm belief that he and the President know what is best; the rest of us are to be patient and they will announce our destiny.

> BARBARA HOWAR, *Laughing All the Way,* 1973.

24 Treaties at best are but complied with so long as interest requires their fulfilment. Consequently, they are virtually binding on the weaker party only; or, in plain truth, they are not binding at all.

> WASHINGTON IRVING, in *Diedrich Knickerbocker's History of New York,* 1809.

25 The moment we engage in confederations, or alliances with any nation we may from that time date the downfall of our republic.

> ANDREW JACKSON, to James Branch, criticizing John Quincy Adams, March 3, 1826, quoted in Robert V. Remini, *Andrew Jackson & the Course of American Freedom,* 1981.

26 Peace, commerce, and honest friendship with all nations, entangling alliances with none.

> THOMAS JEFFERSON, in his first inaugural address, March 4, 1801.

27 We consider the interests of Cuba, Mexico and ours as the same, and that the object of both must be to exclude all European influence from this hemisphere.

THOMAS JEFFERSON, in a letter to William C.C. Claiborne, October, 1808.

28 The less we have to do with the amities or enmities of Europe the better. Not in our day, but at no distant one, we may shake a rod over the heads of all, which may make the stoutest tremble. But I hope our wisdom will grow with our power, and teach us, that the less we use our power the greater it will be.

THOMAS JEFFERSON, in a letter to Thomas Leiper, June 12, 1815.

29 I have ever deemed it fundamental for the United States never to take active part in the quarrels of Europe. Their political interests are entirely distinct from ours. Their mutual jealousies, their balance of power, their complicated alliances, their forms and principles of government, are all foreign to us. They are nations of eternal war.

THOMAS JEFFERSON, in a letter to James Monroe, June 11, 1823.

30 It is a *sine qua non* of successful dealing with Russia that the foreign government in question should remain at all times cool and collected and that its demands on Russian policy should be put forward in such a manner as to leave the way open for a compliance not too detrimental to Russian prestige.

GEORGE F. KENNAN, "The Sources of Soviet Conduct," *Foreign Affairs,* July, 1947.

31 It is clear that the main element of any United States policy toward the Soviet Union must be that of a long-term, patient but firm and vigilant containment of Russian expansive tendencies.

Ibid.

32 Let us never negotiate out of fear, but let us never fear to negotiate.

JOHN F. KENNEDY, in his inaugural address, January 20, 1961.

33 [The Russians] have offered to trade us an apple for an orchard. We don't do that in this country.

JOHN F. KENNEDY, speaking of his meeting with Andrei Gromyko, foreign minister of the USSR, reported in the *New York Times,* October 8, 1961.

34 Acting on our own, by ourselves, we cannot establish justice throughout the world; we cannot ensure its domestic tranquility, or provide for its common defense, or promote its general welfare, or secure the blessings of liberty to ourselves and our posterity. But joined with other free nations, we can do all this and more.

JOHN F. KENNEDY, in a speech at Philadelphia, July 4, 1962, quoted in J. William Fulbright, *Old Myths and New Realities,* 1964.

35 Domestic policy can only defeat us; foreign policy can kill us.

JOHN F. KENNEDY, quoted in Arthur M. Schlesinger, Jr., *The Imperial Presidency,* 1973.

36 No nation has a monopoly of justice or virtue, and none has the capacity to enforce its own conceptions globally.

HENRY KISSINGER, quoted in Richard Valeriani, *Travels with Henry,* 1979.

37 We cannot always assure the future of our friends; we have a better chance of assuring our future if we remember who our friends are.

HENRY KISSINGER, speaking of the Shah of Iran, *White House Years,* 1979.

38 Most foreign policies that history has marked highly, in whatever country, have been originated by leaders who were opposed by experts.

HENRY KISSINGER, *Years of Upheaval,* 1982.

39 The many different strands that make up American thinking on foreign policy have so far proved inhospitable to an approach based on the calculation of the national interest and relationships of power. Americans are comfortable with an idealistic tradition that espouses great causes, such as making the world safe for democracy, or human rights.

Ibid.

40 For a diplomat to think that rival and unfriendly powers cannot be brought to a settlement is to forget what diplomacy is all about. There would be little for diplomats to do if the world consisted of partners, enjoying political intimacy, and responding to common appeals.

WALTER LIPPMANN, *The Cold War,* 1947.

41 An alliance is like a chain. It is not made stronger by adding weak links to it. A great power like the United States gains no advantage and it loses prestige by offering, indeed peddling, its alliances to all and sundry. An alliance should be hard diplomatic currency, valuable and hard to get, and not inflationary paper from the mimeograph machine in the State Department.

> WALTER LIPPMANN, in his column in the *New York Herald Tribune,* August 5, 1952.

42 Much of what Mr. [Henry A.] Wallace calls his global thinking is, no matter how you slice it, still Globaloney.

> CLARE BOOTHE LUCE, in a speech in Congress, February 9, 1943.

43 Today our potential foreign obligations are almost unlimited. We have moved from a position of isolation and rejection of world responsibility to a position of isolated, almost singular responsibility for the whole world.

> EUGENE J. McCARTHY, *The Limits of Power,* 1967.

44 We have a habit of trying to get our fingers into every corner of the globe. I think we do that too often, sometimes too heavily, and perhaps a little restraint in the other direction might be beneficial in the years ahead.

> MIKE MANSFIELD, in a speech in the U.S. Senate, July, 1966, quoted in Eugene McCarthy, *The Limits of Power,* 1967.

45 Our policy is directed not against any country or doctrine but against hunger, poverty, desperation and chaos. Its purpose should be the revival of a working economy in the world so as to permit the emergence of political and social conditions in which free institutions can exist.

> GEORGE C. MARSHALL, describing his plan for European recovery from World War II, in a speech at Harvard University, June 5, 1947.

46 The American continents, by the free and independent condition which they have assumed and maintain, are henceforth not to be considered as subjects for future colonization by any European powers.

> JAMES MONROE, in a message to Congress, now known as the Monroe Doctrine, December 2, 1823.

47 With the existing colonies or dependencies of any European power we have not interfered and shall not interfere. But with the Governments who have declared their independence and maintained it, and whose independence we have, on great consideration and on just principles, acknowledged, we could not view any interposition for the purpose of oppressing them, or controlling in any other manner their destiny, by any European power in any other light than as the manifestation of an unfriendly disposition toward the United States.

> *Ibid.*

48 The favorite cliché of those who advocate summit talks regardless of the circumstances is, "Talking is always better than fighting." This, however, is not the only choice. Talking is not better than not talking when you do not know what you are going to talk about.

> RICHARD M. NIXON, *The Challenges We Face,* 1960.

49 A diplomatic character is the narrowest sphere of society that man can act in. It forbids intercourse by a reciprocity of suspicion; and a diplomatist is a sort of unconnected atom, continually repelling and repelled.

> THOMAS PAINE, *The Rights of Man,* 1791–1792.

50 It is impossible to view Vietnam without taking into consideration where it fits into the gigantic chess game called the cold war. The stakes in that game are no less than our very existence, and only the president has access to all the facts necessary for each move.

> RONALD REAGAN, *Sincerely, Ronald Reagan,* 1976.

51 We built it, we paid for it, it's ours, and we're going to keep it.

> RONALD REAGAN, on the Panama Canal, in a campaign speech in Texas, 1976.

52 There's the one thing no Nation can ever accuse us of and that is Secret Diplomacy. Our Foreign

dealings are an Open Book, generally a Check Book.

> WILL ROGERS, October 21, 1923, quoted in Donald Day, *The Autobiography of Will Rogers*, 1949.

53 There is a small articulate minority in this country which advocates changing our national symbol which is the eagle to that of the ostrich and withdrawing from the United Nations.

> ELEANOR ROOSEVELT, in a speech before the Democratic National Convention, July 22, 1952.

54 We have to face the fact that either all of us are going to die together or we are going to learn to live together and if we are to live together we have to talk.

> ELEANOR ROOSEVELT, quoted in the *New York Times*, October 15, 1960.

55 In the field of world policy I would dedicate this nation to the policy of the good neighbor.

> FRANKLIN D. ROOSEVELT, in his first inaugural address, March 4, 1933.

56 There is a homely old adage which runs: "Speak softly and carry a big stick; you will go far." If the American nation will speak softly and yet build and keep at a pitch of the highest training a thoroughly efficient navy, the Monroe Doctrine will go far.

> THEODORE ROOSEVELT, in a speech at the Minnesota State Fair, September 2, 1901.

57 He who walks in the middle of the road gets hit from both sides.

> GEORGE P. SHULTZ, quoted in Richard M. Nixon, *The Memoirs of Richard Nixon*, 1978.

58 We Americans can't seem to get it that you can't commit rape a little.

> LINCOLN STEFFENS, on U.S. intervention in Mexico in 1914, in *The Autobiography of Lincoln Steffens*, 1931.

59 Diplomacy, for example, is not the art of asserting ever more emphatically that attitudes should not be what they clearly are. It is not the repudiation of actuality, but the recognition of actuality, and the use of actuality to advance our national interests.

> ADLAI E. STEVENSON, *Call to Greatness*, 1954.

60 Just being an American nowadays is not always comfortable. In the sensitive new areas some will denounce American aid as imperialism; but if it is not forthcoming we are denounced for indifference or discrimination. And sometimes if we stand correctly aloof from the local political scene we are accused of supporting reaction and the status quo. But if we don't keep our hands off and indicate some preference for policies or politicians then we are denounced for interfering. We are damned if we do and damned if we don't—at least now and then.

> Ibid.

61 No administration can conduct a sound foreign policy when the future sits in judgment on the past and officials are held accountable as dupes, fools or traitors for anything that goes wrong.

> Ibid.

62 We cannot be any stronger in our foreign policy—for all the bombs and guns we may heap up in our arsenals—than we are in the spirit which rules inside the country. Foreign policy, like a river, cannot rise above its source.

> ADLAI E. STEVENSON, in a speech at New Orleans, December 4, 1954, collected in *What I Think*, 1956.

63 We cannot afford to destroy at home the very liberty which we must sell to the rest of the world as the basis for progress and happiness.

> ROBERT A. TAFT, *A Foreign Policy for Americans*, 1951.

64 My ardent desire is, and my aim has been, to comply strictly with all our engagements, foreign and domestic; but to keep the United States free from political connections with every other country, to see them independent of all and under the influence of none.

> GEORGE WASHINGTON, in a letter to Patrick Henry, October 9, 1795.

65 Why quit our own to stand upon foreign ground? Why by interweaving our destiny with that of any part of Europe, entangle our peace and prosperity in the toils of European ambition, rivalship, interest, humor, or caprice?

GEORGE WASHINGTON, in his Farewell Address, September 17, 1796.

66 It is our true policy to steer clear of permanent alliances with any portion of the foreign world, so far, I mean, as we are now at liberty to do it; for let me not be understood as capable of patronizing infidelity to existing engagements. I hold the maxim no less applicable to public than to private affairs that honesty is always the best policy. I repeat, therefore, let those engagements be observed in their genuine sense.

Ibid.

67 We may well be unable to afford to be the world's policeman, but neither can we afford to fail to live up to the responsibilities that the accidents of a bountiful land and a beneficent fate have placed upon us.

GEN. WILLIAM C. WESTMORELAND, *A Soldier Reports*, 1976.

68 We shall not, I believe, be obliged to alter our policy of watchful waiting.

WOODROW WILSON, annual message to Congress, referring to his administration's refusal to support the reactionary government of Mexico's Gen. Victoriano Huerta, December 2, 1913.

69 No nation is fit to sit in judgment upon any other nation.

WOODROW WILSON, in a speech in New York City, April 20, 1915.

70 A general association of nations must be formed under specific covenants for the purpose of affording mutual guarantees of political independence and territorial integrity to great and small states alike.

WOODROW WILSON, in an address to Congress, the last of the Fourteen Points, January 8, 1918.

69. DIVORCE

See also FAMILY; MARRIAGE

1 Alimony is the most exorbitant of all stud-fees, and the worst feature of it is that you pay it retroactively.

JOHN BARRYMORE, at the end of his second marriage, quoted in Gene Fowler, *Good Night, Sweet Prince*, 1943.

2 Divorce, *n.* A resumption of diplomatic relations and rectification of boundaries.

AMBROSE BIERCE, in Ernest J. Hopkins, *The Enlarged Devil's Dictionary*, 1967.

3 Divorce, *n.* A bugle blast that separates the combatants and makes them fight at long range.

Ibid.

4 Draw up the papers, lawyer, and make 'em
    good and stout,
For things are running crossways, and Betsey
    and I are out.

WILL CARLETON, "Betsey and I Are Out," 1873.

5 Divorce is a disturbing business: to the clergy, to statisticians, to those who engage in it, and to their offspring, but the men and women who lead the lives of quiet desperation rather than resort to it, no matter how grim their condition, contribute little to the general welfare.

ILKA CHASE, *Free Admission*, 1948.

6 So many persons think divorce a panacea for every ill, find out, when they try it, that the remedy is worse than the disease.

DOROTHY DIX, in *Dorothy Dix, Her Book*, 1926.

7 Husbands and wives should never separate if there is no Christian demand for it. It is better to await the logic of events than for a wife precipitately to leave her husband, or for a husband to leave his wife.

MARY BAKER EDDY, *Science and Health*, 1875.

8 If divorce has increased by one thousand percent, don't blame the women's movement. Blame the obsolete sex roles on which our marriages were based.

BETTY FRIEDAN, in a speech in New York City, January 20, 1974.

9 Marriage is the most inviolable and irrevocable of all contracts that were ever formed. Every human compact may be lawful dissolved but this.

JAMES CARDINAL GIBBONS, *The Faith of Our Fathers,* 1876.

10 The married man who wants a change of venue is probably headed for the divorce court.

ELBERT HUBBARD, *The Roycroft Dictionary and Book of Epigrams,* 1923.

11 There are three sides to every question—where a divorce is involved.

Ibid.

12 When one hears the argument that marriage should be indissoluble for the sake of children, one cannot help wondering whether the protagonist is really such a firm friend of childhood, or whether his concern for the welfare of children is merely so much protective coloration for a constitutional and superstitious fear of change.

SUZANNE LaFOLLETTE, *Concerning Women,* 1926.

13 I played Santa Claus many times, and if you don't believe it, check out the divorce settlements awarded my wives.

GROUCHO MARX, *The Groucho Phile,* 1976.

14 Alimony—The ransom that the happy pay to the devil.

H.L. MENCKEN, "Sententiae," in *The Vintage Mencken,* 1955.

70. DRESS

1 A little of what you call frippery is very necessary towards looking like the rest of the world.

ABIGAIL ADAMS, in a letter to John Adams, May 1, 1780.

2 The costume of woman should be suited to her wants and necessities. It should conduce at once to her health, comfort, and usefulness; and, while it should not fail also to conduce to her personal adornment, it should make that end of secondary importance.

AMELIA JENKS BLOOMER, in a letter to Charlotte A. Joy, June 3, 1857.

3 The fair Flora looked up with a pitiful air,
And answered quite promptly, "Why, Harry, *mon cher,*
I should like above all things to go with you there,
But really and truly—I've nothing to wear."

WILLIAM ALLEN BUTLER, "Nothing to Wear," 1857.

4 There is one other reason for dressing well, namely that dogs respect it, and will not attack you in good clothes.

RALPH WALDO EMERSON, entry written in 1870, *Journals,* 1909–1914.

5 It is only when mind and character slumber that the dress can be seen.

RALPH WALDO EMERSON, "Social Aims," *Letters and Social Aims,* 1876.

6 I have heard with admiring submission the experience of the lady who declared that "the sense of being perfectly well dressed gives a feeling of inward tranquility which religion is powerless to bestow."

Ibid.

7 When you incline to have new Cloathes, look first well over the old Ones, and see if you cannot shift with them another year. . . . Remember, a

Patch on your Coat, and Money in your Pocket, is better and more creditable than a Writ on your Back, and no Money to take it off.

> BENJAMIN FRANKLIN, *Poor Richard's Almanack,* 1756.

8 *Fond* Pride of Dress, *is sure a very Curse;*
  E'er Fancy *you consult, consult your Purse.*

> BENJAMIN FRANKLIN, *The Way to Wealth,* 1758.

9 If you wear your cambric ruffles as I do, and take care not to mend the holes, they will come in time to be lace; and feathers, my dear girl, may be had in America from every cock's tail.

> BENJAMIN FRANKLIN, in a letter to his daughter, June 3, 1779.

10 After all, you can't expect men not to judge by appearances.

> ELLEN GLASGOW, *The Sheltered Life,* 1932.

11 Skirts couldn't get any shorter and remain legal.

> AMY GREENE, in *American Way* magazine, June, 1970.

12 The outward forms the inward man reveal,—
  We guess the pulp before we cut the peel.

> OLIVER WENDELL HOLMES, SR., "A Rhymed Lesson," 1846.

13 Some ladies think they may, under the privileges of the *déshabillé,* be loose and negligent of their dress in the morning. But be you, from the moment you rise till you go to bed, as cleanly and properly dressed as at the hours of dinner or tea.

> THOMAS JEFFERSON, in a letter to Martha Jefferson, 1783.

14 Where's the man could ease a heart
  Like a satin gown?

> DOROTHY PARKER, "The Satin Dress," *Enough Rope,* 1927.

15 One wants to be *very* something, *very* great, *very* heroic; or if not that, then at least very stylish and very fashionable.

> HARRIET BEECHER STOWE, "Dress, or Who Makes the Fashions," *Atlantic Monthly,* 1864.

16 No man ever stood the lower in my estimation for having a patch in his clothes; yet I am sure that there is greater anxiety, commonly, to have fashionable, or at least clean and unpatched clothes, than to have a sound conscience.

> HENRY DAVID THOREAU, *Walden,* 1854.

17 Beware of all enterprises that require new clothes.

> Ibid.

---

71. DRINKING

See also WINE & SPIRITS

---

1 There was an old hen
  And she had a wooden leg,
  And every damned morning
  She laid another egg;
  She was the best damned chicken
  On the whole damned farm—
  And another little drink
  Wouldn't do us no harm.

> Folk song.

2 The saloon must go.

> Motto of the Anti-Saloon League, 1895.

3 We advocate the repeal of the Eighteenth Amendment. We urge the enactment of such measures by the several states as will actually promote temperance, effectively prevent the return of the saloon and bring the liquor traffic into the open under complete supervision and control by the states.

> Plank of the Democratic Party national platform, 1932.

4 How dry I am! How dry I am!
  Nobody knows how dry I am!

> Popular song.

5 We, cold water girls and boys,
  Freely renounce the treacherous joys

Of brandy, whiskey, rum, and gin;
The serpent's lure to death and sin.

> Song of the cold water societies, temperance groups composed largely of schoolchildren, c.1840.

6 The water wagon is the place for me.
Last night at twelve I felt immense; Today I feel like thirty cents.
My eyes are bleared, my coppers hot, I'd like to eat but I cannot!
It is no time for mirth and laughter—
The cold, gray dawn of the morning after.

> GEORGE ADE, "Remorse," *The Sultan of Sulu,* 1902.

7 It's a fine experience to have one's staggering done *for,* and not *by* one.

> JOHN BARRYMORE, speaking about rough seas he encountered on a voyage from Naples to Bombay, 1934, quoted in Gene Fowler, *Good Night, Sweet Prince,* 1943.

8 You can't drown yourself in drink. I've tried: you float.

> JOHN BARRYMORE, in a conversation with playwright Ashton Stevens, quoted in Gene Fowler, *Good Night, Sweet Prince,* 1943.

9 Let's get out of these wet clothes and into a dry martini.

> ROBERT BENCHLEY, quoted in Robert E. Drennan, *The Algonquin Wits,* 1968 (also attributed to Alexander Woollcott and Billy Wilder).

10 Drunkenness is a joy reserved for the gods: so men do partake of it impiously, and so they are very properly punished for their audacity.

> JAMES BRANCH CABELL, *Jurgen,* 1919.

11 Ha! see where the wild-blazing Grog-Shop appears,
As the red waves of wretchedness swell,
How it burns on the edge of tempestuous years
The horrible Light-House of Hell!

> McDONALD CLARKE, the "mad poet" of Broadway, in "The Rum Hole."

12 He seldom went up to town without coming down "three sheets in the wind."

> RICHARD HENRY DANA, *Two Years Before the Mast,* 1840.

13 'Twas a balmy Summer evening, and a goodly crowd was there,
Which well-nigh filled Joe's barroom on the corner of the square:
And as songs and witty stories came through the open door
A vagabond crept slowly in and posed upon the floor.

> HUGH ANTOINE D'ARCY, "The Face on the Barroom Floor," 1887 (also titled "The Face upon the Floor").

14 Such men as will get drunk and then abuse their wives do not deserve the name of men, for they have not the principle of men, but may be called the Devil's swill-tub walking upright, and such deserve a dose of eel tea, *i.e.,* spirituous liquor in which a living eel has been slimed.

> LORENZO DOW, *Reflections on Matrimony,* 1833.

15 [Whiskey] doesn't sustain life, but, whin taken hot with wather, a lump iv sugar, a piece iv lemon peel, and just th' dustin' iv the nutmeg-grater, it makes life sustainable.

> FINLEY PETER DUNNE, *Mr. Dooley's Philosophy,* 1900.

16 Alcohol is nicissary f'r a man so that now an' thin he can have a good opinion iv himsilf, ondisturbed be th' facts.

> FINLEY PETER DUNNE, "Mr. Dooley on Alcohol," the *Chicago Tribune,* April 26, 1914.

17 As I was drinkin' gin and water,
And me bein' the One Eyed Riley.

> T.S. ELIOT, *The Cocktail Party,* 1950.

18 There is this to be said in favor of drinking, that it takes the drunkard first out of society, then out of the world.

> RALPH WALDO EMERSON, entry written in 1866, *Journals,* 1909–1914.

19 I never drank anything stronger than beer before I was twelve.

> W.C. FIELDS, quoted in Robert Lewis Taylor, *W.C. Fields, His Follies and Fortunes,* 1949.

20 I exercise extreme self-control. I never drink anything stronger than gin before breakfast.

> Ibid.

21 The hangover became a part of the day as well allowed-for as the Spanish siesta.

> F. Scott Fitzgerald, "My Lost City," in *The Crack-Up,* 1945.

22 He that drinks fast, pays slow.

> Benjamin Franklin, *Poor Richard's Almanack,* 1733.

23 Many Estates are spent in the Getting,
Since Women for Tea forsook Spinning and
  Knitting,
And Men for Punch forsook Hewing and
  Splitting.

> Benjamin Franklin, *Poor Richard's Almanack,* 1758.

24 Count all the trees that crown Jamaica's
  hills,
Count all the stars that through the heavens
  you see,
Count every drop that the wide ocean fills;
Then count the pleasures Bacchus yields to
  me.

> Philip Freneau, "The Jamaica Funeral," published in *Poems,* 1786.

25 We are all desperately afraid of sounding like Carrie Nation. I must take the risk. Any writer who wants to do his best against a deadline should stick to Coca-Cola.

> John Kenneth Galbraith, *Annals of an Abiding Liberal,* 1979.

26 Licker talks mighty loud w'en it git loose fum de jug.

> Attributed to Joel Chandler Harris.

27 I decided to stop drinking with creeps.
I decided to drink only with friends.
I've lost 30 pounds.

> Ernest Hemingway, quoted in *American Way* magazine, August, 1974.

28 Man wants but little drink below,
But wants that little strong.

> Oliver Wendell Holmes, Sr., "A Song of Other Days," 1829. (This is a parody of lines by Oliver Goldsmith: "Man wants but little here below,/Nor wants that little long.")

29 The warm, champagny, old-particular,
  brandy-punchy feeling.

> Oliver Wendell Holmes, Sr., "Nux Postcaenatica," 1848.

30 If wine tells truth,—and so have said the
  wise,—
It makes me laugh to think how brandy lies!

> Oliver Wendell Holmes, Sr., "The Banker's Secret," 1855.

31 A great social and economic experiment, noble in motive and far-reaching in purpose.

> Herbert Hoover, on prohibition, in a letter to Sen. William E. Borah, February 28, 1928.

32 For it's always fair weather
When good fellows get together
With a stein on the table and a good song
  ringing clear.

> Richard Hovey, "A Stein Song," and interlude in the poem "Spring," from *Along the Trail,* 1898.

33 You can't get away from yourself by going to a booze-bazaar.

> Elbert Hubbard, *The Roycroft Dictionary and Book of Epigrams,* 1923.

34 Alcoholic psychosis is nothin' more or less'n ole D.T.'s in a dinner suit.

> Kin Hubbard, *Abe Martin's Broadcast,* 1930.

35 I wish to see this beverage become common instead of the whiskey which kills one-third of our citizens and ruins their families.

> Thomas Jefferson, on beer, in a letter to Charles Yancey, January 6, 1816.

36 My experience through life has convinced me that, while moderation and temperance in all things are commendable and beneficial, abstinence from

spirituous liquors is the best safeguard of morals and health.

GEN. ROBERT E. LEE, in a letter to S.G.M. Miller and others, December 9, 1869.

37 Prohibition will work great injury to the cause of temperance. It is a species of intemperance within itself, for it goes beyond the bounds of reason in that it attempts to control a man's appetite by legislation, and makes a crime out of things that are not crimes. A Prohibition law strikes a blow at the very principles upon which our government was founded.

ABRAHAM LINCOLN, in a speech in the Illinois House of Representatives, December 18, 1840.

38 If we take habitual drunkards as a class, their heads and their hearts will bear an advantageous comparison with those of any other class. There seems ever to have been a proneness in the brilliant and warm-blooded to fall into this vice. The demon of intemperance ever seems to have delighted in sucking the blood of genius and generosity.

ABRAHAM LINCOLN, in a speech to the Washington Temperance Society, Springfield, Illinois, February 22, 1842.

39 Men do not knowingly drink for the effect alcohol produces on the body. What they drink for is the brain-effect; and if it must come through the body, so much the worse for the body.

JACK LONDON, *John Barleycorn,* 1913.

40 All the no-saying and no-preaching in the world will fail to keep men, and youths growing into manhood, away from John Barleycorn when John Barleycorn is everywhere accessible, and where John Barleycorn is everywhere the connotation of manliness, and daring, and great-spiritedness. The only rational thing for the twentieth century folk to do is to cover up the well.

Ibid.

41 Better sleep with a sober cannibal than a drunken Christian.

HERMAN MELVILLE, *Moby-Dick,* 1851.

42 I've made it a rule never to drink by daylight and never to refuse a drink after dark.

H.L. MENCKEN, quoted in the *New York Post,* September 18, 1945.

43 There aint gonna be no whiskey; there aint gonna be no gin;
There aint gonna be no highball to put the whiskey in;
There aint gonna be no cigarettes to make folks pale and thin;
But you can't take away that tendency to sin, sin, sin.

VAUGHN MILLER, "There Ain't Gonna Be No Whiskey," 1919.

44 One more drink and I'll be under the host.

DOROTHY PARKER, quoted in John Keats, *You Might as Well Live,* 1970.

45 Tolerance to my mind has been greatly overrated. . . . I take as much pleasure in detesting the good brothers and sisters of the [Anti-Saloon] League as they have in hating me.

WESTBROOK PEGLER, c.1929, quoted in Oliver Pilat, *Pegler: Angry Man of the Press,* 1963.

46 Drunkenness spoils health, dismounts the mind, and unmans men. It reveals secrets, is quarrelsome, lascivious, impudent, dangerous, and mad.

WILLIAM PENN, *Some Fruits of Solitude,* 1693.

47 Drink the first. Sip the second slowly. Skip the third.

KNUTE ROCKNE, quoted in Jerry Brondfield, *Rockne,* 1976.

48 I ask especially that no state shall, by law or otherwise, authorize the return of the saloon, either in its old form or in some modern guise.

FRANKLIN D. ROOSEVELT, proclamation on repeal of the Eighteenth Amendment, December 5, 1933.

49 To pass prohibitory laws to govern localities where the sentiment does not sustain them is simply equivalent to allowing free liquor, plus lawlessness.

THEODORE ROOSEVELT, in a letter to William Howard Taft, July 16, 1908.

50 The prohibition law, written for weaklings and derelicts, has divided the nation, like Gaul, into three parts—wets, drys, and hypocrites.

FLORENCE SABIN, in a speech, February 9, 1931.

51 At the punch-bowl's brink,
  Let the thirsty think
    What they say in Japan:
  "First the man takes a drink,
  Then the drink takes a drink,
    Then the drink takes the man!"

> EDWARD ROWLAND SILL, "An Adage from the
> Orient," *The Poems of Edward Rowland Sill,*
> 1902.

52 There are two things that will be believed of any man whatsoever, and one of them is that he has taken to drink.

> BOOTH TARKINGTON, *Penrod,* 1914.

53 Water is the only drink for a wise man.

> HENRY DAVID THOREAU, *Walden,* 1854.

54 Prohibition only drives drunkenness behind doors and into dark places, and does not cure it or even diminish it.

> MARK TWAIN, in a letter to the *San Francisco
> Alta California,* May 28, 1867.

55 But for the journalistic monopoly that forbade the slightest revealment of Eastern news till a day after its publication in the California papers, the glorified flag on Mount Davidson would have been saluted and re-saluted, that memorable evening, as long as there was a charge of powder to thunder with; the city would have been illuminated, and every man that had any respect for himself would have got drunk,—as was the custom of the country on all occasions of public moment.

> MARK TWAIN, "The Glorious Flag on
> Davidson," *Roughing It,* 1872.

56 I prefer temperance hotels—altho' they sell worse liquor than any other kind of hotels.

> ARTEMUS WARD, *Artemus Ward's Lecture,* 1869.

57 They drink with impunity, or anybody who invites them.

> ARTEMUS WARD, in the program for his lecture
> at Dodworth Hall, New York City, reprinted in
> *The Complete Works of Artemus Ward,* 1898.

58 Where have you disposed of their carcasses?
  Those drunkards and gluttons of so many
    generations?

Where have you drawn off all the foul liquid
    and meat?

> WALT WHITMAN, "This Compost," 1856.

59 The saloon is the poor man's club.

> BISHOP CHARLES D. WILLIAMS at Michigan,
> c.1900.

60 Said Aristotle unto Plato,
  "Have another sweet potato?"
  Said Plato unto Aristotle,
  "Thank you, I prefer the bottle."

> OWEN WISTER, lines from *Philosophy 4,* 1903.

61 Father, dear father, come home with me
    now,
  The clock in the belfry strikes one.

> HENRY CLAY WORK, "Come Home, Father," a
> famous 19th-century temperance song, 1864.

---

72. DUTY

See also CHARACTER; CONDUCT

---

1 Think of your forefathers! Think of your posterity!

> JOHN QUINCY ADAMS, in a speech in Plymouth,
> Massachusetts, December 22, 1802.

2 He who is false to present duty breaks a thread in the loom, and will find the flaw when he may have forgotten its cause.

> HENRY WARD BEECHER, *Life Thoughts,* 1858.

3 Duty, *n.* That which sternly impels us in the direction of profit, along the line of desire.

> AMBROSE BIERCE, *The Devil's Dictionary,* 1906.

4 There is a moral interference with our fellow creatures at home and abroad, not only to be asserted as a right, but binding as a duty.

> WILLIAM ELLERY CHANNING, in a letter to
> Jonathan Phillips, 1839.

5 No man can always be right. So the struggle is to do one's best; to keep the brain and conscience

clear; never to be swayed by unworthy motives or inconsequential reasons, but to strive to unearth the basic factors involved and then do one's duty.

> DWIGHT D. EISENHOWER, in a letter to Mamie Doud Eisenhower, February 15, 1943.

6 I have my own stern claims and perfect circle. It denies the name of duty to many offices that are called duties.

> RALPH WALDO EMERSON, "Self-Reliance," *Essays,* First Series, 1841.

7 What I must do is all that concerns me, not what the people think.

> Ibid.

8 So nigh is grandeur to our dust,
So near is God to man,
When duty whispers low, *Thou must,*
The youth replies, *I can.*

> RALPH WALDO EMERSON, "Voluntaries," published in the *Atlantic Monthly,* October, 1863.

9 *Noblesse oblige;* or, superior advantages bind you to larger generosity.

> RALPH WALDO EMERSON, "Progress of Culture," *Letters and Social Aims,* 1876.

10 Let thy child's first Lesson be Obedience, and the second will be what thou wilt.

> BENJAMIN FRANKLIN, *Poor Richard's Almanack,* 1739.

11 I shall never ask, never refuse, nor ever resign an office.

> BENJAMIN FRANKLIN, *Autobiography,* 1798.

12 Pressed into service means pressed out of shape.

> ROBERT FROST, "The Self-Seeker," in *North of Boston,* 1914.

13 Let no guilty man escape, if it can be avoided. Be specially vigilant. . . . No personal consideration should stand in the way of performing a public duty.

> ULYSSES S. GRANT, note written on a letter concerning the so-called Whiskey Ring, dated July 29, 1875.

14 In the midst of doubt, in the collapse of creeds, there is one thing I do not doubt, that no man who lives in the same world with most of us can doubt, and that is that the faith is true and adorable which leads a soldier to throw away his life in obedience to a blindly accepted duty, in a cause which he little understands, in a plan of campaign of which he has no notion, under tactics of which he does not see the use.

> OLIVER WENDELL HOLMES, JR., in a speech given at Harvard University, May 30, 1895.

15 A legal duty so-called is nothing but a prediction that if a man does or omits certain things he will be made to suffer in this or that way by judgment of the court.

> OLIVER WENDELL HOLMES, JR., "The Path of the Law," address delivered at the Boston University School of Law, January 8, 1897.

16 I declare my belief that it is not your duty to do anything that is not to your own interest. Whenever it is unquestionably your duty to do a thing, then it will benefit you to perform that duty.

> EDGAR WATSON HOWE, *Country Town Sayings,* 1911.

17 The individual who refuses to defend his rights when called by his Government, deserves to be a slave, and must be punished as an enemy of his country and friend to her foe.

> ANDREW JACKSON, in a proclamation from Mobile, Alabama, to the people of Louisiana, September 21, 1814.

18 The brave man inattentive to his duty, is worth little more to his country, than the coward who deserts her in the hour of danger.

> ANDREW JACKSON, to soldiers who had retreated from their positions on the right bank of the Mississippi River at the battle of New Orleans, January 8, 1815.

19 My duty is to obey orders.

> Attributed to Thomas Jonathan "Stonewall" Jackson.

20 A lively and lasting sense of filial duty is more effectually impressed on the mind of a son or daughter by reading "King Lear," than by all the

dry volumes of ethics and divinity that ever were written.

> THOMAS JEFFERSON, in a letter to Robert Skipwith, August 3, 1771.

21 Only aim to do your duty, and mankind will give you credit where you fail.

> THOMAS JEFFERSON, *The Rights of British America,* 1774.

22 Duty is the sublimest word in our language. Do your duty in all things. You cannot do more. You should never wish to do less.

> GEN. ROBERT E. LEE, lines inscribed beneath his bust in the Hall of Fame at the former campus of New York University.

23 Let us have faith that right makes might, and in that faith let us to the end dare to do our duty as we understand it.

> ABRAHAM LINCOLN, in a speech at Cooper Union, New York City, February 27, 1860.

24 What better fate for a man than to die in the performance of his duty?

> GEN. DOUGLAS MACARTHUR, in response to a complaint that he was working his men to death, c.1946, quoted in William Manchester, *American Caesar,* 1978.

25 If a sense of duty tortures a man, it also enables him to achieve prodigies.

> H.L. MENCKEN, *Prejudices,* First Series, 1919.

26 The duty of man . . . is plain and simple, and consists of but two points. His duty to god, which every man must feel; and with respect to his neighbor, to do as he would be done by.

> THOMAS PAINE, *The Rights of Man,* 1791.

27 As the duty is precisely correspondent to the power, it follows that the richer, the wiser, the more powerful a man is, the greater is the obligation upon him to employ his gifts in lessening the sum of human misery; and this employment constitutes happiness, which the weak and wicked vainly imagine to consist in wealth, finery, or sensual gratification.

> JOHN RANDOLPH, in a letter to his nephew Theodore Dudley, February 15, 1806, quoted in Russell Kirk, *John Randolph of Roanoke,* 1951.

28 It is not a man's duty, as a matter of course, to devote himself to the eradication of any, even the most enormous wrong; he may still properly have other concerns to engage him; but it is his duty, at least, to wash his hands of it, and, if he gives it no thought longer, not to give it practically his support.

> HENRY DAVID THOREAU, "Civil Disobedience," 1849.

29 The only obligation which I have a right to assume is to do at any time what I think right.

> Ibid.

30 Make it a point to do something every day that you don't want to do. This is the golden rule for acquiring the habit of doing your duty without pain.

> MARK TWAIN, "Pudd'nhead Wilson's New Calendar," *Following the Equator,* 1897.

31 Duties are not performed for duty's *sake,* but because their *neglect* would make the man *uncomfortable.* A man performs but *one* duty—the duty of contenting his spirit, the duty of making himself agreeable to himself.

> MARK TWAIN, *What Is Man?* 1906.

32 There is no evil that we cannot either face or fly from, but the consciousness of duty disregarded. A sense of duty pursues us ever. It is omnipresent, like the Deity. If we take to ourselves the wings of the morning, and dwell in the uttermost parts of the sea, duty performed or duty violated is still with us, for our happiness or our misery. If we say the darkness shall cover us, in the darkness as in the light our obligations are yet with us.

> DANIEL WEBSTER, at the trial of John F. Knapp for the murder of a Captain White, 1830.

33 The worst of doing one's duty was that it apparently unfitted one for doing anything else.

> EDITH WHARTON, *The Age of Innocence,* 1920.

34 Simple duty hath no place for fear.

> JOHN GREENLEAF WHITTIER, "Abraham Davenport," *The Tent on the Beach,* 1867.

35 There is no question what the roll of honor in America is. The roll of honor consists of the names of men who have squared their conduct by ideals of duty.

> WOODROW WILSON, in a speech in Washington, D.C., February 27, 1916.

73. ECONOMICS

See also BUSINESS; DEBT; LABOR
MOVEMENT; MONEY; POVERTY; WEALTH

1 There are plenty of good five-cent cigars in the country. The trouble is they cost a quarter. What this country really needs is a good five-cent nickel.

> FRANKLIN P. ADAMS [F.P.A], quoted in Robert E. Drennan, *The Algonquin Wits,* 1968.

2 There are those who believe that if you will only legislate to make the well-to-do prosperous, their prosperity will leak through on those below. The Democratic idea, however, has been that if you make the masses prosperous, their prosperity will find its way up through every class which rests upon them.

> WILLIAM JENNINGS BRYAN, in his "Cross of Gold" speech at the Democratic Party National Convention, Chicago, July 8, 1896.

3 Take back your protection; we are now men, and we can beat the world at the manufacture of steel.

> ANDREW CARNEGIE, testifying at tariff hearings before the House Ways and Means Committee, December 21, 1908.

4 Of all human powers operating on the affairs of mankind, none is greater than that of competition.

> HENRY CLAY, in a speech in the U.S. Senate, February 2, 1832.

5 Trade is a plant which grows wherever there is peace, as soon as there is peace, and as long as there is peace.

> RALPH WALDO EMERSON, "The Young American," *Nature: Addresses and Lectures,* 1849.

6 No man acquires property without acquiring with it a little arithmetic also.

> RALPH WALDO EMERSON, "Montaigne," *Representative Men,* 1850.

7 Necessity never made a good bargain.

> BENJAMIN FRANKLIN, *Poor Richard's Almanack,* 1735.

8 Necessaries of life, that are not foods, and all other conveniences, have their values estimated by the proportion of food consumed while we are employed in procuring them.

> BENJAMIN FRANKLIN, "Positions to be Examined," April 4, 1769.

9 There's no such thing as a free lunch.

> Attributed to Milton Friedman, 1974.

10 In economics, hope and faith coexist with great scientific pretension and also a deep desire for respectability.

> JOHN KENNETH GALBRAITH, in the *New York Times Magazine,* June 7, 1970.

11 Consumer wants can have bizarre, frivolous, or even immoral origins, and an admirable case can still be made for a society that seeks to satisfy them. But the case cannot stand if it is the process of satisfying wants that creates the wants. For then the individual who urges the importance of production to satisfy these wants is precisely in the position of the onlooker who applauds the efforts of the squirrel to keep abreast of the wheel that is propelled by his own efforts.

> JOHN KENNETH GALBRAITH, *The Affluent Society,* 1976.

12 Interest [on capital] springs from the power of increase which the reproductive forces of nature . . . give to capital. It is not an arbitrary, but a natural thing; it is not the result of a particular

social organization, but of laws of the universe which underlie society. It is, therefore, just.

HENRY GEORGE, *Progress and Poverty,* 1879.

13 The fundamental principle of human action— the law that is to political economy what the law of gravitation is to physics—is that men seek to gratify their desires with the least exertion.

Ibid.

14 Demand is not a fixed quantity, that increases only as population increases. In each individual it rises with *his* power of getting the things demanded.

Ibid.

15 Save possibly in educational effects, cooperation can produce no general results that competition will not produce.

Ibid.

16 What is necessary for the use of land is not its private ownership, but the security of improvements. It is not necessary to say to a man, "this land is yours," in order to induce him to cultivate or improve it. It is only necessary to say to him, "whatever your labor or capital produces on this land shall be yours."

Ibid.

17 The value of a thing is the amount of laboring or work that its possession will save to the possessor.

HENRY GEORGE, *The Science of Political Economy,* 1897.

18 The old traditions—the calculus of loss and gain, the cult of efficiency, the assumption that the most profitable use of a resource is the best use—are not only unnecessary. They are profoundly antisocial as well.

MICHAEL HARRINGTON, *Toward a Democratic Left,* 1968.

19 You ought to shoot all the economists and elect a couple of historians.

ERNEST HOLLINGS, quoted in the *New York Times,* June 8, 1983.

20 Except the tax levied for personal consumption, large ownership means investment, and investment means the direction of labor toward the production of the greatest returns—returns that so far as they are great show by that very fact that they are consumed by the many, not alone by the few.

OLIVER WENDELL HOLMES, JR., in a speech in New York City, February 15, 1913.

21 If capital an' labor ever do git t'gether it's good night fer th' rest of us.

Attributed to Kin Hubbard.

22 In 1980, Mr. George Bush, a man with reasonable access to Mr. Reagan, did an analysis of Mr. Reagan's economic plan. Mr. George Bush concluded that Reagan's plan was "voodoo economics." He was right.

JESSE JACKSON, in a speech before the Democratic National Convention, July 16, 1984.

23 Innovating economies expand and develop. Economies that do not add new kinds of goods and services, but continue only to repeat old work, do not expand much nor do they, by definition, develop.

JANE JACOBS, *The Economy of Cities,* 1969.

24 The instinct of ownership is fundamental in man's nature.

WILLIAM JAMES, *The Varieties of Religious Experience,* 1902.

25 The merchants will manage the better, the more they are left free to manage for themselves.

THOMAS JEFFERSON, in a letter to Gideon Granger, August 13, 1800.

26 Agriculture, manufactures, commerce, and navigation, the four pillars of our prosperity, are then most thriving when left most free to individual enterprise. Protection from casual embarrassments, however, may sometimes be seasonably interposed.

THOMAS JEFFERSON, in his first annual message to Congress, December 8, 1801.

27 It used to be said that my knowledge of economics was an argument against universal suffrage.

. . . And I tended to believe that until I started dealing with the economists.

> HENRY KISSINGER, quoted in Richard Valeriani, *Travels with Henry,* 1979.

28 Property is the fruit of labor; Property is desirable, is a positive good in the world. That some should be rich shows that others may become rich, and hence is just encouragement to industry and enterprise. Let not him who is houseless pull down the house of another, but let him work diligently and build one for himself, thus by example assuring that his own shall be safe from violence when built.

> ABRAHAM LINCOLN, reply to a committee from the New York Workingmen's Association, March 21, 1864.

29 The prosperity of any commercial nation is regulated by the prosperity of the rest. If they are poor, she cannot be rich; and her condition, be it what it may, is an index of the height of the commercial tide in other nations.

> THOMAS PAINE, *The Rights of Man,* 1792.

30 This absorption of revenue by all levels of government, the alarming rate of inflation and the rising toll of unemployment all stem from a single source: the belief that government, particularly the federal government, has the answer to our ills, and that the proper method of dealing with social problems is to transfer power from the private to the public sector, and within the public sector from state and local governments to the ultimate power center in Washington. This collectivist, centralizing approach, whatever name or party label it wears, has created our economic problems.

> RONALD REAGAN, in an address to the Chicago Executives Club, September 26, 1975.

31 In this present crisis, government is not the solution to our problem. Government is the problem.

> RONALD REAGAN, speaking of inflation and unemployment, in his first inaugural address, January 20, 1981.

32 A recession is when your neighbor loses his job. A depression is when you lose yours.

> RONALD REAGAN, quoted in Lou Cannon, *Reagan,* 1982.

33 An economist is a man that can tell you . . . what can happen under any given condition, and his guess is liable to be as good as anybody else's, too.

> WILL ROGERS, quoted in Adam Smith, *Paper Money,* 1981.

34 If the nation is living within its income, its credit is good. If in some crisis it lives beyond its income for a year or two it can usually borrow temporarily on reasonable terms. But if, like the spendthrift, it throws discretion to the winds, is willing to make no sacrifice at all in spending, extends its taxing to the limit of the people's power to pay, and continues to pile up deficits, it is on the road to bankruptcy.

> FRANKLIN D. ROOSEVELT, in a speech in Pittsburgh, Pennsylvania, October 19, 1932.

35 The economic royalists complain that we seek to overthrow the institutions of America. What they really complain of is that we seek to take away their power. Our allegiance to American institutions requires the overthrow of this kind of power. In vain they seek to hide behind the flag and the Constitution. In their blindness they forget what the flag and the Constitution stand for.

> FRANKLIN D. ROOSEVELT, in his acceptance speech at the Democratic Party National Convention in Philadelphia, June 27, 1936.

36 I believe, I have always believed, and I will always believe in private enterprise as the backbone of economic well-being in America.

> FRANKLIN D. ROOSEVELT, in a speech in Chicago, October 14, 1936.

37 If we are brought face to face with the naked issue of either keeping or totally destroying a prosperity in which the majority share, but in which some share improperly, why, as sensible men, we must decide that it is a great deal better that some people should prosper too much than that no one should prosper enough.

> THEODORE ROOSEVELT, in a speech in Fitchburg, Massachusetts, September 2, 1902.

38 Wall Street Lays an Egg.

> SIME SILVERMAN, news headline in *Variety,* following the stock market crash in October, 1929.

39 Intractable problems are usually not intractable because there are no solutions, but because there are no solutions without severe side effects. . . . It is only when we demand a solution with no costs that there are no solutions.

> LESTER C. THUROW, *The Zero-Sum Society*, 1980.

40 It is not competition but monopoly that deprives labor of its product.

> BENJAMIN R. TUCKER, *Why I Am an Anarchist*, 1892.

74. EDUCATION

See also BOOKS; EXPERIENCE; KNOWLEDGE; LANGUAGE

1 Education is what you have left over after you have forgotten everything you have learned.

> Anonymous.

2 It is an axiom in political science that unless a people are educated and enlightened it is idle to expect the continuance of civil liberty or the capacity for self-government.

> Texas Declaration of Independence, March 2, 1836.

3 The free school is the promoter of that intelligence which is to preserve us as a free nation; therefore, the state or nation, or both combined, should support free institutions of learning sufficient to afford to every child growing up in the land the opportunity of a good common school education.

> Plank of the Republican Party national platform, 1888.

4 We are opposed to state interference with parental rights and rights of conscience in the education of children as an infringement of the fundamental Democratic doctrine that the largest individual liberty consistent with the rights of others insures the highest type of American citizenship and the best government.

> Plank of the Democratic Party national platform, 1892.

5 Hit's a lot worse to be soul-hungry than to be body-hungry.

> A woman from Kentucky, asking that her granddaughter be admitted to Berea College high school, c.1900, quoted in Alfred Stefferud, *The Wonderful World of Books*, 1953.

6 A teacher affects eternity; he can never tell where his influence stops.

> HENRY ADAMS, *The Education of Henry Adams*, 1907.

7 To furnish the means of acquiring knowledge is . . . the greatest benefit that can be conferred upon mankind.

> JOHN QUINCY ADAMS, in a report on the founding of the Smithsonian Institution, c.1846.

8 The true teacher defends his pupils against his own personal influence.

> A. BRONSON ALCOTT, "Orphic Sayings," published in *The Dial*, 1840–1841.

9 Observation more than books, experience rather than persons, are the prime educators.

> A. BRONSON ALCOTT, *Table Talk*, 1877.

10 The ignorant classes are the dangerous classes. Ignorance is the womb of monsters.

> HENRY WARD BEECHER, *Proverbs from Plymouth Pulpit*, 1870.

11 Education, *n.* That which discloses to the wise and disguises from the foolish their lack of understanding.

> AMBROSE BIERCE, *The Devil's Dictionary*, 1906.

12 Erudition, *n.* Dust shaken out of a book into an empty skull.

> Ibid.

13 Learning, *n.* The kind of ignorance distinguishing the studious.

> Ibid.

14 Lecturer, *n.* One with his hand in your pocket, his tongue in your ear and his faith in your patience.

> Ibid.

15 The trouble with people is not that they don't know but that they know so much that ain't so.

> JOSH BILLINGS, in *Josh Billings' Encyclopedia of Wit and Wisdom,* 1874.

16 Equalizing opportunity through universal higher education subjects the whole population to the intellectual mode natural only to a few. It violates the fundamental egalitarian principle of respect for the differences between people.

> CAROLINE BIRD, *The Case Against College,* 1975.

17 The parents have a right to say that no teacher paid by their money shall rob their children of faith in God and send them back to their homes skeptical, or infidels, or agnostics, or atheists.

> WILLIAM JENNINGS BRYAN, testifying at the Scopes trial, Dayton, Tennessee, July 16, 1925.

18 We may say that if the political education of the average American voter be compared with that of the average voter in Europe, it stands high; but if it be compared with the functions which the theory of the American government lays on him, which its spirit implies, which the methods of its party organization assume, its inadequacy is manifest. This observation, however, is not so much a reproach to the schools . . . as a tribute to the height of the ideal which the American conception of popular rule sets up.

> JAMES BRYCE, *The American Commonwealth,* 1888.

19 Education ought, no doubt, to enlighten a man; but the educated classes, speaking generally, are the property-holding classes, and the possession of property does more to make a man timid than education does to make him hopeful. . . . In the less-educated man a certain simplicity and openness of mind go some way to compensate for the lack of knowledge. He is more apt to be influenced by the authority of leaders; but as, at least in England and America, he is generally shrewd enough to discern between a great man and a demagogue, this is more a gain than a loss.

> Ibid.

20 For the educator, complacent in his ivory tower, to scorn affiliation with a cause he considers to be noble, to refuse to attempt to win disciples from the ranks of students he is in a position to influence, is unmistakably to forswear a democratic responsibility, and to earn for himself the contemptible title of dilettante and solipsist.

> WILLIAM F. BUCKLEY, JR., *God and Man at Yale,* 1951.

21 An expert is one who knows more and more about less and less.

> Attributed to Nicholas Murray Butler.

22 It is with a kind of joy that I attack Harvard College, knowing that Harvard supplies the light and liberalism—hardly elsewhere to be seen in America—by which I am permitted to proceed. I should grieve to have this freedom extinguished, as it would be if the alumni were forbidden to take a critical interest in the institution.

> JOHN JAY CHAPMAN, in a letter to *Science* magazine, November 1, 1909.

23 A university studies politics, but it will not advocate fascism or communism. A university studies military tactics, but it will not promote war. A university studies peace, but it will not organize crusades of pacifism. It will study every question that affects human welfare, but it will not carry a banner in a crusade for anything except freedom of learning.

> LOTUS DELAT COFFMAN, in the *Journal of the American Association of University Women,* January, 1936.

24 He who enters a university walks on hallowed ground.

> JAMES BRYANT CONANT, "Notes on the Harvard Tercentenary," 1936.

25 What is the purpose of a college or university? It is to educate and train, to prepare its student body for the great tasks of life. . . . The last thing in the world a college or university should be concerned with is being number one in football or basketball if the price one pays for that is the corruption of character and the undermining of true student morale on campus.

> HOWARD COSELL, *Like It Is,* 1974.

26 I learned three important things in college—to use a library, to memorize quickly and visually, to drop asleep at any time given a horizontal surface and fifteen minutes. What I could not learn was to think creatively on schedule.

> AGNES DE MILLE, *Dance to the Piper*, 1952.

27 Education is not preparation for life; education is life itself.

> Attributed to John Dewey.

28 The twig is so easily bended
> I have banished the rule and the rod:
> I have taught them the goodness of
>   knowledge,
>   They have taught me the goodness of
>   God:
> My heart is the dungeon of darkness,
>   Where I shut them for breaking the rule;
> My frown is sufficient correction;
>   My love is the law of the school.

> CHARLES MONROE DICKINSON, "The Children," in *The Children and Other Verses*, 1889.

29 "D' ye think th' colledges has much to do with th' progress iv th' wurruld?" asked Mr. Hennessy.
  "D' ye think," said Mr. Dooley, " 'tis th' mill that makes th' wather run?"

> FINLEY PETER DUNNE, *Mr. Dooley's Opinions*, 1900.

30 Parents have become so convinced that educators know what is best for children that they forget that they themselves are really the experts.

> MARIAN WRIGHT EDELMAN, quoted in Margie Casady, "Society's Pushed-Out Children," *Psychology Today*, June, 1975.

31 It is the supreme art of the teacher to awaken joy in creative expression and knowledge.

> Attributed to Albert Einstein.

32 Enter to grow in wisdom.
> Depart to serve better thy country and
>   mankind.

> CHARLES WILLIAM ELIOT, lines inscribed on the 1890 Gate to Harvard Yard.

33 The office of the scholar is to cheer, to raise, and to guide men by showing them facts amidst appearances.

> RALPH WALDO EMERSON, *The American Scholar*, 1837.

34 There is no teaching until the pupil is brought into the same state or principle in which you are: a transfusion takes place; he is you, and you are he; there is a teaching; and by no unfriendly chance or bad company can he ever quite lose the benefit.

> RALPH WALDO EMERSON, "Spiritual Laws," *Essays*, First Series, 1841.

35 Why drag this dead weight of a Sunday-school over the whole Christendom? It is natural and beautiful that childhood should inquire, and maturity should teach; but it is time enough to answer questions when they are asked.

> Ibid.

36 We are students of words: we are shut up in schools, and colleges, and recitation-rooms, for ten or fifteen years, and come out at last with a bag of wind, a memory of words, and do not know a thing.

> RALPH WALDO EMERSON, "The New England Reformers," *Essays*, Second Series, 1844.

37 The intelligent have a right over the ignorant; namely, the right of instructing them.

> RALPH WALDO EMERSON, *Representative Men*, 1850.

38 One of the benefits of a college education is to show the boy its little avail.

> RALPH WALDO EMERSON, "Culture," *The Conduct of Life*, 1860.

39 The idea of a girl's education is whatever qualifies her for going to Europe.

> RALPH WALDO EMERSON, a statement attributed to "an eminent teacher of girls," in *The Conduct of Life*, 1860.

40 If the pupil be of a texture to bear it, the best university that can be recommended to a man of ideas is the gauntlet of the mob.

> RALPH WALDO EMERSON, *Society and Solitude*, 1870.

41 Every scholar is surrounded by wiser men than he.

> Ibid.

42 If this boy passes the examinations he will be admitted; and if the white students choose to withdraw, all the income of the college will be devoted to his education.

> EDWARD EVERETT, president of Harvard, responding to protest against admission of a black student, 1848.

43 Nations have recently been led to borrow billions for war; no nation has ever borrowed largely for education. Probably no nation is rich enough to pay for both war and civilization. We must make our choice; we cannot have both.

> ABRAHAM FLEXNER, *Universities,* 1930.

44 We call our schools free because we are not free to stay away from them until we are sixteen years of age.

> ROBERT FROST, in the introduction to his *Collected Poems,* 1939.

45 Next in importance to freedom and justice is popular education, without which neither freedom nor justice can be permanently maintained.

> JAMES A. GARFIELD, in a letter accepting the Republican nomination for the Presidency, July 12, 1880.

46 Of all horned cattle, the most helpless in a printing-office is a college graduate.

> Attributed to Horace Greeley, c.1860.

47 The right to impart instruction, harmless in itself or beneficial to those who receive it, is a substantial right of property.

> JOHN MARSHALL HARLAN, in a Supreme Court opinion, *Berea College* v. *Kentucky,* 1908.

48 Knowledge and timber shouldn't be much used till they are seasoned.

> OLIVER WENDELL HOLMES, SR., *The Autocrat of the Breakfast-Table,* 1858.

49 A man's ignorance is as much his private property, and as precious in his own eyes, as his family Bible.

OLIVER WENDELL HOLMES, SR., in a lecture in New York City, "The Young Practitioner," March 2, 1871.

50 We need education in the obvious more than investigation of the obscure.

> OLIVER WENDELL HOLMES, JR., in a speech in New York City, February 15, 1913.

51 A college degree does not lessen the length of your ears: it only conceals it.

> ELBERT HUBBARD, *The Roycroft Dictionary and Book of Epigrams,* 1923.

52 Now, owls are not really wise—they only look that way. The owl is a sort of college professor.

> Ibid.

53 The history of scholarship is a record of disagreements.

> CHARLES EVANS HUGHES, in a speech in Washington, D.C., May 7, 1936.

54 Academic freedom is simply a way of saying that we get the best results in education and research if we leave their management to people who know something about them.

> ROBERT M. HUTCHINS, *The Higher Learning in America,* 1936.

55 The policy of the repression of ideas cannot work and never has worked. The alternative to it is the long, difficult road of education. To this the American people have been committed.

> ROBERT M. HUTCHINS, testifying before the Illinois Seditious Activities Investigation Commission, April 21, 1949.

56 It is one of the paradoxes of our time that modern society needs to fear . . . only the educated man.

> ROBERT H. JACKSON, quoted in William F. Buckley, *God and Man at Yale,* 1951.

57 Our colleges ought to have lit up in us a lasting relish for the better kind of man, a loss of appetite for mediocrities.

> WILLIAM JAMES, "The Social Value of the College-Bred," *Memories and Studies,* 1911.

58 Preach, my dear Sir, a crusade against ignorance; establish and improve the law for educating

the common people. Let our countrymen know . . . that the tax which will be paid for this purpose is not more than the thousandth part of what will be paid to kings, priests and nobles, who will rise up among us if we leave the people in ignorance.

THOMAS JEFFERSON, in a letter to George Wythe, August 13, 1786.

59 I have never thought a boy should undertake abstruse or difficult sciences, such as mathematics in general, till fifteen years of age at soonest. Before that time, they are best employed in learning the languages, which is merely a matter of memory.

THOMAS JEFFERSON, in a letter to Ralph Izard, July 17, 1788.

60 If a nation expects to be ignorant and free, in a state of civilization, it expects what never was and never will be.

THOMAS JEFFERSON, in a letter to Charles Yancey, January 6, 1816.

61 We just must not, we just cannot afford the great waste that comes from the neglect of a single child.

LYNDON B. JOHNSON, in a speech before the National Conference on Education Legislation, March 1, 1965.

62 I find that the three major administrative problems on a campus are sex for the students, athletics for the alumni, and parking for the faculty.

CLARK KERR, in a speech at the inauguration of president Charles E. Odegaard, University of Washington, quoted in *Time* magazine, November 17, 1958.

63 What the vast majority of American children need is to stop being pampered, stop being indulged, stop being chauffeured, stop being catered to. In the final analysis it is not what you do for your children but what you have taught them to do for themselves that will make them successful human beings.

ANN LANDERS, *Ann Landers Says Truth Is Stranger . . .,* 1968.

64 [American students] emerge like luggage after a well planned tour covered with labels but with very little acquirement within. The Universities are largely the gifts of the very rich, handed back to the middle class.

SHANE LESLIE, *American Wonderland,* 1936.

65 Upon the subject of education, not presuming to dictate any plan or system respecting it, I can only say that I view it as the most important subject which we, as a people, can be engaged in.

ABRAHAM LINCOLN, in his first recorded public speech, to the people of Sangamon County, Illinois, March 9, 1832.

66 I desire to see the time when education, and by its means, morality, sobriety, enterprise and industry, shall become much more general than at present.

ABRAHAM LINCOLN, in a letter to the *Sangamon Journal,* 1832.

67 Does a College education pay? Does it pay to feed in pork trimmings at five cents a pound in the hopper and draw out nice, cunning, little "country" sausages at the other end? Does it pay to take a steer that's been running loose on the range and living on cactus and petrified wood till he's just a bunch of barb-wire and sole-leather, and feed him corn till he's just a solid hunk of porterhouse steak and oleo oil?

GEORGE HORACE LORIMER, *Letters from a Self-Made Merchant to His Son,* 1902.

68 It was in making education not only common to all, but in some sense compulsory on all, that the destiny of the free republics of America was practically settled.

JAMES RUSSELL LOWELL, "New England Two Centuries Ago," *Among My Books,* 1870.

69 The better part of every man's education is that which he gives himself.

JAMES RUSSELL LOWELL, "Abraham Lincoln," *My Study Windows,* 1871.

70 The fundamental theory of liberty upon which governments in this Union repose excludes any general power of the State to standardize its children by forcing them to accept instruction from public teachers only. The child is not the mere

creature of the state; those who nurture him and direct his destiny have the right, coupled with the high duty, to recognize and prepare him for additional obligations.

> James Clark McReynolds, in a Supreme Court decision, *Pierce* v. *Society of the Sisters,* 1925.

71 Education alone can conduct us to that enjoyment which is, at once, best in quality and infinite in quantity.

> Horace Mann, *Lectures on Education,* 1845.

72 In our country and in our times no man is worthy of the honored name of statesman who does not include the highest practicable education of the people in all his plans of administration.

> Ibid.

73 It is boasted sometimes of a schoolmaster that such a brave man had his education under him, but it is never said how many who might have been brave men have been ruined by him.

> Cotton Mather, *Essays To Do Good,* 1710.

74 A highbrow is a person educated beyond his intelligence.

> Attributed to Brander Matthews.

75 If one cannot state a matter clearly enough so that even an intelligent twelve-year-old can understand it, one should remain within the cloistered walls of the university and laboratory until one gets a better grasp of one's subject matter.

> Margaret Mead, quoted in *Redbook* magazine, July, 1963.

76 The most extraordinary thing about a really good teacher is that he or she transcends accepted educational methods. Such methods are designed to help average teachers approximate the performance of good teachers.

> Margaret Mead, quoted in *Redbook* magazine, September, 1972.

77 If, at my death, my executors, or more properly my creditors, find any precious MSS. in my desk, then here I prospectively ascribe all the honor and the glory to whaling; for a whale ship was my Yale College and my Harvard.

> Herman Melville, *Moby-Dick,* 1851.

78 The average schoolmaster is and always must be essentially an ass, for how can one imagine an intelligent man engaging in so puerile an avocation?

> H.L. Mencken, *Prejudices,* Third Series, 1922.

79 In a free world, if it is to remain free, we must maintain, with our lives if need be, but surely by our lives, the opportunity for a man to learn anything.

> J. Robert Oppenheimer, in the *Journal of the Atomic Scientists,* September, 1956.

80 The teacher's life should have three periods—study until 25, investigation until 40, profession until 60, at which age I would have him retired on a double allowance.

> William Osler, in a speech in Baltimore, Maryland, February 22, 1905.

81 The "thousand profound scholars" may have failed, first, because they were scholars, secondly, because they were profound, and thirdly, because they were a thousand.

> Edgar Allan Poe, "The Rationale of Verse," published in *The Pioneer,* March, 1843.

82 Education is not the means of showing people how to get what they want. Education is an exercise by means of which enough men, it is hoped, will learn to want what is worth having.

> Ronald Reagan, *Sincerely, Ronald Reagan,* 1976.

83 Erudition, like a bloodhound, is a charming thing when held firmly in leash, but it is not so attractive when turned loose upon a defenseless, unerudite public.

> Agnes Repplier, *Points of View,* 1891.

84 The papers today say that illiteracy has decreased. The more that learn how to read the less learn how to make a living. That's one thing about a little education. It spoils you for actual work. The more you know the more you think somebody owes you a living.

> Will Rogers, September 4, 1931, quoted in Donald Day, *The Autobiography of Will Rogers,* 1949.

85 The gains of education are never really lost. Books may be burned and cities sacked, but truth, like the yearning for freedom, lives in the hearts of humble men.

> FRANKLIN D. ROOSEVELT, in his acceptance speech at the Democratic Party National Convention, June 27, 1936.

86 The turgid style of Johnson, the purple glare of Gibbon, and even the studied and thickset metaphors of Junius are all equally unnatural, and should not be admitted into our company.

> BENJAMIN RUSH, *A Plan of a Federal University,* 1788.

87 There is but one method of preventing crimes, and of rendering a republican form of government durable, and that is, by disseminating the seeds of virtue and knowledge through every part of the state by means of proper places and modes of education, and this can be done effectually only by the interference and aid of the Legislature.

> BENJAMIN RUSH, *The Influence of Physical Causes Upon the Moral Faculty,* 1788.

88 The great difficulty in education is to get experience out of ideas.

> GEORGE SANTAYANA, *The Life of Reason,* 1905.

89 True education makes for inequality; the inequality of individuality, the inequality of success; the glorious inequality of talent, of genius; for inequality, not mediocrity, individual superiority, not standardization, is the measure of the progress of the world.

> FELIX E. SCHELLING, *Pedagogically Speaking,* 1929.

90 Education is a private matter between the person and the world of knowledge and experience, and has little to do with school or college.

> LILLIAN SMITH, "Bridges to Other People," *Redbook* magazine, September, 1969.

91 I could undertake to be an efficient pupil if it were possible to find an efficient teacher.

> GERTRUDE STEIN, "Q.E.D.," published in *Fernhurst, Q.E.D., and Other Early Writings,* 1972.

92 I have thought about it a great deal, and the more I think, the more certain I am that obedience is the gateway through which knowledge, yes, and love, too, enter the mind of the child.

> ANNIE SULLIVAN, in a letter, March 11, 1887, quoted in Helen Keller, *The Story of My Life,* 1903.

93 Scholars are wont to sell their birthright for a mess of learning.

> HENRY DAVID THOREAU, *A Week on the Concord and Merrimack Rivers,* 1849.

94 What does education often do? It makes a straight-cut ditch of a free, meandering brook.

> HENRY DAVID THOREAU, entry written in October, 1850, *Journal,* 1906.

95 We do not learn by inference and deduction and the application of mathematics to philosophy, but by direct intercourse and sympathy.

> HENRY DAVID THOREAU, *Excursions,* 1863.

96 Soap and education are not as sudden as a massacre, but they are more deadly in the long run.

> MARK TWAIN, "The Facts Concerning the Recent Resignation," 1867.

97 Training is everything. The peach was once a bitter almond; cauliflower is nothing but cabbage with a college education.

> MARK TWAIN, "Pudd'nhead Wilson's Calendar," *Pudd'nhead Wilson,* 1894.

98 In the first place God made idiots. This was for practice. Then He made School Boards.

> MARK TWAIN, "Puddn'head Wilson's New Calendar," *Following the Equator,* 1897.

99 There is no defense or security for any of us except in the highest intelligence and development of all.

> BOOKER T. WASHINGTON, in an address at the Atlanta Exposition, September 18, 1895.

100 On the diffusion of education among the people rest the preservation and perpetuation of our free institutions.

> DANIEL WEBSTER, in an address in Madison, Indiana, June 1, 1837.

101 The use of a university is to make young gentlemen as unlike their fathers as possible.

> WOODROW WILSON, in an address in Pittsburgh, Pennsylvania, on the 70th anniversary of the YMCA, October 24, 1914.

75. ELECTIONS

See also CAMPAIGN SLOGANS; POLITICS

1 The presidential election, occurring once in four years, throws the country for several months into a state of turmoil, for which there may be no occasion. Perhaps there are no serious party issues to be decided, perhaps the best thing would be that the existing Administration should pursue the even tenor of its way. The Consitution, however, requires an election to be held, so the whole costly and complicated machinery of agitation is put in motion; and if issues do not exist, they have to be created.

> JAMES BRYCE, *The American Commonwealth,* 1888.

2 A presidential election is sometimes . . . a turning-point in history. In form it is nothing more than the choice of an administrator who cannot influence policy otherwise than by refusing his assent to bills. In reality it is the deliverance of the mind of the people upon all such questions as they feel able to decide.

> Ibid.

3 The ordinary American voter does not object to mediocrity. He has a lower conception of the qualities requisite to make a statesman than those who direct public opinion in Europe have. He likes his candidate to be sensible, vigorous, and, above all, what he calls "magnetic," and does not value, because he sees no need for, originality or profundity, a fine culture or a wide knowledge.

> Ibid.

4 He who takes the oath today to preserve, protect, and defend the Constitution of the United States only assumes the solemn obligation which every patriotic citizen . . . should share with him. . . . Your every voter, as surely as your Chief Magistrate, under the same high sanction, though in a different sphere, exercises a public trust.

> GROVER CLEVELAND, in his inaugural address, March 4, 1885.

5 The man who can right himself by a vote will seldom resort to a musket.

> JAMES FENIMORE COOPER, *The American Democrat,* 1838.

6 The first step toward liberation for *any* group is to use the power in hand. . . . And the power in hand is the vote.

> HELEN GAHAGAN DOUGLAS, quoted by Lee Israel in *Ms.* magazine, October, 1973.

7 Voting is the most basic essential of citizenship and I think that any man or woman in this country who fails to avail himself or herself of that right should hide in shame. I truly wish there were some sort of badge of dishonor that a non-voter would have to wear.

> INDIA EDWARDS, *Pulling No Punches,* 1977.

8 Hell, I never vote *for* anybody, I always vote *against.*

> W.C. FIELDS, quoted in Robert Lewis Taylor, *W.C. Fields, His Follies and Fortunes,* 1949.

9 In most places in the country, voting is looked upon as a right and a duty, but in Chicago it's a *sport.* In Chicago not only *your* vote counts, but all kinds of other votes—kids, dead folks, and so on.

> DICK GREGORY, in *Dick Gregory's Political Primer,* 1972.

10 When it comes to persuading the electorate, there is currently nothing more important to a candidate than a wife, kids, and the right kind of animals. Dogs are great assets to candidates, and the feeling seems to be engendered that if a dog loves the candidate, he can't be all that bad.

> Ibid.

11 The freeman, casting with unpurchased hand
The vote that shakes the turret of the land.

OLIVER WENDELL HOLMES, SR., "Poetry: a Metrical Essay," 1836.

12 We will spend and spend, and tax and tax, and elect and elect.

Attributed to Harry L. Hopkins.

13 What they [direct primaries] actually appear to have accomplished is a confusion and vast expenditure of money that have proved to be, if not worse, at all events no better, than the old way of selecting candidates.

ALICE ROOSEVELT LONGWORTH, *Crowded Hours,* 1933.

14 So far as I can see it [woman's suffrage] has made little difference beyond doubling the number of voters. There is no woman's vote as such. They divide up just about as the men do.

Ibid.

15 Electioneering is upon no very pleasant footing anywhere; but with you, where the "base proletarian rout" are admitted to vote, it must be peculiarly irksome and repugnant to the feelings of a gentleman.

JOHN RANDOLPH, in a letter to Francis Scott Key, September 12, 1813.

16 I believe that biennial elections and quadrennial governorships are inventions which deprive the people of power, and at the same time offer prizes to be captured by the corruption of political life.

THOMAS BRACKETT REED, quoted in William Alexander Robinson, *Thomas B. Reed, Parliamentarian,* 1930.

17 An election is both a selection and rejection; it is a choosing up of sides. It matters greatly whether reason or passion guides our choice. Reason will enlighten and elevate our understanding and it will discover in controversy the springs of a new unity. But passion will poison the political atmosphere in which the nation must meet the tests of the future.

ADLAI E. STEVENSON, in a speech at Indianapolis, Indiana, September 18. 1954.

18 If we do justice at the polls to our own conscience and sense of responsibility, then alone can we do justice to the nation we love; then alone can

we make our beloved land a symbol and shrine of hope and faith for all free men.

ADLAI E. STEVENSON, in a speech in New York City, October 30, 1954.

19 Had America every attraction under heaven that nature and social enjoyment can offer, this electioneering madness would make me fly from it in disgust. It engrosses every conversation, it irritates every temper, it substitutes party spirit for personal esteem; and, in fact, vitiates the whole system of society.

FRANCES TROLLOPE, *Domestic Manners of the Americans,* 1832.

20 As long as I count the votes, what are you going to do about it?

WILLIAM MARCY "BOSS" TWEED, commenting on New York City elections, November, 1871.

21 Unless drastic reforms are made we must accept that fact that every four years the United States will be up for sale, and the richest man or family will buy it.

GORE VIDAL, *Reflections upon a Sinking Ship,* 1969.

22 Heroes and philosophers, brave men and vile, have since Rome and Athens tried to make this particular manner of transfer of power work effectively; no people has succeeded at it better, or over a longer period of time, than the Americans. Yet as the transfer of this power takes place, there is nothing to be seen except an occasional line outside a church or school, or a file of people fidgeting in the rain, waiting to enter the booths. No bands play on election day, no troops march, no guns are readied, no conspirators gather in secret headquarters. The noise and the blare, the bands and the screaming, the pageantry and oratory of the long fall campaign, fade on election day. All the planning is over, all effort spent. Now the candidates must wait.

THEODORE H. WHITE, *The Making of the President, 1960,* 1961.

76. ENEMIES

See also ANGER; FRIENDS; INVECTIVE;
REVENGE

1 Enemy, *n.* A designing scoundrel who has done you some service which it is inconvenient to repay. In military affairs, a body of men actuated by the basest motives and pursuing the most iniquitous aim.

AMBROSE BIERCE, entry in Ernest J. Hopkins, *The Enlarged Devil's Dictionary,* 1967.

2 Better make a weak man your enemy than your friend.

JOSH BILLINGS, "Affurisms," *Josh Billings: His Sayings,* 1865.

3 There is no little enemy.

BENJAMIN FRANKLIN, *Poor Richard's Almanack,* 1733.

4 If you attend to your work, and let your enemy alone, some one else will come along some day, and do him up for you.

EDGAR WATSON HOWE, *Country Town Sayings,* 1911.

5 It is an undeniable privilege of every man to prove himself right in the thesis that the world is his enemy; for if he reiterates it frequently enough and makes it the background of his conduct he is bound eventually to be right.

GEORGE F. KENNAN, "The Sources of Soviet Conduct," *Foreign Affairs,* July, 1947.

6 Folks never understand the folks they hate.

JAMES RUSSELL LOWELL, *The Biglow Papers,* Second Series, 1867.

7 I don't have a warm personal enemy left. They've all died off. I miss them terribly because they helped define me.

CLARE BOOTHE LUCE, in a television appearance on *The Dick Cavett Show,* July 21, 1981.

8 Your friends sometimes go to sleep, your enemies never do.

THOMAS BRACKETT REED, in an address, March 6, 1891, quoted in William A. Robinson, *Thomas B. Reed, Parliamentarian,* 1930.

9 I no doubt deserved my enemies, but I don't believe I deserved my friends.

WALT WHITMAN, quoted in Gamaliel Bradford, *Biography and the Human Heart,* 1932.

77. ENGLAND

1 England expects every American to do his duty.

Anonymous anti-British saying during World War I.

2 The extremes of opulence and of want are more remarkable, and more constantly obvious, in this country [England] than in any other that I ever saw.

JOHN QUINCY ADAMS, diary entry, November 8, 1816.

3 A nation of shopkeepers.

SAMUEL ADAMS, characterizing England in an oration believed to have been delivered in Philadelphia, August 1, 1776.

4 An English tourist's preconceived idea of us is a thing he brings over with him on the steamer and carries home again intact.

THOMAS BAILEY ALDRICH, *Ponkapog Papers,* 1903.

5 The Anglo-Saxon carries self-government and self-development with him wherever he goes.

HENRY WARD BEECHER, in a speech in Liverpool, England, October 16, 1863.

6 If there be one test of national genius universally accepted, it is success; and if there be one successful country in the universe for the last millennium, that country is England.

RALPH WALDO EMERSON, *English Traits,* 1856.

7 The sea which, according to Virgil's famous line, divided the poor Britons utterly from the

world, proved to be the ring of marriage with all nations.

> Ibid.

8 Domesticity is the taproot which enables the English to branch wide and high. The motive and end of their trade and empire is to guard the independence and privacy of their homes.

> Ibid.

9 Every one of these islanders is an island himself, safe, tranquil, incommunicable.

> Ibid.

10 English history is aristocracy with the doors open. Who has courage and faculty, let him come in.

> Ibid.

11 An Englishman shows no mercy to those below him in the social scale, as he looks for none from those above him; any forbearance from his superiors surprises him, and they suffer in his good opinion.

> Ibid.

12 Governments of nations of shopkeepers must keep shop also.

> RALPH WALDO EMERSON, entry written in 1862, *Journals,* 1909–1914. (See quotation 3, above.)

13 The greatest benefit of the Eton school, says the report in an English blue book, is the serenity and repose of character which it gives to its graduates, and which, as the document says, without intent of irony, is a well-known trait of the character of the English gentleman.

> RALPH WALDO EMERSON, "Public and Private Education," *Uncollected Lectures,* 1932.

14 This selfish race, from all the world
    disjoin'd,
Perpetual discord spread throughout mankind,
Aim to extend their empire o'er the ball,
Subject, destroy, absorb, and conquer all.

> PHILIP FRENEAU, *The British Prison Ship,* 1781.

15 England and the United States are natural allies, and should be the best of friends.

> ULYSSES S. GRANT, *Personal Memoirs,* 1885.

16 It takes a great deal to produce ennui in an Englishman and if you do, he only takes it as convincing proof that you are well-bred.

> MARGARET HALSEY, *With Malice Toward Some,* 1938.

17 Englishmen are not made of polishable substance.

> NATHANIEL HAWTHORNE, journal entry, February 13, 1854.

18 The Englishman's strong point is his vigorous insularity; that of the American his power of adaptation. Each of these attitudes has its perils. The Englishman stands firmly on his feet, but he who merely does this never advances. The American's disposition is to step forward even at the risk of a fall.

> THOMAS WENTWORTH HIGGINSON, "A Half-Century of American Literature (1857–1907)," in *Carlyle's Laugh and Other Surprises,* 1909.

19 His home!—the Western giant smiles,
    And twirls the spotty globe to find it;—
This little speck the British Isles?
    'Tis but a freckle—never mind it!

> OLIVER WENDELL HOLMES, SR., "A Good Time Going," 1858.

20 The King blew his nose twice, and wiped the royal perspiration repeatedly from a face which is probably the largest uncivilized spot in England.

> OLIVER WENDELL HOLMES, SR., writing of William IV of England, quoted in John T. Morse, *The Life and Letters of Oliver Wendell Holmes,* 1897.

21 By no stretch of charity, and by no violence to grammar can you call the British Nation a Christian people. The British leaders have an itch for dictation, and their chief vice is a thirst for power.

> ELBERT HUBBARD, in *The Philistine* magazine, published from 1895–1915.

22 The sun of her glory is fast descending to the horizon.

> THOMAS JEFFERSON, on Great Britain, in *Notes on the State of Virginia,* 1784.

23 Of all nations on earth, they [the British] require to be treated with the most *hauteur*. They require to be kicked into common good manners.

THOMAS JEFFERSON, in a letter to Col. William Stephens Smith, September 28, 1787.

24 I considered the British as our natural enemies, and as the only nation on earth who wished us ill from the bottom of their souls. And I am satisfied that, were our continent to be swallowed up by the ocean, Great Britain would be in a bonfire from one end to the other.

THOMAS JEFFERSON, in a letter to William Carmichael, December 11, 1787.

25 The real power and property of the [British] government is in the great aristocratical families of the nation. The nest of office being too small for all of them to cuddle into it at once, the contest is eternal which shall crowd the other out. For this purpose they are divided into two parties, the Ins and the Outs.

THOMAS JEFFERSON, in a letter to John Langdon, governor of New Hampshire, March 5, 1810.

26 This is the true character of the English Government, and it presents the singular phenomenon of a nation, the individuals of which are as faithful to their private engagements and duties, as honorable, as worthy as those of any Nation on earth, and yet whose government is the most unprincipled at this day known.

Ibid.

27 The English have been a wise, a virtuous and truly estimable people. But commerce and a corrupt government have rotted them to the core. Every generous, nay, every just sentiment, is absorbed in the thirst for gold. I speak of their cities, which we may certainly pronounce to be ripe for despotism, and fitted for no other government. Whether the leaven of the agricultural body is sufficient to regenerate the residuary mass, and maintain it in a sound state, under any reformation of government, may well be doubted.

THOMAS JEFFERSON, in a letter to James Ogilvie, August 4, 1811.

28 I consider the government of England as totally without morality, insolent beyond bearing, inflated

with vanity and ambition, aiming at the exclusive dominion of the sea, lost in corruption, of deep-rooted hatred towards us, hostile to liberty wherever it endeavors to show its head, and the eternal disturber of the peace of the world.

THOMAS JEFFERSON, in a letter to Thomas Leiper, June, 1815.

29 It has ever appeared to me that the difference between the Whig and the Tory of England is, that the Whig deduces his rights from the Anglo-Saxon source, and the Tory from the Norman.

THOMAS JEFFERSON, in a letter to John Cartwright, June 5, 1824.

30 To no race are we more indebted for the virtues which constitute a great people than to the Anglo-Saxon.

GEN. ROBERT E. LEE, in a letter to W.H. Nettleton, May 21, 1866.

31 Nothing, I am sure, equals my thankfulness when I meet an Englishman who is not like every other.

JAMES RUSSELL LOWELL, "On a Certain Condescension in Foreigners," 1869.

32 Not a Bull of them all but is persuaded he bears Europa upon his back.

Ibid.

33 [England] has a conviction that whatever good there is in us is wholly English, when the truth is that we are worth nothing except so far as we have disinfected ourselves of Anglicism.

Ibid.

34 The New World's Sons, from England's
        breasts we drew
    Such milk as bids remember whence we
        came;
Proud of her Past, wherefrom our Present
        grew,
    This window we inscribe with Raleigh's
        name.

JAMES RUSSELL LOWELL, lines on the Raleigh window, St. Margaret's, Westminster, 1888.

35 France built its best colony on a principle of exclusion, and failed: England reversed the system, and succeeded.

FRANCIS PARKMAN, *Montcalm and Wolfe,* 1884.

36 There is not a more disgusting spectacle under the sun than our subserviency to British criticism. It is disgusting, first, because it is truckling, servile, pusillanimous—secondly, because of its gross irrationality. We know the British to bear us little but ill will—we know this, and yet, day after day, submit our necks to the degrading yoke of the crudest opinion that emanates from the fatherland.

EDGAR ALLAN POE, *Marginalia,* 1844–1849.

37 I once heard it argued . . . by Englishmen, that it was a good thing for us that we have lost the United States. There are some subjects on which there can be no argument, and to an Englishman this is one of them.

CECIL RHODES, *A Draft of Some of My Ideas,* c.1877.

38 England is the paradise of individuality, eccentricity, heresy, anomalies, hobbies, and humors.

GEORGE SANTAYANA, "The British Character," *Soliloquies in England and Later Soliloquies,* 1922.

39 An American whether he be embarked in politics, in literature, or in commerce, desires English admiration, English appreciation of his energy, and English encouragement.

ANTHONY TROLLOPE, "Maine, New Hampshire, and Vermont," *North America,* 1862.

40 The English are mentioned in the Bible: Blessed are the meek, for they shall inherit the earth.

MARK TWAIN, "Pudd'nhead Wilson's New Calendar," *Following the Equator,* 1897.

41 A power which has dotted over the surface of the whole globe with her possessions and military posts, whose morning drum-beat, following the sun, and keeping company with the hours, circles the earth with one continuous and unbroken strain of the martial airs of England.

DANIEL WEBSTER, in a speech, May 7, 1834.

42 Only Anglo-Saxons can govern themselves.

WILLIAM ALLEN WHITE, in the *Emporia Gazette,* March 20, 1899.

43 O Englishmen!—in hope and creed,
   In blood and tongue our brothers!
 We too are heirs of Runnymede;
   And Shakespeare's fame and Cromwell's deed
   Are not alone our mother's.

JOHN GREENLEAF WHITTIER, "To Englishmen," *In War Time and Other Poems,* 1864.

78. EPITAPHS

See also LAST WORDS

Some of the most enduring lines written by Americans are found on gravestones. Many of these memorable epitaphs are whimsical, while others are quite moving. Readers interested in epitaphs will find an outstanding collection in the volume *Quaint Epitaphs,* by Susan Darling Safford, 1898.

1 Here lies the body of Bob Dent;
  He kicked up his heels and to Hell he
    went.

Tombstone near Port Gibson, Mississippi.

2 His faith in the people never wavered.

Grave of Andrew Johnson, Greeneville, Tennessee.

3 Here lies the body of Obadiah Wilkinson
   And Ruth, his wife.
 Their warfare is accomplished.

Gravestone in New Haven, Connecticut.

4 Here lies the bones of Richard Lawton
Whose death alas! was strangely brought
    on.
Trying his corns one day to mow off.
His razor slipped and cut his toe off.
His toe or rather what it grew to,
An inflimation quickly grew to.
Which took alas! to mortifying
And was the cause of Richard's dying.

    Gravestone in Plymouth, Massachusetts.

5 Here lies Cynthia, Steven's wife
She lived six years in calm and strife.
Death came at last and set her free,
I was glad and so was she.

    Gravestone in Hollis, New Hampshire.

6 A thousand ways cut short our days,
None are exempt from death.
A honey-bee by stinging me
Did stop my mortal breath.

    Gravestone in Orange County, New York.

7 A rum cough carried him off.

    Gravestone in Stowe, Vermont.

8 Epitaph, *n.* An inscription on a tomb, showing that virtues acquired by death have a retroactive effect.

    AMBROSE BIERCE, *The Devil's Dictionary,*
    1906.

9 Here Huntington's ashes long have lain
Whose loss is our own eternal gain,
For while he exercised all his powers,
Whatever he gained, the loss was ours.

    AMBROSE BIERCE, epitaph on C.P.
    Huntington, included in the entry for the word
    "loss" in *The Devil's Dictionary,* 1906.

10 Here lies Sir Jenkin Grout, who loved his friend, and persuaded his enemy; what his mouth ate, his hand paid for; what his servants robbed, he restored: if a woman gave him pleasure, he supported her in pain: he never forgot his children: and whoso touched his finger, drew after it his whole body.

Epitaph given by Ralph Waldo Emerson in "Manners," *Essays,* Second Series, 1844.

11   The Body of
        B Franklin Printer,
    (Like the Cover of an old Book
        Its Contents torn out
  And stript of its Lettering & Gilding)
     Lies here, Food for Worms.
    But the Work shall not be lost;
For it will, (as he believ'd) appear once more,
    In a new and more elegant Edition
       Revised and corrected,
        By the Author.

    BENJAMIN FRANKLIN, his own epitaph,
    written in 1728. (Franklin died on April 19,
    1790).

12 Here Skugg
Lies snug
As a bug
In a rug.

    BENJAMIN FRANKLIN, epitaph for Miss
    Georgiana Shipley's pet squirrel, in a letter to
    her, September 26, 1772.

13 And were an epitaph to be my story
I'd have a short one ready for my own.
I would have written of me on my stone:
I had a lover's quarrel with the world.

    ROBERT FROST, "The Lesson for Today,"
    read at Harvard University, June 20,
    1941.

14 He loved his country as no other man has loved her, but no man deserved less at her hands.

    EDWARD EVERETT HALE, epitaph of Philip
    Nolan, *The Man Without a Country,* 1863.

15 When fades at length our lingering day,
Who cares what pompous tombstones
    say?
Read on the hearts that love us still,
Hic jacet Joe. *Hic jacet* Bill.

    OLIVER WENDELL HOLMES, SR., "Bill and
    Joe," 1868.

16 Here was buried Thomas Jefferson, author of the Declaration of American Independence, of the statute of Virginia for religious freedom, and father of the University of Virginia.

> THOMAS JEFFERSON, his own epitaph. (Jefferson died on July 4, 1826.)

17 Over my dead body!

> GEORGE F. KAUFMAN, his own proposed epitaph, quoted in Robert E. Drennan, *The Algonquin Wits,* 1968.

18 If, after I depart this vale, you ever remember me and have thought to please my ghost, forgive some sinner and wink your eye at some homely girl.

> H.L. MENCKEN, his own proposed epitaph, in *Smart Set* magazine, December, 1921.

19 Excuse my dust.
This is on me.

> DOROTHY PARKER, two of her own proposed epitaphs, quoted in Robert E. Drennan, *The Algonquin Wits,* 1968.

20 Unawed by opinion
Unseduced by flattery
Undismayed by disaster
He confronted life with antique courage
And death with Christian hope.

> Epitaph of James Petigru, Charleston, South Carolina, 1863.

21 Warm Summer sun, shine kindly here;
Warm southern wind, blow softly here;
Green sod above, lie light, lie light—
Good night, dear heart, good night, good night.

> MARK TWAIN, epitaph for his daughter, 1896 (adapted from "To Annette," by Robert Richardson, c.1885).

---

79. EQUALITY

See also CIVIL RIGHTS; JUSTICE; WOMEN'S RIGHTS

---

1 The fact is, that the Americans have ignored in all their legislative as in many of their administrative arrangements, the differences of capacity between man and man. They underrate the difficulties of government and overrate the capacities of the man of common sense. Great are the blessings of equality; but what follies are committed in its name!

> JAMES BRYCE, *The American Commonwealth,* 1888.

2 No poor, rural, weak, or black person should ever again have to bear the additional burden of being deprived of the opportunity for an education, a job, or simple justice.

> JIMMY CARTER, inaugural address as governor of Georgia, January 12, 1971.

3 Equality, in a social sense, may be divided into that of condition and that of rights. Equality of condition is incompatible with civilization, and is found only to exist in those communities that are but slightly removed from the savage state. In practice, it can only mean a common misery.

> JAMES FENIMORE COOPER, *The American Democrat,* 1838.

4 The very existence of government at all infers inequality. The citizen who is preferred to office becomes the superior of those who are not, so long as he is the repository of power.

> Ibid.

5 I do not believe that the Almighty ever intended the Negro to be the equal of the white man. If He

did, He has been a long time demonstrating the fact.

> STEPHEN A. DOUGLAS, first Lincoln-Douglas debate, August 21, 1858.

6 Behold th' land iv freedom, where ivry man's as good as ivry other man, on'y th' other man don't know it.

> FINLEY PETER DUNNE, "The New York Custom House," *Mr Dooley's Opinion,* 1901.

7 This [is the] home iv opporchunity where ivry man is th' equal iv ivry other man befure th' law if he isn't careful.

> FINLEY PETER DUNNE, *Dissertations by Mr. Dooley,* 1906.

8 As a man is equal to the Church and equal to the State, so he is equal to every other man.

> RALPH WALDO EMERSON, "New England Reformers," *Essays,* Second Series, 1844.

9 Whilst the rights of all as persons are equal, in virtue of their access to reason, their rights in property are very unequal. One man owns his clothes, and another owns a county.

> RALPH WALDO EMERSON, "Politics," *Essays,* Second Series, 1844.

10 There is a little formula, couched in pure Saxon, which you may hear in the corners of streets and in the yard of the dame's school, from very little republicans: "I'm as good as you be," which contains the essence of the Massachusetts Bill of Rights and of the American Declaration of Independence.

> RALPH WALDO EMERSON, "Boston," *Natural History of Intellect,* 1893.

11 The [15th] amendment nullifies sophisticated as well as simple-minded modes of discrimination.

> FELIX FRANKFURTER, in a Supreme Court decision, *Lane* v. *Wilson,* 1939.

12 Wherever there is a human being, I see God-given rights inherent in that being, whatever may be the sex or complexion.

> WILLIAM LLOYD GARRISON, in *William Lloyd Garrison, 1805–79: The Story of His Life Told by His Children,* 1885–1889.

13 The equal right of all men to the use of land is as clear as their equal right to breathe the air—it is a right proclaimed by the fact of their existence. For we cannot suppose that some men have a right to be in this world, and others no right.

> HENRY GEORGE, *Progress and Poverty,* 1879.

14 The struggle for equal opportunity in America is the struggle for America's soul. The ugliness of bigotry stands in direct contradiction to the very meaning of America.

> HUBERT H. HUMPHREY, *Beyond Civil Rights—A New Day of Equality,* 1968.

15 We have talked long enough in this country about equal rights. We have talked for a hundred years or more. It is time now to write the next chapter—and to write in the books of law.

> LYNDON B. JOHNSON, in his first presidential address to Congress, November 27, 1963.

16 Equality in society beats inequality, whether the latter be of the British-aristocratic sort or of the domestic-slavery sort.

> ABRAHAM LINCOLN, in a speech in Peoria, Illinois, October 16, 1854.

17 I think the authors of that notable instrument [the Declaration of Independence] intended to include all men, but they did not intend to declare all men equal in all respects. They did not mean to say all men were equal in color, size, intellect, moral developments, or social capacity. They defined with tolerable distinctness in what respects they did consider all men created equal—equal with "certain unalienable rights, among which are life, liberty, and the pursuit of happiness."

> ABRAHAM LINCOLN, in a speech on the Dred Scott decision, June 26, 1857.

18 I am an aristocrat; I love liberty, I hate equality.

> JOHN RANDOLPH, quoted in Russell Kirk, *John Randolph of Roanoke,* 1951.

19 We hate to see people standing too much above ourselves; we never endure it patiently. In practical life we never submit to it. We either grow up to the advanced people, or we pull the advanced people down.

THOMAS BRACKETT REED, speaking in the House of Representatives, 1891.

20 No one can make you feel inferior without your consent.

ELEANOR ROOSEVELT, *This Is My Story*, 1937.

21 It is a party of one idea; but that is a noble one, an idea that fills and expands all generous souls; the idea of equality, the equality of all men before human tribunals and human laws, as they all are equal before the divine tribunal and divine laws.

WILLIAM HENRY SEWARD, in a speech in Rochester, New York, October 25, 1858.

22 In a state where the citizens are all practically equal, it becomes difficult for them to preserve their independence against aggressions of power.

ALEXIS DE TOCQUEVILLE, *Democracy in America*, 1835–1840.

23 Americans are so enamored of equality that they would rather be equal in slavery than unequal in freedom.

Ibid.

24 To separate [black children] from others of similar age and qualifications solely because of their race generates a feeling of inferiority as to their status in the community that may affect their hearts and minds in a way unlikely ever to be undone. . . . In the field of public education the doctrine of "separate but equal" has no place. Separate educational facilities are inherently unequal.

EARL WARREN, Supreme Court decision, *Brown v. Board of Education*, 1954.

25 Beneath thy broad, impartial eye,
  How fade the lines of caste and birth!
How equal in their suffering lie
  The groaning multitudes of earth!

JOHN GREENLEAF WHITTIER, "Democracy," 1841, collected in *Songs of Labor*, 1850.

26 The Constitution does not provide for first and second class citizens.

WENDELL L. WILLKIE, *An American Program*, 1944.

27 Goddammit, look! We live here and they live there. We black and they white. They got things and we ain't. They do things and we can't. It's just like living in jail.

RICHARD WRIGHT, *Native Son*, 1940.

80. EVIL

See also AFFLICTION; ANGER; CRIME; PAIN; PUNISHMENT; REVENGE; SIN

1 Some men wish evil and accomplish it
But most men, when they work in that machine
Just let it happen somewhere in the wheels.
The fault is no decisive villainous knife
But the dull saw that is the routine mind.

STEPHEN VINCENT BENÉT, *John Brown's Body*, 1928.

2 If men were basically evil, who would bother to improve the world instead of giving it up as a bad job at the outset?

VAN WYCK BROOKS, *From a Writer's Notebook*, 1958.

3 It is right noble to fight with wickedness and wrong; the mistake is in supposing that spiritual evil can be overcome by physical means.

LYDIA M. CHILD, *Letters from New York*, 1852.

4 The first lesson of history is the good of evil.

RALPH WALDO EMERSON, *The Conduct of Life*, 1860.

5 Evil is here in the world, not because God wants it or uses it here, but because He knows not how at the moment to remove it; or knowing, has not the skill or power to achieve His end. Evil, therefore, is a fact not to be explained away, but to be accepted; and accepted not to be endured, but to be conquered. It is a challenge neither to our reason nor to our patience, but to our courage.

JOHN HAYNES HOLMES, "A Struggling God," in Joseph Fort Newton, *My Idea of God*, 1926.

6 Darkness cannot drive out darkness; only light can do that. Hate cannot drive out hate; only love can do that. Hate multiplies hate, violence multiplies violence, and toughness multiplies toughness in a descending spiral of destruction. . . . The chain reaction of evil—hate begetting hate, wars producing more wars—must be broken, or we shall be plunged into the dark abyss of annihilation.

MARTIN LUTHER KING, JR., *Strength to Love,* 1963.

7 The world loves a spice of wickedness.

HENRY WADSWORTH LONGFELLOW, *Hyperion,* 1839.

8 Evil springs up, and flowers, and bears no
      seed,
   And feeds the green earth with its swift
      decay,
   Leaving it richer for the growth of truth.

JAMES RUSSELL LOWELL, "Prometheus," printed in the *United States Magazine and Democratic Review,* August, 1843.

9 It may be necessary temporarily to accept a lesser evil, but one must never label a necessary evil as good.

MARGARET MEAD, in *Redbook* magazine, November, 1978.

10 All that most maddens and torments; all that stirs up the lees of things; all truth with malice in it; all that cracks the sinews and cakes the brain; all the subtle demonisms of life and thought; all evil, to crazy Ahab, were visibly personified, and made practically assailable in Moby-Dick. He piled upon the whale's white hump the sum of all the general rage and hate felt by his whole race from Adam down; and then, as if his chest had been a mortar, he burst his hot heart's shell upon it.

HERMAN MELVILLE, *Moby-Dick,* 1851.

11 In the collective life of man, at least, most evil arises because finite men involved in the flux of time pretend that they are not so involved. They make claims of virtue, of wisdom, and of power which are beyond their competence as creatures. These pretensions are the source of evil, whether they are expressed by kings and emperors or by commissars and revolutionary statesmen.

REINHOLD NIEBUHR, *The Structure of Nations and Empires,* 1959.

12 No man is justified in doing evil on the ground of expediency.

THEODORE ROOSEVELT, *The Strenuous Life,* 1900.

13 Those who corrupt the public mind are just as evil as those who steal from the public purse.

ADLAI E. STEVENSON, in a speech in Albuquerque, New Mexico, September 12, 1952.

14 There are a thousand hacking at the branches of evil to one who is striking at the root.

HENRY DAVID THOREAU, *Walden,* 1854.

15 We may not pay him [Satan] reverence, for that would be indiscreet, but we can at least respect his talents. A person who has for untold centuries maintained the imposing position of spiritual head of four fifths of the human race, and political head of the whole of it, must be granted the possession of executive abilities of the loftiest order. In his large presence the other popes and politicians shrink to midges for the microscope. I would like to see him. I would rather see him and shake him by the tail than any other member of the European Concert.

MARK TWAIN, "Concerning the Jews," 1892.

---

81. EVOLUTION

See also CHANGE; NATURE; SCIENCE

---

1 The progress of evolution from President Washington to President Grant, was alone evidence enough to upset Darwin.

HENRY ADAMS, *The Education of Henry Adams,* 1907.

2 Evolution is fascinating to watch. To me it is most interesting when one can observe the evolution of a single man.

SHANA ALEXANDER, "Evolution of a Rebel Priest," *The Feminine Eye,* 1970.

3 There are no short cuts in evolution.

LOUIS D. BRANDEIS, speech in Boston, April 22, 1904.

4 There is no more reason to believe that man descended from some inferior animal than there is to believe that a stately mansion has descended from a small cottage.

WILLIAM JENNINGS BRYAN, at Dayton, Tennessee, during the Scopes trial, July 28, 1925.

5 A fire-mist and a planet,
    A crystal and a cell,
 A jellyfish and a saurian,
    And caves where the cavemen dwell;
 Then a sense of law and beauty,
    And a face turned from the clod—
 Some call it Evolution,
    And others call it God.

WILLIAM HERBERT CARRUTH, "Each in his Own Tongue," *Poems,* 1908.

6 I niver cud undherstand why if mankind come down fr'm th' monkey we weren't more janyal.

FINLEY PETER DUNNE, *Mr. Dolley on Making a Will and Other Necessary Evils,* 1919.

7 Cause and effect, means and ends, seed and fruit, cannot be severed; for the effect already blooms in the cause, the end pre-exists in the means, the fruit in the seed.

RALPH WALDO EMERSON, "Compensation," *Essays,* First Series, 1841.

8 Cause and effect are two sides of one fact.

RALPH WALDO EMERSON, "Circles," *Essays,* First Series, 1841.

9 How far off yet is the trilobite! how far the quadruped! how inconceivably remote is man! All duly arrive, and then race after race of men. It is a long way from granite to the oyster; farther yet to Plato and the preaching of the immortality of the soul.

RALPH WALDO EMERSON, "Nature," *Essays,* Second Series, 1844.

10 Each animal or vegetable form remembers the next inferior and predicts the next higher.

RALPH WALDO EMERSON, "Poetry and Imagination," *Letters and Social Aims,* 1876.

11 Recall from Time's abysmal chasm
 That piece of primal protoplasm
 The First Amoeba, strangely splendid,
 From whom we're all of us descended.

ARTHUR GUITERMAN, "Ode to the Amoeba."

12 Children, behold the Chimpanzee;
 He sits on the ancestral tree
 From which we sprang in ages gone.
 I'm glad we sprang: had we held on,
 We might, for aught that I can say,
 Be horrid Chimpanzees to-day.

OLIVER HERFORD, "The Chimpanzee."

13 We seem to be trapped by a civilization that has accelerated many physical aspects of evolution but has forgotten that other vital part of man—his mind and his psyche.

SYBIL LEEK, *ESP—The Magic Within You,* 1971.

14 From what flat wastes of cosmic slime,
    And stung by what quick fire,
 Sunward the restless races climb!—
    Men risen out of mire!

DON MARQUIS, "Unrest," in *Dreams and Dust,* 1915.

15 When you were a tadpole and I was a fish,
    In the Paleozoic time,
 And side by side on the ebbing tide,
 We sprawled through the ooze and
    slime, . . .
 My heart was rife with the joy of life,
    For I loved you even then.

LANGDON SMITH, "Evolution," 1906.

16 I don't believe your old bastard theory of evolution either; I believe it's pure jackass nonsense.

WILLIAM A. "BILLY" SUNDAY, at a revival meeting, c.1912.

17 I believe that our Heavenly Father invented man because he was disappointed in the monkey.

MARK TWAIN, quoted in Bernard De Voto, *Mark Twain in Eruption,* 1940.

82. EXPERIENCE

See also KNOWLEDGE; PHILOSOPHY; WISDOM

1 All experience is an arch, to build upon.

HENRY ADAMS, *The Education of Henry Adams,* 1907.

2 Experience is a good teacher, but she sends in terrific bills.

MINNA ANTRIM, *Naked Truth and Veiled Allusions,* 1902.

3 Once, *adv.* Enough.

AMBROSE BIERCE, *The Devil's Dictionary,* 1906.

4 Twice, *adv.* Once too often.

Ibid.

5 Only so much do I know, as I have lived.

RALPH WALDO EMERSON, *The American Scholar,* 1837.

6 The years teach much which the days never know.

RALPH WALDO EMERSON, "Experience," *Essays,* Second Series, 1844.

7 The finished man of the world must eat of every apple once.

RALPH WALDO EMERSON, *The Conduct of Life,* 1860.

8 A great part of courage is the courage of having done the thing before.

RALPH WALDO EMERSON, "Courage," *Society and Solitude,* 1870.

9 Experience keeps a dear school, yet Fools will learn in no other.

BENJAMIN FRANKLIN, *Poor Richard's Almanack,* 1743.

10 A moment's insight is sometimes worth a life's experience.

OLIVER WENDELL HOLMES, SR., *The Professor at the Breakfast-Table,* 1860.

11 Experience is the name every one gives his mistakes.

ELBERT HUBBARD, *The Roycroft Dictionary and Book of Epigrams,* 1923.

12 One cannot collect all the beautiful shells on the beach.

ANNE MORROW LINDBERGH, *A Gift from the Sea,* 1955.

13 One thorn of experience is worth a whole wilderness of warning.

JAMES RUSSELL LOWELL, "Shakespeare Once More," *Among My Books,* 1870.

14 [Proverbs are] the ready money of human experience.

JAMES RUSSELL LOWELL, *My Study Windows,* 1871.

15 One may almost doubt if the wisest man has learned anything of absolute value by living.

HENRY DAVID THOREAU, *Walden,* 1854.

16 Man's capacities have never been measured; nor are we to judge of what he can do by any precedents, so little has been tried.

Ibid.

17 We should be careful to get out of an experience only the wisdom that is in it—and stop there; lest we be like the cat that sits down on a hot stove-lid. She will never sit down on a hot stove-lid again—and that is well; but also she will never sit down on a cold one any more.

MARK TWAIN, "Pudd'nhead Wilson's New Calendar," *Following the Equator,* 1897.

83. FAILURE

See also ADVERSITY; SUCCESS; TROUBLE

1 Our whole way of life today is dedicated to the removal of risk. Cradle to grave we are supported, insulated, and isolated from the risks of life—and if we fall, our government stands ready with Band-aids of every size.

> SHIRLEY TEMPLE BLACK, in a speech in Texas, June, 1967, quoted in Rodney G. Minott, *The Sinking of The Lollipop,* 1968.

2 And nothing to look backward to with pride,
And nothing to look forward to with hope.

> ROBERT FROST, "The Death of the Hired Man," *North of Boston,* 1914.

3 Who would not rather founder in the fight
Than not have known the glory of the fray?

> RICHARD HOVEY, "Two and Fate," 1898, collected in *Along the Trail,* 1903.

4 A failure is a man who has blundered, but is not able to cash in the experience.

> ELBERT HUBBARD, *The Roycroft Dictionary and Book of Epigrams,* 1923.

5 The *probability* that we may fall in the struggle *ought not* to deter us from the support of a cause we believe to be just; it *shall not* deter me.

> ABRAHAM LINCOLN, "The Sub-Treasury," speech in the House of Representatives at Springfield, Illinois, December 26, 1839.

6 The greatest accomplishment is not in never falling, but in rising again after you fall.

> VINCE LOMBARDI, quoted in Jerry Kramer, *Instant Replay,* 1968.

7 Never mind;
If some of us were not so far behind,
The rest of us were not so far ahead.

> EDWING ARLINGTON ROBINSON, "Inferential," in *The Three Taverns,* 1920.

8 Have you heard that it was good to gain the day?

I also say it is good to fall, battles are lost in the same spirit in which they are won.

> WALT WHITMAN, "Song of Myself," 1855.

9 To those who've fail'd, in aspiration vast,
To unnam'd soldiers fallen in front on the lead,
To calm, devoted engineers—to over-ardent travelers—to pilots on their ships,
To many a lofty song and picture without recognition—I'd rear a laurel-cover'd monument.

> WALT WHITMAN, "To Those Who've Fail'd," 1888.

10 Let the thick curtain fall;
I better know than all
How little I have gained
How vast the unattained.

> JOHN GREENLEAF WHITTIER, "My Triumph," 1870.

84. FAME

See also GREATNESS; IMMORTALITY; MOTION PICTURES; POWER; REPUTATION; SUCCESS; TALENT

1 Famous, *adj.* Conspicuously miserable.

> AMBROSE BIERCE, *The Devil's Dictionary,* 1906.

2 The very agency which first makes the celebrity in the long run inevitably destroys him. . . . There is not even any tragedy in the celebrity's fall, for he is a man returned to his proper anonymous station.

> DANIEL BOORSTIN, *The Image,* 1962.

3 Fame is being paid a lot of money for what people think about you as well as for what you do . . . trying to find yourself while under the scrutiny of thousands of eyes . . . reacting instead of acting, being passive instead of active . . . having people tell you what they want you to do with your life . . . learning to understand what others want from you.

> BILL BRADLEY, *Life on the Run,* 1976.

4 Fame is a fickle food
Upon a shifting plate.

> EMILY DICKINSON, "Fame is a fickle food,"
> published in *The Single Hound,* 1914.

5 The longest wave is quickly lost in the sea.

> RALPH WALDO EMERSON, "Plato,"
> *Representative Men,* 1850.

6 If a man knows the law, people find it out, tho'
he live in a pine shanty, and resort to him. And if
a man can pipe or sing, so as to wrap the prisoned
soul in an elysium; or can paint landscape, and
convey into oils and ochres all enchantments of
Spring and Autumn; or can liberate and intoxicate
all people who hear him with delicious songs and
verses; it is certain that the secret cannot be kept:
the first witness tells it to a second, and men go by
fives and tens and fifties to his door.

> RALPH WALDO EMERSON, entry written in 1855,
> *Journals,* 1909–1914.

7 I trust a good deal to common fame, as we all
must. If a man has good corn, or wood, or boards,
or pigs, to sell, or can make better chairs or knives,
crucibles, or church organs, than anybody else, you
will find a broad, hard-beaten road to his house,
though it be in the woods.

> RALPH WALDO EMERSON, entry written in
> February, 1855, *Journals,* 1909–1914.

8 If a man can write a better book, preach a better
sermon, or make a better mouse-trap than his neighbor, though he builds his house in the woods, the
world will make a beaten path to his door.

> RALPH WALDO EMERSON, quoted in the
> anthology *Borrowings,* issued by the Ladies of the
> First Unitarian Church of Oakland, California,
> 1889.

9 The hater of property and of government takes
care to have his warranty-deed recorded, and the
book written against Fame and learning has the
author's name on the title-page.

> RALPH WALDO EMERSON, entry written in 1857,
> *Journals,* 1909–1914.

10 He pays too high a price
For knowledge and for fame

Who sells his sinews to be wise,
His teeth and bones to buy a name,
And crawls through life a paralytic
To earn the praise of bard and critic.

> RALPH WALDO EMERSON, "Fame," 1867.

11 If you wou'd not be forgotten
As soon as you are dead and rotten,
Either write things worth reading,
Or do things worth the writing.

> BENJAMIN FRANKLIN, *Poor Richard's Almanack,*
> 1738.

12   What madness is ambition!
What is there in that little breath of men
Which they call Fame, that should induce
  the brave
To forfeit ease and that domestic bliss
Which is the lot of happy ignorance?

> PHILIP FRENEAU, "The Pictures of Columbus,"
> in *Miscellaneous Works,* 1788.

13 How patient Nature smiles at Fame!
The weeds, that strewed the victor's way,
Feed on his dust to shroud his name,
Green where his proudest towers decay.

> OLIVER WENDELL HOLMES, SR., "A Roman
> Aqueduct," 1836.

14 Ah, pensive scholar, what is fame?
A fitful tongue of leaping flame;
A giddy whirlwind's fickle gust,
That lifts a pinch of mortal dust;
A few swift years, and who can show
Which dust was Bill, and which was Joe?

> OLIVER WENDELL HOLMES, SR., "Bill and Joe,"
> 1868.

15 Fame is delightful, but as collateral it does not
rank high.

> ELBERT HUBBARD, *The Roycroft Dictionary and
> Book of Epigrams,* 1923.

16 The idol of today pushes the hero of yesterday
out of our recollection; and will, in turn, be supplanted by his successor of tomorrow.

> WASHINGTON IRVING, "Westminster Abbey,"
> *The Sketch Book,* 1819–1820.

17 That you have enemies, you must not doubt, when you reflect that you have made yourself eminent. If you meant to escape malice, you shall have confined yourself within the sleepy line of regular duty. When you transgressed this, and enterprised deeds which will hand down your name with honor to future times, you made yourself a mark for envy and malice to shoot at.

THOMAS JEFFERSON, in a letter to James Steptoe, November 26, 1782.

18 I find in fact that he is happiest of whom the world says least, good or bad.

THOMAS JEFFERSON, in a letter to John Adams, August 27, 1786.

19 One of the reasons that so many people who achieve fame and fortune don't find happiness is because, almost by definition, if you reach that high estate you are going to find yourself surrounded by the lowest hangers-on in the world. It is not that you get cut off from the real people; you just get cut off from the good people. And pretty soon, if you don't watch out, you can start to turn into a creep yourself.

BILLIE JEAN KING, in *Billie Jean,* 1982.

20 Sleep on, O brave-hearted, O wise man that
     kindled the flame—
To live in mankind is far more than to live
     in a name.

VACHEL LINDSAY, "The Eagle That Is Forgotten," *General William Booth Enters into Heaven and Other Poems,* 1913.

21 If cash comes with fame, come fame; if cash comes without fame, come cash.

JACK LONDON, in a letter to his friend Cloudesley Johns, November 1, 1899.

22 Fame comes only when deserved, and then is as inevitable as destiny, for it is destiny.

HENRY WADSWORTH LONGFELLOW, *Hyperion,* 1839.

23 The dog that gets his name in the want-ad columns in the paper because he is lost gets all of the publicity; all the good dogs who find their own way home do not get any publicity in the papers.

KARL MUNDT, before the House Special Subcommittee on Dissemination of Information Abroad, May 20, 1947.

24 A man may write himself out of reputation when nobody else can do it.

THOMAS PAINE, *The Rights of Man,* 1791–1792.

25 The problem of fame is that you get frozen in one frame and nothing you do can alter the name.

JERRY RUBIN, *Growing (Up) at 37,* 1976.

26 At the London airport a few years ago I was interviewed for 10 minutes before I discovered the interviewer thought I was Tallulah Bankhead. And Miss Bankhead had already been dead for three months—if you can believe the *New York Times.*

GLORIA SWANSON, quoted in *American Way* magazine, June, 1973.

27 If you will observe, it doesn't take
A man of giant mould to make
A giant shadow on the wall;
And he who in our daily sight
Seems but a figure mean and small,
Outlined in Fame's illusive light,
May stalk, a silhouette sublime,
Across the canvas of his time.

JOHN TOWNSEND TROWBRIDGE, "Author's Night," in *The Emigrant's Story and Other Poems,* 1874.

28 The cross of the Legion of Honor has been conferred upon me. However, few escape that distinction.

MARK TWAIN, *A Tramp Abroad,* 1880.

29 Celebrities used to be found in clusters, like oysters—and with much the same defensive mechanisms.

BARBARA WALTERS, *How to Talk with Practically Anybody About Practically Anything,* 1970.

30 My foothold is tenon'd and mortis'd in
     granite,
I laugh at what you call dissolution,
And I know the amplitude of time.

WALT WHITMAN, "Song of Myself," 1855.

85. FAMILY

See also AGE; ANCESTRY; DIVORCE;
MARRIAGE; WOMAN; WOMEN'S RIGHTS;
WORK; YOUTH

1 Families mean support and an audience to men.
To women, they just mean more work.

Anonymous, quoted by Gloria Steinem in *Ms.*
magazine, September, 1981.

2 The mother's heart is the child's schoolroom.

HENRY WARD BEECHER, *Life Thoughts,* 1859.

3 Better to be driven out from among men than to
be disliked of children.

RICHARD HENRY DANA, "Domestic Life,"
published in *The Idle Man* magazine, 1821–1822.

4 Discipline is a symbol of caring to a child. He
needs guidance. If there is love, there is no such
thing as being too tough with a child. . . . If you
have never been hated by your child, you have
never been a parent.

BETTE DAVIS, *The Lonely Life,* 1962.

5 Cleaning your house while your kids are still
  growing
 Is like shoveling the walk before it stops
  snowing.

PHYLLIS DILLER, in *Phyllis Diller's
Housekeeping Hints,* 1966.

6 The security and elevation of the family and of
family life are the prime objects of civilization, and
the ultimate ends of all industry.

CHARLES WILLIAM ELIOT, *The Happy Life,*
1896.

7 It is my conviction that the family is God's basic
unit in society. God's most important unit in society. No wonder then . . . we are in a holy war for
the survival of the family. Before a nation collapses
the families of that nation must go down first.
What is a local church? Nothing but a congregation of families.

JERRY FALWELL, speaking at a morning service,
December 2, 1979.

8 Mother Knows Best.

EDNA FERBER, story title, 1927.

9 Total commitment to family and total commitment to career is possible, but fatiguing.

MURIEL FOX, quoted by Barbara Jordan Moore
in *New Woman* magazine, October, 1971.

10 What maintains one Vice would bring up two
Children.

BENJAMIN FRANKLIN, *Poor Richard's Almanack,*
1758.

11 No parent was ever very comfortable with a
child after it had reached twenty-five.

EDGAR WATSON HOWE, *Sinner Sermons,* 1926.

12 The reason grandparents and grandchildren get
along so well is that they have a common enemy.

Attributed to Sam Levenson.

13 What the world needs is not romantic lovers
who are sufficient unto themselves, but husbands
and wives who live in communities, relate to other
people, carry on useful work and willingly give
time and attention to their children.

MARGARET MEAD, in *Redbook* magazine,
November, 1965.

14 Children aren't happy with nothing to ignore,
 And that's what parents were created for.

OGDEN NASH, "The Parent," in *Many Long
Years Ago,* 1945.

15 The family is one of nature's masterpieces.

GEORGE SANTAYANA, *The Life of Reason,*
1905–1906.

16 I have no sympathy with the old idea that children owe such immense gratitude to their parents
that they can never fulfill their obligations to them.
I think the obligation is all on the other side. Parents can never do too much for their children to
repay them for the injustice of having brought them
into the world, unless they have insured them high
moral and intellectual gifts, fine physical health,
and enough money and education to render life
something more than one ceaseless struggle for
necessaries.

ELIZABETH CADY STANTON, diary entry, November 12, quoted in Theodore Stanton and Harriot Stanton Blatch, *Elizabeth Cady Stanton,* 1922.

17 It's clear that most American children suffer too much mother and too little father.

GLORIA STEINEM, writing in the *New York Times,* August 26, 1971.

18 We are always too busy for our children; we never give them the time or interest they deserve. We lavish gifts upon them; but the most precious gift—our personal association, which means so much to them—we give grudgingly.

MARK TWAIN, quoted in Albert Bigelow Paine, *Mark Twain: A Biography,* 1912.

19 With four walk-in-closets to walk in,
Three bushes, two shrubs, and one tree,
The suburbs are good for the children,
But no place for grown-ups to be.

JUDITH VIORST, in *It's Hard to Be Hip Over Thirty and Other Tragedies of Married Life,* 1968.

20 I teach my child to look at life in a thoroughly materialistic fashion. If he escapes and becomes the sort of person I hope he will become, it will be because he sees through the hokum that I hand out.

E.B. WHITE, "Sanitation," *One Man's Meat,* 1944.

21 There are no illegitimate children—only illegitimate parents.

LÉON R. YANKWICH, in a District Court decision, *Zipkin* v. *Mozon,* June, 1928.

---

86. FATE

See also DESTINY; HEART

---

1 The bitterest tragic element in life from an intellectual source is the belief in a brute Fate or Destiny.

RALPH WALDO EMERSON, "The Tragic," published in *The Dial,* April, 1844.

2 We may be partial, but Fate is not.

RALPH WALDO EMERSON, "The Conservative," *Nature; Addresses and Lectures,* 1849.

3 Providence has a wild, rough, incalculable road to its end, and it is of no use to try to whitewash its huge, mixed instrumentalities, or to dress up that terrific benefactor in a clean shirt and white neckcloth of a student in divinity.

RALPH WALDO EMERSON, "Fate," *The Conduct of Life,* 1860.

4 Whatever limits us, we call Fate.

Ibid.

5 'Tis weak and vicious people who cast the blame on Fate.

Ibid.

6 Friends are few, thoughts are few, facts few—only one; only one fact, now tragically, now tenderly, now exaltingly illustrated in sky, in earth, in men and women, Fate, Fate. The universe is all chemistry, with a certain hint of a magnificent *Whence* or *Whereto.*

RALPH WALDO EMERSON, in a letter to Caroline Sturgis Tappan, quoted in Stephen E. Whicher, *Selections from Ralph Waldo Emerson,* 1960.

7 We are spinning our own fates, good or evil, and never to be undone. Every smallest stroke of virtue or of vice leaves its never so little scar. . . . Nothing we ever do is, in strict scientific literalness, wiped out.

WILLIAM JAMES, *The Principles of Psychology,* 1890.

8 Though the mills of God grind slowly, yet
     they grind exceeding small;
Though with patience He stands waiting, with
     exactness grinds He all.

HENRY WADSWORTH LONGFELLOW, "Poetic Aphorisms: Retribution," translated from *The Sinngedichte of Friedrich von Logau,* 1845.

9 All are architects of Fate.
   Working in these walls of Time;
Some with massive deeds and great,
   Some with ornaments of rhyme.

HENRY WADSWORTH LONGFELLOW, "The Builders," 1846, collected in *The Seaside and the Fireside,* 1849.

10 There is no good in arguing with the inevitable. The only argument available with an east wind is to put on your overcoat.

JAMES RUSSELL LOWELL, in a speech in Birmingham, England, October 6, 1884, published in *On Democracy,* 1884.

11 Three were the fates—gaunt Poverty that
     chains,
   Gray Drudgery that grinds the hope away,
   And gaping Ignorance that starves the soul.

EDWIN MARKHAM, "Young Lincoln," 1901, collected in *Poems of Edwin Markham,* 1950.

12 Fate is the Gunman that all gunmen dread;
   Fate stings the Stinger for his roll of green;
   Fate, strong-arm Worker, on the bean
   Of strong-arm workers bumps his pipe of
     lead.

DON MARQUIS, "Proverbs xii, 7," in *Noah an' Jonah an' Cap'n John Smith,* 1921.

13 You can't slink out of life or out of the work life lays on you.

WASHINGTON A. ROEBLING, quoted in David McCullough, *The Great Bridge,* 1972.

14 The outward wayward life we see,
   The hidden springs we may not know. . . .
   It is not ours to separate
   The tangled skein of will and fate.

JOHN GREENLEAF WHITTIER, *Snow-Bound,* 1866.

87. FEAR

See also BRAVERY; CHARACTER; COWARDICE

1 Tell us your phobias and we will tell you what you are afraid of.

ROBERT BENCHLEY, "Phobias," in *My Ten Years in a Quandary, and How They Grew,* 1936.

2 Fear tastes like a rusty knife and do not let her into your house.

JOHN CHEEVER, *The Wapshot Chronicle,* 1957.

3 The first and great commandment is, Don't let them scare you.

ELMER DAVIS, *But We Were Born Free,* 1954.

4 And I will show you something different from
     either
   Your shadow at morning striding behind you
   Or your shadow at evening rising to meet
     you;
   I will show you fear in a handful of dust.

T.S. ELIOT, *The Waste Land,* 1922.

5 I knew a man scared by the rustle of his own hat-band.

RALPH WALDO EMERSON, entry written in 1837, *Journals,* 1909–1914.

6 Fear always springs from ignorance.

RALPH WALDO EMERSON, *The American Scholar,* 1837.

7 Fear is an instructor of great sagacity, and the herald of all revolutions.

RALPH WALDO EMERSON, "Compensation," *Essays,* First Series, 1841.

8 All infractions of love and equity in our social relations are speedily punished. They are punished by fear.

Ibid.

9 We are afraid of truth, afraid of fortune, afraid of death, and afraid of each other.

RALPH WALDO EMERSON, "Self-Reliance," *Essays,* First Series, 1841.

10 He has not learned the lesson of life who does not every day surmount a fear.

RALPH WALDO EMERSON, "Courage," *Society and Solitude,* 1870.

11 Our tragedy today is a general and universal physical fear so long sustained by now that we can even bear it. There are no longer problems of the spirit. There is only the question: When will I be

blown up? . . . The basest of all things is to be afraid.

> WILLIAM FAULKNER, in his Nobel Prize acceptance speech, Stockholm, Sweden, December 10, 1950.

12 A good scare is worth more to a man than good advice.

> EDGAR WATSON HOWE, *Country Town Sayings*, 1911.

13 The thing we fear we bring to pass.

> ELBERT HUBBARD, in *The Philistine* magazine, published from 1895–1915.

14 The atomic bomb is a paper tiger which the U.S. reactionaries use to scare people. It looks terrible, but in fact it isn't.

> MAO TSE-TUNG, to Anna Louise Strong in August, 1960, quoted in Robert Jay Lifton and Nicholas Humphrey, *In a Dark Time*, 1984.

15 Some men have strange antipathies in their natures. . . . There are some who, if a cat accidentally come into the room, though they neither see it, nor are told of it, will presently be in a sweat, and ready to die.

> INCREASE MATHER, *Remarkable Providences*, 1684.

16 The one permanent emotion of the inferior man is fear—fear of the unknown, the complex, the inexplicable. What he wants beyond everything else is safety.

> H.L. MENCKEN, *Prejudices*, Second Series, 1920.

17 And the silken sad uncertain rustling of each purple curtain
Thrilled me—filled me with fantastic terrors never felt before.

> EDGAR ALLAN POE, "The Raven," published in the *New York Evening Mirror*, January 29, 1845.

18 Hear the loud alarum bells, Brazen bells!
What a tale of terror, now, their turbulency tells!
In the startled ear of night

How they scream out their affright!
Too much horrified to speak,
They can only shriek, shriek.

> EDGAR ALLAN POE, "The Bells," published in *Sartain's Union Magazine*, November, 1849.

19 An' the Gobble-uns 'll git you
Ef you
Don't
Watch
Out!

> JAMES WHITCOMB RILEY, "Little Orphant Annie," 1883.

20 Let me assert my firm belief that the only thing we have to fear is fear itself—nameless, unreasoning, unjustified terror which paralyzes needed efforts to convert retreat into advance.

> FRANKLIN D. ROOSEVELT, in his first inaugural address, March 4, 1933.

21 For many years we have suckled on fear and fear alone, and there is no good product of fear. Its children are cruelty and deceit and suspicion germinating in our darkness. And just as surely as we are poisoning the air with our test bombs, so are we poisoned in our souls by fear, faceless, stupid sarcomic terror.

> JOHN STEINBECK, *Once There Was a War*, 1958.

22 Nothing is so much to be feared as fear.

> HENRY DAVID THOREAU, entry dated September 27, 1851, in his *Journal*, 1906.

23 The people of the United States are at the present time dominated and driven by two kinds of officially propagated fear: fear of the Soviet Union and fear of the income tax.

> EDMUND WILSON, *The Cold War and the Income Tax*, 1963.

---

88. FLAG

See also PATRIOTISM

---

1 Off with your hat as the flag goes by!
And let the heart have its say;

You're man enough for a tear in your eye
That you will not wipe away.

> HENRY CUYLER BUNNER, "The Old Flag,"
> 1888.

2 Many a bum show has been saved by the flag.

> GEORGE M. COHAN, in *La Follette's Weekly
> Magazine,* founded 1909.

3 When Freedom from the mountain height
Unfurled her standard to the air,
She tore the azure robe of night,
And set the stars of glory there.
She mingled with its gorgeous dyes
The milky baldric of the skies,
And striped its pure celestial white
With streakings of the morning light;
Then from his mansion in the sun
She called her eagle bearer down,
And gave into his mighty hand
The symbol of her chosen land.

> JOSEPH RODMAN DRAKE, "The American Flag,"
> in *The Culprit Fay, and Other Poems,* 1836.

4 There it is—Old Glory!

> CAPT. WILLIAM DRIVER, sea captain, on seeing
> the American flag raised over his ship off Salem,
> Massachusetts, December, 1831.

5 Ay, tear her tattered ensign down!
Long has it waved on high,
And many an eye has danced to see
That banner in the sky.

> OLIVER WENDELL HOLMES, SR., "Old
> Ironsides," 1830.

6 Oh! say can you see by the dawn's early light
What so proudly we hailed at the twilight's
last gleaming,
Whose stripes and bright stars through the
perilous fight,
O'er the ramparts we watch'd were so
gallantly streaming?
And the rockets' red glare, the bombs bursting
in air,
Gave proof through the night that our flag
was still there;
Oh! say, does that star spangled banner yet
wave,

O'er the land of the free, and the home of
the brave?

> FRANCIS SCOTT KEY, "The Star Spangled
> Banner," published in the *Baltimore Patriot,*
> September 20, 1814.

7 If you have a weak candidate and a weak platform, wrap yourself up in the American flag and talk about the Constitution.

> MATTHEW STANLEY QUAY, political boss of
> Pennsylvania, comment made in 1886.

8 Yes, we'll rally round the flag, boys, we'll
rally once again,
Shouting the battle-cry of Freedom,
We will rally from the hill-side, we'll gather
from the plain,
Shouting the battle-cry of Freedom.
The Union forever, Hurrah boys, hurrah!

> GEORGE FREDERICK ROOT, "The Battle-Cry of
> Freedom," 1861.

9 "Shoot, if you must, this old gray head,
But spare your country's flag," she said.

> JOHN GREENLEAF WHITTIER, "Barbara
> Frietchie," 1864.

89. FLORIDA

1 In God we trust.

> State motto.

2 Physically and socially, Florida has its own North and South, but its northern area is strictly southern and its southern area definitely northern.

> Federal Writers' Project, *Florida: A Guide to the
> Southernmost State,* 1939.

3 The evolution of a tourist into a permanent resident consists of a struggle to harmonize misconceptions and preconceptions of Florida with reality. An initial diversion is to mail northward snapshots of himself reclining under a coconut palm or a beach umbrella, with the hope that they will be delivered in the midst of a blizzard.

At the same time, the tourist checks weather reports from the North, and if his home community is having a mild winter he feels that his Florida trip has been in part a swindle. Nothing short of ten-foot snowdrifts and burst waterpipes at home can make his stay in the southland happy and complete.

> Ibid.

4 What business have healthy people with climates?

> SIDNEY LANIER, *Florida: Its Scenery, Climate and History,* 1875.

5 Friend sun!

> Ibid.

6 The billion-dollar-a-year tourist trade, the fusion of the Old South and the restless North is rapidly producing a new kind of state which is neither Southern nor Northern, Middle Western nor Western, yet with discernible elements of all four. In fact, Florida is to the United States today what the United States was to Europe a hundred years ago—a melting pot, a frontier, a place to improve your health or your luck.

> BUDD SCHULBERG, "Florida," in *American Panorama: East of the Mississippi,* 1960.

7 Florida is the world's greatest amusement park.

> Ibid.

8 Miami is . . . of an unimaginable awfulness—much like other American seaside resorts but on an unprecedented scale: acres of cheap white shops, mountain ranges of white hotels. After lunch, I had a taxi drive me over to Miami Beach. It goes on for miles—thousands of hotels and houses and monotonous lines of palms. I can't imagine how people live here or why so many of them come: it all seems a great insipid vacuum—less amusing than Southern California, because there is no touch of fantasy about anything.

> EDMUND WILSON, in a letter to Elena Wilson, November 26, 1949, quoted in *Letters on Literature and Politics 1912–1972,* 1977.

90. FLOWERS

See also AGRICULTURE; HEALTH; NATURE

1 You cannot forget if you would those golden kisses all over the cheeks of the meadow, queerly called *dandelions.*

> HENRY WARD BEECHER, "A Discourse of Flowers," *Star Papers,* 1855.

2 Flowers are the sweetest things God ever made and forgot to put a soul into.

> HENRY WARD BEECHER, *Life Thoughts,* 1858.

3 Though many a flower in the wood is waking,
  The daffodil is our doorside queen;
She pushes upward the sword already,
  To spot with sunshine the early green.

> WILLIAM CULLEN BRYANT, "An Invitation to the Country," published in *Harper's Weekly,* May, 1857.

4 It is as sprightly as the daffodil, as colorful as the rose, as resolute as the zinnia, as delicate as the chrysanthemum, as aggressive as the petunia, as ubiquitous as the violet, and as stately as the snapdragon. It beguiles the senses and ennobles the spirit of man. . . . Since it is native to America, and nowhere else in the world, and common to every state in the Union, I present the American marigold for designation as the national floral emblem of our country.

> EVERETT M. DIRKSEN, quoted in Neil MacNeil, *Dirksen: Portrait of a Public Man,* 1970.

5 Earth laughs in flowers.

> RALPH WALDO EMERSON, "Hamatreya," in *Poems,* 1847.

6 The Amen! of Nature is always a flower.

> OLIVER WENDELL HOLMES, SR., *The Autocrat of the Breakfast-Table,* 1858.

7 Yellow japanned buttercups and star-disked dandelions—just as we see them lying in the grass, like sparks that have leaped from the kindling sun of summer.

OLIVER WENDELL HOLMES, SR., *The Professor at the Breakfast-Table,* 1860.

8 I walk down the garden paths,
And all the daffodils
Are blowing, and the bright blue squills.
I walk down the patterned garden-paths
In my stiff, brocaded gown.
With my powdered hair, and jewelled fan,
I too am a rare
Pattern. As I wander down
The garden paths.

AMY LOWELL, "Patterns," 1916.

9 A weed is no more than a flower in disguise.

JAMES RUSSELL LOWELL, *A Fable for Critics,* 1848.

10 One of the attractive things about the flowers is their beautiful reserve.

HENRY DAVID THOREAU, entry dated June 17, 1853, in his *Journal,* 1906.

11 In the dooryard fronting an old farm-house
near the white-wash'd palings,
Stands the lilac-bush tall-growing with
heart-shaped leaves of rich green,
With many a pointed blossom rising delicate,
with the perfume strong I love,
With every leaf a miracle—

WALT WHITMAN, "When Lilacs Last in the Dooryard Bloom'd," 1865–1866.

12 All over bouquets of roses,
O death, I cover you over with roses and
early lilies,
But mostly and now the lilac that blooms the
first,
Copious I break, I break the sprigs from the
bushes,
With loaded arms I come, pouring for you,
For you and the coffins all of you, O death.

Ibid.

13 It is the month of June,
The month of leaves and roses,
When pleasant sights salute the eyes
And pleasant scents the noses.

NATHANIEL PARKER WILLIS, "The Month of June," 1844.

91. FOLLY

See also EXPERIENCE; HEART; WISDOM

1 Fool, *n.* A person who pervades the domain of intellectual speculation and diffuses himself through the channels of moral activity. He is omnific, omniform, omnipercipient, omniscient, omnipotent. He it was who invented letters, printing, the railroad, the steamboat, the telegraph, the platitude and the circle of the sciences. He created patriotism and taught the nations war—founded theology, philosophy, law, medicine and Chicago. He established monarchical and republican government. . . . And after the rest of us shall have retired for the night of eternal oblivion he will sit up to write a history of human civilization.

AMBROSE BIERCE, *The Devil's Dictionary,* 1906.

2 As Charms are nonsense, Nonsense is a Charm.

BENJAMIN FRANKLIN, *Poor Richard's Almanack,* 1734.

3 The use of proverbs is characteristic of an unlettered people. They are invaluable treasures to dunces with good memories.

JOHN HAY, *Castilian Days,* 1871.

4 Don't be mean to the fool; put a penny in his cup, as you do for the blind beggar.

EDGAR WATSON HOWE, *Sinner Sermons,* 1926.

5 There's nothing we read of in torture's
inventions
Like a well-meaning dunce with the best of
intentions.

JAMES RUSSELL LOWELL, *A Fable for Critics,* 1848.

6 There is no folly of the beasts of the earth which is not infinitely outdone by the madness of men.

HERMAN MELVILLE, *Moby-Dick,* 1851.

7 People who cannot recognize a palpable absurdity are very much in the way of civilization.

AGNES REPPLIER, *In Pursuit of Laughter,* 1936.

8 The best human intelligence is still decidedly barbarous; it fights in heavy armor and keeps a fool at court.

> GEORGE SANTAYANA, *The Life of Reason,* 1905–1906.

9 The country is a fool, *I* think.

> MARK TWAIN AND CHARLES DUDLEY WARNER, *The Gilded Age,* 1873.

10 Hain't we got all the fools in town on our side? And ain't that a big enough majority in any town?

> MARK TWAIN, *The Adventures of Huckleberry Finn,* 1884.

11 Let us be thankful for the fools. But for them the rest of us could not succeed.

> MARK TWAIN, "Pudd'nhead Wilson's New Calendar," *Following the Equator,* 1897.

---

92. FOOD

See also APPETITE; DRINKING; SEX; WINE & SPIRITS

---

1 Food is our common ground, a universal experience.

> JAMES BEARD, *Beard on Food,* 1974.

2 Grilling, broiling, barbecuing—whatever you want to call it—is an art, not just a matter of building a pyre and throwing on a piece of meat as a sacrifice to the gods of the stomach.

> Ibid.

3 If I were a jolly archbishop
On Fridays I'd eat all the fish up—
Salmon and flounders and smelts;
On other days everything else.

> AMBROSE BIERCE, verse following the definition of "Archbishop," *The Devil's Dictionary,* 1906.

4 Chili's a lot like sex: When it's good it's great, and even when it's bad, it's not so bad.

> BILL BOLDENWECK, quoted in *American Way* magazine, June, 1982.

5 Fake food—I mean those patented substances chemically flavored and mechanically bulked out to kill the appetite and deceive the gut—is unnatural, almost immoral, a bane to good eating and good cooking.

> JULIA CHILD, *Julia Child and Company,* 1978.

6 For those who love it, cooking is at once child's play and adult joy. And cooking done with care is an act of love.

> CRAIG CLAIBORNE, *Craig Claiborne's Kitchen Primer,* 1969.

7 Man is born to eat.

> Ibid.

8 The apple is our national fruit, and I like to see that the soil yields it; I judge of the country so. The American sun paints himself in these glowing balls amid the green leaves. Man would be more solitary, less friended, less supported, if the land yielded only the useful maize and potato, and withheld this ornamental and social fruit.

> RALPH WALDO EMERSON, entry written in 1848, *Journals,* 1909–1914.

9 Salt is white and pure,—there is something holy in salt.

> NATHANIEL HAWTHORNE, entry dated October 4, 1840, *Passages from the American Notebooks,* 1868.

10 There is something in the red of a raspberry pie that looks as good to a man as the red in a sheep looks to a wolf.

> EDGAR WATSON HOWE, *Sinner Sermons,* 1926.

11 The superiority of the article [chocolate] both for health and nourishment will soon give it the same preference over tea and coffee in America which it has in Spain.

> THOMAS JEFFERSON, in a letter to John Adams, November 27, 1785.

12 The American does not drink at meals as a sensible man should. Indeed, he has no meals. He stuffs for ten minutes thrice a day.

> RUDYARD KIPLING, *American Notes,* 1891.

13 Cooking is like love. It should be entered into with abandon or not at all.

HARRIET VAN HORNE, quoted in *Vogue* magazine, October, 1956.

14 A man who has spent much time and money in dreary restaurants moodily chewing filet of sole on the special luncheon is bound to become unmanageable when he discovers that he can produce the main fish course directly, at the edge of his own pasture, by a bit of trickery on a fine morning.

E.B. WHITE, writing about life on the Maine coast, "Salt Water Farm," *One Man's Meat*, 1944.

---

93. FOOTBALL

See also SPORTS

---

1 There is an intensity and a danger in football—as in life generally—which keep us alive and awake. It is a test of our awareness and ability. Like so much of life, it presents us with the choice of responding either with fear or with action and clarity.

JOHN BRODIE, quoted in Rick Telander, *Joe Namath and the Other Guys*, 1976.

2 Football is, after all, a wonderful way to get rid of aggressions without going to jail for it.

HEYWOOD HALE BROUN, *Tumultuous Merriment*, 1979.

3 Football has been rousing emotions for hundreds of years in a variety of forms, all having in common the idea of moving a ball from one place to another with varying degrees of violence as the means of propulsion.

Ibid.

4 Football is much like chess. Match-ups. Harassments. Lines and rules and squares and decisions. Sucker him in and whack him.

MIKE HOLOVAK, football player, *Violence Every Sunday—The Story of a Professional Football Coach*, 1967.

5 Gentlemen, you are about to go forth on the greatest mission of your lives—you are about to play Harvard in football.

TAD JONES, speaking to the Yale team, quoted in Jerry Brondfield, *Rockne*, 1976.

6 Does football keep you from growing up? Oh, my God, yes! One hundred percent yes! I've even heard guys who I thought had no minds at all admit that.

DAVID KNIGHT, quoted in Rick Telander, *Joe Namath and the Other Guys*, 1976.

7 Football is pain and agony, and our kids are prepared to pay the price.

FRANK KUSH, football coach, quoted in James A. Michener, *Sports in America*, 1976.

8 Winning isn't everything. It's the only thing.

VINCE LOMBARDI, quoted in Jerry Kramer, *Instant Replay*, 1968. (James Michener, in *Sports in America*, 1976, quoted Lombardi on this, his best-known comment: "I wish to hell I'd never said the damned thing. . . . I meant the effort. . . . I meant having a goal. . . . I sure as hell didn't mean for people to crush human values and morality.")

9 There are three important things in life: family, religion, and the Green Bay Packers.

VINCE LOMBARDI, quoted in Tom Dowling, *Coach: A Season with Lombardi*, 1970.

10 Football is a game of clichés, and I believe in every one of them.

Ibid.

11 Football isn't a contact sport, it's a collision sport. Dancing is a contact sport.

VINCE LOMBARDI, quoted in James A. Michener, *Sports in America*, 1976.

12 People have started asking me if we've got any talent on this team. Well, I tell them, if we start winning games we'll have talent. But since we're getting beat to death, no, we don't.

JOE NAMATH, quoted in Rick Telander, *Joe Namath and the Other Guys*, 1976.

13 Let's face it, everyone knows the name of the game is "get the quarterback."

> JOE NAMATH, 1978, quoted in Bob Abel and Michael Valenti, *Sports Quotes*, 1983.

14 For when the one Great Scorer comes
To write against your name,
He marks—not that you won or lost—
But how you played the game.

> GRANTLAND RICE, "Alumnus Football," in *The Tumult and the Shouting*, 1954.

15 We count on winning. And if we lose, don't beef. And the best way to prevent beefing is—don't lose.

> KNUTE ROCKNE, quoted in Jerry Brondfield, *Rockne*, 1976.

16 I don't want anybody going out there to die for dear old Notre Dame. Hell, I want you fighting *to stay alive!*

> Ibid.

17 Football is a game played with the arms, legs and shoulders but mostly from the neck up.

> Ibid.

18 Football is good for the country. Every American has that feeling inside him that he'd like to hit somebody. He can't do it in this kind of society. But he comes out to the ballpark and he's almost in the game. It keeps him from going soft. It's the fans' way of fighting for the country.

> TOM ROUSSEL, football player, quoted in Tom Dowling, *Coach: A Season with Lombardi*, 1970.

19 Football doesn't build character. It eliminates the weak ones.

> DARRELL ROYAL, quoted in James A. Michener, *Sports in America*, 1976.

20 I want to win a championship. . . . It's probably what I want right now more than anything else in the world. But if I don't, I'm not going to kill myself. And if I do win a championship, it will probably make me happier than anything else could—right now. But in a few years, it won't make much difference.

> FRAN TARKENTON, quoted in Dick Schaap, *Sport*, 1975.

21 Under the brown California sky, the
fierceness of their struggle brought tears
to the eyes of 90,000 God-fearing fans.
They were twenty-two men who were
somehow more than men.
They were giants, idols, titans. . . .
Behemoths.
They stood for everything Good and True
and Right in the American Spirit.
Because they had guts.
And they yearned for the Ultimate Glory,
the Great Prize, the Final Fruits of a
long and vicious campaign.
Victory in the Super Bowl: $15,000 each.

> HUNTER S. THOMPSON, *Fear and Loathing on the Campaign Trail, '72*, 1973.

---

94. FORCE

See also ARMY; AUTHORITY; CONQUEST; MILITARISM; NAVY; NUCLEAR AGE; POWER; TYRANNY; VICTORY; WAR

---

1 Force can only overcome other force. When it has done this, it has spent itself and other means of influencing conduct have to be employed.

> DEAN ACHESON, *A Democrat Looks at His Party*, 1955.

2 Neither philosophy, nor religion, nor morality, nor wisdom, nor interest will ever govern nations or parties against their vanity, their pride, their resentment or revenge, or their avarice or ambition. Nothing but force and power and strength can restrain them.

> JOHN ADAMS, in a letter to Thomas Jefferson, October 9, 1787.

3 "Force is but might," the teacher said—
"That definition's just."
The boy said naught but thought instead,
Remembering his pounded head: "Force is not might but must!"

> AMBROSE BIERCE, *The Devil's Dictionary*, 1906.

4 There is no force so powerful as an idea whose time has come.

> EVERETT DIRKSEN, referring to the Civil Rights Bill, in a speech in the U.S. Senate, 1964.

5 Force cannot give right.

> THOMAS JEFFERSON, *A Summary View of the Rights of British America,* 1774.

6 Force, the vital principle and immediate parent of despotism.

> THOMAS JEFFERSON, in his first inaugural address, March 4, 1801.

7 You use whatever force is necessary to achieve the purpose, and I would like to feel that there wouldn't be a need for using armed force if we made it apparent that we have the will, if necessary, to do that.

> RONALD REAGAN, quoted in Hedrick Smith et. al., *Reagan the Man, the President,* 1980.

8 There is such a thing as a nation being so right that it does not need to convince others by force that it is right.

> WOODROW WILSON, in a speech at Convention Hall, Philadelphia, May 10, 1915.

9 There is . . . but one response possible from us: force, force to the utmost, force without stint or limit, the righteous and triumphant force which shall make right the law of the world and cast every selfish dominion down in the dust.

> WOODROW WILSON, in an address at Baltimore, Maryland, on the first anniversary of the U.S. entry into World War I, April 6, 1918.

95. FREEDOM

See also AMERICA; CIVIL RIGHTS; DEMOCRACY; EQUALITY; INDEPENDENCE; LIBERTY; RELIGIOUS FREEDOM; TYRANNY

1 Every generation must wage a new war for freedom against new forces that seek through new devices to enslave mankind.

Plank of the platform of the Conference for Progressive Political Action, 1924.

2 Oh, Lord, I want to be free, want to be free;
Rainbow round my shoulder, wings on my feet.

> Folk song, quoted in Howard W. Odum, *Wings on My Feet,* 1929.

3 All men are born free and equal, and have certain natural, essential, and unalienable rights.

> JOHN ADAMS, Constitution of Massachusetts, 1779.

4 When people talk of the freedom of writing, speaking, or thinking, I cannot choose but laugh. No such thing ever existed. No such thing now exists; but I hope it will exist. But it must be hundreds of years after you and I shall write and speak no more.

> JOHN ADAMS, in a letter to Thomas Jefferson, July 15, 1818.

5 The truth is, all might be free if they valued freedom, and defended it as they ought.

> Attributed to Samuel Adams.

6 Driven from every other corner of the earth, freedom of thought and the right of private judgment in matters of conscience direct their course to this happy country as their last asylum.

> SAMUEL ADAMS, in a speech in Philadelphia, August 1, 1776.

7 Free speech is to a great people what winds are to oceans and malarial regions, which waft away the elements of disease, and bring new elements of health. Where free speech is stopped miasma is bred, and death comes fast.

> HENRY WARD BEECHER, *Royal Truths,* 1866.

8 Freedom, *n.* Exemption from the stress of authority in a beggarly half dozen of restraint's infinite multitude of methods. A political condition that every nation supposes itself to enjoy in virtual monopoly. Liberty. The distinction between freedom and liberty is not accurately known; naturalists have never been able to find a living specimen of either.

> AMBROSE BIERCE, *The Devil's Dictionary,* 1906.

9 I am for the First Amendment from the first word to the last. I believe it means what it says.

> HUGO BLACK, in an interview before the American Jewish Congress, April 14, 1962.

10 An unconditional right to say what one pleases about public affairs is what I consider to be the minimum guarantee of the First Amendment.

> HUGO BLACK, in a Supreme Court decision, *New York Times Company* v. *Sullivan*, 1964.

11 Fear of serious injury cannot alone justify suppression of free speech and assembly. Men feared witches and burned women. It is the function of speech to free men from the bondage of irrational fears.

> LOUIS D. BRANDEIS, in a Supreme Court opinion, *Whitney* v. *California*, 1927.

12 We are so concerned to flatter the majority that we lose sight of how very often it is necessary, in order to preserve freedom for the minority, let alone for the individual, to face that majority down.

> WILLIAM F. BUCKLEY, JR., "We Want Our Politicians to Be Hypocrites," October 17, 1964, collected in *The Jeweler's Eye*, 1968.

13 Freedom of expression is the matrix, the indispensable condition, of nearly every other form of freedom.

> BENJAMIN N. CARDOZO, in a Supreme Court opinion, *Palko* v. *Connecticut*, 1937.

14 Freedom is not a luxury that we can indulge in when at last we have security and prosperity and enlightenment; it is, rather, antecedent to all of these, for without it we can have neither security nor prosperity nor enlightenment.

> HENRY STEELE COMMAGER, *Freedom, Loyalty, Dissent*, 1954.

15 We cannot have a society half slave and half free; nor can we have thought half slave and half free. If we create an atmosphere in which men fear to think independently, inquire fearlessly, express themselves freely, we will in the end create the kind of society in which men no longer care to think independently or to inquire fearlessly. If we put a premium on conformity we will, in the end, get conformity.

> HENRY STEELE COMMAGER, *Freedom and Order*, 1966.

16 The justification and the purpose of freedom of speech is not to indulge those who want to speak their minds. It is to prevent error and discover truth. There may be other ways of detecting error and discovering truth than that of free discussion, but so far we have not found them.

> Ibid.

17 To say that a man is free to choose to walk while the only walk he can take will lead him over a precipice is to strain words as well as facts.

> JOHN DEWEY, *Human Nature and Conduct*, 1922.

18 It is not easy to be free men, for to be free you must afford freedom to your neighbor, regardless of race, color, creed, or national origin, and that sometimes, for some, is very difficult.

> HELEN GAHAGAN DOUGLAS, in a speech in Congress, 1945.

19 Freedom has its life in the hearts, the actions, the spirit of men and so it must be daily earned and refreshed—else like a flower cut from its life-giving roots, it will wither and die.

> DWIGHT D. EISENHOWER, in a speech to the English Speaking Union, London, 1944.

20 To preserve his freedom of worship, his equality before the law, his liberty to speak and act as he sees fit subject only to provisions that he trespass not upon similar rights of others, a Londoner will fight. So will a citizen of Abilene.

> DWIGHT D. EISENHOWER, July, 1945, quoted in Richard M. Nixon, *The Challenges We Face*, 1960.

21 Freedom all winged expands,
　Nor perches in a narrow place;
　Her broad van seeks unplanted lands;
　She loves a poor and virtuous race.

> RALPH WALDO EMERSON, "Voluntaries," published in the *Atlantic Monthly*, October, 1863.

22 We grant no dukedoms to the few,
    We hold like rights and shall;
Equal on Sunday in the pew,
    On Monday in the mall.
For what avail the plough or sail,
Or land, or life, if freedom fail?

> RALPH WALDO EMERSON, "Boston," *May-Day and Other Pieces,* 1867.

23 Systems political or religious or racial or national—will not just respect us because we practice freedom, they will fear us because we do.

> WILLIAM FAULKNER, in *Harper's Magazine,* June, 1956.

24 We cannot choose freedom established on a hierarchy of degrees of freedom, on a caste system of equality like military rank. We must be free not because we claim freedom, but because we practice it.

> Ibid.

25 Economic arrangements play a dual role in the promotion of a free society. On the one hand, freedom in economic arrangements is itself a component of freedom broadly understood, so economic freedom is an end in itself. In the second place, economic freedom is also an indispensable means toward the achievement of political freedom.

> MILTON FRIEDMAN, *Capitalism and Freedom,* 1962.

26 Freedom is a tenable objective only for responsible individuals.

> MILTON FRIEDMAN AND ROSE FRIEDMAN, *Free to Choose,* 1979.

27 A society that puts equality . . . ahead of freedom will end up with neither equality nor freedom.

> Ibid.

28 Before every free conscience in America is subpoenaed, please speak up!

> JUDY GARLAND, c.1947, quoted in Anne Edwards, *Judy Garland,* 1975.

29 I hold a jail more roomy in the expression of my judgment and convictions than would be the whole world if I were to submit to repression and be denied the right to express myself.

> SAMUEL GOMPERS, *Seventy Years of Life and Labor,* 1925.

30 The freedom of speech and the freedom of the press have not been granted to the people in order that they may say the things which please, and which are based upon accepted thought, but the right to say the things which displease, the right to say the things which may convey the new and yet unexpected thoughts, the right to say things, even though they do a wrong.

> SAMUEL GOMPERS, reply before being sentenced for contempt of court in the Bucks Stove case, 1908, from *Seventy Years of Life and Labor,* 1925.

31 There have existed, in every age and every country, two distinct orders of men—the lovers of freedom and the devoted advocates of power.

> ROBERT YOUNG HAYNE, in a speech in the U.S. Senate, January 21, 1830.

32 The most stringent protection of free speech would not protect a man in falsely shouting fire in a theater and causing a panic.

> OLIVER WENDELL HOLMES, JR., in a Supreme Court opinion, *Schenck v. United States,* 1919.

33 When a nation is at war many things that might be said in time of peace are such a hindrance to its effort that their utterance will not be endured so long as men fight and no court could regard them as protected by any consitutional right.

> Ibid.

34 If there is any principle of the Constitution that more imperatively calls for attachment than any other it is the principle of free thought—not free thought for those who agree with us but freedom for the thought that we hate.

> OLIVER WENDELL HOLMES, JR., in a Supreme Court opinion, *United States v. Schwimmer,* 1928.

35 Free speech does not live many hours after free industry and free commerce die.

> HERBERT HOOVER, in a speech in New York City, October 22, 1928.

36 We are not free; it was not intended we should be. A book of rules is placed in our cradle, and we never get rid of it until we reach our graves. Then we are free, and only then.

> EDGAR WATSON HOWE, in *E.W. Howe's Monthly,* published from 1911–1937.

37 I express many absurd opinions. But I am not the first man to do it; American freedom consists largely in talking nonsense.

> EDGAR WATSON HOWE, *Preaching from the Audience,* 1926.

38 You often hear that this is a free country, and that a man is at liberty to express his opinions. It is not true.

> EDGAR WATSON HOWE, *The Indignations of E.W. Howe,* 1933.

39 As He died to make men holy,
  Let us die to make men free,
 While God is marching on.

> JULIA WARD HOWE, "The Battle Hymn of the Republic," *Atlantic Monthly,* February, 1862.

40 There is no freedom on earth or in any star for those who deny freedom to others.

> ELBERT HUBBARD, *The Roycroft Dictionary and Book of Epigrams,* 1923.

41 Poverty curtails individual freedom. So do illiteracy, prejudice, lack of education, inability to obtain the basic needs of life.

> HUBERT H. HUMPHREY, *The Cause Is Mankind,* 1964.

42 The opinions of men are not the object of civil government, nor under its jurisdiction.

> THOMAS JEFFERSON, *Virginia Statute of Religious Freedom,* 1779.

43 Is uniformity of opinion desirable? No more than that of face and stature.

> THOMAS JEFFERSON, *Notes on the State of Virginia,* 1784.

44 Subject opinion to coercion: whom will you make your inquisitors? Fallible men; men governed by bad passions, by private as well as public reasons.

> Ibid.

45 Every difference of opinion is not a difference of principle. We have called by different names brethren of the same principle. . . . If there be any among us who would wish to dissolve this Union or to change its republican form, let them stand undisturbed as monuments of the safety with which error of opinion may be tolerated where reason is left free to combat it.

> THOMAS JEFFERSON, in his first inaugural address, March 4, 1801.

46 I tolerate with the utmost latitude the right of others to differ from me in opinion without imputing to them criminality. I know too well the weakness and uncertainty of human reason to wonder at its different results.

> THOMAS JEFFERSON, in a letter to Abigail Adams, September 11, 1804.

47 We are reluctant to admit that we owe our liberties to men of a type that today we hate and fear—unruly men, disturbers of the peace, men who resent and denounce what Whitman called "the insolence of elected persons"—in a word, free men. . . . Freedom is always purchased at a great price, and even those who are willing to pay it have to admit that the price is great.

> GERALD W. JOHNSON, *American Freedom and the Press,* 1958.

48 The defense of freedom is finally grounded in an appreciation of its value. No government, no foreign policy, is more important to the defense of freedom than are the writers, teachers, communication specialists, researchers—whose responsibility it is to document, illustrate, and explain the human consequences of freedom and unfreedom.

> JEANE J. KIRKPATRICK, in an address to the Committee for the Free World, Washington, D.C., January 23, 1982.

49 The cause of freedom is identified with the destinies of humanity, and in whatever part of the world it gains ground, by and by it will be a common gain to all those who desire it.

> LAJOS KOSSUTH, in a speech in New York City, 1851.

50 Private property was the original source of freedom. It still is its main bulwark.

> WALTER LIPPMANN, *The Good Society,* 1937.

51 No! true freedom is to share
All the chains our brothers wear.

> JAMES RUSSELL LOWELL, "Stanzas on Freedom," 1843.

52 And I honor the man who is willing to sink
Half his present repute for the freedom to
        think,
And, when he has thought, be his cause
        strong or weak,
Will risk t' other half for the freedom to
        speak.

> JAMES RUSSELL LOWELL, *A Fable for Critics,* 1848.

53 Freedom needs all her poets: it is they
Who give her aspirations wings,
And to the wiser law of music sway
Her wild imaginings.

> JAMES RUSSELL LOWELL, "To the Memory of Hood," honoring the English poet Thomas Hood, 1848.

54 *What is freedom?* Freedom is the right to choose: the right to create for oneself the alternatives of choice. Without the possibility of choice and the exercise of choice a man is not a man but a member, an instrument, a thing.

> ARCHIBALD MACLEISH, in "A Declaration of Freedom."

55 Freedom is the right to one's dignity as a man.

> Ibid.

56 Since the general civilization of mankind, I believe there are more instances of the abridgment of the freedom of the people by gradual and silent encroachments of those in power than by violent and sudden usurpations.

> JAMES MADISON, in a speech in the Virginia Convention, June 16, 1788.

57 We must not confuse dissent with disloyalty.

> EDWARD R. MURROW, in a report on Sen. Joseph McCarthy, on the television program *See It Now,* March 7, 1954.

58 Our best hope, both of a tolerable political harmony and of an inner peace, rests upon our ability to observe the limits of human freedom even while we responsibly exploit its creative possibilities.

> REINHOLD NIEBUHR, *The Structure of Nations and Empires,* 1959.

59 As long as men are free to ask what they must, free to say what they think, free to think what they will, freedom can never be lost, and science can never regress.

> J. ROBERT OPPENHEIMER, in *Life* magazine, October 10, 1949.

60 There can be no prescription old enough to supersede the Law of Nature and the grant of God Almighty, who has given to all men a natural right to be free, and they have it ordinarily in their power to make themselves so, if they please.

> JAMES OTIS, *The Rights of the British Colonies Asserted and Proved,* 1764.

61 Freedom hath been hunted round the globe. Asia and Africa have long expelled her. Europe regards her like a stranger, and England hath given her warning to depart. Oh, receive the fugitive, and prepare in time an asylum for mankind!

> THOMAS PAINE, *Common Sense,* 1776.

62 Those who expect to reap the blessings of freedom must, like men, undergo the fatigue of supporting it.

> THOMAS PAINE, *The American Crisis,* No. 4, September 12, 1777.

63 Blandishments will not fascinate us, nor will threats of a "halter" intimidate. For, under God, we are determined that wheresoever, whensoever, or howsoever we shall be called to make our exit, we will die free men.

> JOSIAH QUINCY, *Observations on the Boston Port Bill,* 1774.

64 Cabal is the necessary effect of freedom. Where men are left free to act, we must calculate on their being governed by their interests and passions.

> JOHN RANDOLPH, in a letter to Littleton Waller Tazewell, April 21, 1804.

Franklin D. Roosevelt: from "four freedoms" speech, January 6, 1941

This was one of President Roosevelt's annual messages to Congress. He gave his vision of the future of America and the world, enunciating the four basic freedoms all people should possess when the war that had by then engulfed Europe was over. In six months Germany would invade the U.S.S.R. and in less than a year the United States would itself be at war.

. . . In the future days, which we seek to make secure, we look forward to a world founded upon four essential human freedoms.

The first is freedom of speech and expression everywhere in the world.

The second is freedom of every person to worship God in his own way everywhere in the world.

The third is freedom from want, which, translated into world terms, means economic understandings which will secure to every nation a healthy peacetime life for its inhabitants everywhere in the world.

The fourth is freedom from fear—which, translated into world terms, means a worldwide reduction of armaments to such a point and in such a thorough fashion that no nation will be in a position to commit an act of physical aggression against any neighbor—anywhere in the world.

That is no vision of a distant millennium. It is a definite basis for a kind of world attainable in our own time and generation. That kind of world is the very antithesis of the so-called new order of tyranny which the dictators seek to create with the crash of a bomb.

To that new order we oppose the greater conception—the moral order. A good society is able to face schemes of world domination and foreign revolutions alike without fear.

Since the beginning of our American history, we have been engaged in change—in a perpetual peaceful revolution—a revolution which goes on steadily, quietly adjusting itself to changing conditions—without the concentration camp or the quicklime in the ditch. The world order which we seek is the cooperation of free countries, working together in a friendly, civilized society.

This nation has placed its destiny in the hands and hearts of its millions of free men and women, and its faith in freedom under the guidance of God. Freedom means the supremacy of human rights everywhere. Our support goes to those who struggle to gain those rights or keep them. Our strength is in our unity of purpose. To that high concept there can be no end save victory.

65 We have plenty of freedom in this country but not a great deal of independence.

> John W. Raper, *What This World Needs,* 1954.

66 There can be no greater good than the quest for peace, and no finer purpose than the preservation of freedom.

> Ronald Reagan, in a speech to Congress on the Geneva summit meeting, November 21, 1985.

67 Freedom breeds freedom. Nothing else does.

> Anne Roe, *The Making of a Scientist,* 1952.

68 Freedom of conscience, of education, of speech, of assembly are among the very fundamentals of democracy and all of them would be nullified should freedom of the press ever be successfully challenged.

> Franklin D. Roosevelt, in a letter to W.N. Hardy, September 4, 1940.

69 We look forward to a world founded upon four essential human freedoms. The first is freedom of speech and expression everywhere in the world. The second is freedom of every person to worship God in his own way everywhere in the world. The third is freedom from want . . . everywhere in the world. The fourth is freedom from fear . . . anywhere in the world.

> Franklin D. Roosevelt, in a speech to Congress, January 6, 1941.

70 Privacy is absolutely essential to maintaining a free society. The idea that is at the foundation of the notion of privacy is that the citizen is not the tool or the instrument of government—but the reverse. . . . If you have no privacy, it will tend to follow that you have no political freedom, no religious freedom, no freedom of families to make their own decisions [regarding having children]. All these freedoms tend to reinforce one another.

> Benno C. Schmidt, Jr., in an interview in *The Christian Science Monitor,* December 5, 1986.

71 Who ever walked behind anyone to freedom? If we can't go hand in hand, I don't want to go.

> Hazel Scott, quoted in *Ms.* magazine, November, 1974.

72 A hungry man is not a free man.

> Adlai E. Stevenson, in a campaign speech, September 6, 1952.

73 My definition of a free society is a society where it is safe to be unpopular.

> Adlai E. Stevenson, in a speech in Detroit, Michigan, October 7, 1952.

74 Freedom—effective freedom—does not exist as a formula which can be written out by some and then used by others. The freedom that counts is simply what is in the minds and hearts of millions of free people. It is nothing more than the total of the feelings of people as they are expressed in the way we, the people, deal with our own families and our own neighbors and associates.

> Adlai E. Stevenson, in an address before the General Federation of Women's Clubs, Philadelphia, May 24, 1955.

75 If our freedom means ease alone, if it means shirking the hard disciplines of learning, if it means evading the rigors and rewards of creative activity, if it means more expenditure on advertising than education, if it means in the schools the steady cult of the trivial and the mediocre, if it means—worst of all—indifference, or even contempt for all but athletic excellence, we may keep for a time the forms of free society, but its spirit will be dead.

> Adlai E. Stevenson, in an address to the National School Boards Association, San Francisco, California, January 26, 1959.

76 Freedom is not an ideal, it is not even a protection, if it means nothing more than freedom to stagnate, to live without dreams, to have no greater aim than a second car and another television set—and this in a world where half our fellow men have less than enough to eat.

> Adlai E. Stevenson, "Putting First Things First," *Foreign Affairs,* January, 1960.

77 If I want to be free from any other man's dictation, I must understand that I can have no other man under my control.

> William Graham Sumner, in the essay "The Forgotten Man," in *The Forgotten Man and Other Essays,* 1919.

78 What other liberty is there worth having, if we have not freedom and peace in our minds—if our inmost and most private man is but a sour and turbid pool?

> HENRY DAVID THOREAU, entry written on October 26, 1853, *Journal,* 1906.

79 How rarely I meet with a man who can be free, even in thought! We all live according to rule. Some men are bedridden; all world-ridden.

> HENRY DAVID THOREAU, entry written on May 12, 1857, *Journal,* 1906.

80 It is by the goodness of God that in our country we have those three unspeakably precious things: freedom of speech, freedom of conscience, and the prudence never to practice either of them.

> MARK TWAIN, "Pudd'nhead Wilson's New Calendar," *Following the Equator,* 1897.

81 If men are to be precluded from offering their sentiments on a matter which may involve the most serious and alarming consequences that can invite the consideration of mankind, reason is of no use to us; the freedom of speech may be taken away, and dumb and silent we may be led, like sheep to the slaughter.

> GEORGE WASHINGTON, address to officers of the Army, urging moderation in seeking redress of grievances from Congress, March 15, 1783.

82 You can have no wise laws nor free enforcement of wise laws unless there is free expression of the wisdom of the people—and, alas, their folly with it. But if there is freedom, folly will die of its own poison, and the wisdom will survive.

> WILLIAM ALLEN WHITE, *The Editor and His People,* 1924.

83 Freedom exists only where the people take care of the government.

> WOODROW WILSON, in a speech in New York City, September 4, 1912.

84 Only free peoples can hold their purpose and their honor steady to a common end and prefer the interests of mankind to any narrow interest of their own.

> WOODROW WILSON, in his war message to Congress, April 2, 1917.

96. FRIENDS

See also AFFECTION; LOVE

1 Accident counts for much in companionship as in marriage.

> HENRY ADAMS, *The Education of Henry Adams,* 1907.

2 Seneca closed the vast circle of his knowledge by learning that a friend in power was a friend lost.

> Ibid.

3 Friends are born, not made.

> Ibid.

4 One friend in a lifetime is much; two are many; three are hardly possible.

> Ibid.

5 You and I ought not to die before we have explained ourselves to each other.

> JOHN ADAMS, in a letter to Thomas Jefferson, July 15, 1813.

6 The perfect friendship of two men is the deepest and highest sentiment of which the finite mind is capable; women miss the best in life.

> GERTRUDE ATHERTON, *The Conqueror,* 1902.

7 Acquaintance, *n.* A person whom we know well enough to borrow from, but not well enough to lend to. A degree of friendship called slight when its object is poor or obscure, and intimate when he is rich or famous.

> AMBROSE BIERCE, *The Devil's Dictionary,* 1906.

8 Friendless, *adj.* Having no favors to bestow. Destitute of fortune. Addicted to utterance of truth and common sense.

> Ibid.

9 Friendship, *n.* A ship big enough to carry two in fair weather, but only one in foul.

> Ibid.

10 Only solitary men know the full joys of friendship. Others have their family; but to a solitary and an exile his friends are everything.

> WILLA CATHER, *Shadows on the Rock,* 1931.

11 I pretind ivry man is honest, and I believe none iv them ar-re. In that way I keep me friends an' save me money.

> FINLEY PETER DUNNE, "The Christmas Spirit," *American Magazine,* December, 1906.

12 We want but two or three friends, but these we cannot do without, and they serve us in every thought we think.

> RALPH WALDO EMERSON, in a letter to Thomas Carlyle, September 17, 1836.

13 A friend is a person with whom I may be sincere. Before him I may think aloud.

> RALPH WALDO EMERSON, "Friendship," *Essays,* First Series, 1841.

14 A friend may well be reckoned the masterpiece of Nature.

> Ibid.

15 I hate the prostitution of the name of friendship to signify modish and worldly alliances.

> Ibid.

16 Better be a nettle in the side of your friend than his echo.

> Ibid.

17 The only way to have a friend is to be one.

> Ibid.

18 I do then with my friends as I do with my books. I would have them where I can find them, but I seldom use them.

> Ibid.

19 Let me live in my house by the side of the road
And be a friend to man.

> SAM WALTER FOSS, "The House by the Side of the Road," in Hazel Felleman, *Best Loved Poems of the American People,* 1936.

20 There are three faithful friends—an old wife, an old dog, and ready money.

> BENJAMIN FRANKLIN, *Poor Richard's Almanack,* 1738.

21 A Father's a Treasure; a Brother's a Comfort; a Friend is both.

> BENJAMIN FRANKLIN, *Poor Richard's Almanack,* 1747.

22 Friendship increases by visiting Friends, but by visiting seldom.

> BENJAMIN FRANKLIN, *Poor Richard's Almanack,* 1751.

23 Fame is the scentless sunflower, with gaudy crown of gold;
But friendship is the breathing rose, with sweets in every fold.

> OLIVER WENDELL HOLMES, SR., "No Time Like the Old Time," 1865.

24 Probably no man ever had a friend he did not dislike a little; we are all so constituted by nature no one can possibly entirely approve of us.

> EDGAR WATSON HOWE, *The Indignations of E. W. Howe,* 1933.

25 Your friend is the man who knows all about you, and still likes you.

> ELBERT HUBBARD, *The Roycroft Dictionary and Book of Epigrams,* 1923.

26 Wherever you are it is your own friends who make your world.

> WILLIAM JAMES, quoted in Ralph Barton Perry, *The Thought and Character of William James,* 1935.

27 The happiest moments it [my heart] knows are those in which it is pouring forth its affections to a few esteemed characters.

> THOMAS JEFFERSON, in a letter to Eliza House Trist, December 15, 1786.

28 An injured friend is the bitterest of foes.

> THOMAS JEFFERSON, in his "French Treaties Opinion," written for Pres. Washington, April 28, 1793.

29 I find friendship to be like wine, raw when new, ripened with age, the true old man's milk and restorative cordial.

> THOMAS JEFFERSON, in a letter to Benjamin Rush, August 17, 1811.

30 I'm a controversial figure. My friends either dislike me or hate me.

> OSCAR LEVANT, quoted in the introduction to Artemus Ward, *Artemus Ward, His Book,* 1964 edition.

31 I breathed a song into the air,
   It fell to earth, I knew not where. . . .
   And the song, from beginning to end,
   I found again in the heart of a friend.

> HENRY WADSWORTH LONGFELLOW, "The Arrow and the Song," *The Belfry of Bruges and Other Poems,* 1845.

32 A true friend unbosoms freely, advises justly, assists readily, adventures boldy, takes all patiently, defends courageously, and continues a friend unchangeably.

> WILLIAM PENN, *Some Fruits of Solitude,* 1693.

33 There can be no friendship where there is no freedom. Friendship loves a free air, and will not be fenced up in straight and narrow enclosures.

> Ibid.

34 A friend's only gift is himself. . . . To praise the utility of friendship, as the ancients so often did, and to regard it as a political institution justified, like victory or government, by its material results, is to lose one's moral bearings. . . . We are not to look now for what makes friendship useful, but for whatever may be found in friendship that may lend utility to life.

> GEORGE SANTAYANA, *The Life of Reason,* 1905–1906.

35 Friends are generally of the same sex, for when men and women agree, it is only in their conclusions; their reasons are always different.

> Ibid.

36 Grant stood by me when I was crazy, and I stood by him when he was drunk, and now we stand by each other.

> Attributed to William T. Sherman, c.1870.

37 One may discover a new side to his most intimate friend when for the first time he hears him speak in public. He will be stranger to him as he is more familiar to the audience. The longest intimacy could not foretell how he would behave then.

> HENRY DAVID THOREAU, entry written on February 6, 1841, *Journal,* 1906.

38 The most I can do for my friend is simply to be his friend.

> HENRY DAVID THOREAU, entry written on February 7, 1841, *Journal,* 1906.

39 Friends will be much apart. They will respect more each other's privacy than their communion.

> HENRY DAVID THOREAU, entry written on February 22, 1841, *Journal,* 1906.

40 Nothing makes the earth seem so spacious as to have friends at a distance; they make the latitudes and longitudes.

> HENRY DAVID THOREAU, in a letter to Mrs. E. Castleton, May 22, 1843.

41 I never found the companion that was so companionable as solitude.

> HENRY DAVID THOREAU, "Solitude," *Walden,* 1854.

42 A man cannot be said to succeed in this life who does not satisfy one friend.

> HENRY DAVID THOREAU, entry written on February 19, 1857, *Journal,* 1906.

43 The holy passion of Friendship is of so sweet and steady and loyal and enduring a nature that it will last through a whole lifetime, if not asked to lend money.

> MARK TWAIN, "Pudd'nhead Wilson's Calendar," *Pudd'nhead Wilson,* 1894.

44 There is an old time toast which is golden for its beauty. "When you ascend the hill of prosperity may you not meet a friend."

MARK TWAIN, "Pudd'nhead Wilson's New
Calendar," *Following the Equator,* 1897.

45 True friendship is a plant of slow growth, and
must undergo and withstand the shocks of adversity before it is entitled to the appellation.

GEORGE WASHINGTON, in a letter to Bushrod
Washington, January 15, 1783.

46 The rare few, who, early in life, have rid themselves of the friendship of the many.

JAMES ABBOTT MCNEILL WHISTLER, dedication
of *The Gentle Art of Making Enemies,* 1890.

97. GENIUS

See also GREATNESS; INVENTION; WISDOM

1 The sad truth is that excellence makes people
nervous.

SHANA ALEXANDER, "Neglected Kids—the
Bright Ones," *The Feminine Eye,* 1970.

2 These are the prerogatives of genius: to know
without having learned; to draw just conclusions
from unknown premises; to discern the soul of
things.

AMBROSE BIERCE, *Collected Works,* 1911.

3 I do not think America is a good place in which
to be a genius. A genius can never expect to have
a good time anywhere, if he is a genuine article, but
America is about the last place in which life will be
endurable at all for an inspired writer of any kind.

SAMUEL BUTLER, notebook entry, c.1890.

4 Genius is one per cent inspiration and ninety-
nine per cent perspiration.

Attributed to Thomas Edison.

5 In every work of genius we recognize our own
rejected thoughts; they come back to us with a
certain alienated majesty.

RALPH WALDO EMERSON, "Self-Reliance,"
Essays, First Series, 1841.

6 Beware when the great God lets loose a thinker
on this planet.

RALPH WALDO EMERSON, "Circles," *Essays,*
First Series, 1841.

7 Talent finds its models, methods, and ends in
society, exists for exhibition, and goes to the soul
only for power to work. Genius is its own end, and
draws its means and the style of its architecture
from within.

RALPH WALDO EMERSON, "The Method of
Nature," *Nature; Addresses and Lectures,* 1849.

8 Great geniuses have the shortest biographies.
Their cousins can tell you nothing about them.
They lived in their writings, and so their house and
street life was trivial and commonplace.

RALPH WALDO EMERSON, "Plato," *Representative
Men,* 1850.

9 Your man of genius pays dearly for his distinction. His head runs up into a spire, and instead of
a healthy man, merry and wise, he is some mad
dominie.

RALPH WALDO EMERSON, *The Conduct of Life,*
1860.

10 It is a problem that genius can very well solve—
to illuminate every low or trite word you can offer
it. Give your rubbish to Shakespeare, he will give
it all back to you in gold and stars.

RALPH WALDO EMERSON, entry written in 1863,
Journals, 1909–1914.

11 The miracles of genius always rest on profound
convictions which refuse to be analyzed.

RALPH WALDO EMERSON, "Progress of Culture,"
Letters and Social Aims, 1876.

12 A fine genius in his own country, is like gold in
the mine.

BENJAMIN FRANKLIN, *Poor Richard's Almanack,*
1733.

13 Genius will live and thrive without training, but
it does not the less reward the watering pot and
pruning knife.

MARGARET FULLER, diary entry, quoted in
Thomas Wentworth Higginson, *The Life of
Margaret Fuller Ossoli,* 1884.

14 The man or woman of real talent is rare, the born genius rarer still. For every book that survives the merciless judgment of time, there are nine hundred and ninety-nine rotting unread in libraries and nine thousand and ninety-nine that were never written in the first place.

MICHAEL HARRINGTON, *Fragments of the Century,* 1973.

15 Genius melts many ages into one, and thus effects something permanent, yet still with a similarity of office to that of the more ephemeral writer. A work of genius is but the newspaper of a century, or perchance of a hundred centuries.

NATHANIEL HAWTHORNE, *Mosses from an Old Manse,* 1846.

16 Perhaps, moreover, he whose genius appears deepest and truest excels his fellows in nothing save the knack of expression; he throws out occasionally a lucky hint at truths of which every human soul is profoundly though unutterably conscious.

Ibid.

17 Genius is always impatient of its harness; its wild blood makes it hard to train.

OLIVER WENDELL HOLMES, SR., *The Professor at the Breakfast-Table,* 1860.

18 Genius is the ability to act wisely without precedent—the power to do the right thing the first time.

ELBERT HUBBARD, *The Roycroft Dictionary and Book of Epigrams,* 1923.

19 Genius, in truth, means little more than the faculty of perceiving in an unhabitual way.

WILLIAM JAMES, *The Principles of Pyschology,* 1890.

20 Geniuses are commonly believed to excel other men in their power of sustained attention. . . . But it is their genius making them attentive, not their attention making geniuses of them.

WILLIAM JAMES, *The Principles of Psychology,* abridged version, 1892.

21 Towering genius disdains a beaten path. It seeks regions hitherto unexplored.

ABRAHAM LINCOLN, address at the Young Men's Lyceum, Springfield, Illinois, January 27, 1838.

22 Talent is that which is in a man's power; genius is that in whose power a man is.

JAMES RUSSELL LOWELL, "Rousseau and the Sentimentalists," *Among My Books,* 1870.

23 Genius, all over the world, stands hand in hand, and one shock of recognition runs the whole circle round.

HERMAN MELVILLE, "Hawthorne and His Mosses," 1850, quoted in Edmund Wilson, *The Shock of Recognition,* 1943.

24 Genius is the father of a heavenly line; but the mortal mother, that is industry.

THEODORE PARKER, "Of the Culture of the Religious Powers," *Ten Sermons on Religion,* 1852.

25 Men of genius are far more abundant than is supposed. In fact, to appreciate thoroughly the work of what we call genius, is to possess all the genius by which the work was produced.

EDGAR ALLAN POE, *Marginalia,* 1844–1849.

26 What the world calls genius is the state of mental disease arising from the undue predominance of some one of the faculties. The works of such genius are never sound in themselves, and, in especial, always betray the general mental insanity.

EDGAR ALLAN POE, "Fifty Suggestions," in *Graham's Magazine,* May, 1845.

27 Genius . . . is the capacity to see ten things where the ordinary man sees one, and where the man of talent sees two or three, *plus* the ability to register that multiple perception in the material of his art.

EZRA POUND, *Jefferson and/or Mussolini,* 1935.

28 Genius is not a single power. . . . It reasons, but it is not reasoning; it judges, but it is not judgment; it imagines, but it is not imagination; it feels deeply and fiercely, but it is not passion. It is neither, because it is all.

EDWIN PERCY WHIPPLE, "Literature and Life," 1849.

29 Genius is no snob. It does not run after titles or seek by preference the high circles of society.

WOODROW WILSON, in a speech at Hodgenville, Kentucky, September 4, 1916.

98. GEORGIA

1 Wisdom, Justice, Moderation.

>State motto.

2 The average Georgian votes the Democratic ticket, attends the Baptist or Methodist church, goes home to midday dinner, relies greatly on high cotton prices, and is so good a family man that he flings wide his doors to even the most distant of his wife's cousins' cousins.

>Federal Writers' Project, *Georgia: A Guide to Its Towns and Countryside,* 1940.

3 I am determined that at the end of this administration we shall be able to stand up anywhere in the world—in New York, California, or Florida—and say, "I'm a Georgian," and be proud of it.

>JIMMY CARTER, inaugural address as Governor of Georgia, Atlanta, Georgia, January 12, 1971.

4 I heard it said that the "architecture" of Atlanta is rococola. The pun is bad, but what the city would be like without Coca-Cola is hard to conceive. . . . In Atlanta alone Coca-Cola has made at least a thousand millionaires.

>JOHN GUNTHER, *Inside U.S.A.,* 1947.

5 Out of the hills of Habersham,
  Down the valleys of Hall,
I hurry amain to reach the plain
Run the rapid and leap the fall,
Split at the rock, and together again,
Accept my bed, or narrow or wide,
And flee from folly on every side
With a lover's pain to attain the plain
  Far from the hills of Habersham,
  Far from the valleys of Hall.

>SIDNEY LANIER, "Song of the Chattahoochee," 1877.

6 Bring the good old bugle, boys, we'll sing
  another song:
Sing it with a spirit that will start the world
  along,
Sing it as we used to sing it—fifty thousand
  strong,
  As we were marching through Georgia.
"Hurrah! hurrah! we bring the Jubilee!
Hurrah! hurrah! the flag that makes you
  free!"
So they sang the chorus from Atlanta to the
  Sea
  As we were marching through Georgia.

>HENRY CLAY WORK, "Marching through Georgia," 1865.

99. GOLDWYNISMS

See also MOTION PICTURES

Samuel Goldwyn, the Hollywood mogul, may have surpassed Richard Brinsley Sheridan's Mrs. Malaprop in number and inventiveness of outrageous linguistic innovations. Just as Mrs. Malaprop was the creature of the playwright's imagination, however, Goldwyn became legendary largely through the assistance of his Hollywood press agents, who worked valiantly to devise hundreds of what came to be known as Goldwynisms. The following represent a brief sample of sayings ascribed to Samuel Goldwyn.

1 Anybody who goes to see a psychiatrist ought to have his head examined.

2 In two words: im—possible.

3 I read part of it all the way through.

4 I'll write you a blanket check.

5 I don't think anybody should write his autobiography until after he's dead.

6 A verbal contract isn't worth the paper it's written on.

7 I want to make a picture about the Russian secret police—the G.O.P.

8 That's the trouble with directors. Always biting the hand that lays the golden egg.

9 Include me out.

100. GOSSIP

See also CONVERSATION

1 There is so much good in the worst of us,
And so much bad in the best of us,
That it hardly behooves any one of us
To talk about the rest of us.

Anonymous.

2 Everybody says it, and what everybody says must be true.

JAMES FENIMORE COOPER, *Miles Wallingford,* 1844.

3 Do not be so impatient to set the town right concerning the unfounded pretensions and the false reputation of certain men of standing. They are laboring harder to set the town right concerning themselves, and will certainly succeed.

RALPH WALDO EMERSON, "New England Reformers," *Essays,* Second Series, 1844.

4 Hear no ill of a Friend, nor speak any of an Enemy.

BENJAMIN FRANKLIN, *Poor Richard's Almanack,* 1739.

5 Gossip is vice enjoyed vicariously.

ELBERT HUBBARD, in *The Philistine* magazine, published from 1895–1915.

6 Gossip is only the lack of a worthy theme.

ELBERT HUBBARD, *The Roycroft Dictionary and Book of Epigrams,* 1923.

7 If you haven't got anything nice to say about anybody, come sit next to me.

ALICE ROOSEVELT LONGWORTH, motto embroidered on a cushion.

8 Knowing, what all experience serves to show,
No mud can soil us but the mud we throw.

JAMES RUSSELL LOWELL, "Epistle to George William Curtis," 1874.

9 There are two kinds of people who blow
    through life like a breeze,
And one kind is gossipers, and the other kind
    is gossipees.

OGDEN NASH, "I Have It on Good Authority," *I'm a Stranger Here Myself,* 1938.

10 Gossip is news running ahead of itself in a red satin dress.

LIZ SMITH, quoted in *American Way* magazine, September 3, 1985.

101. GOVERNMENT

See also CAMPAIGN SLOGANS; CONGRESS;
CONSTITUTION; DEMOCRACY; DIPLOMACY;
LIBERTY; POLITICS; PRESIDENCY;
PRESIDENTS; STATESMANSHIP; STATES'
RIGHTS; TAXATION; TYRANNY; VICE
PRESIDENCY

1 One might search the whole list of Congress, Judiciary, and Executive during the twenty-five years 1870 to 1895 and find little but damaged reputation.

HENRY ADAMS, quoted in Richard Hofstadter, *The American Political Tradition,* 1948.

2 The most sensible and jealous people are so little attentive to government, that there are no instances of resistance, until repeated, multiplied oppressions have placed it beyond a doubt, that their rulers had formed settled plans to deprive them of their liberties.

JOHN ADAMS, *Novanglus: or, A History of the Dispute with America,* a series of articles published in the *Boston Gazette,* 1774.

3 As the happiness of the people is the sole end of government, so the consent of the people is the only foundation of it, in reason, morality, and the natural fitness of things.

JOHN ADAMS, proclamation adopted by the Council of Massachusetts Bay, 1774.

4 Fear is the foundation of most governments.

> JOHN ADAMS, *Thoughts on Government*, 1776.

5 Mobs will never do to govern states or command armies. Until they're elected.

> JOHN ADAMS, in a letter to Benjamin Hichborn, January 27, 1787.

6 While all other Sciences have advanced, that of Government is at a stand; little better understood; little better practiced now than 3 or 4 thousand years ago.

> JOHN ADAMS, in a letter to Thomas Jefferson, July 9, 1813.

7 I consider biennial elections as a security that the sober, second thought of the people shall be law.

> FISHER AMES, in a speech, January, 1788.

8 A monarchy is a merchantman which sails well, but will sometimes strike on a rock, and go to the bottom; a republic is a raft which will never sink, but then your feet are always in the water.

> FISHER AMES, in a speech in the House of Representatives, 1795.

9 The nation guarantees the nurture, education, and comfortable maintenance of every citizen from the cradle to the grave.

> EDWARD BELLAMY, *Looking Backward, 2000–1887*, 1888.

10 Absolute, *adj.* Independent, irresponsible. An absolute monarchy is one in which the sovereign does as he pleases so long as he pleases the assassins. Not many absolute monarchies are left, most of them having been replaced by limited monarchies, where the sovereign's power for evil (and for good) is greatly curtailed, and by republics, which are governed by chance.

> AMBROSE BIERCE, *The Devil's Dictionary*, 1906.

11 The marvel of all history is the patience with which men and women submit to burdens unnecessarily laid upon them by their governments.

> Attributed to William E. Borah.

12 Since government is not an exact science, prevailing public opinion concerning the evils and the remedy is among the important facts deserving consideration, particularly when the public conviction is both deep-seated and widespread and has been reached after deliberation.

> LOUIS D. BRANDEIS, in a dissenting opinion in *Truax v. Corrigan,* 1921.

13 It is a great merit of American government that it relies very little on officials, and arms them with little power of arbitrary interference.

> JAMES BRYCE, *The American Commonwealth,* 1888.

14 It is a gross error to confound the exercise of sovereign powers with sovereignty itself, or the delegation of such powers with the surrender of them.

> JOHN C. CALHOUN, in a speech in the U.S. Senate, February 15, 1833.

15 The very essence of a free government consists in considering offices as public trusts, bestowed for the good of the country, and not for the benefit of an individual or a party.

> JOHN C. CALHOUN, in a speech, February 13, 1835.

16 What was once a constitutional federal republic is now converted, in reality, into one as absolute as that of the autocrat of Russia, and as despotic in its tendency as any absolute government that ever existed.

> JOHN C. CALHOUN, in a speech in the U.S. Senate, March 4, 1850.

17 Government is a contrivance of human wisdom to provide for human wants. People have the right to expect that these wants will be provided for by this wisdom.

> JIMMY CARTER, in his inaugural address as Governor of Georgia, Atlanta, Georgia, January 12, 1971.

18 A simple and a proper function of government is just to make it easy for us to do good and difficult for us to do wrong.

> JIMMY CARTER, acceptance speech at the Democratic National Convention, New York, July 15, 1976.

19 The office of government is not to confer happiness, but to give men opportunity to work out happiness for themselves.

> WILLIAM ELLERY CHANNING, in a review in the *Christian Examiner,* September-October, 1827.

20 It is to arraign the dispositions of Providence Himself to suppose that He has created beings incapable of governing themselves, and to be trampled on by kings.

> HENRY CLAY, in a speech in the House of Representatives, March 24, 1818.

21 Self-government is the natural government of man.

> Ibid.

22 Government is a trust, and the officers of the government are trustees; and both the trust and the trustees are created for the benefit of the people.

> HENRY CLAY, in a speech at Lexington, Kentucky, May 16, 1829.

23 Public officers are the servants and agents of the people, to execute laws which the people have made and within the limits of a constitution which they have established.

> GROVER CLEVELAND, in a letter accepting nomination for governor of New York, October 7, 1882.

24 Good government . . . has for its objects the protection of every person within its care in the greatest liberty consistent with the good order of society, and his perfect security in the enjoyment of his earnings with the least possible diminution for public needs.

> GROVER CLEVELAND, in his second annual message to Congress, December 6, 1886.

25 Though the people support the Government, the Government should not support the people.

> GROVER CLEVELAND, in a veto message, February 16, 1887.

26 I have considered the pension list of the Republic a roll of honor.

> GROVER CLEVELAND, veto of an act granting a pension to one Mary Ann Dougherty, July 5, 1888.

27 The lessons of paternalism ought to be unlearned and the better lesson taught that while the people should patriotically and cheerfully support their Government its functions do not include the support of the people.

> GROVER CLEVELAND, in his second inaugural address, March 4, 1893.

28 Allow the state to invade the areas of thought, of education, of the press, of religion, of association, and we will have statism. . . . Those who fear statism, as all who are rooted in American history and tradition fear it, must resolutely oppose it where it is most dangerous, precisely in the realm of the mind and the spirit of men. For if once we get a government strong enough to control men's minds, we will have a government strong enough to control everything.

> HENRY STEELE COMMAGER, *Freedom and Order,* 1966.

29 Despotism has forever had a powerful hold upon the world. Autocratic government, not self-government, has been the prevailing state of mankind. It needs to be remembered that the record of past history is the record, not of the success of republics, but of their failure.

> CALVIN COOLIDGE, "The Destiny of America," speech delivered at Northampton, Massachusetts, May 30, 1923.

30 A monarchy is the most expensive of all forms of government, the regal state requiring a costly parade, and he who depends on his own power to rule, must strengthen that power by bribing the active and enterprising whom he cannot intimidate.

> JAMES FENIMORE COOPER, *The American Democrat,* 1838.

31 The principal business of government is to further and promote human strivings.

> WILBUR L. CROSS, interview in the *New York Times,* March 29, 1931.

32 Every government, at some time or other, falls into wrong measures; these may proceed from mistake or passion.—But every such measure does not dissolve the obligation between the governors and

the governed; the mistake may be corrected; the passion may pass over. It is the duty of the governed, to endeavor to rectify the mistake, and appease the passion.

> JOHN DICKINSON, *Letters from a Farmer in Pennsylvania,* 1768.

33 Government has hardened into a tyrannical monopoly, and the human race in general becomes as absolutely property as beasts in the plow.

> JOHN DICKINSON, in a letter to Thomas McKean, November 22, 1802.

34 Under our present system, the chief duty of the governor of Alabama is running an employment agency.

> FRANK DIXON, in his inaugural address as governor of Alabama, January 17, 1938.

35 The less government we have the better—the fewer laws, and the less confided power. The antidote to this abuse of formal government is the influence of private character, the growth of the Individual; the appearance of the principal to supersede the proxy; the appearance of the wise man; of whom the existing government is, it must be owned, but a shabby imitation.

> RALPH WALDO EMERSON, "Politics," *Essays,* Second Series, 1844.

36 In dealing with the State we ought to remember that its institutions are not aboriginal, though they existed before we were born; that they are not superior to the citizen; that every one of them was once the act of a single man; every law and usage was a man's expedient to meet a particular case; that they all are imitable, all alterable; we may make as good; we may make better.

> Ibid.

37 Every actual State is corrupt. Good men must not obey the laws too well.

> Ibid.

38 The State is a poor, good beast who means the best: it means friendly. A poor cow who does well by you,—do not grudge it its hay. It cannot eat bread, as you can; let it have without grudge a little grass for its four stomachs. It will not stint to yield

you milk from its teat. You, who are a man walking cleanly on two feet, will not pick a quarrel with a poor cow. Take this handful of clover and welcome. But if you go to hook me when I walk in the fields, then, poor cow, I will cut your throat.

> RALPH WALDO EMERSON, entry written in 1846, *Journals,* 1909–1914.

39 Government has been a fossil; it should be a plant.

> RALPH WALDO EMERSON, "The Young American," *Nature; Addresses and Lectures,* 1849.

40 If government knew how, I should like to see it check, not multiply the population. When it reaches its true law of action, every man that is born will be hailed as essential.

> RALPH WALDO EMERSON, "Considerations by the Way," *The Conduct of Life,* 1860.

41 For thirty years, the Bible-believing Christians of America have been largely absent from the executive, legislative, and judicial branches of both federal and local government.

> JERRY FALWELL, quoted in William R. Goodman, Jr., and James J.H. Price, *Jerry Falwell: An Unauthorized Profile,* 1981.

42 In Rivers & bad Governments, the lightest Things swim at top.

> BENJAMIN FRANKLIN, *Poor Richard's Almanack,* 1754.

43 To the free man, the country is the collection of individuals who compose it, not something over and above them. He is proud of a common heritage and loyal to common traditions. But he regards government as a means, an instrumentality, neither a grantor of favors and gifts, nor a master or god to be blindly worshipped and served. He recognizes no national goal except as it is the consensus of the goals the citizens severally serve. He recognizes no national purpose except as it is the consensus of the purposes for which the citizens severally strive.

> MILTON FRIEDMAN, *Capitalism and Freedom,* 1962.

44 The prime enemy of the people is the government, save as it involves itself in the exigent and

increasing needs of national defense and those of bankrupt but still meritorious corporations.

JOHN KENNETH GALBRAITH, *Annals of an Abiding Liberal,* 1979.

45 All free governments are managed by the combined wisdom and folly of the people.

JAMES A. GARFIELD, in a letter, April 21, 1880.

46 Businesses which are in their nature monopolies are properly part of the functions of the State, and should be assumed by the State. There is the same reason why Government should carry telegraphic messages as that it should carry letters; that railroads should belong to the public as that common roads should.

HENRY GEORGE, *Progress and Poverty,* 1879.

47 The experience of Russia, more than any theories, has demonstrated that *all* government, whatever its forms or pretenses, is a dead weight that paralyzes the free spirit and activities of the masses.

EMMA GOLDMAN, *My Disillusionment in Russia,* 1923.

48 None of us here in Washington knows all or even half of the answers. You people out there in the fifty states had better understand that. If you love your country, don't depend on handouts from Washington for your information. If you cherish your freedom, don't leave it all up to BIG GOVERNMENT.

BARRY GOLDWATER, *Why Not Victory?* 1962.

49 Haven't you ever noticed how highways always get beautiful near the state capital?

SHIRLEY ANN GRAU, *The Wind Shifting West,* 1973.

50 It is that in all legislative assemblies the greater the number composing them may be, the fewer will be the men who will in fact direct their proceedings.

ALEXANDER HAMILTON, *The Federalist,* 1787–1788.

51 Contracts between a nation and individuals are only binding on the conscience of the sovereign, and have no pretensions to a compulsive force.

Ibid.

52 The people can never err more than in supposing that by multiplying their representatives beyond a certain limit, they strengthen the barrier against the government of a few.

Ibid.

53 Why has government been instituted at all? Because the passions of men will not conform to the dictates of reason and justice, without constraint.

Ibid.

54 A nation that represses social problems with police power will become something of an armed camp—which is not a very happy place for either the wardens or the prisoners.

MICHAEL HARRINGTON, *Toward a Democratic Left,* 1968.

55 We admit of no government by divine right. . . . The only legitimate right to govern is an express grant of power from the governed.

WILLIAM HENRY HARRISON, in his inaugural address, March 4, 1841.

56 The government is mainly an expensive organization to regulate evildoers, and tax those who behave; government does little for fairly respectable people except annoy them.

EDGAR WATSON HOWE, *Notes for My Biographer,* 1926.

57 I am against government by crony.

HAROLD L. ICKES, resigning from Pres. Harry S Truman's cabinet, February, 1946.

58 Our government is founded upon the intelligence of the people.

Attributed to Andrew Jackson.

59 I am of opinion that a good Judiciary lends much to the dignity of a state and the happiness of the people. . . . On the Contrary a bad Judiciary involved in party business is the greatest Curse that can befall a Country.

ANDREW JACKSON, in a letter to William Blount, February 29, 1796.

60 I for one do not despair of the republic; I have great confidence in the virtue of the great majority of the people, and I cannot fear the result.

> ANDREW JACKSON, in a letter to James Hamilton, Jr., June 29, 1828.

61 The duties of all public officers are, or at least admit of being made, so plain and simple that men of intelligence may readily qualify themselves for their performance; and I can not but believe that more is lost by the long continuance of men in office than is generally to be gained by their experience.

> ANDREW JACKSON, in his first message to Congress, December 8, 1829.

62 There are no necessary evils in government. Its evils exist only in its abuses. If it would confine itself to equal protection, and, as Heaven does its rains, shower its favors alike on the high and the low, the rich and the poor, it would be an unqualified blessing.

> ANDREW JACKSON, in a message to Congress, vetoing the bill to recharter the Second Bank of the United States, July 10, 1832.

63 The Government can suffer no rivals in the field of coercion. Liberty requires that coercion be applied to the individual not by other individuals but by the Government after full inquiry into the justification.

> ROBERT H. JACKSON, *The Supreme Court in the American System of Government,* 1955.

64 The legitimate powers of government extend to such acts only as are injurious to others.

> THOMAS JEFFERSON, *Notes on the State of Virginia,* 1784.

65 The influence over government must be shared among all the people. If every individual which composes their mass participates of the ultimate authority, the government will be safe; because the corrupting of the whole mass will exceed any private resources of wealth; and public ones cannot be provided but by levies on the people. In this case every man would have to pay his own price.

> Ibid.

66 Those societies (as the Indians) which live without government, enjoy in their general mass an infinitely greater degree of happiness than those who live under the European governments. Among the former, public opinion is in the place of law, and restrains morals as powerfully as laws ever did anywhere. Among the latter, under pretence of governing, they have divided their nations into two classes, wolves and sheep.

> THOMAS JEFFERSON, in a letter to Edward Carrington, January 16, 1787.

67 But with all the imperfections of our present government, it is without comparison the best existing, or that ever did exist.

> THOMAS JEFFERSON, in a letter to Edward Carrington, August 4, 1787.

68 I was much an enemy to monarchy before I came to Europe. I am ten thousand times more so since I have seen what they are. There is scarcely an evil known in these countries which may not be traced to their king as its source, nor a good which is not derived from the small fibers of republicanism existing among them.

> THOMAS JEFFERSON, in a letter to George Washington, May 2, 1788.

69 It is not the policy of the government in that country [the United States] to give any aid to works of any kind. They let things take their natural course without help or impediment, which is generally the best policy.

> THOMAS JEFFERSON, in a letter to Thomas Digges, June 19, 1788.

70 It would be a dangerous delusion were a confidence in the men of our choice to silence our fears for the safety of our rights; that confidence is everywhere the parent of despotism. Free government is founded in jealousy and not in confidence; it is jealousy, and not confidence which prescribes limited constitutions, to bind down those whom we are obliged to trust with power.

> THOMAS JEFFERSON, lines from the Kentucky Resolutions, November 16, 1798.

71 The will of the people is the only legitimate foundation of any government, and to protect its free expression should be our first object.

> THOMAS JEFFERSON, in a letter to Benjamin Waring, March, 1801.

72 Sometimes it is said that man cannot be trusted with the government of himself. Can he, then, be trusted with the government of others?

> THOMAS JEFFERSON, in his first inaugural address, March 4, 1801.

73 A wise and frugal government, which shall restrain men from injuring one another, shall leave them otherwise free to regulate their own pursuits of industry and improvement, and shall not take from the mouth of labor the bread it has earned. This is the sum of good government, and this is necessary to close the circle of our felicities.

> Ibid.

74 The hand of the people has given the mortal blow to a conspiracy which, in other countries, would have called for an appeal to armies, and has proved that government to be the strongest of which every man feels himself a part.

> THOMAS JEFFERSON, in a letter to Edward Tiffin, February 2, 1807. (Jefferson was referring to the alleged conspiracy of Aaron Burr to separate the western states from the Union.)

75 The ordinary affairs of a nation offer little difficulty to a person of any experience; but the gift of office is the dreadful burden which oppresses him.

> THOMAS JEFFERSON, in a letter to James Sullivan, March 3, 1808.

76 The care of human life and happiness, and not their destruction, is the first and only legitimate object of good government.

> THOMAS JEFFERSON, in a message to the citizens of Washington County, Maryland, March 31, 1809.

77 The only orthodox object of the institution of government is to secure the greatest degree of happiness possible to the general mass of those associated under it.

> THOMAS JEFFERSON, in a letter to F.A. van der Kemp, March 22, 1812.

78 The functionaries of every government have propensities to command at will the liberty and property of their constituents.

> THOMAS JEFFERSON, in a letter to Charles Yancey, January 6, 1816.

79 A single good government becomes thus a blessing to the whole earth, its welcome to the oppressed restraining within certain limits the measure of their oppressions.

> THOMAS JEFFERSON, in a letter to George Flower, September 12, 1817. (Jefferson held that the existence of representative government in the U.S. had a restraining effect on European monarchies.)

80 The science of government is the most abstruse of all sciences; if, indeed, that can be called a science which has but few fixed principles, and practically consists in little more than the exercise of a sound discretion, applied to the exigencies of the state as they arise. It is the science of experiment.

> WILLIAM JOHNSON, in a Supreme Court opinion, *Anderson* v. *Dunn*, 1821.

81 Personal virtue is a good in itself, but it is not a sufficient means to the end of good government.

> JEANE J. KIRKPATRICK, in a speech in Washington, D.C., September 29, 1982.

82 Governments can encourage the cultivation of private virtue. They can provide a framework in which we may pursue virtue (or happiness), but they cannot make us virtuous (or happy), and the effort to use the coercive power of government for that purpose not only fails to produce private morality, it undermines public morality as well.

> Ibid.

83 Everyone is for more openness [in government] and an end to secrecy.

> HENRY KISSINGER, quoted in Richard Valeriani, *Travels with Henry,* 1979.

84 The legitimate object of government is to do for a community of people whatever they need to have done, but cannot do at all, or cannot so well do for themselves in their separate and individual capacities. In all that the people can individually do as well for themselves, government ought not to interfere.

> ABRAHAM LINCOLN, note on government, July 1, 1854.

85 When a white man governs himself, that is self government. But when he governs himself and also governs some other men, that is worse than self government—that is despotism. What I do mean to say is that no man is good enough to govern another man without that other's consent.

ABRAHAM LINCOLN, in a speech in Peoria, Illinois, October 16, 1854.

86 Perpetuity is implied, if not expressed, in the fundamental law of all national governments. It is safe to assert that no government proper ever had a provision in its organic law for its own termination.

ABRAHAM LINCOLN, in his first inaugural address, March 4, 1861.

87 Must a government, of necessity, be too strong for the liberties of its own people, or too weak to maintain its own existence?

ABRAHAM LINCOLN, in a message to Congress in special session, July 4, 1861.

88 The workingmen are the basis of all governments, for the plain reason that they are the more numerous.

ABRAHAM LINCOLN, in a speech in Cincinnati, Ohio, February 12, 1861.

89 A nation may be said to consist of its territory, its people, and its laws. The territory is the only part which is of certain durability.

ABRAHAM LINCOLN, in his annual message to Congress, December 1, 1862.

90 You must not complicate your government beyond the capacity of its electorate to understand it. If you do, it will escape all control, turn corrupt and tyrannical, lose the popular confidence, offer real security to no man, and in the end it will let loose all the submerged antagonisms within the state.

WALTER LIPPMANN, in the *Atlantic Monthly,* October, 1924.

91 If the professors try to run the government, we shall end by having the government run the professors.

WALTER LIPPMANN, in a speech at the University of Rochester, June 15, 1936.

92 In relation to society and government it may be repeated that new ideas are rare; in regard to the latter, perhaps not more than two really large and new ideas have been developed in as many millenniums.

HENRY CABOT LODGE, in a speech in Schenectady, New York, June 9, 1915.

93 The only thing that saves us from the bureaucracy is its inefficiency.

Attributed to Eugene McCarthy.

94 Experience has instructed us that no skill in the science of government has yet been able to discriminate and define, with sufficient certainty, its three great provinces—the legislative, executive, and judiciary; or even the privileges and powers of the different legislative branches. Questions daily occur in the course of practice which prove the obscurity which reigns in these subjects, and which puzzle the greatest adepts in political science.

JAMES MADISON, *The Federalist,* 1787–1788.

95 The idea of a national government involves in it, not only an authority over the individual citizens, but an indefinite supremacy over all persons and things, so far as they are objects of lawful government. Among a people consolidated into one nation, this supremacy is completely vested in the national legislature.

Ibid.

96 The government of the Union . . . is emphatically and truly a government of the people. In form and in substance it emanates from them, its powers are granted by them, and are to be exercised directly on them, and for their benefit.

JOHN MARSHALL, in a Supreme Court opinion, in *McCulloch* v. *Maryland,* 1819.

97 The end of the government being the good of mankind points out its great duties; it is above all things to provide for the security, the quiet, the happy enjoyment of life, liberty, and property.

JAMES OTIS, *The Rights of the British Colonies Asserted and Proved,* 1764.

98 Society in every state is a blessing, but government, even in its best stage, is but a necessary evil; in its worst state an intolerable one.

THOMAS PAINE, *Common Sense,* 1776.

99 All hereditary government is in its nature tyranny. An heritable crown, or an heritable throne, or by what other fanciful name such things may be called, have no other significant explanation than that mankind are heritable property. To inherit a government, is to inherit the people, as if they were flocks and herds.

> THOMAS PAINE, *The Rights of Man,* 1791–1792.

100 Every age and generation must be as free to act for itself, *in all cases,* as the ages and generations which preceded it. The vanity and presumption of governing beyond the grave, is the most ridiculous and insolent of all tyrannies.

> Ibid.

101 Government in a well-constituted republic, requires no belief from man beyond what his reason can give. He sees the *rationale* of the whole system, its origin, and its operation; and as it is best supported when best understood, the human faculties act with boldness, and acquire, under this form of government, a gigantic manliness.

> Ibid.

102 Great part of that order which reigns among mankind is not the effect of government. It has its origin in the principles of society and the natural constitution of man. It existed prior to government, and would exist if the formality of government was abolished.

> Ibid.

103 In fine, society performs for itself almost everything which is ascribed to government.

> Ibid.

104 All the monarchical governments are military. War is their trade, plunder and revenue their objects. While such governments continue, peace has not the absolute security of a day.

> Ibid.

105 Let the people think they govern and they will be governed.

> WILLIAM PENN, *Some Fruits of Solitude,* 1693.

106 No system of government was ever so ill devised that, under proper men, it wouldn't work well enough.

> Ibid.

107 Republics exist only on the tenure of being constantly agitated.

> WENDELL PHILLIPS, in a speech in Boston, January 28, 1852.

108 Everybody knows that government never began anything. It is the whole world that thinks and governs.

> WENDELL PHILLIPS, in a lecture in Boston, October 4, 1859.

109 Governments exist to protect the rights of minorities. The loved and the rich need no protection,—they have many friends and few enemies.

> WENDELL PHILLIPS, in a speech in Boston, December 21, 1860.

110 'Tis a political maxim that all government tends to despotism, and like the human frame brings at its birth the latent seed which finally shall destroy the constitution. This is a melancholy truth—but such is the lot of humanity.

> JOSIAH QUINCY, in a letter to the *Boston Gazette,* 1767.

111 Government, to be safe and to be free, must consist of representatives having a common interest and a common feeling with the represented. . . . No government extending from the Atlantic to the Pacific can be fit to govern me or those whom I represent. There is death in the pot, compound it how you will.

> JOHN RANDOLPH, speaking in Congress, January, 1822.

112 Bureaucracy does not take kindly to being assailed and isn't above using a few low blows and a knee to the groin when it fights back. Knowing this, I have become extremely cautious in dealing with government agencies.

> RONALD REAGAN, *Where's the Rest of Me?* 1965.

113 Government exists to protect rights which are ours from birth; the right to life, to liberty, and the

pursuit of happiness. A man may choose to sit and fish instead of working—that's his pursuit of happiness. He does not have the right to force his neighbors to support him in his pursuit because that interferes with their pursuit of happiness.

> RONALD REAGAN, *Sincerely, Ronald Reagan,* 1976.

114 Government exists to protect us from each other. We can't afford the government it would take to protect us from ourselves.

> RONALD REAGAN, quoted in Laurence I. Barrett, *Gambling with History—Reagan in the White House,* 1983.

115 The best system is to have one party govern and the other party watch, and on general principles I think it would be best for us to govern and the Democrats watch.

> THOMAS BRACKETT REED, in a debate in the House of Representatives, April 22, 1880.

116 Whereas a tightly centralized government tends, by its disproportionate weight and power, to stifle diversity and creativity in both the public and private sectors, a federal system provides room for both infinite variety and creativity in all sectors of national life. This is equally true for political organizations, philanthropic associations, social institutions, or economic enterprises.

> NELSON A. ROCKEFELLER, *The Future of Federalism,* 1962.

117 Grand ideas of government—lofty abstract principles, even the wisest constitutions and laws—depend for their very life and meaning on the willingness of citizens and leaders to apply them and to improve them.

> Ibid.

118 If we do not halt this steady process of building commissions and regulatory bodies and special legislation like huge inverted pyramids over every one of the simple constitutional provisions, we shall soon be spending many billions of dollars more.

> FRANKLIN D. ROOSEVELT, in a radio address, March 2, 1930. (Roosevelt had just noted that the annual federal budget had reached $3,500,000,000.)

119 The only sure bulwark of continuing liberty is a government strong enough to protect the interests of the people, and a people strong enough and well enough informed to maintain its sovereign control over its government.

> FRANKLIN D. ROOSEVELT, in a radio address, April 14, 1938.

120 The government is us; we are the government, you and I.

> THEODORE ROOSEVELT, in a speech in Asheville, North Carolina, September 9, 1902.

121 I do not believe in government ownership of anything which can with propriety be left in private hands, and in particular I should most strenuously object to government ownership of railroads.

> THEODORE ROOSEVELT, in a speech in Raleigh, North Carolina, October 19, 1905.

122 There is something to be said for government by a great aristocracy which has furnished leaders to the nation in peace and war for generations; even a democrat like myself must admit this. But there is absolutely nothing to be said for government by a plutocracy, for government by men very powerful in certain lines and gifted with the "money touch," but with ideals which in their essence are merely those of so many glorified pawnbrokers.

> THEODORE ROOSEVELT, in a letter to Edward Grey, November 15, 1913.

123 Everything is un-American that tends either to government by a plutocracy, or government by a mob. To divide along the lines of section or caste or creed is un-American. All privilege based on wealth, and all enmity to honest men merely because they are wealthy, are un-American—both of them equally so. Americanism means the virtues of courage, honor, justice, truth, sincerity, and hardihood—the virtues that made America. The things that will destroy America are prosperity-at-any-price, peace-at-any-price, safety-first instead of duty-first, the love of soft living, and the get-rich-quick theory of life.

> THEODORE ROOSEVELT, in a letter to S. Stanwood Menken, January 10, 1917.

124 Government neither subsists nor arises because it is good or useful, but solely it is inevitable.

GEORGE SANTAYANA, *The Life of Reason,* 1905.

125 I do not subscribe to the doctrine that the people are the slaves and property of their government. I believe that government is for the use of the people, and not the people for the use of government.

GERRIT SMITH, in a speech in the House of Representatives, June 27, 1854.

126 No government can be free that does not allow all its citizens to participate in the formation and execution of her laws. . . . Every other government is a despotism.

THADDEUS STEVENS, in a speech in the House of Representatives, June 3, 1867.

127 Socialism is the public ownership of the means of production, and no one is proposing that. But as we use the word, it seems to be any government authority we do not like. Of course, things we like—tariffs, subsidies, mail concessions, support prices, tax write-offs, depletion allowances and government aids to particular groups—are rarely denounced as "socialism" except perhaps by the group's competitors.

ADLAI E. STEVENSON, in a paper delivered at the National Business Conference, Harvard Business School, June 6, 1959.

128 When all the fine phrases are stripped away, it appears that the state is only a group of men with human interests, passions, and desires, or, worse yet, the state is only an obscure clerk hidden in some corner of a governmental bureau. In either case the assumption of superhuman wisdom and virtue is proved false.

WILLIAM GRAHAM SUMNER, *Commercial Crises,* 1879.

129 How does it become a man to behave towards the American government today? I answer, that he cannot without disgrace be associated with it.

HENRY DAVID THOREAU, "Civil Disobedience," 1849.

130 I saw that the State was half-witted, that it was timid as a lone woman with her silver spoons, and

that it did not know its friends from its foes, and I lost all my remaining respect for it, and pitied it.

Ibid.

131 There will never be a really free and enlightened State until the State comes to recognize the individual as a higher and independent power, from which all its own power and authority are derived, and treats him accordingly.

Ibid.

132 I went to the store the other day to buy a bolt for our front door, for, as I told the storekeeper, the Governor was coming here. "Aye," said he, "and the Legislature too." "Then I will take two bolts," said I.

HENRY DAVID THOREAU, entry written September 8, 1859, *Journal,* 1906.

133 It is important not to confuse stability with force, or the greatness of a thing with its duration. In democratic republics the power that directs society is not stable, for it often changes hands and assumes a new direction. But whichever way it turns, its force is almost irresistible.

ALEXIS DE TOCQUEVILLE, *Democracy in America,* 1838.

134 Every segment of our population and every individual has the right to expect from our government a fair deal.

HARRY S TRUMAN, in a message to Congress, 1949.

135 Secrecy and a free, democratic government don't mix.

HARRY S TRUMAN, quoted in Merle Miller, *Plain Speaking: An Oral Biography of Harry S Truman,* 1974.

136 Experience has taught us, that men will not adopt and carry into execution measures the best calculated for their own good, without the intervention of a coercive power.

GEORGE WASHINGTON, in a letter to John Jay, August 1, 1786.

137 No man is a warmer advocate for proper restraints and wholesome checks in every department of government than I am; but I have never yet been able to discover the propriety of placing it absolutely out of the power of men to render essential Services, because a possibility remains of their doing ill.

GEORGE WASHINGTON, in a letter to Bushrod Washington, November 10, 1787.

138 The basis of our political systems is the right of the people to make and to alter their constitutions of government. But the constitution which at any time exists, till changed by an explicit and authentic act of the whole people, is sacredly obligatory upon all. The very idea of the power and the right of the people to establish government presupposes the duty of every individual to obey the established government.

GEORGE WASHINGTON, in his Farewell Address, September 17, 1796.

139 Toward the preservation of your government and the permanency of your present happy state, it is requisite not only that you steadily discountenance irregular oppositions to its acknowledged authority, but also that you resist with care the spirit of innovation upon its principles, however specious the pretexts.

Ibid.

140 If, in our case, the Representative system ultimately fail, popular governments must be pronounced impossible. No combination of circumstances more favorable to the experiment can ever be expected to occur. The last hopes of mankind, therefore, rest with us; and if it should be proclaimed, that our example had become an argument against the experiment, the knell of popular liberty would be sounded throughout the earth.

DANIEL WEBSTER, "Address Delivered at the Laying of the Corner Stone of the Bunker Hill Monument," June 17, 1825.

141 The inherent right in the people to reform their government I do not deny; and they have another right, and that is to resist unconstitutional laws without overturning the government.

DANIEL WEBSTER, in his second reply to Robert Y. Hayne during their celebrated Senate debate on the nature of the Union, January 26, 1830.

142 The national government possesses those powers which it can be shown the people have conferred on it, and no more. All the rest belongs to the state governments, or to the people themselves.

Ibid.

143 We have been taught to regard a representative of the people as a sentinel on the watch-tower of liberty.

DANIEL WEBSTER, in a speech in the U.S. Senate, May 7, 1834.

144 I say the mission of government, henceforth in civilized lands, is not repression alone, and not authority alone, not even of law, nor by that favorite standard of the eminent writer, the rule of the best men, the born heroes and captains of the race (as if such ever, or one time out of a hundred, get into the big places, elective or dynastic)—but higher than the highest arbitrary rule, to train communities through all their grades, beginning with individuals and ending there again, to rule themselves.

WALT WHITMAN, *Democratic Vistas,* 1870.

145 There is no indispensable man. The Government will not collapse and go to pieces if any one of the gentlemen who are seeking to be entrusted with its guidance should be left at home.

WOODROW WILSON, in 1912, quoted in the *New York Times Magazine,* June 10, 1956.

146 The firm basis of government is justice, not pity.

WOODROW WILSON, in his first inaugural address, March 4, 1913.

147 No man ever saw the people of whom he forms a part. No man ever saw a government. I live in the midst of the Government of the United States, but I never saw the Government of the United States. Its personnel extends through all the nations, and across the seas, and into every corner of the world in the persons of the representatives of the United States in foreign capitals and in foreign centers of commerce.

WOODROW WILSON, in a speech in Pittsburgh, Pennsylvania, January 29, 1916.

102. GREATNESS

See also FAME; IMMORTALITY; POWER;
REPUTATION; SUCCESS; TALENT

1 If you would be accounted great by your contemporaries, be not too much greater than they.

AMBROSE BIERCE, *Collected Works*, 1909–1912.

2 Greatness, after all, in spite of its name, appears to be not so much a certain size as a certain quality in human lives. It may be present in lives whose range is very small.

PHILLIPS BROOKS, "The Purpose and Use of Comfort," *Sermons*, 1878.

3 The greatest man is he who chooses the right with invincible resolution, who resists the sorest temptations from within and without, who bears the heaviest burdens cheerfully, who is calmest in storms and most fearless under menace and frowns, whose reliance on truth, on virtue, on God, is most unfaltering.

WILLIAM ELLERY CHANNING, "Self-Culture," 1838.

4 They may talk of their Jeffersons and Jacksons, but I set down Washington and Natty Bumppo as the two only really great men of my time.

JAMES FENIMORE COOPER, *Home As Found*, 1838, in which he praises Bumppo, his own paragon of a fictional hero.

5 Is it not better to live in Revolution than to live in dead times? Are we not little and low out of good nature now, when, if our companions were noble, or the crisis fit for heroes, we should be great also?

RALPH WALDO EMERSON, entry written in 1838, *Journals*, 1909–1914.

6 The essence of greatness is the perception that virtue is enough.

RALPH WALDO EMERSON, "Heroism," *Essays*, First Series, 1841.

7 The hero is a mind of such balance that no disturbances can shake his will, but pleasantly and as it were merrily he advances to his own music, alike in frightful alarms and in the tipsy mirth of universal dissoluteness.

Ibid.

8 There is somewhat in great actions which does not allow us to go behind them. Heroism feels and never reasons, and therefore is always right; and although a different breeding, different religion and greater intellectual activity would have modified or even reversed the particular action, yet for the hero that thing he does is the highest deed, and is not open to the censure of philosophers or divines.

Ibid.

9 A foolish consistency is the hobgoblin of little minds, adored by little statesmen and philosophers and divines. With consistency a great soul has simply nothing to do. He may as well concern himself with his shadow on the wall. Speak what you think now in hard words and tomorrow speak what tomorrow thinks in hard words again, though it contradict everything you said today,—"Ah, so you shall be sure to be misunderstood."—Is it so bad then to be misunderstood? Pythagoras was misunderstood, and Socrates, and Jesus, and Luther, and Copernicus, and Galileo, and Newton, and every pure and wise spirit that ever took flesh. To be great is to be misunderstood.

RALPH WALDO EMERSON, "Self-Reliance," *Essays*, First Series, 1841.

10 What I must do is all that concerns me, not what the people think. This rule . . . may serve for the whole distinction between greatness and meanness. It is the harder because you will always find those who think they know what is your duty better than you know it. It is easy in the world to live after the world's opinion; it is easy in solitude to live after our own; but the great man is he who in the midst of the crowd keeps with perfect sweetness the independence of solitude.

Ibid.

11 Great men serve us as insurrections do in bad governments.

RALPH WALDO EMERSON, "Character," *Essays*, Second Series, 1844.

12 It will never make any difference to a hero what the laws are. His greatness will shine and accomplish itself unto the end, whether they second him or not.

> RALPH WALDO EMERSON, "The Conservative," *Nature; Addresses and Lectures,* 1849.

13 Nothing is more simple than greatness; indeed, to be simple is to be great.

> RALPH WALDO EMERSON, "Literary Ethics," *Nature; Addresses and Lectures,* 1849.

14 Works of the intellect are great only by comparison with each other.

> Ibid.

15 I count him a great man who inhabits a higher sphere of thought, into which other men rise with labor and difficulty; he has but to open his eyes to see things in a true light and in large relations, whilst they must make painful corrections and keep a vigilant eye on many sources of error.

> RALPH WALDO EMERSON, "Uses of Great Men," *Representative Men,* 1850.

16 He is great who is what he is from nature, and who never reminds us of others.

> Ibid.

17 When nature removes a great man, people explore the horizon for a successor; but none comes, and none will. His class is extinguished with him. In some other and quite different field, the next man will appear.

> Ibid.

18 Every hero becomes a bore at last. Perhaps Voltaire was not bad-hearted, yet he said of the good Jesus, even, "I pray you, let me never hear that man's name again."

> Ibid.

19 The measure of a master is his success in bringing all men round to his opinion twenty years later.

> RALPH WALDO EMERSON, "Culture," *The Conduct of Life,* 1860.

20 When divine souls appear, men are compelled by their own self-respect to distinguish them.

> RALPH WALDO EMERSON, entry written in 1865, *Journals,* 1909–1914.

21 Each man is a hero and an oracle to somebody.

> RALPH WALDO EMERSON, *Letters and Social Aims,* 1876.

22 A great style of hero draws equally all classes, all the extremes of society, till we say the very dogs believe in him.

> RALPH WALDO EMERSON, "Greatness," *Letters and Social Aims,* 1876.

23 It is a grand mistake to think of being great without goodness; and I pronounce it as certain that there was never yet a truly great man that was not at the same time truly virtuous.

> BENJAMIN FRANKLIN, "The Busy-Body Papers," in the *American Weekly Mercury,* February 18, 1729.

24 But matchless Franklin! What a few
Can hope to rival such as you.
Who seized from kings their sceptred pride
And turned the lighning's dart aside.

> PHILIP FRENEAU, "On the Death of Dr. Benjamin Franklin," 1790.

25 Great men have to be lifted upon the shoulders of the whole world, in order to conceive their great ideas, or perform their great deeds.

> NATHANIEL HAWTHORNE, written May 7, 1850, in *Passages from the American Notebook,* 1868.

26 A hero cannot be a hero unless in an heroic world.

> Ibid.

27 The greatest obstacle to being heroic is the doubt whether one may not be going to prove one's self a fool; the truest heroism is to resist the doubt—and the profoundest wisdom, to know when it ought to be resisted, and when to be obeyed.

> NATHANIEL HAWTHORNE, *The Blithedale Romance,* 1852.

28 Great men are rarely isolated mountainpeaks; they are the summits of ranges.

> THOMAS WENTWORTH HIGGINSON, "A Plea for Culture," *Atlantic Essays,* 1871.

29 Not until the game is over and all of the chips have been counted can you calculate a man's winnings or losses. And not until he stands against the perspective of history can you correctly measure his stature.

> JIMMY HOFFA, *The Trials of Jimmy Hoffa,* 1970.

30 The world's great men have not commonly been great scholars, nor its great scholars great men.

> OLIVER WENDELL HOLMES, SR., *The Autocrat of the Breakfast-Table,* 1858.

31 Everyone is the chief personage, the hero, of his own baptism, his own wedding, and his own funeral.

> OLIVER WENDELL HOLMES, SR., in a farewell lecture at the Harvard University Medical School, November 28, 1882.

32 Little minds are interested in the extraordinary; great minds in the commonplace.

> ELBERT HUBBARD, *The Roycroft Dictionary and Book of Epigrams,* 1923.

33 When the will defies fear, when duty throws the gauntlet down to fate, when honor scorns to compromise with death—this is heroism.

> ROBERT INGERSOLL, in a speech in New York City, May 29, 1882.

34 The people are tired of greatness.

> WALTER LIPPMANN, analyzing the mood of the 1920s, quoted in Michael V. DiSalle, *Second Choice,* 1966.

35 Great Truths are portions of the soul of man; Great souls are portions of Eternity.

> JAMES RUSSELL LOWELL, sonnet No. 6, *A Year's Life,* 1841.

36 A great man is made up of qualities that meet or make great occasions.

> JAMES RUSSELL LOWELL, "Garfield," *My Study Windows,* 1871.

37 If any man seeks for greatness, let him forget greatness and ask for truth, and he will find both.

> HORACE MANN, "On Achieving Greatness."

38 In the years to come . . . what will determine whether Senator Kennedy or I, if I am elected, was a great President? It will not be our ambition . . . because greatness is not something that is written on a campaign poster. It will be determined to the extent that we represent the deepest ideals, the highest feelings and faith of the American people. In other words, the next President as he leads America in the free world can be only great as the American people are great.

> RICHARD M. NIXON, in the final presidential debate with John F. Kennedy, 1960, quoted in Fawn Brodie, *Richard Nixon: The Shaping of His Character,* 1981.

39 To vilify a great man is the readiest way in which a little man can himself attain greatness.

> EDGAR ALLAN POE, *Marginalia,* 1844–1849.

40 We can't all be heroes because somebody has to sit on the curb and clap as they go by.

> Attributed to Will Rogers.

41 To stand upon the ramparts and die for our principles is heroic, but to sally forth to battle and win for our principles is something more than heroic.

> FRANKLIN D. ROOSEVELT, in an address nominating Alfred E. Smith at the Democratic Party's national convention, June, 1928.

42 A great city is that which has the greatest
    men and women,
If it be a few ragged huts, it is still the
    greatest city in the whole world.

> WALT WHITMAN, "Song of the Broad-Axe," 1856.

---

103. HAPPINESS

See also HUMOR; LOVE; MERRIMENT;
SORROW

---

1 At the age of five I had become a skeptic and began to sense that any happiness that came my way might be the prelude to some grim cosmic joke.

> RUSSELL BAKER, *Growing Up,* 1982.

2 The trouble is not that we are never happy—it is that happiness is so episodical.

> RUTH BENEDICT, quoted in Margaret Mead, *An Anthropologist at Work,* 1951.

3 Happiness, *n.* An agreeable sensation arising from contemplating the misery of another.

> AMBROSE BIERCE, *The Devil's Dictionary,* 1906.

4 That is happiness; to be dissolved into something complete and great.

> WILLA CATHER, *My Antonia,* 1918.

5 Men are the constant dupes of names, while their happiness and well-being mainly depend on things.

> JAMES FENIMORE COOPER, *The American Democrat,* 1838.

6 Happiness lies, first of all, in health.

> GEORGE WILLIAM CURTIS, in a letter from the collection *Lotus-Eating,* 1852.

7 His labor is a chant,
   His idleness a tune;
Oh, for a bee's experience
   Of clovers and of noon!

> EMILY DICKINSON, "The Bee," *Poems,* 1890.

8 The best way to secure future happiness is to be as happy as is rightfully possible to-day.

> CHARLES W. ELIOT, *The Happy Life,* 1896.

9 To fill the hour—that is happiness; to fill the hour, and leave no crevice for a repentance or an approval.

> RALPH WALDO EMERSON, "Experience," *Essays,* Second Series, 1844.

10 We find a delight in the beauty and happiness of children, that makes the heart too big for the body.

> RALPH WALDO EMERSON, *The Conduct of Life,* 1860.

11 Happiness means quiet nerves.

> W.C. FIELDS, quoted in Robert Lewis Taylor, *W.C. Fields, His Follies and Fortunes,* 1949.

12 I am glad you are happy—but I never believe much in happiness. I never believe in misery either.

Those are things you see on the stage or the screen or the printed page, they never really happen to you in life.

> F. SCOTT FITZGERALD, in a letter to his daughter, Frances Scott Fitzgerald, August 8, 1933, in Andrew Turnbull *The Letters of F. Scott Fitzgerald,* 1963.

13 Human felicity is produced not so much by great pieces of good fortune that seldom happen, as by little advantages that occur every day.

> BENJAMIN FRANKLIN, in his *Autobiography,* begun in 1771 and published in its present form in 1868.

14 We of the Anglo-Saxon race do not know how to enjoy ourselves; we do not know how to get the most out of this life that flies so rapidly.

> HENRY GEORGE, in the San Francisco *State,* April 12, 1879. (The *State* was a four-page weekly, largely written by George. It expired after eleven issues.)

15 People need joy quite as much as clothing. Some of them need it far more.

> MARGARET COLLIER GRAHAM, *Gifts and Givers,* 1906.

16 Happiness in this world, when it comes, comes incidentally. Make it the object of pursuit, and it leads us a wild-goose chase, and is never attained. Follow some other object, and very possibly we may find that we have caught happiness without dreaming of it.

> NATHANIEL HAWTHORNE, entry written in November, 1852, *Passages from the American Notebooks,* 1868.

17 Perhaps there is no happiness in life so perfect as the martyr's.

> O. HENRY, "The Country of Elusion," *The Trimmed Lamp,* 1907.

18 I care not much for gold or land;—
   Give me a mortgage here and there,—
Some good bank-stock, some note of hand,
   Or trifling railroad share,—
I only ask that Fortune send
A *little* more than I shall spend.

> OLIVER WENDELL HOLMES, SR., "Contentment," *The Autocrat of the Breakfast-Table,* 1858.

19 Happiness is a habit—cultivate it.

ELBERT HUBBARD, *The Roycroft Dictionary and Book of Epigrams,* 1923.

20 Happiness is the only good, reason the only torch, justice the only worship, humanity the only religion, and love the only priest.

ROBERT G. INGERSOLL, "A Tribute to Ebon Ingersoll," June 2, 1879. (Ebenezer Clark Ingersoll was his brother.)

21 How to gain, how to keep, how to recover happiness is in fact for most men at all times the secret motive of all they do, and of all they are willing to endure.

WILLIAM JAMES, *The Varieties of Religious Experience,* 1902.

22 Happiness, like every other emotional state, has blindness and insensibility to opposing facts given it as its instinctive weapon for self-protection against disturbance.

Ibid.

23 If the happiness of the mass of the people can be secured at the expense of a little tempest now and then, or even of a little blood, it will be a precious purchase.

THOMAS JEFFERSON, in a letter to Ezra Stiles, December 24, 1786.

24 It is neither wealth nor splendor, but tranquility and occupation, which give happiness.

THOMAS JEFFERSON, in a letter to his sister, Mrs. Anna Scott Marks, July 12, 1788.

25 The rays of happiness, like those of light, are colorless when unbroken.

HENRY WADSWORTH LONGFELLOW, *Kavanagh,* 1849.

26 Kissing your hand may make you feel very very good but a diamond and safire bracelet lasts forever.

ANITA LOOS, *Gentlemen Prefer Blondes,* 1925.

27 Happiness, to some elation;
Is to others, mere stagnation.

AMY LOWELL, "Happiness," *Sword Blades and Poppy Seeds,* 1911.

28 my life is so romantic
capricious and corybantic
and i m toujours gai toujours gai

DON MARQUIS, "the song of mehitabel," *archy and mehitabel,* 1927.

29 Puritanism—The haunting fear that someone, somewhere, may be happy.

H.L. MENCKEN, "Sententiae," *The Vintage Mencken,* 1955.

30 There is only one way to achieve happiness
on this terrestrial ball,
And that is to have either a clear conscience,
or none at all.

OGDEN NASH, "Interoffice Memorandum," *I'm a Stranger Here Myself,* 1938.

31 Happiness is desired by all men; and moments of it are probably attained by most men. Only moments of it can be attained because happiness is the inner concomitant of neat harmonies of body, spirit and society; and these neat harmonies are bound to be infrequent.

REINHOLD NIEBUHR, *The Irony of American History,* 1962.

32 The foolish man seeks happiness in the
distance;
The wise grows it under his feet.

JAMES OPPENHEIM, "The Wise."

33 Man's real life is happy, chiefly because he is ever expecting that it soon will be so.

EDGAR ALLAN POE, *Marginalia,* 1844–1849.

34 Happiness is a way-station between too little and too much.

CHANNING POLLOCK, *Mr. Moneypenny,* 1928.

35 Happiness is the only sanction of life; where happiness fails, existence remains a mad and lamentable experiment.

GEORGE SANTAYANA, "Reason in Common Sense," *The Life of Reason,* 1905–1906.

36 Happiness Is a Warm Puppy.

CHARLES M. SCHULZ, title of a book, 1962.

37 A happy woman is one who has no cares at all;
a cheerful woman is one who has cares but doesn't
let them get her down.

> BEVERLY SILLS, in a television interview on *60
> Minutes*, 1975.

38 Man is the artificer of his own happiness.

> HENRY DAVID THOREAU, entry written January
> 21, 1838, *Journal*, 1906.

39 What wisdom, what warning can prevail
against gladness? There is no law so strong which
a little gladness may not transgress.

> HENRY DAVID THOREAU, entry written
> January 3, 1853, *Journal*, 1906.

40 Grief can take care of itself, but to get the full
value of a joy you must have somebody to divide it
with.

> MARK TWAIN, "Pudd'nhead Wilson's New
> Calendar," *Following the Equator*, 1897.

41 Too much of a good thing can be wonderful.

> MAE WEST, quoted in Joseph Weintraub, *The
> Wit and Wisdom of Mae West*, 1967.

42 There is that in me—I do not know what it
 is— but I know it is in me. . . .
 I do not know it—it is without name—it is a
  word unsaid,
 It is not in any dictionary, utterance,
  symbol. . . .
 Do you see O my brothers and sisters?
 It is not chaos or death—it is form, union,
  plan— it is eternal life—it is Happiness.

> WALT WHITMAN, "Song of Myself," 1855.

43 The sun and stars that float in the open air,
 The apple-shaped earth, and we upon it,
  surely the drift of them is something
  grand,
 I do not know what it is except that it is
  grand, and that it is happiness.

> WALT WHITMAN, "A Song for Occupations,"
> 1855.

44 I am for those who believe in loose delights,
 I share the midnight orgies of young
  men,

I dance with the dancers and drink with the
 drinkers.

> WALT WHITMAN, "Native Moments," 1860.

45 Happy days are here again,
 The skies above are clear again.
 Let us sing a song of cheer again,
 Happy days are here again!

> JACK YELLEN, "Happy Days Are Here Again,"
> from the musical comedy *Chasing Rainbows*,
> 1929 (used in Franklin D. Roosevelt's presidential
> campaign of 1936 and thereafter in all Democratic
> Party campaigns).

---

104. HAWAII

1 Ua mau ke ea o ka aina i ka pono. (The life of
the land is perpetuated by righteousness.)

> State motto.

2 I cannot help feeling that the chief end of this
meeting is plantation profits, and the prosperity of
the country, the demands of society, the future of
the Hawaiian race only comes secondarily if at all.

> SANFORD B. DOLE, addressing a convention of
> planters in the 1880s, quoted in Francine du
> Plessix Gray, *Hawaii: The Sugar-Coated
> Fortress*, 1972.

3 The spiritual destiny of Hawaii has been shaped
by a Calvinist theory of paternalism enacted by the
descendants of the missionaries who had carried it
there: a will to do good for unfortunates regardless
of what the unfortunates thought about it.

> FRANCINE DU PLESSIX GRAY, *Hawaii: The
> Sugar-Coated Fortress*, 1972.

4 The vast Pacific ocean would always remain the
islanders' great solace, escape and nourishment, the
amniotic fluid that would keep them hedonistic and
aloof, guarded, gentle and mysterious.

> Ibid.

5 The *nicest* thing about Hawaii is that when we
select a beauty queen at the university we don't

have just *one* beauty queen. We have a Polynesian beauty queen, a Chinese beauty queen, a Japanese beauty queen, a Filipino beauty queen, a Portuguese beauty queen, a Puerto Rico beauty queen, a Negro beauty queen, *and* a Caucasian beauty queen. Six, eight beauty queens all in a row. *That's* what I like the best about Hawaii.

> THOMAS HAMILTON, quoted in Francine du Plessix Gray, *Hawaii: The Sugar-Coated Fortress,* 1972.

6 O my people,
Honor thy god;
Respect alike [the rights of] men great and
    humble;
See to it that our aged, our women, and our
    children
Lie down to sleep by the roadside
Without fear of harm.
Disobey, and die.

> KAMEHAMEHA I, "Law of the Splintered Paddle," quoted in the proceedings of the U.S. 91st Congress, 1969.

7 The Hawaiian people have been from time immemorial lovers of poetry and music, and have been apt in improvising historic poems, songs of love, and chants of worship, so that praises of the living or wails over the dead were with them but the natural expression of their feelings.

> LYDIA KAMEKEHA LILIUOKALANI, *Hawaii's Story,* 1898.

8 No alien land in all the world has any deep strong charm for me but that one, no other land could so longingly and so beseechingly haunt me, sleeping and waking, through half a lifetime, as that one has done.

> MARK TWAIN, in Walter F. Frear, *Mark Twain and Hawaii,* 1947.

9 The loveliest fleet of islands that lies anchored in any ocean.

> MARK TWAIN, in a letter to H.P. Wood, secretary of the Hawaii Promotion Committee, quoted in Walter F. Frear, *Mark Twain and Hawaii,* 1947.

105. HEALTH

See also LIFE; MEDICINE; MERRIMENT; PAIN

1 Asking questions in therapy would be so helpful if anyone ever answered them accurately. But no one ever does.

> VIRGINIA MAE AXLINE, *Dibs: In Search of Self,* 1965.

2 The *healthy,* the *strong* individual, is the one who asks for help when he needs it. Whether he's got an abscess on his knee or in his soul.

> RONA BARRETT, *Miss Rona: An Autobiography,* 1974.

3 Thousands upon thousands of persons have studied disease. Almost no one has studied health.

> ADELLE DAVIS, *Let's Eat Right to Keep Fit,* 1954.

4 Health is not a condition of matter, but of Mind; nor can the material senses bear reliable testimony on the subject of health.

> MARY BAKER EDDY, *Science and Health,* 1875.

5 "Cleanliness is next to godliness"; but washing should be only for the purpose of keeping the body clean, and this can be effected without scrubbing the whole surface [of an infant] daily. Water is not the natural habitat of humanity.

> Ibid.

6 Sickness is a belief, which must be annihilated by the divine Mind.

> Ibid.

7 Give me health and a day and I will make the pomp of emperors ridiculous.

> RALPH WALDO EMERSON, "Nature," in *Nature; Addresses and Lectures,* 1849.

8 When I go into my garden with a spade, and dig a bed, I feel such an exhilaration and health that I discover that I have been defrauding myself all this time in letting others do for me what I should have done with my own hands.

RALPH WALDO EMERSON, "Man the Reformer," *Nature; Addresses and Lectures,* 1849.

9 The first wealth is health. Sickness is poor-spirited, and cannot serve any one; it must husband its resources to live. But health . . . runs over, and inundates the neighborhoods and creeks of other men's necessities.

RALPH WALDO EMERSON, "Power," *The Conduct of Life,* 1860.

10 Health is the first muse, and sleep is the condition to produce it.

RALPH WALDO EMERSON, "Resources," *Uncollected Lectures,* 1932.

11 To lengthen thy Life, lessen thy Meals.

BENJAMIN FRANKLIN, *Poor Richard's Almanack,* 1733.

12 Be not sick too late, nor well too soon.

BENJAMIN FRANKLIN, *Poor Richard's Almanack,* 1734.

13 It is ill Jesting with the Joiner's Tools, worse with the Doctor's.

BENJAMIN FRANKLIN, *Poor Richard's Almanack,* 1752.

14 A bodily disease which we look upon as whole and entire within itself, may, after all, be but a symptom of some ailment in the spiritual part.

NATHANIEL HAWTHORNE, *The Scarlet Letter,* 1850.

15 I larnt him to chaw terbacker
To keep his milk-teeth white.

JOHN HAY, "Little Breeches," in *Pike County Ballads and Other Pieces,* 1871.

16 There is only one thing people like that is good for them: a good night's sleep.

EDGAR WATSON HOWE, *Country Town Sayings,* 1911.

17 We have had for three weeks past a warm visit from the sun (my almighty physician) and I find myself almost reestablished.

THOMAS JEFFERSON, in a letter to James Monroe, March 18, 1785.

18 The sovereign invigorator of the body is exercise, and of all the exercises walking is best.

THOMAS JEFFERSON, in a letter to Thomas Mann Randolph, Jr., who later married Jefferson's daughter Martha, August 27, 1786.

19 The most uninformed mind with a healthy body is happier than the wisest valetudinarian.

THOMAS JEFFERSON, in a letter to Thomas Mann Randolph, Jr., July 6, 1787.

20 I am in the habit of going to sea whenever I begin to grow hazy about the eyes, and to be over-conscious of my lungs.

HERMAN MELVILLE, *Moby-Dick,* 1851.

21 There is this noteworthy difference between savage and civilized; that while a sick, civilized man may be six months convalescing, generally speaking, a sick savage is almost half well again in a day.

Ibid.

22 Measure your health by your sympathy with morning and Spring.

HENRY DAVID THOREAU, entry written February 25, 1859, *Journal,* 1906.

23 American lads and lasses are all pale. Men at thirty and women at twenty-five have had all semblance of youth baked out of them. Infants even are not rosy, and the only shades known on the cheeks of children are those composed of brown, yellow, and white. All this comes of those damnable hot-air pipes with which every tenement in America is infested.

ANTHONY TROLLOPE, "Buffalo to New York," *North America,* 1862.

24 He had had much experience of physicians, and said, "The only way to keep your health is to eat what you don't want, drink what you don't like, and do what you'd druther not."

MARK TWAIN, "Pudd'nhead Wilson's New Calendar," *Following the Equator,* 1897.

25 If any thing is sacred, the human body is sacred,
And the glory and sweet of a man is the token of manhood untainted,

And in man or woman a clean, strong,
    firm-fibred body is more beautiful than
    the most beautiful face.

> WALT WHITMAN, "I Sing the Body Electric,"
> 1855.

26 Beneath her torn hat glowed the wealth
    Of simple beauty and rustic health.

> JOHN GREENLEAF WHITTIER, "Maud Muller,"
> 1854.

106. HEART

1 Heart, *n.* An automatic, muscular blood-pump.
Figuratively, this useful organ is said to be the seat
of emotions and sentiments—a very pretty fancy
which, however, is nothing but a survival of a once
universal belief. It is now known that the sentiments and emotions reside in the stomach.

> AMBROSE BIERCE, *The Devil's Dictionary,* 1906.

2 In the desert
    I saw a creature, naked, bestial,
    Who, squatting upon the ground,
    Held his heart in his hands,
    And ate of it.
    I said: "Is it good, friend?"
    "It is bitter—bitter," he answered;
    "But I like it
    Because it is bitter,
    and because it is my heart."

> STEPHEN CRANE, "The Heart," *The Black
> Riders and Other Lines,* 1895.

3 The heart asks pleasure first,
    And then, excuse from pain;
    And then, those little anodynes
    That deaden suffering.
    And then, to go to sleep;
    And then, if it should be
    The will of its Inquisitor,
    The liberty to die.

> EMILY DICKINSON, "The Heart Asks Pleasure
> First," in *Poems,* 1890.

4 Futile the winds
    To a heart in port.

> EMILY DICKINSON, "Wild Nights! Wild
> Nights!" in *Poems,* Second Series, 1891.

5 The heart has its arguments, with which the understanding is not acquainted.

> RALPH WALDO EMERSON, quoting an unnamed
> person, "Worship," *The Conduct of Life,* 1860.

6 The heart of the fool is in his mouth, but the
mouth of the wise man is in his heart.

> BENJAMIN FRANKLIN, *Poor Richard's Almanack,*
> 1733.

7 O hearts that break and give no sign
    Save whitening lips and fading tresses.

> OLIVER WENDELL HOLMES, SR., "The
> Voiceless," 1853.

8 Whatever comes from the brain carries the hue
of the place it came from, and whatever comes from
the heart carries the heat and color of its birthplace.

> OLIVER WENDELL HOLMES, SR., *The Professor
> at the Breakfast-Table,* 1860.

9 Let us, then, be up and doing,
    With a heart for any fate.

> HENRY WADSWORTH LONGFELLOW, "A Psalm
> of Life," 1839.

10 It is the heart, and not the brain,
    That to the highest doth attain.

> HENRY WADSWORTH LONGFELLOW, "The
> Building of the Ship," 1849.

11 The heart hath its own memory, like the
    mind,
    And in it are enshrined
    The precious keepsakes, into which is
      wrought
    The giver's loving thought.

> HENRY WADSWORTH LONGFELLOW, "From My
> Arm-Chair," 1879.

12 All that hath been majestical
    In life or death, since time began,
    Is native in the simple heart of all,
    The angel heart of man.

JAMES RUSSELL LOWELL, published in the *United States Magazine and Democratic Review*, October, 1842.

13 I feel the unutterable longing,
   Thy hunger of the heart is mine;
 I reach and grope for hands in darkness,
   My ear grows sharp for voice or sign.

JOHN GREENLEAF WHITTIER, "To Lydia Maria Child," 1870.

---

107. HISTORY

See also EXPERIENCE; KNOWLEDGE

---

1 No honest historian can take part with—or against—the forces he has to study. To him even the extinction of the human race should be merely a fact to be grouped with other vital statistics.

HENRY ADAMS, *The Education of Henry Adams,* 1907.

2 The public history of all countries, and all ages, is but a sort of mask, richly colored. The interior working of the machinery must be foul.

JOHN QUINCY ADAMS, in a diary entry written November 9, 1822.

3 With the loss of tradition we have lost the thread which safely guided us through the vast realms of the past, but this thread was also the chain fettering each successive generation to a predetermined aspect of the past. It could be that only now will the past open up to us with unexpected freshness and tell us things that no one as yet had ears to hear.

HANNAH ARENDT, quoted in Carl J. Frederich, *Nomos I, Authority,* 1958.

4 On no other stage are the scenes shifted with a swiftness so like magic as on the great stage of history when once the hour strikes.

EDWARD BELLAMY, *Looking Backward: 2000–1887,* 1888.

5 It's always seemed to me . . . that legends and yarns and folktales are as much a part of the real history of a country as proclamations and provisos and constitutional amendments.

STEPHEN VINCENT BENÉT, quoted in Charles A. Fenton, *Stephen Vincent Benét: The Life and Times of an American Man of Letters,* 1958.

6 Bismarck, when asked what was the most important fact in modern history, replied: "The fact that North America speaks English."

GURNEY BENHAM, *Benham's Book of Quotations,* 1948.

7 Historian, *n.* A broad-gauge gossip.

AMBROSE BIERCE, *The Devil's Dictionary,* 1906.

8 History, *n.* An account mostly false, of events mostly unimportant, which are brought about by rulers mostly knaves, and soldiers mostly fools.

Ibid.

9 History is the torch that is meant to illuminate the past to guard us against the repetition of our mistakes of other days. We cannot join in the rewriting of history to make it conform to our comfort and convenience.

CLAUDE G. BOWERS, in the introduction to F. Jay Taylor, *The United States and the Spanish Civil War,* 1956.

10 History selects its heroes and its villains, and few of us resist participation either at the parade or at the guillotine.

WILLIAM F. BUCKLEY, JR., *The Jeweler's Eye,* 1968.

11 The history of every country begins in the heart of a man or a woman.

WILLA CATHER, *O Pioneers!* 1913.

12 The history of the earth! Doth it present anything but crimes of the most heinous nature, committed from one end of the world to the other? We observe avarice, rapine, and murder, equally prevailing in all parts. History perpetually tells us of millions of people abandoned to the caprice of the maddest princes, and of whole nations devoted to the blind fury of tyrants. . . . If one corner breathes in peace for a few years, it is, in turn subjected, torn, and leveled; one would almost believe the

principles of action in man, considered as the first agent of this planet, to be poisoned in their most essential parts.

> MICHEL GUILLAUME JEAN DE CRÈVECOEUR, *Letters from an American Farmer,* 1782.

13 Like a good many people that I know th' Muse iv Histhry . . . has a long mim'ry but 'tis inaccrate. Tis like a cousin iv mine that cud remimber things that happened forty years ago, but they were niver so.

> FINLEY PETER DUNNE, *Mr. Dooley on Making a Will and Other Necessary Evils,* 1919.

14 There is no history. There is only Biography. The attempt to perpetrate, to fix a thought or principle, fails continually . . . your action is good only whilst it is alive,—whilst it is in you. The awkward imitation of it by your child or your disciple is not a repetition of it, is not the same thing, but another thing. The new individual must work out the whole problem of science, letters and theology for himself; can owe his fathers nothing. There is no history; only biography.

> RALPH WALDO EMERSON, entry written May 28, 1839, *Journals,* 1909–1914.

15 This human mind wrote history, and this must read it. The Sphinx must solve her own riddle. If the whole of history is in one man, it is all to be explained from individual experience.

> RALPH WALDO EMERSON, "History," *Essays,* First Series, 1841.

16 As crabs, goats, scorpions, the balance, and the waterpot lose their meanness when hung as signs in the zodiac, so I can see my own vices without heat in the distant persons of Solomon, Alcibiades, and Catiline.

> Ibid.

17 I have no expectation that any man will read history aright, who thinks that what was done in a remote age, by men whose names have resounded far, has any deeper sense than what he is doing today.

> Ibid.

18 I am ashamed to see what a shallow village tale our so-called History is.

> Ibid.

19 Conspicuous is the preponderance of nature over will. . . . There is less intention in history than we ascribe to it. We impute deep-laid, far-sighted plans to Caesar and Napoleon; but the best of their power was in nature, not in them.

> RALPH WALDO EMERSON, "Spiritual Laws," *Essays,* First Series, 1841.

20 The world always had the same bankrupt look, to foregoing ages as to us,—as of a failed world just re-collecting its old withered forces to begin again and try to do a little business.

> RALPH WALDO EMERSON, "Past and Present," in *The Dial,* July, 1843.

21 The two parties which divide the state, the party of Conservatism and that of Innovation, are very old, and have disputed the possession of the world ever since it was made. This quarrel is the subject of civil history.

> RALPH WALDO EMERSON, "The Conservative," *Nature; Addresses and Lectures,* 1849.

22 Most of the great results of history are brought about by discreditable means.

> RALPH WALDO EMERSON, "Considerations By the Way," *The Conduct of Life,* 1860.

23 The history of man is a series of conspiracies to win from Nature some advantage without paying for it.

> RALPH WALDO EMERSON, "Demonology," *Lectures and Biographical Sketches,* 1883.

24 History is bunk.

> Attributed to Henry Ford. (In 1919, in a libel suit brought against the *Chicago Tribune,* Ford denied that he had used the word "bunk.")

25 There is no inevitability in history except as men make it.

> FELIX FRANKFURTER, quoted by J.M. Brown in the *Saturday Review,* October 30, 1954.

26 Historians relate, not so much what is done, as what they would have believed.

BENJAMIN FRANKLIN, *Poor Richard's Almanack,*
1739.

27 The Golden Age never was the present Age.

BENJAMIN FRANKLIN, *Poor Richard's Almanack,*
1750.

28 "History" is not a divine force; it is the instrument of those who make it.

J. WILLIAM FULBRIGHT, *Old Myths and New
Realities,* 1964.

29 The illusion that the times that were are better than those that are, has probably pervaded all ages.

HORACE GREELEY, *The American Conflict,*
1864–1866.

30 History is bright and fiction dull with homely men who have charmed women.

O. HENRY, "Next to Reading Matter," *Roads of
Destiny,* 1909.

31 I know of no way of judging the future but by the past.

PATRICK HENRY, in a speech in the Virginia
Convention, March 23, 1775.

32 Upon this point a page of history is worth a volume of logic.

OLIVER WENDELL HOLMES, JR., in a Supreme Court
opinion in *New York Trust Co. v. Eisner,* 1921.

33 History fades into fable, facts become clouded with doubt and controversy, the inscription moulders from the tablet, the statue falls from the pedestal. Columns, arches, pyramids—what are they but heaps of sand? and their epitaphs, but characters written in the dust?

WASHINGTON IRVING, "Westminster Abbey,"
The Sketch-Book, 1819–1820.

34 The historian, essentially, wants more documents than he can really use; the dramatist only wants more liberties than he can really take.

HENRY JAMES, in the preface to vol. XII of the
New York Edition of *The Novels and Tales of
Henry James,* 1907–1909.

35 If every nation gets the government it deserves, every generation writes the history which corresponds with its view of the world.

ELIZABETH JANEWAY, in *Between Myth and
Morning,* 1974.

36 History, by apprizing [men] of the past, will enable them to judge of the future; it will avail them of the experience of other times and other nations; it will qualify them as judges of the actions and designs of men; it will enable them to know ambition under every disguise it may assume; and knowing it, to defeat its views.

THOMAS JEFFERSON, *Notes on the State of
Virginia,* 1784.

37 History, in general, only informs us what bad government is.

THOMAS JEFFERSON, in a letter to John Norvell,
June 11, 1807.

38 I like the dreams of the future better than the history of the past—so, good night!

THOMAS JEFFERSON, in a letter to John Adams,
August 1, 1816.

39 A morsel of genuine history, a thing so rare as to be always valuable.

THOMAS JEFFERSON, in a letter to John Adams,
September 8, 1817.

40 History is a better guide than good intentions.

JEANE J. KIRKPATRICK, "Dictatorship and
Double Standards," *Commentary* magazine,
November, 1979.

41 History knows no resting places and no plateaus.

HENRY KISSINGER, *White House Years,* 1979.

42 History is not, of course, a cookbook offering pretested recipes. It teaches by analogy, not by maxims. It can illuminate the consequences of actions in comparable situations, yet each generation must discover for itself what situations are in fact comparable.

Ibid.

43 If history teaches anything it is that there can be no peace without equilibrium and no justice without restraint.

Ibid.

44 It is history that teaches us to hope.

> GEN. ROBERT E. LEE, in a letter to Charles Marshall, c.1866.

45 The time is not come for impartial history. If the truth were told just now it would not be credited.

> GEN. ROBERT E. LEE, c.1868, quoted in David MaCrae, *The Americans at Home,* 1870.

46 The history of an oppressed people is hidden in the lies and the agreed-upon myth of its conquerors.

> MERIDEL LE SUEUR, *Crusaders,* 1955.

47 The dogmas of the quiet past are inadequate to the stormy present.

> ABRAHAM LINCOLN, in his second annual message to Congress, December 1, 1862.

48 Consult the dead upon things that were,
But the living only on things that are.

> HENRY WADSWORTH LONGFELLOW, *The Golden Legend,* 1851.

49 Nor deem the irrevocable Past
  As wholly wasted, wholly vain,
If, rising on its wrecks, at last
  To something nobler we attain.

> HENRY WADSWORTH LONGFELLOW, "The Ladder of St. Augustine," 1858.

50 Old events have modern meanings; only that survives
Of past history which finds kindred in all hearts and lives.

> JAMES RUSSELL LOWELL, "Mahmood the Image-Breaker," 1850.

51 Safe in the hallowed quiets of the past.

> JAMES RUSSELL LOWELL, "The Cathedral," 1870.

52 The Don Quixote of one generation may live to hear himself called the savior of society by the next.

> JAMES RUSSELL LOWELL, "Don Quixote," an address delivered in London c.1882–1884, published in *Democracy and Other Addresses,* 1887.

53 The course of life is like the sea;
Men come and go; tides rise and fall;
And that is all of history.

> JOAQUIN MILLER, *The Sea of Fire,* 1902.

54 America was discovered accidentally by a great seaman who was looking for something else; when discovered it was not wanted; and most of the exploration for the next fifty years was done in the hope of getting through or around it. America was named after a man who discovered no part of the New World. History is like that, very chancy.

> SAMUEL ELIOT MORISON, *The Oxford History of the American People,* 1965.

55 History is a realm in which human freedom and natural necessity are curiously intermingled.

> REINHOLD NIEBUHR, *The Structure of Nations and Empires,* 1959.

56 There is no reason to repeat bad history.

> ELEANOR HOLMES NORTON, in Robin Morgan, *Sisterhood Is Powerful,* 1970.

57 Half a continent had changed hands at the scratch of a pen.

> FRANCIS PARKMAN, on the treaty ending the French and Indian Wars, in *Montcalm and Wolfe,* 1884.

58 Thy Naiad airs have brought me home
To the glory that was Greece,
And the grandeur that was Rome.

> EDGAR ALLAN POE, "To Helen," 1831.

59 The Past is a bucket of ashes.

> CARL SANDBURG, "Prairie," in *Cornhuskers,* 1918.

60 Far from offering a short cut to clairvoyance, history teaches us that the future is full of surprises and outwits all our certitudes. For the study of history issues not in scientific precision nor in moral finality but in irony.

> ARTHUR M. SCHLESINGER, JR., *The Bitter Heritage: Vietnam and American Democracy, 1941–1966,* 1967.

61 The only antidote to a shallow knowledge of history is a deeper knowledge, the knowledge

which produces not dogmatic certitude but diagnostic skill, not clairvoyance but insight.

Ibid.

62 Far from unveiling the secret of things to come, history bestows a different gift: it makes us—or should make us—understand the extreme difficulty, the intellectual peril, the moral arrogance of supposing that the future will yield itself so easily to us.

Ibid.

63 History, by putting crisis in perspective, supplies the antidote to every generation's illusion that its own problems are uniquely oppressive.

ARTHUR M. SCHLESINGER, JR., "The Challenge of Change," in the *New York Times Magazine*, July 27, 1986.

64 All history is modern history.

WALLACE STEVENS, "Adagia," *Opus Posthumous*, 1957.

65 All history is only one long story to this effect: men have struggled for power over their fellowmen in order that they might win the joys of earth at the expense of others, and might shift the burdens of life from their own shoulders upon those of others.

WILLIAM GRAHAM SUMNER, *The Forgotten Man*, 1883.

66 This lament for a golden age is only a lament for golden men.

HENRY DAVID THOREAU, entry written April 5, 1841, *Journal*, 1906.

67 Many are concerned about the monuments of the West and the East—to know who built them. For my part, I should like to know who in those days did not build them.

HENRY DAVID THOREAU, *Walden*, 1854.

68 Men make history and not the other way round. In periods where there is no leadership, society stands still. Progress occurs when courageous, skillful leaders seize the opportunity to change things for the better.

HARRY S TRUMAN, in *This Week* magazine, February 22, 1959.

69 The only thing new in the world is the history you don't know.

HARRY S TRUMAN, quoted in Merle Miller, *Plain Speaking*, 1982.

70 I am content to define history as the past events of which we have knowledge and refrain from worrying about those of which we have none—until, that is, some archeologist digs them up.

BARBARA W. TUCHMAN, "When Does History Happen?" the *New York Times Book Review*, March 8, 1964.

71 What his imagination is to the poet, facts are to the historian. His exercise of judgment comes in their selection, his art in their arrangement. His method is narrative. His subject is the story of man's past. His function is to make it known.

Ibid.

72 The history of the world is the record of a man in quest of his daily bread and butter.

HENDRIK WILLEM VAN LOON, *The Story of Mankind*, 1921.

73 The past, at least, is secure.

DANIEL WEBSTER, in his second speech of reply in the U.S. Senate to Sen. Robert Y. Hayne, January 26, 1830.

74 I respect Assyria, China, Teutonia, and the
    Hebrews,
I adopt each theory, myth, god and demi-
    god,
I see that the old accounts, bibles,
    genealogies, are true, without exception,
I assert that all past days were what they
    must have been.

WALT WHITMAN, "With Antecedents," 1860.

75 The Past—the dark, unfathom'd retrospect!
The teeming gulf—the sleepers and the
    shadows!
The past! the infinite greatness of the past!
For what is the present after all but a growth
    out of the past?

WALT WHITMAN, *Passage to India*, 1871.

108. HOLLYWOOD

See also MOTION PICTURES

1 It's a great place to live—if you're an orange.

> FRED ALLEN, on Los Angeles and Hollywood, quoted in Max Wilk, *The Wit and Wisdom of Hollywood,* 1971.

2 What I like about Hollywood is that one can get along by knowing two words of English—*swell* and *lousy.*

> Attributed to Vicki Baum, c.1933.

3 When I departed Hollywood forever, in 1940, I thought that getting away from the place would automatically cure me of its pestiferous disease, playfully referred to there as "going Hollywood." I retired first to my father's home in Wichita, but there I found that the citizens could not decide whether they despised me for having once been a success away from home or for now being a failure in their midst.

> LOUISE BROOKS, *Lulu in Hollywood,* 1982.

4 When I was under contract to Paramount in 1928, [I] complained about being forced to hang around Hollywood waiting to make some film. "That's what we are paying you for—your time," was the harsh comment of the front office. "You mean my life," I said to myself.

> Ibid.

5 As an adjective, the very word "Hollywood" has long been pejorative and suggestive of something referred to as "the System," a phrase delivered with the same sinister emphasis that James Cagney once lent to "the Syndicate." The System not only strangles talent but poisons the soul, a fact supported by rich webs of lore.

> JOAN DIDION, "I Can't Get That Monster Out of My Mind," 1964, from *Slouching Towards Bethlehem,* 1968.

6 It's a mining town in lotus land.

> F. SCOTT FITZGERALD, *The Last Tycoon,* 1941.

7 This is the only town where you can wake up in the morning and listen to the birds c-coughing in the trees.

> JOE FRISCO, a comedian who habitually stuttered while delivering his lines, quoted in Max Wilk, *The Wit and Wisdom of Hollywood,* 1971.

8 With a mental equipment which allows me to tell the difference between hot and cold, I stand out in this community like a modern-day Cicero. Dropped into any other city of the world, I'd rate as a possibly adequate night watchman.

> ANITA LOOS, *No Mother to Guide Her,* 1961.

9 "Childish" is the word with which the intelligentsia once branded Hollywood. And yet, those movies, which depicted Life as life can never be, were fairy tales for the adult. Today there are no fairy tales for us to believe in.

> Ibid.

10 Hollywood always had a streak of the totalitarian in just about everything it did.

> SHIRLEY MACLAINE, *You Can Get There from Here,* 1975.

11 Hollywood's queens and kings lived far more luxuriously than most of the reigning families in Europe. Most of them tossed their money around as though they manufactured it themselves in the cellar. They went in for solid gold bathtubs, chauffeur-driven Rolls Royces, champagne for breakfast and caviar every fifteen minutes. It was the kind of world that today only exists in the pages of movie magazines and for the sons of a few Latin American dictators.

> GROUCHO MARX, *Groucho and Me,* 1959.

12 A trip through a sewer in a glass-bottomed boat.

> WILSON MIZNER, quoted in Alva Johnston, *The Incredible Mizners,* 1953.

13 Hollywood is a carnival where there are no concessions.

> WILSON MIZNER, quoted in Max Wilk, *The Wit and Wisdom of Hollywood,* 1971.

14 A dreary industrial town controlled by hoodlums of enormous wealth.

> Attributed to S.J. Perelman.

15 In Hollywood, if you didn't sing or dance, you would end up as an after-dinner speaker, so they made me an after-dinner speaker.

>   RONALD REAGAN, quoted in Hedrick Smith et al., *Reagan the Man, the President,* 1980.

16 They know only one word of more than one syllable here, and that is *fillum.*

>   Attributed to Louis Sherwin, c.1920.

17 A place where the inmates are in charge of the asylum.

>   Attributed to Laurence Stallings, c.1930.

18 By its adherence, over so long a period of years, to a standard of living well in excess of anything known in the lives of its audience, it has at last communicated to its audience a feeling of actually living in this dream world and a conviction that the standards of this world are the norm.

>   E.B. WHITE, "Movies," *One Man's Meat,* 1944.

19 It is disturbing to realize that even after we have been reduced to Hollywood's low, we are still rolling in the sort of luxury which eventually destroyed Rome.

>   E.B. WHITE, describing the stage set for an ordinary home, in "Movies," *One Man's Meat,* 1944.

20 All Hollywood corrupts; and absolute Hollywood corrupts absolutely.

>   EDMUND WILSON, "Old Antichrist's Sayings," May, 1938, quoted in *Letters on Literature and Politics 1912–1972,* 1977.

---

109. HOME

See also FAMILY

---

1 Home is where the heart is.

>   Anonymous.

2 Any old place I hang my hat is home, sweet home to me.

>   Anonymous.

3 I long for rural and domestic scenes, for the Warbling of Birds and the Prattle of my children. . . . As much as I Converse with Sages or Heroes, they have very little of my Love or Admiration. I should prefer the Delights of a Garden to the Dominion of a World.

>   JOHN ADAMS, in a letter to his wife, March 16, 1777.

4 My home is in whatever town I'm booked.

>   POLLY ADLER, *A House Is Not a Home,* 1953.

5 That is an honest house which has the owner's honor built into its apartments, and whose appointments are his proper ornaments.

>   A. BRONSON ALCOTT, *Tablets,* 1868.

6 House, *n.* A hollow edifice erected for the habitation of man, rat, mouse, beetle, cockroach, fly, mosquito, flea, bacillus and microbe.

>   AMBROSE BIERCE, *The Devil's Dictionary,* 1906.

7 Hovel, *n.* The fruit of a flower called the Palace.

>   Ibid.

8 It was a terrible, strange-looking hotel. But Little Sunshine stayed on: it was his rightful home, he said, for if he went away, as he had once upon a time, other voices, other rooms, voices lost and clouded, strummed his dreams.

>   TRUMAN CAPOTE, *Other Voices, Other Rooms,* 1948.

9 Dark is the night, and fitful and drearily
>   Rushes the wind, like the waves of the sea!
>   Little care I, as here I sit cheerily,
>   Wife at my side and my baby on knee:
>   King, king, crown me the king:
>   Home is the kingdom and love is the king!

>   WILLIAM RANKIN DURYEA, "A Song for Hearth and Home," the *New York Home Journal,* 1866.

10 Good-bye to Flattery's fawning face;
>   To Grandeur with his wise grimace:
>   To upstart Wealth's averted eye;
>   To supple Office, low and high;
>   To crowded halls, to court and street;
>   To frozen hearts and hasting feet;

To those who go, and those who come;
Good-bye, proud world! I'm going home.

RALPH WALDO EMERSON, "Good-bye," 1839.

11 Happy is the house that shelters a friend!

RALPH WALDO EMERSON, "Friendship," *Essays,*
First Series, 1841.

12 The house is a castle which the king cannot
enter.

RALPH WALDO EMERSON, "Wealth," *English
Traits,* 1856.

13 Cleave to thine acre; the round year
Will fetch all fruits and virtues here:
Fool and foe may harmless roam,
Loved and lovers bide at home.

RALPH WALDO EMERSON, "Considerations by the
Way," *The Conduct of Life,* 1860.

14 Every spirit makes its house; but afterwards the
house confines the spirit.

RALPH WALDO EMERSON, "Fate," *The Conduct
of Life,* 1860.

15 A house kept to the end of prudence is laborious
without joy; a house kept to the end of display is
impossible to all but a few women, and their success is dearly bought.

RALPH WALDO EMERSON, "Domestic Life,"
Society and Solitude, 1870.

16 The household is a school of power.

RALPH WALDO EMERSON, "Education," *Lectures
and Biographical Sketches,* 1883.

17 Home is the place to do the things you want to
do. Here we eat just when we want to. Breakfast
and luncheon are extremely moveable feasts. It's
terrible to allow conventional habits to gain a hold
on a whole household; to eat, sleep and live by clock
ticks.

ZELDA FITZGERALD, in an interview in the
Baltimore Sun, 1923.

18 Way down upon de Swanee Ribber,
Far, far away,
Dere's wha my heart is turning ebber,
Dere's wha de old folks stay.

All up and down de whole creation,
Sadly I roam,
Still longing for de old plantation,
And for de old folks at home.

STEPHEN COLLINS FOSTER, "Old Folks at
Home," 1851.

19 [Husband]
"Home is the place where, when you have to
go there,
They have to take you in."
[Wife]
"I should have called it
Something you somehow haven't to deserve."

ROBERT FROST, "The Death of the Hired Man,"
North of Boston, 1914.

20 It takes a heap o' livin' in a house t' make it
home.

EDGAR A. GUEST, "Home," in *The Collected
Verse of Edgar A. Guest,* 1934.

21 Home, in one form or another, is the great object of life.

JOSIAH GILBERT HOLLAND, "Home," *Gold-Foil
Hammered from Popular Proverbs,* 1859.

22 No genuine observer can decide otherwise than
that the homes of a nation are the bulwarks of
personal and national safety.

Ibid.

23 Goethe once said, "He is happiest, king or peas-
ant, who finds happiness at home." And Goethe
knew—because he never found it.

ELBERT HUBBARD, *The Roycroft Dictionary and
Book of Epigrams,* 1923.

24 It takes a hundred men to make an encamp-
ment, but one woman can make a home.

ROBERT G. INGERSOLL, "Woman," speech at
Peoria, Illinois, April 29, 1870.

25 The happiness of the domestic fireside is the first
boon of Heaven; and it is well it is so, since it is that
which is the lot of the mass of mankind.

THOMAS JEFFERSON, in a letter to John
Armstrong, February 8, 1813.

26 In happy homes he saw the light
Of household fires gleam warm and bright.

> HENRY WADSWORTH LONGFELLOW, "Excelsior," 1841.

27 O fortunate, O happy day,
When a new household finds its place
Among the myriad homes of earth,
Like a new star just sprung to birth,
And rolled on its harmonious way
Into the boundless realms of space!

> HENRY WADSWORTH LONGFELLOW, "The Hanging of the Crane," 1874.

28 Stay, stay at home, my heart, and rest;
Home-keeping hearts are happiest,
For those that wander they know not where
Are full of trouble and full of care;
To stay at home is best.

> HENRY WADSWORTH LONGFELLOW, "Song," 1877.

29 Housework isn't bad in itself—the trouble with it is that it's inhumanly lonely.

> PAT LOUD, *Pat Loud: A Woman's Story,* 1974.

30 To learn such a simple lesson,
Need I go to Paris and Rome,
That the many make the household,
But only one the home?

> JAMES RUSSELL LOWELL, "The Dead House," the *Atlantic Monthly,* October, 1858.

31 Joy dwells beneath a humble roof;
Heaven is not built of country seats
But little queer suburban streets.

> CHRISTOPHER MORLEY, "To the Little House," in *Songs for a Little House,* 1917.

32 It takes a heap of other things besides
A heap o' livin' to make a home out of a house.
To begin with, it takes a heap o' payin'.

> OGDEN NASH, "A Heap o' Livin'." (See quotation 20, above.)

33 Mid pleasures and palaces tho we may roam,
Be it ever so humble, there's no place like home;

A charm from the sky seems to hallow us there,
Which, seek through the world, is ne'er met with elsewhere.
Home, home, sweet, sweet home!
There's no place like home! there's no place like home!

> JOHN HOWARD PAYNE, "Home, Sweet Home," from his opera *Clari, the Maid of Milan,* 1823.

34 I have been very happy with my homes, but homes really are no more than the people who live in them.

> NANCY REAGAN, *Nancy,* 1980.

35 Our lives are domestic in more senses than we think. From the hearth, the field is a great distance. It would be well, perhaps, if we were to spend more of our days and nights without any obstruction between us and the celestial bodies, if the poet did not speak so much from under a roof, or the saint dwell there so long. Birds do not sing in caves, nor do doves cherish their innocence in dovecotes.

> HENRY DAVID THOREAU, *Walden,* 1854.

36 I had three chairs in my house: one for solitude, two for friendship, three for society.

> Ibid.

37 Almost any man worthy of his salt would fight to defend his home, but no one ever heard of a man going to war for his boarding house.

> MARK TWAIN, quoted in Bernard DeVoto, *Mark Twain in Eruption,* 1940.

38 One face to the world, another at home makes for misery.

> AMY VANDERBILT, *New Complete Book of Etiquette,* 1963.

39 I read within a poet's book
A word that starred the page:
"Stone walls do not a prison make,
Nor iron bars a cage!"
Yes, that is true, and something more:
You'll find, where'er you roam,
That marble floors and gilded walls
Can never make a home.

But every house where Love abides,
And Friendship is a guest,
Is surely home, and home-sweet-home:
For there the heart can rest.

HENRY VAN DYKE, "A Home Song," collected in
The Poems of Henry Van Dyke, 1911.

---

110. HOPE

1 When hope is taken away from a people moral
degeneration follows swiftly after.

PEARL S. BUCK, in a letter to the *New York
Times,* November 15, 1941.

2 Hope is the thing with feathers,
That perches in the soul,
And sings the tune without the words,
And never stops at all.

EMILY DICKINSON, "Hope," in *Poems,* Second
Series, 1891.

3 He that lives upon Hope, dies farting.

BENJAMIN FRANKLIN, *Poor Richard's Almanack,*
1736.

4 There is nothing so well known as that we
should not expect something for nothing—but we
all do and call it Hope.

EDGAR WATSON HOWE, *Country Town Sayings,*
1911.

5 I suppose it can be truthfully said that Hope is
the only universal liar who never loses his reputation for veracity.

ROBERT G. INGERSOLL, in a speech at the
Manhattan Liberal Club, published in the
Truth-Seeker, a New York weekly, February 28,
1892.

6 The setting of a great hope is like the setting of
the sun. The brightness of our life is gone.

HENRY WADSWORTH LONGFELLOW, *Hyperion,*
1839.

7 'Tis always morning somewhere.

HENRY WADSWORTH LONGFELLOW, "The Birds
of Killingworth," *Tales of a Wayside Inn,* 1886.

8 But the nearer the dawn the darker the night,
And by going wrong all things come right;
Things have been mended that were worse,
And the worse, the nearer they are to mend.

HENRY WADSWORTH LONGFELLOW, "The Baron
of St. Castine," *Tales of a Wayside Inn,* 1886.

9 Behind the cloud the starlight lurks,
Through showers the sunbeams fall;
For God, who loveth all His works,
Has left His hope with all!

JOHN GREENLEAF WHITTIER, "A Dream of
Summer," 1847.

10 Alas for him who never sees
The stars shine through his cypress-trees,
Who, hopeless, lays his dead away,
Nor looks to see the breaking day
Across the mournful marbles play!

JOHN GREENLEAF WHITTIER, *Snow-Bound: A
Winter Idyll,* 1866.

---

111. HORSE RACING

See also SPORTS

---

1 Losers walking around with money in their pock-
ets are always dangerous, not to be trusted. Some
horse always reaches out and grabs them.

BILL BARICH, *Laughing in the Hills,* 1980.

2 Horse racing means loud clothes.

MRS. HEYWOOD HALE BROUN, quoted in
Heywood Hale Broun, *Tumultuous Merriment,*
1979.

3 Well, I'd say I lost a few million here and there.

CAB CALLOWAY, describing his betting luck,
quoted in *American Way* magazine, March, 1977.

4 Gwine to run all night!
Gwine to run all day!
I bet my money on de bob-tail nag,
Somebody bet on de bay.

STEPHEN COLLINS FOSTER, "Camptown Races,"
1850.

5 The only man who makes money following the races is the one who does so with a broom and shovel.

ELBERT HUBBARD, *The Roycroft Dictionary and Book of Epigrams*, 1923.

6 You can take an ol' mule and run him and feed him and train him and get him in the best shape of his life, but you ain't going to win the Kentucky Derby!

PEPPER MARTIN, quoted in Heywood Hale Broun, *Tumultuous Merriment*, 1979.

---

112. HUMANKIND

See also HEART; MAN; WOMAN

---

1 Of all the animals on earth, man has shown himself to be the most cruel and brutal. He is the only animal that will create instruments of death for his own destruction. Man is the only animal on all the earth that has ever been known to burn its young as a sacrifice to appease the wrath of some imaginary deity. He is the only one that will build homes, towns and cities at such a cost in sacrifice and suffering and turn around and destroy them in war.

Attributed to "an American hill-country philosopher" by J. William Fulbright in *Old Myths and New Realities*, 1964.

2 Man is a soul informed by divine ideas, and bodying forth their image. His mind is the unit and measure of things visible and invisible.

A. BRONSON ALCOTT, *Tablets*, 1868.

3 Man, *n.* An animal so lost in rapturous contemplation of what he thinks he is as to overlook what he undubitably ought to be. His chief occupation is extermination of other animals and his own species, which, however, multiplies with such insistent rapidity as to infest the whole habitable earth and Canada.

AMBROSE BIERCE, *The Devil's Dictionary*, 1906.

4 A man is the sum of his ancestors; to reform him you must begin with a dead ape and work downward through a million graves. He is like the lower end of a suspended chain; you can sway him slightly to the right or the left, but remove your hand and he falls into line with the other links.

AMBROSE BIERCE, *Collected Works*, 1911.

5 Man is stumbling blindly through a spiritual darkness while toying with the precarious secrets of life and death. The world has achieved brilliance without wisdom, power without conscience. We know more about war than we know about peace, more about killing than we know about living.

GEN. OMAR BRADLEY, in an address in Boston, November 10, 1948.

6 Men are like plants; the goodness and flavor of the fruit proceeds from the peculiar soil and exposition in which they grow. We are nothing but what we derive from the air we breathe, the climate we inhabit, the government we obey, the system of religion we profess, and the nature of our employment.

MICHEL GUILLAUME JEAN DE CRÈVECOEUR, *Letters from an American Farmer*, 1782.

7 Man is not matter: he is not made up of brain, blood, bones, and other material elements. The Scriptures inform us that man is made in the image and likeness of God. Matter is not that likeness.

MARY BAKER EDDY, *Science and Health*, 1875.

8 Human kind
Cannot bear very much reality.

T.S. ELIOT, "Burnt Norton," *Four Quartets*, 1935.

9 That is the vice—that no one feels himself called to act for man, but only as a fraction of man.

RALPH WALDO EMERSON, "Man the Reformer," published in *The Dial* magazine, April, 1841.

10 An institution is the lengthened shadow of one man . . . and all history resolves itself very easily into the biography of a few stout and earnest persons.

RALPH WALDO EMERSON, "Self-Reliance," *Essays*, First Series, 1841.

11 Not in nature but in man is all the beauty and worth he sees. The world is very empty, and is indebted to this gilding, exalting soul for all its pride.

> RALPH WALDO EMERSON, "Spiritual Laws," *Essays,* First Series, 1841.

12 Let us treat men and women well; treat them as if they were real; perhaps they are.

> RALPH WALDO EMERSON, "Experience," *Essays,* Second Series, 1844.

13 I like man, but not men.

> RALPH WALDO EMERSON, entry written in March, 1846, *Journals,* 1909–1914.

14 I believe that man will not merely endure; he will prevail. He is immortal, not because he alone among creatures has an inexhaustible voice, but because he has a soul, a spirit capable of compassion and sacrifice and endurance.

> WILLIAM FAULKNER, in his Nobel Prize acceptance speech, Stockholm, Sweden, December 10, 1950.

15 There are only two kinds of people in the world that really count. One kind's wheat and the other kind's emeralds.

> EDNA FERBER, *So Big,* 1924.

16 Mankind are very odd Creatures: One Half censure what they practice, the other half practice what they censure; the rest always say and do as they ought.

> BENJAMIN FRANKLIN, *Poor Richard's Almanack,* 1752.

17 Man is not an ox, who, when he had eaten his fill, lies down to chew the cud; he is the daughter of the horse leech, who constantly asks for more.

> HENRY GEORGE, *Progress and Poverty,* 1879.

18 Take mankind in general: they are vicious, their passions may be operated upon.

> ALEXANDER HAMILTON, in a speech at the Constitutional Convention, Philadelphia, Pennsylvania, June 22, 1787.

19 One great error is that we suppose mankind more honest than they are.

> Ibid.

20 Mankind are earthen jugs with spirits in them.

> NATHANIEL HAWTHORNE, entry written in 1842, *Passages from the American Notebooks,* 1868.

21 Man is not made for defeat.

> ERNEST HEMINGWAY, *The Old Man and the Sea,* 1952.

22 The world is made up of a great mob, and nothing will influence it so much as the lash.

> EDGAR WATSON HOWE, *Success Easier Than Failure,* 1917.

23 We are creatures of the moment; we live from one little space to another; and only one interest at a time fills these.

> WILLIAM DEAN HOWELLS, *A Hazard of New Fortunes,* 1890.

24 It is man who sanctifies a place, and it is work that sanctifies a man.

> ELBERT HUBBARD, *The Roycroft Dictionary and Book of Epigrams,* 1923.

25 The history of the world shows that when a mean thing was done, man did it; when a good thing was done, man did it.

> ROBERT G. INGERSOLL, in a speech in Pittsburgh, October 14, 1879.

26 Man passes away; his name perishes from record and recollection; his history is as a tale that is told, and his very monument becomes a ruin.

> WASHINGTON IRVING, "Westminster Abbey," *The Sketch Books,* 1819–1820.

27 The concrete man has but one interest—to be right. That to him is the art of all arts, and all means are fair which help him to it.

> WILLIAM JAMES, *The Sentiment of Rationality,* 1882.

28 In many respects man is the most ruthlessly ferocious of beasts. . . . We, the lineal representatives of the successful enactors of one scene of slaughter after another, must, whatever more pacific virtues we may also possess, still carry about with us, ready at any moment to burst into flame, the smouldering and sinister traits of character by

means of which they lived through so many massacres, harming others, but themselves unharmed.

WILLIAM JAMES, *The Principles of Psychology,* 1890.

29 The mass of men are neither wise nor good.

JOHN JAY, in a letter to George Washington, June 27, 1786.

30 The bulk of mankind are schoolboys through life.

THOMAS JEFFERSON, "Notes on a Money Unit," 1784.

31 Experience declares that man is the only animal which devours his own kind; for I can apply no milder term to the governments of Europe, and to the general prey of the rich on the poor.

THOMAS JEFFERSON, in a letter to Col. Edward Carrington, January 16, 1787.

32 What a Bedlamite is man!

THOMAS JEFFERSON, in a letter to John Adams, January 22, 1821.

33 I have no high opinion of human beings: they are always going to fight and do nasty things to each other. They are always going to be part animal, governed by their emotions and subconscious drives rather than by reason.

GEORGE F. KENNAN, in an interview with George Urban published in *Encounter* magazine, September, 1976.

34 Vaster is Man than his works.

ROCKWELL KENT, caption for an illustration.

35 Man is man because he is free to operate within the framework of his destiny. He is free to deliberate, to make decisions, and to choose between alternatives. He is distinguished from animals by his freedom to do evil or to do good and to walk the high road of beauty or tread the low road of ugly degeneracy.

MARTIN LUTHER KING, JR., *The Measures of Man,* 1959.

36 O suffering, sad humanity!
    O ye afflicted ones, who lie
    Steeped to the lips in misery,

Longing, and yet afraid to die,
    Patient, though sorely tried!

HENRY WADSWORTH LONGFELLOW, "The Goblet of Life," 1841.

37 Before Man made us citizens, great Nature made us men.

JAMES RUSSELL LOWELL, "On the Capture of Certain Fugitive Slaves Near Washington," published in the *Boston Courier,* July 19, 1845.

38 Console yourself, dear man and brother, whatever else you may be sure of, be sure at least of this, that you are dreadfully like other people. Human nature has a much greater genius for sameness than for originality, or the world would be at a sad pass shortly.

JAMES RUSSELL LOWELL, "On a Certain Condescension in Foreigners," 1869.

39 Women, it is true, make human beings, but only men can make men.

MARGARET MEAD, *Male and Female,* 1948.

40 Seat thyself sultanically among the moons of Saturn, and take high abstracted man alone, and he seems a wonder, a grandeur, and a woe. But from the same point take mankind in mass, and for the most part they seem a mob of unnecessary duplicates, both contemporary and hereditary.

HERMAN MELVILLE, *Moby-Dick,* 1851.

41 If men cease to believe that they will one day become gods then they will surely become worms.

HENRY MILLER, *The Colossus of Maroussi,* 1941.

42 A human being; an ingenious assembly of portable plumbing.

CHRISTOPHER MORLEY, *Human Being,* 1932.

43 The dignity and beauty of man rests in the human spirit which makes him more than simply a physical being. This spirit must never be suppressed for exploitation by others. As long as the people recognize the beauty of their human spirits and move against suppression and exploitation, they will be carrying out one of the most beautiful

ideas of all time. Because the human whole is much greater than the sum of its parts.

> HUEY P. NEWTON, quoted in Francine du Plessix Gray, *Hawaii: The Sugar-Coated Fortress*, 1972.

44 Man is that curious creature who, though partly determined and limited by the necessities of nature, also possesses a rational freedom which enables him to harness the forces of nature in the world and to transmute the natural appetites and drives in his own nature so that he can conceive ends and entertain ambitions which exceed the limits which pure nature sets for all her creatures except man.

> REINHOLD NIEBUHR, *The Structures of Nations and Empires*, 1959.

45 Man's unique reward, however, is that while animals survive by adjusting themselves to their background, man survives by adjusting his background to himself.

> AYN RAND, *For the New Intellectual*, 1961.

46 The life of reason is no fair reproduction of the universe, but the expression of man alone.

> GEORGE SANTAYANA, *The Life of Reason*, 1905–1906.

47 We are not really native to this world, except in respect to our bodies.

> GEORGE SANTAYANA, *The Genteel Tradition at Bay*, 1931.

48 Man is distinctly more aggressive, cruel, and relentless than any of the other apes.

> BENJAMIN SPOCK, *Decent and Indecent*, 1970.

49 There is a sort of competition between the head and the heart for the control of each human being's actions. If the head becomes too dominant, by upbringing and education, the heart dries up.

> Ibid.

50 Man is a spiritual being in that—unless he is badly corrupted—he responds powerfully to nonmaterial stimuli: the beauty in nature or in art, the trust of children, the needs of helpless people, the death of a friend even though long absent.

> Ibid.

51 Man can be the most affectionate and altruistic of creatures, yet he's potentially more vicious than any other. He is the only one who can be persuaded to hate millions of his own kind whom he has never seen and to kill as many as he can lay his hands on in the name of his tribe or his God.

> Ibid.

52 I love mankind, but I hate the institutions of the dead unkind.

> HENRY DAVID THOREAU, *A Week on the Concord and Merrimack Rivers*, 1849.

53 Man is the great poet, and not Homer nor Shakespeare; and our language itself, and the common arts of life, are his work.

> Ibid.

54 The civilized man is a more experienced and wiser savage.

> HENRY DAVID THOREAU, *Walden*, 1854.

55 Man's capacities have never been measured; nor are we to judge of what he can do by any precedents, so little has been tried.

> Ibid.

56 Man and his affairs, church and state and school, trade and commerce, and manufactures and agriculture, even politics, the most alarming of them all—I am pleased to see how little space they occupy in the landscape.

> HENRY DAVID THOREAU, "Walking," *Excursions*, 1863.

57 There are times when one would like to hang the whole human race, and finish the farce.

> MARK TWAIN, *A Connecticut Yankee at King Arthur's Court*, 1889.

58 Man is the only animal that blushes. Or needs to.

> MARK TWAIN, "Pudd'nhead Wilson's New Calendar," *Following the Equator*, 1897.

59 I have no race prejudices, and I think I have no color prejudices nor creed prejudices. Indeed, I

know it. I can stand any society. All I care to know is that a man is a human being—that is enough for me; he can't be any worse.

> MARK TWAIN, "Concerning the Jews," 1899.

60 The fact that man knows right from wrong proves his *intellectual* superiority to the other creatures; but the fact that he can *do* wrong proves his *moral* inferiority to any creatures that *cannot*.

> MARK TWAIN, *What Is Man?* 1906.

61 There is no escape—man drags man down, or man lifts man up.

> Attributed to Booker T. Washington.

62 You can't hold a man down without staying down with him.

> Ibid.

63 Each of us inevitable,
Each of us limitless—each of us with his or
   her right upon the earth,
Each of us allow'd the eternal purports of
   the earth,
Each of us here as divinely as any is here.

> WALT WHITMAN, "Salut au Monde," originally titled "Poem of Salutation," 1856.

64 Of Life immense in passion, pulse, and
   power,
Cheerful, for freest action form'd under the
   laws divine,
The Modern Man I sing.

> WALT WHITMAN, "One's-Self I Sing," 1867.

65 In thy lone and long night-watches, sky
   above and wave below,
Thou didst learn a higher wisdom than the
   babbling schoolmen know;
God's stars and silence taught thee, as His
   angels only can,
That the one sole sacred thing beneath the
   scope of heaven is Man!

> JOHN GREENLEAF WHITTIER, "The Branded Hand," 1846.

113. HUMOR

See also MERRIMENT

1 I have gotten a lot of letters about my work, most of them from criminals and subhumans, who want to sell ideas. I can rarely use them as they're in the worst possible taste, but sometimes funny in a grotesque sort of way. Some of the worst come from a minister in Georgia.

> CHARLES ADDAMS, in a letter to James Thurber, quoted in James Thurber, *The Years with Ross,* 1957.

2 Sheer madness is, of course, the highest possible brow in humor.

> ROBERT BENCHLEY, 1926, quoted in Walter Blair and Hamlin Hill, *America's Humor,* 1978.

3 The world would not be in such a snarl
If Marx had been Groucho instead of Karl.

> IRVING BERLIN, birthday message to Groucho Marx, quoted in Groucho Marx, *The Groucho Phile,* 1976.

4 Humorist, *n.* A plague that would have softened down the hoar austerity of Pharaoh's heart and persuaded him to dismiss Israel with his best wishes, cat-quick.

> AMBROSE BIERCE, *The Devil's Dictionary,* 1906.

5 Laughter, *n.* An interior convulsion, producing a distortion of the features and accompanied by inarticulate noises. It is infectious and, though intermittent, incurable. Liability to attacks of laughter is one of the characteristics distinguishing man from the animals.

> Ibid.

6 Wit, *n.* The salt with which the American humorist spoils his intellectual cookery by leaving it out.

> Ibid.

7 Witticism, *n.* A sharp and clever remark, usually quoted and seldom noted; what the Philistine is pleased to call a "joke."

> Ibid.

8 Being a funny person does an awful lot of things to you. You feel that you mustn't get serious with people. They don't expect it from you, and they don't want to see it. You're not entitled to be serious, you're a clown, and they only want you to make them laugh.

> FANNY BRICE, quoted in Norman Katkov, *The Fabulous Fanny,* 1952.

9 I never saw a Purple Cow,
I never hope to see one;
But I can tell you, anyhow,
I'd rather see than be one.

> GELETT BURGESS, "The Purple Cow," published in *The Lark* magazine, 1895.

10 Ah, yes, I wrote the "Purple Cow"—
I'm sorry, now, I wrote it!
But I can tell you anyhow,
I'll kill you if you quote it.

> GELETT BURGESS, "Reply" of "Après Cinq Ans," 1914.

11 Men will confess to treason, murder, arson, false teeth, or a wig. How many of them will own up to a lack of humor?

> FRANK MOORE COLBY, *The Colby Essays,* 1926.

12 The essence of all jokes, of all comedy, seems to be an honest or well-intended halfness; a non-performance of that which is pretended to be performed, at the same time that one is giving loud pledges of performance. The balking of the intellect, the frustrated expectation, the break of continuity in the intellect, is comedy and it announces itself in the pleasant spasms we call laughter.

> RALPH WALDO EMERSON, "The Comic," *Letters and Social Aims,* 1876.

13 Wit makes its own welcome, and levels all distinctions. No dignity, no learning, no force of character, can make any stand against good wit.

> Ibid.

14 Humor is one of God's most marvelous gifts. Humor gives us smiles, laughter, and gaiety. Humor reveals the roses and hides the thorns. Humor makes our heavy burdens light and smooths the rough spots in our pathways. Humor endows us with the capacity to clarify the obscure, to simplify the complex, to deflate the pompous, to chastise the arrogant, to point a moral, and to adorn a tale.

> SAM J. ERVIN, JR., *Humor of a Country Lawyer,* 1983.

15 An ounce of revealing humor often has more power to reveal, convince, or ridicule than do many tons of erudite argument.

> Ibid.

16 For reasons I have never understood, Alexandria, Virginia, is screamingly funny to Washingtonians, while the great city of Oakland never fails to get a chuckle out of San Franciscans. And Bismarck, North Dakota, is funny anywhere in the United States.

> W.C. FIELDS, quoted in Robert Lewis Taylor, *W.C. Fields, His Follies and Fortunes,* 1949.

17 I never saw anything funny that wasn't terrible. If it causes pain, it's funny; if it doesn't, it isn't. I try to hide the pain with embarrassment, and the more I do that, the better they like it. But that doesn't mean they are unsympathetic. Oh no, they laugh often with tears in their eyes.

> W.C. FIELDS, quoted in Walter Blair and Hamlin Hill, *America's Humor,* 1978.

18 Where humor is concerned, there are no standards—no one can say what is good or bad, although you can be sure that everyone will. Only a very foolish man will use a form of language that is wholly uncertain in its effect. And that is the nature of humor.

> JOHN KENNETH GALBRAITH, *Annals of an Abiding Liberal,* 1979.

19 I never dare to write
As funny as I can.

> OLIVER WENDELL HOLMES, SR., "The Height of the Ridiculous," 1830.

20 People that make puns are like wanton boys that put coppers on the railroad tracks.

> OLIVER WENDELL HOLMES, SR., *The Autocrat of the Breakfast-Table,* 1858.

21 Wit that is kindly is not very witty.

> EDGAR WATSON HOWE, *Sinner Sermons,* 1926.

22 The first thing any comedian does on getting an unscheduled laugh is to verify the state of his buttons; the second is to look around and see if a cat has walked out on the stage.

> ALVA JOHNSTON, quoted in Robert Lewis Taylor, *W.C. Fields, His Follies and Fortunes,* 1949.

23 Ultimately, all jokes, parables, lies, and in fact all fictions and fables of whatever sort are simply the decorative showcases of their tellers' anxieties, their repressions, and generally of their neuroses.

> GERSHON LEGMAN, *No Laughing Matter,* 1982.

24 I'll meet you tonight under the moon. Oh, I can see you now—you and the moon. You wear a necktie so I'll know you.

> GROUCHO MARX, in *The Cocoanuts,* 1929, quoted in Groucho Marx, *The Groucho Phile,* 1976.

25 One morning I shot an elephant in my pajamas. How he got in my pajamas, I'll never know.

> GROUCHO MARX, in *Animal Crackers,* 1930, quoted in Groucho Marx, *The Groucho Phile,* 1976.

26 Laughter is man's most distinctive emotional expression. Man shares the capacity for love and hate, anger and fear, loyalty and grief, with other living creatures. But humor, which has an intellectual as well as an emotional element, belongs to man.

> MARGARET MEAD, in *Redbook* magazine, March, 1963.

27 It always withers in the presence of the messianic delusion, like justice and truth in front of patriotic passion.

> H.L. MENCKEN, on the sense of humor, *Prejudices,* First Series, 1919.

28 Among animals, *one* has a sense of humor.
Humor saves a few steps, it saves years.

> MARIANNE MOORE, "The Pangolin," 1941.

29 Wit has truth in it; wisecracking is simply calisthenics with words.

> DOROTHY PARKER, quoted in the *Paris Review,* Summer, 1956.

30 There is not one female comic who was beautiful as a little girl.

> JOAN RIVERS, quoted by Lydia Lane in the *Los Angeles Times,* May 10, 1974.

31 Everything is funny as long as it is happening to somebody else.

> WILL ROGERS, *The Illiterate Digest,* 1924.

32 A comedian can only last till he either takes himself serious or his audience takes him serious.

> WILL ROGERS, in his newspaper column, June 28, 1931.

33 The reason that there are so few women comics is that so few women can bear being laughed at.

> ANNA RUSSELL, quoted in the London *Sunday Times,* August 25, 1957.

34 He killed the noble Mudjokivis.
Of the skin he made him mittens,
Made them with the fur side inside,
Made them with the skin side outside.
He, to get the warm side inside,
Put the inside skin side outside;
He, to get the cold side outside,
Put the warm side fur side inside.
That's why he put the fur side inside,
Why he put the skin side outside,
Why he turned them inside outside.

> GEORGE A. STRONG, "The Song of Milkanwatha," in Franklin P. Adams, *Innocent Merriment,* 1942.

35 You never see a frog so modest and straightfor'ard as he was, for all he was so gifted.

> MARK TWAIN, "The Celebrated Jumping Frog of Calaveras County," 1865.

36 Guides cannot master the subtleties of the American joke.

> MARK TWAIN, *Innocents Abroad,* 1869.

37 Everything human is pathetic. The secret source of Humor itself is not joy but sorrow. There is no humor in heaven.

> MARK TWAIN, "Pudd'nhead Wilson's New Calendar," *Following the Equator,* 1897.

38 Wit is the only wall
Between us and the dark.

> MARK VAN DOREN, "Wit," in *A Winter Diary and Other Poems,* 1935.

39 Why is this thus? What is the reason of this thusness?

> ARTEMUS WARD, *Artemus Ward's Lecture,* 1869.

40 It's hard to be funny when you have to be clean.

> MAE WEST, quoted in Joseph Weintraub, *The Wit and Wisdom of Mae West,* 1967.

41 Whatever else an American believes or disbelieves about himself, he is absolutely sure he has a sense of humor.

> E.B. WHITE, "Some Remarks on Humor," *The Second Tree from the Corner,* 1954.

---

114. IDAHO

---

1 Esto perpetua. (May she endure forever.)

> State motto.

2 Dice 'em, hash 'em, boil 'em, mash 'em! Idaho, Idaho, Idaho!

> Former Idaho football cheer, quoted in Charles Kuralt, *Dateline America,* 1979.

3 Idaho is torn, above all, between two other states; between the pull of Washington in the north, that of Utah in the south. Half of Idaho belongs to Spokane, I heard it said, and the other half to the Mormon church.

> JOHN GUNTHER, *Inside U.S.A.,* 1947.

4 I asked an Idaho patriot why the potatoes were so big. Answer: "We fertilize 'em with cornmeal, and irrigate with milk."

> Ibid.

5 There were two small hotels in Ketchum, and a group of nice cabins built around a hot-water pool. The business section consisted of one block: two grocery stores, three restaurants, one drugstore, and

twelve combination saloons and gambling halls. These were called "clubs." Gambling was not legal in Idaho, and neither was liquor by the drink, but nobody in Ketchum paid any attention. Everything was wide open.

> ERNIE PYLE, *Home Country,* 1947.

6 At the gambling casinos in Ketchum they took the big beautiful wheels off the roulette tables at the end of play every night and locked them up. Why? Because if they didn't people would come in and paste numbers on the wheel—say three or four 27s—and then play that number the following night, and it would be quite a while before the dealer realized what had happened.

> Ibid.

---

115. ILLINOIS

See also CHICAGO

---

1 State sovereignty—national union.

> State motto.

2 Although the geographical center of the United States is 500 miles to the west, Illinois is the axis of the nation, the hub and vortex of all the wonderful and eccentric hullabaloo that comprises our sweet land of liberty.

> CLYDE BRION DAVIS, "Illinois," in *American Panorama: East of the Mississippi,* 1960.

3 Illinois is perhaps the most American of all the states. It's the U.S.A. in a capsule. Here our virtues and our faults are most exaggerated and magnified. Here somehow the heroes seem more heroic, the villains more villainous, the buffoons more comic. Here violence is more unrestrained, and the capacity for greatness is as limitless as the sweep of the unending cornfields.

> Ibid.

4 A dismal swamp, on which the half-built houses rot away; . . . a hotbed of disease, an ugly sepulchre, a grave uncheered by any gleam of promise: a place

without one single quality, in earth or air or water, to commend it: such is this dismal Cairo [Illinois].

CHARLES DICKENS, *American Notes,* 1842.

5 No one, not in my situation, can appreciate my feeling of sadness at this parting. To this place, and the kindness of these people, I owe everything. Here I have lived a quarter of a century, and have passed from a young to an old man. Here my children have been born, and one is buried. I now leave, not knowing when or whether ever I may return.

ABRAHAM LINCOLN, in his farewell address at Springfield, Illinois, February 11, 1861.

116. IMMIGRANTS

See also AMERICA; AMERICANS; AMERICA
SEEN FROM ABROAD; RELIGIOUS FREEDOM

1 Foreign immigration, which in the past has added so much to the wealth, development of resources, and increase of power to this nation, the asylum of the oppressed of all nations, should be fostered and encouraged by a liberal and just policy.

Platform plank of the National Union
[Republican] Party, 1864.

2 Hereafter no State court or court of the United States shall admit Chinese to citizenship.

Chinese Exclusion Act, Section 14, May 6, 1882.

3 We heartily approve all legitimate efforts to prevent the United States from being used as the dumping ground for the known criminals and professional paupers of Europe.

Platform plank of the Democratic National Party, 1892.

4 For the protection of the equality of our American citizenship and of the wages of our workingmen, against the fatal competition of low-priced labor, we demand that the immigration laws be thoroughly enforced, and so extended as to exclude from entrance to the United States those who can neither read nor write.

Platform plank of the Republican National Party, 1896.

5 Wide open and unguarded stand our gates,
And through them presses a wild, motley
    throng—
Men from the Volga and the Tartar steppes,
Featureless faces from the Huang-Ho,
Malayan, Scythian, Teuton, Kelt and Slav,
Flying the Old World's poverty and scorn;
These bringing with them unknown Gods and
    rites,
Those, tiger passions here to stretch their
    claws.
In street and alley, what strange tongues are
    these,
Accents of menace alien to our air,
Voices that once the Tower of Babel knew!
O Liberty, white Goddess! Is it well
To leave the gates unguarded?

THOMAS BAILEY ALDRICH, "The Unguarded
Gates," published in the *Atlantic Monthly,* 1892.

6 Immigrant, *n.* An unenlightened person who thinks one country better than another.

AMBROSE BIERCE, *The Devil's Dictionary,* 1906.

7 Foreigners ourselves, and mostly unable to speak English, we had Americanized the system of providing clothes for the American woman of moderate or humble means. . . . We had done away with prohibitive prices and greatly improved the popular taste. Indeed, the Russian Jew had made the average American girl a "tailor-made" girl.

ABRAHAM CAHAN, *The Rise of David Levinsky,*
1917.

8 The admitted right of a government to prevent the influx of elements hostile to its internal peace and security may not be questioned, even where there is not treaty stipulation on the subject.

GROVER CLEVELAND, in his first annual message
to Congress, December 8, 1885.

9 He is an American who, leaving behind him all his ancient prejudices and manners, receives new ones from the new mode of life he has embraced, the new government he obeys, and the new rank he holds.

Michel Guillaume Jean de Crèvecoeur, *Letters from an American Farmer,* 1782.

10 The great number of European emigrants, yearly coming over here, informs us that the severity of taxes, the injustice of laws, the tyranny of the rich, and the oppressive avarice of the church are as intolerable as ever. Will these calamities have no end? Are not the great rulers of the earth afraid of losing, by degrees, their most useful subjects? This country, providentially intended for the general asylum of the world, will flourish by the oppression of their people; they will every day become better acquainted with the happiness we enjoy, and seek for the means of transporting themselves here, in spite of all obstacles and laws.

Ibid.

11 I watched a small man with thick calluses on both hands work 15 and 16 hours a day. I saw him once literally bleed from the bottoms of his feet, a man who came here uneducated, alone, unable to speak the language, who taught me all I needed to know about faith and hard work by the simple eloquence of his example. I learned about our kind of democracy from my father. I learned about our obligation to each other from him and from my mother. They asked only for a chance to work and to make the world better for their children and they asked to be protected in those moments when they would not be able to protect themselves. This nation and this nation's government did that for them.

Mario Cuomo, in the keynote address at the Democratic National Convention, July 16, 1984.

12 Every ship that comes to America got its chart from Columbus.

Ralph Waldo Emerson, "On the Uses of Great Men," *Representative Men,* 1850.

13 The German and Irish millions, like the Negro, have a great deal of guano in their destiny. They are ferried over the Atlantic, and carted over America, to ditch and to drudge, to make corn cheap, and then to lie down prematurely to make a spot of green grass on the prairie.

Ralph Waldo Emerson, "Fate," *The Conduct of Life,* 1860.

14 Once I thought to write a history of the immigrants in America. Then I discovered that the immigrants *were* American history.

Oscar Handlin, *The Uprooted,* 1951.

15 What has become of the descendants of the irresponsible adventurers, the scapegrace sons, the bond servants, the redemptionists and the indentured maidens, the undesirables, and even the criminals, which made up, not all, of course, but nevertheless a considerable part of, the earliest emigrants to these virgin countries? They have become the leaders of the thought of the world, the vanguard in the march of progress, the inspirers of liberty, the creators of national prosperity, the sponsors of universal education and enlightenment.

William Randolph Hearst, testifying before the American Crime Study Commission, May 19, 1929.

16 Give me your tired, your poor,
Your huddled masses yearning to breathe free,
The wretched refuse of your teeming shore,
Send these, the homeless, tempest tossed to me,
I lift my lamp beside the golden door!

Emma Lazarus, "The New Colossus," 1883.

17 We are a nation of immigrants. It is immigrants who brought to this land the skills of their hands and brains to make of it a beacon of opportunity and of hope for all men.

Herbert H. Lehman, testifying before the House Subcommittee on Immigration and Naturalization, July 2, 1947.

18 Yes, we have a good many poor tired people here already, but we have plenty of mountains, rivers, woods, lots of sunshine and air, for tired people to rest in. . . . So give us as many as come— we can take it, and take care of them.

Mary Margaret McBride, *America for Me,* 1941.

19 My opinion, with respect to emigration, is, that, except of useful Mechanics and some particular descriptions of men or professions, there is no need of encouragement: while the policy or advantage of

its taking place in a body (I mean the settling of them in a body) may be much questioned; for, by so doing, they retain the Language, habits and principles (good or bad) which they bring with them.

> GEORGE WASHINGTON, in a letter to John Adams, November 15, 1794.

117. IMMORTALITY

See also DEATH; LIFE; RELIGION

1 I cannot conceive that [God] could make such a species as the human merely to live and die on this earth. If I did not believe in a future state, I should believe in no God.

> JOHN ADAMS, in a letter to Thomas Jefferson, December 8, 1818.

2 The insatiableness of our desires asserts our personal imperishableness.

> A. BRONSON ALCOTT, *Tablets,* 1868.

3 If there be anything in me that is of permanent worth and service to the universe, the universe will know how to preserve it. Whatsoever in me is not of permanent worth and service, neither can nor should be preserved.

> HORACE JAMES BRIDGES, "Concerning God," in Joseph Fort Newton, *My Idea of God,* 1926.

4 [Walt] Whitman once said to me that he would as soon hope to argue a man into good health as to argue him into a belief in immortality. He said he *knew* it was so without proof; but I never could light my candle at his great torch.

> JOHN BURROUGHS, quoted in Clara Barrus, *Life and Letters of John Burroughs,* 1925.

5 The truth is, no one really believes in immortality. Belief must mean something more than desire or hope.

> CLARENCE DARROW, *The Story of My Life,* 1932.

6 When we abandon the thought of immortality we at least have cast out fear. We gain a certain dignity and self-respect. We regard our fellow travelers as companions in the pleasures and tribulations of life. . . . We gain kinship with the world.

> Ibid.

7 The only secret people keep
  Is Immortality.

> EMILY DICKINSON, "Reticence," in *Poems,* Third Series, 1896.

8 My life closed twice before its close;
  It yet remains to see
  If Immortality unveil
  A third event to me.

> EMILY DICKINSON, "Parting," in *Poems,* Third Series, 1896.

9 *Immortality.* I notice that as soon as writers broach this question they begin to quote. I hate quotations. Tell me what you know.

> RALPH WALDO EMERSON, entry written in May, 1849, *Journals,* 1909–1914.

10 The blazing evidence of immortality is our dissatisfaction with any other solution.

> RALPH WALDO EMERSON, entry written in July, 1855, *Journals,* 1909–1914.

11 I am a better believer, and all serious souls are better believers, in immortality than we can give grounds for.

> RALPH WALDO EMERSON, "Immortality," *Letters and Social Aims,* 1876.

12 Here is my Creed. I believe in one God, Creator of the Universe. That He governs it by his Providence. That He ought to be worshiped. That the most acceptable service we render Him is doing good to His other children. That the soul of Man is immortal, and will be treated with justice in another life respecting its conduct in this.

> BENJAMIN FRANKLIN, in a letter to Ezra Stiles, March 9, 1790.

13 There is no Death! What seems so is transition;
  This life of mortal breath
  Is but a suburb of the life elysian,
  Whose portal we call Death.

HENRY WADSWORTH LONGFELLOW, "Resignation," in *The Seaside and the Fireside,* 1849.

14 The few little years we spend on earth are only the first scene in a Divine Drama that extends on into Eternity.

EDWIN MARKHAM, speaking at the funeral of Adam Willis Wagnalls, September, 1924.

15 Immortality is not a gift,
Immortality is an achievement;
And only those who strive mightily
Shall possess it.

EDGAR LEE MASTERS, "The Village Atheist," *Spoon River Anthology,* 1915.

16 The universe is a stairway leading nowhere unless man is immortal.

EDGAR YOUNG MULLINS, "The Father Almighty," quoted in Joseph Fort Newton, *My Idea of God,* 1926.

17 I content myself with believing, even to positive conviction, that the power that gave me existence is able to continue it, in any form and manner he pleases, either with or without this body; and it appears more probable to me that I shall continue to exist hereafter than that I should have had existence, as I now have, before that existence began.

THOMAS PAINE, *The Age of Reason,* 1794.

18 We go wondering about immortality, unconscious that we are ourselves immortality.

DONALD CULROSS PEATTIE, *The Road of a Naturalist,* 1941.

19 The fact of having been born is a bad augury for immortality.

GEORGE SANTAYANA, *The Life of Reason,* 1905–1906.

20 I swear I think now that every thing without
    exception has an eternal soul!
The trees have, rooted in the ground! the
    weeds of the sea have! the animals!

WALT WHITMAN, "To Think of Time," 1881.

21 Happy he whose inward ear
  Angel comfortings can hear,
    O'er the rabble's laughter;

And while Hatred's fagots burn,
Glimpses through the smoke discern
  Of the good hereafter.

JOHN GREENLEAF WHITTIER, "Barclay of Ury," 1847.

---

118. INDEPENDENCE

See also FREEDOM; INDIVIDUALITY; LIBERTY

---

1 So live that you can look any man in the eye and tell him to go to hell.

Attributed to an engineer working on the Panama Canal and used by John D. Rockefeller, Jr., in a speech at Dartmouth College, June, 1930.

2 Within our own borders we possess all the means of sustenance, defense, and commerce; at the same time, these advantages are so distributed among the different states of this continent as if nature had in view to proclaim to us—be united among yourselves, and you will want nothing from the rest of the world.

SAMUEL ADAMS, in a speech on American Independence, July 4, 1776.

3 I would rather choose to be a plumber or a peddler in the hope to find that modest degree of independence still available under present circumstances.

ALBERT EINSTEIN, in a letter acknowledging award of a membership card in a plumber's union, November, 1954.

4 Whoso would be a man, must be a Nonconformist.

RALPH WALDO EMERSON, "Self-Reliance," *Essays,* First Series, 1841.

5 We walk alone in the world. Friends, such as we desire, are dreams and fables.

RALPH WALDO EMERSON, "Friendship," *Essays,* First Series, 1841.

6 You don't need a lot of bureaucrats looking over your shoulder and telling you how to run your life

or how to run your business. We are a people who declared our independence 200 years ago, and we are not about to lose it now to paper shufflers and computers.

> GERALD R. FORD, in a speech in Chicago, Illinois, August 25, 1975.

7 Studious of Ease, and fond of humble Things,
   Below the Smiles, below the Frowns of
       Kings:
Thanks to my Stars, I prize the Sweets of
       Life,
No sleepness Nights I count, no Days of
       Strife.
I rest, I wake, I drink, I sometimes love,
I read, I write, I settle, or I rove;
Content to live, content to die unknown,
Lord of myself, accountable to none.

> BENJAMIN FRANKLIN, *Poor Richard's Almanack*, 1742.

8 My apple trees will never get across
And eat the cones under his pines, I tell him.
He only says, "Good fences make good
       neighbors."

> ROBERT FROST, "Mending Wall," *North of Boston*, 1914.

9 It's easy to be independent when you've got money. But to be independent when you haven't got a thing—that's the Lord's test.

> MAHALIA JACKSON, in *Movin' On Up*, with Evan McLoud Wylie, 1966.

10 Neither the clamor of the mob nor the voice of power will ever turn me by the breadth of a hair from the course I mark out for myself, guided by such knowledge as I can obtain, and controlled and directed by a solemn conviction of right and duty.

> ROBERT M. LAFOLLETTE, SR., in a speech in the U.S. Senate, October 6, 1917.

11 His brow is wet with honest sweat,
   He earns whate'er he can,
And looks the whole world in the face,
   For he owes not any man.

> HENRY WADSWORTH LONGFELLOW, "The Village Blacksmith," *Ballads and Other Poems*, 1841.

12 It is easy to be independent when all behind you agree with you, but the difficulty comes when nine hundred and ninety-nine of your friends think you wrong.

> WENDELL PHILLIPS, *Speeches, Lectures and Letters*, 1863.

13 The self-evident truths announced in the Declaration of Independence are not truths at all, if taken literally; and the practical conclusions contained in the same passage of that Declaration prove that they were never designed to be so received.

> WILLIAM PINKNEY, in a speech in the U.S. Senate, February 15, 1820.

14 [The State] is not armed with superior wit or honesty, but with superior physical strength. I was not born to be forced. I will breathe after my own fashion. Let us see who is the strongest. . . . If a plant cannot live according to its nature, it dies; and so a man.

> HENRY DAVID THOREAU, "Civil Disobedience," 1849.

15 I would rather sit on a pumpkin and have it all to myself than be crowded on a velvet cushion. I would rather ride on earth in an ox cart, with a free circulation, than go to heaven in the fancy car of an excursion train and breathe a malaria all the way.

> HENRY DAVID THOREAU, *Walden*, 1854.

16 It is my living sentiment, and by the blessing of God it shall be my dying sentiment,—Independence now and Independence forever!

> DANIEL WEBSTER, in a eulogy for John Adams and Thomas Jefferson given on August 2, 1826.

17 Jefferson's Declaration of Independence is a practical document for the use of practical men. It is not a thesis for philosophers, but a whip for tyrants; it is not a theory of government, but a program of action.

> WOODROW WILSON, in a speech at Indianapolis, Indiana, April 13, 1911.

18 There is something better, if possible, that a man can give than his life. That is his living spirit

to a service that is not easy, to resist counsels that are hard to resist, to stand against purposes that are difficult to stand against.

> WOODROW WILSON, in a speech at Suresnes Cemetery, France, May 30, 1919.

119. INDIANA

1 The crossroads of America.

> State motto.

2 Oh the moonlight's fair tonight along the
>   Wabash,
> From the fields there comes the breath of
>   new-mown hay;
> Thro' the sycamores the candle lights are
>   gleaming,
> On the banks of the Wabash far away.

> PAUL DRESSER, in the song "On the Banks of the Wabash Far Away," 1897.

3 When an Eastern man is cheated by a Hoosier he is said to be *Wabashed.*

> RALPH WALDO EMERSON, entry written in 1860, *Journals,* 1909–1914.

4 Blest Indiana! in whose soil
> Men seek the sure rewards of toil,
> And honest poverty and worth
> Find here the best retreat on earth,
> While hosts of Preachers, Doctors, Lawyers,
> All independent as wood-sawyers,
> With men of every hue and fashion,
> Flock to the rising "Hoosier" nation.

> JOHN FINLEY, "The Hoosier's Nest," published as the "Address of the Carrier of the *Indianapolis Journal,*" January 1, 1833.

5 I come from Indiana, the home of more first-rated second-class men than any state in the Union.

> THOMAS R. MARSHALL, *Recollections,* 1925.

120. INDIVIDUALITY

See also CHARACTER; FREEDOM; INDEPENDENCE; LIBERTY

1 I'm a ragged individualist.

> Attributed to Jane Ace, in Goodman Ace, *The Fine Art of Hypochondria,* 1966.

2 If I smashed the traditions it was because I knew no traditions.

> MAUDE ADAMS, quoted in Ada Patterson, *Maude Adams: A Biography,* 1907.

3 Individualism, we are entitled to say, is, if not truth, the nearest thing we have to truth, no closer thing to truth in the field of social relations having appeared on the horizon.

> WILLIAM F. BUCKLEY, JR., *God and Man at Yale,* 1951.

4 Individuality is the aim of political liberty. By leaving to the citizen as much freedom of action and of being as comports with order and the rights of others, the institutions render him truly a freeman. He is left to pursue his means of happiness in his own manner.

> JAMES FENIMORE COOPER, *The American Democrat,* 1838.

5 Human diversity makes tolerance more than a virtue; it makes it a requirement for survival.

> RENÉ DUBOS, *Celebrations of Life,* 1981.

6 Any power must be an enemy of mankind which enslaves the individual by terror and force, whether it arises under the Fascist or the Communist flag. All that is valuable in human society depends upon the opportunity for development accorded to the individual.

> ALBERT EINSTEIN, in a statement in England, September 15, 1933.

7 *The true value of a human being* is determined primarily by the measure and the sense in which he has attained to liberation from the self.

> ALBERT EINSTEIN, *The World as I See It,* 1934.

8 Is it not the chief disgrace in the world, not to be an unit—not to be reckoned one character—not to yield that peculiar fruit which each man was created to bear, but to be reckoned in the gross, in the hundred, or the thousand, of the party, the section, to which we belong; and our opinion predicated geographically, as the north, or the south?

> RALPH WALDO EMERSON, *The American Scholar,* 1837.

9 The great majority of men are not original, for they are not primary, have not assumed their own vows, but are secondaries—grow up and grow old in seeming and following; and when they die they occupy themselves to the last with what others will think, and whether Mr. A and Mr. B will go to their funeral.

> RALPH WALDO EMERSON, entry written in 1841, *Journals,* 1909–1914.

10 Whoso would be a man, must be a Nonconformist.

> RALPH WALDO EMERSON, "Self-Reliance," *Essays,* First Series, 1841.

11 Good and bad are but names very readily transferable to that or this; the only right is what is after my constitution, the only wrong what is against it.

> Ibid.

12 Nature never rhymes her children, nor makes two men alike.

> RALPH WALDO EMERSON, "Character," *Essays,* Second Series, 1844.

13 We fancy men are individuals; so are pumpkins; but every pumpkin in the field goes through every point of pumpkin history.

> RALPH WALDO EMERSON, "Nominalist and Realist," *Essays,* Second Series, 1844.

14 You must pay for conformity. All goes well as long as you run with conformists. But you, who are honest men in other particulars, know that there is alive somewhere a man whose honesty reaches to this point also, that he shall not kneel to false gods, and, on the day when you meet him, you sink into the class of counterfeits.

> RALPH WALDO EMERSON, *English Traits,* 1856.

15 Singularity in right hath ruined many: Happy those who are convinced of the general Opinion.

> BENJAMIN FRANKLIN, *Poor Richard's Almanack,* 1757.

16 It is easier to live through someone else than to become complete yourself.

> BETTY FRIEDAN, *The Feminine Mystique,* 1963.

17 How little does heredity count as compared with conditions. This one, we say, is the result of a thousand years of European progress, and that one of a thousand years of Chinese petrifaction; yet, placed an infant in the heart of China, and but for the angle of the eye or the shade of the hair, the Caucasian would grow up as those around him, using the same speech, thinking the same thoughts, exhibiting the same tastes. Change Lady Vere de Vere in her cradle with an infant of the slums, and will the blood of a hundred earls give you a refined and cultured woman?

> HENRY GEORGE, *Progress and Poverty,* 1879.

18 I cannot and will not cut my conscience to fit this year's fashions.

> LILLIAN HELLMAN, in a letter to the House Committee on Un-American Activities, May 19, 1952.

19 If a man is in a minority of one we lock him up.

> OLIVER WENDELL HOLMES, JR., in a speech, "Law and the Court," New York City, February 15, 1913.

20 The American system of rugged individualism.

> HERBERT HOOVER, in a speech in New York City, October 22, 1928. (Hoover later made it clear that he had not originated the phrase, which had been in use for many years.)

21 Imitator: A man who succeeds in being an imitation.

> ELBERT HUBBARD, *The Roycroft Dictionary and Book of Epigrams,* 1923.

22 I never submitted the whole system of my opinions to the creed of any party of men whatever, in religion, in philosophy, in politics or in anything else, where I was capable of thinking for myself. Such an addiction is the last degradation of a free

and moral agent. If I could not go to Heaven but with a party, I would not go there at all.

> THOMAS JEFFERSON, in a letter to Francis Hopkinson, March 13, 1789.

23 I am of a sect by myself, as far as I know.

> THOMAS JEFFERSON, in a letter to Ezra Stiles, June 25, 1819.

24 One day our descendants will think it incredible that we paid so much attention to things like the amount of melanin in our skin or the shape of our eyes or our gender instead of the unique identities of each of us as complex human beings.

> FRANKLIN THOMAS, quoted in Gloria Steinem, *Outrageous Acts and Everyday Rebellions,* 1983.

25 I think that we should be men first, and subjects afterward.

> HENRY DAVID THOREAU, "Civil Disobedience," 1849.

26 Public opinion is a weak tyrant compared with our own private opinion. What a man thinks of himself, that it is which determines, or rather indicates, his fate.

> HENRY DAVID THOREAU, *Walden,* 1854.

27 The man who goes alone can start today; but he who travels with another must wait till that other is ready, and it may be a long time before they get off.

> Ibid.

28 If a man does not keep pace with his companions, perhaps it is because he hears a different drummer. Let him step to the music which he hears, however measured or far away.

> Ibid.

29 I celebrate myself, and sing myself.

> WALT WHITMAN, "Song of Myself," 1855.

30 Individuality, the pride and centripetal isolation of a human being in himself—personalism. . . . It forms, or is to form, the compensating balance-wheel of the successful working machinery of aggregate America.

> WALT WHITMAN, *Democratic Vistas,* 1871.

31 Must not the virtue of modern Individualism, continually enlarging, usurping all, seriously affect, perhaps keep down entirely, in America, the like of the ancient virtue of Patriotism, the fervid and absorbing love of general country?

> WALT WHITMAN, in a note to *Democratic Vistas,* 1871.

121. INSANITY

1 Mad, *adj.* Affected with a high degree of intellectual independence; not conforming to standards of thought, speech and action derived by the conformants from study of themselves; at odds with the majority; in short, unusual. It is noteworthy that persons are pronounced mad by officials destitute of evidence that themselves are sane.

> AMBROSE BIERCE, *The Devil's Dictionary,* 1906.

2 The lunatic asylum of the solar system.

> SAMUEL PARKES CADMAN, on the planet Earth, in a speech in New York City, November 17, 1935.

3 Much madness is divinest sense
  To a discerning eye;
Much sense the starkest madness.
  'Tis the majority
In this, as all, prevails.
  Assent, and you are sane;
Demur,—you're straightway dangerous,
  And handled with a chain.

> EMILY DICKINSON, "Much madness is divinest sense," in *Poems,* 1890.

4 I proceed, gentlemen, briefly to call attention to the present state of insane persons, confined within this Commonwealth, in cages, closets, cellars, stalls, pens! Chained, naked, beaten with rods, and lashed into obedience.

> DOROTHEA DIX, *Memorial to the Legislature of Massachusetts,* 1843.

5 Insanity is often the logic of an accurate mind overtaxed.

OLIVER WENDELL HOLMES, SR., *The Autocrat of the Breakfast-Table,* 1858.

6 It has at last become possible for large numbers of people to pass from the cradle to the grave without ever having had a pang of genuine fear. Many of us need an attack of mental disease to teach us the meaning of the word. Hence the possibility of so much blindly optimistic philosophy and religion.

WILLIAM JAMES, *The Principles of Psychology,* 1890.

7 Not so much of thee is left among us
As the hum outliving the hushed bell.

JAMES RUSSELL LOWELL, writing about his mother, in "The Darkened Mind," 1868.

8 Man's insanity is heaven's sense; and wandering from all mortal reason, man comes at last to that celestial thought, which, to reason, is absurd and frantic; and weal or woe, feels then uncompromised, indifferent as his God.

HERMAN MELVILLE, *Moby-Dick,* 1851.

9 Who in the rainbow can draw the line where the violet tint ends and the orange tint begins? Distinctly we see the difference of the colors, but where exactly does the one first blendingly enter into the other? So with sanity and insanity.

HERMAN MELVILLE, *Billy Budd,* 1924.

10 True!—nervous—very, very dreadfully nervous I had been and am; but why *will* you say that I am mad? The disease had sharpened my senses—not destroyed—not dulled them. Above all was the sense of hearing acute. I heard all things in the heaven and in the earth. I heard many things in hell. How, then, am I mad?

EDGAR ALLAN POE, "The Tell-Tale Heart," 1843.

11 There is nothing in the world so enjoyable as a thorough-going monomania.

AGNES REPPLIER, in "The Decay of Sentiment," *Books and Men,* 1888.

12 Sanity is a madness put to good uses.

GEORGE SANTAYANA, *Little Essays,* 1920.

122. INVECTIVE

See also LANGUAGE; ORATORY; SPEECH

1 God damn your god damned old hellfired god damned soul to hell god damn you and goddam your god damned family's god damned hellfired god damned soul to hell and god damnation god damn them and god damn your god damn friends to hell.

Text of a letter received by Abraham Lincoln, November 25, 1860.

2 Sir, Divine Providence takes care of his own Universe. Moral monsters cannot propagate. . . . Impotent of everything but malevolence of purpose, they can no otherwise multiply miseries than by blaspheming all that is pure and prosperous and happy. Could demon propagate demon, the Universe might become a Pandemonium; but I rejoice that the Father of Lies can never become the Father of Liars.

TRISTAM BURGES, attacking John Randolph on the subject of Randolph's impotence, quoted in William Cabell Bruce, *John Randolph of Roanoke,* 1922.

3 No thank you, I don't engage in criminal practice.

ROSCOE CONKLING, refusing to campaign for James G. Blaine, the Republican presidential candidate, 1884.

4 He has all the characteristics of a dog—except loyalty.

Attributed to Sam Houston, referring to Thomas Jefferson Green.

5 A sharp tongue is the only edged tool that grows keener with constant use.

WASHINGTON IRVING, "Rip Van Winkle," *The Sketch Book,* 1820.

6 Never trust a man who combs his hair straight from his left armpit.

ALICE ROOSEVELT LONGWORTH, referring to Douglas MacArthur, quoted in Michael Teague,

Mrs. L: Conversations with Alice Roosevelt Longworth, 1981.

7 Let them call me rebel, and welcome, I feel no concern from it; but I should suffer the misery of devils, were I to make a whore of my soul by swearing allegiance to one whose character is that of a sottish, stupid, stubborn, worthless, brutish man. I conceive likewise a horrid idea in receiving mercy from a being, who at the last day shall be shrieking to the rocks and mountains to cover him, and fleeing with terror from the orphan, the widow, and the slain of America.

THOMAS PAINE, *Common Sense,* January 10, 1776.

8 He is a man of splendid abilities, but utterly corrupt. He shines and stinks like rotten mackerel by moonlight.

JOHN RANDOLPH, on Edward Livingston, quoted in W. Cabell Bruce, *John Randolph of Roanoke,* 1922.

9 I will say to the gentleman that if I ever "made light" of his remarks, it is more than he ever made of them himself.

THOMAS BRACKETT REED, to William M. Springer of Illinois, in the House of Representatives, 1881.

10 You take the lies out of him, and he'll shrink to the size of your hat; you take the malice out of him, and he'll disappear.

MARK TWAIN, *Life on the Mississippi,* 1883.

11 He is useless on top of the ground; he ought to be under it, inspiring the cabbages.

MARK TWAIN, "Pudd'nhead Wilson's Calendar," *Pudd'nhead Wilson,* 1894.

---

123. INVENTION

See also GENIUS

---

1 A tool is but the extension of a man's hand, and a machine is but a complex tool. And he that in-vents a machine augments the power of a man and the well-being of mankind.

HENRY WARD BEECHER, "Business," *Proverbs from Plymouth Pulpit,* 1870.

2 Inventor, *n.* A person who makes an ingenious arrangement of wheels, levers and springs, and believes it civilization.

AMBROSE BIERCE, *The Devil's Dictionary,* 1906.

3 Telephone, *n.* An invention of the devil which abrogates some of the advantages of making a disagreeable person keep his distance.

Ibid.

4 In trying to make something new, half the undertaking lies in discovering whether it can be done. Once it has been established that it can, duplication is inevitable.

HELEN GAHAGAN DOUGLAS, *A Full Life,* 1982.

5 'Tis frivolous to fix pedantically the date of particular inventions. They have all been invented over and over fifty times. Man is the arch machine, of which all these shifts drawn from himself are toy models.

RALPH WALDO EMERSON, "Fate," *The Conduct of Life,* 1860.

6 Only an inventor knows how to borrow, and every man is or should be an inventor.

RALPH WALDO EMERSON, "Quotation and Originality," *Letters and Social Aims,* 1876.

7 Five thousand balloons, capable of raising two men each, could not cost more than five ships of the line; and where is the prince who can afford so to cover his country with troops for its defense as that 10,000 men descending from the clouds might not in many places do an infinite deal of mischief before a force could be brought together to repel them?

BENJAMIN FRANKLIN, in a letter to Jan Ingenhousz, January 16, 1784.

8 Now, boys, we have got her done, let's start her up and see why she doesn't work.

Attributed to John Fritz, engineer, upon building a new machine, quoted in David McCullough, *The Path Between the Seas,* 1978.

9 God forgives those who invent what they need.

LILLIAN HELLMAN, *The Little Foxes,* 1936.

10 I look upon the invention of Mr. Bessemer as almost the greatest invention of the ages. I do not mean measured by its chemical or mechanical attributes. I mean by virtue of its great results upon the structure of society and government. It is the great enemy of privilege. It is the great destroyer of monopoly. It will be the great equalizer of wealth.

ABRAM HEWITT, 1892, quoted in Elting E. Morison, *Men, Machines, and Modern Times,* 1966.

11 A man likes marvelous things; so he invents them, and is astonished.

EDGAR WATSON HOWE, *Sinner Sermons,* 1926.

12 Attention, the universe! By kingdoms, right wheel!

SAMUEL F.B. MORSE, message said to have been sent during an early demonstration of the telegraph, New York City, c.1837. (Morse was probably not the orginator of the message.)

13 All Wrigley had was an idea. He was the first man to discover that American jaws must wag. So why not give them something to wag against?

WILL ROGERS, on the invention of chewing gum, *The Illiterate Digest,* 1924.

14 What hath God wrought!

ALFRED VAIL, using a phrase from Numbers, in the first long-distance message sent by Morse telegraph from Washington, D.C., to Baltimore, Maryland, May 24, 1844.

15 Success. Four flights Thursday morning. All against twenty-one-mile wind. Started from level with engine power alone. Average speed through air thirty-one miles. Longest fifty-nine seconds. Inform press. Home Christmas.

ORVILLE AND WILBUR WRIGHT, in a telegram from Kitty Hawk, North Carolina, to their father, Rev. Milton Wright, December 17, 1903.

---

124. IOWA

---

1 Our liberties we prize and our rights we will maintain.

State motto.

2 Iowa spells agriculture, and agriculture in this part of the world spells corn. This is the heart of agrarian America.

JOHN GUNTHER, *Inside U.S.A.,* 1947.

3 The gold mines and the diamond mines of the world are cheap and trivial compared to the produce that Iowa breeds out of its land every year. Iowa could buy out the world's diamond production every year with hunks of ham and buckets of lard. Iowa would still have most of its produce left.

PHIL STONG, *Hawkeyes,* 1940.

4 The character of Iowa is essentially bucolic in the best senses of the word (and, to be quite honest, occasionally in some of the worst).

Ibid.

---

125. JOURNALISM

See also BOOKS; LITERATURE; WRITERS

---

1 A newspaper is a private enterprise, owing nothing to the public, which grants it no franchise. It is therefore affected with no public interest. It is emphatically the property of its owner, who is selling a manufactured product at his own risk.

Editorial comment in the *Wall Street Journal,* January 20, 1925.

2 The liberty of the press is essential to the security of freedom in a state.

JOHN ADAMS, in the Massachusetts Bill of Rights, 1780.

3 [Journalists] are a sort of assassins who sit with loaded blunderbusses at the corner of streets and fire them off for hire or for sport at any passenger they select.

> JOHN QUINCY ADAMS, diary entry, September 7, 1820.

4 To a newspaperman a human being is an item with the skin wrapped around it.

> Attributed to Fred Allen.

5 Newspapers are the schoolmasters of the common people. That endless book, the newspaper, is our national glory.

> HENRY WARD BEECHER, "The Press," *Proverbs from Plymouth Pulpit,* 1870.

6 I tell the honest truth in my paper, and I leave the consequences to God.

> JAMES GORDON BENNETT, SR., in the *New York Herald,* May 10, 1836.

7 What is to prevent a daily newspaper from being made the greatest organ of social life? Books have had their day—the theaters have had their day—the temple of religion has had its day. A newspaper can be made to take the lead of all these in the great movements of human thought and of human civilization.

> JAMES GORDON BENNETT, SR., in an editorial in the *New York Herald,* August 19, 1836.

8 The organs of opinion seem almost as numerous as the people themselves, and they are all engaged in representing their own view as that of the "people." Like other valuable articles, genuine opinion is surrounded by many counterfeits.

> JAMES BRYCE, *The American Commonwealth,* 1888.

9 The sovereign press for the most part acknowledges accountability to no one except its owners and publishers.

> ZECHARIAH CHAFEE, JR., "The Press Under Pressure," in the *Nieman Reports,* April, 1948.

10 The press, like fire, is an excellent servant, but a terrible master.

> JAMES FENIMORE COOPER, *The American Democrat,* 1838.

11 A man may utter with impunity that which he cannot publish with impunity. The distinction arises from the greater circulation, and the greater power to injure, of a published libel than of a spoken slander. The editor of a journal, therefore, does not possess the same immunities as an editor that he possesses as a private citizen.

> Ibid.

12 It is often made a matter of boasting, that the United States contain so many public journals. It were wiser to make it a cause of mourning, since the quality, in this instance, diminishes in an inverse ratio to the quantity.

> Ibid.

13 Journalism consists in buying white paper at two cents a pound and selling it at ten cents a pound.

> Attributed to Charles A. Dana.

14 When a dog bites a man that is not news, but when a man bites a dog, that is news.

> CHARLES A. DANA, "What is News?" in the *New York Sun,* 1882.

15 Th' newspaper does ivrything f'r us. It runs th' polis foorce an' th' banks, commands th' milishy, conthrols th' ligislachure, baptizes th' young, marries th' foolish, comforts th' afflicted, afflicts th' comfortable, buries th' dead an' roasts thim aftherward.

> FINLEY PETER DUNNE, *Observations by Mr. Dooley,* 1902.

16 I, like every soldier of America, will die for the freedom of the press, even for the freedom of newspapers that call me everything that is a good deal less than being a gentleman.

> DWIGHT D. EISENHOWER, in a press conference at Moscow, August 14, 1945.

17 I hate to be defended in a newspaper. As long as all that is said is said against me, I feel a certain assurance of success. But as soon as honeyed words of praise are spoken for me, I feel as one that lies unprotected before his enemies.

> RALPH WALDO EMERSON, "Compensation," *Essays,* First Series, 1841.

18 It doesn't matter what the press says about you. The press has always been traditionally . . . on the wrong side of most issues. . . . Don't let the press bother you. We've got a commitment here to do right if hell freezes over.

> JERRY FALWELL, at a rally in Arkansas, April, 1980.

19 Printers are educated in the belief that when men differ in opinion both sides ought equally to have the advantage of being heard by the public; and that when truth and error have fair play, the former is always an overmatch for the latter: hence they cheerfully serve all contending writers that pay them well, without regarding on which side they are of the question in dispute.

> BENJAMIN FRANKLIN, "Apology for Printers," in *The Pennsylvania Gazette,* June 10, 1731.

20 It is . . . unreasonable what some assert, "that printers ought not to print anything but what they approve"; since if all of that business should make such a resolution, and abide by it, an end would thereby be put to free writing, and the world would afterwards have nothing to read but what happen'd to be the opinions of printers.

> Ibid.

21 Backward ran sentences until reeled the mind.

> WOLCOTT GIBBS, parodying the writing style of *Time* magazine in "Time . . . Fortune . . . Life . . . Luce," in the *New Yorker,* November 28, 1936.

22 According to American principle and practice the public is the ruler of the State, and in order to rule rightly it should be informed correctly.

> WILLIAM RANDOLPH HEARST, quoted in the *New York Journal-American,* November 11, 1954.

23 The relationship between Government and the press in the nation's capital is so intimate as to be almost incestuous. Where newspapers in other parts of the world see it as their responsibility to lay a mine field for authority to walk through, the pundits and bureau chiefs of Washington's press corps often seem to regard it as their business instead to lay out a red carpet.

> ANTHONY HOWARD, quoted in Eugene J. McCarthy, *The Year of the People,* 1969.

24 Muckraker: One who sits on the fence and defames American enterprise as it marches by.

> ELBERT HUBBARD, *The Roycroft Dictionary and Book of Epigrams,* 1923.

25 The basis of our government's being the opinion of the people, the very first object should be to keep that right; and were it left to me to decide whether we should have a government without newspapers, or newspapers without a government, I should not hesitate a moment to prefer the latter.

> THOMAS JEFFERSON, in a letter to Col. Edward Carrington, January 16, 1787.

26 No government ought to be without censors; and where the press is free, no one ever will.

> THOMAS JEFFERSON, in a letter to George Washington, September 9, 1792. (Jefferson used "censor" to mean one who criticizes or censures the government.)

27 I have so completely withdrawn myself from these spectacles of usurpation and misrule, that I do not take a single newspaper, nor read one a month; and I feel myself infinitely the happier for it.

> THOMAS JEFFERSON, expressing unhappiness over events in Europe in a letter to Tench Coxe, May 1, 1794.

28 At a very early period of my life I determined never to put a sentence into any newspaper. I have religiously adhered to the resolution through my life, and have great reason to be contented with it.

> THOMAS JEFFERSON, in a letter to Samuel Smith, August 22, 1798.

29 [Newspapers] serve as chimneys to carry off noxious vapors and smoke.

> THOMAS JEFFERSON, in a letter to Tadeusz Kosciusko, April 2, 1802.

30 No experiment can be more interesting than that we are now trying, and which we trust will end in establishing the fact, that man may be governed by reason and truth. Our first object should therefore be, to leave open to him all the avenues to

truth. The most effectual hitherto found, is the freedom of the press. It is, therefore, the first shut up by those who fear the investigation of their actions.

THOMAS JEFFERSON, in a letter to Judge John Tyler, June 28, 1804.

31 It is a melancholy truth, that a suppression of the press could not more completely deprive the nation of its benefits, than is done by its abandoned prostitution to falsehood. Nothing can now be believed which is seen in a newspaper.

THOMAS JEFFERSON, in a letter to John Norvell, June 11, 1807.

32 The man who never looks into a newspaper is better informed than he who reads them; inasmuch as he who knows nothing is nearer to truth than he whose mind is filled with falsehoods and errors. He who reads nothing will still learn the great facts, and the details are all false.

Ibid.

33 Perhaps an editor might begin a reformation in some such way as this. Divide his paper into four chapters, heading the 1st, Truths. 2d, Probabilities. 3d, Possibilities. 4th, Lies.

Ibid.

34 Where the press is free, and every man able to read, all is safe.

THOMAS JEFFERSON, in a letter to Charles Yancey, January 6, 1816.

35 I read no newspaper now but Ritchie's, and in that chiefly the advertisements, for they contain the only truths to be relied on in a newspaper.

THOMAS JEFFERSON, in a letter to Nathaniel Macon, January 12, 1819.

36 [The press is] the best instrument for enlightening the mind of man, and improving him as a rational, moral, and social being.

THOMAS JEFFERSON, in a letter to A. Coray, October 31, 1823.

37 The only security of all is in a free press. The force of public opinion cannot be resisted, when permitted freely to be expressed. The agitation it produces must be submitted to. It is necessary, to keep the waters pure.

THOMAS JEFFERSON, in a letter to the Marquis de Lafayette, November 4, 1823.

38 Even though we never like it, and even though we wish they didn't write it, and even though we disapprove, there isn't any doubt at all that we could not do the job at all in a free society without a very, very active press.

JOHN F. KENNEDY, "Conversation with President Kennedy," December 17, 1962, in *Public Papers,* 1962.

39 Behold the whole huge earth sent to me hebdomadally in a brown-paper wrapper!

JAMES RUSSELL LOWELL, *The Biglow Papers,* First Series, 1848.

40 I du believe with all my soul
In the gret Press's freedom,
To pint the people to the goal
An' in the traces lead 'em.

Ibid.

41 In a world of daily—nay, almost hourly—journalism every clever man, every man who thinks himself clever, or whom anybody else thinks clever, is called upon to deliver his judgment point-blank and at the word of command on every conceivable subject of human thought.

JAMES RUSSELL LOWELL, address given October 6, 1884, in Birmingham, England, from *On Democracy,* 1884.

42 A popular Government, without popular information, or the means of acquiring it, is but a prologue to a farce or a tragedy; or, perhaps both.

JAMES MADISON, in a letter to W.T. Barry, August 4, 1832.

43 The freedom of the press is one of the great bulwarks of liberty, and can never be restrained but by despotic governments.

GEORGE MASON, in the Virginia Bill of Rights, June 12, 1776.

44 All successful newspapers are ceaselessly querulous and bellicose. They never defend anyone or

anything if they can help it; if the job is forced upon them, they tackle it by denouncing someone or something else.

H.L. MENCKEN, *Prejudices,* First Series, 1919.

45 You won't have Nixon to kick around anymore, because, gentlemen, this is my last press conference.

RICHARD M. NIXON, speaking to reporters after conceding defeat in his campaign for governor of California, November 7, 1962.

46 The media are far more powerful than the President in creating public awareness and shaping public opinion, for the simple reason that the media always have the last word.

RICHARD M. NIXON, *The Memoirs of Richard Nixon,* 1978.

47 There isn't another writer that has a worse reputation for inaccuracy, indecency, for recklessness, for malice, for hatred, for viciousness, for besmirching people's characters and destroying them.

LOUIS NIZER, on Westbrook Pegler, in his summation to the jury at Pegler's trial for libel against Quentin Reynolds, 1953, quoted in Oliver Pilat, *Pegler: Angry Man of the Press,* 1963.

48 All the news that's fit to print.

ADOLPH S. OCHS, motto of the *New York Times,* 1896.

49 It will be my earnest aim that the *New York Times* give the news, all the news, in concise and attractive form, in language that is permissible in good society, and give it early, if not earlier, than it can be learned through any other medium. To give the news impartially, without fear or favor, regardless of party, sect, or interest involved; to make the columns of the *New York Times* a forum for the consideration of all public questions of public importance, and, to that end, to invite intelligent discussion from all shades of opinion.

ADOLPH S. OCHS, in his salutary in the *New York Times,* August 18, 1896.

50 I am afraid I couldn't be trusted around Mr. Roosevelt. For the first time in my life in this business, I might find myself squabbling for a chance to carry the champion's water-bucket.

WESTBROOK PEGLER, on Franklin D. Roosevelt, c.1933, quoted in Oliver Pilat, *Pegler: Angry Man of the Press,* 1963.

51 My hates have always occupied my mind much more actively and have given greater spiritual satisfactions than my friendships. . . . The wish to favor a friend is not as active as the instinct to annoy some person or institution I detest.

WESTBROOK PEGLER, in his column "Fair Enough," quoted in Oliver Pilat, *Pegler: Angry Man of the Press,* 1963.

52 Of all the fantastic fog-shapes that have risen off the swamp of confusion since the big war, the most futile, and, at the same time, the most pretentious is the deep-thinking, hair-trigger columnist or commentator who knows all the answers offhand and can settle great affairs with absolute finality three days or even six days a week.

Ibid.

53 We live under a government of men and morning newspapers.

Attributed to Wendell Phillips.

54 An institution that should always fight for progress and reform, never tolerate injustice or corruption, always fight demagogues of all parties, never belong to any party, always oppose privileged classes and public plunderers, never lack sympathy with the poor, always remain devoted to the public welfare, never be satisfied with merely printing news, always be drastically independent, never be afraid to attack wrong, whether by predatory plutocracy or predatory poverty.

JOSEPH PULITZER, editorial on becoming publisher of the *New York World,* May 10, 1883.

55 Nothing less than the highest ideals, the most scrupulous anxiety to do right, the most accurate knowledge of the problems it has to meet, and a sincere sense of moral responsibility will save journalism from a subservience to business interests, seeking selfish ends, antagonistic to public welfare.

JOSEPH PULITZER, "The College of Journalism," in the *North American Review,* May, 1904.

56 I write from the worm's-eye point of view.

ERNIE PYLE, *Here Is Your War,* 1943.

57 That potent engine, the dread of tyrants, and of villains, but the shield of freedom and of worth.

> JOHN RANDOLPH, on the press, in a speech in Congress, January 29, 1805.

58 All I know is what I see in the papers.

> WILL ROGERS, remark he used in several speeches and articles, c.1928.

59 It is very difficult to have a free, fair and honest press anywhere in the world. . . . As a rule, papers are largely supported by advertising, and that immediately gives the advertisers a certain hold over the medium which they use.

> ELEANOR ROOSEVELT, *If You Ask Me,* 1946.

60 The men with the muckrakes are often indispensable to the well-being of society; but only if they know when to stop raking the muck, and look upward to the celestial crown above them, to the crown of worthy endeavor. There are beautiful things above and round about them; and if they gradually grow to feel that the whole world is nothing but muck, their power of usefulness is gone.

> THEODORE ROOSEVELT, in an address in Washington, D.C., April 14, 1906.

61 In our country I am inclined to think that almost, if not quite, the most important profession is that of the newspaper man, including the man of the magazines, especially the cheap magazines, and the weeklies.

> THEODORE ROOSEVELT, in a speech in Milwaukee, Wisconsin, September 7, 1910.

62 *The New Yorker* will not be edited for the old lady from Dubuque.

> HAROLD ROSS, on the founding of the magazine he edited for so long, 1925.

63 I ain't no lady. I'm a newspaperwoman.

> HAZEL BRANNON SMITH, quoted by T. George Harris in *Look* magazine, November 16, 1965.

64 He had discovered that there was room at the bottom and with sensational news sensationally written and pictured, he did reach for and get the people. He was a demagogue; he was pro-labor. I

cannot describe the hate of those days for Hearst except to say that it was worse than it is now.

> LINCOLN STEFFENS, writing about William Randolph Hearst in *The Autobiography of Lincoln Steffens,* 1931.

65 The sources of information are the springs from which democracy drinks.

> ADLAI E. STEVENSON, in a speech in Cincinnati, Ohio, October 19, 1956.

66 Your typewriter is a public trust. The sound may be the most beautiful noise you know. But it has meaning and justification only if it is a part of the gloriously discordant symphony of a free society.

> ADLAI E. STEVENSON, in a speech in Washington, D.C., December 12, 1960.

67 Newspapers, television networks, and magazines have sometimes been outrageously abusive, untruthful, arrogant, and hypocritical. But it hardly follows that elimination of a strong and independent press is the way to eliminate abusiveness, untruth, arrogance, or hypocrisy from government itself.

> POTTER STEWART, in a speech at Yale University Law School, 1974.

68 Here shall the Press the People's right
  maintain,
  Unawed by influence and unbribed by gain;
  Here patriot Truth her glorious precepts
  draw,
  Pledged to Religion, Liberty, and Law.

> JOSEPH STORY, motto of the *Salem Register,* Massachusetts, 1802.

69 The vital measure of a newspaper is not its size but its spirit—that is its responsibility to report the news fully, accurately and fairly.

> ARTHUR HAYS SULZBERGER, accepting an award from Temple Israel to the *New York Times,* Boston, May 9, 1956.

70 To a philosopher all *news,* as it is called, is gossip, and they who edit and read it are old women over their tea.

> HENRY DAVID THOREAU, *Walden,* 1854.

71 In order to enjoy the inestimable benefits that the liberty of the press ensures, it is necessary to submit to the inevitable evils that it creates.

ALEXIS DE TOCQUEVILLE, *Democracy in America,* 1835.

72 The average consumption of newspapers by an American must amount to about three a day.

ANTHONY TROLLOPE, "Education and Religion," *North America,* 1862.

73 I have been reading the morning paper. I do it every morning—well knowing that I shall find in it the usual depravities and basenesses and hypocrisies and cruelties that make up civilization, and cause me to put in the rest of the day pleading for the damnation of the human race.

MARK TWAIN, in a letter to William Dean Howells, 1899.

74 Get your facts first, and then you can distort 'em as much as you please.

MARK TWAIN, to Rudyard Kipling, quoted in Rudyard Kipling, *From Sea to Sea,* 1899.

75 There are only two forces that can carry light to all corners of the globe—the sun in the heavens and the Associated Press.

MARK TWAIN, in a speech at the annual dinner of the Associated Press, New York City, September 18, 1906.

76 Women, wampum, and wrongdoing are always news.

STANLEY WALKER, *City Editor,* 1938.

77 The press in our free country is reliable and useful not because of its good character but because of its great diversity. As long as there are many owners, each pursuing his own brand of truth, we the people have the opportunity to arrive at the truth and to dwell in the light. . . . There is safety in numbers: the papers expose each other's follies and peccadillos, correct each other's mistakes, and cancel out each other's biases. The reader is free to range around in the whole editorial bouillabaisse and explore it for the one clam that matters—the truth.

E.B. WHITE, in a letter to W.B. Jones, January 30, 1976, collected in Dorothy Lobrano Guth, *The Letters of E.B. White,* 1976.

78 In America the president reigns for four years, and journalism governs for ever and ever.

OSCAR WILDE, *The Soul of Man under Socialism,* 1891.

79 There is a serious profession of journalism, and it involves its own special problems. To write what you are interested in writing, and to succeed in getting editors to pay for it, is a feat that may require pretty close calculation and a good deal of ingenuity.

EDMUND WILSON, in *Letters on Literature and Politics 1912–1972,* 1977.

---

126. JUSTICE

See also CIVIL RIGHTS; CRIME; EQUALITY; FREEDOM; LAW; PUNISHMENT; REVENGE

---

1 Facts are stubborn things; and whatever may be our wishes, our inclinations, or the dictates of our passions, they cannot alter the state of facts and evidence.

JOHN ADAMS, arguing in defense of the British soldiers involved in the Boston Massacre, December, 1770.

2 Justice, though due to the accused, is due to the accuser also. The concept of fairness must not be strained till it is narrowed to a filament. We are to keep the balance true.

BENJAMIN N. CARDOZO, in a Supreme Court opinion, *Snyder* v. *Commonwealth of Massachusetts,* 1934.

3 When a just cause reaches its flood tide . . . whatever stands in the way must fall before its overwhelming power.

CARRIE CHAPMAN CATT, in a speech in Stockholm, Sweden, "Is Woman Suffrage Progressing?" 1911.

4 As long as the world shall last there will be wrongs, and if no man objected and no man rebelled, those wrongs would last forever.

> CLARENCE DARROW, speaking to a jury in Chicago, 1920, quoted in Arthur Weinberg, *Attorney for the Damned,* 1957.

5 There is no such thing as justice—in or out of court.

> CLARENCE DARROW, in an interview in the *New York Times,* April 19, 1936.

6 Hogan's r-right whin he says: "Justice is blind." Blind she is, an' deef an' dumb an' has a wooden leg.

> FINLEY PETER DUNNE, *Mr. Dooley's Opinions,* 1900.

7 One man's justice is another's injustice; one man's beauty another's ugliness; one man's wisdom another's folly as one beholds the same objects from a higher point. One man thinks justice consists in paying debts, and has no measure in his abhorrence of another who is very remiss in his duty and makes the creditor wait tediously. But that second man has his own way of looking at things; asks himself Which debt must I pay first, the debt to the rich, or the debt to the poor? the debt of money, or the debt of thought to mankind, of genius to nature?

> RALPH WALDO EMERSON, "Circles," *Essays,* First Series, 1841.

8 The judge weighs the arguments and puts a brave face on the matter, and, since there must be a decision, decides as he can, and hopes he has done justice and given satisfaction to the community.

> RALPH WALDO EMERSON, *The Conduct of Life,* 1860.

9 Whoever fights, whoever falls,
Justice conquers evermore, . . .
And he who battles on her side,
God, though he were ten times slain,
Crowns him victor glorified,
Victor over death and pain.

> RALPH WALDO EMERSON, "Voluntaries," published in the *Atlantic Monthly,* 1863.

10 Capital punishment is as fundamentally wrong as a cure for crime as charity is wrong as a cure for poverty.

> Attributed to Henry Ford.

11 A Mob's a Monster; Heads enough, but no Brains.

> BENJAMIN FRANKLIN, *Poor Richard's Almanack,* 1747.

12 That which is unjust can really profit no one; that which is just can really harm no one.

> HENRY GEORGE, *The Irish Land Question,* 1881.

13 For every social wrong there must be a remedy. But the remedy can be nothing less than the abolition of the wrong.

> HENRY GEORGE, *Social Problems,* 1884.

14 That justice is the highest quality in the moral hierarchy I do not say, but that it is the first. That which is above justice must be based on justice, and include justice, and be reached through justice.

> Ibid.

15 How long we shall continue to blunder along without the aid of unpartisan and authoritative scientific assistance in the administration of justice, no one knows; but all fair persons not conventionalized by provincial legal habits of mind ought, I should think, unite to effect some such change.

> LEARNED HAND, in an opinion, *Parke, Davis & Co. v. H.K. Mulford Co.,* 1911.

16 There is no surer way to misread any document than to read it literally. . . . As nearly as we can, we must put ourselves in the place of those who uttered the words, and try to divine how they would have dealt with the unforeseen situation; and, although their words are by far the most decisive evidence of what they would have done, they are by no means final.

> LEARNED HAND, in an opinion, *Giuseppi v. Walling,* 1944.

17 Justice, I think, is the tolerable accommodation of the conflicting interests of society, and I don't believe there is any royal road to attain such accommodations concretely.

LEARNED HAND, quoted in Philip Hamburger, *The Great Judge,* 1946.

18 Generosity is the flower of justice.

NATHANIEL HAWTHORNE, entry written December 19, 1850, in *Passages from the American Notebooks,* 1868.

19 The founders of a new colony, whatever Utopia of human virtue and happiness they might originally project, have invariably recognized it among their earliest practical necessities to allot a portion of virgin soil as a cemetery, and another portion as the site of a prison.

NATHANIEL HAWTHORNE, *The Scarlet Letter,* 1850.

20 Mob law does not become due process of law by securing the assent of a terrorized jury.

OLIVER WENDELL HOLMES, JR., in a dissenting Supreme Court opinion, *Frank v. Mangum,* 1915.

21 Justice: A system of revenge where the State imitates the criminal.

ELBERT HUBBARD, *The Roycroft Dictionary and Book of Epigrams,* 1923.

22 There is but one blasphemy, and that is injustice.

ROBERT G. INGERSOLL, in a speech in Chicago, Illinois, September 20, 1880.

23 We must remember that we have to make judges out of men, and that by being made judges their prejudices are not diminished and their intelligence is not increased.

ROBERT G. INGERSOLL, in a speech in Washington, D.C., October 22, 1883.

24 Justice is always the same, whether it be due from one man to a million, or from a million to one man.

Attributed to John Jay.

25 An individual, thinking himself injured, makes more noise than a State.

THOMAS JEFFERSON, in a letter to the Georgia delegates in Congress, December 22, 1785.

26 [It is] more dangerous that even a guilty person should be punished without the forms of law than that he should escape.

THOMAS JEFFERSON, in a letter to William Carmichael, May 27, 1788. (Jefferson was discussing a group of armed people acting to prevent the lynching of a physician accused of robbing graves.)

27 The sword of the law should never fall but on those whose guilt is so apparent as to be pronounced by their friends as well as foes.

THOMAS JEFFERSON, in a letter to Sarah Mease, March, 1801.

28 I believe . . . that [justice] is instinct and innate, that the moral sense is as much a part of our constitution as that of feeling, seeing, or hearing.

THOMAS JEFFERSON, in a letter to John Adams, October 14, 1816.

29 Injustice anywhere is a threat to justice everywhere.

MARTIN LUTHER KING, JR., in a letter written from his jail cell in Birmingham, Alabama, published in the *Atlantic Monthly,* August, 1963.

30 Why should there not be a patient confidence in the ultimate justice of the people? Is there any better or equal hope in the world?

ABRAHAM LINCOLN, in his first inaugural address, March 4, 1861.

31 A jury too frequently has at least one member more ready to hang the panel than to hang the traitor.

ABRAHAM LINCOLN, in a letter to Erastus Corning *et al.,* June 12, 1863.

32 He reminds me of the man who murdered both his parents, and then, when sentence was about to be pronounced, pleaded for mercy on the grounds that he was an orphan.

Attributed to Abraham Lincoln. (The same idea was expressed by Artemus Ward in the newspaper sketch "A Hard Case.")

33 Man is unjust, but God is just; and finally justice triumphs.

HENRY WADSWORTH LONGFELLOW, *Evangeline,* 1847.

34 Exact justice is commonly more merciful in the long run than pity, for it tends to foster in men those stronger qualities which make them good citizens.

> JAMES RUSSELL LOWELL, "Dante," *Among My Books,* 1876.

35 Justice is the end of government. It is the end of civil society. It ever has been and ever will be pursued until it be obtained, or until liberty be lost in the pursuit.

> JAMES MADISON, *The Federalist,* No. 51, 1787–1788.

36 Injustice is relatively easy to bear; what stings is justice.

> H.L. MENCKEN, *Prejudices,* Third Series, 1922.

37 Judge—a law student who marks his own examination-papers.

> H.L. MENCKEN, "Sententiae," *The Vintage Mencken,* 1955.

38 Man's capacity for justice makes democracy possible, but man's inclination to injustice makes democracy necessary.

> REINHOLD NIEBUHR, *The Children of Light and the Children of Darkness,* 1944.

39 Any modern community which establishes a tolerable justice is the beneficiary of the ironic triumph of the wisdom of common sense over the foolishness of its wise men.

> REINHOLD NIEBUHR, *The Irony of American History,* 1962.

40 A few men may make a mob as well as many.

> WENDELL PHILLIPS, in a speech on the murder by a mob of Elijah P. Lovejoy, delivered in Boston, December 8, 1837.

41 Our judges have been, on the whole, both able and upright public servants. . . . But their whole training and the aloofness of their position on the bench prevent their having, as a rule, any real knowledge of, or understanding sympathy with, the lives and needs of the ordinary hard-working toiler.

> THEODORE ROOSEVELT, in a speech in Santiago, Chile, November 22, 1913.

42 There is a higher law than the Constitution.

> WILLIAM H. SEWARD, in a speech in the U.S. Senate, March 11, 1850.

43 Communism is the corruption of a dream of justice.

> ADLAI E. STEVENSON, in a speech in Urbana, Illinois, 1951.

44 A government in which the majority rule in all cases cannot be based on justice, even as far as men understand it.

> HENRY DAVID THOREAU, "Civil Disobedience," 1849.

45 If the injustice is part of the necessary friction of the machine of government, let it go, let it go; perchance it will wear smooth—certainly the machine will wear out.

> Ibid.

46 Under a government which imprisons any unjustly, the true place for a just man is also a prison.

> Ibid.

47 The jury system puts a ban upon intelligence and honesty, and a premium upon ignorance, stupidity, and perjury.

> MARK TWAIN, *Roughing It,* 1872.

48 Are you going to hang him *anyhow*—and try him afterwards?

> Ibid.

49 If it had not been for these thing, I might have live out my life talking at street corners to scorning men. I might have die, unmarked, unknown, a failure. Now we are not a failure. This is our career and our triumph. Never in our full life could we hope to do such work for tolerance, for joostice, for man's understanding of men as now we do by accident. Our words—our lives—our pains—nothing! The taking of our lives—lives of a good shoemaker and a poor fish-peddler—all! That last moment belongs to us—that agony is our triumph.

BARTOLOMEO VANZETTI, in a statement on the death sentences imposed on him and Nicola Sacco for the 1920 killing of a paymaster, April 9, 1927.

50 The administration of justice is the firmest pillar of government.

GEORGE WASHINGTON, in a letter to Edmund Randolph, September 27, 1789.

51 There is no happiness, there is no liberty, there is no enjoyment of life, unless a man can say, when he rises in the morning, I shall be subject to the decision of no unwise judge today.

DANIEL WEBSTER, in a speech in New York City, March 10, 1831.

52 Justice, sir, is the great interest of man on earth. It is the ligament which holds civilized beings and civilized nations together.

DANIEL WEBSTER, in a funeral address for Joseph Story, September 12, 1845.

53 Judging from the main portions of the history of the world, so far, justice is always in jeopardy.

WALT WHITMAN, *Democratic Vistas*, 1870.

54 The hope of all who suffer,
The dread of all who wrong.

JOHN GREENLEAF WHITTIER, characterizing the Union cause in the Civil War, in "The Mantle of St. John De Matha," 1865.

55 Justice has nothing to do with expediency. Justice has nothing to do with any temporary standard whatever. It is rooted and grounded in the fundamental instincts of humanity.

WOODROW WILSON, in a speech in Washington, D.C., February 26, 1916.

127. KANSAS

1 Ad astra per aspera. (To the stars through difficulties.)

State motto.

2 Happy is the man who wakens to find he has wandered from Kansas only in a dream.

Attributed to Foster Dwight Coburn, 1881.

3 First in Freedom, First in Wheat.

Kansas slogan, quoted in Dwight D. Eisenhower, *Eisenhower Speaks,* 1948.

4 The roosters lay eggs in Kansas.
The roosters lay eggs as big as beer kegs.
And the hair grows on their legs in Kansas.

Popular song, c.1880.

5 Raise less corn and more *Hell.*

Advice to the farmers of Kansas, attributed to Mary Elizabeth (mistakenly called Mary Ellen) Lease, but possibly "coined by a hostile reporter," according to Roger Butterfield, in *The American Past,* 1957.

6 To understand why people say "Dear old Kansas!" is to understand that Kansas is no mere geographical expression, but a state of mind, a religion, and a philosophy in one.

CARL LOTUS BECKER, "Kansas," 1910.

7 There is no monument under heaven on which I would rather have my name inscribed than on this goodly state of Kansas.

HENRY WARD BEECHER, in a speech at Emporia, Kansas, 1883.

8 Kansas, in sum, is one of our finest states and lives a sane, peaceful, and prosperous life.

PEARL S. BUCK, *America,* 1971.

9 Kansas is the navel of the nation. Diagonals drawn from Duluth to Galveston, from Washington to San Francisco, from Tallahassee to Olympia, from Sacramento to Augusta, intersect it in its center.

JOHN JAMES INGALLS, in a speech in the U.S. Senate, c.1885.

10 We preferred the comparatively simple but more intelligent life of Kansas to Washington. There are some intelligent people in Washington. More of 'em in Kansas.

ALFRED M. "ALF" LANDON, speaking of his decision not to run for the Senate after his defeat in the 1936 presidential race, quoted in *American Heritage* magazine, April, 1970.

11 If I ever wander in my affection for freedom, I shall come up here [to Kansas] and renew it. Men will yet come to Kansas as they came of old to Jerusalem.

> WILLIAM H. SEWARD, in an address at Lawrence, Kansas, 1860.

12 The Crime Against Kansas.

> CHARLES SUMNER, title given his antislavery speech in the Senate, containing invective aimed at Sen. Andrew P. Butler of South Carolina and other Southerners, May 19–20, 1856. (The speech triggered the notorious caning of Sumner by Butler's nephew, Preston Brooks, on the Senate floor on May 22, 1856.)

13 What's the Matter With Kansas?

> WILLIAM ALLEN WHITE, title of his best-known editorial, in the *Emporia Gazette,* August 15, 1896.

14 We have an old mossback Jacksonian who snorts and howls because there is a bathtub in the State House; we are running that old jay for Governor. We have another shabby, wild-eyed, rattle-brained fanatic who has said openly in a dozen speeches that "the rights of the user are paramount to the rights of the owner"; we are running him for Chief Justice, so that capital will come tumbling over itself to get into the state. We have raked the old ash heap of failure in the state and found an old human hoop skirt who has failed as a businessman, who has failed as an editor, who has failed as a preacher, and we are going to run him for Congressman-at-Large.

> Ibid.

15 Kansas is the child of Plymouth Rock.

> WILLIAM ALLEN WHITE, *Autobiography,* 1946.

128. KENTUCKY

1 United we stand, divided we fall.

> State motto.

2 Here's to old Kentucky,
  The State where I was born,
Where the corn is full of kernels,
  And the Colonels full of corn.

> A Kentucky toast.

3 There are children lucky from dawn till dusk,
But never a child so lucky!
For I cut my teeth on "Money Musk"
In the Bloody Ground of Kentucky!

> STEPHEN VINCENT BENÉT, "The Ballad of William Sycamore," 1922, collected in *Selected Works of Stephen Vincent Benét,* 1942.

4 She was bred in old Kentucky,
  Where the meadow grass is blue,
There's the sunshine of the country
  In her face and manner, too;
She was bred in old Kentucky,
Take her, boy, you're mighty lucky,
  When you marry a girl like Sue.

> HARRY BRAISTED, "She Was Bred in Old Kentucky," 1898.

5 [Louisville] is regular and cheerful: the streets being laid out at right angles, and planted with young trees. The buildings are smoky and blackened, from the use of bituminous coal, but an Englishman is well used to that appearance, and indisposed to quarrel with it. There did not appear to be much business stirring; and some unfinished buildings and improvements seemed to intimate that the city had been overbuilt in the ardor of "going ahead," and was suffering under the reaction consequent upon such feverish forcing of its powers.

> CHARLES DICKENS, *American Notes,* 1842.

6 The sun shines bright in the old Kentucky
  Home.

> Stephen Collins Foster, "My Old Kentucky
> Home," 1853.

7 Weep no more, my lady;
  Oh, weep no more today!
  We will sing one song for the old Kentucky
  Home,
  For the old Kentucky Home, far away.

> Ibid.

8 Here's a health to old Kentucky,
  Where the fathers, through the years,
  Hand down the courtly graces
  To the sons of cavaliers;
  Where the golden age is regnant,
  And each succeeding morn
  Finds "the corn is full of kernels,
  And the Colonels full of corn."

> William J. Lampton, "To Old Kentucky."

9 The moonlight is the softest, in Kentucky;
  Summer days come oftest, in Kentucky;
  Friendship is the strongest,
  Love's fires glow the longest,
  Yet a wrong is always wrongest,
  In Kentucky.

> James H. Mulligan, "In Kentucky."

10 Great, tall, raw-boned Kentuckians, attired in
hunting-shirts, and trailing their loose joints over a
vast extent of territory, with the easy lounge peculiar to the race.

> Harriet Beecher Stowe, Uncle Tom's Cabin,
> 1852.

11 Hurrah for Old Kentucky! That's the way to
do it. Give 'em hell, damn 'em.

> Zachary Taylor, to the 2nd Kentucky
> Regiment at the Battle of Buena Vista, Mexico,
> February 23, 1847.

129. KNOWLEDGE

See also Books; Education; Experience;
Perception; Philosophy; Science;
Wisdom

1 Curiosity killed the cat.

> Popular saying (frequently completed with "but
> satisfaction brought it back").

2 I'm astounded by people who want to "know"
the universe when it's hard enough to find your way
around Chinatown.

> Attributed to Woody Allen.

3 We don't know a millionth of one percent about
anything.

> Attributed to Thomas Edison.

4 Of all kinds of knowledge that we can ever obtain, the knowledge of God and the knowledge of
ourselves are the most important.

> Jonathan Edwards, Freedom of Will, 1754.

5 No facts are to me sacred; none are profane; I
simply experiment, an endless seeker with no Past
at my back.

> Ralph Waldo Emerson, "Circles," Essays,
> First Series, 1841.

6 You shall not know too much. There is a difference between a judge's and a deputy sheriff's
knowledge of the world, and again between that of
the last and a burglar's.

> Ralph Waldo Emerson, entry written in 1845,
> Journals, 1909–1914.

7 Knowledge is the knowing that we cannot know.

> Ralph Waldo Emerson, "Montaigne,"
> Representative Men, 1850.

8 Our knowledge is the amassed thought and experience of innumerable minds: our language, our
science, our religion, our opinions, our fancies we
inherited.

> Ralph Waldo Emerson, "Quotation and
> Originality," Letters and Social Aims, 1876.

9 To be proud of Knowledge is to be blind with Light.

BENJAMIN FRANKLIN, *Poor Richard's Almanack,* 1756.

10 To know is not less than to feel.

OLIVER WENDELL HOLMES, JR., in conversation with William James, c.1866.

11 I was at that age when a man knows least and is most vain of his knowledge; and when he is extremely tenacious in defending his opinion upon subjects about which he knows nothing.

WASHINGTON IRVING, "Buckthorne; or, the Young Man of Great Expectations," *Tales of a Traveller,* 1824.

12 If we could first know where we are, and whither we are tending, we could better judge what to do, and how to do it.

ABRAHAM LINCOLN, in a speech at Springfield, Illinois, June 16, 1858.

13 Ignorance is of a peculiar nature; once dispelled, it is impossible to re-establish it. It is not originally a thing of itself, but is only the absence of knowledge; and though man may be *kept* ignorant, he cannot be *made* ignorant.

THOMAS PAINE, *The Rights of Man,* 1791–1792.

14 Yet these men had no need to travel to be as wise as Solomon in all his glory, so similar are the lives of men in all countries, and fraught with the same homely experiences. One half the world *knows* how the other half lives.

HENRY DAVID THOREAU, *A Week on the Concord and Merrimack Rivers,* 1849.

15 What is most of our boasted so-called knowledge but a conceit that we know something, which robs us of the advantage of our actual ignorance? What we call knowledge is often our positive ignorance; ignorance our negative knowledge.

HENRY DAVID THOREAU, "Walking," the *Atlantic Monthly,* June, 1862.

16 A man's ignorance sometimes is not only useful, but beautiful,—while his knowledge, so called, is oftentimes worse than useless, besides being ugly.

Ibid.

17 It is better to ask some of the questions than to know all the answers.

JAMES THURBER, "The Scotty Who Knew Too Much," *Fables for Our Time,* 1940.

18 I am thankful that the good God created us all ignorant. I am glad that when we change His plans in this regard we have to do it at our own risk.

MARK TWAIN, in a letter to the *San Francisco Alta California,* May 28, 1867.

19 Although kingdoms and provinces may be wrested from the hands that hold them . . . it is the glorious prerogative of the empire of knowledge, that what it gains it never loses. On the contrary, it increases by the multiple of its own power; all its ends become means; all its attainments, helps to new conquests.

DANIEL WEBSTER, in an address at the laying of the cornerstone of the Bunker Hill Monument, June 17, 1825.

20 Knowledge, in truth, is the great sun in the firmament. Life and power are scattered with all its beams.

Ibid.

21 Thoughts may be bandits. Thoughts may be raiders. Thoughts may be invaders. Thoughts may be disturbers of international peace.

WOODROW WILSON, in an address to the National Press Club, May 16, 1916.

---

130. KOREAN WAR

See also WAR

---

1 Red China is not the powerful nation seeking to dominate the world. Frankly, in the opinion of the Joint Chiefs of Staff, this strategy would involve us in the wrong war, at the wrong place, at the wrong time, and with the wrong enemy.

GEN. OMAR BRADLEY, testifying before a Senate committee on the desirability of widening the Korean War, May 15, 1951.

2 I shall go to Korea.

> DWIGHT D. EISENHOWER, in a statement in
> Detroit, Michigan, during his presidential
> campaign, October 24, 1952.

3 [Chinese military intervention] created a new war and an entirely new situation, a situation not contemplated when our forces were committed against the North Korean invaders; a situation which called for new decisions in the diplomatic sphere to permit the realistic adjustment of military strategy. Such decisions have not been forthcoming.

> GEN. DOUGLAS MACARTHUR, in his address to a
> joint session of Congress, April 19, 1951.

4 Of the nations of the world, Korea alone, up to now, is the sole one which has risked its all against communism. The magnificence of the courage and fortitude of the Korean people defies description.

> Ibid.

5 I have just left your fighting sons in Korea. They have met all tests there, and I can report to you without reservation that they are splendid in every way. It was my constant effort to preserve them and end this savage conflict honorably and with the least loss of time and a minimum sacrifice of life. Its growing bloodshed has caused me the deepest anguish and anxiety. Those gallant men will remain often in my thoughts, and in my prayers always.

> Ibid.

6 It isn't just dust that is settling in Korea, Senator, it is American blood.

> GEN. DOUGLAS MACARTHUR, remark during
> Senate hearings, quoted in *Time* magazine, May
> 14, 1951.

7 Our first line of defense for Western Europe is not the Elbe, it is not the Rhine—it is the Yalu.

> GEN. DOUGLAS MACARTHUR, in a speech in
> 1951, quoted in William Manchester, *American
> Caesar,* 1978.

8 It is fatal to enter any war without the will to win it.

> GEN. DOUGLAS MACARTHUR, in a speech to the
> Republican National Convention, July 7, 1952.

9 In the final analysis, the issue now joined right here in Korea is whether Communism or individual freedom shall prevail; whether the plight of fear-driven people we have witnessed here shall be checked, or shall at some future time, however distant, engulf our own loved ones in all its misery and despair.

> GEN. MATTHEW B. RIDGWAY, in a message to
> the U.S. Eighth Army, January 21, 1951.

10 The willingness to settle for a stalemate . . . was all that brought peace to Korea. . . . We had finally come to realize that military victory was not what it had been in the past—that it might even elude us forever if the means we used to achieve it brought wholesale devastation to the world or led us down the road of international immorality past the point of no return.

> GEN. MATTHEW B. RIDGWAY, *The Korean
> War,* 1967.

11 The attack upon Korea makes it plain beyond all doubt that Communism has passed beyond the use of subversion to conquer independent nations and will now use armed invasion and war.

> HARRY S TRUMAN, in a statement to the press,
> June 27, 1950.

12 I wasn't going to let this attack on the Republic of Korea . . . go forward. Because if it wasn't stopped, it would lead to a third world war, and I wasn't going to let that happen. Not while I was President.

> HARRY S TRUMAN, quoted in Merle Miller,
> *Plain Speaking,* 1974.

13 This was a police action, a limited war, whatever you want to call it to stop aggression and to prevent a big war. And that's all it ever was.

> Ibid.

14 I fired him because he wouldn't respect the authority of the President. That's the answer to that. I didn't fire him because he was a dumb son of a bitch, although he was, but that's not against the law for generals. If it was, half to three-quarters of them would be in jail.

> HARRY S TRUMAN, on his dismissal of Gen.
> Douglas MacArthur, quoted in Merle Miller,
> *Plain Speaking,* 1974.

15 If we had not persuaded the United Nations to back up the free Republic of Korea, Western Europe would have gone into the hands of the Communists.

> HARRY S TRUMAN, *The Autobiography of Harry S Truman,* 1980.

---

131. LABOR MOVEMENT

See also BUSINESS; ECONOMICS; MONEY; POVERTY; WEALTH

---

1 The working class and the employing class have nothing in common. There can be no peace so long as hunger and want are found among millions of working people and the few, who make up the employing class, have all the good things of life. Between these two classes a struggle must go on until all the toilers come together on the political, as well as on the industrial field, and take and hold that which they produce by their labor, through an economic organization of the working class without affiliation with any political party.

> Preamble to the constitution of the Industrial Workers of the World, ratified in Chicago, June, 1905.

2 A living wage includes not merely decent maintenance for the present but also a reasonable provision for such future needs as sickness, invalidity, and old age.

> Pastoral Letter of the Roman Catholic Archbishops and Bishops of the United States, February 22, 1920.

3 It is the law of nature between master and servant that the servant shall spoil or plunder the master.

> JOHN QUINCY ADAMS, in his diary, December 17, 1810.

4 The rights and interests of the laboring man will be protected and cared for—not by labor agitators, but by the Christian men to whom God in His infinite wisdom has given the control of the property interests of the country.

> GEORGE F. BAER, in a letter to the president of the Philadelphia and Reading Railway, July 17, 1902.

5 The prosecution of modern wars rests completely upon the operation of labor in mines, mills and factories, so that labor fights there just as truly as the soldiers do in the trenches.

> MARY BEARD, *A Short History of the American Labor Movement,* 1920.

6 Neither the common law nor the Fourteenth Amendment confers the absolute right to strike.

> LOUIS D. BRANDEIS, in a Supreme Court opinion, *Dorchy v. Kansas,* 1926.

7 The golf links lie so near the mill
  That almost every day
The laboring children can look out
  And see the men at play.

> SARAH N. CLEGHORN, "The Golf Links Lie So Near the Mill," first published in Franklin P. Adams's column "The Conning Tower," in the *New York Tribune,* 1919.

8 [The wage earner] relies for work upon the ventures of confident and contented capital. This failing him, his condition is without alleviation, for he can neither prey on the misfortune of others nor hoard his labor.

> GROVER CLEVELAND, in a message to Congress, August 8, 1893.

9 There is no right to strike against the public safety by anybody, anywhere, any time.

> CALVIN COOLIDGE, in a telegram to Samuel Gompers, president of the American Federation of Labor, regarding the Boston police strike, September 14, 1919.

10 Whoever employs, with the right to command, is a master; and, whoever serves, with an obligation to obey, a servant.

> JAMES FENIMORE COOPER, *The American Democrat,* 1838.

11 The workers are the saviors of society, the redeemers of the race.

> EUGENE V. DEBS, in a speech in New York City, December 10, 1905.

12 The American workman who strikes ten blows with his hammer, while the foreign workman only strikes one, is really vanquishing that foreigner, as if the blows were aimed at and told on his person.

RALPH WALDO EMERSON, "Worship," *The Conduct of Life,* 1860.

13 [Eugene V. Debs] was *an agitator,* born of the first national awakening of American labor. The shame of servitude and the glory of struggle were emblazoned in the mind of every worker who heard Debs.

ELIZABETH GURLEY FLYNN, *Debs, Haywood, Ruthenberg,* 1939.

14 Capital is a result of labor, and is used by labor to assist it in further production. Labor is the active and initial force, and labor is therefore the employer of capital.

HENRY GEORGE, *Progress and Poverty,* 1879.

15 The methods by which a trade union can alone act are necessarily destructive; its organization is necessarily tyrannical.

Ibid.

16 For as labor cannot produce without the use of land, the denial of the equal right to the use of land is necessarily the denial of the right of labor to its own produce.

Ibid.

17 It is but a truism that labor is most productive where its wages are largest. Poorly paid labor is inefficient labor, the world over.

Ibid.

18 The man who gives me employment, which I must have or suffer, that man is my master, let me call him what I will.

HENRY GEORGE, *Social Problems,* 1884.

19 The labor of women in the house, certainly, enables men to produce more wealth than they otherwise could; and in this way women are economic factors in society. But so are horses.

CHARLOTTE PERKINS GILMAN, *Women and Economics,* 1898.

20 As to the great mass of working girls and women, how much independence is gained if the narrowness and lack of freedom of the home are exchanged for the narrowness and lack of freedom of the factory, sweatshop, department store, or office?

EMMA GOLDMAN, "The Tragedy of Women's Emancipation," *Anarchism and Other Essays,* 1911.

21 The labor of a human being is not a commodity or article of commerce. You can't weigh the soul of a man with a bar of pig iron.

SAMUEL GOMPERS, *Seventy Years of Life and Labor,* 1925.

22 Labor disgraces no man; unfortunately you occasionally find men disgrace labor.

ULYSSES S. GRANT, in a speech in Birmingham, England, October, 1877.

23 While Labor builds far more sumptuous mansions in our day than of old, . . . the laborer who builds those mansions lives oftenest in a squalid lodging . . . and . . . while the demands for labor, the uses of labor, the efficiency of labor, are multiplied and extended on every side by the rush of invention and the growth of luxury around us, . . . the temperate, efficient, upright worker often finds the comfortable maintenance and proper education of his children beyond his ability.

HORACE GREELEY, "An Address to the Printers of New York," January 17, 1850.

24 The only true foundation of any right to property is man's labor. That is property, and that alone, which labor of man has made such.

GALUSHA A. GROW, in a speech in the House of Representatives, 1852.

25 I looked up at Nye,
    And he gazed upon me;
  And he rose with a sigh,
    And said, "Can this be?
  We are ruined by Chinese cheap labor,"—
    And he went for that heathen Chinee.

BRET HARTE, "Plain Language from Truthful James," 1870.

26 We are here to confederate the workers of this country into a working-class movement that shall have for its purpose the emancipation of the working class from the slave bondage of capitalism. . . . This organization will be formed, based and founded on the class struggle, having in view no compromise and no surrender, and but one object and one purpose and that is to bring the workers of this country into the possession of the full value of their toil.

> WILLIAM D. "BIG BILL" HAYWOOD, opening the Continental Congress of the Working Class, which founded the Industrial Workers of the World, Chicago, June 27, 1905.

27 Work and pray, live on hay,
You'll get pie in the sky when you die.

> JOE HILL, in a labor song, "The Preacher and the Slave," c.1910.

28 The American labor force is composed of the most uncommon collection of rugged individualists ever assembled for mutual cause. They like to do their own griping and to solve their own problems. They do not want outside help and instinctively resist it. They were never "joiners"—and that included unions.

> JIMMY HOFFA, in *The Trials of Jimmy Hoffa*, 1970.

29 In the old days all you needed was a handshake. Nowadays you need forty lawyers.

> JIMMY HOFFA, in *Hoffa: The Real Story*, 1975.

30 They all know I'm back, very much back, and that I will be the general president again come hell or high water. I'm not a guy who believes in limited warfare, so the rats better start jumping the ship.

> Ibid.

31 When we oppose labor and capital, labor means the group that is selling its product, and capital all the other groups that are buying it.

> OLIVER WENDELL HOLMES, JR., in a speech in New York City, February 15, 1913.

32 Labor is the foundation of all, and those that labor are the Caryatides that support the structure and glittering dome of civilization and progress.

> ROBERT G. INGERSOLL, "How to Reform Mankind," 1896.

33 No tin hat brigade of goose-stepping vigilantes or Bible-babbling mob of blackguarding and corporation-paid scoundrels will prevent the onward march of labor.

> JOHN L. LEWIS, quoted in *Time* magazine, September 9, 1937.

34 The genesis of this campaign against labor in the House of Representatives is not hard to find. . . . It runs across to the Senate of the United States and emanates there from a labor-baiting, poker-playing, whiskey-drinking, evil old man whose name is [John Nance] Garner.

> JOHN L. LEWIS, addressing a Congressional committee, August, 1939.

35 In the early days of the world, the Almighty said to the first of our race, "In the sweat of thy face shalt thou eat bread"; and since then, if we except the light and the air of heaven, no good thing has been, or can be enjoyed by us, without having first cost labor.

> ABRAHAM LINCOLN, fragment of a discussion on tariffs, dated December 1, 1847.

36 I am glad to see that a system of labor prevails in New England under which laborers can strike when they want to, where they are not obliged to work under all circumstances, and are not tied down and obliged to labor whether you pay them or not. I like the system which lets a man quit when he wants to, and wish it might prevail everywhere.

> ABRAHAM LINCOLN, in an address in New Haven, Connecticut, March 6, 1860.

37 Labor is prior to and independent of capital. Capital is only the fruit of labor, and could never have existed if labor had not first existed. Labor is the superior of capital, and man deserves much the higher consideration.

> ABRAHAM LINCOLN, in his first annual message to Congress, December 3, 1861.

38 The effort to build up unions is as much the work of pioneers as the extension of civilization

into the wilderness. The unions are the first feeble effort to conquer the industrial jungle for democratic life.

> WALTER LIPPMANN, *Drift and Mastery,* 1914.

39 Laborin' man an' laborin' woman
   Hev one glory an' one shame.
   Ev'ythin' thet's done inhuman
   Injers all on 'em the same.

> JAMES RUSSELL LOWELL, *The Biglow Papers,*
> First Series, 1848.

40 The working class is loyal to friends, not ideas.

> NORMAN MAILER, *The Armies of the Night,*
> 1968.

41 How will it be with kingdoms and with
      kings—
   With those who shaped him to the thing he
      is—
   When this dumb Terror shall rise to judge
      the world,
   After the silence of the centuries?

> EDWIN MARKHAM, "The Man with the Hoe,"
> 1899.

42 The worker has the right to refuse to work, that is, to strike, and to induce by peaceful and lawful methods others to strike with him.

> WILLIAM CARDINAL O'CONNELL, in a pastoral
> letter, November 23, 1912.

43 The maintenance of a home is the minimum wage dictated by the law of nature, and prompted by the highest public policy. It is the clear right of the wage-earner, and to protect this right he may make use of all legitimate means.

> Ibid.

44 I feel that the true way of dealing with the matter is by a force which is overwhelming and prevents any attempts at resistance.

> RICHARD OLNEY, U.S. Attorney General and a
> director of the Burlington and Santa Fe Railroads,
> ordering the bloody breakup of the Pullman strike,
> June 30, 1894.

45 When I get thinking about this dangerous union thing, this empire of the irresponsible which

President Roosevelt has set up in this country, I find that I am more afraid of that than of Hitler.

> WESTBROOK PEGLER, in his column "Fair
> Enough," c.1943.

46 We affirm, as a fundamental principle, that labor, the creator of wealth, is entitled to all it creates.

> WENDELL PHILLIPS, in a resolution at the
> Labor-Reform Convention, Boston, September,
> 1870.

47 Short hours, better education, cooperation in the end, and in the meantime a political movement that will concentrate the thought of the country upon this thing.

> WENDELL PHILLIPS, in an address, "The
> Foundation of the Labor Movement," October
> 31, 1871. (Phillips was expressing what he termed
> "the motto of the workingmen of the United
> States.")

48 Large consumption is at the basis of saving in manufacture, and hence high wages contribute their share to progress.

> THOMAS BRACKETT REED, in a speech in the
> House of Representatives, November 1, 1894.

49 No labor leader can deliver the vote. If any labor leader says he can deliver the vote he is kidding you or himself. He can influence and try to mobilize his people around issues, and they will deliver the vote.

> WALTER REUTHER, in *The Nation* magazine,
> December 3, 1952.

50 I see an America where the workers are really free and through their great unions, undominated by any outside force or any dictator within, can take their proper place in the council tables with the owners and managers of business.

> FRANKLIN D. ROOSEVELT, in his acceptance
> speech at the Democratic National Convention,
> June 27, 1936.

51 It is essential that there should be organization of labor. This is an era of organization. Capital organizes and therefore labor must organize.

> THEODORE ROOSEVELT, in a speech in
> Milwaukee, Wisconsin, October 14, 1912.

52 Never forget that men who labor cast the votes, set up and pull down governments.

> Attributed to Elihu Root.

53   The single clenched fist lifted and ready,
Or the open asking hand held out and
     waiting.
       Choose:
For we meet by one or the other.

> CARL SANDBURG, "Choose," *Chicago Poems,*
> 1916.

54 I do not believe that a shorter work year will be achieved through a four-day week for most people—I am not sure that wives want their husbands underfoot that much.

> GEORGE P. SHULTZ, in *American Way* magazine,
> February, 1970.

55 There is no boon in nature. All the blessings we enjoy are the fruits of labor, toil, self-denial, and study.

> WILLIAM GRAHAM SUMNER, "The Boon of
> Nature," in *The Independent* magazine, October
> 27, 1887.

56 Men have become the tools of their tools.

> HENRY DAVID THOREAU, *Walden,* 1854.

57 Unemployed purchasing power means unemployed labor and unemployed labor means human want in the midst of plenty. This is the most challenging paradox of modern times.

> HENRY A. WALLACE, in a speech, 1934.

58 Labor in this country is independent and proud. It has not to ask the patronage of capital, but capital solicits the aid of labor.

> DANIEL WEBSTER, in a speech in the House of
> Representatives, April 2, 1824.

59 The eight-hour day now undoubtedly has the sanction of the judgment of society in its favor and should be adopted as a basis for wages even where the actual work to be done cannot be completed within eight hours.

> WOODROW WILSON, speaking to the press,
> August 19, 1916.

132. LANGUAGE

See also BOOKS; EDUCATION; INVECTIVE;
KNOWLEDGE; LITERATURE; ORATORY;
SPEECH

1 Expletive deleted.

> Term used to replace vulgarity in the transcripts
> of the White House recordings of conversations
> related to the Watergate affair, released to the
> public April 30, 1974.

2 English is destined to be in the next and succeeding centuries more generally the language of the world than Latin was in the last or French is in the present age.

> JOHN ADAMS, in a letter to the President of
> Congress, September 5, 1780.

3 Devotees of grammatical studies have not been distinguished for any very remarkable felicities of expression.

> A. BRONSON ALCOTT, *Tablets,* 1868.

4 All words are pegs to hang ideas on.

> HENRY WARD BEECHER, "The Human Mind,"
> *Proverbs from Plymouth Pulpit,* 1870.

5 Slang, *n.* The grunt of the human hog (*Pignoramus intolerabilis*) with an audible memory.

> AMBROSE BIERCE, *The Devil's Dictionary,* 1906.

6 The search is for the just word, the happy phrase, that will give expression to the thought, but somehow the thought itself is transfigured by the phrase when found.

> BENJAMIN N. CARDOZO, *The Growth of the
> Law,* 1924.

7 As always, the British especially shudder at the latest American vulgarity, and then they embrace it with enthusiasm two years later.

> ALISTAIR COOKE, quoted in *American Way*
> magazine, March, 1975.

8 The common faults of American language are an ambition of effect, a want of simplicity, and a turgid abuse of terms.

JAMES FENIMORE COOPER, *The American Democrat,* 1838.

9 She dealt her pretty words like blades,
As glittering they shone,
And every one unbared a nerve
Or wantoned with a bone.

EMILY DICKINSON, "She dealt her pretty words like blades," in *Further Poems,* 1929.

10 Faith, whin us free born Americans get through with th' English language we'll make it look as though it had been run over be a musical comedy.

FINLEY PETER DUNNE, "Mr. Dooley on Slang," in the *Boston Globe,* August 13, 1913.

11 I learn immediately from any speaker how much he has already lived, through the poverty or the splendor of his speech. Life lies behind us as the quarry from whence we get tiles and copestones for the masonry of today. This is the way to learn grammar. Colleges and books only copy the language which the fields and the work-yard made.

RALPH WALDO EMERSON, *The American Scholar,* 1837.

12 It seems as if the present age of words should naturally be followed by an age of silence, when men shall speak only through facts, and so regain their health. We die of words. We are hanged, drawn, and quartered by dictionaries.

RALPH WALDO EMERSON, entry written in 1838, *Journals,* 1909–1914.

13 We infer the spirit of the nation in great measure from the language, which is a sort of monument to which each forcible individual in a course of many hundred years has contributed a stone.

RALPH WALDO EMERSON, "Nominalist and Realist," *Essays,* Second Series, 1844.

14 Every word was once a poem. Every new relation is a new word.

RALPH WALDO EMERSON, "The Poet," *Essays,* Second Series, 1844.

15 The poets made all the words, and therefore language is the archives of history, and, if we must say it, a sort of tomb of the muses. For though the origin of most of our words is forgotten, each word was at first a stroke of genius.

Ibid.

16 Language is fossil poetry.

Ibid.

17 There is no more welcome gift to men than a new symbol that satiates, transports, converts them. They assimilate themselves to it, deal with it in all ways, and it will last a hundred years. Then comes a new genius, and brings another.

RALPH WALDO EMERSON, "Poetry and Imagination," *Letters and Social Aims,* 1876.

18 *Saying* and *Doing,* have quarrel'd and parted.

BENJAMIN FRANKLIN, *Poor Richard's Almanack,* 1756.

19 As our alphabet now stands, the bad spelling, or what is called so, is generally the best, as conforming to the sound of the letters and of the words.

BENJAMIN FRANKLIN, in a letter to Mrs. Jane Mecom, July 4, 1786.

20 Nouns and verbs are almost pure metal; adjectives are cheaper ore.

MARIE GILCHRIST, quoted by Leonora Speyer in *The Saturday Review of Literature,* 1946.

21 Language—human language—after all, is but little better than the croak and cackle of fowls, and other utterances of brute nature—sometimes not so adequate.

NATHANIEL HAWTHORNE, entry written July 14, 1850, in *Passages from the American Notebooks,* 1868.

22 Life and language are alike sacred. Homicide and *verbicide*—that is, violent treatment of a word with fatal results to its legitimate meaning, which is its life—are alike forbidden.

OLIVER WENDELL HOLMES, SR., *The Autocrat of the Breakfast-Table,* 1858.

23 Every language is a temple, in which the soul of those who speak it is enshrined.

OLIVER WENDELL HOLMES, SR., *The Professor at the Breakfast-Table,* 1860.

24 Language! the blood of the soul, sir, into which our thoughts run, and out of which they grow.

> Ibid.

25 I would never use a long word where a short one would answer the purpose. I know there are professors in this country who "ligate" arteries. Other surgeons only tie them, and it stops the bleeding just as well.

> OLIVER WENDELL HOLMES, SR., in a lecture at Harvard University, November 6, 1867.

26 A word is not a crystal, transparent and unchanging, it is the skin of a living thought and may vary greatly in color and content according to the circumstances and time in which it is used.

> OLIVER WENDELL HOLMES, JR., in a Supreme Court decision, *Towne* v. *Eisner,* January 7, 1918.

27 Language gradually varies, and with it fade away the writings of authors who have flourished their allotted time.

> WASHINGTON IRVING, *The Sketch-Book,* 1819–1820.

28 I'm glad you like adverbs—I adore them; they are the only qualifications I really much respect.

> HENRY JAMES, in a letter to Miss M. Betham Edwards, January 5, 1912.

29 No instance exists of a person's writing two languages perfectly. That will always appear to be his native language which was most familiar to him in his youth.

> THOMAS JEFFERSON, in a letter to John Bannister, Jr., October 15, 1785.

30 You will learn to speak better from women and children in three months, than from men in a year.

> THOMAS JEFFERSON, on the French language, in a letter to Thomas Mann Randolph, Jr., July 6, 1787.

31 The new circumstances under which we are placed call for new words, new phrases, and for the transfer of old words to new objects. An American dialect will therefore be formed.

> THOMAS JEFFERSON, in a letter to John Waldo, August 16, 1813.

32 He can compress the most words into the smallest ideas of any man I ever met.

> ABRAHAM LINCOLN, on a fellow lawyer, quoted in Abraham Gross, *Lincoln's Own Stories,* 1912.

33 History is condensed in the catchwords of the people.

> HENRY DEMAREST LLOYD, *Wealth Against Commonwealth,* 1894.

34 Deeds are better things than words are,
Actions mightier than boastings.

> HENRY WADSWORTH LONGFELLOW, *The Song of Hiawatha,* 1855.

35 It is remarkable how very debased the language has become in a short period in America.

> FREDERICK MARRYAT, *A Diary in America, with Remarks on Its Institutions,* 1839.

36 In point of naked syntactical accuracy, the English of America is not at all inferior to that of England; but we do not discriminate so precisely in the meaning of words.

> GEORGE PERKINS MARSH, *Lectures on the English Language,* 1860.

37 As there is now nothing new to be learned from the dead languages, all the useful books being already translated, the languages are becoming useless, and the time expended in teaching and learning them is wasted. So far as the study of languages may contribute to the progress and communication of knowledge, it is only in the living languages that new knowledge is to be found.

> THOMAS PAINE, *The Age of Reason* 1794–1796.

38 A definition is no proof.

> WILLIAM PINKNEY, in a speech in the U.S. Senate, February 15, 1820.

39 Good swearing is used as a form of punctuation, not necessarily as a response to pain or insult, and is utilized by experts to lend a sentence a certain zest, like a sprinkling of paprika.

> GEORGE PLIMPTON, *Paper Lion,* 1965.

40 A definition is that which so describes its object as to distinguish it from all others; it is no definition

of any one thing if its terms are applicable to any one other.

EDGAR ALLAN POE, "The Rationale of Verse," published in *The Pioneer*, March, 1843.

41 Grammar is the analysis of language.

Ibid.

42 A man's grammar, like Caesar's wife, must not only be pure, but above suspicion of impurity.

EDGAR ALLAN POE, *Marginalia*, 1844–1849.

43 The phraseology of every nation has a taint of drollery about it to the ears of every nation speaking a different tongue.

Ibid.

44 How very commonly we hear it remarked that such and such thoughts are beyond the compass of words. I do not believe that any thought, properly so called, is out of the reach of language. . . . I have never had a thought which I could not set down in words.

Ibid.

45 Only where there is language is there world.

ADRIENNE RICH, "The Demon Lover," *Leaflets*, 1969.

46 One of our defects as a nation is a tendency to use what have been called "weasel words." When a weasel sucks eggs the meat is sucked out of the egg. If you use a "weasel word" after another there is nothing left of the other. You can have universal training, or you can have voluntary training, but when you use the word "voluntary" to qualify the word "universal" you are making a "weasel word"; it has sucked all the meaning out of "universal."

THEODORE ROOSEVELT, ridiculing Woodrow Wilson's phrase "universal voluntary military training," in a speech in St. Louis, Missouri, May 31, 1916.

47 Every immigrant who comes here should be required within five years to learn English or leave the country.

THEODORE ROOSEVELT, in an article in the *Kansas City Star*, April 27, 1918.

48 Language, like all art, becomes pale with years; words and figures of speech lose their contagious and suggestive power.

GEORGE SANTAYANA, *The Life of Reason*, 1905.

49 One must be chary of words because they turn into cages.

VIOLA SPOLIN, quoted by Barry Hyams in the *Los Angeles Times*, May 26, 1974.

50 Vigorous writing is concise. A sentence should contain no unnecessary words, a paragraph no unnecessary sentences, for the same reason that a drawing should have no unnecessary lines and a machine no unnecessary parts. This requires not that the writer make all his sentences short, or that he avoid all detail and treat his subjects only in outline, but that every word tell.

WILLIAM STRUNK, JR., *The Elements of Style*, 1918.

51 Language is the most perfect work of art in the world. The chisel of a thousand years retouches it.

HENRY DAVID THOREAU, entry written in 1840, *Journal*, 1906.

52 We are armed with language adequate to describe each leaf in the field, but not to describe human character.

HENRY DAVID THOREAU, entry written in 1851, *Journal*, 1906.

53 Some of those old American words *do* have a kind of a bully swing to them; a man can *express* himself with 'em—a man can get at what he wants to *say*, dontchuknow.

MARK TWAIN, conversation of a fellow American in Europe, in *A Tramp Abroad*, 1880.

54 As to the adjective, when in doubt strike it out.

MARK TWAIN, "Pudd'nhead Wilson's Calendar," *Pudd'nhead Wilson*, 1894.

55 An average English word is four letters and a half. By hard, honest labor I've dug all the large words out of my vocabulary and shaved it down till the average is three and a half. . . . I never write "metropolis" for seven cents, because I can get the same money for "city." I never write "policeman,"

because I can get the same price for "cop." I never write "valetudinarian" at all, for not even hunger and wretchedness can humble me to the point where I will do a word like that for seven cents; I wouldn't do it for fifteen.

> MARK TWAIN, in a speech at the annual dinner of the Associated Press, New York City, September 18, 1906.

56 Numerous local causes, such as a new country, new associations of people, new combinations of ideas in arts and sciences, and some intercourse with tribes wholly unknown in Europe, will introduce new words into the American tongue. These causes will produce, in a course of time, a language in North America as different from the future language of England as the modern Dutch, Danish and Swedish are from the German, or from one another.

> NOAH WEBSTER, *Dissertations on the English Language,* 1789.

57 Language is the expression of ideas, and if the people of one country cannot preserve an identity of ideas they cannot retain an identity of language.

> NOAH WEBSTER, in the preface to *An American Dictionary of the English Language,* 1828.

58 Language, as well as the faculty of speech, was the immediate gift of God.

> Ibid.

59 The Americans are going to be the most fluent and melodious-voiced people in the world—and the most perfect users of words. The new world, the new times, the new people, the new vistas need a new tongue according—yes, what is more, they will have such a new tongue—will not be satisfied until it is evolved.

> WALT WHITMAN, *An American Primer,* 1904.

60 View'd freely, the English language is the accretion and growth of every dialect, race, and range of time, and is both the free and compacted composition of all.

> WALT WHITMAN, "Slang in America," in the *North American Review,* November, 1885.

61 Language . . . is not an abstract construction of the learned, or of dictionary-makers, but is something arising out of the work, needs, ties, joys, affections, tastes, of long generations of humanity, and has its bases broad and low, close to the ground.

> Ibid.

62 A tendency to slang, to colloquial inelegancies, and even vulgarities, is the besetting sin against which we, as Americans, have especially to guard and to struggle.

> WILLIAM DWIGHT WHITNEY, *Language and the Study of Language,* 1867.

63 God fills the gaps of human need,
Each crisis brings its word and deed.

> JOHN GREENLEAF WHITTIER, "The Lost Occasion," 1880.

64 From purest wells of English undefiled
None deeper drank than he, the New
World's Child.

> JOHN GREENLEAF WHITTIER, "James Russell Lowell," 1891.

65 We have really everything in common with America nowadays, except, of course, language.

> OSCAR WILDE, *The Canterville Ghost,* 1888.

66 I have heard in this country . . . and see daily . . . errors in grammar, improprieties, and vulgarisms which hardly any person of the same class in point of rank and literature would have fallen into in Great Britain.

> JOHN WITHERSPOON, "The Druid," in the *Pennsylvania Journal and Weekly Advertiser,* May 9, 1781.

67 The word Americanism, which I have coined . . . is exactly similar in its formation and signification to the word Scotticism.

> Ibid.

68 I love smooth words, like gold-enameled fish
Which circle slowly with a silken swish,
And tender ones, like downy-feathered birds:
Words shy and dappled, deep-eyed deer in
herds.

> ELINOR WYLIE, "Pretty Words," in *Collected Poems of Elinor Wylie,* 1932.

133. LAST WORDS

See also DEATH; EPITAPHS

The accuracy of reports of famous people's last words is often difficult to establish. Some of these may constitute improvements upon history.

1 Thomas Jefferson still survives.

> JOHN ADAMS, July 4, 1826, the 50th anniversary of the Declaration of Independence. (Adams was wrong. Jefferson had died a few hours earlier, but also on the Fourth. On the day before, concerned that he might die before the anniversary, Jefferson had uttered his last words: "Is it the Fourth?" and then slipped into a coma.)

2 This is the last of earth. I am content.

> JOHN QUINCY ADAMS, died February 23, 1848, quoted in Josiah Quincy, *Memoir of the Life of John Quincy Adams*, 1858.

3 Waiting, are they? Waiting, are they? Well, goddam 'em, let 'em wait.

> ETHAN ALLEN, responding to his physician's observation: "General, I fear the angels are waiting for you," February 12, 1789.

4 I am reconciled to death but detest the mode. It will be but a moment's pang. I pray you bear witness that I met my fate like a brave man.

> MAJOR JOHN ANDRÉ, about to be hanged as a British spy during the American Revolution, October 2, 1780. (Major Benjamin Tallmadge said of André awaiting execution: "By heavens . . . I never saw a man whose fate I foresaw whom I so sincerely pitied. . . . He seems to be as cheerful as if he was going to an assembly.)

5 I would rather be a servant in the house of the Lord than sit in the seat of the mighty.

> ALBEN BARKLEY, former vice-president of the United States, stricken while addressing a student political convention at Washington and Lee University, April 30, 1956.

6 How were the circus receipts today at Madison Square Garden?

> P. T. BARNUM, circus showman, died April 7, 1891.

7 Is everybody happy? I want everybody to be happy. I know I'm happy.

> ETHEL BARRYMORE, died June 18, 1959.

8 Now comes the mystery.

> HENRY WARD BEECHER, clergyman, died March 8, 1887.

9 Goodbye, kid. Hurry back.

> HUMPHREY BOGART, to his wife, Lauren Bacall, as she left the room for a moment, January 14, 1957.

10 Tell mother—tell mother—I died for my country. My hands—useless—useless.

> JOHN WILKES BOOTH, Lincoln's assassin, himself killed, perhaps by pursuers, perhaps by his own hand, April 26, 1865.

11 I am ready at any time. Do not keep me waiting.

> JOHN BROWN, to the hangman, December 2, 1859.

12 On that subject I am coy.

> AARON BURR, asked if he was ready for salvation, September 14, 1836.

13 The South, the poor South! God knows what will become of her.

> JOHN C. CALHOUN, died March 31, 1850.

14 I have tried so hard to do the right.

> GROVER CLEVELAND, died June 24, 1908.

15 Gentlemen, the battle is done. The victory is ours.

> GEORGE DEWEY, January 16, 1917 (almost 20 years after his great naval victory at Manila Bay).

16 Nay, first a child; then a young man; then a strong man, before an elder of Jesus Christ.

Quaker martyr Mary Dyer, on being asked at her execution in Boston for the crime of sedition whether a church elder should be asked to pray for her, 1660.

17 To my friends: My work is done. Why wait?

GEORGE EASTMAN, in a suicide note, March 14, 1932.

18 It is very beautiful over there.

THOMAS EDISON, died October 18, 1931.

19 A dying man can do nothing easy.

BENJAMIN FRANKLIN, April 17, 1790, responding to a request from his daughter to turn over so he might breathe more easily. Another version has it that she was praying he would live many more years, and he replied, "I hope not."

20 Why fear death? It is the most beautiful adventure in life.

CHARLES FROHMAN, Broadway producer of J.M. Barrie's Peter Pan, 1904, going down on the *Lusitania,* May 7, 1915. (His words are from the play.)

21 Glory hallelujah! I am going to the Lordy! I come. Ready. Go!

CHARLES JULIUS GUITEAU, assassin of James A. Garfield, on the gallows in Washington, D.C., June 30, 1882.

22 I only regret that I have but one life to lose for my country.

NATHAN HALE, about to be hanged as a spy by the British during the American Revolution, September 22, 1776.

23 I know that I am going where Lucy is.

RUTHERFORD B. HAYES, certain of reunion with his wife, January 17, 1893.

24 Turn up the lights. I don't want to go home in the dark.

O. HENRY, on his deathbed, June 5, 1910, reported in C. Alphonso Smith, *O. Henry,* 1916. (The words are sometimes given as: "Put up the shades. I don't want to go home

in the dark." The final sentence evokes the words of a popular song of the time: "I'm afraid to go home in the dark.")

25 Lot of damn foolery.

OLIVER WENDELL HOLMES, SR., seeing that an oxygen tent was being readied for him, October 7, 1894.

26 I strike my flag!

ISAAC HULL, once commander of the U.S.S. *Constitution* (Old Ironsides), February 13, 1843.

27 Let us cross over the river and rest under the trees.

STONEWALL JACKSON, Confederate general, May 10, 1863. (He had been mortally wounded at Chancellorsville the week before.)

28 Ben, make sure you play "Precious Lord, Take My Hand." Play it real pretty for me.

MARTIN LUTHER KING, JR., speaking to Ben Branch, a friend, seconds before King was struck by an assassin's bullet, April 4, 1968.

29 Strike the tent.

ROBERT E. LEE, died October 12, 1870.

30 Is this dying? Is this all? Is this all that I feared when I prayed against a hard death? Oh! I can bear this. I can bear it. I can bear it.

COTTON MATHER, Puritan clergyman, died February 13, 1728.

31 Don't baby me so.

J. P. MORGAN, died March 31, 1913.

32 I knew it. I knew it. Born in a hotel room—and God damn it—died in a hotel room.

EUGENE O'NEILL, shortly before his death in the Shelton Hotel, Boston, Massachusetts, November 27, 1953.

33 I have lived an honest and useful life to mankind; my time has been spent in doing good; and I die in perfect composure and resignation to the will of my Creator.

THOMAS PAINE, from his last will, 1809.

34 Lord, help my poor soul.

EDGAR ALLAN POE, died October 7, 1849.

35 What is the answer? In that case, what is the question?

GERTRUDE STEIN, responding to the question "What is the answer?" put to her by Alice B. Toklas, July 27, 1946.

36 Folks are better than angels.

Attributed to Edward Thompson Taylor, a Boston clergyman, responding to assurances from friends that he would soon be with the angels, April 5, 1871.

37 I did not know we had ever quarreled, Aunt.

HENRY DAVID THOREAU, responding to his Aunt Louisa, when asked whether he had made his peace with God, May 6, 1862. (A few days before, when a visitor said to Thoreau that he seemed "so near the brink of the dark river, that [I] almost wonder how the opposite shore may appear to you," Thoreau answered, "One world at a time." Edward Wagenknecht, in *Henry David Thoreau, What Manner of Man?* 1981, reported that Thoreau's final words, to his sister Sophie, were "Now comes good sailing.")

38 Death, the only immortal who treats us all alike, whose pity and whose peace and whose refuge are for all—the soiled and the pure, the rich and the poor, the loved and the unloved.

MARK TWAIN, in a memorandum written before his death, April 21, 1910.

39 'Tis well.

GEORGE WASHINGTON, after being told his secretary understood Washington's burial instructions, December 14, 1799. (Washington then said to his doctor, "I die hard, but I am not afraid to go.")

40 I have made many mistakes, but I love my country, and have labored for the youth of my country, and I trust no precept of mine has taught any dear youth to sin.

NOAH WEBSTER, died May 28, 1843.

41 If I should have any property at the time of my death, which I most seriously doubt will be the case, I bequeath and devise it to my beloved wife.

JOSEPH WILSON, quoted in Sam J. Ervin, Jr., *Humor of a Country Lawyer,* 1983.

134. LAW

See also CIVIL RIGHTS; CRIME; EQUALITY; JUSTICE; PUNISHMENT

1 Three Philadelphia lawyers are a match for the Devil.

Popular saying, early nineteenth century.

2 I will not counsel or maintain any suit or proceeding which shall appear to me to be unjust, nor any defense except such as I believe to be honestly debatable under the law of the land.

American Bar Association, model oath for candidates seeking admission to the bar, c.1925.

3 Law is merely the expression of the will of the strongest for the time being, and therefore laws have no fixity, but shift from generation to generation.

BROOKS ADAMS, *The Law of Civilization and Decay,* 1895.

4 The law, in all vicissitudes of government, fluctuations of the passions or flights of enthusiasm, will preserve a steady, undeviating course; it will not bend to the uncertain wishes, imaginations and wanton tempers of men. . . . On the one hand it is inexorable to the cries and lamentations of the prisoners. On the other it is deaf, deaf as an adder to the clamors of the populace.

JOHN ADAMS, defending the British soldiers in the Boston Massacre trials, December 4, 1770.

5 The sober second thought of the people shall be law.

FISHER AMES, in a speech in Congress, 1788.

6 One thing I supplicate your majesty: that you will give orders, under a great penalty, that no bachelors of law should be allowed to come here [to the New World]; for not only are they bad themselves, but they also make and contrive a thousand iniquities.

VASCO NUÑEZ DE BALBOA, to King Ferdinand V of Spain, 1513.

7 We bury men when they are dead, but we try to embalm the dead body of laws. . . . It usually takes a hundred years to make a law; and then, after it has done its work, it usually takes a hundred years to get rid of it.

HENRY WARD BEECHER, *Life Thoughts,* 1858.

8 Laws and institutions are constantly tending to gravitate. Like clocks, they must be occasionally cleansed, and wound up, and set to true time.

Ibid.

9 Laws are not masters but servants, and he rules them who obeys them.

HENRY WARD BEECHER, *Proverbs from Plymouth Pulpit,* 1870.

10 Court Fool, *n.* The plaintiff.

AMBROSE BIERCE, *The Devil's Dictionary,* 1906.

11 Lawful, *adj.* Compatible with the will of a judge having jurisdiction.

Ibid.

12 Lawyer, *n.* One skilled in circumvention of the law.

Ibid.

13 Litigant, *n.* A person about to give up his skin for the hope of retaining his bones.

Ibid.

14 Litigation, *n.* A machine which you go into as a pig and come out of as a sausage.

Ibid.

15 Oath, *n.* In law, a solemn appeal to the Deity, made binding upon the conscience by a penalty for perjury.

Ibid.

16 The term Rule of Law, like the phrases: "Love of God" and "Brotherhood of Man," is a short and simple expression of one of the few most sublime concepts that the mind and spirit of man has yet achieved.

GEORGE H. BOLDT, in a speech on Law Day USA, Tacoma, Washington, May 1, 1958.

17 The law is not an end in itself, nor does it provide ends. It is preeminently a means to serve what we think is right.

WILLIAM J. BRENNAN, in a Supreme Court opinion, *Roth* v. *United States,* 1957.

18 Law cannot stand aside from the social changes around it.

Ibid.

19 No people is shrewder than the American in perceiving when a law works ill, nor prompter in repealing it.

JAMES BRYCE, *The American Commonwealth,* 1888.

20 Law is whatever is boldly asserted and plausibly maintained.

AARON BURR, quoted in James Parton, *The Life and Times of Aaron Burr,* 1857.

21 No written law has ever been more binding than unwritten custom supported by popular opinion.

CARRIE CHAPMAN CATT, in a speech on women's suffrage before the U.S. Senate, February 13, 1900.

22 Law is the expression and the perfection of common sense.

Attributed to Joseph Hodges Choate.

23 No man has ever yet been hanged for breaking the spirit of a law.

GROVER CLEVELAND, quoted in James Ford Rhodes, *History of the United States,* 1893–1906.

24 Jurisprudence, in effect, is a special branch of the science of transcendental nonsense.

> FELIX S. COHEN, *Transcendental Nonsense and the Functional Approach,* 1935.

25 I don't want to know what the law is, I want to know who the judge is.

> ROY COHN, a favorite saying, quoted by Tom Wolfe in the *New York Times Book Review,* April 3, 1988.

26 One with the law is a majority.

> CALVIN COOLIDGE, in his acceptance speech upon nomination for the vice presidency, Republican National Convention, July 27, 1920.

27 Free government has no greater menace than disrespect for authority and continual violation of law. It is the duty of a citizen not only to observe the law but to let it be known that he is opposed to its violation.

> CALVIN COOLIDGE, in a message to Congress, December 6, 1923.

28 The law, unfortunately, has always been retained on the side of power; laws have uniformly been enacted for the protection and perpetuation of power.

> THOMAS COOPER, *Liberty of the Press,* 1830.

29 The government of the United States is and always has been a lawyer's government.

> CHAUNCEY DEPEW, in a speech, 1898.

30 Our defense is not in armaments, nor in science, nor in going underground. Our defense is in law and order.

> ALBERT EINSTEIN, quoted by Ralph E. Lapp in the *New York Times Magazine,* August 2, 1964.

31 Let a man keep the law,—any law,—and his way will be strewn with satisfactions.

> RALPH WALDO EMERSON, "Prudence," *Essays,* First Series, 1841.

32 The wise know that foolish legislation is a rope of sand which perishes in the twisting; that the State must follow and not lead the character and progress of the citizen.

> RALPH WALDO EMERSON, "Politics," *Essays,* Second Series, 1844.

33 Things have their laws, as well as men; and things refuse to be trifled with.

> Ibid.

34 The law may in a mad freak say that all shall have power except the owners of property; they shall have no vote. Nevertheless, by a higher law, the property will, year after year, write every statute that respects property.

> Ibid.

35 Any laws but those which men make for themselves are laughable.

> Ibid.

36 The favorite phrase of English law is "a custom whereof the memory of man runneth not back to the contrary."

> RALPH WALDO EMERSON, *English Traits,* 1856.

37 The good lawyer is not the man who has an eye to every side and angle of contingency, and qualifies all his qualifications, but who throws himself on your part so heartily, that he can get you out of a scrape.

> RALPH WALDO EMERSON, "Power," *The Conduct of Life,* 1860.

38 God works wonders now & then;
Behold! a Lawyer, an honest Man.

> BENJAMIN FRANKLIN, *Poor Richard's Almanack,* 1733.

39 *Laws* like to *Cobwebs,* catch small Flies,
Great ones break thro' before your eyes.

> BENJAMIN FRANKLIN, *Poor Richard's Almanack,* 1734.

40 A Lean award is better than a fat Judgment.

> BENJAMIN FRANKLIN, *Poor Richard's Almanack,* 1753.

41 Laws *too gentle* are seldom *obeyed; too severe,* seldom *executed.*

> BENJAMIN FRANKLIN, *Poor Richard's Almanack,* 1756.

42 The best public measures are seldom adopted from previous wisdom, but forc'd by the occasion.

> BENJAMIN FRANKLIN, in his *Autobiography*, 1798.

43 The law of society is, each for all, as well as all for each.

> HENRY GEORGE, *Progress and Poverty*, 1879.

44 I know no method to secure the repeal of bad or obnoxious laws so effective as their stringent execution.

> ULYSSES S. GRANT, in his inaugural address, March 4, 1869.

45 I am the law.

> FRANK HAGUE, major of Jersey City, New Jersey, quoted in the *New York Times*, November 11, 1937.

46 When any people are ruled by laws in framing which they have no part, that are to bind them to all intents and purposes, without, in the same manner, binding the legislators themselves, they are, in the strictest sense, slaves; and the government, with respect to them, is despotic.

> ALEXANDER HAMILTON, *The Farmer Refuted*, 1775.

47 It is essential to the idea of a law that it be attended with a sanction; or, in other words, a penalty or punishment for disobedience.

> ALEXANDER HAMILTON, *The Federalist*, 1787–1788.

48 Laws are a dead letter without courts to expound and define their true meaning and operation.

> Ibid.

49 It will be of little avail to the people that the laws are made by men of their own choice, if the laws be so voluminous that they cannot be read, or so incoherent that they cannot be understood; if they be repealed or revised before they are promulgated, or undergo such incessant changes that no man, who knows what the law is today, can guess what it will be tomorrow.

> ALEXANDER HAMILTON OR JAMES MADISON, *The Federalist*, 1787–1788.

50 It is of course true that any kind of judicial legislation is objectionable on the score of the limited interests which a Court can represent, yet there are wrongs which in fact legislatures cannot be brought to take an interest in, at least not until the Courts have acted.

> LEARNED HAND, in a letter to Louis D. Brandeis, January 22, 1919.

51 If the prosecution of crime is to be conducted with so little regard for that protection which centuries of English law have given to the individual, we are indeed at the dawn of a new era; and much that we have deemed vital to our liberties, is a delusion.

> LEARNED HAND, in an opinion reversing a lower court decision in *United States* v. *Di Re,* in which arrest and evidence were illegally obtained, 1947.

52 There is in this country no superior, dominant, ruling class of citizens. There is no caste here. Our Constitution is color-blind, and neither knows nor tolerates classes among citizens. In respect of civil rights, all citizens are equal before the law.

> JOHN MARSHALL HARLAN, in a dissenting Supreme Court opinion, *Plessy* v. *Ferguson,* 1896.

53 It is only rogues who feel the restraint of law.

> JOSIAH GILBERT HOLLAND, "Perfect Liberty," *Gold-Foil,* 1859.

54 Come, you of the law, who can talk, if you
    please,
Till the man in the moon will allow it's a
    cheese.

> OLIVER WENDELL HOLMES, SR., "Lines Recited at the Berkshire Jubilee," August 23, 1844.

55 The life of the law has not been logic; it has been experience.

> OLIVER WENDELL HOLMES, JR., *The Common Law,* 1881.

56 Great cases like hard cases make bad law. For great cases are called great not by reason of their real importance in shaping the law of the future but because of some accident of immediate overwhelming interest which appeals to the feelings and dis-

torts the judgment. These immediate interests exercise a kind of hydraulic pressure which makes what previously was clear seem doubtful, and before which even well-settled principles of law will bend.

> Oliver Wendell Holmes, Jr., in a dissenting Supreme Court opinion in *Northern Securities Company* v. *United States,* 1904.

57 The case is decided upon an economic theory. . . . I strongly believe that my agreement or disagreement [with that theory] has nothing to do with the right of a majority to embody their opinions in law.

> Oliver Wendell Holmes, Jr., dissenting Supreme Court opinion, *Lochner* v. *New York,* 1905.

58 General propositions do not decide concrete cases.

> Ibid.

59 Every opinion tends to become a law.

> Ibid.

60 May God twist my tripes, if I string out the obvious for the delectation of fools!

> Oliver Wendell Holmes, Jr., on being requested to deliver longer opinions, c.1911, quoted in Catherine Drinker Bowen, *Yankee from Olympus,* 1944.

61 While there still is doubt, while opposite convictions still keep a battlefront against each other, the time for law has not come.

> Oliver Wendell Holmes, Jr., in a speech in New York City, February 15, 1913.

62 It is our duty to declare lynch law as little valid when practiced by a regularly drawn jury as when administered by one elected by a mob intent on death.

> Oliver Wendell Holmes, Jr., in a dissenting Supreme Court opinion, *Frank* v. *Mangum,* 1914. (This was the appeal of the conviction of Leo Frank for murder.)

63 Pretty much all law consists in forbidding men to do some things that they want to do.

> Oliver Wendell Holmes, Jr., in a dissenting Supreme Court opinion, *Adkins* v. *Children's Hospital,* 1922.

64 If the law is upheld only by government officials, then all law is at an end.

> Herbert Hoover, in a message to Congress, 1929.

65 Nearly every lawsuit is an insult to the intelligence of both plaintiff and defendant.

> Edgar Watson Howe, *Sinner Sermons,* 1926.

66 Laws that do not embody public opinion can never be enforced.

> Elbert Hubbard, *The Roycroft Dictionary and Book of Epigrams,* 1923.

67 Law: 1. A scheme for protecting the parasite and prolonging the life of the rogue, averting the natural consequences which would otherwise come to them. 2. The crystallization of public opinion.

> Ibid.

68 Lawyer: 1. A person who takes this from that, with the result that That hath not where to lay his head. 2. An unnecessary evil. 3. The only man in whom ignorance of the law is not punished.

> Ibid.

69 Law is what a judge dispenses. The judge, however, is no representative of the average man's common sense. A certain remoteness from the experiences of everyday life and a certain rigidity of viewpoint are essential to his role as judge.

> Gerhart Husserl, legal scholar, writing in the *Journal of Social Philosophy,* July, 1940.

70 Laws spring from the instinct of self-preservation.

> Robert G. Ingersoll, "Some Mistakes of Moses," 1879.

71 Young lawyers attend the courts, not because they have business there but because they have no business anywhere else.

> Washington Irving, *Salmagundi,* 1807–1808.

72 I did believe, and ever will believe, that just laws can make no distinction of privilege between the rich and poor, and that when men of high standing attempt to trample upon the rights of the weak, they are the fittest objects for example and

punishment. In general, the great can protect themselves, but the poor and humble require the arm and shield of the law.

> ANDREW JACKSON, in a letter to John Quincy Adams, August 26, 1821.

73 Were it made a question, whether no law, as among the savage Americans, or too much law, as among the civilized Europeans, submits man to the greatest evil, one who has seen both conditions of existence would pronounce it to be the last; and that the sheep are happier of themselves, than under the care of wolves.

> THOMAS JEFFERSON, *Notes on the State of Virginia,* 1784.

74 Ignorance of the law is no excuse, in any country. If it were, the laws would lose their effect, because it can be always pretended.

> THOMAS JEFFERSON, in a letter to André Limozin, December 22, 1787.

75 The execution of the laws is more important than the making them.

> THOMAS JEFFERSON, in a letter to the Abbé Arnoud, July 19, 1789.

76 The study of the law is useful in a variety of points of view. It qualifies a man to be useful to himself, to his neighbors and to the public. It is the most certain stepping-stone to preferment in the political line.

> THOMAS JEFFERSON, in a letter to Thomas Mann Randolph, May 30, 1790.

77 I consider all the encroachments made on the Constitution heretofore as nothing, as mere retail stuff, compared with the wholesale doctrine that there is a Common Law in force in the United States, of which, and of all the cases within its provisions, their courts have cognizance.

> THOMAS JEFFERSON, in a letter to Charles Pinckney, October, 1799.

78 A strict observance of the written laws is doubtless *one* of the high duties of a good citizen, but it is not *the highest*. The laws of necessity, of self-preservation, of saving our country when in danger, are of higher obligation.

> THOMAS JEFFERSON, in a letter to John B. Colvin, September 20, 1810.

79 This corporeal globe, and everything upon it, belong to its present corporeal inhabitants, during their generation. They alone have a right to direct what is the concern of themselves alone, and to declare the law of that direction.

> THOMAS JEFFERSON, in a letter to Samuel Kercheval, July 12, 1816.

80 Laws are made for men of ordinary understanding, and should therefore be construed by the ordinary rules of common sense. Their meaning is not to be sought for in metaphysical subtleties, which may make anything mean everything or nothing, at pleasure.

> THOMAS JEFFERSON, in a letter to William Johnson, June 12, 1823.

81 Every form of bigotry can be found in ample supply in the legal system of our country. It would seem that Justice (usually depicted as a woman) is indeed blind to racism, sexism, war, and poverty.

> FLORYNCE R. KENNEDY, quoted in Robin Morgan, *Sisterhood Is Powerful,* 1970.

82 Laws are felt only when the individual comes into conflict with them.

> SUZANNE LAFOLLETTE, "The Beginnings of Emancipation," *Concerning Women,* 1926.

83 Never, never, never, on cross-examination ask a witness a question you don't already know the answer to, was a tenet I absorbed with my baby-food. Do it, and you'll often get an answer you don't want, an answer that might wreck your case.

> HARPER LEE, *To Kill a Mockingbird,* 1960.

84 Let me not be understood as saying that there are no bad laws, or that grievances may not arise for the redress of which no legal provisions have been made. I mean to say no such thing. But I do mean to say that although bad laws, if they exist, should be repealed as soon as possible, still, while they continue in force, for the sake of example they should be religiously observed.

> ABRAHAM LINCOLN, in the address "The Perpetuation of Our Political Institutions," Springfield, Illinois, January 27, 1837.

85 There is no grievance that is a fit object of redress by mob rule.

> Ibid.

86 Discourage litigation. Persuade your neighbors to compromise whenever you can. . . . As a peacemaker the lawyer has a superior opportunity of being a good man. There will still be business enough.

> ABRAHAM LINCOLN, in lecture notes, July 1, 1850.

87 The government of the United States has been emphatically termed a government of laws, and not of men. It will certainly cease to deserve this high appellation, if the laws furnish no remedy for the violation of a vested legal right.

> JOHN MARSHALL, in a Supreme Court opinion, *Marbury* v. *Madison,* 1803.

88 A law not repealed continues in force, not because it cannot be repealed, but because it is not repealed, and the non-repealing passes for consent.

> THOMAS PAINE, *The Rights of Man,* 1791.

89 The best use of good laws is to teach men to trample bad laws under their feet.

> WENDELL PHILLIPS, in a speech, April 12, 1852.

90 The law must be stable, but it must not stand still.

> ROSCOE POUND, *Introduction to the Philosophy of Law,* 1922.

91 We are always saying let the law take its course, but what we mean is "Let the law take our course."

> WILL ROGERS, February 19, 1935, quoted in Donald Day, *The Autobiography of Will Rogers,* 1949.

92 It is difficult to make our material condition better by the best law, but it is easy enough to ruin it by bad laws.

> THEODORE ROOSEVELT, in a speech in Providence, Rhode Island, August 23, 1902.

93 Damn the law! I want the [Panama] canal built.

> Attributed to Theodore Roosevelt, 1903.

94 No man is above the law and no man is below it; nor do we ask any man's permission when we require him to obey it. Obedience to the law is demanded as a right, not asked as a favor.

> THEODORE ROOSEVELT, in a message to Congress, January, 1904.

95 Why is there always a secret singing
When a lawyer cashes in?
Why does a hearse horse snicker
Hauling a lawyer away?

> CARL SANDBURG, "The Lawyers Know Too Much," *Smoke and Steel,* 1920.

96 [The law] is a jealous mistress, and requires a long and constant courtship. It is not to be won by trifling favors, but by lavish homage.

> JOSEPH STORY, in his inaugural address as Dane Professor of Law at Harvard University, August 15, 1829.

97 Blundering experiments in legislation cannot be simply abandoned if they do not work well; even if they are set aside, they leave their effects behind; and they create vested interests which make it difficult to set them aside.

> WILLIAM GRAHAM SUMNER, "Federal Legislation on Railroads," in *The Independent,* January 20, 1887.

98 Somehow strangely the vice of men gets well represented and protected but their virtue has none to plead its cause—nor any charter of immunities and rights. The Magna Charta is not chartered rights—but chartered wrongs.

> HENRY DAVID THOREAU, entry written March 16, 1842, *Journals,* 1906.

99 I think that we should be men first, and subjects afterward. It is not desirable to cultivate a respect for the law, so much as for the right.

> HENRY DAVID THOREAU, "Civil Disobedience," 1849.

100 Unjust laws exist: shall we be content to obey them, or shall we endeavor to amend them, and obey them until we have succeeded, or shall we transgress them at once? Men generally, under such a government as this, think that they ought to

wait until they have persuaded the majority to alter them. They think that, if they should resist, the remedy would be worse than the evil. But it is the fault of the government itself that the remedy *is* worse than the evil.

Ibid.

101 The law will never make men free; it is men who have got to make the law free. They are the lovers of law and order who observe the law when the government breaks it.

HENRY DAVID THOREAU, "Slavery in Massachusetts," 1854.

102 Is it not possible that an individual may be right and a government wrong? Are laws to be enforced simply because they are made? or declared by any number of men to be good, if they are *not* good?

HENRY DAVID THOREAU, "A Plea for Captain John Brown," 1859.

103 Any fool can make a rule.

HENRY DAVID THOREAU, entry written February 3, 1860, *Journal,* 1906.

104 The deference of the Americans to the laws has been justly applauded; but it must be added that in America legislation is made by the people and for the people. Consequently, in the United States the law favors those classes that elsewhere are most interested in evading it.

ALEXIS DE TOCQUEVILLE, *Democracy in America,* 1835.

105 When a people lose respect for one bad law, it is but a short step before they include the good laws with the bad and are shortly in rebellion against all law.

OSCAR W. UNDERWOOD, *Drifting Sands of Party Politics,* 1928.

106 Next to the confrontation between two highly trained, finely honed batteries of lawyers, jungle warfare is a stately minuet.

BILL VEECK, *The Hustler's Handbook,* 1965.

107 Greed vs. greed makes for the kind of lawsuits that are settled between the lawyers as soon as both sides decide to take what they can get. Principle vs. principle is a holy war, and no holy war has ever been settled out of court.

BILL VEECK, *Thirty Tons a Day,* 1972.

108 It is the spirit and not the form of law that keeps justice alive.

EARL WARREN, in *Fortune* magazine, November, 1955.

109 Tell me a man is dishonest, and I will answer he is no lawyer. He cannot be, because he is careless and reckless of justice; the law is not in his heart, is not the standard and rule of his conduct.

DANIEL WEBSTER, in a speech in Charleston, South Carolina, May 10, 1847.

110 Most good lawyers live well, work hard, and die poor.

Ibid.

111 There is plenty of law at the end of a night-stick.

Attributed to Grover A. Whalen.

112 No doubtful balance of rights and wrongs,
Nor weary lawyers with endless tongues.

JOHN GREENLEAF WHITTIER, *Maud Muller,* 1854.

113 Law is the crystallization of the habit and thought of society.

WOODROW WILSON, in a lecture at Princeton University, 1893.

114 What we seek is the reign of law, based upon the consent of the governed and sustained by the organized opinion of mankind.

WOODROW WILSON, on the League of Nations, in a speech at Mount Vernon, July 4, 1918.

135. LIBERTY

See also DEMOCRACY; EQUALITY; FREEDOM;
INDEPENDENCE; TYRANNY

1 Things have come to a hell of a pass
When a man can't wallop his own jackass.

Anonymous, c.1900.

2 Liberty Is Always Unfinished Business.

American Civil Liberties Union, title of its annual
report, 1955–1956.

3 I would define liberty to be a power to do as we
would be done by. The definition of liberty to be
the power of doing whatever the law permits,
meaning the civil laws, does not seem satisfactory.

JOHN ADAMS, to J.H. Tiffany, March 31, 1819.

4 The proposition that the people are the best keepers of their own liberties is not true. They are the
worst conceivable, they are no keepers at all; they
can neither judge, act, think, or will, as a political
body.

JOHN ADAMS, in *Defence of the Constitution of
the United States of America against the Attack
of Mr. Turgot,* 1787.

5 Individual liberty is individual power, and as the
power of a community is a mass compounded of
individual powers, the nation which enjoys the
most freedom must necessarily be in proportion to
its numbers the most powerful nation.

JOHN QUINCY ADAMS, in a letter to James
Lloyd, October 1, 1822.

6 Our liberty depends on our education, our laws,
and habits to which even prejudices yield; on the
dispersion of our people on farms and on the almost
equal diffusion of property.

FISHER AMES, in an address in Boston,
Massachusetts, February 8, 1800.

7 The things required for prosperous labor, prosperous manufactures, and prosperous commerce are
three. First, liberty; second, liberty; third, liberty.

HENRY WARD BEECHER, in a speech in
Liverpool, England, October 16, 1863.

8 Liberty, *n.* One of Imagination's most precious
possessions.

AMBROSE BIERCE, *The Devil's Dictionary,* 1906.

9 Experience should teach us to be most on our
guard to protect liberty when the government's
purposes are beneficent. Men born to freedom are
naturally alert to repel invasion of their liberty by
evil-minded rulers. The greatest dangers to liberty
lurk in insidious encroachment by men of zeal,
well-meaning but without understanding.

LOUIS D. BRANDEIS, in a dissenting Supreme
Court opinion, *Olmstead* v. *United States,* 1928.

10 We have had so many years of prosperity, we
have passed through so many difficulties and dangers without the loss of liberty—that we begin to
think that we hold it by divine right from heaven
itself. . . . It is harder to preserve than to obtain
liberty.

JOHN C. CALHOUN, in a speech in the U.S.
Senate, January, 1848.

11 People do not understand liberty or majorities.
The will of the majority is the will of a rabble.
. . . Democracy is levelling—this is inconsistent
with true liberty.

JOHN C. CALHOUN, quoted in John S. Jenkins,
The Life of John Caldwell Calhoun, 1850.

12 Attack another's rights and you destroy your
own.

JOHN JAY CHAPMAN, on imperialism, in a letter,
1897.

13 Liberty like charity must begin at home.

JAMES BRYANT CONANT, "Our Unique
Heritage," in an address at Harvard College,
June 30, 1942.

14 You can only protect your liberties in this world
by protecting the other man's freedom. You can
only be free if I am free.

CLARENCE DARROW, addressing a jury in
Chicago, 1920, quoted in Arthur Weinberg,
Attorney for the Damned, 1957.

15 The whole history of the progress of human
liberty shows that all concessions yet made to her

august claims, have been made of earnest struggle.
. . . If there is no struggle, there is no progress.
Those who profess to favor freedom yet deprecate
agitation, are men who want crops without plowing
up the ground, they want rain without thunder and
lightning. They want the ocean without the awful
roar of its many waters. Power concedes nothing
without a demand. It never did and it never will.
. . . The limits of tyrants are prescribed by the
endurance of those whom they oppress.

> FREDERICK DOUGLASS, in a speech in
> Canandaigua, New York, August 3, 1857.

16 The cost of liberty is less than the price of
repression.

> W.E.B. DuBois, *John Brown,* 1909.

17 Liberty trains for liberty. Responsibility is the
first step in responsibility.

> Ibid.

18 Don't put no constrictions on da people. Leave
'em ta hell alone.

> JIMMY DURANTE, quoted in Nelson A.
> Rockefeller, *Unity, Freedom and Peace: A
> Blueprint for Tomorrow,* 1968.

19 The word *liberty* in the mouth of Mr. [Daniel]
Webster sounds like the word *love* in the mouth of
a courtesan.

> RALPH WALDO EMERSON, entry written in 1851,
> *Journals,* 1909–1914.

20 Nothing is more disgusting than the crowing
about liberty by slaves, as most men are, and the
flippant mistaking for freedom of some paper preamble like a Declaration of Independence or the
statute right to vote, by those who have never dared
to think or to act.

> RALPH WALDO EMERSON, "Fate," *The Conduct
> of Life,* 1860.

21 They that can give up essential liberty to purchase a little temporary safety, deserve neither liberty nor safety.

> BENJAMIN FRANKLIN, motto of the *Historical
> Review of Pennsylvania,* 1759.

22 It is a common observation here that our cause
is *the cause of all mankind,* and that we are fighting for their liberty in defending our own.

> BENJAMIN FRANKLIN, in a letter from Paris to
> Samuel Cooper, 1777.

23 Where liberty dwells, there is my country.

> BENJAMIN FRANKLIN, in a letter to B. Vaughan,
> March 14, 1783. (This Latin aphorism was also
> the motto of James Otis.)

24 Our country has liberty without license, and
authority without despotism.

> JAMES CARDINAL GIBBONS, in a speech in Rome,
> March 25, 1887.

25 Liberty is worth whatever country is worth. It
is by liberty that a man has a country; it is by liberty
he has rights.

> HENRY GILES, *The Worth of Liberty,* 1847.

26 I would remind you that extremism in the defense of liberty is no vice. And let me remind you
also that moderation in the pursuit of justice is no
virtue.

> BARRY M. GOLDWATER, in his speech accepting
> the Republican presidential nomination,
> Republican National Convention, San Francisco,
> California, July 16, 1964.

27 Natural liberty is a gift of the beneficent Creator to the whole human race.

> ALEXANDER HAMILTON, *The Farmer Refuted,*
> 1775.

28 Real liberty is neither found in despotism or the
extremes of democracy, but in moderate governments.

> ALEXANDER HAMILTON, in the debates of the
> Federal Convention, June 26, 1787.

29 The liberty of the press consists, in my idea, in
publishing the truth, from good motives and for
justifiable ends, though it reflect on the government, on magistrates, or individuals.

> ALEXANDER HAMILTON, in a speech in New
> York City, 1804.

30 Liberty lies in the hearts of men and women;
when it dies there, no constitution, no law, no court

can save it; no constitution, no law, no court can even do much to help it. While it lies there it needs no constitution, no law, no court to save it. And what is this liberty which must lie in the hearts of men and women? It is not the ruthless, the unbridled will; it is not freedom to do as one likes. That is the denial of liberty, and leads straight to its overthrow.

> LEARNED HAND, "The Spirit of Liberty," in a speech in New York City, May 21, 1944.

31 The spirit of liberty is the spirit which is not too sure that it is right; the spirit of liberty is the spirit which seeks to understand the minds of other men and women; the spirit of liberty is the spirit which weighs their interests alongside its own without bias; the spirit of liberty remembers that not even a sparrow falls to earth unheeded; the spirit of liberty is the spirit of Him who, near two thousand years ago, taught mankind that lesson it has never learned, but has never quite forgotten: that there is a kingdom where the least shall be heard and considered side by side with the greatest.

> Ibid.

32 Liberty is a beloved discipline.

> GEORGE C. HOMANS, *The Human Group,* 1950.

33 Liberty: 1. A password in universal use, and hence of no value. 2. The slogan of a party or sect that seeks to enslave some other party or sect.

> ELBERT HUBBARD, *The Roycroft Dictionary and Book of Epigrams,* 1923.

34 The liberty of the press is not confined to newspapers and periodicals. It necessarily embraces pamphlets and leaflets. These indeed have been historic weapons in the defense of liberty, as the pamphlets of Thomas Paine and others in our own history abundantly attest.

> CHARLES EVANS HUGHES, in a Supreme Court opinion, *Lovell* v. *City of Griffin,* 1938.

35 What light is to the eyes—what air is to the lungs—what love is to the heart, liberty is to the soul of man. Without liberty, the brain is a dungeon, where the chained thoughts die with their pinions pressed against the hingeless doors.

> ROBERT G. INGERSOLL, "Progress," lecture delivered in Peoria, Illinois, May 14, 1866.

36 There is no slavery but ignorance. Liberty is the child of intelligence.

> ROBERT G. INGERSOLL, "The Liberty of Man, Woman, and Child," 1877.

37 No people ever lost their liberties unless they themselves first became corrupt. . . . The people are the safeguards of their own liberties, and I rely wholly on them to guard themselves.

> ANDREW JACKSON, to a Presbyterian clergyman in Pennsylvania, 1824, quoted in Robert V. Remini, *Andrew Jackson and the Course of American Freedom,* 1981.

38 Liberty is not the mere absence of restraint, it is not a spontaneous product of majority rule, it is not achieved merely by lifting underprivileged classes to power, nor is it the inevitable by-product of technological expansion. It is achieved only by a rule of law.

> ROBERT H. JACKSON, *The Supreme Court in the American System of Government,* 1955

39 The God who gave us life, gave us liberty at the same time.

> THOMAS JEFFERSON, *A Summary View of the Rights of British America,* 1774.

40 My God! how little do my countrymen know what precious blessings they are in possession of, and which no other people on earth enjoy.

> THOMAS JEFFERSON, in a letter from Paris to James Monroe, June 17, 1785.

41 The people are the only censors of their governors; and even their errors will tend to keep these to the true principles of their institution. To punish these errors too severely would be to suppress the only safeguard of the public liberty.

> THOMAS JEFFERSON, in a letter to Col. Edward Carrington, January 16, 1787.

42 The tree of liberty must be refreshed from time to time, with the blood of patriots and tyrants. It is its natural manure.

> THOMAS JEFFERSON, in a letter to Col. William S. Smith, November 13, 1787.

Patrick Henry: "Give me liberty, or give me death" speech, March 23, 1775

Though one of the most famous speeches in American history, Patrick Henry's oration to the Virginia convention was not transcribed as given but reconstructed from memory.

Mr. President, it is natural to man to indulge in the illusions of hope. We are apt to shut our eyes against a painful truth and listen to the song of that siren, till she transforms us into beasts. Is this the part of wise men, engaged in a great and arduous struggle for liberty? Is it that insidious smile with which our petition has been lately received? Trust it not, sir; it will prove a snare to your feet. Suffer not yourselves to be betrayed with a kiss. Ask yourselves how this gracious reception of our petition comports with those warlike preparations which cover our waters and darken our land. Are fleets and armies necessary to a work of love and reconciliation? Have we shown ourselves so unwilling to be reconciled that force must be called in to win back our love? Let us not deceive ourselves, sir. These are the implements of war and subjugation—the last arguments to which kings resort. I ask gentlemen, sir, what means this martial array, if its purpose be not to force us to submission? Can gentlemen assign any other possible motive for it? Has Great Britain any enemy in this quarter of the world to call for all this accumulation of navies and armies? No, sir, she has none. They are meant for us; they can be meant for no other. They are sent over to bind and rivet upon us those chains which the British Ministry have been so long forging.

And what have we oppose to them? Shall we try argument? Sir, we have been trying that for the last ten years. Have we anything new to offer upon the subject? Nothing. We have held the subject up in every light of which it is capable; but it has been all in vain. Shall we resort to entreaty and humble supplication? What terms shall we find which have not been already exhausted? Let us not, I beseech you, sir, deceive ourselves longer. Sir, we have done everything that could be done to avert the storm which is now coming on. We have petitioned; we have remonstrated; we have supplicated; we have prostrated ourselves before the throne and have implored its interposition to arrest the tyrannical hands of the Ministry and Parliament. Our petitions have been slighted; our remonstrances have produced additional violence and insult; our supplications have been disregarded; and we have been spurned, with contempt, from the foot of the throne. In vain, after these things, may we indulge the fond hope of peace and reconciliation.

There is no longer any room for hope. If we wish to be free; if we mean to preserve inviolate those inestimable privileges for which we have been so long contending; if we mean not basely to abandon the noble struggle in which we have been so long engaged, and which we have pledged ourselves never to abandon, until the glorious object of our contest shall be obtained; we must fight! I repeat it, sir, we must fight!! An appeal to arms and to the God of hosts is all that is left us!

They tell us, sir, that we are weak, unable to cope with so formidable an adversary. But when shall we be stronger. Will it be the next week or the next year? Will it be when we are totally disarmed, and when a British guard shall be stationed in every house? Shall we gather strength by irresolution and inaction? Shall we acquire the means of effectual resistance by lying supinely on our backs and hugging the delusive phantom of hope, until our enemies shall have bound us hand and foot? Sir, we are not weak if we make a proper use of those means which the God of nature has placed in our power. Three millions of people armed in the holy cause of liberty and in such a country as that which we possess are invincible by any force which our enemy can send against us.

Besides, sir, we shall not fight our battles alone. There is a just God who presides over the destinies of nations, and who will raise up friends to fight our battles for us. The battle, sir, is not to the strong alone; it is to the vigilant, the active, the brave. Besides, sir, we have no election. If we were base enough to desire it, it is now too late to retire from the contest. There is no retreat but in submission and slavery! Our chains are forged. Their clanking may be heard on the plains of Boston! The war is inevitable—and let it come!! I repeat it, sir, let it come!!!

It is vain, sir, to extenuate the matter. Gentlemen may cry, peace, peace; but there is no peace. The war is actually begun! The next gale that sweeps from the north will bring to our ears the clash of resounding arms! Our brethren are already in the field! Why stand we here idle? What is it that gentlemen wish? What would they have? Is life so dear or peace so sweet as to be purchased at the price of chains and slavery?

Forbid it, Almighty God—I know not what course others may take; but as for me, give me liberty, or give me death!

43 The natural progress of things is for liberty to yield and government to gain ground.

> THOMAS JEFFERSON, in a letter to Col. Edward Carrington, May 27, 1788.

44 You are too well informed a politician, too good a judge of men, not to know, that the ground of liberty is to be gained by inches, that we must be contented to secure what we can get, from time to time, and eternally press forward for what is yet to get. It takes time to persuade men to do even what is for their own good.

> THOMAS JEFFERSON, in a letter to Rev. Charles Clay, January 27, 1790.

45 We are not to expect to be translated from despotism to liberty in a featherbed.

> THOMAS JEFFERSON, in a letter to the Marquis de Lafayette, urging him to save his own head during the French Revolution, April 2, 1790.

46 Let us restore to social intercourse that harmony and affection without which liberty and even life itself are but dreary things.

> THOMAS JEFFERSON, in his first inaugural address, March 4, 1801.

47 The boisterous sea of liberty is never without a wave.

> THOMAS JEFFERSON, in a letter to Richard Rush, October 20, 1820.

48 Liberty in the wild and freakish hands of fanatics has once more, as frequently in the past, proved the effective helpmate of autocracy and the twin brother of tyranny.

> OTTO KAHN, in a speech at the University of Wisconsin, January 14, 1918.

49 The deadliest foe of democracy is not autocracy but liberty frenzied. Liberty is not foolproof. For its beneficent working it demands self-restraint.

> Ibid.

50 Liberty without learning is always in peril and learning without liberty is always in vain.

> JOHN F. KENNEDY, in a speech in celebration of the ninetieth anniversary of the founding of Vanderbilt University, March 18, 1963.

51 Our reliance is in the love of liberty which God has planted in us. Our defense is in the spirit which primed liberty as the heritage of all men, in all lands everywhere. Destroy this spirit and you have planted the seeds of despotism at your door. Familiarize yourselves with the chains of bondage and you prepare your own limbs to wear them. Accustomed to trample on the rights of others, you have lost the genius of your own independence and become the fit subjects of the first cunning tyrant who rises among you.

> ABRAHAM LINCOLN, in a speech in Edwardsville, Illinois, September 13, 1858.

52 The world has never had a good definition of the word "liberty," and the American people, just now, are much in want of one. . . . With some, the word "liberty" may mean for each man to do as he pleases with himself and the product of his labor; while with others, the same word may mean for some men to do as they please with other men and the product of other men's labor. Here are two, not only different, but incompatible things, called by the same name—liberty. And it follows that each of the things is, by the respective parties, called by two different and incompatible names,—liberty and tyranny.

> ABRAHAM LINCOLN, in a speech in Baltimore, Maryland, April 18, 1864.

53 Liberty, as it is conceived by current opinion, has nothing inherent about it; it is a sort of gift or trust bestowed on the individual by the state pending *good behavior*.

> MARY MCCARTHY, "The Contagion of Ideas," a talk given in 1952.

54 Liberty is to faction what air is to fire, an aliment without which it instantly expires. But it could not be less folly to abolish liberty, which is essential to political life, because it nourishes faction, than it would be to wish the annihilation of air, which is essential to animal life, because it imparts to fire its destructive agency.

> JAMES MADISON, *The Federalist*, 1787–1788.

55 All government, of course, is against liberty.

> Attributed to H.L. Mencken.

56 He that would make his own liberty secure must guard even his enemy from oppression.

> THOMAS PAINE, *Dissertation on First Principles of Government*, 1795.

57 Eternal vigilance is the price of liberty; power is ever stealing from the many to the few. The manna of popular liberty must be gathered each day or it is rotten. The living sap of today outgrows the dead rind of yesterday. The hand entrusted with power becomes, either from human depravity or *esprit de corps*, the necessary enemy of the people. Only by continued oversight can the democrat in office be prevented from hardening into a despot; only by unintermitted agitation can a people be sufficiently awake to principle not to let liberty be smothered in material prosperity.

> WENDELL PHILLIPS, speaking at Harvard University in 1852, quoted in Ralph Korngold, *Two Friends of Man,* 1950.

58 Whether in chains or in laurels, Liberty knows nothing but victories.

> WENDELL PHILLIPS, "The Lesson of the Hour," an address at Plymouth Church, Brooklyn, New York, November 1, 1859.

59 The legislature of the United States shall pass no law on the subject of religion nor touching or abridging the liberty of the press.

> CHARLES PINCKNEY, in a resolution presented before the Constitutional Convention, 1787.

60 I am not for a return of that definition of liberty under which for many years a free people were being gradually regimented into the service of the privileged few.

> FRANKLIN D. ROOSEVELT, in a Fireside Chat, September 30, 1934.

61 Liberty . . . is meek and reasonable. She admits that she belongs to all—to the high and the low, the rich and the poor, the black and the white—and that she belongs to them all equally.

> GERRIT SMITH, in a speech in the House of Representatives, June 27, 1854.

62 Civil liberty is the status of the man who is guaranteed by law and civil institutions the exclu-

sive employment of all his own powers for his own welfare.

WILLIAM GRAHAM SUMNER, *The Forgotten Man*, 1883.

63 When I say liberty I do not simply mean what is referred to as "free enterprise." I mean liberty of the individual to think his own thoughts and live his own life as he desires to think and to live; the liberty of the family to decide how they wish to live, what they want to eat for breakfast and for dinner, and how they wish to spend their time; liberty of a man to develop his ideas and get other people to teach those ideas, if he can convince them that they have some value to the world; liberty of every local community to decide how its children shall be educated, how its local services shall be run, and who its local leaders shall be; liberty of a man to choose his own occupation; and liberty of a man to run his own business as he thinks it ought to be run, as long as he does not interfere with the right of other people to do the same thing.

ROBERT A. TAFT, *A Foreign Policy for Americans*, 1951.

64 He who would save liberty must put his trust in democracy.

NORMAN THOMAS, in the *Saturday Review of Literature*, June 7, 1930.

65 It is not the fact of liberty but the way in which liberty is exercised that ultimately determines whether liberty itself survives.

DOROTHY THOMPSON, "What Price Liberty?" *Ladies Home Journal*, May, 1958.

66 When liberty is taken away by force it can be restored by force. When it is relinquished voluntarily by default it can never be recovered.

DOROTHY THOMPSON, "New Caspar Milquetoasts," *Ladies Home Journal*, August, 1958.

67 I had reasoned this out in my mind, there was two things I had a right to, liberty and death. If I could not have one, I would have the other, for no man should take me alive.

HARRIET TUBMAN, c.1868, quoted by Marcy Galen in *Ms.* magazine, August, 1973.

68 Liberty, when it begins to take root, is a plant of rapid growth.

GEORGE WASHINGTON, in a letter to James Madison, March 2, 1788.

69 If the true spark of religious and civil liberty be kindled, it will burn. Human agency cannot extinguish it. Like the earth's central fire, it may be smothered for a time; the ocean may overwhelm it; mountains may press it down; but its inherent and unconquerable force will heave both the ocean and the land, and at some time or other, in some place or other, the volcano will break out and flame up to heaven.

DANIEL WEBSTER, in an address at Bunker Hill Monument, June 17, 1825.

70 Liberty and Union, now and forever, one and inseparable.

DANIEL WEBSTER, in a speech in the U.S. Senate, January 26, 1830.

71 God grants liberty only to those who love it, and are always ready to guard and defend it.

DANIEL WEBSTER, in a speech in the U.S. Senate, June 3, 1834.

72 Liberty exists in proportion to wholesome restraint; the more restraint on others to keep off from us, the more liberty we have.

DANIEL WEBSTER, in a speech in Charleston, South Carolina, May 10, 1847.

73 While I trust that liberty and free institutions, as we have experienced them, may ultimately spread over the globe, I am by no means sure that all people are fit for them; nor am I desirous of imposing or forcing our peculiar forms upon any other nation that does not wish to embrace them.

DANIEL WEBSTER, in a speech at Springfield, Massachusetts, September 29, 1847.

74 Liberty is the only thing you cannot have unless you are willing to give it to others.

WILLIAM ALLEN WHITE, in the *Emporia Gazette*, October 24, 1940.

75 To the States or any one of them, or any city of the States, *Resist much, obey little,*

Once unquestioning obedience, once fully
    enslaved,
Once fully enslaved, no nation, state, city of
    this earth, ever afterward resumes its
    liberty.

    WALT WHITMAN, "To the States," 1860.

76 The only soil in which liberty can grow is that
of a united people. We must have faith that the
welfare of one is the welfare of all. We must know
that the truth can only be reached by the expression
of our free opinions, without fear and without ran-
cor. . . . We must learn to abhor those disruptive
pressures, whether religious, political, or economic,
that the enemies of liberty employ.

    WENDELL WILLKIE, in his speech accepting the
    Republican presidential nomination, August 17,
    1940.

77 Happiness must be achieved through liberty
rather than in spite of liberty.

    Ibid.

78 Liberty has never come from the government.
Liberty has always come from the subjects of it.
The history of liberty is a history of resistance. The
history of liberty is a history of limitations of governmental power, not the increase of it.

    WOODROW WILSON, in a speech at the New
    York Press Club, September 9, 1912.

79 I would rather belong to a poor nation that was
free than to a rich nation that had ceased to be in
love with liberty. We shall not be poor if we love
liberty.

    WOODROW WILSON, in a speech in Mobile,
    Alabama, October 27, 1912.

80 Liberty does not consist . . . in mere declarations
of the rights of man. It consists in the translation
of those declarations into definite actions.

    WOODROW WILSON, in a speech on July 4, 1914.

81 I have always summed up for myself individual
liberty and business liberty and every other kind of
liberty in the phrase that is common in the sporting
world—"A free field and no favor."

    WOODROW WILSON, in a speech to the Electric
    Railway Association, in Washington, D.C.,
    January 29, 1915.

82 Civil or federal liberty is the proper end and
object of authority, and cannot exist without it; and
it is a liberty to do that only which is good, just, and
honest.

    JOHN WINTHROP, in his *Journal,* 1635.

---

136. LIFE

See also DEATH

---

1 Our days begin with trouble here,
    Our life is but a span,
And cruel death is always near,
    So frail a thing is man.

    The New England Primer, c.1683.

2 Gosh! I feel like a real good cry!
    Life, he says, is a cheat, a fake.
Well, I agree with the grouchy guy—
    The best you get is an even break.

    FRANKLIN P. ADAMS, "Ballade of Schopenhauer's
    Philosophy," in *The Melancholy Lute,* 1936.

3 I am one of those people who just can't help
getting a kick out of life—even when it's a kick in
the teeth.

    POLLY ADLER, *A House Is Not a Home,* 1953.

4 One must have lived greatly whose record would
bear the full light of day from beginning to its
close.

    A. BRONSON ALCOTT, "Learning," *Table Talk,*
    1877.

5 Now I am beginning to live a little, and feel less
like a sick oyster at low tide.

    LOUISA MAY ALCOTT, quoted in Edna D.
    Cheney, *Louisa May Alcott: Her Life, Letters,
    and Journals,* 1889.

6 I have three phobias which, could I mute them,
would make my life as slick as a sonnet, but as dull
as ditch water: I hate to go to bed, I hate to get up,
and I hate to be alone.

    TALLULAH BANKHEAD, in *Tallulah,* 1952.

7 I am convinced that the world is not a mere bog in which men and women trample themselves in the mire and die. Something magnificent is taking place here amid the cruelties and tragedies, and the supreme challenge to intelligence is that of making the noblest and best in our curious heritage prevail.

CHARLES A. BEARD, quoted in Will Durant, *On the Meaning of Life,* 1932.

8 We sleep, but the loom of life never stops and the pattern which was weaving when the sun went down is weaving when it comes up tomorrow.

HENRY WARD BEECHER, *Life Thoughts,* 1858.

9 Life is like a mountain: after climbing up one side and sliding down the other, put up the sled.

JOSH BILLINGS, in *Josh Billings' Encyclopedia of Wit and Wisdom,* 1874.

10 Life is a copycat and can be bullied into following the master artist who bids it come to heel.

HEYWOOD BROUN, "Nature the Copycat," *It Seems to Me,* 1935.

11 Life is a struggle, but not a warfare.

JOHN BURROUGHS, *The Summit of the Years,* 1913.

12 There are only two or three human stories, and they go on repeating themselves as fiercely as if they had never happened before.

WILLA CATHER, *O Pioneers!* 1913.

13 Whoso does not see that genuine life is a battle and a march has poorly read his origin and his destiny.

LYDIA MARIA CHILD, *Letters from New York,* 1843–1845.

14 A man said to the universe:
"Sir, I exist!"
"However," replied the universe,
"The fact has not created in me
A sense of obligation."

STEPHEN CRANE, *War Is Kind,* 1899.

15 I have a rendezvous with Life
In days I hope will come
Ere youth has sped, and strength of mind,
Ere voices sweet grow dumb. . . .

Though wet, nor blow, nor space, I fear,
Yet fear I deeply, too,
Lest Death should greet and claim me ere
I keep Life's rendezvous.

COUNTEE CULLEN, "I Have a Rendezvous with Life," in *Caroling Dusk,* 1927.

16 None meet life honestly and few heroically.

Attributed to Clarence Darrow.

17 I took one draught of life,
I'll tell you what I paid,
Precisely an existence—
The market-price, they said.

EMILY DICKINSON, "I took one draught of life," *Further Poems,* 1929.

18 That it will never come again
Is what makes life so sweet.

EMILY DICKINSON, *Bolts of Melody,* 1945.

19 Life is a God-damned, stinking, treacherous game, and nine hundred and ninety-nine men out of every thousand are bastards.

THEODORE DREISER, quoting an unidentified newspaper editor, in *A Book About Myself,* 1922.

20 If ye live enough befure thirty ye won't care to live at all afther fifty.

FINLEY PETER DUNNE, *Mr. Dooley's Opinion,* 1900.

21 Life'd not be worth livin' if we didn't keep our inimies.

FINLEY PETER DUNNE, *Mr. Dooley in Peace and in War,* 1900.

22 Only a life lived for others is the life worth while.

ALBERT EINSTEIN, quoted in the *New York Times,* June 20, 1932.

23 What is the meaning of human life, or of organic life altogether? To answer this question at all implies a religion. Is there any sense then, you ask, in putting it? I answer, the man who regards his own life and that of his fellow creatures as meaningless is not merely unfortunate but almost disqualified for life.

ALBERT EINSTEIN, *The World as I See It,* 1934.

24 I have measured out my life with coffee spoons.

> T.S. ELIOT, *The Love Song of J. Alfred Prufrock,* first published in *Poetry* magazine, 1915.

25 Yet we have gone on living,
Living and partly living.

> T.S. ELIOT, *Murder in the Cathedral,* 1935.

26 We are always getting ready to live, but never living.

> RALPH WALDO EMERSON, entry written April 13, 1834, *Journals,* 1909–1914.

27 My life is not an apology, but a life. It is for itself and not for a spectacle. I much prefer that it should be of a lower strain, so it be genuine and equal, than that it should be glittering and unsteady.

> RALPH WALDO EMERSON, "Self-Reliance," *Essays,* First Series, 1841.

28 Life is a festival only to the wise. Seen from the nook and chimney-side of prudence, it wears a ragged and dangerous front.

> RALPH WALDO EMERSON, "Heroism," *Essays,* First Series, 1841.

29 Life is a series of surprises. We do not guess today the mood, the pleasure, the power of tomorrow, when we are building up our being.

> RALPH WALDO EMERSON, "Circles," *Essays,* First Series, 1841.

30 All life is an experiment. The more experiments you make the better.

> RALPH WALDO EMERSON, entry written in November, 1842, *Journals,* 1909–1914.

31 We live amid surfaces, and the true art of life is to skate well on them.

> RALPH WALDO EMERSON, "Experience," *Essays,* Second Series, 1844.

32 The life of man is the true romance, which, when it is valiantly conducted, will yield the imagination a higher joy than any fiction.

> RALPH WALDO EMERSON, "New England Reformers," *Essays,* Second Series, 1844.

33 Man's life is but seventy salads long.

> RALPH WALDO EMERSON, "Nature," *Essays,* Second Series, 1844.

34 Life is too short to waste
In critic peep or cynic bark,
Quarrel or reprimand;
    'Twill soon be dark;
Up! mind thine own aim and
    God save the mark!

> RALPH WALDO EMERSON, "To J.W.," from *Poems,* 1847.

35 Life consists in what man is thinking of all day.

> RALPH WALDO EMERSON, entry written in 1847, *Journals,* 1909–1914.

36 Life is eating us up. We shall be fables presently. Keep cool: it will be all one a hundred years hence.

> RALPH WALDO EMERSON, "Montaigne," *Representative Men,* 1850.

37 Life is March weather, savage and serene in one hour.

> Ibid.

38 No power of genius has ever yet had the smallest success in explaining existence. The perfect enigma remains.

> RALPH WALDO EMERSON, "Plato," *Representative Men,* 1850.

39 Life is a boundless privilege, and when you pay for your ticket, and get into the car, you have no guess what good company you will find there.

> RALPH WALDO EMERSON, "Considerations by the Way," *The Conduct of Life,* 1860.

40 It is the depth at which we live and not at all the surface extension that imports.

> RALPH WALDO EMERSON, "Works and Days," *Society and Solitude,* 1870.

41 Fill my hour, ye gods, so that I may not say, whilst I have done this, "Behold, also, an hour of my life is gone,"—but rather, "I have lived an hour."

> Ibid.

42 Life is good only when it is magical and musical, a perfect timing and consent, and when we do not anatomize it. You must treat the days respectfully, you must be a day yourself, and not interrogate it like a college professor. The world is enigmatical,—everything said, and everything known or done,—and must not be taken literally, but genially.

Ibid.

43 We live by desire to live; we live by choice; by will, by thought, by virtue, by the vivacity of the laws which we obey, and obeying share their life,—or we die by sloth, by disobedience, by losing hold of life, which ebbs out of us.

RALPH WALDO EMERSON, "Immortality," *Letters and Social Aims,* 1876.

44 Sooner or later that which is now life shall be poetry, and every fair and manly trait shall add a richer strain to the song.

RALPH WALDO EMERSON, "Poetry and Imagination," *Letters and Social Aims,* 1876.

45 One moment of a man's life is a fact so stupendous as to take the lustre out of all fiction.

RALPH WALDO EMERSON, "Demonology," *Lectures and Biographical Sketches,* 1883.

46 Listen, you son of a bitch, life isn't all a goddamn football game! You won't always get the girl! Life is rejection and pain and loss.

FREDERICK EXLEY, in *A Fan's Notes,* 1977.

47 I don't want to live—I want to love first, and live incidentally.

ZELDA FITZGERALD, in a letter to F. Scott Fitzgerald, 1919, quoted in Nancy Mitford, *Zelda,* 1970.

48 Wish not so much to live long as to live well.

BENJAMIN FRANKLIN, *Poor Richard's Almanack,* 1738.

49 A life of leisure, and a life of laziness, are two things.

BENJAMIN FRANKLIN, *Poor Richard's Almanack,* 1746.

50 Were it offered to my choice, I should have no objection to a repetition of the same life from its beginning, only asking the advantages authors have in a second edition to correct some faults of the first.

BENJAMIN FRANKLIN, *Autobiography,* 1798.

51 A noble life, crowned with heroic death, rises above and outlives the pride and pomp and glory of the mightiest empire of the earth.

JAMES A. GARFIELD, in a speech in the House of Representatives, December 9, 1858.

52 We are but shadows: we are not endowed with real life, and all that seems most real about us is but the thinnest substance of a dream,—till the heart be touched. That touch creates us—then we begin to be—thereby we are beings of reality and inheritors of eternity.

NATHANIEL HAWTHORNE, entry written October 4, 1840, in *Passages from the American Notebooks,* 1868.

53 Life is made up of marble and mud.

NATHANIEL HAWTHORNE, *The House of the Seven Gables,* 1851.

54 The world is a fine place and worth fighting for.

ERNEST HEMINGWAY, *For Whom the Bell Tolls,* 1940.

55 You know, we're kicking our way into adolescence from the minute we're born. Gradually you form your own ideas of how you should lead your life. It's strange, but when you get hurt—really hurt, I mean—you're willing to throw those ideas aside for another set that now make sense to you and calm your hurt.

ERNEST HEMINGWAY, quoted in Carlos Baker, *Ernest Hemingway—A Life Story,* 1969.

56 Life is made up of sobs, sniffles, and smiles, with sniffles predominating.

O. HENRY, "The Gift of the Magi," *The Four Million,* 1906.

57 Without discipline, there's no life at all.

KATHARINE HEPBURN, in a television appearance on the Dick Cavett Show, April 4, 1975.

58 Like phantoms painted on the magic slide,
Forth from the darkness of the past we glide,
As living shadows for a moment seen
In airy pageant on the eternal screen,
Traced by a ray from one unchanging flame,
Then seek the dust and stillness whence we
    came.

> OLIVER WENDELL HOLMES, SR., "A Rhymed
> Lesson," 1846.

59 Our brains are seventy-year clocks. The angel
of life winds them up once for all, then closes the
case, and gives the key into the hands of the angel
of the resurrection.

> OLIVER WENDELL HOLMES, SR., *The Autocrat of
> the Breakfast-Table,* 1858.

60 Life is a great bundle of little things.

> OLIVER WENDELL HOLMES, SR., *The Professor
> at the Breakfast-Table,* 1860.

61 Life is a fatal complaint, and an eminently contagious one.

> OLIVER WENDELL HOLMES, SR., *The Poet at the
> Breakfast-Table,* 1872.

62 Life is an end in itself, and the only question as
to whether it is worth living is whether you have
enough of it.

> OLIVER WENDELL HOLMES, JR., in a speech at
> the Bar Association dinner, Boston,
> Massachusetts, 1900.

63 Life is a romantic business. It is painting a picture, not doing a sum.

> OLIVER WENDELL HOLMES, JR., in a letter to
> Oswald Ryan, June 5, 1911.

64 All life is an experiment. Every year if not every
day we have to wager our salvation upon some
prophecy based upon imperfect knowledge.

> OLIVER WENDELL HOLMES, JR., in a dissenting
> Supreme Court opinion, *Abrams* v. *United States,*
> 1919.

65 To live is to function. That is all there is in
living.

> OLIVER WENDELL HOLMES, JR., in a speech on
> his 91st birthday, Washington, D.C., March 8,
> 1932.

66 Life is a preparation for the future; and the best
preparation for the future is to live as if there were
none.

> ELBERT HUBBARD, in *The Philistine* magazine,
> published from 1895–1915.

67 Every life is its own excuse for being, and to
deny or refute the untrue things that are said of you
is an error in judgment. All wrong recoils upon the
doer, and the man who makes wrong statements
about others is himself to be pitied, not the man he
vilifies. It is better to be lied about than to lie. At
the last no one can harm us but ourselves.

> ELBERT HUBBARD, *The Roycroft Dictionary and
> Book of Epigrams,* 1923.

68 Do not take life too seriously—you will never
get out of it alive.

> Ibid.

69 Life is just one damn thing after another.

> Ibid.

70 Life is a shadowy, strange, and winding road.

> ROBERT G. INGERSOLL, in a speech in Chicago,
> Illinois, November 26, 1882.

71 Live all you can; it's a mistake not to. It doesn't
so much matter what you do in particular so long
as you have your life.

> HENRY JAMES, *The Ambassadors,* 1903.

72 Be not afraid of life. Believe that life *is* worth
living, and your belief will help create the fact.

> HENRY JAMES, "Is Life Worth Living?" *The
> Will to Believe,* 1897.

73 Life has its heroes and its villains, its soubrettes
and its ingenues, and all roles may be acted well.

> JOSEPH WOOD KRUTCH, *The Modern Temper,*
> 1929.

74 Life is what happens while you are making
other plans.

> Attributed to John Lennon.

75 One day nearer the grave, Thurber.

> M.B. "BILL" LEVICK, daily greeting to James
> Thurber at the *New Yorker,* quoted in James
> Thurber, *The Years with Ross,* 1957.

76 Life is a loom, weaving illusion.

> VACHEL LINDSAY, "The Chinese Nightingale,"
> 1917.

77 Life is the west-going dream-storms' breath,
Life is a dream, the sigh of the skies,
The breath of the stars, that nod on their
    pillows
With their golden hair mussed over their
    eyes.

> VACHEL LINDSAY, "The Ghost of the Buffaloes,"
> 1917.

78 Tell me not, in mournful numbers,
    Life is but an empty dream!—
For the soul is dead that slumbers,
    And things are not what they seem.
Life is real! Life is earnest!
    And the grave is not its goal;
Dust thou art, to dust returnest,
    Was not spoken of the soul.

> HENRY WADSWORTH LONGFELLOW, "A Psalm
> of Life," 1839.

79 Art is long, and Time is fleeting,
    And our hearts, though stout and brave,
Still, like muffled drums, are beating
    Funeral marches to the grave.

> Ibid.

80 Lives of great men all remind us
    We can make our lives sublime,
And, departing, leave behind us
    Footprints on the sands of time.

> Ibid.

81 Take them, O great Eternity!
    Our little life is but a gust
That bends the branches of thy tree,
    And trails its blossoms in the dust!

> HENRY WADSWORTH LONGFELLOW, "Suspiria,"
> 1849.

82 For gentleness and love and trust
Prevail o'er angry wave and gust;
And in the wreck of noble lives
Something immortal still survives.

> HENRY WADSWORTH LONGFELLOW, "The
> Building of the Ship," 1849.

83 Our ingress into the world
    Was naked and bare;
Our progress through the world
    Is trouble and care.
Our egress from the world
    Will be nobody knows where:
But if we do well here
    We shall do well there.

> HENRY WADSWORTH LONGFELLOW, "The
> Student's Tale," *Tales of a Wayside Inn,*
> 1863–1874.

84 Ships that pass in the night, and speak each
        other in passing,
    Only a signal shown and a distant voice in
        the darkness;
So on the ocean of life, we pass and speak
        one another,
    Only a look and a voice, then darkness again
        and a silence.

> HENRY WADSWORTH LONGFELLOW, "The
> Theologian's Tale," *Tales of a Wayside Inn,*
> 1863–1874.

85 Most men make the voyage of life as if they
carried sealed orders which they were not to open
till they were fairly in mid-ocean.

> JAMES RUSSELL LOWELL, "Dante," *Among My
> Books,* 1876.

86 But life is sweet, though all that makes it
        sweet
    Lessen like sound of friends' departing feet.

> JAMES RUSSELL LOWELL, in the postscript to
> "Epistle to George William Curtis," 1887.

87 A little while the tears and laughter,
    The willow and the rose;
A little while, and what comes after
    No man knows.
An hour to sing, to love and linger,
    Then lutanist and lute
Will fall on silence, song and singer
    Both be mute.

> DON MARQUIS, "A Little While," in Burton
> Egbert Stevenson, *The Home Book of Verse,*
> 1953.

88 Degenerate sons and daughters,
Life is too strong for you—
It takes life to love life.

> EDGAR LEE MASTERS, "Lucinda Matlock," *Spoon River Anthology,* 1915.

89 None but a good man is really a living man, and the more good any man does, the more he really lives. All the rest is death, or belongs to it.

> COTTON MATHER, *Bonifacius: An Essay Upon the Good,* 1710.

90 Born in throes, 'tis fit that man should live in pains and die in pangs.

> HERMAN MELVILLE, *Moby-Dick,* 1851.

91 There are certain queer times and occasions in this strange mixed affair we call life when a man takes this whole universe for a vast practical joke, though the wit thereof he but dimly discerns, and more than suspects that the joke is at nobody's expense but his own.

> Ibid.

92 All men live enveloped in whale-lines. All are born with halters around their necks; but it is only when caught in the swift, sudden turn of death, that mortals realize the silent, subtle everpresent perils of life.

> Ibid.

93 Life's a voyage that's homeward bound.

> HERMAN MELVILLE, quoted in John Cournos, *A Modern Plutarch,* 1928.

94 The basic fact about human existence is not that it is a tragedy, but that it is a bore.

> H.L. MENCKEN, *Prejudices,* 1919–1927.

95 Unrest of spirit is a mark of life.

> KARL MENNINGER, in *This Week* magazine, October 16, 1958.

96 My candle burns at both ends;
It will not last the night;
But, oh, my foes, and oh, my friends—
It gives a lovely light.

> EDNA ST. VINCENT MILLAY, "First Flag," *A Few Figs from Thistles,* 1920.

97 The past belongs to God: the present only is ours. And short as it is, there is more in it, and of it, than we can well manage.

> DONALD GRANT MITCHELL, *Reveries of a Bachelor,* 1850.

98 Life's a tough proposition, and the first hundred years are the hardest.

> Attributed to Wilson Mizner.

99 Life is a foreign language; all men mispronounce it.

> CHRISTOPHER MORLEY, *Thunder on the Left,* 1925.

100 We do not live to extenuate the miseries of the past nor to accept as uncurable those of the present.

> FAIRFIELD OSBORN, *The Limits of the Earth,* 1953.

101 Whatever life is (and nobody can define it) it is something forever changing shape, fleeting, escaping us into death. Life is indeed the only thing that can die, and it begins to die as soon as it is born, and never ceases dying. Each of us is constantly experiencing cellular death. For the renewal of our tissues means a corresponding death of them, so that death and rebirth become, biologically, right and left hand of the same thing. All growing is at the same time a dying away from that which lived yesterday.

> DONALD CULROSS PEATTIE, *The Road of a Naturalist,* 1941.

102 Tell me not in mournful wish-wash
Life's a sort of sugared dish-wash.

> EZRA POUND, "L'Homme Moyen Sensuel," in *Personae,* 1926. (See quotation 78, above.)

103 When I consider life and its few years—
A wisp of fog betwixt us and the sun;
A call to battle, and the battle done
Ere the last echo dies within our ears;
A rose choked in the grass; an hour of fears;
The gusts that past a darkening shore do
beat;

The burst of music down an unlistening
    street—
I wonder at the idleness of tears.

> LIZETTE WOODWORTH REESE, "Tears,"
> published in *Scribner's Magazine,* November,
> 1899.

104 An awful lot of life on this planet is one man's
assessment of the other.

> WALT W. ROSTOW, quoted in Hugh Sidey, *John
> F. Kennedy, President: A Reporter's Inside Story,*
> 1963.

105 A life without surrender is a life without commitment.

> JERRY RUBIN, *Growing (Up) at 37,* 1976.

106 All life is six to five against.

> Attributed to Damon Runyon.

107 That life is worth living is the most necessary
of assumptions, and, were it not assumed, the most
impossible of conclusions.

> GEORGE SANTAYANA, "Reason in Common
> Sense," *The Life of Reason,* 1905–1906.

108 Nothing can be meaner than the anxiety to live
on, to live on anyhow and in any shape; a spirit with
any honor is not willing to live except in its own
way, and a spirit with any wisdom is not over-eager
to live at all.

> GEORGE SANTAYANA, *Winds of Doctrine,* 1913.

109 There is no cure for birth and death save to
enjoy the interval.

> GEORGE SANTAYANA, "War Shrines," *Soliloquies
> in England and Later Soliloquies,* 1922.

110   From a boy
I gloated on existence. Earth to me
Seemed all-sufficient and my sojourn there
One trembling opportunity for joy.

> ALAN SEEGER, "I Loved . . ." *Poems,* 1916.

111 There are two things to aim at in life: first to
get what you want; and, after that, to enjoy it. Only
the wisest of mankind achieve the second.

> LOGAN PEARSALL SMITH, *Afterthoughts,* 1931.

112 Waves of serener life pass over us from time
to time, like flakes of sunlight over the fields in
cloudy weather.

> HENRY DAVID THOREAU, *A Week on the
> Concord and Merrimack Rivers,* 1849.

113 My life is like a stroll upon the beach,
    As near the ocean's edge as I can go.

> Ibid.

114 The art of life, of a poet's life, is, not having
anything to do, to do something.

> HENRY DAVID THOREAU, entry dated April 29,
> 1852, in his *Journal,* 1906.

115 Our life is frittered away by detail . . .
Simplify, simplify.

> HENRY DAVID THOREAU, "Where I Lived, and
> What I Lived For," *Walden,* 1854.

116 The mass of men lead lives of quiet desperation. What is called resignation is confirmed desperation. From the desperate city you go into the
desperate country, and have to console yourself
with the bravery of minks and muskrats. A stereotyped but unconscious despair is concealed even
under what are called the games and amusements
of mankind. There is no play in them, for this
comes after work. But it is a characteristic of wisdom not to do desperate things.

> HENRY DAVID THOREAU, "Economy," *Walden,*
> 1854.

117 He is blessed over all mortals who loses no
moment of the passing life in remembering the
past.

> HENRY DAVID THOREAU, *Excursions,*
> 1863.

118 Let us endeavour so to live that when we come
to die even the undertaker will be sorry.

> MARK TWAIN, "Pudd'nhead Wilson's Calendar,"
> *Pudd'nhead Wilson,* 1894.

119 Why is it that we rejoice at a birth and grieve
at a funeral? It is because we are not the person
involved.

> Ibid.

120 All say, "How hard it is to die"—a strange complaint from people who have had to live. Pity is for the living, envy for the dead.

> Ibid.

121 Life is like an overlong drama through which we sit being nagged by the vague memories of having read the reviews.

> JOHN UPDIKE, *The Coup,* 1978.

122 An unhatched egg is to me the greatest challenge in life.

> E.B. WHITE, in a letter to Reginald Allen, March 5, 1973.

123 I do not snivel that snivel the world over,
> That months are vacuums, and the ground
> > but wallow and filth.

> WALT WHITMAN, "Song of Myself," 1855.

124 O I see now that life cannot exhibit all to
> me, as the day cannot,
> I see that I am to wait for what will be
> > exhibited by death.

> WALT WHITMAN, "Night on the Prairies," 1860.

125 Thanks in old age—thanks ere I go,
> For health, the midday sun, the impalpable
> > air—for life, mere life.

> WALT WHITMAN, "Thanks in Old Age," 1888.

126 My advice to you is not to inquire why or whither, but just enjoy your ice cream while it's on your plate—that's my philosophy.

> THORNTON WILDER, *The Skin of Our Teeth,* 1942.

127 The cost of living is going up and the chance of living is going down.

> FLIP WILSON, quoted in Eric Lax, *On Being Funny,* 1975.

137. ABRAHAM LINCOLN

See also CAMPAIGN SLOGANS; CIVIL WAR; CONGRESS; CONSTITUTION; DEMOCRACY; EQUALITY; GOVERNMENT; POLITICS; SLAVERY

1 Blackguard and buffoon as he is, he has pursued his end with an energy as untiring as an Indian, and a singleness of purpose that might almost be called patriotic.

> Unidentified author, on Lincoln, in the *Charleston Mercury,* January 10, 1865.

2 His mind works in the right directions but seldom works clearly and cleanly. His bread is of unbolted flour, and much straw, too, mixes in the bran, and sometimes gravel stones.

> HENRY WARD BEECHER, in a letter to Salmon P. Chase, December, 1863.

3 Lincoln, six feet one in his stocking feet,
> The lank man, knotty and tough as a hickory
> > rail,
> Whose hands were always too big for
> > white-kid gloves,
> Whose wit was a coonskin sack of dry, tall
> > tales,
> Whose weathered face was homely as a
> > plowed field.

> STEPHEN VINCENT BENÉT, *John Brown's Body,* 1928.

4 No king this man, by grace of God's intent;
> No, something better, freeman,—President!
> A nature, modeled on a higher plan,
> Lord of himself, an inborn gentleman!

> GEORGE HENRY BOKER, "Our Heroic Themes," read at Harvard University, July 20, 1865.

5 This man's appearance, his pedigree, his coarse low jokes and anecdotes, his vulgar similes and his frivolity are a disgrace to the seat he holds.

> Attributed to John Wilkes Booth, 1864.

6 Oh, slow to smite and swift to spare,
> Gentle and merciful and just!

Who, in the fear of God, didst bear
  The sword of power, a nation's trust!

> WILLIAM CULLEN BRYANT, "Abraham Lincoln,"
> April, 1865.

7 O Uncommon Commoner! may your name
Forever lead like a living flame!
Unschooled scholar! how did you learn
The wisdom a lifetime may not earn?

> EDMUND VANCE COOKE, "The Uncommon
> Commoner."

8 In Washington the most striking thing is the absence of personal loyalty to the President. It does not exist. He has no admirers, no enthusiastic supporters, none to bet on his head. If a Republican convention were to be held tomorrow, he would not get the vote of a state.

> RICHARD HENRY DANA, JR., in a letter to
> Charles Francis Adams, March, 1863.

9 Lincoln is one of those peculiar men who perform with admirable skill everything which they undertake.

> STEPHEN A. DOUGLAS, in the first
> Lincoln-Douglas debate, Ottawa, Illinois,
> August 21, 1858.

10 I am sure if this man had ruled in a period of less facility of printing, he would have become mythological in a very few years, like Aesop or Pilpay, or one of the Seven Wise Masters, by his fables and proverbs.

> RALPH WALDO EMERSON, "Abraham Lincoln,"
> 1865, published in *Miscellanies,* 1884.

11 His heart was as great as the world, but there was no room in it to hold the memory of a wrong.

> RALPH WALDO EMERSON, "Greatness," *Letters
> and Social Aims,* 1876.

12 I should be glad if I could flatter myself that I came as near to the central idea of the occasion in two hours as you did in two minutes.

> EDWARD EVERETT, in a note to Abraham Lincoln
> the day after Lincoln delivered his famous address
> at Gettysburg, Pa., November 20, 1863. (Lincoln
> responded to Everett's note, "In our respective
> parts yesterday, you could not have been excused
> to make a short address, nor I a long one. I am

pleased to know that, in your judgment, the little I did say was not entirely a failure." Everett was the featured speaker at Gettysburg, but Lincoln's address is the one remembered.)

13 Lincoln had faith in time, and time has justified his faith.

> BENJAMIN HARRISON, in an address on Lincoln
> Day, Chicago, 1898.

14 The President last night had a dream. He was in a party of plain people and as it became known who he was they began to comment on his appearance. One of them said, "He is a common-looking man." The President replied, "Common-looking people are the best in the world: that is the reason the Lord makes so many of them."

> JOHN HAY, diary entry, December 23, 1863.

15 It is absurd to call him a modest man. No great man was ever modest. . . . I consider Lincoln republicanism incarnate—with all its faults and all its virtues.

> JOHN HAY, on Abraham Lincoln, quoted in
> William H. Herndon, *Lincoln: The True Story of
> a Great Life,* 1889.

16 He ought to hang somebody, and get up a name for will or decision—for character. Let him hang some child or woman, if he has not courage to hang a man.

> WILLIAM H. HERNDON, junior partner in
> Lincoln's law firm, in a letter to Lyman
> Trumbull, November 20, 1861.

17 Lincoln was not a type. He stands alone—no ancestors, no fellows, no successors.

> ROBERT G. INGERSOLL, "Abraham Lincoln,"
> 1894.

18 Strange mingling of mirth and tears, of the tragic and grotesque, of cap and crown, of Socrates and Rabelais, of Aesop and Marcus Aurelius— Lincoln, the gentlest memory of the world.

> Ibid.

19 Hundreds of people are now engaged in smoothing out the lines on Lincoln's face—forcing all features to the common mold—so that he may be

known, not as he really was, but, according to their poor standard, as he should have been.

> Ibid.

20 Lincoln's words have become the common covenant of our public life. Let us now get on with his work.

> LYNDON B. JOHNSON, address at the Lincoln Memorial in Washington, February 12, 1964.

21 I presume you all know who I am. I am humble Abraham Lincoln. I have been solicited by many friends to become a candidate for the legislature. My politics are short and sweet, like the old woman's dance. . . . I am in favor of the internal improvements system and a high protective tariff. These are my sentiments and political principles. If elected, I shall be thankful; if not it will be all the same. . . . If the good people, in their wisdom, shall see fit to keep me in the background, I have been too familiar with disappointments to be very much chagrined.

> ABRAHAM LINCOLN, in his first recorded speech, March 9, 1832.

22 Whatever woman may cast her lot with mine, should any ever do so, it is my intention to do all in my power to make her happy and contented; and there is nothing I can imagine that would make me more unhappy than to fail in the effort.

> ABRAHAM LINCOLN, in a letter to Mary Owens, May 7, 1837.

23 I have now come to the conclusion never again to think of marrying, and for this reason: I can never be satisfied with anyone who would be blockhead enough to have me.

> ABRAHAM LINCOLN, in a letter to Mrs. O.H. Browning, written after Mary Owens refused his proposal of marriage, April 1, 1838.

24 Nothing new here except my marrying, which to me is a matter of profound wonder.

> ABRAHAM LINCOLN, in a letter to Samuel Marshall, November 11, 1842.

25 It is a great piece of folly to attempt to make anything out of me or my early life. It can all be condensed into a single sentence, and that sentence you will find in Gray's "Elegy": "The short and simple annals of the poor."

> ABRAHAM LINCOLN, speaking with John L. Scripps, Lincoln's first biographer, June, 1860.

26 As to whiskers, having never worn any, do you not think people would call it a piece of silly affectation if I were to begin it now?

> ABRAHAM LINCOLN, in a letter to Grace Bedell, October 19, 1860.

27 I have been selected to fill an important office for a brief period, and am now, in your eyes, invested with an influence which will soon pass away; but should my administration prove to be a very wicked one, or what is more probable, a very foolish one, if you, the people, are true to yourselves and the Constitution, there is but little harm I can do, thank God.

> ABRAHAM LINCOLN, in a speech at Lawrenceburg, Indiana, February 28, 1861.

28 I take the official oath today with no mental reservations, and with no purpose to construe the Constitution or laws by any hypercritical rules.

> ABRAHAM LINCOLN, in his first inaugural address, March 4, 1861.

29 With my own ability, I cannot succeed, without the sustenance of Divine Providence, and of the great free, happy and intelligent people. Without these I cannot hope to succeed; with them, I cannot fail.

> ABRAHAM LINCOLN, in a speech in Newark, New Jersey, February 21, 1861.

30 I claim not to have controlled events, but confess plainly that events have controlled me.

> ABRAHAM LINCOLN, in a letter to A.G. Hodges, April 4, 1864.

31 I desire so to conduct the affairs of this administration that if at the end, when I come to lay down the reins of power, I have lost every other friend on earth, I shall at least have one friend left, and that friend shall be down inside of me.

> ABRAHAM LINCOLN, in a reply to a committee urging a peace settlement with the Confederacy, 1864.

32 You can fool all the people some of the time and
some of the people all of the time, but you can't fool
all of the people all of the time.

>   ABRAHAM LINCOLN, in a speech at Clinton,
>   Illinois, September 8, 1858, collected in *Lincoln's
>   Complete Works,* 1905.

33 A bronzed, lank man! His suit of ancient
        black,
    A famous high top-hat and plain worn shawl
    Make him the quaint great figure that men
        love,
    The prairie-lawyer, master of us all.

>   VACHEL LINDSAY, "Abraham Lincoln Walks at
>   Midnight," *The Congo and Other Poems,* 1914.

34 His head is bowed. He thinks of men and
        kings.
    Yea, when the sick world cries, how can he
        sleep?
    Too many peasants fight, they know not
        why;
    Too many homesteads in black terror weep.

>   Ibid.

35 Here was a man to hold against the world,
    A man to match the mountains and the sea.

>   EDWIN MARKHAM, "Lincoln, the Man of the
>   People," 1901.

36 The color of the ground was in him, the red
        earth;
    The smack and tang of elemental things.

>   Ibid.

37 Up from Log cabin to the Capitol,
    One fire was on his spirit, one resolve—
    To send the keen axe to the root of wrong,
    Clearing a free way for the feet of God.

>   Ibid.

38 He held his place—
    Held the long purpose like a growing tree—
    Held on through blame and faltered not at
        praise.
    And when he fell in whirlwind, he went
        down
    As when a lordly cedar, green with boughs,

Goes down with a great shout upon the hills,
And leaves a lonesome place against the sky.

>   Ibid.

39 Our big, gaunt, homely brother—
    Our huge Atlantic coast-storm in a shawl,
    Our cyclone in a smile—our President.

>   James Oppenheim, "The Lincoln-Child."

40 Mr. Lincoln was deficient in those little links
which make up the chain of woman's happiness.

>   MARY OWENS, on her decision not to accept
>   Lincoln's marriage proposal, in a letter to William
>   H. Herndon, May 22, 1866.

41 [Lincoln] is a first-rate second-rate man. He is
one of the best specimens of a second-rate man, and
he is honestly waiting, like any other servant, for
the people to come and send him on any errand they
wish.

>   WENDELL PHILLIPS, in a speech, August 2, 1862,
>   quoted in Ralph Korngold, *Two Friends of Man,*
>   1950.

42 For he, to whom we had applied
    Our shopman's test of age and worth,
    Was elemental when he died,
    As he was ancient at his birth:
    The saddest among kings of earth,
    Bowed with a galling crown, this man
    Met rancor with a cryptic mirth,
    Laconic—and Olympian.

>   EDWIN ARLINGTON ROBINSON, "The Master,"
>   *The Town Down the River,* 1910.

43 He worked for me, but was always reading and
thinking. I used to get mad at him for it. I say he
was awfully lazy. He would laugh and talk—crack
jokes and tell stories all the time; didn't love work
half as much as pay. He said to me one day that his
father taught him to work; but he never taught him
to love it.

>   JOHN ROMINE, neighbor of the Lincoln family
>   during Lincoln's boyhood near Gentryville,
>   Indiana, in William H. Herndon, *Herndon's
>   Lincoln,* 1889.

44 When Abraham Lincoln was shoveled into
        the tombs, he forgot the copperheads and

Abraham Lincoln: Gettysburg Address, November 19, 1863

This, the most famous speech in American history, took only three minutes to deliver. It ranks with the Declaration of Independence and the Constitution as among the most enduring statements of American liberty and freedom.

Four score and seven years ago our fathers brought forth on this continent a new nation, conceived in liberty and dedicated to the proposition that all men are created equal.

Now we are engaged in a great civil war, testing whether that nation or any nation so conceived and so dedicated can long endure. We are met on a great battlefield of that war. We have come to dedicate a portion of that field as a final resting place for those who here gave their lives that that nation might live. It is altogether fitting and proper that we should do this.

But, in a larger sense, we cannot dedicate—we cannot consecrate—we cannot hallow—this ground. The brave men, living and dead, who struggled here have consecrated it far above our poor power to add or detract. The world will little note nor long remember what we say here, but it can never forget what they did here. It is for us, the living, rather, to be dedicated here to the unfinished work which they who fought here have thus far so nobly advanced.

It is rather for us to be here dedicated to the great task remaining before us—that from these honored dead we take increased devotion to that cause for which they gave the last full measure of devotion; that we here highly resolve that these dead shall not have died in vain; that this nation, under God, shall have a new birth of freedom; and that government of the people, by the people, for the people shall not perish from the earth.

the assassin . . . in the dust, in the cool tombs.

CARL SANDBURG, "Cool Tombs," 1918.

45 Not often in the story of mankind does a man arrive on earth who is both steel and velvet, who is as hard as rock and soft as drifting fog, who holds in his heart and mind the paradox of terrible storm and peace unspeakable and perfect.

CARL SANDBURG, opening sentence of his address to a joint session of Congress on the 150th anniversary of Lincoln's birth, February 12, 1959.

46 I will make a prophecy that may now sound peculiar. In fifty years, perhaps much sooner, Lincoln's name will be inscribed close to Washington's on this Republic's roll of honor.

CARL SCHURZ, in a letter to Theodor Petrasch, October 12, 1864.

47 Now he belong to the ages.

EDWIN M. STANTON, at the death of Lincoln, April 15, 1865.

48 The Union, with him, in sentiment rose to the sublimity of a religious mysticism, while his ideas

of its structure and formation, in logic, rested upon nothing but the subtleties of a sophism!

> ALEXANDER H. STEPHENS, in *A Constitutional View of the Late War Between the States,* 1868–1870.

49 Someone asked me, as I came in, down on the street, how I felt and I was reminded of a story that a fellow townsman of ours used to tell—Abraham Lincoln. They asked him how he felt once after an unsuccessful election. He said he felt like a little boy who had stubbed his toe in the dark. He said that he was too old to cry, but it hurt too much to laugh.

> ADLAI E. STEVENSON, commenting on his defeat in the presidential election, November 5, 1952.

50 No Caesar he whom we lament,
A man without a precedent,
Sent, it would seem, to do
His work, and perish, too.
One of the people! born to be
Their curious epitome;
To share, yet rise above
Their shifting hate and love.

> RICHARD HENRY STODDARD, *Abraham Lincoln: An Horatian Ode,* 1865.

51 Beside this corpse, that bears for winding
sheet
The Stars and Stripes he lived to rear
anew,
Between the mourners at his head and feet,
Say, scurril jester, is there room for *you?*

Yes, he had lived to shame me from my
sneer,
To lame my pencil and confute my pen—
To make me own this hind of Princes peer,
This rail-splitter a true-born king of men.

> TOM TAYLOR, author of the play Lincoln was watching when he was shot, in "Abraham Lincoln," *Punch* magazine, May 6, 1865.

52 He has doctrines, not hatreds, and is without ambition except to do good and serve his country.

> ELIHU B. WASHBURNE, speaking in the House of Representatives on Lincoln's nomination for the presidency, May 29, 1860.

53 I never see that man without feeling that he is one to become personally attach'd to, for his combination of purest, heartiest tenderness, and native western form of manliness.

> WALT WHITMAN, "The Inauguration," March 4, 1865, in *Specimen Days and Collect,* 1882.

54 O comrade lustrous with silver face in the
night.

> WALT WHITMAN, "When Lilacs Last in the Dooryard Bloom'd," 1865–1866.

55 O Captain! my Captain! our fearful trip is
done,
The ship has weathered every rack, the prize
we sought is won,
The port is near, the bells I hear, the people
all exulting.
While follow eyes the steady keel, the vessel
grim and daring;
But O heart! heart! heart!
O the bleeding drops of red,
Where on the deck my Captain lies,
Fallen cold and dead.

> WALT WHITMAN, "O Captain! My Captain!" 1865–1866.

56 No more for him life's stormy conflicts,
Nor victory, nor defeat—no more time's dark
events,
Charging like ceaseless clouds across the sky.

> WALT WHITMAN, "Hush'd Be the Camps Today," 1865–1866.

57 This dust was once the man,
Gentle, plain, just and resolute, under whose
cautious hand,
Against the foulest crime in history known in
any land or age,
Was saved the Union of these States.

> WALT WHITMAN, "This Dust Was Once a Man," 1865–1866.

58 In my opinion Carl Sandburg is the worst thing that has happened to Lincoln since Booth shot him.

> EDMUND WILSON, in a letter to John Dos Passos, April 30, 1953, quoted in *Letters on Literature and Politics: 1912–1972,* 1977.

59 Lincoln was a very normal man with very normal gifts, but all upon a great scale, all knit together in loose and natural form, like the great frame in which he moved and dwelt.

WOODROW WILSON, in an address in Chicago, February 12, 1909.

---

138. LITERATURE

See also BOOKS; JOURNALISM; LANGUAGE; POET; POETRY; WRITERS

---

1 Literature has been the charm of my life, and, could I have carved out my own fortunes, to literature would my whole life have been devoted.

JOHN QUINCY ADAMS, diary entry, December 25, 1820.

2 The curious have observed that the progress of humane literature (like the sun) is from the East to the West; thus has it traveled thro' Asia and Europe, and now is arrived at the eastern shore of America.

NATHANIEL AMES, 1758, in *Astronomical Diary and Almanack,* 1725–1764.

3 When you were living a tale you did not have time to color it as it should be colored—your mind stuck on odd useless trifles—the teeth of a man you struck—the feel of an iron bar—the shape of a sail against the stars. Besides, in life you were hungry and thirsty and had to make water—things which did not happen in a tale, or, if they did, assumed heroic proportions.

STEPHEN VINCENT BENÉT, *Spanish Bayonet,* 1926.

4 American muse, whose strong and diverse heart
So many men have tried to understand
But only made it smaller with their art
Because you are as various as your land.

STEPHEN VINCENT BENÉT, "Invocation," *John Brown's Body,* 1928.

5 Who cares about spelling? Milton spelt *dog* with two *g's.* The American Milton, when he comes,

may spell it with three, while all the world wonders, if he is so minded.

AUGUSTINE BIRRELL, *Men, Women and Books,* 1894.

6 Studying literature at Harvard is like learning about women at the Mayo Clinic.

Attributed to Roy Blount, Jr.

7 If the Americans did not speak English they would evidently feel called on to create more high literature for themselves. Many books which America might produce are not produced because the men qualified to write them know that there are already English books on the same subject; and the higher such men's standard is, the more apt are they to overrate the advantages which English authors enjoy as compared with themselves.

JAMES BRYCE, *The American Commonwealth,* 1888.

8 Self-expression must pass into communication for its fulfillment.

PEARL S. BUCK, quoted in Helen Hull, *The Writer's Book,* 1950.

9 The tendinous part of the mind, so to speak, is more developed in winter; the fleshy, in summer. I should say winter had given the bone and sinew to literature, summer the tissues and the blood.

JOHN BURROUGHS, "The Snow-Walkers," in *Winter Sunshine,* 1875.

10 Criticism means an attempt to find out what something is, not for the purpose of judging it, or imitating it, nor for the purpose of illustrating something else nor for any other ulterior purpose whatever.

JOHN JAY CHAPMAN, *Emerson, and Other Essays,* 1898.

11 Every novel should have a beginning, a muddle, and an end.

Attributed to Peter De Vries.

12 I had better never see a book than to be warped by its attraction clean out of my own orbit, and made a satellite instead of a system.

RALPH WALDO EMERSON, *The American Scholar,* 1837.

13 Literature is the effort of man to indemnify himself for the wrongs of his condition.

> RALPH WALDO EMERSON, "Walter Savage Landor," published in *The Dial*, 1841.

14 Could Shakespeare give a theory of Shakespeare?

> RALPH WALDO EMERSON, "Spiritual Laws," *Essays*, First Series, 1841.

15 All writing is by the grace of God. People do not deserve to have good writing, they are so pleased with bad.

> RALPH WALDO EMERSON, entry written in 1841, *Journals*, 1909–1914.

16 Good writing is a kind of skating which carries off the performer where he would not go, and is only right admirable when to all its beauty and speed a subserviency to the will, like that of walking, is added.

> RALPH WALDO EMERSON, entry written in 1847, *Journals*, 1909–1914.

17 All literature is yet to be written. Poetry has scarce chanted its first song. The perpetual admonition of nature to us is, "The world is new, untried. Do not believe the past. I give you the universe a virgin today."

> RALPH WALDO EMERSON, "Literary Ethics," *Addresses and Lectures*, 1849.

18 Writing is more and more a terror to old scribes.

> RALPH WALDO EMERSON, entry written in 1864, *Journals*, 1909–1914.

19 How far off from life and manners and motives the novel still is! Life lies about us dumb; the day, as we know it, has not yet found a tongue.

> RALPH WALDO EMERSON, "Books," *Society and Solitude*, 1870.

20 Literature is not, in itself, a means of solving problems; these can be solved only by action, by social and political action.

> JAMES T. FARRELL, in *Harper's Magazine*, October, 1954.

21 American literature, in order to be great, must be national, and in order to be national, must deal with conditions peculiar to our own land and climate. Every genuinely American writer must deal with the life he knows best and for which he cares the most.

> HAMLIN GARLAND, *A Son of the Middle Border*, 1917.

22 I permit myself to think that American literature should somehow be considered quite apart from its effect on the sale of underwear or safety razors. . . . [not as] a narrow rill of text meandering down a wide plain of advertising.

> HAMLIN GARLAND, writing in *Bookman* magazine, May, 1924, quoted in Jean Holloway, *Hamlin Garland*, 1960.

23 Literature is a noble calling, but only when the call obeyed by the aspirant issues from a world to be enlightened and blessed, not from a void stomach clamoring to be gratified and filled.

> HORACE GREELEY, in a letter to Robert Dale Owen, March 5, 1860.

24 All modern American literature comes from one book by Mark Twain called *Huckleberry Finn*.

> ERNEST HEMINGWAY, *Green Hills of Africa*, 1935.

25 Realism is nothing more and nothing less than the truthful treatment of material.

> WILLIAM DEAN HOWELLS, *Criticism and Fiction*, 1891.

26 Literature: The art of saying a thing by saying something else just as good.

> ELBERT HUBBARD, *The Roycroft Dictionary and Book of Epigrams*, 1923.

27 It takes a great deal of history to produce a little literature.

> HENRY JAMES, *Hawthorne*, 1879.

28 The time-honored bread sauce of the happy ending.

> HENRY JAMES, *Theatricals*, Second Series, 1894–1895.

29 It is through the ghost[writer] that the great gift of knowledge which the inarticulate have for the world can be made available.

ELIZABETH JANEWAY, quoted in Helen Hull, *The Writer's Book,* 1950.

30 What is called style, in writing or speaking is formed very early in life, while the imagination is warm, and impressions are permanent.

THOMAS JEFFERSON, in a letter to J. Bannister, Jr., October 15, 1785.

31 No republic has more zeal than that of letters.

THOMAS JEFFERSON, in a letter to Noah Webster, December 4, 1790.

32 I concur entirely with you in opposition to Purists, who would destroy all strength and beauty of style by subjecting it to a rigorous compliance with their rules. Fill up all the ellipses and syllepses of Tacitus, Sallust, Livy, &c. and the elegance and force of their sententious brevity are extinguished.

THOMAS JEFFERSON, in a letter to John Waldo, August 16, 1813.

33 I have always very much despised the artificial canons of criticism. When I have read a work in prose or poetry, or seen a painting, a statue, &c., I have only asked myself whether it gives me pleasure, whether it is animating, interesting, attaching? If it is, it is good for these reasons.

THOMAS JEFFERSON, in a letter to William Wirt, 1816.

34 Literature is my Utopia. Here I am not disfranchised. No barrier of the senses shuts me out from the sweet, gracious discourse of my book friends. They talk to me without embarrassment or awkwardness.

HELEN KELLER, *The Story of My Life,* 1902.

35 As the blood of all nations is mingling with our own, so will their thoughts and feelings finally mingle in our literature. We shall draw from the Germans, tenderness; from the Spaniards, passion; from the French, vivacity; to mingle more and more with our English solid sense.

HENRY WADSWORTH LONGFELLOW, *Kavanagh,* 1849.

36 Many readers judge of the power of a book by the shock it gives their feelings.

Ibid.

37 Critics are sentinels in the grand army of letters, stationed at the corners of newspapers and reviews, to challenge every new author.

Ibid.

38 A wise skepticism is the first attribute of a good critic.

JAMES RUSSELL LOWELL, *Among My Books,* 1870.

39 The benignities of literature defy fortune and outlive calamity. They are beyond the reach of thief or moth or rust. As they cannot be inherited, so they cannot be alienated.

JAMES RUSSELL LOWELL, in a talk in Chelsea, Massachusetts, December 22, 1885.

40 Every novel was suckled at the breast of older novels, and great mothers are often prolific of anemic offspring.

JOHN MACY, *The Spirit of American Literature,* 1913.

41 A man with his belly full of the classics is an enemy of the human race.

HENRY MILLER, *Tropic of Cancer,* 1934.

42 The people must grant a hearing to the best poets they have else they will never have better.

HARRIET MONROE, quoted in Hope Stoddard, *Famous American Women,* 1970.

43 [Harold Ross, editor of *The New Yorker*] was an almost impossible man to work for—rude, ungracious and perpetually dissatisfied with what he read; and I admire him more than anyone I have met in professional life. Only perfection was good enough for him, and on the rare occasions he encountered it, he viewed it with astonished suspicion.

OGDEN NASH, quoted in James Thurber, *The Years with Ross,* 1957.

44 Longfellow was complaining the other day of a decline in the interest in literature and in the taste for it. Nor was he mistaken,—this generation is given over to the making and spending of money, and is losing the capacity of thought. It wants to be amused, and the magazines amuse it.

CHARLES ELIOT NORTON, in a letter to Thomas Carlyle, November 16, 1873.

45 The two worst sins of bad taste in fiction are pornography and sentimentality. One is too much sex and the other too much sentiment.

FLANNERY O'CONNOR, in a letter to Eileen Hall, March 10, 1956, quoted in Sally Fitzgerald, *The Habit of Being: Letters of Flannery O'Connor,* 1979.

46 The novel is an art form and when you use it for anything other than art, you pervert it.

FLANNERY O'CONNOR, in a letter to Father John McCown, May 9, 1956, quoted in Sally Fitzgerald, *The Habit of Being: Letters of Flannery O'Connor,* 1979.

47 It took me quite a while to realize that there were fashions in literary criticism and that they shifted and changed much like the fashions in women's hats.

ANN PETRY, quoted in Helen Hull, *The Writer's Book,* 1950.

48 Take the whole range of imaginative literature, and we are all wholesale borrowers. In every matter that relates to invention, to use, or beauty, or form, we are borrowers.

WENDELL PHILLIPS, "The Lost Arts," an address given in 1838.

49 We are becoming boisterous and arrogant in the pride of a too speedily assumed literary freedom. . . . So far from being ashamed of the many disgraceful literary failures to which our own inordinate vanities and misapplied patriotism have lately given birth, and so far from deeply lamenting that these daily puerilities are of home manufacture, we adhere pertinaciously to our original blindly conceived idea, and thus often find ourselves involved in the gross paradox of liking a stupid book the better, because, sure enough, its stupidity is American.

EDGAR ALLAN POE, "Review of Poems by Drake and Halleck," *Southern Literary Messenger* magazine, April, 1836.

50 Great literature is simply language charged with meaning to the utmost possible degree.

EZRA POUND, *How to Read,* 1931.

51 Literature is news that stays news.

Ibid.

52 You *can't* quit. This isn't a magazine—it's a Movement!

HAROLD ROSS, to E.B. White, when White threatened to leave *The New Yorker,* quoted in James Thurber, *The Years with Ross,* 1957.

53 To turn events into ideas is the function of literature.

GEORGE SANTAYANA, *Little Essays,* 1920.

54 What are the classics but the noblest recorded thoughts of man? They are the only oracles which are not decayed.

HENRY DAVID THOREAU, *Walden,* 1854.

55 Shakespeare, Madam, is obscene, and thank God, we are sufficiently advanced to have found it out!

FRANCES TROLLOPE, quoting a remark made to her by an American, in *Domestic Manners of the Americans,* 1832.

56 To be a bestseller is not necessarily a measure of quality, but it *is* a measure of communication.

BARBARA W. TUCHMAN, in an address to the American Historical Association, December, 1966.

57 The public is the only critic whose opinion is worth anything at all.

MARK TWAIN, "A General Reply," in *The Galaxy* magazine, November, 1870.

58 Delicacy—a sad, sad false delicacy—robs literature of the two best things among its belongings: Family-circle narratives and obscene stories.

MARK TWAIN, in a letter to William Dean Howells, September 19, 1877.

59 *Classic.* A book which people praise and don't read.

MARK TWAIN, "Pudd'nhead Wilson's New Calendar," *Following the Equator,* 1897.

60 I don't believe any of you have ever read *Paradise Lost,* and you don't want to. That's something that you just want to take on trust. It's a classic, just as Professor Winchester says, and it meets his def-

inition of a classic—something that everybody wants to have read and nobody wants to read.

> MARK TWAIN, "The Disappearance of Literature," an address given on November 20, 1900. (Caleb T. Winchester was a professor at Wesleyan University, a lecturer, and a writer. Among his works was the volume *Some Principles of Literary Criticism,* 1904.)

61 Literature becomes free institutions. It is the graceful ornament of civil liberty, and a happy restraint on the asperities which political controversies sometimes occasion.

> DANIEL WEBSTER, in a speech in Plymouth, Massachusetts, December 22, 1820.

62 Fiction reveals truths that reality obscures.

> JESSAMYN WEST, quoted in the *Reader's Digest,* April, 1973.

63 I don't know which is more discouraging, literature or chickens.

> E.B. WHITE, in a letter to James Thurber, November 18, 1938.

64 In a free country it is the duty of writers to pay no attention to duty. Only under a dictatorship is literature expected to exhibit an harmonious design or an inspirational tone. A despot doesn't fear eloquent writers preaching freedom—he fears a drunken poet who may crack a joke that will take hold. His gravest concern is lest gaiety, or truth in sheep's clothing, somewhere gain a foothold, lest joy in some unguarded moment be unconfined.

> E.B. WHITE, "Salt Water Farm," *One Man's Meat,* 1944.

65 The art of art, the glory of expression and the sunshine of the light of letters, is simplicity.

> WALT WHITMAN, in the preface to *Leaves of Grass,* 1855.

66 Our fundamental want today in the United States, with closest, amplest reference to present conditions, and to the future, is of a class, and the clear idea of a class, of native authors, literatuses, far different, far higher in grade, than any yet known, sacerdotal, modern, fit to cope with our occasions, lands, permeating the whole mass of

American mentality, taste, belief, breathing into it a new breath of life, giving it decision.

> WALT WHITMAN, *Democratic Vistas,* 1870.

67 Literature, strictly consider'd, has never recognized the People, and, whatever may be said, does not today. Speaking generally, the tendencies of literature, as hitherto pursued, have been to make mostly critical and querulous men. It seems as if, so far, there were some natural repugnance between a literary and professional life and the rude rank spirit of the democracies.

> Ibid.

68 I cannot divest my appetite of literature.

> WALT WHITMAN, *Specimen Days and Collect,* 1882.

69 I was always keenly aware that literature demands not only all one can give it but also all one can get other people to give it.

> EDMUND WILSON, in a letter to T.S. Matthews, 1960, quoted in *Letters on Literature and Politics 1912–1972,* 1977.

70 Income tax returns are the most imaginative fiction being written today.

> Attributed to Herman Wouk.

---

139. LOUISIANA

See also NEW ORLEANS

---

1 Union, justice, and confidence.

> State motto.

2 But where is that favored land?—It is in this great continent.—It is, reader, in Louisiana that these bounties of nature are in the greatest perfection.

> JOHN JAMES AUDUBON, *The Birds of America,* 1827–1838.

3 In 1803 Louisiana was an unmanned, undefended empire embracing the whole watershed of the Mississippi and comprising the present states of

Louisiana, Arkansas, Oklahoma, Missouri, both Dakotas, Iowa, Nebraska, Kansas, Minnesota, Colorado, Wyoming, and Montana—a third of North America.

> ALISTAIR COOKE, *America,* 1973.

4 Such are the great features of Louisiana; a country, that in the course of human events, is perhaps destined to be amongst the most remarkable upon which the happiness or misery of mankind have ever been, or will be felt.

> WILLIAM DARBY, *A Geographical Description of the State of Louisiana, the Southern Part of the State of Mississippi, and Territory of Alabama,* 1817.

5 In Louisiana the live-oak is the king of the forest, and the magnolia is its queen; and there is nothing more delightful to one who is fond of the country than to sit under them on a clear, calm spring morning like this.

> JOSEPH JEFFERSON, *The Autobiography of Joseph Jefferson,* 1917.

6 Concede that the new government of Louisiana is only what it should be as the egg is to the fowl, we shall sooner have the fowl by hatching the egg than by smashing it. . . . Can Louisiana be brought into proper practical relation with the Union sooner by sustaining or by discarding her new State government?

> ABRAHAM LINCOLN, urging acceptance of Louisiana's postwar constitution in his last public speech, April 11, 1865.

7 We have lived long, but this is the noblest work of our lives.

> ROBERT LIVINGSTON, on the signing of the Louisiana Purchase, quoted in John Keats, *Eminent Domain: The Louisiana Purchase and the Making of America,* 1973.

8 A four-hundred-dollar suit on old Uncle Earl would look like socks on a rooster.

> EARL K. LONG, in a campaign speech, quoted in A.J. Liebling, *The Earl of Louisiana,* 1970.

9 And it is here, under this oak where Evangeline waited for her lover, Gabriel, who never came. This oak is an immortal spot, made so by Longfellow's poem, but Evangeline is not the only one who has waited here in disappointment. Where are the schools that you have waited for your children to have, that have never come? Where are the roads and highways that you send your money to build, that are no nearer now than before? Where are the institutions to care for the sick and the disabled? Evangeline wept bitter tears in her disappointment, but it lasted through only one lifetime. Your tears in this country, around this oak, have lasted for generations. Give me the chance to dry the tears of those who still weep here!

> HUEY P. LONG, in a speech, 1927, quoted by T. Harry Williams in *Huey Long,* 1969.

10 I have sir; just like you would a load of potatoes.

> HUEY P. LONG, responding to the question, "Governor, do you mean to tell us that you bought and paid for our Representative?" Quoted in the *Official Journal of the House of Representatives, State of Louisiana,* begun March 20, 1929.

11 Here no hungry winter congeals our blood
>   like the rivers;
> Here no stony ground provokes the wrath of
>   the farmer.
> Smoothly the ploughshare runs through the
>   soil, as a keel through the water.
> All the year round the orange-groves are in
>   blossom; and grass grows
> More in a single night than a whole
>   Canadian summer.
> Here, too, numberless herds run wild and
>   unclaimed in the prairies;
> Here, too, lands may be had for the asking,
>   and forests of timber
> With a few blows of the axe are hewn and
>   framed into houses.
> After your houses are built, and your fields
>   are yellow with harvests,
> No King George of England shall drive you
>   away from your homesteads,
> Burning your dwellings and barns, and
>   stealing your farms and your cattle.

> HENRY WADSWORTH LONGFELLOW, *Evangeline, A Tale of Acadie,* 1847.

12 As a society, we're a banana republic. What we ought to do is declare bankruptcy, secede from the union and declare ourselves a banana republic and file for foreign aid. We're just about as illiterate and just about as progressive as a Latin American country.

> KEVIN REILLY, quoted in the Louisiana State University *Daily Reveille,* June 18, 1985.

13 In Louisiana they vote by electricity. It's a marvelous way to vote, but Huey [Long] runs the switchboard, so it don't matter which button they boys press, all the answers come out yes.

> WILL ROGERS, January 29, 1935, quoted in Donald Day, *The Autobiography of Will Rogers,* 1949.

14 Sir Walter Scott is probably responsible for the Capitol building; for it is not conceivable that this little sham castle would ever have been built if he had not run the people mad, a couple of generations ago, with his medieval romances. . . . It is pathetic enough that a whitewashed castle, with turrets and things—materials all ungenuine within and without, pretending to be what they are not—should ever have been built in this otherwise honorable place; but it is much more pathetic to see this architectural falsehood undergoing restoration and perpetuation in our day, when it would have been so easy to let dynamite finish what a charitable fire began, and then devote this restoration money to the building of something genuine.

> MARK TWAIN, on the State Capitol building in Baton Rouge, in *Life on the Mississippi,* 1883.

---

140. LOVE

See also AFFECTION; FRIENDS; MARRIAGE

---

1 Love 'em and leave 'em.

> Folk wisdom on treatment of women.

2 If even worms are inclined to be in love with one another, how can we expect people not to do so?

> Pawnee Indian song.

3 Fifty million Frenchmen can't be wrong.

> Saying of American soldiers in France, 1917–1918.

4 Romance cannot be put into quantity production—the moment love becomes casual, it becomes commonplace.

> FREDERICK LEWIS ALLEN, *Only Yesterday,* 1931.

5 To be loved is to be fortunate, but to be hated is to achieve distinction.

> MINNA ANTRIM, *Naked Truth and Veiled Allusions,* 1902.

6 The fate of love is that it always seems too little or too much.

> AMELIA E. BARR, *The Belle of Bowling Green,* 1904.

7 To love I must have something I can put my arms around.

> HENRY WARD BEECHER, *Royal Truths,* 1862.

8 Love is more just than justice.

> HENRY WARD BEECHER, *Proverbs from Plymouth Pulpit,* 1870.

9 In expressing love we belong among the undeveloped countries.

> Attributed to Saul Bellow.

10 Women in love are less ashamed than men. They have less to be ashamed of.

> AMBROSE BIERCE, example supplied in the definition of the word "epigram," *The Devil's Dictionary,* 1906.

11 Love is a delightful day's journey. At the farther end kiss your companion and say farewell.

> AMBROSE BIERCE, *Collected Works,* 1909–1912.

12 The ability to make love frivolously is the thing which distinguishes human beings from the beasts.

> HEYWOOD BROUN, quoted in Robert E. Drennan, *The Algonquin Wits,* 1968.

13 I am Tarzan of the Apes. I want you. I am yours. You are mine. We will live here together always in my house. I will bring you the best fruits,

the tenderest deer, the finest meats that roam the jungle. I will hunt for you. I am the greatest of the jungle hunters. I will fight for you. I am the mightiest of the jungle fighters. You are Jane Porter, I saw it in your letter. When you see this you will know that it is for you and that Tarzan of the Apes loves you.

> EDGAR RICE BURROUGHS, *Tarzan of the Apes,* 1914.

14 Love alone can lend young people rapture, however transiently, in a world wherein the result of every human endeavor is transient, and the end of all is death.

> JAMES BRANCH CABELL, *Jurgen,* 1919.

15 A kiss is now attestedly a quite innocuous performance, with nothing very fearful about it one way or the other. It even has its pleasant side.

> Ibid.

16 The true beloveds of this world are in their lover's eyes lilac opening, ship lights, school bells, a landscape, remembered conversations, friends, a child's Sunday, lost voices, one's favorite suit, autumn and all seasons, memory, yes, it being the earth and water of existence, memory.

> TRUMAN CAPOTE, *Other Voices, Other Rooms,* 1948.

17 So blind is life, so long at last is sleep,
  And none but Love to bid us laugh or
    weep.

> WILLA CATHER, "Evening Song," in *April Twilights,* 1903.

18 *Is* there more? More than Love and Death? Then tell me its name!

> EMILY DICKINSON, in a letter to Mrs. J.G. Holland, 1883.

19 Love is anterior to life,
  Posterior to death.

> EMILY DICKINSON, "Love," *Poems,* Third Series, 1896.

20 Nobody wants to kiss when they are hungry.

> Attributed to Dorothy Dix.

21 So long as little children are allowed to suffer, there is no true love in this world.

> ISADORA DUNCAN, "Memoirs," *This Quarter* magazine, Autumn, 1929.

22 To infinite, ever-present Love, all is Love, and there is no error, no sin, sickness, nor death.

> MARY BAKER EDDY, *Science and Health,* 1875.

23 The doctrine of hatred must be preached as the counteraction of the doctrine of love, when that pules and whines.

> RALPH WALDO EMERSON, "Self-Reliance," *Essays,* First Series, 1841.

24 All mankind love a lover.

> RALPH WALDO EMERSON, "Love," *Essays,* First Series, 1841.

25 No man ever forgot the visitation of that power to his heart and brain, which created all things anew; which was the dawn in him of music, poetry and art; which made the face of nature radiant with purple light, the morning and the night varied enchantments; when a single tone of one voice could make the heart bound.

> Ibid.

26 Love, which is the essence of God, is not for levity, but for the total worth of man.

> RALPH WALDO EMERSON, "Friendship," *Essays,* First Series, 1841.

27 Thou art to me a delicious torment.

> Ibid.

28 The accepted and betrothed lover has lost the wildest charm of his maiden in her acceptance of him. She was heaven whilst he pursued her as a star; she cannot be heaven if she stoops to such a one as he.

> RALPH WALDO EMERSON, "Nature," *Essays,* Second Series, 1844.

29 Lovers should guard their strangeness.

> RALPH WALDO EMERSON, "Manners," *Essays,* Second Series, 1844.

30 The power of love, as the basis of a State, has never been tried.

RALPH WALDO EMERSON, "Politics," *Essays, Second Series,* 1844.

31 The sense of the world is short,—
Long and various the report,—
    To love and be beloved;
Men and gods have not outlearned it;
And, how oft soe'er they've turned it,
    'Tis not to be improved.

RALPH WALDO EMERSON, "Eros," 1847.

32 The way to a man's heart is through his stomach.

FANNY FERN, in "Willis Parton."

33 If you would be loved, love and be loveable.

BENJAMIN FRANKLIN, *Poor Richard's Almanack,* 1755.

34 Love is an irresistible desire to be irresistibly desired.

Attributed to Robert Frost.

35 Earth's the right place for love: I don't know where it's likely to go better.

ROBERT FROST, "Birches," 1916.

36 There are only three things worthwhile—fighting, drinking, and making love.

KATHERINE GEROULD, "The Tortoise," *Vain Oblations,* 1914.

37 Love is man's natural endowment, but he doesn't know how to use it. He refuses to recognize the power of love because of his love of power.

DICK GREGORY, *The Shadow that Scares Me,* 1968.

38 What a sweet reverence is that when a young man deems his mistress a little more than mortal and almost chides himself for longing to bring her close to his heart.

NATHANIEL HAWTHORNE, *The Marble Faun,* 1860.

39 To be loved is very demoralizing.

KATHARINE HEPBURN, appearing on television in the Dick Cavett Show, April 4, 1975.

40 The old, old story,—fair, and young,
    And fond,—and not too wise,—
That matrons tell, with sharpened tongue,
    To maids with downcast eyes.

OLIVER WENDELL HOLMES, SR., "Agnes," 1855.

41 The sound of a kiss is not so loud as that of cannon, but its echo lasts a great deal longer.

OLIVER WENDELL HOLMES, SR., *The Professor at the Breakfast-Table,* 1860.

42 Soft is the breath of a maiden's Yes:
Not the light gossamer stirs with less;
But never a cable that holds so fast
Through all the battles of wave and blast.

OLIVER WENDELL HOLMES, SR., "Dorothy Q.," 1871.

43 There is no sorrow like a love denied
Nor any joy like love that has its will.

RICHARD HOVEY, *The Marriage of Guenevere,* 1891.

44 If there is any one thing that a man should do in private, it is his loving.

EDGAR WATSON HOWE, *Country Town Sayings,* 1911.

45 Love affairs have always greatly interested me, but I do not greatly care for them in books or moving pictures. In a love affair I wish to be the hero, with no audience present.

EDGAR WATSON HOWE, *Sinner Sermons,* 1926.

46 If a woman doesn't chase a man a little, she doesn't love him.

Ibid.

47 We cannot permit love to run riot; we must build fences around it, as we do around pigs.

EDGAR WATSON HOWE, *Preaching from the Audience,* 1926.

48 Love is the third rail for Life's Empire State Express.

ELBERT HUBBARD, *The Roycroft Dictionary and Book of Epigrams,* 1923.

49 Lovers are fools, but Nature makes them so.

Ibid.

50 Love goes to those who are deserving—not to those who set snares for it and who lie in wait. The life of strife and contest never wins.

> Ibid.

51 Love, we say, is life; but love without hope and faith is agonizing death.

> Ibid.

52 I'll believe it when girls of twenty with money marry male paupers, turned sixty.

> Ibid.

53 Good-nature is the cheapest commodity in the world, and love is the only thing that will pay ten per cent to both borrower and lender.

> ROBERT G. INGERSOLL, "The Liberty of Man, Woman, and Child," 1877.

54 To a man the disappointment of love may occasion some bitter pangs—it wounds some feelings of tenderness—it blasts some prospects of felicity; but he is an active being—he may dissipate his thoughts in the whirl of varied occupation; or may plunge into the tide of pleasure. Or if the scene of disappointment be too full of painful associations, he can shift his abode at will. . . . But woman's is comparatively a fixed, a secluded, and meditative life. . . . Her lot is to be wooed and won; and if unhappy in her love, her heart is like some fortress that has been captured, and sacked, and abandoned, and left desolate.

> WASHINGTON IRVING, "The Broken Heart," *The Sketch Book,* 1819–1820.

55 I find as I grow older that I love those most whom I loved first.

> THOMAS JEFFERSON, in a letter to Mary Jefferson Bolling, July 23, 1787.

56 The emotion of love, in spite of the romantics, is not self-sustaining; it endures only when the lovers love many things together, and not merely each other.

> WALTER LIPPMANN, *A Preface to Morals,* 1929.

57 O, there is nothing holier, in this life of ours, than the first consciousness of love—the first fluttering of its silken wings.

> HENRY WADSWORTH LONGFELLOW, *Hyperion,* 1839.

58 Love keeps the cold out better than a cloak. It serves for food and raiment.

> HENRY WADSWORTH LONGFELLOW, *The Spanish Student,* 1843.

59 It is difficult to know at what moment love begins; it is less difficult to know that it has begun.

> HENRY WADSWORTH LONGFELLOW, *Kavanagh,* 1849.

60 Love, that of every woman's heart
Will have the whole, and not a part,
That is to her, in Nature's plan,
More than ambition is to man,
Her light, her life, her very breath,
With no alternative but death.

> HENRY WADSWORTH LONGFELLOW, *The Golden Legend,* 1851.

61 Day by day he gazed upon her,
Day by day he sighed with passion,
Day by day his heart within him
Grew more hot with love and longing.

> HENRY WADSWORTH LONGFELLOW, *The Song of Hiawatha,* 1855.

62 True Love is but a humble, low-born thing,
And hath its food served up in earthen ware;
It is a thing to walk with, hand in hand,
Through the everydayness of this workday
world.

> JAMES RUSSELL LOWELL, "Love," 1840.

63 Love, in reason's terms, answers nothing. We say that *Amor vincit omnia* but in truth love conquers nothing—certainly not death—certainly not chance.

> ARCHIBALD MACLEISH, in *Time* magazine, December 22, 1958.

64 He drew a circle that shut me out—
Heretic, rebel, a thing to flout.
But Love and I had the wit to win:
We drew a circle that took him in!

> EDWIN MARKHAM, "Outwitted," in *The Shoes of Happiness and Other Poems,* 1915.

65 To be in love is merely to be in a state of perceptual anesthesia—to mistake an ordinary young man
for a Greek god or an ordinary young woman for
a goddess.

> H.L. MENCKEN, *Prejudices,* First Series, 1919.

66 A man always remembers his first love with
special tenderness. But after that he begins to
bunch them.

> H.L. MENCKEN, *Sententiae,* in *The Vintage
> Mencken,* 1955.

67 Love is born of faith, lives on hope, and dies of
charity.

> GIAN CARLO MENOTTI, notebook jottings for his
> opera *Maria Golovin,* 1958.

68 And if I loved you Wednesday,
Well what is that to you?
I do not love you Thursday—
So much is true.

> EDNA ST. VINCENT MILLAY, "Thursday," in *A
> Few Figs from Thistles,* 1920.

69 This have I known always: Love is no more
Than the wide blossom which the wind
    assails,
Than the great tide that treads the shifting
    shore,
Strewing fresh wreckage gathered in the
    gales;
Pity me that the heart is slow to learn
What the swift mind beholds at every turn.

> EDNA ST. VINCENT MILLAY, "Pity me not,"
> from *The Harp-Weaver and Other Poems,* 1923.

70 I know I am but summer to your heart,
And not the full four seasons of the year;
And you must welcome from another part
Such noble moods as are not mine, my dear.

> EDNA ST. VINCENT MILLAY, "I know I am but
> summer," in *The Harp-Weaver and Other
> Poems,* 1923.

71 Romantic love is the privilege of emperors,
kings, soldiers and artists; it is the butt of democrats, traveling salesmen, magazine poets, and the
writers of American novels.

> GEORGE JEAN NATHAN, *Testament of a Critic,*
> 1931.

72 What I cannot love, I overlook. Is that real
friendship?

> ANAÏS NIN, "San Francisco," *The Diary of Anaïs
> Nin,* 1974.

73 'Tis that delightsome transport we can feel
Which painters cannot paint, nor words
    reveal,
Nor any art we know of can conceal.

> THOMAS PAINE, "What Is Love?" c.1800.

74 Hell's afloat in lovers' tears.

> Attributed to Dorothy Parker.

75 Scratch a lover, and find a foe.

> DOROTHY PARKER, "Ballade of a Great
> Weariness," *Enough Rope,* 1927.

76 Men seldom make passes
At girls who wear glasses.

> DOROTHY PARKER, "News Item," *Enough Rope,*
> 1927.

77 Thou wast all that to me, love,
    For which my soul did pine:
A green isle in the sea, love,
    A fountain and a shrine.

> EDGAR ALLAN POE, "To One in Paradise," 1834.

78 It was many and many a year ago,
    In a kingdom by the sea,
That a maiden there lived whom you may
    know
    By the name of Annabel Lee;
And this maiden she lived with no other
    thought
    Than to love and be loved by me.

She was a child and I was a child,
    In this kingdom by the sea,
But we loved with a love that was more than
    love,—
    I and my Annabel Lee;
With a love that the winged seraphs of
    heaven
    Coveted her and me.

EDGAR ALLAN POE, "Annabel Lee," published in the *New York Tribune,* October 9, 1849.

79 Love is an expression and assertion of self-esteem, a response to one's own values in the person of another. One gains a profoundly personal, selfish joy from the mere existence of the person one loves. It is one's own personal, selfish happiness that one seeks, earns, and derives from love.

AYN RAND, *The Virtue of Selfishness,* 1964.

80 Love means giving one's self to another person fully, not just physically. When two people really love each other, this helps them to stay alive and grow. One must really be loved to grow. Love's such a precious and fragile thing that when it comes we have to hold on tightly. And when it comes, we're very lucky because for some it never comes at all. If you have love, you're wealthy in a way that can never be measured. Cherish it.

NANCY REAGAN, in *Nancy,* 1980.

81 Love that's wise
Will not say all it means.

EDWIN ARLINGTON ROBINSON, *Tristram,* 1927.

82 Were it not for love,
Poor life would be a ship not worth the
launching.

Ibid.

83 It takes a woman twenty years to make a man of her son, and another woman twenty minutes to make a fool of him.

HELEN ROWLAND, *Reflections of a Bachelor Girl,* 1903.

84 A husband is what is left of the lover after the nerve has been extracted.

HELEN ROWLAND, *The Rubaiyat of a Bachelor,* 1915.

85 Take any streetful of people buying clothes and groceries, cheering a hero or throwing confetti and blowing tin horns . . . tell me if the lovers are losers . . . tell me if any get more than the lovers . . . in the dust . . . in the cool tombs.

CARL SANDBURG, "Cool Tombs," 1918.

86 Even the inconstant flame may burn brightly, if the soul is naturally combustible.

GEORGE SANTAYANA, *The Life of Reason,* 1905–1906.

87 Love is only half the illusion; the lover, but not his love, is deceived.

Ibid.

88 Love means not ever having to say you're sorry.

ERICH SEGAL, *Love Story,* 1970.

89 Sometimes love is stronger than a man's convictions.

ISAAC BASHEVIS SINGER, quoted in the *New York Times Magazine,* November 26, 1978.

90 Love is the vital essence that pervades and permeates, from the center to the circumference, the graduating circles of all thought and action. Love is the talisman of human weal and woe—the open sesame to every human soul.

ELIZABETH CADY STANTON, speech at Tenth National Woman's Rights Convention, New York City, May 10, 1860.

91 All that a man has to say or do that can possibly concern mankind, is in some shape or other to tell the story of his love—to sing, and, if he is fortunate and keeps alive, he will be forever in love.

HENRY DAVID THOREAU, entry dated May 6, 1854, in his *Journal,* 1906.

92 Love is the strange bewilderment which overtakes one person on account of another person.

JAMES THURBER AND E.B. WHITE, *Is Sex Necessary?* 1929.

93 Love is much nicer to be in than an automobile accident, a tight girdle, a higher tax bracket, or a holding pattern over Philadelphia.

JUDITH VIORST, "What IS This Thing Called Love?" *Redbook* magazine, February, 1975.

94 Will you love me in December as you do in
May,
Will you love me in the good old fashioned
way?
When my hair has all turned gray,
Will you kiss me then and say,

That you love me in December as you do in
 May?

JAMES J. WALKER, "Will You Love Me in
December as You Do in May?" verse set to music
by Ernest R. Ball, 1905.

95 She may strike the pouncing eagle, but she
 dares not harm the dove;
And every gate she bars to Hate shall open
 wide to Love!

JOHN GREENLEAF WHITTIER, "Brown of
Osawatomie," 1859.

96 Oh, rank is good, and gold is fair,
 And high and low mate ill;
But love has never known a law
 Beyond its own sweet will!

JOHN GREENLEAF WHITTIER, "Amy
Wentworth," 1862.

97 For still in mutual sufferance lies
 The secret of true living;
Love scarce is love that never knows
 The sweetness of forgiving.

JOHN GREENLEAF WHITTIER, "Among the
Hills," 1869.

98 And all things that were true and fair
 Lay closely to my loving eye,
With nothing shadowy between—
 I was a boy of seventeen.

NATHANIEL PARKER WILLIS, "Melanie,"
Melanie and Other Poems, 1835.

99 I've played the traitor
Over and over;
I'm a good hater,
But a bad lover.

ELINOR WYLIE, "Peregrine," *Black Armour,*
1923.

100 His love life seems as mixed up as a dog's
breakfast.

HAYDIE EAMES YATES, writing about an
unidentified celebrity, quoted in James Thurber,
The Years with Ross, 1957.

141. LUCK

1 Fortune, in its workings, has something in common with the slot-machine. There are those who
can bait it forever and never get more than an odd
assortment of lemons for their pains; but once in a
while there will come a man for whom all the
grooves will line up, and when that happens there's
no end to the showering down.

DOROTHY BAKER, *Young Man With a Horn,*
1938.

2 I don't know anything about luck. I've never
banked on it, and I'm afraid of people who do.
Luck to me is something else: hard work—and
realizing what is opportunity and what isn't.

LUCILLE BALL, quoted in Eleanor Harris, *The
Real Story of Lucille Ball,* 1954.

3 Shallow men believe in luck, believe in circumstances. . . . Strong men believe in cause and effect.

RALPH WALDO EMERSON, "Worship," *The
Conduct of Life,* 1860.

4 Human felicity is produced not so much by great
pieces of good fortune that seldom happen, as by
little advantages that occur every day.

BENJAMIN FRANKLIN, in his *Autobiography,*
1798.

5 The only sure thing about luck is that it will
change.

BRET HARTE, "The Outcasts of Poker Flat,"
1869.

6 We all have something to fall back on, and I
never knew a phony who didn't land on it eventually.

Attributed to Wilson Mizner.

7 Luck is the residue of design.

BRANCH RICKEY, quoted in Howard Cosell, *Like
It Is,* 1974.

8 Luck is what happens when preparation meets
opportunity.

DARRELL ROYAL, quoted in James A. Michener, *Sports in America,* 1976.

9 The first half of life consists of the capacity to enjoy without the chance; the last half consists of the chance without the capacity.

MARK TWAIN, in a letter to Edward L. Dimmitt, July 19, 1901.

142. MAINE

1 Dirigo. (I direct.)

State motto.

2 As Maine goes, so goes the nation.

Political maxim.

3 Don't ever ask directions of a Maine native. . . . Somehow we think it is funny to misdirect people and we don't smile when we do it, but we laugh inwardly. It is our nature.

A Maine native, quoted by John Steinbeck in *Travels with Charley,* 1962.

4 As Maine goes, so goes Vermont.

JAMES A. FARLEY, after the 1936 presidential election, in which the Democrats swept all the states except Maine and Vermont.

5 There are only two things that ever make the front page in Maine papers. One is a forest fire and the other is when a New Yorker shoots a moose instead of the game warden.

GROUCHO MARX, in a letter to *Variety,* August 23, 1934, quoted in Groucho Marx, *The Groucho Phile,* 1976.

6 Here's to the state of Maine, the land of the bluest skies, the greenest earth, the richest air, the strongest, and what is better, the sturdiest men, the fairest, and what is best of all, the truest women under the sun.

THOMAS BRACKETT REED, in a speech at Portland, Maine, August 7, 1900.

7 Did you ever see a place that looks like it was built just to enjoy? Well, this whole state of Maine looks that way. If it's not a beautiful lake, it's a beautiful tree, or a pretty green hay meadow, And beautiful old time houses, with barns built right in with the kitchens.

WILL ROGERS, July 13, 1934, quoted in Donald Day, *The Autobiography of Will Rogers,* 1949.

8 This is what you might call a brand-new country; the only roads were of Nature's making, and the few houses were camps. Here, then, one could no longer accuse institutions and society, but must front the true source of evil.

HENRY DAVID THOREAU, *The Maine Woods,* 1850.

9 Woods and fields encroach everywhere [in Maine], creeping to within a few feet of the neon and the court, and the experienced traveler into this land is always conscious that just behind the garish roadside stand, in its thicket of birch and spruce, stands the delicate and well-proportioned deer; just beyond the overnight cabin, in the pasture of granite and juniper, trots the perfectly designed fox.

E. B. WHITE, "Home-Coming," 1955, in *Essays of E. B. White,* 1977.

10 I am lingering in Maine this winter, to fight wolves and foxes. The sun here is less strong than Florida's, but so is the spirit of development.

E. B. WHITE, "A Report in January," 1958, in *Essays of E. B. White,* 1977.

143. MAJORITY RULE

See also DEMOCRACY; GOVERNMENT

1 The minority of a country is never known to agree, except in its efforts to reduce and oppress the majority.

JAMES FENIMORE COOPER, *The American Democrat,* 1838.

2 Neither current events nor history show that the majority rules, or ever did rule.

JEFFERSON DAVIS, in a letter to James Frazier Jacquess and James R. Gilmore, July 17, 1864.

3 The history of most countries has been that of majorities—mounted majorities, clad in iron, armed with death, treading down the tenfold more numerous minorities.

> OLIVER WENDELL HOLMES, SR., in an address to the Massachusetts Medical Society, May 30, 1860.

4 I not only believe majority rule is just, I believe it is best. All men know more than a few; all experience is better than new and untried theory.

> EDGAR WATSON HOWE, *Success Easier Than Failure,* 1917.

5 It is my principle that the will of the majority should always prevail.

> THOMAS JEFFERSON, in a letter to James Madison, December 20, 1787.

6 I readily . . . suppose my opinion wrong, when opposed by the majority.

> THOMAS JEFFERSON, in a letter to James Madison, July 31, 1788.

7 One, on God's side, is a majority.

> WENDELL PHILLIPS, on John Brown, in a speech in Brooklyn, New York, November 1, 1859.

---

144. MAN

See also HUMANKIND; WOMAN

---

1 Men are often false to their country and their honor, false to duty and even to their interest, but multitudes of men are never long false or deaf to their passions.

> FISHER AMES, in a speech in Boston, February 8, 1800.

2 A man is a god in ruins.

> RALPH WALDO EMERSON, *Nature,* 1836.

3 A man must have aunts and cousins; must buy carrots and turnips, must have barn and woodshed, must go to market and to the blacksmith's shop, must saunter and sleep and be inferior and silly.

> RALPH WALDO EMERSON, entry written June 8, 1838, *Journals,* 1909–1914.

4 Men are not made like boxes, a hundred or thousand to order, and all exactly alike, of known dimension, and all their properties known; but no, they come into nature through a nine months' astonishment, and of a character, each one, incalculable, and of extravagant possibilities.

> RALPH WALDO EMERSON, entry written in 1838, *Journals,* 1909–1914.

5 Every true man is a cause, a country, and an age; requires infinite spaces and numbers and time fully to accomplish his design;—and posterity seems to follow his steps as a train of clients. A man Caesar is born, and for ages after we have a Roman Empire. Christ is born, and millions of minds so grow and cleave to his genius that he is confounded with virtue and the possible of man.

> RALPH WALDO EMERSON, "Self-Reliance," *Essays,* First Series, 1841.

6 A man is a golden impossibility.

> RALPH WALDO EMERSON, "Experience," *Essays,* Second Series, 1844.

7 Men are not philosophers, but are rather very foolish children, who, by reason of their partiality, see everything in the most absurd manner, and are the victims at all times of the nearest object.

> RALPH WALDO EMERSON, "The Conservative," *Nature; Addresses and Lectures,* 1849.

8 Man can paint, or make, or think nothing but man.

> RALPH WALDO EMERSON, "Uses of Great Men," *Representative Men,* 1850.

9 A man ought to compare advantageously with a river, an oak, a mountain.

> RALPH WALDO EMERSON, "Fate," *The Conduct of Life,* 1860.

10 Very few of our race can be said to be yet finished men. We still carry sticking to us some remains of the preceding inferior quadruped organization. We call these millions men; but they are not yet men.

> RALPH WALDO EMERSON, "Culture," *The Conduct of Life,* 1860.

11 Man's conclusions are reached by toil. Woman arrives at the same by sympathy.

> RALPH WALDO EMERSON, entry written in 1866, *Journals,* 1909–1914.

12 The natural man has a difficult time getting along in this world. Half the people think he is a scoundrel because he is not a hypocrite.

> EDGAR WATSON HOWE, *Sinner Sermons,* 1926.

13 A man is as good as he has to be, and a woman as bad as she dares.

> ELBERT HUBBARD, *The Roycroft Dictionary and Book of Epigrams,* 1923.

14 If a man hasn't discovered something that he will die for, he isn't fit to live.

> MARTIN LUTHER KING, JR., in a speech in Detroit, June 23, 1963.

15 It is difficult to make a man miserable while he feels he is worthy of himself and claims kindred to the great God who made him.

> ABRAHAM LINCOLN, in a speech, August 14, 1862.

16 I'm no better than the best,
> And whether worse than the rest
> Of my fellow-men who knows?

> HENRY WADSWORTH LONGFELLOW, *The Divine Tragedy: The Third Passover,* 1871.

17 Nature they say, doth dote,
And cannot make a man
Save on some worn-out plan,
Repeating us by rote.

> JAMES RUSSELL LOWELL, "Ode Recited at the Harvard Commemoration," July 21, 1865.

18 Man's role is uncertain, undefined, and perhaps unnecessary.

> MARGARET MEAD, *Male and Female,* 1948.

19 Titles are but nicknames, and every nickname is a title. The thing is perfectly harmless in itself, but it marks a sort of foppery in the human character which degrades it. It renders man diminutive in things which are great, and the counterfeit of woman in things which are little.

> THOMAS PAINE, *The Rights of Man,* 1791.

20 What is human and the same about the males and females classified as *Homo sapiens* is much greater than the differences.

> ESTELLE R. RAMEY, quoted in Francine Klagsbrun, *The First Ms. Reader,* 1972.

21 All assemblages of men are different from the men themselves. Neither intelligence nor culture can prevent a mob from acting as a mob. The wise man and the knave lose their identity and merge themselves into a new being.

> THOMAS BRACKETT REED, in a speech at Bowdoin College, Maine, July 25, 1902.

22 I have no hostility towards men. Some of my best friends are men. I married a man, and my father was a man.

> JILL RUCKELSHAUS, quoted by Frederic A. Birmingham in the *Saturday Evening Post,* March 3, 1973.

23 It's not the men in my life that counts—it's the life in my men.

> MAE WEST, in the film *I'm No Angel,* 1933.

24 I only like two kinds of men: domestic and foreign.

> Attributed to Mae West.

---

145. MARRIAGE

See also DIVORCE; FAMILY; LOVE

---

1 Marriage is a condition most women aspire to and most men submit to.

> Anonymous.

2 When a man makes a mistake in his first marriage, the victim is his second wife.

> Anonymous.

3 The difference between a wife and a mistress is that the wife makes a better bargain.

> Anonymous.

4 I want (who does not want?) a wife
   Affectionate and fair,
To solace all the woes of life
   And all its days to share;
Of temper sweet, of yielding will,
   Of firm yet placid mind,
With all my faults to love me still,
   With sentiments refined.

> JOHN QUINCY ADAMS, "The Wants of Man,"
> c.1787.

5 The women who take husbands not out of love
but out of greed, to get their bills paid, to get a fine
house and clothes and jewels; the women who
marry to get out of a tiresome job, or to get away
from disagreeable relatives, or to avoid being called
an old maid—these are whores in everything but
name. The only difference between them and my
girls is that my girls gave a man his money's worth.

> POLLY ADLER, *A House Is Not a Home,* 1953.

6 When two people marry they become in the eyes
of the law one person, and that one person is the
husband!

> SHANA ALEXANDER, in the introduction to the
> *State-by-State Guide to Women's Legal Rights,*
> 1975.

7 I married beneath me. All women do.

> NANCY ASTOR, quoted in Marjorie P. Weiser and
> Jean S. Arbeiter, *Womanlist,* 1981.

8 When archaeologists discover the missing arms
of Venus de Milo, they will find that she was wearing boxing-gloves.

> JOHN BARRYMORE, on marriage, quoted in Gene
> Fowler, *Good Night, Sweet Prince,* 1943.

9 Well-married, a man is winged: ill-matched, he
is shackled.

> HENRY WARD BEECHER, *Proverbs from
> Plymouth Pulpit,* 1870.

10 They stood before the altar and supplied
   The fire themselves in which their fat was
     fried.

> AMBROSE BIERCE, lines from the definition of the
> word "altar," *The Devil's Dictionary,* 1906.

11 Bride, *n.* A woman with a fine prospect of happiness behind her.

> AMBROSE BIERCE, *The Devil's Dictionary,* 1906.

12 Husband, *n.* One who, having dined, is charged
with the care of the plate.

> Ibid.

13 Marriage, *n.* The state of condition of a community consisting of a master, a mistress, and two
slaves, making in all, two.

> Ibid.

14 Widow, *n.* A pathetic figure that the Christian
world has agreed to take humorously, although
Christ's tenderness toward widows was one of the
most marked features of His character.

> Ibid.

15 If ever two were one, then surely we.
If ever man were lov'd by wife, then thee;
If ever wife was happy in a man,
Compare with me ye women if you can.

> ANNE BRADSTREET, "To My Dear and Loving
> Husband," 1678.

16 Marriage is not just spiritual communion and
passionate embraces; marriage is also three-meals-a-
day and remembering to carry out the trash.

> DR. JOYCE BROTHERS, "When Your Husband's
> Affection Cools," *Good Housekeeping* magazine,
> May, 1972.

17 Our troth had been plighted,
   Not by moonbeam, or starbeam, or fountain
     or grove,
   But in a front parlor most brilliantly lighted,
   Beneath the gas-fixtures we whispered our
     love;
   Without any romance, or rapture, or sighs,
   Without any tears in Miss Flora's blue eyes,
   Or blushes or transports, or such silly
     actions,
   It was one of the quietest business
     transactions.

> WILLIAM ALLEN BUTLER, *Nothing to Wear,*
> 1857.

18 People marry through a variety of other reasons, and with varying results; but to marry for love is to invite inevitable tragedy.

JAMES BRANCH CABELL, *The Cream of the Jest*, 1917.

19 The very fact that we make such a to-do over golden weddings indicates our amazement at human endurance. The celebration is more in the nature of a reward for stamina.

ILKA CHASE, *Free Admission*, 1948.

20 I am a woman meant for a man, but I never found a man who could compete.

Attributed to Bette Davis.

21 Many a sensible man . . . has saved up all his weakness for his choice of a wife.

JOHN W. DE FOREST, *Seacliff or The Mystery of the Westervelts*, 1859.

22 Any intelligent woman who reads the marriage contract, and then goes into it, deserves all the consequences.

ISADORA DUNCAN, *My Life*, 1927.

23 Is not marriage an open question, when it is alleged, from the beginning of the world, that such as are in the institution wish to get out, and such as are out wish to get in?

RALPH WALDO EMERSON, "Montaigne," *Representative Men*, 1850.

24 Where there's Marriage without Love, there will be Love without Marriage.

BENJAMIN FRANKLIN, *Poor Richard's Almanack*, 1734.

25 Wedlock, as old Men note, hath likened been
　Unto a publick Crowd or common Rout;
Where those that are without would fain get in,
And those that are within would fain get out.
Grief often treads upon the Heels of
　Pleasure,
Marry'd in Haste, we oft repent at Leisure;
Some by Experience find these Words
　misplac'd,
Marry'd at Leisure, they repent in Haste.

Ibid.

26 You cannot pluck roses without fear of
　thorns,
Nor enjoy a fair wife without danger of
　horns.

Ibid.

27 Keep thy eyes wide open before marriage, and half shut afterwards.

BENJAMIN FRANKLIN, *Poor Richard's Almanack*, 1738.

28 One good Husband is worth two good Wives; for the scarcer things are the more they're valued.

BENJAMIN FRANKLIN, *Poor Richard's Almanack*, 1742.

29 It is the man and woman united that make the complete human being. Separate, she wants his force of body and strength of reason; he, her softness, sensibility and acute discernment. Together, they are most likely to succeed in the world.

BENJAMIN FRANKLIN, "Advice to a Young Man on the Choice of a Mistress," June 25, 1745.

30 A single man has not nearly the value he would have in the state of union. He is an incomplete animal. He resembles the odd half of a pair of scissors.

Ibid.

31 An undutiful Daughter will prove an unmanageable Wife.

BENJAMIN FRANKLIN, *Poor Richard's Almanack*, 1752.

32 The greatest thing in family life is to take a hint when a hint is intended—and not to take a hint when a hint isn't intended.

Attributed to Robert Frost.

33 As to marriage, I think the intercourse of heart and mind may be fully enjoyed without entering into this partnership of daily life.

MARGARET FULLER, in a letter to her sister, 1848.

34 A man in love is incomplete until he has married. Then he's finished.

ZSA ZSA GABOR, quoted in *Newsweek* magazine, March 28, 1960.

35 Husbands are like fires. They go out when unattended.

> Ibid.

36 If men knew how women pass the time when they are alone, they'd never marry.

> O. HENRY, "Memoirs of a Yellow Dog," *The Four Million,* 1906.

37 If a man really loves a woman, of course he wouldn't marry her for the world if he were not quite sure that he was the best person she could by any possibility marry.

> OLIVER WENDELL HOLMES, SR., *The Autocrat of the Breakfast-Table,* 1858.

38 I should like to see any kind of a man, distinguishable from a gorilla, that some good and even pretty woman could not shake a husband out of.

> OLIVER WENDELL HOLMES, SR., *The Professor at the Breakfast-Table,* 1860.

39 Husband and wife come to look alike at last.

> Ibid.

40 I believe that we all should wise up and recognize that a marriage is a small business and that married couples are business partners.

> DAVID HOPKINSON, clinical psychologist, quoted in *American Way* magazine, May 14, 1985.

41 A man should be taller, older, heavier, uglier, and hoarser than his wife.

> EDGAR WATSON HOWE, *Country Town Sayings,* 1911.

42 A honeymoon is a good deal like a man laying off to take an expensive vacation, and coming back to a different job.

> EDGAR WATSON HOWE, *Sinner Sermons,* 1926.

43 Marriage: A legal or religious ceremony by which two persons of the opposite sex solemnly agree to harass and spy on each other for ninety-nine years, or until death do them join.

> ELBERT HUBBARD, *The Roycroft Dictionary and Book of Epigrams,* 1923.

44 Wife: 1. In good society, a publicity agent who advertises her husband's financial status through conspicuous waste and conspicuous leisure. 2. In the submerged tenth, a punchingbag and something handy for batting up flies.

> Ibid.

45 It is a fortunate wife who can deal with her husband honestly instead of diplomatically.

> Ibid.

46 Marriage is love's demi-tasse.

> Ibid.

47 While a live husband may be a necessity, a dead one is a luxury.

> Ibid.

48 The trouble with many married people is that they are trying to get more out of marriage than there is in it.

> Ibid.

49 Old maids rush in where widows fear to tread.

> Ibid.

50 A widow who marries the second time doesn't deserve to be one.

> Ibid.

51 The French rule is wise, that no lady dances after marriage. This is founded in solid physical reasons, gestation and nursing leaving little time to a married lady when this exercise can be either safe or innocent.

> THOMAS JEFFERSON, in a letter to N. Burwell, March 14, 1818.

52 I think the best thing I can do is to be a distraction.

> JACQUELINE KENNEDY, reflecting on her role as a U.S. Senator's wife, quoted in the *New York Post,* March 25, 1957.

53 Marrying a man is like buying something you've been admiring for a long time in a shop window. You may love it when you get it home, but it doesn't always go with everything else in the house.

> JEAN KERR, "The Ten Worst Things about a Man," *The Snake Has All the Lines,* 1958.

54 'Tis sad when you think of her wasted life,
    For youth cannot mate with age,
And her beauty was sold for an old man's
    gold—
    She's a bird in a gilded cage.

    ARTHUR J. LAMB, "A Bird in a Gilded Cage,"
    1900.

55 Marriage is neither Heaven nor Hell. It is simply Purgatory.

    Attributed to Abraham Lincoln, 1864.

56 Mark was a Pill. His little Dame had
        Class . . .
One of those Unions that neglect to
        Une . . .
She was a Saint! He was a Hound! Alas,
That such a Peach should marry such a
        Prune!
Why did she stick? Who knows the inward
        tune
To which these women march? We know, at
        least,
Mark had a Wad, and bought her gowns and
        shoon . . .
Also, one eats or one is soon deceased. . . .
Mayhap it was a case of Booty and the
        Beast!

    DON MARQUIS, "Tristram and Isolt," in Burton
    Egbert Stevenson, *The Home Book of Modern
    Verse,* 1953.

57 Some people claim that marriage interferes with romance. There's no doubt about it. Anytime you have a romance, your wife is bound to interfere.

    GROUCHO MARX, *The Groucho Phile,* 1976.

58 There is no place like a bed for confidential disclosures between friends. Man and wife, they say, there open the very bottom of their souls to each other; and some old couples often lie and chat over old times till nearly morning.

    HERMAN MELVILLE, *Moby-Dick,* 1851.

59 Who are happy in marriage? Those with so little imagination that they cannot picture a better state, and those so shrewd that they prefer quiet slavery to hopeless rebellion.

    H.L. MENCKEN, *Prejudices,* Second Series, 1920.

60 For one American husband who maintains a chorus girl in Levantine luxury around the corner, there are hundreds who are as true to their oaths, year in and year out, as so many convicts in the deathhouse.

    H.L. MENCKEN, *In Defense of Women,* 1922.

61 Adultery is the application of democracy to love.

    H.L. MENCKEN, "Sententiae," in *The Vintage
    Mencken,* 1955.

62 I wonder what Adam and Eve think of it by this time.

    MARIANNE MOORE, "Marriage," 1935.

63 The man who never in his life
Has washed the dishes with his wife
Or polished up the silver plate—
He still is largely celibate.

    CHRISTOPHER MORLEY, "Washing the Dishes,"
    in *Songs for a Little House,* 1917.

64 With children no longer the universally accepted reason for marriage, marriages are going to have to exist on their own merits.

    ELEANOR HOLMES NORTON, quoted in Robin
    Morgan, *Sisterhood is Powerful,* 1970.

65 Hear the mellow wedding bells,
    Golden bells!
What a world of happiness their harmony
    foretells!

    EDGAR ALLAN POE, "The Bells," published in
    Sartain's Union Magazine, November, 1849.

66 Maybe I am old-fashioned, but believing in true love, saving yourself for that true love, and having one husband for all of your life just seems to me how things should be, although I know it doesn't always work out that way.

    NANCY REAGAN, *Nancy,* 1980.

67 I believe in marriage and the marriage contract, and I couldn't live any other way. I believe in standing up and committing yourself before God, the law, and your family and friends to another person and a way of life. Anything less is playing house. I've always wanted to belong to somebody

and to love someone who belonged to me. I always wanted someone to take care of me, someone I could take care of.

> Ibid.

68 The honeymoon is not actually over until we cease to stifle our sighs and begin to stifle our yawns.

> HELEN ROWLAND, quoted in Franklin P. Adams et al., *The Book of Diversion,* 1925.

69 Successful marriage is an art that can only be learned with difficulty. But it gives pride and satisfaction, like any other expertness that is hard won. . . . I would say that the surest measures of a man's or woman's maturity is the harmony, style, joy, dignity he creates in his marriage, and the pleasure and inspiration he provides for his spouse. An immature person may achieve great success in a career but never in marriage.

> BENJAMIN SPOCK, *Decent and Indecent,* 1968.

70 Our marriage is, in many cases, a mere outward tie, impelled by custom, policy, interest, necessity; founded not even in friendship, to say nothing of love; with every possible inequality of condition and development. In these heterogeneous unions, we find youth and old age, beauty and deformity, refinement and vulgarity, virtue and vice, the educated and the ignorant, angels of grace and goodness, with devils of malice and malignity: and the sum of all this is human wretchedness and despair; cold fathers, sad mothers, and hapless children, who shiver at the hearthstone, where the fires of love have all gone out.

> ELIZABETH CADY STANTON, speech at the Tenth National Woman's Rights Convention, New York City, May 10, 1860.

71 In the best condition of marriage, as we now have it, to woman come all the penalties and sacrifices. A man, in the full tide of business or pleasure, can marry and not change his life one iota; he can be husband, father, and everything beside; but in marriage, woman gives up all.

> Ibid.

72 The War Between Men and Women.

> JAMES THURBER, title of a cartoon series.

73 There is an absurd idea disseminated in novels, that the happier a girl is with another man, the happier it makes the old lover she has blighted. Don't allow yourself to believe any such nonsense as that. The more cause that girl finds to regret that she did not marry you, the more comfortable you will feel over it.

> MARK TWAIN, "Answers to Correspondents," *Sketches New and Old,* 1875.

74 Hence arises a most touching question—where are the girls of my youth? Some are married—some would like to be. Oh my Maria! Alas, she married another. They frequently do. I hope she is happy—because I am.

> ARTEMUS WARD, *Artemus Ward's Lecture,* 1869.

75 Brigham Young has two hundred wives. . . . He loves not wisely but two hundred well. He is dreadfully married. He's the most married man I ever saw in my life.

> Ibid.

76 Marriage was instituted by God himself for the purpose of preventing promiscuous intercourse of the sexes, for promoting domestic felicity, and for securing the maintenance and security of children.

> NOAH WEBSTER, *An American Dictionary of the English Language,* 1828.

77 Maud Muller looked and sighed: "Ah me!
That I the Judge's bride might be!
He would dress me up in silks so fine,
And praise and toast me at his wine."

> JOHN GREENLEAF WHITTIER, "Maud Muller," 1854.

78 The best part of married life is the fights. The rest is merely so-so.

> THORNTON WILDER, *The Matchmaker,* 1954.

79 The world well tried—the sweetest thing in life
Is the unclouded welcome of a wife.

> NATHANIEL PARKER WILLIS, "Lady Jane," 1844.

80 Take my wife . . . please!

> HENNY YOUNGMAN, his best-known comedy line.

146. MARYLAND

1 Fatti maschii, parole femine. (Manly deeds, womanly words.)

    State motto.

2 In truth, he had never seen a finished landscape; but Maryland was raggedness of a new kind.

    HENRY ADAMS, *The Education of Henry Adams,* 1907.

3 For more than a century Baltimore was known throughout the nation under the unsavory name of "Mobtown." The title owed its origin to the speed and frequency with which the citizenry found excuse to riot.

    FRANCIS F. BEIRNE, *The Amiable Baltimoreans,* 1968.

4 Wonderful little Baltimore, in which, whether when perched on a noble eminence or passing from one seat of the humanities, one seat of hospitality, to another—a process mainly consisting indeeed, as it seemed to me, of prompt drives through romantic parks and woodlands that were all suburban yet all Arcadian—I caught no glimpse of traffic, however mild, nor spied anything "tall" at the end of any vista.

    HENRY JAMES, *The American Scene,* 1907.

5 Admirable I found them, the Maryland boughs, and so immediately disposed about the fortunate town [Baltimore] by parkside and lonely lane, by trackless hillside and tangled copse, that the depth of rural effect becomes at once bewildering. You wonder at the absent transitions, you look in vain for the shabby fringes.

    Ibid.

6 You have never seen, on the lap of nature, so large a burden so neatly accommodated. Baltimore sits there as some quite robust but almost unnaturally good child might sit on the green apron of its nurse, with no concomitant crease or crumple, no

uncontrollable "mess," by the nursery term, to betray its temper.

    Ibid.

7 The old charm, in truth, still survives in the town [Baltimore], despite the frantic efforts of the boosters and boomers who, in late years, have replaced all its ancient cobblestones with asphalt, and bedizened it with Great White Ways and suburban boulevards, and surrounded it with stinking steel plants and oil refineries, and increased its population from 400,000 to 800,000.

    H. L. MENCKEN, in *Prejudices: Fifth Series,* 1926.

8 A Baltimorean is not merely John Doe, an isolated individual of *Homo sapiens,* exactly like every other John Doe. He is John Doe of a certain place—of Baltimore, of a definite *house* in Baltimore.

    H. L. MENCKEN, *Prejudices: Fifth Series,* 1926.

9 The despot's heel is on thy shore,
    Maryland!
His touch is at thy temple door,
    Maryland!
Avenge the patriotic gore
That flecked the streets of Baltimore,
And be the battle queen of yore,
    Maryland! My Maryland!

Hark to a wand'ring son's appeal,
    Maryland!
My mother State! to thee I kneel,
    Maryland!
For life and death, for woe and weal,
Thy peerless chivalry reveal,
And gird thy beauteous limbs with steel,
    Maryland! My Maryland!

    JAMES RYDER RANDALL, the first two stanzas of "Maryland, My Maryland," 1861.

10 Our summer in Maryland was delightful. . . . In no part of North America are the natural productions of the soil more various, or more beautiful. Strawberries of the richest flavor sprung beneath our feet; and when these passed away, every grove,

every lane, every field looked like a cherry orchard, offering an inexhaustible profusion of fruit to all who would take the trouble to gather it.

> FRANCES TROLLOPE, *Domestic Manners of the Americans,* 1832.

---

147. MASSACHUSETTS

---

1 Ense petit placidam sub libertate quietem. (By the sword she seeks peaceful quiet under liberty.)

> State motto.

2 It shall be the duty of the legislatures and magistrates . . . to countenance and inculcate the principles of humanity and general benevolence, public and private charity, industry and frugality, honesty and punctuality in their dealings; sincerity, good humor, and all social affections and generous sentiments among the people.

> Constitution of Massachusetts, 1780.

3 Have faith in Massachusetts!

> CALVIN COOLIDGE, in a speech in the Massachusetts legislature, January 7, 1914.

4 [The Puritans] were a very wonderful people. . . . If they were narrow it was not a blighting and destructive narrowness, but a vital and productive narrowness.

> CALVIN COOLIDGE, in a speech in Watertown, Massachusetts, 1930.

5 the Cambridge ladies who live in furnished
>   souls
are unbeautiful and have comfortable minds.

> E.E. CUMMINGS, "Realities," 1923.

6 Massachusetts is Italy upside down.

> RALPH WALDO EMERSON, quoting William Ellery Channing in a journal entry dated November 19, 1848, *Journals,* 1909–1914.

7 Down to the Plymouth Rock, that had been
>   to their feet as a doorstep

Into a world unknown,— the corner-stone of
>   a nation!

> HENRY WADSWORTH LONGFELLOW, on Plymouth Rock, in *The Courtship of Miles Standish,* 1858.

8 Nantucket! Take out your map and look at it—a mere hillock, and elbow of sand; all beach, without a background. Some gamesome wights will tell you that they have to plant weeds there, they don't grow naturally; that pieces of wood in Nantucket are carried about like bits of the true cross in Rome; that one blade of grass makes an oasis, three blades in a day's walk a prairie.

> HERMAN MELVILLE, *Moby-Dick,* 1851.

9 The rock underlies all America: it only crops out here.

> WENDELL PHILLIPS, in a speech at Plymouth, Massachusetts, December 21, 1855.

10 The first public love of my heart is the Commonwealth of Massachusetts.

> JOSIAH QUINCY, in a speech in the House of Representatives, January 14, 1811.

11 I shall enter on no encomium upon Massachusetts; she needs none. There she is. Behold her, and judge for yourselves. There is her history; the world knows it by heart. The past, at least, is secure. There is Boston and Concord and Lexington and Bunker Hill; and there they will remain forever.

> DANIEL WEBSTER, in his second reply in the Webster-Hayne debate, January 26, 1830.

12 No slave-hunt in our borders,— no pirate on
>   our strand!
No fetters in the Bay State— no slave upon
>   our land!

> JOHN GREENLEAF WHITTIER, "Massachusetts to Virginia," 1843.

148. MEDICINE

See also HEALTH; LIFE; MERRIMENT

1 Medicine, *n.* A stone flung down the Bowery to kill a dog in Broadway.

AMBROSE BIERCE, *The Devil's Dictionary,* 1923.

2 Physician, *n.* One upon whom we set out hopes when ill and our dogs when well.

Ibid.

3 It is simply absurd that without modern science painless childbirth does not exist as a matter of course.

ISADORA DUNCAN, *My Life,* 1927.

4 If th' Christyan Scientists had some science an' th' doctors more Christianity, it wudden't make anny diff'rence which ye called in—if ye had a good nurse.

FINLEY PETER DUNNE, "Christian Science," *Mr. Dooley's Opinions,* 1900.

5 How do drugs, hygiene, and animal magnetism heal? It may be affirmed that they do not heal, but only relieve suffering temporarily, exchanging one disease for another.

MARY BAKER EDDY, *Science and Health,* 1875.

6 Homeopathy is insignificant as an art of healing, but of great value as criticism on the hygeia or medical practice of the time.

RALPH WALDO EMERSON, "Nominalist and Realist," *Essays,* Second Series, 1844.

7 Some day when you have time, look into the business of prayer, amulets, baths, and poultices, and discover for yourself how much valuable therapy the medical profession has cast out of the window.

Attributed to Martin H. Fischer.

8 He's the best physician that knows the worthlessness of the most medicines.

BENJAMIN FRANKLIN, *Poor Richard's Almanack,* 1733.

9 God heals and the Doctor takes the Fees.

BENJAMIN FRANKLIN, *Poor Richard's Almanack,* 1736.

10 I firmly believe that if the whole *materia medica,* as now used, could be sunk to the bottom of the sea, it would be all the better for mankind, and all the worse for the fishes.

OLIVER WENDELL HOLMES, SR., in a speech to the Massachusetts Medical Society, Boston, May 30, 1860.

11 What I call a good patient is one who, having found a good physician, sticks to him till he dies.

OLIVER WENDELL HOLMES, SR., in a lecture in New York City, March 2, 1871.

12 The indigent sick of this city and its environs, without regard to sex, age or color, who may require surgical or medical treatment, and who can be received into the hospital without peril to the other inmates, and the poor of this city and state, of all races, who are stricken down by any casualty, shall be received into the hospital, without charge, for such period of time and under such regulations as you may prescribe.

JOHNS HOPKINS, in a letter instructing the first trustees of the Johns Hopkins Hospital, Baltimore, Maryland, March, 1873.

13 The worse about medicine is that one kind makes another necessary.

ELBERT HUBBARD, in *The Philistine* magazine, published from 1895–1915.

14 I believe we may safely affirm, that the inexperienced and presumptuous band of medical tyros let loose upon the world, destroys more of human life in one year, than all the Robinhoods, Cartouches, and Macheaths do in a century. It is in this part of medicine that I wish to see a reform, an abandonment of hypothesis for sober facts, the first degree of value set on clinical observation, and the lowest on visionary theories. I would wish the young practitioner, especially, to have deeply impressed on his mind, the real limits of his art, and that when the state of his patient gets beyond these, his office is to be watchful, but quiet spectator of the operations of nature.

THOMAS JEFFERSON, in a letter to Dr. Caspar Wistar, June 21, 1807.

15 Who ever said that doctors are truthful or even intelligent? You're getting a lot if they know their profession.

MARJORIE KARMEL, *Thank You, Dr. Lamaze,* 1959.

16 Forth then issued Hiawatha,
Wandered eastward, wandered westward,
Teaching men the use of simples
And the antidotes for poisons,
And the cure of all diseases.
Thus was first made known to mortals
All the mystery of Medamin,
All the sacred art of healing.

HENRY WADSWORTH LONGFELLOW, *The Song of Hiawatha,* 1855.

17 Medical doctors strike me as ignorant as to how a *healthy* body works. They know how to control or repair some diseased bodies, but their medicine is often worse than the disease. And what about the pressure and competitiveness of the pharmaceutical industry and the make-profits-quick motives of the food corporations? Medical doctors put little or no emphasis on nutrition, exercise, and energy balance. They are paid when we are sick, not when we are well.

JERRY RUBIN, *Growing (Up) at 37,* 1976.

18 Consider the deference which is everywhere paid to a doctor's opinion. Nothing more strikingly betrays the credulity of mankind than medicine. Quackery is a thing universal, and universally successful. In this case it becomes literally true that no imposition is too great for the credulity of men.

HENRY DAVID THOREAU, *A Week on the Concord and Merrimack Rivers,* 1849.

19 It is wonderful that the physician should ever die, and that the priest should ever live. Why is it that the priest is never called to consult with the physician? It is because men believe practically that matter is independent of spirit. But what is quackery? It is commonly an attempt to cure the diseases of a man by addressing his body alone. There is need of a physician who shall minister to both soul

and body at once, that is to man. Now he falls between two stools.

Ibid.

149. MERRIMENT

See also HAPPINESS

1 An onion can make people cry, but there's no vegetable that can make them laugh.

Anonymous.

2 Laughter, the Best Medicine.

A department in *Reader's Digest* magazine featuring humorous anecdotes.

3 Laffing iz the sensation ov pheeling good all over, and showing it principally in one spot.

JOSH BILLINGS, *Josh Billings' Comical Lexicon,* 1877.

4 Indecency and fun are old cronies.

SAMUEL SULLIVAN COX, *Why We Laugh,* 1876.

5 Eat, drink and be leary.

O. HENRY, "The Man Higher Up," *The Gentle Grafter,* 1908.

6 Mirth's concussions rip the outward case,
And plant the stitches in a tenderer place.

OLIVER WENDELL HOLMES, SR., "A Rhymed Lesson," 1846.

7 Laughter and tears are meant to turn the wheels of the same machinery of sensibility; one is a wind-power and the other water-power, that is all.

OLIVER WENDELL HOLMES, SR., *The Autocrat of the Breakfast-Table,* 1858.

8 Laughing has always been considered by theologians as a crime.

ROBERT G. INGERSOLL, in a speech in Chicago, Illinois, November 26, 1882.

9 The Marquesan girls dance all over, as it were; not only do their feet dance, but their arms, hands,

fingers, ay, their very eyes seem to dance in their heads.

HERMAN MELVILLE, *Typee,* 1846.

10 Popularity is exhausting. The life of the party almost always winds up in a corner with an overcoat over him.

Attributed to Wilson Mizner.

11 He had a broad face,
   And a round little belly
That shook when he laughed,
   Like a bowlful of jelly.

CLEMENT CLARKE MOORE, "A Visit from St. Nicholas," 1823.

12 Drink and dance and laugh and lie,
   Love, the reeling midnight through,
For tomorrow we shall die! (But, alas, we
   never do.)

DOROTHY PARKER, "The Flaw in Paganism," *Death and Taxes,* 1931.

---

150. MICHIGAN

---

1 Si quaeris peninsulam amoenam circumspice. (If you seek a pleasant peninsula, look around you.)

State motto.

2 Michigan is perhaps the strangest state in the Union, a place where the past, the present, and the future are all tied up together in a hard knot. . . . It is the skyscraper, the mass-production line, and the frantic rush into what the machine will some day make of all of us, and at the same time it is golden sand, blue water, green pine trees on empty hills, and a wind that comes down from the cold spaces, scented with the forests that were butchered by hard-handed men in checked flannel shirts and floppy pants. It is the North Country wedded to the force that destroyed it.

BRUCE CATTON, "Michigan," in *American Panorama: East of the Mississippi,* 1960.

3 We lived less than three hundred miles from Detroit, which seemed to be a door looking into the future, showing unimaginable things; and three hundred miles in the other direction, off into the desolate north country, lay the bleak spine of the upper peninsula of Michigan, a reef of the oldest rocks on earth—pre-Cambrian rocks, laid down before there were any living creatures to be fossilized, rocks dead since the hour of creation.

BRUCE CATTON, *Waiting for the Morning Train,* 1972.

4 There was a rich man and he lived in
      Detroitium,
   Glory hallelujah, heirojarum.
And all the workers he did exploitium,
   Glory hallelujah, heirojarum.

WOODY GUTHRIE, "There Was a Rich Man and He Lived in Detroitium," collected in *Hard Hitting Songs for Hard-Hit People,* 1967.

5 You can slip up on Detroit in the dead of night, consider it from any standpoint, and it's still hell on wheels.

GEORGE SESSIONS PERRY, *Cities of America,* 1947.

6 I had forgotten how rich and beautiful is the countryside—the deep topsoil, the wealth of great trees, the lake country of Michigan handsome as a well-made woman, and dressed and jeweled. It seemed to me that the earth was generous and outgoing here in the heartland, and perhaps the people took a cue from it.

JOHN STEINBECK, *Travels with Charley,* 1962.

---

151. THE MIDWEST

See also individual states

---

1 The Great Prairies . . . resemble the steppes of Tartary more than any other known portion of the world; being, in fact, a vast country, incapable of sustaining a dense population.

JAMES FENIMORE COOPER, *The Prairie,* 1827.

2 The Midwest is exactly what one would expect from a marriage between New England puritanism and *rich* soil.

> JOHN GUNTHER, *Inside U.S.A.,* 1947.

3 You get damn few good guys in the Middle West.

> ERNEST HEMINGWAY, to Waldo Peirce, on Hemingway's month-long stay in Piggott, Arkansas, in 1928.

4 It isn't necessary to have relatives in Kansas City to be unhappy.

> GROUCHO MARX, in a letter to Goodman Ace, January 18, 1951.

5 The Michiganers are calld Woolfverines, the Illinois Suckers, the Indianians Hooshers, and the Missourians Pukes, and the N. Yorkers Eels, and the People of Detroit Hollow Heads. Although there is many Peculiarities in their manners they all appear to be very friendly to Strangers.

> MORRIS SLEIGHT, a sea captain, in a letter to his wife, July 9, 1834, quoted in Paul M. Angle, *Prairie State,* 1968.

6 Almost on crossing the Ohio line it seemed to me that people were more open and more outgoing. The waitress in a roadside stand said good morning before I had a chance to, discussed breakfast as though she liked the idea, spoke with enthusiasm about the weather, sometimes even offered some information about herself without my delving. Strangers talked freely to one another without caution.

> JOHN STEINBECK, *Travels with Charley,* 1962.

---

152. MILITARISM

See also ARMY; FORCE; NAVY

---

1 We oppose militarism. It means conquest abroad and intimidation and oppression at home. It means the strong arm which has ever been fatal to free institutions. It is what millions of our citizens have fled from in Europe. It will impose upon our peace loving people a large standing army and unnecessary burden of taxation, and will be a constant menace to their liberties.

> Plank of the Democratic Party national platform, 1900.

2 In the councils of government, we must guard against the acquisition of unwarranted influence, whether sought or unsought, by the military-industrial complex. The potential for the disastrous rise of misplaced power exists and will persist. We must never let the weight of this combination endanger our liberties or democratic processes.

> DWIGHT D. EISENHOWER, in his presidential farewell message, January 17, 1961.

3 Militarism is the great preserver of our ideals of hardihood, and human life with no use for hardihood would be contemptible.

> WILLIAM JAMES, "The Moral Equivalent of War," 1910.

4 Pride, arrogance, and the lust of conquest are the natural and bitter fruits of military preparation—fruits fatal to national peace and happiness.

> JOHN JAY, "A Review of the Causes and Consequences of the Mexican War," 1849.

5 The spirit of this country is totally adverse to a large military force.

> THOMAS JEFFERSON, in a letter to Chandler Price, February 28, 1807.

6 For a people who are free, and who mean to remain so, a well-organized and armed militia is their best security.

> THOMAS JEFFERSON, in his eighth annual message to Congress, November 8, 1808.

7 We must train and classify the whole of our male citizens, and make military instruction a regular part of collegiate education. We can never be safe till this is done.

> THOMAS JEFFERSON, in a letter to James Monroe, June 18, 1813.

8 The [early] Greeks and Romans had no standing armies, yet they defended themselves. The Greeks, by their laws, and the Romans, by the spirit of their

people, took care to put into the hands of their rulers no such engine of oppression as a standing army. Their system was to make every man a soldier, and oblige him to repair to the standard of his country whenever that was reared. This made them invincible, and the same remedy will make us so.

THOMAS JEFFERSON, in a letter to Dr. Thomas Cooper, September 10, 1814.

9 A nation that continues year after year to spend more money on military defense than on programs of social uplift is approaching spiritual death.

MARTIN LUTHER KING, JR., *Where Do We Go From Here? Chaos or Community,* 1967.

10 I have heard . . . of your recently saying that both the army and the government needed a dictator. . . . Only those generals who gain successes can set up dictators.

ABRAHAM LINCOLN, in a letter to Joseph Hooker, January 26, 1863.

11 We may not be in the slightest danger of invasion, but if in an armed world we disarm, we shall count less and less in the councils of nations.

WALTER LIPPMANN, "A Cure for Militarism," in the *Metropolitan* magazine, February, 1915.

12 No one can claim to be called Christian who gives money for the building of warships and arsenals.

BELVA ANN LOCKWOOD, in a speech in London, England, c.1886.

13 They talk about conscription as being a democratic institution. Yes; so is a cemetery.

MEYER LONDON, in a speech in the House of Representatives, April 25, 1917.

14 A warlike spirit, which alone can create and civilize a state, is absolutely essential to national defense and to national perpetuity.

GEN. DOUGLAS MACARTHUR, in the *Infantry Journal,* March, 1927.

15 If we are forced to fight, we must have the means and the determination to prevail or we will not have what it takes to secure the peace.

RONALD REAGAN, quoted in Hedrick Smith et al., *Reagan the Man, the President,* 1980.

16 In this country of ours, the man who has not raised himself to be a soldier, and the woman who has not raised her boy to be a soldier for the right, neither one of them is entitled to citizenship in the Republic.

THEODORE ROOSEVELT, in a speech at Camp Upton, Yaphank, New York, November 18, 1917.

17 If there is one basic element in our Constitution, it is civilian control of the military.

HARRY S TRUMAN, *Memoirs,* 1955.

18 When men are irritated and their passions inflamed they fly hastily and cheerfully to arms, but after the first emotions are over, to expect among such people as compose the bulk of an army that they are influenced by any other principles than those of interest is to look for what never did and I fear never will happen.

GEORGE WASHINGTON, in a letter to the president of Congress, September 24, 1776.

19 A free people ought not only be armed, but disciplined.

GEORGE WASHINGTON, in his first annual address to Congress, January 8, 1790.

20 [The several sections of the country, united under one government] will avoid the necessity of those overgrown military establishments which, under any form of government, are inauspicious to liberty, and which are to be regarded as particularly hostile to republican liberty.

GEORGE WASHINGTON, in his Farewell Address, September 19, 1796.

21 The whole present system of the officering and personnel of the army and navy of these States, and the spirit and letter of their trebly-aristocratic rules and regulations, is a monstrous exotic, a nuisance and revolt, and belongs here just as much as orders of nobility, or the pope's council of cardinals. I say if the present theory of our army and navy is sensible and true, then the rest of America is an unmitigated fraud.

WALT WHITMAN, in a footnote in *Democratic Vistas,* 1870.

153. MINNESOTA

1 L'étoile du Nord. (The star of the North.)

State motto.

2 To understand Minnesota it is necessary . . . that one respond to youth, forgiving its occasional awkwardness and egoism for the sake of its healthy vigor, its color, its alternating self-confidence and self-distrust, its eagerness for experiment. One will not expect to find here the mellowness of cities, villages, and countrysides in the older states.

Federal Writers' Project, *Minnesota: A State Guide,* 1938.

3 What a glorious new Scandinavia might not Minnesota become! . . . The climate, the situation, the character of the scenery, agrees with our people better than that of any other of the American states, and none of them appear to me to have a greater or more beautiful future before them than Minnesota.

FREDRIKA BREMER, *Homes of the New World,* 1853.

4 May your soul be forever tormented by fire and your bones be dug up by dogs and dragged through the streets of Minneapolis.

GARRISON KEILLOR, *Happy to Be Here,* 1982.

5 Duluth! the word fell upon my ear with a peculiar and indescribable charm, like the gentle murmur of a low fountain stealing forth in the midst of roses; or the soft, sweet accents of an angel's whisper in the bright, joyous dream of sleeping innocence.

JAMES PROCTOR KNOTT, in a speech in the House of Representatives, January 21, 1871.

6 Yet, sir, had it not been for this map, kindly furnished me by the Legislature of Minnesota, I might have gone down to my obscure and humble grave in an agony of despair, because I could nowhere find Duluth. Had such been my melancholy fate, I have no doubt that with the last feeble pulsation of my breaking heart, with the last faint exhalation of my fleeting breath, I should have whispered, "Where is Duluth?"

Ibid.

7 Minnesotans are just different, that's all. On the day of which I speak, with the wind-chill factor hovering at fifty-seven below, hundreds of them could be perceived through the slits in my ski mask out ice fishing on this frozen lake. It was cold out there, bitter, biting, cutting, piercing, hyperborean, marmoreal cold, and there were all these Minnesotans running around outdoors, happy as lambs in the spring.

CHARLES KURALT, *Dateline America,* 1979.

8 The state seal shows a farmer, a waterfall, a forest, and an Indian riding into the sunset. It should be changed to ice cubes rampant on a field of white, a grinning, barefoot Swede in a Grain Belt Beer T-shirt riding a snowmobile, and a shivering visitor whose stricken breath is freezing into ice crystals.

Ibid.

154. MISSISSIPPI

1 Virtute et armis. (By valor and arms.)

State motto.

2 Mississippi begins in the lobby of a Memphis, Tennessee, hotel and extends south to the Gulf of Mexico. It is dotted with little towns concentric about the ghosts of the horses and mules once tethered to the hitch-rail enclosing the county courthouse and it might almost be said to have only two directions, north and south, since until a few years ago it was impossible to travel east or west in it unless you walked or rode one of the horses or mules.

WILLIAM FAULKNER, "Mississippi," *American Panorama: East of the Mississippi,* 1960.

3 Mississippi will drink wet and vote dry—so long as any citizen can stagger to the polls.

Attributed to Will Rogers.

155. MISSISSIPPI RIVER

1 The Father of Waters.

> Popular nickname for the Mississippi. (The word Mississippi comes from the Algonquian words for "great river.")

2 But what words shall describe the Mississippi, great father of rivers, who (praise be to Heaven) has no young children like him! An enormous ditch, sometimes two or three miles wide, running liquid mud, six miles an hour: its strong and frothy current choked and obstructed everywhere.

> CHARLES DICKENS, *American Notes,* 1842.

3 Ol' man river, dat ol' man river,
  He must know sumpin', but don't say nothin',
  He just keeps rollin', he keeps on rollin'
      along.

> OSCAR HAMMERSTEIN II, "Ol' Man River," in *Showboat,* 1927.

4 The Father of Waters again goes unvexed to the sea.

> ABRAHAM LINCOLN, on the capture of Vicksburg, Mississippi, July 4, 1863, and the reopening of river traffic, in a letter to James C. Conkling, August 26, 1863.

5 The Mississippi is well worth reading about. It is not a commonplace river, but on the contrary is in all ways remarkable. Considering the Missouri its main branch, it is the longest river in the world—four thousand three hundred miles. It seems safe to say that it is also the crookedest river in the world, since in one part of its journey it uses up one thousand three hundred miles to cover the same ground that the crow would fly over in six hundred and seventy-five.

> MARK TWAIN, *Life on the Mississippi,* 1883.

6 When I was a boy, there was but one permanent ambition among my comrades in our village on the west bank of the Mississippi River. That was, to be a steamboatman. We had transient ambitions of other sorts, but they were only transient. . . . These ambitions faded out, each in its turn; but the ambition to be a steamboatman always remained.

> Ibid.

7 The face of the water, in time, became a wonderful book—a book that was a dead language to the uneducated passenger, but which told its mind to me without reserve, delivering its most cherished secrets as clearly as if it uttered them with a voice. And it was not a book to be read once and thrown aside, for it had a new story to tell every day.

> Ibid.

8 If I have seemed to love my subject, it is no surprising thing, for I have loved the profession far better than any I have followed since, and I took a measureless pride in it. The reason is plain: a pilot, in those days, was the only unfettered and entirely independent human being that lived in the earth.

> Ibid.

9 The Mississippi is a just and equitable river; it never tumbles one man's farm overboard without building a new farm just like it for that man's neighbor. This keeps down hard feelings.

> Ibid.

156. MISSOURI

1 Salus populi suprema lex esto. (The welfare of the people shall be the supreme law.)

> State motto.

2 Be from Missouri, of course; but for God's sake forget it occasionally.

> ELBERT HUBBARD, *The Roycroft Dictionary and Book of Epigrams,* 1923.

3 A Missourian gets used to Southerners thinking him a Yankee, a Northerner considering him a cracker, a Westerner sneering at his effete Easternness, and the Easterner taking him for a cowhand.

> WILLIAM LEAST HEAT MOON, *Blue Highways,* 1982.

4 In all the years since I left the White House, I have wondered why so many people come from so far away and take so much trouble to look at the house where I live. Perhaps it is because once a man has been President he becomes an object of curiosity like those other notorious Missouri characters, Mark Twain and Jesse James.

> HARRY S TRUMAN, *Mr. Citizen*, 1960.

5 The first time I ever saw St. Louis I could have bought it for six million dollars, and it was the mistake of my life that I did not do it.

> MARK TWAIN, *Life on the Mississippi*, 1883.

6 I'm from Missouri, you've got to show me.

> Attributed to Willard D. Vandiver, in a speech in Philadelphia, 1899. (There have been many other claims concerning the origin of the saying. One stated that when Missouri miners went to work in Colorado mines they used the phrase to indicate their unfamiliarity with local mine operations.)

---

157. MONEY

See also BUSINESS; DEBT; ECONOMICS; POVERTY; WEALTH

---

1 Money never goes to jail.

> Anonymous wisdom.

2 Money isn't important, but it's the only way to keep score.

> Anonymous, quoted in Jerry Kramer, *Farewell to Football*, 1969.

3 Money isn't everything, but lack of money isn't anything.

> FRANKLIN P. ADAMS [F.P.A.], quoted in Robert E. Drennan, *The Algonquin Wits*, 1968.

4 I cannot afford to waste my time making money.

> Attributed to Louis Agassiz, turning down an offer for a series of lectures.

5 Where there is money, there is fighting.

> MARIAN ANDERSON, quoted in Kosti Vehanen, *Marian Anderson, a Portrait*, 1941.

6 Each dollar is a soldier that does your bidding.

> Vincent Astor, quoted in Harvey O'Connor, *The Astors*, 1941.

7 No one can earn a million dollars honestly.

> Attributed to William Jennings Bryan.

8 You shall not press down upon the brow of labor this crown of thorns. You shall not crucify mankind upon a cross of gold!

> WILLIAM JENNINGS BRYAN, in an address to the Democratic National Convention, July 8, 1896.

9 A power has risen up in the government greater than the people themselves, consisting of many and various and powerful interests combined in one mass, and held together by the cohesive power of the vast surplus in the banks.

> JOHN C. CALHOUN, in a speech in the U.S. Senate, May 28, 1836.

10 Learn how to cook! That's the way to save money.

> JULIA CHILD, in *Julia Child's Kitchen*, 1975.

11 The dealers in money have always, since the days of Moses, been the dangerous class.

> Attributed to Peter Cooper.

12 Money is so unlike every other article that I believe a man has neither a legal or a moral right to take all that he can get.

> PETER COOPER, quoted by U.S. Attorney General A.J. Cummings, in an address at the American Federation of Labor Convention in Philadelphia, December, 1892.

13 If a man is wise, he gets rich, an' if he gets rich, he gets foolish, or his wife does. That's what keeps the money movin' around.

> FINLEY PETER DUNNE, *Observations by Mr. Dooley*, 1902.

14 Money doesn't talk, it swears.

> BOB DYLAN, quoted in Jerry Rubin, *Growing (Up) at 37*, 1976.

15 Ah, my poor countrymen! Yankees and Dollars have such inextricable association that the words ought to rhyme.

> RALPH WALDO EMERSON, entry written in 1840, *Journals*, 1909–1914.

16 Money, which represents the prose of life, and which is hardly spoken of in parlors without an apology, is, in its effects and laws, as beautiful as roses.

> RALPH WALDO EMERSON, "Nominalist and Realist," *Essays*, Second Series, 1844.

17 An Englishman who has lost his fortune is said to have died of a broken heart.

> RALPH WALDO EMERSON, *English Traits*, 1856.

18 A dollar in Florida is not worth a dollar in Massachusetts. A dollar is not value, but representative of value, and, at last, of moral values.

> RALPH WALDO EMERSON, "Wealth," *The Conduct of Life*, 1860.

19 Can anybody remember when the times were not hard, and money not scarce?

> RALPH WALDO EMERSON, "Works and Days," *Society and Solitude*, 1870.

20 Money is everything in this world to some people and more than the next to other poor souls.

> AUGUSTA EVANS, *Beulah*, 1859.

21 The hold which controllers of money are able to maintain on productive forces is seen to be more powerful when it is remembered that, although money is supposed to represent the real wealth of the world, there is always much more wealth than there is money, and real wealth is often compelled to wait upon money, thus leading to that most paradoxical situation—a world filled with wealth but suffering want.

> HENRY FORD, *My Life and Work*, 1923.

22 There are two fools in this world. One is the millionaire who thinks that by hoarding money he can somehow accumulate real power, and the other is the penniless reformer who thinks that if only he can take the money from one class and give it to another, all the world's ills will be cured.

> Ibid.

23 Money, after all, is extremely simple. It is a part of our transportation system. It is a simple and direct method of conveying goods from one person to another. Money is in itself most admirable. It is essential. It is not intrinsically evil. It is one of the most useful devices in social life. And when it does what it was intended to do, it is all help and no hindrance.

> Ibid.

24 Money is like an arm or a leg—use it or lose it.

> HENRY FORD, in an interview in the *New York Times*, November 8, 1931.

25 Nothing but Money,
Is sweeter than Honey.

> BENJAMIN FRANKLIN, *Poor Richard's Almanack*, 1735.

26 Lend Money to an Enemy, and thou'lt gain him, to a Friend, and thou'lt lose him.

> BENJAMIN FRANKLIN, *Poor Richard's Almanack*, 1740.

27 Remember that money is of a prolific generating nature. Money can beget money, and its offspring can beget more.

> BENJAMIN FRANKLIN, in a letter to "My Friend, A.B.," 1748.

28 He that is of Opinion Money will do every Thing, may well be suspected of doing every Thing for Money.

> BENJAMIN FRANKLIN, *Poor Richard's Almanack*, 1753.

29 A Change of *Fortune* hurts a wise Man no more than a Change of the *Moon*.

> BENJAMIN FRANKLIN, *Poor Richard's Almanack*, 1756.

30 If you would know the Value of Money, go and try to borrow some.

> BENJAMIN FRANKLIN, *Poor Richard's Almanack*, 1758.

31 A man is sometimes more generous when he has but a little money than when he has plenty, perhaps thro' fear of being thought to have but little.

> BENJAMIN FRANKLIN, *Autobiography*, 1798.

32 Whoever controls the volume of money in any country is absolute master of all industry and commerce.

> Attributed to James A. Garfield.

33 I am an advocate of paper money, but that paper money must represent what it professes on its face. I do not wish to hold in my hands the printed lies of the government.

> JAMES A. GARFIELD, speaking in Congress, 1866.

34 Any party which commits itself to paper money will go down amid the general disaster, covered with the curses of a ruined people.

> Ibid.

35 How many men are there who fairly earn a million dollars?

> HENRY GEORGE, *Progress and Poverty,* 1879.

36 I haven't any time to make money, and I don't want any anyhow. Money is more trouble than it's worth.

> Attributed to Horace Greeley.

37 This bank-note world.

> FITZ-GREENE HALLECK, "Alnwick Castle," in *Alnwick Castle, with Other Poems,* 1827.

38 What I know about money, I learned the hard way—by having had it.

> MARGARET HALSEY, *The Folks at Home,* 1952.

39 Put not your trust in money, but put your money in trust.

> OLIVER WENDELL HOLMES, SR., *The Autocrat of the Breakfast-Table,* 1858.

40 When a man says money can do anything, that settles it: he hasn't any.

> EDGAR WATSON HOWE, *Sinner Sermons,* 1923.

41 When a fellow says it hain't the money but the principle o' the thing, it's th' money.

> KIN HUBBARD, *Hoss Sense and Nonsense,* 1926.

42 No government can afford to be a clipper of coin.

> ROBERT G. INGERSOLL, in a speech in New York City, October 23, 1880.

43 The almighty dollar, that great object of universal devotion throughout our land, seems to have no genuine devotees in these peculiar villages.

> WASHINGTON IRVINGTON, "The Creole Village," *Wolfert's Roost and Miscellanies,* 1855.

44 A great deal of small change is useful in a state, and tends to reduce the prices of small articles.

> THOMAS JEFFERSON, "Notes on the Establishment of a Money Unit, and of a Coinage for the United States," 1784.

45 Money, and not morality, is the principle of commerce and commercial nations.

> THOMAS JEFFERSON, in a letter to John Langdon, March 5, 1810.

46 The typical American believes that no necessity of the soul is free and that there are precious few, if any, which cannot be bought.

> JOSEPH WOOD KRUTCH, "The European Visitor," *If You Don't Mind My Saying So,* 1964.

47 I cried all the way to the bank.

> LIBERACE, *An Autobiography,* 1973.

48 The urbane activity with which a man receives money is really marvelous, considering that we so earnestly believe money to be the root of all earthly ills, and that on no account can a monied man enter heaven. Ah! how cheerfully we consign ourselves to perdition!

> HERMAN MELVILLE, *Moby-Dick,* 1851.

49 Americans relate all effort, all work, and all of life itself to the dollar. Their talk is of nothing but dollars.

> NANCY MITFORD, *Noblesse Oblige,* 1956.

50 Certainly there are lots of things in life that
   money won't buy, but it's very funny—
Have you ever tried to buy them without
   money?

> OGDEN NASH, "The Terrible People," *Happy Days,* 1933.

51 Americans want action for their money. They are fascinated by its self-reproducing qualities.

> PAULA NELSON, *The Joy of Money,* 1975.

52 Money can be translated into the beauty of living, a support in misfortune, an education, or future security. It also can be translated into a source of bitterness.

> SYLVIA PORTER, in *Sylvia Porter's Money Book,* 1975.

53 The money changers have fled from their high seats in the temple of our civilization. We may now restore that temple to the ancient truths. The measure of the restoration lies in the extent to which we apply social values more noble than mere monetary profit. Happiness lies not in the mere possession of money; it lies in the joy of achievement, in the thrill of creative effort.

> FRANKLIN D. ROOSEVELT, in his first inaugural address, March 4, 1933.

54 If you rub up against money long enough, some of it may rub off on you.

> DAMON RUNYON, "A Very Honorable Guy," *Furthermore,* 1938.

55 Money is power, freedom, a cushion, the root
>   of all evil, the sum of blessings. . . .
> Money breeds money.
> Money rules the world.

> CARL SANDBURG, *The People, Yes,* 1936.

56 All money is a matter of belief.

> ADAM SMITH, *Paper Money,* 1981.

57 I am for gold dollars as against balony dollars.

> ALFRED E. SMITH, in an interview in New York City, November 24, 1933.

58 Banks are failing all over the country, but not the sand banks, solid and warm and streaked with bloody blackberry vines. You may run on them as much as you please, even as the crickets do, and find their account in it. They are the stockholders in these banks, and I hear them creaking their content. In these banks, too, and such as these, are my funds deposited, funds of health and enjoyment. Invest in these country banks. Let your capital be simplicity and contentment.

> HENRY DAVID THOREAU, entry dated October 14, 1859, in his *Journal,* 1906.

59 The ways by which you may get money almost without exception lead downward.

> HENRY DAVID THOREAU, *Life Without Principle,* 1863.

60 You want 21 percent risk free? Pay off your credit cards.

> ANDREW TOBIAS, quoted in *American Way* magazine, November, 1982.

61 Anyone who tries to understand the money question goes crazy.

> Attributed to Frank Vanderlip.

62 Let us all be happy and live within our means, even if we have to borrer the money to do it with.

> ARTEMUS WARD, "Science and Natural History," *Artemus Ward in London, and Other Papers,* 1867.

63 My friends, money is not all. It is not money that will mend a broken heart or reassemble the fragments of a dream. Money cannot brighten the hearth nor repair the portals of a shattered home. I refer, of course, to Confederate money.

> ARTEMUS WARD, quoted in the introduction to *Artemus Ward, His Book,* 1964 edition.

64 It is not a custom with me to keep money to look at.

> GEORGE WASHINGTON, in a letter to John Parke Custis, January, 1780.

65 Too great a quantity of cash in circulation is a much greater evil than too small a quantity.

> NOAH WEBSTER, in a letter to the *Maryland Journal,* August 9, 1785.

158. MONTANA

1 Oro y plata. (Gold and silver.)

> State motto.

2 [Butte] is the toughest, bawdiest town in America, with the possible exception of Amarillo, Texas.

... I heard it called "the only electric-lit cemetery in the United States."

JOHN GUNTHER, *Inside U.S.A.,* 1947.

3 Montana is as big as Illinois, Michigan, and Indiana. It is bigger than Italy and Japan. To say that it is the third American state in size does not, perhaps, make its enormousness tangible; say instead that one out of every twenty-five American square miles is Montanan.

Ibid.

4 Montana: High, Wide, and Handsome.

JOSEPH KINSEY HOWARD, title of a book, 1943.

5 Butte is the black heart of Montana, feared and distrusted.... Butte is a sooty memorial to personal heroism, to courage and vigor even in rascality; and it is a monument to a wasted land.

JOSEPH KINSEY HOWARD, *Montana: High, Wide, and Handsome,* 1943.

6 Colorado is high, having more peaks within its borders than any other state. Wyoming is wide, with the breadth of the plains between the Big Horns and the Grand Tetons. California is handsome, with a splendor of success. It takes all three adjectives to describe Montana.

DONALD CULROSS PEATTIE, *The Road of a Naturalist,* 1941.

7 I am in love with Montana. For other states I have admiration, respect, recognition, even some affection, but with Montana it is love.... It seems to me that Montana is a great splash of grandeur. The scale is huge but not overpowering. The land is rich with grass and color, and the mountains are the kind I would create if mountains were ever put on my agenda.

JOHN STEINBECK, *Travels with Charley,* 1962.

8 Montana seems to me to be what a small boy would think Texas is like from hearing Texans.

Ibid.

159. MOTION PICTURES

See also GOLDWYNISMS; HOLLYWOOD

1 The technique of murder must be presented in a way that will not inspire imitation.

Code approved by the Motion Picture Producers and Distributors of America, March 31, 1930.

2 Scenes of passion ... should not be introduced when not essential to the plot. ... In general, passion should be so treated that these scenes do not stimulate the lower and baser element.

Ibid.

3 Boy meets girl, boy loses girl, boy gets girl.

Hollywood producers' formula for movie plots.

4 People have been modeling their lives after films for years, but the medium is somehow unsuited to moral lessons, cautionary tales, or polemics of any kind.

RENATA ADLER, *A Year in the Dark,* 1969.

5 Any little pinhead who makes one picture is a "star."

HUMPHREY BOGART, quoted in Richard Schickel, *The Stars,* 1962.

6 The only thing you owe the public is a good performance.

HUMPHREY BOGART, quoted in Max Wilk, *The Wit and Wisdom of Hollywood,* 1971.

7 There was no other occupation in the world [in Hollywood's heyday] that so closely resembled enslavement as the career of a film star.

LOUISE BROOKS, *Lulu in Hollywood,* 1982.

8 Studio contracts were always a joke, as far as actors were concerned. Studios could break them at will; the actors were bound by their fear of impoverishing lawsuits and permanent unemployment.

Ibid.

9 Every actor has a natural animosity toward every other actor, present or absent, living or dead. Most

Hollywood directors did not understand that, any more than they understood why an actor might be tempted to withhold the rapt devotion to the master which they considered essential to their position of command.

> Ibid.

10 Movies suddenly became "film" and "cinema" an "art form" and terribly chic. . . . Film criticism became the means whereby a stream of young intellectuals could go straight from the campus film society into the professionals' screening room without managing to get a glimpse of the real world in between.

> Judith Crist, *The Private Eye, the Cowboy and the Very Naked Girl,* 1968.

11 I've got the celluloid in my blood.

> W.C. Fields, quoted in Robert Lewis Taylor, *W.C. Fields, His Follies and Fortunes,* 1949.

12 I never said, "I want to be alone." I only said, "I want to be *left* alone." There is all the difference.

> Greta Garbo, quoted in John Bainbridge, *Garbo,* 1955.

13 [Metro-Goldwyn-Mayer] had us working days and nights on end. They'd give us pep-up pills to keep us on our feet long after we were exhausted. Then they'd take us to the studio hospital and knock us cold with sleeping pills. . . . Then after four hours they'd wake us up and give us the pep-up pills again so we could work another seventy-two hours in a row.

> Judy Garland, quoted in Anne Edwards, *Judy Garland,* 1975.

14 The convictions of Hollywood and television are made of boiled money.

> Lillian Hellman, *An Unfinished Woman,* 1969.

15 You ain't heard nothin' yet, folks.

> Al Jolson, in *The Jazz Singer,* 1927.

16 Movies have been doing so much of the same thing—in slightly different ways—for so long that few of the possibilities of this great hybrid art have yet been explored.

> Pauline Kael, *Going Steady,* 1968.

17 Good movies make you care, make you believe in possibilities again.

> Ibid.

18 The lowest action trash is preferable to wholesome family entertainment. When you clean them up, when you make movies respectable, you kill them.

> Ibid.

19 Any girl can be glamorous. All you have to do is stand still and look stupid.

> Hedy Lamarr, quoted in Richard Schickel, *The Stars,* 1962.

20 That's the trouble, a sex symbol becomes a thing. I just hate being a thing.

> Marilyn Monroe, in an interview published a week before her suicide, quoted in Richard Schickel, *The Stars,* 1962.

21 She runs the gamut of emotions from A to B.

> Attributed to Dorothy Parker, commenting on a performance by Katharine Hepburn.

22 You call this a script? Give me a couple of $5,000-a-week writers and I'll write it myself!

> Joseph Pasternak, quoted in Max Wilk, *The Wit and Wisdom of Hollywood,* 1971.

23 I left the screen because I didn't want what happened to Chaplin to happen to me. When he discarded the little tramp, the little tramp turned around and killed him.

> Mary Pickford, quoted by Aljean Harmetz in the *New York Times,* March 28, 1971.

24 To be completely candid, I think most movies nowadays are trash, and many strike me as unhealthy. The explicit sex, pointless violence, and crude language appeal only to our lowest instincts. They have taken away our idealism, our sense of fun and joy. It's chic to be cynical and tear our heroes down. What has happened to us? And what are we doing to our young people?

> Nancy Reagan, *Nancy,* 1980.

25 So much of our profession is taken up with pretending, with the interpretation of never-never roles, that an actor must spend at least half his waking hours in fantasy, in rehearsal or shooting. If he is only an actor, I feel, he is much like I was in *King's Row,* only half a man—no matter how great his talents.

> RONALD REAGAN, *Where's the Rest of Me?* 1965.

26 The Communist plan for Hollywood was remarkably simple. It was merely to take over the motion picture business. Not only for its profit, as the hoodlums had tried—but also for a grand worldwide propaganda base.

> Ibid.

27 You can't spring a new plot on an audience the first time and expect it to go. It takes a Movie audience years to get on to a new plot.

> WILL ROGERS, 1920, quoted in Donald Day, *The Autobiography of Will Rogers,* 1949.

28 There is only one thing that can kill the Movies and that is education.

> Ibid.

29 The real thing with which you are corrupting the world is the anarchism of Hollywood. There you put a string of heroes in front of people and all of them are anarchists, and the one answer to anything annoying or to any breach of the law or to any expression which he considers unmanly, is to give the other person a sock in the jaw. I wonder you don't prosecute the people who produce these continual strings of gentlemen who, when they are not kissing the heroine, are socking the jaw of somebody else. It is a criminal offense to sock a person in the jaw.

> GEORGE BERNARD SHAW, in an address before the Academy of Political Science, New York City, April 11, 1933.

30 My only problem is finding a way to play my fortieth fallen female in a different way from my thirty-ninth.

> BARBARA STANWYCK, in an interview with Hedda Hopper, 1953.

31 Leave them when you're looking good and thank God for the trust funds Mama set up.

> CONSTANCE TALMADGE, to her sister Norma, announcing her retirement from the movies at the advent of sound, quoted in Richard Schickel, *The Stars,* 1962.

32 All Americans born between 1890 and 1945 wanted to be movie stars.

> GORE VIDAL, "Scott's Case," *New York Review of Books,* May 1, 1980.

33 I wouldn't pay $50,000 for any damn book, any time.

> JACK WARNER, turning down the chance to film *Gone With the Wind,* quoted in Max Wilk, *The Wit and Wisdom of Hollywood,* 1971.

34 Talk low, talk slow, and don't say too much.

> Advice on acting, attributed to John Wayne.

35 Come up and see me sometime.

> MAE WEST, in *Diamond Lil,* 1932.

36 Goodness had nothing to do with it, dearie.

> MAE WEST, to a hatcheck girl who said, "Goodness, what beautiful diamonds," in the film *Night After Night,* 1932.

---

160. MUSIC

See also SONGS

---

1 I said as I sat by the edge of the sea,
A music-hall show would look bully to me;
I thought as I walked by the edge of the dunes,
Why should the Devil have all the good tunes?

> FREDERICK LEWIS ALLEN, "Familiar Quotations," in *Harper's Monthly,* December, 1922.

2 Man, if you gotta ask you'll never know.

> Attributed to Louis Armstrong, when asked to define jazz.

3 Blessed Cecilia, appear in visions
   To all musicians, appear and inspire;
   Translated Daughter, come down and startle
   Composing mortals with immortal fire.

   > W.H. AUDEN, "Hymn to St. Cecilia" (patron
   > saint of music), set to music by Benjamin Britten,
   > 1942.

4 The Americans are almost ignorant of the art of
music, one of the most elevating, innocent and refining of human tastes, whose influence on the habits and morals of a people is of the most beneficial
tendency.

   > JAMES FENIMORE COOPER, *The American
   > Democrat,* 1838.

5 The truest expression of a people is in its dances
and its music.

   > AGNES DE MILLE, "Do I Hear a Waltz?" in the
   > *New York Times Magazine,* May 11, 1975.
   > ("Do I Hear a Waltz" was also the title of a
   > popular song of the time.)

6 The best, most beautiful, and most perfect way
that we have of expressing a sweet concord of mind
to each other is by music.

   > JONATHAN EDWARDS, *Miscellaneous Observations
   > on Important Theological Subjects,* 1747.

7 What omniscience has music! So absolutely im-
personal, and yet every sufferer feels his secret sorrow soothed.

   > RALPH WALDO EMERSON, entry written in 1864,
   > *Journals,* 1909–1914.

8 All the sounds of the earth are like music.

   > OSCAR HAMMERSTEIN, II, "Oh, What a
   > Beautiful Mornin'," the opening song of
   > *Oklahoma!* 1943.

9 People don't understand the kind of fight it takes
to record what you want to record the way you
want to record it.

   > BILLIE HOLIDAY, *Lady Sings the Blues,* with
   > William Dufty, 1956.

10 You think they are crusaders, sent
      From some infernal clime,
   To pluck the eyes of Sentiment,
      And dock the tail of Rhyme,

   To crack the voice of Melody,
      And break the legs of Time.

   > OLIVER WENDELL HOLMES, SR., "The
   > Music-Grinders," 1830.

11 A few can touch the magic string,
      And noisy Fame is proud to win them:—
   Alas for those that never sing,
      But die with all their music in them!

   > OLIVER WENDELL HOLMES, SR., "The
   > Voiceless," 1853.

12 When people hear good music, it makes them
homesick for something they never had, and never
will have.

   > EDGAR WATSON HOWE, *Country Town Sayings,*
   > 1911.

13 Music is the only one of the arts that can not be
prostituted to a base use.

   > ELBERT HUBBARD, *The Roycroft Dictionary and
   > Book of Epigrams,* 1923.

14 American Ragtime or "Jazz," which is Ragtime
raised to the nth power, is scorned as fit only for the
musical wastebasket. Naturally much that jazz has
brought has been hopelessly cheap and artificial,
but behind it there is a gem of something wonderful, which the composer with ears made in America
may well build into the master music of tomorrow.

   > RUPERT HUGHES, in *Etude* magazine, May,
   > 1920.

15 It is from the blues that all that may be called
American music derives its most distinctive characteristic.

   > JAMES WELDON JOHNSON, *Black Manhattan,*
   > 1930.

16   But presently
   A velvet flute-note fell down pleasantly
   Upon the bosom of that harmony,
   And sailed and sailed incessantly.

   > SIDNEY LANIER, "The Symphony," 1875.

17 Music is Love in search of a word.

   > SIDNEY LANIER, "The Symphony," 1875.

18 Ragtime is a type of music substantially new in
musical history. . . . I am sure that many a native

composer could save his soul if he would open his ears to this folk music of the American city.

> HIRAM K. MODERWELL, in the *New Republic,* October 16, 1915.

19 If I could dwell
> Where Israfel
> > Hath dwelt, and he where I,
> He might not sing so wildly well
> > A mortal melody,
> While a bolder note than this might swell
> > From my lyre within the sky.

> EDGAR ALLAN POE, "Israfel," 1831.

20 It is in music, perhaps, that the soul most nearly attains the great end for which, when inspired by the Poetic Sentiment, it struggles—the creation of supernal Beauty.

> EDGAR ALLAN POE, in "The Poetic Principle," 1850.

21 Hear the sledges with the bells,
> > Silver bells!
> What a world of merriment their melody
> > foretells!
> How they tinkle, tinkle, tinkle,
> > In the icy air of night!
> While the stars, that oversprinkle
> All the heavens, seem to twinkle
> > With a crystalline delight;
> Keeping time, time, time,
> In a sort of Runic rhyme
> To the tintinnabulation that so musically
> > wells
> From the bells, bells, bells, bells,
> > Bells, bells, bells—
> From the jingling and the tinkling of the
> > bells.

> EDGAR ALLAN POE, "The Bells," published in *Sartain's Union Magazine,* November, 1849.

22 Music rots when it gets too far from the dance.

> EZRA POUND, *How to Read,* 1931.

23 Drum on your drums, batter on your banjos,
> > sob on the long cool winding
> > saxophones.
> Go to it, O jazzmen.

> CARL SANDBURG, "Jazz Fantasia," in *Smoke and Steel,* 1920.

24 A musical education is necessary for musical judgment. What most people relish is hardly music; it is rather a drowsy revery relieved by nervous thrills.

> GEORGE SANTAYANA, "Reason in Art," *The Life of Reason,* 1905–1906.

25 Music has always had its own syntax, its own vocabulary and symbolic means. Indeed, it is with mathematics the principal language of the mind when the mind is in a condition of non-verbal feeling.

> GEORGE STEINER, "The Retreat from the Word," *Language and Silence,* 1958.

26 Music is feeling, then, not sound.

> WALLACE STEVENS, "Peter Quince at the Clavier," 1923.

27 All music is only a sweet striving to express character.

> HENRY DAVID THOREAU, entry dated November 12, 1841, in his *Journal,* 1906.

28 Music hath caught a higher pace than any virtue that I know. It is the arch-reformer; it hastens the sun to its setting; it invites him to his rising; it is the sweetest reproach, a measured satire.

> HENRY DAVID THOREAU, entry dated January 8, 1842, in his *Journal,* 1906.

29 When I hear music, I fear no danger. I am invulnerable. I see no foe. I am related to the earliest times, and to the latest.

> HENRY DAVID THOREAU, entry dated January 13, 1857, in his *Journal,* 1906.

30 Wagner's music is better than it sounds.

> Attributed to Mark Twain (also to Bill Nye and others).

31 The tongues of violins,
> (I think O tongues ye tell this heart, that
> > cannot tell itself,
> This brooding yearning heart, that cannot tell
> > itself.)

> WALT WHITMAN, *Proud Music of the Storm,* 1870.

161. NATURE

See also AGRICULTURE; ANIMALS; AUTUMN;
FLOWERS; POLLUTION; SPRING; SUMMER;
WEATHER; WINTER

1 The lightning bug is a wondrous sight,
  But you'd think it has no mind;
  It pumps around in the darkest night,
  With its headlight on behind.

  Anonymous

2 I have devoted my whole life to the study of
Nature, and yet a single sentence may express all
that I have done. I have shown that there is a
correspondence between the succession of Fishes in
geological times and the different stages of their
growth in the egg—this is all.

  LOUIS AGASSIZ, *Methods of Study in Natural
  History,* 1863.

3 Of all formal things in the world, a clipped
hedge is the most formal; and of all the informal
things in the world, a forest tree is the most informal.

  HENRY WARD BEECHER, *Royal Truths,* 1862.

4 Of all man's works of art, a cathedral is greatest.
A vast and majestic tree is greater than that.

  HENRY WARD BEECHER, *Proverbs from
  Plymouth Pulpit,* 1870.

5 Nature never makes any blunders; when she
makes a fool, she means it.

  JOSH BILLINGS, "Affurisms," in *Josh Billings:
  His Sayings,* 1865.

6 When I behold the heavens as in their prime,
  And then the earth (though old) still clad in
      green,
  The stones and trees, insensible to time,
  Nor age nor wrinkle on their front are seen;
  If winter come, and greenness then do fade,
  A Spring returns, and they more youthful
      made;
  But Man grows old, lies down, remains where
      once he's laid.

  ANNE BRADSTREET, "Contemplations," *The
  Tenth Muse,* 1678.

7 Shall I then praise the heavens, the trees, the
      earth
  Because their beauty and their strength last
      longer
  Shall I wish there, or never to had birth,
  Because they're bigger, and their bodies
      stronger?
  Nay, they shall darken, perish, fade and die,
  And when unmade, so ever shall they lie,
  But man was made for endless immortality.

  Ibid.

8 To him who in the love of Nature holds
  Communion with her visible forms, she speaks
  A various language; for his gayer hours
  She has a voice of gladness, and a smile
  And eloquence of beauty, and she glides
  Into his darker musings, with a mild
  And healing sympathy, that steals away
  Their sharpness, ere he is aware.

  WILLIAM CULLEN BRYANT, "Thanatopsis,"
  1821.

9 Go forth, under the open sky, and list
  To Nature's teachings, while from all
      around—
  Earth and her waters, and the depths of air—
  Comes a still voice.

  Ibid.

10 The groves were God's first temples.

  WILLIAM CULLEN BRYANT, "A Forest Hymn,"
  1825.

11 Loveliest of lovely things are they,
  One earth, that soonest pass away.
  The rose that lives its little hour
  Is prized beyond the sculptured flower.

  WILLIAM CULLEN BRYANT, "A Scene on the
  Banks of the Hudson," 1828.

12 There are no sermons in stones. It is easier to get
a spark out of a stone than a moral.

  JOHN BURROUGHS, *Time and Change,* 1912.

13 The "control of nature" is a phrase conceived in arrogance, born of the Neanderthal age of biology and the convenience of man.

> RACHEL CARSON, *Silent Spring,* 1962.

14 I like trees because they seem more resigned to the way they have to live than other things do.

> WILLA CATHER, *O Pioneers!* 1913.

15 That sort of beauty which is called natural, as of vines, plants, trees, etc., consists of a very complicated harmony; and all the natural motions, and tendencies, and figures of bodies in the universe are done according to proportion, and therein is their beauty.

> JONATHAN EDWARDS, "Notes on the Mind," written c.1718.

16 Nature never wears a mean appearance. Neither does the wisest man extort her secret and lose his curiosity by finding out all her perfection. Nature never became a toy to a wise spirit.

> RALPH WALDO EMERSON, *Nature,* 1836.

17 Every natural action is graceful.

> Ibid.

18 The first steps in Agriculture, Astronomy, Zoölogy (those first steps which the farmer, the hunter, and the sailor take), teach that Nature's dice are always loaded; that in her heaps and rubbish are concealed sure and useful results.

> RALPH WALDO EMERSON, *Nature,* 1836.

19 Who leaves the pine-tree, leaves his friend,
  Unnerves his strength, invites his end.

> RALPH WALDO EMERSON, "Woodnotes," first printed in *The Dial* magazine, 1841.

20 Nature is a mutable cloud, which is always and never the same.

> RALPH WALDO EMERSON, "History," *Essays,* First Series, 1841.

21 Nature is an endless combination and repetition of a very few laws. She hums the old well-known air through innumerable variations.

> Ibid.

22 The man who has seen the rising moon break out of the clouds at midnight has been present like an archangel at the creation of light and of the world.

> Ibid.

23 Nature hates monopolies and exceptions.

> RALPH WALDO EMERSON, "Compensation," *Essays,* First Series, 1841.

24 There are no fixtures in nature. The universe is fluid and volatile.

> RALPH WALDO EMERSON, "Circles," *Essays,* First Series, 1841.

25 The sky is the daily bread of the eyes.

> RALPH WALDO EMERSON, entry written May 25, 1843, *Journals,* 1909–1914.

26 He who knows what sweet and virtues are in the ground, the waters, the plants, the heavens, and how to come at these enchantments, is the rich and royal man.

> RALPH WALDO EMERSON, "Nature," *Essays,* Second Series, 1844.

27 Plants are the young of the world, vessels of health and vigor; but they grope ever upward towards consciousness; the trees are imperfect men, and seem to bemoan their imprisonment, rooted in the ground.

> Ibid.

28 Nature hates calculators.

> RALPH WALDO EMERSON, "Experience," *Essays,* Second Series, 1844.

29 Nature, as we know her, is no saint.

> Ibid.

30 Nature tells every secret once.

> RALPH WALDO EMERSON, "Behavior," *The Conduct of Life,* 1860.

31 See thou bring not to field or stone
  The fancies found in books;
Leave authors' eyes, and fetch your own,
  To brave the landscape's looks.

> RALPH WALDO EMERSON, "Waldeinsamkeit," *May Day and Other Poems,* 1867.

32 Nature has made up her mind that what cannot defend itself shall not be defended.

> RALPH WALDO EMERSON, "Courage," *Society and Solitude,* 1870.

33 How cunningly nature hides every wrinkle of her inconceivable antiquity under roses and violets and morning dew!

> RALPH WALDO EMERSON, "Progress of Culture," *Letters and Social Aims,* 1876.

34 Nature encourages no looseness, pardons no errors.

> RALPH WALDO EMERSON, "The Superlative," *Lectures and Biographical Sketches,* 1883.

35 In America nature is autocratic, saying "I am not arguing, I am telling you."

> ERIK H. ERIKSON, *Childhood and Society,* 1950.

36 Something there is that doesn't love a wall.

> ROBERT FROST, "Mending Wall," *North of Boston,* 1914.

37 The trail has taught me much. I know now the varied voices of the coyote—the wizard of the mesa. I know the solemn call of herons and the mocking cry of the loon. I remember a hundred lovely lakes, and recall the fragrant breath of pine and fir and cedar and poplar trees. The trail has strung upon it, as upon a thread of silk, opalescent dawns and saffron sunsets. It has given me blessed release from care and worry and the troubled thinking of our modern day. It has been a return to the primitive and the peaceful. Whenever the pressure of our complex city life thins my blood and benumbs my brain, I seek relief in the trail; and when I hear the coyote wailing to the yellow dawn, my cares fall from me—I am happy.

> HAMLIN GARLAND, "Hitting the Trail," published in *McClure's* magazine, February, 1899.

38 A river seems a magic thing. A magic, moving, living part of the very earth itself—for it is from the soil, both from its depth and from its surface, that a river has its beginning.

> LAURA GILPIN, *The Rio Grande,* 1949.

39 Nature is not affected by finance. If someone offered you ten thousand dollars to let them touch you on your eyeball without you blinking, you would never collect the money. At the very last moment, Nature would force you to blink your eye. Nature will protect her own.

> DICK GREGORY, *The Shadow that Scares Me,* 1968.

40 Mountains are earth's undecaying monuments.

> NATHANIEL HAWTHORNE, *The Notch of the White Mountains,* 1868.

41 The sea is feline. It licks your feet—its huge flanks purr very pleasant for you; but it will crack your bones and eat you, for all that, and wipe the crimsoned foam from its jaws as if nothing had happened.

> OLIVER WENDELL HOLMES, SR., *The Autocrat of the Breakfast-Table,* 1858.

42 Our old mother nature has pleasant and cheery tones enough for us when she comes in her dress of blue and gold over the eastern hilltops; but when she follows us upstairs to our beds in her suit of black velvet and diamonds, every creak of her sandals and every whisper of her lips is full of mystery and fear.

> OLIVER WENDELL HOLMES, SR., *The Professor at the Breakfast-Table,* 1860.

43 Nature is profoundly imperturbable. We may adjust the beating of our hearts to her pendulum if we will and can, but we may be very sure that she will not change the pendulum's rate of going because our hearts are palpitating.

> OLIVER WENDELL HOLMES, SR., in a speech to the Massachusetts Medical Society, Boston, May 30, 1860.

44 Nature: The Unseen Intelligence which loved us into being, and is disposing of us by the same token.

> ELBERT HUBBARD, *The Roycroft Dictionary and Book of Epigrams,* 1923.

45 Nature punishes for most sins, but sacrilege, heresy, and blasphemy are not in her calendar, so man has to look after them.

> Ibid.

46 Nature has no one distinguishable ultimate tendency with which it is possible to feel a sympathy.

> WILLIAM JAMES, *The Varieties of Religious Experience*, 1902.

47 There is not a sprig of grass that shoots uninteresting to me, nor any thing that moves.

> THOMAS JEFFERSON, in a letter to Martha Jefferson Randolph, December 23, 1790.

48 I think that I shall never see
A poem lovely as a tree.

> JOYCE KILMER, "Trees," 1914.

49 Ye marshes, how candid and simple and
    nothing-withholding and free
Ye publish yourselves to the sky and offer
    yourselves to the sea!

> SIDNEY LANIER, "The Marshes of Glynn," 1878.

50 Conservation is a state of harmony between men and land.

> ALDO LEOPOLD, *A Sand County Almanac*, 1949.

51 Beneath some patriarchal tree
    I lay upon the ground;
His hoary arms uplifted he,
And all the broad leaves over me
Clapped their little hands in glee,
    With one continuous sound.

> HENRY WADSWORTH LONGFELLOW, "Prelude," *Voices of the Night*, 1839.

52 This is the forest primeval. The murmuring
    pines and the hemlocks,
Bearded with moss, and in garments green,
    indistinct in the twilight,
Stand like Druids of eld, with voices sad and
    prophetic,
Stand like harpers hoar, with beards that rest
    on their bosoms.

> HENRY WADSWORTH LONGFELLOW, *Evangeline*, 1847.

53 Silently, one by one, in the infinite meadows
    of heaven,
Blossomed the lovely stars, the forget-me-nots
    of the angels.

> Ibid.

54 It glimmers on the forest tips,
And through the dewy foliage drips
In little rivulets of light,
And makes the heart in love with night.

> HENRY WADSWORTH LONGFELLOW, describing moonlight, in *The Golden Legend*, 1851.

55 "Come, wander with me," she said,
    "Into regions yet untrod;
And read what is still unread
    In the manuscripts of God."

> HENRY WADSWORTH LONGFELLOW, "The Fiftieth Birthday of Agassiz," read by Longfellow at a dinner for Louis Agassiz, May 28, 1857.

56 The birch, most shy and ladylike of trees.

> JAMES RUSSELL LOWELL, "An Indian Summer Reverie," 1846.

57 The pine is the mother of legends.

> JAMES RUSSELL LOWELL, "The Growth of a Legend," 1847.

58 Every clod feels a stir of might,
    An instinct within it that reaches and
        towers,
And, groping blindly above it for light,
    Climbs to a soul in grass and flowers.

> JAMES RUSSELL LOWELL, *The Vision of Sir Launfal*, 1848.

59 Oh, horrible vulturism of earth! from which not the mightiest whale is free.

> HERMAN MELVILLE, *Moby-Dick*, 1851.

60 Woodman, spare that tree!
    Touch not a single bough!
In youth it sheltered me,
    And I'll protect it now.

> GEORGE POPE MORRIS, "Woodman, Spare That Tree," 1830.

61 In God's wildness lies the hope of the world— the great fresh unblighted, unredeemed wilderness.

> JOHN MUIR, note from Alaska, 1890.

62 The clearest way into the Universe is through a forest wilderness.

> JOHN MUIR, *John of the Mountains*, 1938.

63 O'er folded blooms,
   On swirls of musk,
The beetle booms adown the glooms
And bumps along the dusk.

> JAMES WHITCOMB RILEY, "Dusk Song—The
> Beetle," *The Complete Poetical Works of James
> Whitcomb Riley,* 1941.

64 What nature delivers to us is never stale. Because what nature creates has eternity in it.

> ISAAC BASHEVIS SINGER, quoted by Richard
> Burgh in the *New York Times Magazine,*
> November 26, 1978.

65 Nature will bear the closest inspection. She invites us to lay our eye level with her smallest leaf, and take an insect view of it plain.

> HENRY DAVID THOREAU, entry dated October
> 22, 1839, in his *Journal,* 1906.

66 The universe is so aptly fitted to our organization, that the eye wanders and reposes at the same time. On every side there is something to soothe and refresh this sense. Look up at the tree-tops and see how finely Nature finishes off her work there. See how the pines spire without end higher and higher, and make a graceful fringe to the earth. And who shall count the finer cobwebs that soar and float away from their utmost tops, and the myriad insects that dodge between them. Leaves are of more various forms than the alphabets of all languages put together; of the oaks alone there are hardly two alike, and each expresses its own character.

> HENRY DAVID THOREAU, *A Week on the
> Concord and Merrimack Rivers,* 1849.

67 Art can never match the luxury and superfluity of Nature. In the former all is seen; it cannot afford concealed wealth, and is niggardly in comparison; but Nature, even when she is scant and thin outwardly, satisfies us still by the assurance of a certain generosity at the roots.

> Ibid.

68 The bluebird carries the sky on his back.

> HENRY DAVID THOREAU, entry dated April 3,
> 1852, in his *Journal,* 1906.

69 We need the tonic of wildness—to wade sometimes in marshes where the bittern and the meadow hen lurk, and hear the booming of the snipe; to smell the whispering sedge where only some wilder and more solitary fowl builds her nest, and the mink crawls with its belly close to the ground. At the same time that we are earnest to explore and learn all things, we require that all things be mysterious and unexplorable, that land and sea be infinitely wild, unsurveyed and unfathomed by us because unfathomable. We can never have enough of nature.

> HENRY DAVID THOREAU, *Walden,* 1854.

70 Nature is full of genius, full of the divinity; so that not a snowflake escapes its fashioning hand.

> HENRY DAVID THOREAU, entry dated January 5,
> 1856, in his *Journal,* 1906.

71 In Wildness is the preservation of the World.

> HENRY DAVID THOREAU, "Walking," published
> in the *Atlantic Monthly,* June, 1862.

72 For I had rather be thy child
   And pupil, in the forest wild
   Than be the king of men elsewhere
   And most sovereign slave of care
   To have one moment of thy dawn
   Than share the city's year forlorn.

> HENRY DAVID THOREAU, "Nature," *Poems of
> Nature,* 1895.

73 To own a bit of ground, to scratch it with a hoe, to plant seeds, and watch the renewal of life—this is the commonest delight of the race, the most satisfactory thing a man can do.

> CHARLES DUDLEY WARNER, *My Summer in a
> Garden,* 1870.

74 A child said, *What is the grass?* fetching it
      to me with full hands;
   How could I answer the child? I do not
      know what it is any more than he.

> WALT WHITMAN, "Song of Myself," 1855.

75 I believe a leaf of grass is no less than the journey-work of the stars.

> Ibid.

76 The sharp-hoof'd moose of the north, the cat
      on the house-sill, the chickadee, the
      prairie-dog,

The litter of the grunting sow as they tug at
her teats,
The brood of the turkey-hen, and she with
her half-spread wings,
I see in them and myself the same old law.

Ibid.

77 Sea of stretch'd ground-swells,
Sea breathing broad and convulsive breaths,
Sea of the brine of life and of unshovell'd yet
always-ready graves,
Howler and scooper of storms, capricious and
dainty sea,
I am integral with you, I too am of one
phase and of all phases.

Ibid.

78 Lo, the moon ascending,
Up from the east, the silvery round moon,
Beautiful over the house-tops, ghastly,
phantom moon,
Immense and silent moon.

WALT WHITMAN, "Dirge for Two Veterans,"
1865.

79 In this broad earth of ours,
Amid the measureless grossness and the slag,
Enclosed and safe within its central heart,
Nestles the seed perfection.

WALT WHITMAN, "Song of the Universal," 1881.

80 After you have exhausted what there is in business, politics, conviviality, and so on—have found
that none of these finally satisfy, or permanently
wear—what remains? Nature remains.

WALT WHITMAN, "New Themes Entered
Upon," *Specimen Days and Collect,* 1882.

81 "Is this," I cried,
"The end of prayer and preaching?
Then down with pulpit, down with priest,
And give us Nature's teaching!"

JOHN GREENLEAF WHITTIER, "A Sabbath
Scene," 1850.

82 Nature speaks in symbols and in signs,
And through her pictures human fate divines.

JOHN GREENLEAF WHITTIER, "To Charles
Sumner," 1854.

83 The harp at Nature's advent strung
Has never ceased to play;
The song the stars of morning sung
Has never died away.

JOHN GREENLEAF WHITTIER, "The Worship of
Nature," 1867.

---

162. NAVY

See also ARMY; FORCE; MILITARISM

---

1 It is no part of our policy to create and maintain
a navy able to cope with that of the other great
powers of the world.

CHESTER A. ARTHUR, in his third annual message
to Congress, December 4, 1883.

2 Admiral, *n.* That part of a warship which does
the talking while the figurehead does the thinking.

AMBROSE BIERCE, *The Devil's Dictionary,* 1906.

3 If you wish to avoid foreign collision, you had
better abandon the ocean—surrender your commerce; give up all your prosperity.

HENRY CLAY, in a speech in the House of
Representatives, January 22, 1812.

4 To aim at such a navy as the greater European
nations possess would be a foolish and wicked
waste of the energies of our countrymen. It would
be to pull on our own heads that load of military
expense which makes the European laborer go supperless to bed, and moistens his bread with the
sweat of his brows.

THOMAS JEFFERSON, *Notes on the State of
Virginia,* 1784.

5 A naval force can never endanger our liberties,
nor occasion bloodshed; a land force would do both.

THOMAS JEFFERSON, in a letter to James Monroe,
August 11, 1786.

6 Sea power in the broad sense . . . includes not
only the military strength afloat, that rules the sea
or any part of it by force of arms, but also the
peaceful commerce and shipping from which alone

a military fleet naturally and healthfully springs, and on which it securely rests.

> ALFRED THAYER MAHAN, *The Influence of Sea Power upon History, 1660–1783,* 1890.

7 Even had the United States a great national shipping, it may be doubted whether a sufficient navy would follow; the distance which separates her from other great powers, in one way a protection, is also a snare.

> Ibid.

8 Sighted sub, sank same.

> DONALD F. MASON, U.S. Navy pilot, who sent this four-word message after attacking a German submarine with aerial depth charges, January 28, 1942.

9 No matter what the atomic age brings, America will always need sailors and ships and shipborne aircraft to preserve her liberty, her communications with the free world, even her existence. If the deadly missiles with their apocalyptic warheads are ever launched at America, the Navy will still be out on blue water fighting for her, and the nation or alliance that survives will be the one that retains command of the oceans.

> SAMUEL ELIOT MORISON, *The Two-Ocean War,* 1963.

10 Don't give up the ship.

> OLIVER HAZARD PERRY, words inscribed on his battle flag at the Battle of Lake Erie, September 10, 1813. (Perry took these words from Capt. James Lawrence, who is believed to have uttered them after being mortally wounded in an engagement between his ship, *Chesapeake,* and the British frigate *Shannon* off Boston Harbor, June 1, 1813.)

11 We have met the enemy and they are ours—two ships, two brigs, one schooner and one sloop.

> OLIVER HAZARD PERRY, message dated September 19, 1813, to Gen. William Henry Harrison, reporting Perry's victory at the Battle of Lake Erie on September 10.

12 Our American merchant ships must be protected by our American Navy. It can never be doubted that the goods *will* be delivered by this nation, whose Navy believes in the tradition of "Damn the torpedoes; full speed ahead!"

> FRANKLIN D. ROOSEVELT, in his Navy Day address, October 27, 1941.

13 We have never had as many ships as a nation of such size and such vast interests really needs; but still by degrees we have acquired a small fleet of battleships, cruisers, gunboats, and torpedo boats, all excellent of their class.

> THEODORE ROOSEVELT, "Admiral Dewey," *McClure's Magazine,* October, 1899.

14 A thoroughly good navy takes a long time to build up. . . . Ships take years to build, crews take years before they become thoroughly expert, while the officers not only have to pass their early youth in a course of special training, but cannot possibly rise to supreme excellence in their profession unless they make it their life-work.

> Ibid.

15 We need to keep in a condition of preparedness, especially as regards our navy, not because we want war, but because we desire to stand with those whose plea for peace is listened to with respectful attention.

> THEODORE ROOSEVELT, in a speech in New York City, November 11, 1902.

16 To an active external Commerce, the protection of a Naval force is indispensable.

> GEORGE WASHINGTON, in his eighth annual address to Congress, December 7, 1796.

17 It is in our own experience that the most sincere neutrality is not a sufficient guard against the depredations of nations at war. To secure respect to a neutral flag requires a naval force organized and ready to vindicate it from insult or aggression. This may even prevent the necessity of going to war.

> Ibid.

18 Absolute freedom of navigation upon the seas, outside territorial waters, alike in peace and in war, except as the seas may be closed in whole or in part by international action for the enforcement of international covenants.

> WOODROW WILSON, the second of his Fourteen Points, in a speech to Congress, January 8, 1918.

163. NEBRASKA

1 Equality before the law.

> State motto.

2 Hurrah for Greer county! The land of the free,
The land of the bedbug, grasshopper and flea;
I'll sing of its praises, I'll tell of its fame,
While starving to death on my government claim.

> Nebraska pioneer song, c.1870.

3 Here the Middle West merges with the West. The farms and small towns in the eastern half suggest the rich, more densely populated country of Iowa and Illinois. The cities have much of the fast tempo and businesslike ways that prevail in the larger cities of the Midwest. But, in western Nebraska, fields give way to the great cattle ranches of the sandhill area, life is more leisurely, and manners are more relaxed. Something of the Old West still survives.

> Federal Writers' Project, *Nebraska: A Guide to the Cornhusker State,* 1939.

4 The names given by the Indians are always remarkably appropriate: and certainly none was ever more so than that which they have given to this stream—the Nebraska, or Shallow River.

> JOHN C. FRÉMONT, writing about the Platte River, which flows east into the Missouri, and has also been called "the Mile-Wide and Inch-Deep," quoted in the *Nebraska Blue Book, 1984–1985,* 1985. (Artemus Ward, the humorist, said the Platte would be a good river if set on edge.)

5 Omaha, Nebraska, was but a halting place on the road to Chicago, but it revealed to me horrors that I would not willingly have missed. The city to casual investigations seemed to be populated entirely by Germans, Poles, Slavs, Hungarians, Croats, Magyars, and all the scum of Eastern European States, but it must have been laid out by the Americans. No other people would cut the traffic of a main street with two streams of railway lines, each some eight or nine tracks wide, and cheerfully drive tramcars across the metals. Every now and again they have horrible railway crossing accidents at Omaha, but nobody seems to think of building an overhead bridge. That would interfere with the vested interests of the undertakers.

> RUDYARD KIPLING, *American Notes,* 1891.

6 Barns back east have weather vanes on them to show which way the wind is blowing, but out here there's no need. . . . Farmers just look out the window to see which way the barn is leaning. Some farmers . . . attach a logging chain to a stout pole. They can tell the wind direction by which way the chain is blowing. They don't worry about high wind until the chain starts whipping around and links begin snapping off. Then they know it's likely the wind will come up before morning.

> CHARLES KURALT, *Dateline America,* 1979.

7 In regard to this extensive section of the country, I do not hesitate in giving the opinion that it is almost wholly unfit for cultivation, and of course uninhabitable by a people depending on agriculture for their subsistence.

> MAJ. STEPHEN H. LONG, an early explorer of Nebraska, c.1820, quoted in James C. Olson, *History of Nebraska,* 1966.

8 We were at sea—there is no other adequate expression—on the plains of Nebraska. . . . It was a world almost without a feature; an empty sky, an empty earth; front and back, the line of railway stretched from horizon to horizon, like a cue across a billiard-board; on either hand, the green plain ran till it touched the skirts of heaven.

> ROBERT LOUIS STEVENSON, *Across the Plains,* 1892.

164. NEVADA

1 All for our country.

> State motto.

2 It occurred to some charitable people [moving west in 1849] who could still muse as they staggered that you couldn't get word back to a man's family that he had died nowhere. So they created place names, and wherever the trail turned or there was a new vista they marked a stick and planted it. . . . I have an old, yellowing automobile map that still peppers the wilderness of Nevada with such names as Fortitude, Desolation, Last Gasp.

ALISTAIR COOKE, *America,* 1973.

3 Nevada is mostly desert, mountains, and fabulous natural resources. It is one of the friendliest states I know, and it lives on four things, mining, livestock, the divorce trade, and gambling.

JOHN GUNTHER, *Inside U.S.A.,* 1947.

4 Look at Utah and Nevada from an airplane. They are indistinguishable. You could not possibly tell where one stops and the other begins. Yet the two states differ so enormously that they might belong to different worlds. Utah is a creature of the Mormon Church. . . . Nevada was settled . . . by miners and prospectors and gamblers who found California too tame. Utah is the most staid and respectable of states; Nevada is, by common convention at least, the naughtiest.

Ibid.

5 If an unknown individual arrived, they did not inquire if he was capable, honest, industrious, but—had he killed his man? If he had not, he gravitated to his natural and proper position, that of a man of small consequence; if he had, the cordiality of his reception was graduated according to the number of his dead.

MARK TWAIN, *Roughing It,* 1872.

6 The cheapest and easiest way to become an influential man and be looked up to by the community at large was to stand behind a bar, wear a cluster-diamond pin, and sell whisky. I am not sure but that the saloon-keeper held a shade higher rank than any other member of society.

Ibid.

165. NEW ENGLAND

See also individual states

1 The great vice of this New England people is their adoration of Mammon. And rooted as it is in the character, the tree has now attained immense luxuriance and bids fair to overshadow us all.

CHARLES FRANCIS ADAMS, in his *Diary,* October 6, 1833.

2 The one great poem of New England is her Sunday.

HENRY WARD BEECHER, *Proverbs from Plymouth Pulpit,* 1870.

3 Yankee, *n.* In Europe, an American. In the Northern States of our Union, a New Englander. In the Southern States the word is unknown. (See Damyank.)

AMBROSE BIERCE, *The Devil's Dictionary,* 1906.

4 New England is a legitimate child of *Old* England. . . . It is England and Scotland again in miniature and in childhood.

CALVIN COLTON, *Manual for Emigrants to America,* 1832.

5 Of course what the man from Mars will find out first about New England is that it is neither new nor very much like England.

JOHN GUNTHER, *Inside U.S.A.,* 1947.

6 He comes of the *Brahmin caste of New England.* This is the harmless, inoffensive, untitled aristocracy.

OLIVER WENDELL HOLMES, SR., *Elsie Venner,* 1861.

7 Those New England States, I do believe, will be the noblest country in the world in a little while. They will be the salvation of that very great body with a very little soul, the rest of the United States; they are the pith and marrow, heart and core, head and spirit of that country.

FANNY KEMBLE, *A Year of Consolation,* 1847.

Mayflower Compact, November 11, 1620

Sometimes called America's first constitution, the Mayflower Compact was a self-governing agreement that foreshadowed independence from Great Britain.

In the name of God, Amen. We whose names are underwritten, the loyal subjects of our dread sovereign lord, King James, by the grace of God, of Great Britain, France, and Ireland, King, Defender of the Faith, etc.

Having undertaken for the glory of God, and advancement of the Christian faith and honor of our king and country, a voyage to plant the first colony in the northern parts of Virginia, do by these present, solemnly and mutually, in the presence of God and one of another, covenant and combine ourselves together into a civil body politic, for our better ordering and preservation and furtherance of the ends aforesaid; and by virtue hereof to enact, constitute, and frame such just and equal laws, ordinances, acts, constitutions, offices from time to time as shall be thought most meet and convenient for the general good of the colony; unto which we promise all due submission and obedience. In witness whereof we have hereunder subscribed our names, Cape Cod, 11th of November, in the year of the reign of our sovereign lord, King James, of England, France, and Ireland 18, and of Scotland 54. Anno Domini 1620.

---

8 Oliver Wendell Holmes says that Yankee Schoolmarms, the cider, and the salt codfish of the Eastern states are responsible for what he calls a nasal accent.

> RUDYARD KIPLING, *From Sea to Sea,* 1899.

9 The most serious charge which can be brought against New England is not Puritanism but February.

> JOSEPH WOOD KRUTCH, *The Twelve Seasons,* 1949.

10 I believe no one attempts to praise the climate of New England.

> HARRIET MARTINEAU, *Retrospect of Western Travel,* 1838.

11 The New Englanders are a people of God, settled in those which were once the Devil's territories.

> COTTON MATHER, *The Wonders of the Invisible World,* 1692.

12 The Hottentots and Kickapoos are very well in their way. The Yankees alone are preposterous.

> EDGAR ALLAN POE, "The Philosophy of Furniture," published in *Burton's Gentleman's Magazine,* May, 1840.

13 The people of New England are by nature patient and forbearing but there are some things which they will not stand. Every year they kill a lot of poets for writing about "Beautiful Spring." These are generally casual visitors who bring their notions of spring from somewhere else.

> MARK TWAIN, in a speech to the New England Society, December, 1876.

14 I wonder if anybody ever reached the age of thirty-five in New England without wanting to kill himself.

BARRETT WENDELL, in *Barrett Wendell and his Letters,* 1924.

---

166. NEW HAMPSHIRE

1 Live free or die.

State motto.

2 The God who made New Hampshire
Taunted the lofty land
With little men.

RALPH WALDO EMERSON, "Ode Inscribed to W.H. Channing," 1846.

3 I like your nickname, the "Granite State." It shows the strength of character, firmness of principle and restraint that have long characterized New Hampshire.

GERALD R. FORD, in a speech at Concord, New Hampshire, April 17, 1975.

4 Just specimens is all New Hampshire has,
One each of everything as in a show-case
Which naturally she doesn't care to sell.

ROBERT FROST, "New Hampshire," 1923.

5 She's one of the two best states in the Union. Vermont's the other.

Ibid.

6 The Vermont mountains stretch extended
straight;
New Hampshire mountains curl up in a coil.

Ibid.

7 The glorious bards of Massachusetts seem
To want to make New Hampshire people
over.
They taunt the lofty land with little men.

Ibid.

---

167. NEW JERSEY

1 Liberty and prosperity.

State motto.

2 Like China, New Jersey absorbs the invader.

Federal Writers' Project, *New Jersey: A Guide to Its Present And Past,* 1939.

3 New Jersey has always been a useful "no man's land" between the arrogance of New York and the obstinacy of Pennsylvania. The time it takes to traverse it diagonally permits a cooling off, coming or going.

STRUTHERS BURT, *Philadelphia: Holy Experiment,* 1945.

4 [New Jersey resembles] a beer barrel, tapped at both ends, with all the live beer running into Philadelphia and New York.

Attributed to Benjamin Franklin by Abram Browning, in an address at the Centennial Exposition in Philadelphia in 1876, quoted in Miriam V. Studley, *Historic New Jersey Through Visitors' Eyes,* 1964.

5 Of the great unbroken city that will one day reach at least from Boston to Richmond, this section [New Jersey] is already built.

JOHN MCPHEE, *The Pine Barrens,* 1968.

---

168. NEW MEXICO

1 It grows as it goes.

State motto.

2 Space is the keynote of the land—vast, limitless stretches of plain, desert, and lofty mountains, with buttes and mesas and purple distances to rest the eye.

Federal Writers' Project, *New Mexico: A Guide to the Colorful State,* 1940.

3 At the fiesta at San Ildefonso
I saw
Among the gay throng,
A Taos man,
Head swathed in white robe,
Black eyes peering out at the world,
Body wrapped in a white blanket
Standing white and brown and black,
Immobile, silent
Against a white adobe wall.
Taos, New Mexico.

> INA SIZER CASSIDY, "Fiesta," in Gerta Aison,
> *American States Anthology,* 1936.

4 A sweep of red carnelian-colored hills lying at the foot of the mountains came into view; they curved like two arms about a depression in the plain; and in that depression was Santa Fé, at last! A thin, wavering adobe town . . . a green plaza . . . at one end a church with two earthen towers that rise high above the flatness. The long main street began at the church, the town seemed to flow from it like a stream from a spring.

> WILLA CATHER, *Death Comes for the
> Archbishop,* 1927.

5 In the spring of 1943 a very small dribble of odd-looking tourists arrived at Santa Fé, New Mexico, the first capital of New Spain in North America. . . . They were a secret team of refugees and native American and British scientists who had gathered at Santa Fé before being driven off thirty miles northwest to Los Alamos. There, in the loneliness of the desert, they would brew the Apocalypse.

> ALISTAIR COOKE, *America,* 1973.

6 That New Mexico, which has given life to art from ancient Indian rain dances to a story like [D.H.] Lawrence's "The Woman Who Rode Away," should also have given birth to the atomic bomb, is perhaps an irony that measures the gamut of our civilization.

> JOHN GUNTHER, *Inside U.S.A.,* 1947.

7 Most of the artists seemed to be genuine people, living normal lives, though there were freaks and pretenders—people who like to dress up like Indi-

ans and stare into fireplaces. Many people who go to Santa Fé stay sane. Some go to pot. Some go what you might call native, and don't take baths any more, and ride to cocktail parties on spotted ponies, and dress like Spaniards, and collect pink mice, and live in tents as the Indians used to do. . . . But I regret to say that all the artists and writers I met were as fine people as you'd ever wish to see—intelligent, serious, good. I tried to find some of the freaks, so I could do stories about them, but they all must have been out picking huckleberries.

> ERNIE PYLE, describing the Santa Fé artistic
> community of the 1930s, *Home Country,* 1947.

169. NEW ORLEANS

1 No city perhaps on the globe, in an equal number of human beings, presents a greater contrast of national manners, language, and complexion, than does New Orleans.

> WILLIAM DARBY, *A Geographical Description of
> the State of Louisiana, the Southern Part of the
> State of Mississippi, and Territory of Alabama,*
> 1817.

2 Hedonistic, complacent, extravagant where amusement is concerned, soft to the point sometimes of insincerity, tolerant to the point sometimes of decadence; but always vivacious, good-natured, well dressed and well mannered—these are the characteristics of a typical New Orleanian. You might think, perhaps, that his vices outweigh his virtues; it depends on what you believe is important, but there is no denying that he is an easy fellow to get along with.

> OLIVER EVANS, *New Orleans,* 1959.

3 In some ways gaudy old New Orleans very much resembles an alluring, party-loving woman who is neither as virtuous as she might be nor as young as she looks, who has a come-hither eye, an engaging trace of accent in her speech, and a weakness for the pleasures both of the table and the couch—a *femme fatale* who has known great ecstasy and tragedy, but still laughs and loves excitement, and who,

after each bout of sinning, does duly confess and perhaps partially repent.

GEORGE SESSIONS PERRY, *Cities of America,* 1947.

4 It is a town where an architect, a gourmet, or a roué is in hog heaven.

Ibid.

5 New Orleans, in spring-time, just when the orchards were flushing over with peach-blossoms, and the sweet herbs came to flavor the juleps—seemed to me the city of the world where you can eat and drink the most and suffer the least.

WILLIAM MAKEPEACE THACKERAY, *Roundabout Papers,* 1862.

6 This Mardi-Gras pageant was the exclusive possession of New Orleans until recently. . . . It is a thing which could hardly exist in the practical North.

MARK TWAIN, *Life on the Mississippi,* 1883.

7 New Orleans is the most cosmopolitan of provincial cities.

CHARLES DUDLEY WARNER IN *Harper's New Monthly Magazine,* 1887.

---

170. NEW YORK

See also NEW YORK CITY

---

1 Excelsior. (Ever upward.)

State motto.

2 Refusal to conform is a cardinal sin to the upstater. He will not let himself be called pretentious by his neighbors. . . . Once I heard an upstater admit to a group of friends that he felt that he had done "a pretty good job" on a project. The remark caused a shocked silence.

CARL CARMER, "Upstate Is a Country," *My Kind of Country,* 1966.

3 The beauty and freshness of this calm retreat [West Point], in the very dawn and greenness of summer—it was then the beginning of June—were exquisite indeed. Leaving it upon the sixth, and returning to New York, to embark for England on the succeeding day, I was glad to think that among the last memorable beauties which had glided past us, and softened in the bright perspective, were those whose pictures, traced by no common hand, are fresh in most men's minds; not easily to grow old, or fade beneath the dust of Time: The Kaatskill Mountains, Sleepy Hollow, and the Tappaan Zee.

CHARLES DICKENS, *American Notes,* 1842.

4 Those who are in Albany escaped Sing Sing, and those who are in Sing Sing were on their way to Albany.

ELBERT HUBBARD, *The Roycroft Dictionary and Book of Epigrams,* 1923.

5 Whoever has made a voyage up the Hudson must remember the Kaatskill mountains. They are a dismembered branch of the great Appalachian family, and are seen away to the west of the river, swelling up to a noble height, and lording it over the surrounding country.

WASHINGTON IRVING, opening sentences of "Rip Van Winkle," *The Sketch Book,* 1819–1820.

6 It is in such little retired Dutch valleys, found here and there embosomed in the great State of New York, that population, manners, and customs, remain fixed; while the great torrent of migration and improvement, which is making such incessant changes in other parts of this restless country, sweeps by them unobserved.

WASHINGTON IRVING, "The Legend of Sleepy Hollow," *The Sketch Book,* 1819–1820.

7 Minds so earnest and helpless that it takes them half-an-hour to get from one idea to its immediately adjacent next neighbor, and then they lie down on it . . . like a cow on a doormat, so that you can get neither in nor out with them.

WILLIAM JAMES, in a letter to his wife, describing his audience at a Chautauqua lecture, July, 1896, quoted in Gay Wilson Allen, *William James,* 1968.

8 Niagara Falls is very nice. It's like a large version of the old Bond sign on Times Square. I'm very glad I saw it, because from now on if I am asked whether I have seen Niagara Falls I can say yes, and be telling the truth for once.

> JOHN STEINBECK, *Travels with Charley*, 1962.

9 I was disappointed with Niagara—most people must be disappointed with Niagara. Every American bride is taken there, and the sight of the stupendous waterfall must be one of the earliest, if not the keenest disappointments in American married life.

> OSCAR WILDE, *Impressions of America*, 1883.

171. NEW YORK CITY

1 It's a nice place to visit, but I wouldn't want to live there.

> Anonymous.

2 A thoroughfare that begins in a graveyard and ends in a river.

> Description of Wall Street.

3 All its inhabitants ascend to heaven right after their deaths, having served their full term in hell right on Manhattan Island.

> *The Barnard Bulletin*, September 22, 1967.

4 New York is where I *have* to be. I wish I knew why.

> A secretary, quoted in Jack Olsen, *The Girls in the Office*, 1972.

5 When an American stays away from New York too long, something happens to him. Perhaps he becomes a little provincial, a little dead, a little afraid.

> SHERWOOD ANDERSON, quoted in Mike Marqusee and Bill Harris, *New York*, 1985.

6 If 1,668,172 people . . . are to be set down in one narrow strip of land between two quiet rivers, you can hardly improve on this solid mass of buildings and the teeming organism of human life that streams through them. For better or for worse, this is real.

> BROOKS ATKINSON, in the *New York Times*, March 17, 1964.

7 My life had begun . . . in the invincible and indescribable squalor of Harlem. . . . In that ghetto I was tormented. I felt caged, like an animal. I wanted to escape. I felt if I did not get out I would slowly strangle.

> JAMES BALDWIN, in a television narrative based on his life, June 1, 1964.

8 You can take a boy out of Brooklyn, but you can never get Brooklyn out of the boy.

> W[ILLIS] T[ODHUNTER] BALLARD, *Say Yes to Murder*, 1942.

9 The trouble with New York is it's so convenient to everything I can't afford.

> JACK BARRY, quoted in the *Reader's Digest*, December, 1952.

10 After 20 annual visits, I am still surprised each time to return to see this giant asparagus bed of alabaster and rose and green skyscrapers.

> CECIL BEATON, *It Gives Me Great Pleasure*, 1955.

11 New York, the hussy, was taken in sin again!

> THOMAS BEER, *The Mauve Decade*, 1926.

12 What is barely hinted at in other American cities is condensed and enlarged in New York.

> SAUL BELLOW, quoted in Mike Marqusee and Bill Harris, *New York*, 1985.

13 I regard it [Manhattan] as a curiosity: I don't let myself get caught in the wheels.

> LUDWIG BEMELMANS, quoted in *Time* magazine, July 2, 1951.

14 Everybody ought to have a lower East Side in their life.

> IRVING BERLIN, quoted in *Vogue* magazine, November 1, 1962.

15 Mammon, *n.* The god of the world's leading religion. His chief temple is in the holy city of New York.

> AMBROSE BIERCE, *The Devil's Dictionary*, 1906.

16 Nowhere is [success] pursued more ardently than in the city of New York.

> STEPHEN BIRMINGHAM, *Holiday* magazine, March, 1961.

17 East Side, West Side, all around the town,
  The tots sang "Ring-a-rosie," "London
    Bridge is falling down";
  Boys and girls together, me and Mamie
    O'Rourke,
  Tripped the light fantastic on the sidewalks
    of New York.

> JAMES W. BLAKE, "The Sidewalks of New York," 1894.

18 I like the rough impersonality of New York, where human relations are oiled by jokes, complaints, and confessions—all made with the assumption of never seeing the other person again. I like New York because there are enough competing units to make it still seem a very mobile society. I like New York because it engenders high expectations simply by its pace.

> BILL BRADLEY, *Life on the Run,* 1976.

19 The present in New York is so powerful that the past is lost.

> JOHN J. CHAPMAN, in a letter, 1909.

20 The food of the city's most celebrated dining salons, with one or perhaps two exceptions, is neither predictably elegant nor superb. More often than not it is predictably commonplace.

> CRAIG CLAIBORNE, in the *New York Times,* September 1, 1963.

21 Give My Regards to Broadway.

> GEORGE M. COHAN, song title and refrain, 1904.

22 O Sleepless as the river under thee,
  Vaulting the sea, the prairies' dreaming sod,
  Unto us lowliest sometime sweep, descend
  And of the curveship lend a myth to God.

> HART CRANE, "To Brooklyn Bridge," *The Bridge,* 1930.

23 absitively posolutely dead
  like coney island in winter.

> E. E. CUMMINGS, *Tulips and Chimneys,* 1923.

24 There is and has long been—perhaps this is something of a boast on my part, but I say it as I feel it—there has been a special bond between New York and me. . . . How often, at difficult moments, I looked to New York, I listened to New York, to find out what you were thinking and feeling here, and always I found a comforting echo.

> CHARLES DE GAULLE, at a luncheon given in his honor, quoted in the *New York Times,* April 27, 1960.

25 New York is full of people . . . with a feeling for the tangential adventure, the risky adventure, the interlude that's not likely to end in any double-ring ceremony.

> JOAN DIDION, in *Mademoiselle* magazine, February, 1961.

26 New York is a sucked orange.

> RALPH WALDO EMERSON, "Culture," *The Conduct of Life,* 1860.

27 New York is a different country. Maybe it ought to have a separate government. Everybody thinks differently, acts differently. They just don't know what the hell the rest of the United States is.

> HENRY FORD, quoted in the *Reader's Digest,* October, 1973.

28 [Hell is] New York City with all the escape hatches sealed.

> JAMES R. FRAKES, quoted in the *New York Times,* May 19, 1974.

29 Stream of the living world
    Where dash the billows of strife!—
  One plunge in the mighty torrent
    Is a year of tamer life!
  City of glorious days,
    Of hope, and labor and mirth,
  With room and to spare, on thy splendid
    bays,
    For the ships of all the earth!

> RICHARD WATSON GILDER, "The City."

30 New York . . . that unnatural city where every one is an exile, none more so than the American.

> CHARLOTTE PERKINS GILMAN, *The Living of Charlotte Perkins Gilman,* 1935.

31 Prostitution is the only business that isn't leaving the city.

> ROY GOODMAN, speaking to the New York Press Club, October 24, 1976.

32 Those lions still are rude and wild,
    For while they pose as meek and mild,
        To keep their fierceness hid,
    Down from their pedestals they'd leap,
    As soon as New York went to sleep—
    If New York ever did!

> ARTHUR GUITERMAN, poem celebrating the stone lions at the entrance to the New York Public Library, *The New York Public Library in Fiction, Poetry, and Children's Literature,* 1950.

33 It is one of the great charms of New York that at the Met one may still see bejeweled Grandes Dames, rouged like crazy, wearing what at first glance appear to be black fur stoles, but then turn out to be their enervated sons slung across their mamas' magnificent shoulders; one may still see Elderly Patricians hanging from boxes by the heels, with their opera glasses pointing like guns right *down* the décolletage of a huge soprano; one may still see swarms of Liveried Chauffeurs waiting to escort their Employers to their cars, to place fur wraps about their aged shanks, to touch their caps respectfully at the words, "Home, James, and don't spare the Rolls."

> TYRONE GUTHRIE, "The 'Grand' Opera Behind Grand Opera," the *New York Times Magazine,* January 5, 1958.

34 The city of right angles and tough, damaged people.

> PETE HAMILL, writing in the *New York Daily News,* November 15, 1978.

35 New York was the only city in the United States that did not need a booster organization. . . . In New York we simply assumed that we were the best—in baseball as well as intellect, in brashness and in subtlety, in everything—and it would have been unseemly to remark upon such an obvious fact.

> MICHAEL HARRINGTON, *Fragments of the Century,* 1973.

36 The lusts of the flesh can be gratified anywhere; it is not this sort of license that distinguishes New York. It is, rather, a lust of the total ego for recognition, even for eminence. More than elsewhere, everybody here wants to be Somebody.

> SYDNEY J. HARRIS, *Strictly Personal,* 1953.

37 The great big city's a wondrous toy
    Just made for a girl and boy.
    We'll turn Manhattan
    Into an isle of joy.

> LORENZ HART, "Manhattan," 1925.

38 The only credential the city asked was the boldness to dream. For those who did, it unlocked its gates and its treasures, not caring who they were or where they came from.

> MOSS HART, *Act One,* 1959.

39 This city drives me crazy, or, if you prefer, crazier; and I have no peace of mind or rest of body till I get out of it. Nobody can find any body, nothing seems to be anywhere, everything seems to be mathematics and geometry and enigmatics and riddles and confusion worse confounded: architecture and mechanics run mad. . . . I think an earthquake might produce some improvement.

> LAFCADIO HEARN, letter to Joseph Tumson, 1889.

40 Little old Bagdad-on-the-Subway.

> O. HENRY, "A Madison Square Arabian Night," *The Trimmed Lamp,* 1907.

41 You'd think New York people was all wise; but no. They don't get a chance to learn. Everything's too compressed. Even the hayseeds are baled hayseeds. But what else can you expect from a town that's shut off from the world by the ocean on one side and New Jersey on the other?

> O. HENRY, "A Tempered Wind," *The Gentle Grafter,* 1908.

42 The city gave him what he demanded and then branded him with its brand. . . . He acquired that charming insolence, that irritating completeness, that sophisticated crassness, that overbalanced poise that makes the Manhattan gentleman so delightfully small in his greatness.

O. HENRY, "The Defeat of the City," *The Voice of the City,* 1908.

43 George Washington, with his right arm upraised, sits on his iron horse at the lower corner of Union Square. . . . Should the General raise his left hand as he has raised his right, it would point to a quarter of the city that forms a haven for the oppressed and suppressed of foreign lands. In the cause of national or personal freedom they have found a refuge here, and the patriot who made it for them sits on his steed, overlooking their district, while he listens through his left ear to vaudeville that caricatures the posterity of his protégés.

O. HENRY, "A Philistine in Bohemia," *The Voice of the City,* 1908.

44 The Yappian Way.

O. HENRY, "Modern Rural Sports," *The Gentle Grafter,* 1908.

45 It couldn't have happened anywhere but in little old New York.

O. HENRY, "A Little Local Colour," *Whirligigs,* 1910.

46 Well, little old Noisyville-on-the-Subway is good enough for me. It's giving me mine.

O. HENRY, "The Duel," *Strictly Business,* 1910.

47 Far below and around lay the city like a ragged purple dream. The irregular houses were like the broken exteriors of cliffs lining deep gulches and winding streams. Some were mountainous; some lay in long, monotonous rows like the basalt precipices hanging over desert cañons. Such was the background of the wonderful, cruel, enchanting, bewildering, fatal, great city.

Ibid.

48 [Like] most native New Yorkers I was born out of town, Cedar Rapids, Iowa, to be specific.

HARRY HERSHFIELD, toastmaster and columnist known as "Mr. New York," quoted in the *New York Times,* December 5, 1965.

49 The Bow'ry, the Bow'ry!
They say such things, and they do strange
things

On the Bow'ry, the Bow'ry!
I'll never go there any more!

CHARLES H. HOYT, "The Bowery," 1891.

50 New York: The posthumous revenge of the Merchant of Venice.

ELBERT HUBBARD, *The Roycroft Dictionary and Book of Epigrams,* 1923.

51 Melting pot Harlem—Harlem of honey and chocolate and caramel and rum and vinegar and lemon and lime and gall . . . where the subway from the Bronx keeps right on downtown.

LANGSTON HUGHES, quoted in *Freedomways,* Summer, 1963.

52 We have had all the reform that we want in this city for some time to come.

JOHN F. HYLAN, Mayor of New York, in a speech to the Civil Service Reform Association, January 10, 1918.

53 Tammany Hall bears the same relation to a penitentiary as a Sunday-school to the church.

ROBERT G. INGERSOLL, speaking in Indianapolis, Indiana, September 21, 1876. (Tammany Hall was the name given the Democratic political machine that controlled city politics—and, therefore, the city—for decades.)

54 The renowned and ancient city of Gotham.

WASHINGTON IRVING, *Salmagundi,* 1807–1808. (This is said to be the earliest reference to New York City as "Gotham.")

55 One of the things that amaze me is the amount of energy that's in New York. You get no energy from the earth because the earth is all covered up with cement and bricks. There's no place to walk on the earth unless you go to Central Park. The energy all comes from human beings.

PHIL JACKSON, basketball player, quoted in Bill Bradley, *Life on the Run,* 1976.

56 New York, like London, seems to be a cloaca of all the depravities of human nature.

THOMAS JEFFERSON, in a letter to William Short, 1823.

57 The main reason why the unlighted streets were not turned into a dark and steaming jungle was the reaction of the community. . . . In the dark all men were the same color. In the dark our fellow man was seen more clearly than in the normal light of a New York night.

> STEPHEN KENNEDY, on the surprisingly low crime rate during a blackout of one of Manhattan's most densely populated areas, quoted in *Time* magazine, August 31, 1959.

58 The world is grand, awfully big and astonishingly beautiful, frequently thrilling. But I love New York.

> DOROTHY KILGALLEN, *Girl Around the World*, 1936.

59 The more one studied it, the more grotesquely bad it grew—bad in its paving, bad in its streets, bad in its street-police, and but for the kindness of the tides, would be worse than bad in its sanitary arrangements.

> RUDYARD KIPLING, "From Tideway to Tideway," 1892.

60 To start with, there's the alien accent. "Tree" is the number between two and four. "Jeintz" is the name of the New York professional football team. A "fit" is a bottle measuring seven ounces less than a quart. This exotic tongue has no relationship to any of the approved languages at the United Nations, and is only slightly less difficult to master than Urdu.

> FLETCHER KNEBEL, in *Look* magazine, March 26, 1963.

61 No other city in the United States can divest the visitor of so much money with so little enthusiasm. In Dallas, they take away with gusto; in New Orleans, with a bow; in San Francisco, with a wink and a grin. In New York, you're lucky if you get a grunt.

> Ibid.

62 New York is a place where I think in general the houses are better built than in Boston. They are generally of brick and three stories high with the largest kind of windows. Their churches are grand; their college, workhouse, and hospitals most excellently situated and also exceedingly commodious, their principal streets much wider than ours. The people—why, the people are magnificent: in their equipages which are numerous, in their house furniture which is fine, in their pride and conceit which are inimitable, in their profaneness which is intolerable, in the want of principle which is prevalent, in their Toryism which is insufferable, and for which they must repent in dust and ashes.

> HENRY KNOX, in a letter to his wife Lucy, January 5, 1776, quoted in George F. Scheer and Hugh Rankin, *Rebels and Redcoats*, 1957.

63 My first qualification for this great office is my monumental personal ingratitude!

> FIORELLO LAGUARDIA, disposing of office seekers following his election as mayor of New York, 1934, quoted in Ernest Cuneo, *Life With Fiorello*, 1955.

64 Not like the brazen giant of Greek fame,
  With conquering limbs astride from land to
    land;
  Here at our sea-washed, sunset gates shall
    stand
  A mighty woman with a torch, whose flame
  Is the imprisoned lightning, and her name
  Mother of exiles.

> EMMA LAZARUS, on the Statue of Liberty, in "The New Colossus," 1883.

65 A hundred times have I thought New York is a catastrophe and fifty times: It is a beautiful catastrophe.

> LE CORBUSIER, quoted in the *New York Herald Tribune*, August 6, 1961.

66 New York has total depth in every area. Washington has only politics; after that, the second biggest thing is white marble.

> JOHN LINDSAY, *Vogue* magazine, August, 1963.

67 Some day this old Broadway shall climb to
    the skies,
  As a ribbon of cloud on a soul-wind shall
    rise,
  And we shall be lifted, rejoicing by night,
  Till we join with the planets who choir their
    delight.

The signs in the streets and the signs in the
    skies
Shall make a new Zodiac, guiding the wise,
And Broadway make one with that
    marvelous stair
That is climbed by the rainbow-clad spirits of
    prayer.

> VACHEL LINDSAY, "Rhyme about an Electrical
> Advertising Sign," in *Collected Poems,* 1925.

68 Robinson Crusoe, the self-sufficient man, could
not have lived in New York City.

> WALTER LIPPMANN, in *Newsweek* magazine,
> February 26, 1968.

69 New York attracts the most talented people in
the world in the arts and professions. It also attracts
them in other fields. Even the bums are talented.

> EDMUND LOVE, *Subways Are for Sleeping,* 1957.

70 There are only about four hundred people in
New York society.

> WARD MCALLISTER, in an interview with
> Charles H. Crandall, in the *New York Tribune,*
> 1888.

71 [New York is] humanity in microcosm; reflect-
ing the infinite variety as well as the infinite capacity for good or evil of the human race.

> DIOSDADO MACAPAGAL, during a visit to the
> United States, 1964.

72 Terrible things happen to young girls in New
York City.

> MARY MARGARET MCBRIDE, *A Long Way from
> Missouri,* 1959.

73 A car is useless in New York, essential everywhere else. The same with good manners.

> MIGNON MCLAUGHLIN, *The Second Neurotic's
> Notebook,* 1966.

74 The inhabitants are in general brisk and lively,
kind to strangers, dress very gay; the fair sex are in
general handsome, and said to be very obliging.

> PATRICK M'ROBERTS, on New York City, *Tour
> Through Part of the North Provinces of America,*
> 1775.

75 The ills of New York cannot be solved by
money. New York will be ill until it is magnificent.
For New York must be ready to show the way to
the rest of Western civilization. Until it does, it
will be no more than the victim of the technological
revolution no matter how much money it receives
in its budget. Money bears the same relation to
social solutions that water does to blood.

> NORMAN MAILER, quoted in the *New York
> Times Magazine,* May 18, 1965.

76 I never tire of singing my own "Manhattan
Magnificat." . . . I pray for all the worry-weary
souls . . . and the glad and gay ones, too. For there
is gaiety in this sprawling metropolis. You hear it
in the cheep of sparrows in the park, the laughter
of children in playgrounds, the banter of taxi drivers lightly insulting other motorists, and it is a truer
gaiety than that which glitters in the night spots of
theaters, where visitors so often seek it.

> SISTER MARYANNA OF THE DOMINICAN
> ACADEMY, quoted in the *New York Daily News,*
> April 9, 1960.

77 Every great wave of popular passion that rolls
up on the prairies is dashed to spray when it strikes
the hard rocks of Manhattan.

> H. L. MENCKEN, *Prejudices,* Fourth Series,
> 1925.

78 New York is not all bricks and steel. . . . It is
the place where all the aspirations of the Western
World meet to form one vast master aspiration.
. . . It is the icing on the pie called Christian Civilization.

> H. L. MENCKEN, *Prejudices,* Sixth Series, 1927.

79 He speaks English with the flawless imperfection of a New Yorker.

> GILBERT MILLSTEIN, on restaurant owner André
> Surmain, quoted in *Esquire* magazine, January,
> 1962.

80 I like living here. Brooklyn has given me pleasure, has helped to educate me; has afforded me, in
fact, the kind of tame excitement on which I thrive.

> MARIANNE MOORE, "Brooklyn from Clinton
> Hill," *A Marianne Moore Reader,* 1961.

81 The nation's thyroid gland.

> CHRISTOPHER MORLEY, quoted in the *New York Times,* March 2, 1970.

82 The Bronx?
No thonx.

> OGDEN NASH, originally in *The New Yorker,* 1931.

83 I wrote those lines, "The Bronx? No
     thonx";
I shudder to confess them.
Now I'm an older, wiser man
I cry, "The Bronx? God bless them!"

> OGDEN NASH, on the occasion of the Bronx golden jubilee, 1964, printed in the *New York Times,* May 27, 1964.

84 The Great White Way.

> ALBERT BIGELOW PAINE, title of a play, 1901.

85 Who that has known thee but shall burn
     In exile till he come again
To do thy bitter will, O stern
     Moon of the tides of men!

> JOHN REED, "Proud New York," in *Poetry* magazine, April, 1919.

86 Hardly a day goes by, you know, that some innocent bystander ain't shot in New York City. All you got to do is be innocent and stand by and they're gonna shoot you. The other day, there was four people shot in one day—four innocent people—in New York City. Amazing. It's kind of hard to *find* four innocent people in New York. That's why a policeman don't have to aim. He just shoots anywhere. Whoever he hits, that's the right one.

> WILL ROGERS, quoted in the *Reader's Digest,* June, 1972.

87 That's the New York thing, isn't it. People who seem absolutely crazy going around telling you how crazy they used to be before they had therapy.

> JUDITH ROSSNER, *Any Minute I Can Split,* 1972.

88 Every person on the streets of New York is a type. The city is one big theater where everyone is on display.

> JERRY RUBIN, *Growing (Up) at 37,* 1976.

89 A sallow waiter brings me beans and
     pork . . .
Outside there's fury in the firmament.
Ice-cream, of course, will follow; and I'm
     content.
O Babylon! O Carthage! O New York!

> SIEGFRIED SASSOON, "Storm on Fifth Avenue," in the *London Mercury* magazine, April, 1921.

90 Genghis Khan conquered Asia with an army only half the size of New York City's civil service.

> EMANUEL SAVAS, deputy city administrator, quoted in the *New York Times Magazine,* October 8, 1972.

91 The upper East Side of Manhattan . . . is the province of Let's Pretend.

> GAIL SHEEHY, *Hustling,* 1971.

92 Wall Street Lays an Egg.

> SIME SILVERMAN, founder and editor of *Variety,* headline on the stock market crash, October, 1929.

93 There's a tree that grows in Brooklyn. Some people call it the Tree of Heaven. No matter where its seed falls, it makes a tree which struggles to reach the sky.

> BETTY SMITH, *A Tree Grows in Brooklyn,* 1943.

94 Just where the Treasury's marble front
     Looks over Wall Street's mingled nations,
Where Jews and Gentiles most are wont
     To throng for trade and last quotations;
Where, hour, by hour, the rates of gold
     Outrival, in the ears of people,
The quarter-chimes, serenely tolled
     From Trinity's undaunted steeple.

> EDMUND CLARENCE STEDMAN, "Pan in Wall Street," *The Blameless Prince,* 1869.

95 This city's got the right name—New York. Nothing ever gets old around here.

> RALPH STEPHENSON, a counterman in Pennsylvania Station, commenting on demolition

work at the station, quoted in the *New York Times,* October 29, 1963.

96 The thing which in the subway is called congestion is highly esteemed in the night spots as intimacy.

SIMEON STRUNSKY, *No Mean City,* 1944.

97 The pneumatic noisemaker is becoming the emblematic sound of New York, the way the bells of Big Ben are the sound of London.

HORACE SUTTON, referring to the jackhammer, quoted in the *Saturday Evening Post,* March 11, 1961.

98 I have two faults to find with it [New York]. In the first place, there is nothing to see; and, in the second place, there is no mode of getting about to see anything.

ANTHONY TROLLOPE, *North America,* 1862.

99 Situated on an island, which I think it [New York] will one day cover, it rises like Venice, from the sea, and like the fairest of cities in the days of her glory, receives into its lap tribute of all the riches of the earth.

FRANCES TROLLOPE, *Domestic Manners of the Americans,* 1832.

100 Here I was in New York, city of prose and fantasy, of capitalist automatism, its streets a triumph of cubism, its moral philosophy that of the dollar. New York impressed me tremendously because, more than any other city in the world, it is the fullest expression of our modern age.

LEON TROTSKY, *My Life,* 1930.

101 Skyscraper National Park.

KURT VONNEGUT, *Slapstick,* 1976.

102 It can destroy an individual, or it can fulfill him, depending a good deal on luck. No one should come to New York to live unless he is willing to be lucky.

E. B. WHITE, *Here Is New York,* 1949.

103 [Through office windows] you can see in pantomime the puppets fumbling with their slips of paper (but you don't hear the rustle), see them pick up their phone (but you don't hear the ring), see the

noiseless, ceaseless moving about of so many passers of pieces of paper: New York, the capital of memoranda, in touch with Calcutta, in touch with Reykjavik, and always fooling with something.

Ibid.

104 New York is to the nation what the white church spire is to the village—the visible symbol of aspiration and faith, the white plume saying the way is up!

E. B. WHITE, quoted in *Mental Health in the Metropolis,* 1962.

105 Not the pageants of you, not your shifting
         tableaus, your spectacles, repay me,
Not the interminable rows of your houses,
         nor the ships at the wharves,
Nor the processions in the streets, nor the
         bright windows with goods in them,
Nor to converse with learn'd persons, or
         bear my share in the soiree or feast;
Not those, but as I pass O Manhattan, your
         frequent and swift flash of eyes offering
         me love,
Offering response to my own—these repay
         me,
Lovers, continual lovers, only repay me.

WALT WHITMAN, "City of Orgies," 1860.

106 My own Manhattan, with spires and the
         sparkling and hurrying tides, and the
         ships.

WALT WHITMAN, "When Lilacs Last in the Dooryard Bloom'd," 1865–1866.

107 City of hurried and sparkling waters! city of
         spires and masts!
City nested in bays! my city!

WALT WHITMAN, "Mannahatta," 1860.

108 A little strip of an island with a row of wellfed folks up and down the middle, and a lot of hungry folks on each side.

HARRY LEON WILSON, *The Spenders,* 1902.

109 But now the train was slowing to a halt. Long tongues of cement now appeared, and faces, swarming figures, running forms beside the train. And all these faces, forms, and figures slowed to instancy,

were held there in the alertness of expectant movement. There was a grinding screech of brakes, a
slight jolt, and, for a moment, utter silence. At this
moment there was a terrific explosion. It was New
York.

> THOMAS WOLFE, *The Web and the Rock,*
> 1939.

110 There is a wonderful, secret thrill of some
impending ecstasy on a frozen winter's night. On
one of these nights of frozen silence when the cold
is so intense that it numbs one's flesh, and the sky
above the city flashes with one deep jewelry of cold
stars, the whole city, no matter how ugly its parts
may be, becomes a proud, passionate, Northern
place: everything about it seems to soar up with an
aspirant, vertical, glittering magnificence to meet
the stars. One hears the hoarse notes of the great
ships in the river, and one remembers suddenly the
princely girdle of proud, potent tides that bind the
city, and suddenly New York blazes like a magnificent jewel in its fit setting of sea, and earth, and
stars.

> Ibid.

111 It was a cruel city, but it was a lovely one; a
savage city, yet it had such tenderness; a bitter,
harsh, and violent catacomb of stone and steel and
tunneled rock, slashed savagely with light, and
roaring, fighting a constant ceaseless warfare of
men and of machinery; and yet it was so sweetly
and so delicately pulsed, as full of warmth, of passion, and of love, as it was full of hate.

> Ibid.

112 We plant a tub and call it Paradise. . . . New
York is the great stone desert.

> ISRAEL ZANGWILL, *The Melting Pot,* 1908.

---

172. NORTH CAROLINA

---

1 Esse quam videri. (To be rather than seem.)

> State motto.

2 A vale of humility between two mountains of
conceit.

> Anonymous description of North Carolina. (Also
> given as "a valley of humiliation. . . . " The
> so-called mountains are the states of Virginia and
> South Carolina.)

3 First at Bethel, furthest at Gettysburg, and last
at Appomattox.

> Anonymous, describing North Carolina.

4 I'm a Tar Heel born,
I'm a Tar Heel bred,
And when I die
I'll be a Tar Heel dead.

> University of North Carolina fight song.

5 In my honest and unbiased judgment, the Good
Lord will place the Garden of Eden in North Carolina when He restores it to earth. He will do this
because He will have so few changes to make in
order to achieve perfection.

> SAM J. ERVIN, JR., *Humor of a Country Lawyer,*
> 1983.

6 We have discovered the main to be the goodliest
soil under the cope of heaven, so abounding with
sweet trees, that bring such sundry rich and pleasant gums, grapes of such greatness, yet wild, as
France, Spain, or Italy have no greater, so many
sorts of Apothecary drugs, such several kinds of
flax, and one kind like silk.

> RALPH LANE, head of the Roanoke Island colony,
> in a letter to Sir Richard Hakluyt, September 3,
> 1585.

7 Inhabitants of Carolina, through the Richness of
the Soil, live an easy and pleasant Life . . . under
one of the mildest Governments in the World.

> JOHN LAWSON, in his account of a 39-day trip
> from Charleston through the Carolinas, *A New
> Voyage to Carolina,* 1709.

8 North Carolina begins with the brightness of sea
sands and ends with the loneliness of the Smokies
reaching in chill and cloud to the sky.

> OVID WILLIAMS PIERCE, quoted in Richard
> Walser, *The North Carolina Miscellany,* 1962.

9 The Land of the Sky.

> CHRISTIAN REID, the title of her novel set in the North Carolina mountains, 1876.

173. NORTH DAKOTA

1 Liberty and union, now and forever, one and inseparable.

> State motto.

2 North Dakota is a doomed state. In twenty years it will revert to the Indian and the buffalo. We must be moving on.

> AN EARLY SETTLER, quoted in Frank P. Stockbridge, "The North Dakota Man Crop," *World's Work* magazine, November, 1912.

3 Freely admitted is the rural character of the State, and there is seldom an attempt to cover native crudities with a veneer of eastern culture.

> Federal Writers' Project, *North Dakota: A Guide to the Northern Prairie State,* 1938.

4 A State of unbounded plains and hills and Badlands—elbowroom. Superb sunsets. High winds and tumbleweed. Farms and plows and sweeping fields. . . . Little towns crowded on Saturday night, and busy cities shipping out the products of North Dakota and supplying the needs of the producers. . . . The sad, slow wail of a coyote on the still prairie.

> Ibid.

5 I like the democracy of North Dakota, the state without a millionaire and with fewest paupers; where rich and poor find a common meeting ground in the fight for improvements in the home state. . . . There is something of the broadness of its prairies in the mental makeup of its people. A radical is not so radical nor a conservative so conservative in this rather free-and-easy non-eastern state.

> MART CONNOLLY, quoted in Elwyn B. Robinson, *History of North Dakota,* 1966.

6 All this country is still youthful. Man has not labored long enough there to thoroughly humanize it, and often you continue to find a savor of the desert or wilderness. . . . The long broad slope between the Rocky Mountains and the Mississippi River which includes North Dakota is destined to be in most ways an ideal farming section that for extent and fertility will be unrivaled the world over.

> CLIFTON JOHNSON, *Highways and Byways of the Rocky Mountains,* 1910.

7 I would never have been President if it had not been for my experiences in North Dakota.

> THEODORE ROOSEVELT, quoted in Elwyn B. Robinson, *History of North Dakota,* 1966.

8 The children of these prairies do not grow up expecting that all the bonbons of this world are going to be fed them with a runcible spoon by pampering destiny. Here you sweat by summer and shiver by winter and work and pay for everything you get, so that by the time you are an adult you are spiritually prepared for more hard work. North Dakota life has been meant to make of you a tough fighter, a hard worker.

> DR. CARROLL E. SIMCOX, commencement address at the University of North Dakota, 1961.

9 Someone must have told me about the Missouri River at Bismarck, North Dakota, or I must have read about it. In either case, I hadn't paid attention. I came on it in amazement. . . . Here is the boundary between east and west. On the Bismarck side it is eastern landscape, eastern grass, with the look and smell of eastern America. Across the Missouri on the Mandan side, it is pure west, with brown grass and water scorings and small outcrops. The two sides of the river might be a thousand miles apart.

> JOHN STEINBECK, *Travels with Charley,* 1962.

10 If you will take a map of the United States and fold it in the middle, eastern edge against western, and crease it sharply, right in the crease will be Fargo. . . . That may not be a very scientific method for finding the east-west middle of the country, but it will do.

> Ibid.

174. NUCLEAR AGE

See also MILITARISM; WAR

1 Behind the black portent of the new atomic age lies a hope which, seized upon with faith, can work our salvation. If we fail, then we have damned every man to be the slave of fear.

> BERNARD BARUCH, in a speech before the United Nations Atomic Energy Commission, June 14, 1946.

2 If we fight a war and win it with H-bombs, what history will remember is *not* the ideals we were fighting for but the method we used to accomplish them.

> HANS BETHE, in *Scientific American* magazine, c.1950, quoted in Robert Jungk, *Brighter than a Thousand Suns,* 1958.

3 We have grasped the mystery of the atom and rejected the Sermon on the Mount.

> GEN. OMAR BRADLEY, in a speech in Boston, November 10, 1948.

4 The world has achieved brilliance without wisdom, power without conscience. Ours is a world of nuclear giants and ethical infants.

> Ibid.

5 I went over the complete inventory of U.S. nuclear warheads, which is really a sobering experience.

> JIMMY CARTER, diary entry, December 28, 1977.

6 Science has brought forth this danger, but the real problem is in the minds and hearts of men.

> ALBERT EINSTEIN, quoted in the *New York Times Magazine,* June 23, 1946.

7 It should not be forgotten that the atomic bombs were made in this country as a preventive measure. It was to head off its use by the Germans if they discovered it. We are in effect making the low standards of the enemy in the last war our own for the present.

> ALBERT EINSTEIN, in a statement to the press, 1947, quoted in Robert Jungk, *Brighter than a Thousand Suns,* 1958.

8 If I had known that the Germans would not succeed in constructing the atom bomb, I would never have lifted a finger.

> Ibid.

9 Radioactive poisoning of the atmosphere and hence annihilation of any life on earth has been brought within the range of technical possibilities. The ghostlike character of this development [the hydrogen bomb] lies in its apparently compulsory trend. Every step appears as the unavoidable consequence of the preceding one. In the end there beckons more and more clearly general annihilation.

> Ibid.

10 Thirty seconds after the explosion came, first the air blast pressing hard against people and things, to be followed almost immediately by the strong, sustained awesome roar which warned of doomsday and made us feel that we puny things were blasphemous to dare tamper with the forces heretofore reserved to The Almighty.

> THOMAS FARRELL, in an official report on the first atom bomb test, Alamogordo, New Mexico, July 16, 1945.

11 We have one foot in genesis and the other in apocalypse, and annihilation is always one immediate option.

> MICHAEL HARRINGTON, *Toward a Democratic Left,* 1968.

12 What are we to make of terms like "nuclear exchange," "escalation," "nuclear yield," "counterforce," "megatons," or of "the window of vulnerability" or (ostensibly much better) "window of opportunity." Quite simply, these words provide a way of talking about nuclear weapons without really talking about them. In them we find nothing about billions of human beings being incinerated or literally melted, nothing about millions of corpses. Rather, the weapons come to seem ordinary and manageable or even mildly pleasant: a "nuclear exchange" sounds something like mutual gift-giving.

Robert Jay Lifton, *Indefensible Weapons,*
1982.

13 Atomic energy bears that same duality that has
faced man from time immemorial, a duality expressed in the Book of Books thousands of years
ago: "See, I have set before thee this day life and
good and death and evil . . . therefore choose life."

David E. Lilienthal, *This I Do Believe,* 1949.

14 Massive atomic deterring power can win us
years of grace, years in which to wrench history
from its present course and direct it toward the
enshrinement of human brotherhood.

Brien McMahon, in a speech in the U.S.
Senate, September 18, 1951.

15 We knew the world would not be the same.

J. Robert Oppenheimer, speaking of the first
atom bomb test at Alamogordo, New Mexico,
July 16, 1945.

16 Nature is neutral. Man has wrested from nature
the power to make the world a desert or to make
the deserts bloom. There is no evil in the atom;
only in men's souls.

Adlai E. Stevenson, in a speech at Hartford,
Connecticut, September 18, 1952.

17 With the unlocking of the atom, mankind
crossed one of the great watersheds of history. We
have entered uncharted lands. The maps of strategy and diplomacy by which we guided ourselves
until yesterday no longer reveal the way. Fusion
and fission revolutionized the entire foundation of
human affairs.

Adlai E. Stevenson, in an address before the
General Federation of Women's Clubs,
Philadelphia, May 24, 1955.

18 Every effort is being bent toward assuring that
this weapon and the new field of science that stands
behind it will be employed wisely in the interests
of the security of peace-loving nations and the well-
being of the world.

Henry L. Stimson, in a statement on the
dropping of the atomic bomb on Hiroshima on
August 6, 1945.

19 It won't be until the bombs get so big that they
can annihilate everything that people will really

become terrified and begin to take a reasonable line
in politics. Those who oppose the hydrogen bomb
are behaving like ostriches if they think they are
going to promote peace in that way.

Edward Teller, quoted in Robert Jungk,
Brighter than a Thousand Suns, 1958.

20 It took us eighteen months to build the first
nuclear power generator; it now takes twelve years;
that's progress.

Edward Teller, quoted in Milton and Rose
Friedman, *Free to Choose,* 1979.

21 A mushroom of boiling dust up to 20,000 feet.

Paul W. Tibbets, describing the explosion of
the atomic bomb at Hiroshima on August 6, 1945.

22 This weapon is to be used against Japan between now and August 10th. . . . It seems to be the
most terrible thing ever discovered, but it can be
made the most useful.

Harry S Truman, in his diary, July 25, 1945.

23 The release of atomic energy constitutes a new
force too revolutionary to consider in the framework of old ideas.

Harry S Truman, in a message to Congress,
October 3, 1945.

24 The experience of the scientists who have
worked on the atomic bomb has indicated that in
any investigation of this kind the scientist ends by
putting unlimited powers in the hands of the people
whom he is least inclined to trust with their use. It
is perfectly clear also that to disseminate information about a weapon in the present state of our
civilization is to make it practically certain that that
weapon will be used.

Norbert Wiener, quoted in Robert Jungk,
Brighter than a Thousand Suns, 1958.

175. OHIO

1 With God, all things are possible.

State motto.

2 Ohio is the farthest west of the east and the farthest north of the south.

LOUIS BROMFIELD, quoted in John Gunther, *Inside U.S.A.,* 1947.

3 Cincinnati is a beautiful city; cheerful, thriving, and animated. I have not often seen a place that commends itself so favorably and pleasantly to a stranger at the first glance as this does: with its clean houses of red and white, its well-paved roads, and footways of bright tile. Nor does it become less prepossessing on a closer acquaintance. The streets are broad and airy, the shops extremely good, the private residences remarkable for their elegance and neatness.

CHARLES DICKENS, *American Notes,* 1842.

4 Basically, Ohio is nothing more nor less than a giant carpet of agriculture studded by great cities.

JOHN GUNTHER, *Inside U.S.A.,* 1947.

5 I know of no other metropolis with quite so impressive a record in the practical application of good citizenship to government.

JOHN GUNTHER, on Cleveland, *Inside U.S.A.,* 1947.

---

176. OKLAHOMA

---

1 Labor omnia vincit. (Work conquers all things.)

State motto.

2 [In 1889] the last big tract of Indian land was declared open for settlement, in Oklahoma. The claimants and the speculators mounted their horses and lined up like trotters waiting for a starting gun. The itchy ones jumped the gun and were ever after known as Sooners—as Oklahoma was thereafter called the Sooner State.

ALISTAIR COOKE, *America,* 1973.

3 "Okla-homa," he explained . . . "That's Choctaw. Okla-people. Humma-red. Red People. That's what they called it when the Indians came here to live."

EDNA FERBER, *Cimarron,* 1930.

4 Oil. Nothing else mattered. Oklahoma, the dry, the wind-swept, the burning, was a sea of hidden oil. The red prairies, pricked, ran black and slimy with it. The work of years was undone in a day. . . . Compared to that which now took place the early days following the Run in '89 were idyllic. They swarmed on Oklahoma from every state in the Union.

Ibid.

5 The state that Oklahoma most resembles is of course Texas, if only because it too does everything with color and originality, but tell an Oklahoman that his state is a "dependency" of Texas and he will bite your eyes out.

JOHN GUNTHER, *Inside U.S.A.,* 1947.

6 Tall tales come out of Oklahoma just as out of Texas, one favorite describes the "crowbar hole." This is a hole through the wall that many houses have, designed to check the weather. You shove a crowbar through the hole; if it bends, the wind velocity outside is normal; if the bar breaks off, "it is better to stay in the house."

Ibid.

7 Tulsa, "oil capital of the world," as it calls itself, is a tough, get-rich-quick, heady town about as sensitive as corduroy.

Ibid.

8 On a single day [during the Dust Bowl disaster of 1935], I heard, fifty million *tons* of soil were blown away. People sat in Oklahoma City, with the sky invisible for three days in a row, holding dust masks over their faces and wet towels to protect their mouths at night, while the farms blew by.

Ibid.

9 Oklahoma,
   Where the wind comes sweepin' down the
      plain,
   And the wavin' wheat
   Can sure smell sweet
   When the wind comes right behind the rain.

OSCAR HAMMERSTEIN II, "Oklahoma," from the musical *Oklahoma!* 1943.

10 Oklahoma is one of the friendliest states in the Union. Taxi drivers open the front door, so you can ride up front. If there's just one passenger he always rides with the driver, and they talk.

ERNIE PYLE, *Home Country,* 1947.

11 Oklahoma City is an especially friendly town. People there have a pride about their town—not a silly civic pride, but that same feeling that exists in San Francisco and New Orleans. They just wouldn't live anywhere else, that's all.

Ibid.

12 Okie use' ta mean you was from Oklahoma. Now it means you're a dirty son-of-a-bitch. Okie means you're scum. Don't mean nothing itself, it's the way they say it.

JOHN STEINBECK, *The Grapes of Wrath,* 1939.

---

177. ORATORY

See also INVECTIVE; LANGUAGE; SPEECH

---

1 Oratory, *n.* A conspiracy between speech and action to cheat the understanding. A tyranny tempered by stenography.

AMBROSE BIERCE, *The Devil's Dictionary,* 1906.

2 An orator is a man who says what he thinks and feels what he says.

WILLIAM JENNINGS BRYAN, quoted in Paxton P. Hibben, *The Peerless Leader,* 1929.

3 No man ever made a great speech on a mean subject.

Attributed to Eugene V. Debs.

4 A man cannot speak but he judges himself.

RALPH WALDO EMERSON, "Compensation," *Essays,* First Series, 1841.

5 A course of mobs is good practice for orators.

RALPH WALDO EMERSON, "Power, *The Conduct of Life,* 1860.

6 Condense some daily experience into a glowing symbol, and an audience is electrified.

RALPH WALDO EMERSON, "Eloquence," *Letters and Social Aims,* 1876.

7 Here comes the Orator! with his Flood of Words, and his Drop of Reason.

BENJAMIN FRANKLIN, *Poor Richard's Almanack,* 1735.

8 A powerful preacher is open to the same sense of enjoyment—an awful, tremulous, gooseflesh sort of state, but still enjoyment—that a great tragedian feels when he curdles the blood of his audience.

OLIVER WENDELL HOLMES, SR., *The Guardian Angel,* 1867.

9 Oratory: The lullaby of the Intellect.

ELBERT HUBBARD, *The Roycroft Dictionary and Book of Epigrams,* 1923.

10 Amplification is the vice of modern oratory. It is an insult to an assembly of reasonable men, disgusting and revolting instead of persuading. Speeches measured by the hour, die with the hour.

THOMAS JEFFERSON, in a letter to David Harding, president of the Jefferson Debating Society of Hingham, April 20, 1824.

11 Where judgment has wit to express it there's the best orator.

WILLIAM PENN, *Some Fruits of Solitude,* 1693.

12 [William Jennings] Bryan is a personally honest and rather attractive man, a real orator and a born demagogue, who has every crank, fool and putative criminal in the country behind him, and a large proportion of the ignorant honest class.

THEODORE ROOSEVELT, in a letter to Anna Roosevelt Cowles, July 19, 1896.

13 I thank God that, if I am gifted with little of the spirit which is able to raise mortals to the skies, I have yet none, as I trust, of that other spirit which would drag angels down.

DANIEL WEBSTER, in a speech in the U.S. Senate, January 26, 1830.

178. OREGON

1 The Union.

> State motto.

2 The cowards never started—and the weak died along the way.

> Attributed to pioneers who survived the journey west on the Oregon Trail, quoted by Bruce Catton in *This Week* magazine, March 11, 1955.

3 Or lose thyself in the continuous woods
Where rolls the Oregon, and hears no sound,
Save his own dashings.

> WILLIAM CULLENT BRYANT, *Thanatopsis,* 1817.

4 Oregon was settled by New Englanders in the first instance, and has a native primness, a conservatism, much like that of New Hampshire or Vermont. It is, indeed, one of the most astonishing things in America that Portland, Oregon, should be almost indistinguishable from Portland, Maine.

> JOHN GUNTHER, *Inside U.S.A.,* 1947.

5 Portland produces lumber and jig-saw fittings for houses, and beer and buggies, and bricks and biscuit; and, in case you should miss the fact, there are glorified views of the town hung up in public places with the value of the products set down in dollars. All this is excellent and exactly suitable to the opening of a new country; but when a man tells you it is civilization, you object.

> RUDYARD KIPLING, *American Notes,* 1891.

6 Portland is so busy that it can't attend to its own sewage or paving, and the four-story brick blocks front cobble-stones and plank sidewalks and other things much worse. I saw a foundation being dug out. The sewage of perhaps twenty years ago, had thoroughly soaked into the soil, and there was a familiar and Oriental look about the compost that flew up with each shovel-load. Yet the local papers, as was just and proper, swore there was no place like Portland, Oregon, U.S.A.

> Ibid.

7 Oregon is seldom heard of. Its people believe in the Bible, and hold that all radicals should be lynched. It has no poets and no statesmen.

> H.L. MENCKEN, in the *American Mercury,* 1925.

179. PAIN

See also AFFLICTION; SORROW; TROUBLE

1 Next to ingratitude, the most painful thing to bear is gratitude.

> HENRY WARD BEECHER, *Proverbs from Plymouth Pulpit,* 1870.

2 Pain, *n.* An uncomfortable frame of mind that may have a physical basis in something that is being done to the body, or may be purely mental, caused by the good fortune of another.

> AMBROSE BIERCE, *The Devil's Dictionary,* 1906.

3 The sufferers parade their miseries, tear the lint from their bruises, reveal their indictable crimes, that you may pity them. They like sickness, because physical pain will extort some show of interest from the bystanders, as we have seen children, who, finding themselves of no account when grown people come in, will cough till they choke, to draw attention.

> RALPH WALDO EMERSON, "Culture," *The Conduct of Life,* 1860.

4 Pain is superficial, and therefore fear is. The torments of martyrdoms are probably most keenly felt by the bystanders. The torments are illusory. The first suffering is the last suffering, the later hurts being lost on insensibility.

> RALPH WALDO EMERSON, "Courage," *Society and Solitude,* 1870.

5 Pain wastes the Body; Pleasures the Understanding.

> BENJAMIN FRANKLIN, *Poor Richard's Almanack,* 1735.

6 The honest Man takes Pains, and then enjoys Pleasures; the Knave takes Pleasure, and then suffers Pains.

BENJAMIN FRANKLIN, *Poor Richard's Almanack,* 1755.

7 I find the pain of a little censure, even when it is unfounded, is more acute than the pleasure of much praise.

THOMAS JEFFERSON, in a letter to Francis Hopkinson, March 13, 1789.

8 I do not agree that an age of pleasure is no compensation for a moment of pain.

THOMAS JEFFERSON, in a letter to John Adams, August 1, 1816.

9 It's odd that you can get so anesthetized by your own pain or your own problem that you don't quite fully share the hell of someone close to you.

LADY BIRD JOHNSON, *A White House Diary,* 1970.

10 No pain, no palm; no thorns, no throne; no gall, no glory; no cross, no crown.

WILLIAM PENN, *No Cross, No Crown,* 1669.

11 The sickness—the nausea—
   The pitiless pain—
Have ceased with the fever
   That maddened my brain—
With the fever called "Living"
   That burned in my brain.

EDGAR ALLAN POE, "For Annie," 1849.

---

180. PATRIOTISM

See also AMERICANS; FLAG

---

1 Patriotism in the female sex is the most disinterested of all virtues. . . . Deprived of a voice in legislation, obliged to submit to those laws which are imposed upon us, is it not sufficient to make us indifferent to the public welfare? Yet all history and every age exhibit instances of patriotic virtue in the female sex; which considering our situation equals the most heroic of yours.

ABIGAIL ADAMS, in a letter to John Adams, June 17, 1782.

2 I can never join with my voice in the toast which I see in the papers attributed to one of our gallant naval heroes. I cannot ask of heaven success, even for my country, in a cause where she should be in the wrong. *Fiat justitia, pereat caelum.* [Let justice be done though the heavens fall.] My toast would be, may our country be always successful, but whether successful or otherwise, always right.

JOHN QUINCY ADAMS, referring to Stephen Decatur's toast, "our country, right or wrong," in a letter to John Adams, August 1, 1816.

3 Patriot, *n.,* One to whom the interests of a part seem superior to those of the whole. The dupe of statesmen and the tool of conquerors.

AMBROSE BIERCE, *The Devil's Dictionary,* 1906.

4 Patriotism, *n.* Combustible rubbish ready to the torch of any one ambitious to illuminate his name. In Dr. Johnson's famous dictionary patriotism is defined as the last resort of a scoundrel. With all due respect to an enlightened but inferior lexicographer I beg to submit that it is the first.

Ibid.

5 Un-American, *adj.* Wicked, intolerable, heathenish.

Ibid.

6 Patriotism is a mighty precious thing when it costs nothing, but the mass of mankind consider it a very foolish thing when it curtails their self-indulgence.

JOHN BROCKENBROUGH, in a letter concerning the Embargo Act of 1807, to John Randolph, 1808.

7 Protection and patriotism are reciprocal.

JOHN C. CALHOUN, in a speech in the House of Representatives, 1812.

8 We join ourselves to no party that does not carry the flag and keep step to the music of the Union.

RUFUS CHOATE, in a letter to the Whig Convention, October 1, 1855.

9 Who are the really disloyal? Those who inflame racial hatreds, who sow religious and class dissensions. Those who subvert the Constitution by violating the freedom of the ballot box. Those who make a mockery of majority rule by the use of the filibuster. Those who impair democracy by denying equal educational facilities. Those who frustrate justice by lynch law or by making a farce of jury trials. Those who deny freedom of speech and of the press and of assembly. Those who demand special favors against the interest of the commonwealth. Those who regard public office merely as a source of private gain. Those who would exalt the military over the civil. Those who for selfish and private purposes stir up national antagonisms and expose the world to the ruin of war.

> HENRY STEELE COMMAGER, *Freedom, Loyalty, Dissent,* 1954.

10 Patriotism is easy to understand in America. It means looking out for yourself by looking out for your country.

> CALVIN COOLIDGE, in a speech in Northampton, Massachusetts, May 30, 1923.

11 Treason is in the air around us everywhere. It goes by the name of patriotism.

> THOMAS CORWIN, in a letter from Washington, D.C., January 16, 1861. (Corwin was a moderate Republican who opposed the radical abolitionists but also opposed the expansion of slavery.)

12 Our country! In her intercourse with foreign nations, may she always be in the right; but our country, right or wrong.

> STEPHEN DECATUR, in a toast offered at Norfolk, Virginia, April, 1816.

13 You can't prove you're an American by waving Old Glory.

> HELEN GAHAGAN DOUGLAS, *A Full Life,* 1982.

14 "Th' American nation in th' Sixth Ward is a fine people," he says. "They love th' eagle," he says, "on th' back iv a dollar."

> FINLEY PETER DUNNE, "Oratory on Politics," *Mr. Dooley in Peace and War,* 1898.

15 Nationalism is an infantile disease. It is the measles of mankind.

> ALBERT EINSTEIN, to George Sylvester Viereck, 1921.

16 Any relation to the land, the habit of tilling it, or mining it, or even hunting on it, generates the feeling of patriotism.

> RALPH WALDO EMERSON, "The Young American," *Nature; Addresses and Lectures,* 1849.

17 Nations have lost their old omnipotence; the patriotic tie does not hold. Nations are getting obsolete; we go and live where we will.

> RALPH WALDO EMERSON, *English Traits,* 1856.

18 Our country is the world—our countrymen are mankind.

> WILLIAM LLOYD GARRISON, motto of the abolitionist journal *The Liberator,* 1831–1865.

19 Remember . . . that behind all these men you have to do with, behind officers and Government and people even, there is the Country Herself, your Country, and that you belong to Her as you belong to your own mother.

> EDWARD EVERETT HALE, *The Man Without a Country,* 1863.

20 To be radical is, in the best and only decent sense of the word, patriotic.

> MICHAEL HARRINGTON, *Fragments of the Century,* 1973.

21 He serves his party best who serves the country best.

> RUTHERFORD B. HAYES, in his inaugural address, March 5, 1877.

22 What we need are critical lovers of America—patriots who express their faith in their country by working to *improve* it.

> HUBERT H. HUMPHREY, *Beyond Civil Rights: A New Day of Equality,* 1968.

23 He loves his country best who strives to make it best.

> ROBERT G. INGERSOLL, in a speech in New York City, May 29, 1882.

24 Our federal Union; it must be preserved.

> ANDREW JACKSON, in a toast at the Jefferson Birthday Celebration, 1830.

25 Patriotism is a centrifugal emotion intensifying at the outskirts.

> ALICE JAMES, in a letter to her sister-in-law, Mrs. William James, December 10, 1888.

26 My affections were first for my own country, and then, generally, for all mankind.

> THOMAS JEFFERSON, in a letter to Thomas Law, January 15, 1811.

27 I look upon the whole world as my fatherland. . . . I look upon true patriotism as the brotherhood of man and the service of all to all.

> HELEN KELLER, in the *New York Call,* December 20, 1915.

28 The mystic chords of memory, stretching from every battlefield and patriot grave to every living heart and hearthstone all over this broad land.

> ABRAHAM LINCOLN, in his first inaugural address, March 4, 1861.

29 There is something magnificent in having a country to love. It is almost like what one feels for a woman. Not so tender, perhaps, but to the full as self-forgetful.

> JAMES RUSSELL LOWELL, in a letter to Charles Eliot Norton, April 13, 1865.

30 Certainly it is no shame to a man that he should be as nice about his country as about his sweetheart. . . . Yet it would hardly be wise to hold every one an enemy who could not see her with our own enchanted eyes. It seems to be the common opinion of foreigners that Americans are *too* tender upon this point.

> JAMES RUSSELL LOWELL, "On a Certain Condescension in Foreigners," 1869.

31 Whenever you hear a man speak of his love for his country it is a sign that he expects to be paid for it.

> H.L. MENCKEN, "Sententiae," in *The Vintage Mencken,* 1955.

32 Patriotism is often an arbitrary veneration of real estate above principles.

> GEORGE JEAN NATHAN, *Testament of a Critic,* 1931.

33 There are not wanting men so weak as to suppose that their approbation of warlike measures is a proof of personal gallantry, and that opposition to them indicates a want of that spirit which becomes a friend of his country; as if it required more courage and patriotism to join in the acclamation of the day, than steadily to oppose one's self to the mad infatuation to which every people and all governments have, at some time or other, given way.

> JOHN RANDOLPH, opposing war with England, in an open letter, published in Virginia newspapers, dated May 30, 1812.

34 A man who is good enough to shed his blood for his country is good enough to be given a square deal afterwards. More than that no man is entitled to, and less than that no man shall have.

> THEODORE ROOSEVELT, in a speech in Springfield, Illinois, June 4, 1903.

35 The pacifist is as surely a traitor to his country and to humanity as is the most brutal wrongdoer.

> THEODORE ROOSEVELT, in a speech in Pittsburgh, July 27, 1917.

36 There can be no fifty-fifty Americanism in this country. There is room here for only 100% Americanism, only for those who are Americans and nothing else.

> THEODORE ROOSEVELT, in a speech at the State Republican Party Convention, Saratoga, New York, July 19, 1918.

37 The man who loves other countries as much as his own stands on a level with the man who loves other women as much as he loves his own wife.

> THEODORE ROOSEVELT, in an address in New York City, on the anniversary of the first Battle of the Marne, September 6, 1918.

38 Patriotism is just loyalty to friends, people, families.

> ROBERT SANTOS, quoted in Al Santoli, *Everything We Had: An Oral History of the Vietnam War by Thirty-three American Soldiers Who Fought It,* 1981.

39 Our country, right or wrong. When right, to be kept right; when wrong, to be put right.

CARL SCHURZ, in a speech in the U.S. Senate, January 17, 1872.

40 I feel that this do-or-die, my-country-right-or-wrong kind of patriotism is not merely out of place in a nuclear armed world, it is criminal egotism on a monstrous scale. The world won't be safe until people in all countries recognize it for what it is and, instead of cheering the leader who talks that way, impeach him.

BENJAMIN SPOCK, *Decent and Indecent,* 1968.

41 I venture to suggest that patriotism is not a short and frenzied outburst of emotion but the tranquil and steady dedication of a lifetime.

ADLAI E. STEVENSON, in a speech at the American Legion Convention, August 27, 1952.

42 There is the National flag. He must be cold, indeed, who can look upon its folds rippling in the breeze without pride of country. If in a foreign land, the flag is companionship, and country itself, with all its endearments.

CHARLES SUMNER, in an address entitled "Are We a Nation?" delivered at the Cooper Institute, New York City, November 19, 1867.

43 The name of American, which belongs to you in your national capacity, must always exalt the just pride of patriotism more than any appellation derived from local discriminations.

GEORGE WASHINGTON, in his Farewell Address, September 17, 1796.

44 Let our object be, our country, our whole country, and nothing but our country.

DANIEL WEBSTER, in his address delivered at the laying of the cornerstone of the Bunker Hill Monument, June 17, 1825.

45 Thank God. I—I also—am an American!

DANIEL WEBSTER, in his address upon the completion of Bunker Hill Monument, June 17, 1843.

46 I shall know but one country. The ends I aim at shall be my country's, my God's, and Truth's. I was born an American; I will live an American; I shall die an American.

DANIEL WEBSTER, in a speech, July 17, 1850.

47 There would never be a moment, in war or in peace, when I wouldn't trade all the patriots in the country for one tolerant man. Or when I wouldn't swap the vitamins in a child's lunchbox for a jelly glass of magnanimity.

E.B. WHITE, "Coon Hunt," *One Man's Meat,* 1944.

48 I hold that it would be improper for any committee or any employer to examine my conscience. They wouldn't know how to get into it, they wouldn't know what to do when they got in there, and I wouldn't let them in anyway. Like other Americans, my acts and my words are open to inspection—not my thoughts or my political affiliation.

E.B. WHITE, in a letter to the *New York Herald Tribune,* dated November 29, 1947.

49 The principle of demanding an expression of political conformity as the price of a job is the principle of hundred percentism. It is not new and it is blood brother of witch burning.

E.B. WHITE, in a letter to the *New York Herald Tribune,* dated December 4, 1947.

50 The lines of red are lines of blood, nobly and unselfishly shed by men who loved the liberty of their fellowmen more than they loved their own lives and fortunes.

WOODROW WILSON, in a speech on Flag Day, May 7, 1915.

---

181. PEACE

See also WAR

---

1 Peace, *n.* In international affairs, a period of cheating between two periods of fighting.

AMBROSE BIERCE, *The Devil's Dictionary,* 1906.

2 Thank God for peace! Thank God for peace, when the great gray ships come in!

GUY WETMORE CARRYL, "When the Great Gray Ships Come In," dated August 20, 1898.

3 War is an invention of the human mind. The human mind can invent peace with justice.

NORMAN COUSINS, *Who Speaks for Man?* 1952.

4 God and the politicians willing, the United States can declare peace upon the world, and win it.

ELY CULBERTSON, *Must We Fight Russia?* 1946.

5 Mankind will never win lasting peace so long as men use their full resources only in tasks of war. While we are yet at peace, let us mobilize the potentialities, particularly the moral and spiritual potentialities, which we ususally reserve for war.

JOHN FOSTER DULLES, *War or Peace,* 1950.

6 A peaceful world is a world in which differences are tolerated, and are not eliminated by violence.

Ibid.

7 You have to take chances for peace, just as you must take chances in war. . . . The ability to get to the verge without getting into the war is the necessary art. If you try to run away from it, if you are scared to go to the brink, you are lost.

JOHN FOSTER DULLES, quoted by James Shepley in *Life* magazine, January 16, 1956.

8 Unless the cause of peace based on law gathers behind it the force and zeal of a religion, it hardly can hope to succeed.

ALBERT EINSTEIN, quoted in the *Atlantic Monthly,* 1947.

9 I say we are going to have peace even if we have to fight for it.

DWIGHT D. EISENHOWER, in a speech at Frankfurt-am-Main, Germany, June 10, 1945.

10 The peace we seek is nothing less than the fulfillment of our whole faith among ourselves and in our dealings with others. This signifies more than the stilling of guns, easing the sorrow of war. More than an escape from death, it is a way of life. More than a haven for the weary, it is a hope for the brave.

DWIGHT D. EISENHOWER, in his first inaugural address, January 20, 1953.

11 Nothing can bring you peace but yourself. Nothing can bring you peace but the triumph of principles.

RALPH WALDO EMERSON, "Self-Reliance," *Essays,* First Series, 1841.

12 The real and lasting victories are those of peace, and not of war.

RALPH WALDO EMERSON, "Worship," *The Conduct of Life,* 1860.

13 The god of Victory is said to be one-handed, but Peace gives victory to both sides.

RALPH WALDO EMERSON, entry written in 1867, *Journals,* 1909–1914.

14 Even peace may be purchased at too high a price.

Attributed to Benjamin Franklin.

15 I have never known a peace made, even the most advantageous, that was not censured as inadequate, and the makers condemned as injudicious or corrupt. "Blessed are the peacemakers" is, I suppose, to be understood in the other world; for in this they are frequently cursed.

BENJAMIN FRANKLIN, in a letter to John Adams, October 12, 1781.

16 May we never see another war! For in my opinion, there never was a good war or a bad peace.

BENJAMIN FRANKLIN, in a letter to Josiah Quincy, September 11, 1783.

17 Let us have peace.

ULYSSES S. GRANT, in his speech accepting the Republican presidential nomination, May 29, 1868.

18 [Peace:] An idea which seems to have originated in Switzerland but has never caught hold in the United States. Supporters of this idea are frequently accused of being unpatriotic and trying to create civil disorder.

DICK GREGORY, *Dick Gregory's Political Primer,* 1972.

19 Peace: A monotonous interval between fights.

ELBERT HUBBARD, *The Roycroft Dictionary and Book of Epigrams,* 1923.

20 Peace and friendship with all mankind is our wisest policy, and I wish we may be permitted to pursue it.

> THOMAS JEFFERSON, in a letter to Charles William Frederick Dumas, May 6, 1786.

21 In this age when there can be no losers in peace and no victors in war, we must recognize the obligation to match national strength with national restraint.

> LYNDON B. JOHNSON, addressing a joint session of Congress, November 27, 1963.

22 No man should think that peace comes easily. Peace does not come by merely wanting it, or shouting for it, or marching down Main Street for it. Peace is built brick by brick, mortared by the stubborn effort and the total energy and imagination of able and dedicated men. And it is built in the living faith that, in the end, man can and will master his own destiny.

> LYNDON B. JOHNSON, *The Vantage Point: Perspectives of the Presidency, 1963–1969,* 1971.

23 Nonviolence is the answer to the crucial political and moral questions of our time; the need for man to overcome oppression and violence without resorting to oppression and violence. Man must evolve for all human conflict a method which rejects revenge, aggression and retaliation. The foundation of such a method is love.

> MARTIN LUTHER KING, JR., in his speech accepting the Nobel Peace Prize, Stockholm, Sweden, December 11, 1964.

24 Peace! and no longer from its brazen portals
　　The blast of War's great organ shakes the
　　　　skies!
But beautiful as songs of the immortals,
　　The holy melodies of love arise.

> HENRY WADSWORTH LONGFELLOW, "The Arsenal at Springfield," 1845.

25 Buried was the bloody hatchet,
Buried was the dreadful war-club,
Buried were all warlike weapons,
And the war-cry was forgotten,
There was peace among the nations.

> HENRY WADSWORTH LONGFELLOW, *The Song of Hiawatha,* 1855.

26 Ef you want peace, the thing you've gut to
　　du
Is jes' to show you're up to fightin', tu.

> JAMES RUSSELL LOWELL, *The Biglow Papers,* Second Series, 1866.

27 Wars are bred by poverty and oppression. Continued peace is possible only in a relatively free and prosperous world.

> Attributed to George C. Marshall.

28 There is only one threat to world peace, the one that is presented by the internationalist communist conspiracy.

> RICHARD M. NIXON, in a commencement address at Whittier College, June 12, 1954.

29 Our goal will be peace. Our instrument for achieving peace will be law and justice. Our hope will be that, under these conditions, the vast energies now devoted to weapons of war will instead be used to clothe, house, and feed the entire world. This is the only goal worthy of our aspirations. Competing in this way, nobody will lose, and mankind will gain.

> RICHARD M. NIXON, in *The Challenges We Face,* 1960.

30 If there must be trouble let it be in my day, that my child may have peace.

> THOMAS PAINE, *The American Crisis,* No. 1, published in the *Pennsylvania Journal,* December 19, 1776.

31 It isn't enough to talk about peace. One must believe in it. And it isn't enough to believe in it. One must work at it.

> ELEANOR ROOSEVELT, in a Voice of America broadcast, November 11, 1951.

32 More than an end to war, we want an end to the beginnings of all wars.

> FRANKLIN D. ROOSEVELT, in a speech intended for broadcast on April 13, 1945. (Roosevelt died the day before.)

33 Peace is normally a great good, and normally it coincides with righteousness, but it is righteousness and not peace which should bind the conscience of

a nation as it should bind the conscience of an individual; and neither a nation nor an individual can surrender conscience to another's keeping.

> THEODORE ROOSEVELT, in his sixth annual message to Congress, December 4, 1906.

34 We should do all in our power to hasten the day when there shall be peace among the nations—a peace based upon justice and not upon cowardly submission to wrong.

> Ibid.

35 For lo! the days are hastening on,
>   By prophet-bards foretold,
> When with the ever-circling years,
>   Comes round the age of gold;
> When Peace shall over all the earth
>   Its ancient splendors fling
> And the whole world send back the song
>   Which now the angels sing.

> EDMUND HAMILTON SEARS, "It Came Upon the Midnight Clear," 1850.

36 Peace is not the work of a single day, nor will it be the consequence of a single act. Yet every constructive act contributes to its growth; every omission impedes it. Peace will come, in the end, if it comes at all, as a child grows to maturity —slowly, imperceptibly, until we realize one day in incredulous surprise that the child is almost grown.

> ADLAI E. STEVENSON, in a speech at New Orleans, December 4, 1954.

37 Our first, our greatest, our most relentless purpose is peace. For without peace there is nothing.

> ADLAI E. STEVENSON, in a speech at Chicago, November 19, 1955.

38 Peace will never be entirely secure until men everywhere have learned to conquer poverty without sacrificing liberty or security.

> Attributed to Norman Thomas.

39 I want peace and I'm willing to fight for it.

> HARRY S TRUMAN, in his diary, May 22, 1945, quoted in Robert H. Ferrell, *Off the Record*, 1980.

40 The Marshall Plan will go down in history as one of America's greatest contributions to the peace of the world.

> HARRY S TRUMAN, "Years of Trial and Hope," from *Memoirs*, 1955.

41 To discerning men, nothing can be more evident, than that a peace on the principles of dependence, however limited . . . would be to the last degree dishonorable and ruinous.

> GEORGE WASHINGTON, in a letter to John Bannister, April 21, 1778.

42 There is nothing so likely to produce peace as to be well prepared to meet an enemy.

> GEORGE WASHINGTON, in a letter to Elbridge Gerry, January 29, 1780.

43 Would to god, the harmony of nations was an object that lay nearest to the hearts of Sovereigns; and that the incentives to peace . . . might be daily encreased!

> GEORGE WASHINGTON, in a letter to the Marquis de Lafayette, January 10, 1788.

44 To be prepared for war is one of the most effectual means of preserving peace.

> GEORGE WASHINGTON, in his first annual message to Congress, January 8, 1790.

45 If we desire to avoid insult, we must be able to repel it; if we desire to secure peace, one of the most powerful instruments of our rising prosperity, it must be known that we are at all times ready for war.

> GEORGE WASHINGTON, in his fifth annual message to Congress, December 3, 1793.

46 Peace with all the world is my sincere wish. I am sure it is our true policy, and am persuaded it is the ardent desire of the government.

> GEORGE WASHINGTON, in a letter to the Rev. Jonathan Boucher, August 15, 1798.

47 Peace is always beautiful.

> WALT WHITMAN, "The Sleepers," 1855.

48 Beautiful that war and all its deeds of
>   carnage must in time be utterly lost,

That the hands of the sisters Death and
    Night incessantly softly wash again, and
    ever again, this soiled world.

> WALT WHITMAN, "Reconciliation," *Drum-Taps,*
> 1865.

49 But dream not helm and harness
    The sign of valor true;
Peace hath higher tests of manhood
    Than battle ever knew.

> JOHN GREENLEAF WHITTIER, "The Hero,"
> 1853.

50 The example of America must be the example
not merely of peace because it will not fight, but of
peace because peace is the healing and elevating
influence of the world, and strife is not. There is
such a thing as a man being too proud to fight.
There is such a thing as a nation being so right that
it does not need to convince others by force that it
is right.

> WOODROW WILSON, in a speech in Convention
> Hall, Philadelphia, May 10, 1915.

51 There is a price which is too great to pay for
peace, and that price can be put in one word. One
cannot pay the price of self-respect.

> WOODROW WILSON, in a speech in Des Moines,
> Iowa, February 1, 1916.

52 There must be, not a balance of power, but a
community of power; not organized rivalries, but
an organized common peace.

> WOODROW WILSON, in an address before the
> U.S. Senate, January 22, 1917.

53 A steadfast concert for peace can never be maintained except by a partnership of democratic nations.

> WOODROW WILSON, in his war message to
> Congress, April 2, 1917.

54 Open covenants of peace, openly arrived at.

> WOODROW WILSON, the beginning of the first of
> his Fourteen Points, in his message to Congress,
> January 8, 1918.

182. PENNSYLVANIA

1 Virtue, liberty and independence.

> State motto.

2 Pennsylvania is the keystone of the democratic
arch.

> Pennsylvania Democratic Committee, 1803.

3 [In colonial Pennsylvania] they have no lawyers.
Everyone is to tell his own case, or some friend for
him. . . . 'Tis a blessed country.

> An anonymous European visitor, quoted in
> Francis R. Aumann, *The Colonial Legal System,*
> 1940.

4 The Pennsylvania mind, as minds go, was not
complex; it reasoned little and never talked; but in
practical matters it was the steadiest of all American types; perhaps the most efficient; certainly the
safest.

> HENRY ADAMS, *The Education of Henry Adams,*
> 1918.

5 As to the Philadelphians, damnation seize them,
body and soul!

> WILLIAM COBBETT, in a letter to William
> Thornton, 1800.

6 Nowhere in this country, from sea to sea, does
nature comfort us with such assurance of plenty,
such rich and tranquil beauty as in those unsung,
unpainted hills of Pennsylvania.

> REBECCA HARDING DAVIS, *Bits of Gossip,*
> 1904.

7 [Philadelphia] is a handsome city, but distractingly regular. After walking about it for an hour or
two, I felt that I would have given the world for
a crooked street.

> CHARLES DICKENS, *American Notes,* 1842.

8 Pittsburgh is like Birmingham in England; at
least its townspeople say so. Setting aside the
streets, the shops, the houses, wagons, factories,
public buildings, and population, perhaps it may be.

It certainly has a great quantity of smoke hanging around it, and is famous for its ironworks.

> Ibid.

9 On the whole I'd rather be in Philadelphia.

> Attributed to W.C. Fields, a proposed inscription for his tombstone.

10 Pennsylvania had produced but two great men: Benjamin Franklin, of Massachusetts, and Albert Gallatin, of Switzerland.

> Attributed to John James Ingalls.

11 The cradle of toleration and freedom of religion.

> THOMAS JEFFERSON, in a letter to Thomas Cooper, November 2, 1822.

12 Philadelphia is so admirably supplied with water from the Schuykill waterworks that every house has it laid on from the attic to the basement; and all day long they wash windows, doors, marble steps, and pavements in front of the houses. Indeed they have so much water that they can afford to be very liberal to passers-by.

> FREDERICK MARRYAT, *A Diary in America,* 1839.

13 After many waitings, watchings, solicitings, and disputes in Council, this day my country was confirmed to me under the great seal of England, with large powers and privileges, by the name of Pennsylvania, a name the king would give it in honor of my father.

> WILLIAM PENN, in a letter to Robert Turner, March 14, 1681.

14 Philadelphia, a metropolis sometimes known as the City of Brotherly Love, but more accurately as the City of Bleak November Afternoons.

> S.J. PERELMAN, *Westward Ha!* 1948.

15 Six months' residence here would justify suicide.

> HERBERT SPENCER, during a visit to Pittsburgh with Andrew Carnegie, September 18–19, 1882.

183. PERCEPTION

See also EXPERIENCE; KNOWLEDGE; PHILOSOPHY; WISDOM

1 An optimist sees opportunity in every calamity. A pessimist sees calamity in every opportunity.

> Anonymous.

2 All the world is queer but me and thee, dear; and sometimes I think thee is a little queer.

> Attributed to a Quaker addressing his wife.

3 I really believe there are things nobody would see if I didn't photograph them.

> DIANE ARBUS, in *Diane Arbus,* 1972.

4 Cynic, *n.* A blackguard whose faulty vision sees things as they are, not as they ought to be.

> AMBROSE BIERCE, *The Devil's Dictionary,* 1906.

5 Mind, *n.* A mysterious form of matter secreted by the brain. Its chief activity consists in the endeavor to ascertain its own nature, the futility of the attempt being due to the fact that it has nothing but itself to know itself with.

> Ibid.

6 Optimist, *n.* A proponent of the doctrine that black is white.

> Ibid.

7 Positivism, *n.* A philosophy that denies our knowledge of the Real and affirms our ignorance of the Apparent.

> Ibid.

8 Reality, *n.* The dream of a mad philosopher.

> Ibid.

9 Understanding, *n.* A cerebral secretion that enables one having it to know a house from a horse by the roof on the house. Its nature and laws have been exhaustively expounded by Locke, who rode a house, and Kant, who lived in a horse.

> Ibid.

10 The optimist proclaims that we live in the best of all possible worlds; and the pessimist fears this is true.

JAMES BRANCH CABELL, *The Silver Stallion*, 1926.

11 We can all perceive the difference between ourselves and our inferiors, but when it comes to a question of the difference between us and our superiors we fail to appreciate merits of which we have no proper conceptions.

JAMES FENIMORE COOPER, *The American Democrat*, 1838.

12 I never saw a Moor—
I never saw the Sea—
Yet know I how the Heather looks
And what a Billow be.

EMILY DICKINSON, *Poems*, 1890.

13 The mind, let it stretch its conceptions ever so far, can never so much as bring itself to conceive of a state of perfect nothing.

JONATHAN EDWARDS, "Notes on Natural Science," written c.1718.

14 The least change in our point of view gives the whole world a pictorial air. A man who seldom rides needs only to get into a coach and traverse his own town, to turn the street into a puppet-show.

RALPH WALDO EMERSON, *Nature*, 1836.

15 The world is his who can see through its pretension.

RALPH WALDO EMERSON, in a Phi Beta Kappa oration delivered August 31, 1837.

16 Good and bad are but names very readily transferable to that or this.

RALPH WALDO EMERSON, "Self-Reliance," *Essays*, First Series, 1841.

17 Every excess causes a defect; every defect an excess. Every sweet hath its sour; every evil its good. Every faculty which is a receiver of pleasure has an equal penalty put on its abuse. It is to answer for its moderation with its life.

RALPH WALDO EMERSON, "Compensation," *Essays*, First Series, 1841.

18 One man's justice is another's injustice; one man's beauty another's ugliness; one man's wisdom another's folly.

RALPH WALDO EMERSON, "Circles," *Essays*, First Series, 1841.

19 How can we speak of the action of the mind under any divisions, as of its knowledge, of its ethics, of its works, and so forth, since it melts will into perception, knowledge into act? Each becomes the other. Itself alone is.

RALPH WALDO EMERSON, "Intellect," *Essays*, First Series, 1841.

20 Nothing astonishes men so much as common sense and plain dealing.

RALPH WALDO EMERSON, "Art," *Essays*, First Series, 1841.

21 The new molecular philosophy shows astronomical interspaces betwixt atom and atom, shows that the world is all outside; it has no inside.

RALPH WALDO EMERSON, "Experience," *Essays*, Second Series, 1844.

22 I suppose you could never prove to the mind of the most ingenious mollusk that such a creature as a whale was possible.

RALPH WALDO EMERSON, entry written in May, 1848, *Journals*, 1909–1914.

23 Fancy is a wilful, imagination a spontaneous act; fancy, a play as with dolls and puppets which we choose to call men and women; imagination, a perception and affirming of a real relation between a thought and some material fact. Fancy amuses; imagination expands and exalts us.

RALPH WALDO EMERSON, "Poetry and Imagination," *Letters and Social Aims*, 1876.

24 What is a weed? A plant whose virtues have not yet been discovered.

RALPH WALDO EMERSON, *Fortune of the Republic*, 1878.

25 The illusion that times that were are better than those that are, has probably pervaded all ages.

HORACE GREELEY, *The American Conflict*, 1864–1866.

26 We must think things, not words.

> OLIVER WENDELL HOLMES, JR., 1899, quoted in
> Catherine Drinker Bowen, *Yankee from
> Olympus,* 1944.

27 An idea that is not dangerous is unworthy of
being called an idea at all.

> ELBERT HUBBARD, *The Roycroft Dictionary and
> Book of Epigrams,* 1923.

28 As in the night all cats are gray, so in the darkness of metaphysical criticism all causes are obscure.

> WILLIAM JAMES, *The Principles of Psychology,*
> 1890.

29 [Consciousness] is nothing jointed; it flows. A
"river" or a "stream" is the metaphor by which it
is most naturally described. *In talking of it hereafter, let us call it the stream of thought, of consciousness, or of subjective life.*

> Ibid.

30 The blindness in human beings . . . is the blindness with which we all are afflicted in regard to the
feelings of creatures and people different from ourselves.

> WILLIAM JAMES, "On a Certain Blindness in
> Human Beings," an address published in *Talks to
> Teachers on Pyschology,* 1899.

31 An idea, to be suggestive, must come to the
individual with the force of a revelation.

> WILLIAM JAMES, *The Varieties of Religious
> Experience,* 1902.

32 A sensation is rather like a client who has given
his case to a lawyer and then has passively to listen
in the courtroom to whatever account of his affairs,
pleasant or unpleasant, the lawyer finds it most
expedient to give.

> WILLIAM JAMES, *Pragmatism,* 1907.

33 The moment a person forms a theory, his imagination sees, in every object, only the traits which
favor that theory.

> THOMAS JEFFERSON, in a letter to Charles
> Thomson, September 20, 1787.

34 I see a green tree. And to me it is green. And
you would call the tree green also. And we would
agree on this. But is the color you see as green the
same color I see as green? Or say we both call a
color black. But how do we know that what you see
as black is the same color I see as black?

> CARSON MCCULLERS, *The Member of the
> Wedding,* 1946.

35 To enjoy bodily warmth, some small part of you
must be cold, for there is no quality in this world
that is not what it is merely by contrast. Nothing
exists in itself. If you flatter yourself that you are
all over comfortable, and have been so a long time,
then you cannot be said to be comfortable any
more.

> HERMAN MELVILLE, *Moby-Dick,* 1851.

36 One step above the sublime makes the ridiculous, and one step above the ridiculous makes the
sublime again.

> THOMAS PAINE, *The Age of Reason,* 1794–1795.

37 Rosiness is not a worse windowpane than
gloomy gray when viewing the world.

> GRACE PALEY, *Enormous Changes at the Last
> Minute,* 1960.

38 All that we see or seem
Is but a dream within a dream.

> EDGAR ALLAN POE, "A Dream Within a
> Dream," 1827.

39 The worm's eye point of view.

> ERNIE PYLE, in *Here Is Your War,* 1943.

40 It is a very lonely life that a man leads, who
becomes aware of truths before their time.

> THOMAS BRACKETT REED, in an address c.1899,
> quoted in William Alexander Robinson, *Thomas
> B. Reed, Parliamentarian,* 1930.

41 Everything we do not know anything about always looks big. The human creature is imaginative.
If he sees a tail disappearing over a fence, he images
the whole beast and usually images the wrong
beast. . . . Whenever we take a trip into the realms
of fancy, we see a good many things that never
were.

THOMAS BRACKETT REED, quoted in Samuel Walker McCall, *The Life of Thomas Brackett Reed,* 1914.

42 An ideal cannot wait for its realization to prove its validity.

GEORGE SANTAYANA, *The Life of Reason,* 1905.

43 In imagination, not in perception, lies the substance of experience, while knowledge and reason are but its chastened and ultimate form.

Ibid.

44 Rose is a rose is a rose is a rose.

GERTRUDE STEIN, "Sacred Emily," 1913.

45 Thinking implies disagreement; and disagreement implies nonconformity; and nonconformity implies heresy; and heresy implies disloyalty—so, obviously, thinking must be stopped.

ADLAI E. STEVENSON, *Call to Greatness,* 1954.

46 The perception of beauty is a moral test.

HENRY DAVID THOREAU, entry dated June 21, 1852, in his *Journal,* 1906.

47 Honor wears different coats to different eyes.

BARBARA TUCHMAN, *The Guns of August,* 1962.

48 Nothing out of its place is good and nothing in its place is bad.

WALT WHITMAN, in the preface to *Leaves of Grass,* 1855.

49 Every cubic inch of space is a miracle.

WALT WHITMAN, "Miracles," 1881.

---

184. PHILOSOPHY

See also EXPERIENCE; KNOWLEDGE; PERCEPTION; RELIGION; WISDOM

---

1 One who knows less and less about more and more.

Definition of a philosopher.

2 My definition [of a philosopher] is of a man up in a balloon, with his family and friends holding the ropes which confine him to the earth and trying to haul him down.

LOUISA MAY ALCOTT, quoted in Edna D. Cheney, *Louisa May Alcott: Her Life, Letters and Journals,* 1889.

3 It is a very good world for the purposes for which it was built; and that is all anything is good for.

HENRY WARD BEECHER, *Royal Truths,* 1866.

4 Philosophy, *n.* A route of many roads leading from nowhere to nothing.

AMBROSE BIERCE, *The Devil's Dictionary,* 1906.

5 Reason is experimental intelligence, conceived after the pattern of science, and used in the creation of social arts; it has something to do. It liberates man from the bondage of the past, due to ignorance and accident hardened into custom. It projects a better future and assists man in its realization. And its operation is always subject to test in experience. . . . Intelligence is not something possessed once for all. It is in constant process of forming, and its retention requires constant alertness in observing consequences, an open-minded will to learn and courage in re-adjustment.

JOHN DEWEY, *Reconstruction in Philosophy,* 1920.

6 Philosophy accepts the hard and hazardous task of dealing with problems not yet open to the methods of science—problems like good and evil, beauty and ugliness, order and freedom, life and death.

WILL DURANT, *The Story of Philosophy,* 1926.

7 Beware when the great God lets loose a thinker on this planet.

RALPH WALDO EMERSON, "Circles," *Essays,* First Series, 1841.

8 There is no philosopher who is a philosopher at all times.

RALPH WALDO EMERSON, "The Conservative," 1842, published in *Nature; Addresses and Lectures,* 1849.

9 Philosophy is the account which the mind gives to itself of the constitution of the world.

RALPH WALDO EMERSON, "Plato,"
Representative Men, 1850.

10 Great men are they who see that spiritual is stronger than any material force, that thoughts rule the world.

RALPH WALDO EMERSON, "Progress of Culture," an address given July 18, 1867, published in *Letters and Social Aims,* 1876.

11 A philosophy requiring a large volume is too much; a hundred pages is enough.

EDGAR WATSON HOWE, *Preaching from the Audience,* 1926.

12 Metaphysics: 1. An attempt to define a thing and by so doing escape the bother of understanding it. 2. The explanation of a thing by a person who does not understand it.

ELBERT HUBBARD, *The Roycroft Dictionary and Book of Epigrams,* 1923.

13 Philosophy: Our highest conception of life, its duties and its destinies.

Ibid.

14 All our scientific and philosophic ideals are altars to unknown gods.

WILLIAM JAMES, "The Dilemma of Determinism," in the *Unitarian Review,* September, 1884.

15 The philosophic climate of our time inevitably forces its own clothing on us.

WILLIAM JAMES, *The Varieties of Religious Experience,* 1902.

16 [Consciousness] is the name of a nonentity, and has no right to a place among first principles. Those who still cling to it are clinging to a mere echo, the faint rumor left behind by the disappearing "soul" upon the air of philosophy.

WILLIAM JAMES, *Essays in Radical Empiricism,* 1912.

17 I too am an Epicurean. I consider the genuine (not the imputed) doctrines of Epicurus as containing everything rational in moral philosophy which Greece and Rome have left us.

THOMAS JEFFERSON, in a letter to William Short, October 31, 1819.

18 There are philosophies which are unendurable not because men are cowards, but because they are men.

LUDWIG LEWISOHN, *The Modern Drama,* 1915.

19 When men can no longer be theists, they must, if they are civilized, become humanists.

WALTER LIPPMANN, *A Preface to Morals,* 1929.

20 I have a simple philosophy. Fill what's empty. Empty what's full. And scratch where it itches.

ALICE ROOSEVELT LONGWORTH, quoted in Peter Russell and Leonard Ross, *The Best,* 1974.

21 Philosophy drips gently from his tongue
Who hath three meals a day in guarantee.

CHRISTOPHER MORLEY, "So This Is Arden," in *Parson's Pleasure,* 1923.

22 Between the laughing and the weeping philosopher there is no opposition: *the same facts* that make one laugh make one weep. No whole-hearted man, no sane art, can be limited to either mood.

GEORGE SANTAYANA, *Persons and Places,* 1944–1953.

23 To be a philosopher is not merely to have subtle thoughts, nor even to found a school, but so to love wisdom as to live according to its dictates, a life of simplicity, independence, magnanimity, and trust.

HENRY DAVID THOREAU, *Walden,* 1854.

---

185. THE POET

See also BOOKS; LITERATURE; POETRY; WRITERS

---

1 You will never be alone with a poet in your pocket.

JOHN ADAMS, in a letter to John Quincy Adams, May 14, 1781.

2 Nobody loves a poet.

> IRVING BABBITT, *Rousseau and Romanticism,*
> 1919.

3 I reckon, when I count at all,
First Poets—then the Sun—
Then Summer—then the Heaven of God—
And then the list is done.
But looking back—the first so seems
To comprehend the whole—
The others look a needless show,
So I write Poets—All.

> EMILY DICKINSON, *Further Poems,* 1929.

4 To the poet, to the philosopher, to the saint, all
things are friendly and sacred, all events profitable,
all days holy, all men divine.

> RALPH WALDO EMERSON, "History," *Essays,*
> First Series, 1841.

5 Homer's words are as costly and admirable to
Homer as Agamemnon's victories are to Agamemnon.

> RALPH WALDO EMERSON, "The Poet," *Essays,*
> Second Series, 1844.

6 The sign and credentials of the poet are that he
announces that which no man foretold.

> Ibid.

7 The experience of each new age requires a new
confession, and the world seems always waiting for
its poet.

> Ibid.

8 All men are poets at heart. They serve nature for
bread, but her loveliness overcomes them sometimes.

> RALPH WALDO EMERSON, "Literary Ethics,"
> *Nature; Addresses and Lectures,* 1849.

9 Sunshine cannot bleach the snow,
Nor time unmake what poets know.

> RALPH WALDO EMERSON, "The Test," published
> in the *Atlantic Monthly,* January, 1861.

10 There was never poet who had not the heart in
the right place.

> RALPH WALDO EMERSON, "Success," *Society and
> Solitude,* 1870.

11 The poet is never the poorer for his song.

> RALPH WALDO EMERSON, "Works and Days,"
> *Society and Solitude,* 1870.

12 There are two classes of poets—the poets by
education and practice, these we respect; and poets
by nature, these we love.

> RALPH WALDO EMERSON, *Parnassus,* 1874.

13 The test of the poet is the power to take the
passing day, with its news, its cares, its fears, as he
shares them, and hold it up to a divine reason, till
he sees it to have a purpose and beauty. . . . Then
the dry twig blossoms in his hand.

> RALPH WALDO EMERSON, "Poetry and
> Imagination," *Letters and Social Aims,* 1876.

14 The poet gives us the eminent experiences
only,—a god stepping from peak to peak, nor planting his foot but on a mountain.

> Ibid.

15 [Ezra] Pound's crazy. All poets are. . . . They
have to be. You don't put a poet like Pound in the
loony bin. For history's sake we shouldn't keep him
there.

> ERNEST HEMINGWAY, commenting on Pound's
> incarceration in St. Elizabeths Hospital in
> Washington, D.C., quoted by Leonard Lyons in
> the *New York Post,* January 24, 1957.

16 We call those poets who are first to mark
Through earth's dull mist the coming of the
dawn,—
Who see in twilight's gloom the first pale
spark,
While others only note that day is gone.

> OLIVER WENDELL HOLMES, SR., "Shakespeare,"
> 1864.

17 There is no mere earthly immortality that I
envy so much as the poet's. If your name is to live
at all, it is so much better to have it live in people's
hearts than only in their brains!

> OLIVER WENDELL HOLMES, SR., *The Poet at the
> Breakfast-Table,* 1872.

18 Poets are prophets whose prophesying never
comes true.

Edgar Watson Howe, *Country Town Sayings,* 1911.

19 Poet: A person born with the instinct to poverty.

Elbert Hubbard, *The Roycroft Dictionary and Book of Epigrams,* 1923.

20 Next to being a great poet, is the power of understanding one.

Henry Wadsworth Longfellow, *Hyperion,* 1839.

21 The bards sublime,
  Whose distant footsteps echo
  Through the corridors of Time.

Henry Wadsworth Longfellow, "The Day Is Done," 1845.

22 Read from some humbler poet,
  Whose songs gushed from his heart,
  As showers from the clouds of summer,
  Or tears from the eyelids start.

Ibid.

23 All that is best in the great poets of all countries is not what is national in them, but what is universal.

Henry Wadsworth Longfellow, *Kavanagh,* 1849.

24 For voices pursue him by day,
  And haunt him by night,
  And he listens, and needs must obey,
  When the Angel says, "Write!"

Henry Wadsworth Longfellow, "L'Envoi," *Ultima Thule,* 1880.

25 Could I but speak it and show it,
  This pleasure more sharp than pain,
  That baffles and lures me so,
  The world should once more have a poet,
  Such as it had
  In the ages glad, Long ago!

James Russell Lowell, "In the Twilight," published in the *Atlantic Monthly,* January, 1868.

26 gods i am pent in a cockroach
  i with the soul of a dante
  am mate and companion of fleas

i with the gift of a homer
must smile when a mouse calls me pal
tumble bugs are my familiars
this is the punishment meted
because i have written vers libre

Don Marquis, "the wail of archy," *archy and mehitabel,* 1927.

27 Nine-tenths of the best poetry of the world has been written by poets less than thirty years old; a great deal more than half of it has been written by poets under twenty-five.

H.L. Mencken, *Prejudices,* Third Series, 1922.

28 Blake, Homer, Job, and you,
  Have made old wine-skins new.
  Your energies have wrought
  Stout continents of thought.

Marianne Moore, "That Harp You Play So Well," 1915.

29 The degree in which a poet's imagination dominates reality is, in the end, the exact measure of his importance and dignity.

George Santayana, *The Life of Reason,* 1905–1906.

30 The poet who does not revere his art, and believe in its sovereignty, is not born to wear the purple.

Edmund Clarence Stedman, *The Poets of America,* 1885.

31 A poet looks at the world as a man looks at a woman.

Wallace Stevens, "Adagia," in *Opus Posthumous,* 1957.

32 The poet speaks only those thoughts that come unbidden like the wind that stirs the trees—and men cannot help but listen. He is not listened to but heard.

Henry David Thoreau, entry dated May 9, 1841, in his *Journal,* 1906.

33 An old poet comes at last to watching his moods as narrowly as a cat does a mouse.

Henry David Thoreau, entry dated August 28, 1851, in his *Journal,* 1906.

34 The proof of a poet is that his country absorbs him as affectionately as he has absorbed it.

> WALT WHITMAN, in his preface to *Leaves of Grass*, 1855.

35 [The poet] judges not as the judge judges but as the sun falling around a helpless thing.

> Ibid.

36 I sound my barbaric yawp over the roofs of the world.

> WALT WHITMAN, "Song of Myself," 1855.

186. POETRY

See also BOOKS; LITERATURE; POET; WRITERS

1 Poetry is that art which selects and arranges the symbols of thought in such a manner as to excite the imagination the most powerfully and delightfully.

> WILLIAM CULLEN BRYANT, in a lecture, "The Nature of Poetry," April, 1825.

2 Poetry is the worst mask in the world behind which folly and stupidity could attempt to hide their features.

> Ibid.

3 In my own experience of the appreciation of poetry I have always found that the less I knew about the poet and his work, before I began to read it, the better.

> T.S. ELIOT, *Dante*, 1929.

4 The true poem is the poet's mind.

> RALPH WALDO EMERSON, "History," *Essays*, First Series, 1841.

5 Poetry must be as new as foam, and as old as the rock.

> RALPH WALDO EMERSON, entry written in March, 1845, *Journals*, 1909–1914.

6 The finest poetry was first experience.

> RALPH WALDO EMERSON, "Shakespeare," *Representative Men*, 1850.

7 Poetry teaches the enormous force of a few words.

> RALPH WALDO EMERSON, *Parnassus*, 1874.

8 Poetry is a way of taking life by the throat.

> Attributed to Robert Frost.

9 Writing free verse is like playing tennis with the net down.

> ROBERT FROST, in a talk at the Milton [Massachusetts] Academy, May, 17, 1935.

10 Like a piece of ice on a hot stove a poem must ride on its own melting. A poem may be worked over once it is in being, but may not be worried into being.

> ROBERT FROST, in the introduction to his *Collected Poems*, 1939.

11 When a thought takes one's breath away, a lesson on grammar seems an impertinence.

> THOMAS WENTWORTH HIGGINSON, in the preface to Emily Dickinson's *Poems*, 1890.

12 A poem is no place for an idea.

> EDGAR WATSON HOWE, *Country Town Sayings*, 1911.

13 Poetry is the bill and coo of sex.

> ELBERT HUBBARD, *The Roycroft Dictionary and Book of Epigrams*, 1923.

14 When power leads man toward arrogance, poetry reminds him of his limitations. When power narrows the areas of man's concern, poetry reminds him of the richness and diversity of his existence. When power corrupts, poetry cleanses, for art establishes the basic human truths which must serve as the touchstone of our judgment.

> JOHN F. KENNEDY, in a speech at Amherst College, October 26, 1963.

15 Glorious indeed is the world of God around us, but more glorious the world of God within us. There lies the Land of Song; there lies the poet's native land.

HENRY WADSWORTH LONGFELLOW, *Hyperion,* 1839.

16 Great is the art of beginning, but greater the
      art is of ending;
   Many a poem is marred by a superfluous
      verse.

   HENRY WADSWORTH LONGFELLOW, "Elegiac
   Verse," 1881.

17 A poem should not mean
   But be.

   ARCHIBALD MACLEISH, *Ars Poetica,* 1926.

18 Poetry is a comforting piece of fiction set to
   more or less lascivious music.

   H.L. MENCKEN, *Prejudices,* Third Series,
   1922.

19 Poetry has done enough when it charms, but
   prose must also convince.

   Ibid.

20 Poetry, men attain
   By subtler pain
   More flagrant in the brain—
   An honesty unfeigned,
   A heart unchained,
   A madness well restrained.

   CHRISTOPHER MORLEY, "At the Mermaid
   Cafeteria," in *Chimneysmoke,* 1921.

21 With me poetry has been not a purpose, but a
   passion; and the passions should be held in reverence: they must not—they cannot at will be excited, with an eye to the paltry compensations, or
   the more paltry commendations, of mankind.

   EDGAR ALLAN POE, in his preface to *The Raven
   and Other Poems,* 1845.

22 I hold that a long poem does not exist. I maintain that the phrase "a long poem" is simply a flat
   contradiction in terms.

   EDGAR ALLAN POE, "The Poetic Principle,"
   1850.

23 I would define, in brief, the Poetry of words as
   the Rhythmical Creation of Beauty. Its sole arbiter
   is Taste. With the Intellect or with the Conscience

it has only collateral relations. Unless incidentally,
it has no concern whatever either with Duty or
with Truth.

   Ibid.

24 Poetry atrophies when it gets too far from
   music.

   EZRA POUND, *How to Read,* 1931.

25 Poetry is the journal of a sea animal living on
   land, wanting to fly in the air. Poetry is a search for
   syllables to shoot at the barriers of the unknown
   and the unknowable. Poetry is a phantom script
   telling how rainbows are made and why they go
   away.

   CARL SANDBURG, "Poetry Considered," in the
   Atlantic Monthly, March, 1923.

26 Poetry is an art, and chief of the fine arts: the
   easiest to dabble in, the hardest in which to reach
   true excellence.

   EDMUND CLARENCE STEDMAN, *Victorian Poets,*
   1887.

27 Poetry must resist the intelligence almost successfully.

   WALLACE STEVENS, "Adagia," *Opus Posthumous,*
   1957.

28 My life hath been the poem I would have
      writ,
   But I could not both live, and live to utter it.

   HENRY DAVID THOREAU, entry dated August 28,
   1841, in his *Journal,* 1906.

29 It is the characteristic of great poems that they
   will yield of their sense in due proportion to the
   hasty and the deliberate reader. To the practical
   they will be common sense, and to the wise wisdom; as either the traveler may wet his lips, or an
   army may fill its water-casks at a full stream.

   HENRY DAVID THOREAU, *A Week on the
   Concord and Merrimack Rivers,* 1849.

30 Poetry implies the whole truth, philosophy expresses a particle of it.

   HENRY DAVID THOREAU, entry dated June 26,
   1852, in his *Journal,* 1906.

31 The works of the great poets have never yet been read by mankind, for only great poets can read them. They have only been read as the multitude have read the stars, at most astrologically, not astronomically.

> HENRY DAVID THOREAU, "Reading," *Walden,* 1854.

32 That may be very good Dutch Flat poetry, but it won't do in the metropolis. It is too smooth and blubbery; it reads like buttermilk gurgling from a jug.

> MARK TWAIN, "Answers to Correspondents," *Sketches New and Old,* 1875.

33 I think there is no such thing as a long poem. If it is long it isn't a poem; it is something else. A book like *John Brown's Body,* for instance, is not a poem—it is a series of poems tied together with cord. Poetry is intensity, and nothing is intense for long.

> E.B. WHITE, "Poetry," *One Man's Meat,* 1944.

34   I love the old melodious lays
  Which softly melt the ages through,
     The songs of Spenser's golden days,
  Arcadian Sidney's silver phrase,
     Sprinkling our noon of time with freshest
        morning dew.

> JOHN GREENLEAF WHITTIER, in the proem to *Poems,* 1849.

---

187. POLITICS

See also CONGRESS; CONSTITUTION; DEMOCRACY; DIPLOMACY; ELECTIONS; GOVERNMENT

---

1 Will it play in Peoria?

> Traditional rhetorical question of American politics (implying that a political action, in order to work, must have the support of the citizens of the so-called average American town).

2 A mugwump is a fellow with his mug on one side of the fence and his wump on the other.

> Political saying, describing Republicans who crossed party lines and supported Grover Cleveland, the Democratic candidate, in the presidential election of 1884.

3 The trend of Democracy is toward socialism, while the Republican party stands for a wise and regulated individualism. Socialism would destroy wealth; Republicanism would prevent its abuse. Socialism would give to each an equal right to take; Republicanism would give to each an equal right to earn. Socialism would offer an equality of possession which would soon leave no one anything to possess; Republicanism would give equality of opportunity.

> Plank of the Republican Party national platform, 1908.

4 Liberals! They're not leaders! If they were real leaders they'd understand that their style of politicking and self-aggrandizement is what's destroying the capacity of any of us to get anywhere.

> BELLA ABZUG, quoted in Mel Ziegler, *Bella!* 1972.

5 The establishment is made up of little men, very frightened.

> Ibid.

6 Knowledge of human nature is the beginning and end of political education.

> HENRY ADAMS, *The Education of Henry Adams,* 1907.

7 Modern politics is, at bottom, a struggle not of men but of forces.

> Ibid.

8 I agree with you that in politics the middle way is none at all.

> JOHN ADAMS, in a letter to Horatio Gates, March 23, 1776.

9 No sooner has one Party discovered or invented an Amelioration of the Condition of Man or the order of Society, than the opposite Party belies it, misconstrues it, misrepresents it, ridicules it, insults it, and persecutes it.

> JOHN ADAMS, in a letter to Thomas Jefferson, July 9, 1813.

10 Politics, *n.* A strife of interests masquerading as a contest of principles. The conduct of public affairs for private advantage.

AMBROSE BIERCE, *The Devil's Dictionary,* 1906.

11 Politician, *n.* An eel in the fundamental mud upon which the superstructure of organized society is reared. When he wriggles he mistakes the agitation of his tail for the trembling of the edifice. As compared with the statesman, he suffers the disadvantage of being alive.

Ibid.

12 Stalwart Republicans.

JAMES G. BLAINE, describing a faction within the Republican Party known for political patronage and domination of the civil service, 1877.

13 A liberal is a man who leaves the room when the fight starts.

HEYWOOD BROUN, quoted in Robert E. Drennan, *The Algonquin Wits,* 1968.

14 It is into the hands of the parties that the working of the government has fallen. Their ingenuity, stimulated by incessant rivalry, has turned many provisions of the Constitution to unforeseen uses, and given to the legal institutions of the country no small part of their present color.

JAMES BRYCE, *The American Commonwealth,* 1888.

15 The American parties now continue to exist, because they have existed. The mill has been constructed, and its machinery goes on turning, even when there is no grist to grind.

Ibid.

16 Blindfold me, spin me about like a top, and I will walk up to the single liberal in the room without zig or zag and find him even if he is hiding behind the flowerpot.

WILLIAM F. BUCKLEY, JR., "Notes Toward an Empirical Definition of Conservatism," October, 1963.

17 We are Republicans, and don't propose to leave our party and identify ourselves with the party whose antecedents have been Rum, Romanism, and Rebellion.

SAMUEL D. BURCHARD, to James G. Blaine, October 29, 1884.

18 The Democratic party is like a man riding backward in a carriage. It never sees a thing until it has gone by.

Attributed to Benjamin F. Butler, c.1870.

19 [Ronald] Reagan is different from me in almost every basic element of commitment and experience and promise to the American people, and the Republican party now is sharply different from what the Democratic party is. And I might add parenthetically that the Republican party is sharply different under Reagan from what it was under Gerald Ford and Presidents all the way back to Eisenhower.

JIMMY CARTER, speaking in Independence, Missouri, September 2, 1980.

20 We shall not note our increase of virtue too much by seeing more crooks in Sing Sing, as by seeing fewer of them in drawing rooms.

JOHN JAY CHAPMAN, in the periodical *The Political Nursery,* published between 1897–1901.

21 A politician thinks of the next election; a statesman thinks of the next generation.

Attributed to James Freeman Clarke.

22 The other side can have a monopoly of all the dirt in this campaign.

GROVER CLEVELAND, comment made while destroying documents gathered to smear James G. Blaine, during the 1884 Presidential campaign, quoted in Allan Nevins, *Grover Cleveland,* 1932.

23 Party honesty is party expediency.

GROVER CLEVELAND, quoted in the *New York Commercial Advertiser,* September 19, 1889.

24 Contact with the affairs of state is one of the most corrupting of the influences to which men are exposed.

JAMES FENIMORE COOPER, *The American Democrat,* 1838.

25 The demagogue is usually sly, a detractor of others, a professor of humility and disinterestedness, a great stickler for equality as respects all

above him, a man who acts in corners, and avoids open and manly expositions of his course, calls blackguards gentlemen, and gentlemen folks, appeals to passions and prejudices rather than to reason, and is in all respects, a man of intrigue and deception, of sly cunning and management.

> Ibid.

26 Party leads to vicious, corrupt and unprofitable legislation, for the sole purpose of defeating party.

> Ibid.

27 You may say for me that offices will be held by politicians.

> RICHARD CROKER, boss of Tammany Hall, speaking to the press after a New York City mayoral election, January 4, 1893.

28 a politician is an arse upon which everyone
> has sat except a man.

> E.E. CUMMINGS, "a politician," in *1 x 1,* 1944.

29 The difference between Democrats and Republicans has always been measured in courage and confidence. The Republicans believe the wagon train will not make it to the frontier unless some of our old, some of our young, and some of our weak are left behind by the side of the trail. The strong will inherit the land! We Democrats believe that we can make it all the way with the whole family intact.

> MARIO CUOMO, in the keynote address to the Democratic National Convention, July 16, 1984.

30 We believe that while survival of the fittest may be a good working description of the process of evolution, a government of humans should elevate itself to a higher order, one which fills the gaps left by chance or a wisdom we don't understand.

> Ibid.

31 The Democratic party is like a mule. It has neither pride of ancestry nor hope of posterity.

> IGNATIUS DONNELLY, in a speech in the Minnesota Legislature, 1860.

32 Such pipsqueaks as [Richard M.] Nixon and [Joseph R.] McCarthy are trying to get us so frightened of Communism that we'll be afraid to turn out the lights at night.

> HELEN GAHAGAN DOUGLAS, 1950, quoted by Lee Israel in *Ms.* magazine, October, 1973.

33 Th' dimmycratic party ain't on speakin' terms with itsilf.

> FINLEY PETER DUNNE, *Mr. Dooley's Opinions,* 1900.

34 I think we ought to let him hang there. Let him twist slowly, slowly in the wind.

> JOHN EHRLICHMAN, speaking to White House counsel John Dean about acting FBI director L. Patrick Gray, early in the investigation of the Watergate scandal, March 7–8, 1973. (Gray resigned a month later, after it was revealed that he had destroyed documents given him by Dean.)

35 My life is a mixture of politics and war. The latter is bad enough—but I've been trained for it! The former is straight and unadulterated venom! But I have to devote lots of my time, and much more of my good disposition, to it.

> DWIGHT D. EISENHOWER, in a letter to Mamie Doud Eisenhower, September 27, 1943.

36 Many people seem astounded that I'd have no slightest interest in politics. I can't understand them.

> DWIGHT D. EISENHOWER, in a letter to Mamie Doud Eisenhower, May 23, 1945.

37 Politics is a profession; a serious, complicated and, in its true sense, a noble one.

> DWIGHT D. EISENHOWER, in a letter to Leonard V. Finder, January 22, 1948.

38 Politics . . . excites all that is selfish and ambitious in man.

> DWIGHT D. EISENHOWER, in a letter to Sid Richardson, June 20, 1951.

39 A Sect or Party is an elegant incognito, devised to save a man from the vexation of thinking.

> RALPH WALDO EMERSON, entry written in June, 1831, *Journals,* 1909–1914.

40 Government has come to be a trade, and is managed solely on commercial principles. A man

plunges into politics to make his fortune, and only cares that the world should last his days.

RALPH WALDO EMERSON, in a letter to Thomas Carlyle, October 7, 1835.

41 A party is perpetually corrupted by personality.

RALPH WALDO EMERSON, "Politics," *Essays,* Second Series, 1844.

42 The spirit of our American radicalism is destructive and aimless. It is not loving; it has no ulterior and divine ends, but is destructive only out of hatred and selfishness.

Ibid.

43 Men are conservatives when they are least vigorous, or when they are most luxurious. They are conservatives after dinner, or before taking their rest; when they are sick, or aged.

RALPH WALDO EMERSON, "New England Reformers," *Essays,* Second Series, 1844.

44 There is always a certain meanness in the argument of conservatism, joined with a certain superiority in its fact.

RALPH WALDO EMERSON, "The Conservative," *Nature; Addresses and Lectures,* 1849.

45 There is a certain satisfaction in coming down to the lowest ground of politics, for we get rid of cant and hypocrisy.

RALPH WALDO EMERSON, "Napoleon," *Representative Men,* 1850.

46 Politics is a deleterious profession, like some poisonous handicrafts. Men in power have no opinions, but may be had cheap for any opinion, for any purpose.

RALPH WALDO EMERSON, "Power," *The Conduct of Life,* 1860.

47 There are always two parties, the party of the Past and the party of the Future; the Establishment and the Movement.

RALPH WALDO EMERSON, "Life and Letters in New England," *Lectures and Biographical Sketches,* 1883.

48 The first Mistake in Publick business, is the going into it.

BENJAMIN FRANKLIN, *Poor Richard's Almanack,* 1758.

49 We cannot safely leave politics to politicians, or political economy to college professors.

HENRY GEORGE, *Social Problems,* 1883.

50 A liberal is a man who is willing to spend somebody else's money.

CARTER GLASS, in an interview with the Associated Press, September 24, 1938.

51 I never said all Democrats were saloon-keepers. What I said was that all saloon-keepers are Democrats.

HORACE GREELEY, c.1860.

52 There are two major kinds of promises in politics: the promises made by candidates to the voters and the promises made by the candidates to persons and groups able to deliver the vote. Promises falling into the latter category are loosely called "patronage," and promises falling into the former category are most frequently called "lies."

DICK GREGORY, in *Dick Gregory's Political Primer,* 1972.

53 [A politician is] a person skilled in the art of compromise. Usually an elected offical who has compromised to get nominated, compromised to get elected, and compromised repeatedly to stay in office. When election time rolls around again, the process is recycled. In times of crisis a politician flexes his muscle to solve problems.

Ibid.

54 Political promises are much like marriage vows. They are made at the beginning of the relationship between candidate and voter, but are quickly forgotten. When voters catch a candidate breaking political promises, they try to overlook it.

Ibid.

55 There are no generalizations in American politics that vested selfishness cannot cut through.

JOHN GUNTHER, *Inside U.S.A.,* 1947.

56 In politics, as in religion, it is equally absurd to aim at making proselytes by fire and sword.

Heresies in either can rarely be cured by persecution.

ALEXANDER HAMILTON, *The Federalist,* No. 1, 1787–1788.

57 Men often oppose a thing merely because they have had no agency in planning it, or because it may have been planned by those whom they dislike.

ALEXANDER HAMILTON, *The Federalist,* No. 70, 1787–1788.

58 A politician will do anything to keep his job—even become a patriot.

WILLIAM RANDOLPH HEARST, in an editorial, August 28, 1933.

59 Politics is the science of who gets what, when, and why.

Attributed to Sidney Hillman.

60 They are playing politics at the expense of human misery.

HERBERT HOOVER, speaking of congressmen who were sponsoring bills for relief of the unemployed, December 9, 1930.

61 You can't adopt politics as a profession and remain honest.

LOUIS MCHENRY HOWE, in a speech, at Columbia University, January 17, 1933.

62 A Conservative: One who is opposed to the things he is in favor of.

ELBERT HUBBARD, *The Roycroft Dictionary and Book of Epigrams,* 1923.

63 Like an armed warrior, like a plumed knight, James G. Blaine marched down the halls of the American Congress and threw his shining lance full and fair against the brazen foreheads of the defamers of his country and the maligners of his honor.

ROBERT G. INGERSOLL, in a speech nominating James G. Blaine for president at the Republican Convention, June 15, 1876.

64 The greatest superstition now entertained by public men is that hypocrisy is the royal road to success.

ROBERT G. INGERSOLL, in a speech at a Thirteen Club dinner, New York City, December 13, 1886.

65 Talk about our corruption! It is a mere fly-speck of superficiality compared with the rooted and permanent forces of corruption that exist in the European states. The only serious permanent force of corruption in America is party spirit.

WILLIAM JAMES, alluding to the Dreyfus affair, in a letter, 1899, quoted in Justin Kaplan, *Lincoln Steffens: A Biography,* 1974.

66 Whenever a man has cast a longing eye on offices, a rottenness begins in his conduct.

THOMAS JEFFERSON, in a letter to Tench Coxe, 1799.

67 Politics are such a torment that I would advise every one I love not to mix with them.

THOMAS JEFFERSON, in a letter to Martha Jefferson Randolph, February 11, 1800.

68 Politics, like religion, hold up the torches of martyrdom to the reformers of error.

THOMAS JEFFERSON, in a letter to James Ogilvie, August 4, 1811.

69 Men by their constitutions are naturally divided into two parties: 1. Those who fear and distrust the people, and wish to draw all powers from them into the hands of the higher classes. 2. Those who identify themselves with the people, have confidence in them, cherish and consider them as the most honest and safe, although not the most wise depository of the public interests. In every country these two parties exist; and in every one where they are free to think, speak, and write, they will declare themselves.

THOMAS JEFFERSON, in a letter to Henry Lee, August 10, 1824.

70 If you're going to play the game properly, you'd better know every rule.

BARBARA JORDAN, quoted by Charles L. Sanders in *Ebony* magazine, February, 1975.

71 There is rarely political risk in supporting the President and rarely political advantage in disagree-

ment—unless and until a particular policy appears a failure.

> NICHOLAS D. KATZENBACH, in the *New York Times Book Review*, February 18, 1973.

72 Politics is property.

> MURRAY KEMPTON, quoted by Norman Mailer in *Miami and the Siege of Chicago*, 1968.

73 The secret of the Kennedy successes in politics was not money but meticulous planning and organization, tremendous effort, and the enthusiasm and devotion of family and friends.

> ROSE FITZGERALD KENNEDY, *Times to Remember*, 1974.

74 In politics it is difficult sometimes to decide whether the politicians are humorless hypocrites or hypocritical humorists.

> FRANK RICHARDSON KENT, in the *Baltimore Sun*, July 24, 1932.

75 The brains trust.

> JAMES M. KIERAN, characterizing the group of Columbia University professors who advised Franklin D. Roosevelt on his campaign speeches, in a conversation with Roosevelt, 1932. (The phrase caught on and soon became "brain trust.")

76 The public life of every political figure is a continual struggle to rescue an element of choice from the pressure of circumstance.

> HENRY KISSINGER, *White House Years*, 1979.

77 The outsider thinks in terms of absolutes; for him right and wrong are defined in their conception. The political leader does not have this luxury. He rarely can reach his goal except in stages; any partial step is inherently morally imperfect and yet morality cannot be approximated without it.

> Ibid.

78 I've never belonged to any political party for more than fifteen minutes.

> FIORELLO H. LAGUARDIA, quoted in John Gunther, *Inside U.S.A.*, 1947.

79 Why do good public servants break with political parties? It's so simple. The political people never ask you to do anything that's right—and

that's what you're going to do anyway! No. What they want you to do is all the things that are wrong.

> Ibid.

80 What this country needs is more unemployed politicians.

> EDWARD LANGLEY, quoted by Charles McCabe in the *San Francisco Chronicle*, October 24, 1980.

81 Mr. Chairman, this work is exclusively the work of politicians; a set of men who have interests aside from the interests of the people, and who, to say the most of them, are, taken as a mass, at least one long step removed from honest men. I say this with the greater freedom, because, being a politician myself, none can regard it as personal.

> ABRAHAM LINCOLN, speaking in the Illinois legislature against a proposed investigation of the management of the state bank, January 11, 1837.

82 Republicans . . . are for both the *man* and the *dollar;* but in cases of conflict, the man *before* the dollar.

> ABRAHAM LINCOLN, in a letter to H.L. Pierce et al., April 6, 1859.

83 What is conservatism? Is it not adherence to the old and tried, against the new and untried?

> ABRAHAM LINCOLN, in a speech at Cooper Union, New York City, February 27, 1860.

84 I do not allow myself to suppose that either the convention or the League have concluded to decide that I am either the greatest or the best man in America, but rather they have concluded that it is not best to swap horses while crossing the river, and have further concluded that I am not so poor a horse that they might not make a botch of it in trying to swap.

> ABRAHAM LINCOLN, speaking to a delegation of the National Union League, on his renomination as President, June 9, 1864.

85 I have not been able to convince myself that one policy, one party, one class, or one set of tactics, is as fertile as human need.

> WALTER LIPPMANN, *Drift and Mastery*, 1914.

86 The effort to calculate exactly what the voters want at each particular moment leaves out of account the fact that when they are troubled the thing the voters most want is to be told what to want.

> WALTER LIPPMANN, "The Bogey of Public Opinion," *Vanity Fair* magazine, December, 1931.

87 In a political fight, when you've got nothing in favor of your side, start a row in the opposition camp.

> HUEY P. LONG, quoted in T. Harry Williams, *Huey Long*, 1969.

88 I understand the rules of war in politics. No one has practiced them more.

> HUEY P. LONG, speaking to reporters, July, 1933, quoted in T. Harry Williams, *Huey Long*, 1969.

89 The man who pulls the plow gets the plunder in politics.

> HUEY P. LONG, in a speech in the U.S. Senate, January 30, 1934.

90 Ez to my princerples, I glory
  In hevin' nothin' o' the sort;
I aint a Whig, I aint a Tory,
  I'm jest a canderdate, in short.

> JAMES RUSSELL LOWELL, *The Biglow Papers*, First Series, 1848.

91 At present, trust a man with making constitutions on less proof of competence than we should demand before we gave him our shoe to patch.

> JAMES RUSSELL LOWELL, "On a Certain Condescension in Foreigners," published in the *Atlantic Monthly*, January, 1869.

92 It is the mark of the successful politician that he faces the inevitable, and then takes credit for it. Jumping on the bandwagon can be made to look like leadership if the move is made dexterously enough.

> CHARLES MCCABE, quoted in Edmund G. Brown, *Reagan: The Political Chameleon*, 1976.

93 Our differences are policies, our agreements principles.

> WILLIAM MCKINLEY, in a speech in Des Moines, Iowa, 1901.

94 There is always some basic principle that will ultimately get the Republican party together. If my observations are worth anything, that basic principle is the cohesive power of public plunder.

> A.J. MCLAURIN, in a speech in the U.S. Senate, May, 1906.

95 Politics quarantines one from history; most of the people who nourish themselves in the political life are in the game not to make history but to be diverted from the history which is being made.

> NORMAN MAILER, *Some Honorable Men: Political Conventions, 1960–1972*, 1976.

96 A political convention is after all not a meeting of a corporation's board of directors; it is a fiesta, a carnival, a pig-rooting, horse-snorting, band-playing, voice-screaming medieval get-together of greed, practical lust, compromised idealism, career-advancement, meeting, feud, vendetta, conciliation, of rabble-rousers, fist fights (as it used to be), embraces, drunks (again as it used to be) and collective rivers of animal sweat.

> Ibid.

97 Socialism, indeed, is simply the degenerate capitalism of bankrupt capitalists. Its one genuine object is to get more money for its professors; all its other grandiloquent objects are afterthoughts, and most of them are bogus.

> H.L. MENCKEN, *Prejudices,* Third Series, 1922.

98 The believing mind reaches its perihelion in the so-called Liberals. They believe in each and every quack who sets up his booth on the fair-grounds, including the Communists. The Communists have some talents too, but they always fall short of believing in the Liberals.

> H.L. MENCKEN, "Sententiae," in *The Vintage Mencken*, 1955.

99 A good [politician] is quite as unthinkable as an honest burglar.

> H.L. MENCKEN, quoted in *Newsweek* magazine, September 12, 1955.

100 Any party which takes credit for the rain must not be surprised if its opponents blame it for the drought.

DWIGHT W. MORROW, in a campaign speech, October, 1930.

101 Waving the bloody shirt.

> Attributed to Oliver P. Morton, alluding to memories of the Civil War evoked in the Presidential campaign of 1876.

102 Political success comes from a combination of hard work and breaks. But unless you have the guts to take chances when the breaks come your way, and the determination and stamina to work hard, you will never amount to much more than a political hack and a perennial "almost-ran" in your political career.

> RICHARD M. NIXON, quoted in Earl Mazo, *Richard Nixon: A Political and Personal Portrait,* 1959.

103 Politics is an art and a science. Politicians are, in the main, honorable, above average in their intellectual equipment, and effective in getting action on problems that less practical people only talk or write about. An individual has to be a politician before he can be a statesman.

> Ibid.

104 The man who deliberately weakens his party almost invariably ends up by weakening hinmself.

> Ibid.

105 I think, perhaps, as I look back at those who shaped my own life—and there are a great deal of similarities between the game of football and the game of politics—that I learned a great deal from a football coach who not only taught his players how to win but also taught them that when you lose you don't quit, that when you lose you fight harder the next time.

> RICHARD M. NIXON, *Public Papers,* July 30, 1971.

106 The Democrats let it all out and love to shout and laugh and have fun. The Republicans have fun but they don't want people to see it. The Democrats, even when they are not having fun, like to appear to be having fun.

> RICHARD M. NIXON, entry from his diary, 1973.

107 Politics is the science of exigencies.

> THEODORE PARKER, "Of Truth and the Intellect," *Ten Sermons of Religion,* 1852.

108 If more politicians in this country were thinking about the next generation instead of the next election, it might be better for the United States and the world.

> CLAUDE PEPPER, quoted in the *Orlando Sentinel-Star,* Decemver 29, 1946.

109 Politics is but the common pulse-beat, of which revolution is the fever-spasm.

> WENDELL PHILLIPS, "The Philosophy of the Abolition Movement," a speech in Boston, January 27, 1853.

110 Civilization dwarfs political machinery.

> WENDELL PHILLIPS, "Lincoln's Election," a speech in Boston, November 7, 1860.

111 The politican who steals is worse than a thief. He is a fool. With the grand opportunities all around for a man with political pull, there's no excuse for stealin' a cent.

> GEORGE WASHINGTON PLUNKITT, quoted in *Time* magazine, August 22, 1955.

112 I must say acting was good training for the political life which lay ahead for us.

> NANCY REAGAN, *Nancy,* 1980.

113 Something the liberal will have to explain and stand trial for is his inability to see the Communist as he truly is and not as some kind of Peck's Bad Boy of liberalism who is basically all right but just a bit overboard and rough-edged. This ideological myopia is even true of some who have met the Reds in philosophical combat and who should have learned something from crossing swords.

> RONALD REAGAN, *Where's the Rest of Me?* 1965.

114 Sadly I have come to realize that a great many so-called liberals aren't liberal—they will defend to the death your right to agree with them.

> Ibid.

115 [The Democratic party is] a hopeless assortment of discordant differences, as incapable of positive action as it is capable of infinite clamor.

THOMAS BRACKETT REED, "Two Congresses Contrasted," the *North American Review,* August, 1892.

116 Politics is mostly pill-taking.

THOMAS BRACKETT REED, in a letter to John Dalzell, August 1, 1896.

117 A good party is better than the best man that ever lived.

THOMAS BRACKETT REED, quoted in William Alexander Robinson, *Thomas B. Reed, Parliamentarian,* 1930.

118 Politics is not a vocation. It is not even an avocation. It's an incurable disease. If it ever gets in one's blood, it can never be eradicated.

JOSEPH T. ROBINSON, in a speech at Charlotte, North Carlina, 1928.

119 Politics is the life blood of democracy. To call politics "dirty" is to call democracy "dirty."

NELSON A. ROCKEFELLER, *The Future of Federalism,* 1962.

120 Politics, of course, requires sweat, work, combat, and organization. But these should not be ugly words for any free people.

Ibid.

121 I tell you Folks, all Politics is Apple Sauce.

WILL ROGERS, in *The Illiterate Digest,* 1924.

122 The Republicans have their splits right after election and Democrats have theirs just before an election.

WILL ROGERS, in his newspaper column, December 29, 1930.

123 Politics has got so expensive that it takes lots of money to even get beat with.

WILL ROGERS, in his newspaper column, June 28, 1931.

124 Politics is the best show in America. I love animals and I love politicians and I love to watch both of 'em play, either back home in their native state or after they have been captured and sent to the zoo or to Washington.

WILL ROGERS, quoted in the *New York Times,* January 28, 1984.

125 I have spent many years of my life in opposition and I rather like the role.

ELEANOR ROOSEVELT, in a letter to Bernard Baruch, November 18, 1952.

126 If we can "boondoggle" ourselves out of this depression, that word is going to be enshrined in the hearts of the American people for years to come.

FRANKLIN D. ROOSEVELT, in a speech to the New Jersey State Emergency Council, in Newark, New Jersey, January 18, 1936.

127 A radical is a man with both feet firmly planted—in the air. A conservative is a man with two perfectly good legs who, however, has never learned to walk forward. A reactionary is a somnambulist walking backward. But a liberal is a man who uses his legs and his hands at the behest—at the command—of his head.

FRANKLIN D. ROOSEVELT, in a radio speech, October 26, 1939.

128 I wish in this campaign to do . . . whatever is likely to produce the best results for the Republican ticket. I am as strong as a bull moose and you can use me up to the limit.

THEODORE ROOSEVELT, in a letter to Mark Hanna, June 27, 1900.

129 The leader works in the open, and the boss in covert. The leader leads, and the boss drives.

THEODORE ROOSEVELT, in a speech in Binghamton, New York, October 24, 1910.

130 My hat is in the ring.

THEODORE ROOSEVELT, declaring his candidacy for the Republican presidential nomination, Cleveland, Ohio, February 21, 1912.

131 The old parties are husks, with no real soul within either, divided on artificial lines, boss-ridden and privilege-controlled, each a jumble of incongruous elements, and neither daring to speak out wisely and fearlessly on what should be said on the vital issues of the day.

THEODORE ROOSEVELT, in a speech at the Progressive party convention, Chicago, August 6, 1912.

132 Politicians cannot afford to deal in finalities and ultimate truths; they abide, by and large, by probabilities and reasonable assumptions and the law of averages.

RICHARD ROVERE, *Senator Joe McCarthy,* 1959.

133 The spoils system, that practice which turns public offices, high and low, from public trusts into objects of prey and booty for the victorious party, may without extravagance of language be called one of the greatest criminals in our history, if not the greatest. In the whole catalogue of our ills there is none more dangerous to the vitality of our free institutions.

CARL SCHURZ, in a speech in Chicago, December 12, 1894.

134 I have come home to look after my fences.

JOHN SHERMAN, after almost 40 years in Congress, speaking of the condition of his farm to neighbors and constituents, c.1877 (thought to be the origin of the political term "fence-mending").

135 Let's look at the record.

ALFRED E. SMITH, a phrase he used repeatedly in his presidential campaign, 1928.

136 No matter how thin you slice it, it's still baloney.

ALFRED E. SMITH, a phrase he used in speeches against Franklin D. Roosevelt and the New Deal, 1936.

137 Nobody shoots at Santa Claus.

Ibid.

138 Make politics a sport, as they do in England, or a profession, as they do in Germany. . . . But don't try to reform politics with the banker, the lawyer, and the drygoods merchant, for these are businessmen.

LINCOLN STEFFENS, "Great Types of Modern Business-Politics," first published in *Ainslee's* magazine, October, 1901.

139 The corruption that shocks us in public affairs we practice in our private concerns. There is no essential difference between the pull that gets your wife into society or for your book a favorable notice and that which gets a heeler into office, a thief out

of jail, and a rich man's son on the board of directors.

LINCOLN STEFFENS, in his introduction to *The Shame of the Cities,* 1904.

140 We mean by "politics" the people's business— the most important business there is.

ADLAI E. STEVENSON, in a speech at Chicago, November 19, 1955.

141 After lots of people who go into politics have been in it for a while they find that to stay in politics they have to make all sorts of compromises to satisfy their supporters and that it becomes awfully important for them to keep their jobs because they have nowhere else to go.

ADLAI E. STEVENSON, in an interview, 1958.

142 A new race of men is springing up to govern the nation; they are the hunters after popularity, men ambitious, not of the honor so much as of the profits of office—the demagogues, whose principles hang laxly upon them, and who follow not so much what is right as what leads to a temporary vulgar applause.

JOSEPH STORY, *Commentaries on the Constitution of the United States,* 1833.

143 Skilled professional liars are as much in demand in politics as they are in the advertising business . . . and the main function of any candidate's press secretary is to make sure the press gets nothing but Upbeat news.

HUNTER S. THOMPSON, *Fear and Loathing on the Campaign Trail, '72,* 1973.

144 Politics . . . are but as the cigar-smoke of a man.

HENRY DAVID THOREAU, "Walking," 1862.

145 Politics is, as it were, the gizzard of society, full of grit and gravel, and the two political parties are its two opposite halves—sometimes split into quarters, it may be, which grind on each other. Not only individuals, but states, have thus a confirmed dyspepsia.

HENRY DAVID THOREAU, "Life Without Principle," 1863.

146 Ninety-eight percent of the adults in this country are decent, hard-working, honest Americans. It's the other lousy two percent that get all the publicity. But then—we elected them.

> Attributed to Lily Tomlin.

147 A leader has to lead, or otherwise he has no business in politics.

> HARRY S TRUMAN, quoted in Merle Miller, *Plain Speaking: An Oral Biography of Harry S Truman,* 1974.

148 If you can't stand the heat, get out of the kitchen.

> HARRY S TRUMAN, a favorite saying.

149 I think I can say, and say with pride, that we have some legislatures that bring higher prices than any in the world.

> MARK TWAIN, in an address, "Americans and the English," July 4, 1872.

150 When I want to buy up any politicians I always find the anti-monopolists the most purchasable. They don't come so high.

> WILLIAM HENRY VANDERBILT, reported in the *Chicago Daily News,* October 9, 1882.

151 Hamilton and Jefferson were, first, men of extraordinary brilliance and, second, they believed passionately in their own theory of government. . . . The collision between Jefferson and Hamilton struck real sparks. Each was a sort of monster driven by vanity, but each was also an intellectual philosopher of government, and each thought he was creating a perfect or perfectable system of government. Our politicians have not thought about such matters for half a century.

> GORE VIDAL, in "A Conversation with Myself," Book-of-the-Month Club *News,* November, 1973.

152 I'm not a politician and my other habits air good also.

> ARTEMUS WARD, "Fourth of July Oration," *Artemus Ward, His Book,* 1862.

153 Hearto4, as I hav numerously obsarved, I have abstrained from having any sentimunts or principles, my pollertics, like my religion, bein of a exceedin accommodation character.

> ARTEMUS WARD, "The Crisis," in *Artemus Ward, His Book,* 1862.

154 Politics makes strange bedfellows.

> CHARLES DUDLEY WARNER, *My Summer in a Garden,* 1871.

155 [The spirit of party] serves always to distract the public councils and enfeeble the public administration. It agitates the community with ill-founded jealousies and false alarms; kindles the animosity of one part against another; foments occasionally riot and insurrection.

> GEORGE WASHINGTON, in his Farewell Address, September 17, 1796.

156 There is an opinion that parties in free countries are useful checks upon the administration of the government, and serve to keep alive the spirit of liberty. This within certain limits is probably true; and in governments of a monarchical cast patriotism may look with indulgence, if not with favor, upon the spirit of party. But in those of the popular character, in governments purely elective, it is a spirit not to be encouraged.

> Ibid.

157 All dressed up, with nowhere to go.

> WILLIAM ALLEN WHITE, characterizing the Progressive Party after Theodore Roosevelt had withdrawn from the Presidential campaign, 1916.

158 Celebrity, not mastery, is the fruit of victory.

> GEORGE F. WILL, on the Jimmy Carter White House, March 6, 1978, in *The Pursuit of Virtue and Other Tory Notions,* 1982.

159 Marxism is the opium of the intellectuals.

> EDMUND WILSON, in *Letters on Literature and Politics 1912–1972,* 1977.

160 A radical is one of whom people say "He goes too far." A conservative, on the other hand, is one who "doesn't go far enough." Then there is the reactionary, "one who doesn't go at all." All these terms are more or less objectionable, wherefore we have coined the term "progressive." I should say

that a progressive is one who insists upon recognizing new facts as they present themselves—one who adjusts legislation to these new facts.

> WOODROW WILSON, in a speech to the
> Kansas Society of New York, New York City,
> January 29, 1911.

161 Politics I conceive to be nothing more than the science of the ordered progress of society along the lines of greatest usefulness and convenience to itself.

> WOODROW WILSON, in an address to the
> Pan-American Scientific Congress, Washington,
> D.C., January 6, 1916.

162 He was learning for himself the truth of the saying "A liberal is a conservative who has been arrested."

> TOM WOLFE, *The Bonfire of the Vanities,* 1987.

---

188. POLLUTION

See also CITIES; NATURE; TECHNOLOGY

---

1 One person's trash basket is another's living space.

> National Academy of Sciences, "Waste
> Management and Control," 1965.

2 DDT is one of the safest pesticides being used.

> JAMES M. BROWN, of the National Cotton
> Council of America, in a letter in *American Way*
> magazine, June, 1970.

3 Over increasingly large areas of the United States, spring now comes unheralded by the return of the birds, and the early mornings are strangely silent where once they were filled with the beauty of bird song.

> RACHEL CARSON, *Silent Spring,* 1962.

4 As crude a weapon as the cave man's club, the chemical barrage has been hurled against the fabric of life.

> Ibid.

5 Science is triumphant with far-ranging success, but its triumph is somehow clouded by growing difficulties in providing for the simple necessities of human life on the earth.

> BARRY COMMONER, *Science and Survival,* 1966.

6 Because we depend on so many detailed and subtle aspects of the environment, *any* change imposed on it for the sake of some economic benefit has a price. . . . Sooner or later, wittingly or unwittingly, we must pay for every intrusion on the natural environment.

> Ibid.

7 We have been massively intervening in the environment without being aware of many of the harmful consequences of our acts until they have been performed and the effects—which are difficult to understand and sometimes irreversible—are upon us. Like the sorcerer's apprentice, we are acting upon dangerously incomplete knowledge. We are, in effect, conducting a huge experiment *on ourselves.*

> Ibid.

8 The family which takes its mauve and cerise, air-conditioned, power-steered and power-braked automobile out for a tour passes through cities that are badly paved, made hideous by litter, blighted buildings, billboards and posts for wires that should long since have been put underground. They pass on into a countryside that has been rendered largely invisible by commercial art. . . . They picnic on exquisitely packaged food from a portable icebox by a polluted stream and go on to spend the night at a park which is a menace to public health and morals. Just before dozing off on an air mattress, beneath a nylon tent, amid the stench of decaying refuse, they may reflect vaguely on the curious unevenness of their blessings. Is this, indeed, the American genius?

> JOHN KENNETH GALBRAITH, *The Affluent
> Society,* 1976.

9 Ruin is the destination toward which all men rush, each pursuing his own best interest in a society that believes in the freedom of the commons. Freedom in a commons brings ruin to all.

GARRETT HARDIN, "The Tragedy of the Commons," *Science,* December 13, 1968.

10 Water is the most precious, limited natural resource we have in this country. . . . But because water belongs to no one—except the people—special interests, including government polluters, use it as their private sewers.

RALPH NADER, in his introduction to David Zwick and Marcy Benstock, *Water Wasteland,* 1971.

11 A tree is a tree—how many more do you need to look at?

RONALD REAGAN, in a speech to the Western Wood Products Association, September 12, 1965.

12 We travel together, passengers on a little spaceship, dependent on its vulnerable reserves of air and soil; all committed for our safety to its security and peace; preserved from annihilation only by the care, the work and, I will say, the love we give our fragile craft.

ADLAI E. STEVENSON, quoted in Garrett Hardin, *Exploring New Ethics for Survival,* 1972.

13 Industrial vomit . . . fills our skies and seas. Pesticides and herbicides filter into our foods. Twisted automobile carcasses, aluminum cans, non-returnable glass bottles and synthetic plastics form immense kitchen middens in our midst as more and more of our detritus resists decay. We do not even begin to know what to do with our radioactive wastes—whether to pump them into the earth, shoot them into outer space, or pour them into the oceans. Our technological powers increase, but the side effects and potential hazards also escalate.

ALVIN TOFFLER, *Future Shock,* 1970.

14 Although I'm sometimes pessimistic about man's future, I don't believe him to be innately evil. I'm more worried about his insatiable curiosity than I am about his poor character: his preoccupation with the moon is disturbing to me, particularly since his own rivers run dirty and his air is getting fouler every year.

E.B. WHITE, in a letter to Judith W. Preusser, February 25, 1966.

189. POVERTY

See also BUSINESS; DEBT; ECONOMICS; MONEY; WEALTH

1 I cannot understand how we can put together all those programs for sending food across the oceans when at home we have people who are slowly starving to death. We could use less foreign aid and more home aid.

PEARL BAILEY, *Pearl's Kitchen,* 1973.

2 Hungry people cannot be good at learning or producing anything, except perhaps violence.

Ibid.

3 Poverty is not a misfortune to the poor only who suffer it, but it is more or less a misfortune to all with whom he deals.

HENRY WARD BEECHER, in a speech in Liverpool, England, October 16, 1863.

4 Beggar, *n.* One who has relied on the assistance of his friends.

AMBROSE BIERCE, *The Devil's Dictionary,* 1906.

5 Poverty is one ov them kind ov misfortunes that we all ov us dread but none ov us pitty.

JOSH BILLINGS, *Josh Billings' Encyclopedia of Wit and Wisdom,* 1874.

6 Squeamishness was never yet bred in an empty pocket.

JAMES BRANCH CABELL, *The Cream of the Jest,* 1917.

7 Over the hill to the poor-house I'm trudgin' my weary way.

WILL CARLETON, "Over the Hill to the Poorhouse," *Farm Ballads,* 1873.

8 Poverty breeds lack of self-reliance.

DANIEL DELEON, *Two Pages from Roman History,* 1903.

9 Rich men never whistle, poor men always do; bird-songs are in the hearts of the people.

STEPHEN BENTON ELKINS, in a speech, 1906.

10 Poverty demoralizes.

> RALPH WALDO EMERSON, *The Conduct of Life*, 1860.

11 Want is a growing giant whom the coat of Have was never large enough to cover.

> Ibid.

12 Poverty consists in feeling poor.

> RALPH WALDO EMERSON, "Domestic Life," *Society and Solitude*, 1870.

13 The greatest man in history was the poorest.

> Ibid.

14 Light purse, heavy heart.

> BENJAMIN FRANKLIN, *Poor Richard's Almanack*, 1733.

15 For one poor Man there are an hundred indigent.

> BENJAMIN FRANKLIN, *Poor Richard's Almanack*, 1746.

16 Having been poor is no shame, but being ashamed of it, is. Poverty often deprives a man of all spirit and virtue.

> BENJAMIN FRANKLIN, *Poor Richard's Almanack*, 1749.

17 *Laziness* travels so slowly, that *Poverty* soon overtakes him.

> BENJAMIN FRANKLIN, *Poor Richard's Almanack*, 1756.

18 The children who go to bed hungry in a Harlem slum or a West Virginia mining town are not being deprived because no food can be found to give them; they are going to bed hungry because, despite all our miracles of invention and production, we have not yet found a way to make the necessities of life available to all of our citizens—including those whose failure is not a lack of personal industry or initiative, but only an unwise choice of parents.

> J. WILLIAM FULBRIGHT, *Old Myths and New Realities*, 1964.

19 It is an elementary mark of sophistication always to mistrust the man who blames on revolutionaries what should be attributed to deprivation.

> JOHN KENNETH GALBRAITH, "Poverty and the Way People Behave," 1965.

20 The association of poverty with progress is the great enigma of our times—it is the riddle which the Sphinx of fate puts to our civilization, and which, not to answer, is to be destroyed.

> HENRY GEORGE, *Progress and Poverty*, 1879.

21 Paupers will raise paupers, even if the children be not their own, just as familiar contact with criminals will make criminals of the children of virtuous parents.

> Ibid.

22 We in America today are nearer to the final triumph over poverty than ever before in the history of any land. The poorhouse is vanishing from among us. We have not yet reached the goal, but given a chance to go forward with the policies of the last eight years, and we shall soon, with the help of God, be within sight of the day when poverty shall be banished from this nation.

> HERBERT HOOVER, in his speech accepting the Republican Presidential nomination, August 11, 1928.

23 It's no disgrace t' be poor, but it might as well be.

> KIN HUBBARD, *Abe Martin's Sayings and Sketches*, 1915.

24 Poverty is now an inhuman anachronism.

> HUBERT H. HUMPHREY, *Beyond Civil Rights: A New Day of Equality*, 1968.

25 I had rather be a beggar and spend my last dollar like a king, than be a king and spend my money like a beggar.

> ROBERT G. INGERSOLL, "Liberty of Man, Woman and Child," an address given in Troy, New York, December 17, 1877.

26 Poverty indeed *is* the strenuous life—without brass bands, or uniforms, or hysteric popular applause, or lies, or circumlocutions.

> WILLIAM JAMES, *The Varieties of Religious Experience*, 1902.

27 The prevalent fear of poverty among the educated classes is the worst moral disease from which our civilization suffers.

> Ibid.

28 This administration today, here and now, declares unconditional war on poverty in America. I urge this Congress and all Americans to join with me in that effort. It will not be a short or easy struggle—no single weapon or strategy will suffice—but we shall not rest until that war is won.

> LYNDON B. JOHNSON, in a State of the Union message, January 8, 1964.

29 The curse of poverty has no justification in our age. It is socially as cruel and blind as the practice of cannibalism at the dawn of civilization, when men ate each other because they had not yet learned to take food from the soil or to consume the abundant animal life around them. The time has come for us to civilize ourselves by the total, direct and immediate abolition of poverty.

> MARTIN LUTHER KING, JR., *Where Do We Go from Here? Chaos or Community,* 1967.

30 It is the world's one crime its babes grow dull,
Its poor are ox-like, limp and leaden-eyed.
Not that they starve, but starve so dreamlessly, . . .
Not that they sow, but that they seldom reap, . . .
Not that they die, but that they die like sheep.

> VACHEL LINDSAY, "The Leaden-Eyed," in *Collected Poems,* 1925.

31 There is nothing perfectly secure but poverty.

> HENRY WADSWORTH LONGFELLOW, in a letter, November 13, 1872.

32 Poverty pays with its person the chief expenses of war, pestilence, and famine.

> JAMES RUSSELL LOWELL, "On Democracy," an address given in Birmingham, England, October 6, 1884.

33 I am for lifting everyone off the social bottom. In fact, I am for doing away with the social bottom altogether.

CLARE BOOTHE LUCE, quoted in *Time* magazine, February 14, 1964.

34 Thru this dread shape humanity betrayed,
Plundered, profaned and disinherited,
Cries protest to the Judges of the World.

> EDWIN MARKHAM, "The Man with the Hoe," 1899.

35 Poverty is a soft pedal upon all branches of human activity, not excepting the spiritual.

> H.L. MENCKEN, *A Book of Prefaces,* 1917.

36 We shall never solve the paradox of want in the midst of plenty by doing away with plenty.

> OGDEN MILLS, in a speech in New York City, March 21, 1934.

37 Unless the system in which you have political freedom proves that it is the most effective in bringing about economic progress, Communism is going to gain increasing adherents throughout the world. We have to bear in mind this essential fact: the terrible poverty and misery that so many people suffer cannot continue to be endured. They know there must be a way out, and they are going to take the way that they think is the quickest and surest, in the long run.

> RICHARD M. NIXON, quoted in Earl Mazo, *Richard Nixon: A Political and Personal Portrait,* 1959.

38 We hold that the moral obligation of providing for old age, helpless infancy, and poverty, is far superior to that of supplying the invented wants of courtly extravagance, ambition and intrigue.

> THOMAS PAINE, "Address and Declaration of the Friends of Universal Peace and Liberty," August, 1791.

39 How the Other Half Lives.

> JACOB RIIS, the title of one of his books, 1890.

40 The forgotten man at the bottom of the economic pyramid.

> FRANKLIN D. ROOSEVELT, in a radio speech, April 7, 1932.

41 I see one-third of a nation ill-housed, ill-clad, ill-nourished.

> FRANKLIN D. ROOSEVELT, in his second inaugural address, January 20, 1937.

42 God help the rich; the poor can sleep with their windows shut.

> BERT LESTON TAYLOR, *The So-Called Human Race,* 1922.

43 It [poverty] is life near the bone, where it is sweetest.

> HENRY DAVID THOREAU, *Walden,* 1854.

44 The town's poor seem to me often to live the most independent lives of any.

> Ibid.

45 Cultivate poverty like a garden herb, sage.

> Ibid.

46 Happy must be the State
Whose ruler heedeth more
The murmurs of the poor
Than flatteries of the great.

> JOHN GREENLEAF WHITTIER, "King Solomon and the Ants," 1877.

47 The basic cure for poverty is money.

> GEORGE A. WILEY, in a statement to the Democratic Party platform committee, Chicago, 1968.

48 No one can love his neighbor on an empty stomach.

> WOODROW WILSON, in a speech in New York City, May 23, 1912.

49 Hunger does not breed reform; it breeds madness, and all the ugly distempers that make an ordered life impossible.

> WOODROW WILSON, in a speech to Congress, November 11, 1918.

190. POWER

See also ARMY; AUTHORITY; CONQUEST; MILITARISM; NAVY; NUCLEAR AGE; TYRANNY; VICTORY; WAR

1 I am more and more convinced that man is a dangerous creature; and that power, whether vested in many or a few, is ever grasping, and like the grave, cries "Give, give!"

> ABIGAIL ADAMS, in a letter to John Adams, November 27, 1775.

2 The effect of power and publicity on all men is the aggravation of self, a sort of tumor that ends by killing the victim's sympathies.

> HENRY ADAMS, *The Education of Henry Adams,* 1907.

3 Power when wielded by abnormal energy is the most serious of facts.

> Ibid.

4 The balance of power in a society accompanies the balance of property in land.

> JOHN ADAMS, in a letter to James Sullivan, May 26, 1776.

5 The fundamental article of my political creed is that despotism, or unlimited sovereignty, or absolute power, is the same in a majority of a popular assembly, an aristocratical council, an oligarchical junto, and a single emperor.

> JOHN ADAMS, in a letter to Thomas Jefferson, November 13, 1815.

6 Power must never be trusted without a check.

> JOHN ADAMS, in a letter to Thomas Jefferson, February 2, 1816.

7 It is defeat that turns bone to flint; it is defeat that turns gristle to muscle; it is defeat that makes men invincible.

> HENRY WARD BEECHER, *Royal Truths,* 1862.

8 We are in jail, we insist, because we would neither remain silent nor passive before the pathology

of naked power, which rules our country and dominates half the world, which shamelessly wastes resources as well as people, which leaves in its wake racism, poverty, foreign exploitation, and war. In face of this we felt, free men cannot remain free and silent, free men cannot confess their powerlessness by doing nothing.

> DANIEL AND PHILIP BERRIGAN, quoted in Daniel Berrigan, *America Is Hard to Find,* 1972.

9 Power intoxicates men. It is never voluntarily surrendered. It must be taken from them.

> JAMES F. BYRNES, quoted in the *New York Times,* May 15, 1956.

10 The arts of power and its minions are the same in all countries and in all ages. It marks its victim; denounces it; and excites the public odium and the public hatred, to conceal its own abuses and encroachments.

> HENRY CLAY, in a speech in the U.S. Senate, March 14, 1834.

11 Power always has most to apprehend from its own illusions. Monarchs have incurred more hazards from the follies of their own that have grown up under the adulation of parasites, than from the machinations of their enemies.

> JAMES FENIMORE COOPER, *The American Democrat,* 1838.

12 There is a strain in a man's heart that will sometime or other run out to excess, unless the Lord restrain it, but it is not good to venture it: It is necessary therefore, that all power that is on earth be limited, Church-power or other: If there be power given to speak great things, then look for great blasphemies, look for a licentious abuse of it. It is counted a matter of danger to the State to limit Prerogatives; but it is a further danger not to have them limited.

> JOHN COTTON, in a sermon, "Limitation of Government," quoted in Perry Miller and Thomas H. Johnson, *The Puritans,* 1963.

13 Power politics is the diplomatic name for the law of the jungle.

> ELY CULBERTSON, *Must We Fight Russia?* 1946.

14 All the kings of the earth, before God, are as grasshoppers; they are nothing, and less than nothing: both their love and their hatred is to be despised.

> JONATHAN EDWARDS, in the sermon "Sinners in the Hands of an Angry God," delivered July 8, 1741.

15 Men, such as they are, very naturally seek money or power; and power because it is as good as money.

> RALPH WALDO EMERSON, *The American Scholar,* 1837.

16 You shall have joy, or you shall have power, said God; you shall not have both.

> RALPH WALDO EMERSON, entry written in October, 1842, *Journals,* 1909–1914.

17 The imbecility of men is always inviting the impudence of power.

> RALPH WALDO EMERSON, "On the Uses of Great Men," *Representative Men,* 1850.

18 Power is the first good.

> RALPH WALDO EMERSON, "Inspiration," *Letters and Social Aims,* 1876.

19 The power to do good is also the power to do harm; those who control the power today may not tomorrow; and, more important, what one man regards as good, another may regard as harm.

> MILTON FRIEDMAN, *Capitalism and Freedom,* 1962.

20 Concentrated power is not rendered harmless by the good intentions of those who create it.

> Ibid.

21 The lust for power is not rooted in strength but in weakness.

> ERICH FROMM, *Escape from Freedom,* 1941.

22 [Power is] exerted energy and capacity for action. When followed by the word *structure,* it refers to a group which includes America's most wealthy and influential citizens. When prefixed by the word *black,* it creates terror in the minds of the power structure.

DICK GREGORY, in *Dick Gregory's Political Primer,* 1972.

23 In the general course of human nature, a power over a man's subsistence amounts to a power over his will.

ALEXANDER HAMILTON, *The Federalist,* 1787–1788.

24 One precedent in favor of power is stronger than an hundred against it.

THOMAS JEFFERSON, *Notes on the State of Virginia,* 1784.

25 I have never been so well pleased, as when I could shift power from my own, on the shoulders of others; nor have I ever been able to conceive how any rational being could propose happiness to himself from the exercise of power over others.

THOMAS JEFFERSON, in a letter to Monsieur Destutt de Tracy, January 26, 1811.

26 Power at its best is love implementing the demands of justice. Justice at its best is love correcting everything that stands against love.

MARTIN LUTHER KING, JR., *Where Do We Go from Here? Chaos or Community,* 1967

27 Power . . . is not an end in itself, but is an instrument that must be used toward an end.

JEANE J. KIRKPATRICK, in an address to the National Urban League, Washington, D.C., July 20, 1981.

28 Power is the great aphrodisiac.

HENRY KISSINGER, in the *New York Times,* January 19, 1971.

29 The management of a balance of power is a permanent undertaking, not an exertion that has a foreseeable end.

HENRY KISSINGER, *White House Years,* 1979.

30 Power should not be concentrated in the hands of so few, and powerlessness in the hands of so many.

MAGGIE KUHN, quoted in *Ms.* magazine, June, 1975.

31 The supreme issue, involving all others, is the encroachment of the powerful few upon the rights of the many.

Attributed to Robert M. La Follette, Sr.

32 From the summit of power men no longer turn their eyes upward, but begin to look about them.

JAMES RUSSELL LOWELL, "New England," *Among My Books,* 1870.

33 Power in defense of freedom is greater than power in behalf of tyranny and oppression.

MALCOLM X, in a speech in New York City, 1965.

34 Goodness, armed with power, is corrupted; and pure love without power is destroyed.

REINHOLD NIEBUHR, *Beyond Tragedy,* 1938.

35 Men and nations must use their power with the purpose of making it an instrument of justice and a servant of interests broader than their own.

REINHOLD NIEBUHR, *The Irony of American History,* 1962.

36 The hand entrusted with power becomes, either from human depravity or *esprit de corps,* the necessary enemy of the people.

WENDELL PHILLIPS, in a speech to the Anti-Slavery Society, Boston, January 28, 1852.

37 Power is ever stealing from the many to the few.

Ibid.

38 Oppression is but another name for irresponsible power.

WILLIAM PINKNEY, in a speech, February 15, 1820.

39 Isolation from reality is inseparable from the exercise of power.

GEORGE REEDY, quoted in Arthur M. Schlesinger, *The Imperial Presidency,* 1973.

40 The economic royalists complain that we seek to overthrow the institutions of America. What they really complain of is that we seek to take away their power. Our allegiance to American institutions requires the overthrow of this kind of power.

FRANKLIN D. ROOSEVELT, in his acceptance speech at the Democratic Party National Convention, June 27, 1936.

41 The power to define the situation is the ultimate power.

JERRY RUBIN, *Growing (Up) at 37,* 1976.

42 We in America are fighting the money power; but if men can elsewhere get the power without money, what do they care about money? Power is what men seek, and any group that gets it will abuse it.

LINCOLN STEFFENS, to Upton Sinclair, quoted in *Exposé* magazine, February, 1956.

43 Power can be taken, but not given. The process of the taking is empowerment in itself.

GLORIA STEINEM, in *Ms.* magazine, July, 1978.

44 Since the beginning of time, governments have been mainly engaged in kicking people around. The astonishing achievement in modern times in the Western world is the idea that the citizen should do the kicking.

ADLAI E. STEVENSON, *What I Think,* 1956.

45 Wherever there is a force in human society the problem is to use it and regulate it; to get the use and prevent the abuse of it. The state is no exception; on the contrary, it is the chief illustration.

WILLIAM GRAHAM SUMNER, "The Bequests of the Nineteenth Century to the Twentieth," 1901, published in the *Yale Review,* Summer, 1933.

46 The way to have power is to take it.

Attributed to William Marcy "Boss" Tweed.

47 What do I care about the law. Hain't I got the power?

CORNELIUS VANDERBILT, quoted in Robert L. Heilbroner, *The Worldly Philosophers,* 1972.

48 Arbitrary power is most easily established on the ruins of liberty abused to licentiousness.

GEORGE WASHINGTON, "Circular to the States," June 8, 1783.

49 Power *naturally* and *necessarily* follows property.

DANIEL WEBSTER, in a speech to the Massachusetts Convention, 1820.

50 There are many objects of great value to man which cannot be attained by unconnected individuals, but must be attained, if attained at all, by association.

DANIEL WEBSTER, in a speech in Pittsburgh, Pennsylvania, July, 1833.

191. PREDICTIONS

See also PROGRESS

1 Those most dedicated to the future are not always the best prophets.

ELINOR HAYS, *Morning Star,* 1961.

2 I think it probable that civilization somehow will last as long as I care to look ahead—perhaps with smaller numbers, but perhaps also bred to greatness and splendor by science. I think it not improbable that man, like the grub that prepares a chamber for the winged thing it never has seen but is to be—that man may have cosmic destinies that he does not understand. And so beyond the vision of battling races and an impoverished earth I catch a dreaming glimpse of peace.

OLIVER WENDELL HOLMES, JR., in an address given at a Harvard Law School dinner in New York City, February, 1913.

3 I sometimes believe we're heading very fast for Armageddon right now.

RONALD REAGAN, quoted in James L. Franklin, "The Religious Right and the New Apocalypse," *Boston Globe,* May 2, 1982.

4 I do not know how many future generations we can count on before the Lord returns.

JAMES WATT, quoted by James L. Franklin in the *Boston Globe,* May 2, 1982.

5 I have read the Book of Revelation and, yes, I believe the world is going to end—by an act of God, I hope—but every day I think that time is running out.

CASPAR WEINBERGER, in an interview in the *New York Times*, August 23, 1982.

6 I expect the human generations of the future to be as superior to ourselves in education, in the mastery of techniques, in the comprehensiveness of their mental range, and in their capacity for organized cooperation as we are to the prehistoric cliff dwellers whose caves I went over to see in the Frijoles Canyon yesterday.

EDMUND WILSON, in a letter to Allen Tate, July 20, 1931.

192. PRESIDENCY

See also CONGRESS; CONSTITUTION; ELECTIONS; GOVERNMENT; LINCOLN; PRESIDENTS; STATESMANSHIP; VICE PRESIDENCY; WASHINGTON

1 In Britain the government has to come down in front of Parliament every day to explain its actions, but here the President never answers directly to Congress.

BELLA ABZUG, June 17, 1971, quoted in Mel Ziegler, *Bella!* 1972.

2 Young man, I have lived in this house many years and seen the occupants of that White House across the square come and go, and nothing that you minor officials or the occupants of that house can do will affect the history of the world for long.

HENRY ADAMS, to Assistant Secretary of the Navy Franklin D. Roosevelt during Woodrow Wilson's administration, quoted in Richard Hofstadter, *The American Political Tradition*, 1948.

3 You are apprehensive of monarchy; I, of aristocracy. I would therefore have given more power to the President and less to the Senate.

JOHN ADAMS, in a letter to Thomas Jefferson, November 16, 1787.

4 No man who ever held the office of President would congratulate a friend on obtaining it. He will make one man ungrateful, and a hundred men his enemies, for every office he can bestow.

JOHN ADAMS, after the election of his son, John Quincy Adams, to the Presidency, 1824.

5 In a country where there is no hereditary throne nor hereditary aristocracy, an office raised far above all other offices offers too great a stimulus to ambition. This glittering prize, always dangling before the eyes of prominent statesmen, has a power stronger than any dignity under a European crown to lure them . . . from the path of straightforward consistency.

JAMES BRYCE, *The American Commonwealth*, 1888.

6 Great men are not chosen President, firstly, because great men are rare in politics; secondly, because the method of choice does not bring them to the top; thirdly, because they are not, in quiet times, absolutely needed.

Ibid.

7 I had rather be right than be President.

HENRY CLAY, upon being advised that his defense of slavery on economic grounds would do mortal damage to his chances of becoming President, 1839. (Fifty years later, during an 1890 House debate, Congressman William Springer of Illinois declared that, like Clay, he too would "rather be right than be President." House Speaker Thomas Brackett Reed interrupted him, saying, "The gentleman need not be disturbed. He will never be either.")

8 When I was a boy I was told that anybody could become President; I'm beginning to believe it.

Attributed to Clarence Darrow.

9 The White House is another world. Expediency is everything.

JOHN DEAN, quoted by Mary McGrory in the *New York Post*, June 18, 1973.

10 Since studying this subject I am convinced that the office of the Presidency is not such a very difficult one to fill, his duties being mainly to execute the laws of Congress. Should I be chosen for this exalted position, I would execute the laws of Congress as faithfully as I have always executed the orders of my superiors.

GEORGE DEWEY, announcing his intention to run for the Presidency, April 3, 1900.

11 A man is old enough to vote whin he can vote, he's old enough to wurruk whin he can wurruk. And he's old enough to be prisidint whin he becomes prisidint. If he ain't, 'twill age him.

FINLEY PETER DUNNE, *Mr. Dooley's Opinions,* 1901.

12 The farmer imagines power and place are fine things. But the President has paid dear for his White House. It has commonly cost him all his peace and the best of his manly attributes. To preserve for a short time so conspicuous an appearance before the world, he is content to eat dust before the real masters who stand erect behind the throne.

RALPH WALDO EMERSON, "Compensation," *Essays,* First Series, 1841.

13 To me the Presidency and the Vice Presidency were not prizes to be won but a duty to be done.

GERALD R. FORD, *A Time to Heal,* 1979.

14 An executive is less dangerous to the liberties of the people when in office during life, than for seven years.

ALEXANDER HAMILTON, speaking at the Constitutional Convention, June 18, 1787.

15 Every vital question of state will be merged in the question "Who will be the next President?"

ALEXANDER HAMILTON, *The Federalist,* 1787–1788.

16 My God, this is a hell of a job! I have no trouble with my enemies. I can take care of my enemies all right. But my damn friends, my goddamn friends. . . . They're the ones that keep me walking the floor nights!

WARREN G. HARDING, speaking to William Allen White, reported in White's *Autobiography,* 1946.

17 Americans expect their Presidents to do what no monarch by Divine Right could ever do—resolve for them all the contradictions and complexities of life. And those who seek the Presidency invariably promise—and perhaps really believe—

that they can handle our problems for us, at least better than the other guy.

ROBERT T. HARTMANN, *Palace Politics: An Inside Account of the Ford Years,* 1980.

18 It would be supremely dangerous if a President were to believe in the myth of his own omnipotence. Fortunately, a new President is soon disabused.

Ibid.

19 The Executive of the Union has, ever since the commencement of the present Government, been grasping after power, and in many instances, exercised powers, that he was not constitutionally invested with.

ANDREW JACKSON, in a letter to John Overton, February 24, 1797.

20 As the meeting of Congress approaches, my labors increase. I am engaged preparing for them, and this with my other labors, employs me day and night. I can with truth say mine is a situation of dignified slavery.

ANDREW JACKSON, in a letter to Robert J. Chester, November 30, 1829.

21 The perpetual reeligibility of the President, I fear, will make an office for life, and then hereditary.

THOMAS JEFFERSON, in a letter to George Washington, March 4, 1788.

22 I know well that no man will ever bring out of that office the reputation which carries him into it. The honeymoon would be as short in that case as in any other, and its moments of ecstasy would be ransomed by years of torment and hatred.

THOMAS JEFFERSON, in a letter to Edward Rutledge, December 27, 1796.

23 With experience enough in subordinate offices to have seen the difficulties of this the greatest of all, I have learned to expect that it will rarely fall to the lot of imperfect man to retire from this station with the reputation and the favor which bring him into it.

THOMAS JEFFERSON, in his first inaugural address, March 4, 1801.

24 The danger is that the indulgence and attachments of the people will keep a man in the chair after he becomes a dotard.... General Washington set the example of voluntary retirement after eight years. I shall follow it. And a few more precedents will oppose the obstacle of habit to any one after awhile who shall endeavor to extend his term.

> THOMAS JEFFERSON, in a letter to John Taylor, January 6, 1805.

25 The American Presidency is a formidable, exposed, and somewhat mysterious institution.

> Attributed to John F. Kennedy.

26 This is a most Presidential country. The tone and example set by the President have a tremendous effect on the quality of life in America. The President is like the conductor of a big symphony orchestra—and a new conductor can often get different results with the same score and the same musicians.

> WALTER LIPPMANN, quoted by William Attwood in *Look* magazine, April 25, 1961.

27 They set up a President only to attack and vilify him, just as some African savages make an idol that they may kick and cuff while they pretend to pray to it.

> CHARLES MACKAY, *Life and Liberty in America, 1857–1858*, 1859.

28 What kind of world view the American President has, how well he understands the uses of power and the nuances of diplomacy, whether he has a strategic vision and the will and shrewdness to carry it out—all these are vital, even indispensable, elements.

> RICHARD M. NIXON, *The Real War*, 1980.

29 You can always get the truth from an American statesman after he has turned seventy, or given up all hope of the Presidency.

> WENDELL PHILLIPS, in an address in Boston, November 7, 1860.

30 No President who performs his duties faithfully and conscientiously can have any leisure.

> JAMES K. POLK, in his diary, September 1, 1847.

31 We'll all do the job as if there will never be another election. In other words ... we'll take no actions or make no decisions that are based on how they might bear on or affect an election. Whatever we do will be based on what we believe, to the best of our ability, is best for the people of this country.

> RONALD REAGAN, speaking at his first Cabinet meeting, March 30, 1981, quoted in Rowland Evans and Robert Novak, *The Reagan Revolution*, 1981.

32 There is far less to the presidency, in terms of essential activity, than meets the eye. A president moves through his days surrounded by literally hundreds of people whose relationship to him is that of a doting mother to a spoiled child. Whatever he wants is brought to him immediately— food, drink, helicopters, airplanes, people, in fact, everything but relief from his political problems.

> GEORGE REEDY, *The Twilight of the Presidency*, 1970.

33 It is preeminently a place of moral leadership.

> FRANKLIN D. ROOSEVELT, quoted by Anne O'Hare McCormick in the *New York Times*, September 11, 1932.

34 It is the duty of the President to propose and it is the privilege of the Congress to dispose.

> FRANKLIN D. ROOSEVELT, in a press conference, July 23, 1937.

35 I have a very definite philosophy about the Presidency. I think it should be a very powerful office, and I think the President should be a very strong man who uses without hesitation every power that the position yields; but because of this fact I believe that he should be sharply watched by the people [and] held to a strict accountability by them.

> THEODORE ROOSEVELT, in a letter to Henry Cabot Lodge, July 19, 1908.

36 I took the Canal Zone and let Congress debate, and while the debate goes on the canal does also.

> THEODORE ROOSEVELT, in a speech in Berkeley, California, March 23, 1911.

37 My view was that every executive officer ... was a steward of the people, bound actively and affir-

matively to do all he could for the people, and not to content himself with the negative merit of keeping his talents undamaged in a napkin.

> THEODORE ROOSEVELT, in his *Autobiography*, 1913.

38 Oh, if I could only be President and Congress, too, for just ten minutes.

> THEODORE ROOSEVELT, speaking to young Franklin D. Roosevelt, recalled in a letter from FDR to Robert M. Ashburn, August 18, 1928.

39 The advance planning and sense stimuli employed to capture a $10 million cigarette or soap market are nothing compared to the brainwashing and propaganda blitzes used to ensure control of the largest cash market in the world: the Executive Branch of the United States Government.

> PHYLLIS SCHLAFLY, *A Choice Not an Echo*, 1964.

40 The American democracy must discover a middle ground between making the President a czar and making him a puppet. The problem is to devise means of reconciling a strong and purposeful Presidency with equally strong and purposeful forms of democratic control. Or, to put it succinctly, we need a strong Presidency—but a strong Presidency *within the Constitution.*

> ARTHUR M. SCHLESINGER, JR., *The Imperial Presidency*, 1973.

41 If forced to choose between the penitentiary and the White House for four years . . . I would say the penitentiary, thank you.

> WILLIAM T. SHERMAN, in a letter to Gen. Henry W. Halleck, September, 1864.

42 I will not accept if nominated and will not serve if elected.

> WILLIAM T. SHERMAN, in a telegram to the Republican Party National Convention, June 5, 1884.

43 A career politician finally smelling the White House is not much different from a bull elk in the rut. He will stop at nothing, trashing anything that gets in his way; and anything he can't handle personally he will hire out—or, failing that, make a deal. It is a difficult syndrome for most people to understand, because few of us ever come close to the kind of Ultimate Power and Achievement that the White House represents to a career politician.

> HUNTER S. THOMPSON, *Fear and Loathing On the Campaign Trail, '72.* 1973.

44 In my opinion eight years as President is enough and sometimes too much for any man to serve in that capacity. There is a lure in power. It can get into a man's blood just as gambling and lust for money have been known to do.

> HARRY S TRUMAN, in a memorandum, April 16, 1950.

45 It is an entirely personal office. What the President of today decides becomes the issue of tomorrow. He calls the dance.

> THEODORE H. WHITE, *The Making of the President, 1960,* 1961.

46 Whether a man is burdened by power or enjoys power; whether he is trapped by responsibility or made free by it; whether he is moved by other people and outer forces or moves them—this is of the essence of leadership.

> Ibid.

47 From 40 to 60 per cent of the Presidential office is not in administration but in morals, politics, and spiritual leadership. . . . As President of the United States and servant of God, he has much more to do than to run a desk at the head of the greatest corporation in the world. He has to guide a people in the greatest adventure ever undertaken on the planet.

> WILLIAM ALLEN WHITE, *Selected Letters,* 1947.

---

193. PRESIDENTS

See also CONGRESS; CONSTITUTION; ELECTIONS; GOVERNMENT; LINCOLN; PRESIDENCY; STATESMANSHIP; VICE PRESIDENCY; WASHINGTON

---

1 To err is Truman.

> A joke popular in 1946.

John F. Kennedy: Inaugural Address, January 20, 1961

Containing the famous "Ask not what your country can do for you—ask what you can do for your country," this stirring speech was delivered by the youngest man ever elected to the presidency. Kennedy's assassination on November 22, 1963, engraved his words even more deeply on the hearts and minds of all Americans.

We observe today not a victory of party but a celebration of freedom—symbolizing an end as well as a beginning—signifying renewal as well as change. For I have sworn before you and Almighty God the same solemn oath our forebears prescribed nearly a century and three-quarters ago.

The world is very different now. For man holds in his mortal hands the power to abolish all forms of human poverty and all forms of human life. And yet the same revolutionary beliefs for which our forebears fought are still at issue around the globe—the belief that the rights of man come not from the generosity of the state but from the hand of God.

We dare not forget today that we are the heirs of that first revolution. Let the word go forth from this time and place, to friend and foe alike, that the torch has been passed to a new generation of Americans—born in this century, tempered by war, disciplined by a hard and bitter peace, proud of our ancient heritage—and unwilling to witness or permit the slow undoing of those human rights to which this nation has always been committed, and to which we are committed today at home and around the world.

Let every nation know, whether it wishes us well or ill, that we shall pay any price, bear any burden, meet any hardship, support any friend, oppose any foe to assure the survival and the success of liberty.

This much we pledge—and more.

To those old allies whose cultural and spiritual origins we share, we pledge the loyalty of faithful friends. United, there is little we cannot do in a host of cooperative ventures. Divided, there is little we can do—for we dare not meet a powerful challenge at odds and split asunder.

To those new states whom we welcome to the ranks of the free, we pledge our word that one form of colonial control shall not have passed away merely to be replaced by a far more iron tyranny. We shall not always expect to find them supporting our view. But we shall always hope to find them strongly supporting their own freedom—and to remember that, in the past, those who foolishly sought power by riding the back of the tiger ended up inside.

To those people in the huts and villages of half the globe struggling to break the bonds of mass misery, we pledge our best efforts to help them help themselves, for whatever period is required—not because the Communists may be doing it, not because we seek their votes, but because it is right. If a free society cannot help the many who are poor, it cannot save the few who are rich.

To our sister republics south of our border, we offer a special pledge—to convert our good words into good deeds—in a new alliance for progress—to assist free men and free governments in casting off the chains of poverty. But this peaceful revolution of hope cannot become the prey of hostile powers. Let all our neighbors know that we shall join with them to oppose aggression or subversion anywhere in the Americas. And let every other power know that this hemisphere intends to remain the master of its own house.

To that world assembly of sovereign states, the United Nations, our last best hope in an age where the instruments of war have far outpaced the instruments of peace, we renew our pledge of support—to prevent it from becoming merely a forum for invective—to strengthen its shield of the new and the weak—and to enlarge the area in which its writ may run.

Finally, to those nations who would make themselves our adversary, we offer not a pledge but a request—that both sides begin anew the quest for peace before the dark powers of destruction unleashed by science engulf all humanity in planned or accidental self-destruction. We dare not tempt them with weakness. For only when our arms are sufficient beyond doubt can we be certain beyond doubt that they will never be employed.

But neither can two great and powerful groups of nations take comfort from our present course—both sides overburdened by the cost of modern weapons, both rightly alarmed by the steady spread of the deadly atom, yet both racing to alter that uncertain balance of terror that stays the hand of mankind's final war.

So let us begin anew—remembering on both sides that civility is not a sign of weakness, and sincerity is always subject to proof. Let us never negotiate out of fear. But let us never fear to negotiate.

Let both sides explore what problems unite us instead of belaboring those problems which divide us.

Let both sides, for the first time, formulate serious and precise proposals for the inspection and control of arms—and bring the absolute power to destroy other nations under the absolute control of all nations.

Let both sides seek to invoke the wonders of science instead of its terrors. Together let us explore the stars, conquer the deserts, eradicate disease, tap the ocean depths, and encourage the arts and commerce.

Let both sides unite to heed in all corners of the earth the command of Isaiah—to "undo the heavy burdens . . . [and] let the oppressed go free."

And if a beachhead of cooperation may push back the jungle of suspicion, let both sides join in creating a new endeavor, not a new balance of power but a new world of law, where the strong are just and the weak secure and the peace preserved.

All this will not be finished in the first 100 days. Nor will it be finished in the first 1,000 days, nor in the life of this administration, nor even perhaps in our lifetime on this planet. But let us begin.

In your hands, my fellow citizens, more than mine, will rest the final success or failure of our course. Since this country was founded, each generation of Americans has been summoned to give testimony to its national loyalty. The graves of young Americans who answered the call to service surround the globe.

Now the trumpet summons us again—not as a call to bear arms, though arms we need—not as a call to battle, though embattled we are—but a call to bear the burden of a long twilight struggle, year in and year out, "rejoicing in hope, patient in tribulation"—a struggle against the common enemies of man: tyranny, poverty, disease, and war itself.

Can we forge against these enemies a grand and global alliance, North and South, East and West, that can assure a more fruitful life for all mankind? Will you join in that historic effort?

In the long history of the world, only a few generations have been granted the role of defending freedom in its hour of maximum danger. I do not shrink from this responsibility—I welcome it. I do not believe that any of us would exchange places with any other people or any other generation. The energy, the faith, the devotion which we bring to this endeavor will light our country and all who serve it—and the glow from that fire can truly light the world.

And so, my fellow Americans—ask not what your country can do for you—ask what you can do for your country.

My fellow citizens of the world—ask not what America will do for you but what together we can do for the freedom of man.

Finally, whether you are citizens of America or citizens of the world, ask of us here the same high standards of strength and sacrifice which we ask of you. With a good conscience our only sure reward, with history the final judge of our deeds, let us go forth to lead the land we love, asking His blessing and His help, but knowing that here on earth God's work must truly be our own.

2 Hey, hey, LBJ, how many kids did you kill today?

> Chant of Vietnam War protesters, mid-1960s.

3 Grover Cleveland was a man of honor, courage, and integrity. He followed the right as he saw it. But he saw it through a conservative and conventional cast of mind.

> DEAN G. ACHESON, *A Democrat Looks at His Party,* 1955.

4 I pray Heaven bestow the best of blessings on this House and all that shall hereafter inhabit it. May none but honest and wise men ever rule under this roof.

> JOHN ADAMS, in a prayer he offered as the first occupant of the White House, November 2, 1800. (Franklin D. Roosevelt had the prayer carved above the fireplace in the State Dining Room in 1934.)

5 I would take no one step to advance or promote pretensions to the Presidency. If that office was to be the prize of cabal and intrigue, of purchasing newspapers, bribing by appointments, or bargaining for foreign missions, I had no ticket in that lottery. Whether I had the qualifications necessary for a President of the United States, was, to say the least, very doubtful to myself. But that I had no talents for obtaining the office by such means was perfectly clear.

> JOHN QUINCY ADAMS, in his diary, February 25, 1821.

6 Van Buren is a demagogue with a tincture of artistocracy—an amalgamated metal of lead and copper.

> JOHN QUINCY ADAMS, in his diary, October, 1834.

7 Such is human nature in the gigantic intellect, the envious temper, the ravenous ambition, and the rotten heart of Daniel Webster. His treatment of me has been, is, and will be an improved edition of Andrew Jackson's gratitude.

> JOHN QUINCY ADAMS, in his diary, September 17, 1841.

8 After two years in what is usually described as the world's most difficult job, after one bullet in his lung, the oldest President in American history looked more fit than he did while running for the office. He insisted on conducting the presidency according to his own metabolism. Reagan the man was as much an anomaly in the White House as Reagan the ism was in American history.

> LAURENCE I. BARRETT, *Gambling with History,* 1983.

9 I too would allow that Ronald Reagan is undoubtedly a sincere man. I also believe that he is in reality what he appears to be: a simple man. His ideas, his philosophy, his perceptions, his comprehension of human affairs and society are also neatly confined to a simple framework of thought and action that permits no doubts and acknowledges no sobering complexities. No wonder his manner is

that of a man with utter confidence in his own fundamentalist purity and integrity, the efficient missionary dedicated to eradicating evil. Unfortunately, in these times the simple man or the simple answer is not enough.

> EDMUND G. "PAT" BROWN, *Reagan: The Political Chameleon,* 1976.

10 Ronald Reagan's election to the Presidency would be a national disaster.

> Ibid.

11 Who now knows or cares to know anything about the personality of James K. Polk or Franklin Pierce? The only thing remarkable about them is that being so commonplace they should have climbed so high.

> JAMES BRYCE, *The American Commonwealth,* 1914.

12 On balance, Carter was not good at public relations. He did not fire enthusiasm in the public or inspire fear in his adversaries. He was trusted, but—very unfairly—that trust was in him as a person but not in him as a leader. He had ambitious goals for this nation, both at home and abroad, and yet he did not succeed in being seen as a visionary or in captivating the nation's imagination. His personal qualities—honesty, integrity, religious conviction, compassion—were not translated in the public mind into statesmanship with a historical sweep.

> ZBIGNIEW BRZEZINSKI, *Power and Principle,* 1983.

13 If you are as happy, my dear sir, on entering this house as I am in leaving it and returning home, you are the happiest man in this country.

> JAMES BUCHANAN, to Abraham Lincoln on Lincoln's arrival at the White House as the new president, March 4, 1861.

14 He keeps his ear so close to the gound it's full of grasshoppers.

> Attributed to Joseph Cannon, speaking of William McKinley.

15 If I'm elected, at the end of four years or eight years I hope people will say, "You know, Jimmy Carter made a lot of mistakes, but he never told me a lie."

> JIMMY CARTER, in an interview with Bill Moyers, May 6, 1976.

16 As President I will not be able to provide everything that every one of you might like. I am sure to make many mistakes. But I can promise you that you will never have the feeling that your needs are being ignored, or that we have forgotten who put us in office.

> JIMMY CARTER, in a televised address, February 1, 1977.

17 Our policy is based on an historical vision of America's role. Our policy is derived from a larger view of global change. Our policy is rooted on our moral values, which never change. Our policy is reinforced by our material wealth and by our military power. Our policy is designed to serve mankind. And it is a policy that I hope will make you proud to be Americans.

> JIMMY CARTER, in a commencement address at Notre Dame University, May 22, 1977.

18 I planted four trees in the White House garden. I hope Reagan doesn't cut them down.

> JIMMY CARTER, quoted in Zbigniew Brzezinski, *Power and Principle,* 1983.

19 [Richard M. Nixon] has a deeper concern for his place in history than for the people he governs. And history will not fail to note that fact.

> SHIRLEY CHISHOLM, *The Good Fight,* 1973.

20 He [John Quincy Adams] has peculiar powers as an assailant, and almost always, even when attacked, gets himself into that attitude by making war upon his accuser; and he has, withal, an instinct for the jugular and the carotid artery, as unerring as that of any carnivorous animal.

> RUFUS CHOATE, quoted in Samuel Gilman Brown, *Memoir of Rufus Choate,* 1862.

21 Tell the truth.

> GROVER CLEVELAND, on being asked by his campaign managers what to do about the scandal centering on his liaison with Maria Halpin, quoted in *Harper's Weekly,* August 16, 1884.

22 There are now three projects on foot to serve me up and help people to breast or dark meat, with or without stuffing.

> GROVER CLEVELAND, in a letter to Richard Watson Gilder, November 20, 1896.

23 I feel like a locomotive hitched to a boy's express wagon.

> GROVER CLEVELAND, on being asked in 1897 how he felt without the burden of presidential responsibility, quoted in Robert McElroy, *Grover Cleveland*, 1923.

24 He will hew to the line of right, let the chips fly where they may.

> ROSCOE CONKLING, in a speech supporting the nomination of Ulysses S. Grant for a third term, at the Republican National Convention, Chicago, June 5, 1880.

25 A fitting representative of the common aspirations of his fellow citizens.

> CALVIN COOLIDGE, speaking of Warren G. Harding in his speech accepting nomination as Harding's running mate, at the Republican National Convention, July 27, 1920.

26 I do not choose to run for President in 1928.

> CALVIN COOLIDGE, in a statement to the press, August 2, 1927.

27 I should like to be known as a former president who tries to mind his own business.

> CALVIN COOLIDGE, in *Cosmopolitan* magazine, May, 1930.

28 the only man woman or child who wrote a
   simple declarative sentence with seven
   grammatical errors "is dead"

> E.E. CUMMINGS, on Warren G. Harding, in *ViVa*, 1931.

29 The convention will be deadlocked, and after the other candidates have gone their limit, some twelve or fifteen men, worn out and bleary-eyed for lack of sleep, will sit down, about two o'clock in the morning, around a table in a smoke-filled room in some hotel, and decide the nomination. When that time comes, Harding will be selected.

> HARRY M. DAUGHERTY, Harding's campaign manager, accurately predicting the circumstances of Harding's becoming the Republican presidential nominee in 1920.

30 In the strongest language you can command you can state that I have no political ambitions at all. Make it even stronger than that if you can.

> DWIGHT D. EISENHOWER, commenting in Abilene, Kansas, June 22, 1945, quoted in *Eisenhower Speaks*, 1948.

31 I believe Dick Nixon to be an honest man. I am confident that he will place all the facts before the American people fairly and squarely.

> DWIGHT D. EISENHOWER, statement made during the presidential campaign, September 1952. (It had been revealed that Nixon, while a U.S. Senator, had accepted money from wealthy constituents.)

32 There was no more unlikely leader of a political revolution than this septuagenarian who had become known to the nation as a Grade B movie actor. Sometimes, he seemed more improbable as a national leader viewed at first hand than he did as a personality dimly viewed through the news media.

> ROWLAND EVANS AND ROBERT NOVAK, writing of President Reagan early in his first administration, *The Reagan Revolution*, 1981.

33 Truman's very ordinariness has today made him something of a folk hero: a plain-speaking, straight-talking, ordinary fellow who did what he saw as his duty without turning his obligation into an opportunity for personal gain.

> ROBERT H. FERRELL, *Truman: A Centenary Remembrance*, 1984.

34 I am a Ford, not a Lincoln.

> GERALD R. FORD, upon being sworn in as Vice-President, December 6, 1973.

35 He wanted everyone with him all the time, and when they weren't, it broke his heart.

> MAX FRANKEL, describing Lyndon B. Johnson, in Richard Harwood and Haynes Johnson, *Lyndon*, 1973.

36 [The President is] the last person in the world to know what the people really want and think.

> Attributed to James A. Garfield.

37 My God! What is there in this place [the White House] that a man should ever want to get into it?

> JAMES A. GARFIELD, quoted in *Time* magazine, April 24, 1950.

38 [Lyndon Johnson was] an extraordinarily gifted President who was the wrong man from the wrong place at the wrong time under the wrong circumstances.

> ERIC GOLDMAN, *The Tragedy of Lyndon Johnson,* 1969.

39 We'll stand pat!

> MARK HANNA, using a poker term to describe William McKinley's reelection campaign, 1900.

40 Now look! That damned cowboy is President of the United States.

> Attributed to Mark Hanna, on hearing of William McKinley's death and Theodore Roosevelt's accession to the presidency, September 14, 1901.

41 I can see but one word written over the head of my husband if he is elected, and the word is "Tragedy."

> MRS. WARREN G. HARDING, quoted in Robert K. Murray, *The Harding Era,* 1969.

42 We drew to a pair of deuces and filled.

> WARREN G. HARDING, on hearing he had won the Republican nomination for President, June 12, 1920.

43 Higgledy-piggledy,
Benjamin Harrison,
Twenty-third President
Was, and, as such
Served between Clevelands, and
Save for this trivial
Idiosyncrasy,
Didn't do much.

> JOHN HOLLANDER, "Historical Reflections," *Jiggery-Pokery,* 1966.

44 He [Theodore Roosevelt] was very likeable, a big figure, a rather ordinary intellect, with extraordinary gifts, a shrewd and I think pretty unscrupulous politician. He played all his cards—if not more.

> OLIVER WENDELL HOLMES, JR., in a letter to Sir Frederick Pollock, quoted in Catherine Drinker Bowen, *Yankee from Olympus,* 1944.

45 You are in a war, Mr. President. I was in a war, too. And in a war there is only one rule: *Form your battalions and fight.*

> OLIVER WENDELL HOLMES, JR., speaking with Franklin D. Roosevelt, March 8, 1933, quoted in Catherine Drinker Bowen, *Yankee from Olympus,* 1944.

46 I have no fears for the future of our country. It is bright with hope.

> HERBERT HOOVER, in his inaugural address, March 4, 1929.

47 There are only two occasions when Americans respect privacy, especially in Presidents. Those are prayer and fishing.

> HERBERT HOOVER, in the *New York Herald Tribune,* May 19, 1947.

48 I was in favor of giving former Presidents a seat in the Senate until I passed 75 years. Since then I have less taste for sitting on hard-bottomed chairs during long addresses.

> HERBERT HOOVER, in *This Week* magazine, February 7, 1960.

49 I am ready to serve our country in any capacity from office boy up.

> HERBERT HOOVER, message to Lyndon B. Johnson, 1963.

50 Richard Nixon [is] one of the finest young men, both in character and ability, that I have ever had the opportunity of having in my classes. He is a superior student, alert, aggressive, a fine speaker and one who can do an exceptionally good piece of research when called upon to do so. His position with his fellows is shown by the fact that he is this year president of the Duke Bar Association.

H. CLAUDE HORACK, in a letter to J. Edgar Hoover, May 3, 1937.

51 Brought up under the tyranny of Britain—altho young embarked in the struggle for our liberties, in which I lost every thing that was dear to me . . . for which I have been amply repaid by living under the mild administration of a republican government. To maintain this, and the independent rights of our nation is a duty that I have ever owed to my country to myself and posterity, and when I do all I can to it support, I have only done my duty.

ANDREW JACKSON, to William Blount, January 4, 1813, quoted in Robert V. Remini, *Andrew Jackson and the Course of American Empire,* 1977.

52 I cannot be intimidated from doing that which my judgment and conscience tells me is right by any earthly power.

ANDREW JACKSON, to Andrew J. Donelson, April 27, 1824, quoted in Robert V. Remini, *Andrew Jackson and the Course of American Freedom,* 1981.

53 I had retired from the bustle of public life to my farm, there to repair an enfeebled constitution, worn out in the service of my country. The people of their own mere will brought my name before the nation for the office of President of these U. States. They have sustained me against all the torrents of slander that corruption and wickedness could invent . . . and by a large majority of the virtuous yeomanry of the U. States have elected me to fill the presidential chair. . . . I accept the office given me by the free and unbiased suffrage, of a virtuous people, with the feelings of the highest gratitude.

ANDREW JACKSON, in a memorandum, 1828, quoted in Robert V. Remini, *Andrew Jackson and the Course of American Freedom,* 1981.

54 John Marshall has made his decision: now let him enforce it!

ANDREW JACKSON, referring to the conflict between the executive and the judiciary branches following the Supreme Court decision in *Worcester* v. *Georgia,* upholding the rights of the Cherokee Indians to stay on their land, March 3, 1832.

55 I cannot die in a better cause than in perpetuating our republican system.

ANDREW JACKSON, to Martin Van Buren, September 22, 1840, quoted in Robert V. Remini, *Andrew Jackson and the Course of American Democracy,* 1984.

56 He is vain, irritable, and a bad calculator of the force and probable effect of the motives which govern men. This is all the ill which can possibly be said of him. He is as disinterested as the Being who made him: he is profound in his view; and accurate in his judgment, except where knowledge of the world is necessary to form a judgment.

THOMAS JEFFERSON, on John Adams, in a letter to James Madison, January 30, 1787.

57 I have no ambition to govern men. It is a painful and thankless office.

THOMAS JEFFERSON, in a letter to John Adams, December 28, 1796.

58 Called upon to undertake the duties of the first executive office of our country, I avail myself of the presence of that portion of my fellow citizens which is here assembled, to express my grateful thanks for the favor with which they have been pleased to look toward me, to declare a sincere consciousness that the task is above my talents, and that I approach it with those anxious and awful presentiments which the greatness of the charge and the weakness of my powers so justly inspire.

THOMAS JEFFERSON, in his first inaugural address, March 4, 1801.

59 I am tired of an office where I can do no more good than many others who would be glad to be employed in it. To myself, personally, it brings nothing but unceasing drudgery and daily loss of friends.

THOMAS JEFFERSON, in a letter to John Dickinson, January 13, 1807.

60 I have the consolation . . . of having added nothing to my private fortune during my public service, and of retiring with hands as clean as they are empty.

THOMAS JEFFERSON, in a letter to Count Diodati, March 29, 1807.

Franklin D. Roosevelt: from First Inaugural Address, March 4, 1933

President Roosevelt's ringing words and bold course of action, outlined in this famous inaugural address, helped revive hope and confidence in the future among millions of Americans shattered by economic collapse.

I am certain that my fellow Americans expect that on my induction into the presidency I will address them with a candor and a decision which the present situation of our nation impels. This is preeminently the time to speak the truth, the whole truth, frankly and boldly. Nor need we shrink from honestly facing conditions in our country today. This great nation will endure as it has endured, will revive and will prosper.

So, first of all, let me assert my firm belief that the only thing we have to fear is fear itself—nameless, unreasoning, unjustified terror which paralyzes needed efforts to convert retreat into advance. In every dark hour of our national life a leadership of frankness and vigor has met with that understanding and support of the people themselves which is essential to victory. I am convinced that you will again give that support to leadership in these critical days.

In such a spirit on my part and on yours we face our common difficulties. They concern, thank God, only material things. Values have shrunken to fantastic levels; taxes have risen; our ability to pay has fallen; government of all kinds is faced by serious curtailment of income; the means of exchange are frozen in the currents of trade; the withered leaves of industrial enterprise lie on every side; farmers find no markets for their produce; the savings of many years in thousands of families are gone.

More important, a host of unemployed citizens face the grim problem of existence, and an equally great number toil with little return. Only a foolish optimist can deny the dark realities of the moment.

Yet our distress comes from no failure of substance. We are stricken by no plague of locusts. Compared with the perils which our forefathers conquered because they believed and were not afraid, we have still much to be thankful for. Nature still offers her bounty, and human efforts have multiplied it. Plenty is at our doorstep, but a generous use of it languishes in the very sight of the supply. Primarily this is because the rulers of the exchange of mankind's goods have failed, through their own stubbornness and their own incompetence, have admitted their failure, and abdicated. Practices of the unscrupulous money changers stand indicted in the court of public opinion, rejected by the hearts and minds of men. . . .

Our greatest primary task is to put people to work. This is no unsolvable problem if we face it wisely and courageously. It can be accomplished in part by direct recruiting by the government itself, treating the task as we would treat the emergency of a war, but, at the same time, through this employment, accomplishing greatly needed projects to stimulate and reorganize the use of our natural resources.

Hand in hand with this we must frankly recognize the overbalance of population in our industrial centers and, by engaging on a national scale in a redistribution, endeavor to provide a better use of the land for those best fitted for the land. The task can be helped by definite efforts to raise the values of agricultural products and with this the power to purchase the output of our cities. It can be helped by preventing realistically the tragedy of the growing loss through foreclosure of our small homes and our farms. It can be helped by insistence that the federal, state, and local governments act forthwith on the demand that their cost be drastically reduced. It can be helped by the unifying of relief activities which today are often scattered, uneconomical, and unequal. It can be helped by national planning for and supervision of all forms of transportation and of communications and other utilities which have a definitely public character. There are many ways in which it can be helped, but it can never be helped merely by talking about it. We must act and act quickly.

Finally, in our progress toward a resumption of work, we require two safeguards against a return of the evils of the old order: there must be a strict supervision of all banking and credits and investments; there must be an end to speculation with other people's money, and there must be provision for an adequate but sound currency. . . .

Our Constitution is so simple and practical that it is possible always to meet extraordinary needs by changes in emphasis and arrangement without loss of essential form. That is why our constitutional system has proved itself the most superbly enduring political mechanism the modern world has produced. It has met every stress of vast expansion of territory, of foreign wars, of bitter internal strife, of world relations.

It is to be hoped that the normal balance of executive and legislative authority may be wholly adequate to meet the unprecedented task before us. But it may be that an unprecedented demand and need for undelayed action may call for temporary departure from that normal balance of public procedure.

I am prepared under my constitutional duty to recommend the measures that a stricken nation in the midst of a stricken world may require. These measures, or such other measures as the Congress may build out of its experience and wisdom, I shall seek, within my constitutional authority, to bring to speedy adoption.

But in the event that the Congress shall fail to take one of these two courses, and in the event that the national emergency is still critical, I shall not evade the clear course of duty that will then confront me. I shall ask the Congress for the one remaining instrument to meet the crisis—broad executive power to wage a war against the emergency, as great as the power that would be given to me if we were in fact invaded by a foreign foe.

For the trust reposed in me I will return the courage and the devotion that befit the time. I can do no less.

We face the arduous days that lie before us in the warm courage of national unity; with the clear consciousness of seeking old and precious moral values; with the clean satisfaction that comes from the stern performance of duty by old and young alike. We aim at the assurance of a rounded and permanent national life.

We do not distrust the future of essential democracy. The people of the United States have not failed. In their need they have registered a mandate that they want direct, vigorous action. They have asked for discipline and direction under leadership. They have made me the present instrument of their wishes. In the spirit of the gift I take it.

In this dedication of a nation we humbly ask the blessing of God. May He protect each and every one of us. May He guide me in the days to come.

61 I have the consolation to reflect that during the period of my administration not a drop of the blood of a single fellow citizen was shed by the sword of war or of the law.

> THOMAS JEFFERSON, in a letter to papal nuncio Count Dugnani, February 14, 1818.

62 This was one of those terrific, pummeling White House days that can stretch and grind and use you—even I, who only live on the periphery. So what must it be like for Lyndon!

> LADY BIRD JOHNSON, in an entry dated March 14, 1968, *A White House Diary,* 1970.

63 Gerry Ford is a nice guy, but he played too much football with his helmet off.

> Attributed to Lyndon B. Johnson.

64 [Gerald Ford] can't fart and chew gum at the same time.

> Attributed to Lyndon B. Johnson.

65 I know I've got a heart big enough to be President. I know I've got guts enough to be President. But I wonder whether I've got intelligence and ability enough to be President—I wonder if any man does.

> LYNDON B. JOHNSON, in a remark to Hugh Sidey, Spring, 1960, quoted in Sidey's *A Very Personal Presidency: Lyndon Johnson in the White House,* 1968.

66 All I have I would have given gladly not to be standing here today.

> LYNDON B. JOHNSON, in his first Presidential address to Congress, November 27, 1963.

67 A President's hardest task is not to do what is right but to know what is right.

> LYNDON B. JOHNSON, in his State of the Union message, January 4, 1965.

68 Now there are many, many people who can recommend and advise, and a few of them consent, but there is only one who has been chosen by the American people to decide.

> LYNDON B. JOHNSON, in a speech at Omaha, Nebraska, June 30, 1966.

69 I shall not seek, and I will not accept, the nomination of my party for another term as your President.

> LYNDON B. JOHNSON, speaking to the nation on television, March 31, 1968.

70 The good Lord endowed me with a wonderful constitution, twenty hours a day; I was plenty sturdy and tough, I had reasonable perception and astuteness, I was not a temple of wisdom or a fountain of justice, but I could comprehend things. No one ever said I was a goddamn boob, no one from Bobby [Kennedy] up or down ever said that.

> LYNDON B. JOHNSON, in Doris Kearns, *Lyndon Johnson and the American Dream,* 1976.

71 I knew from the start if I left a woman I really loved—the Great Society—in order to fight that bitch of a war . . . then I would lose everything at home. My hopes . . . my dreams.

> Ibid.

72 A flaw in a diamond stands out while the blemish on a pebble is unnoticed.

> REBEKAH BAINES JOHNSON, writing of press criticism of her son Lyndon B. Johnson, in a letter to him, March 22, 1958.

73 Let the word go forth from this time and place, to friend and foe alike, that the torch has been passed to a new generation of Americans—born in this century, tempered by war, disciplined by a hard and bitter peace, proud of our ancient heritage—and unwilling to witness or permit the slow undoing of those human rights to which this nation has always been committed, and to which we are committed today at home and around the world. Let every nation know, whether it wishes us well or ill, that we shall pay any price, bear any burden, meet any hardship, support any friend, oppose any foe to assure the survival and the success of liberty.

> JOHN F. KENNEDY, in his inaugural address, January 20, 1961.

74 My fellow Americans: ask not what your country can do for you—ask what you can do for your country.

> Ibid.

75 I have tried to make the whole tone and thrust of this office and this administration one that will demand a higher standard of excellence from every individual.

> JOHN F. KENNEDY, in a letter to Alicia Patterson, publisher of *Newsday,* May 11, 1961.

76 I do not think it altogether inappropriate to introduce myself. I am the man who accompanied Jacqueline Kennedy to Paris, and I have enjoyed it.

> JOHN F. KENNEDY, speaking to the press during his state visit to France, June, 1961, quoted in Evelyn Lincoln, *My Twelve Years with John F. Kennedy,* 1965.

77 When I ran for the Presidency of the United States, I knew that this country faced serious challenges, but I could not realize, nor could any man realize who does not bear the burdens of this office, how heavy and constant would be those burdens.

> JOHN F. KENNEDY, in an address to the nation on the Berlin crisis, July 25, 1961.

78 I think this is the most extraordinary collection of talent, of human knowledge, that has ever been gathered together at the White House, with the possible exception of when Thomas Jefferson dined alone.

> JOHN F. KENNEDY, in a speech honoring Nobel Prize winners at the White House, April 29, 1962.

79 The President . . . is rightly described as a man of extraordinary powers. Yet it is also true that he must wield those powers under extraordinary limitations—and it is these limitations which so often give the problem of choice its complexity and even poignancy. Lincoln, Franklin Roosevelt once remarked, "was a sad man because he couldn't get it all at once. And nobody can."

> JOHN F. KENNEDY, in the foreword to Theodore C. Sorenson, *Decision-Making in the White House,* 1963.

80 I had plenty of problems when I came into office. But wait until the fellow who follows me sees what he will inherit.

> JOHN F. KENNEDY, in Hugh Sidey, *John F. Kennedy, President: A Reporter's Inside Story,* 1963.

81 What extraordinary vehicles destiny selects to accomplish its design. This man, so lonely in his hour of triumph, so ungenerous in some of his motivations, had navigated our nation through one of the most anguishing periods in its history. Not by nature courageous, he had steeled himself to conspicuous acts of rare courage. Not normally outgoing, he had forced himself to rally his people to its challenge. He had striven for a revolution in American foreign policy so that it would overcome the disastrous oscillations between overcommitment and isolation. Despised by the Establishment, ambiguous in his human perceptions, he had yet held fast to a sense of national honor and responsibility, determined to prove that the strongest free country had no right to abdicate.

> HENRY KISSINGER, on Richard M. Nixon, in *White House Years,* 1979.

82 It often seems that American Presidents come out of regional offices of Central Casting: If Jimmy Carter's Georgia accent and demeanor frequently seemed to remind Americans of some of their clichés about the rural South; John Kennedy's urbane humor, voice, and style seemed to fit their preconceptions about upper crust Boston; Lyndon Johnson was almost a caricature cowboy of Texas, big, masculine, and sometimes vulgar; Richard Nixon suggested a nouveau riche California, slightly insecure, on the make, and as trustworthy as a Los Angeles car dealer, some critics would say. Ronald Reagan represents other sides to some of those clichés upon which people have built their images of California; he was the handsome movie star, an immigrant from Middle America, like millions of other Californians who came west during the 1930s to seek their fortunes and brought with them small-town conservative Middle Western values.

> ROBERT LINDSEY, "Creating the Role," in Hedrick Smith et al., *Reagan the Man, the President,* 1980.

83 I think everyone must feel that the brevity of his tenure of office was a mercy to him and to the country. Harding was not a bad man. He was just a slob.

ALICE ROOSEVELT LONGWORTH, *Crowded Hours,* 1933.

84 Though I yield to no one in my admiration for Mr. Coolidge, I do wish he did not look as if he had been weaned on a pickle.

ALICE ROOSEVELT LONGWORTH, quoting a remark made to her doctor by one of his patients, in *Crowded Hours,* 1933.

85 Since the days when Jefferson expounded his code of political philosophy, the whole world has become his pupil.

MICHAEL MACWHITE, in a speech at the University of Virginia, April, 1931.

86 Nixon was the artist who had discovered the laws of vibration in all the frozen congelations of the mediocre.

NORMAL MAILER, *St. George and the Godfather,* 1972.

87 What kind of President would Nixon be? Well, to begin with, he would be perhaps the hardest-driving chief executive and the most controversial since Theodore Roosevelt. There would be nothing haphazard, nothing bland about his administration, nor any doubt about its political identity.

EARL MAZO, *Richard Nixon: A Political and Personal Portrait,* 1959.

88 Ronald Reagan is the most ignorant President since Warren Harding.

RALPH NADER, quoted in the *Pacific Sun,* March 21, 1981.

89 I have sacrificed everything in my life that I consider precious in order to advance the political career of my husband.

PAT NIXON, quoted in Betty Medsger, *Women at Work,* 1975.

90 I don't think that you can lead from a position of vacillation. If you are going to lead, you've got to decide in advance whether the issue is one that you feel is worth fighting about. If it isn't, then you take no position at all. But if it is worth fighting about, you've got to take a clear-cut position and get all of the advantage that comes from being out in front.

RICHARD M. NIXON, quoted in Earl Mazo, *Richard Nixon: A Political and Personal Portrait,* 1959.

91 You won't have Nixon to kick around anymore because, gentlemen, this is my last press conference.

RICHARD M. NIXON, speaking to reporters after conceding defeat in his campaign for governor of California, November 7, 1962.

92 I don't give a shit what happens. I want you all to stonewall it, let them plead the Fifth Amendment, cover-up or anything else, if it'll save it— save the plan. That's the whole point.

RICHARD M. NIXON, speaking to John Dean, John Ehrlichman, Robert Haldeman, and John Mitchell in the President's office in the Executive Office Building, recorded in the so-called Watergate tapes, March 22, 1973.

93 This office is a sacred trust and I am determined to be worthy of that trust.

RICHARD M. NIXON, speaking of the Presidency in a televised address, April 30, 1973.

94 I made my mistakes, but in all my years of public life I have never profited, never profited from public service. I've earned every cent. And in all of my years in public life I have never obstructed justice. . . . I welcome this kind of examination because people have got to know whether or not their President is a crook. Well, I'm not a crook. I've earned everything I've got.

RICHARD M. NIXON, in Orlando, Florida, responding to newspaper editors' questions about his tax returns, November 17, 1973.

95 When the President does it, that means that it is not illegal.

RICHARD M. NIXON, in a television interview, May 20, 1977.

96 Our Presidents *want* publicity, but above all, they want results. We should applaud rather than condemn them when they resist the insatiable demands of the media in order to do the job they were elected to do.

RICHARD M. NIXON, *The Real War,* 1980.

97 It has been the political career of this man to begin with hypocrisy, proceed with arrogance, and finish in contempt.

> THOMAS PAINE, speaking of John Adams in an open letter, "To the Citizens of the United States," published in the *National Intelligencer,* November 22, 1802.

98 How could they tell?

> Attributed to Dorothy Parker, responding to news that Calvin Coolidge had died on January 5, 1933.

99 [Thomas Jefferson was] a gentleman of thirty-two who could calculate an eclipse, survey an estate, tie an artery, plan an edifice, try a cause, break a horse, dance a minuet, and play the violin.

> JAMES PARTON, in *Thomas Jefferson,* 1874.

100 He wouldn't commit himself to the time of day from a hatful of watches.

> WESTBROOK PEGLER, on Herbert Hoover, c.1929, quoted in Oliver Pilat, *Pegler: Angry Man of the Press,* 1963.

101 The quality of his being one with the people, of having no artificial or natural barriers between him and them, made it possible for him to be a leader without ever being, or thinking of being, a dictator.

> FRANCES PERKINS, on Franklin D. Roosevelt, in *The Roosevelt I Knew,* 1946.

102 We have exchanged the Washingtonian dignity for the Jeffersonian simplicity, which in due time came to be only another name for the Jacksonian vulgarity.

> HENRY CODMAN POTTER, in a speech on the centennial of George Washington's inauguration, April 30, 1889.

103 He rowed to his objective with muffled oars.

> JOHN RANDOLPH, speaking of Martin Van Buren, quoted in W. Cabell Bruce, *John Randolph of Roanoke,* 1923.

104 I don't know anyone who is as vain or more selfish than Lyndon Johnson.

> SAM RAYBURN, quoted in Robert A. Caro, *The Path to Power,* 1982.

105 I had been lauded as a star in sports and had been praised in movies: in politics I found myself misrepresented, cursed, vilified, denounced, and libeled. Yet it was by far the most fascinating part of my life.

> RONALD REAGAN, *Where's the Rest of Me?* 1965.

106 For many years now, you and I have been shushed like children and told there are no simple answers to the complex problems that are beyond our comprehension. Well, the truth is there are simple answers. There are just not easy ones.

> RONALD REAGAN, in his inaugural address as Governor of California, January, 1967.

107 I have long believed there was a divine plan that placed this land here to be found by people of a special kind, that we have a rendezvous with destiny. Yes, there is a spirit moving in this land and a hunger in the people for a spiritual revival. If the task I seek should be given to me, I would pray only that I could perform it in a way that would serve God.

> RONALD REAGAN, in a letter written when campaigning for the Republican presidential nomination in 1976, quoted in Helene von Damm, *Sincerely, Ronald Reagan,* 1981.

108 We have to move ahead, but we are not going to leave *anyone* behind.

> RONALD REAGAN, in his acceptance speech at the Republican Party's National Convention, July, 1980.

109 [He has] the backbone of a chocolate éclair.

> THOMAS BRACKETT REED, describing William McKinley, April, 1898. (Also attributed to Theodore Roosevelt on McKinley.)

110 He does not concentrate on thinking programs through but in getting them through.

> JAMES RESTON, on Lyndon B. Johnson, quoted in Michael V. DiSalle, *Second Choice,* 1966.

111 Franklin had a good way of simplifying things. He made people feel that he had a real understanding of things and they felt they had about the same understanding.

> ELEANOR ROOSEVELT, in an interview in the newspaper *PM,* April 6, 1947.

112 I doubt if Eisenhower can stand a second term and I doubt if the country can stand Nixon as President.

> ELEANOR ROOSEVELT, in a letter to Lord Elibank, January 20, 1956, quoted in Joseph P. Lash, *Eleanor: The Years Alone,* 1972.

113 I feel like a bull moose. I'm ashamed of myself to be so sound and well.

> THEODORE ROOSEVELT, quoted in Lincoln Steffens, "Theodore Roosevelt, Governor," *McClure's Magazine,* May, 1899.

114 It would be simple nonsense to try to prevent it [an assassination attempt] for, as Lincoln said, though it would be safer for a President to live in a cage, it would interfere with his business.

> THEODORE ROOSEVELT, in a letter to Henry Cabot Lodge, August 6, 1906.

115 I've often thought with Nixon that if he'd made the football team, his life would have been different.

> ADELA ROGERS ST. JOHNS, quoted by Joyce Haber in the *Los Angeles Times,* October 13, 1974.

116 I have always tried to treat white-collar criminals like other criminals. It still bothers me that Richard Nixon escaped that equal treatment. I feel that if he had been convicted in my court, I would have sent him to jail. . . . If Nixon had had the character of President Eisenhower, or any other honest president, this scandal [the Watergate break-in and subsequent cover-up] would never have happened. . . . I hope no political party will ever stoop so low as to embrace the likes of Richard Nixon again.

> JOHN J. SIRICA, *To Set the Record Straight,* 1979.

117 His life has been so sudden and his fighting so aggressive, that most people think he never thinks, that every act is born of the impulse of the moment. The public man is the private man, and his friends have no advantage in acquaintance with him over strangers.

> LINCOLN STEFFENS, on Theodore Roosevelt in "The Real Roosevelt," *Ainslee's* magazine, December, 1898.

118 This is a man of many masks. Who can say they have seen his real face?

> ADLAI E. STEVENSON, speaking of Richard M. Nixon, 1956.

119 I have come to the conclusion that the major part of the work of a President is to increase the gate receipts of expositions and fairs and bring tourists into the town.

> WILLIAM HOWARD TAFT, quoted in Archibald W. Butt, *Taft and Roosevelt,* 1930.

120 I would rather be Chief Justice of the United States, and a quieter life than that which comes at the White House is more in keeping with my temperament, but when taken into consideration that I go into history as a President, and my children and children's children are the better placed on account of that fact, I am inclined to think that to be President well compensates one for all the trials and criticisms he has to bear and undergo.

> Ibid.

121 Last night the moon, the stars and all the planets fell on me. If you fellows ever pray, pray for me.

> HARRY S TRUMAN, speaking to reporters on the day after succeeding to the presidency, April 13, 1945.

122 I never think of anyone as the President but Mr. Roosevelt.

> HARRY S TRUMAN, in a letter to Eleanor Roosevelt, nearly six months after FDR's death, quoted in Robert H. Ferrell, *Off the Record,* 1980.

123 Well all the President is, is a glorified public relations man who spends his time flattering, kissing, and kicking people to get them to do what they are supposed to do anyway.

> HARRY S TRUMAN, in a letter to his sister, Mary Jane Truman, November 14, 1947, quoted in Robert H. Ferrell, *Off the Record,* 1980.

124 I would rather have peace in the world than be President.

> HARRY S TRUMAN, in his annual Christmas message, Independence, Missouri, December 24, 1948.

125 The President of the United States is two people—he's the President and he's a human being.

> HARRY S TRUMAN, in a speech to the National Association of Broadcasters, December 14, 1950.

126 A President needs political understanding to *run* the government, but he may be *elected* without it.

> HARRY S TRUMAN, *Years of Trial and Hope,* from *Memoirs,* 1955.

127 As long as I have been in the White House, I can't help waking at 5 A.M. and hearing the old man at the foot of the stairs calling and telling me to get out and milk the cows.

> HARRY S TRUMAN, to Sen. George Aiken, quoted in Robert J. Donovan, *Conflict and Crisis,* 1977.

128 Nixon is a shifty-eyed goddamn liar. . . . He's one of the few in the history of this country to run for high office talking out of both sides of his mouth at the same time and lying out of both sides.

> HARRY S TRUMAN, quoted by Leo Rosten, *Infinite Riches,* 1978.

129 I tried never to forget who I was and where I'd come from and where I was going back to.

> HARRY S TRUMAN, quoted in Merle Miller, *Plain Speaking,* 1982.

130 I tread in the footsteps of illustrious men, whose superiors it is our happiness to believe are not found on the executive calendar of any country.

> MARTIN VAN BUREN, in his inaugural address, March 4, 1837.

131 In receiving from the people the sacred trust twice confided to my illustrious predecessor [Andrew Jackson], and which he has discharged so faithfully and so well, I know that I can not expect to perform the arduous task with equal ability and success.

> MARTIN VAN BUREN, in his inaugural address, March 4, 1837.

132 I wouldn't want a professional screen actor to be President of the United States, no matter how nice or bright he is because he's spent his entire life being moved about like a piece of furniture. He's used to being used. . . . I couldn't imagine an actor as president, I could imagine a director. After all, he's a hustler, a liar, a cheat—plainly presidential.

> GORE VIDAL, quoted in *American Film,* April, 1977.

133 By God, he had rather be on his farm than to be made emperor of the world.

> Attributed to George Washington, speaking of Thomas Jefferson.

134 If he was a freak, God and the times needed one.

> WILLIAM ALLEN WHITE, writing of Theodore Roosevelt, in *Masks in a Pageant,* 1928.

135 His walk was a shoulder-shaking, assertive, heel-clicking, straight-away gait, rather consciously rapid as one who is habitually about his master's business.

> WILLIAM ALLEN WHITE, describing Theodore Roosevelt, quoted in David McCullough, *The Path Between the Seas,* 1978.

136 [Lyndon B.] Johnson might play politics in the North, but he did not come to the South [to secure civil rights for blacks] with vindictiveness in his heart; there might be a little Scalawag in him but a Carpetbagger he could never be.

> TOM WICKER, *JFK and LBJ,* 1968.

137 Lyndon Johnson came into office seeking a Great Society in America and found instead an ugly little war that consumed him.

> Ibid.

138 Reagan the actor never made anyone forget Barrymore, but Reagan the President, serenely confident and not apt to panic, is going to try to make Washington forget where others found the limits of the possible.

> GEORGE F. WILL, *The Pursuit of Virtue and Other Tory Notions,* 1982.

139 I think that Lincoln, Wilson, and F.D.R. were all carried into war by the power drive be-

hind them—though they all must have had moments, Woodrow Wilson especially, when they hoped that it might be avoided. I don't believe that it is possible to be President and not be willing to lead the country into war. Nobody can get to be President who has not himself a strong drive to power.

> EDMUND WILSON, in a letter to Barbara Deming, April 11, 1962, in *Letters on Literature and Politics, 1912–1972,* 1977.

140 The immortality of Thomas Jefferson does not lie in any one of his achievements, or in the series of his achievements, but in his attitude toward mankind.

> WOODROW WILSON, address at Jefferson Day banquet, Washington, D.C., April 13, 1916.

141 The President can never again be the mere domestic figure he has been throughout so large a part of our history. The nation has risen to the first rank in power and resources. The other nations of the world look askance upon her, half in envy, half in fear, and wonder with a deep anxiety what she will do with her vast strength. Our President must always, henceforth, be one of the great powers of the world, whether he act greatly, or wisely, or not. He must stand always at the front of our affairs, and the office will be as big and as influential as the man who occupies it.

> WOODROW WILSON, quoted in Nelson A. Rockefeller, *Unity, Freedom and Peace: A Blueprint for Tomorrow,* 1968.

142 His philosophical approach is superficial, overly simplistic, one-dimensional. What he preaches is pure economic pap, glossed over with uplifting homilies and inspirational chatter. Yet so far the guy is making it work. Appalled by what seems to me a lack of depth, I stand in awe nevertheless of his political skill. I am not sure that I have seen its equal.

> JIM WRIGHT, on Ronald Reagan, in his diary, June 11, 1981.

194. PRINCIPLE

See also CHARACTER; CONDUCT; DUTY; INDIVIDUALITY; REPUTATION

1 Principles . . . become modified in practice, by facts.

> JAMES FENIMORE COOPER, *Democrat,* 1838.

2 The value of a principle is the number of things it will explain.

> RALPH WALDO EMERSON, "The Preacher," *Lectures and Biographical Sketches,* 1883.

3 Moral perfection in death is a luxury most men can do without.

> GARRETT HARDIN, *Exploring New Ethics for Survival,* 1972.

4 Every honest man will suppose honest acts to flow from honest principles, and the rogues may rail without intermission.

> THOMAS JEFFERSON, in a letter to Benjamin Rush, December 20, 1801.

5 Important principles may and must be flexible.

> ABRAHAM LINCOLN, in an address in Washington, D.C., April 11, 1865.

6 It is never right to compromise with dishonesty.

> HENRY CABOT LODGE, JR., in a 1952 conversation with Republican leaders, quoted in Richard Norton Smith, *Thomas E. Dewey and His Times,* 1982.

7 The truly important ingredients of life are still the same as they always have been—true love and real friendship, honesty and faithfulness, sincerity, unselfishness and selflessness, the concept that it is better to give than to receive, to do unto others as you would have them do unto you. These principles are still around, they haven't gone away.

> NANCY REAGAN, *Nancy,* 1980.

8 One, with God, is always a majority, but many a martyr has been burned at the stake while the votes were being counted.

THOMAS BRACKETT REED, in a speech in the House of Representatives, 1885.

9 You are so afraid of losing your moral sense that you are not willing to take it through anything more dangerous than a mud-puddle.

GERTRUDE STEIN, "Q.E.D," published in *Fernhurst, Q.E.D., and Other Early Writings,* 1972.

---

195. PROGRESS

See also CHANGE; EVOLUTION; HISTORY; INVENTION; KNOWLEDGE; NUCLEAR AGE; PREDICTIONS; SCIENCE; SPACE EXPLORATION; SUCCESS; TECHNOLOGY

---

1 A savage is a man of one story, and that one story a cellar.... The civilized man is thirty stories deep.

HENRY WARD BEECHER, in a speech in Liverpool, England, October 16, 1863.

2 All thoughtful men agree that the present aspect of society is portentous of great changes. The only question is, whether they will be for the better or the worse.... *Looking Backward* was written in the belief that the Golden Age lies before us and not behind us, and is not far away. Our children will surely see it, and we, too, who are already men and women, if we deserve it by our faith and by our works.

EDWARD BELLAMY, in the postscript to *Looking Backward: 2000–1887,* 1888.

3 Weep not that the world changes—did it keep
    A stable, changeless state, it were cause indeed
        to weep.

WILLIAM CULLEN BRYANT, "Mutation," 1824.

4 The objector and the rebel who raises his voice against what he believes to be the injustice of the present and the wrongs of the past is the one who hunches the world along.

CLARENCE DARROW, addressing a trial jury in Chicago, 1920, quoted in Arthur Weinberg, *Attorney for the Damned,* 1957.

5 We do make progress but it's the same kind Julyus Caesar made an' ivry wan has made befure or since an' in this age iv masheenery we're still burrid be hand.

FINLEY PETER DUNNE, *Observations by Mr. Dooley,* 1902.

6 The civilized man has built a coach, but has lost the use of his feet. He is supported on crutches, but lacks so much support of muscle. He has a fine Geneva watch, but he fails of the skill to tell the hour by the sun.

RALPH WALDO EMERSON, "Self-Reliance," *Essays,* First Series, 1841.

7 All our progress is an unfolding, like the vegetable bud. You have first an instinct, then an opinion, then a knowledge, as the plant has root, bud, and fruit. Trust the instinct to the end, though you can render no reason.

RALPH WALDO EMERSON, "Intellect," *Essays,* First Series, 1841.

8 We think our civilization near its meridian, but we are yet only at the cock-crowing and the morning star.

RALPH WALDO EMERSON, "Politics," *Essays,* Second Series, 1844.

9 To accomplish anything excellent, the will must work for catholic and universal ends.

RALPH WALDO EMERSON, "Civilization," *Society and Solitude,* 1870.

10 Progress robs us of past delights.

SAM J. ERVIN, JR., *Humor of a Country Lawyer,* 1983.

11 So long as all the increased wealth which modern progress brings, goes but to build up great fortunes, to increase luxury, and make sharper the contest between the House of Have and the House of Want, progress is not real and cannot be permanent.

HENRY GEORGE, *Progress and Poverty,* 1879.

12 Social progress makes the well-being of all more and more the business of each; it binds all closer

and closer together in bonds from which none can escape.

> HENRY GEORGE, *Social Problems,* 1884.

13 Cost is the father and compensation is the mother of progress.

> JOSIAH GILBERT HOLLAND, *Plain Talks,* 1866.

14 I do not pin my dreams for the future to my country or even to my race. I think it probable that civilization somehow will last as long as I care to look ahead.

> OLIVER WENDELL HOLMES, JR., in a speech in New York City, February 15, 1913.

15 The slogan of progress is changing from the full dinner pail to the full garage.

> HERBERT HOOVER, in a speech in New York City, October 22, 1928.

16 Progress needs the brakeman, but the brakeman should not spend all his time putting on the brakes.

> ELBERT HUBBARD, *The Roycroft Dictionary and Book of Epigrams,* 1923.

17 The history of progress is written in the lives of infidels.

> ROBERT G. INGERSOLL, in a speech in New York City, May 1, 1881.

18 Laws and institutions must go hand in hand with the progress of the human mind. As that becomes more developed, more enlightened, as new discoveries are made, new truths disclosed, and manners and opinions change with the change of circumstances, institutions must advance also, and keep pace with the times.

> THOMAS JEFFERSON, in a letter to Samuel Kercheval, July 12, 1816.

19 Harsh and brutal systems slowly give place to gentler ones. The stars in their courses have all along fought against Sisera and his kind. The way of the transgressor has proved to be not only difficult but impossible. The universe is against it.

> RUFUS MATTHEW JONES, "The Eternal Goodness," in Joseph Fort Newton, *My Idea of God,* 1926. (Sisera, a Canaanite general, oppressed the Israelites, but was slain by Deborah and Barak.)

20 Actually, time itself is neutral; it can be used either destructively or constructively. More and more I feel that the people of ill will have used time much more effectively than have the people of good will. . . . Human progress never rolls in on wheels of inevitability; it comes through the tireless efforts of men willing to be co-workers with God, and without this hard work, time itself becomes an ally of the forces of social stagnation. We must use time creatively, in the knowledge that the time is always ripe to do right.

> MARTIN LUTHER KING, JR., in "Letter from Birmingham Jail," April 16, 1963.

21 Every generation must go further than the last or what's the use in it?

> MERIDEL LE SUEUR, *Salute to Spring,* 1940.

22 I do not mean to say we are bound to follow implicitly in whatever our fathers did. To do so would be to discard all the lights of current experience—to reject all progress, all improvement.

> ABRAHAM LINCOLN, in a Cooper Union address, New York City, February 27, 1860.

23 He who is firmly seated in authority soon learns to think security, and not progress, the highest lesson of statecraft.

> JAMES RUSSELL LOWELL, *Among My Books,* 1870.

24 Not a change for the better in our human housekeeping has ever taken place that wise and good men have not opposed it—have not prophesied that the world would wake up to find its throat cut in consequence.

> JAMES RUSSELL LOWELL, "On Democracy," an address in Birmingham, England, October 6, 1884.

25 Progress might have been all right once but it has gone on too long.

> Attributed to Ogden Nash.

26 Every step of progress the world has made has been from scaffold to scaffold, and from stake to stake.

> WENDELL PHILLIPS, in a speech in Worcester, Massachusetts, October 15, 1851.

27 The reason why the race of man moves slowly is because it must move all together.

> THOMAS BRACKETT REED, in a speech in Waterville, Maine, July 30, 1885.

28 We make more progress by owning our faults than by always dwelling on our virtues.

> THOMAS BRACKETT REED, quoted in Samuel Walker McCall, *The Life of Thomas Brackett Reed,* 1914.

29 Progress, far from consisting in change, depends on retentiveness. When change is absolute there remains no being to improve and no direction is set for possible improvement: and when experience is not retained, as among savages, infancy is perpetual. Those who cannot remember the past are condemned to repeat it.

> GEORGE SANTAYANA, *The Life of Reason,* 1905–1906.

30 All progress has resulted from people who took unpopular positions.

> ADLAI E. STEVENSON, in a speech at Princeton University, New Jersey, March 22, 1954.

31 Most of the luxuries, and many of the so-called comforts of life, are not only not indispensable, but positive hindrances to the elevation of mankind.

> HENRY DAVID THOREAU, *Walden,* 1854.

32 I have no doubt that it is a part of the destiny of the human race, in its gradual improvement, to leave off eating animals, as surely as the savage tribes have left off eating each other when they came in contact with the more civilized.

> Ibid.

33 Five years ago, lodged in an attic; live in a swell house now, with a mansard roof, and all the modern inconveniences.

> MARK TWAIN, *Life on the Mississippi,* 1883.

34 Life means progress, and progress means suffering.

> HENDRIK WILLEM VAN LOON, *Tolerance,* 1925.

35 The eager and often inconsiderate appeals of reformers and revolutionists are indispensable, to counterbalance the inertness and fossilism making so large a part of human institutions.

> WALT WHITMAN, *Democratic Vistas,* 1870.

36 And step by step, since time began,
I see the steady gain of man.

> JOHN GREENLEAF WHITTIER, "The Chapel of the Hermits," 1851.

---

196. THE PUBLIC

See also AMERICANS; DEMOCRACY; SOCIETY

---

1 There's a sucker born every minute.

> Attributed to P.T. Barnum.

2 To do as the people do is a tribute to the people's majesty.

> JAMES BRYCE, *The American Commonwealth,* 1888.

3 But to the great mass of mankind in all places, public questions come in the third or fourth rank among the interests of life, and obtain less than a third or a fourth of the leisure available for thinking. It is therefore rather sentiment than thought that the mass can contribute; and the soundness and elevation of their sentiment will have more to do with their taking their stand on the side of justice, honor, and peace, than any reasoning they can apply to the sifting of the multifarious facts thrown before them, and to the drawing of the legitimate inferences therefrom.

> Ibid.

4 In a free country more especially, ten men who care are worth a hundred who do not.

> Ibid.

5 The world is governed much more by opinion than by laws. It is not the judgment of courts, but the moral judgment of individuals and masses of men, which is the chief wall of defense round property and life.

> WILLIAM ELLERY CHANNING, in a letter to Jonathan Phillips, 1839.

6 Nothing is more uncertain than a dependence upon public bodies. They are moved like the wind, but rather more uncertain.

> ABRAHAM CLARK, in a letter to James Caldwell, March 7, 1777.

7 The constant appeals to public opinion in a democracy, though excellent as a corrective of public vices, induce private hypocrisy, causing men to conceal their own convictions when opposed to those of the mass, the latter being seldom wholly right, or wholly wrong.

> JAMES FENIMORE COOPER, *The American Democrat,* 1838.

8 A mob is a society of bodies voluntarily bereaving themselves of reason, and traversing its work. The mob is man voluntarily descending to the nature of the beast.

> RALPH WALDO EMERSON, "Compensation," *Essays,* First Series, 1841.

9 A mob cannot be a permanency; everybody's interest requires that it should not exist.

> RALPH WALDO EMERSON, "Politics," *Essays,* Second Series, 1844.

10 Leave this hypocritical prating about the masses. Masses are rude, lame, unmade, pernicious in their demands and influence, and need not to be flattered but to be schooled. I wish not to concede anything to them, but to tame, drill, divide and break them up, and draw individuals out of them. The worst of charity is that the lives you are asked to preserve are not worth preserving.

> RALPH WALDO EMERSON, "Considerations by the Way," *The Conduct of Life,* 1860.

11 The people are to be taken in very small doses.

> RALPH WALDO EMERSON, *Society and Solitude,* 1870.

12 The real political issues of the day declare themselves, and come out of the depths of that deep which we call public opinion.

> JAMES A. GARFIELD, in a speech in Boston, September 10, 1878.

13 I shall on all subjects have a policy to recommend, but none to enforce against the will of the people.

> ULYSSES S. GRANT, in his first inaugural address, March 4, 1869.

14 Public opinion is the judgment of the incapable many opposed to that of the discerning few.

> ELBERT HUBBARD, *The Roycroft Dictionary and Book of Epigrams,* 1923.

15 When public opinion changes, it is with the rapidity of thought.

> THOMAS JEFFERSON, in a letter to Charles Yancey, January 6, 1816.

16 It may be true, and I suspect it is, that the mass of people everywhere are normally peace-loving and would accept many restraints and sacrifices in preference to the monstrous calamities of war. But I also suspect that what purports to be public opinion in most countries that consider themselves to have popular government is often not really the consensus of the feelings of the mass of the people at all but rather the expression of the interests of special highly vocal minorities—politicians, commentators, and publicity-seekers of all sorts: people who live by their ability to draw attention to themselves and die, like fish out of water, if they are compelled to remain silent.

> GEORGE F. KENNAN, *American Diplomacy, 1900–1950,* 1951.

17 No one ever went broke underestimating the taste of the American public.

> Attributed to H.L. Mencken.

18 The public, with its mob yearning to be instructed, edified and pulled by the nose, demands certainties.

> H.L. MENCKEN, *Prejudices,* First Series, 1919.

19 Common sense, in so far as it exists, is all for the bourgeoisie. Nonsense is the privilege of the aristocracy. The worries of the world are for the common people.

> GEORGE JEAN NATHAN, *Autobiography of an Attitude,* 1925.

20 In America, public opinion is the leader.

> FRANCES PERKINS, *People at Work*, 1934.

21 There is no tyranny so despotic as that of public opinion among a free people.

> DONN PIATT, "Lincoln," *Memories of the Men Who Saved the Union*, 1887.

22 It is an ancient axiom of statecraft that you can always give the public anything but you can never take away what you once have given, without enormous trouble.

> WALTER BOUGHTON PITKIN, *Twilight of the American Mind*, 1928.

23 The nose of a mob is its imagination. By this, at any time, it can be quietly led.

> EDGAR ALLAN POE, *Marginalia*, 1844–1849.

24 There is . . . one tremendous ruler of the human race—and that ruler is that combination of the opinions of all, the leveling up of universal sense which is called public sentiment.

> THOMAS BRACKETT REED, in a speech in Waterville, Maine, July 30, 1885.

25 [Public sentiment is] in its essence nothing more or less than the expression of the average intelligence and average ignorance of mankind [and constitutes] the ever-present regulator and police of humanity. . . . Let a man proclaim a new principle. Public sentiment will surely be on the other side.

> THOMAS BRACKETT REED, quoted in William Alexander Robinson, *Thomas B. Reed, Parliamentarian*, 1930.

26 I am the people—the mob—the crowd—the mass.
Do you know that all the great work of the world is done through me?

> CARL SANDBURG, "I Am the People, the Mob," 1916.

27 Vox populi, vox humbug. [The voice of the people is the voice of humbug.]

> WILLIAM T. SHERMAN, in a letter to his wife, June 2, 1863.

28 Who is . . . the Forgotten Man? He is the clean, quiet, virtuous, domestic citizen, who pays his debts and his taxes and is never heard of out of his little circle.

> WILLIAM GRAHAM SUMNER, "The Forgotten Man," in *The Forgotten Man and Other Essays*, 1919.

29 Whenever A and B put their heads together and decide what A, B and C must do for D, there is never any pressure on A and B. They consent to it and like it. There is rarely any pressure on D because he does not like it and contrives to evade it. The pressure all comes on C. Now, who is C? He is always the man who, if let alone, would make a reasonable use of his liberty without abusing it. He would not constitute any social problem at all and would not need any regulation. He is the Forgotten Man.

> Ibid.

30 The public be damned.

> WILLIAM H. VANDERBILT, replying to a reporter who asked whether he was working for the public or his stockholders, 1883.

31 Public opinion is stronger than the legislature, and nearly as strong as the Ten Commandments.

> CHARLES DUDLEY WARNER, *My Summer in a Garden*, 1871.

32 The people at large are governed much by custom. To acts of legislation or civil authority they have been ever taught to yield a willing obedience, without reasoning about their propriety. On those of military power, whether immediate or derived originally from another source, they have ever looked with a jealous and suspicious eye.

> GEORGE WASHINGTON, in a letter to the President of the Continental Congress, December 14, 1777.

33 In a free and republican government, you cannot restrain the voice of the multitude; every man will speak as he thinks, or more properly without thinking, consequently will judge of effects without attending to the causes.

> GEORGE WASHINGTON, in a letter to the Marquis de Lafayette, September 1, 1778.

34 The power under the Constitution will always be in the people.

> GEORGE WASHINGTON, in a letter to Bushrod Washington, November 10, 1787.

35 It is on great occasions only, and after time has been given for cool and deliberate reflection, that the real voices of the people can be known.

> GEORGE WASHINGTON, in a letter to Edward Carrington, May 1, 1796.

36 In proportion as the structure of a government gives force to public opinion, it is essential that public opinion should be enlightened.

> GEORGE WASHINGTON, in his Farewell Address, September 19, 1796.

---

197. PUNISHMENT

See also CRIME; JUSTICE; LAW

---

1 The sheriff took Frankie to the gallows,
Hung her until she died;
They hung her for killing Johnny,
And the undertaker waited outside;
She killed her man, 'cause he done her wrong.

> From the folk ballad "Frankie and Johnny," c.1875.

2 If any shall be heard to swear, curse, or blaspheme the name of God, the commander is strictly enjoined to punish them for every offense by causing them to wear a wooden collar or some shameful badge, for so long a time as he shall judge proper.

> JOHN ADAMS, *Rules for the Regulation of the Navy of the United Colonies,* 1775.

3 You simply cannot hang a millionaire in America.

> BOURKE COCKRAN, quoted in Shane Leslie, *American Wonderland,* 1936.

4 Jails and prisons are designed to break human beings, to convert the population into specimens in a zoo—obedient to our keepers, but dangerous to each other.

> ANGELA DAVIS, *An Autobiography,* 1974.

5 Many people are unaware of the fact that jail and prison are two entirely different institutions. People in prison have already been convicted. Jails are primarily for pretrial confinement, holding places until prisoners are either convicted or found innocent. More than half of the jail population have never been convicted of anything, yet they languish in those cells.

> Ibid.

6 Crime and punishment grow out of one stem. Punishment is a fruit that unsuspected ripens within the flower of the pleasure which concealed it.

> RALPH WALDO EMERSON, "Compensation," *Essays,* First Series, 1841.

7 What other dungeon is so dark as one's own heart! What jailer so inexorable as one's self!

> NATHANIEL HAWTHORNE, *The House of the Seven Gables,* 1851.

8 Only the man who has enough good in him to feel the justice of the penalty can be punished; the others can only be hurt.

> WILLIAM ERNEST HOCKING, *The Coming World Civilization,* 1957.

9 The greatest punishment is to be despised by your neighbors, the world, and members of your family.

> EDGAR WATSON HOWE, in *E.W. Howe's Monthly,* published from 1911–1937.

10 We are not punished for our sins, but by them.

> ELBERT HUBBARD, *The Roycroft Dictionary and Book of Epigrams,* 1923.

11 Punishment should fit the criminal, not the crime.

> Ibid.

12 Whosoever committeth murder by way of duel shall suffer death by hanging; and if he were the challenger, his body, after death, shall be gibbetted. He who removeth it from the gibbet shall be guilty of a misdemeanor, and the officer shall see that it be replaced.

THOMAS JEFFERSON, "A Bill for proportioning
Crimes and Punishments, in cases heretofore
Capital," 1779.

13 Nations, like individuals, are subjected to punishments and chastisements in this world.

ABRAHAM LINCOLN, "Proclamation for a
National Fast-Day," March 30, 1863.

14 I'd horsewhip you if I had a horse.

GROUCHO MARX, in *Horse Feathers,* 1932.

15 You have put me in here a cub, but I will come
out roaring like a lion, and I will make all hell
howl!

CARRY NATION, referring to her imprisonment,
c.1901, quoted in Carleton Beals, *Cyclone Carry,*
1962.

16 Every unpunished murder takes away something from the security of every man's life.

DANIEL WEBSTER, arguing in a murder trial in
Salem, Massachusetts, August, 1830.

---

198. REBELLION

See also AMERICAN REVOLUTION;
AUTHORITY; CIVIL WAR; FREEDOM;
LIBERTY; REVOLUTION

---

1 Insurrection, *n.* An unsuccessful revolution.
Disaffection's failure to substitute misrule for bad
government.

AMBROSE BIERCE, *The Devil's Dictionary,* 1906.

2 Rebel, *n.* A proponent of a new misrule who has
failed to establish it.

Ibid.

3 When an insurrection is justifiable, an answer
can seldom be given beforehand. The result decides. When treason prospers, none dare call it
treason.

JAMES BRYCE, on the question of the South's right
to secede from the Union, in *The American
Commonwealth,* 1888.

4 The revolt against any oppression usually goes to
an opposite extreme for a time; and that is right and
necessary.

TENNESSEE CLAFLIN, in *Woodhull and Claflin's
Weekly,* 1871.

5 When the appeal is made to the sword, highly
probable it is that the punishment will exceed the
offense; and the calamities attending on war outweigh those preceding it. These considerations of
justice and prudence, will always have great influence with good and wise men.

JOHN DICKINSON, *Letters from a Farmer in
Pennsylvania,* 1768.

6 Never strike a king unless you are sure you shall
kill him.

RALPH WALDO EMERSON, entry written in
September, 1843, *Journals,* 1909–1914.

7 Political agitation, by the passions it arouses or
the convictions it engenders, may in fact stimulate
men to the violation of law. Detestation of existing
policies is easily transformed into forcible resistance
of the authority which puts them in execution, and
it would be folly to disregard the causal relation
between the two. Yet to assimilate agitation, legitimate as such, with direct incitement to violent resistance, is to disregard the tolerance of all methods
of political agitation which in normal times is a
safeguard of free government.

LEARNED HAND, in a Federal district court
opinion, *Masses Publishing Co.* v. *Patten,* 1917.

8 I hold it, that a little rebellion, now and then, is
a good thing, and as necessary in the political world
as storms in the physical. Unsuccessful rebellions,
indeed, generally establish the encroachments on
the rights of the people, which have produced them.
An observation of this truth should render honest
republican governors so mild in their punishment
of rebellions, as not to discourage them too much.
It is a medicine necessary for the sound health of
government.

THOMAS JEFFERSON, in a letter to James
Madison, January 30, 1787.

9 The spirit of resistance to government is so valuable on certain occasions that I wish it to be always

kept alive. It will often be exercised when wrong, but better so than not to be exercised at all. I like a little rebellion now and then.

THOMAS JEFFERSON, in a letter to Abigail Adams, February 22, 1787.

10 I will quote the motto of one, I believe, of the regicides of Charles I, "Rebellion to tyrants is obedience to God."

THOMAS JEFFERSON, in a letter to Edward Everett, February 24, 1823.

11 Show me the man who makes war on the government, and fires on its vessels, and I will show you a traitor. If I were President of the United States, I would have all such arrested, and when tried and convicted, by the Eternal God I would hang them.

ANDREW JOHNSON, in a public statement, March 2, 1861.

12 The limitation of riots, moral questions aside, is that they cannot win and their participants know it. Hence, rioting is not revolutionary but reactionary because it invites defeat. It involves an emotional catharsis, but it must be followed by a sense of futility.

MARTIN LUTHER KING, JR., *The Trumpet of Conscience,* 1967.

13 No doubt but it is safe to dwell
     Where ordered duties are;
No doubt the cherubs earn their wage
     Who wind each ticking star;
No doubt the system is quite right!—
     Sane, ordered, regular;
But how the rebel fires the soul
     Who dares the strong gods' ire!

DON MARQUIS, "The Rebel," in *Dreams and Dust,* 1915.

14 It doesn't take a majority to make a rebellion; it takes only a few determined leaders and a sound cause.

H.L. MENCKEN, *Prejudices,* Fifth Series, 1926.

15 The only justification of rebellion is success.

THOMAS BRACKETT REED, speaking in the House of Representatives, April 12, 1878.

16 If the injustice is part of the necessary friction of the machine of government, let it go, let it go: perchance it will wear smooth—certainly the machine will wear out. . . . Perhaps you may consider whether the remedy will not be worse than the evil; but if it is of such a nature that it requires you to be the agent of injustice to another, then, I say, break the law. Let your life be a counter friction to stop the machine.

HENRY DAVID THOREAU, "Civil Disobedience," 1849.

199. REFORM

See also CHANGE; PROGRESS

1 With most men reform is a trade. . . . Reform for its own sake seldom thrives.

JOHN QUINCY ADAMS, in a letter, April 21, 1837.

2 When Dr. Johnson defined patriotism as the last refuge of a scoundrel, he ignored the enormous possibilities of the word reform.

ROSCOE CONKLING, quoted in David M. Jordan, *Roscoe Conkling of New York,* 1971.

3 A man that'd expect to thrain lobsters to fly in a year is called a loonytic; but a man that thinks men can be tu-rrned into angels be an illiction is called a rayformer an' remains at large.

FINLEY PETER DUNNE, *Mr. Dooley's Opinions,* 1900.

4 We are reformers in Spring and Summer; in Autumn and Winter we stand by the old; reformers in the morning, conservers at night.

RALPH WALDO EMERSON, "The Conservative," *Nature; Addresses and Lectures,* 1849.

5 Reform has no gratitude, no prudence, no husbandry.

Ibid.

6 Reform must come from within, not from without. You cannot legislate for virtue.

JAMES CARDINAL GIBBONS, in a speech in Baltimore, Maryland, September 13, 1909.

7 Most reformers wore rubber boots and stood on glass when God sent a current of Commonsense through the Universe.

ELBERT HUBBARD, *The Roycroft Dictionary and Book of Epigrams,* 1923.

8 'Tis not too late to build our young land right,
Cleaner than Holland, courtlier than Japan,
Devout like early Rome with hearths like hers,
Hearths that will recreate the breed called man.

VACHEL LINDSAY, "To Reformers in Despair," *Collected Poems,* 1923.

9 Change is not reform.

JOHN RANDOLPH, speaking at the Virginia Constitutional Convention, December, 1829.

10 Nothing so needs reforming as other people's habits.

MARK TWAIN, "Pudd'nhead Wilson's Calendar," *Pudd'nhead Wilson,* 1894.

11 A reformer is a guy who rides through a sewer in a glass-bottomed boat.

Attributed to Jimmy Walker, c.1928.

---

200. RELIGION

See also BELIEF; EVIL; PERCEPTION; PHILOSOPHY; RELIGIOUS FREEDOM; SIN

---

1 Now I lay me down to sleep;
I pray the Lord my soul to keep.
If I should die before I wake,
I pray the Lord my soul to take.

Anonymous, from *The New England Primer,* compiled and published by Benjamin Harris, c.1690.

2 Job feels the rod,
Yet blesses God.

Ibid.

3 It takes a rubber ball to bounce,
It takes a baseball to roll,
But it takes a dam' good preacher
To send salvation to my soul.

Folk song, quoted in Howard W. Odum, *Wings on My Feet,* 1929.

4 Work for the Lord, pay is small, retirement benefits are out of this world.

A sign outside Chuck Meyer's House of Television, Phoenix, Arizona, reported in Bill Bradley, *Life on the Run,* 1976.

5 The frightful engines of ecclesiastical councils, of diabolical malice, and Calvinistical good-nature never failed to terrify me exceedingly whenever I thought of preaching.

JOHN ADAMS, in a letter to Richard Cranch, August 29, 1756.

6 Here is every Thing which can lay hold of the Eye, Ear, and Imagination. Every Thing which can charm and bewitch the simple and ignorant. I wonder how Luther ever broke the spell.

JOHN ADAMS, describing his visit to a Roman Catholic church in Philadelphia, in a letter to Abigail Adams, October 9, 1774.

7 I believe in God in his wisdom and benevolence: and I cannot conceive that such a Being could make such a species as the human merely to live and die on this earth. If I did not believe [in] a future state, I should believe in no God.

JOHN ADAMS, in a letter to Thomas Jefferson, December 8, 1818.

8 There is in the clergy of all the Christian denominations a time-serving, cringing, subservient morality, as wide from the spirit of the Gospel as it is from the intrepid assertion and vindication of truth.

JOHN QUINCY ADAMS, in his diary, May 27, 1838.

9 How can I believe in God when just last week I got my tongue caught in the roller of an electric typewriter?

WOODY ALLEN, "Selections from the Allen Notebooks," in *Without Feathers,* 1975.

10 Religion tends to speak the language of the heart, which is the language of friends, lovers, children, and parents.

> EDWARD SCRIBNER AMES, "My Conception of God," in Joseph Fort Newton, *My Idea of God,* 1926.

11 If a religion is unpatriotic, it ain't right.

> HARRIETTE ARNOW, *The Dollmaker,* 1954.

12 The Bible is the most betrashed book in the world. Coming to it through commentaries is much like looking at a landscape through garret windows, over which generations of unmolested spiders have spun their webs.

> HENRY WARD BEECHER, *Life Thoughts,* 1858.

13 We not only live among men, but there are airy hosts, blessed spectators, sympathetic lookers-on, that see and know and appreciate our thoughts and feelings and acts.

> HENRY WARD BEECHER, *Royal Truths,* 1866.

14 I hope those old water-logged saints that died soaking in damp stone cells were taken to Heaven. They had Hell enough on earth.

> Ibid.

15 Plenty well, no pray; big bellyache, heap God.

> AMBROSE BIERCE, quoting "the simple Red Man of the western wild," in the definition of "indigestion" in *The Devil's Dictionary,* 1906.

16 Brahma, *n.* He who created the Hindoos, who are preserved by Vishnu and destroyed by Siva—a rather neater division of labor than is found among the deities of some other nations.

> AMBROSE BIERCE, *The Devil's Dictionary,* 1906.

17 Christian, *n.* One who believes that the New Testament is a divinely inspired book admirably suited to the spiritual needs of his neighbor. One who follows the teachings of Christ in so far as they are not inconsistent with a life of sin.

> Ibid.

18 Clergyman, *n.* A man who undertakes the management of our spiritual affairs as a method of bettering his temporal ones.

> Ibid.

19 Miracle, *n.* An act or event out of the order of nature and unaccountable, as beating a normal hand of four kings and an ace with four aces and a king.

> Ibid.

20 Piety, *n.* Reverence for the Supreme Being, based upon His supposed resemblance to man.
> The pig is taught by sermons and epistles
> To think the God of Swine has snout and
>   bristles.

> Ibid.

21 Pray, *n.* To ask that the laws of the universe be annulled in behalf of a single petitioner confessedly unworthy.

> Ibid.

22 Saint, *n.* A dead sinner revised and edited.

> Ibid.

23 The religion of Hell is patriotism, and the government is an enlightened democracy.

> JAMES BRANCH CABELL, *Jurgen,* 1919.

24 The trouble with born-again Christians is that they are an even bigger pain the second time around.

> HERB CAEN, writing in the *San Francisco Chronicle,* July 20, 1981.

25 It is only when men begin to worship that they begin to grow.

> CALVIN COOLIDGE, in a speech at Fredericksburg, Virginia, July 6, 1922.

26 In America the taint of sectarianism lies broad upon the land. Not content with acknowledging the supremacy of the Deity, and with erecting temples in his honor, where all can bow down with reverence, the pride and vanity of human reason enter into and pollute our worship, and the houses that should be of God and for God, alone, where he is to be honored with submissive faith, are too often merely schools of metaphysical and useless distinctions. The nation is sectarian, rather than Christian.

> JAMES FENIMORE COOPER, *The American Democrat,* 1838.

27 I do not consider it an insult, but rather a compliment to be called an agnostic. I do not pretend to know where many ignorant men are sure—that is all that agnosticism means.

> CLARENCE DARROW, speaking at the Scopes trial, Dayton, Tennessee, July 13, 1925.

28 I don't believe in God because I don't believe in Mother Goose.

> CLARENCE DARROW, in a speech in Toronto, Canada, 1930.

29 When Wall Street yells war, you may rest assured every pulpit in the land will yell war.

> EUGENE V. DEBS, in a speech in Canton, Ohio, June 16, 1918.

30 It is the final proof of God's omnipotence that he need not exist in order to save us.

> PETER DE VRIES, *Mackeral Plaza,* 1958.

31 Somewhere, and I can't find where, I read about an Eskimo hunter who asked the local missionary priest, "If I did not know about God and sin, would I go to hell?" "No," said the priest, "not if you did not know." "Then why," asked the Eskimo earnestly, "did you tell me?"

> ANNIE DILLARD, *Pilgrim at Tinker Creek,* 1974.

32 Men may believe what they cannot prove. They may not be put to the proof of their religious doctrines or beliefs. Religious experiences which are as real as life to some may be incomprehensible to others.

> WILLIAM O. DOUGLAS, in a Supreme Court opinion, *United States* v. *Ballard,* 1944.

33 If I were personally to define religion I would say that it is a bandage that man has invented to protect a soul made bloody by circumstance.

> Attributed to Theodore Dreiser.

34 God is Love.

> MARY BAKER EDDY, *Science and Health, with Key to the Scriptures,* 1875.

35 Experience teaches us that we do not always receive the blessings we ask for in prayer.

> Ibid.

36 Christian Science reveals incontrovertibly that Mind is All-in-all, that the only realities are the divine Mind and idea.

> Ibid.

37 Sickness, sin, and death, being inharmonious, do not originate in God nor belong to His government.

> Ibid.

38 How would you define Christian Science? As the law of God, the law of good, interpreting and demonstrating the divine Principle and rule of universal harmony.

> MARY BAKER EDDY, *Rudimental Divine Science,* 1891.

39 I do not believe that any type of religion should ever be introduced into the public schools of the United States.

> Attributed to Thomas A. Edison.

40 Resolved, Never to utter any thing that is sportive, or matter of laughter, on a Lord's day.

> JONATHAN EDWARDS, resolution dated December 23, 1722, *Works,* 1829.

41 We find it easy to tread on and crush a worm that we see crawling on the earth; so it is as easy for us to cut or singe a slender thread that any thing hangs by: thus easy is it for God, when he pleases, to cast his enemies down to hell.

> JONATHAN EDWARDS, in the sermon "Sinners in the Hands of an Angry God," 1741.

42 The God that holds you over the pit of Hell, much as one holds a spider, or some loathsome insect over the fire, abhors you, and is dreadfully provoked; his wrath towards you burns like fire; he looks upon you as worthy of nothing else, but to be cast into the fire; he is of purer eyes than to bear to have you in his sight; you are ten thousand times more abominable in his eyes than the most hateful venomous serpent is in ours.

> Ibid.

43 The way to Heaven is ascending; we must be content to travel up hill, though it be hard and

tiresome, and contrary to the natural bias of our flesh.

> JONATHAN EDWARDS, in the sermon "The Christian Pilgrim," c.1745.

44 He that sees the beauty of holiness, or true moral good, sees the greatest and most important thing in the world. . . . There is no other true excellence or beauty.

> JONATHAN EDWARDS, *Treatise of Religious Affections,* 1746.

45 We are justified only by faith in Christ and not by any manner of virtue or goodness of our own. . . . Christ alone performs the condition of our justification and salvation. . . . Christ suffered the punishment of sin, not as a private person, but as our surety.

> JONATHAN EDWARDS, quoted in Sereno E. Dwight, *The Works of President Edwards,* 1808.

46 The first and last lesson of religion is, "The things that are seen are temporal; the things that are unseen are eternal." It puts an affront upon nature.

> RALPH WALDO EMERSON, *Nature,* 1836.

47 The test of a religion or philosophy is the number of things it can explain: so true is it. But the religion of our churches explains neither art nor society nor history, but itself needs explanation.

> RALPH WALDO EMERSON, entry written in 1838, *Journals,* 1909–1914.

48 The very word Miracle, as pronounced by Christian churches, gives a false impression; it is a Monster. It is not one with the blowing clover and the falling rain.

> RALPH WALDO EMERSON, in an address at Harvard Divinity School, Cambridge, Massachusetts, July 15, 1838.

49 What greater calamity can fall upon a nation than the loss of worship? Then all things go to decay.

> Ibid.

50 I like a church; I like a cowl;
> I love a prophet of the soul;
> And on my heart monastic aisles

Fall like sweet strains, or pensive smiles;
Yet not for all his faith can see
Would I that cowled churchman be.

> RALPH WALDO EMERSON, "The Problem," printed in *The Dial* magazine, July, 1840.

51 Jesus astonishes and overpowers sensual people. They cannot unite him to history, or reconcile him with themselves.

> RALPH WALDO EMERSON, "History," *Essays,* First Series, 1841.

52 I like the silent church before the service begins, better than any preaching.

> RALPH WALDO EMERSON, "Self-Reliance," *Essays,* First Series, 1841.

53 For every Stoic was a Stoic; but in Christendom where is the Christian?

> Ibid.

54 Our young people are diseased with the theological problems of original sin, origin of evil, predestination and the like. . . . These are the soul's mumps and measles and whooping-coughs, and those who have not caught them cannot describe their health or prescribe the cure.

> RALPH WALDO EMERSON, "Spiritual Laws," *Essays,* First Series, 1841.

55 Begin where we will, we are pretty sure in a short space to be mumbling our ten commandments.

> RALPH WALDO EMERSON, "Prudence," *Essays,* First Series, 1841.

56 The simplest person who in his integrity worships God, becomes God.

> RALPH WALDO EMERSON, "The Over-Soul," *Essays,* First Series, 1841.

57 We can never see Christianity from the catechism: —from the pastures, from a boat in the pond, from amidst the songs of wood-birds we possibly may.

> RALPH WALDO EMERSON, "Circles," *Essays,* First Series, 1841.

58 Belief consists in accepting the affirmations of the soul; unbelief, in denying them.

RALPH WALDO EMERSON, "Montaigne," *Representative Men,* 1850.

59 No people, at the present day, can be explained by their national religion. They do not feel responsible for it; it lies far outside of them.

RALPH WALDO EMERSON, *English Traits,* 1856.

60 God builds his temple in the heart on the ruins of churches and religions.

RALPH WALDO EMERSON, "Worship," *The Conduct of Life,* 1860.

61 Heaven always bears some proportion to earth. The god of the cannibals will be a cannibal, of the crusaders, a crusader, and of the merchants a merchant.

Ibid.

62 Wonderful verse of the gods,
Of one import, of varied tone;
They chant the bliss of their abodes
To man imprisoned in his own.

RALPH WALDO EMERSON, "My Garden," 1867.

63 The sect of the Quakers in their best representatives appear to me to have come nearer to the sublime history and genius of Christ than any other of the sects.

RALPH WALDO EMERSON, in an address on natural religion, Boston, April 4, 1869.

64 The Bible is like an old Cremona; it has been played upon by the devotion of thousands of years until every word and particle is public and tunable.

RALPH WALDO EMERSON, "Quotation and Originality," *Letters and Social Aims,* 1876.

65 God himself does not speak prose, but communicates with us by hints, omens, inference and dark resemblances in objects lying all around us.

RALPH WALDO EMERSON, "Poetry and Imagination," *Letters and Social Aims,* 1876.

66 The religions we call false were once true. They also were affirmations of the conscience correcting the evil customs of their times.

RALPH WALDO EMERSON, "Character," *Lectures and Biographical Sketches,* 1883.

67 The religion of one age is the literary entertainment of the next.

Ibid.

68 The clergy are as like as peas.

RALPH WALDO EMERSON, "The Preacher," *Lectures and Biographical Sketches,* 1883.

69 Religious faith is not a storm cellar to which men and women can flee for refuge from the storms of life. It is, instead, an inner spiritual strength which enables them to face those storms with hope and serenity. Religious faith has the miraculous power to lift ordinary human beings to greatness in seasons of stress.

SAM J. ERVIN, JR., *Humor of a Country Lawyer,* 1983.

70 My own introduction to the unspeakable depths to which human beings can sink was not made through theaters, uncensored billboards, or evil-minded companions, but solely through an unrestricted access to my sainted grandmother's Bible.

CHARLES FLANDRAU, in the *St. Paul Pioneer Press,* January 14, 1917.

71 I believe there is one supreme most perfect Being, Author and Father of the gods themselves. For I believe that man is not the most perfect being but one, rather that as there are many degrees of beings his inferiors, so there are many degrees of beings superior to him.

BENJAMIN FRANKLIN, "Articles of Belief and Acts of Religion," November 20, 1728.

72 I imagine it great vanity in me to suppose that the Supremely Perfect does in the least regard such an inconsiderable nothing as man. More especially, since it is impossible for me to have any positive clear idea of that which is infinite and incomprehensible, I cannot conceive otherwise than that He, the Infinite Father, expects or requires no worship or praise from us, but that He is even infinitely above it.

Ibid.

73 None preaches better than the ant, and she says nothing.

BENJAMIN FRANKLIN, *Poor Richard's Almanack,* 1736.

74 Many a long dispute among Divines may be thus abridg'd, It is so, It is not so; It is so, It is not so.

BENJAMIN FRANKLIN, *Poor Richard's Almanack,* 1743.

75 I believe in one God, creator of the universe. That He governs it by His providence. That He ought to be worshiped. That the most acceptable service we render to Him is doing good to His other children. That the soul of man is immortal and will be treated with justice in another life respecting its conduct in this. These I take to be the fundamental principles of all sound religion.

BENJAMIN FRANKLIN, in a letter to Ezra Stiles, president of Yale, March 9, 1790.

76 As to Jesus of Nazareth . . . I think the system of morals and His religion, as He left them to us, the best the world ever saw or is likely to see; but I apprehend it has received various corrupting changes, and I have, with most of the present dissenters in England, some doubts as to His divinity.

Ibid.

77 The religion which allies itself with injustice to preach down the natural aspirations of the masses is worse than atheism.

HENRY GEORGE, *The Irish Land Question,* 1881.

78 It is the fool who saith in his heart there is no God. But what shall we call the man who tells us that with this sort of a world God bids us be content?

HENRY GEORGE, *Social Problems,* 1884.

79 The Catholic Church teaches that there is but one God, who is infinite in knowledge, in power, in goodness, and in every other perfection; who created all things by His omnipotence, and governs them by His Providence.

JAMES CARDINAL GIBBONS, *The Faith of Our Fathers,* 1877.

80 It cannot be denied that corruption of morals prevailed in the sixteenth century to such an extent as to call for a sweeping reformation, and that laxity of discipline invaded even the sanctuary.

Ibid.

81 A competent religious guide must be clear and intelligible to all, so that every one may fully understand the true meaning of the instructions it contains. Is the Bible a book intelligible to all? Far from it; it is full of obscurities and difficulties not only for the illiterate, but even for the learned.

Ibid.

82 A civil ruler dabbling in religion is as reprehensible as a clergyman dabbling in politics. Both render themselves odious as well as ridiculous.

Ibid.

83 Religious paintings are the catechism of the ignorant.

Ibid.

84 Leave the matter of religion to the family altar, the church, and the private school, supported entirely by private contributions. Keep the church and the State forever separate.

ULYSSES S. GRANT, in a speech in Des Moines, Iowa, 1875.

85 No priestcraft can longer make man content with misery here in the hope of compensation hereafter.

G. STANLEY HALL, *Senescence,* 1922.

86 We do ourselves wrong, and too meanly estimate the Holiness above us, when we deem that any act or enjoyment good in itself, is not good to do religiously.

NATHANIEL HAWTHORNE, *The Marble Faun,* 1860.

87 That religion, or the duty which we owe to our Creator, and the manner of discharging it, can be directed only by reason and conviction, not by force or violence; and therefore all men are equally entitled to the free exercise of religion, according to the dictates of conscience; and that it is the mutual duty of all to practice Christian forbearance, love, and charity towards each other.

PATRICK HENRY, Virginia Bill of Rights, June 12, 1776.

88 He was not ill-looking, according to the village standard, parted his hair smoothly, tied his white cravat carefully, was fluent, plausible, had a gift in prayer, was considered eloquent, was fond of listening to their spiritual experiences, and had a sickly wife.

OLIVER WENDELL HOLMES, SR., describing a clergyman, in *The Guardian Angel,* 1867.

89 People think the confessional is unknown in our Protestant churches. It is a great mistake. The principal change is, that there is no screen between the penitent and the father confessor.

OLIVER WENDELL HOLMES, SR., *The Guardian Angel,* 1867.

90 The enduring value of religion is in its challenge to aspiration and hope in the mind of man.

ERNEST MARTIN HOPKINS, quoted in Will Durant, *On the Meaning of Life,* 1932.

91 Religion is not an intelligence test, but a faith.

EDGAR WATSON HOWE, *Sinner Sermons,* 1926.

92 God: The John Doe of philosophy and religion.

ELBERT HUBBARD, *The Roycroft Dictionary and Book of Epigrams,* 1923.

93 Heaven: The Coney Island of the Christian imagination.

Ibid.

94 If your religion does not change you, then you had better change your religion.

Ibid.

95 We are all children in the kindergarten of God.

Ibid.

96 Missionaries are sincere, self-deceived persons suffering from meddler's itch.

Ibid.

97 Religions are many and diverse, but reason and goodness are one.

Ibid.

98 To know but one religion is not to know that one.

Ibid.

99 A creed is an ossified metaphor.

Ibid.

100 God will not look you over for medals, degrees, or diplomas, but for scars.

Ibid.

101 As a career, the business of an orthodox preacher is about as successful as that of a celluloid dog chasing an asbestos cat through Hell.

Ibid.

102 A religious dogma is a metaphor frozen stiff.

Ibid.

103 We never ask God to forgive anybody except where we haven't.

Ibid.

104 The only way you can get into the Kingdom of Heaven is to carry the Kingdom of Heaven in your own heart.

Ibid.

105 Formal religion was organized for slaves: it offered them consolation which earth did not provide.

ELBERT HUBBARD, in *The Philistine* magazine, published from 1895–1915.

106 We, too, have our religion, and it is this: Help for the living, hope for the dead.

Attributed to Robert G. Ingersoll.

107 An honest God is the noblest work of man.

ROBERT G. INGERSOLL, "The Gods," 1872, in *The Gods, and Other Lectures,* 1876.

108 The inspiration of the Bible depends upon the ignorance of him who reads.

ROBERT G. INGERSOLL, in a speech, "Some Reasons Why," in New York City, April 25, 1881.

109 Miracles are the children of mendacity.

Ibid.

110 Every pulpit is a pillory in which stands a convict; every member of the church stands over him with a club, called a creed.

> ROBERT G. INGERSOLL, in a speech in New York City, April 16, 1882.

111 The day that this country ceases to be free for irreligion it will cease to be free for religion—except for the sect that can win political power.

> ROBERT H. JACKSON, in a dissenting Supreme Court opinion, *Zorach v. Clauson,* 1952.

112 The prophet has drunk more deeply than anyone of the cup of bitterness, but his countenance is so unshaken and he speaks such mighty words of cheer that his will becomes our will, and our life is kindled at his own.

> WILLIAM JAMES, *The Principles of Psychology,* 1890.

113 Religion, whatever it is, is a man's total reaction upon life.

> WILLIAM JAMES, *The Varieties of Religious Experience,* 1902.

114 The highest flights of charity, devotion, trust, patience, bravery to which the wings of human nature have spread themselves have been flown for religious ideals.

> Ibid.

115 The pivot round which the religious life, as we have traced it, revolves, is the interest of the individual in his private personal destiny. Religion, in short, is a monumental chapter in the history of human egotism.

> Ibid.

116 I myself believe that the evidence for God lies primarily in inner personal experiences.

> WILLIAM JAMES, *Pragmatism,* 1907.

117 No man has the right to abandon the care of his salvation to another.

> THOMAS JEFFERSON, "Notes on Locke and Shaftesbury," written in 1776.

118 If thinking men would have the courage to think for themselves, and to speak what they think, it would be found they do not differ in religious opinion as much as is supposed.

> THOMAS JEFFERSON, in a letter to John Adams, August 22, 1813.

119 I must ever believe that religion substantially good which produces an honest life, and we have been authorized by One whom you and I equally respect, to judge of the tree by its fruit. Our particular principles of religion are a subject of accountability to our God alone. I inquire after no man's, and trouble none with mine; nor is it given to us in this life to know whether yours or mine, our friends or our foes, are exactly the right. Nay, we have heard it said that there is not a Quaker or a Baptist, a Presbyterian or an Episcopalian, a Catholic or a Protestant in heaven; that, on entering that gate, we leave those badges of schism behind, and find ourselves united in those principles only in which God has united us all. Let us not be uneasy then about the different roads we may pursue . . . to that our last abode.

> THOMAS JEFFERSON, in a letter to Miles King, September 26, 1814.

120 A professorship of Theology should have no place in our institution [the University of Virginia].

> THOMAS JEFFERSON, in a letter to Thomas Cooper, October 7, 1814.

121 I have ever judged of the religion of others by their lives. . . . It is in our lives, and not from our words, that our religion must be read. By the same test the world must judge me. But this does not satisfy the priesthood. They must have a positive, a declared assent to all their interested absurdities. My opinion is that there would never have been an infidel, if there had never been a priest. The artificial structures they have built on the purest of all moral systems, for the purpose of deriving from it pence and power, revolt those who think for themselves, and who read in that system only what is really there.

> THOMAS JEFFERSON, in a letter to Mrs. M. Harrison Smith, August 6, 1816.

122 It is, I think, an error to believe that there is any need of religion to make life seem worth living.

Sinclair Lewis, quoted in Will Durant, *On the Meaning of Life,* 1932.

123 We, on our side, are praying Him to give us victory, because we believe we are right; but those on the other side pray Him, too, for victory, believing they are right. What must He think of us?

Abraham Lincoln, remark to Rev. Byron Sunderland, December, 1862.

124 In great contests each party claims to act in accordance with the will of God. Both may be, and one must be wrong. God cannot be for and against the same thing at the same time.

Abraham Lincoln, in a memorandum dated September 30, 1862.

125 In regard to this Great Book, I have but to say, it is the best gift God has given to man. All the good the Savior gave to the world was communicated through this book. But for it we could not know right from wrong.

Abraham Lincoln, "Reply to Loyal Colored People of Baltimore upon Presentation of a Bible," September 7, 1864.

126 Morality without religion is only a kind of dead reckoning—an endeavor to find our place on a cloudy sea by measuring the distance we have run, but without any observation of the heavenly bodies.

Henry Wadsworth Longfellow, *Kavanagh,* 1849.

127 And folks are beginning to think it looks
        odd,
    To choke a poor scamp for the glory of
        God.

James Russell Lowell, *A Fable for Critics,* 1848.

128 The only faith that wears well and holds its color in all weathers is that which is woven of conviction and set with the sharp mordant of experience.

James Russell Lowell, "Abraham Lincoln," *My Study Windows,* 1871.

129 Each individual is either a sinner or a saint. It is impossible to be both; it is impossible to be neutral; there is no half-way business in God.

Aimee Semple McPherson, *This Is That,* 1923.

130 Often God has to shut a door in our face, so that He can subsequently open the door through which He wants us to go.

Catherine Marshall, *A Man Called Peter,* 1951.

131 Quakers are under the strong delusion of Satan.

Increase Mather, *Remarkable Providences,* 1684.

132 If the gods think to speak outright to man, they will honorably speak outright; not shake their heads, and give an old wife's darkling hint.

Herman Melville, *Moby-Dick,* 1851.

133 A chaplain is the minister of the Prince of Peace serving in the host of the God of War—Mars. As such, he is as incongruous as a musket would be on the altar at Christmas.

Herman Melville, *Billy Budd,* first published in 1924.

134 The mystery of God may be unfathomable, His power and majesty beyond reckoning, His ways not as our ways; but if He is a God, He is not absolute or infinite.

Paul Elmer More, *Pages from an Oxford Diary,* 1937.

135 As to religion, I hold it to be the indispensable duty of all government to protect all conscientious professors thereof, and I know of no other business which government has to do therewith. . . . For myself, I fully and conscientiously believe that it is the will of the Almighty that there should be diversity of religious opinions among us. It affords a larger field for our Christian kindness. Were we all of one way of thinking, our religious dispositions would want matter for probation; and on this liberal principle I look on the various denominations among us to be like children of the same family, differing only in what are called their Christian names.

Thomas Paine, *Common Sense,* 1776.

136 Persecution is not an original feature in *any* religion; but it is always the strongly-marked fea-

ture of all law-religions, or religions established by law.

THOMAS PAINE, *The Rights of Man,* 1791–1792.

137 My country is the world, and my religion is to do good.

Ibid.

138 Every religion is good that teaches man to be good; and I know of none that instructs him to be bad.

Ibid.

139 As to the Christian system of faith, it appears to me as a species of atheism—a sort of religious denial of God. It professes to believe in a man rather than in God. It is a compound made up chiefly of manism with but little deism, and is as near to atheism as twilight is to darkness.

THOMAS PAINE, *The Age of Reason,* 1794–1795.

140 I believe in one God, and no more; and I hope for happiness beyond this life. I believe in the equality of man; and I believe that religious duties consist in doing justice; loving mercy, and endeavoring to make our fellow-creatures happy.

Ibid.

141 I do not believe in the creed professed by the Jewish church, by the Roman church, by the Greek church, by the Turkish church, by the Protestant church, nor by any church that I know of. My own mind is my own church.

Ibid.

142 Whenever we read the obscene stories, the voluptuous debaucheries, the cruel and torturous executions, the unrelenting vindictiveness, with which more than half the Bible is filled, it would be more consistent that we called it the word of a demon, than the word of God. It is a history of wickedness, that has served to corrupt and brutalize mankind.

Ibid.

143 The only idea man can affix to the name of God is that of a *first cause,* the cause of all things. And incomprehensible and difficult as it is for a man to conceive what a first cause is, he arrives at

the belief of it from the tenfold greater difficulty of disbelieving it.

Ibid.

144 Take away from Genesis the belief that Moses was the author, on which only the strange belief that it is the word of God has stood, and there remains nothing of Genesis but an anonymous book of stories, fables, and traditionary or invented absurdities, or of downright lies.

Ibid.

145 The most detestable wickedness, the most horrid cruelties, and the greatest miseries that have afflicted the human race have had their origin in this thing called revelation, or revealed religion. It has been the most dishonorable belief against the character of the Divinity, the most destructive to morality and the peace and happiness of man, that ever was propagated since man began to exist.

Ibid.

146 Religion without joy—it is no religion.

THEODORE PARKER, "Of Conscious Religion," *Ten Sermons of Religion,* 1855.

147 To the mind of the Puritan, heaven was God's throne; but no less was the earth His footstool: and each in its degree and kind had its demand on man. He held it a duty to labor and to multiply; and, building on the Old Testament quite as much as on the New, thought that a reward on earth as well as in heaven awaited those who were faithful to the law. . . . On the other hand, those who shaped the character, and in great measure the destiny, of New France had always on their lips the nothingness and the vanity of life. For them, time was nothing but a preparation for eternity, and the highest virtue consisted in a renunciation of all the cares, toils, and interests of earth.

FRANCIS PARKMAN, *The Jesuits in North America in the Seventeenth Century,* 1867.

148 The instinct of domination is a weed that grows rank in the shadow of the temple, climbs over it, possesses it, covers its ruin, and feeds on its decay. The unchecked sway of priests has always been the most mischievous of human tyrannies; and

even were they all well-meaning and sincere, it would be so still.

> Ibid.

149 That Religion cannot be right, that a Man is the worse for having.

> WILLIAM PENN, *Some Fruits of Solitude*, 1693.

150 Religion itself is nothing else but Love to God and man.

> Ibid.

151 Difference of religion breeds more quarrels than difference of politics.

> WENDELL PHILLIPS, in a speech, November 7, 1860.

152 So the filthy little atheist [Thomas Paine] had to stay in prison, "where he amused himself with publishing a pamphlet against Jesus Christ." There are infidels and infidels; Paine belonged to the variety—whereof America possesses at present one or two shining examples—that apparently esteems a bladder of dirty water as the proper weapon with which to assail Christianity.

> THEODORE ROOSEVELT, in *Gouverneur Morris*, 1888.

153 The true Christian is the true citizen, lofty of purpose, resolute in endeavor, ready for a hero's deeds, but never looking down on his task because it is cast in the day of small things.

> THEODORE ROOSEVELT, in a speech, "Christian Citizenship," in New York City, December 30, 1900.

154 That fear first created the gods is perhaps as true as anything so brief could be on so great a subject.

> GEORGE SANTAYANA, *The Life of Reason*, 1905–1906.

155 Religion in its humility restores man to his only dignity, the courage to live by grace.

> GEORGE SANTAYANA, *Dialogues in Limbo*, 1925.

156 The memory of my own suffering has prevented me from ever shadowing one young soul with the superstitions of the Christian religion.

> ELIZABETH CADY STANTON, *Eighty Years and More*, 1898.

157 If there is no Hell, a good many preachers are obtaining money under false pretenses.

> Attributed to William A. "Billy" Sunday.

158 The church is a sort of hospital for men's souls, and as full of quackery as the hospitals for their bodies.

> HENRY DAVID THOREAU, "Sunday," *A Week on the Concord and Merrimack Rivers*, 1849.

159 The mason asks but a narrow shelf to spring his brick from; man requires only an infinitely narrower one to spring his arch of faith from.

> HENRY DAVID THOREAU, entry dated January 31, 1852, in his *Journal*, 1906.

160 There is no very important difference between a New-Englander's religion and a Roman's. We both worship in the shadow of our sins: they erect the temples for us. Jehovah has no superiority to Jupiter.

> HENRY DAVID THOREAU, entry dated June 6, 1853, in his *Journals*, 1906.

161 The tavern will compare favorably with the church. The church is the place where prayers and sermons are delivered, but the tavern is where they are to take effect, and if the former are good, the latter cannot be bad.

> HENRY DAVID THOREAU, "The Landlord," *Excursions*, 1863.

162 A remarkably handsome man when he is in the full tide of sermonizing, and his face is lit up with animation, but he is as homely as a singed cat when he isn't doing anything.

> MARK TWAIN, on Henry Ward Beecher, in a letter to the *San Francisco Alta California*, February 18, 1867.

163 A solemn, unsmiling, sanctimonious old iceberg that looked like he was waiting for a vacancy in the Trinity.

> MARK TWAIN, describing a passenger aboard the *Quaker City* en route to the Holy Land who asked whether the ship would stop at sea to observe the Sabbath, in a letter to the *San Francisco Alta California*, June 6, 1867.

164 Adam was but human—this explains it all. He did not want the apple for the apple's sake, he wanted it only because it was forbidden. The mistake was in not forbidding the serpent; then he would have eaten the serpent.

> MARK TWAIN, "Pudd'nhead Wilson's Calendar," *Pudd'nhead Wilson,* 1894.

165 Religion, like water, may be free, but when they pipe it to you, you've got to help pay for the piping. And the piper!

> ABIGAIL VAN BUREN, in her newspaper column, "Dear Abby," April 28, 1974.

166 Who seeks for Heaven alone to save his
    soul
  May keep the path, but will not reach the
    goal;
  While he who walks in love may wander
    far,
  Yet God will bring him where the blessed
    are.

> HENRY VAN DYKE, *The Story of the Other Wise Man,* 1896.

167 Jesus loves me—this I know,
  For the Bible tells me so.

> ANNA BARTLETT WARNER, "The Love of Jesus," 1858.

168 When you speak of God, or his attributes, let it be seriously, in reverence.

> GEORGE WASHINGTON, "Rules of Civility," maxims copied by Washington when a schoolboy, c. 1748, quoted in *Maxims of Washington,* 1942.

169 To trust altogether in the justice of our cause without our own utmost exertions would be tempting Providence.

> GEORGE WASHINGTON, in a letter to Jonathan Trumbull, August 7, 1776.

170 It is the duty of all nations to acknowledge the providence of Almighty God, to obey his will, to be grateful for his benefits, and humbly to implore his protection and favor.

> GEORGE WASHINGTON, in a Thanksgiving proclamation, October 3, 1789.

171 If such talents as I possess have been called into action by great events, and those events have terminated happily for our country, the glory should be ascribed to the manifest interposition of an overruling Providence.

> GEORGE WASHINGTON, in a letter to the Synod of the Reformed Dutch Church in North America, October 9, 1789.

172 Happily the Government of the United States, which gives to bigotry no sanction, to persecution no assistance, requires only that they who live under its protection should demean themselves as good citizens in giving it on all occasions their effectual support.

> GEORGE WASHINGTON, in a letter to the congregation of Touro Synagogue, Newport, Rhode Island, 1790.

173 Of all the animosities which have existed among mankind, those which are caused by a difference of sentiments in religion appear to be the most inveterate and distressing, and ought most to be deprecated.

> GEORGE WASHINGTON, in a letter to Edward Newenham, October 20, 1792.

174 Of all the dispositions and habits which lead to political prosperity, religion and morality are indispensable supports. In vain would that man claim the tribute of patriotism who should labor to subvert these great pillars of human happiness, these firmest props of the duties of men and citizens.

> GEORGE WASHINGTON, in his Farewell Address, September 17, 1796.

175 Let us with caution indulge the supposition that morality can be maintained without religion. Whatever may be conceded to the influence of refined education on minds of peculiar structure, reason and experience both forbid us to expect that national morality can prevail in exclusion of religious principle.

> Ibid.

176 The ways of Providence are unscrutable, and mortals must submit.

> GEORGE WASHINGTON, in a letter to Thaddeus Kosciuszko, August 31, 1797.

177 Whatever makes men good Christians, makes them good citizens.

> DANIEL WEBSTER, in a speech in Plymouth, New Hampshire, December 22, 1820.

178 The Bible is a book of faith, and a book of doctrine, and a book of morals, and a book of religion, of especial revelation from God; but it is also a book which teaches man his own individual responsibility, his own dignity, and his equality with his fellow-man.

> DANIEL WEBSTER, in an address on the completion of the Bunker Hill Monument, June 17, 1843.

179 Each is not for its own sake,
 I say the whole earth and all the stars in the sky are for religion's sake.
 I say no man has ever yet been half devout enough,
 None has ever yet adored or worship'd half enough,
 None has begun to think how divine he himself is, and how certain the future is.
 I say that the real and permanent grandeur of these States must be their religion,
 Otherwise there is no real and permanent grandeur;
 (Nor character nor life worthy the name without religion,
 Nor land nor man or woman without religion).

> WALT WHITMAN, "Starting from Paumanok," 1860.

180 Even in religious fervor there is a touch of animal heat.

> WALT WHITMAN, *Democratic Vistas,* 1870.

181 I swear I think now that everything without exception has an eternal soul!
 The trees have, rooted in the ground! the weeds of the sea have! the animals!

> WALT WHITMAN, "To Think of Time," 1881.

182 Bear witness, O Thou wronged and
 merciful One!

That Earth's most hateful crimes have in
 Thy name been done!

> JOHN GREENLEAF WHITTIER, "The Gallows," 1842.

183 Through this dark and stormy night
Faith beholds a feeble light
 Up the blackness streaking;
Knowing God's own time is best,
In a patient hope I rest
 For the full day-breaking!

> JOHN GREENLEAF WHITTIER, "Barclay of Ury," 1847.

184 I bow my forehead to the dust,
 I veil mine eyes for shame,
And urge, in trembling self-distrust,
 A prayer without a claim.

> JOHN GREENLEAF WHITTIER, "The Eternal Goodness," 1867.

185 I know not where His islands lift
 Their fronded palms in air;
I only know I cannot drift
 Beyond His love and care.

> Ibid.

186 We search the world for truth; we cull
The good, the pure, the beautiful,
From graven stone and written scroll,
From all old flower fields of the soul;
And, weary seekers of the best,
We come back laden from our quest,
To find that all the sages said
Is in the Book our mothers read.

> JOHN GREENLEAF WHITTIER, "Miriam," 1871.

187 Before me, even as behind,
 God is, and all is well.

> JOHN GREENLEAF WHITTIER, "My Birthday," 1871.

188 Let God be magnified,
 Whose everlasting strength
Upholds me under sufferings
 Of more than ten years' length.

> MICHAEL WIGGLESWORTH, *The Day of Doom,* 1662.

189 I think one would go crazy if he did not believe in Providence. It would be a maze without a clue. Unless there were some supreme guidance we would despair of the results of human counsel.

> WOODROW WILSON, reply to a committee of the National Council of Evangelical Free Churches, London, England, December 28, 1918.

190 Our religion is simply the truth. It is all said in this one expression—it embraces all truth, wherever found in all the works of God and man.

> Attributed to Brigham Young.

---

201. RELIGIOUS FREEDOM

See also FREEDOM; RELIGION

---

1 Noe person or persons whatsoever within this Province, or the Islands, Ports, Harbors, Creekes, or havens thereunto belonging professing to believe in Jesus Christ, shall from henceforth bee any waies troubled, Molested or discountenanced for or in respect of his or her religion nor in the free exercise thereof within this Province or the Islands thereunto belonging nor any way compelled to the beliefe or exercise of any other Religion against his or her consent.

> Anonymous, Maryland Toleration Act, April 21, 1649.

2 It is the right as well as the duty of all men in society, publicly, and at stated seasons, to worship the Supreme Being, the Great Creator and Preserver of the universe. And no subject shall be hurt, molested, or restrained, in his person, liberty, or estate, for worshipping God in the manner and season most agreeable to the dictates of his own conscience.

> Anonymous, Massachusetts Bill of Rights, 1780.

3 All religions united with government are more or less inimical to liberty. All, separated from government, are compatible with liberty.

> HENRY CLAY, in a speech in the House of Representatives, March 24, 1818.

4 I would no more quarrel with a man because of his religion than I would because of his art.

> MARY BAKER EDDY, "Harvest," published in *The Independent,* November, 1906.

5 The idea of religion and politics don't mix was invented by the Devil to keep Christians from running their own country. If any place in the world we need Christianity, it's in Washington. And that's why preachers long since, need to get over that intimidation forced upon us by liberals, that if we mention anything about politics, we are degrading our ministry.

> JERRY FALWELL, in a special religious service, July 4, 1976.

6 If we had nothing else to boast of, we could claim with justice that first among the nations we of this country made it an article of organic law that the relations between man and his Maker were a private concern into which other men had no right to intrude.

> DAVID DUDLEY FIELD, in an address in Chicago, 1893.

7 Religious factions will go on imposing their will on others unless the decent people connected to them recognize that religion has no place in public policy. They must learn to make their views known without trying to make their views the only alternatives.

> BARRY GOLDWATER, in a speech, 1981.

8 I would suggest that the Quakers have done their share to make the country what it is . . . and that I had not supposed hitherto that we regretted our inability to expel them because they believe more than some of us do in the teachings of the Sermon on the Mount.

> OLIVER WENDELL HOLMES, JR., on conscientious objection, in a dissenting Supreme Court opinion, *United States* v. *Schwimmer,* 1929.

9 I may grow rich by an art I am compelled to follow; I may recover health by medicines I am compelled to take against my own judgment; but I cannot be saved by a worship I disbelieve and abhor.

> THOMAS JEFFERSON, notes for a speech, c.1776.

10 Millions of innocent men, women, and children, since the introduction of Christianity, have been burnt, tortured, fined, imprisoned; yet we have not advanced one inch towards uniformity. What has been the effect of coercion? To make one half the world fools and the other half hypocrites.

> THOMAS JEFFERSON, *Notes on the State of Virginia,* 1784.

11 I am for freedom of religion and against all maneuvers to bring about a legal ascendancy of one sect over another.

> THOMAS JEFFERSON, in a letter to Elbridge Gerry, January 26, 1799.

12 I never will, by any word or act, bow to the shrine of intolerance, or admit a right of inquiry into the religious opinions of others.

> THOMAS JEFFERSON, in a letter to Edward Dowse, April 19, 1803.

13 I am really mortified to be told that, *in the United States of America,* a fact like this can become a subject to inquiry, and of criminal inquiry too, as an offence against religion; that a question about the sale of a book can be carried before the civil magistrate. Is this then our freedom of religion?

> THOMAS JEFFERSON, in a letter to N. G. Dufief, April 19, 1814. (Jefferson was referring to the legal problems attending the issuance of a scientific work by a French author, M. de Becourt, on the creation of the world.)

14 It is not the legitimate province of the legislature to determine what religion is true, or what is false.

> RICHARD M. JOHNSON, in his second *Report on the Transportation of the Mail on Sundays,* 1830.

15 I believe in an America where the separation of church and state is absolute—where no Catholic prelate would tell the President (should he be a Catholic) how to act and no Protestant minister would tell his parishioners for whom to vote—where no church or church school is granted any public funds or political preference—and where no man is denied public office merely because his religion differs from the President who might appoint him or the people who might elect him.

> JOHN F. KENNEDY, in a speech before the Greater Houston Ministerial Association, Houston, Texas, September 12, 1960.

16 There are few Jews in the United States; in Maryland there are very few. But if there were only one—to that one, we ought to do justice.

> THOMAS KENNEDY, urging a change in the Maryland State Constitution clause that required officials to declare their belief in Christianity, c.1823.

17 The church must be reminded that it is not the master or the servant of the state, but rather the conscience of the state. It must be the guide and the critic of the state, and never its tool. If the church does not recapture its prophetic zeal, it will become an irrelevant social club without moral or spiritual authority.

> MARTIN LUTHER KING, JR., *Strength to Love,* 1963.

18 Is it not strange that the descendants of those Pilgrim Fathers who crossed the Atlantic to preserve their own freedom of opinion have always proved themselves intolerant of the spiritual liberty of others?

> ROBERT E. LEE, in a letter to his wife, December 27, 1856.

19 The wall of separation ensures the government's freedom from religion and the individual's freedom of religion. The second probably cannot flourish without the first.

> LEONARD W. LEVY, *The Establishment Clause: Religion and the First Amendment,* 1986.

20 We will be a better country when each religious group can trust its members to obey the dictates of their own religious faith without assistance from the legal structure of the country.

> MARGARET MEAD, in *Redbook* magazine, February, 1963.

21 Persecution is not an original feature in *any* religion; but it is always the strongly-marked feature of all law-religions, or religions established by

law. Take away the law-establishment, and every religion re-assumes its original benignity.

> THOMAS PAINE, *The Rights of Man,* 1791–1792.

22 The adulterous connection of church and state.

> THOMAS PAINE, *The Age of Reason,* 1794–1795.

23 I believe we are descendid from the Puritins, who nobly fled from a land of despitism to a land of freedim, where they could not only enjoy their own religion, but prevent everybody else from enjoyin *his.*

> ARTEMUS WARD, "Introduction to the Club," a letter to *Punch,* 1866, in *The Works of Artemus Ward,* 1898.

24 He that is willing to tolerate any religion, or discrepant way of religion, besides his own, unless it be in matters merely indifferent, either doubts of his own, or is not sincere in it.

> NATHANIEL WARD, *The Simple Cobler of Aggawam,* 1647.

25 I have often expressed my sentiments, that every man, conducting himself as a good citizen, and being accountable to God alone for his religious opinions, ought to be protected in worshipping the Deity according to the dictates of his own conscience.

> GEORGE WASHINGTON, in a letter to the United Baptist Churches in Virginia, May, 1789.

26 Government being, among other purposes, instituted to protect the consciences of men from oppression, it certainly is the duty of Rulers, not only to abstain from it themselves, but according to their stations, to prevent it in others.

> GEORGE WASHINGTON, in a letter to the Religious Society called Quakers, September 28, 1789.

27 It is now no more that toleration is spoken of as if it was by the indulgence of one class of the people that another enjoyed the exercise of their inherent natural rights. For happily the Government of the United States, which gives to bigotry no sanction, to persecution no assistance, requires only that those who live under its protection should demean themselves as good citizens in giving it, on all occasions, their effectual support.

> GEORGE WASHINGTON, in a letter to the congregation of Touro Synagogue, Newport, Rhode Island, August, 1790.

28 It is the will and command of God that . . . a permission of the paganish, Jewish, Turkish, or anti-Christian consciences and worships be granted to all men in all nations and countries; and they are only to be fought against with that sword which is only (in soul matters) able to conquer, to wit, the sword of God's spirit, the Word of God.

> ROGER WILLIAMS, *The Bloudy Tenent of Persecution,* 1644.

---

202. REPUTATION

See also CHARACTER; CONDUCT; FAME; GREATNESS

---

1 A man's personal defects will commonly have, with the rest of the world, precisely that importance which they have to himself. If he makes light of them, so will other men.

> RALPH WALDO EMERSON, *English Traits,* 1856.

2 How many people live on the reputation of the reputation they might have made!

> OLIVER WENDELL HOLMES, SR., *The Autocrat of the Breakfast-Table,* 1858.

3 What people say behind your back is your standing in the community in which you live.

> EDGAR WATSON HOWE, *Sinner Sermons,* 1926.

4 I had laid it down as a law to myself, to take no notice of the thousand calumnies issued against me, but to trust my character to my own conduct, and the good sense and candor of my fellow citizens.

> THOMAS JEFFERSON, in a letter to Wilson C. Nicholas, June 13, 1809.

5 Until you've lost your reputation, you never realize what a burden it was or what freedom really is.

> MARGARET MITCHELL, *Gone with the Wind,* 1936.

6 One man lies in his work, and gets a bad reputation; another in his manners, and enjoys a good one.

> HENRY DAVID THOREAU, entry dated June 25, 1852, in his *Journal,* 1906.

7 The good opinion of honest men, friends to freedom and well-wishers to mankind, wherever they may be born or happen to reside, is the only kind of reputation a wise man would ever desire.

> GEORGE WASHINGTON, in a letter to Edward Pemberton, June 20, 1788.

203. REVENGE

See also CRIME; JUSTICE; PUNISHMENT

1 I've labored long and hard for bread
For honor and for riches
But on my corns too long you've tred,
You fine-haired sons of bitches.

> CHARLES E. BOLTON, in a note left behind after he robbed a Wells Fargo stagecoach, quoted in Joseph H. Jackson, *Bad Company,* 1949.

2 There's small Revenge in Words, but Words may be greatly revenged.

> BENJAMIN FRANKLIN, *Poor Richard's Almanack,* 1735.

3 'Tis more noble to forgive, and more manly to despise, than to revenge an Injury.

> BENJAMIN FRANKLIN, *Poor Richard's Almanack,* 1752.

4 For mere vengeance I would do nothing. This nation is too great to look for mere revenge. But for the security of the future I would do everything.

> JAMES A. GARFIELD, in a speech on the assassination of Lincoln, New York City, April 15, 1865.

5 Nobuddy ever fergits where he buried a hatchet.

> KIN HUBBARD, *Abe Martin's Broadcast,* 1930.

204. REVOLUTION

See also AMERICAN REVOLUTION; REBELLION

1 An oppressed people are authorized, whenever they can, to rise and break their fetters.

> HENRY CLAY, addressing the U.S. House of Representatives, March 24, 1818.

2 The right to revolt has sources deep in our history.

> WILLIAM O. DOUGLAS, *An Almanac of Liberty,* 1954.

3 Every revolution was first a thought in one man's mind.

> RALPH WALDO EMERSON, "History," *Essays,* First Series, 1841.

4 Revolution is the negation of the existing, a violent protest against man's inhumanity to man with all the thousand and one slaveries it involves. It is the destroyer of dominant values upon which a complex system of injustice, oppression, and wrong has been built up by ignorance and brutality.

> EMMA GOLDMAN, *My Disillusionment in Russia,* 1925.

5 The ultimate end of all revolutionary social change is to establish the sanctity of human life, the dignity of man, the right of every human being to liberty and well-being.

> Ibid.

6 The right of revolution is an inherent one. When people are oppressed by their government, it is a natural right they enjoy to relieve themselves of the oppression, if they are strong enough, either by withdrawal from it, or by overthrowing it and substituting a government more acceptable.

> ULYSSES S. GRANT, in his *Personal Memoirs,* 1885–1886.

7 Revolutions are not made by men in spectacles.

> OLIVER WENDELL HOLMES, SR., in a lecture, "The Young Practitioner," New York City, March 2, 1871.

8 The history of mankind is one long record of giving revolution another trial, and limping back at last to sanity, safety, and work.

EDGAR WATSON HOWE, *Preaching from the Audience,* 1926.

9 What country can preserve its liberties, if its rulers are not warned from time to time that this people preserve the spirit of resistance? Let them take arms.

THOMAS JEFFERSON, in a letter to William S. Smith, November 13, 1787.

10 Those who make peaceful revolution impossible will make violent revolution inevitable.

JOHN F. KENNEDY, speaking to Latin American diplomats at the White House, March 12, 1962.

11 Revolutions conducted in the name of liberty more often than not refine new tools of authority.

HENRY KISSINGER, *White House Years,* 1979.

12 To be a true revolutionary one requires a monstrous self-confidence. Who else would presume to impose on his followers the inevitable deprivations of revolutionary struggle, except one monomaniacally dedicated to the victory of his convictions and free of doubt about whether they justified the inevitable suffering?

Ibid.

13 Any people anywhere, being inclined and having the power, have the right to rise up, and shake off the existing government, and form a new one that suits them better. This is a most valuable, a most sacred right, a right which we hope and believe is to liberate the world. Nor is this right confined to cases in which the whole people of an existing government may choose to exercise it. Any portion of such people that can, may revolutionize and make their own of so much of the territory as they inhabit. More than this, a majority of any portion of such people may revolutionize, putting down a minority, intermingled with, or near about them, who may oppose their movement.

ABRAHAM LINCOLN, in a speech in the U.S. House of Representatives, January 12, 1848.

14 Be not deceived. Revolutions do not go backward.

ABRAHAM LINCOLN, in a speech, May 19, 1856. (This idea was also expressed by William H. Seward in a speech on October 25, 1858, and by Wendell Phillips in a speech on February 17, 1861.)

15 If by the mere force of numbers a majority should deprive a minority of any clearly written constitutional right, it might, in a moral point of view, justify revolution—certainly would if such a right were a vital one.

ABRAHAM LINCOLN, in his first inaugural address, March 4, 1861.

16 This country, with its institutions, belongs to the people who inhabit it. Whenever they shall grow weary of the existing government, they can exercise their constitutional right of amending it, or their revolutionary right to dismember or overthrow it.

Ibid.

17 It is not the insurrections of ignorance that are dangerous, but the revolts of intelligence.

JAMES RUSSELL LOWELL, "On Democracy," a lecture given at Birmingham, England, October 6, 1884.

18 Revolution is bloody, revolution is hostile, revolution knows no compromise, revolution overturns and destroys everything that gets in its way.

MALCOLM X, "Message to the Grass Roots," November, 1963.

19 How will it be with kingdoms and with
        kings—
With those who shaped him to the thing he
        is—
When this dumb terror shall rise to judge
        the world,
After the silence of the centuries?

EDWIN MARKHAM, "The Man With the Hoe," 1899.

20 John Birch may not be merely another murmur in the drugged sleep of a conquered people. It may be the first outcry in a grand revolution—led not

by one general but by a hundred of the best generals and admirals that the country has yet produced.

> WESTBROOK PEGLER, writing about the John Birch Society, c.1961, quoted in Oliver Pilat, *Pegler: Angry Man of the Press,* 1963.

21 Revolutions are not made: they come. A revolution is as natural a growth as an oak. It comes out of the past. Its foundations are laid far back.

> WENDELL PHILLIPS, in a speech in Boston, January 28, 1852.

22 Insurrection of thought always precedes insurrection of arms.

> WENDELL PHILLIPS, on John Brown, in a speech at Harper's Ferry, November 1, 1859.

23 We live in an age of revolution and explosion: exploding bombs, exploding population, revolutionary wars, revolutionary wants. In such an age, we have only two choices, no more. We shall learn to be masters of circumstance—or we shall be its victims.

> NELSON A. ROCKEFELLER, *Unity, Freedom and Peace: A Blueprint for Tomorrow,* 1968.

24 A single revolutionary spark may kindle a fire that, smoldering for a time, may burst into a sweeping and destructive conflagration. It cannot be said that the state is acting arbitrarily or unreasonably when, in the exercise of its judgment as to the measures necessary to protect the public peace and safety, it seeks to extinguish the spark without waiting until it has enkindled the flame or blazed into the conflagration.

> EDWARD TERRY SANFORD, in a Supreme Court opinion, *Gitlow* v. *People of New York,* 1925.

25 Revolutions are ambiguous things. Their success is generally proportionate to their power of adaptation and to the reabsorption within them of what they rebelled against.

> GEORGE SANTAYANA, *The Life of Reason,* 1905–1906.

26 Revolutions appeal to those who have not; they have to be imposed on those who have.

> GILBERT SELDES, *Against Revolution,* 1932.

27 It was like a trip into the future. I could write a mile and not tell all that makes me glad these days. I have seen the future; and it works.

> LINCOLN STEFFENS, in a letter to Marie Howe, written during his visit to Russia, April 3, 1919. (William C. Bullitt, who traveled to Russia with Steffens and later represented the United States as ambassador there, said Steffens coined it days before he laid eyes on the revolution.)

28 What current leaders and theoreticians define as revolution is usually little more than taking over the army and the radio stations.

> GLORIA STEINEM, in *Ms.* magazine, September, 1979.

29 All men recognize the right of revolution: that is, the right to refuse allegiance to, and to resist, the government when its tyranny or its inefficiency is great and unendurable.

> HENRY DAVID THOREAU, "Civil Disobedience," 1849.

30 The great wheel of political revolution began to move in America.

> DANIEL WEBSTER, "Address Delivered at the Laying of the Corner Stone of the Bunker Hill Monument," June 17, 1825.

31 Repression is the seed of revolution.

> DANIEL WEBSTER, in a speech, 1845.

32 Our own revolution has ended the need for revolution forever.

> GEN. WILLIAM C. WESTMORELAND, in an address to the Daughters of the American Revolution, quoted in Daniel Berrigan, *America Is Hard to Find,* 1972.

---

205. RHODE ISLAND

---

1 Hope.

> State motto.

2 Newport was charming, but it asked for no education and gave none. What it gave was much

gayer and pleasanter, and one enjoyed it amazingly; but friendships in that society were a kind of social partnership, like the classes at college; not education but the subjects of education. All were doing the same thing, and asking the same question of the future. None could help. Society seemed founded on the law that all was for the best New Yorkers in the best of Newports, and that all young people were rich if they could waltz. It was a new version of the Ant and Grasshopper.

> HENRY ADAMS, *The Education of Henry Adams,* 1918.

3 Newport had once been a haven for religious dissenters out of Massachusetts and later a capital port of the slave trade. One hundred years after the Declaration that "all men are created equal," there began to gather in Newport a colony of the rich, determined to show that some Americans were conspicuously more equal than others.

> ALISTAIR COOKE, *America,* 1973.

4 The uniqueness of Rhode Island lies in its size; [James] Bryce wrote that it might become the first American "city-state." Everybody is packed close together; almost everybody knows everybody else. An administrator—the governor, say—is at the beck and call of anybody; he must go and see for himself in an emergency, because everything is within fifty miles of his office.

> JOHN GUNTHER, *Inside U.S.A.,* 1947.

5 One views it as placed there, by some refinement in the scheme of nature, just as a touchstone of taste—with a beautiful little sense to be read into it by a few persons, and nothing at all to be made of it, as to its essence, by most others.

> HENRY JAMES, describing Aquidneck Island, site of Newport, in *The American Scene,* 1907.

6 Where bay and tranquil river blend,
  And leafy hillsides rise,
  The spires of Providence ascend
  Against the ancient skies,

  And in the narrow winding ways
  That climb o'er slope and crest,
  The magic of forgotten days
  May still be found to rest.

> H.P. LOVECRAFT, "Providence," quoted in L. Sprague De Camp, *Lovecraft: A Biography,* 1975.

7 There is no question of illusion or disillusion about Providence—I know what it is, and have never mentally dwelt anywhere else. . . . Providence is part of me—I *am* Providence.

> H.P. LOVECRAFT, in a letter to Lillian Clark, March 27, 1926, quoted in L. Sprague De Camp, *Lovecraft: A Biography,* 1975.

8 Rhode Island was settled and is made up of people who found it unbearable to live anywhere else in New England.

> WOODROW WILSON, in a speech in New York City, January 29, 1911.

206. SAN FRANCISCO

1 North Beach to Tenderloin, over Russian
      Hill,
  The grades are something giddy, and the
      curves are fit to kill!
  All the way to Market Street, climbing up the
      slope,
  Down upon the other side, hanging to the
      rope;
  But the sight of San Francisco, as you take
      the lurching dip!
  There is plenty of excitement on the Hyde
      Street Grip!

> GELETT BURGESS, "The Hyde Street Grip," in *A Gage of Youth,* 1901.

2 If California ever becomes a prosperous country, this bay [San Francisco Bay] will be the center of its prosperity.

> RICHARD HENRY DANA, JR., in *Two Years Before the Mast,* 1840.

3 The San Francisco fog has never been sufficiently glorified. It has neither the impenetrable yellow murkiness of the London variety nor the heavy stifling sootiness of the mist that rolls in on New York across the Hudson. The fogs are pure

sea water condensed by the clean hot breath of the interior valleys and blown across the peninsula by the trade winds. They come in, not an enveloping blanket but a luminous drift, conferring a magic patina on the most commonplace structures, giving them an air of age and mystery.

ARNOLD GENTHE, *As I Remember,* 1930.

4 I have seen purer liquors, better segars, finer tobacco, truer guns and pistols, larger dirks and bowie knives, and prettier courtezans, here in San Francisco, than in any other place I have ever visited; and it is my unbiased opinion that California can and does furnish the best bad things that are obtainable in America.

HINTON R. HELPER, *Land of Gold: Reality Versus Fiction,* 1855.

5 Protect me from the wrath of an outraged community if these letters be ever read by American eyes. San Francisco is a mad city—inhabited for the most part by perfectly insane people whose women are of a remarkable beauty.

RUDYARD KIPLING, *American Notes,* 1891.

6 San Francisco has only one drawback. 'Tis hard to leave.

Ibid.

7 I passed out of the house. Day was trying to dawn through the smoke-pall. A sickly light was creeping over the face of things. Once only the sun broke through the smoke-pall, blood-red and showing quarter its usual size. The smoke-pall itself, viewed from beneath, was a rose-color that pulsed and fluttered with lavender shades. Then it turned to mauve and yellow and dun. There was no sun. And so dawned the second day on stricken San Francisco.

JACK LONDON, on the San Francisco earthquake and fire, April 18–19, 1906, in "The Story of an Eye-Witness," 1906.

8 San Francisco has the feeling of a Graustark devised by Bret Harte, Mark Twain, Jack London, and Robert Louis Stevenson, plus a couple of dashes of Saroyan—all of whose imaginations are woven into the emotional fabric of the town.

GEORGE SESSIONS PERRY, *Cities of America,* 1947. (*Graustark,* 1901, a romance by George Barr McCutcheon, was set in the mythical kingdom of Graustark.)

9 When I was a child growing up in Salinas we called San Francisco "the City." Of course it was the only city we knew, but I still think of it as the City, and so does everyone else who has ever associated with it.

JOHN STEINBECK, *Travels with Charley,* 1962.

10 I have compiled the following almanac expressly for the latitude of San Francisco:
Oct. 17.—Weather hazy; atmosphere murky and dense. An expression of profound melancholy will be observable upon most countenances.
Oct. 18.—Slight earthquake. Countenances grow more melancholy. . . .
Oct. 23.—Mild, balmy earthquakes.
Oct. 24.—Shaky.
Oct. 25.—Occasional shakes, followed by light showers of bricks and plastering. N.B.—Stand from under!
Oct. 26.—Considerable phenomenal atmospheric foolishness. About this time expect more earthquakes; but do not look for them, on account of the bricks.

MARK TWAIN, "A Page from a Californian Almanac," 1865.

11 San Francisco, a truly fascinating city to live in, is stately and handsome at a fair distance, but close at hand one notes that the architecture is mostly old-fashioned, many streets are made up of decaying, smoke-grimed, wooden houses, and the barren sand-hills toward the outskirts obtrude themselves too prominently. Even the kindly climate is sometimes pleasanter when read about than personally experienced, for a lively, cloudless sky wears out its welcome by and by.

MARK TWAIN, *Roughing It,* 1872.

12 O when in San Francisco do
As natives do: they sit and stare
And smile and stare again. The view
Is visible from anywhere.

Here hills are white with houses whence,
Across a multitude of sills,
The owners, lucky residents,
See other houses, other hills.

JOHN UPDIKE, "Scenic," *The Carpentered Hen and Other Tame Creatures,* 1958.

---

207. SCIENCE

See also INVENTION; KNOWLEDGE;
MEDICINE; NUCLEAR AGE; POLLUTION;
PROGRESS; SPACE EXPLORATION;
TECHNOLOGY

---

1 Man has mounted science and is now run away with. I firmly believe that before many centuries more, science will be the master of man. The engines he will have invented will be beyond his strength to control. Some day science shall have the existence of mankind in its power, and the human race commit suicide by blowing up the world.

HENRY ADAMS, in a letter to his brother, April 11, 1862.

2 With the monstrous weapons man already has, humanity is in danger of being trapped in this world by its moral adolescents. Our knowledge of science has already outstripped our capacity to control it. We have many men of science, too few men of God.

GEN. OMAR BRADLEY, in an address in Boston, November 10, 1948.

3 There is no personal salvation; there is no national salvation, except through science.

Attributed to Luther Burbank.

4 If we take science as our sole guide, if we accept and hold fast that alone which is verifiable, the old theology must go.

JOHN BURROUGHS, *The Light of Day,* 1900.

5 Science: The Endless Frontier.

VANNEVAR BUSH, the title of a book, 1945.

6 In recent times, modern science has developed to give mankind, for the first time in the history of the human race, a way of securing a more abundant life which does not simply consist in taking away from someone else.

KARL TAYLOR COMPTON, in a speech before the American Philosophical Society, 1938.

7 It is always observable that the physical and exact sciences are the last to suffer under despotisms.

RICHARD HENRY DANA, JR., *To Cuba and Back,* 1859.

8 Every great advance in science has issued from a new audacity of imagination.

JOHN DEWEY, *The Quest For Certainty,* 1929.

9 I pull a flower from the woods,—
A monster with a glass
Computes the stamens in a breath,
And has her in a class.

EMILY DICKINSON, "Old-Fashioned," in *Poems,* Second Series, 1891.

10 Natural science has outstripped moral and political science. That is too bad; but it is a fact, and the fact does not disappear because we close our eyes to it.

JOHN FOSTER DULLES, *War or Peace,* 1950.

11 Every science begins as philosophy and ends as art.

WILL DURANT, *The Story of Philosophy,* 1926.

12 The whole of science is nothing more than a refinement of everyday thinking.

ALBERT EINSTEIN, "Physics and Reality," 1936.

13 It seems hard to sneak a look at God's cards. But that he plays dice and uses "telepathic" methods (as the present quantum theory requires of him) is something that I cannot believe for a single moment.

ALBERT EINSTEIN, in a letter to Cornelius Lanczos, February 14, 1938, quoted in Helen Dukas and Banesh Hoffman, *The Human Side,* 1979.

14 Concern for man himself and his fate must always form the chief interest of all technical endeav-

ors. . . . Never forget this in the midst of your diagrams and equations.

> ALBERT EINSTEIN, quoted in Robert S. Lynd, *Knowledge for What?* 1939.

15 Science without religion is lame, religion without science is blind.

> ALBERT EINSTEIN, *Out of My Later Years*, 1950.

16 Science is a wonderful thing if one does not have to earn one's living at it.

> ALBERT EINSTEIN, in a letter to a California college student, March 24, 1951, quoted in Helen Dukas and Banesh Hoffman, *Albert Einstein: The Human Side*, 1979.

17 'Tis a short sight to limit our faith in laws to those of gravity, of chemistry, of botany, and so forth.

> RALPH WALDO EMERSON, "Worship," *The Conduct of Life*, 1860.

18 Men love to wonder, and that is the seed of our science; and such is the mechanical determination of our age, and so recent are our best contrivances, that use has not dulled our joy and pride in them; and we pity our fathers for dying before steam and galvanism, sulphuric ether and ocean telegraphs, photograph and spectroscope arrived, as cheated out of half their human estate. These arts open great gates of a future, promising to make the world plastic and to lift human life out of its beggary to a godlike ease and power.

> RALPH WALDO EMERSON, "Works and Days," *Society and Solitude*, 1870.

19 All human science is but the increment of the power of the eye.

> JOHN FISKE, *The Destiny of Man Viewed in the Light of His Origin*, 1884.

20 Science has radically changed the conditions of human life on earth. It has expanded our knowledge and our power but not our capacity to use them with wisdom.

> J. WILLIAM FULBRIGHT, *Old Myths and New Realities*, 1964.

21 Science is a first-rate piece of furniture for a man's upper chamber, if he has common sense on the ground floor.

> OLIVER WENDELL HOLMES, SR., *The Poet at the Breakfast-Table*, 1872.

22 Science is the topography of ignorance.

> OLIVER WENDELL HOLMES, SR., *Medical Essays*, 1883.

23 The church saves sinners, but science seeks to stop their manufacture.

> ELBERT HUBBARD, *The Roycroft Dictionary and Book of Epigrams*, 1923.

24 Every science has been an outcast.

> ROBERT G. INGERSOLL, "Liberty of Man, Woman and Child," an address given in Troy, New York, December 17, 1877.

25 Science, like life, feeds on its own decay. New facts burst old rules; then newly divined conceptions bind old and new together into a reconciling law.

> WILLIAM JAMES, *The Will to Believe*, 1897.

26 If science produces no better fruits than tyranny, murder, rapine, and destitution of national morality, I would rather wish our country to be ignorant, honest, and estimable, as our neighboring savages are.

> THOMAS JEFFERSON, in a letter to John Adams, January 21, 1812.

27 It's as important an event as would be the transfer of the Vatican from Rome to the New World. The Pope of Physics has moved and the United States will now become the center of the natural sciences.

> PAUL LANGEVIN, on Albert Einstein's moving from Berlin to Princeton in 1933, quoted in Robert Jungk, *Brighter than a Thousand Suns*, 1958.

28 Both the man of science and the man of art live always at the edge of mystery, surrounded by it. Both, as the measure of their creation, have always had to do with the harmonization of what is new with what is familiar, with the balance between novelty and synthesis, with the struggle to make

partial order in total chaos. . . . This cannot be an easy life.

> J. ROBERT OPPENHEIMER, in a lecture, c.1954, quoted in Robert Jungk, *Brighter than a Thousand Suns,* 1958.

29 It is a fraud of the Christian system to call the sciences human invention; it is only the application of them that is human. Every science has for its basis a system of principles as fixed and unalterable as those by which the universe is regulated and governed. Man cannot make principles; he can only discover them.

> THOMAS PAINE, *The Age of Reason,* 1794–1795.

30 Science is nothing but developed perception, interpreted intent, common sense rounded out and minutely articulated.

> GEORGE SANTAYANA, *The Life of Reason,* 1905–1906.

31 Even heavy automobile traffic out of New York City on a summer weekend minutely unbalances the earth as it rotates.

> PAUL SIPLE, *90 Degrees South,* 1959.

32 Mystics always hope that science will some day overtake them.

> BOOTH TARKINGTON, *Looking Forward,* 1926.

33 Science, testing absolutely all thoughts, all works, has already burst well upon the world—a sun, mounting, most illuminating, most glorious—surely never again to set.

> WALT WHITMAN, *Democratic Vistas,* 1870.

34 The great scientists have been occupied with values—it is only their vulgar followers who think they are not. If scientists like Descartes, Newton, Einstein, Darwin, and Freud don't "look deeply into experience," what do they do? They have imaginations as powerful as any poet's and some of them were first-rate writers as well. How do you draw the line between *Walden* and *The Voyage of the Beagle?* The product of the scientific imagination is a new vision of relations—like that of the artistic imagination.

> EDMUND WILSON, in a letter to Allen Tate, July 20, 1931, quoted in *Letters on Literature and Politics, 1912–1972,* 1977.

---

208. SEX

See also CHASTITY; FAMILY; LOVE; MARRIAGE

---

1 Women's Liberation calls it enslavement but the real truth about the sexual revolution is that it has made of sex an almost chaotically limitless and therefore unmanageable realm in the life of women.

> MIDGE DECTER, *The New Chastity and Other Arguments Against Women's Liberation,* 1972.

2 I hear America swinging,
  The carpenter with his wife or the mason's wife, or even the mason,
  The mason's daughter in love with the boy next door, who is in love with the boy next door to him,
  Everyone free, comrades in arms together, freely swinging.

> PETER DE VRIES, "I Hear America Swinging," 1976.

3 Instead of fulfilling the promise of infinite orgastic bliss, sex in the America of the feminine mystique is becoming a strangely joyless national compulsion, if not a contemptuous mockery.

> BETTY FRIEDAN, *The Feminine Mystique,* 1963.

4 Women complain about sex more often than men. Their gripes fall into two major categories: (1) Not enough, (2) Too much.

> ANN LANDERS, in *Ann Landers Says Truth Is Stranger . . .,* 1968.

5 Wilful sterility is, from the standpoint of the nation, from the standpoint of the human race, the one sin for which the penalty is national death, race death; a sin for which there is no atonement. . . . No man, no woman, can shirk the primary duties of life, whether for love of ease and pleasure, or for any other cause, and retain his or her self-respect.

> THEODORE ROOSEVELT, in his sixth annual message to Congress, December 3, 1906.

6 Of the delights of *this* world man cares *most* for sexual intercourse. He will go any length for it—risk fortune, character, reputation, life itself. And what do you think he has done? In a thousand years you would never guess—*He has left it out of his heaven! Prayer takes its place.*

> MARK TWAIN, to Albert Bigelow Paine, December, 1906, published in *Mark Twain's Notebook,* 1935.

7 Sex contains all, bodies, souls,
   Meanings, proofs, purities, delicacies, results,
      promulgations,
   Songs, commands, health, pride, the maternal
      mystery, the seminal milk,
   All hopes, benefactions, bestowals, all the
      passions, loves, beauties, delights of the
      earth.

> WALT WHITMAN, "A Woman Waits For Me," 1856.

8 Be composed—be at ease with me—I am
      Walt Whitman, liberal and lusty as
      Nature,
   Not till the sun excludes you do I exclude
      you,
   Not till the waters refuse to glisten for you
      and the leaves to rustle for you, do my
      words refuse to glisten and rustle for you.

> WALT WHITMAN, "To a Common Prostitute," 1860.

209. SIN

See also EVIL; RELIGION

1 In Adam's Fall
   We sinned all.

> Anonymous, in *The New England Primer,* compiled and published by Benjamin Harris, c.1690.

2 It takes two bodies to make one seduction.

> GUY WETMORE CARRYL, quoted in Thomas Beer, *The Mauve Decade,* 1926.

3 I've looked on a lot of women with lust. I've committed adultery in my heart many times. This is something that God recognizes I will do—and I have done it—and God forgives me for it.

> JIMMY CARTER, quoted in *Playboy* magazine, October, 1976.

4 He said he was against it.

> Attributed to Calvin Coolidge, on being asked what was said by a clergyman who had preached on sin, c.1925.

5 Every sin is the result of a collaboration.

> Attributed to Stephen Crane.

6 It is not the great temptations that ruin us; it is the little ones.

> JOHN W. DE FOREST, *Seacliff, or The Mystery of the Westervelts,* 1859.

7 Vice . . . is a creature of such heejous mien . . . that th' more ye see it th' betther ye like it.

> FINLEY PETER DUNNE, "The Crusade Against Vice," *Mr. Dooley's Opinion,* 1900.

8 Prayer is not to be used as a confessional, to cancel sin.

> MARY BAKER EDDY, *Science and Health, with Key to the Scriptures,* 1875.

9 Sin kills the sinner and will continue to kill him as long as he sins.

> Ibid.

10 Sin makes its own hell, and goodness its own heaven.

> Ibid.

11 Sin brought death, and death will disappear with the disappearance of sin.

> Ibid.

12 Your wickedness makes you, as it were, heavy as lead, and to tend downwards with great weight and pressure towards Hell; and if God should let you go, you would immediately sink and swiftly descend and plunge into the bottomless gulf, and your healthy constitution, and your own care and prudence, and best contrivance, and all your righ-

teousness, would have no more influence to uphold you and keep you out of Hell than a spider's web would have to stop a falling rock.

> JONATHAN EDWARDS, "Sinners in the Hands of an Angry God," sermon given July 8, 1741.

13 Some men spend their whole lives, from their infancy to their dying day, in going down the broad way to destruction.

> JONATHAN EDWARDS, "The Christian Pilgrim," c. 1745.

14 That which we call sin in others is experiment for us.

> RALPH WALDO EMERSON, "Experience," *Essays, Second Series,* 1844.

15 Demonology is the shadow of theology.

> RALPH WALDO EMERSON, "Demonology," *Lectures and Biographical Sketches,* 1883.

16 Sin is not hurtful because it is forbidden, but it is forbidden because it's hurtful.

> BENJAMIN FRANKLIN, *Poor Richard's Almanack,* 1739.

17 Not to be deficient in this particular, the author has provided himself with a moral—the truth, namely, that the wrongdoing of one generation lives into the successive ones.

> NATHANIEL HAWTHORNE, *The House of the Seven Gables,* 1851.

18 Fashions in sin change.

> LILLIAN HELLMAN, *Watch on the Rhine,* 1941.

19 Sin has many tools, but a lie is the handle which fits them all.

> OLIVER WENDELL HOLMES, SR., *The Autocrat of the Breakfast-Table,* 1858.

20 Who are those who will eventually be damned? Oh, the others, the others, the others!

> ELBERT HUBBARD, *The Roycroft Dictionary and Book of Epigrams,* 1923.

21 We should be judged, not by our acts, but by our temptations.

> Ibid.

22 The only sure-enough sinner is the man who congratulates himself that he is without sin.

> Ibid.

23 He is a sinner who nails a man because he is another.

> Ibid.

24 As a rule the devils have been better friends to man than the gods.

> ROBERT G. INGERSOLL, in a speech in Boston, April 23, 1880.

25 The biggest sin is sitting on your ass.

> FLORYNCE R. KENNEDY, quoted by Gloria Steinem in *Ms.* magazine, March, 1973.

26 Soldiers! we have sinned against Almighty God. We have forgotten His signal mercies, and have cultivated a revengeful, haughty, and boastful spirit. We have not remembered that the defenders of a just cause should be pure in His eyes.

> GEN. ROBERT E. LEE, in his orders to the Army of Northern Virginia, August 13, 1863.

27 It is the duty of nations as well as of men to own their dependence upon the overruling power of God, to confess their sins and transgressions in humble sorrow, yet with assured hope that genuine repentance will lead to mercy and pardon.

> ABRAHAM LINCOLN, in a proclamation, March 30, 1863.

28 That there is a Devil is a thing doubted by none but such as are under the influences of the Devil. For any to deny the being of a Devil must be from an ignorance or profaneness worse than diabolical.

> COTTON MATHER, *The Wonders of the Invisible World,* 1693.

29 Home is heaven and orgies are vile
But you need an orgy, once in a while.

> OGDEN NASH, "Home, 99 44/100% Sweet Home," *The Primrose Path,* 1935.

30 Let him rebuke who ne'er has known the pure Platonic grapple,
Or hugged two girls at once behind a chapel.

> EZRA POUND, "L'Homme moyen sensuel," *Personae,* 1926.

31 Well, there's a Book that says we're all sinners and I at least chose a sin that's made quite a few people happier than they were before they met me.

SALLY STANFORD, *The Lady of the House,* 1966.

32 The only deadly sin I know is cynicism.

HENRY L. STIMSON, *On Active Service in Peace and War,* 1948.

33 I's wicked, I is.

HARRIET BEECHER STOWE, *Uncle Tom's Cabin,* 1852.

34 We cannot well do without our sins; they are the highway of our virtue.

HENRY DAVID THOREAU, entry dated March 22, 1842, in his *Journal,* 1906.

35 When women go wrong, men go right after them.

MAE WEST, quoted in Joseph Weintraub, *The Wit and Wisdom of Mae West,* 1967.

36 Sin, every day, takes out a new patent for some new invention.

EDWIN PERCY WHIPPLE, "The Romance of Rascality," *Essays and Reviews,* 1848–1849.

37 But Adam's guilt our souls hath spilt,
    His fault is charg'd upon us;
And that alone hath overthrown,
    And utterly undone us.

MICHAEL WIGGLESWORTH, *The Day of Doom,* 1662.

38 But the sin forgiven by Christ in heaven
By man is cursed alway!

NATHANIEL PARKER WILLIS, "Unseen Spirits," 1843.

39 But he who never sins can little boast
Compared to him who goes and sins no
        more!
The "sinful Mary" walks more white in
        heaven
Than some who never "sinn'd and were
        forgiven"!

NATHANIEL PARKER WILLIS, "The Lady Jane," *The Poems, Sacred, Passionate, and Humorous,* 1868.

40 All the things I really like to do are either immoral, illegal, or fattening.

ALEXANDER WOOLLCOTT, quoted in Robert F. Drennan, *The Algonquin Wits,* 1968.

41 How impure are the channels through which trade hath a conveyance! How great is that danger to which poor lads are now exposed, when placed on shipboard to learn the art of sailing!

JOHN WOOLMAN, in his *Journal,* 1774.

---

210. SLAVERY

See also BLACK AMERICANS; CIVIL RIGHTS; CIVIL WAR; EQUALITY; LINCOLN

---

1 Go down, Moses,
  'Way down in Egypt land;
  Tell ole Pharaoh
  To let my people go.

Spiritual, c.1840.

2 The importation of Negroes of the African race, from any foreign country, other than the slaveholding states or territories of the United States of America, is hereby forbidden; and Congress is required to pass such laws as shall effectually prevent the same.

Constitution of the Confederate States of America, Art. I, Sec. 9, March 11, 1861.

3 Slavery is the great and foul stain upon the North American Union, and it is a contemplation worthy of the most exalted soul whether its total abolition is or is not practicable.

JOHN QUINCY ADAMS, in his diary, February 24, 1820.

4 The men and women of the North are slaveholders, those of the South slaveowners. The guilt rests on the North equally with the South.

SUSAN B. ANTHONY, in a speech "No Union with Slaveholders," 1857.

5 If those laws of the southern states, by virtue of which slavery exists there and is what it is, are not wrong, nothing is wrong.

> LEONARD BACON, *Slavery Discussed,* 1846.

6 Looking upon African slavery from the same standpoint held by the noble framers of our Constitution, I have ever considered it one of the greatest blessings (both for themselves and us) that God ever bestowed upon a favorite nation.

> JOHN WILKES BOOTH, in a letter written before his assassination of President Lincoln, 1865.

7 There never has yet existed a wealthy and civilized society in which one portion of the community did not, in point of fact, live on the labor of the other. Broad and general as is this assertion, it is fully borne out by history.

> JOHN C. CALHOUN, in a pro-slavery speech in the U.S. Senate, 1837.

8 No more slave states and no more slave territory.

> SALMON P. CHASE, in a resolution adopted by the Free-Soil Party National Convention, August 9, 1848.

9 If slavery is as disagreeable to Negroes as we think it is, why don't they all march over the border, where they would be received with open arms? It all amazes me. I am always studying these creatures. They are to me inscrutable in their way and past finding out.

> MARY BOYKIN CHESNUT, entry dated July 27, 1861, in *A Diary from Dixie,* 1905.

10 We first crush people to the earth, and then claim the right of trampling on them forever, because they are prostrate.

> LYDIA MARIA CHILD, *An Appeal on Behalf of That Class of Americans Called Africans,* 1833.

11 They [the slaves] have stabbed themselves for freedom—jumped into the waves for freedom—starved for freedom—fought like very tigers for freedom! But they have been hung, and burned, and shot—and their tyrants have been their historians!

> Ibid.

12 Slavery is no more sinful, by the Christian code, than it is sinful to wear a whole coat, while another is in tatters, to eat a better meal than a neighbor, or otherwise to enjoy ease and plenty, while our fellow creatures are suffering and in want.

> JAMES FENIMORE COOPER, *The American Democrat,* 1838.

13 Abolitionism proposes to destroy the right and extinguish the principle of self-government for which our forefathers waged a seven years' bloody war, and upon which our whole system of free government is founded.

> STEPHEN A. DOUGLAS, in a speech in the U.S. Senate, March 3, 1854.

14 Slaves are generally expected to sing as well as to work.

> FREDERICK DOUGLASS, *Narrative of the Life of Frederick Douglass,* 1845.

15 Every tone [sung by slaves] was a testimony against slavery, and a prayer to God for deliverance from chains.

> Ibid.

16 You have seen how a man was made a slave; you shall see how a slave was made a man.

> Ibid.

17 You profess to believe that "of one blood God made all nations of men to dwell on the face of all the earth"—and hath commanded all men, everywhere, to love one another—yet you notoriously hate (and glory in your hatred!) all men whose skins are not colored like your own!

> FREDERICK DOUGLASS, "What to the Slave Is the Fourth of July?" a speech at Rochester, New York, July 4, 1852.

18 If you put a chain around the neck of a slave, the other end fastens itself around your own.

> RALPH WALDO EMERSON, "Compensation," *Essays,* First Series, 1841.

19 I think we must get rid of slavery or we must get rid of freedom.

> RALPH WALDO EMERSON, "The Assault upon Mr. Sumner's Speech," May 26, 1856. (Sumner

often spoke out against slavery. See Sumner quotations, below.)

20 Slavery it is that makes slavery; freedom, freedom.

> RALPH WALDO EMERSON, "Woman," a lecture given in 1855, published in *Miscellanies,* 1884.

21 I *will* be as harsh as truth and as uncompromising as justice. On this subject, I do not wish to think, or speak, or write, with moderation. No! No! Tell a man whose house is on fire to give a moderate alarm; tell him to moderately rescue his wife from the hands of the ravisher; tell the mother to gradually extricate her babe from the fire into which it has fallen; but urge me not to use moderation in a cause like the present.

> WILLIAM LLOYD GARRISON, in the first issue of the *Liberator,* January 1, 1831.

22 I am in earnest—I will not equivocate—I will not excuse—I will not retreat a single inch—AND I WILL BE HEARD.

> Ibid.

23 Resolved, That the compact which exists between the North and the South is a covenant with death and an agreement with hell; involving both parties in atrocious criminality, and should be immediately annulled.

> WILLIAM LLOYD GARRISON, resolution passed by the Massachusetts Anti-Slavery Society, Boston, January 27, 1843. (The compact to which Garrison referred was the Constitution of the United States.)

24 Slavery always has, and always will, produce insurrections wherever it exists, because it is a violation of the natural order of things.

> ANGELINA GRIMKÉ, "Appeal to the Christian Women of the South," in *The Anti-Slavery Examiner,* September, 1836.

25 Whatever difference of opinion may exist as to the effect of slavery on national wealth and prosperity, if we may trust to experience, there can be no doubt that it has never yet produced any injurious effect on individual or national character.

> ROBERT YOUNG HAYNE, in a speech in the U.S. Senate, January 21, 1830.

26 Slavery destroys, or vitiates, or pollutes, whatever it touches. No interest of society escapes the influence of its clinging curse. It makes Southern religion a stench in the nostrils of Christendom: it makes Southern politics a libel upon all the principles of republicanism; it makes Southern literature a travesty upon the honorable profession of letters.

> HINTON ROWAN HELPER, *The Impending Crisis of the South: How to Meet It,* 1857.

27 The whole commerce between master and slave is a perpetual exercise of the most boisterous passions, the most unremitting despotism on the one part, and degrading submissions on the other. Our children see this, and learn to imitate it; for man is an imitative animal. This quality is the germ of all education in him. From his cradle to his grave he is learning to do what he sees others do. . . . The man must be a prodigy who can retain his manners and morals undepraved by such circumstances.

> THOMAS JEFFERSON, *Notes on the State of Virginia,* 1784.

28 In a warm climate, no man will labor for himself who can make another labor for him. This is so true, that of the proprietors of slaves a very small proportion indeed are ever seen to labor. And can the liberties of a nation be thought secure when we have removed their only firm basis, a conviction in the minds of the people that these liberties are of the gift of God? That they are not to be violated but with His wrath? Indeed I tremble for my country when I reflect that God is just.

> Ibid.

29 This abomination must have an end, and there is a superior bench reserved in Heaven for those who hasten it.

> THOMAS JEFFERSON, in a letter to Edward Rutledge, July 14, 1787.

30 Emancipation was a Proclamation but not a fact.

> LYNDON B. JOHNSON, quoted in Martin Luther King, Jr., *Why We Can't Wait,* 1963.

31 In this enlightened age there are few, I believe, but what will acknowledge that slavery as an institution is a moral and political evil in any country.

ROBERT E. LEE, in a letter to his wife, December 27, 1856.

32 I hold it to be a paramount duty of us in the free states, due to the Union of the States, and perhaps to liberty itself (paradox though it may seem), to let the slavery of the other states alone; while, on the other hand, I hold it to be equally clear that we should never knowingly lend ourselves, directly or indirectly, to prevent that slavery from dying a natural death.

ABRAHAM LINCOLN, in a letter to Williamson Durley, October 3, 1845.

33 Although volume upon volume is written to prove slavery a very good thing, we never hear of the man who wishes to take the good of it, by being a slave himself.

ABRAHAM LINCOLN, in a note on slavery, July 1, 1854.

34 This declared indifference, but, as I must think, covert real zeal, for the spread of slavery, I cannot but hate. I hate it because of the monstrous injustice of slavery itself. I hate it because it deprives our republican example of its just influence in the world; enables the enemies of free institutions with plausibility to taunt us as hypocrites; causes the real friends of freedom to doubt our sincerity; and especially because it forces so many good men among ourselves into an open war with the very fundamental principles of civil liberty.

ABRAHAM LINCOLN, in a reply to Stephen Douglas, Peoria, Illinois, October 16, 1854.

35 If the Negro is a man, why then my ancient faith teaches me that "all men are created equal," and that there can be no moral right in connection with one man's making a slave of another.

Ibid.

36 The Autocrat of all the Russias will resign his crown and proclaim his subjects free republicans sooner than will our American masters voluntarily give up their slaves.

ABRAHAM LINCOLN, in a letter to George Robertson, August 15, 1855.

37 I now do no more than oppose the extension of slavery. I am not a Know-nothing; that is certain. How could I be? How can anyone who abhors the oppression of Negroes be in favor of degrading classes of white people? Our progress in degeneracy appears to me to be pretty rapid. As a nation, we began by declaring that *all men are created equal.* We now practically read it, *all men are created equal except Negroes.* When the Know-nothings get control, it will read, *all men are created equal except Negroes and foreigners and Catholics.* When it comes to this I shall prefer emigrating to some country where they make no pretense of loving liberty—to Russia, for instance, where despotism can be taken pure, and without the base alloy of hypocrisy.

ABRAHAM LINCOLN, in a letter to Joshua F. Speed, August 24, 1855.

38 We will make converts day by day; we will grow strong by calmness and moderation; we will grow strong by the violence and injustice of our adversaries. And, unless truth be a mockery and justice a hollow lie, we will be in the majority after a while, and then the revolution which we will accomplish will be none the less radical from being the result of pacific measures. The battle of freedom is to be fought out on principle.

ABRAHAM LINCOLN, in the so-called "lost speech," at Bloomington, Illinois, May 29, 1856. (The speech was not recorded at the time, but was reconstructed from notes in 1896 by H.C. Whitney and first published in *McClure's Magazine,* in September of that year.)

39 Do not mistake that the ballot is stronger than the bullet. Therefore, let the legions of slavery use bullets; but let us wait patiently . . . and fire ballots at them in return; and by that peaceful policy, I believe we shall ultimately win.

Ibid.

40 "A house divided against itself cannot stand." I believe this government cannot endure permanently half slave and half free. I do not expect the Union to be dissolved; I do not expect the house to fall; but I do expect it will cease to be divided. It will become all one thing, or all the other. Either the opponents of slavery will arrest the further

spread of it, and place it where the public mind shall rest in the belief that it is in the course of ultimate extinction, or its advocates will push it forward till it shall become alike lawful in all the States, old as well as new, North as well as South.

ABRAHAM LINCOLN, in a speech at the Illinois Republican State Convention, June 17, 1858.

41 I leave you, hoping that the lamp of liberty will burn in your bosoms, until there shall no longer be a doubt that all men are created free and equal.

ABRAHAM LINCOLN, in a speech in Chicago, July 10, 1858.

42 I have no purpose, either directly or indirectly, to interfere with the institution of slavery in the States where it exists. I believe I have no lawful right to do so, and I have no inclination to do so.

ABRAHAM LINCOLN, in his first debate with Stephen Douglas, Ottawa, Illinois, August 21, 1858.

43 This is a world of compensations; and he who would *be* no slave, must consent to *have* no slave. Those who deny freedom to others, deserve it not for themselves; and, under a just God, can not long retain it.

ABRAHAM LINCOLN, in a letter to H.L. Pierce et al., April 6, 1859.

44 Every State wherein slavery now exists which shall abolish the same therein at any time or times before the first day of January, A.D. 1900, shall receive compensation from the United States. . . . The President of the United States shall deliver to every such State bonds of the United States bearing interest at the rate of _____ per cent per annum to an amount equal to the aggregate sum of _____ for each slave shown to have been therein by the Eighth Census.

ABRAHAM LINCOLN, proposal for compensated emancipation, in his second annual message to Congress, December 1, 1862.

45 In giving freedom to the slave we assure freedom to the free—honorable alike in what we give and what we preserve. We shall nobly save or meanly lose the last, best hope of earth.

Ibid.

46 I do order and declare that all persons held as slaves within said designated states and parts of states are, and henceforward shall be, free; and that the executive government of the United States, including the military and naval authorities thereof, will recognize and maintain the freedom of said persons.

ABRAHAM LINCOLN, in the Emancipation Proclamation, January 1, 1863. (The proclamation, issued "as a fit and necessary war measure," freed all slaves in the states or parts of states that were in armed rebellion as of January 1, 1863.)

47 I am naturally antislavery. If slavery is not wrong, nothing is wrong. I cannot remember when I did not so think and feel.

ABRAHAM LINCOLN, in a letter to A.G. Hodges, April 4, 1864.

48 Men! whose boast it is that ye
  Come of fathers brave and free,
  If there breathe on earth a slave,
  Are ye truly free and brave?

JAMES RUSSELL LOWELL, "Stanzas on Freedom," 1843.

49 What claim has slavery to immunity from discussion? We are told that discussion is dangerous. Dangerous to what? . . . The advocates of slavery have taken refuge in the last covert of desperate sophism, and affirm that their institution is of Divine ordination, that its bases are laid in the nature of man. Is anything, then, of God's contriving endangered by inquiry? Was it the system of the universe, or the monks, that trembled at the telescope of Galileo?

JAMES RUSSELL LOWELL, "The American Tract Society," 1858, in *Political Essays,* 1871.

50 Today we are not put up on the platforms and sold at the courthouse square. But we are forced to sell our strength, our time, our souls during almost every hour that we live. We have been freed from one kind of slavery only to be delivered into another.

CARSON MCCULLERS, *The Heart Is a Lonely Hunter,* 1940.

Abraham Lincoln: Emancipation Proclamation, January 1, 1863

As the Civil War progressed, and its bloody battles made the sacrifice on both sides more profound and the outcome more uncertain, Lincoln, never an abolitionist, recognized the military necessity of freeing the slaves in states still in rebellion against the Union. It was not, however, until ratification of the Thirteenth Amendment on December 2, 1865, eight months after the assassination of President Lincoln, that slaves became legally free throughout the United States.

Whereas, on the 22nd day of September, in the year of our Lord 1862, a proclamation was issued by the President of the United States, containing, among other things, the following, to wit:

> That on the 1st day of January, in the year of our Lord 1863, all persons held as slaves within any state or designated part of a state, the people whereof shall then be in rebellion against the United States, shall be then, thenceforward, and forever free; and the executive government of the United States, including the military and naval authority thereof, will recognize and maintain the freedom of such persons and will do no act or acts to repress such persons, or any of them, in any efforts they may make for their actual freedom.

> That the executive will, on the 1st day of January aforesaid, by proclamation, designate the states and parts of states, if any, in which the people thereof, respectively, shall then be in rebellion against the United States;

and the fact that any state or the people thereof shall on that day be in good faith represented in the Congress of the United States by members chosen thereto at elections wherein a majority of the qualified voters of such states shall have participated shall, in the absence of strong countervailing testimony, be deemed conclusive evidence that such state and the people thereof are not then in rebellion against the United States.

Now, therefore, I, Abraham Lincoln, President of the United States, by virtue of the power in me vested as commander in chief of the Army and Navy of the United States, in time of actual armed rebellion against the authority and government of the United States, and as a fit and necessary war measure for suppressing said rebellion, do, on this 1st day of January, in the year of our Lord 1863, and in accordance with my purpose so to do, publicly proclaimed for the full period of 100 days from the day first above mentioned, order and designate as the states and parts of states wherein the people thereof, respectively, are this day in rebellion against the United States the following, to wit:

Arkansas, Texas, Louisiana (except the parishes of St. Bernard, Plaquemines, Jefferson, St. John, St. Charles, St. James, Ascension, Assumption, Terrebonne, Lafourche, St. Mary, St. Martin, and Orleans, including the city of New Orleans), Mississippi, Alabama, Florida, Georgia, South Carolina, North Carolina, and Virginia (except the forty-eight counties designated as West Virginia, and also the counties of Berkeley, Accomac, Northampton, Elizabeth City, York, Princess Anne, and Norfolk, including the cities of Norfolk and Portsmouth), and which excepted parts are for the present left precisely as if this proclamation were not issued.

And, by virtue of the power and for the purpose aforesaid, I do order and declare that all persons held as slaves within said designated states and parts of states are, and henceforward shall be, free; and that the executive government of the United States, including the military and naval authorities thereof, will recognize and maintain the freedom of said persons.

And I hereby enjoin upon the people so declared to be free to abstain from all violence, unless in necessary self-defense; and I recommend to them that, in all cases when allowed, they labor faithfully for reasonable wages.

And I further declare and make known that such persons of suitable condition will be received into the armed service of the United States to garrison forts, positions, stations, and other places, and to man vessels of all sorts in said service.

And upon this act, sincerely believed to be an act of justice, warranted by the Constitution upon military necessity, I invoke the considerate judgment of mankind and the gracious favor of Almighty God.

---

51 It is to be hoped that by expressing a national disapprobation of this [slave] trade we may destroy it, and make ourselves free from reproaches, and our posterity from the imbecility ever attendant on a country filled with slaves.

JAMES MADISON, in a speech in the U.S. House of Representatives, May 13, 1789.

52 I would as soon return my own brother or sister into bondage as I would return a fugitive slave. Before God, and Christ, and all Christian men, they are my brothers and sisters.

HORACE MANN, in a speech in Boston, February 15, 1850.

53 Slavery is in flagrant violation of the institutions of America—direct government—over all the people, by all the people, for all the people.

THEODORE PARKER, in a sermon delivered at Boston, July 4, 1858.

54 It is an irrepressible conflict between opposing and enduring forces, and it means that the United States must and will, sooner or later, become either entirely a slave-holding nation, or entirely a free-labor nation.

WILLIAM H. SEWARD, in a speech in Rochester, New York, October 25, 1858.

55 Did any property class ever reform itself? Did the patricians in old Rome, the noblesse or clergy in France? The landholders in Ireland? The landed aristocracy in England? Does the slave-holding class even seek to beguile you with such a hope? Has it not become rapacious, arrogant, defiant?

WILLIAM S. SEWARD, in a speech during the Republican primary campaign of 1860, quoted in Catherine Drinker Bowen, *Yankee from Olympus*, 1944.

56 Our new government's foundations are laid, its cornerstone rests upon the great truth that the Negro is not equal to the white man, that slavery—subordination to the superior race—is his natural and normal condition.

ALEXANDER H. STEPHENS, in a speech in Savannah, Georgia, March 21, 1861.

57 So long as the law considers all these human beings, with beating hearts and living affections, only as so many *things* belonging to the master—so long as the failure, or misfortune, or imprudence, or death of the kindest owner, may cause them any day to exchange a life of kind protection and indulgence for one of hopeless misery and toil—so long it is impossible to make anything beautiful or desirable in the best-regulated administration of slavery.

HARRIET BEECHER STOWE, *Uncle Tom's Cabin,* 1852.

58 Poets, with voices of melody, sing for freedom. Who could tune for slavery?

CHARLES SUMNER, in a speech in the U.S. Senate, August 26, 1852.

59 By the Law of Slavery, man, created in the image of God, is divested of the human character, and declared to be a mere chattel.

CHARLES SUMNER, in a speech in New York City, May 9, 1859.

60 Where slavery is, there liberty cannot be; and where liberty is, there slavery cannot be.

CHARLES SUMNER, in a speech in New York City, November 5, 1864.

61 The right of property in a slave is distinctly and expressly affirmed in the Constitution. . . . No word can be found in the Constitution which gives Congress a greater power over slave property or which entitles property of that kind to less protection than property of any other description.

ROGER BROOKE TANEY, in a Supreme Court opinion in *Dred Scott* v. *Sandford,* March 6, 1857.

62 Under a government which imprisons any unjustly, the true place for a just man is also a prison . . . on that separate, but more free and honorable, ground, where the State places those who are not *with* her, but *against* her—the only house in a slave State in which a free man can abide with honor.

HENRY DAVID THOREAU, "Civil Disobedience," 1849.

63 Lincoln's proclamation . . . not only set the black slaves free, but set the white man free also.

MARK TWAIN, Independence Day speech, London, England, July 4, 1907.

64 In my schoolboy days I had no aversion to slavery. I was not aware that there was anything wrong about it. No one arraigned it in my hearing; the local papers said nothing against it; the local pulpit taught us that God approved it, that it was a holy thing, and that the doubter need only look in the Bible if he wished to settle his mind—and then the texts were read aloud to us to make the matter sure.

MARK TWAIN, *Autobiography,* 1924.

65 I vividly remember seeing a dozen black men and women chained to one another, once, and lying in a group on the pavement, awaiting shipment to the Southern slave market. Those were the saddest faces I have ever seen.

Ibid.

66 Up from Slavery.

BOOKER T. WASHINGTON, the title of his autobiography, 1901.

67 There is not a man living who wishes more sincerely than I do to see a plan adopted for the abolition of it [slavery]. But there is only one proper way and effectual mode by which it can be accomplished, and that is by legislative authority; and this, as far as my suffrage will go, shall never be wanting.

GEORGE WASHINGTON, in a letter to Robert Morris, April 12, 1786.

68 Some petitions were presented to the Assembly, at its last session, for the abolition of slavery, but they could scarcely obtain a reading. To set them afloat at once would, I really believe, be productive of much inconvenience and mischief; but by degrees it certainly might, and assuredly ought to be effected; and that too by legislative authority.

GEORGE WASHINGTON, in a letter to the Marquis de Lafayette, May 10, 1786.

69 I never mean (unless some particular circumstance should compel me to it) to possess another slave by purchase; it being among my first wishes

to see some plan adopted by which slavery in this country may be abolished by slow, sure, and imperceptible degrees.

GEORGE WASHINGTON, in a letter to John Francis Mercer, September 9, 1786.

70 Upon the decease [of] my wife, it is my Will and desire, th[at] all the Slaves which I hold in [my] *own right,* shall receive their free[dom.]

GEORGE WASHINGTON, in his Will, July 9, 1790.

71 In God's own might
We gird us for the coming fight,
And, strong in Him whose cause is ours
In conflict with unholy powers,
We grasp the weapons He has given,—
The Light, and Truth, and Love of Heaven.

JOHN GREENLEAF WHITTIER, on the gathering storm over slavery in "The Moral Warfare," 1836.

72 Our fellow-countrymen in chains!
Slaves, in a land of light and law!
Slaves, crouching on the very plains
Where rolled the storm of Freedom's war!

JOHN GREENLEAF WHITTIER, "Expostulation," 1834.

73 What! mothers from their children riven!
What! God's own image bought and sold!
Americans to market driven,
And bartered as the brute for gold!

Ibid.

211. SOCIETY

See also AMERICANS; PUBLIC

1 Civilization degrades the many to exalt the few.

A. BRONSON ALCOTT, *Table Talk,* 1877.

2 There may be said to be two classes of people in the world; those who constantly divide the people of the world into two classes and those who do not.

ROBERT BENCHLEY, quoted in Robert E. Drennan, *The Algonquin Wits,* 1968.

3 Ours is an individualistic society, indeed, and the state must do for the individual what family does in the older civilizations.

PEARL S. BUCK, *The Child Who Never Grew,* 1950.

4 A society that seduces the conscience by sweet reason is one thing, but ours is developing into a society that harpoons the conscience and tows it right into the maws of the mother vessel, there to be macerated and stuffed into a faceless can.

WILLIAM F. BUCKLEY, JR., "We Want Our Politicians to Be Hypocrites," *The Jeweler's Eye,* October 17, 1964.

5 The social duties of a gentleman are of a high order. The class to which he belongs is the natural repository of the manners, tastes, tone, and, to a certain extent, of the principles of a country.

JAMES FENIMORE COOPER, *The American Democrat,* 1838.

6 The pedigree of honey
Does not concern the bee;
A clover, any time, to him
Is aristocracy.

EMILY DICKINSON, "The pedigree of honey," in *Poems,* 1890.

7 Our civilization is still in the middle stage: scarcely beast, in that it is no longer wholly guided by instinct; scarcely human, in that it is not yet wholly guided by reason.

THEODORE DREISER, *Sister Carrie,* 1900.

8 The great men of the day are on a plane so low as to be thoroughly intelligible to the vulgar. Nevertheless, as God maketh the world forevermore, whatever the devils may seem to do, so the thoughts of the best minds always become the last opinion of Society.

RALPH WALDO EMERSON, in a letter to Thomas Carlyle, November 20, 1834.

9 Society everywhere is in conspiracy against the manhood of every one of its members. Society is a joint-stock company, in which the members agree, for the better security of his bread to each shareholder, to surrender the liberty and culture of the

eater. The virtue in most request is conformity. Self-reliance is its aversion. It loves not realities and creators, but names and customs.

Ralph Waldo Emerson, "Self-Reliance,"
Essays, First Series, 1841.

10 Society never advances. It recedes as fast on one side as it gains on the other.

Ibid.

11 Introduce a base person among gentlemen; it is all to no purpose; he is not their fellow. Every society protects itself. The company is perfectly safe, and he is not one of them, though his body is in the room.

Ralph Waldo Emerson, "Spiritual Laws,"
Essays, First Series, 1841.

12 Society will pardon much to genius and special gifts, but, being in its nature a convention, it loves what is conventional, or what belongs to coming together.

Ralph Waldo Emerson, "Manners," *Essays,*
Second Series, 1844.

13 Coolness and absence of heat and haste indicate fine qualities. A gentleman makes no noise; a lady is serene.

Ibid.

14 Society is frivolous, and shreds its day into scraps, its conversation into ceremonies and escapes.

Ralph Waldo Emerson, "Character," *Essays,*
Second Series, 1844.

15 The worthless and offensive members of society, whose existence is a social pest, invariably think themselves the most ill-used people alive, and never get over their astonishment at the ingratitude and selfishness of their contemporaries.

Ralph Waldo Emerson, *Representative Men,*
1850.

16 'T is the fine souls who serve us, and not what is called fine society. Fine society is only a self-protection against the vulgarities of the street and the tavern. Fine society, in the common acceptation, has neither ideas nor aims. . . . It is an unprinci-

pled decorum; an affair of clean linen and coaches, of gloves, cards and elegance in trifles. There are other measures of self-respect for a man than the number of clean shirts he puts on every day.

Ralph Waldo Emerson, "Considerations by the Way," *The Conduct of Life,* 1860.

17 Solitude is impracticable, and society fatal. We must keep our head in the one and our hands in the other. The conditions are met, if we keep our independence, yet do not lose our sympathy.

Ralph Waldo Emerson, "Society and
Solitude," *Society and Solitude,* 1870.

18 The highest civility has never loved the hot zones. Wherever snow falls there is usually civil freedom. Where the banana grows the animal system is indolent and pampered at the cost of higher qualities; man is sensual and cruel.

Ralph Waldo Emerson, "Civilization," *Society
and Solitude,* 1870.

19 The true test of civilization is not the census, nor the size of cities, nor the crops—no, but the kind of man the country turns out.

Ibid.

20 Of all the cordials known to us, the best, safest, and most exhilarating, with the least harm, is society.

Ralph Waldo Emerson, "Clubs," *Society and
Solitude,* 1870.

21 The cocktail party or dinner party is, essentially, a fair, more refined and complex than those at which embroidery or livestock are entered in competition but for the same ultimate purpose of displaying and improving the craftsmanship or breed. The cleanliness of the house, the excellence of the garden, the taste, quality and condition of the furnishings and the taste, quality and imagination of the food and intoxicants and the deftness of their service are put on display before the critical eye of those invited to appraise them. Comparisons are made with other exhibitors. Ribbons are not awarded, but the competent administrator is duly proclaimed a good housekeeper, a gracious hostess, a clever manager or, more simply, a really good wife.

JOHN KENNETH GALBRAITH, *Annals of an Abiding Liberal,* 1979.

22 The ideal of Socialism is grand and noble . . . but such a state of society cannot be manufactured—it must grow. Society is an organism, not a machine.

HENRY GEORGE, *Progress and Poverty,* 1879.

23 The law of society is, each for all, as well as all for each. No one can keep to himself the good he may do, any more than he can keep the bad.

Ibid.

24 It is not from top to bottom that societies die; it is from bottom to top.

Ibid.

25 It is still in the lap of the gods whether a society can succeed which is based on "civil liberties and human rights" conceived as I have tried to describe them; but of one thing at least we may be sure: the alternatives that have so far appeared have been immeasurably worse.

LEARNED HAND, "A Fanfare for Prometheus," quoted in Irving F. Dilliard, *The Spirit of Liberty,* 1955.

26 There are some things that should never be mentioned in polite society—f'r instance, the doings of Polite Society.

ELBERT HUBBARD, *The Roycroft Dictionary and Book of Epigrams,* 1923.

27 The true civilization is where every man gives to every other every right that he claims for himself.

ROBERT G. INGERSOLL, in an interview in the *Washington Post,* November 14, 1880.

28 Life is of no value but as it brings us gratifications. Among the most valuable of these is rational society. It informs the mind, sweetens the temper, cheers our spirits, and promotes health.

THOMAS JEFFERSON, in a letter to James Madison, February 20, 1784.

29 Without society, and a society to our taste, men are never contented.

THOMAS JEFFERSON, in a letter to James Monroe, December 18, 1786.

30 Those who wallow in the imperfections of their society or turn them into an excuse for a nihilistic orgy usually end up by eroding all social and moral restraints; eventually in their pitiless assault on all beliefs they multiply suffering.

HENRY KISSINGER, *White House Years,* 1979.

31 A town that boasts inhabitants like me
Can have no lack of good society!

HENRY WADSWORTH LONGFELLOW, "The Birds of Killingworth," *Tales of a Wayside Inn,* 1886.

32 Solitude is as needful to the imagination as society is wholesome for the character.

JAMES RUSSELL LOWELL, "Dryden," *Among My Books,* 1870.

33 Those who hold and those who are without property have ever formed distinct interests in society. . . . A landed interest, a manufacturing interest, a mercantile interest, a moneyed interest, with many lesser interests, grow up of necessity in civilized nations, and divide them into different classes, actuated by different sentiments and views.

JAMES MADISON, *The Federalist,* 1787–1788.

34 Gentlemen: Please accept my resignation. I don't care to belong to any social organization that will accept me as a member.

GROUCHO MARX, in a letter of resignation to the Friars Club of Beverly Hills, *The Groucho Phile,* 1976.

35 What is wrong with the old Adam Smith philosophy and what should be completely unacceptable to any American (and I would say this particularly to my fellow Republicans) is the idea of the survival of the fittest. Let's put it this way: The fittest should survive, and also the fit should survive. Those who are "unfit" you have to have a social consciousness about, to take care of them. The "survival of the fittest" assumes "the hell with the rest of them." This is wrong, morally and socially, apart from being completely wrong politically.

RICHARD M. NIXON, quoted in Earl Mazo, *Richard Nixon: A Political and Personal Portrait,* 1959.

36 No one man is capable, without the aid of society, of supplying his own wants; and those wants acting upon every individual, impel the whole of them into society, as naturally as gravitation acts to a center.

THOMAS PAINE, *The Rights of Man,* 1791–1792.

37 I doubt very much if Civilization (so called) has helped generosity. I bet the old cave man would divide his raw meat with you as quick as one of us will ask a down-and-out to go in and have a meal with us. Those old boys and girls would rip off a wolf skin breech-clout and give you half of it, quicker than a Ph.D. would slip you his umbrella. . . . Civilization has taught us to eat with a fork, but even now if nobody is around we use our fingers.

WILL ROGERS, January 20, 1935, quoted in Donald Day, *The Autobiography of Will Rogers,* 1949.

38 Society is like the air, necessary to breathe, but insufficient to live on.

GEORGE SANTAYANA, *Little Essays,* 1920.

39 It is the tendency of all social burdens to crush out the middle class, and to force the society into an organization of only two classes, one at each social extreme.

WILLIAM GRAHAM SUMNER, "What Makes the Rich Richer and the Poor Poorer?" *Popular Science Monthly,* January, 1887.

40 What men call social virtue, good fellowship, is commonly but the virtue of pigs in a litter, which lie close together to keep each other warm.

HENRY DAVID THOREAU, entry dated October 23, 1852, in his *Journal,* 1906.

41 Society is always diseased, and the best is the most so.

HENRY DAVID THOREAU, *Excursions,* 1863.

42 In some respects a trailer park is a Utopian society, for it consists of persons each of whom is occupying the same amount of space in the community, and none of whom is working very hard at anything in particular, and all of whom are engaged in perfecting the art of living; and although trailer society, like every other society I have ever examined, has its little caste system, economically it is rather a success: every day is a holiday and every night is bingo.

E.B. WHITE, "Trailer Park," *One Man's Meat,* 1944.

43 High society is for those who have stopped working and no longer have anything important to do.

WOODROW WILSON, in an address in Washington, D.C., February 24, 1915.

---

212. SONGS

See also MUSIC

---

1 Around her neck she wore a yellow ribbon;
    She wore it in September, and in the month of May;
And when I asked her where the hell she got it—
    She got it from a lover who is far, far away.

Anonymous.

2 Casey Jones, he mounted to the cabin,
Casey Jones, with his orders in his hand!
Casey Jones, he mounted to the cabin,
Took his farewell trip into the promised land.

Anonymous.

3 Frankie and Johnny were lovers, lordee, and how they could love,
Swore to be true to each other, true as the stars above;
He was her man, but he done her wrong.

Anonymous, "Frankie and Johnny," c.1850.

4 Oh, Shenandoah, I long to hear you,
Away, you rolling river!
Oh, Shenandoah, I long to hear you,
Ah-ha, we're bound away,
Across the wide Missouri!

Anonymous, "Shenandoah."

5 Ha-ha-ha, you and me,
  Little brown jug, don't I love thee!

> Anonymous, "The Little Brown Jug."

6 There is a tavern in the town,
  And there my true love sits him down,
  And drinks his wine with laughter free,
  And never, never thinks of me.

> Anonymous, "There Is a Tavern in the Town."

7 Yankee Doodle came to town
    Riding on a pony;
  Stuck a feather in his cap
    And called it Macaroni.

> Anonymous, "Yankee Doodle."

8 Come on and hear, come on and hear, Alexander's Ragtime Band.

> IRVING BERLIN, "Alexander's Ragtime Band," 1911.

9 John Brown's body lies a-mouldering in the
    grave,
  His soul goes marching on.

> THOMAS BRIGHAM BISHOP, "John Brown's Body," 1860. (The song is also attributed to Charles Sprague Hall.)

10 Gold, glory, greed! I loved you not for long;
   Wine, Women, war! seductive, but not
     strong;
   One passion lasts—the deathless lust of Song.

> EDMUND VANCE COOKE, "David," *From the Book of Extenuations,* 1926.

11 Daisy, Daisy, give me your answer, do!
   I'm half crazy, all for the love of you!
   It won't be a stylish marriage,
   I can't afford a carriage,
   But you'll look sweet upon the seat
   Of a bicycle built for two!

> HARRY DACRE, "Daisy Bell," 1892.

12 Y'ought to hyeah dat gal a-wa'blin',
   Robins, la'ks an' all dem things,
   Heish dey moufs an' hides dey faces
   When Malindy sings.

> PAUL LAURENCE DUNBAR, "When Malindy Sings," 1903.

13 Homer's harp is broken and Horace's lyre is unstrung, and the voices of the great singers are hushed; but their songs—their songs are immortal. . . . The singer belongs to a year, his song to all time.

> EUGENE FIELD, *The Love Affairs of a Bibliomaniac,* 1896.

14 Oh! Susanna, oh, don't you cry for me;
   I've come from Alabama wid my banjo on
     my knee.

> STEPHEN FOSTER, "Oh! Susanna," 1848.

15 Way down upon de Swanee ribber,
   Far, far away,
   Dere's where my heart is turning ebber,
   Dere's where de old folks stay.

> STEPHEN FOSTER, "Old Folks at Home," 1851.

16 Many a heart is aching, if you could read
     them all,
   Many the hopes that have vanished, after the
     ball.

> CHARLES K. HARRIS, "After the Ball," 1892.

17 What is the voice of song, when the world lacks the ear of taste?

> NATHANIEL HAWTHORNE, "Canterbury Pilgrims," from *The Snow-Image and Other Twice Told Tales,* 1851.

18 Blues are the songs of despair, but gospel songs are the songs of hope.

> MAHALIA JACKSON, *Movin' On Up,* with Evan McLoud Wylie, 1966.

19 How you gonna keep 'em down on the farm after they've seen Paree?

> SAM M. LEWIS AND JOE YOUNG, refrain of their song of the same title, 1919. (The allusion is to the doughboys returning from their victory in Europe.)

20 I shot an arrow into the air,
   It fell to earth, I knew not where;
   For, so swiftly it flew, the sight
   Could not follow it in its flight.

   I breathed a song into the air,
   It fell to earth, I knew not where;

For who has sight so keen and strong,
That it can follow the flight of song?

> HENRY WADSWORTH LONGFELLOW, "The
> Arrow and the Song," 1845.

21 When he sang, the village listened;
All the warriors gathered round him,
All the women came to hear him:
Now he stirred their souls to passion,
Now he melted them to pity.

> HENRY WADSWORTH LONGFELLOW, *The Song of
> Hiawatha,* 1855.

22 The leaguèd might of futile things
Wars with the heart that dares and sings.

> DON MARQUIS, "The Singer," in *Dreams and
> Dust,* 1915.

23 I care not who writes the laws of a country so
long as I may listen to its songs.

> GEORGE JEAN NATHAN, *The World in Falseface,*
> 1923.

24 In Heaven a spirit doth dwell
Whose heart-strings are a lute;
None sing so wildly well
As the angel Israfel.

> EDGAR ALLAN POE, "Israfel," 1831.

25 Songs are like people, animals, plants. They
have genealogies, pedigrees, thoroughbreds, cross-
breeds, mongrels, strays, and often a strange love-
child.

> CARL SANDBURG, *The American Songbag,* 1927.

26 In the sweet by-and-by,
We shall meet on that beautiful shore.

> IRA DAVID SANKEY, "Sweet By-and-By," *Sacred
> Songs,* 1873.

27 Meet me in St. Louis, Louis,
Meet me at the fair.

> ANDREW B. STERLING, "Meet Me in St. Louis,"
> 1904.

28 I can't sing. As a singist I am not a success. I
am saddest when I sing. So are those who hear me.
They are sadder even than I am.

> Artemus Ward, *Artemus Ward's Lectures,* 1869.

213. SORROW

See also AFFLICTION; DEATH; HAPPINESS;
MERRIMENT; PAIN; TROUBLE

1 When a man has a great sorrow, he should be
indulged in all sorts of vagaries till he has lived it
down.

> LOUISA MAY ALCOTT, *Little Women,* 1868.

2 It is only in sorrow bad weather masters us; in joy
we face the storm and defy it.

> AMELIA BARR, *Jan Vedder's Wife,* 1885.

3 Parting is all we know of heaven,
And all we need of hell.

> EMILY DICKINSON, "Parting," *Poems,* Third
> Series, 1896.

4 Tragedy is in the eye of the observer, and not in
the heart of the sufferer.

> RALPH WALDO EMERSON, "The Tragic,"
> published in *The Dial* magazine, April, 1844.

5 *Yes,* he thought, *between grief and nothing I
will take grief.*

> WILLIAM FAULKNER, *The Wild Palms,* 1939.

6 If of all words of tongue and pen,
The saddest are, "It might have been,"
More sad are these we daily see,
"It is, but it hadn't ought to be."

> BRET HARTE, "Mrs. Judge Jenkins," *East and
> West Poems,* 1871. (See quotation 20, below.)

7 If you suffer, thank God!—it is a sure sign that
you are alive.

> ELBERT HUBBARD, *The Roycroft Dictionary and
> Book of Epigrams,* 1923.

8 The sorrow for the dead is the only sorrow from
which we refuse to be divorced. Every other wound
we seek to heal, every other affliction to forget; but
this wound we consider it a duty to keep open, this
affliction we cherish and brood over in solitude.

> WASHINGTON IRVING, "Rural Funerals," *The
> Sketch-Book,* 1819–1820.

9 In the deepest heart of all of us there is a corner in which the ultimate mystery of things works sadly.

> WILLIAM JAMES, "Is Life Worth Living?" *The Will to Believe,* 1897.

10 A lean sorrow is hardest to bear.

> SARA ORNE JEWETT, *The Life of Nancy,* 1895.

11 Oh, fear not in a world like this,
    And thou shalt know erelong,
  Know how sublime a thing it is
    To suffer and be strong.

> HENRY WADSWORTH LONGFELLOW, "The Light of Stars," *Voices of the Night,* 1839.

12 Believe me, every man has his secret sorrows, which the world knows not; and oftentimes we call a man cold when he is only sad.

> HENRY WADSWORTH LONGFELLOW, *Hyperion,* 1839.

13 Be still, sad heart! and cease repining;
  Behind the clouds is the sun still shining;
  Thy fate is the common fate of all,
  Into each life some rain must fall,
    Some days must be dark and dreary.

> HENRY WADSWORTH LONGFELLOW, "The Rainy Day," *Ballads and Other Poems,* 1842.

14 A feeling of sadness comes o'er me
    That my soul cannot resist:
  A feeling of sadness and longing,
    That is not akin to pain,
  And resembles sorrow only
    As the mist resembles the rain.

> HENRY WADSWORTH LONGFELLOW, "The Day is Done," *The Belfry of Bruges and Other Poems,* 1846.

15 Not indolence, nor pleasure, nor the fret
    Of restless passions that would not be
      stilled,
  But sorrow, and a care that almost killed,
  Kept me from what I may accomplish yet.

> HENRY WADSWORTH LONGFELLOW, "Mezzo Cammin," *The Belfry of Bruges and Other Poems,* 1846.

16 If we could read the secret history of our enemies, we should find in each man's life sorrow and suffering enough to disarm all hostility.

> HENRY WADSWORTH LONGFELLOW, "Table-Talk," *Driftwood,* 1857.

17 Sorrow, the great idealizer.

> JAMES RUSSELL LOWELL, "Spenser," *Among My Books,* 1876.

18 When I was a child people simply looked about them and were moderately happy; today they peer beyond the seven seas, bury themselves waist deep in tidings, and by and large what they see and hear makes them unutterably sad.

> E.B. WHITE, "Removal," *One Man's Meat,* 1944.

19 Earth to a chamber of mourning turns—I
    hear the o'er weening, mocking voice,
  *Matter is conqueror—matter, triumphant
    only, continues onward.*

> WALT WHITMAN, "Yet, Yet, Ye Downcast Hours," 1860.

20 For of all sad words of tongue or pen,
  The saddest are these: "It might have been!"

> JOHN GREENLEAF WHITTIER, "Maud Muller," 1854.

---

214. THE SOUTH

See also individual states

---

1 Southerners are, of course, a mythological people. . . . Lost by choice in dreaming of high days gone and big house burned, now we cannot even wish to escape.

> JONATHAN DANIELS, *A Southerner Discovers the South,* 1938.

2 Den I wish I was in Dixie, Hooray! Hooray!
    In Dixie land I'll take my stand,
  And lib and die in Dixie.
    Away! Away!
  Away down south in Dixie!

> DANIEL D. EMMETT, "Dixie," 1859.

3 No hardier republicanism was generated in New England than in the slave states of the South, which produced so many great statesmen of America.

> WILLIAM E. GLADSTONE, "Kin Beyond the Sea," published in the *North American Review,* September, 1878.

4 Southerners can never resist a losing cause.

> MARGARET MITCHELL, *Gone with the Wind,* 1936.

5 In the South the war is what A.D. is elsewhere; they date from it.

> MARK TWAIN, *Life on the Mississippi,* 1883.

6 O magnet-South! O glistening, perfumed South! my South!

O quick mettle, rich blood, impulse and love! Good and evil! O all dear to me!

> WALT WHITMAN, "O Magnet-South," 1860.

215. SOUTH CAROLINA

1 Animis opibusque parati (Prepared in mind and resources).
Dum spiro spero (While I breathe, I hope).

> State mottoes.

2 South Carolinians are among the rare folk in the South who have no secret envy of Virginians.

Robert E. Lee: farewell to his army, April 10, 1865

The surrender of General Robert E. Lee to General Ulysses S. Grant on the day before had been marked by generosity. Grant allowed all soldiers to keep their horses and the officers to keep their sidearms as well. The Civil War was over.

After four years of arduous service, marked by unsurpassed courage and fortitude, the Army of Northern Virginia has been compelled to yield to overwhelming numbers and resources. I need not tell the survivors of so many hard-fought battles, who have remained steadfast to the last, that I have consented to this result from no distrust of them; but, feeling that valor and devotion could accomplish nothing that could compensate for the loss that would have attended the continuation of the contest, I have determined to avoid the useless sacrifice of those whose past services have endeared them to their countrymen.

By the terms of the agreement, officers and men can return to their homes and remain there until exchanged. You will take with you the satisfaction that proceeds from the consciousness of duty faithfully performed; and I earnestly pray that a merciful God will extend to you His blessing and protection.

With an increasing admiration of your constancy and devotion to your country, and a grateful remembrance of your kind and generous consideration of myself, I bid you an affectionate farewell.

Federal Writers' Project, *South Carolina: A Guide to the Palmetto State,* 1941.

3 The South Carolinian has fire in his head, comfort in his middle, and a little lead in his feet. Proud of his past, often scornful of innovations, he is not willing to adapt unless thoroughly convinced that it is a good thing. . . . He knows his faults, at least many of them. He will discuss them and propose remedies—but woe to the outsider who reminds him of them. The faults of his State are as personal to him as a wart on his nose.

Ibid.

4 Gentlemen, there are Hottentots and there are Cottontots. A cottontot I take to be a person who, growing nothing but cotton, has to buy every earthly thing that he uses or consumes, consequently rarely if ever saves anything, and finds himself at the last of the year the property of his commission merchant—himself the property of the Northern man.

GEORGE WILLIAM BAGBY, in a speech in Charleston, South Carolina, 1877.

5 In South Carolina the spirit and the links of social life are aristocratic to a degree which I cannot approve of, however much I may like certain people there. And aristocracy there has this in common with aristocracies of the present time; that, while the aristocratic virtues and greatness have vanished, merely the pretension remains.

FREDERIKA BREMER, *The Homes of the New World: Impressions of America,* 1853.

6 We were taught to be South Carolinians, Ca-ro-li-ni-ans, mind you, and not, please God, the Tarheel slur, Calinians.

WILLIAM FRANCIS GUESS, "South Carolina," in *American Panorama: East of the Mississippi,* 1960.

7 An old Charlestonian may think of his city first and last, his heart bound to the palm-lined Battery, where echoes linger from the blasts of the guns his forebears trained on two meddling foreign powers—Great Britain and the United States.

Ibid.

8 South Carolina is too small for a republic and too large for a lunatic asylum.

Attributed to James Louis Petigru, on being asked if he would support South Carolina's secession from the Union, 1860.

9 The manners of the inhabitants of Charleston are as different from those of the other North American cities as are the products of their soil. . . . There prevails here a finer manner of life, and on the whole there are more evidences of courtesy than in the northern cities.

JOHANN DAVID SCHOEPF, *Travels in the Confederation, 1783–1784,* 1911.

---

216. SOUTH DAKOTA

---

1 Under God the people rule.

State motto.

2 Hard work is a legacy of the generations who settled the prairie, broke the soil, built the sod houses, fought the droughts and grasshoppers and penny-a-pound prices for their products. It is a legacy that even those of us who leave carry with us. All of this work has produced what may be the single largest collection of powerful hands in the world.

TOM BROKAW, quoted in John Milton, *South Dakota: A Bicentennial History,* 1977.

3 I guess it's the physical and cultural remoteness of South Dakota that compels everyone to memorize almost every South Dakotan who has left the state and achieved some recognition. As a child I would pore over magazines and newspapers, looking for some sign that the rest of the world knew we existed.

Ibid.

4 Mountain, plain or prairie fields,
Summer heat or snows,
South Dakota's people are
The grandest crop she grows.

BADGER CLARK, quoted in Robert F. Karolevitz, *Challenge: The South Dakota Story,* 1981.

5 It never is verboten for any South Dakotan
To laugh and talk as freely as he votes,
And if they haven't riches to carry in their
    britches,
They always carry laughter in their throats.

Ibid.

6 A part of hell with the fires burnt out.

GEORGE ARMSTRONG CUSTER, describing the South Dakota Bad Lands, quoted in John Gunther, *Inside U.S.A.,* 1947.

7 As the Christian looks forward with hope and faith to that land of pure delight, so the miner looks forward to the Black Hills, a region of fabulous wealth, where the rills repose on beds of gold and the rocks are studded with precious metal.

CLEMENT A. LOUNSBERRY, newspaper editor, in the *Bismarck Tribune,* June, 1874.

8 What frightens me . . . is that our nation's urban majority don't understand a place like South Dakota. They don't connect what they consider to be the country's "boondocks" with the food they need for survival. . . . Often I think we are all Indians here, in as much danger of losing our land as the Sioux of one hundred years ago. And if it happens, I fear we will meet with the same massive national indifference.

KATHLEEN NORRIS, quoted in John Milton, *South Dakota: A Bicentennial History,* 1977.

9 I was not prepared for the Bad Lands. They deserve this name. They are like the work of an evil child. Such a place the Fallen Angels might have built as a spite to Heaven, dry and sharp, desolate and dangerous, and for me filled with foreboding. A sense comes from it that it does not like or welcome humans.

JOHN STEINBECK, *Travels with Charley,* 1962.

217. SPACE EXPLORATION

See also SCIENCE; TECHNOLOGY

1 Houston, Tranquillity Base here. The Eagle has landed.

NEIL ARMSTRONG, first words from the moon, July 20, 1969.

2 That's one small step for a man, one giant leap for mankind.

NEIL ARMSTRONG, on becoming the first person to stand on the moon, July 20, 1969.

3 Reaching the Moon by three-man vessels in one long bound from Earth is like casting a thin thread across space. The main effort, in the coming decades, will be to strengthen this thread; to make it a cord, a cable, and, finally, a broad highway.

ISAAC ASIMOV, "The Coming Decades in Space," *The Beginning and the End,* 1977.

4 Man must have bread and butter, but he must also have something to lift his heart. This program is clean. We are not spending the money to kill people. We are not harming the environment. We are helping the spirit of man. We are unlocking secrets billions of years old.

FAROUK EL BAZ, quoted in "Skylab: Next Great Moment in Space," *American Way* magazine, April, 1973.

5 Since I've been back on earth, I feel at home. No matter where I am on earth, I feel completely relaxed. I do not feel foreign. I do not feel alien.

Attributed to astronaut Jim Irwin, December, 1974.

6 I believe that this nation should commit itself to achieving a goal, before this decade is out, of landing a man on the moon and returning him safely to the earth.

JOHN F. KENNEDY, in a special message to Congress, May 25, 1961.

7 Because of what you have done the heavens have become a part of man's world, and as you talk to

us from the Sea of Tranquillity, it inspires us to redouble our efforts to bring peace and tranquillity to earth.

> RICHARD M. NIXON, in an earth-moon communication with Neil Armstrong, July 20, 1969.

8 Advanced civilizations—if they exist—aren't breaking their backs to save us before we destroy ourselves. Personally, I think that makes for a more interesting universe.

> CARL SAGAN, quoted in *American Way* magazine, June, 1978.

9 Excelsior! We're Going to the Moon! Excelsior!

> KURT VONNEGUT, title of an essay in *Wampeters, Foma, and Granfalloons,* 1974.

10 "One sacred memory from childhood is perhaps the best education," said Feodor Dostoevski. I believe that, and I hope that many Earthling children will respond to the first human footprint on the moon as a sacred thing. We need sacred things.

> Ibid.

11 The right stuff was not bravery in the simple sense of being willing to risk your life (by riding on top of a Redstone or Atlas rocket). Any fool could do that (and many fools would no doubt volunteer, given the opportunity), just as any fool could throw his life away in the process. No, the idea (as all *pilots* understood) was that a man should have the ability to go up in a hurtling piece of machinery and put his hide on the line and have the moxie, the reflexes, the experience, the coolness, to pull it back at the last yawning moment.

> TOM WOLFE, *The Right Stuff,* 1979.

12 Alan Shepard finally got his turn on May 5 [1961]. He was inserted in the capsule, on top of a Redstone rocket. . . . All across the eastern half of the country people were doing the usual, turning on their radios and television sets, rolling the knobs in search of something to give the nerve endings a little tingle—and what suspense awaited them! An astronaut sat on the tip of a rocket, preparing to get himself blown to pieces.

> Ibid.

218. SPANISH-AMERICAN WAR

See also WAR

1 Remember the Maine!

> Slogan coined after the sinking of the U.S. battleship *Maine* in the harbor of Havana, Cuba, February 15, 1898.

2 "Well, here's to the Maine, and I'm sorry for Spain,"
Said Kelly and Burke and Shea.

> J.I.C. CLARKE, "The Fighting Race," in Burton E. Stevenson, *The Home Book of Verse,* 1953.

3 Someone has said that "God takes care of drunken men, sailors, and the United States." This expedition apparently relied on the probability that that axiom would prove true.

> RICHARD HARDING DAVIS, describing the U.S. expedition to Cuba, in *The Cuban and Porto Rican Campaigns,* 1898.

4 This is God Almighty's war, and we are only His agents.

> RICHARD HARDING DAVIS, quoting an unidentified U.S. general, in *The Cuban and Porto Rican Campaigns,* 1898.

5 You may fire when you are ready, Gridley.

> COMMODORE GEORGE DEWEY, to Capt. Charles V. Gridley, commander of Dewey's flagship, *Olympia,* during the battle of Manila Bay, May 1, 1898.

6 It has been a splendid little war; begun with the highest motives, carried on with magnificent intelligence and spirit, favored by that Fortune which loves the brave. It is now to be concluded, I hope, with that fine good nature, which is, after all, the distinguishing trait of the American character.

> JOHN HAY, in a letter to Theodore Roosevelt, July 27, 1898.

7 You furnish the pictures, and I'll furnish the war.

WILLIAM RANDOLPH HEARST, in a cable to Frederic Remington, *New York Journal* artist in Havana, Cuba, March, 1898.

8 Ye who remembered the Alamo,
Remember the Maine!
Ye who unfettered the slave,
Break a free people's chain!

RICHARD HOVEY, "The Word of the Lord from Havana," *Along the Trail,* 1903.

9 Remember the Maine—
That all the world as well as Spain
May know that God has given us the sword
To punish crime and vindicate his word.

RICHARD HOVEY, "The Call of the Bugles," *Along the Trail,* 1903.

10 We want no war of conquest. . . . War should never be entered upon until every agency of peace has failed.

WILLIAM MCKINLEY, in his inaugural address, March 4, 1897.

11 I have already transmitted to Congress the report of the naval court of inquiry on the destruction of the battleship *Maine* in the harbor of Havana during the night of the 15th of February. The destruction of that noble vessel has filled the national heart with inexpressible horror. Two hundred and fifty-eight brave sailors and marines and two officers of our Navy, reposing in the fancied security of a friendly harbor, have been hurled to death, grief and want brought to their homes and sorrow to the nation. . . . The destruction of the *Maine,* by whatever exterior cause, is a patent and impressive proof of a state of things in Cuba that is intolerable. That condition is thus shown to be such that the Spanish Government can not assure safety and security to a vessel of the American Navy in the harbor of Havana on a mission of peace, and rightfully there.

WILLIAM MCKINLEY, in his war message to Congress, April 11, 1898.

12 I ask the Congress to authorize and empower the President to take measures to secure a full and final termination of hostilities between the government of Spain and the people of Cuba, and to secure in the island the establishment of a stable government, capable of maintaining order and observing its international obligations, insuring peace and tranquility and the security of its citizens as well as our own, and to use the military and naval forces of the United States as may be necessary for these purposes.

Ibid.

13 Oh, dewy was the morning
Upon the first of May,
And Dewey was the admiral
Down in Manila Bay,
And dewy were the Regent's eyes,
Them orbs of royal blue,
And dew we feel discouraged?
I dew not think we dew.

EUGENE WARE, untitled verse, published in the *Topeka* [Kansas] *Capital,* May 10, 1898.

---

219. SPEECH

See also INVECTIVE; LANGUAGE; ORATORY

---

1 Gentlemen, there comes a tide in the affairs of bastards when no amount of cursing will suffice. Let us merely observe a moment of silence, like a deaf-mute who has just hit his fingers with a hammer.

JOHN BARRYMORE, quoted in Gene Fowler, *Good Night, Sweet Prince,* 1943.

2 When we talk about ourselves we almost invariably use Latin words, and when we talk about our neighbors we use Saxon words.

HENRY WARD BEECHER, *Royal Truths,* 1866.

3 Talk, *v.t.* To commit an indiscretion without temptation, from an impulse without purpose.

AMBROSE BIERCE, *The Devil's Dictionary,* 1906.

4 I realize that . . . there are certain limitations placed upon the right of free speech. I must be exceedingly careful, prudent, as to what I say, and even more careful and prudent as to how I say it.

I may not be able to say all I think, but I am not going to say anything I do not think.

> EUGENE V. DEBS, in an address at Canton, Ohio, June 16, 1918.

5 Congress is really the home of the split infinitive, where it finds its finest fruition. This is the place where the dangling participle is certainly nourished. This is the home of the broken sentence.

> EVERETT M. DIRKSEN, quoted in Neil MacNeil, *Dirksen: Portrait of a Public Man,* 1970.

6 I confess to some pleasure from the stinging rhetoric of a rattling oath in the mouth of truckmen and teamsters. How laconic and brisk it is by the side of a page of the *North American Review.* Cut these words and they would bleed; they are vascular and alive; they walk and run. Moreover they who speak them have this elegancy, that they do not trip in their speech. It is a shower of bullets, whilst Cambridge men and Yale men correct themselves and begin again at every half sentence.

> RALPH WALDO EMERSON, entry written in 1840, *Journals,* 1909–1914.

7 Better things are said, more incisive, more wit and insight are dropped in talk and forgotten by the speaker, than get into books.

> RALPH WALDO EMERSON, in a lecture in Boston, December 18, 1864.

8 Spartans, stoics, heroes, saints and gods use a short and positive speech.

> RALPH WALDO EMERSON, "The Superlative," *Lectures and Biographical Sketches,* 1883.

9 Write with the learned, pronounce with the vulgar.

> BENJAMIN FRANKLIN, *Poor Richard's Almanack,* 1738.

10 Speak little, do much.

> BENJAMIN FRANKLIN, *Poor Richard's Almanack,* 1755.

11 [The English] do not talk, as so many Americans do, to make a good impression on themselves by making a good impression on somebody else. They have already made a good impression on themselves and talk simply because they think sound is more manageable than silence.

> MARGARET HALSEY, *With Malice Toward Some,* 1938.

12 Articulate words are a harsh clamor and dissonance. When man arrives at his highest perfection, he will again be dumb. For I suppose he was dumb at the Creation, and must go around an entire circle in order to return to that blessed state.

> NATHANIEL HAWTHORNE, entry written in April, 1841, in *Passages from the American Notebooks,* 1868.

13 Words lead to things; a scale is more
    precise,—
Coarse speech, bad grammar, swearing,
    drinking, vice.

> OLIVER WENDELL HOLMES, SR., "A Rhymed Lesson," 1846.

14 Talking is like playing on the harp; there is as much in laying the hands on the strings to stop their vibrations as in twanging them to bring out their music.

> OLIVER WENDELL HOLMES, SR., *The Autocrat of the Breakfast-Table,* 1858.

15 With effervescing opinions, as with champagne, the quickest way to let them get flat is to let them get exposed to the air.

> OLIVER WENDELL HOLMES, JR., in a letter to the Harvard Liberal Club, January 12, 1920.

16 In a country and government like ours, eloquence is a powerful instrument, well worthy of the special pursuit of our youth.

> THOMAS JEFFERSON, in a letter to George W. Summers and John B. Garland, February 27, 1822.

17 Words can destroy. What we call each other ultimately becomes what we think of each other, and it matters.

> JEANE J. KIRKPATRICK, "Israel as Scapegoat," an address before the Anti-Defamation League, February 11, 1982.

18 Speaking words of endearment where words of comfort availed not.

HENRY WADSWORTH LONGFELLOW, *Evangeline,* 1847.

19 Why don't you speak for yourself, John?

HENRY WADSWORTH LONGFELLOW, *The Courtship of Miles Standish,* 1858.

20 Peter Piper picked a peck of pickled peppers.

JAMES KIRKE PAULDING, quoted in Allan Keller, *Life Along the Hudson,* 1976.

21 Look out how you use proud words,
When you let proud words go, it is not easy
    to call them back.

CARL SANDBURG, "Primer Lesson," 1922.

22 A people who are prosperous and happy, optimistic and progressive, will produce much slang; it is a case of play; they amuse themselves with the language.

WILLIAM GRAHAM SUMNER, A.G. Keller and M.R. Davie, *The Science of Society,* 1927.

23 We love eloquence for its own sake, and not for any truth which it may utter, or any heroism it may inspire.

HENRY DAVID THOREAU, "Civil Disobedience," 1849.

24 I very seldom during my whole stay in the country heard a sentence elegantly turned and correctly pronounced from the lips of an American.

FRANCES TROLLOPE, *Domestic Manners of the Americans,* 1832.

25 When I speak my native tongue in its utmost purity an Englishman can't understand me at all.

MARK TWAIN, "Concerning the American Language," 1882.

26 A Southerner talks music. . . . The educated Southerner has no use for an *r,* except at the beginning of a word.

MARK TWAIN, *Life on the Mississippi,* 1883.

27 In certain trying circumstances, urgent circumstances, desperate circumstances, profanity furnishes a relief denied even to prayer.

MARK TWAIN, quoted in Albert Bigelow Paine, *Mark Twain: A Biography,* 1912.

28 True eloquence does not consist in speech. . . . It must consist in the man, in the subject, and in the occasion. It comes, if it comes at all, like the outbreaking of a fountain from the earth, or the bursting forth of volcanic fires, with spontaneous, original, native force.

DANIEL WEBSTER, in an address in Boston, August 2, 1826.

29 My voice goes after what my eyes cannot
    reach,
With the twirl of my tongue I encompass
    worlds and volumes of worlds.
Speech is the twin of my vision, it is unequal
    to measure itself,
It provokes me forever, it says sarcastically,
*Walt you contain enough, why don't you let
    it out then?*

WALT WHITMAN, "Song of Myself," 1855.

30 A call in the midst of the crowd,
My own voice, orotund, sweeping, and final.

Ibid.

31 Slang, profoundly consider'd, is the lawless germinal element, below all words and sentences, and behind all poetry, and proves a certain perennial rankness and protestantism in speech.

WALT WHITMAN, "Slang in America," 1885.

32 The propensity to approach a meaning not directly and squarely, but by circuitous styles of expression, seems a born quality of the common people everywhere, evidenced by nicknames.

Ibid.

33 If a man is a fool the best thing to do is to encourage him to advertise the fact by speaking.

WOODROW WILSON, in a speech in Paris, France, May 10, 1919.

220. SPORTS

See also BASEBALL; BERRAISMS; FOOTBALL; HORSE RACING

1 Golf matches are not won on the fairways or greens. They are won on the tee—the first tee.

> Anonymous, quoted in Bobby Riggs, *Court Hustler,* 1973.

2 Sport develops not character, but characters.

> Anonymous, quoted in James A. Michener, *Sports in America,* 1976.

3 Float like a butterfly, sting like a bee.

> MUHAMMAD ALI, on his boxing style, coined by his associate, Drew "Bundini" Brown.

4 Not only do I knock 'em out, I pick the round.

> MUHAMMAD ALI, in a statement to the press, December, 1962.

5 Fighters were not supposed to be human or intelligent. Just brutes that exist to entertain and to satisfy a crowd's thirst for blood.

> MUHAMMAD ALI, *The Greatest,* 1975.

6 I hated the sight on TV of big, clumsy, lumbering heavyweights plodding, stalking each other like two Frankenstein monsters, clinging, slugging toe to toe. I knew I could do it better. I would be as fast as a lightweight, circle, dance, shuffle, hit and move, zip-zip-pop-pop, hit and move back and dance again and make an art out of it.

> Ibid.

7 Champions aren't made in gyms. Champions are made from something they have deep inside them—a desire, a dream, a vision. They have to have last-minute stamina, they have to be a little faster, they have to have the skill and the will. But the will must be stronger than the skill.

> Ibid.

8 Every time you win, you're reborn; when you lose, you die a little.

> GEORGE ALLEN, quoted in James A. Michener, *Sports in America,* 1976.

9 There has never been a great athlete who died not knowing what pain is.

> BILL BRADLEY, quoted in John McPhee, *A Sense of Where You Are,* 1965.

10 A professional basketball player must be able to run six miles in a game, a hundred games a year—jumping and pivoting under constant physical contact. My body becomes so finely tuned that three days without workouts makes a noticeable difference in timing, wind, and strength. I believe that basketball is the most physically grueling of all professional sports.

> BILL BRADLEY, *Life on the Run,* 1976.

11 Sports do not build character. They reveal it.

> HEYWOOD HALE BROUN, quoted in James A. Michener, *Sports in America,* 1976.

12 Golf is not, on the whole, a game for realists. By its exactitudes of measurement it invites the attention of perfectionists.

> HEYWOOD HALE BROUN, *Tumultuous Merriment,* 1979.

13 Boxers have those quick, automatic, reflexive insights that enable them to decipher an opponent's vulnerabilities and to strike at them with immediacy. They can amaze you with their perception, and, even though they're in a brutal sport, with their sensitivity and concern for others.

> HOWARD COSELL, *Like It Is,* 1974.

14 People are frustrated these days. The times are vexing, the inflation ever escalating, the problems of daily living overwhelming. Sports, for the masses, are a prime means of escape from those problems. It is at the playing arena that people can let their emotions loose, or at least so they think.

> Ibid.

15 Honey, I just forgot to duck.

> JACK DEMPSEY, speaking to his wife over the telephone from his dressing room after losing the heavyweight title to Gene Tunney, September 23, 1926.

16 What'd he want me to do, write him a letter?

> JACK DEMPSEY, talking with reporters after knocking out Jack Sharkey, who had been

protesting to the referee about four consecutive low blows when Dempsey threw the final punch, July 21, 1927.

17 "How you play the game" is for college boys. When you're playing for money, winning is the only thing that matters. Show me a good loser in professional sports, and I'll show you an idiot. Show me a sportsman, and I'll show you a player I'm looking to trade to Oakland.

LEO DUROCHER, *Nice Guys Finish Last,* 1975.

18 If you're in professional sports, buddy, and you don't care whether you win or lose, you are going to finish last.

Ibid.

19 Good shot, bad luck, and hell are the five basic words to be used in a game of tennis.

VIRGINIA GRAHAM, *Say Please,* 1949.

20 Anyone who will tear down sports will tear down America. Sports and religion have made America what it is today.

WOODY HAYES, quoted in Bill Bradley, *Life on the Run,* 1976.

21 A race track swarms with sweaty oafs intent on getting something for nothing and sullen if they fail. A fight crowd is exciting and excited, and vaguely pathologic. But a baseball crowd, excepting the stray cranks and exhibitionists, is a neighborly lot.

JOHN K. HUTCHENS, quoted in the *New York Times Magazine,* July 14, 1946.

22 We wuz robbed.

JOE JACOBS, after his fighter, Max Schmeling, lost the heavyweight title to Jack Sharkey on a foul, June 21, 1932.

23 You've got to win in sports—that's talent—but you've also got to learn how to remind everybody how you did win, and how often. That comes with experience.

BILLIE JEAN KING, *Billie Jean,* 1982.

24 It's really impossible for athletes to grow up. As long as you're playing, no one will let you. On the one hand, you're a child, still playing a game. And everybody around you acts like a kid, too. But on the other hand, you're a superhuman hero that everyone dreams of being. No wonder we have such a hard time understanding who we are.

Ibid.

25 It's easy to have faith in yourself and have discipline when you're a winner, when you're number one. What you got to have is faith and discipline when you're not a winner.

VINCE LOMBARDI, quoted in Tom Dowling, *Coach: A Season with Lombardi,* 1970.

26 He can run, but he can't hide.

JOE LOUIS, before his first heavyweight title fight with the light-heavyweight champion, Billy Conn, June 19, 1941.

27 In this country, when you finish second, no one knows your name.

FRANK MCGUIRE, basketball coach, quoted in James A. Michener, *Sports in America,* 1976.

28 Prizefighting offers a profession to men who might otherwise commit murder in the street.

NORMAN MAILER, *The Fight,* 1975.

29 In my book a tennis player is the complete athlete. He has to have the speed of a sprinter, the endurance of a marathon runner, the agility of a boxer or fencer and the gray matter of a good football quarterback. Baseball, football, basketball players are good athletes, but they don't need all these attributes to perform well.

BOBBY RIGGS, *Court Hustler,* 1973.

30 Win this one for the Gipper.

Attributed to Knute Rockne, exhorting his Notre Dame football team before a big game of 1921. ("The Gipper" was the nickname of one of Rockne's players, George Gipp, an All-American fullback who had died on December 4, 1920, after the end of the football season.)

31 As I emphatically disbelieve in seeing Harvard or any other college turn out mollycoddles instead of vigorous men, I may add that I do not in the least object to a sport because it is rough.

THEODORE ROOSEVELT, in a speech in Cambridge, Massachusetts, February 23, 1907.

32 I zigged when I should have zagged.

> JACK ROPER, heavyweight boxer, after recovering from a knockout by Joe Louis, April 17, 1939.

33 Professional sports add something to the spirit and vitality of a city. They are a reflection of the city's image of itself. I don't simply believe that; I know it. A winning team can bring a city together, and even a losing team can provide a bond of common misery.

> BILL VEECK, *Thirty Tons a Day,* 1972.

---

221. SPRING

See also NATURE; WEATHER

---

1 Spring comes laughing down the valley
All in white, from the snow
Where the winter's armies rally
Loth to go.

> AMELIA JOSEPHINE BURR, "New Life," *Life and Living,* 1916.

2 April is the cruellest month, breeding
Lilacs out of the dead land, mixing
Memory and desire, stirring
Dull roots with spring rain.

> T.S. ELIOT, *The Waste Land,* 1922.

3 Daughter of Heaven and Earth, coy Spring,
With sudden passion languishing,
Teaching barren moors to smile,
Painting pictures mile on mile,
Holds a cup of cowslip-wreaths,
Whence a smokeless incense breathes.

> RALPH WALDO EMERSON, "May-Day," 1867.

4 When the trellised grapes their flowers
unmask,
And the new-born tendrils twine,
The old wine darkling in the cask
Feels the bloom on the living vine,
And bursts the hoops at hint of spring.

> Ibid.

5 The air
Made love to all it touched as if its care
Were all to spare;
The earth
Prickled with lust of birth;
The woodland streams
Babbled the incoherence of the thousand
dreams
Wherewith the warm sun teems.

> RICHARD HOVEY, "Spring: An Ode," 1898.

6 Spring in the world!
And all things are made new.

> Ibid.

7 For surely in the blind deep-buried roots
Of all men's souls to-day
A secret quiver shoots.

> Ibid.

8 Spring's not to be mistaken.
When her first far flute-notes blow
Across the snow,
Bird, beast, and blossom know
That she is there.

> Ibid.

9 The swallow is come!
The swallow is come!
  O, fair are the seasons, and light
Are the days that she brings,
With her dusky wings,
  And her bosom snowy white!

> HENRY WADSWORTH LONGFELLOW, *Hyperion,* 1839.

10 Came the Spring with all its splendor,
  All its birds and all its blossoms,
  All its flowers and leaves and grasses.

> HENRY WADSWORTH LONGFELLOW, *The Song of Hiawatha,* 1855.

11 The lovely town was white with
    apple-blooms,
  And the great elms o'erhead
Dark shadows wove on their aerial looms,
  Shot through with golden thread.

> HENRY WADSWORTH LONGFELLOW, "Hawthorne," 1855.

12 The word May is a perfumed word. It is an illuminated initial. It means youth, love, song, and all that is beautiful in life.

> HENRY WADSWORTH LONGFELLOW, journal entry, May 1, 1861.

13 Then came the lovely spring with a rush of blossoms and music,
  Flooding the earth with flowers, and the air with melodies vernal.

> HENRY WADSWORTH LONGFELLOW, "The Theologian's Tale," *Tales of a Wayside Inn,* 1863–1874.

14 Then seems to come a hitch—things lag behind,
  Till some fine mornin' Spring makes up her mind. . . .
  Then all the waters bow themselves an' come,
  Suddin, in one gret slope o' shedderin' foam,
  Jes' so our Spring gits everythin' in tune
  An' gives one leap from Aperl into June:
  Then all comes crowdin' in; afore you think,
  Young oak-leaves mist the side-hill woods with pink.

> JAMES RUSSELL LOWELL, section entitled "Spring" in "Sunthin' in the Pastoral Line," *The Biglow Papers,* Second Series, 1867.

15 Wag the world how it will,
  Leaves must be green in Spring.

> HERMAN MELVILLE, "Malvern Hill," in *Battle-Pieces and Aspects of the War,* 1866.

16 Spring rides no horses down the hill,
  But comes on foot, a goose-girl still.
  And all the loveliest things there be
  Come simply so, it seems to me.

> EDNA ST. VINCENT MILLAY, "The Goose-Girl," in *The Harp-Weaver and Other Poems,* 1923.

17 Winter lingered so long in the lap of Spring, that it occasioned a great deal of talk.

> Attributed to Bill Nye.

18 Spring, with that nameless pathos in the air
  Which dwells with all things fair,
  Spring, with her golden suns and silver rain,
  Is with us once again.

> HENRY TIMROD, "Spring," 1862.

19 Again the blackbirds sing; the streams
  Wake, laughing, from their winter dreams,
  And tremble in the April showers
  The tassels of the maple flowers.

> JOHN GREENLEAF WHITTIER, "The Singer," written in memory of poet Alice Cary, 1871.

---

222. STATESMANSHIP

See also DIPLOMACY; GOVERNMENT; POLITICS; PRESIDENCY

---

1 We must not . . . take her statesmen as types of the highest or strongest American manhood. The national qualities come out fully in them, but not always in their best form.

> JAMES BRYCE, *The American Commonwealth,* 1888.

2 A statesman cannot afford to be a moralist.

> Attributed to Will Durant.

3 The opportunist thinks of me and today. The statesman thinks of us and tomorrow.

> DWIGHT D. EISENHOWER, in an address at Lafayette College, Easton, Pennsylvania, November 1, 1946.

4 [Statesman:] One who cannot compromise with what he knows to be right or make political deals which will allow a form of evil or injustice to be even temporarily victorious. Usually not an elected public official. In times of crisis, the statesman flexes his mind and not his muscle.

> DICK GREGORY, *Dick Gregory's Political Primer,* 1972.

5 [Statesmanship:] The art of uncompromising devotion to humanity, the alleviation of suffering, and the creation of a decent and peaceful environment throughout the world.

> Ibid.

6 Any statesman is in part the prisoner of necessity. He is confronted with an environment he did not create, and is shaped by a personal history he can no longer change.

HENRY KISSINGER, *White House Years,* 1979.

7 Even in the best of times, no judgment is more tenuous than an assessment of the significance of a statesman's actions.

HENRY KISSINGER, *Years of Upheaval,* 1982.

8 Statesman create; ordinary leaders consume. The ordinary leader is satisfied with ameliorating the environment, not transforming it; a statesman must be a visionary and an educator.

Ibid.

9 The politician says: "I will give you what you want." The statesman says: "What you think you want is this. What it is possible for you to get is that. What you really want, therefore, is the following."

WALTER LIPPMANN, *A Preface to Morals,* 1929.

10 The statesman who is surest that he can divine the future most urgently invites his own retribution.

ARTHUR M. SCHLESINGER, JR., *The Bitter Heritage: Vietnam and American Democracy, 1941–1966,* 1967.

11 The true statesman does not despise any wisdom, howsoever lowly may be its origin.

MARK TWAIN, *A Connecticut Yankee in King Arthur's Court,* 1889.

12 In statesmanship get the formalities right, never mind about the moralities.

MARK TWAIN, "Pudd'nhead Wilson's New Calendar," *Following the Equator,* 1897.

13 I've been a statesman without salary for many years, and I have accomplished great and widespread good. I don't know that it has benefited anybody very much, even if it was good; but I do know that it hasn't harmed me very much, and it hasn't made me any richer.

MARK TWAIN, in an address, "Municipal Corruption," January 4, 1901.

14 Why don't you show us a statesman who can rise up to the Emergency, and cave in the Emergency's head?

ARTEMUS WARD, "Things in New York," *The Works of Artemus Ward,* 1898.

---

223. STATES' RIGHTS

See also CIVIL WAR; CONSTITUTION; DEMOCRACY; GOVERNMENT; MAJORITY RULE

---

1 My hopes of the long continuance of this Union are extinct. The people must go the way of all the world, and split up into an uncertain number of rival communities, enemies in war, in peace friends.

JOHN QUINCY ADAMS, in his diary, July 30, 1834.

2 What were the states before the Union? The hope of their enemies, the fear of their friends, and arrested only by the Constitution from becoming the shame of the world.

HORACE BINNEY, *Eulogy on the Life and Character of John Marshall,* 1835.

3 So far from lamenting as a fault, though an unavoidable fault, of their Federal system, the State independence I have described, the Americans are inclined to praise it as a merit. They argue, not merely that the best way on the whole is to leave a State to itself, but that this is the only way in which a permanent cure of its diseases will be effected. They are consistent not only in their Federal principles but in their democratic principles.

JAMES BRYCE, *The American Commonwealth,* 1888.

4 The Americans, like the English, have no love for scientific arrangement. Although the [State] Constitutions have been drafted by lawyers, and sometimes by the best lawyers of each State, logical classification and discrimination have not been sought after.

Ibid.

5 I never use the word "Nation" in speaking of the United States; I always use the word "Union" or "Confederacy." We are not a Nation, but a Union, a confederacy of equal and sovereign States.

> JOHN C. CALHOUN, in a letter to Oliver Dyer, January 1, 1849.

6 I owe a paramount allegiance to the whole Union—a subordinate one to my own State.

> HENRY CLAY, in a speech in the U.S. Senate, July 22, 1850.

7 The local interests of a state ought in every case to give way to the interests of the Union; for when a sacrifice of one or the other is necessary, the former becomes only an apparent, partial interest, and should yield, on the principle that the small good ought never to oppose the great one.

> ALEXANDER HAMILTON, in a speech in Poughkeepsie, New York, June 24, 1788.

8 Who . . . are the true friends of the Union? Those who would confine the federal government strictly within the limits prescribed by the Constitution; who would preserve to the states and the people all powers not expressly delegated; who would make this a federal and not a national Union.

> ROBERT YOUNG HAYNE, in a speech in the U.S. Senate, January 21, 1830.

9 If the Federal government, in all, or any, of its departments, is to prescribe the limits of its own authority, and the states are bound to submit to the decision, and are not to be allowed to examine and decide for themselves, when the barriers of the Constitution shall be overleaped, this is practically "a government without limitation of powers." The states are at once reduced to mere petty corporations.

> Ibid.

10 Tell . . . the Nullifiers for me that they can talk and write resolutions and print threats to their heart's content. But if one drop of blood be shed . . . in defiance of the laws of the United States, I will hang the first man of them I can get my hands on to the first tree I can find.

> Attributed to Andrew Jackson, referring to the doctrine of nullification, which held that a state could declare an act of Congress invalid if it exceeded constitutional restrictions on federal power.

11 Secession, like any other revolutionary act, may be morally justified by the extremity of oppression; but to call it a constitutional right is confounding the meaning of terms, and can only be done through gross error or to deceive those who are willing to assert a right, but would pause before they made a revolution or incur the penalties consequent on a failure.

> ANDREW JACKSON, in a proclamation to the people of South Carolina, December 10, 1832.

12 My idea is that we should be made one nation in every case concerning foreign affairs, and separate ones in whatever is merely domestic.

> THOMAS JEFFERSON, in a letter to John Blair, August 13, 1787.

13 The states should be left to do whatever acts they can do as well as the general government.

> THOMAS JEFFERSON, in a letter to John Harvie, Jr., July 25, 1790.

14 What an augmentation of the field for jobbing, speculating, plundering, office-building and office-hunting would be produced by an assumption of all the State powers into the hand of the General Government! The true theory of our Constitution is surely the wisest and best, that the states are independent as to everything within themselves and united as to everything respecting foreign nations. Let the General Government be reduced to foreign concerns only.

> THOMAS JEFFERSON, in a letter to Gideon Granger, August 13, 1800.

15 The maintenance inviolate of the rights of the States, and especially the right of each State to order and control its own domestic institutions according to its own judgment exclusively, is essential to that balance of powers on which the perfection and endurance of our political fabric depend.

> ABRAHAM LINCOLN, in a letter to Duff Green, December 28, 1860.

16 Our States have neither more nor less power than that reserved to them in the Union by the Constitution, no one of them ever having been a State *out* of the Union.

> ABRAHAM LINCOLN, in a message to Congress, July 4, 1861.

17 Much has been said about the "sovereignty" of the States, but the word even is not in the National Constitution, nor, as is believed, in any of the State constitutions.

> Ibid.

18 The States have their status in the Union, and they have no other legal status. . . . The Union, and not themselves separately, procured their independence and their liberty. By conquest or purchase the Union gave each of them whatever of independence and liberty it has. The Union is older than any of the States, and, in fact, it created them as States.

> Ibid.

19 The States have no power, by taxation or otherwise, to retard, impede, burden, or in any manner control the operations of the constitutional laws enacted by Congress to carry into execution the powers vested in the general government.

> JOHN MARSHALL, in a Supreme Court opinion, *McCulloch* v. *Maryland,* 1819.

20 Asking one of the states to surrender part of her sovereignty is like asking a lady to surrender part of her chastity.

> JOHN RANDOLPH, quoted in Russell Kirk, *John Randolph of Roanoke,* 1951.

21 States' rights should be preserved when they mean the people's rights, but not when they mean the people's wrongs; not, for instance, when they are invoked to prevent the abolition of child labor, or to break the force of the laws which prohibit the importation of contract labor to this country.

> THEODORE ROOSEVELT, in a speech to the Harvard Union, Cambridge, Massachusetts, February 23, 1907.

22 I say the right of a state to annul a law of Congress cannot be maintained but on the ground of the inalienable right of man to resist oppression; that is to say, upon the ground of revolution.

> DANIEL WEBSTER, in a speech in the U.S. Senate, January 26, 1830.

224. SUCCESS

See also FAILURE; TALENT

1 You can't steal second base and keep one foot on first.

> An unidentified aging junior executive, quoted in Derek Evans and David Fulwiler, *Who's Nobody in America,* 1981.

2 The American dream, I think, was that within this system every man could become an owner. . . . It has been said that every soldier of Napoleon carried in his knapsack a marshal's baton, and in the early days of this century it seems to have been thought that every young American carried in his lunch box a roll of ticker tape.

> DEAN ACHESON, in an address to the Law Club of Chicago, January 22, 1937.

3 Success is full of promise till men get it; and then it is a last-year's nest from which the birds have flown.

> HENRY WARD BEECHER, *Life Thoughts,* 1859.

4 Achievement, *n.* The death of endeavor and the birth of disgust.

> AMBROSE BIERCE, *The Devil's Dictionary,* 1906.

5 Success, *n.* The one unpardonable sin against one's fellows.

> Ibid.

6 Have little care that Life is brief,
And less that Art is long.
Success is in the silences
Though Fame is in the song.

> BLISS CARMAN, "Envoy," *Songs from Vagabondia,* 1894.

7 How to Win Friends and Influence People.

> DALE CARNEGIE, the title of his best-selling book, 1938.

8 I have found some of the best reasons I ever had for remaining at the bottom simply by looking at the men at the top.

> FRANK COLBY, *The Colby Essays,* 1926.

9 Success is counted sweetest
By those who ne'er succeed.

> EMILY DICKINSON, "Success," *Poems,* 1890.

10 Try not to become a man of success but rather try to become a man of value.

> ALBERT EINSTEIN, quoted in *Life* magazine, May 2, 1955.

11 The reward of a thing well done is to have done it.

> RALPH WALDO EMERSON, "New England Reformers," *Essays,* Second Series, 1844.

12 All successful men have agreed in one thing—they were *causationists.* They believed that things went not by luck, but by law; that there was not a weak or a cracked link in the chain that joins the first and last of things.

> RALPH WALDO EMERSON, "Power," *The Conduct of Life,* 1860.

13 Often a certain abdication of prudence and foresight is an element of success.

> RALPH WALDO EMERSON, "Demonology," *Lectures and Biographical Sketches,* 1883.

14 I remember riding in a taxi one afternoon between very tall buildings under a mauve and rosy sky; I began to bawl because I had everything I wanted and knew I would never be so happy again.

> F. SCOTT FITZGERALD, "My Lost City," in *The Crack-Up,* 1945.

15 Success has ruin'd many a Man.

> BENJAMIN FRANKLIN, *Poor Richard's Almanack,* 1752.

16 The success of any great moral enterprise does not depend upon numbers.

> WILLIAM LLOYD GARRISON, quoted in *William Lloyd Garrison, 1805–79: The Story of His Life Told by His Children,* 1885–1889.

17 He started to sing as he tackled the thing
That couldn't be done, and he did it.

> EDGAR A. GUEST, "It Couldn't be Done," in *Collected Verse of Edgar A. Guest,* 1934.

18 Success has killed more men than bullets.

> Attributed to Texas Guinan.

19 Of course everybody likes and respects self-made men. It is a great deal better to be made in that way than not to be made at all.

> OLIVER WENDELL HOLMES, SR., *The Autocrat of the Breakfast-Table,* 1858.

20 When a man succeeds, he does it in spite of everybody, and not with the assistance of everybody.

> EDGAR WATSON HOWE, *Country Town Sayings,* 1911.

21 In order to stand success you must be of a very stern fiber, with all the gods on your side.

> ELBERT HUBBARD, *The Roycroft Dictionary and Book of Epigrams,* 1923.

22 Success: A subtle contrivance of Nature for bringing about a man's defeat.

> Ibid.

23 Success consists in the climb.

> Ibid.

24 All success consists in this: You are doing something for somebody—benefiting humanity—and the feeling of success comes from the consciousness of this.

> Ibid.

25 Behind every man who achieves success
Stand a mother, a wife, and the IRS.

> ETHEL JACOBSON, quoted in the *Reader's Digest,* April, 1973.

26 Self-esteem = $\dfrac{\text{Success}}{\text{Pretensions}}$

> WILLIAM JAMES, *The Principles of Psychology,* abridged edition, 1892.

27 The moral flabbiness born of the exclusive worship of the bitch-goddess SUCCESS. That—with the squalid cash interpretation put on the word success—is our national disease.

> WILLIAM JAMES, in a letter to H.G. Wells, September 11, 1906.

28 He said he'd bring home the bacon, and the honey boy has gone and done it.

> "TINY" JOHNSON, when her son, boxer Jack Johnson, knocked out Jim Jeffries, July 4, 1910.

29 It ain't enough to get the breaks. You gotta know how to use 'em.

> HUEY P. LONG, a favorite saying.

30 Not in the clamor of the crowded street,
Not in the shouts and plaudits of the throng,
But in ourselves, are triumph and defeat.

> HENRY WADSWORTH LONGFELLOW, "The Poets," 1876.

31 I must admit that I personally measure success in terms of the contributions an individual makes to her or his fellow human beings.

> MARGARET MEAD, in *Redbook* magazine, November, 1978.

32 Be nice to people on your way up because you'll meet 'em on your way down.

> Attributed to Wilson Mizner.

33 There is only one success—to be able to spend your life in your own way.

> CHRISTOPHER MORLEY, *Where the Blue Begins,* 1922.

34 It is obvious that people like to play winners, they like to be with winners. Winners get favorable treatment. Losers are scorned.

> RICHARD M. NIXON, quoted in Earl Mazo, *Richard Nixon: A Political and Personal Portrait,* 1959.

35 Our self-made men are the glory of our institutions.

> WENDELL PHILLIPS, in a speech in Boston, December 21, 1860.

36 The man who never tells an unpalatable truth "at the wrong time" (the right time has yet to be discovered) is the man whose success in life is fairly well assured.

> AGNES REPPLIER, *Under Dispute,* 1923.

37 Success is having a baked potato come out of the oven just right. Not raw and not overdone. Success to me is having ten honeydew melons and eating only the top half of each one.

> BARBRA STREISAND, quoted in *Life* magazine, September 20, 1963.

38 Only he is successful in his business who makes that pursuit which affords him the highest pleasure sustain him.

> HENRY DAVID THOREAU, entry dated January 10, 1851, in his *Journal,* 1906.

39 The man with a new idea is a Crank until the idea succeeds.

> MARK TWAIN, "Pudd'nhead Wilson's New Calendar," *Following the Equator,* 1897.

40 Not to the swift, the race:
Not to the strong, the fight:
Not to the righteous, perfect grace:
Not to the wise, the light.

> HENRY VAN DYKE, "Reliance," in *The Poems of Henry Van Dyke,* 1911.

41 A man is never so on trial as in the moment of excessive good fortune.

> LEW WALLACE, *Ben Hur: A Tale of the Christ,* 1880.

42 I have learned that success is to be measured not so much by the position that one has reached in life as by the obstacles which he has overcome while trying to succeed.

> BOOKER T. WASHINGTON, in his autobiography, *Up from Slavery,* 1901.

43 Oft, when the wine in his glass was red,
He longed for the wayside well instead;
And closed his eyes on his garnished rooms
To dream of meadows and clover-blooms.
And the proud man sighed, with a secret
        pain,
"Ah, that I were free again!"

John Greenleaf Whittier, "Maud Muller," *The Panorama and Other Poems,* 1856.

44 You have to want it [success] bad. You can find geniuses on any skid row and average intellects as presidents of banks. It's what pushes you from inside.

Charley Winner, football coach, quoted in Rick Telander, *Joe Namath and the Other Guys,* 1976.

225. SUMMER

See also Nature; Weather

1 The Long Hot Summer.

Title of a motion picture, 1958. (The screenplay was based on William Faulkner's novel *The Hamlet,* 1940, one section of which is entitled "The Long Summer.")

2 Do what we can, summer will have its flies.

Ralph Waldo Emerson, "Prudence," *Essays,* First Series, 1841.

3 O summer day beside the joyous sea!
O summer day so wonderful and white,
So full of gladness and so full of pain!
Forever and forever shalt thou be
To some the gravestone of a dead delight,
To some the landmark of a new domain.

Henry Wadsworth Longfellow, "A Summer Day by the Sea," 1874.

4 And what is so rare as a day in June?
Then, if ever, come perfect days;
Then Heaven tries earth if it be in tune,
And over it softly her warm ear lays.

James Russell Lowell, *The Vision of Sir Launfal,* 1848.

5 'Long about knee-deep in June,
'Bout the time strawberries melts
On the vine.

James Whitcomb Riley, "Knee-Deep in June," 1883.

6 In the good old summer time,
In the good old summer time,
Strolling thro' the shady lanes,
With your baby mine;
You hold her hand and she holds yours,
And that's a very good sign
That she's your tootsey-wootsey
In the good old summer time.

Ren Shields, "In the Good Old Summer Time," set to music by George Evans, 1902.

7 O, softly on yon banks of haze,
Her rosy face the Summer lays!

John Townsend Trowbridge, "Midsummer," *Poetical Works,* 1903.

226. TALENT

See also Success

1 I think knowing what you can *not* do is more important than knowing what you can do. In fact, that's good taste.

Lucille Ball, quoted in Eleanor Harris, *The Real Story of Lucille Ball,* 1954.

2 Every natural power exhilarates; a true talent delights the possessor first.

Ralph Waldo Emerson, "The Scholar," *Lectures and Biographical Sketches,* 1883.

3 The peril of every fine faculty is the delight of playing with it for pride. Talent is commonly developed at the expense of character, and the greater it grows, the more is the mischief. . . . Talent is mistaken for genius, a dogma or system for truth, ambition for greatness, ingenuity for poetry, sensuality for art.

Ibid.

4 Everyone has talent. What is rare is the courage to follow the talent to the dark place where it leads.

Erica Jong, quoted in Francine Klagsbrun, *The First Ms. Reader,* 1972.

5 Man's capacities have never been measured; nor are we to judge of what he can do by any precedent, so little has been tried.

HENRY DAVID THOREAU, *Walden,* 1854.

227. TAXATION

See also CONGRESS; DEBT; ECONOMICS; GOVERNMENT; MONEY; POVERTY; WEALTH

1 It is inseparably essential to the freedom of a people, and the undoubted right of Englishmen, that no taxes be imposed on them but with their own consent, given personally, or by their representatives.

Resolution of the Stamp Act Congress, New York City, October 19, 1765.

2 It is an essential, unalterable right, in nature, engrafted into the British Constitution, as a fundamental law, and ever held sacred and irrevocable by the subjects within the realm, that what a man has honestly acquired is absolutely his own, which he may freely give, but cannot be taken from him without his consent.

SAMUEL ADAMS, in the "Massachusetts Circular Letter," February 11, 1768.

3 Tariff, *n.* A scale of taxes on imports, designed to protect the domestic producer against the greed of his consumer.

AMBROSE BIERCE, *The Devil's Dictionary,* 1906.

4 Collecting more taxes than is absolutely necessary is legalized robbery.

Attributed to Calvin Coolidge.

5 We cannot be happy without being free; we cannot be free without being secure in our property; we cannot be secure in our property if, without our consent, others may, as by right, take it away.

JOHN DICKINSON, on taxation imposed by the British Parliament on the American colonies, in *Letters from a Farmer in Pennsylvania to the Inhabitants of the British Colonies,* published in the *Pennsylvania Chronicle,* 1767–1768.

6 Of all debts, men are least willing to pay the taxes. What a satire is this on government!

RALPH WALDO EMERSON, "Politics," *Essays,* Second Series, 1844.

7 Idleness and pride tax with a heavier hand than kings and parliaments; if we can get rid of the former we may easily bear the latter.

BENJAMIN FRANKLIN, in a letter to Charles Thomson, July 11, 1765.

8 In this world nothing can be said to be certain, except death and taxes.

BENJAMIN FRANKLIN, in a letter to Jean-Baptiste Leroy, November 13, 1789.

9 The tax upon land values is . . . the most just and equal of all taxes. It falls only upon those who receive from society a peculiar and valuable benefit, and upon them in proportion to the benefit they receive. It is the taking by the community, for the use of the community, of that value which is the creation of the community. It is the application of the common property to common uses.

HENRY GEORGE, *Progress and Poverty,* 1879.

10 [Taxation] must not take from individuals what rightfully belongs to individuals.

HENRY GEORGE, *The Condition of Labor,* 1891.

11 [Taxation] must not repress industry. It must not check commerce. It must not punish thrift. It must offer no impediment to the largest production and the fairest division of wealth.

Ibid.

12 Taxes are what we pay for civilized society.

OLIVER WENDELL HOLMES, JR., in a Supreme Court opinion, *Compañía de Tabacos v. Collector,* 1904.

13 The power to tax is not the power to destroy while this court sits.

OLIVER WENDELL HOLMES, JR., in a dissenting Supreme Court opinion, *Panhandle Oil Co. v. Mississippi,* 1930.

14 The purse of the people is the real seat of sensibility. It is to be drawn upon largely, and they will

then listen to truths which could not excite them through any other organ.

> THOMAS JEFFERSON, in a letter to A.H. Rowan, September 26, 1798.

15 Sound principles will not justify our taxing the industry of our fellow citizens to accumulate treasure for wars to happen we know not when, and which might not, perhaps, happen but from the temptations offered by that treasure.

> THOMAS JEFFERSON, in his first annual message to Congress, December 8, 1801.

16 Taxes should be continued by annual or biennial reenactments, because a constant hold, by the nation, of the strings of the public purse is a salutary restraint from which an honest government ought not to wish, nor a corrupt one to be permitted, to be free.

> THOMAS JEFFERSON, in a letter to John Wayles Eppes, September 11, 1813.

17 The beggar is taxed for a corner to die in.

> JAMES RUSSELL LOWELL, "The Vision of Sir Launfal," 1848.

18 That the power to tax involves the power to destroy; that the power to destroy may defeat and render useless the power to create; that there is a plain repugnance, in conferring on one government a power to control the constitutional measures of another, which other, with respect to those very measures, is declared to be supreme over that which exerts the control, are propositions not to be denied.

> JOHN MARSHALL, in a Supreme Court opinion, *McCulloch* v. *Maryland,* 1819. (This ruling denied the right of the State of Maryland to impose a tax on the Bank of the United States. Marshall's wording reflected that of Daniel Webster in arguing before the court in this case: "An unlimited power to tax involves, necessarily, the power to destroy.")

19 As the Chinese poet, Ah Ling, put it (in the
wastebasket):
The more the moolah
You make in your racket,
The quicker you go
In a higher bracket.

> GROUCHO MARX, *Many Happy Returns,* 1942.

20 Taxation without representation is tyranny.

> Attributed to James Otis, 1763.

21 I'm sure everyone feels sorry for the individual who has fallen by the wayside or who can't keep up in our competitive society, but my own compassion goes beyond that to those millions of unsung men and women who get up every morning, send the kids to school, go to work, try to keep up the payments on their house, pay exorbitant taxes to make possible compassion for the less fortunate, and as a result have to sacrifice many of their own desires and dreams and hopes. Government owes them something better than always finding a new way to make them share the fruit of their toils with others.

> RONALD REAGAN, *Sincerely, Ronald Reagan,* 1976.

22 Taxes are paid in the sweat of every man who labors because they are a burden on production and can be paid only by production. If excessive, they are reflected in idle factories, tax-sold farms, and, hence, in hordes of the hungry tramping the streets and seeking jobs in vain. Our workers may never see a tax bill, but they pay in deductions from wages, in increased cost of what they buy, or (as now) in broad cessation of employment.

> FRANKLIN D. ROOSEVELT, in a speech in Pittsburgh, Pennsylvania, October 19, 1932.

23 The state and municipality go to great expense to support policemen and sheriffs and judicial officers, to protect people against themselves, that is, against the results of their own folly, vice, and recklessness. Who pays for it? Undoubtedly the people who have not been guilty of folly, vice, or recklessness.

> WILLIAM GRAHAM SUMNER, "The Forgotten Man," *The Forgotten Man and Other Essays,* 1919.

24 We've got so much taxation. I don't know of a single foreign product that enters this country untaxed except the answer to prayer.

> MARK TWAIN, in an address, "When in Doubt, Tell the Truth," March 9, 1906.

25 The thing generally raised on city land is taxes.

CHARLES DUDLEY WARNER, *My Summer in a Garden*, 1870.

26 What is it we are contending against? Is it against paying the duty of three pence per pound on tea because burthensome? No, it is the right only we have all along disputed.

GEORGE WASHINGTON, in a letter to Bryan Fairfax, July 20, 1774.

27 I think the Parliament of Great Britain hath no more right to put their hands into my pocket, without my consent, than I have to put my hands into yours for money.

Ibid.

---

228. TECHNOLOGY

See also POLLUTION; PROGRESS; SCIENCE; SPACE EXPLORATION; TELEVISION & RADIO

---

1 Despite the dazzling successes of modern technology and the unprecedented power of modern military systems, they suffer from a common and catastrophic fault. While providing us with a bountiful supply of food, with great industrial plants, with high-speed transportation, and with military weapons of unprecedented power, they threaten our very survival.

BARRY COMMONER, *Science and Survival*, 1966.

2 Why does this magnificent applied science which saves work and makes life easier bring us so little happiness? The simple answer runs: Because we have not yet learned to make sensible use of it.

ALBERT EINSTEIN, in an address at the California Institute of Technology, February, 1931.

3 America's technology has turned in upon itself; its corporate form makes it the servant of profits, not the servant of human needs.

ALICE EMBREE, quoted in Robin Morgan, *Sisterhood is Powerful*, 1970.

4 It is all one to me if a man comes from Sing Sing or Harvard. We hire a man, not his history.

Attributed to Henry Ford.

5 Technology, while adding daily to our physical ease, throws daily another loop of fine wire around our souls. It contributes hugely to our mobility, which we must not confuse with freedom. The extensions of our senses, which we find so fascinating, are not adding to the discrimination of our minds, since we need increasingly to take the reading of a needle on a dial to discover whether we think something is good or bad, or right or wrong.

ADLAI E. STEVENSON, "My Faith in Democratic Capitalism," in *Fortune* magazine, October, 1955.

6 That great, growling engine of change—technology.

ALVIN TOFFLER, *Future Shock*, 1970.

7 Technology feeds on itself. Technology makes more technology possible.

Ibid.

8 Each new machine or technique, in a sense, changes all existing machines and techniques, by permitting us to put them together into new combinations. The number of possible combinations rises exponentially as the number of new machines or techniques rises arithmetically. Indeed, each new combination may, itself, be regarded as a new super-machine.

Ibid.

---

229. TELEVISION & RADIO

---

1 I thought television would be a great journalistic tool for the future and wrote the guy who was head of it at NBC, in 1947, suggesting he might be interested in my services when I left Moscow for United Press. Never heard from him.

WALTER CRONKITE, quoted in *American Way* magazine, January, 1976.

2 Television pollutes identity.

> NORMAN MAILER, *St. George and the Godfather*, 1972.

3 When television is good, nothing—not the theater, not the magazines or newspapers—nothing is better. But when television is bad, nothing is worse. I invite you to sit down in front of your television set when your station goes on the air and stay there without a book, magazine, newspaper, profit-and-loss sheet, or rating book to distract you, and keep your eyes glued to that set until the station signs off. I can assure you that you will observe a vast wasteland.

> NEWTON MINOW, in a speech to the National Association of Broadcasters, May 9, 1961.

4 Television is not so effective now as it was in 1952. The novelty has worn off. There is a very early point of diminishing returns in using television. Both parties did too much of it in the 1956 campaign. People probably got tired of seeing favorite programs thrown off for political speeches.

> RICHARD M. NIXON, quoted in Earl Mazo, *Richard Nixon: A Political and Personal Portrait*, 1959.

5 I guess television just has more power than any of us know.

> RONALD REAGAN, in *Sincerely, Ronald Reagan*, 1976.

6 I have long had a suspicion that an entire generation of Americans grew up feeling inferior to just the *names* of the guys on the radio. Pierre André. Harlow Wilcox. Vincent Pelletier. Truman Bradley. Westbrook Van Voorhees. André Baruch. Norman Brokenshire. There wasn't a Charlie Schmidlap in the lot.

> JEAN SHEPHERD, *In God We Trust, All Others Pay Cash*, 1966.

7 There is no boredom or misery to equal the pursuit of distraction alone. We do not slip into happiness. It is strenuously sought and earned. A nation glued to the television screen is not simply at a loss before the iron pioneers of the new collective society. It isn't even having a good time.

> ADLAI E. STEVENSON, in an address to the National School Boards Association, San Francisco, California, January 26, 1959.

8 Remember please, for the next day or so, the terrible lesson you learned tonight: That grinning, glowing, globular invader of your livingroom is an inhabitant of the Punkin Patch, and if your doorbell rings and nobody's there, that was no Martian—it's Halloween!

> ORSON WELLES, concluding remarks on the Mercury Theater of the Air radio production of "The War of the Worlds," October 30, 1938.

9 One of the chief pretenders to the throne of God is radio itself, which has acquired a sort of omniscience. I live in a strictly rural community, and people here speak of "The Radio" in the large sense, with an over-meaning. When they say "The Radio" they don't mean a cabinet, an electrical phenomenon, or a man in a studio, they refer to a pervading and somewhat godlike presence which has come into their lives and homes.

> E.B. WHITE, "Sabbath Morn," February, 1939.

10 Chewing gum for the eyes.

> Attributed to Frank Lloyd Wright, describing television.

---

230. TENNESSEE

---

1 Agriculture and Commerce.

> Unofficial state motto, from the wording on the state seal. (In 1965 the Tennessee legislature adopted "Tennessee—America at Its Best" as the state's official slogan.)

2 Tennesseans' lives are unhurried. Though they may complain about weather, poor crops, bad business and politics, beneath all is a certain feeling of security. The farmer will leave his plowing, the attorney his lawsuit, the business man his accounts, for a moment's or an hour's conversation with stranger or friend. With his good-tempered easiness of manners, the Tennessean has a democratic feeling of equality. His mind, unlike his bed, does not

have to be made up each morning, for his judgment and dignity proceed from himself. Whether of farm, mountain, or city, he is like the Tennessee farmer who, after hearing Martin Van Buren speak, stepped up, shook the President's hand, and invited him "to come out and r'ar around with the boys."

> Federal Writers' Project, *Tennessee: A Guide to the State,* 1939.

3 There's only one place worth living in, and that's Middle Tennessee. When I get out I'm going back there. I'm going to marry a Nashville gal. I'm going to buy some Middle Tennessee land and raise Tennessee Walking Horses and Tennessee babies. I'm going to cure Tennessee hams with Tennessee hickory, and I'm not going to drink anything but old Jack Daniel sour-mash Tennessee whisky. And if my wife ever talks about leaving Middle Tennessee, I'll drag her clean over to the Tennessee River and drown her. Hell, I'm so homesick I could root for the University and I'm a Vanderbilt man.

> A homesick young airman from Tennessee, quoted by Hodding Carter in "Tennessee," *American Panorama: East of the Mississippi,* 1960.

4 Take of London fog 30 parts; malaria 10 parts; gas leaks 20 parts; dewdrops gathered in a brickyard at sunrise 25 parts; odor of honeysuckle 15 parts. Mix. The mixture will give you an approximate conception of a Nashville drizzle.

> O. HENRY, "A Municipal Report," *Strictly Business,* 1910.

5 What you need for breakfast, they say in east Tennessee, is a jug of good corn liquor, a thick beefsteak, and a hound dog. Then you feed the beefsteak to the hound dog.

> CHARLES KURALT, *Dateline America,* 1979.

6 The way the government interferes with private business is enough to drive a fellow crazy. That old government moved into Tennessee and bought a lot of hilly land. Then they signed a proclamation making this land into the Great Smokies National Park. And thereby ruined the finest settlement of moonshiners in the U.S.A.

> ERNIE PYLE, *Home Country,* 1947.

7 I came South for my health, I will go back on the same errand, and suddenly. Tennesseean journalism is too stirring for me.

> MARK TWAIN, "Journalism in Tennessee," *Sketches New and Old,* 1875.

---

231. TEXAS

---

1 Friendship.

> State motto.

2 Remember the Alamo!

> Battle cry at San Jacinto, Texas, April 21, 1836.

3 Congress doth consent that the territory properly included within, and rightfully belonging to the Republic of Texas, may be erected into a new State, to be called the State of Texas.

> Joint Resolution of Congress for the annexation of Texas, March 1, 1845.

4 I like the story, doubtless antique, that I heard near San Antonio. A child asks a stranger where he comes from, whereupon his father rebukes him gently, "Never do that, son. If a man's from Texas, he'll tell you. If he's not, why embarrass him by asking?"

> JOHN GUNTHER, *Inside U.S.A.,* 1947.

5 Texas could wear Rhode Island as a watch fob.

> PAT NEFF, quoted in John Gunther, *Inside U.S.A.,* 1947.

6 If I owned Texas and Hell, I would rent out Texas and live in Hell.

> PHILIP H. SHERIDAN, at Fort Clark, Texas, in 1855.

7 Texas is a state of mind. Texas is an obsession. Above all, Texas is a nation in every sense of the word. . . . A Texan outside of Texas is a foreigner.

> JOHN STEINBECK, *Travels with Charley,* 1962.

232. THANKSGIVING

1 Yes ma'am, no ma'am,
   Thank you ma'am, please.
   Open up the turkey's butt
   And fork out the peas.

> Facetious Thanksgiving grace, recalled in Hennig
> Cohen and Tristram Peter Coffin, *The Folklore of
> American Holidays,* 1987.

2 Heap high the board with plenteous cheer and
      gather to the feast,
   And toast that sturdy Pilgrim band whose
      courage never ceased.
   Give praise to that All Gracious One by
      whom their steps were led,
   And thanks unto the harvest's Lord who
      sends our "daily bread."

> ALICE WILLIAMS BROTHERTON, "The First
> Thanksgiving Day," in Mildred Harrington and
> Josephine Thomas, *Our Holidays in Poetry,*
> 1929.

3 Over the river and through the wood,
      To grandfather's house we go;
         The horse knows the way
         To carry the sleigh
      Through the white and drifted snow.

> LYDIA MARIA CHILD, "Thanksgiving Day,"
> *Flowers for Children,* 1844–1846.

4 Over the river and through the wood,
      Now grandmother's cap I spy!
         Hurrah for the fun!
         Is the pudding done?
      Hurrah for the pumpkin pie!

> Ibid.

5 'Twas founded be th' Puritans to give thanks f'r
   bein' presarved fr'm th' Indyans, an' . . . we keep
   it to give thanks we are presarved fr'm th' Puritans.

> FINLEY PETER DUNNE, "Thanksgiving," *Mr.
> Dooley's Opinions,* 1900.

6 The year that is drawing toward its close has
been filled with the blessings of fruitful fields and
healthful skies. To these bounties, which are so
constantly enjoyed that we are prone to forget the
source from which they come, others have been
added which are of so extraordinary a nature that
they cannot fail to penetrate and soften even the
heart which is habitually insensible to the ever-
watchful providence of Almighty God. . . . I do,
therefore, invite my fellow-citizens, in every part of
the United States, and also those who are at sea,
and those who are sojourning in foreign lands, to
set apart and observe the last Thursday of November next as a day of thanksgiving and praise to our
beneficent Father who dwelleth in the heavens.

> ABRAHAM LINCOLN, Thanksgiving Day
> Proclamation, October 3, 1863.

7 Let us, on the day set aside for this purpose, give
thanks to the Ruler of the universe for the strength
which He has vouchsafed us to carry on our daily
labors and for the hope that lives within us of the
coming of a day when peace and the productive
activities of peace shall reign on every continent.

> FRANKLIN D. ROOSEVELT, Thanksgiving Day
> Proclamation, October 31, 1939.

8 It having pleased the Almighty ruler of the Universe propitiously to defend the cause of the United
American States and finally by raising us up a powerful friend among the princes of the earth to establish our liberty and independence upon lasting
foundations, it becomes us to set apart a day for
gratefully acknowledging the divine goodness and
celebrating the important event which we owe to
His benign Interposition.

> GEORGE WASHINGTON, in orders to his troops,
> May 5, 1778.

9 Ah! on Thanksgiving day, when from East
      and from West,
   From North and from South come the pilgrim
      and guest. . . .
   What moistens the lip and what brightens the
      eye?
   What calls back the past, like the rich
      Pumpkin pie?

> JOHN GREENLEAF WHITTIER, "The Pumpkin,"
> 1844.

10 Who murmurs at his lot today?
    Who scorns his native fruit and bloom?
    Or sighs for dainties far away,
      Beside the bounteous board of home?

> JOHN GREENLEAF WHITTIER, "For an Autumn Festival," 1859.

11 Brave and high-souled Pilgrims, you who
      knew no fears,
    How your words of thankfulness go ringing
      down the years;
    May we follow after; like you, work and
      pray,
    And with hearts of thankfulness keep
      Thanksgiving Day.

> ANNETTE WYNNE, "Thanksgiving Day," For Days and Days, 1919.

---

233. THEATER

---

1 People wouldn't know a good actor if they saw one, but they can recognize a good part. . . . If you have a good part in a hit, your whole life will change, you will become a success, and you will pay a price for that success. You will play the same part all the rest of your life under different names.

> GEORGE ABBOTT, quoted in Heywood Hale Broun, Tumultuous Merriment, 1979.

2 There is less in this than meets the eye.

> TALLULAH BANKHEAD, commenting on a play by Maurice Maeterlinck, January 3, 1922.

3 It's one of the tragic ironies of the theater that only one man in it can count on steady work—the night watchman.

> TALLULAH BANKHEAD, Tallulah, 1952.

4 That's all there is, there isn't any more.

> ETHEL BARRYMORE, in a curtain call at the end of the play Sunday, New York City, 1904.

5 For an actress to be a success she must have the face of Venus, the brains of Minerva, the grace of Terpsichore, the memory of Macaulay, the figure of Juno, and the hide of a rhinoceros.

> ETHEL BARRYMORE, quoted in George Jean Nathan, The Theatre in the Fifties, 1953.

6 Audiences? No, the plural is impossible. Whether it be in Butte, Montana, or Broadway, it's an audience. The same great hulking monster with four thousand eyes and forty thousand teeth.

> JOHN BARRYMORE, to playwright Ashton Stevens, April, 1906, quoted in Gene Fowler, Good Night, Sweet Prince, 1943.

7 The Great Actor always must act. He must make a ceremony of waking up in the morning. He must sit in his room and act so that his whole body vibrates to the thrill of it. Forever he must be a poseur. Every last second of his life must be pose and posture.

> LIONEL BARRYMORE, 1904, quoted in Gene Fowler, Good Night, Sweet Prince, 1943.

8 Your audience gives you everything you need. . . . There is no director who can direct you like an audience.

> FANNY BRICE, quoted in Norman Katkov, The Fabulous Fanny, 1952.

9 Your true right tragedy is enacted on the stage of a man's soul, and with the man's reason as lone auditor.

> JAMES BRANCH CABELL, The Cream of the Jest, 1917.

10 Give My Regards to Broadway.

> GEORGE M. COHAN, title of one of his best-known songs, 1904.

11 When you are away from old Broadway you are only camping out.

> GEORGE M. COHAN, quoted in Fred J. Ringel, America as Americans See It, 1932.

12 Actors are a nuisance in the earth, the very offal of society.

> TIMOTHY DWIGHT, Essay on the Stage, published posthumously in 1824.

13 Generally speaking, the American theater is the aspirin of the middle classes.

> WOLCOTT GIBBS, More in Sorrow, 1958.

14 Behind the curtain's mystic fold
The glowing future lies unrolled.

> BRET HARTE, speaking at the opening of the
> California Theatre, San Francisco, January 19,
> 1870.

15 An actress's life is so transitory—suddenly
you're a building.

> HELEN HAYES, speaking of the Broadway theater
> named for her, November, 1955.

16 One can play comedy; two are required for
melodrama; but a tragedy demands three.

> ELBERT HUBBARD, *The Roycroft Dicitionary and
> Book of Epigrams,* 1923.

17 Satire is what closes on Saturday night.

> GEORGE S. KAUFMAN, quoted in Robert E.
> Drennan, *The Algonquin Wits,* 1968.

18 Comedians on the stage are invariably suicidal
when they get home.

> ELSA LANCHESTER, *Charles Laughton and I,*
> 1938.

19 Coughing in the theater is not a respiratory ailment. It is a criticism.

> ALAN JAY LERNER, *The Street Where I Live,*
> 1978.

20 In all ages the drama, through its portrayal of
the acting and suffering spirit of man, has been
more closely allied than any other art to his deeper
thoughts concerning his nature and his destiny.

> LUDWIG LEWISOHN, *The Modern Drama,* 1915.

21 A farce or a comedy is best played; a tragedy is
best read at home.

> ABRAHAM LINCOLN, after a performance by
> Edwin Booth in *The Merchant of Venice,*
> 1863.

22 Actors begin where militia colonels, Fifth Avenue rectors and Rotary orators leave off. The most
modest of them (barring, perhaps, a few unearthly
traitors to the craft) matches the conceit of the
solitary pretty girl on a slow ship.

> H.L. MENCKEN, *Damn! A Book of Calumny,*
> 1918.

23 The theater is no place for painful speculation;
it is a place for diverting representation.

> H.L. MENCKEN, *Prejudices,* First Series, 1919.

24 Great drama is the reflection of a great doubt in
the heart and mind of a great, sad, gay man.

> GEORGE JEAN NATHAN, *Materia Critica,* 1924.

25 Drama—what literature does at night.

> GEORGE JEAN NATHAN, *Testament of a Critic,*
> 1931.

26 The basis of the dramatic form of entertainment
is the emotional catharsis experienced by the audience. . . . We've kept a little stardust in our mun-
dane lives by identifying with make-believe characters in make-believe adventures in the house of
illusion—the theater.

> RONALD REAGAN, *Where's the Rest of Me?* 1965.

27 Just know your lines and don't bump into the
furniture.

> SPENCER TRACY, on the two things an actor
> needs to know.

---

234. TIME

---

1 Time is a river without banks.

> Anonymous.

2 Time cuts down all,
Both great and small.

> *The New England Primer,* compiled and
> published by Benjamin Harris, c.1690.

3 Well, time wounds all heels.

> Attributed to Jane Ace in Goodman Ace, *The
> Fine Art of Hypochondria,* 1966.

4 My stern chase after time is, to borrow a simile
from Tom Paine, like the race of a man with a
wooden leg after a horse.

> JOHN QUINCY ADAMS, in his diary, March 25,
> 1844.

5 See childhood, youth, and manhood pass,
  And age with furrowed brow;
Time was—Time shall be—drain the glass—
  But where in Time is now?

  JOHN QUINCY ADAMS, "The Hour Glass," 1848.

6 Time is one's best friend, teaching best of all the wisdom of silence.

  A. BRONSON ALCOTT, *Table Talk*, 1877.

7 Backward, flow backward, O tide of the years!
I am so weary of toil and of tears—
Toil without recompense, tears all in vain—
Take them and give me my childhood again!
I have grown weary of dust and decay,
Weary of flinging my soul-wealth away,
Weary of sowing for others to reap;
Rock me to sleep, mother—rock me to sleep!

  ELIZABETH AKERS ALLEN, "Rock Me to Sleep," 1860.

8 Give me no changeless hours, for I know
Moments on earth are sweeter that they go.

  HERVEY ALLEN, "Moments," in Burton Egbert Stevenson, *The Home Book of Modern Verse*, 1953.

9 Time does not become sacred to us until we have lived it, until it has passed over us and taken with it a part of ourselves.

  JOHN BURROUGHS, "The Spell of the Past," in *Literary Values and Other Papers*, 1902.

10 Little drops of water, little grains of sand,
  Make the mighty ocean, and the pleasant
    land.
So the little minutes, humble though they be,
Make the mighty ages of eternity.

  JULIA CARNEY, "Little Things," 1845.

11 A faded boy in sallow clothes
Who drove a lonesome cow
To pastures of oblivion—
A statesman's embryo.

The boys that whistled are extinct,
The cows that fed and thanked
Remanded to a ballad's barn
Or clover's retrospect.

EMILY DICKINSON, "A faded boy," in *Bolts of Melody*, 1945.

12 Softened by Time's consummate plush,
  How sleek the woe appears
That threatened childhood's citadel
  And undermined the years!

  EMILY DICKINSON, "Childish Griefs," in *Poems*, Third Series, 1896.

13 Time is a test of trouble,
  But not a remedy.
If such it prove, it prove too
  There was no malady.

  EMILY DICKINSON, "They say that 'time assuages,'" in *Poems*, Third Series, 1896.

14 Time present and time past
Are both perhaps present in time future,
And time future contained in time past.
If all time is eternally present
All time is unredeemable.
What might have been is an abstraction
Remaining a perpetual possibility
Only in a world of speculation.

  T.S. ELIOT, "Burnt Norton," in *Four Quartets*, 1943.

15 This time, like all times, is a very good one, if we but know what to do with it.

  RALPH WALDO EMERSON, *The American Scholar*, 1837.

16 Time dissipates to shining ether the solid angularity of facts.

  RALPH WALDO EMERSON, "History," *Essays*, First Series, 1841.

17 I know a song which is more hurtful than strychnine or the kiss of the asp. It blasts those who hear it, changes their color and shape, and dissipates their substance. It is called Time.

  RALPH WALDO EMERSON, entry written in 1856, *Journals*, 1909–1914.

18 Daughters of time, the hypocritic days,
Muffled and dumb like barefoot dervishes,
And marching single in an endless file,
Bring diadems and faggots in their hands.

RALPH WALDO EMERSON, "Days," published in the first issue of the *Atlantic Monthly,* November, 1857.

19 The surest poison is time.

RALPH WALDO EMERSON, "Old Age," *Society and Solitude,* 1870.

20 The days are ever divine as to the first Aryans. They are of the least pretension, and of the greatest capacity of anything that exists. They come and go like muffled and veiled figures sent from a distant friendly party; but they say nothing, and if we do not use the gifts they bring, they carry them as silently away.

RALPH WALDO EMERSON, "Works and Days," *Society and Solitude,* 1870.

21 Time is an herb that cures all Diseases.

BENJAMIN FRANKLIN, *Poor Richard's Almanack,* 1738.

22 Lost Time is never found again.

BENJAMIN FRANKLIN, *Poor Richard's Almanack,* 1748.

23 Remember that time is money.

BENJAMIN FRANKLIN, "Advice to a Young Tradesman," 1748.

24 You may delay, but *Time* will not.

BENJAMIN FRANKLIN, *Poor Richard's Almanack,* 1758.

25 But *dost thou love Life, then do not squander Time, for that's the Stuff Life is made of.*

Ibid.

26 Time flies over us, but leaves its shadow behind.

NATHANIEL HAWTHORNE, *The Marble Faun,* 1860.

27 Pick my left pocket of its silver dime,
But spare the right—it holds my golden time!

OLIVER WENDELL HOLMES, SR., "A Rhymed Lesson," 1846.

28 Old time, in whose banks we deposit our notes,

Is a miser who always wants guineas for groats;
He keeps all his customers still in arrears
By lending them minutes and charging them years.

OLIVER WENDELL HOLMES, SR., "Our Banker," 1874.

29 Time has upset many fighting faiths.

OLIVER WENDELL HOLMES, JR., in a dissenting Supreme Court opinion, *Abrams et al.* v. *the United States,* 1919.

30 A time filled with varied and interesting experiences seems short in passing, but long as we look back. On the other hand, a tract of time empty of experience seems long in passing, but in retrospect short.

WILLIAM JAMES, *The Principles of Psychology,* 1890.

31 No person will have occasion to complain of the want of time who never loses any.

THOMAS JEFFERSON, in a letter to his daughter, May 5, 1787.

32 Th' incalculable Up-and-Down of Time.

SIDNEY LANIER, "Clover," in *Poems,* 1877.

33 Time! what an empty vapor 'tis!
And days, how swift they are:
Swift as an Indian arrow—
Fly on like a shooting star;
The present moment just is here,
Then slides away in haste,
That we can never say they're ours,
But only say they're past.

ABRAHAM LINCOLN, poem copied in his notebook, author unknown, c.1828.

34 Look not mournfully into the Past. It comes not back again. Wisely improve the Present. It is thine. Go forth to meet the shadowy Future, without fear, and with a manly heart.

HENRY WADSWORTH LONGFELLOW, *Hyperion,* 1839.

35 What is time? The shadow on the dial, the striking of the clock, the running of the sand, day

and night, summer and winter, months, years, centuries—these are but arbitrary and outward signs, the measure of Time, not Time itself. Time is the Life of the soul.

Ibid.

36 It is not till time, with reckless hand, has torn out half the leaves from the Book of Human Life, to light the fires of passion with, from day to day, that man begins to see that the leaves which remain are few in number.

Ibid.

37 The day is done, and the darkness
    Falls from the wings of night,
As a feather is wafted downward
    From an eagle in his flight.

HENRY WADSWORTH LONGFELLOW, "The Day Is Done," *The Belfry of Bruges and Other Poems,* 1846.

38 Somewhat back from the village street
Stands the old-fashioned country seat.
Across its antique portico
Tall poplar-trees their shadows throw;
And from its station in the hall
An ancient timepiece says to all—
    "Forever—never!
    Never—forever!"

HENRY WADSWORTH LONGFELLOW, "The Old Clock on the Stairs," *The Belfry of Bruges and Other Poems,* 1846.

39   Time has laid his hand
Upon my heart, gently, not smiting it,
But as a harper lays his open palm
Upon his harp, to deaden its vibrations.

HENRY WADSWORTH LONGFELLOW, "The Cloisters," *The Golden Legend,* 1851.

40 Time is a great legalizer, even in the field of morals.

H.L. MENCKEN, *A Book of Prefaces,* 1917.

41 I've been on a calendar, but never on time.

MARILYN MONROE, quoted in *Look* magazine, January 16, 1962.

42 Time is a flowing river. Happy those who allow themselves to be carried, unresisting, with the current.

CHRISTOPHER MORLEY, *Where the Blue Begins,* 1922.

43   Time softly there
Laughs through the abyss of radiance with
    the gods.

WILLIAM VAUGHN MOODY, *The Fire Bringer,* 1904.

44 This is a world that goes slowly, because it has an eternity to go in.

THOMAS BRACKETT REED, in a speech in Philadelphia, April 9, 1890.

45 What comes of all your visions and your
    fears?
Poets and kings are but the clerks of Time,
Tiering the same dull webs of discontent,
Clipping the same sad alnage of the years.

EDWING ARLINGTON ROBINSON, "The Clerks," *The Children of the Night,* 1897. ("Alnage" means measurement.)

46 The small intolerable drums
    Of Time are like slow drops descending.

EDWIN ARLINGTON ROBINSON, "The Poor Relation," *The Man Against the Sky,* 1916.

47 I never yet talked to the man who wanted to save time who could tell me what he was going to do with the time he saved.

WILL ROGERS, quoted in Garrett Hardin, *Exploring New Ethics for Survival,* 1972.

48 Time is but the stream I go a-fishing in.

HENRY DAVID THOREAU, *Walden,* 1854.

49 The future is no more uncertain than the present.

WALT WHITMAN, "Song of the Broad-Axe," 1856.

235. TRAVEL

1 This ain't the Waldorf; if it was you wouldn't be here.

>   Humorous notice found in country hotels, c.1900.

2 See America First.

>   Advertising slogan, c.1914.

3 The traveled mind is the catholic mind educated from exclusiveness and egotism.

>   A. BRONSON ALCOTT, *Table Talk,* 1877.

4 Traveling is no fool's errand to him who carries his eyes and itinerary along with him.

>   Ibid.

5 In America there are two classes of travel—first class and with children.

>   ROBERT BENCHLEY, quoted in Robert E.
>   Drennan, *The Algonquin Wits,* 1968.

6 It is for want of self-culture that the superstition of Traveling, whose idols are Italy, England, Egypt, retains its fascination for all educated Americans. They who made England, Italy, or Greece venerable in the imagination, did so by sticking fast where they were, like an axis of the earth. . . . The soul is no traveler; the wise man stays at home.

>   RALPH WALDO EMERSON, "Self-Reliance,"
>   *Essays,* First Series, 1841.

7 He who travels to be amused, or to get somewhat which he does not carry, travels away from himself, and grows old even in youth among old things.

>   Ibid.

8 Traveling is a fool's paradise.

>   Ibid.

9 Railway aids traveling by getting rid of all avoidable obstructions of the road, and leaving nothing to be conquered but pure space.

>   RALPH WALDO EMERSON, "Manners," *Essays,*
>   Second Series, 1844.

10 There are three wants which can never be satisfied: that of the rich, who wants something more; that of the sick, who wants something different; and that of the traveler, who says, "Anywhere but here."

>   RALPH WALDO EMERSON, "Considerations by the
>   Way," *The Conduct of Life,* 1860.

11 The power which the sea requires in a sailor makes a man of him very fast, and the change of shores and population clears his head of much nonsense of his wigwam.

>   RALPH WALDO EMERSON, "Civilization," *Society
>   and Solitude,* 1870.

12 The time will come when people will travel in stages moved by steam engines, from one city to another, almost as fast as birds fly, fifteen or twenty miles an hour.

>   OLIVER EVANS, *Patent Right Oppression
>   Exposed,* 1813.

13 Visits should be short, like a winter's day,
   Lest you're too troublesome, hasten away.

>   BENJAMIN FRANKLIN, *Poor Richard's Almanack,*
>   1733.

14 Fish & Visitors stink in 3 days.

>   BENJAMIN FRANKLIN, *Poor Richard's Almanack,*
>   1736.

15 Traveling is one way of lengthening life, at least in appearance.

>   BENJAMIN FRANKLIN, in a letter to Mary
>   Stevenson, September 14, 1767.

16 I journeyed fur, I journeyed fas'; I glad I
   foun' de place at las'!

>   JOEL CHANDLER HARRIS, *Nights with Uncle
>   Remus,* 1883.

17 I am fevered with the sunset,
   I am fretful with the bay,
   For the wander-thirst is on me
   And my soul is in Cathay.

>   RICHARD HOVEY, "The Sea Gipsy," in *More
>   Songs from Vagabondia,* 1896.

18 I must forth again to-morrow!
   With the sunset I must be

Hull down on the trail of rapture
In the wonder of the Sea.

Ibid.

19 Drop anchor anywhere and the anchor will drag—that is, if your soul is a limitless, fathomless sea, and not a dogpound.

ELBERT HUBBARD, *The Roycroft Dictionary and Book of Epigrams,* 1923.

20 Someday the sun is going to shine down on me in some faraway place.

MAHALIA JACKSON, quoted in the *Reader's Digest,* March, 1973.

21 [Traveling] makes men wiser, but less happy. When men of sober age travel, they gather knowledge which they may apply usefully for their country; but they are subject ever after to recollections mixed with regret.

THOMAS JEFFERSON, in a letter to Peter Carr, August 10, 1787.

22 Are you lost daddy I arsked tenderly.
Shut up he explained.

RING LARDNER, *The Young Immigrunts,* 1920.

23 Travelers are always discoverers, especially those who travel by air. There are no signposts in the sky to show a man has passed that way before.

ANNE MORROW LINDBERGH, *North to the Orient,* 1935.

24 Is there *anything* as horrible as *starting* on a trip? Once you're off, that's all right, but the last moments are earthquake and convulsion, and the feeling that you are a snail being pulled off your rock.

ANNE MORROW LINDBERGH, *Hour of Gold, Hour of Lead,* 1973.

25 It's little I know what's in my heart,
What's in my mind it's little I know,
But there's that in me must up and start,
And it's little I care where my feet go.

EDNA ST. VINCENT MILLAY, "Departure," *The Harp-Weaver and Other Poems,* 1923.

26 I was going to stay on the three million miles of bent and narrow rural American two-lane, the roads to Podunk and Toonerville. Into the sticks, the boondocks, the burgs, backwaters, jerkwaters, the wide-spots-in-the-road, the don't-blink-or-you'll-miss-it towns. Into those places where you say, "My god! What if you lived here!" The Middle of Nowhere.

WILLIAM LEAST HEAT MOON, *Blue Highways,* 1982.

27 I think that to get under the surface and really appreciate the beauty of any country, one has to go there poor.

GRACE MOORE, *You're Only Human Once,* 1944.

28 "Potter hates Potter, and Poet hates Poet,"—so runs the wisdom of the ancients—but tourist hates tourist with a cordial Christian animosity that casts all Pagan prejudices in the shade.

AGNES REPPLIER, *Compromises,* 1904.

29 I could never test it [the warning that Maine natives deliberately misdirect travelers] because through my own efforts I am lost most of the time without any help from anyone.

JOHN STEINBECK, *Travels with Charley,* 1962.

30 I sought trains; I found passengers.

PAUL THEROUX, in *The Great Railway Bazaar,* 1975.

31 I have had enough of sights and shows, and noise and bustle, and confusion, and now I want to disperse. I am ready to go.

MARK TWAIN, in a letter to the *San Francisco Alta California,* June 6, 1867.

32 Travel is fatal to prejudice, bigotry, and narrow-mindedness, and many of our people need it sorely on these accounts. Broad, wholesome, charitable views of men and things cannot be acquired by vegetating in one little corner of the earth all one's lifetime.

MARK TWAIN, *The Innocents Abroad,* 1869.

33 I have found out that there ain't no surer way to find out whether you like people or hate them, than to travel with them.

MARK TWAIN, *Tom Sawyer Abroad,* 1894.

34 Afoot and light-hearted I take to the open road,
  Healthy, free, the world before me,
  The long brown path before me leading wherever I choose.
  Henceforth I ask not good-fortune, I myself am good-fortune,
  Henceforth I whimper no more, postpone no more, need nothing,
  Done with indoor complaints, libraries, querulous criticisms,
  Strong and content I travel the open road.

WALT WHITMAN, "Song of the Open Road," 1856.

236. TROUBLE

See also ADVERSITY; AFFLICTION; PAIN; SORROW

1 You can't unscramble scrambled eggs.

American proverb.

2 Nobody knows the trouble I've seen,
  Nobody knows but Jesus.

Spiritual, c.1845.

3 Calamity, *n.* A more than commonly plain and unmistakable reminder that the affairs of this life are not of our own ordering. Calamities are of two kinds: misfortune to ourselves, and good fortune to others.

AMBROSE BIERCE, *The Devil's Dictionary,* 1906.

4 Distress, *n.* A disease incurred by exposure to the prosperity of a friend.

Ibid.

5 Misfortune, *n.* The kind of fortune that never misses.

Ibid.

6 It is a matter of much satisfaction and gratitude with me to observe how heroically most of us endure the misfortunes of other people.

JOHN W. DE FOREST, *Seacliff or The Mystery of the Westervelts,* 1859.

7 I know not why it is, but a letter is scarcely welcome to me. I expect to be lacerated by it, and if I come safe to the end of it, I feel like one escaped.

RALPH WALDO EMERSON, entry written in 1836, *Journals,* 1909–1914.

8 Some of your griefs you have cured,
  And the sharpest you still have survived;
  But what torments of pain you endured
  From evils that never arrived!

RALPH WALDO EMERSON, translation of a French poem, in "Considerations by the Way," *The Conduct of Life,* 1860.

9 The worst wheel of the cart makes the most noise.

BENJAMIN FRANKLIN, *Poor Richard's Almanack,* 1737.

10 If Man could Half his Wishes, he would double his Troubles.

BENJAMIN FRANKLIN, *Poor Richard's Almanack,* 1752.

11 For want of a Nail the Shoe is lost; for want of a Shoe, the Horse is lost; for want of a Horse the Rider is lost.

Ibid.

12 If pleasures are greatest in anticipation, just remember that this is also true of trouble.

ELBERT HUBBARD, *The Roycroft Dictionary and Book of Epigrams,* 1923.

13 When trouble comes, wise men take to their work: weak men take to the woods.

Ibid.

14 How much pain have cost us the evils which have never happened.

THOMAS JEFFERSON, "A Decalogue of Canons for observation in personal life," in a letter to Thomas Jefferson Smith, February 21, 1825.

15 Such was the wreck of the Hesperus,
  In the midnight and the snow!
Christ save us all from a death like this,
  On the reef of Norman's Woe!

> HENRY WADSWORTH LONGFELLOW, "The Wreck of the Hesperus," *Ballads and Other Poems,* 1841.

16 He saves me trouble, and that is a saving I would rather buy dear than any other. Beyond meat and drink, it is the only use I have ever discovered for money.

> JAMES RUSSELL LOWELL, speaking of an old servant, in a letter to Thomas Bailey Aldrich, May 28, 1873.

17 Let us be of good cheer, however, remembering that the misfortunes hardest to bear are those which never come.

> JAMES RUSSELL LOWELL, "On Democracy," address deliverd in Birmingham, England, October 6, 1884, published in *Democracy and Other Addresses,* 1887.

18 there is always
  a comforting thought
  in time of trouble when
  it is not our trouble

> DON MARQUIS, "comforting thoughts," *archy does his part,* 1935.

19 Death and taxes and childbirth! There's never any convenient time for any of them!

> MARGARET MITCHELL, *Gone with the Wind,* 1936.

20 Troubles impending always seem worse than troubles surmounted, but this does not prove that they really are.

> ARTHUR M. SCHLESINGER, JR., "The Challenge of Change," in the *New York Times Magazine,* July 27, 1986.

21 Everybody knows if you are too careful you are so occupied in being careful that you are sure to stumble over something.

> GERTRUDE STEIN, *Everybody's Autobiography,* 1937.

22 Ya got trouble,
  Right here in River City,

With a capital T
And that rhymes with P
And that stands for Pool.

> MEREDITH WILLSON, "Ya Got Trouble," from *The Music Man,* 1957.

237. TRUTH

See also BELIEF; EXPERIENCE; KNOWLEDGE; PERCEPTION; RELIGION; WISDOM

1 I had rather starve and rot and keep the privilege of speaking the truth as I see it, than of holding all the offices that capital has to give from the presidency down.

> BROOKS ADAMS, *The Degradation of the Democratic Dogma,* 1919.

2 The deepest truths are best read between the lines, and, for the most part, refuse to be written.

> A. BRONSON ALCOTT, *Concord Days,* 1872.

3 Truth is inclusive of all the virtues, is older than sects or schools, and, like charity, more ancient than mankind.

> A. BRONSON ALCOTT, *Table Talk,* 1877.

4 Even a liar tells a hundred truths to one lie; he has to, to make the lie good for anything.

> HENRY WARD BEECHER, *Proverbs from Plymouth Pulpit,* 1870.

5 It is better to know nothing than to know what ain't so.

> Attributed to Josh Billings.

6 As scarce as truth is, the supply has always been in excess of the demand.

> JOSH BILLINGS, "Affurisms," *Josh Billings: His Sayings,* 1865.

7 For truth there is no deadline.

> HEYWOOD BROUN, in *The Nation,* December 30, 1939.

8 Truth, crushed to earth, shall rise again;
  Th' eternal years of God are hers;
  But Error, wounded, writhes in pain,
  And dies among his worshippers.

> WILLIAM CULLEN BRYANT, "The Battlefield,"
> 1839.

9 The most casual student of history knows that, as a matter of fact, truth does *not* necessarily vanquish. What is more, truth can *never* win unless it is promulgated. Truth does not carry within itself an antitoxin to falsehood. The cause of truth must be championed, and it must be championed dynamically.

> WILLIAM F. BUCKLEY, JR., *God and Man at Yale,* 1951.

10 To [William Jennings] Bryan, truth lay only in holy scripture, and scripture comprised two books: the Bible and the Constitution of the United States.

> ALISTAIR COOKE, *America,* 1973.

11 The ability to discriminate between that which is true and that which is false is one of the last attainments of the human mind.

> JAMES FENIMORE COOPER, *The American Democrat,* 1838.

12 The truth has always been dangerous to the rule of the rogue, the exploiter, the robber. So the truth must be ruthlessly suppressed.

> EUGENE V. DEBS, in a speech in Canton, Ohio, June 16, 1918.

13 I like a look of agony,
  Because I know it's true;
  Men do not sham convulsion,
  Nor simulate a throe.

> EMILY DICKINSON, "Real," in *Poems,* 1890.

14 Truth, Life, and Love are a law of annihilation to everything unlike themselves, because they declare nothing but God.

> MARY BAKER EDDY, *Science and Health with Key to the Scriptures,* 1875.

15 Truth is what stands the test of experience.

> ALBERT EINSTEIN, *Out of My Later Years,* 1950.

16 God offers to every mind its choice between truth and repose. Take which you please—you can never have both.

> RALPH WALDO EMERSON, "Intellect," *Essays,* First Series, 1841.

17 Every violation of truth is not only a sort of suicide in the liar, but is a stab at the health of human society.

> RALPH WALDO EMERSON, "Prudence," *Essays,* First Series, 1841.

18 Truth is the summit of being; justice is the application of it to affairs.

> RALPH WALDO EMERSON, "Character," *Essays,* Second Series, 1844.

19 Truth is such a fly-away, such a sly-boots, so untransportable and unbarrelable a commodity, that it is as bad to catch as light.

> RALPH WALDO EMERSON, "Literary Ethics," *Nature; Addresses and Lectures,* 1849.

20 In a contempt for the gabble of today's opinions the secret of the world is to be learned.

> Ibid.

21 The highest compact we can make with our fellow is—"Let there be truth between us two forevermore."

> RALPH WALDO EMERSON, "Behavior," *The Conduct of Life,* 1860.

22 Every truth leads in another. The bud extrudes the old leaf, and every truth brings that which will supplant it.

> RALPH WALDO EMERSON, "The Sovereignty of Ethics," *Lectures and Biographical Sketches,* 1883.

23 Men of the world value truth, in proportion to their ability; not by its sacredness, but for its convenience.

> RALPH WALDO EMERSON, "The Superlative," *Lectures and Biographical Sketches,* 1883.

24 The Sting of a Reproach, is the Truth of it.

> BENJAMIN FRANKLIN, *Poor Richard's Almanack,* 1746.

25 Half the Truth is often a great Lie.

> BENJAMIN FRANKLIN, *Poor Richard's Almanack,* 1758.

26 Most of the change we think we see in life
Is due to truths being in and out of favor.

> ROBERT FROST, "The Black Cottage," 1914.

27 It is astonishing what force, purity, and wisdom it requires for a human being to keep clear of falsehoods.

> MARGARET FULLER, in a letter to William Henry Channing, July, 1842.

28 He who sees the truth, let him proclaim it, without asking who is for it or who is against it.

> HENRY GEORGE, *The Land Question,* 1881.

29 And fierce though the fiends may fight, and long though the angels hide,
I know that truth and right have the universe on their side.

> WASHINGTON GLADDEN, *Ultima Veritas,* 1912.

30 In fact, there's nothing that keeps its youth,
So far as I know, but a tree and truth.

> OLIVER WENDELL HOLMES, SR., "The Deacon's Masterpiece," published in the *Atlantic Monthly,* 1858.

31 Truth is tough. It will not break, like a bubble, at a touch; nay, you may kick it about all day, like a foot-ball, and it will be round and full at evening.

> OLIVER WENDELL HOLMES, SR., *The Professor at the Breakfast-Table,* 1860.

32 The best test of truth is the power of the thought to get itself accepted in the competition of the market.

> OLIVER WENDELL HOLMES, JR., in a dissenting Supreme Court opinion, *Abrams* v. *United States,* 1919.

33 A lie travels by the Marconi route, while Truth goes by slow freight and is often ditched at the first water-tank.

> ELBERT HUBBARD, *The Roycroft Dictionary and Book of Epigrams,* 1923.

34 It is a good policy to leave a few things unsaid.

> Ibid.

35 Truth, in its struggles for recognition, passes through four distinct stages. First, we say it is damnable, dangerous, disorderly, and will surely disrupt society. Second, we declare it is heretical, infidelic and contrary to the Bible. Third, we say it is really a matter of no importance either one way or the other. Fourth, we aver that we have always upheld and believed it.

> Ibid.

36 Live truth instead of professing it.

> Ibid.

37 Truth lies at the end of a circle.

> Ibid.

38 The man who finds a truth lights a torch.

> ROBERT G. INGERSOLL, "The Truth," 1897.

39 There is no worse lie than a truth misunderstood by those who hear it.

> WILLIAM JAMES, *The Varieties of Religious Experience,* 1902.

40 "The true," to put it very briefly, is only the expedient in the way of our thinking, just as "the right" is only the expedient in the way of our behaving.

> WILLIAM JAMES, *Pragmatism,* 1907.

41 It is error alone which needs the support of government. Truth can stand by itself.

> THOMAS JEFFERSON, *Notes on the State of Virginia,* 1784.

42 Ignorance is preferable to error; and he is less remote from the truth who believes nothing, than he who believes what is wrong.

> Ibid.

43 We are not afraid to follow truth wherever it may lead, nor to tolerate any error so long as reason is left free to combat it.

> THOMAS JEFFERSON, in a letter to William Roscoe, December 27, 1820.

44 The truth is sometimes a poor competitor in the market place of ideas—complicated, unsatisfying,

full of dilemmas, always vulnerable to misinterpretation and abuse.

> GEORGE F. KENNAN, *American Diplomacy, 1900–1950,* 1951.

45 I believe it is an established maxim in morals that he who makes an assertion without knowing whether it is true or false is guilty of falsehood, and the accidental truth of the assertion does not justify or excuse him.

> ABRAHAM LINCOLN, in a letter to the editor of the *Illinois Gazette,* dated August 11, 1846.

46 We better know there is fire whence we see much smoke rising than we could know it by one or two witnesses swearing to it. The witnesses may commit perjury, but the smoke cannot.

> ABRAHAM LINCOLN, in a letter to J.R. Underwood and Henry Grider, October 26, 1864.

47 Truth is generally the best vindication against slander.

> ABRAHAM LINCOLN, in a letter to Edwin M. Stanton, July 14, 1864.

48 Why entreat me, why upbraid me,
When the steadfast tongues of truth
And the flattering hopes of youth
Have all deceived me and betrayed me?

> HENRY WADSWORTH LONGFELLOW, *The Golden Legend,* 1851.

49 We cannot sever right from wrong;
Some falsehood mingles with all truth.

> Ibid.

50   Who dares
To say that he alone has found the truth?

> HENRY WADSWORTH LONGFELLOW, "John Endicott," *The New England Tragedies,* 1868.

51   The nimble lie
Is like the second-hand upon a clock;
We see it fly, while the hour-hand of truth
Seems to stand still, and yet it moves unseen,
And wins at last, for the clock will not strike
Till it has reached the goal.

> HENRY WADSWORTH LONGFELLOW, "Macello De' Corvi," *Michael Angelo: A Fragment,* 1881.

52 Get but the truth once uttered, and 'tis like
A star new-born, that drops into its place,
And which, once circling in its placid round,
Not all the tumult of the earth can shake.

> JAMES RUSSELL LOWELL, "A Glance Behind the Curtain," 1843.

53 Who speaks the truth stabs Falsehood to the heart.

> JAMES RUSSELL LOWELL, "L'Envoi," 1843.

54 I do not fear to follow out the truth,
Albeit along the precipice's edge.

> JAMES RUSSELL LOWELL, "A Glance Behind the Curtain," 1843.

55 Truth forever on the scaffold, Wrong forever
on the throne,—
Yet that scaffold sways the future, and,
behind the dim unknown,
Standeth God within the shadow, keeping
watch above his own.

> JAMES RUSSELL LOWELL, "The Present Crisis," 1844.

56 Truth, after all, wears a different face to everybody, and it would be too tedious to wait till all were agreed.

> JAMES RUSSELL LOWELL, "On Democracy," delivered in Birmingham, England, October 6, 1884, collected in *Democracy and Other Addresses,* 1887.

57 Style will find readers and shape convictions, while mere truth only gathers dust on the shelf.

> JAMES RUSSELL LOWELL, *Political Essays,* 1888.

58 It should seem that there is, perhaps, nothing on which so little reliance is to be placed as facts, especially when related by those who saw them.

> Ibid.

59 Truth is the silliest thing under the sun. Try to get a living by the Truth—and go to the Soup Societies. Heavens! Let any clergyman try to preach the Truth from its very stronghold, the pulpit, and they would ride him out of his church on his own pulpit banister.

> HERMAN MELVILLE, in a letter to Nathaniel Hawthorne, June, 1851.

60 Nine times out of ten, in the arts as in life, there is actually no truth to be discovered; there is only error to be exposed.

H.L. Mencken, *Prejudices,* Third Series, 1922.

61 The smallest atom of truth represents some man's bitter toil and agony; for every ponderable chunk of it there is a brave truth-seeker's grave upon some lonely ash-dump and a soul roasting in hell.

Ibid.

62 Truth is not a diet
But a condiment.

Christopher Morley, "Veritas vos Damnabit," in *Translations from the Chinese,* 1922.

63 Half-truths to which men are accustomed are so much easier to pass than the golden mintage they rarely encounter!

Christopher Morley, *Religio Journalistici,* 1924.

64 The truth is America's most potent weapon. We cannot enlarge upon the truth. But we can and must intensify our efforts to make that truth more shining.

Richard M. Nixon, *The Challenges We Face,* 1960.

65 The People have a right to the Truth as they have a right to life, liberty and the pursuit of happiness. It is *not* right that they be exploited and deceived with false views of life, false characters, false sentiment, false morality, false history, false philosophy, false emotions, false heroism, false notions of self-sacrifice, false views of religion, of duty, of conduct and manners.

Frank Norris, *The Responsibilities of the Novelist,* 1903.

66 The mind, in discovering truths, acts in the same manner as it acts through the eye in discovering objects; when once any object has been seen, it is impossible to put the mind back to the same condition it was in before it saw it.

Thomas Paine, *The Rights of Man,* 1791–1792.

67 Such is the irresistible nature of truth that all it asks, and all it wants, is the liberty of appearing.

Ibid.

68 Mystery is the antagonist of truth. It is a fog of human invention that obscures truth, and represents it in distortion.

Thomas Paine, *The Age of Reason,* 1794–1795.

69 Truth never yet fell dead in the streets; it has such affinity with the soul of man, the seed however broadcast will catch somewhere and produce its hundredfold.

Theodore Parker, *A Discourse of Matters Pertaining to Religion,* 1842.

70 Truth stood on one side and Ease on the other; it has often been so.

Ibid.

71 Inquiry is human; blind obedience brutal. Truth never loses by the one but often suffers by the other.

William Penn, *Some Fruits of Solitude,* 1693.

72 Truth is one forever, absolute; but opinion is truth filtered through the moods, the blood, the disposition of the spectator.

Wendell Phillips, "Against Idolatry," an address given in Boston, October 4, 1859.

73 It is the nature of truth in general, as of some ores in particular, to be richest when most superficial.

Edgar Allan Poe, "The Rationale of Verse," published in *The Pioneer* magazine, March, 1843.

74 Man passes away; generations are but shadows; there is nothing stable but truth.

Josiah Quincy, Jr., in a speech in Boston, September 17, 1830.

75 Truth is given the eternal years of God because she needs them every one.

Thomas Brackett Reed, in a speech at Bowdoin College, Maine, July 25, 1902.

76 The best of us only pass from one inaccuracy to another, and so do the worst, but on the whole,

the last inaccuracy is nearer the truth than the old one.

> THOMAS BRACKETT REED, quoted in Samuel Walker McCall, *The Life of Thomas Brackett Reed,* 1914.

77 The truth survives, the untruth perishes. Men have but little capacity for the recognition of truth at first sight, and of a hundred things which seem plausible, it is fortunate if one be true. Hence it is well that all things should be held at arm's length and stand the scrutiny of our prejudices and interests, of our religion and our skepticism.

> Ibid.

78 Truth is a jewel which should not be painted over; but it may be set to advantage and shown in a good light.

> GEORGE SANTAYANA, *The Life of Reason,* 1905–1906.

79 We shall seek the truth and endure the consequences.

> CHARLES SEYMOUR, quoted in William F. Buckley, *God and Man at Yale,* 1951.

80 Man may burn his brother at the stake, but he cannot reduce truth to ashes; he may murder his fellow man with a shot in the back, but he does not murder justice; he may slay armies of men, but as it is written, "Truth beareth off the victory."

> ADLAI STEVENSON, in a speech at Alton, Illinois, November 9, 1952.

81 Nothing from man's hands, nor law, nor constitution, can be final. Truth alone is final.

> CHARLES SUMNER, in a speech in the U.S. Senate, August 26, 1852.

82 It takes two to speak the truth—one to speak, and another to hear.

> HENRY DAVID THOREAU, *A Week on the Concord and Merrimack Rivers,* 1849.

83 Rather than love, than money, than fame, give me truth.

> HENRY DAVID THOREAU, *Walden,* 1854.

84 Some circumstantial evidence is very strong, as when you find a trout in the milk.

> HENRY DAVID THOREAU, entry dated November 11, 1854, in his *Journal,* 1906.

85 "Truth is mighty and will prevail"—the most majestic compound fracture of fact which any of woman born has yet achieved.

> MARK TWAIN, in an address, "Advice to Youth," c.1882.

86 Tell the truth or trump—but get the trick.

> MARK TWAIN, "Pudd'nhead Wilson's Calendar," *Pudd'nhead Wilson,* 1894.

87 One of the most striking differences between a cat and a lie is that a cat has only nine lives.

> Ibid.

88 When in doubt tell the truth.

> MARK TWAIN, "Pudd'nhead Wilson's New Calendar," *Following the Equator,* 1897.

89 Truth is the most valuable thing we have. Let us economize it.

> Ibid.

90 Truth is stranger than fiction—to some people, but I am measurably familiar with it.

> Ibid.

91 Truth is stranger than Fiction, but it is because Fiction is obliged to stick to possibilities; Truth isn't.

> Ibid.

92 Figures often beguile me, particularly when I have the arranging of them myself; in which case the remark attributed to Disraeli would often apply with justice and force: "There are three kinds of lies: lies, damned lies, and statistics."

> MARK TWAIN, *Autobiography,* 1924.

93 Serious misfortunes originating in misrepresentation frequently flow and spread before they can be dissipated by truth.

> GEORGE WASHINGTON, in a letter to John Jay, May 8, 1796.

94 There is nothing so powerful as truth; and often nothing so strange.

> DANIEL WEBSTER, arguing in a murder trial, April 6, 1830.

95 Falsehoods which we spurn today
    Were the truths of long ago;
Let the dead boughs fall away,
    Fresher shall the living grow.

> JOHN GREENLEAF WHITTIER, "Calef in Boston,"
> 1849.

---

238. TYRANNY

See also AMERICAN REVOLUTION;
AUTHORITY; DEMOCRACY; FORCE;
GOVERNMENT; INDEPENDENCE; MAJORITY
RULE; REBELLION; REVOLUTION

---

1 The worst tyrants are those which establish themselves in our own breasts.

> WILLIAM ELLERY CHANNING, in a sermon,
> "Spiritual Freedom," 1830.

2 The world is made up for the most part of morons and natural tyrants, sure of themselves, strong in their own opinions, never doubting anything.

> CLARENCE DARROW, "Personal Liberty," 1928.

3 If you would rule the world quietly, you must keep it amused.

> RALPH WALDO EMERSON, offering a maxim for
> tyrants, in "New England Reformers," *Essays*,
> Second Series, 1844.

4 The moment a man says, "Give up your rights, here is money," there is tyranny. It comes masquerading in monks' cowls and in citizens' coats; comes savagely or comes politely. But it is tyranny.

> RALPH WALDO EMERSON, entry written in 1851,
> *Journals*, 1909–1914.

5 With reasonable men, I will reason; with humane men I will plead; but to tyrants I will give no quarter, nor waste arguments where they will certainly be lost.

> WILLIAM LLOYD GARRISON, quoted in *William
> Lloyd Garrison, 1805–79: The Story of His Life
> Told by His Children*, 1885–1889.

6 Some boast of being friends to government; I am a friend to righteous government, to a government founded upon the principles of reason and justice; but I glory in publicly avowing my eternal enmity to tyranny.

> JOHN HANCOCK, in a speech on the Boston
> Massacre, Boston, March 5, 1774.

7 The evils of tyranny are rarely seen but by him who resists it.

> JOHN HAY, *Castilian Days*, 1871.

8 Every tyrant who has lived has believed in freedom—for himself.

> ELBERT HUBBARD, in *The Philistine* magazine,
> published from 1895–1915.

9 How hard the tyrants die!

> ELBERT HUBBARD, *The Roycroft Dictionary and
> Book of Epigrams*, 1923.

10 He who endeavors to control the mind by force is a tyrant, and he who submits is a slave.

> ROBERT G. INGERSOLL, in a lecture, "Some
> Mistakes of Moses," 1879.

11 The time to guard against corruption and tyranny is before they shall have gotten hold of us. It is better to keep the wolf out of the fold than to trust to drawing his teeth and claws after he shall have entered.

> THOMAS JEFFERSON, *Notes on the State of
> Virginia*, 1784.

12 There is no king, who, with a sufficient force, is not always ready to make himself absolute.

> THOMAS JEFFERSON, in a letter to George
> Wythe, August 13, 1786.

13 It is the old practice of despots to use a part of the people to keep the rest in order.

> THOMAS JEFFERSON, in a letter to John Taylor,
> June 1, 1798.

14 I have sworn upon the altar of God, eternal hostility against every form of tyranny over the mind of man.

> THOMAS JEFFERSON, in a letter to Benjamin
> Rush, September 23, 1800.

15 Enlighten the people generally, and tyranny and oppressions of body and mind will vanish like evil spirits at the dawn of day.

THOMAS JEFFERSON, in a letter to Pierre Samuel
Du Pont de Nemours, April 24, 1816.

16 Man is capable of self-government, and only
rendered otherwise by the moral degradation de-
signedly super-induced on him by the wicked acts
of his tyrants.

THOMAS JEFFERSON, in a letter to the Marquis de
Barbé-Marbois, June 14, 1817.

17 Tyranny and anarchy are alike incompatible
with freedom, security, and the enjoyment of opportunity.

JEANE J. KIRKPATRICK, in a statement before the
Third Committee of the United Nations General
Assembly, November 24, 1981.

18 "You work and toil and earn bread, and I'll eat
it." No matter in what shape it comes, whether
from the mouth of a king who seeks to bestride the
people of his own nation and live by the fruit of
their labor, or from one race of men as an apology
for enslaving another race, it is the same tyrannical
principle.

ABRAHAM LINCOLN, in the final Lincoln-Douglas
Debate, Alton, Illinois, October 15, 1858.

19 Thus dwelt together in love these simple
      Acadian farmers,
   Dwelt in the love of God and of man. Alike
      were they free from
   Fear, that reigns with the tyrant, and envy,
      the vice of republics.

HENRY WADSWORTH LONGFELLOW, Evangeline,
1847.

20 Bureaucracy, the rule of no one, has become the
modern form of despotism.

MARY MCCARTHY, in The New Yorker
magazine, October 18, 1958.

21 The accumulation of all powers, legislative, executive, and judiciary, in the same hands, whether
of one, a few, or many, and whether hereditary,
self-appointed, or elective, may justly be pronounced the very definition of tyranny.

JAMES MADISON, The Federalist, No. 47,
1787–1788.

22 Since the general civilization of mankind, I believe there are more instances of the abridgment of
the freedom of the people, by gradual and silent
encroachments of those in power, than by violent
and sudden usurpations: but on a candid examination of history, we shall find that turbulence, violence and abuse of power, by the majority trampling on the rights of the minority, have produced
factions and commotions, which, in republics, have
more frequently than any other cause, produced
despotism.

JAMES MADISON, "General Defense of the
Constitution," a speech in the Virginia
Convention, June 6, 1788.

23 there is bound to be a certain amount of
   trouble running any country
   if you are president the trouble happens to
      you
   but if you are a tyrant you can arrange things
      so
   that most of the trouble happens to other
      people

DON MARQUIS, "archy's newest deal," archy does
his part, 1935.

24 Tyranny brings ignorance and brutality with it.
It degrades men from their just rank into the class
of brutes; it damps their spirits; it suppresses arts;
it extinguishes every spark of noble ardor and generosity in the breasts of those who are enslaved by
it; it makes naturally strong and great minds feeble
and little, and triumphs over the ruins of virtue and
humanity.

JONATHAN MAYHEW, A Discourse Concerning
Unlimited Submission and Non-Resistance to the
Higher Powers, 1750.

25 Tyranny, like hell, is not easily conquered; yet
we have this consolation with us, that the harder
the conflict, the more glorious the triumph. What
we obtain too cheap, we esteem too lightly:—'Tis
dearness only that gives every thing its value.

THOMAS PAINE, in the first of a series of
pamphlets, The American Crisis, published in the
Pennsylvania Journal, December 19, 1776.

26 There is no tyranny so hateful as a vulgar and
anonymous tyranny. It is all-permeating, all-

thwarting; it blasts every budding novelty and sprig of genius with its omnipresent and fierce stupidity. Such a headless people has the mind of a worm and the claws of a dragon.

GEORGE SANTAYANA, *The Life of Reason,* 1905–1906.

27 Tyranny is the normal pattern of government. It is only by intense thought, by great effort, by burning idealism and unlimited sacrifice that freedom has prevailed as a system of government. And the efforts which were first necessary to create it are fully as necessary to sustain it in our own day.

ADLAI E. STEVENSON, "The Political Relevance of Moral Principle," a lecture given in Washington, D.C., January 18, 1959.

28 Passive resistance, the most potent weapon ever wielded by man against oppression.

BENJAMIN R. TUCKER, "Refusal to Pay Rent," *Instead of a Book, By a Man Too Busy To Write One,* 1893.

29 There is a natural and necessary progression, from the extreme of anarchy to the extreme of tyranny; and . . . arbitrary power is most easily established on the ruins of liberty abused to licentiousness.

GEORGE WASHINGTON, in a circular to the States, June 8, 1783.

30 When a people shall have become incapable of governing themselves, and fit for a master, it is of little consequence from what quarter he comes.

GEORGE WASHINGTON, in a letter to the Marquis de Lafayette, April 28, 1788.

---

239. UTAH

---

1 Industry.

State motto.

2 Even if there had been no background of Joseph Smith, Angel Moroni, and the Book of Mormon, Utahns would have been incomprehensible, misun-

derstood and lied about, because they set down in the book of Western history the most stubbornly cross-grained chapter it contains. . . . Utah has always had a way of doing things different. The rest of the country has never quite got over it.

Federal Writers' Project, *Utah: A Guide to the State,* 1941.

3 Water in Utah is precious, savored as champagne might be in another land. Life does not come easy. Perhaps some of the especial flavor of Utah comes from this quality of things coming hard. Its beauty is not wholehearted; always there is something withheld. Utah's loveliness is a desert loveliness, unyielding and frequently sterile.

Ibid.

4 One must thank the genius of Brigham Young for the creation of Salt Lake City,—an inestimable hospitality to the Overland Emigrants, and an efficient example to all men in the vast desert, teaching how to subdue and turn it to a habitable garden.

RALPH WALDO EMERSON, entry written in October, 1863, *Journals,* 1909–1914.

5 Jews in Utah, being non-Mormon, are theoretically subject to classification as Gentiles, which gave rise to the well-known remark that "Utah is the only place in the world where Jews are Gentiles."

JOHN GUNTHER, *Inside U.S.A.,* 1947.

6 I am concerned for the sake of Mr. Phil Robinson, his soul. You will remember that he wrote a book called *Saints and Sinners* in which he proved very prettily that the Mormon was almost altogether an estimable person. Ever since my arrival at Salt Lake I have been wondering what made him write that book. On mature reflection, and after a long walk round the city, I am inclined to think it was the sun, which is very powerful hereabouts.

RUDYARD KIPLING, *American Notes,* 1891.

7 What's in the Great Salt Lake? . . . Salt. Eight billion tons of salt, worth about fifty billion dollars. Also gypsum, magnesium, lithium, sulfur, boron, and potash. . . . Swimmers like the Great Salt Lake. Nonswimmers are absolutely knocked out by it

because they can't sink. There is no record of anybody ever having gone swimming and drowned in the Great Salt Lake. The best life preserver, they say, is a ten-pound weight tied to your feet, to keep your feet down and your head up.

CHARLES KURALT, *Dateline America,* 1979.

8 [Salt Lake City] lies in the edge of a level plain as broad as the state of Connecticut, and crouches close down to the ground under a curving wall of mighty mountains whose heads are hidden in the clouds, and whose shoulders bear relics of the snows of winter all the summer long. Seen from one of these dizzy heights, twelve or fifteen miles off, Great Salt Lake City is toned down and diminished till it is suggestive of a child's toy village reposing under the majestic protection of the Chinese wall.

MARK TWAIN, *Roughing It,* 1872.

9 Salt Lake City was healthy—an extremely healthy city. They declared that there was only one physician in the place and he was arrested every week regularly and held to answer under the vagrant act for having "no visible means of support."

Ibid.

10 I girdid up my Lions & fled the Seen. I packt up my duds & Left Salt Lake, which is a 2nd Soddum & Germorrer, inhabitid by as theavin & onprincipled a set of retchis as ever drew Breth in eny spot on the Globe.

ARTEMUS WARD, "A Visit to Brigham Young," *Artemus Ward, His Book,* 1862.

11 There are no ravishingly beautiful women present, and no positively ugly ones. The men are fair to middling. They will never be slain in cold blood for their beauty, nor shut up in jail for their homeliness.

ARTEMUS WARD, on a visit to the Mormon Tabernacle, "Great Salt Lake City," *The Works of Artemus Ward,* 1898.

12 Brigham Young says the devil has monopolized the good music long enough, and it is high time the Lord had a portion of it. Therefore trombones are tooted on Sundays in Utah as well as on other days; and there are some splendid musicians there.

ARTEMUS WARD, "Great Salt Lake City," *The Works of Artemus Ward,* 1898.

240. VERMONT

1 Freedom and unity.

State motto.

2 To specify each locality in Vermont possessing attractions to the summer tourist, or inducements to one wishing to build a summer home, would require nearly a complete description of each town.

Vermont Board of Agriculture publication of 1892, quoted in Noel Perrin, *Third Person Rural,* 1983.

3 Vermont is a country unto itself. Indeed for fourteen years after the declaration of independence, the State refused to join the Union and remained an independent republic.

PEARL S. BUCK, *Pearl Buck's America,* 1971.

4 All in all, Vermont is a jewel state, small but precious.

Ibid.

5 Blaze the mountains in the windless Autumn, Frost-clear, blue-nooned, apple-ripening days.

SARAH N. CLEGHORN, "Vermont," in *Portraits and Protests,* 1917.

6 I love Vermont because of her hills and valleys, her scenery and invigorating climate, but most of all, because of her indomitable people. They are a race of pioneers who have almost beggared themselves to serve others. If the spirit of liberty should vanish in other parts of the union, and support of our institutions should languish, it could all be replenished from the generous store held by the people of this brave little state of Vermont.

CALVIN COOLIDGE, in an address at Bennington, Vermont, September 9, 1928.

7 Vermonters are really something quite special and unique. . . . This state bows to nothing: the first

legislative measure it ever passed was "to adopt the laws of God . . . until there is time to frame better."

JOHN GUNTHER, *Inside U.S.A.,* 1947.

8 There is no cure for Vermont weather. It is consistent only in its inconsistency.

NOEL PERRIN, *Third Person Rural,* 1983.

9 Statistics prove that no Vermonter ever left the State unless transportation was furnished in advance. She is what you call a "Hard Boiled State." The principal ingredients are Granite, Rock Salt and Republicans. The last being the hardest of the three.

WILL ROGERS, March 29, 1925, quoted in Donald Day, *The Autobiography of Will Rogers,* 1949.

10 My heart is where the hills fling up
　　Green garlands to the day;
　'T is where the blue lake brims her cup,
　　The sparkling rivers play.
　My heart is on the mountains still
　　Where'er my steps may be;
　Vermont, O maiden of the hills,
　　My heart is there with thee!

WENDELL PHILLIPS STAFFORD, first stanza of "Song of Vermont," *The Land We Love,* 1916.

11 We have no populous towns, seaports, or large manufactories, to collect the people together. They are spread over the whole country, forming small and separate settlements.

SAMUEL WILLIAMS, *The Natural and Civil History of Vermont,* 1794.

241. VICE PRESIDENCY

See also GOVERNMENT; POLITICS

1 My country has in its wisdom contrived for me the most insignificant office that ever the invention of man contrived or his imagination conceived.

JOHN ADAMS, in a letter to Abigail Adams, December 19, 1793.

2 I personally believe the Vice President of the United States should never be a nonentity. I believe he should be used. I believe he should have a very useful job.

DWIGHT D. EISENHOWER, quoted in Nelson A. Rockefeller, *Unity, Freedom and Peace: A Blueprint for Tomorrow,* 1968.

3 Let me assure the distinguished Vice President of the United States that I have absolutely no designs on his job.

GERALD R. FORD, speaking at a Gridiron Club Dinner, 1968.

4 A spare tire on the automobile of government.

JOHN NANCE GARNER, characterizing the office of Vice President, June 19, 1934.

5 The Vice President will be and is what the President wants him to be.

HUBERT H. HUMPHREY, quoted in Michael V. DiSalle, *Second Choice,* 1966.

6 The second office of the government is honorable and easy, the first is but a splendid misery.

THOMAS JEFFERSON, in a letter to Elbridge Gerry, May 13, 1797.

7 If you are very active as Vice President, everyone in America knows your name. But that is your only property. It is not the same thing as real power—more like being a movie star.

NORMAN MAILER, *Miami and the Siege of Chicago,* 1968.

8 The Vice President of the United States is like a man in a cataleptic state: he cannot speak; he cannot move; he suffers no pain; and yet he is perfectly conscious of everything that is going on about him.

Attributed to Thomas R. Marshall.

9 There were once two brothers. One ran away to sea. The other was elected Vice President and neither was heard of again.

THOMAS R. MARSHALL, quoted in Dick Gregory, *Dick Gregory's Political Primer,* 1972.

10 I think the Vice President should do anything the President wants him to do.

> RICHARD M. NIXON, quoted in Earl Mazo, *Richard Nixon: A Political and Personal Portrait,* 1959.

11 Will you please tell me what you do with all the Vice Presidents a Bank has? I guess that's to get you more discouraged before you can see the President. Why, the United States is the biggest Business institution in the World and they only have one Vice President and nobody has ever found anything for him to do.

> WILL ROGERS, in a speech to the International Bankers Association, 1922.

12 The opportunities afforded by the Vice Presidency, particularly the Presidency of the Senate, do not come—they are there to be seized. Here is one instance in which it is the man who makes the office, not the office the man.

> HARRY S TRUMAN, *Years of Decision,* 1955.

13 I do not propose to be buried until I am really dead.

> DANIEL WEBSTER, on being offered the Whig nomination for Vice President, 1848.

14 There is very little to be said about the Vice President. . . . His importance consists in the fact that he may cease to be Vice President.

> WOODROW WILSON, *Congressional Government—A Study in American Politics,* 1885.

---

242. VICTORY

See also CONQUEST; WAR

---

1 Force complete, absolute, overpowering, was applied until the enemy's will to resist and capacity to exist as a nation were broken. This was victory.

> DEAN G. ACHESON, *Powers and Diplomacy,* 1958.

2 We learned that military power is primarily effective against opposing military power and, by

overawing and overcoming it, enhances acceptance of its possessor's will and purposes. But physical force soon runs into limitations in imposing acceptance on minds not wholly governed by reason or fear of physical suffering. . . . So when people say that our soldiers win wars only to have our diplomats lose the peace, the truths which puzzle them are that military force is not so potent as they had thought, and people are more intractable.

> DEAN G. ACHESON, address at the University of Indiana, March 5, 1965, published in *This Vast External Realm,* 1973.

3 The winning team like the conquering army claims everything in its path and seems to say that only winning is important. Yet like getting into a college of your choice or winning an election or marrying a beautiful mate victory is fraught with as much danger as glory. Victory has very narrow meanings and, if exaggerated or misused, can become a destructive force.

> BILL BRADLEY, *Life on the Run,* 1976.

4 If fight we must, let's go in there and shoot the works for victory with everything at our disposal.

> GEN. MARK CLARK, in testimony before Congress, c.1954, quoted in Dean Acheson, *Power and Diplomacy,* 1958.

5 Sometimes it's worse to win a fight than to lose.

> BILLIE HOLIDAY, *Lady Sings the Blues,* 1956.

6 I wonder whether even in the past total victory was not really an illusion from the standpoint of the victors. In a sense, there is not total victory short of genocide, unless it be a victory over the minds of men. But the total military victories are rarely victories over the minds of men.

> GEORGE F. KENNAN, *American Diplomacy, 1900–1950,* 1951.

7 They see nothing wrong in the rule, that to the victors belong the spoils of the enemy.

> WILLIAM L. MARCY, speech in the U.S. Senate, January 21, 1832.

8 We have met the enemy and they are ours—two ships, two brigs, one schooner and one sloop.

OLIVER HAZARD PERRY, message dated September 19, 1813, to Gen. William Henry Harrison, reporting Perry's victory at the Battle of Lake Erie on September 10.

9 What red-blooded American could oppose so shining a concept as victory? It would be like standing up for sin against virtue.

GEN. MATTHEW B. RIDGWAY, *The Korean War,* 1967.

10 Defeat would be bad enough, but victory would be intolerable.

HUNTER S. THOMPSON, describing the dilemma faced by Florida police on the eve of a Vietnam veterans' march on the 1972 Republican Party National Convention, in *Fear and Loathing on the Campaign Trail, '72,* 1973.

---

243. VIETNAM WAR

See also WAR

---

1 The corner has definitely been turned toward victory in Vietnam.

Defense Department announcement, May, 1963.

2 Whereas naval units of the Communist regime in Vietnam, in violation of the principles of the Charter of the United Nations and of international law, have deliberately and repeatedly attacked United States naval vessels . . . and Whereas these attacks are part of a deliberate and systematic campaign of aggression . . . and Whereas the United States is assisting the peoples of southeast Asia to protect their freedom and has no territorial, military or political ambitions in that area. . . Now, therefore, be it Resolved by the Senate and the House of Representatives of the United States of America in Congress assembled, that the Congress approves and supports the determination of the President, as Commander in Chief, to take all necessary measures to repel any armed attack against the forces of the United States and to prevent further aggression.

Gulf of Tonkin Resolution, passed by Congress on August 7, 1964.

3 It became necessary to destroy the town to save it.

An unidentified U.S. Army major, explaining to an Associated Press reporter the decision to bomb and shell Bentre, Vietnam, February 7, 1968.

4 I felt sorry. I don't know why I felt sorry. John Wayne never felt sorry.

An American soldier who had knifed a Viet Cong soldier to death, quoted in Robert Jay Lifton, *Home from the War,* 1974.

5 Only You Can Prevent Forests.

Sign in the ready room of U.S. airmen spraying defoliants in Vietnam, quoted in Gen. William Westmoreland, *A Soldier Reports,* 1976.

6 The United States could well declare unilaterally that this stage of the Vietnam War is over— that we have "won" in the sense that our armed forces are in control of most of the field and no potential enemy is in a position to establish its authority over South Vietnam. . . . It may be a far-fetched proposal, but nothing else has worked.

SEN. GEORGE D. AIKEN, in a call for a "unilateral declaration of military victory," October 19, 1966.

7 We got in more trouble for killing water buffalo than we did for killing people. That was something I could never adjust to.

LEE CHILDRESS, quoted in Al Santoli, *Everything We Had: An Oral History of the Vietnam War by Thirty-Three American Soldiers Who Fought It,* 1981.

8 Whether history will judge this war to be different or not, we cannot say. But this we can say with certainty: a government and a society that silences those who dissent is one that has lost its way. This we can say: that what is essential in a free society is that there should be an atmosphere where those who wish to dissent and even to demonstrate can do so without fear of recrimination or vilification.

HENRY STEELE COMMAGER, *Freedom and Order,* 1966.

9 You have a row of dominoes set up, you knock over the first one, and what will happen to the last one is . . . that it will go over very quickly.

> DWIGHT D. EISENHOWER, on the strategic importance of Indochina, in a press conference, April 7, 1954.

10 If force is going to do the bidding, you must commit the amount of force necessary to bring the conflict to a successful conclusion.

> DWIGHT D. EISENHOWER, in a remark at a White House meeting on Vietnam with Pres. Lyndon B. Johnson, 1966.

11 [President] Johnson condemned his officials who worked on Vietnam to the excruciating mental task of holding reality and the official version of reality together as they moved farther and farther apart.

> FRANCES FITZGERALD, *Fire in the Lake,* 1972.

12 I think it is reasonable that if we must continue to fight wars, they ought to be fought by those people who really want to fight them. Since it seems to be the top half of the generation gap that is the most enthusiastic about going to war, why not send the Old Folks Brigade to Vietnam—with John Wayne leading them?

> DICK GREGORY, in *Dick Gregory's Political Primer,* 1972.

13 The battle against Communism must be joined in Southeast Asia with strength and determination . . . or the United States, inevitably, must surrender the Pacific and take up our defenses on our own shores.

> LYNDON B. JOHNSON, 1961, quoted in Stanley Karnow, *Vietnam: A History,* 1983.

14 We still seek no wider war.

> LYNDON B. JOHNSON, in a speech just after the Gulf of Tonkin incident, August 4, 1964. (The Gulf of Tonkin Resolution was passed by Congress on August 7. See quotation 2, above.)

15 In that region there is nothing that we covet. There is nothing we seek. There is no territory or no military position or no political ambition. Our one desire and our one determination is that the people of Southeast Asia be left in peace to work out their own destinies in their own ways.

> LYNDON B. JOHNSON, on the Vietnam War, in a press conference, March 13, 1965.

16 No commander in chief could meet face to face with these soldiers without asking himself: What is it they are doing there? . . . They are there to keep aggression from succeeding. They are there to stop one nation from taking over another nation by force. They are there to help people who do not want to have an ideology pushed down their throats and imposed upon them. They are there because somewhere, and at some place, the free nations of the world must say again to the militant disciples of Asian communism: This far and no further. The time is now, and the place is Vietnam.

> LYNDON B. JOHNSON, remarks recorded in Manila, Philippines, for broadcast to the American people, October 27, 1966.

17 Our objective in South Vietnam has never been the annihilation of the enemy. It has been to bring about a recognition in Hanoi that its objective— taking over the South by force—could not be achieved.

> LYNDON B. JOHNSON, address to the nation, March 31, 1968.

18 I believe that a peaceful Asia is far nearer to reality because of what America has done in Vietnam.

> Ibid.

19 This was a war of no fixed front. The "enemy" might be two or three divisions at one time, as at Khe Sanh, or two or three armed men sneaking into a village at night to murder the village chief. It was a war of subversion, terror, and assassination, of propaganda, economic disruption, and sabotage. It was a political war, an economic war, and a fighting war—all at the same time.

> LYNDON B. JOHNSON, *The Vantage Point: Perspectives of the Presidency, 1963–1969,* 1971.

20 Pouring money, materiel and men into the jungles [of Vietnam] without at least a remote prospect of victory would be dangerously futile and self-destructive.

JOHN F. KENNEDY, in a speech in the U.S. Senate, April 6, 1954.

21 The troops will march in, the bands will play, the crowds will cheer, and in four days everyone will have forgotten. Then we will be told we have to send in more troops. It's like taking a drink. The effect wears off, and you have to take another.

JOHN F. KENNEDY, on military intervention in South Vietnam, quoted in Stanley Karnow, *Vietnam: A History,* 1983.

22 We have a problem in making our power credible, and Vietnam is the place.

JOHN F. KENNEDY, remark to James Reston, 1961, quoted in Stanley Karnow, *Vietnam: A History,* 1983.

23 We can protect these countries by our guarantees against outright military invasion. We can assist them through economic assistance to improve the life of their people. We can assist them through defense support in strengthening their armed forces against internal guerrilla activity. But, in the final analysis . . . they have to organize the political and social life of the country in such a way that they maintain the support of their people. There is a limit beyond which our efforts cannot go.

JOHN F. KENNEDY, press conference, May 5, 1961.

24 In the final analysis, it is their war. They are the ones who have to win it or lose it. We can help them, we can give them equipment, we can send our men out there as advisers, but they have to win it, the people of Vietnam.

JOHN F. KENNEDY, press conference, September 3, 1963.

25 The bombs in Vietnam explode at home; they destroy the hopes and possibilities for a decent America.

MARTIN LUTHER KING, JR., *Where Do We Go from Here? Chaos or Community,* 1967.

26 Somehow this madness must cease. We must stop now. I speak as a child of God and brother to the suffering poor of Vietnam. I speak for those whose land is being laid waste, whose homes are being destroyed, whose culture is being subverted.

I speak for the poor of America who are paying the double price of smashed hopes at home and death and corruption in Vietnam. I speak as a citizen of the world, for the world as it stands aghast at the path we have taken. I speak as an American to the leaders of my own nation. The great initiative in this war is ours. The initiative to stop it must be ours.

MARTIN LUTHER KING, JR., *The Trumpet of Conscience,* 1967.

27 Psychologists or sociologists may explain some day what it is about that distant monochromatic land, of green mountains and fields merging with an azure sea, that for millennia has acted as a magnet for foreigners who sought glory there and found frustration, who believed that in its rice fields and jungles some principle was to be established and entered them only to recede in disillusion.

HENRY KISSINGER, *White House Years,* 1979.

28 The time has come to stop beating our heads against stone walls under the illusion that we have been appointed policeman to the human race.

WALTER LIPPMANN, on U.S. foreign policy in Indochina, in his column in the *New York Herald Tribune,* February 2, 1965.

29 Vietnam is a military problem. Vietnam is a political problem; and as the war goes on it has become more clearly a moral problem.

EUGENE J. McCARTHY, *The Limits of Power,* 1967.

30 It is said that we must carry on the war in Vietnam in order to preserve and defend our national honor. Our national honor is not at stake, and should not so readily be offered. In every other great war of the century, we have had the support of what is generally accepted as the decent opinion of mankind. We do not have that today. We cannot, of course, depend only on this opinion to prove our honor; it may not be sound. But always in the past we have not only had this support, but we have used it as a kind of justification for our actions.

Ibid.

31 America today is more isolated than it has been since the heyday of isolationism, not by our with-

drawal from the world but by the withdrawal of most of the world from us.

EUGENE J. MCCARTHY, *The Year of the People,* 1969.

32 Napalm has become "Incinderjell," which makes it sound like Jello. And defoliants are referred to as weed-killers—something you use in your driveway. The resort to euphemism denotes, no doubt, a guilty conscience or—the same thing nowadays—a twinge in the public-relations nerve.

MARY MCCARTHY, *Vietnam,* 1967.

33 And it's one, two, three,
    What're we fightin' for?
Don't ask me, I don't give a damn,
    Next stop is Vietnam.
And it's five, six, seven,
    Open up the pearly gates.
There ain't no time to wonder why,
    Whoopee! we're all gonna die.

JOE MCDONALD, rock composer, refrain from the song "I Feel Like I'm Fixin' to Die Rag," Country Joe and the Fish, 1967.

34 We seem bent upon saving the Vietnamese from Ho Chi Minh, even if we have to kill them and demolish their country to do it. . . . I do not intend to remain silent in the face of what I regard as a policy of madness which, sooner or later, will envelop my son and American youth by the millions for years to come.

GEORGE MCGOVERN, in a speech in the U.S. Senate, April 25, 1967.

35 The war in Vietnam was bad for America because it was a bad war, as all wars are bad if they consist of rich boys fighting poor boys when the rich boys have an advantage in the weapons.

NORMAN MAILER, *The Armies of the Night,* 1968.

36 If the Devil was devoted to destroying all belief in conservative values among the intelligent and prosperous, he could not have picked a finer instrument to his purpose than the war in Vietnam.

NORMAN MAILER, *St. George and the Godfather,* 1972.

37 Vietnam was our longest, costliest, and, as it went on, our least popular war; it was also the least understood. And the more attempts were made to explain it, the more puzzling it became.

MERLE MILLER, *Lyndon: An Oral Biography,* 1980.

38 We did a fine job there. If it happened in World War II, they still would be telling stories about it. But it happened in Vietnam, so nobody knows about it. They don't even tell recruits about it today. Marines don't talk about Vietnam. We lost. They never talk about losing. So it's just wiped out, all of that's off the slate, it doesn't count. It makes you a little bitter.

JOHN MUIR, quoted in Al Santoli, *Everything We Had: An Oral History of the Vietnam War by Thirty-Three American Soldiers Who Fought It,* 1981.

39 If in order to avoid further Communist expansion in Asia and particularly in Indo-China, if in order to avoid it we must take the risk by putting American boys in, I believe that the executive branch of the government has to take the politically unpopular position of facing up to it and doing it, and I personally would support such a decision.

RICHARD M. NIXON, in a speech, April 16, 1954.

40 What the United States wants for South Vietnam is not the important thing. What North Vietnam wants for South Vietnam is not the important thing. What is important is what the people of South Vietnam want for South Vietnam.

RICHARD M. NIXON, address to the nation, May 14, 1969.

41 Let me be quite blunt. Our fighting men are not going to be worn down; our mediators are not going to be talked down; and our allies are not going to be let down.

Ibid.

42 The defense of freedom is everybody's business—not just America's business. And it is particularly the responsibility of the people whose freedom is threatened. In the previous administration, we Americanized the war in Vietnam. In this administration, we are Vietnamizing the search for peace.

Richard M. Nixon, address to the nation, November 3, 1969.

43 I want to end the war to save the lives of those brave young men in Vietnam. But I want to end it in a way which will increase the chance that their younger brothers and their sons will not have to fight in some future Vietnam someplace in the world.

Ibid.

44 Tonight, American and South Vietnamese units will attack the headquarters for the entire Communist military operation in South Vietnam. . . . We take this action not for the purpose of expanding the war into Cambodia, but for the purpose of ending the war in Vietnam, and winning the just peace we all desire.

Richard M. Nixon, in a televised address on what was called a U.S. and South Vietnamese incursion into Cambodia, April 30, 1970.

45 My fellow Americans, we live in an age of anarchy, both abroad and at home.

Ibid.

46 Lyndon Johnson told the Nation
Have no fear of escalation,
I am trying everyone to please.
And though it isn't really war,
We're sending 50,000 more
To help save Vietnam from Vietnamese.

Tom Paxton, in the song "Lyndon Johnson Told the Nation," 1965.

47 We should declare war on North Vietnam. We could pave the whole place over by noon and be home for dinner.

Ronald Reagan, quoted in Edmund G. Brown, *Reagan: The Political Chameleon,* 1976.

48 You know, if I thought of a child dying, that's the way it was. That's war. Children die. You kill them, they kill you. Women kill you, you kill them. That's it. There's no Geneva Convention. There's no rules. There's nothing.

Gayle Smith, quoted in Al Santoli, *Everything We Had: An Oral History of the Vietnam War*

by Thirty-Three American Soldiers Who Fought It, 1981.

49 I'd rather see America save her soul than her face.

Norman Thomas, speaking to antiwar demonstrators in Washington, D.C., November 27, 1965.

50 Press and television had created an aura not of victory but of defeat, which, coupled with the vocal antiwar elements, profoundly influenced timid officials in Washington. It was like two boxers in a ring, one having the other on the ropes, close to a knock-out, when the apparent winner's second inexplicably throws in the towel.

Gen. William C. Westmoreland, *A Soldier Reports,* 1976.

51 Even though American resolve fell short in the end, it remains a fact that few countries have ever engaged in such idealistic magnanimity; and no gain or attempted gain for human freedom can be discounted.

Ibid.

244. VIRGINIA

1 Sic semper tyrannis. (Thus always to tyrants.)

State motto.

2 This country [Virginia] wants nothing but to be peopled with a well-born race to make it one of the best colonies in the world.

Aphra Behn, *The Widow Ranter, or The History of Bacon in Virginia,* 1690.

3 Carry me back to old Virginny,
There's where the cotton and the corn and taters grow.

James A. Bland, "Carry Me Back to Old Virginny," 1875.

4 That, without any fear of succeeding, the intrepid native Virginian will dauntlessly attempt to conceal his superiority to everybody else, remains a

tribal virtue which has not escaped the comment of anthropologists.

> James Branch Cabell, *Let Me Live,*
> 1947.

5 The higher Virginians seem to venerate themselves as men.

> John Davis, *Travels of Four Years and a Half in the United States of America,* 1803.

6 The Virginia idea, it must be clearly understood, was not what is today called the American Dream. The Virginian did not dream of a democracy, with its literal meaning of the rule of the people. His dream was to found an aristocratic republic, in which superior individuals would emerge to rule the many.

> Clifford Dowdey, "Virginia," in *American Panorama: East of the Mississippi,* 1960.

7 All eastern Virginians are Shintoists under the skin. Genealogy makes history personal to them in terms of family. Kinship to the eighth degree usually is recognized. . . . A pleasant society it is, one that does not adventure rashly into new acquaintanceship but welcomes with a certain stateliness of manner those who come with letters from friends.

> Douglas Southall Freeman, "The Spirit of Virginia," in Federal Writers' Project, *Virginia: A Guide to the Old Dominion,* 1940.

8 Our society is neither scientific nor splendid, but independent, hospitable, correct, and neighborly.

> Thomas Jefferson, in a letter to Nathaniel Bowditch, October 26, 1818.

9 The good Old Dominion [Virginia], the blessed mother of us all.

> Thomas Jefferson, "Thoughts on Lotteries," 1826.

10 You can work for Virginia, to build her up again, to make her great again. You can teach your children to live and cherish her.

> Robert E. Lee, to the daughter of Dr. Prosser Tabb, May, 1870.

245. WAR

See also Conquest; Militarism; Nuclear Age; Victory; and individual wars

1 What Price Glory?

> Maxwell Anderson, the title of a play, 1924.

2 There's a consensus out that it's OK to kill when your government decides who to kill. If you kill inside the country you get in trouble. If you kill outside the country, right time, right season, latest enemy, you get a medal.

> Joan Baez, *Daybreak,* 1966.

3 Take the profit out of war.

> Bernard M. Baruch, a statement he made many times. (Baruch's article "Taking the Profit out of War" appeared in the *Atlantic Monthly,* in January, 1926.)

4 War, *n.* A by-product of the arts of peace. The most menacing political condition is a period of international amity. . . . "In time of peace prepare for war" has a deeper meaning than is commonly discerned; it means, not merely that all things earthly have an end—that change is the one immutable and eternal law—but that the soil of peace is thickly sown with seeds of war and singularly suited to their germination and growth. . . . War loves to come like a thief in the night; professions of eternal amity provide the night.

> Ambrose Bierce, *The Devil's Dictionary,* 1906.

5 What this country needs—what every country needs occasionally—is a good hard bloody war to revive the vice of patriotism on which its existence as a nation depends.

> Ambrose Bierce, in a letter, February 15, 1911.

6 It is no longer possible to shield ourselves with arms alone against the ordeal of attack. For modern war visits destruction on the victor and vanquished alike. . . . The way to win an atomic war is to make certain it never starts.

> Gen. Omar Bradley, in an address in Boston, November 10, 1948.

7 In war there is no second prize for the runner-up.

> GEN. OMAR BRADLEY, in the *Military Review*,
> February, 1950.

8 We are now speeding inexorably towards a day when even the ingenuity of our scientists may be unable to save us from the consequences of a single rash act or a lone reckless hand upon the switch of an uninterceptible missile. . . . Have we already gone too far in this search for peace through the accumulation of peril? Is there any way to halt this trend—or must we push on with new devices until we inevitably come to judgment before the atom?

> GEN. OMAR BRADLEY, in a speech in
> Washington, D.C., November 5, 1957.

9 No nation ever had an army large enough to guarantee it against attack in time of peace or insure it victory in time of war.

> CALVIN COOLIDGE, in a speech, October 6, 1925.

10 They were going to look at war, the red animal—war, the blood-swollen god.

> STEPHEN CRANE, *The Red Badge of Courage*,
> 1895.

11 Great is the battle-god, and his kingdom—
A field where a thousand corpses lie.

> STEHEN CRANE, "War Is Kind," 1899.

12 Mother whose heart hung humble as a
        button
On the bright splendid shroud of your son,
Do not weep.
War is kind.

> Ibid.

13 Sooner or later every war of trade becomes a war of blood.

> EUGENE V. DEBS, in a speech at Canton, Ohio,
> June 16, 1918.

14 The master class has always declared the wars; the subject class has always fought the battles. The master class has had all to gain and nothing to lose, while the subject class has had nothing to gain and all to lose—especially their lives.

> Ibid.

15 The working class who fight all the battles, the working class who make the supreme sacrifices, the working class who freely shed their blood and furnish the corpses, have never yet had a voice in either declaring war or making peace. It is the ruling class that invariably does both. They alone declare war and they alone make peace.

> Ibid.

16 The more horrible a depersonalized scientific mass war becomes, the more necessary it is to find universal ideal motives to justify it.

> JOHN DEWEY, *Human Nature and Conduct*,
> 1922.

17 As long as armies exist, any serious conflict will lead to war. A pacifism which does not actively fight against the armament of nations is and must remain impotent.

> ALBERT EINSTEIN, *The World as I See It*, 1934.

18 To my mind, to kill in war is not a whit better than to commit ordinary murder.

> ALBERT EINSTEIN, in *Kaizo,* a Japanese magazine,
> Autumn, 1952.

19 War creates such a strain that all the pettiness, jealousy, ambition, greed, and selfishness begin to leak out the seams of the average character. On top of this are the problems created by the enemy, by weather, by international politics, including age-old racial and nationalistic animosities, by every conceivable kind of difficulty, and, finally, just by the nature of war itself.

> DWIGHT D. EISENHOWER, in a letter to Mamie
> Doud Eisenhower, December 16, 1942.

20 In war there is no substitute for victory.

> DWIGHT D. EISENHOWER, in a letter to Mamie
> Doud Eisenhower, August 2, 1944. (Douglas
> MacArthur used the same phrase in his speech to
> Congress in 1951, during the Korean War. See
> quotation 61, below.)

21 Men acquainted with the battlefield will not be found among the numbers that glibly talk of another war.

> DWIGHT D. EISENHOWER, in an address at
> Chicago, June 2, 1946.

22 War is not only destructive, it is sterile of positive result. The most that military victory can do is to provide opportunity to attempt anew the establishment of durable international peace.

> Ibid.

23 War is no longer a lively adventure or expedition into romance, matching man against man in a test of the stout-hearted. Instead, it is aimed against the cities mankind has built. Its goal is their total destruction and devastation.

> DWIGHT D. EISENHOWER, in a speech in Edinburgh, Scotland, October 3, 1946.

24 I hate war as only a soldier who has lived it can, only as one who has seen its brutality, its futility, its *stupidity*.

> DWIGHT D. EISENHOWER, quoted in John Gunther, *Eisenhower: The Man and the Symbol*, 1952.

25 War gratifies, or used to gratify, the combative instinct of mankind, but it gratifies also the love of plunder, destruction, cruel discipline, and arbitrary power.

> CHARLES WILLIAM ELIOT, *Five American Contributions to Civilization*, 1897.

26 The cannon will not suffer any other sound to be heard for miles and for years around it.

> RALPH WALDO EMERSON, entry written in 1864, *Journals*, 1909–1914.

27 War, to sane men at the present day, begins to look like an epidemic insanity, breaking out here and there like the cholera or influenza, infecting men's brains instead of their bowels.

> RALPH WALDO EMERSON, "War," *Miscellanies*, 1884.

28 War educates the senses, calls into action the will, perfects the physical constitution, brings men into such swift and close collision in critical moments that man measures man.

> Ibid.

29 Get there first with the most men.

> Attributed to Gen. Nathan Bedford Forrest.

30 Either man is obsolete or war is.

> BUCKMINSTER FULLER, *I Seem to Be a Verb*, 1970.

31 A nation is not worthy to be saved if, in the hour of its fate, it will not gather up all its jewels of manhood and life, and go down into the conflict, however bloody and doubtful, resolved on measureless ruin or complete success.

> JAMES A. GARFIELD, in a speech in the House of Representatives, June 25, 1864.

32 Nations do not arm for war. They arm to keep themselves from war.

> BARRY M. GOLDWATER, *Why Not Victory?* 1962.

33 The art of war is simple enough. Find out where your enemy is. Get at him as soon as you can. Strike at him as hard as you can and as often as you can, and keep moving on.

> Attributed to Ulysses S. Grant.

34 We in America should see that no man is ever given, no matter how gradually, or how noble and excellent the man, the power to put this country into a war which is now being prepared and brought closer each day with all the premeditation of a long-planned murder. For when you give power to an executive you do not know who will be filling that position when the time of crisis comes.

> ERNEST HEMINGWAY, "Notes on the Next War: A Serious Letter," in *Esquire* magazine, September, 1935.

35 I do not . . . think that a philosophic view of the world would regard war as absurd.

> OLIVER WENDELL HOLMES, JR., in a dissenting Supreme Court opinion, *United States* v. *Schwimmer*, 1928.

36 Older men declare war. But it is youth that must fight and die. And it is youth who must inherit the tribulation, the sorrow, and the triumphs that are the aftermath of war.

> HERBERT HOOVER, in a speech at the Republican Party National Convention, Chicago, June 27, 1944.

37 So long as governments set the example of killing their enemies, private individuals will occasionally kill theirs.

ELBERT HUBBARD, *The Roycroft Dictionary and Book of Epigrams,* 1923.

38 War: The sure result of the existence of armed men.

Ibid.

39 A soldier is a slave—he does what he is told to do—everything is provided for him—his head is a superfluity. He is only a stick used by men to strike other men; and he is often tossed to Hell without a second thought.

Ibid.

40 The power to wage war is the power to wage war successfully.

CHARLES EVANS HUGHES, *The Supreme Court of the United States,* 1928.

41 That wars and rumors of wars are the great threats to political stability and to liberty needs no demonstration. Total war means total subjection of the individual to the state.

ROBERT H. JACKSON, *The Supreme Court in the American System of Government,* 1955.

42 What we now need to discover in the social realm is the moral equivalent of war: something heroic that will speak to men as universally as war does, and yet will be as compatible with their spiritual selves as war has proved itself to be incompatible.

WILLIAM JAMES, *The Varieties of Religious Experience,* 1902.

43 War . . . is not the most favorable moment for divesting the monarchy of power. On the contrary, it is the moment when the energy of a single hand shows itself in the most seducing form.

THOMAS JEFFERSON, in a letter to Michel Guillaume Jean de Crèvecoeur, August 9, 1788.

44 [We] prefer war in all cases to tribute under any form, and to any people whatever.

THOMAS JEFFERSON, in a letter to Thomas Barclay, May 13, 1791.

45 I have seen enough of one war never to wish to see another.

THOMAS JEFFERSON, in a letter to John Adams, April 25, 1794.

46 I love peace, and I am anxious that we should give the world still another useful lesson, by showing to them other modes of punishing injuries than by war, which is as much a punishment to the punisher as to the sufferer.

THOMAS JEFFERSON, in a letter to Tench Coxe, May 1, 1794.

47 Of my disposition to maintain peace until its condition shall be made less tolerable than that of war itself, the world has had proofs, and more, perhaps, than it has approved. I hope it is practicable, by improving the mind and morals of society, to lessen the disposition to war; but of its abolition I despair.

THOMAS JEFFERSON, in a letter to Noah Worcester, November 26, 1817.

48 Our chiefs are killed. . . . The old men are all dead. . . . The little children are freezing to death. My people, some of them have run away to the hills and have no blankets, no food. No one knows where they are, perhaps freezing to death. I want to have time to look for my children and see how many of them I can find. Maybe I can find them among the dead. Hear me, my chiefs. My heart is sick and sad. From where the sun now stands I will fight no more forever.

CHIEF JOSEPH, to the Nez Percé tribe after surrendering to Gen. Nelson A. Miles in Montana, October, 1877.

49 A war regarded as inevitable or even probable, and therefore much prepared for, has a very good chance of eventually being fought.

GEORGE F. KENNAN, *The Cloud of Danger,* 1977.

50 [A] nuclear disaster, spread by winds and waters and fear, could well engulf the great and the small, the rich and the poor, the committed and the uncommitted alike. Mankind must put an end to war or war will put an end to mankind.

JOHN F. KENNEDY, in an address to the United Nations, September 25, 1961.

51 Today, every inhabitant of this planet must contemplate the day when it may no longer be habitable. Every man, woman, and child lives under a nuclear sword of Damocles, hanging by the slenderest of threads, capable of being cut at any moment by accident, miscalculation, or madness. The weapons of war must be abolished before they abolish us.

Ibid.

52 The greatest danger of war seems to me not to be in the deliberate actions of wicked men, but in the inability of harassed men to manage events that have run away with them.

HENRY KISSINGER, quoted in *The Middlesex News,* September 22, 1985.

53 One of the miseries of war is that there is no Sabbath, and the current of work and strike has no cessation. How can we be pardoned for all our offenses?

GEN. ROBERT E. LEE, in a letter to his daughter Annie, December 8, 1861.

54 It is well that war is so terrible—we should grow too fond of it.

GEN. ROBERT E. LEE, to James Longstreet at the Battle of Fredericksburg, December 13, 1862.

55 What a cruel thing is war: to separate and destroy families and friends, and mar the purest joys and happiness God has granted us in this world; to fill our hearts with hatred instead of love for our neighbors, and to devastate the fair face of this beautiful world!

GEN. ROBERT E. LEE, in a letter to his wife, December 25, 1862.

56 He had grown up in a country run by politicians who sent the pilots to man the bombers to kill the babies to make the world safer for children to grow up in.

URSULA K. LE GUIN, *The Lathe of Heaven,* 1971.

57 The question so often asked, "Would the survivors envy the dead?" may turn out to have a simple answer. No, they would be incapable of such feel-

ings. They would not so much envy as, inwardly and outwardly, resemble the dead.

ROBERT JAY LIFTON AND KAI ERIKSON, "Nuclear War's Effect on the Mind," in the *New York Times,* March 15, 1982.

58 I don't think old men ought to promote wars for young men to fight. I don't like warlike old men.

WALTER LIPPMANN, in a television interview, May, 1961, quoted in Ronald Steel, *Walter Lippmann and the American Century,* 1980.

59 Ef you take a sword an' dror it,
    An' go stick a feller thru,
Guv'ment ain't to answer for it,
    God'll send the bill to you.

Ez fer war, I call it murder—
    Ther you hev it plain and flat;
I don't want to go no furder
    Than my Testyment fer that. . . .

JAMES RUSSELL LOWELL, *The Biglow Papers,* First Series, 1848.

60 I know war as few other men now living know it, and nothing to me is more revolting. I have long advocated its complete abolition, as its very destructiveness on both friend and foe has rendered it useless as a method of settling international disputes.

GEN. DOUGLAS MACARTHUR, in a speech to Congress, April 19, 1951.

61 War's very object is victory, not prolonged indecision. In war there is no substitute for victory.

GEN. DOUGLAS MACARTHUR, in his address to a joint session of Congress, April 19, 1951.

62 I listen vainly, but with thirsty ear, for the witching melody of faint bugles blowing reveille, of far drums beating the long roll. In my dreams I hear again the crash of guns, the rattle of musketry, the strange, mournful mutter of the battlefield.

GEN. DOUGLAS MACARTHUR, in speech at West Point, May 12, 1962.

63 Now deeper roll the maddening drums,
    And the mingling host like ocean heaves;

While from the midst a horrid wailing
    comes,
  And high above the fight the lonely bugle
    grieves!

> GRENVILLE MELLEN, "Ode on the Celebration of
> the Battle of Bunker Hill," June 17, 1825.

64 There is no record in history of a nation that
ever gained anything valuable by being unable to
defend itself.

> H.L. MENCKEN, *Prejudices,* Fifth Series, 1926.

65 War is the only sport that is genuinely amusing.
And it is the only sport that has any intelligible use.

> Ibid.

66 Preparation for war is a constant stimulus to
suspicion and ill will.

> JAMES MONROE, on the signing of the
> Rush-Bagot Convention, April 28, 1818. (The
> agreement called for the mutual demilitarization of
> the Great Lakes by the U.S. and Great Britain.)

67 The muffled drum's sad roll has beat
    The soldier's last tattoo;
  No more on Life's parade shall meet
    That brave and fallen few.
  On Fame's eternal camping-ground
    Their silent tents are spread,
  And Glory guards, with solemn round,
    The bivouac of the dead.

> THEODORE O'HARA, "The Bivouac of the
> Dead," 1847.

68 Wars may be fought with weapons, but they are
won by men. It is the spirit of the men who follow
and of the man who leads that gains the victory.

> GEN. GEORGE S. PATTON, in the *Cavalry
> Journal,* September, 1933.

69 A pint of sweat will save a gallon of blood.

> GEN. GEORGE S. PATTON, in a message to his
> troops en route to North Africa, October, 1942.

70 Battle is the most magnificent competition in
which a human being can indulge. It brings out all
that is best; it removes all that is base. All men are
afraid in battle. The coward is the one who lets his
fear overcome his sense of duty. Duty is the essence
of manhood.

> GEN. GEORGE S. PATTON, in a message to his
> troops, 1943.

71 The only war I ever approved of was the Trojan
War; it was fought over a woman and the men
knew what they were fighting for.

> WILLIAM LYON PHELPS, in a sermon in
> Riverside Church, New York City, June 25,
> 1933.

72 The surest way to prevent war is not to fear it.

> JOHN RANDOLPH, speaking in the House of
> Representatives, March 5, 1806.

73 As a woman I can't go to war, and I refuse to
send anyone else.

> JEANNETTE RANKIN, quoted in Hannah
> Josephson, *Jeannette Rankin: First Lady in
> Congress,* 1974.

74 You can no more win a war than you can win
an earthquake.

> Ibid.

75 War means an ugly mob-madness, crucifying
the truthtellers, choking the artists, sidetracking
reforms, revolutions, and the working of social
forces.

> JOHN REED, "Whose War?" published in the
> *Masses,* April, 1917.

76 Great horror as war itself is, every honest soldier
knows that it has its moments of joy—joy in the
fellowship of one's fighting comrades, joy and pride
in the growth of a fighting spirit and the conviction
of invincibility that shines out of the faces of well-
led and well-disciplined troops; and the small but
treasured joy of a warm fire and a plain hot meal
at the end of a cold and difficult day.

> GEN. MATTHEW B. RIDGWAY, *The Korean
> War,* 1967.

77 I have seen war. I have seen war on land and
sea. I have seen blood running from the wounded.
I have seen men coughing out their gassed lungs.
I have seen the dead in the mud. I have seen
cities destroyed. . . . I have seen children starving.

I have seen the agony of mothers and wives. I hate war.

> FRANKLIN D. ROOSEVELT, in a speech at Chautauqua, New York, August 14, 1936.

78 The epidemic of world lawlessness is spreading. . . . War is a contagion.

> FRANKLIN D. ROOSEVELT, in a speech in Chicago, October 5, 1937.

79 War is not merely justifiable, but imperative, upon honorable men, upon an honorable nation, where peace can only be obtained by the sacrifice of conscientious conviction or of national welfare.

> THEODORE ROOSEVELT, in his annual message to Congress, December 4, 1906.

80 A just war is in the long run far better for a nation's soul than the most prosperous peace obtained by acquiescence in wrong or injustice. Moreover, though it is criminal for a nation not to prepare for war, so that it may escape the dreadful consequences of being defeated in war, yet it must always be remembered that even to be defeated in war may be far better than not to have fought at all.

> Ibid.

81 A really great people, proud and high-spirited, would face all the disasters of war rather than purchase that base prosperity which is bought at the price of national honor.

> THEODORE ROOSEVELT, in an address at Harvard University, February 23, 1907.

82 Sometime they'll give a war and nobody will come.

> CARL SANDBURG, *The People, Yes*, 1936.

83 To call war the soil of courage and virtue is like calling debauchery the soil of love.

> GEORGE SANTAYANA, *The Life of Reason*, 1905–1906.

84 If the people raise a great howl against my barbarity and cruelty, I will answer that war is war, and not popularity-seeking.

> GEN. WILLIAM T. SHERMAN, in a letter to Gen. Henry W. Halleck, September 4, 1864.

85 You cannot qualify war in harsher terms than I will. War is cruelty, and you cannot refine it.

> GEN. WILLIAM T. SHERMAN, in a letter to James M. Calhoun and others, Atlanta, Georgia, September 12, 1864. (Calhoun, mayor of Atlanta, headed a group that had asked Sherman to rescind his order for the evacuation of the city.)

86 There is many a boy here today who looks on war as all glory, but, boys, it is all hell. You can bear this warning voice to generations yet to come. I look upon war with horror.

> GEN. WILLIAM T. SHERMAN, in a speech before the Grand Army of the Republic Convention, August 11, 1880.

87 War crushes with bloody heel all justice, all happiness, all that is God-like in man. In our age there can be no peace that is not honorable; there can be no war that is not dishonorable.

> CHARLES SUMNER, in a speech, "The True Grandeur of Nations," Boston, July 4, 1845.

88 The four great motives which move men to social activity are hunger, love, vanity, and fear of superior powers. If we search out the causes which have moved men to war we find them under each of these motives or interests.

> WILLIAM GRAHAM SUMNER, "War," in *War and Other Essays*, 1911.

89 War and revolution never produce what is wanted, but only some mixture of the old evils with new ones; what is wanted is a peaceful and rational solution of problems and situations—but that requires great statesmanship and great popular sense and virtue. In the past the work has been done by war and revolution, with haphazard results and great attendant evils.

> Ibid.

90 If you want a war, nourish a doctrine. Doctrines are the most fearful tyrants to which men ever are subject, because doctrines get inside of a man's own reason and betray him against himself. Civilized men have done their fiercest fighting for doctrines.

> Ibid.

91 There is no state of readiness for war; the notion calls for never-ending sacrifices. . . . A wiser rule would be to make up your mind soberly what you want, peace or war, and then to get ready for what you want; for what we prepare for is what we shall get.

Ibid.

92 War, undertaken even for justifiable purposes, such as to punish aggression in Korea, has often had the principal results of wrecking the country intended to be saved and spreading death and destruction among an innocent civilian population.

ROBERT A. TAFT, *A Foreign Policy for Americans,* 1951.

93 Far from establishing liberty throughout the world, war has actually encouraged and built up the development of dictatorships and has only restored liberty in limited areas at the cost of untold hardship, of human suffering, of death and destruction beyond the conception of our fathers.

Ibid.

94 The soldier is applauded who refuses to serve in an unjust war by those who do not refuse to sustain the unjust government which makes the war; is applauded by those whose own act and authority he disregards and sets at naught; as if the State were penitent to that degree that it hired one to scourge it while it sinned, but not to that degree that it left off sinning for a moment.

HENRY DAVID THOREAU, "Civil Disobedience," 1849.

95 O Lord our God, help us to tear their soldiers to bloody shreds with our shells; help us to cover their smiling fields with the pale forms of their patriot dead; help us to drown the thunder of the guns with the shrieks of their wounded, writhing in pain. . . . For our sakes who adore Thee, Lord, blast their hopes, blight their lives, protract their bitter pilgrimage, make heavy their steps, water their way with tears, stain the white snow with the blood of their wounded feet!

MARK TWAIN, "The War Prayer," written in 1905 but publication delayed to 1923.

96 That no man should scruple, or hesitate a moment to use arms in defense of so valuable a blessing [as freedom], on which all the good and evil of life depends, is clearly my opinion; yet arms . . . should be the last resource.

GEORGE WASHINGTON, in a letter to George Mason, April 5, 1769.

97 My first wish is to see this plague to mankind banished from off the earth, and the sons and daughters of this world employed in more pleasing and innocent amusements, than in preparing implements and exercising them for the destruction of mankind.

GEORGE WASHINGTON, in a letter to David Humphrey, July 25, 1785.

98 The friends of humanity will deprecate war, wheresoever it may appear; and we have experienced enough of its evil in this country to know that it should not be wantonly or unnecessarily entered upon.

GEORGE WASHINGTON, in a letter to the merchants and traders of Philadelphia, May 17, 1793.

99 I believe it [the Mexican War] to be a war of pretexts, a war in which the true motive is not distinctly avowed, but in which pretenses, afterthoughts, evasions and other methods are employed to put a case before the community which is not the true case.

DANIEL WEBSTER, in a speech in Springfield, Massachusetts, September 29, 1847.

100 There comes a time in every battle—in every war—when both sides become discouraged by the seemingly endless requirement for more effort, more resources, and more faith. At this point the side which presses on with renewed vigor is the one to win.

GEN. WILLIAM C. WESTMORELAND, speaking at the Honolulu Conference, February, 1966.

101 As the soldier prays for peace he must be prepared to cope with the hardships of war and to bear its scars.

GEN. WILLIAM C. WESTMORELAND, *A Soldier Reports,* 1976.

102 Away with themes of war! Away with war
  itself!
  Hence from my shuddering sight to never
    more return that show of blacken'd,
    mutilated corpses!
  That hell unpent and raid of blood, fit for
    wild tigers or for lop-tongued wolves,
    not reasoning men.

> WALT WHITMAN, "Song of the Exposition,"
> 1871.

103   Soldier, be strong, who fightest
    Under a Captain stout;
  Dishonor not thy conquering Head
    By basely giving out.
  Endure a while, bear up,
  And hope for better things.
  War ends in peace, and morning light
    Mounts upon midnight's wings.

> MICHAEL WIGGLESWORTH, *Meat Out of the
> Eater,* 1670.

246. GEORGE WASHINGTON

See also AMERICAN REVOLUTION;
PRESIDENTS

1 There has scarcely appeared a really great man
whose character has been more admired in his lifetime, or less correctly understood by his admirers.

> FISHER AMES, "Eulogy on Washington," address
> delivered in Boston, February 8, 1800.

2 His example: *that* let us endeavor, by delineat-
ing, to impart to mankind. Virtue will place it in
her temple, Wisdom in her treasury.

> Ibid.

3 The father of his country.

> FRANCIS BAILEY, caption under the portrait of
> Washington, in the *Nord Americanische
> Kalender,* Lancaster, Pennsylvania, 1779.

4 The head of Washington hangs in my dining-
room for a few days past, and I cannot keep my eyes
off of it. It has a certain Appalachian strength, as

if it were truly the first-fruits of America, and expressed the Country. The heavy, leaden eyes turn
on you, as the eyes of an ox in a pasture. And the
mouth has gravity and depth of quiet, as if this
MAN had absorbed all the serenity of America,
and left none for his restless, rickety, hysterical
countrymen.

> RALPH WALDO EMERSON, entry written in 1852,
> *Journals,* 1909–1914.

5 The character, the counsels, the example of our
Washington . . . will guide us through the doubts
and difficulties that beset us; they will guide our
children and our children's children in the paths of
prosperity and peace.

> EDWARD EVERETT, "Washington Abroad and at
> Home," a speech in Boston, July 5, 1858.

6 Here [in Europe] you would know, and enjoy,
what posterity will say of Washington. For 1000
leagues have nearly the same effect with 1000 years.

> BENJAMIN FRANKLIN, in a letter to George
> Washington, from Paris, March 5, 1780.

7 His memory will be adored while liberty shall
have votaries, his name will triumph over time and
will in future ages assume its just station among the
most celebrated worthies of the world.

> THOMAS JEFFERSON, on George Washington, in
> *Notes on the State of Virginia,* 1784.

8 [Washington] errs as other men do, but errs with
integrity.

> THOMAS JEFFERSON, in a letter to William B.
> Giles, December 31, 1795.

9 His mind was great and powerful, without being
of the very first order; his penetration strong,
though not so acute as that of a Newton, Bacon, or
Locke; and as far as he saw, no judgment was ever
sounder. It was slow in operation, being little aided
by invention or imagination, but sure in conclusion.

> THOMAS JEFFERSON, in a letter to Walter Jones,
> January 2, 1814.

10 He was incapable of fear, meeting personal dangers with the calmest unconcern. Perhaps the
strongest feature in his character was prudence,
never acting until every circumstance, every consid-

eration, was maturely weighed. . . . His integrity was most pure, his justice the most inflexible I have ever known, no motives of interest or consanguinity, of friendship, or hatred, being able to bias his decision. He was, indeed, in every sense of the words, a wise, a good, and a great man.

Ibid.

11 On the whole his character was, in its mass, perfect, in nothing bad, in few points indifferent; and it may truly be said that never did nature and fortune combine more perfectly to make a man great.

Ibid.

12 First in war, first in peace, first in the hearts of his countrymen.

HENRY "LIGHT-HORSE HARRY" LEE, in a eulogy in the House of Representatives, December 26, 1799.

13 Washington is the mightiest name of earth— *long since* mightiest in the cause of civil liberty; *still* mightiest in moral reformation. On that name an eulogy is expected. It cannot be. To add brightness to the sun, or glory to the name of Washington, is alike impossible. Let none attempt it. In solemn awe pronounce the name, and in its naked deathless splendor, leave it shining on.

ABRAHAM LINCOLN, in an address in Springfield, Illinois, February 22, 1842.

14 That nation has not lived in vain which has given the world Washington and Lincoln, the best great men and the greatest good men whom history can show.

HENRY CABOT LODGE, in a speech to the Massachusetts Legislature, February 12, 1909.

15 Firmly erect, he towered above them all,
The incarnate discipline that was to free
With iron curb that armed democracy.

JAMES RUSSELL LOWELL, on Washington, in "Under the Old Elm," from "Three Memorial Poems," 1875.

16 O, Washington! thou hero, patriot sage,
Friend of all climes, and pride of every age!

Attributed to Thomas Paine.

17 The character and services of this gentleman are sufficient to put all those men called kings to shame. While they are receiving from the sweat and labors of mankind a prodigality of pay to which neither their abilities nor their services can entitle them, he is rendering every service in his power, and refusing every precuniary reward. He accepted no pay as commander-in-chief; he accepts none as President of the United States.

THOMAS PAINE, *The Rights of Man,* 1791–1792.

18 As to you, sir, treacherous to private friendship (for so you have been to me, and that in the day of danger) and a hypocrite in public life, the world will be puzzled to decide whether you are an apostate or an impostor, whether you have abandoned good principles or whether you ever had any.

THOMAS PAINE, referring to what he saw as Washington's abandonment of Paine to imprisonment in France, 1793–1794, in a letter to Washington, July 30, 1796.

19 Sit down, Mr. Washington; your modesty is equal to your valor, and that surpasses the power of any language that I possess.

JOHN ROBINSON, seeing that Washington could not find words after hearing himself praised in the Virginia House of Burgesses, 1759.

20 There were features in his face totally different from what I had observed in any other human being. . . . All his features were indicative of the strongest passions; yet like Socrates his judgment and self-command made him appear a man of different cast in the eyes of the world.

GILBERT STUART, c.1797, quoted in James Thomas Flexner, *Gilbert Stuart,* 1955.

21 G. Washington was about the best man this world ever sot eyes on. He was a clear-heded, warm-harted, and stiddy goin man. He never slopt over! The prevailin weakness of most public men is to SLOP OVER! . . . Washington never slopt over. That wasn't George's stile. He luved his country dearly. He wasn't after the spiles. He was a human angil in a 3 kornered hat and knee britches.

ARTEMUS WARD, "Fourth of July Oration," *Artemus Ward, His Book,* 1862.

George Washington: from Farewell Address, September 17, 1796

Certainly the most quoted American political document, the Farewell Address is remembered today chiefly for its remarks about America's role in international affairs. An extract is given here.

Friends and Fellow Citizens:

The period for a new election of a citizen to administer the executive government of the United States being not far distant, and the time actually arrived when your thoughts must be employed in designating the person who is to be clothed with that important trust, it appears to me proper, especially as it may conduce to a more distinct expression of the public voice, that I should now apprise you of the resolution I have formed to decline being considered among the number of those out of whom a choice is to be made.

I beg you, at the same time, to do me the justice to be assured that this resolution has not been taken without a strict regard to all the considerations appertaining to the relation which binds a dutiful citizen to his country; and that, in withdrawing the tender of service which silence in my situation might imply, I am influenced by no diminution of zeal for your future interest, no deficiency of grateful respect for your past kindness. . . .

The great rule of conduct for us, in regard to foreign nations, is in extending our commercial relations to have with them as little political connection as possible. So far as we have already formed engagements, let them be fulfilled with perfect good faith. Here let us stop.

Europe has a set of primary interests which to us have none, or a very remote relation. Hence she must be engaged in frequent controversies, the causes of which are essentially foreign to our concerns. Hence, therefore, it must be unwise in us to implicate ourselves, by artificial ties, in the ordinary vicissitudes of her politics or the ordinary combinations and collisions of her friendships or enmities.

Our detached and distant situation invites and enables us to pursue a different course. If we remain one people, under an efficient government, the period is not far off when we may defy material injury from external annoyance; when we may take such an attitude as will cause the neutrality we may at any time resolve upon to be scrupulously respected; when belligerent nations, under the impossibility of making acquisitions upon us, will not lightly hazard the giving us provocation; when we may choose peace or war, as our interest guided by our justice shall counsel.

Why forgo the advantages of so peculiar a situation? Why quit our own to stand upon foreign ground? Why, by interweaving our destiny with that of any part of Europe, entangle our peace and prosperity in the toils of European ambition, rivalship, interest, humor, or caprice?

It is our true policy to steer clear of permanent alliances with any portion of the foreign world. So far, I mean, as we are now at liberty to do it, for let me not be understood as capable of patronizing infidelity to existing engagements (I hold the maxim no less applicable to public than to private affairs that honesty is always the best policy). I repeat it, therefore: let those engagements be observed in their genuine sense. But, in my opinion, it is unnecessary and would be unwise to extend them.

Taking care always to keep ourselves, by suitable establishments, on a respectably defensive posture, we may safely trust to temporary alliances for extraordinary emergencies.

Harmony, liberal intercourse with all nations are recommended by policy, humanity, and interest. But even our commercial policy should hold an equal and impartial hand, neither seeking nor granting exclusive favors or preferences; consulting the natural course of things; diffusing and diversifying by gentle means the streams of commerce but forcing nothing; establishing with powers so disposed, in order to give to trade a stable course, to define the rights of our merchants, and to enable the government to support them, conventional rules of intercourse, the best that present circumstances and mutual opinion will permit, but temporary and liable to be from time to time abandoned or varied, as experience and circumstances shall dictate; constantly keeping in view that it is folly in one nation to look for disinterested favors from another; that it must pay with a portion of its independence for whatever it may accept under that character; that, by such acceptance, it may place itself in the condition of having given equivalents for nominal favors and yet of being reproached with ingratitude for not giving more. There can be no greater error than to expect, or calculate, upon real favors from nation to nation. It is an illusion which experience must cure, which a just pride ought to discard.

In offering to you, my countrymen, these counsels of an old and affectionate friend, I dare not hope they will make the strong and lasting impression I could wish; that they will control the usual current of the passions or prevent our nation from running the course which has hitherto marked the destiny of nations. But if I may even flatter myself that they may be productive of some partial benefit, some occasional good; that they may now and then recur to moderate the fury of party-spirit, to warn against the mischiefs of foreign intrigue, to guard against the impostures of pretended patriotism, this hope will be a full recompense for the solicitude for your welfare by which they have been dictated.

In relation to the still subsisting war in Europe, my proclamation of the 22nd of April, 1793, is the index to my plan. Sanctioned by your approving voice and by that of your representatives in both houses of Congress, the spirit of that measure has continually governed me—uninfluenced by any attempts to deter or divert me from it.

After deliberate examination with the aid of the best lights I could obtain, I was well satisfied that our country, under all the circumstances of the case, had a right to take, and was bound in duty and interest to take, a neutral position. Having taken it, I determined, as far as should depend upon me, to maintain it, with moderation, perseverance, and firmness. . . .

The inducements of interest for observing that conduct will best be referred to your own reflections and experience. With me, a predominant motive has been to endeavor to gain time to our country to settle and mature its yet recent institutions, and to progress without interruption to that degree of strength and consistency which is necessary to give it, humanly speaking, the command of its own fortune.

Though, in reviewing the incidents of my administration, I am unconscious of intentional error, I am nevertheless too sensible of my defects not to think it probable that I may have committed many errors. Whatever they may be, I fervently beseech the Almighty to avert or mitigate the evils to which they may tend. I shall also carry with me the hope that my country will never cease to view them with indulgence, and that, after forty-five years of my life dedicated to its service, with an upright zeal, the faults of incompetent abilities will be consigned to oblivion as myself must soon be to the mansions of rest.

Relying on its kindness in this as in other things, and actuated by that fervent love toward it which is so natural to a man who views in it the native soil of himself and his progenitors for several generations, I anticipate with pleasing expectations that retreat in which I promise myself to realize, without alloy, the sweet enjoyment of partaking, in the midst of my fellow citizens, the benign influence of good laws under a free government, the ever favorite object of my heart, and the happy reward, as I trust, of our mutual cares, labors, and dangers.

22 If I should conceive myself in a manner constrained to accept, I call Heaven to witness, that this very act [acceptance of the presidency] would be the greatest sacrifice of my personal feelings and wishes that ever I have been called upon to make.

> GEORGE WASHINGTON, referring to the Presidency, in a letter to Benjamin Lincoln, October 26, 1788.

23 My movements to the chair of Government will be accompanied by feelings not unlike those of a culprit who is going to the place of his execution.

> GEORGE WASHINGTON, in a letter to Henry Knox, April 1, 1789.

24 Among the vicissitudes incident to life no event could have filled me with greater anxieties than that of which the notification was transmitted by your order.... The magnitude and difficulty of the trust to which the voice of my country called me, being sufficient to awaken in the wisest and most experienced of her citizens a distrustful scrutiny into his qualifications, could not but overwhelm with despondence one, who, inheriting inferior endowments from nature and unpracticed in the duties of civil administration, ought to be peculiarly conscious of his own deficencies.

> GEORGE WASHINGTON, in his election to the presidency, in his first inaugural address, April 30, 1789.

25 America has furnished to the world the character of Washington. And if our American institutions had done nothing else, that alone would have entitled them to the respect of mankind.

> DANIEL WEBSTER, in his address on completion of Bunker Hill Monument, June 17, 1843.

26 Looking at his father with the sweet face of youth brightened with the inexpressible charm of all-conquering truth, he bravely cried out, "I can't tell a lie, Pa; you know I can't tell a lie. I did cut it with my hatchet."

> MASON LOCKE WEEMS, the apocryphal cherry tree story, in the fifth edition of *The Life and Memorable Actions of George Washington,* 1806.

27 The indomitable heart and arm—proofs of
the never-broken line,

Courage, alertness, patience, faith, the same
—e'en in defeat defeated not, the same.

> WALT WHITMAN, "Washington's Monument, February, 1885," *November Boughs,* 1888.

28 The real Washington was as thoroughly an American as Jackson or Lincoln. What we take for lack of passion in him was but the reserve and self-mastery natural to a man of his class and breeding in Virginia. He was no parlor politician, either. He had seen the frontier, and far beyond it where the French forts lay. He knew the rough life of the country as few other men could. His thoughts did not live at Mount Vernon. He knew difficulty as intimately and faced it always with as quiet a mastery as William the Silent.

> WOODROW WILSON, *Mere Literature,* 1896.

---

247. WASHINGTON, D.C.

---

1 Justitia omnibus. (Justice for all.)

> Official motto.

2 The United States is the only great country in the world which has no capital. . . . By Capital I mean a city which is not only the seat of political government, but is also by the size, wealth, and character of its people the head and center of its country.

> JAMES BRYCE, *The American Commonwealth,* 1888.

3 There are a number of things wrong with Washington. One of them is that everyone has been too long away from home.

> Attributed to Dwight D. Eisenhower, Presidential press conference, May 11, 1955. (This quotation is not in the official transcript in Eisenhower's Public Papers.)

4 Washington, where an insignificant individual may trespass on a nation's time.

> RALPH WALDO EMERSON, "Social Aims," *Uncollected Lectures,* 1932.

5 The cocktail party remains a vital Washington institution, the official intelligence system.

BARBARA HOWAR, *Laughing All the Way*, 1973.

6 [In Washington] is to be seen in constant whirl the balance-wheel, such as it is, of the most complicated political machine on earth.

ALEXANDER MACKAY, *The Western World*, 1849.

7 Washington is, for one thing, the news capital of the world. And for another, it is a company town. Most of the interesting people in Washington either work for the government or write about it.

SALLY QUINN, *We're Going to Make You a Star*, 1975.

8 Washington isn't a city, it's an abstraction.

DYLAN THOMAS, in an interview, quoted in John Malcolm Brinnin, *Dylan Thomas in America*, 1956.

9 Why, when I think of those multitudes of clerks and congressmen—whole families of them—down there slaving away and keeping the country together, why then I know in my heart there is something so good and motherly about Washington, that grand old benevolent National Asylum for the Helpless.

MARK TWAIN, *The Gilded Age*, 1873.

10 It is easy enough to see why a man goes to the poor house or the penitentiary. It's becawz he can't help it. But why he should woluntarily go and live in Washinton, is intirely beyond my comprehension, and I can't say no fairer nor that.

ARTEMUS WARD, "Interview with the Prince Napoleon," *Artemus Ward, His Book*, 1862.

11 Washington, D.C., is the Capital of "our once happy country"—if I may be allowed to koin a frase! The D.C. stands for Desprit Cusses, a numerosity which abounds here.

ARTEMUS WARD, "Artemus Ward in Washington," *The Works of Artemus Ward*, 1898.

12 A friend of mine says that every man who took office in Washington either grew or swelled, and

when I give a man an office, I watch him carefully to see whether he is swelling or growing.

WOODROW WILSON, in a speech to the National Press Club, Washington, D.C., May 15, 1916.

13 Things get very lonely in Washington sometimes. The real voice of the great people of America sometimes sounds faint and distant in that strange city. You hear politics until you wish that both parties were smothered in their own gas.

WOODROW WILSON, in a speech in St. Louis, Missouri, September 5, 1919.

248. WASHINGTON STATE

1 Alki. (Chinook, "by and by.")

State motto.

2 Rainier, from Puget Sound, is a sight for the gods, and when one looks upon him he feels that he is in the presence of the gods.

PAUL FOUNTAIN, *The Eleven Eaglets of the West*, 1905.

3 When you pick up the [Seattle] newspapers . . . you realize, once and for all, that Seattle is a screwy place, because the papers keep talking Alaska this and Alaska that. Anybody knows that Alaska belongs not all over the morning papers but in geography books. Yet it turns out that Alaska is virtually an outlying ward of Seattle.

GEORGE SESSIONS PERRY, *Cities of America*, 1947.

4 In this city of hills and waterways, surrounded by visible, snowy mountain peaks, it is almost impossible to build a house without a view.

GEORGE SESSIONS PERRY, describing Seattle, in *Cities of America*, 1947.

5 The prairies are all right. The mountains are all right. The forests and the deserts and the clear clean air of the heights, they're all right. But what a bewitching thing is a city of the sea. It was good to be in Seattle—to hear the foghorns on the Sound,

and the deep bellow of departing steamers; to feel the creeping fog all around you, the fog that softens things and makes a velvet trance out of nighttime.

ERNIE PYLE, *Home Country,* 1947.

6 Everybody in Portland is crazy about Portland. They rave about it. They don't like chamber of commerce folders; they don't talk about their industries and their schools and their crops; they roar about what a wonderful place Portland is, just to live in.

Ibid.

7 I remembered Seattle as a town sitting on hills beside a matchless harborage—a little city of space and trees and gardens, its houses matched to such a background. It is no longer so. . . . This Seattle was not something changed that I once knew. It was a new thing. Set down there not knowing it was Seattle, I could not have told where I was. Everywhere frantic growth, a carcinomatous growth.

JOHN STEINBECK, *Travels with Charley,* 1962.

---

249. WEALTH

See also AVARICE; BUSINESS; DEBT; ECONOMICS; MONEY; POVERTY

---

1 Them as has, gits.

Popular saying.

2 He frivols through the livelong day,
    He knows not Poverty, her pinch.
His lot seems light, his heart seems gay,
    He has a cinch.

FRANKLIN P. ADAMS [F.P.A.], "The Rich Man," *The Melancholy Lute,* 1936.

3 Rich, *adj.* Holding in trust and subject to an accounting the property of the indolent, the incompetent, the unthrifty, the envious, and the luckless. That is the view that prevails in the underworld, where the Brotherhood of Man finds its most logical development and candid advocacy. To deni-

zens of the midworld the word means good and wise.

AMBROSE BIERCE, *The Devil's Dictionary,* 1906.

4 The problem of our age is the proper administration of wealth, that the ties of brotherhood may still bind together the rich and poor in harmonious relationship.

ANDREW CARNEGIE, "The Gospel of Wealth," 1889. (The essay was first published under the title "Wealth" in the *North American Review.*)

5 This . . . is held to be the duty of the man of wealth: To set an example of modest, unostentatious living, shunning display or extravagance; to provide moderately for the legitimate wants of those dependent upon him; and, after doing so, to consider all surplus revenues which come to him simply as trust funds.

Ibid.

6 The day is not far distant when the man who dies leaving behind him millions of available wealth, which was free to him to administer during life, will pass away "unwept, unhonored, and unsung," no matter to what uses he leaves the dross which he cannot take with him. Of such as these the public verdict will then be: "The man who dies thus rich dies disgraced."

Ibid.

7 To be prosperous is not to be superior, and should form no barrier between men. Wealth ought not to secure to the prosperous the slightest consideration.

WILLIAM ELLERY CHANNING, *Lectures on the Elevation of the Labouring Portion of the Community,* 1840.

8 Communism is a hateful thing and a menace to peace and organized government; but the communism of combined wealth and capital, the outgrowth of overweening cupidity and selfishness, which insidiously undermines the justice and integrity of free institutions, is not less dangerous than the communism of oppressed poverty and toil.

GROVER CLEVELAND, in his annual message to Congress, December 3, 1888.

9 He mocks the people who proposes that the Government shall protect the rich and that they in turn will care for the laboring poor.

Ibid.

10 It is the right of the possessor of property to be placed on an equal footing with all his fellow citizens, in every respect. If he is not to be exalted on account of his wealth, neither is he to be denounced.

JAMES FENIMORE COOPER, *The American Democrat,* 1838.

11 I am absolutely convinced that no wealth in the world can help humanity forward, even in the hands of the most devoted worker in this cause. The example of great and pure personages is the only thing that can lead us to fine ideas and noble deeds. Money only appeals to selfishness and always irresistibly tempts its owners to abuse it.

ALBERT EINSTEIN, *The World as I See It,* 1934.

12 Ah! if the rich were rich as the poor fancy riches!

RALPH WALDO EMERSON, "Nature," *Essays,* Second Series, 1844.

13 Without a rich heart, wealth is an ugly beggar.

RALPH WALDO EMERSON, "Manners," *Essays,* Second Series, 1844.

14 By right or wrong,
Lands and goods go to the strong.
Property will brutely draw
Still to the proprietor;
Silver to silver creep and wind,
And kind to kind.

RALPH WALDO EMERSON, "Initial Daemonic and Celestial Love," *Poems,* 1847.

15 *Riches.* Neither will poverty suit every complexion. Socrates and Franklin may well go hungry and in plain clothes, if they like; but there are people who cannot afford this, but whose poverty of nature needs wealth of food and clothes to make them decent.

RALPH WALDO EMERSON, entry written in 1849, *Journals,* 1909–1914.

16 Wealth is in applications of mind to nature; and the art of getting rich consists not in industry, much less in saving, but in a better order in timeliness, in being at the right spot.

RALPH WALDO EMERSON, "Wealth," *The Conduct of Life,* 1860.

17 To be rich is to have a ticket of admission to the master-works and chief men of each race.

Ibid.

18 The pulpit and the press have many commonplaces denouncing the thirst for wealth; but if men should take these moralists at their word and leave off aiming to be rich, the moralists would rush to rekindle at all hazards this love of power in the people, lest civilization should be undone.

Ibid.

19 Let me tell you about the very rich. They are different from you and me. They possess and enjoy early, and it does something to them, makes them soft where we are hard, and cynical where we are trustful, in a way that, unless you were born rich, it is very difficult to understand. They think, deep in their hearts, that they are better than we are because we had to discover the compensations and refuges of life for ourselves. Even when they enter deep into our world or sink below us, they still think that they are better than we are. They are different.

F. SCOTT FITZGERALD, "The Rich Boy," in the collection *Babylon Revisited,* 1960.

20 He does not possess wealth; it possesses him.

BENJAMIN FRANKLIN, *Poor Richard's Almanack,* 1734.

21 Wealth is not his that has it, but his that enjoys it.

BENJAMIN FRANKLIN, *Poor Richard's Almanack,* 1736.

22 Now I've a sheep and a cow, every body bids me good-morrow.

Ibid.

23 The Poor have little, Beggars none;
The Rich too much, enough not one.

BENJAMIN FRANKLIN, *Poor Richard's Almanack,*
1740.

24 He who multiplies Riches multiplies Cares.

BENJAMIN FRANKLIN, *Poor Richard's Almanack,*
1744.

25 If your Riches are yours, why don't you take
them with you to t'other World?

BENJAMIN FRANKLIN, *Poor Richard's Almanack,*
1751.

26 Many a Man would have been worse, if his
Estate had been better.

Ibid.

27 Wealth is not without its advantages and the
case to the contrary, although it has often been
made, has never proved widely persuasive.

JOHN KENNETH GALBRAITH, *The Affluent
Society,* 1958.

28 Wealth can be accumulated but to a slight degree, and . . . communities really live, as the vast
majority of individuals live, from hand to mouth.
Wealth will not bear much accumulation; except in
a few unimportant forms it will not keep.

HENRY GEORGE, *Progress and Poverty,* 1879.

29 Nature laughs at a miser. He is like the squirrel
who buries his nuts and refrains from digging them
up again.

Ibid.

30 Great wealth always supports the party in
power, no matter how corrupt it may be. It never
exerts itself for reform, for it instinctively fears
change.

HENRY GEORGE, *Social Problems,* 1884.

31 The ideal social state is not that in which each
gets an equal amount of wealth, but in which each
gets in proportion to his contribution to the general
stock.

Ibid.

32 Their vices are probably more favorable to the
prosperity of the state, than those of the indigent;
and partake less of moral depravity.

ALEXANDER HAMILTON, on the rich, in a speech
at the New York Ratifying Convention,
Poughkeepsie, June 21, 1788.

33 It is almost as difficult to reconcile the principles
of republican society with the existence of billionaires as of dukes.

Attributed to Thomas Wentworth Higginson.

34 It cannot be repeated too often that the safety
of great wealth with us lies in obedience to the new
version of the Old World axiom—*Richesse oblige.*

OLIVER WENDELL HOLMES, SR., *A Mortal
Antipathy,* 1855.

35 There is that glorious Epicurean paradox, uttered by my friend, the Historian, in one of his
flashing moments:—"Give us the luxuries of life,
and we will dispense with its necessaries."

OLIVER WENDELL HOLMES, SR., quoting John
Lothrop Motley, in *The Autocrat of the
Breakfast-Table,* 1858.

36 Wealth: A cunning device of Fate whereby
men are made captive, and burdened with responsibilities from which only Death can file their fetters.

ELBERT HUBBARD, *The Roycroft Dictionary and
Book of Epigrams,* 1923.

37 Few rich men own their own property. The
property owns them.

ROBERT G. INGERSOLL, in a speech in New York
City, October 29, 1896.

38 The opposition between the men who have and
the men who are is immemorial.

WILLIAM JAMES, *The Varieties of Religious
Experience,* 1902.

39 Misplaced emphasis occurs . . . when you think
that everything is going well because your car
drives so smoothly, and your new suit fits you so
well, and those high-priced shoes you bought make
your feet feel so good; and you begin to believe that
these things, these many luxuries all around, are the
really important matters of your life.

MARTIN LUTHER KING, SR., *Daddy King,* 1980.

40 That some should be rich, shows that others may become rich, and, hence, is just encouragement to industry and enterprise.

> ABRAHAM LINCOLN, reply to the New York Workingmen's Association, March 21, 1864.

41 The rich man's son inherits cares;
    The bank may break, the factory burn,
A breath may burst his bubble shares,
    And soft white hands could hardly earn
A living that would serve his turn.

> JAMES RUSSELL LOWELL, "The Heritage," *Poems,* 1843.

42 The most valuable of all human possessions, next to a superior and disdainful air, is the reputation of being well to do.

> H.L. MENCKEN, *Prejudices,* Third Series, 1922.

43 Bankers Are Just Like Anybody Else, Except Richer.

> OGDEN NASH, the title of a poem, in *I'm a Stranger Here Myself,* 1938.

44 Pat and I have the satisfaction that every dime that we've got is honestly ours. I should say this, that Pat doesn't have a mink coat. But she does have a respectable Republican cloth coat, and I always tell her that she would look good in anything.

> RICHARD M. NIXON, in his "Checkers" speech, a reply to the revelation that he had accepted money from wealthy constituents while serving in the U.S. Senate, September 23, 1952.

45 The blind pursuit of wealth, for the sake of hoarding, is a species of insanity. There are spirits, and not the least worthy, who, content with an humble mediocrity, leave the field of wealth and ambition open to more active, perhaps more guilty, competitors. Nothing can be more respectable than the independence that grows out of self-denial.

> JOHN RANDOLPH, in a letter to Theodore Dudley, December 30, 1821.

46 Some men like to stand erect, and some men, even after they are rich and in high place, like to crawl.

THOMAS BRACKETT REED, quoted in Samuel Walker McCall, *The Life of Thomas Brackett Reed,* 1914.

47 God gave me my money.

> JOHN D. ROCKEFELLER, SR., quoted in John Thomas Flynn, *God's Gold: The Story of Rockefeller and His Times,* 1932.

48 In the place of the palace of privilege we seek to build a temple out of faith and hope and charity.

> FRANKLIN D. ROOSEVELT, in his acceptance speech after renomination at the Democratic Party National Convention, Philadelphia, June 27, 1936.

49 This concentration of wealth and power has been built upon other people's money, other people's business, other people's labor. Under this concentration independent business was allowed to exist only by sufferance. It has been a menace to the social system as well as to the economic system which we call American democracy.

> FRANKLIN D. ROOSEVELT, in a campaign speech, October 14, 1936.

50 Probably the greatest harm done by vast wealth is the harm that we of moderate means do ourselves when we let the vices of envy and hatred enter deep into our own natures.

> THEODORE ROOSEVELT, in a speech in Providence, Rhode Island, August 23, 1902.

51 Wealth must justify itself in happiness.

> GEORGE SANTAYANA, *The Life of Reason,* 1905–1906.

52 The reason why I defend the millions of the millionaire is not that I love the millionaire, but that I love my own wife and children, and that I know no way in which to get the defense of society for my hundreds, except to give my help, as a member of society, to protect his millions.

> WILLIAM GRAHAM SUMNER, "The Family and Property," in the *Independent* magazine, June 14 and July 19, 1888.

53 The poor rich man! all he has is what he has bought. What I see is mine.

> HENRY DAVID THOREAU, *A Week on the Concord and Merrimack Rivers,* 1849.

54 None can be an impartial or wise observer of human life but from the vantage ground of what *we* should call voluntary poverty.

HENRY DAVID THOREAU, *Walden,* 1854.

55 A man is rich in proportion to the number of things which he can afford to let alone.

Ibid.

56 Superfluous wealth can buy superfluities only. Money is not required to buy one necessary of the soul.

Ibid.

57 That man is the richest whose pleasures are the cheapest.

HENRY DAVID THOREAU, entry dated March 11, 1856, in his *Journal,* 1906.

58 I know of no country . . . where the love of money has taken stronger hold on the affections of men and where a profounder contempt is expressed for the theory of the permanent equality of property. But wealth circulates with inconceivable rapidity, and experience shows that it is rare to find two succeeding generations in the full enjoyment of it.

ALEXIS DE TOCQUEVILLE, *Democracy in America,* 1835.

59 Prosperity is the surest breeder of insolence I know.

MARK TWAIN, in a letter to the *San Francisco Alta California,* February 23, 1867.

60 Inherited wealth is a big handicap to happiness. It is as certain death to ambition as cocaine is to morality.

WILLIAM K. VANDERBILT, in an interview, 1905.

61 Conspicuous consumption of valuable goods is a means of reputability to the gentleman of leisure.

THORSTEIN VEBLEN, *The Theory of the Leisure Class,* 1899.

62 The people of this country are not jealous of fortunes, however great, which have been built up by the honest development of great enterprises, which have been actually earned by business energy and sagacity; they are jealous only of speculative wealth, of the wealth which has been piled up by no effort at all, but only by shrewd wits playing on the credulity of others, taking advantage of the weakness of others, trading in the necessities of others. This is "predatory wealth."

WOODROW WILSON, "Law or Personal Power," a speech delivered in New York City, April 13, 1908.

250. WEATHER

See also AUTUMN; NATURE; SPRING; SUMMER; WINTER

1 The yellow fog that rubs its back upon the window panes.

T.S. ELIOT, "The Love Song of J. Alfred Prufrock," 1915.

2 The hard soil and four months of snow make the inhabitant of the northern temperate zones wiser and abler than his fellow who enjoys the fixed smile of the tropics.

RALPH WALDO EMERSON, "Prudence," *Essays,* First Series, 1841.

3 Nature seems a dissipated hussy. She seduces us from all work; listen to her rustling leaves—to the invitations which each blue peak and rolling river and fork of woodland road offers—and we should never wield the shovel or the trowel.

RALPH WALDO EMERSON, entry written in 1845, *Journals,* 1909–1914.

4 It ain't a fit night out for man or beast.

W.C. FIELDS, in "The Fatal Glass of Beer," 1933.

5 The fact is, the American climate is thoroughly and irredeemably bad—the very worst in the world . . . and I conceive nothing can make up for this dreadful and important defect.

THOMAS H. JAMES, *Rambles in the United States and Canada During the Year 1845.*

6 I prefer much the climate of the United States to that of Europe. I think it a more cheerful one. It is our cloudless sky which has eradicated from our constitutions all disposition to hang ourselves, which we might otherwise have inherited from our English ancestors.

THOMAS JEFFERSON, in a letter to C.F.C. de Volney, February 8, 1805.

7 Oh, what a blamed uncertain thing
     This pesky weather is!
It blew and snew and then it thew
     And now, by jing, it's friz!

Attributed to Philander Johnson.

8 Every dewdrop and raindrop had a whole heaven within it.

HENRY WADSWORTH LONGFELLOW, *Hyperion*, 1839.

9 How beautiful is the rain!
     After the dust and heat,
     In the broad and fiery street,
     In the narrow lane,
How beautiful is the rain!

HENRY WADSWORTH LONGFELLOW, "Rain in Summer," 1844.

10 When descends on the Atlantic
     The gigantic
Storm-wind of the equinox,
Landward in his wrath he scourges
     The toiling surges,
Laden with seaweed from the rocks.

HENRY WADSWORTH LONGFELLOW, "Seaweed," 1844.

11 Thunders are observed oftener to break upon churches than upon any other buildings.

COTTON MATHER, *The Wonders of the Invisible World,* 1693.

12 Thunderstorms are often caused by Satan, and sometimes by good angels. Thunder is the voice of God, and, therefore, to be dreaded.

INCREASE MATHER, *Remarkable Providences,* 1684.

13 They sicken of the calm, who knew the storm.

DOROTHY PARKER, "Fair Weather," in *Sunset Gun,* 1928.

14 It hain't no use to grumble and complane;
     It's jest as cheap and easy to rejoice.—
When God sorts out the weather and sends rain,
     W'y, rain's my choice.

JAMES WHITCOMB RILEY, "Wet-Weather Talk," 1883.

15 The fog comes
on little cat feet.

It sits looking
over the harbor and city
on silent haunches
and then moves on.

CARL SANDBURG, "Fog," 1916.

16 Thank heavens, the sun has gone in, and I don't have to go out and enjoy it.

LOGAN PEARSALL SMITH, *Afterthoughts,* 1931.

17 There is a sumptuous variety about the New England weather that compels the stranger's admiration—and regret. The weather is always doing something there; always attending strictly to business; always getting up new designs and trying them on the people to see how they will go. But it gets through more business in spring than in any other season. In the spring I have counted one hundred and thirty-six different kinds of weather inside of four-and-twenty hours.

MARK TWAIN, in an after-dinner speech at the New England Society, New York City, December 22, 1876.

18 No weather will be found in this book. This is an attempt to pull a book through without weather. . . . Of course weather is necessary to a narrative of human experience. That is conceded. But it ought to be put where it will not be in the way; where it will not interrupt the flow of the narrative. . . . This weather will be found over in the back part of the book, out of the way. *See Appendix.* The reader is requested to turn over and help himself from time to time as he goes along.

MARK TWAIN, "The Weather in this Book," prefatory note, *The American Claimant,* 1892.

19 Thunder is good, thunder is impressive; but it is lightning that does the work.

MARK TWAIN, in a letter, 1908.

20 Everybody talks about the weather, but nobody does anything about it.

CHARLES DUDLEY WARNER, in an editorial in the *Hartford Courant,* August 24, 1897.

21 I got a letter from a lightning rod company this morning trying to put the fear of God in me, but with small success. Lightning seems to have lost its menace. Compared to what is going on on earth today, heaven's firebrands are penny fireworks with wet fuses.

E.B. WHITE, "Removal," in *One Man's Meat,* 1944.

22 The sun, that brief December day,
Rose cheerless over hills of gray,
And, darkly circled, gave at noon
A sadder light than waning moon.
Slow tracing down the thickening sky
Its mute and ominous prophecy,
A portent seeming less than threat,
It sank from sight before it set.

JOHN GREENLEAF WHITTIER, *Snow-Bound,* 1866.

251. THE WEST

See also individual states

1 Ain't no law west of St. Louis, ain't no God west of Fort Smith [Arkansas].

Saying of nineteenth-century trappers and settlers.

2 Home, home on the range,
Where the deer and the antelope play;
Where seldom is heard a discouraging word,
And the skies are not cloudy all day.

Cowboy song, "Home on the Range," 1873.

3 Oh, bury me not on the lone prairie,
Where the wild coyote will howl over me,
In a narrow grave just six by three,
Oh, bury me not on the lone prairie!

Cowboy song, c.1875.

4 Fifty-four forty, or fight.

Attributed to Sen. William Allen, speaking in the U.S. Senate on the Oregon boundary question, 1844. (Allen was referring to the northern boundary of the Oregon territory, longitude 54° 40′ N, which expansionists sought to establish as the northwestern border between the U.S. and Canada.)

5 Westward the course of empire takes its way;
The four first acts already past,
A fifth shall close the drama with the day:
Time's noblest offspring is the last.

GEORGE BERKELEY, "Verses On the Prospect of Planting Arts and Learning in America," 1752.

6 Nature and Time seem to have conspired to make the development of the Mississippi basin and the Pacific slope the swiftest, easiest, completest achievement in the whole record of the civilizing progress of mankind since the founder of the Egyptian monarchy gathered the tribes of the Nile under one government.

JAMES BRYCE, *The American Commonwealth,* 1888.

7 Out where the handclasp's a little stronger,
Out where the smile dwells a little longer,
That's where the West begins.

ARTHUR CHAPMAN, "Out Where the West Begins," 1917.

8 Where the West begins depends when you asked the question. In the nineteenth century Charles Dickens got no farther than St. Louis, nine hundred miles short even of the Rockies. He went home convinced he had seen the West, and he declared it to be a fraud.

ALISTAIR COOKE, *America,* 1973.

9 The achieved West had given the United States something that no people had ever had before, an internal, domestic empire.

BERNARD DE VOTO, *The Year of Decision,* 1943.

10 Only remember—West of the Mississippi it's a little more look, see, act. A little less rationalize, comment, talk.

> F. Scott Fitzgerald, in a letter to Andrew Turnbull, summer, 1934.

11 In one sense California, Oregon, and Washington are not "the West" at all. In Portland I actually heard a lady say that she was "going West" on a brief trip—and she meant Utah! People on the Pacific Coast think of themselves as belonging to the "coast"; the "West" is quite something else again.

> John Gunther, *Inside U.S.A.,* 1947.

12 Our manifest destiny to overspread the continent allotted by Providence for the free development of our yearly multiplying millions.

> John L. O'Sullivan, in an editorial supporting the annexation of Texas, *United States Magazine and Democratic Review,* July-August, 1845.

13 Go west, young man.

> John L.B. Soule, phrase used in an editorial in the *Terre Haute Express,* 1851. (Horace Greeley was so impressed with the editorial that he reprinted it in the *New York Tribune* and expanded on the phrase: "Go west, young man, and grow up with the country.")

14 What the Mediterranean Sea was to the Greeks, breaking the bond of custom, offering new experiences, calling out new institutions and activities, that the ever retreating Great West has been to the eastern United States directly, and to the nations of Europe more remotely.

> Frederick Jackson Turner, "The Significance of the Frontier in American History," a paper read before the American Historical Association, Chicago, July, 1893.

15 Where population is sparse, where the supports of conventions and of laws are withdrawn and men are thrown upon their own resources, courage becomes a fundamental and essential attribute in the individual. The Western man of the old days had little choice but to be courageous.

> Walter Prescott Webb, *The Great Plains,* 1931.

16 What can we do with the western coast, a coast of 3,000 miles, rockbound cheerless, uninviting, and not a harbor on it? What use have we for such a country? I will never vote one cent from the public treasury to place the Pacific Ocean one inch nearer Boston than it is now.

> Daniel Webster, quoted in Nancy Wilson Ross, *Farthest Reach,* 1944.

17 Come my tan-faced children,
  Follow well in order, get your weapons
    ready,
  Have you your pistols? have you your
    sharp-edged axes?
  Pioneers! O pioneers!

> Walt Whitman, "Pioneers! O Pioneers!", 1865.

---

252. WEST VIRGINIA

---

1 Montani semper liberi. (Mountaineers are always freemen.)

> State motto.

2 Almost Heaven.

> Slogan on West Virginia bumper stickers, c.1976.

3 Here is hard-core unemployment, widespread and chronic; here is a region of shacks and hovels for housing; here are cliffs and ravines without standing room for a cow or chickens. In this region of steep mountains a person is exceptionally fortunate if he is able to hack out two or three ten-foot rows of land for potatoes or beans.

> Erskine Caldwell, describing Mingo, McDowell, and Wyoming counties of West Virginia, in *Around About America,* 1964.

4 Country roads, take me home
  To the place I belong,
  West Virginia, mountain momma
  Take me home, country roads.

> John Denver, Bill Danoff, and Taffy Nivert, "Take Me Home, Country Roads," 1971.

5 The state is one of the most mountainous in the country; sometimes it is called the "little Switzerland" of America, and I once heard an irreverent local citizen call it the "Afghanistan of the United States."

JOHN GUNTHER, *Inside U.S.A.,* 1947.

6 We West Virginians are very tired of being considered inhabitants of just a dominion of the Old Dominion; we would like to make it clear that our state has been independent for ninety years. Some residents take a very strong line about this and always refer to it in conversation as "*West*—By God—Virginia!"

JOHN KNOWLES, "West Virginia," in *American Panorama: East of the Mississippi,* 1960.

7 On the map my state is probably the funniest-looking state in the Union; it resembles a pork chop with the narrow end splayed.

Ibid.

8 Whether or not mountaineers were always free, they were almost always poor.

JOHN ALEXANDER WILLIAMS, *West Virginia,* 1976.

---

253. WINE & SPIRITS

See also DRINKING

---

1 Wine, *n.* Fermented grape-juice known to the Women's Christian Union as "liquor," sometimes as "rum." Wine, madam, is God's next best gift to man.

AMBROSE BIERCE, *The Devil's Dictionary,* 1906.

2 It [corn whiskey] smells like gangrene starting in a mildewed silo, it tastes like the wrath to come, and when you absorb a deep swig of it you have all the sensations of having swallowed a lighted kerosene lamp. A sudden, violent jolt of it has been known to stop the victim's watch, snap his suspenders and crack his glass eye right across.

Attributed to Irvin S. Cobb.

3 A man will be eloquent if you give him good wine.

RALPH WALDO EMERSON, "Montaigne," *Representative Men,* 1850.

4 The advantages of whiskey over dogs are legion. Whiskey does not need to be periodically wormed, it does not need to be fed, it never requires a special kennel, it has no toenails to be clipped or coat to be stripped. Whiskey sits quietly in its special nook until you want it. True, whiskey has a nasty habit of running out, but then so does a dog.

W.C. FIELDS, quoted in Ronald J. Fields, *W.C. Fields by Himself,* 1973.

5 Take counsel in wine, but resolve afterwards in water.

BENJAMIN FRANKLIN, *Poor Richard's Almanack,* 1733.

6 Fill every beaker up, my men, pour forth the
  cheering wine:
There's life and strength in every drop—
  thanksgiving to the vine!

ALBERT GORTON GREENE, "The Baron's Last Banquet," in Edmund Clarence Stedman, *An American Anthology,* 1906.

7 Never delay kissing a pretty girl or opening a bottle of whiskey.

ERNEST HEMINGWAY, quoted in Carlos Baker, *Ernest Hemingway: A Life Story,* 1969.

8 Wine: An infallible antidote to commonsense and seriousness; an excuse for deeds otherwise unforgivable.

ELBERT HUBBARD, *The Roycroft Dictionary and Book of Epigrams,* 1923.

9 Take that liquor away; I never touch strong drink. I like it too well to fool with it.

STONEWALL JACKSON, responding to an offer of a mint julep, quoted by George E. Pickett, in a letter to his wife, June 3, 1864.

10 No nation is drunken where wine is cheap; and none sober where the dearness of wine substitutes ardent spirits as the common beverage. It is, in truth, the only antidote to the bane of whiskey.

THOMAS JEFFERSON, in a letter to M. de
Neuville, December 12, 1818.

11 I like it: I always did, and that is the reason I
never use it.

> Attributed to Robert E. Lee, when advised by his
> physician to drink whiskey, c.1850.

12   This song of mine
        Is a Song of the Vine
      To be sung by the glowing embers
        Of wayside inns,
        When the rain begins
      To darken the drear Novembers.

> HENRY WADSWORTH LONGFELLOW, "Catawba
> Wine," 1854.

13 When you ask one friend to dine,
    Give him your best wine!
    When you ask two,
    The second best will do!

> HENRY WADSWORTH LONGFELLOW, quoted in
> Brander Matthews, *Recreations of an Anthologist,*
> 1896.

14 Candy
      is dandy
    But liquor
      is quicker.

> OGDEN NASH, "Reflection on Ice-Breaking,"
> 1931.

15 I get no kick from champagne.
    Mere alcohol doesn't thrill me at all.

> COLE PORTER, "I Get a Kick Out of You," in
> *Anything Goes,* 1934.

16 It's a naive domestic Burgundy without any
breeding, but I think you'll be amused by its presumption.

> JAMES THURBER, caption for a *New Yorker*
> cartoon, collected in *Men, Women and Dogs,*
> 1944.

17 One of the oldest and quietest roads to contentment lies through the conventional trinity of wine,
woman, and song.

> REXFORD GUY TUGWELL, in a speech at the
> Women's National Democratic Club,
> Washington, D.C., May, 1934.

18 Give an Irishman lager for a month, and he's a
dead man. An Irishman is lined with copper, and
the beer corrodes it. But whiskey polishes the copper and is the saving of him.

> MARK TWAIN, *Life on the Mississippi,* 1883.

---

254. WINTER

See also NATURE; WEATHER

---

1 When the short day is brightest, with frost
        and fire,
    The brief sun flames the ice, on pond and
        ditches,
    In windless cold that is the heart's beat,
    Reflecting in a watery mirror
    A glare that is blindness in the early
        afternoon.

> T.S. ELIOT, "Little Gidding," *Four Quartets,*
> 1943.

2 Announced by all the trumpets of the sky,
    Arrives the snow, and, driving o'er the fields,
    Seems nowhere to alight: the whited air
    Hides hills and woods, the river, and the
        heaven,
    And veils the farm-house at the garden's end.
    The sled and traveler stopped, the courier's
        feet
    Delayed, all friends shut out, the housemates
        sit
    Around the radiant fireplace, enclosed
    In a tumultuous privacy of storm.

> RALPH WALDO EMERSON, "The Snow-Storm,"
> published in *The Dial* magazine, January, 1841.

3 Come see the north wind's masonry.
    Out of an unseen quarry evermore
    Furnished with tile, the fierce artificer
    Curves his white bastions with projected roof
    Round every windward stake, or tree, or
        door. . . .
    And when his hours are numbered, and the
        world
    Is all his own, retiring, as he were not,

Leaves, when the sun appears, astonished Art
To mimic in slow structures, stone by stone,
Built in an age, and mad wind's night-work,
The frolic architecture of the snow.

> Ibid.

4 An hour of winter day might seem too short
To make it worth life's while to wake and
sport.

> ROBERT FROST, "A Winter Eden," in
> *West-Running Brook,* 1928.

5 Through woods and mountain passes
The winds, like anthems, roll.

> HENRY WADSWORTH LONGFELLOW, "Midnight
> Mass for the Dying Year," 1839.

6 Oh the long and dreary Winter!
Oh the cold and cruel Winter!

> HENRY WADSWORTH LONGFELLOW, *The Song of
> Hiawatha,* 1855.

7 There seems to be so much more winter than we
need this year.

> KATHLEEN NORRIS, *Bread into Roses,* 1936.

8 Winter is icumen in,
Lhude sing Goddamm,
Raineth drop and staineth slop
And how the wind doth ramm!
Sing: Goddamm.

> EZRA POUND, "Ancient Music," parody of the
> 13th-century "Cuckoo Song": Sumer is icumen in,
> Lhude sing cuccu! Groweth sed, and bloweth
> med, And springth the wude nu.

9 Such is a winter eve. Now for a merry fire, some
old poet's pages, or else serene philosophy, or even
a healthy book of travels to last far into the night,
eked out perhaps with the walnuts which we gathered in November.

> HENRY DAVID THOREAU, entry dated December
> 9, 1856, in his *Journal,* 1906.

10 Unwarmed by any sunset light
The gray day darkened into night,
A night made hoary with the swarm
And whirl-dance of the blinding storm,

As zigzag, wavering to and fro,
Crossed and recrossed the winged snow.

> JOHN GREENLEAF WHITTIER, *Snow-Bound,*
> 1866.

11 We looked upon a world unknown,
On nothing we could call our own.
Around the glistening wonder bent
The blue walls of the firmament,
No cloud above, no earth below,—
A universe of sky and snow!

> JOHN GREENLEAF WHITTIER, *Snow-Bound,*
> 1866.

255. WISCONSIN

1 Forward.

> State motto.

2 Wisconsin is the soul of a great people. She mani-
fests the spirit of the conqueror, whose strength has
subdued the forest, quickened the soil, harnessed
the forces of Nature and multiplied production.
From her abundance she serves food to the world.

> FRED L. HOLMES, *Old World Wisconsin,* 1944.

3 Wisconsin's politics have traditionally been uproar politics—full of the yammer, the squawk, the
accusing finger, the injured howl. Every voter is an
amateur detective, full of zeal to get out and nip a
little political iniquity in the bud.

> GEORGE SESSIONS PERRY, *Cities of America,* 1947.

4 I had heard of the Wisconsin Dells but was not
prepared for the weird country sculptured by the
Ice Age, a strange, gleaming country of water and
carved rock, black and green. To awaken here
might make one believe it a dream of some other
planet, for it has a non-earthly quality, or else the
engraved record of a time when the world was
much younger and much different.

> JOHN STEINBECK, *Travels with Charley,* 1962.

5 By cheese factories and creameries they direct the
stranger in rural Wisconsin, for cheese factories

and creameries are the most striking landmarks of that country. His most striking impression is that the entire landscape of southern Wisconsin is as picturesquely suggestive of dairying as the skyline of Pittsburgh is of the steel industry.

Frank Parker Stockbridge, "The Grand Old Man of Wisconsin," in *The World's Work* magazine, January, 1913.

256. WISDOM

See also Advice; Education; Experience; Folly; Knowledge; Perception; Philosophy

1 God pity the man or the nation wise in proverbs ... for there is much error gone into the collecting of such a store.

Kenneth Burke, *Towards a Better Life,* 1932.

2 The invariable mark of wisdom is to see the miraculous in the common.

Ralph Waldo Emerson, *Nature,* 1836.

3 Nothing astonishes men so much as common sense and plain dealing.

Ralph Waldo Emerson, "Art," *Essays,* First Series, 1841.

4 Much of the wisdom of the world is not wisdom, and the most illuminating class of men are no doubt superior to literary fame and are not writers.

Ralph Waldo Emerson, "The Over-Soul," *Essays,* First Series, 1841.

5 To finish the moment, to find the journey's end in every step of the road, to live the greatest number of good hours, is wisdom.

Ralph Waldo Emerson, "Experience," *Essays,* Second Series, 1844.

6 The wise through excess of wisdom is made a fool.

Ibid.

7 Wisdom attempts nothing enormous and disproportioned to its powers, nothing which it cannot perform or nearly perform.

Ralph Waldo Emerson, "The Conservative," *Nature; Addresses and Lectures,* 1849.

8 There needs but one wise man in a company and all are wise, so rapid is the contagion.

Ralph Waldo Emerson, "Uses of Great Men," *Representative Men,* 1850.

9 Some are weatherwise, some are otherwise.

Benjamin Franklin, *Poor Richard's Almanack,* 1735.

10 Of learned Fools I have seen ten times ten,
Of unlearned wise men I have seen a
    hundred.

Ibid.

11 Tim was so learned, that he could name a Horse in nine Languages. So ignorant that he bought a Cow to ride on.

Benjamin Franklin, *Poor Richard's Almanack,* 1750.

12 Where Sense is wanting, every thing is wanting.

Benjamin Franklin, *Poor Richard's Almanack,* 1754.

13 The Doors of Wisdom are never shut.

Benjamin Franklin, *Poor Richard's Almanack,* 1755.

14 Bromidic though it may sound, some questions *don't* have answers, which is a terribly difficult lesson to learn.

Katharine Graham, quoted by Jane Howard in *Ms.* magazine, October, 1974.

15 A thought is often original, though you have uttered it a hundred times.

Oliver Wendell Holmes, Sr., *The Autocrat of the Breakfast-Table,* 1858.

16 Wit throws a single ray, separated from the rest—red, yellow, blue, or any intermediate shade—upon an object; never white light; that is the province of wisdom.

Ibid.

17 Why can't somebody give us a list of things that everybody thinks and nobody says, and another list of things that everybody says and nobody thinks?

> OLIVER WENDELL HOLMES, SR., *The Professor at the Breakfast-Table,* 1860.

18 It is the province of knowledge to speak, and it is the privilege of wisdom to listen.

> OLIVER WENDELL HOLMES, SR., *The Poet at the Breakfast-Table,* 1872.

19 Common sense is compelled to make its way without the enthusiasm of anyone; all admit it grudgingly.

> EDGAR WATSON HOWE, *The Indignations of E.W. Howe,* 1933.

20 Wisdom: A term Pride uses when talking of Necessity.

> ELBERT HUBBARD, *The Roycroft Dictionary and Book of Epigrams,* 1923.

21 Wise Man: One who sees the storm coming before the clouds appear.

> Ibid.

22 To know when to be generous and when firm—this is wisdom.

> Ibid.

23 Every man is a damn fool for at least five minutes every day. Wisdom consists in not exceeding the limit.

> Ibid.

24 The art of being wise is the art of knowing what to overlook.

> WILLIAM JAMES, *The Principles of Psychology,* 1890.

25 The wise know too well their weakness to assume infallibility; and he who knows most, knows best how little he knows.

> THOMAS JEFFERSON, in a legal brief, July 31, 1810.

26 Every man's own reason must be his oracle.

> THOMAS JEFFERSON, in a letter to Dr. Benjamin Rush, March 6, 1813.

27 God, give us the serenity to accept what
>> cannot be changed;
> Give us the courage to change what should
>> be changed;
> Give us the wisdom to distinguish one from
>> the other.

> REINHOLD NIEBUHR, "Serenity Prayer," 1951. (Various versions had earlier gained currency.)

28 Knowledge is the treasure, but judgment the treasurer of a wise man. He that has more knowledge than judgment is made for another man's use more than his own.

> WILLIAM PENN, *Some Fruits of Solitude,* 1693.

29 Nine-tenths of wisdom consists in being wise in time.

> THEODORE ROOSEVELT, in a speech in Lincoln, Nebraska, June 14, 1917.

30 Wisdom comes by disillusionment.

> GEORGE SANTAYANA, *The Life of Reason,* 1905–1906.

31 Knowledge alone is not enough. It must be leavened with magnanimity before it becomes wisdom.

> ADLAI E. STEVENSON, *Call to Greatness,* 1954.

32 The fickle person is he that does not know what is true or right absolutely—who has not an ancient wisdom for a lifetime—but a new prudence for every hour.

> HENRY DAVID THOREAU, entry dated May 6, 1841, in his *Journal,* 1906.

33 In general we must have a catholic and universal wisdom—wiser than any particular—and be prudent enough to defer to it always. We are literally wiser than we know. Men do not fail for want of knowledge—but for want of prudence to give wisdom the preference.

> Ibid.

34 The wisest man preaches no doctrines; he has no scheme; he sees no rafter, not even a cobweb, against the heavens. It is clear sky.

> HENRY DAVID THOREAU, *A Week on the Concord and Merrimack Rivers,* 1849.

35 A man is wise with the wisdom of his time only, and ignorant with its ignorance.

> HENRY DAVID THOREAU, entry dated January 31, 1853, in his *Journal*, 1906.

36 It is a characteristic of wisdom not to do desperate things.

> HENRY DAVID THOREAU, *Walden*, 1854.

37 A grain of gold will gild a great surface, but not so much as a grain of wisdom.

> HENRY DAVID THOREAU, "Life Without Principle," published posthumously in the *Atlantic Monthly*, October, 1863.

38 Behold, the fool saith, "Put not all thine eggs in the one basket"—which is but a manner of saying, "Scatter your money and your attention"; but the wise man saith, "Put all your eggs in the one basket and—WATCH THAT BASKET."

> MARK TWAIN, "Pudd'nhead Wilson's Calendar," *Pudd'nhead Wilson*, 1894.

39 Here is the test of wisdom,
Wisdom is not finally tested in schools,
Wisdom cannot be pass'd from one having it
  to another not having it,
Wisdom is of the soul, is not susceptible of
  proof, is its own proof,
Applies to all stages and objects and qualities
  and is content,
Is the certainty of the reality and immortality
  of things, and the excellence of things.

> WALT WHITMAN, "Song of the Open Road," 1856.

40 Oh, thriftlessness of dream and guess!
Oh, wisdom which is foolishness!
Why idly seek from outward things
The answer inward silence brings?
Why stretch beyond our proper sphere
And age, for that which lies so near?

> JOHN GREENLEAF WHITTIER, "Questions of Life," 1852.

257. WOMAN

See also DIVORCE; FAMILY; HUMANKIND; MAN; MARRIAGE; WOMEN'S RIGHTS

1 Men of sense in all ages abhor those customs which treat us only as the vassals of your sex.

> ABIGAIL ADAMS, in a letter to John Adams, March 31, 1776.

2 I regret the trifling narrow contracted education of the females of my own country.

> ABIGAIL ADAMS, in a letter to John Adams, June 30, 1778.

3 Whenever serious intellectuals—psychologists, sociologists, practicing physicians, Nobel Prize novelists—take time off from their more normal pursuits to scrutinize and appraise the Modern American Woman they turn in unanimously dreary reports. They find her uninformed, intellectually lazy, lacking in ambition, and disgustingly docile in the presence of dominating males.

> GRACE ADAMS, in *Harper's Magazine*, March, 1939.

4 I must not write a word to you about politics, because you are a woman.

> JOHN ADAMS, in a letter to Abigail Adams, February 13, 1779.

5 Divination seems heightened and raised to its highest power in woman.

> A. BRONSON ALCOTT, *Concord Days*, 1872.

6 Where women are, the better things are implied if not spoken.

> A. BRONSON ALCOTT, "Conversation," *Table Talk*, 1877.

7 When a woman ceases to alter the fashion of her hair, you guess that she has passed the crisis of her experience.

> MARY AUSTIN, *The Land of Little Rain*, 1903.

8 Woman's great mission is to train immature, weak, and ignorant creatures to obey the laws of God.

CATHARINE ESTHER BEECHER, *Woman Suffrage,* 1871.

9 A woman absent is a woman dead.

AMBROSE BIERCE, line under the definition of "absent," *The Devil's Dictionary,* 1906.

10 Femininity appears to be one of those pivotal qualities that are so important no one can define it.

CAROLINE BIRD, *Born Female,* 1968.

11 Let Greeks be Greeks, and women what they are.

ANNE BRADSTREET, *The Tenth Muse,* 1650.

12 The basic discovery about any people is the discovery of the relationship between its men and women.

PEARL S. BUCK, *Of Men and Women,* 1941.

13 No lady is ever a gentleman.

JAMES BRANCH CABELL, *Something About Eve,* 1927.

14 "Why do
You thus devise
Evil against her?" "For that
She is beautiful, delicate.
Therefore."

ADELAIDE CRAPSEY, "Susanna and the Elders," *Verse,* 1915.

15 A lady is one who never shows her underwear unintentionally.

LILLIAN DAY, *Kiss and Tell,* 1931.

16 Some women are like Pompeii; some are like Verdun; some are like Kokomo, Ind., on a Sunday afternoon.

BENJAMIN DE CASSERES, *Fantasia Impromptu: The Adventures of an Intellectual Faun,* 1937.

17 A pessimist is a man who thinks all women are bad. An optimist is one who hopes they are.

Attributed to Chauncey M. Depew.

18 What soft, cherubic creatures
These gentlewomen are!
One would as soon assault a plush
Or violate a star.

EMILY DICKINSON, "What Soft, Cherubic Creatures," in *Poems,* Third Series, 1896.

19 No woman has ever told the truth of her life. The autobiographies of most famous women are a series of accounts of the outward existence, of petty details and anecdotes which give no realization of their real life. For the great moments of joy or agony they remain strangely silent.

ISADORA DUNCAN, *My Life,* 1927.

20 Women have a less accurate measure of time than men. There is a clock in Adam: none in Eve.

RALPH WALDO EMERSON, entry written February 8, 1836, *Journals,* 1909–1914.

21 A beautiful woman is a picture which drives all beholders nobly mad.

RALPH WALDO EMERSON, "Art," *Essays,* First Series, 1841.

22 A beautiful woman is a practical poet, taming her savage mate, planting tenderness, hope, and eloquence in all whom she approaches.

RALPH WALDO EMERSON, "Beauty," *The Conduct of Life,* 1860.

23 A sufficient measure of civilization is the influence of good women.

RALPH WALDO EMERSON, "Civilization," *Society and Solitude,* 1870.

24 Women, despite the fact that nine out of ten of them go through life with a death-bed air either of snatching-the-last-moment or with martyr-resignation, do not die tomorrow—or the next day. They have to live on to any one of many bitter ends.

ZELDA FITZGERALD, "Eulogy on the Flapper," in the *Metropolitan* magazine, June, 1922.

25 There is hardly such a thing to be found as an old woman who is not a good woman.

BENJAMIN FRANKLIN, in a letter to a young man, June 25, 1745.

26 Women like to sit down with trouble as if it were knitting.

ELLEN GLASGOW, *The Sheltered Life,* 1932.

27 There is no sea-wave without salt;
There is no woman without fault.

> JOHN HAY, *Castilian Days,* 1871.

28 Plain women know more about men than beautiful ones do.

> KATHARINE HEPBURN, quoted by Charles Higham in *Kate,* 1975.

29 The typical American woman is not, and never has been, a beer-drinking or a wine-drinking woman; and to this fact mainly we attribute her wealth of loveliness.

> JOSIAH GILBERT HOLLAND *Every-Day Topics,* First Series, 1876.

30 Man has his will—but woman has her way!

> OLIVER WENDELL HOLMES, SR., *The Autocrat of the Breakfast-Table,* 1858.

31 Nature is in earnest when she makes a woman.

> Ibid.

32 The brain-women never interest us like the heart-women; white roses please less than red.

> OLIVER WENDELL HOLMES, SR., *The Professor at the Breakfast-Table,* 1860.

33 I LOVE YOU is all the secret that many, nay, most women have to tell. When that is said, they are like China-crackers on the morning of the fifth of July.

> Ibid.

34 Women rather take to terrible people; prize-fighters, pirates, highwaymen, rebel generals, Grand Turks, and Bluebeards generally have a fascination for the sex; your virgin has a natural instinct to saddle your lion.

> OLIVER WENDELL HOLMES, SR., *The Guardian Angel,* 1867.

35 A woman never forgets her sex. She would rather talk with a man than an angel, any day.

> OLIVER WENDELL HOLMES, SR., *The Poet at the Breakfast-Table,* 1872.

36 There never lived a woman who did not wish she were a man. There never lived a man who wished he were a woman.

> EDGAR WATSON HOWE, *Country Town Sayings,* 1911.

37 Even the proudest of women are willing to accept orders when the time is ripe; and I am fully convinced that to be domineered over by the right man is a thing all good women warmly desire.

> ELBERT HUBBARD, *The Roycroft Dictionary and Book of Epigrams,* 1923.

38 The blaming of woman for all the ills of the world is the crowning blunder of certain creeds.

> Ibid.

39 When a woman works, she gets a woman's wage; but when she sins she gets a man's pay—and then some.

> Ibid.

40 To know the right woman is a liberal education.

> Ibid.

41 Young women with ambitions should be very crafty and cautious, lest mayhap they be caught in the soft, silken mesh of a happy marriage, and go down to oblivion, dead to the world.

> Ibid.

42 Women are all alike in this: they are all different, and most of them are different every hour.

> Ibid.

43 A woman is known by the man she keeps.

> Ibid.

44 If it was woman who put man out of Paradise it is still woman, and woman only, who can lead him back.

> Ibid.

45 I had rather live with the woman I love in a world full of trouble, than to live in heaven with nobody but men.

> ROBERT G. INGERSOLL, "Liberty of Man, Woman and Child," an address given in Troy, New York, December 17, 1877.

46 There is in every true woman's heart a spark of heavenly fire which lies dormant in the broad day-

light of prosperity; but which kindles up, and beams and blazes in the dark hour of adversity.

> WASHINGTON IRVING, "The Wife," *The Sketch Book,* 1819–1820.

47 A woman's whole life is a history of the affections.

> WASHINGTON IRVING, "The Broken Heart," *The Sketch Book,* 1819–1820.

48 I believe that all women, but especially housewives, tend to think in lists. . . . The idea of a series of items, following one another docilely, forms the only possible reasonable approach to life if you have to live it with a home and a husband and children, none of whom would dream of following one another docilely.

> SHIRLEY JACKSON, *Life Among the Savages,* 1953.

49 In those days, it didn't matter: you could be a Wimbledon champion, Phi Beta Kappa, Miss America, Nobel Peace Prize winner, but if they asked you about marriage and you didn't at least have a hot prospect ready to get down on one knee, you knew you were considered to be no more than half a woman.

> BILLIE JEAN KING, in *Billie Jean,* 1982.

50 The woman was not taken
  From Adam's head, we know,
To show she must not rule him—
  'Tis evidently so.

The woman she was taken
  From under Adam's arm,
So she must be protected
  From injuries and harm.

> ABRAHAM LINCOLN, "Adam and Eve's Wedding Song," written before 1830.

51 By and large, mothers and housewives are the only workers who do not have regular time off. They are the great vacationless class.

> ANNE MORROW LINDBERGH, *Gift from the Sea,* 1955.

52 Standing with reluctant feet,
  Where the brook and river meet.
Womanhood and childhood fleet!

> HENRY WADSWORTH LONGFELLOW, "Maidenhood," 1841.

53 As unto the bow the cord is,
  So unto the man is woman;
Though she bends him, she obeys him,
Though she draws him, yet she follows;
Useless each without the other!

> HENRY WADSWORTH LONGFELLOW, *The Song of Hiawatha,* 1855.

54 Do I not know
The life of woman is full of woe?
Toiling on and on and on,
With breaking heart, and tearful eyes,
And silent lips, and in the soul
The secret longings that arise,
Which this world never satisfies!
Some more, some less, but of the whole
Not one quite happy, no, not one!

> HENRY WADSWORTH LONGFELLOW, *The Golden Legend,* 1872.

55 Beautiful in form and feature,
  Lovely as the day,
Can there be so fair a creature
  Formed of common clay?

> HENRY WADSWORTH LONGFELLOW, "The Masque of Pandora," 1875.

56 When you educate a man you educate an individual; when you educate a woman you educate a whole family.

> Attributed to Charles D. McIver, in a speech at North Carolina College for Women.

57 Ah, wonderful women! Just give me a comfortable couch, a dog, a good book, and a woman. Then if you can get the dog to go somewhere and read the book, I might have a little fun!

> GROUCHO MARX, in a comedy routine he performed for men and women serving in World War II, c.1943.

58 Women hate revolutions and revolutionists. They like men who are docile, and well-regarded at the bank, and never late at meals.

> H.L. MENCKEN, *Prejudices,* Fourth Series, 1924.

59 When women kiss it always reminds one of prize-fighters shaking hands.

> H.L. MENCKEN, "Sententiae," from *The Vintage Mencken*, 1955.

60 All elegant women have acquired a technique of weeping which has no . . . fatal effect on the makeup.

> ANAÏS NIN, *Winter of Artifice*, 1939.

61 What I consider my weaknesses are feminine traits: incapacity to destroy, ineffectualness in battle.

> ANAÏS NIN, entry dated January, 1943, in *The Diary of Anaïs Nin*, Vol. III, 1969.

62 Prince, a precept I'd leave for you,
> Coined in Eden, existing yet:
> Skirt the parlor, and shun the zoo—
> Women and elephants never forget.

> DOROTHY PARKER, *Death and Taxes*, 1931.

63 He may go forward like a stoic Roman
> Where pangs and terrors in his pathway lie—
> Or, seizing the swift logic of a woman,
> Curse God and die.

> EDWIN ARLINGTON ROBINSON, "The Man Against the Sky," 1916.

64 Though nowadays he's not so much for
> women:
> "So few of them," he says, "are worth the
> guessing."

> EDWIN ARLINGTON ROBINSON, "Ben Jonson Entertains a Man from Stratford," 1916.

65 I never expected to see the day when the girls would get sunburned in the places they do now.

> Attributed to Will Rogers.

66 Biological *possibility* and desire are not the same as biological *need*. Women have child-bearing equipment. For them to choose not to use the equipment is no more blocking what is instinctive than it is for a man who, muscles or no, chooses not to be a weightlifter.

> BETTY ROLLIN, "Motherhood: Who Needs It?" *Look* magazine, May 16, 1971.

67 Women have crucified the Mary Wollstone-crafts, the Fanny Wrights, and the George Sands of all ages. Men mock us with the fact and say we are ever cruel to each other.

> ELIZABETH CADY STANTON, in a letter to Lucretia Mott, April 1, 1872.

68 A mind always in contact with children and servants, whose aspirations and ambitions rise no higher than the roof that shelters it, is necessarily dwarfed in its proportions.

> ELIZABETH CADY STANTON, *History of Woman Suffrage*, with Susan B. Anthony and Mathilda Gage, 1881.

69 Some of us are becoming men we wanted to marry.

> Attributed to Gloria Steinem.

70 A liberated woman is one who has sex before marriage and a job after.

> GLORIA STEINEM, quoted in *Newsweek* magazine, March 28, 1960.

71 I have met brave women who are exploring the outer edge of human possibility, with no history to guide them, and with a courage to make themselves vulnerable that I find moving beyond the words to express it.

> GLORIA STEINEM, in *Ms.* magazine, April, 1972.

72 Women may be the one group that grows more radical with age.

> GLORIA STEINEM, in *Ms.* magazine, September, 1979.

73 Childbirth is more admirable than conquest, more amazing than self-defense, and as courageous as either one.

> GLORIA STEINEM, in *Ms.* magazine, April, 1981.

74 In the East, women religiously conceal that they have faces; in the West, that they have legs. In both cases they make it evident that they have but little brains.

> HENRY DAVID THOREAU, entry dated January 31, 1852, in his *Journal*, 1906.

75 From birth to age eighteen, a girl needs good parents. From eighteen to thirty-five, she needs

good looks. From thirty-five to fifty-five, she needs a good personality. From fifty-five on, she needs good cash.

> Attributed to Sophie Tucker.

76 They say that man is mighty,
   He governs land and sea,
   He wields a mighty scepter
   O'er lesser powers that be;
   But a mightier power and stronger
   Man from his throne has hurled,
   For the hand that rocks the cradle
   Is the hand that rules the world.

> WILLIAM ROSS WALLACE, "The Hand That Rocks the Cradle," c.1866.

77 The female woman is one of the greatest institooshuns of which this land can boste.

> ARTEMUS WARD, "Woman's Rights," *Artemus Ward, His Book,* 1862.

78 She was born to make hash of men's buzzums & other wimin mad.

> ARTEMUS WARD, "Piccolomini," *Artemus Ward, His Book,* 1862.

79 The world is full of care, much like unto a bubble;
   Women and care, and care and women, and women and care and trouble.

> NATHANIEL WARD, *The Simple Cobler of Aggawam in America,* 1647.

80 Mrs. Ballinger is one of the ladies who pursue Culture in bands, as though it were dangerous to meet it alone.

> EDITH WHARTON, in *Xingu and Other Stories,* 1916.

81 The dream of the American male is for a female who has an essential languor which is not laziness, who is unaccompanied except by himself, and who does not let him down. He desires a beautiful, but comprehensible, creature who does not destroy a perfect situation by forming a complete sentence.

> E.B. WHITE, "Notes on our Times," *The Second Tree from the Corner,* 1954.

82 Be not ashamed, women, your privilege
      encloses the rest and is the exit of the
      rest,
   You are the gates of the body, and you are
      the gates of the soul.

> WALT WHITMAN, "I Sing the Body Electric," 1855.

83 A man is a great thing upon the earth and
      through eternity, but every jot of the
      greatness of man is unfolded out of
      woman;
   First the man is shaped in the woman, he can
      then be shaped in himself.

> WALT WHITMAN, "Unfolded Out of the Folds," 1856.

84 Women sit or move to and fro, some old,
      some young,
   The young are beautiful—but the old are
      more beautiful than the young.

> WALT WHITMAN, "Beautiful Women," 1860.

85 Oh, woman wronged can cherish hate
   More deep and dark than manhood may!

> JOHN GREENLEAF WHITTIER, "Mogg Megone," 1836.

86 The sweetest woman ever Fate
   Perverse denied a household mate,
   Who, lonely, homeless, not the less
   Found peace in love's unselfishness,
   And welcome wheresoe'er she went.

> JOHN GREENLEAF WHITTIER, *Snow-Bound,* 1866.

87 Love and grief and motherhood,
      Fame and mirth and scorn—
   These are all shall befall
      Any woman born.

> MARGARET WIDDEMER, "A Cyprian Woman."

88 I was, being human, born alone;
   I am, being woman, hard beset;
   I live by squeezing from a stone
   The only nourishment I get.

> ELINOR WYLIE, "Let No Charitable Hope," 1923.

89 In a thousand of her [the 20th-century American mother] there is not sex appeal enough to budge a hermit ten paces off a rock ledge.

PHILIP WYLIE, *Generation of Vipers,* 1942.

258. WOMEN'S RIGHTS

See also DIVORCE; EQUALITY; FAMILY;
MARRIAGE; WOMAN

1 In the new code of laws which I suppose it will be necessary for you to make I desire you would remember the ladies and be more generous and favorable to them than your ancestors.

ABIGAIL ADAMS, in a letter to John Adams, March 31, 1776.

2 Do not put such unlimited power into the hands of the husbands. Remember all men would be tyrants if they could. If particular care and attention is not paid to the ladies we are determined to foment a rebellion, and will not hold ourselves bound by any laws in which we have no voice, or representation.

Ibid.

3 I believe that it is as much a right and duty for women to do something with their lives as for men and we are not going to be satisfied with such frivolous parts as you give us.

LOUISA MAY ALCOTT, *Rose in Bloom,* 1876.

4 Men their rights and nothing more; women their rights and nothing less.

SUSAN B. ANTHONY, motto of the women's suffrage newspaper *The Revolution,* 1868.

5 Join the union, girls, and together say *Equal Pay for Equal Work.*

SUSAN B. ANTHONY, in *The Revolution,* March 18, 1869.

6 Woman must not depend upon the protection of man, but must be taught to protect herself.

SUSAN B. ANTHONY, in a speech in San Francisco, July, 1871.

7 Within the stable economy it's necessary to eliminate all forms of sexual discrimination, and to provide women for the first time in our history with economic opportunities equal to those of men.

JIMMY CARTER, in a speech at the Women's Agenda Conference, Washington, D.C., October 2, 1976.

8 Sensible and responsible women do not want to vote. The relative positions to be assumed by man and woman in the working out of our civilization were assigned long ago by a higher intelligence than ours.

GROVER CLEVELAND, in the *Ladies' Home Journal,* April, 1905.

9 Every argument for the emancipation of the colored man was equally one for that of women; and I was surprised that all Abolitionists did not see the similarity in the condition of the two classes.

EMILY COLLINS, quoted in Elizabeth Cady Stanton, Susan B. Anthony, and Mathilda Gage, *History of Woman Suffrage,* 1881.

10 Women have made enormous strides in the last decade, but they still do not seem to understand what a power they could be if they took more interest in government on all levels. If they realized how much government affected their lives and those of their children, they could not resist having a stronger voice in the affairs of the nation, the states and their home communities. We are not a minority but we still are treated as though we were one, and a small one at that.

INDIA EDWARDS, *Pulling No Punches,* 1977.

11 The problem that has no name—which is simply the fact that American women are kept from growing to their full human capacities—is taking a far greater toll on the physical and mental health of our country than any known disease.

BETTY FRIEDAN, *The Feminine Mystique,* 1963.

12 A girl should not expect special privileges because of her sex, but neither should she "adjust" to prejudice and discrimination. She must learn to compete then, not as a woman, but as a human being.

Ibid.

13 A woman is handicapped by her sex, and handicaps society, either by slavishly copying the pattern of man's advance in the professions, or by refusing to compete with man at all. But with the vision to make a new like plan of her own, she can fulfill a commitment to profession and politics, and to marriage and motherhood with equal seriousness.

Ibid.

14 Ye cannot believe it, men; but the only reason why women ever assume what is more appropriate to you is because you prevent them from finding out what is fit for themselves.

MARGARET FULLER, in an untitled essay collected in Alice Rossi, *The Feminist Papers,* 1973.

15 If men could get pregnant, abortion would be a sacrament.

FLORYNCE R. KENNEDY, quoted by Gloria Steinem in *Ms.* magazine, March, 1973.

16 If people believed that women crack under pressure when men don't, they'd believe that women as a group are not as capable or as gutsy as men. I just had to win.

BILLIE JEAN KING, on her tennis match with Bobby Riggs, quoted in *American Way* magazine, June, 1974.

17 I go for all sharing the privileges of the government who assist in bearing its burdens. Consequently, I go for admitting all whites to the right of suffrage who pay taxes or bear arms (by no means excluding females).

ABRAHAM LINCOLN, in a letter to the *Sangamon Journal,* New Salem, Illinois, June 13, 1836.

18 Male supremacy has kept her [woman] down. It has not knocked her out.

CLARE BOOTHE LUCE, in the *Saturday Review/World,* August 24, 1974.

19 Suddenly enfranchised, hastily given the keys of all cities and all liberties, women resemble one of the new states created after a war. We have not owned our freedom long enough to know exactly how it should be used.

PHYLLIS MCGINLEY, *The Province of the Heart,* 1959.

20 It is of very doubtful value to enlist the gifts of women if bringing women into fields that have been defined as male frightens the men, unsexes the women, muffles and distorts the contribution women could make, either because their presence excludes men from the occupation or because it changes the quality of the men who enter it.

MARGARET MEAD, *Male and Female,* 1948.

21 The male form of a female liberationist is a male liberationist—a man who realizes the unfairness of having to work all his life to support a wife and children so that someday his widow may live in comfort, a man who points out that commuting to a job he doesn't like is just as oppressive as his wife's imprisonment in a suburb, a man who rejects his exclusion, by society and most women, from participation in childbirth and the engrossing, delightful care of young children—a man, in fact, who wants to relate himself to people and the world around him as a person.

MARGARET MEAD, in *Redbook* magazine, August, 1975.

22 Women's chains have been forged by men, not by anatomy.

ESTELLE R. RAMEY, in *The First Ms. Reader,* 1972.

23 The equal rights of women have but just reached the region of possibilities. Men have only just left off sneering and have but just begun to consider. Every step of progress from the harem and the veil to free society and property holding has been steadily fought by the vanity, selfishness and indolence, not only of mankind but of womankind also.

THOMAS BRACKETT REED, quoted in Samuel Walker McCall, *The Life of Thomas Brackett Reed,* 1914.

24 The pitfall of the feminist is the belief that the interests of men and women can ever be severed; that what brings sufferings to the one can leave the other unscathed.

AGNES REPPLIER, *Points of Friction,* 1920.

Seneca Falls Declaration on Women's Rights, July 19, 1848

Echoing the Declaration of Independence, the ringing Declaration on Women's Rights launched the feminist movement in the United States. The first national convention of women, held at Seneca Falls, New York, was organized by two famous abolitionists, Lucretia Mott and Elizabeth Cady Stanton, who had been denied their rights to participate fully in antislavery conventions.

When, in the course of human events, it becomes necessary for one portion of the family of man to assume among the people of the earth a position different from that which they have hitherto occupied, but one to which the laws of nature and of nature's God entitle them, a decent respect to the opinions of mankind requires that they should declare the causes that impel them to such a course.

We hold these truths to be self-evident: that all men and women are created equal; that they are endowed by their Creator with certain inalienable rights; that among these are life, liberty, and the pursuit of happiness; that to secure these rights governments are instituted, deriving their just powers from the consent of the governed. Whenever any form of government becomes destructive of these ends, it is the right of those who suffer from it to refuse allegiance to it, and to insist upon the institution of a new government, laying its foundation on such principles, and organizing its powers in such form, as to them shall seem most likely to effect their safety and happiness.

Prudence, indeed, will dictate that governments long established should not be changed for light and transient causes; and, accordingly, all experience has shown that mankind are more disposed to suffer, while evils are sufferable, than to right themselves by abolishing the forms to which they were accustomed. But when a long train of abuses and usurpations, pursuing invariably the same object, evinces a design to reduce them under absolute despotism, it is their duty to throw off such government and to provide new guards for their future security. Such has been the patient sufferance of the women under this government, and such is now the necessity which constrains them to demand the equal station to which they are entitled.

The history of mankind is a history of repeated injuries and usurpations on the part of man toward woman, having in direct object the establishment of an absolute tyranny over her. To prove this, let facts be submitted to a candid world.

He has never permitted her to exercise her inalienable right to the elective franchise.

He has compelled her to submit to laws in the formation of which she had no voice.

He has withheld from her rights which are given to the most ignorant and degraded men, both natives and foreigners.

Having deprived her of this first right of a citizen, the elective franchise, thereby leaving her without representation in the halls of legislation, he has oppressed her on all sides.

He has made her, if married, in the eye of the law, civilly dead.

He has taken from her all right in property, even to the wages she earns.

He has made her, morally, an irresponsible being, as she can commit many crimes with impunity, provided they be done in the presence of her husband. In the covenant of marriage, she is compelled to promise obedience to her husband, he becoming, to all intents and purposes, her master—the law giving him power to deprive her of her liberty and to administer chastisement.

He has so framed the laws of divorce, as to what shall be the proper causes and, in case of separation, to whom the guardianship of the children shall be given, as to be wholly regardless of the happiness of women—the law, in all cases, going upon a false supposition of the supremacy of man and giving all power into his hands.

After depriving her of all rights as a married woman, if single and the owner of property, he has taxed her to support a government which recognizes her only when her property can be made profitable to it.

He has monopolized nearly all the profitable employments, and from those she is permitted to follow, she receives but a scanty remuneration. He closes against her all the avenues to wealth and distinction which he considers most honorable to himself. As a teacher of theology, medicine, or law, she is not known.

He has denied her the facilities for obtaining a thorough education, all colleges being closed against her.

He allows her in church, as well as state, but a subordinate position, claiming apostolic authority for her exclusion from the ministry, and, with some exceptions, from any public participation in the affairs of the church.

He has created a false public sentiment by giving to the world a different code of morals for men and women, by which moral delinquencies which exclude women from society are not only tolerated but deemed of little account in man.

He has usurped the prerogative of Jehovah himself, claiming it as his right to assign for her a sphere of action, when that belongs to her conscience and to her God.

He has endeavored, in every way that he could, to destroy her confidence in her own powers, to lessen her self-respect, and to make her willing to lead a dependent and abject life.

Now, in view of this entire disfranchisement of one-half the people of this country, their social and religious degradation, in view of the unjust laws above mentioned, and because women do feel themselves aggrieved, oppressed, and fraudulently deprived of their most sacred rights, we insist that they have immediate admission to all the rights and privileges which belong to them as citizens of the United States.

In entering upon the great work before us, we anticipate no small amount of misconception, misrepresentation, and ridicule; but we shall use every instrumentality within our power to effect our object. We shall employ agents, circulate tracts, petition the state and national legislatures, and endeavor to enlist the pulpit and the press in our behalf. We hope this Convention will be followed by a series of conventions embracing every part of the country.

RESOLUTIONS

Whereas, the great precept of nature is conceded to be that "man shall pursue his own true and substantial happiness." Blackstone in his *Commentaries* remarks that this law of nature, being coeval with mankind and dictated by God himself, is, of course, superior in obligation to any other. It is binding over all the globe, in all countries and at all times; no human laws are of any validity if contrary to this, and such of them as are valid derive all their force, and all their validity, and all their authority, mediately and immediately, from this original; therefore,

Resolved, That such laws as conflict, in any way, with the true and substantial happiness of woman, are contrary to the great precept of nature and of no validity, for this is "superior in obligation to any other."

Resolved, that all laws which prevent woman from occupying such a station in society as her conscience shall dictate, or which place her in a position inferior to that of man, are contrary to the great precept of nature and therefore of no force or authority.

Resolved, that woman is man's equal, was intended to be so by the Creator, and the highest good of the race demands that she should be recognized as such.

Resolved, that the women of this country ought to be enlightened in regard to the laws under which they live, that they may no longer publish their degradation by declaring themselves satisfied with their present position, nor their ignorance, by asserting that they have all the rights they want.

Resolved, that inasmuch as man, while claiming for himself intellectual superiority, does accord to woman moral superiority, it is preeminently his duty to encourage her to speak and teach, as she has an opportunity, in all religious assemblies.

Resolved, that the same amount of virtue, delicacy, and refinement of behavior that is required of woman in the social state should also be required of man, and the same transgressions should be visited with equal severity on both man and woman.

Resolved, that the objection of indelicacy and impropriety, which is so often brought against woman when she addresses a public audience, comes with a very ill grace from those who encourage, by their attendance, her appearance on the stage, in the concert, or in feats of the circus.

Resolved, that woman has too long rested satisfied in the circumscribed limits which corrupt customs and a perverted application of the Scriptures have marked out for her, and that it is time she should move in the enlarged sphere which her great Creator has assigned her.

Resolved, that it is the duty of the women of this country to secure to themselves their sacred right to the elective franchise.

Resolved, that the equality of human rights results necessarily from the fact of the identity of the race in capabilities and responsibilities.

Resolved, that the speedy success of our cause depends upon the zealous and untiring efforts of both men and women for the overthrow of the monopoly of the pulpit, and for the securing to woman an equal participation with men in the various trades, professions, and commerce.

Resolved, therefore, that, being invested by the Creator with the same capabilities and the same consciousness of responsibility for their exercise, it is demonstrably the right and duty of woman, equally with man, to promote every righteous cause by every righteous means; and especially in regard to the great subjects of morals and religion, it is self-evidently her right to participate with her brother in teaching them, both in private and in public, by writing and by speaking, by any instrumentalities proper to be used, and in any assemblies proper to be held; and this being a self-evident truth growing out of the divinely implanted principles of human nature, any custom or authority adverse to it, whether modern or wearing the hoary sanction of antiquity, is to be regarded as a self-evident falsehood, and at war with mankind.

25 The single most impressive fact about the attempt by American women to obtain the right to vote is how long it took.

> ALICE ROSSI, *The Feminist Papers,* 1973.

26 The claim that American women are downtrodden and unfairly treated is the fraud of the century.

> PHYLLIS SCHLAFLY, quoted in *Ms.* magazine, March, 1974.

27 We hold these truths to be self-evident, that all men and women are created equal.

> ELIZABETH CADY STANTON, at the first Woman's Rights Convention, Seneca Falls, New York, July 19–20, 1848.

28 Resolved, That it is the duty of the women of this country to secure to themselves their sacred right to the elective franchise.

> Ibid.

29 Woman's degradation is in man's idea of his sexual rights. Our religion, laws, customs, are all founded on the belief that woman was made for man.

> ELIZABETH CADY STANTON, in a letter to Susan B. Anthony, June 14, 1860.

30 The prolonged slavery of women is the darkest page in human history.

> ELIZABETH CADY STANTON, *History of Woman Suffrage,* 1881.

31 The only trouble with sexually liberating women is that there aren't enough sexually liberated men to go around.

> GLORIA STEINEM, in *Esquire* magazine, 1962.

32 I can sometimes deal with men as equals and therefore can afford to like them for the first time.

> GLORIA STEINEM, "Sisterhood," in *Ms.* magazine, 1972.

33 The status quo protects itself by punishing all challengers, especially women whose rebellion strikes at the most fundamental social organization: the sex roles that convince half the population that its identity depends on being first in work or in war, and the other half that it must serve as docile, unpaid, or underpaid labor.

> Ibid.

34 Any woman who chooses to behave like a full human being should be warned that the armies of the status quo will treat her as something of a dirty joke. That's their natural and first weapon.

> Ibid.

---

259. WORK

See also BUSINESS; DEBT; ECONOMICS; LABOR MOVEMENT; MONEY; POVERTY; WEALTH

---

1 When God wanted sponges and oysters, He made them, and put one on a rock, and the other in the mud. When He made man, He did not make him to be a sponge or an oyster; He made him with feet, and hands, and head, and heart, and vital blood, and a place to use them, and said to him, "Go work!"

> HENRY WARD BEECHER, *Royal Truths,* 1866.

2 In the ordinary business of life industry can do anything which genius can do, and very many things which it cannot.

> HENRY WARD BEECHER, *Proverbs from Plymouth, Pulpit,* 1870.

3 I do most of my work sitting down; that's where I shine.

> Attributed to Robert Benchley.

4 Labor, *n.* One of the processes by which A acquires property for B.

> AMBROSE BIERCE, *The Devil's Dictionary,* 1906.

5 Whatever I engage in, I must push inordinately.

> ANDREW CARNEGIE, in his diary, quoted in Matthew Josephson, *The Robber Barons,* 1934.

6 It is mind which does the work of the world, so that the more there is of mind, the more work will be accomplished.

> WILLIAM ELLERY CHANNING, "Self-Culture," 1838.

7 A truly American sentiment recognizes the dignity of labor and the fact that honor lies in honest toil.

> GROVER CLEVELAND, in a letter accepting nomination for President, August 18, 1884.

8 American labor, which is the capital of our workingmen.

> GROVER CLEVELAND, in his first annual message to Congress, December 8, 1885.

9 One of the chief arguments used in support of the policy of an open shop is that every man has an inalienable and constitutional right to work. I never found that in the Constitution.

> CLARENCE DARROW, writing in *The Railroad Trainman,* November, 1909.

10 Every man has the inalienable right to work.

> Attributed to Eugene V. Debs.

11 I never did anything worth doing by accident, nor did any of my inventions come by accident; they came by work.

> Attributed to Thomas A. Edison.

12 There is no substitute for hard work.

> THOMAS A. EDISON, quoted in the *Golden Book* magazine, April, 1931.

13 What is the hardest task in the world? To think.

> RALPH WALDO EMERSON, "Intellect," *Essays,* First Series, 1841.

14 The Yankee means to make moonlight work, if he can.

> RALPH WALDO EMERSON, entry written in 1846, *Journals,* 1909–1914.

15 The wonder is always new that any sane man can be a sailor.

> RALPH WALDO EMERSON, *English Traits,* 1856.

16 The high prize of life, the crowning fortune of a man, is to be born with a bias to some pursuit which finds him in employment and happiness.

> RALPH WALDO EMERSON, "Considerations by the Way," *The Conduct of Life,* 1860.

17 I look on that man as happy, who, when there is question of success, looks into his work for a reply.

> RALPH WALDO EMERSON, "Worship," *The Conduct of Life,* 1860.

18 The sum of wisdom is, that the time is never lost that is devoted to work.

> RALPH WALDO EMERSON, "Success," *Society and Solitude,* 1870.

19 It is not work that men object to, but the element of drudgery. We must drive out drudgery wherever we find it. We shall never be wholly civilized until we remove the treadmill from the daily job.

> HENRY FORD, *My Life and Work,* 1923.

20 He that riseth late must trot all day, and shall scarce overtake his business at night.

> BENJAMIN FRANKLIN, *Poor Richard's Almanack,* 1742.

21 The busy man has few idle visitors; to the boiling pot the flies come not.

> BENJAMIN FRANKLIN, *Poor Richard's Almanack,* 1752.

22 He that hath a trade hath an estate.

> BENJAMIN FRANKLIN, *Poor Richard's Almanack,* 1757.

23 At the workingman's house hunger looks in but dares not enter.

> BENJAMIN FRANKLIN, *The Way to Wealth,* 1758.

24 Diligence is the mother of good luck, and God gives all things to industry. Then plough deep while sluggards sleep, and you shall have corn to sell and to keep.

> Ibid.

25 The eye of the master will do more work than both his hands.

> BENJAMIN FRANKLIN, *Poor Richard's Almanack,* 1758.

26 Handle your tools without mittens.

> Ibid.

27 "Men work together," I told him from the
heart,
"Whether they work together or apart."

> ROBERT FROST, "The Tuft of Flowers,"
> published in the *Derry* (New Hampshire)
> *Enterprise,* March 9, 1906.

28 Man must be doing something, or fancy that he
is doing something, for in him throbs the creative
impulse; the mere basker in the sunshine is not a
natural, but an abnormal man.

> HENRY GEORGE, *Progress and Poverty,* 1879.

29 To love what you do and feel that it matters—
how could anything be more fun?

> KATHARINE GRAHAM, quoted by Jane Howard in
> *Ms.* magazine, October, 1974.

30 What the world eminently requires is some wise
adjustment, some remodeling of the Social machinery, diminishing its friction whereby *every person
willing to work shall assuredly have work to do,
and the just reward of that work in the articles
most essential to his sustenance and comfort.*

> HORACE GREELEY, in "An Address to the
> Printers of New York," January 17, 1850.

31 Labor is the curse of the world, and nobody can
meddle with it without becoming proportionately
brutified.

> NATHANIEL HAWTHORNE, entry written August
> 12, 1841, in *Passages from the American
> Notebooks,* 1868.

32 Busy as a one-armed man with the nettle-rash
pasting on wallpaper.

> O. HENRY, "The Ethics of Pig," *The Gentle
> Grafter,* 1908.

33 If you would die fagged to death like a crow
with the king birds after him—be a school-master;
if you would wax thin and savage, like a half-fed
spider—be a lawyer; if you would go off like an
opium-eater in love with your starving delusions—
be a doctor.

> OLIVER WENDELL HOLMES, SR., in a letter to
> Phineas Barnes, March, 1831.

34 Run, if you like, but try to keep your breath;
Work like a man, but don't be worked to
death.

> OLIVER WENDELL HOLMES, SR., "A Rhymed
> Lesson," 1846.

35 Work: 1. That which keeps us out of trouble.
2. A plan of God to circumvent the Devil.

> ELBERT HUBBARD, *The Roycroft Dictionary and
> Book of Epigrams,* 1923.

36 Blessed is that man who has found his work.

> Ibid.

37 Any man who has a job has a chance.

> Ibid.

38 Give us this day our daily work.

> Ibid.

39 One machine can do the work of fifty ordinary
men. No machine can do the work of one extraordinary man.

> Ibid.

40 Every child should be taught that useful work
is worship and that intelligent labor is the highest
form of prayer.

> ROBERT G. INGERSOLL, "How to Reform
> Mankind," 1896.

41 Never fear the want of business. A man who
qualifies himself well for his calling, never fails of
employment in it.

> THOMAS JEFFERSON, in a letter to Peter Carr,
> June 22, 1792.

42 It is wonderful how much may be done if we are
always doing.

> THOMAS JEFFERSON, in a letter to Martha
> Jefferson, May 5, 1787.

43 Few can be induced to labor exclusively for
posterity, and none will do it enthusiastically. Posterity has done nothing for us; and theorize on it as
we may, practically we shall do very little for it
unless we are made to think we are, at the same
time, doing something for ourselves.

> ABRAHAM LINCOLN, in a speech in Springfield,
> Illinois, February 22, 1842.

44 The lady—bearer of this—says she has two sons who want to work. Set them at it, if possible. Wanting to work is so rare a merit that it should be encouraged.

> ABRAHAM LINCOLN, in a letter to Major D. Ramsay, October 17, 1861.

45 The strongest bond of human sympathy, outside of the family relation, should be one uniting all working people, of all nations, and tongues, and kindreds.

> ABRAHAM LINCOLN, in his reply to a committee from the New York Workingmen's Association, March 21, 1864.

46 Let us, then, be up and doing,
>   With a heart for any fate;
> Still achieving, still pursuing,
>   Learn to labor and to wait.

> HENRY WADSWORTH LONGFELLOW, "A Psalm of Life," 1839.

47 One half of the world must sweat and groan that the other half may dream.

> HENRY WADSWORTH LONGFELLOW, *Hyperion*, 1839.

48 Under a spreading chestnut tree
>   The village smithy stands;
> The smith, a mighty man is he,
>   With large and sinewy hands.

> HENRY WADSWORTH LONGFELLOW, "The Village Blacksmith," *Ballads and Other Poems*, 1841.

49 His brow is wet with honest sweat,
>   He earns whate'er he can,
> And looks the whole world in the face,
>   For he owes not any man.

> Ibid.

50 Toiling—rejoicing—sorrowing,
>   Onward through life he goes;
> Each morning sees some task begin,
>   Each evening sees it close;
> Something attempted, something done,
>   Has earned a night's repose.

> Ibid.

51 Taste the joy
That springs from labor.

> HENRY WADSWORTH LONGFELLOW, "The Masque of Pandora," 1875.

52 No man is born into the world, whose work
Is not born with him; there is always work,
And tools to work withal, for those who will:
And blessed are the horny hands of toil!

> JAMES RUSSELL LOWELL, "A Glance Behind the Curtain," printed in *The Democratic Review*, September, 1843.

53 Bad work follers ye ez long's ye live.

> JAMES RUSSELL LOWELL, *The Biglow Papers*, Second Series, 1866.

54 And but two ways are offered to our will,
Toil with rare triumph, ease with safe disgrace,
The problem still for us and all of human race.

> JAMES RUSSELL LOWELL, "Under the Old Elm: Poem Read at Cambridge on the Hundredth Anniversary of Washington's Taking Command of the American Army, 3d July, 1775," 1875.

55 Slave of the wheel of labor, what to him
Are Plato and the swing of Pleiades?
What the long reaches of the peaks of song,
The rift of dawn, the reddening of the rose?

> EDWIN MARKHAM, "The Man with the Hoe," 1899.

56 A man who gets his board and lodging on this ball in an ignominious way is inevitably an ignominious man.

> H.L. MENCKEN, *Prejudices*, Fourth Series, 1924.

57 I go on working for the same reason that a hen goes on laying eggs.

> H.L. MENCKEN, quoted in Will Durant, *On the Meaning of Life*, 1932.

58 Our place is beside the poor, behind the working man. They are our people.

> GEORGE CARDINAL MUNDELEIN of Chicago, in an address, January 2, 1938.

59 One-third of the people in the United States promote, while the other two-thirds provide.

> WILL ROGERS, *The Illiterate Digest,* 1924.

60 I don't pity any man who does hard work worth doing. I admire him. I pity the creature who does not work, at whichever end of the social scale he may regard himself as being.

> THEODORE ROOSEVELT, in a speech in Chattanooga, Tennessee, September 8, 1902.

61 Far and away the best prize that life offers is the chance to work hard at work worth doing.

> THEODORE ROOSEVELT, in a Labor Day speech in Syracuse, New York, September 7, 1903.

62 The men who start out with the notion that the world owes them a living generally find that the world pays its debt in the penitentiary or the poorhouse.

> WILLIAM GRAHAM SUMNER, "Earth Hunger," in *Earth Hunger and Other Essays,* 1913.

63 So far I've found that most high-level executives prefer the boardroom to the Bahamas. They don't really enjoy leisure time; they feel their work is their leisure.

> WILLIAM THEOBALD, college professor, quoted in *American Way* magazine, February 5, 1985.

64 Good for the body is the work of the body, good for the soul the work of the soul, and good for either the work of the other.

> HENRY DAVID THOREAU, entry dated January 23, 1841, in his *Journal,* 1906.

65 It is not necessary that a man should earn his living by the sweat of his brow, unless he sweats easier than I do.

> HENRY DAVID THOREAU, *Walden,* 1854.

66 As for *work,* we haven't any of any consequence. We have the Saint Vitus' dance, and cannot possibly keep our heads still.

> Ibid.

67 The callous palms of the laborer are conversant with finer tissues of self-respect and heroism, whose touch thrills the heart, than the languid fingers of idleness.

> HENRY DAVID THOREAU, "Walking," *Excursions,* 1863.

68 Most men would feel insulted if it were proposed to employ them in throwing stones over a wall, and then in throwing them back, merely that they might earn their wages. But many are no more worthily employed now.

> HENRY DAVID THOREAU, "Life Without Principle," published posthumously in the *Atlantic Monthly,* October, 1863.

69 The aim of the laborer should be, not to get his living, to get "a good job," but to perform well a certain work. . . . Do not hire a man who does your work for money, but him who does it for the love of it.

> Ibid.

70 Work consists of whatever a body is *obliged* to do, and . . . Play consists of whatever a body is not obliged to do.

> MARK TWAIN, *The Adventures of Tom Sawyer,* 1876.

71 There are wealthy gentlemen in England who drive four-horse passenger-coaches twenty or thirty miles on a daily line, in the summer, because the privilege costs them considerable money; but if they are offered wages for the service, that would turn it into work and then they would resign.

> Ibid.

72 Let us be grateful to Adam, our benefactor. He cut us out of the "blessing" of idleness and won for us the "curse" of labor.

> MARK TWAIN, "Pudd'nhead Wilson's New Calendar," *Following the Equator,* 1897.

73 Heaven is blest with perfect rest, but the blessing of Earth is toil.

> HENRY VAN DYKE, *The Toiling of Felix,* 1898.

74 Nothing ever comes to one, that is worth having, except as a result of hard work.

> BOOKER T. WASHINGTON, *Up from Slavery,* 1901.

75 No race can prosper till it learns that there is as much dignity in tilling a field as in writing a poem.

Ibid.

76 Employment gives health, sobriety, and morals. Constant employment and well-paid labor produce, in a country like ours, general prosperity, content, and cheerfulness.

DANIEL WEBSTER, in a speech in the U.S. Senate, July 25, 1846.

77 We should all do what, in the long run, gives us joy, even if it is only picking grapes or sorting the laundry.

E.B. WHITE, in a letter to Judith W. Preusser, November 10, 1963.

78 There is no trade or employment but the young man following it may become a hero.

WALT WHITMAN, "Song of Myself," 1855.

79 Heeding truth alone, and turning
    From the false and dim,
Lamp of toil or altar burning
    Are alike to Him.

JOHN GREENLEAF WHITTIER, "The Lumbermen," *Songs of Labor and Reform,* 1850.

80 Up! up! in nobler toil than ours
    No craftsmen bear a part:
We make of Nature's giant powers
    The slaves of human Art.

JOHN GREENLEAF WHITTIER, "The Ship-Builders," *Songs of Labor and Reform,* 1850.

---

260. WORLD WAR I

See also WAR

---

1 In the judgment of this government, loans by American bankers to any foreign nation at war are inconsistent with the true spirit of neutrality.

WILLIAM JENNINGS BRYAN, in a statement to the press, August 15, 1914.

2 Come on, you sons of bitches! Do you want to live forever?

Attributed to a U.S. Marine sergeant at the battle of Belleau Wood, June 6, 1918.

3 Our plutocracy, our junkers, would have us believe that all the junkers are confined to Germany. It is precisely because we refuse to believe this that they brand us as disloyalists. They want our eyes focused on the junkers in Berlin so that we will not see those within our own borders.

EUGENE V. DEBS, in a speech at Canton, Ohio, June 16, 1918.

4 The purpose of the Allies is exactly the purpose of the Central Powers, and that is the conquest and spoliation of the weaker nations that has always been the purpose of war.

Ibid.

5 Wake up America.

AUGUSTUS P. GARDNER, in a speech, October 16, 1916.

6 I find a hundred thousand sorrows touching my heart, and there is ringing in my ears like an admonition eternal, an insistent call, "It must not be again!"

WARREN G. HARDING, speaking in Hoboken, New Jersey, at a service for American soldiers killed in World War I, May 23, 1921.

7 In a wood they call the Rouge Bouquet,
    There is a new-made grave today,
    Built by never a spade nor pick,
    Yet covered with earth ten meters thick.
    There lie many fighting men,
        Dead in their youthful prime.
    Never to laugh nor love again
        Nor taste the Summertime.

JOYCE KILMER, "Rouge Bouquet," dated March 7, 1918.

8 There's a long, long trail a-winding
    Into the land of my dreams,
    Where the nightingales are singing
    And a white moon beams;
    There's a long, long night of waiting
    Until my dreams all come true,

Till the day when I'll be going down that
Long, long trail with you.

> STODDARD KING AND ZO ELLIOTT, "There's a
> Long, Long Trail," 1913.

9 I maintain that Congress has the right and the
duty to declare the object of the war, and the people
have the right and the obligation to discuss it.

> ROBERT M. LAFOLLETTE, SR., in a speech in the
> U.S. Senate, October 6, 1917.

10 In 1917, we entered World War I in order to
preserve Western civilization, specifically the civilization of Western Europe, from German domination; to defend and protect our declared neutral
rights, especially that of freedom of the seas; and to
preserve our national honor.

> EUGENE J. MCCARTHY, *The Limits of Power,*
> 1967.

11 Hell, Heaven or Hoboken by Christmas.

> Attributed to Gen. John J. Pershing, 1918.

12 We are fighting in the quarrel of civilization
against barbarism, of liberty against tyranny. Germany has become a menace to the whole world. She
is the most dangerous enemy of liberty now existing.

> THEODORE ROOSEVELT, in a speech at Oyster
> Bay, Long Island, April, 1917.

13 The man who does not think it was America's
duty to fight for her own sake in view of the infamous conduct of Germany toward us stands on a
level with a man who wouldn't think it necessary
to fight in a private quarrel because his wife's face
was slapped.

> Ibid.

14 Germany has reduced savagery to a science, and
this great war for the victorious peace of justice
must go on until the German cancer is cut clean out
of the world body.

> THEODORE ROOSEVELT, in a speech in Johnstown,
> Pennsylvania, September 30, 1917.

15 Lafayette, we are here.

> COL. CHARLES E. STANTON, in a speech at the
> grave of Lafayette, in Paris, France, July 4, 1917.

16 It was said in the First World War that the
French fought for their country, the British fought
for freedom of the seas, and the Americans fought
for souvenirs.

> HARRY S TRUMAN, quoted in Margaret Truman,
> *Harry S Truman,* 1973.

17 The United States must be neutral in fact as
well as in name during these days that are to try
men's souls. We must be impartial in thought as
well as in action, must put a curb upon our sentiments as well as upon every transaction that might
be construed as a preference of one party to the
struggle before another.

> WOODROW WILSON, in a proclamation of
> neutrality, August 18, 1914.

18 Our whole duty, for the present, at any rate, is
summed up in this motto: "America first."

> WOODROW WILSON, in a speech in New York
> City, April 20, 1915.

19 The basis of neutrality . . . is not indifference;
it is not self-interest. The basis of neutrality is
sympathy for mankind. It is fairness, it is good will
at bottom. It is impartiality of spirit and of judgment.

> Ibid.

20 It must be a peace without victory. . . . Victory
would mean peace forced upon the loser, a victor's
terms imposed upon the vanquished. It would be
accepted in humiliation, under duress, at an intolerable sacrifice, and would leave a sting, a resentment, a bitter memory upon which terms of peace
would rest, not permanently, but only as upon
quicksand. Only a peace between equals can last.
Only a peace the very principle of which is equality
and a common participation in a common benefit.

> WOODROW WILSON, in a speech to the U.S.
> Senate, January 22, 1917.

21 Since it has unhappily proved impossible to safeguard our neutral rights by diplomatic means
against the unwarranted infringements they are
suffering at the hands of Germany, there may be no
recourse but to *armed* neutrality.

> WOODROW WILSON, in a speech before Congress,
> February 26, 1917.

22 It is a war against all nations. . . . There has been no discrimination. The challenge is to all mankind. Each nation must decide for itself how it will meet it. . . . We must put excited feeling away. Our motive will not be revenge or the victorious assertion of the physical might of the nation, but only the vindication of right, of human right, of which we are only a single champion.

> Woodrow Wilson, in his war message to Congress, April 2, 1917.

23 With a profound sense of the solemn and even tragical character of the step I am taking and of the grave responsibilities which it involves, but in unhesitating obedience to what I deem my constitutional duty, I advise that the Congress declare the recent course of the Imperial German Government to be in fact nothing less than war against the government and people of the United States; that it formally accept the status of belligerent which has thus been thrust upon it.

> Ibid.

24 The world must be made safe for democracy. Its peace must be planted upon the tested foundations of political liberty. We have no selfish ends to serve. We desire no conquest, no dominion. We seek no indemnities for ourselves, no material compensation for the sacrifices we shall freely make.

> Ibid.

25 It is a fearful thing to lead this great peaceful people into war, into the most terrible and disastrous of all wars, civilization itself seeming to be in the balance. But the right is more precious than peace, and we shall fight for the things which we have always carried nearest our hearts.

> Ibid.

26 What we demand in this war . . . is nothing peculiar to ourselves. It is that the world be made fit and safe to live in; and particularly that it be made safe for every peace-loving nation which, like our own, wishes to live its own life, determine its own institutions, be assured of justice and fair dealing by the other peoples of the world as against force and selfish aggression. All the peoples of the world are in effect partners in this interest, and for our own part we see very clearly that unless justice be done to others it will not be done to us.

> Woodrow Wilson, in his address to Congress, enumerating the Fourteen Points for world peace, January 8, 1918.

27 The moral climax of this, the culminating and final war for human liberty, has come.

> Ibid.

28 I tell you, fellow citizens, that the war was won by the American spirit. . . . You know what one of our American wits said, that it took only half as long to train an American army as any other, because you only had to train them to go one way.

> Woodrow Wilson, in an address in Kansas City, Missouri, September 6, 1919.

---

261. WORLD WAR II

See also War

---

1 We're the battling bastards of Bataan:
No mama, no papa, no Uncle Sam,
No aunts, no uncles, no nephews, no nieces,
No rifles, no planes, or artillery pieces,
And nobody gives a damn.

> Sung by U.S. troops defending the Philippines, 1942.

2 We sure liberated the hell out of this place.

> An American soldier, commenting on a French village that had been heavily damaged, 1944, quoted in Max Miller, *The Far Shore,* 1945.

3 While the rest of the world came out bruised and scarred and nearly destroyed, we came out with the most unbelievable machinery, tools, manpower, money. The war was fun for America. . . . And the rest of the world was bleeding and in pain.

> Paul Edwards, quoted in Studs Terkel, *The Good War,* 1984.

4 This war is serious—we'll never preserve our accustomed ways of living in the U.S.—free

Franklin D. Roosevelt: message to Congress asking for war against Japan, December 8, 1941

On December 7, in the midst of negotiations between the United States and Japan over ways to solve problems in the Far East, Japan deceitfully struck Pearl Harbor in Hawaii as well as many other targets in the Pacific. President Roosevelt's message to Congress the next day was a never-to-be-forgotten call to arms.

Yesterday, December 7, 1941—a date which will live in infamy—the United States of America was suddenly and deliberately attacked by naval and air forces of the Empire of Japan.

The United States was at peace with that nation, and, at the solicitation of Japan, was still in conversation with its government and its emperor looking toward the maintenance of peace in the Pacific. Indeed, one hour after Japanese air squadrons had commenced bombing in Oahu, the Japanese ambassador to the United States and his colleague delivered to the secretary of state a formal reply to a recent American message. While this reply stated that it seemed useless to continue the existing diplomatic negotiations, it contained no threat or hint of war or armed attack.

It will be recorded that the distance of Hawaii from Japan makes it obvious that the attack was deliberately planned many days or even weeks ago. During the intervening time the Japanese government has deliberately sought to deceive the United States by false statements and expressions of hope for continued peace.

The attack yesterday on the Hawaiian Islands has caused severe damage to American naval and military forces. Very many American lives have been lost. In addition, American ships have been reported torpedoed on the high seas between San Francisco and Honolulu.

Yesterday the Japanese government also launched an attack against Malaya.

Last night Japanese forces attacked Hong Kong.

Last night Japanese forces attacked Guam.

Last night Japanese forces attacked the Philippine Islands.

Last night the Japanese attacked Wake Island.

This morning the Japanese attacked Midway Island.

Japan has, therefore, undertaken a surprise offensive extending throughout the Pacific area. The facts of yesterday speak for themselves. The people of the United States have already formed their opinions and well understand the implications to the very life and safety of our nation.

As commander in chief of the Army and Navy I have directed that all measures be taken for our defense.

Always will we remember the character of the onslaught against us. No matter how long it may take us to overcome this premeditated invasion, the American people, in their righteous might, will win through to absolute victory. I believe I interpret the will of the Congress and of the people when I assert that we will not only defend ourselves to the uttermost but will make very certain that this form of treachery shall never endanger us again.

Hostilities exist. There is no blinking at the fact that our people, our territory, and our interests are in grave danger.

With confidence in our armed forces—with the unbounded determination of our people—we will gain the inevitable triumph—so help us God.

I ask that the Congress declare that since the unprovoked and dastardly attack by Japan on Sunday, December 7, a state of war has existed between the United States and the Japanese Empire.

speech—press—and right to worship—unless we all turn in now and fight and work!!

> DWIGHT D. EISENHOWER, in a letter to Mamie Doud Eisenhower, June 30, 1943.

5 More than any other war in history, this war has been an array of the forces of evil against those of righteousness. It had to have its leaders and it had to be won—but no matter what the sacrifice, no matter what the suffering of populations, no matter what the cost, the war had to be won.

> DWIGHT D. EISENHOWER, in a speech at Frankfurt-am-Main, Germany, June 10, 1945.

6 Never have soldiers been called upon to endure longer sustained periods of contact with a vicious enemy nor greater punishment from weather or terrain. The American has been harassed by rifle and automatic weapons, pounded by hand grenades, by artillery and rocket shells, attacked by tanks and airplane bombs! He has faced the hazards of countless mines and booby traps and every form of static obstacle. He has conquered them all!

> DWIGHT D. EISENHOWER, in an address before a joint session of Congress, June 18, 1945.

7 Praise the Lord and pass the ammunition.

> Attributed to Howell M. Forgy, at Pearl Harbor, December 7, 1941.

8 The war's over. One or two of those things, and Japan will be finished.

> GEN. LESLIE R. GROVES, to his deputy after the first test of the atomic bomb, July 16, 1945.

9 Truman did not so much say "yes" as not say "no." It would indeed have taken a lot of nerve to say "no" at that time.

> GEN. LESLIE R. GROVES, on the decision to use the atomic bomb, quoted in Robert Jungk, *Brighter than a Thousand Suns*, 1958.

10 The Third Fleet's sunken and damaged ships have been salvaged and are retiring at high speed toward the enemy.

> ADM. WILLIAM F. HALSEY, JR., in a radio dispatch to Adm. Chester Nimitz, October 15, 1944. (The Japanese were reporting that Halsey's Third Fleet had been destroyed.)

11 If CINCPAC [Commander-in-Chief, Pacific] would let me, I'd send them my latitude and longitude.

> ADM. WILLIAM F. HALSEY, JR., after he had been told that Radio Manila had dared listeners to "ask where Halsey is," October 30, 1944.

12 Catch-22 says they [military authorities] have a right to do anything we can't stop them from doing.

> JOSEPH HELLER, *Catch-22*, 1955.

13 Though a man of decisive mind in immediate issues, General Eisenhower is far too easily swayed and diverted to be a great commander-in-chief.

> SIR IAN JACOB, in his diary, December 12, 1942.

14 Here is a victor announcing the verdict to the prostrate enemy. He can exact his pound of flesh if he so chooses. He can impose a humiliating penalty if he so desires. And yet he pleads for freedom, tolerance, and justice.

261. WORLD WAR II

TOSHIKAZU KASE, on Douglas MacArthur at the Japanese surrender, *Journey to the 'Missouri'*, 1950.

15 As long as Europe prepares for war, America must prepare for neutrality.

WALTER LIPPMANN, in his column in the *New York Herald Tribune,* May 17, 1934.

16 The President of the United States ordered me to break through the Japanese lines . . . for the purpose, as I understand it, of organizing the American offensive against Japan, a primary object of which is the relief of the Philippines. I came through and I shall return.

GEN. DOUGLAS MACARTHUR, in a statement to the press after his arrival in Australia from Corregidor, March 20, 1942.

17 I have returned. By the grace of Almighty God, our forces stand again on Philippine soil.

GEN. DOUGLAS MACARTHUR, following the U.S. landing on Leyte, October 20, 1944.

18 I see that the old flagpole still stands. Have your troops hoist the colors to its peak, and let no enemy ever haul them down.

GEN. DOUGLAS MACARTHUR, to the troops who recaptured Corregidor, March 2, 1945.

19 Nuts!

GEN. ANTHONY MCAULIFFE, published reply to the German demand for the surrender of U.S. forces at Bastogne, December 22, 1944. (The original form of the message was somewhat different.)

20 The refusal of the British and Russian people to accept what appeared to be inevitable defeat was the great factor in the salvage of our civilization.

GEN. GEORGE C. MARSHALL, in the Biennial Report of the Chief of Staff, United States Army, September 1, 1945.

21 I feel like a fugitive from th' law of averages.

BILL MAULDIN, in a cartoon caption, *Up Front,* 1944.

22 Look at an infantryman's eyes and you can tell how much war he has seen.

Ibid.

23 Uncommon valor was a common virtue.

Attributed to Adm. Chester Nimitz, characterizing the U.S. Marines at Iwo Jima, 1945.

24 There is one great thing you men will be able to say after this war is all over and you are at home once again. And you may thank God for it. You may be thankful that twenty years from now when you are sitting by the fireplace with your grandson on your knee and he asks you what you did in the great World War II, you won't have to cough, shift him to the other knee and say, "Well, your Granddaddy shoveled shit in Louisiana." No Sir! You can look him straight in the eye and say, "Son, your Granddaddy rode with the great Third Army and a son-of-a-bitch named Georgie Patton."

GEN. GEORGE S. PATTON, in a speech to troops of the Sixth Armored Division, May 31, 1944.

25 We are having one hell of a war.

GEN. GEORGE S. PATTON, in a letter to A.D. Surles, December 15, 1944.

26 We must be the great arsenal of democracy.

FRANKLIN D. ROOSEVELT, a phrase originally used by French official Jean Monnet in a conversation with Felix Frankfurter, first said by Roosevelt in a Fireside Chat, December 29, 1940.

27 Yesterday, December 7, 1941—a date which will live in infamy—the United States of America was suddenly and deliberately attacked by naval and air forces of the Empire of Japan. . . . Japan has . . . undertaken a surprise offensive extending throughout the Pacific area. The facts of yesterday speak for themselves. The people of the United States have already formed their opinions and well understand the implications to the very life and safety of our nation. . . . Always will we remember the character of the onslaught against us. . . . I ask that the Congress declare that since the unprovoked and dastardly attack by Japan on Sunday, December 7, a state of war has existed between the United States and the Japanese Empire.

FRANKLIN D. ROOSEVELT, in his war message to Congress, December 8, 1941.

28 We are now in this war. We are all in it—all the way. Every single man, woman and child is a

partner in the most tremendous undertaking of our American history.

> FRANKLIN D. ROOSEVELT, in his war broadcast to the nation, December 9, 1941.

29 We are now in the midst of a war, not for conquest, not for vengeance, but for a world in which this nation, and all that this nation represents, will be safe for our children. . . . We are going to win the war and we are going to win the peace that follows.

> Ibid.

30 During 1943 and part of 1944 our greatest worry was the possibility that Germany would perfect an atomic bomb before the invasion of Europe. . . . In 1945, when we ceased worrying about what the Germans might do to us, we began to worry about what the government of the United States might do to other countries.

> LEO SZILARD, quoted in Robert Jungk, *Brighter than a Thousand Suns,* 1958.

31 This is a solemn but glorious hour. I only wish that Franklin D. Roosevelt had lived to witness this day. General Eisenhower informs me that the forces of Germany have surrendered to the United Nations. The flags of freedom fly all over Europe.

> HARRY S TRUMAN, in his VE-Day (Victory in Europe Day) message to the nation, delivered from the Radio Room at the White House, 9 a.m., May 8, 1945.

32 Sixteen hours ago an American airplane dropped one bomb on Hiroshima, an important Japanese Army base. That bomb had more power than 20,000 tons of TNT. It had more than two thousand times the blast power of the British "Grand Slam," which is the largest bomb ever yet used in the history of warfare. . . . It is an atomic bomb. It is a harnessing of the basic power of the universe. The force from which the sun draws its powers has been loosed against those who brought war to the Far East.

> HARRY S TRUMAN, in a message to the nation, August 6, 1945.

33 I should imagine today would be a discouraging day for the northern France correspondent of Friends of the Land. The organic matter now being added to French soil is of a most embarrassing nature. Until we quit composting our young men we shall not get far with a program of conservation.

> E.B. WHITE, on the waste of life in war, in "Compost," June, 1940.

34 They Were Expendable.

> WILLIAM LINDSAY WHITE, the title of a book, 1942.

---

262. WRITERS

See also BOOKS; LITERATURE; POET; POETRY

---

1 He writes so well he makes me feel like putting my quill back in my goose.

> Attributed to Fred Allen.

2 At this time I had decided the only thing I was fit for was to be a writer, and this notion rested solely on my suspicion that I would never be fit for real work, and that writing didn't require any.

> RUSSELL BAKER, *Growing Up,* 1982.

3 It took me fifteen years to discover that I had no talent for writing, but I couldn't give it up because by that time I was too famous.

> Attributed to Robert Benchley.

4 Your complete literary chap is a writing animal; and when he dies he leaves a cocoon as large as a hay stack, in which every breath he has drawn is recorded in writing.

> JOHN JAY CHAPMAN, *Greek Genius and Other Essays,* 1915.

5 While the light burning within may have been divine, the outer case of the lamp was assuredly cheap enough. Whitman was, from first to last, a boorish, awkward *poseur.*

> REBECCA HARDING DAVIS, on Walt Whitman, in *Bits of Gossip,* 1904.

6 Your reading you may use in conversation, but your writing should stop with your own thought.

> RALPH WALDO EMERSON, entry written in 1841, *Journals,* 1909–1914.

7 Like the New England soil, my talent is good only whilst I work it. If I cease to task myself, I have no thoughts. This is a poor sterile Yankeeism. What I admire and love is the generous and spontaneous soil which flowers and fruits at all seasons.

> RALPH WALDO EMERSON, entry written in 1849, *Journals,* 1909–1914.

8 It has come to be practically a sort of rule in literature that a man, having once shown himself capable of original writing, is entitled thenceforth to steal from the writings of others at discretion.

> RALPH WALDO EMERSON, "Shakspeare," *Representative Men,* 1850.

9 What point of morals, of manners, of economy, of philosophy, of religion, of taste, of the conduct of life, has he not settled? What mystery has he not signified his knowledge of? What office, or function, or district of man's work, has he not remembered? What maiden has not found him finer than her delicacy? What lover has he not outloved? What sage has he not outseen?

> Ibid.

10 Talent alone cannot make a writer. There must be a man behind the book.

> RALPH WALDO EMERSON, "Goethe," *Representative Men,* 1850.

11 I find it the most extraordinary piece of wit and wisdom that America has yet contributed. . . . I greet you at the beginning of a great career.

> RALPH WALDO EMERSON, writing of *Leaves of Grass,* in a letter to Walt Whitman, July 21, 1855.

12 The art of the writer is to speak his fact and have done. Let the reader find that he cannot afford to omit any line of your writing, because you have omitted every word that he can spare.

> RALPH WALDO EMERSON, entry written in 1862, *Journals,* 1909–1914.

13 Next to the originator of a good sentence is the first quoter of it.

> RALPH WALDO EMERSON, "Eloquence," *Letters and Social Aims,* 1876.

14 The writer, like a priest, must be exempted from secular labor. His work needs a frolic health; he must be at the top of his condition.

> RALPH WALDO EMERSON, "Poetry and Imagination," *Letters and Social Aims,* 1876.

15 All good writing is swimming under water and holding your breath.

> F. SCOTT FITZGERALD, in an undated letter.

16 Your life has been a disappointment, as mine has been too. But we haven't gone through this sweat for nothing.

> F. SCOTT FITZGERALD, in a letter to his wife, Zelda, October 6, 1939, in *The Letters of F. Scott Fitzgerald,* 1963.

17 Writing is easy. All you do is stare at a blank sheet of paper until drops of blood form on your forehead.

> Attributed to Gene Fowler.

18 I have heard that nothing gives an Author so great Pleasure, as to find his Works respectfully quoted by other learned Authors.

> BENJAMIN FRANKLIN, *Poor Richard's Almanack,* 1758.

19 The next thing like living one's life again seems to be a recollection of that life, and to make that recollection as durable as possible by putting it down in writing.

> BENJAMIN FRANKLIN, *Autobiography,* 1798.

20 No tears in the writer, no tears in the reader. No surprise for the writer, no surprise for the reader.

> ROBERT FROST, "The Figure a Poem Makes," preface to *Collected Poems,* 1939.

21 Originality is something that is easily exaggerated, especially by authors contemplating their own work.

> JOHN KENNETH GALBRAITH, *The Affluent Society,* 1976.

22 The essential tragedy and hopelessness of most human life under the conditions into which our society was swiftly hardening embittered me, called for expression, but even then I did not know that I had found my theme. I had no intention at the moment of putting it into fiction.

HAMLIN GARLAND, *A Son of the Middle Border,* 1917.

23 Nothing remains but to go on doggedly making books, although I am perfectly aware that none of them will appeal to the casual reader with greater power than those I have already published. . . . I am told that my books go into libraries and will be studied after my death as social records, but these younger opportunists build castles and buy yachts with the royalties on their tales of lust and war. To be read after one's death is cold comfort—but what if even that is denied me?

HAMLIN GARLAND, *Afternoon Neighbors,* 1934.

24 The average contributor to this magazine is semi-literate; that is, he is ornate to no purpose, full of senseless and elegant variations, and can be relied on to use three sentences where a word would do.

WOLCOTT GIBBS, "Theory and Practice of Editing *New Yorker* Articles," first published in James Thurber, *The Years with Ross,* 1957.

25 If a man have no heroism in his soul, no animating purpose beyond living easily and faring sumptuously, I can imagine no greater mistake on his part than that of resorting to authorship as a vocation.

HORACE GREELEY, in a letter to Robert Dale Owen, March 5, 1860.

26 Bees are sometimes drowned (or suffocated) in the honey which they collect. So some writers are lost in their collected learning.

NATHANIEL HAWTHORNE, entry written in 1842, *Passages from the American Notebooks,* 1868.

27 America is now wholly given over to a damned mob of scribbling women.

NATHANIEL HAWTHORNE, in a letter, 1855, quoted in Caroline Ticknor, *Hawthorne and His Publisher,* 1913.

28 No author, without a trial, can conceive of the difficulty of writing a romance about a country where there is no shadow, no antiquity, no mystery, no picturesque and gloomy wrong, nor anything but a commonplace prosperity, in broad and simple daylight, as is happily the case with my dear native land.

NATHANIEL HAWTHORNE, *The Marble Faun,* 1860.

29 Mr. Whitman's muse is at once indecent and ugly, lascivious and gawky, lubricious and coarse.

LAFCADIO HEARN, on Whitman's *Leaves of Grass,* in the *New Orleans Times-Democrat,* July 30, 1882.

30 He's teaching me to write, and I'm teaching him to box.

ERNEST HEMINGWAY, speaking about Ezra Pound, 1922, quoted in Carlos Baker, *Ernest Hemingway—A Life Story,* 1969.

31 The great thing is to last and get your work done and see and hear and learn and understand; and write when there is something that you know; and not before; and not too damned much after.

ERNEST HEMINGWAY, *Death in the Afternoon,* 1932.

32 The hardest thing to do is to write straight honest prose on human beings. First you have to know the subject; then you have to know how to write. Both take a lifetime to learn, and anybody is cheating who takes politics as a way out. All the outs are too easy, and the thing itself is too hard to do.

ERNEST HEMINGWAY, in *Esquire* magazine, December, 1934.

33 Shells are all much the same. If they don't hit you, there's no story, and if they do, you don't have to write it.

ERNEST HEMINGWAY, in a dispatch for the North American Newspaper Alliance during the Spanish Civil War, October 7, 1937.

34 There are events which are so great that if a writer has participated in them his obligation is to write truly rather than assume the presumption of altering them with invention.

ERNEST HEMINGWAY, in a preface written in April, 1940, for Gustav Regler, *The Great Crusade,* 1940.

35 For a true writer each book should be a new beginning where he tries again for something that is beyond attainment. He should always try for something that has never been done or that others have tried and failed. Then sometimes, with great luck, he will succeed. How simple the writing of literature would be if it were only necessary to write in another way what has been well written. It is because we have had such great writers in the past that a writer is driven far out past where he can go, out to where no one can help him.

ERNEST HEMINGWAY, in an address recorded for the Nobel Prize Committee, accepting the Nobel Prize for literature, 1954.

36 Whitman does not in any measure deserve the great attention we are giving him. He has not enriched American literature with any such congruous material as will enter into it and become a portion of the common stock appropriated by the public taste or the public need. You might strike out of existence all he has written, and the world would not be consciously poorer.

JOSIAH GILBERT HOLLAND, in a letter to Richard Watson Gilder, September 19, 1880.

37 I never saw an author in my life—saving, perhaps, one—that did not purr as audibly as a full-grown domestic cat . . . on having his fur smoothed the right way by a skilful hand.

OLIVER WENDELL HOLMES, SR., *The Autocrat of the Breakfast-Table,* 1858.

38 Nature, when she invented, manufactured, and patented her authors, contrived to make critics out of the chips that were left.

OLIVER WENDELL HOLMES, SR., *The Professor at the Breakfast-Table,* 1860.

39 A writing man is something of a black sheep, like the village fiddler. Occasionally a fiddler becomes a violinist, and is a credit to his family, but as a rule he would have done better had his tendency been toward industry and saving.

EDGAR WATSON HOWE, *The Blessing of Business,* 1918.

40 Emerson, Longfellow, Lowell, Holmes—I knew them all and all the rest of our sages, poets, seers, critics, humorists; they were like one another and like other literary men; but Clemens was sole, incomparable, the Lincoln of our literature.

WILLIAM DEAN HOWELLS, the last sentence of *My Mark Twain,* 1910.

41 The poor writers we have always with us—if we take the daily paper.

ELBERT HUBBARD, *The Roycroft Dictionary and Book of Epigrams,* 1923.

42 Writers seldom write the things they think. They simply write the things they think other folks think they think.

Ibid.

43 There is always this to be said for the literary profession—like life itself, it provides its own revenges and antidotes.

ELIZABETH JANEWAY, quoted in Helen Hull, *The Writer's Book,* 1950.

44 I'm not an author, but before I became mayor, I wasn't a mayor.

EDWARD KOCH, quoted in *Publishers Weekly,* January 25, 1985.

45 A good many young writers make the mistake of enclosing a stamped, self-addressed envelope, big enough for the manuscript to come back in. This is too much of a temptation to the editor.

RING LARDNER, *How to Write Short Stories,* 1924.

46 Every compulsion is put upon writers to become safe, polite, obedient, and sterile. In protest, I declined election to the National Institute of Arts and Letters some years ago, and now I must decline the Pulitzer Prize.

SINCLAIR LEWIS, in a letter declining the Pulitzer Prize for his novel *Arrowsmith,* 1926.

47 Some of our English cousins have undertaken to hold Walt Whitman up as the herald of the coming literature of American democracy, merely because he departed from all received forms, and indulged

in barbarous eccentricities. They mistake difference for originality.

HENRY CABOT LODGE, *Colonialism in the United States,* 1884.

48 If you once understand an author's character, the comprehension of his writings becomes easy.

HENRY WADSWORTH LONGFELLOW, *Hyperion,* 1839.

49 Look, then, into thine heart and write!

HENRY WADSWORTH LONGFELLOW, "Prelude," *Voices of the Night,* 1839.

50 What a writer asks of his reader is not so much to *like* as to *listen.*

HENRY WADSWORTH LONGFELLOW, in a letter to J.S. Dwight, December 10, 1847.

51 The Poet paramount.

HENRY WADSWORTH LONGFELLOW, "Shakespeare," in *The Masque of Pandora and Other Poems,* 1875.

52 There comes Emerson first, whose rich
        words, every one,
    Are like gold nails in temples to hang
        trophies on,
    Whose prose is grand verse, while his verse,
        the lord knows,
    Is some of it pr—No, 'tis not even prose.

JAMES RUSSELL LOWELL, *A Fable for Critics,* 1848.

53 To meet such a primitive Pagan as he,
    In whose mind all creation is duly respected
    As parts of himself—just a little projected;
    And who's willing to worship the stars and
        the sun,
    A convert to—nothing but Emerson.

Ibid.

54 Life, nature, love, God, and affairs of that
        sort,
    He looks at as merely ideas; in short,
    As if they were fossils stuck round in a
        cabinet,
    Of such vast extent that our earth's a mere
        dab in it;

Composed just as he is inclined to conjecture
        her,
    Namely, one part pure earth, ninety-nine
        parts pure lecturer.

Ibid.

55 There comes Poe, with his raven, like
        Barnaby Rudge,
    Three fifths of him genius and two fifths
        sheer fudge.

Ibid.

56 Nature fits all her children with something to
        do,
    He who would write and can't write, can
        surely review;
    Can set up a small booth as critic and sell us
        his
    Petty conceit and his pettier jealousies.

Ibid.

57 America is no place for an artist: to be an artist is to be a moral leper, an economic misfit, a social liability. A corn-fed hog enjoys a better life than a creative writer, painter, or musician. To be a rabbit is better still.

HENRY MILLER, *The Air-Conditioned Nightmare,* 1945.

58 When you steal from one author, it's plagiarism; if you steal from many, it's research.

Attributed to Wilson Mizner.

59 There is no such thing as a dirty theme. There are only dirty writers.

GEORGE JEAN NATHAN, *Testament of a Critic,* 1931.

60 The presence alone of Faulkner in our midst makes a great difference in what the writer can and cannot permit himself to do. Nobody wants his mule and wagon stalled on the same track the Dixie Limited is roaring down.

FLANNERY O'CONNOR, "Some Aspects of the Grotesque in Southern Fiction," quoted in Sally and Robert Fitzgerald, *Mystery and Manners,* 1969.

61 The affair between Margot Asquith and Margot Asquith will live as one of the prettiest love stories in all literature.

> DOROTHY PARKER, reviewing Margot Asquith's *Autobiography,* in *The New Yorker,* 1922.

62 The only "ism" she believes in is plagiarism.

> DOROTHY PARKER, quoted in *Publishers Weekly,* June 19, 1967.

63 When we attend less to "authority" and more to principles, when we look less at merit and more at demerit . . . we shall then be better critics than we are.

> EDGAR ALLAN POE, *Marginalia,* 1844–1849.

64 God have mercy on the sinner
Who must write with no dinner,
No gravy and no grub,
No pewter and no pub,
No belly and no bowels,
Only consonants and vowels.

> JOHN CROWE RANSOM, "Survey of Literature," in *Selected Poems,* 1963.

65 Every misused word revenges itself forever upon a writer's reputation.

> AGNES REPPLIER, *Points of Friction,* 1920.

66 Our authors and scholars are generally men of business, and make their literary pursuits subservient to their interests.

> BENJAMIN RUSH, in a letter April 16, 1790.

67 What I like in a good author is not what he says, but what he whispers.

> LOGAN PEARSALL SMITH, *Afterthoughts,* 1931.

68 The great struggle of a writer is to learn to write as he would talk.

> Attributed to Lincoln Steffens, in Justin Kaplan, *Lincoln Steffens: A Biography,* 1974.

69 You are all a lost generation.

> GERTRUDE STEIN, in a letter to Ernest Hemingway, 1926.

70 When I face the desolate impossibility of writing five hundred pages a sick sense of failure falls on me and I know I can never do it. This happens every time. Then gradually I write one page and then another. One day's work is all I can permit myself to contemplate and I eliminate the possibility of ever finishing.

> JOHN STEINBECK, *Travels with Charley,* 1962.

71 There is probably some long-standing "rule" among writers, journalists, and other word-mongers that says: "When you start stealing from your own work you're in bad trouble." And it may be true.

> HUNTER S. THOMPSON, *Fear and Loathing on the Campaign Trail, '72,* 1973.

72 Unfortunately many things have been omitted which should have been recorded in our journal, for though we made it a rule to set down all our experiences therein, yet such a resolution is very hard to keep, for the important experience rarely allows us to remember such obligations, and so indifferent things get recorded, while that is frequently neglected. It is not easy to write in a journal what interests us at any time, because to write it is not what interests us.

> HENRY DAVID THOREAU, *A Week on the Concord and Merrimack Rivers,* 1849.

73 You do not get a man's most effective criticism until you provoke him. Severe truth is expressed with some bitterness.

> HENRY DAVID THOREAU, entry dated March 15, 1854, in his *Journal,* 1906.

74 I like to think that among his most fervent prayers there must have been one that went: "O Lord, please give all our contributors a million bucks and don't let them bother me about dough again. Keep them productive, Lord, and lead them not into laziness, but deliver them from booze and dames and such. Amen. P.S. Please let Thurber get the system through his head; he doesn't know what goes on around here. And send me a man to make some sense out of this place. Done and done, Lord."

> JAMES THURBER, on Harold Ross, in *The Years with Ross,* 1957.

William Faulkner: Nobel Prize acceptance speech, December 10, 1950

Faulkner's famous address evokes the American credo of sacrifice, duty, compassion, and endurance in the face of the demeaning fear engendered by depression, war, and the atomic bomb. In reality his words were an affirmation of life against death, and Americans saw it not as a message directed only to writers and artists but as an appeal to all.

I feel that this award was not made to me as a man, but to my work—a life's work in the agony and sweat of the human spirit, not for glory and least of all for profit, but to create out of the materials of the human spirit something which did not exist before. So this award is only mine in trust. It will not be difficult to find a dedication for the money part of it commensurate with the purpose and significance of its origin. But I would like to do the same with the acclaim too, by using this moment as a pinnacle from which I might be listened to by the young men and women already dedicated to the same anguish and travail, among whom is already that one who will someday stand where I am standing.

Our tragedy today is a general and universal physical fear so long sustained by now that we can even bear it. There are no longer problems of the spirit. There is only the question: When will I be blown up? Because of this, the young man or woman writing today has forgotten the problems of the human heart in conflict with itself which alone can make good writing because only that is worth writing about, worth the agony and the sweat.

He must learn them again. He must teach himself that the basest of all things is to be afraid; and, teaching himself that, forget it forever, leaving no room in his workshop for anything but the old verities and truths of the heart, the old universal truths lacking which any story is ephemeral and doomed—love and honor and pity and pride and compassion and sacrifice. Until he does so, he labors under a curse. He writes not of love but of lust, of defeats in which nobody loses anything of value, of victories without hope and, worst of all, without pity or compassion. His griefs grieve on no universal bones, leaving no scars. He writes not of the heart but of the glands.

Until he relearns these things, he will write as though he stood among and watched the end of man. I decline to accept the end of man. It is easy enough to say that man is immortal simply because he will endure; that when the last ding-dong of doom has clanged and faded from the last worthless rock hanging tideless in the last red and dying evening, that even then there will still be one more sound: that of his puny, inexhaustible voice, still talking.

I refuse to accept this. I believe that man will not merely endure: he will prevail. He is immortal, not because he alone among creatures has an inexhaustible voice, but because he has a soul, a spirit capable of compassion and sacrifice and endurance. The poet's, the writer's duty is to write about these things. It is his privilege to help man endure by lifting his heart, by reminding him of the courage and honor and hope and pride and compassion and pity and sacrifice which have been the glory of his past. The poet's voice need not merely be the record of man; it can be one of the props, the pillars to help him endure and prevail.

75 He resigned the way other men went home to dinner.

> JAMES THURBER, on Alexander Woollcott, in *The Years with Ross,* 1957.

76 He loved to make everybody mad, and used insults the way other people use simple declarative sentences.

> Ibid.

77 Write without pay until somebody offers pay. If nobody offers within three years the candidate may look upon his circumstances with the most implicit confidence as the sign that sawing wood is what he was intended for.

> MARK TWAIN, "A General Reply," published in *The Galaxy* magazine, November, 1870.

78 It takes a heap of sense to write good nonsense.

> MARK TWAIN, in a note written to himself c.1879, quoted in Walter Blair and Hamlin Hill, *America's Humor,* 1978.

79 You don't know about me without you have read a book by the name of *The Adventures of Tom Sawyer;* but that ain't no matter. That book was made by Mr. Mark Twain, and he told the truth, mainly. There was things which he stretched, but mainly he told the truth.

> MARK TWAIN, opening lines of *The Adventures of Huckleberry Finn,* 1884.

80 There ain't nothing more to write about, and I am rotten glad of it, because if I'd a knowed what a trouble it was to make a book I wouldn't a tackled it, and ain't agoing to no more.

> MARK TWAIN, in the final paragraph of *The Adventures of Huckleberry Finn,* 1884.

81 We are nothing if not permissive. We've all had to get used to what I call demotic writing, where any word is as good as any other word, and garrulity, since it is so common in life, must then be virtuous in literature.

> GORE VIDAL, quoted in Bernard F. Dick, *The Apostate Angel,* 1974.

82 Teaching has ruined more American novelists than drink.

> GORE VIDAL, quoted in Beverly Kempton, "Conversation with Gore Vidal," *Oui* magazine, April, 1975.

83 It was most injudicious in [Samuel] Johnson to select Shakespeare as one of his principal authorities. Play-writers, in describing low scenes and vulgar characters, use low language, language unfit for decent company; and their ribaldry has corrupted our speech, as well as the public morals.

> NOAH WEBSTER, in a letter to Thomas Dawes, August 5, 1809.

84 Writing fiction is an interior affair. Novels and stories always will be put down little by little out of personal feeling and personal beliefs arrived at alone and at firsthand over a period of time as time is needed. To go outside and beat the drum is only to interrupt, interrupt, and so finally to forget and to lose. Fiction has, and must keep, a private address.

> EUDORA WELTY, *The Eye of the Story,* 1979.

85 Writing is so difficult that I often feel that writers, having had their hell on earth, will escape all punishment hereafter.

> JESSAMYN WEST, *To See the Dream,* 1956.

86 A writer is like a bean plant—he has his little day, and then gets stringy.

> E.B. WHITE, in a letter to Harold Ross, September 9, 1938.

87 I am inordinately proud these days of the quill, for it has shown itself, historically, to be the hypodermic which inoculates men and keeps the germ of freedom always in circulation, so that there are individuals in every time in every land who are the carriers, the Typhoid Mary's, capable of infecting others by mere contact and example. These persons are feared by every tyrant—who shows his fear by burning the books and destroying the individuals.

> E.B. WHITE, "Freedom," written in July, 1940, *One Man's Meat,* 1944.

88 I am beginning to feel a little more like an author now that I have had a book banned. The literary life, in this country, begins in jail.

E.B. WHITE, on the banning by the Army and Navy of his book *One Man's Meat,* in a letter to his brother, Stanley Hart White, June, 1944.

89 Margaret Mitchell once remarked: "It is a full-time job to be the author of 'Gone with the Wind.'" This remark greatly impressed me, as being an admission of defeat, American style. (Miss Mitchell, incidentally, was not overstating the matter—she never produced another book.) I don't want being the author of "Charlotte's Web" to be a full-time job or even a part-time job. It seems to me that *being an author* is a silly way to spend one's day.

E.B. WHITE, writing to a librarian who was offended by White's complaint that he was too busy answering letters from children to write another book for them, May 7, 1961.

90 I was a writing fool when I was eleven years old and have been tapering off ever since.

E.B. WHITE, in a letter to Judith W. Preusser, November 10, 1963.

91 I was interested in your remarks about the writer as poser, because, of course, all writing is both a mask and an unveiling, and the question of honesty is uppermost, particularly in the case of the essayist, who must take his trousers off without showing his genitals. (I got my training in the upper berths of Pullman cars long ago.)

E.B. WHITE, in a letter to Scott Elledge, February 16, 1964.

92 I never understood why the slightest fuss was made over G. Stein, whose contribution to letters strikes me as very close to zero.

E.B. WHITE, on Gertrude Stein, in a letter to Howard Cushman, June 21, 1967.

93 Three questions are essential to all just criticism: What is the author's object? How far has he accomplished it? How far is that object worthy of approbation?

NATHANIEL PARKER WILLIS, *Pencillings by the Way,* 1835.

94 Emerson and Thoreau were the real artists among the New England group, and you are likely to underestimate both their intellectual abilities and their style unless you actually read them. Emerson and the first and last chapters of *Walden* still communicate very vividly the real exhilaration in the air of the time. It was a sort of mystic exaltation of the spiritual life in the individual above the debasements of the practical life and the complications of society.

EDMUND WILSON, in a letter to John Peale Bishop, September 6, 1923.

95 He [John Dos Passos] is perhaps the first really important writer to have succeeded in using colloquial American for a novel of the highest artistic seriousness.

EDMUND WILSON, review of *The 42nd Parallel,* in *The New Republic,* 1930.

---

263. WYOMING

1 Equal rights.

State motto.

2 Wyoming is a land of great open spaces with plenty of elbow room. . . . There are sections of the State where it is said you can look farther and see less than any other place in the world.

Federal Writers' Project, *Wyoming: A Guide to Its History, Highways, and People,* 1941.

3 Here is America high, naked, and exposed; this is a massive upland almost like Bolivia.

JOHN GUNTHER, *Inside U.S.A.,* 1947.

4 Almost all the great western rivers are born in or near Wyoming: the Snake (which becomes the Columbia), the Green (Colorado), North Platte, and Yellowstone.

Ibid.

5 About the only thing that will make a Wyoming cattleman reach for his gun nowadays is to call him a "farmer." A "rancher," he wants it clearly understood, drinks only canned milk, never eats vegetables, and grows nothing but hay and whiskers.

Ibid.

6 I have been through the Yellowstone National Park in a buggy, in the company of an adventurous old lady from Chicago and her husband, who disapproved of [the] scenery as being "ongodly." I fancy it scared them.

RUDYARD KIPLING, *American Notes*, 1891.

7 On either side of us were hills from a thousand to fifteen hundred feet high and wooded from heel to crest. As far as the eye could range forward were columns of steam in the air, misshapen lumps of lime, most like preadamite monsters, still pools of turquoise blue, stretches of blue cornflowers, a river that coiled on itself twenty times, boulders of strange colors, and ridges of glaring, staring white.

Ibid.

8 I looked into a gulf seventeen hundred feet deep with eagles and fish hawks circling far below. And the sides of that gulf were one wild welter of color—crimson, emerald, cobalt, ochre, amber, honey splashed with port wine, snow white, vermilion, lemon, and silver grey, in wide washes. The sides did not fall sheer, but were graven by time and water and air into monstrous heads of kings, dead chiefs, men and women of the old time. So far below that no sound of its strife could reach us, the Yellowstone River ran—a finger-wide strip of jade green. The sunlight took those wondrous walls and gave fresh hues to those that nature had already laid there.

Ibid.

9 Hour after hour it was the same unhomely and unkindly world about our onward path; tumbled boulders, cliffs that drearily imitate the shape of monuments and fortifications—how drearily, how tamely, none can tell who has not seen them; not a tree, not a patch of sward, not one shapely or commanding mountain form; sagebrush, eternal sagebrush; over all, the same weariful and gloomy coloring, greys warming into brown, greys darkening towards black; and for sole sign of life, here and there a few fleeing antelopes; here and there, but at incredible intervals, a creek running in a cañon. The plains have a grandeur of their own; but here there is nothing but a contorted smallness.

ROBERT LOUIS STEVENSON, describing the Black Hills, *Across the Plains*, 1892.

---

264. YOUTH

See also AGE; FAMILY

---

1 A boy is an appetite with a skin pulled over it.

Anonymous.

2 Young men have a passion for regarding their elders as senile.

HENRY ADAMS, *The Education of Henry Adams*, 1918.

3 What one knows is, in youth, of little moment; they know enough who know how to learn.

Ibid.

4 Perhaps I may record here my protest against the efforts, so often made, to shield children and young people from all that has to do with death and sorrow, to give them a good time at all hazards on the assumption that the ills of life will come soon enough. Young people themselves often resent this attitude on the part of their elders; they feel set aside and belittled as if they were denied the common human experiences.

JANE ADDAMS, *Twenty Years at Hull House*, 1910.

5 Backward, turn backward, O Time, in your flight,
Make me a child again, just for tonight!

ELIZABETH AKERS ALLEN, "Rock Me to Sleep," 1860.

6 When you're young, the silliest notions seem the greatest achievements.

PEARL BAILEY, *The Raw Pearl*, 1968.

7 Young blood! Youth will be served!

STEPHEN VINCENT BENÉT, "Young Blood," *Young Adventure*, 1918.

8 Childhood, *n.* The period of human life intermediate between the idiocy of infancy and the folly of youth—two removes from the sin of manhood and three from the remorse of age.

AMBROSE BIERCE, *The Devil's Dictionary,* 1906.

9 The hatred of the youth culture for adult society is not a disinterested judgment but a terror-ridden refusal to be hooked into the . . . ecological chain of birthing, growing, and dying. It is the demand, in other words, to remain children.

MIDGE DECTER, *The New Chastity and Other Arguments Against Women's Liberation,* 1972.

10 All children are by nature children of wrath, and are in danger of eternal damnation in Hell.

Attributed to Jonathan Edwards.

11 O Youth: Do you know that yours is not the first generation to yearn for a life full of beauty and freedom? Do you know that all your ancestors felt as you do—and fell victim to trouble and hatred? Do you know, also, that your fervent wishes can only find fulfillment if you succeed in attaining love and understanding of men, and animals, and plants, and stars, so that every joy becomes your joy and every pain your pain? Open your eyes, your heart, your hands, and avoid the poison your forebears so greedily sucked in from History. Then will all the earth be your fatherland, and all your work and effort spread forth blessings.

ALBERT EINSTEIN, entry written in an album at Caputh, Germany, 1932.

12 Fortunately for us and our world, youth is not easily discouraged. Youth with its clear vista and boundless faith and optimism is uninhibited by the thousands of considerations that always bedevil man in his progress. The hopes of the world rest on the flexibility, vigor, capacity for new thought, the fresh outlook of the young.

DWIGHT D. EISENHOWER, in a commencement address at Gettysburg College, May 27, 1946.

13 "And youth is cruel, and has no remorse
    And smiles at situations which it cannot see."
 I smile, of course,
 And go on drinking tea.

T.S. ELIOT, "Portrait of a Lady," 1917.

14 Children are all foreigners.

RALPH WALDO EMERSON, entry written in 1839, *Journals,* 1909–1914.

15 The child with his sweet pranks the fool of his senses, commanded by every sight and sound, without any power to compare and rank his sensations, abandoned to a whistle or a painted chip, to a lead dragoon or a gingerbread-dog, individualizing everything, generalizing nothing, delighted with every new thing, lies down at night overpowered by the fatigue which this day of continual pretty madness has incurred. But Nature has answered her purpose with the curly, dimpled lunatic.

RALPH WALDO EMERSON, "Nature," *Essays,* Second Series, 1844.

16 What art can paint or gild any object in afterlife with the glow which nature gives to the first baubles of childhood! St. Peter's cannot have the magical power over us that the red and gold covers of our first picture-book possessed.

RALPH WALDO EMERSON, "Domestic Life," *Society and Solitude,* 1870.

17 Respect the child. Be not too much his parent. Trespass not on his solitude.

RALPH WALDO EMERSON, "Education," *Lectures and Biographical Sketches,* 1883.

18 [Boys] know truth from counterfeit as quick as the chemist does. They detect weakness in your eye and behavior a week before you open your mouth, and have given you the benefit of their opinion quick as a wink.

Ibid.

19 The number-one thing young people in America—indeed, young people around the world—have going for them is their sense of honesty, morality, and ethics. Young people refuse to accept the lies and rationalizations of the established order.

DICK GREGORY, in *Dick Gregory's Political Primer,* 1972.

20 Over the trackless past, somewhere,
    Lie the lost days of our tropic youth,
    Only regained by faith and prayer,

Only recalled by prayer and plaint:
Each lost day has its patron saint!

BRET HARTE, "The Lost Galleon," 1867.

21 Mom and Pop were just a couple of kids when they got married. He was eighteen, she was sixteen, and I was three.

BILLIE HOLIDAY, the opening lines of her autobiography, *Lady Sings the Blues,* 1958.

22 There is no time like the old time, when you and I were young.

OLIVER WENDELL HOLMES, SR., "No Time Like the Old Time," 1865.

23 Our Gilded Youths should be packed off to coal and iron mines, to freight trains, to fishing fleets in December, to dishwashing and clothes-washing, to road building and tunnel making, according to their choice, to get the childishness knocked out of them, and to come back into society with healthier sympathies and soberer ideas.

WILLIAM JAMES, "The Moral Equivalent of War," 1910.

24 Youth comes but once in a lifetime.

HENRY WADSWORTH LONGFELLOW, *Hyperion,* 1839.

25 Oh, thou child of many prayers!
Life hath quicksands—life hath snares!
Care and age come unawares!

HENRY WADSWORTH LONGFELLOW, "Maidenhood," *Ballads and Other Poems,* 1842.

26 Childhood is the bough, where slumbered
Birds and blossoms many-numbered.

Ibid.

27 And my youth comes back to me.
And a verse of a Lapland song
Is haunting my memory still:
"A boy's will is the wind's will,
And the thoughts of youth are long, long
    thoughts."

HENRY WADSWORTH LONGFELLOW, "My Lost Youth," 1855.

28 Between the dark and the daylight,
    When the night is beginning to lower,
Comes a pause in the day's occupations
    That is known as the children's hour.

HENRY WADSWORTH LONGFELLOW, "The Children's Hour," 1860.

29 There was a little girl, she had a little curl
    Right in the middle of her forehead;
And when she was good, she was very, very,
        good,
    And when she was bad, she was horrid.

Attributed to Henry Wadsworth Longfellow, untitled poem, 1871.

30 How beautiful is youth! how bright it gleams
With its illusions, aspirations, dreams!
Book of Beginnings, Story without End,
Each maid a heroine, and each man a friend!

HENRY WADSWORTH LONGFELLOW, "Morituri Salutamus," 1875.

31 Youth condemns; maturity condones.

AMY LOWELL, *Tendencies in Modern American Poetry,* 1917.

32 If youth be a defect, it is one that we outgrow only too soon.

JAMES RUSSELL LOWELL, in a speech in Cambridge, Massachusetts, November 8, 1886.

33 Where is the world we roved, Ned Bunn?
    Hollows thereof lay rich in shade
By voyagers old inviolate thrown
    Ere Paul Pry cruised with Pelf and Trade.
To us old lads some thoughts come home
Who roamed a world young lads no more
        shall roam.

HERMAN MELVILLE, "To Ned," in *John Marr and Other Sailors,* 1888.

34 The children are always the chief victims of social chaos.

AGNES MEYER, *Out of These Roots,* 1953.

35 This be our solace: that it was not said
When we were young and warm and in our
        prime,

Upon our couch we lay as lie the dead,
Sleeping away the unreturning time.

> EDNA ST. VINCENT MILLAY, sonnet XXVIII, in *Fatal Interview*, 1931.

36 Childhood knows the human heart.

> EDGAR ALLAN POE, "Tamerlane," 1827.

37 Oh! the old swimmin' hole! When I last saw the place,
The scenes was all changed, like the change in my face.

> JAMES WHITCOMB RILEY, "The Old Swimmin' Hole," 1883.

38 Youth sees too far to see how near it is
To seeing farther.

> EDWIN ARLINGTON ROBINSON, *Tristram,* 1927.

39 I confess to pride in this coming generation. You are working out your own salvation; you are more in love with life; you play with fire openly, where we did in secret, and few of you are burned!

> FRANKLIN D. ROOSEVELT, in a speech at Milton Academy, Milton, Massachusetts, May, 1926, published as *Whither Bound?* 1926.

40 Our youth is like a rustic at the play
That cries aloud in simple-hearted fear,
Curses the villain, shudders at the fray,
And weeps before the maiden's wreathed bier.

> GEORGE SANTAYANA, "The Rustic at the Play."

41 Consider well the proportions of things. It is better to be a young June-bug than an old bird of paradise.

> MARK TWAIN, "Pudd'nhead Wilson's Calendar," *Pudd'nhead Wilson,* 1894.

42 Blessings on thee, little man,
Barefoot boy, with cheek of tan! . . .

From my heart I give thee joy—
I was once a barefoot boy!

> JOHN GREENLEAF WHITTIER, "The Barefoot Boy," 1856.

43 Oh, for boyhood's painless play,
Sleep that wakes in laughing day,
Health that mocks the doctor's rules,
Knowledge never learned of schools.

> Ibid.

44 I mourn no more my vanished years:
Beneath a tender rain,
An April rain of smiles and tears,
My heart is young again.

> JOHN GREENLEAF WHITTIER, "My Psalm," 1859.

45 In America the young are always ready to give to those who are older than themselves the full benefits of their inexperience.

> OSCAR WILDE, "The American Invasion," in *Court and Society Review,* March, 1887.

46 You cannot have ecstasy and divine vision without bitterness and despair, and both of these are the property of youth. . . . For the young are not always lighthearted; youth bears a heavy heart. The earth quakes beneath his tread; the stars are combined against him; he is the battleground for a menagerie which is ready to spring at his throat. And when in the midst of these disasters he finds a moment of calm or freedom, his heart goes up like a rocket to the farthest reaches of the sky.

> EDMUND WILSON, in a letter to Christian Gauss, April 25, 1922.

47 The most conservative persons I ever met are college undergraduates.

> WOODROW WILSON, in a speech in New York City, November 19, 1905.

Index

Age *(cont'd)*

    our brains are seventy-year clocks, 136:59

    respectful hearin' whin ∼ further impaired mind, 7:16

    see childhood, youth, and manhood pass, and ∼ with furrowed brow, 234:5

    surest sign of ∼ is loneliness, 7:5

    thanks in old ∼—thanks ere I go, 136:125

    to know whether human is young or old, offer food at short intervals, 20:8

    truth from American statesman after turned seventy, 192:29

    when girls of twenty with money marry paupers, turned sixty, 140:52

    whom gods love die young, 63:35

    who travels to be amused, grows old, 235:7

    will you love me in December as you do in May?, 140:94

    women one group grows more radical with ∼, 257:72

    women's needs according to, 257:75

    young may die; but old must, 63:54

    young women beautiful—but old more beautiful, 257:84

    youth cannot mate with ∼, 145:54

Ages

    belongs to the ∼, 137:47

Agitation

    tolerance of ∼ in normal times safeguard of free government, 198:7

Agnew, Spiro T.

    on civil rights, 50:3

Agnostic

    compliment to be called ∼, 200:27

Agony

    like look of ∼, because I know it's true, 237:13

Agree

    men have gone to war and cut throats because could not ∼, 22:16

    more we arg'ed question, more we didn't ∼, 22:4

Agriculture, 8:1–23

    anything will grow there [California], 40:17

    blessed be ∼! if one does not have too much of it, 8:18

    Iowa spells ∼, 124:2

    Iowa's productivity, 124:3

no pursuit more [important] to country than improving its ∼, 8:19

    we cultivate and irrigate, but God who exaggerates, 40:3

Aid

    could use less foreign ∼ and more home ∼, 189:1

Aiken, George D.

    on Vietnam War, 243:6

Aim

    not failure, but low ∼ is crime, 11:16

    two things to ∼ at in life, 11:20

Air

    ∼ fouler every year, 188:14

    ∼ made love to all it touched, 221:5

    dependent on vulnerable reserves of ∼ and soil, 188:12

    Devil impregnates ∼ with malignant salts, 6:7

Airplane

    Success. Inform press. Home Christmas, 123:15

Airy

    there are ∼ hosts that see and know and appreciate our thoughts, 200:13

Alabama, 9:1–10

    ∼ bad name even among those who reside in it, 9:2

    come from ∼ with banjo on my knee, 9:8

    governor of ∼ is running employment agency, 101:34

    loveliness of backwoods architects of ∼, 9:4

    stars fell on ∼, 9:3

    state motto, 9:1

Alamo

    remember the ∼, 231:2

Alaska, 10:1–11

    bridge to Asia, 10:4

    God grew tired and that was how ∼ happened, 10:6

    outlying ward of Seattle, 248:3

    state motto, 10:1

    white silence, 10:5

Alcohol

    ∼ is nicissary f'r man so now an' thin he can have good opinion iv himsilf, 71:16

    mere ∼ doesn't thrill me at all, 253:15

Alcoholic

    ∼ psychosis ole D.T.'s in dinner suit, 71:34

Alcott, A. Bronson

    on adversity, 3:2

    on age, 7:5

    on ancestry, 17:1

on books, 35:1–4

    on civilization, 211:1

    on conversation, 59:4, 59:5

    on education, 74:8, 74:9

    on home, 109:5

    on humankind, 112:2

    on immortality, 117:2

    on language, 133:3

    on life, 136:4

    on temperament, 43:3, 43:4

    on time, 234:6

    on travel, 235:3, 235:4

    on truth, 237:2, 237:3

    on women, 257:5, 257:6

Alcott, Louisa May

    on character, 43:5

    on Christmas, 48:2

    on life, 136:5

    on November, 28:1

    on philosopher, 184:2

    on sorrow, 213:1

    on women's advice, 4:8

    on women's rights, 258:3

Aldrich, Thomas Bailey

    on beauty, 31:3

    on English tourist, 77:4

    on immigration, 116:5

    on soldier's death, 25:6

Alexander

    ∼'s Ragtime Band, 212:8

Alexander, Shana

    on evolution, 81:2

    on excellence, 97:1

    on marriage, 145:6

Algren, Nelson

    on advice, 4:9

Ali, Muhammad

    on being Black American, 34:1

    on boxing, 220:3–7

Alien

    American sovereign in probationary state, 15:4

Alike

    Nature never makes two men ∼, 120:12

Alimony

    ∼ most exorbitant of stud-fees, 69:1

    ∼—ransom that happy pay to devil, 69:14

Alive

    do not take life seriously—you never get out ∼, 136:68

All

    that's ∼ there is, isn't any more, 233:4

Allen, Elizabeth Akers

    on time, 234:7

    on youth, 264:5

Allen, Ethan

    at Ticonderoga, 14:15

    last words, 133:3

Allen, Fred
    on Boston (Mass.), 36:6
    on California, 40:4
    on Hollywood, 108:1
    on journalism, 125:4
    on writing, 262:1
Allen, Frederick Lewis
    on love, 140:4
    on music, 160:1
Allen, George
    on sports, 220:8
Allen, Hervey
    on time, 234:8
Allen, William
    on Oregon Territory, 251:4
Allen, Woody
    on death, 63:5
    on knowledge, 129:2
    on religion, 200:9
Alliance
    ⌣ should be hard diplomatic
        currency, 68:41
    entangling ⌣s with none, 68:26
    moment engage in ⌣s date
        downfall of republic, 68:25
    our true policy to steer clear of
        permanent ⌣s, 68:66
    young state should stay at home
        and wait suitors for ⌣, 68:17
Alms
    no true ⌣ which hand can hold,
        44:12
    who gives himself with his ⌣
        feeds three, 44:13
Alone
    better ⌣ than in bad company,
        4:60
    man who goes ⌣ can start today,
        120:27
    never said "I want to be ⌣",
        159:12
    right to be let ⌣—most
        comprehensive of rights, 50:6
    we walk ⌣ in world, 118:5
Ambition, 11:1–25
    ⌣ has disappointments to sour
        us, 11:6
    ⌣, vilified by enemies and made
        ridiculous by friends, 11:4
    Christmas is over. Uncork your
        ⌣, 48:1
    common ⌣ strains for elevations,
        11:24
    history will enable to know ⌣
        under every disguise it may
        assume, 107:36
    inherited wealth certain death to
        ⌣, 11:22, 249:60
    little spice of ⌣ I had in younger
        days has long since evaporated,
        11:11

mind whose ⌣s rise no higher
    than roof that shelters it,
    257:68
most would succeed in small
    things if not troubled with
    great ⌣s, 11:14
one wants to be *very* something,
    70:15
some of us becoming men we
    wanted to marry, 257:69
what madness is ⌣, 84:12
wisdom attempts nothing it
    cannot perform, 256:7
without ⌣ except to do good and
    serve country, 137:52
young women with ⌣s should be
    crafty and cautious, 257:41
Ambitious
    [pyramids] tomb for ⌣ booby,
        11:21
America, 12:1–123
almost a continent and hardly a
    nation, 12:85
⌣! ⌣! God shed His grace on
    thee, 12:9
⌣ body of free men, 12:118
⌣ cannot be ostrich with head in
    sand, 12:121
⌣ died of delusion she had moral
    leadership, 12:87
⌣ discovered accidentally by
    great seaman looking for
    something else, 107:54
⌣ does not consist of groups,
    15:54
⌣ excites admiration which must
    be felt on spot, 16:6
⌣ first, 260:18
⌣ for me, 12:105
⌣ has new delicacy, 16:11
⌣ is a hurricane, 12:77
⌣ is American, 12:49
⌣ is country of young men,
    12:31
⌣ is God's great Melting-Pot,
    16:60
⌣ is greatest of opportunities and
    worst of influences, 12:91
⌣ is only place where man
    full-grown, 12:42
⌣ is promise, 12:86
⌣ is rather like life, 16:17
⌣ is tune, 12:64
⌣ is vast conspiracy to make you
    happy, 12:104
⌣ land of overrated child, 16:22
⌣ land of wonders, 12:98
⌣ large friendly dog in small
    room, 16:46
⌣ last abode of romance, 12:70
⌣ means opportunity, freedom,
    power, 12:33

⌣ no place for artist, 262:57
⌣ one long expectoration, 16:54
⌣ only idealist nation in world,
    12:122
⌣ owes debt of justice, 12:62
⌣ owes social prejudices to
    different sects instrumental in
    establishing colonies, 12:18
⌣ proved it practicable to elevate
    mass of mankind, 12:108
⌣ quilt—many patches, pieces,
    colors, sizes held by common
    thread, 15:20
⌣'s duty to fight, 260:13
⌣ will tolerate taking of human
    life without second thought,
    12:40
⌣ would be England viewed
    through solar microscope, 16:14
⌣ woven of many strands, 12:27
⌣ young country with old
    mentality, 12:89
business of ⌣ is business, 39:20
can make poetry out of material
    things, 16:19
considered unhealthy in ⌣ to
    remember mistakes, 15:15
could not live in country so
    miserable as to possess no
    castles, 16:33
distinct national character for
    knavery, 16:38
don't read your reviews, ⌣,
    12:103
emotionally I know she is better
    than every other country, 12:65
English of ⌣ not at all inferior
    to that of England, 132:36
enthusyasm iv this country makes
    me think iv bonfire on ice-floe,
    12:23
European rarely able to see ⌣
    except in caricature, 15:29
everybody in ⌣ is soft, and hates
    conflict, 43:16
family of ⌣, 15:6
genius not be compared with
    Prussians, Austrians, or
    French, 16:39
genuine belief seems to have left
    us, 12:115
good things are football, kindness,
    and jazz bands, 12:90
government by free consent of
    governed, 12:97
government of naive, for naive,
    by naive, 12:81
great ardor for gain; but passion
    for rights of man, 12:118
greatest single achievement of
    European civilization, 16:32
Great Society, 12:54

~s always considering themselves as standing alone, 66:98

~s going to be most melodious-voiced people in world, 132:59

~s have power to baffle England, 14:24

~ society is sort of fresh-water pond, 12:4

~s rather be equal in slavery than unequal in freedom, 79:23

~ system of rugged individualism, 120:20

~ village is small edition of whole country, 16:34

born an ~; live an ~; die an ~, 180:46

can't prove you're ~ by waving Old Glory, 180:13

[Chicago] greatest and most typically ~, 46:7

Chicago last of great ~ cities, 46:11

Chicago most typically ~, 46:5

destiny of colored ~ is destiny of America, 34:6

destiny of republican government entrusted to hands of ~ people, 12:106

divine rights of common man heart of ~ faith, 12:26

do not propose to make merchandise of ~ principles, 39:19

every ~ owns all America, 15:16

every generation of ~s wanted more luxury for next generation, 12:24

every genuine ~ writer must deal with life he knows best, 138:21

fighting against superstitious valuation of Europe, 15:21

God will save good ~, 15:7

government as filled with love as are ~ people, 12:14

he is ~, leaving behind ancient prejudices, receives new ones, 12:20

if ~ condemned to confine activity to own affairs, 16:41

if I were an ~, 14:73

I—I also—an ~, 180:45

in America for month before I saw an ~, 16:55

in four quarters of globe, who reads an ~ book?, 16:37

isn't single human characteristic that can be labeled as "~", 12:101

just being ~ nowadays not always comfortable, 68:60

making of ~ begins where he rejects all other ties, 15:3

mixed ancestry of, 17:5

much cant in ~ moralism, 12:38

name of ~ always exalt pride of patriotism, 180:43

never saw anything like this 100 percent ~, 16:36

no man living will see instance of ~ removing to settle in Europe, 15:22

no second acts in ~ lives, 15:13

not Virginian but ~, 14:46

real ~ will be fusion of all races, 16:61

reservoir of good will toward ~ people, 12:117

slang, even vulgarities, besetting sin against which ~s have to guard, 132:62

soldiers of America have killed more ~s than foreign foes, 25:11

solitude is un-~, 12:58

some of those old ~ words *do* have bully swing, 132:53

springs of ~ civilization lie revealed in clear light of History, 12:84

stuffs for ten minutes thrice a day, 92:12

the ~ doctrinaire is converse of American demagogue, 66:14

ugly pages of ~ history obscured and forgotten, 12:62

un-~, wicked, intolerable, heathenish, 180:5

willing to love all mankind, *except an* ~, 16:21

American Indian

~ is of the soil, 13:13

belongs just as buffalo belonged, 13:13

if [white man] came cold and naked would clothe, 44:10

American Indians, 13:1–16 (*See also* Indian)

ask even chance to live as other men live, 13:9

cannot be fought with poetry, 13:15

Indians have not been without excuse for their evil deeds, 13:1

is it wrong for me to love my own?, 13:12

now you are many, and we are getting very few, 13:10

United States needs its Indians and their culture, 13:16

Americanism

~ means imperative duty to be nobler, 12:72

can be no fifty-fifty ~, 180:36

I hate this shallow ~, 12:32

word ~, 132:67

American (Know-Nothing) Party campaign slogans, 41:7, 41:8

Abraham Lincoln on, 210:37

American League

Washington last in ~, 30:2

American Revolution, 14:1–91

~ fought to preserve liberties Americans already had, 14:59

~ worth while if produced nothing but Declaration of Independence, 14:60

ended need for revolution, 204:32

heroes of ~ are actual, romantic image, debunked, 14:31

no men less revolutionary than heroes of ~, 14:18

Americans, 15:1–54

~ almost ignorant of music, 160:4

~ always assumed all problems can be solved, 15:47

~ always take their heroes from criminal classes, 16:56

~ appear insatiable of praise, 16:44

~ are queer people; they can't rest, 16:27

~ as gregarious as school-boys, 16:29

~ chosen people—Israel of our time, 15:31

~ dirtiest, most contemptible cowardly dogs, 16:59

~ eminently prophets, 15:44

~ getting like Ford car, 15:38

~ invented range of hackneyed phrases, 59:29

~ possessed of sense of humor and proportion, 15:40

~ see history as straight line, 15:14

~ stimulated by big job, 15:23

combined capacity for affairs with devotion to ideal, 15:41

desire to see our brethren secured in blessings enjoyed by ourselves, 15:19

earned slogan, 'Yanks, go home!', 15:52

good ~, when they die, go to Paris, 15:2

great average bulk, unprecedentedly great, 15:51

hard to divide along class lines, 15:37

heart has gone out to them; I cannot tell why, 16:24

I do not like ~ of lower orders, 16:47

Americans *(cont'd)*
  interest is their faith, Money their
    God, 16:51
  let us all be ⁓, 15:27
  most ⁓ are born drunk, 16:13
  no room in country for
    hyphenated ⁓, 15:43
  nothing matter with ⁓ except
    their ideals, 16:12
  old ⁓ drive themselves to death
    with huge cars, 15:49
  our great title is ⁓, 15:36
  race of convicts, 16:20
  ready to bite somebody to get
    what we want, 15:39
  run about world without caring to
    learn the language before hand,
    15:18
  some ⁓ need hyphens in names,
    15:53
  to ⁓ America something more
    than promise and expectation,
    15:30
  vainly imagined all blessings
    produced by superior wisdom
    and virtue of our own, 15:26
  we are puny and fickle folk, 15:9
  whenever confronted with threat
    to our security we are ⁓,
    15:34
  wince if breeze blows over them,
    unless tempered with adulation,
    16:49

**America Seen from Abroad,
  16:1–61** *(See also specific city
  and state names)*
  all men make money their
    pursuit, 29:8
  American does not drink at
    meals, 92:12
  average consumption of
    newspapers, three a day,
    125:72
  cities alike, both great and small,
    49:2
  cities enormous agglomerations,
    49:1
  economic situation of Negroes
    pathological, 34:25
  electioneering madness would
    make me fly from [America] in
    disgust, 75:19
  have everything in common
    except language, 132:65
  if great revolutions, will be
    brought about by black race,
    34:26
  in no country does one find so
    many men of eminent capacity
    for business, 39:10
  lads and lasses are all pale,
    105:23

men and women do not beg in
  the States, 16:48
more one studied [New York
  City], more grotesquely bad it
  grew, 171:59
[New York City] rises like
  Venice from sea, 171:99
New York fullest expression of
  modern age, 171:100
next Augustan age will dawn on
  other side of Atlantic, 16:50
no other country where love of
  money taken stronger hold,
  249:58
not good to be Negro in land of
  free, 34:15
nothing to see and no way to see
  it [in New York City], 171:98
remarkable how debased language
  has become in short period,
  132:35
seldom heard sentence elegantly
  turned, 219:24
South produced great statesmen,
  214:3
talk is of nothing but dollars,
  157:49
young always ready to give to
  older full benefits of
  inexperience, 264:45
Ames, Edward Scribner
  on religion, 200:10
Ames, Fisher
  on America, 12:6
  on elections, 101:7
  on George Washington, 246:1,
    246:2
  on government, 101:8
  on law, 134:5
  on liberty, 135:6
  on men, 144:1
Ames, Nathaniel
  on literature, 138:2
Ammunition
  praise Lord and pass ⁓, 261:7
Amoeba
  First ⁓, from whom we're all
    descended, 81:11
Amusement park
  Florida world's greatest ⁓, 89:7
Anarchism
  ⁓ of Hollywood, 159:29
  [Constitution] charter of ⁓, 57:35
Anarchy
  democracy runs to ⁓, 66:22
  we live in age of ⁓, 243:45
Anatomy
  women's chains forged by men,
    not ⁓, 258:22
Ancestor
  ⁓s never boast of descendants
    who boast of ⁓s, 17:17

democracy makes every man
  forget his ⁓s, 66:98
descent from ⁓ who did not care
  to trace own [genealogy], 17:3
every man is quotation from all
  his ⁓s, 17:9
how shall man escape from his
  ⁓s, 17:10
if my ⁓s look down they might
  upbraid me, 17:5
man is sum of his ⁓s, 112:4
no king has not had slave [nor slave
  king] among his ⁓s, 17:13
Ancestry, 17:1–21
  ⁓ and environment determine
    behavior, 17:4
  genius descends from long lines
    of ⁓, 17:1
  mule has neither pride of ⁓ nor
    hope of posterity, 19:1
  worthwhile to have behind him
    generations of honest,
    hard-working ⁓, 17:16
Anchor
  drop ⁓ anywhere and ⁓ will
    drag, 235:19
Anderson, Marian
  on money, 157:5
Anderson, Maxwell
  on war, 245:1
Anderson, Sherwood
  on New York City, 171:5
André, John
  last words, 133:4
Angel
  ⁓ visited green earth, and took
    flowers away, 63:49
  to hear ⁓s sing, 48:8
Angelou, Maya
  on being Black American, 34:2
Anger, 18:1–13
  ⁓ and folly walk cheek by jowl,
    18:7
  ⁓ is expensive luxury, 18:3
  ⁓ is never without reason, but
    seldom with good one, 18:10
  begun in ⁓ ends in shame, 18:6
Anglo-Saxon
  ⁓ carries self-government and
    self-development with him
    wherever he goes, 77:5
  only ⁓s can govern themselves,
    77:42
  to no race are we more indebted
    than to ⁓, 77:30
  we of ⁓ race do not know how
    to enjoy ourselves, 103:14
Angry
  never forget what man has said
    when ⁓, 18:2
  when ⁓ count four; when very
    ⁓, swear, 18:13

~ needs no religion beyond his
work, 26:24

~s must be sacrificed to their art,
26:18

~s never know much, 26:45

every ~ dips brush in own soul,
26:2

every ~ was first amateur, 26:19

great ~ can paint great picture
on small canvas, 26:56

great ~s never puritans, 26:39

scratch ~ and surprise a child,
26:27

thing that marks true ~ is clear
perception and firm, bold hand,
26:23

torpid ~ seeks inspiration at any
cost, 26:14

Artistic
deplore action which denies ~
talent opportunity because of
prejudice against race, 26:54

Ashes
people who fight fire with fire
end up with ~, 4:59

Asimov, Isaac
on space exploration, 217:3

Ask
~ not what your country can do
for you, 193:74

if you gotta ~ you'll never
know, 160:2

Aspiration
~s are my only friends, 11:15

Asquith, Margot
affair between ~ and ~, 262:61

Assimilation
mission of United States is
benevolent ~, 56:10

Associated Press
two forces carry light to corners
of globe—sun and ~, 125:75

Aster
frosty ~s like smoke upon hills,
28:8

withered tufts of ~s nod,
28:18

Astor, Nancy
on marriage, 145:7

Astor, Vincent
on money, 157:6

Astronaut
sat on tip of rocket, preparing to
get himself blown to pieces,
217:13

Astronomer
when I heard ~, 58:13

Asylum
~ for mankind, 14:65, 95:61

Atheism
Christian system near to ~ as
twilight to darkness, 200:139

Atheist
filthy little ~ [Thomas Paine],
200:152

Atherton, Gertrude
on friends, 96:6

Athlete
impossible for ~s to grow up,
220:24

never been great ~ did not know
what pain is, 220:9

tennis player complete ~, 220:29

Atkinson, Brooks
on New York City, 171:6

Atlanta (Ga.)
architecture of ~ is rococola, 98:4

Atom
come to judgment before the ~,
245:8

grasped mystery of ~ and
rejected Sermon on Mount,
174:3

if I had known Germans would
not succeed in constructing ~
bomb, 174:8

no evil in ~, 174:16

with unlocking of ~, mankind
crossed watershed of history,
174:17

Atomic
~ bomb paper tiger, 87:14

~ bombs made as preventive
measure, 174:7

~ deterring power can win years
of grace, 174:14

~ energy bears same duality that
has faced man from time
immemorial, 174:13

behind black portent of new ~
age lies hope, 174:1

harnessing basic power of
universe, 261:32

way to win ~ war make certain
it never starts, 245:6

weapon most terrible thing ever
discovered, 174:22

Auctioneer
~, man who picked pocket with
tongue, 39:4

Auden, W.H.
on America, 12:7

on music, 160:3

Audience
condense experience into glowing
symbol and ~ electrified, 177:6

gives you everything you need,
233:8

monster with four thousand eyes
and forty thousand teeth, 233:6

Audubon, John James
on Louisiana, 139:2

Austin, Mary
on women, 257:7

Author
~ of several books against world
in general, 35:36

beginning to feel little more like
~ now I have book banned,
262:88

being ~ is silly way to spend
one's day, 262:89

fundamental want is class of
native ~s, 138:66

good ~, not what he says, but
what he whispers, 262:67

if you understand ~'s character,
comprehension of his writings
becomes easy, 262:48

I'm not ~, but before I became
mayor, I wasn't a mayor,
262:44

never saw ~ that did not purr,
262:37

no ~ can conceive of difficulty of
writing romance about country
where there is no shadow,
262:28

no greater mistake than ~ship as
vocation, 262:25

nothing gives ~ so great
pleasure, as to find his words
respectfully quoted, 262:18

originality easily exaggerated,
especially by ~s contemplating
own work, 262:21

our ~s generally men of
business, 262:66

steal from one ~, it's plagiarism;
from many, it's research, 262:58

whatever ~ puts between covers
of his book is public property,
35:38

what is ~'s object?, 262:93

Authority, 27:1–9
all ~ belongs to the people, 27:7

~ based on ignorance of many
and knowledge of few, 27:4

Deity has not given any order of
men ~ over others, 27:2

firmly seated in ~ learns to think
security, and not progress, 27:8

firmly seated in ~ learns to think
security highest lesson of
statecraft, 195:23

men in ~ will always think that
criticism of their policies is
dangerous, 27:5

where people possess no ~, their
rights obtain no respect, 27:3

Autobiographies
~ ought to begin with Chapter
Two, 35:65

Autobiography
nobody should write ~ until
after he's dead, 99:5

Automobile
  Americans getting like Ford car,
    15:38
  old Americans drive themselves to
    death with huge cars, 15:49
  slogan of progress changing from
    full dinner pail to full garage,
    195:15
  Truman's advice on care of, 4:53
Autumn, 28:1–18 *(See also*
  specific months)
  ∼ leaves lie dead, 28:4
  incessant piped the quails, 28:15
  no richer gift has ∼ poured,
    8:22
  reconciling days to graduate ∼
    into winter, 28:12
  skies put on old sophistries of
    June, 28:11
  some call it ∼, others call it
    God, 28:10
  so mercifully dealing with
    growths of summer, 28:6
  these dark days of ∼ rain are
    beautiful, 28:13
  tints of ∼ blossoming under
    spell, 28:17
  withered tufts of asters nod,
    28:18
Avarice, 29:1–10
  ∼ and happiness never saw each
    other, 29:3
Axe
  Lizzie Borden took ∼, 61:1
Axline, Virginia Mae
  on therapy, 105:1

Babbitt, Irving
  on poet, 185:2
Bacchus
  count pleasures ∼ yields to me,
    71:24
Back
  ∼ to normalcy, 41:20
  on his ∼ burden of world,
    189:34
Backbone
  has ∼ of chocolate eclair,
    193:109
Backward
  ∼, flow ∼, O tide of years,
    234:7
Bacon, Leonard
  on slavery, 210:5
Bad
  ∼ times have scientific value, 3:5
  good and ∼ but names readily
    transferable, 183:16
  nothing in its place is ∼, 183:48
  so much ∼ in best of us, 43:1,
    100:1

Baer, George F.
  on labor, 131:4
Baez, Joan
  on war, 245:2
Bagby, George William
  on cottontot, 215:4
Bailey, Francis
  on George Washington, 246:3
Bailey, Pearl
  on America, 12:8
  on poverty, 189:1, 189:2
  on youth, 264:6
Baker, Dorothy
  on luck, 141:1
Baker, Russell
  on happiness, 103:1
  on own writing, 262:2
Balance
  ∼ of power accompanies ∼ of
    property, 190:4
  management of ∼ of power
    permanent undertaking, 190:29
Balboa, Vasco Nuñez de
  on lawyers, 134:6
Baldwin, James
  on Americans, 15:3
  on being Black American, 34:3,
    34:4
  on Harlem, 171:7
Ball
  after the ∼, 212:16
Ball, Lucille
  on luck, 141:2
  on talent, 226:1
Ballard, W.T.
  on Brooklyn, 171:8
Ball game
  leave ∼ in ball park, 30:43
  take me out to ∼, 30:28
  three strikes you're out at old ∼,
    30:29
Balloon
  five thousand ∼s could not cost
    more than five ships, 123:7
Ballot
  ∼ is stronger than bullet, 66:63,
    210:39
  ∼s are rightful successors of
    bullets, 66:66
Baloney
  how thin slice it, still ∼, 187:136
Baltimore (Md.)
  amusing for week, 16:57
  ∼ sits as robust but unnaturally
    good child on green apron of
    nurse, 146:6
  John Doe of definite *house* in ∼,
    146:8
  Johns Hopkins on medical care,
    148:12
  look in vain for shabby fringes,
    146:5

  old charm survives despite frantic
    efforts of boosters, 146:7
  romantic parks and woodlands,
    146:4
  unsavory name of "Mobtown,"
    146:3
Banana
  as society, we're ∼ republic,
    139:12
  where ∼ grows man sensual and
    cruel, 211:18
Bancroft, George
  on authority, 27:3
  on democracy, 66:3
Bandwagon
  jumping on ∼ can look like
    leadership, 187:92
Banjo
  wid ∼ on my knee, 212:14
Bank
  ∼s are failing all over country,
    but not the sand ∼s,
    157:58
  I cried all way to ∼, 157:47
  on ∼s of the Wabash, 119:2
  power of vast surplus in ∼s,
    39:13, 157:9
  since South Sea Bubble I have
    been afraid of ∼s, 39:39
Banker
  ∼s like anybody else, except
    richer, 249:43
Bankhead, Tallulah
  Gloria Swanson on, 84:26
  on own character, 43:6
  on own chastity, 45:1
  on phobias, 136:6
  on theater, 233:2, 233:3
Banking
  ∼ establishments more dangerous
    than standing armies, 64:12
Bankruptcy
  [nation] on road to ∼ [when]
    continues to pile up deficits,
    73:34
Banner
  many eye has danced to see that
    ∼ in sky, 88:5
  star spangled ∼ yet wave, 88:6
Barber
  beware old ∼, 4:19
Bard
  ∼s sublime whose distant
    footsteps echo, 185:21
Barefoot
  ∼ boy, with cheek of tan,
    264:42
Bargain
  necessity never made good ∼,
    73:7
Barich, Bill
  on horse racing, 111:1

Blackout
  New York City, 171:57
Blacksmith
  under spreading chestnut tree,
    259:48
Blaine, James G.
  armed warrior, plumed knight,
    187:63
  campaign slogan, 41:12
  liar from state of Maine, 41:12
  on politics, 187:12
  on trusts, 39:9
  Roscoe Conkling on, 122:3
Blake, James W.
  on New York City, 171:17
Bland
  ⌒ lead the ⌒, 42:8
Bland, James A.
  on Virginia, 244:3
Blease, Coleman L.
  on Constitution, 57:1
Blemish
  flaw in diamond stands out while
    ⌒ on pebble is unnoticed,
    193:72
Bless
  Job feels rod, yet ⌒es God,
    200:2
Blessing
  ⌒s on thee, little man, 264:42
Blindness
  ⌒ to feelings of creatures
    different from ourselves, 183:30
  glare that is ⌒ in early afternoon,
    254:1
Blonde
  gentlemen prefer ⌒s, 47:11
Blood
  ⌒ is destiny, 17:1
  ⌒ will tell but often tells too
    much, 17:17
  lines of red lines of ⌒, nobly
    shed, 180:50
  pint of sweat will save gallon of
    ⌒, 245:69
  smoke and ⌒ is mix of steel,
    39:60
  talk about their Pilgrim ⌒,
    17:14
  war, red animal—war, ⌒-swollen
    god, 245:10
  waving ⌒y shirt, 187:101
Bloomer, Amelia Jenks
  on dress, 70:2
Blossom
  trails its ⌒s in dust, 136:81
Blount, Ray, Jr.
  on literature, 138:6
Blue laws
  ⌒, laying it down that laws of
    God should be law of land,
    55:6

Blues
  ⌒ are songs of despair, 212:18
  from ⌒ that American music
    derives most distinctive
    characteristic, 160:15
Blush
  man only animal that ⌒es,
    112:58
Boarding house
  no one heard of going to war for
    ⌒, 109:37
Boas, Franz
  on ancestry, 17:4
Boat
  rides through sewer in
    glass-bottomed ⌒, 199:11
  trip through sewer in
    glass-bottomed ⌒, 108:12
Body
  strong, firm-fibred ⌒ beautiful as
    most beautiful face, 105:25
Bogart, Humphrey
  last words, 133:9
  on motion pictures, 159:5,
    159:6
Boiling
  to ⌒ pot flies come not, 259:21
Boker, George Henry
  on Abraham Lincoln, 137:4
  on death, 63:6
  on soldier's death, 25:7
Boldenweck, Bill
  on chili, 92:4
Boldt, George H.
  on law, 134:16
Bolton, Charles E.
  on revenge, 203:1
Bonds
  opposed to interest-bearing ⌒ in
    time of peace, 64:1
Bone
  life near ⌒, 189:43
  roll dem ⌒s, 63:31
Book
  any ⌒ which serves to lower
    human gaiety is moral
    delinquent, 35:63
  average shelf life of trade ⌒
    somewhere between milk and
    yogurt, 35:74
  bequest of wings was but a ⌒,
    35:13
  ⌒ highest delight in highest
    civilization, 35:30
  ⌒ of moonlight not written yet,
    35:67
  ⌒ ought to be though eccentric,
    yet its own, 35:59
  bring not to field or stone fancies
    found in ⌒s, 161:31
  "Classic." ⌒ people praise and
    don't read, 138:59

covers of this ⌒ are too far apart,
    35:7
dating new era in life from
    reading ⌒, 35:72
don't join ⌒ burners, 35:17
English dictionary most
    interesting ⌒ in our language,
    35:60
foolishest ⌒ is leaky boat on sea
    of wisdom, 35:42
for every ⌒ that survives
    judgment of time, nine
    hundred and ninety-nine rotting
    unread, 97:14
good ⌒ is opened with
    expectation and closed with
    profit, 35:3
if I'd knowed trouble it was to
    make ⌒ I wouldn't a tackled
    it, 262:80
I had better never see ⌒ than be
    warped by its attraction,
    138:12
men over forty are no judges of
    ⌒ written in new spirit, 35:32
must be man behind ⌒, 262:10
no ⌒ of much importance, 35:44
no frigate like ⌒ to take us lands
    away, 35:14
no girl ever ruined by ⌒, 35:75
no weather will be found in this
    ⌒, 250:18
pages of my ⌒ is my funeral urn,
    35:11
reader became ⌒, 35:68
readers judge power of ⌒ by
    shock it gives, 138:36
security in old ⌒, 35:55
that ⌒ was made by Mr. Mark
    Twain, and he told truth,
    mainly, 262:79
'tis good reader that makes good
    ⌒, 35:24
to produce mighty ⌒, choose
    mighty theme, 35:56
wear old coat and buy new ⌒,
    35:61
whatever author puts between
    covers of his ⌒ is public
    property, 35:38
what is best in any ⌒ is
    translatable, 35:26
who touches this [⌒] touches a
    man, 35:77
would never read ⌒ if possible to
    talk with man who wrote it,
    35:78
wouldn't pay $50,000 for any
    damn ⌒, 159:33
Books, 35:1–78
  a good book is fruitful of other
    ⌒, 35:1

British (*See also* England; English)
~ leaders have itch for dictation, and chief vice is thirst for power, 77:21
~ refusal to accept defeat [World War II], 261:20
~ require to be kicked into common good manners, 77:23
considered ~ our natural enemies, 77:24
not a more disgusting spectacle under sun than our subserviency to ~ criticism, 77:36

British Isles
little speck ~? 'Tis but freckle, 77:19

Broadway
give my regards to ~, 171:21, 233:10
Great White Way, 171:84
some day old ~ shall climb to skies, 233:22
when away from old ~ only camping out, 233:11

Brock, Lou
on baseball, 30:8

Brockenbrough, John
on patriotism, 180:6

Brodie, John
on football, 93:1

Brogan, Denis William
on American militarism, 16:3, 16:4

Brokaw, Tom
on South Dakota, 216:2, 216:3

Bromfield, Louis
on Ohio, 175:2

Bronx
the ~? God bless them, 171:83
the ~? no thonx, 171:82

Brooke, Edward W.
on Congress, 54:14

Brooke, Rupert
on American class structure, 16:5

Brooklyn
~ afforded tame excitement, 171:80
can take boy out of ~, 171:8
tree grows in ~, 171:93

Brooklyn Bridge
Hart Crane on, 171:22
John A. Roebling on, 21:10

Brooklyn Dodgers
when ~ left, things have never been same, 30:6

Brooks, Louise
on Hollywood, 108:3, 108:4
on motion pictures, 159:7–9

Brooks, Phillips
on Christmas, 48:4
on greatness, 102:2

Brooks, Van Wyck
on authority, 27:4
on evil, 80:2

Brotherhood
crown thy good with ~, 12:9
don't believe in ~ with anybody who doesn't want ~ with me, 53:19
will sit down together at table of ~, 50:26

Brothers, Joyce
on marriage, 145:16

Brotherton, Alice Williams
on Thanksgiving Day, 232:2

Broun, Heywood
on conversation, 59:9
on life, 136:10
on love, 140:12
on politics, 187:13
on truth, 237:7

Broun, Heywood Hale
on football, 93:2, 93:3
on golf, 220:12
on sports, 220:11

Broun, Mrs. Heywood Hale
on horse racing, 111:2

Brown, Edmund G.
on diplomacy, 68:7
on Ronald Reagan, 193:9

Brown, James M.
on pesticides, 188:2

Brown, John
Herman Melville on, 51:46
last words, 133:11
on cowardice, 60:2

Browning, Robert
on Chicago (Ill.), 46:4

Brutal
of all animals, man most ~, 112:1

Bryan, William Jennings
Alistair Cooke on, 237:10
campaign slogans, 41:14, 41:16
Daniel Moynihan on, 39:49
on Americans, 15:5
on belief, 32:2, 32:3
on civil rights, 50:7
on democracy, 66:5
on destiny, 67:1
on economics, 73:2
on evolution, 81:4
on gold, 157:8
on money, 157:7
on oratory, 177:2
on public education, 74:17
on World War I, 260:1
Theodore Roosevelt on, 177:12

Bryant, William Cullen
on Abraham Lincoln, 137:6
on adversity, 3:3, 3:4
on autumn, 28:3–7
on death, 63:8–11

on flowers, 90:3
on nature, 161:8–11
on Oregon, 178:3
on poetry, 186:1, 186:2
on progress, 195:3
on truth, 237:8

Bryce, James
on American emphasis on size, 16:7
on American individualism, 16:9
on American optimism, 16:8
on American Revolution, 14:18
on American spirit, 16:6
on business, 39:10–12
on California, 40:5
on Chicago (Ill.), 46:5
on cities, 49:2
on Civil War, 51:9
on Constitution, 57:2
on democracy, 66:6
on education, 74:19
on elections, 75:1–3
on equality, 79:1
on Franklin Pierce, 193:11
on government, 101:13
on James K. Polk, 193:11
on journalism, 125:8
on law, 134:19
on literature, 138:7
on political education, 74:18
on politics, 187:14, 187:15
on presidency, 54:15, 192:5, 192:6
on rebellion, 198:3
on statesmen, 222:1
on states' rights, 223:3, 223:4
on the public, 196:2–4
on the West, 251:6
on Washington (D.C.), 247:2

Brzezinski, Zbigniew
on diplomacy, 68:8
on Jimmy Carter, 193:12

Buchanan, James
on leaving presidency, 193:13

Buck, Pearl S.
on age, 7:11
on books, 35:8
on hope, 110:1
on Kansas, 127:8
on literature, 138:8
on male-female relations, 257:12
on society, 211:3
on Vermont, 240:3, 240:4

Buckingham, J. S.
on Alabama, 9:2

Buckley, William F., Jr.
on democracy, 66:7
on education, 74:20
on freedom, 95:12
on history, 107:10
on individuality, 120:3
on politics, 187:16

on society, 211:4
on truth, 237:9
Bug
 lies snug as ⁓ in rug, 78:12
 lightning ⁓ wondrous sight,
   161:1
Bugle
 high above fight lonely ⁓ grieves,
   245:63
Build
 ah, to ⁓, to ⁓!, 21:7
 ⁓ thee more stately mansions, O
   my soul, 43:49
 not too late to ⁓ young land
   right, 199:8
Builder
 ⁓s wrought with greatest care,
   21:6
Building
 better hand in pulling down than
   ⁓, 14:6
 real ⁓ one on which eye can
   light and stay lit, 21:9
Built
 we ⁓ it, we paid for it, 68:51
Bull
 not ⁓ of them all but is
   persuaded he bears Europa
   upon his back, 77:32
Bull moose
 I am strong as ⁓, 187:128
 I feel like ⁓, 193:113
Bums
 even the ⁓ are talented [in New
   York City], 171:69
Bunner, Henry Cuyler
 on flag, 88:1
Burbank, Luther
 on science, 207:3
Burchard, Samuel D.
 on politics, 187:17
Burden
 how heavy and constant would be
   those ⁓s, 193:77
 on back ⁓ of world, 8:12
Bureaucracy
 ⁓ does not take kindly to being
   assailed, 101:112
 ⁓ modern form of despotism,
   238:20
 only thing that saves us from ⁓
   is its inefficiency, 101:93
 shall soon be spending billions of
   dollars more, 101:118
Bureaucrat
 don't need lot of ⁓s looking over
   your shoulder, 118:6
Burges, Tristam
 on John Randolph, 122:2
Burgess, Gelett
 on San Francisco (Calif.), 206:1

Purple Cow remark, 113:9,
   113:10
Burgoyne, John
 on American Revolution, 14:19
Buried
 ⁓ was bloody hatchet, 181:25
 do not propose to be ⁓ until
   really dead, 241:13
 here was ⁓ Thomas Jefferson,
   78:16
 nobuddy ever fergits where ⁓
   hatchet, 203:5
Burke, Edmund
 on American commerce, 16:10
 on American Revolution, 14:20,
   14:21
Burke, Kenneth
 on choice, 47:3
 on wisdom, 256:1
Burn
 candle ⁓s at both ends, 136:96
Burr, Aaron
 last words, 133:12
 on action, 1:2
 on Constitution, 57:3
 on law, 134:20
Burr, Amelia Josephine
 on spring, 221:1
Burroughs, Edgar Rice
 on love, 140:13
Burroughs, John
 on immortality, 117:4
 on life, 136:11
 on literature, 138:9
 on nature, 161:12
 on science, 207:4
 on time, 234:9
Burt, Struthers
 on New Jersey, 167:3
Bury
 ⁓ me not on the lone prairie, 251:3
Bush, Vannevar
 on science, 207:5
Business, 39:1–71
 American dream every man could
   become an owner, 224:2
 as much conscience as any man in
   ⁓ can afford, 39:62
 big ⁓ "nothing but collection of
   organized appetites", 39:49
 ⁓es properly part of functions of
   state, 101:46
 ⁓ has to prosper before anybody
   can benefit from it, 39:58
 ⁓ underlies everything in our
   national life, 39:70
 chase and kill as much fun as
   prize, 39:16
 drive thy ⁓ *let not that drive*
   thee, 39:31
 employer puts his money into ⁓
   and workman his life, 39:23

free speech does not live many
   hours after free industry and
   commerce die, 95:35
 he that riseth late shall scarce
   overtake his ⁓, 259:20
 let each part of your ⁓ have its
   time, 39:32
 man's success in ⁓ turns upon
   his power of getting people to
   believe he has something they
   want, 39:43
 marriage is a small ⁓, 145:40
 most men are individuals no
   longer so far as their ⁓,
   39:69
 never fear want of ⁓, 259:41
 no better ballast for keeping mind
   steady on its keel than ⁓,
   39:47
 no ⁓ which depends on paying
   less than living wages has right
   to continue, 39:54
 nothing is illegal if hundred
   ⁓men decide to do it, 39:71
 notion that a ⁓ is clothed with
   public interest is little more
   than fiction, 39:37
 object of ⁓ is to make money in
   honorable manner, 39:22
 of America is ⁓, 39:20
 only he successful in his ⁓ who
   makes pursuit which affords
   him highest pleasure, 224:38
 opposition between the people and
   big ⁓ has disappeared, 39:45
 politics the people's ⁓, 187:140
 prostitution only ⁓ that isn't
   leaving [New York City],
   171:31
 revolting character United States
   produced was Christian ⁓man,
   39:48
 so many men of eminent capacity
   for ⁓, 39:10
 this world is place of ⁓, 39:64
 we demand that big ⁓ give
   people square deal, 39:59
 when ⁓ is good it pays to
   advertise, 39:1
 whole curse of trade attaches to
   ⁓, 39:63
Busy
 ⁓ as one-armed man pasting on
   wallpaper, 259:32
 ⁓ man has few idle visitors,
   259:21
Butler, Benjamin F.
 on politics, 187:18
Butler, Nicholas Murray
 on education, 74:21
Butler, Samuel
 on genius, 97:3

Butler, William Allen
  on dress, 70:3
  on marriage, 145:17
Butte (Mont.)
  ~ toughest, bawdiest town in America, 158:2
  monument to wasted land, 158:5
Buttercup
  yellow japanned ~s, 90:7
By-and-by
  in the sweet ~, 212:26
Byrnes, James F.
  on power, 190:9

Cabell, James Branch
  on drinking, 71:10
  on kiss, 140:15
  on love, 140:14
  on marriage, 145:18
  on perception, 183:10
  on poverty, 189:6
  on religion, 200:23
  on theater, 233:9
  on Virginia, 244:4
  on women, 257:13
Cabots
  ~ can't see Kabotschniks, 37:2
  ~ speak only to God, 37:1
  Cohns taking up ~, 37:4
Cadman, Samuel Parkes
  on insanity, 121:2
Caen, Herb
  on religion, 200:24
Cahan, Abraham
  on immigrant clothing industry, 116:7
Caine, Lynn
  on death, 63:12
Cairo (Ill.)
  dismal swamp, on which half-built houses rot away, 115:4
Calamities
  ~ will become lighter, 14:26
Calamity
  two kinds: misfortune to ourselves, and good fortune to others, 236:3
Caldwell, Erskine
  on West Virginia, 252:3
Caldwell, James
  on American Revolution, 14:22
Calhoun, John C.
  last words, 133:13
  on banks' power, 157:9
  on business, 39:13
  on government, 101:14–16
  on liberty, 135:10, 135:11
  on patriotism, 180:7
  on slavery, 210:7
  on states' rights, 223:5

California, 40:1–27
  all scenery in ~ requires *distance*, 40:26
  attraction and superiority of ~ are in its days, 40:8
  ~ can furnish best bad things obtainable, 206:4
  ~ great place—if you happen to be orange, 40:4
  ~ has turned back on world, 40:15
  ~ is country by itself, 40:5
  ~ is tragic country—like every Promised Land, 40:13
  can fall asleep under rose bush in full bloom and freeze to death, 40:9
  men proud, and extravant; women little education, beauty, and morality is none of best, 40:7
  Mojave as though nature tested man for endurance to get to ~, 40:24
  Mount Shasta sudden and solitary from black forests of Northern ~, 40:19
  Nixon on gubernatorial defeat in, 193:91
  no one allowed to attend dinner for Old Settlers of ~ unless in State two and one half years, 40:21
  shame to take away from rattlesnakes, 40:10
  state motto, 40:1
  whatever starts in ~ has inclination to spread, 40:6
  where Creator keeps his treasures, 40:17
Californian
  ~s are race of people, 40:11
  ~ scoundrels invariably lighthearted, 40:14
  how many ~s does it take to change light bulb?, 40:2
Calloway, Cab
  on horse racing, 111:3
Cambodia
  not expanding war into ~, 243:44
Cambridge (Mass.)
  ~ ladies who live in furnished souls, 147:5
Camelot
  "Bridgeport?" said I, pointing. "~," said he, 55:9
Campaign
  monopoly of all dirt in this ~, 187:22
Campaign Slogans, 41:1–39
Candidate
  dogs great assets to ~s, 75:10

Candle
  my ~ burns at both ends, 136:96
Candy
  ~ is dandy but liquor is quicker, 253:14
Cannon
  ~ not suffer other sound to be heard, 245:26
Cannon, Joseph G.
  on ancestry, 17:5
  on William McKinley, 193:14
Capacities
  man's ~ never been measured, 82:16, 226:5
Capital
  ~ all other groups buying [labor's product], 131:31
  ~ only fruit of labor, 131:37
  ~ organizes and labor must organize, 131:51
  ~ result of labor, used by labor, 131:14
  ~ solicits aid of labor, 131:58
  if ~ an' labor git t'gether it's good night fer rest of us, 73:21
  let your ~ be simplicity and contentment, 157:58
  only great country in world which has no ~, 247:2
  whatever ~ you divest to shiftless person is so much diverted from somebody else, 44:18
  whatever your ~ produces is yours, 73:16
Capitalism
  not sufficient condition for political freedom, 39:33
  socialism is degenerate ~, 187:97
Capitalists
  ~ generally act harmoniously to fleece people, 39:44
Capital punishment (*See also* Gallows; Hang)
  ~ as fundamentally wrong as cure for crime as charity for poverty, 126:10
  smaller penalty fewer crimes, 61:11
Capote, Truman
  on belief, 32:4
  on crime, 61:9
  on death, 63:13
  on home, 109:8
  on love, 140:16
Captain
  O ~! my ~, 137:55
Carabillo, Toni
  on police surveillance, 61:10
Cardozo, Benjamin N.
  on free speech, 95:13
  on justice, 126:2
  on language, 132:6

Children *(cont'd)*
suburbs are good for ⌒, 85:19
two classes of travel—first class
and with ⌒, 235:5
what maintains one vice would
bring up two ⌒, 85:10
world needs husbands and wives
who give attention to their ⌒,
85:13

Childress, Lee
on Vietnam War, 243:7

Chili
⌒'s like sex, 92:4

Chimpanzee
behold ⌒ from which we sprang
in ages gone, 81:12

China
open door policy, 68:22

Chinese
no State court or court of the
United States shall admit ⌒ to
citizenship, 116:2

Chips
let ⌒ fly where may, 193:24

Chisholm, Shirley
on Congress, 54:16
on Richard M. Nixon, 193:19

Choate, Joseph Hodges
on law, 134:22

Choate, Rufus
on Declaration of Independence,
51:11
on John Quincy Adams, 193:20
on patriotism, 180:8

Chocolate
Harlem of honey and ⌒, 171:51
superiority of ⌒, 92:11

Choice, 47:1–13
among our gains must be reckoned
possibility   of   ⌒,   47:13
⌒ not echo, 41:36
cultural constraints limit our ⌒s,
62:7
if decisions were ⌒ between
alternatives, decisions would
come easy, 47:3
society clamoring for ⌒ will give
each generation no peace, 47:12
struggle to rescue ⌒ from
pressure of circumstance,
187:76
without possibility of ⌒ man not
man but thing, 95:54

Choose
I do not ⌒ to run, 193:26
will is that by which mind ⌒s
anything, 47:5

Christ
justified only by faith in ⌒,
200:45
Quakers come nearer to ⌒ than
any other sect, 200:63

Christian
Bible-believing ⌒s have been
largely absent from
government, 101:41
born-again ⌒s bigger pain second
time around, 200:24
⌒ endeavor hard on female
pulchritude, 31:28
⌒ follows teachings of Christ so
far as not inconsistent with life
of sin, 200:17
⌒ system species of atheism,
200:139
fraud of ⌒ system to call
sciences human invention,
207:29
in Christendom where is the ⌒?,
200:53
nation is sectarian, rather than ⌒,
200:26
revolting character produced was
⌒ businessman, 39:48
suffering prevented me from
shadowing young soul with
superstitions of ⌒ religion,
200:156
true ⌒ is true citizen, 200:153
whatever makes good ⌒s makes
good citizens, 200:177

Christianity
can never see ⌒ from catechism,
200:57
I don't equate America with ⌒,
12:34
if any place in world need ⌒, it's
in Washington, 201:5
infidel esteems bladder of dirty
water as proper weapon to
assail ⌒, 200:152
since introduction of ⌒, coercion
[made] one half world fools
and other half hypocrites,
201:10

Christian Science
Mind is All-in-all, 200:36
if ⌒ had some science, 148:4
law of God, interpreting and
demonstrating rule of universal
harmony, 200:38
Mary Baker Eddy on, 148:5

Christmas, 48:1–8
carols, 48:4, 48:6, 48:8
⌒ is over. Uncork your ambition,
48:1
⌒ spirit [comes] to head like boil
once a year, 48:3
⌒ won't be ⌒ without presents,
48:2
I heard bells on ⌒ Day, 48:6
jest 'fore ⌒ I'm as good as I kin
be, 48:5
'twas night before ⌒, 48:7

Church
adulterous connection of ⌒ and
state, 201:22
⌒ must be reminded it is not
master or servant of state,
201:17
hospital for men's souls,
200:158
I like silent ⌒ better than
preaching, 200:52
keep ⌒ and State forever
separate, 200:84
local ⌒ nothing but congregation
of families, 85:7
own mind is own ⌒, 200:141
tavern will compare favorably
with ⌒, 200:161
thunders oftener break upon ⌒es,
250:11

Cigar
five-cent ⌒s cost a quarter, 73:1
politics are but as ⌒-smoke of a
man, 187:144

Cincinnati (Ohio)
beautiful city; cheerful, thriving,
and animated, 175:3

Circus
how were ⌒ receipts today?,
133:6

Cities, 49:1–16 *(See also names of
specific cities)*
American ⌒ like badger holes,
ringed with trash, 49:13
⌒ alike, both great and small,
49:2
⌒ give us collision, 49:4
⌒ in whose dark recesses
elevators ascending and
descending, 49:1
⌒ of America inexpressibly
tedious, 16:57
⌒ too big and rich for beauty,
49:10
filthy streets, 49:12
if ⌒ built by sound of music,
21:4
mobs of great ⌒ add to pure
government as sores to human
body, 49:6
New Orleans most cosmopolitan
of provincial ⌒, 169:7
tumultuous populace of large ⌒
to be dreaded, 49:14
what barely hinted at in other ⌒
is condensed and enlarged in
New York, 171:12
whatever events shall disgust men
with ⌒ will render service to
continent, 49:3

Citizen
humblest ⌒ is stronger than all
hosts of error, 66:5

Constitution, The *(cont'd)*
   should states reject this excellent
      ⌒, next will be drawn in
      blood, 57:37
   some men look at ⌒s [as] too
      sacred to be touched, 57:18
   state ⌒s not logical, 223:4
   [Supreme Court] sapping
      foundations of ⌒, 57:21
   to Hell with ⌒, 57:1
   trust man with making ⌒s on
      less proof of competence,
      187:91
   very good articles in it, and very
      bad, 57:15
Consul
   ⌒, failed to secure office from
      people given one by
      Administration on condition
      that he leave country, 68:5
Consumer
   ⌒ wants can have immoral
      origins, 73:11
Consumption
   conspicuous ⌒ means of
      reputability to gentleman of
      leisure, 249:61
Containment
   policy toward Soviet Union must
      be long-term ⌒, 68:31
Contemplation, 58:1–13
   all civil mankind agreed in
      leaving one day for ⌒, 58:3
   ice is interesting subject for ⌒,
      58:10
   no place have more difficulty to
      indulge in reverie, than in
      America, 16:29
Contemporaries
   resemble ⌒ more than
      progenitors, 17:8
Contend
   men ⌒ more furiously over road
      to heaven than visible walks on
      earth, 22:17
Content
   I am ⌒, 133:2
Contention
   no man can spare time for
      personal ⌒, 4:45
Contentment
   oldest and quietest roads to ⌒
      through trinity of wine,
      woman, and song, 253:17
Contract
   ⌒s between nation and
      individuals have no pretensions
      to compulsive force, 101:51
   marriage most irrevocable of all
      ⌒s, 69:9
   verbal ⌒ isn't worth paper
      written on, 99:6

Contradict
   let me never fall into mistake of
      dreaming I am persecuted
      whenever I am ⌒ed, 22:6
   whatever Pro claimed to know
      old Con would ⌒ him, 22:13
Contradiction
   to hazard ⌒—freedom is
      necessary, 47:6
Control
   government strong enought to ⌒
      men's minds, government
      strong enough to ⌒ everything,
      101:28
Controversial
   ⌒ proposals, once accepted,
      become hallowed, 42:3
   I'm ⌒ figure. My friends either
      dislike me or hate me, 96:30
Conventional
   society loves what is ⌒, 211:12
Conversation, 59:1–33
   carry on amusing ⌒ without
      giving reflection to what they
      are saying, 59:29
   ⌒ is art in which man has all
      mankind for his competitors,
      59:13
   ⌒ is feminine, 59:4
   ⌒ last flower of civilization, 59:16
   ⌒'s got to have some root in
      past, 59:24
   five minutes' ⌒ gives arc long
      enough to determine whole
      curve, 59:22
   in ⌒ game is, to say something
      new with old words, 59:12
   inject few raisins of ⌒ into
      tasteless dough of existence,
      59:19
   lettuce like ⌒: must be fresh and
      crisp, 59:33
   single ⌒ with wise man better
      than ten years' study of books,
      59:25
   three cannot take part in ⌒,
      59:11
   tried to top everybody, but
      realized it was killing ⌒, 59:28
Converse
   many can argue, not many ⌒,
      59:5
Convict
   ⌒ No. 9653 for President, 41:22
Cook
   learn to ⌒ to save money, 157:10
   muses starve in ⌒'s shop, 20:6
Cook, Joseph
   on democracy, 66:10
Cooke, Alistair
   on America, 12:17
   on business, 39:16

on consumer goods, 39:17
on language, 132:7
on Louisiana territory, 139:3
on Nevada, 164:2
on Newport (R.I.), 205:3
on Oklahoma, 176:2
on Santa Fé (N.M.), 168:5
on the West, 251:8
on William Jennings Bryan,
   237:10
Cooke, Edmund Vance
   on Abraham Lincoln, 137:7
   on song, 212:10
Cooking
   ⌒ act of love, 92:6
   ⌒ child's play and adult joy, 92:6
   ⌒ like love, 92:13
Cool
   keep ⌒ with Coolidge, 41:23
Coolidge, Calvin
   Alice Roosevelt Longworth on,
      193:84
   campaign slogan, 41:23
   Dorothy Parker on, 193:98
   on belief, 32:5
   on business, 39:18, 39:20
   on civil rights, 50:8
   on commerce with Soviet Union,
      39:19
   on democracy, 66:11
   on government, 101:29
   on labor, 131:9
   on law, 134:26, 134:27
   on League of Nations, 68:11
   on Massachusetts, 147:3
   on military, 25:8
   on own presidency, 193:26,
      193:27
   on patriotism, 180:10
   on Puritans, 147:4
   on religion, 200:25
   on Senate, 54:17
   on sin, 209:4
   on speech, 59:10
   on taxation, 227:4
   on Vermont, 240:6
   on war, 245:9
   on war debt, 64:4
   on Warren G. Harding, 193:25
Cooper, James Fenimore
   Mark Twain on, 13:15
   on America, 12:18
   on ancestry, 17:6
   on business, 39:21
   on conduct, 53:3
   on Congress, 54:18
   on democracy, 66:12–17
   on elections, 75:5
   on equality, 79:3, 79:4
   on gossip, 100:2
   on greatness, 102:4
   on happiness, 103:5

Courage *(cont'd)*
~ is resistance to fear, not absence of fear, 38:27
~ of tiger is one, and of horse another, 38:11
~ takes many forms, 38:3
~ to change what should be changed, 256:27
~ to follow talent, 226:4
~ without conscience is wild beast, 38:14
far less ~ to kill yourself than to wake up one more time, 38:22
few men's ~ proof against protracted meditation, 38:19
great part of ~ is ~ of having done thing before, 82:8
moral ~ sometimes in short supply in fighting army, 25:24
red badge of ~, 51:13
true ~ perfect sensibility of measure of danger and willingness to endure it, 38:24

Course
neither clamor of mob nor voice of power will ever turn me from ~ I mark out for myself, 118:10

Court
crowded ~ docket is surest sign trade is brisk, 61:27
laws are dead letter without ~s to expound true meaning, 134:48
no such thing as justice—in or out of ~, 126:5
wrongs which legislatures cannot take interest in until ~s have acted, 134:50

Courteous
~ to all, intimate with few, 53:25

Cousins, Norman
on peace, 181:3

Covet
to make man ~ thing, necessary to make thing difficult to obtain, 29:10

Cow
ah, yes, I wrote 'Purple ~', 113:10
I never saw Purple ~, 113:9

Coward
better to be soldier's widow than ~'s wife, 25:6
~s never started—weak died along way, 178:2
except creature be part ~ not compliment to say it is brave, 38:27
fearless man more dangerous than ~, 60:7

Republic not established by ~s, 60:4

Cowardice, 60:1-8
caution is word of ~, 60:2
~ lack of ability to suspend imagination, 60:6
~ surest protection against temptation, 60:8

Cowboy
damned ~ is President, 193:40

Cox, James M.
~ and cocktails, 41:21

Cox, Samuel Sullivan
on fun, 149:4

Cradle
hand that rocks ~ rules world, 257:76
robbed ~ and grave, 51:21

Craftsman
in nobler toil than ours no ~ bears part, 259:80

Crane, Hart
on Brooklyn Bridge, 171:22

Crane, Stephen
on Civil War, 51:13
on heart, 106:2
on life, 136:14
on sin, 209:5
on war, 245:10-12

Crank
if man doesn't believe as we do, say he is ~, 32:19

Crapsey, Adelaide
on books, 35:11
on women, 257:14

Crazy
people who seem ~ telling how they used to be before therapy, 171:87
Pound's ~. All poets are, 185:15
this city drives me ~, 171:39

Create
glory of farmer is to ~, 8:3

Creative
could not learn in college to think ~ly on schedule, 74:26
~ genius and critics, 26:8

Creature
we are ~s of the moment, 112:23

Credit
cherish public ~, 64:17
want 21 percent risk free?, 157:60

Credulity
not a crime, 32:12

Creed
ossified metaphor, 200:99
put ~ into deed, 4:15

Crèvecoeur, Michel Guillaume de
on agriculture, 8:2
on America, 12:19, 12:20, 12:21

on American Revolution, 14:26
on books, 35:12
on history, 107:12
on humankind, 112:6
on immigration, 116:9, 116:10

Crime, 61:1-29
Americans always take their heroes from criminal classes, 16:56
capital punishment as fundamentally wrong as cure for ~ as charity for poverty, 126:10
commit ~, and earth is made of glass, 61:15
creating ~s to punish them, 61:21
~ and punishment grow out of one stem, 197:6
~ is contagious, 61:8
Earth's most hateful ~s have in Thy name been done, 200:182
habeas corpus, writ by which man taken out of jail when confined for wrong ~, 61:7
New York City, 171:86
New York City blackouts' low rate of, 171:57
punishment should fit criminal, not ~, 197:11
reason of ~ is deferring of our hopes, 61:17
smaller penalty fewer ~s, 61:11
two kinds of ~s: those committed by people who are caught and those by people who are not, 61:19
when is ~ not ~?, 61:24

Criminal
American jurisprudence wheel of fortune fixed in favor of ~, 61:9
contact with ~s make ~s of children of virtuous parents, 189:21
new type of ~ commits crimes under circumstances that make it impossible for him to know he is doing wrong, 61:4
no distinctly American ~ class except Congress, 54:59
tried to treat white-collar ~s like other ~s, 193:116

Crisis
each ~ brings its word and deed, 132:63

Crist, Judith
on culture, 62:2
on motion pictures, 159:10

Critic
and creativity, 26:8
Boston audience—4000 ~s, 36:34

crawls through life paralytic to
earn praise of bard and ～,
84:10
～s are sentinels to grand army of
letters, 138:37
Nature, when she invented
authors, contrived to make ～s
out of chips left, 262:38
public is only ～ whose opinion is
worth anything, 138:57
set up small booth as ～ and sell
his petty conceit, 262:56
when we attend more to
principles, we shall be better
～s, 262:63
wise skepticism is first attribute of
good ～, 138:38
work of ～ is of secondary
importance, 1:18
Criticism
always despised artificial canons
of ～, 138:33
coughing in theater is ～,
233:19
could Shakespeare give theory of
Shakespeare?, 138:14
～ attempt to find out what
something is, 138:10
darkness of metaphysical ～,
183:28
do not get effective ～ until you
provoke, 262:73
fashions in literary ～ shifted
much like fashions in women's
hats, 138:47
men in authority will always find
～ subversive, 27:5
three questions essential to all ～,
262:93
Crockett, Davy
on advice, 4:11
on Arkansas, 24:4
Croker, Richard
on politics, 187:27
Cronkite, Walter
on television, 229:1
Crook
Chicago full of ～s as saw with
teeth, 46:8
I'm not a ～, 193:94
seeing fewer ～s in drawing
rooms, 187:20
Cross
crucify mankind on ～ of gold,
157:8
no ～, no crown, 179:10
no ～ of gold, 41:14
Cross, Wilbur L.
on government, 101:31
Crowded
nobody goes there, it's too ～,
33:5

Crown
no ～ of thorns, no cross of gold,
41:14
Cry
too old to ～ but hurt too much
to laugh, 137:49
Cuba
most interesting addition which
could ever be made to our
system of states, 56:9
Culbertson, Ely
on peace, 181:4
on power, 190:13
Cullen, Countee
on life, 136:15
Cultivate
～ poverty like garden herb, 189:45
Cultivation
race of cultivators, our ～
unrestrained, 12:19
Cultural
～ constraints condition and limit
our choices, 62:7
～ drought, 62:2
Culture, 62:1–9
～ is only ～ when owner not
aware, 62:6
～ rapidly creating class of
supercilious infidels, 62:9
ends in head-ache, 62:3
few first-class poets, philosophs,
and authors, 62:8
ladies who pursue ～ in bands,
257:80
men who pride themselves on
their ～ haven't any, 62:5
next Augustan age will dawn on
other side of Atlantic, 16:50
Sydney Smith on lack of
American, 16:37
United States needs its Indians
and their ～, 13:16
veneer, rouge, aestheticism, art
museums, that make America
impotent, 12:90
Cummings, E.E.
on America, 12:22
on Cambridge (Mass.) women,
147:5
on Coney Island, 171:23
on politics, 187:28
on Warren G. Harding, 193:28
Cunningham, Imogen
on beauty, 31:4
Cuomo, Mario
on Americans, 15:6
on immigration, 116:11
on politics, 187:29, 187:30
Cuppy, Will
on becoming extinct, 19:5
Curiosity
～ killed cat, 129:1

Curse
trade ～s everything it handles,
39:63
when massa ～, 18:1
Cursing
comes tide when no amount of ～
will suffice, 219:1
Curtain
behind ～'s mystic fold, 233:14
Curtis, George William
on anger, 18:3
on happiness, 103:6
Custer, George A.
on South Dakota, 216:6
Custom
no written law more binding than
unwritten ～, 134:21
world edited by ～s, 62:1
Cynic
～ never sees good quality and
never fails to see bad one,
43:11
～, sees things as are and not as
ought to be, 43:12
sees things as are, 183:4
Cynicism
only deadly sin is ～, 209:32

Dacre, Harry
song by, 212:11
Daffodil
～ doorside queen, 90:3
Daisy
～, ～, give me your answer, do,
212:11
Damn
～ the torpedoes, 51:17
Damned
～ if we do and ～ if we don't,
68:60
public be ～, 196:30
who are those eventually ～?,
209:20
Damyank
"Connecticut Yankee" came to be
pronounced "～", 55:8
Dana, Charles A.
on journalism, 125:13, 125:14
Dana, Richard Henry
on Abraham Lincoln, 137:8
on California, 40:7
on Civil War, 51:14
on drinking, 71:12
on families, 85:3
on San Francisco (Calif.), 206:2
on science, 207:7
Dance
drink and ～ and laugh and lie,
149:12
eyes seem to ～ in their heads,
149:9

Dance *(cont'd)*
    music rots when gets too far from
      ⁓, 160:22
    truest expression of a people is in
      its ⁓s, 160:5
Dandelion
    golden kisses all over cheeks of
      meadow, 90:1
    star-disked ⁓s, 90:7
Daniels, Jonathan
    on the South, 214:1
Daniels, Josephus
    on chastity, 45:2
Darby, William
    on Louisiana, 139:4
    on New Orleans (La.), 169:1
D'Arcy, Hugh Antoine
    on drinking, 71:13
Dark
    between ⁓ and daylight,
      264:28
    I am ⁓ Cavalier, 63:94
    I don't want to go home in ⁓,
      133:24
Darkness
    ⁓ cannot drive out ⁓, 80:6
Darrow, Clarence
    on age, 7:13
    on argument, 22:5
    on business and labor, 39:23
    on crime, 61:12, 61:13
    on death penalty, 61:11
    on immortality, 117:5, 117:6
    on justice, 126:4, 126:5
    on liberty, 135:14
    on life, 136:16
    on presidency, 192:8
    on progress, 195:4
    on religion, 200:27, 200:28
    on tyranny, 238:2
    on work, 259:9
Daugherty, Harry M.
    on Warren G. Harding,
      193:29
Daughter
    undutiful ⁓ prove unmanageable
      wife, 145:31
Davis, Adelle
    on health, 105:3
Davis, Angela
    on penal system, 197:4, 197:5
Davis, Bette
    on marriage, 145:20
    on parenthood, 85:4
Davis, Clyde Brion
    on Illinois, 115:2, 115:3
Davis, David
    on Constitution, 57:6
Davis, Elmer
    on bravery, 38:4
    on fear, 87:3
    on national honor, 60:4

Davis, Jefferson
    on Civil War, 51:15, 51:16
    on majority rule, 143:2
Davis, John
    on Virginia, 244:5
Davis, Rebecca Harding
    on Pennsylvania, 182:6
    on Walt Whitman, 262:5
Davis, Richard Harding
    on Spanish-American War, 218:3,
      218:4
Dawes, Charles G.
    on diplomacy, 68:12
Dawn
    at ⁓ of all we long for so, 63:63
    by ⁓'s early light, 88:6
    nearer ⁓ darker night, 3:9, 110:8
Day
    ⁓ is done, and darkness falls,
      234:37
    ⁓s are ever divine, 234:20
    every ⁓ is Doomsday, 4:16
    melancholy ⁓s are come, saddest
      of year, 28:4
Daylight
    all-night ⁓ in Alaska, 10:10
Day, Lillian
    on being lady, 257:15
DDT
    ⁓ one of safest pesticides, 188:2
Dead
    bivouac of ⁓, 63:64
    bodies that made such noise when
      alive, when ⁓, lie as quietly as
      any others, 63:18
    brave and fallen few, 245:67
    breeding lilacs out of ⁓ land,
      63:19
    Carlyle is incontestably ⁓ at last,
      63:40
    consult ⁓ upon things that were,
      107:48
    ⁓ have no rights, 63:44
    ⁓ in youthful prime, 260:7
    ⁓ like Coney Island in winter,
      171:23
    early to rise and to bed makes
      male ⁓, 4:52
    earth belongs to living, not to ⁓,
      64:12
    eternal, unstirring paralysis, and
      ⁓ly, hopeless trance, 63:60
    fallen cold and ⁓, 137:55
    glad Old Masters are all ⁓,
      26:55
    I shall have more to say when I
      am ⁓, 63:72
    let ⁓ Past bury its ⁓, 1:12
    no flock but one ⁓ lamb is there,
      63:51
    only good Indians were ⁓, 13:11
    over my ⁓ body, 78:17

    pity is for living, envy for ⁓,
      136:120
    ramparts of ⁓, 51:24
    soft falls dew on face of ⁓, 51:7
    sorrow for ⁓ only sorrow from
      which we refuse to be divorced,
      213:8
    th'⁓ are always pop'lar, 44:4
Dean, John
    on presidency, 192:9
Death, 63:1–95
    Adam, first benefactor, brought
      ⁓ into world, 63:81
    all is Love, and there is no ⁓,
      140:22
    all soon stagnation, cold, and
      darkness, 63:33
    all victory ends in defeat of ⁓,
      63:65
    because I could not stop for ⁓,
      63:14
    caught in swift, sudden turn of
      ⁓, 136:92
    chamber in silent halls of ⁓,
      63:10
    come lovely and soothing ⁓,
      63:89
    comin' for to carry me home, 63:4
    [Coolidge] how could they tell?,
      193:98
    cruel ⁓ always near, 136:1
    Dark Cavalier, 63:94
    ⁓ alone can seal the title of any
      man, 63:42
    ⁓ and mangling of couple
      thousand men a small affair,
      51:52
    ⁓ and taxes and childbirth never
      convenient time, 236:19
    ⁓ disappear with disappearance
      of sin, 209:11
    ⁓ is mother of beauty, 63:77
    ⁓ is spongy wall, 63:61
    ⁓ most beautiful adventure in
      life, 133:20
    ⁓ never takes one alone, but
      two, 63:57
    ⁓ observes no ceremony, 63:95
    ⁓, only immortal who treats us
      all alike, 133:38
    ⁓ softens all resentments, 63:92
    ⁓ the consoler, 63:50
    delicious near-by freedom of ⁓,
      7:77
    dull nights go over, 63:87
    each of us is experiencing cellular
      ⁓, 136:101
    fever called "Living" is
      conquered at last, 63:70
    for man who has done natural
      duty, ⁓ is as natural as sleep,
      63:75

Decter, Midge
on sexual revolution, 208:1
on youth culture, 264:9
Deed
~s better than words, 132:34
put creed into ~, 4:15
Defeat
~ makes men invincible, 190:7
~ would be bad enough, but
victory would be intolerable,
242:10
in ourselves, 43:66
in ourselves triumph and ~,
224:30
to be ~ed in war may be better
than not to have fought, 245:80
Defect
every excess causes ~, 183:17
man's personal ~s have
importance [to] world they
have to himself, 202:1
Defender
nation which forgets its ~s will
be itself forgotten, 25:8
Defense
~ of freedom is everybody's
business, 243:42
our ~ is in law and order,
134:30
warlike spirit essential to national
~, 152:14
Deficit
stop ~s, 64:15
Definition
~ no proof, 132:38
~ that which describes object to
distinguish it, 132:40
De Forest, John W.
on marriage, 145:21
on misfortune, 236:6
on temptation, 209:6
De Gaulle, Charles
on New York City, 171:24
Delaware, 65:1–6
~ always disposed to
counter-revolution, 65:5
~ans close traders, 65:2
~ has invariably bowed to Du
Pont's benevolent paternalism,
65:3
~ is like diamond, having
inherent value, 65:6
state motto, 65:1
three counties when tide is out,
two when in, 65:4
Delay
do not ~, 1:13
never ~ kissing pretty girl or
opening bottle of whiskey,
253:7
DeLeon, Daniel
on poverty, 189:8

Delicacy
false ~ robs literature of two
best things, 138:58
Delicious
~ torment, 140:27
Delight
I am for those who believe in
loose ~s, 103:44
Deloria, Vine, Jr.
on American Indians, 13:3
Demagogue
~s follow what leads to
temporary vulgar applause,
187:142
usually sly, detractor of others,
187:25
Demand
increases as population increases,
73:14
De Mille, Agnes
on being in college, 74:26
on music, 160:5
Democracies
ancient ~ never possessed one
feature of good government,
66:33
besetting vice of ~ to substitute
public opinion for law, 66:17
~ slow to make war, but equally
slow to make peace, 66:77
right-wing autocracies do
sometimes evolve into ~,
66:58
slow debates in public assemblies
of ~, 54:57
tendency of all ~ is to
mediocrity, 66:12
Democracy, 66:1–109
adultery is application of ~ to
love, 145:61
air of ~ agrees better with
mere talent than with genius,
66:81
all ills of ~ can be cured by
more ~, 66:90
arsenal of ~, 261:26
beauty of ~ is that you never can
tell when youngster is born
what he is going to do with
himself, 66:108
can't see why ~ means
everybody but me, 66:36
characteristic of ~: ability to shift
ideological attitudes overnight,
66:55
cure evils of ~ by evils of
Fascism! Funny therapeutics,
66:61
dangers of trying to be world's
midwife to ~, 66:57
deadliest foe of ~ is liberty
frenzied, 66:52, 135:49

death of ~ will be slow
extinction from apathy and
undernourishment, 66:37
~ become government of bullies,
66:23
~ can face and live with truth
about itself, 66:35
~ can thrive only when it enlists
devotion of common people,
66:84
~ developed dangerous tendency
to enslave through tyranny of
majorities, 66:62
~ gives every man right to be his
own oppressor, 66:69
~ has given ordinary worker
more dignity than he ever had,
66:60
~ has given to conscience
absolute liberty, 66:3
~, I do not conceive that God
did ordain as fit government,
66:18
~ is direct self-government, over
all the people, for all the
people, by all the people,
66:79
~ is government of all the
people, by all the people, for
all the people, 66:78
~ is levelling, inconsistent with
true liberty, 135:11
~ is morose, 66:22
~ is on trial, 66:19
~ is peace-loving, 66:54
~ is practical necessity, 66:34
~ is raft, 66:10
~ is recurrent suspicion that
more than half people right
more than half time, 66:102
~ is theory that common people
know what they want and
deserve it, 66:75
~ means as equal participation in
rights as is practicable, 66:16
~ most expensive and nefarious
kind of government, 66:76
~ most of all affiliates with open
air, 66:106
~ which fails to concentrate
authority in emergency falls
into confusion, 66:67
essentials of ~ no one has
personal liberty to do what
majority has declared shall not
be done, 66:51
evils we experience flow from
excess of ~, 66:30
exploitation by majority as
repugnant as exploitation by
oligarchy, and ~ loses half its
supposed superiority, 66:91

government of [Hell] is
enlightened ∼, 200:23

he who would save liberty must
put his trust in ∼, 135:64

I believe in ∼ because it releases
energies of every human being,
66:107

if ∼ to flourish, it must have
criticism, 66:9

I like ∼ of North Dakota,
173:5

in America I sought image of ∼,
66:97

inclined to confuse freedom and
∼, 66:28

in ∼ military policy dependent
on public opinion, 66:72

in ∼ people meet and exercise
government in person, 66:71

I say that ∼ can never prove
itself until it founds its own
forms, displacing all that exists,
66:105

learned about ∼ from my father,
116:11

man's inclination to injustice
makes ∼ necessary, 126:38

most popular man under ∼ is
most despotic, 66:74

not only does ∼ make every man
forget his ancestors, it hides his
descendants, 66:98

only a country that is rich and
safe can afford to be ∼, 66:76

political power in hands of men
degraded by poverty is to tie
firebrands to foxes, 66:29

principal advantage of ∼ is
elevation in character of people,
66:15

Puritanism laid egg of ∼, 66:70

real liberty is neither found in
despotism or extremes of ∼,
135:28

right to be wrong in ∼, 66:80

sail, sail thy best, ship of ∼,
12:116

Ship of ∼ may sink through
mutiny, 66:8

sources of information are springs
from which ∼ drinks, 125:65

speak pass-word primeval—I give
sign of ∼, 66:103

to call politics dirty is to call ∼
dirty, 187:119

trend of ∼ is toward socialism,
187:3

unless people understand and
participate, no long-term
program can endure, 66:93

unthinking fatalism surest poison
of ∼, 66:7

vigorous ∼ would never succumb
to communism, 66:20

world made safe for ∼, 260:24

Democrat

∼ is young conservative, 66:25

∼s even when not having fun,
like to appear to be, 187:106

difference between ∼s and
Republicans measured in
courage and confidence, 187:29

I am all kinds of a ∼, 66:109

never said all ∼s were
saloon-keepers, 187:51

Republicans have splits after
election and ∼s just before,
187:122

we ∼s make it all the way with
family intact, 187:20

Democratic

conscription as ∼. So is cemetery,
152:13

∼ government presupposes free
public education, 66:82

drawing shadow of doubt over
validity of ∼ institutions,
66:53

Fathers of Republic did not, and
did not want to, establish ∼
government, 66:92

health of ∼ society measured by
quality of functions performed
by private citizens, 66:96

no force so ∼ as force of ideal,
32:5

price of ∼ survival is to give up
some of ∼ luxuries of past,
66:27

rule in ∼ society which limits
what voters will sacrifice for
public good, 66:68

soundness of ∼ institutions
depends on determination of
government to give
employment to idle men, 66:83

too ∼ for liberty, 12:6

we must work like dogs to justify
faith in ∼ methods, 66:21

Democratic Party

against immigration, 116:3

against militarism, 152:1

ain't on speakin' terms with itsilf,
187:33

assortment of discordant
differences, 187:115

campaign slogans, 41:3, 41:5,
41:11, 41:12, 41:14, 41:19,
41:21, 41:27, 41:30, 41:32–34,
41:39

cancellation of debts by foreign
nations, 64:2

∼ is like mule, 187:31

favors League of Nations, 68:2

for repeal of Prohibition, 71:3

never sees thing until it has gone
by, 187:18

on state interference in education,
74:4

oppose interest-bearing bonds in
time of peace, 64:1

Richard M. Nixon on, 187:106

Rum, Romanism, and Rebellion,
187:17

Thomas Reed on, 187:115

Demonology

∼ is shadow of theology,
209:15

Dempsey, Jack

on boxing, 220:15, 220:16

Denny, Ludwell

on imperialism, 56:5

Denomination

∼s children of same family,
differing only in Christian
names, 200:135

Denver, John

on West Virginia, 252:4

Denver (Colo.)

pulse like rushing wind, 52:4

self-sufficient, self-contained, and
complacent, 52:3

Depew, Chauncey

on law, 134:29

on male-female relations, 257:17

Deportment

refined simplicity characteristic of
high bred ∼, 53:3

Depression

action not ∼, 1:8

boondoggle ourselves out of ∼,
187:126

∼ is when you lose your [job],
73:32

Deprivation

mistrust man who blames on
revolutionaries what should be
attributed to ∼, 189:19

Derby, George

on Arizona, 23:4

Descended

recall First Amoeba from whom
we're all ∼, 81:11

Desert

great stone ∼, 171:112

Deserve

way to ∼ [applause] is to be
good, 43:55

Desire

belief means something more than
∼, 117:5

insatiableness of ∼s asserts
personal imperishableness,
117:2

Desperation

lives of quiet ∼, 136:116

Divorce, 69:1–14
  better to await logic of events, 69:7
  ~, bugle blast that separates the combatants, 69:3
  ~, resumption of diplomatic relations, 69:2
  if ~ has increased, don't blame women's movement, 69:8
  lives of quiet desperation rather than resort to it, 69:5
  married man who wants change of venue headed for ~ court, 69:10
  played Santa Claus many times, check out ~ settlements, 69:13
  remedy worse than disease, 69:6
  three sides to every question—where ~ is involved, 69:11

Dix, Dorothea
  on insane asylums, 121:4

Dix, Dorothy
  on age, 7:14
  on divorce, 69:6
  on kissing, 140:20

Dixie
  I wish I was in ~, 214:2

Dixon, Frank
  on Alabama government, 101:34

Do
  ~ others or they will ~ you, 4:2
  ~ unto others by no means golden rule, 53:22
  never ~ today what you can ~ tomorrow, 1:2

Doctor
  beware young ~, 4:19
  God heals and ~ takes fees, 148:9
  if th' ~s [had] more Christianity, 148:4
  if you would go off like opium-eater in love with delusions—be ~, 259:33
  it is ill jesting with joiner's tools, worse with ~'s, 105:13
  medical ~s ignorant as to how *healthy* body works, 148:17
  who said ~s are truthful or even intelligent?, 148:15

Doctrinaire
  American ~ deals in poetry and [demagogue] in cant, 66:14

Doctrine
  civilized men have done fiercest fighting for ~s, 245:90

Dodo
  never had chance, 19:5

Dog
  advantages of whiskey over ~s legion, 253:4

  better give path to ~ than be bitten in contesting right, 4:45
  ~s great assets to candidates, 75:10
  ~s will not attack you in good clothes, 70:4
  ~ teaches boy to turn around three times before lying down, 19:4
  ~ with bone always in danger, 29:1
  door is what ~ is perpetually on the wrong side of, 19:15
  fleas good fer ~, 19:23
  has all characteristics of ~—except loyalty, 122:4
  if pick up starving ~ and make him prosperous, he will not bite you, 19:20
  more I see of men, more I like ~s, 19:2
  when man bites ~, that is news, 125:14

Dogmas
  ~ of quiet past inadequate to stormy present, 42:14, 107:47

Dole, Charles Fletcher
  on democracy, 66:19

Dole, Sanford B.
  on Hawaii, 104:2

Dollar
  almighty ~, 157:43
  Americans relate all of life to the ~, 157:49
  ~ diplomacy, 68:1
  each ~ is soldier that does your bidding, 157:6
  gold ~s as against balony ~s, 157:57
  how many men fairly earn million ~s, 157:35
  no one can earn million ~s honestly, 157:7
  not value, but representative of value, 157:18
  Republicans for man before ~, 187:82
  'they love th' eagle on back iv ~', 180:14
  Yankees and ~s ought to rhyme, 157:15

Dollarism
  power of ~, 12:78

Domestic
  happiness of ~ fireside first boon of heaven, 109:25
  I long for rural and ~ scenes, 109:3
  our lives are ~ in more senses than we think, 109:35

Domesticity
  ~ is taproot which enables English to branch wide and high, 77:8

Dominoes
  row of ~ set up, knock over first, last will go over quickly, 243:9

Done
  how much may be ~ if we are always doing, 259:42
  tackled thing that couldn't be ~, and did it, 224:17
  to say a thing has never yet been ~, 42:16
  well ~ is better than well said, 1:5

Donnelly, Ignatius
  on politics, 187:31

Don't
  ~ baby me so, 133:31
  ~ give up the ship, 162:10
  ~ you stay at home of evenings?, 7:36

Doomsday
  awesome roar which warned of ~, 174:10
  every day is ~, 4:16

Door
  beaten path to his ~, 84:8
  ~ is what dog is perpetually on the wrong side of, 19:15
  I lift my lamp beside the golden ~, 116:16
  men go by fives and tens and fifties to his ~, 84:6

Dos Passos, John
  Edmund Wilson on, 262:95

Doubt
  truest heroism is to resist ~, 102:27
  when in ~ tell truth, 237:88

Douglas, Helen Gahagan
  on character, 43:19
  on democracy, 66:20
  on elections, 75:6
  on freedom, 95:18
  on invention, 123:4
  on patriotism, 180:13
  on politics, 187:32

Douglas, Michael
  on Chicago (Ill.), 46:6

Douglas, Stephen A.
  on Abraham Lincoln, 137:9
  on racial equality, 79:5
  on slavery, 210:13

Douglas, William O.
  on book banning, 35:15
  on Fifth Amendment, 57:7
  on religion, 200:32
  on revolution, 204:2

Douglass, Frederick
    on Black Americans, 34:6, 34:7
    on civil rights, 50:9
    on liberty, 135:15
    on slavery, 210:14–17
Dow, Dorothy
    on age, 7:15
Dow, Lorenzo
    on drinking, 71:14
Dowdey, Clifford
    on Virginia, 244:6
Down
    can't hold man ⁓ without
        staying ⁓ with him, 50:39
Downtrodden
    claim that women are ⁓ fraud of
        century, 258:26
Draft
    democratic like cemetery, 152:13
    rich man's war and poor man's
        fight, 51:3
Drake, Joseph Rodman
    on flag, 88:3
    on soldier's death, 25:9
Drama
    allied to deeper thoughts
        concerning [man's] nature and
        destiny, 233:20
    baseball is ⁓, 30:20
    great ⁓ reflection of great doubt
        of great man, 233:24
    what literature does at night,
        233:25
Dramatist
    ⁓ wants more liberties than he
        can really take, 107:34
Dream
    all books are either ⁓s or swords,
        35:53
    all we see but ⁓ within ⁓,
        183:38
    half the world must sweat that
        other half may ⁓, 259:47
    [Hollywood] living in ⁓ world,
        108:18
    I have ⁓, 43:59, 50:26
    into land of my ⁓s, 260:8
    regrets take place of ⁓s, 7:6
    voices lost and clouded, strummed
        his ⁓s, 109:8
Dreiser, Theodore
    on Americans, 15:7
    on art, 26:6
    on civilization, 211:7
    on life, 136:19
    on religion, 200:33
Dress, 70:1–17
    all ⁓ed up, with nowhere to go,
        187:157
    be cleanly and properly ⁓ed
        from moment you rise till you
        go to bed, 70:13

being perfectly well ⁓ed gives
    inward tranquility, 70:6
⁓ to please others, 4:22
four-hundred-dollar suit on old
    Uncle Earl, 139:8
indeed, the Russian Jew had
    made the average American girl
    a "tailor-made" girl, 116:7
only when mind and character
    slumber ⁓ can be seen, 70:5
Pat [Nixon] does have respectable
    Republican cloth coat, 249:44
pride of ⁓ is curse, 70:8
Dresser, Paul
    on Wabash River, 119:2
Drink
    American does not ⁓ at meals,
        92:12
    can't drown yourself in ⁓: you
        float, 71:8
    ⁓ and dance and laugh and lie,
        149:12
    ⁓ first. Sip second slowly. Skip
        third, 71:47
    first man takes a ⁓, then the ⁓
        takes a ⁓, then the ⁓ takes
        the man, 71:51
    he that ⁓s fast, pays slow, 71:22
    McKinley ⁓s soda water, Bryan
        ⁓s rum, 41:16
    men ⁓ for brain-effect, 71:39
    Mississippi, ⁓ wet, vote dry, 154:3
    most Americans are born drunk,
        16:13
    never to ⁓ by daylight and never
        to refuse ⁓ after dark, 71:42
    New Orleans where can eat and
        ⁓ most and suffer least, 169:5
    one more ⁓ and I'll be under the
        host, 71:44
    straw that stirs ⁓, 30:25
    tell me brand of whiskey Grant
        ⁓s, 51:40
    they ⁓ with impunity, or anybody
        who invites them, 71:57
    two things believed of any man,
        and one is he has taken to ⁓,
        71:52
    wants but little ⁓ but wants that
        little strong, 71:28
    water is only ⁓ for wise man,
        71:53
Drinking, 71:1–61
    as I was ⁓ gin and water, 71:17
    decided to stop ⁓ with creeps.
        I've lost 30 pounds, 71:27
    in favor of ⁓ that it takes
        drunkard out of world, 71:18
    keep mouth wet, feet dry, 4:20
    many estates are spent in getting,
        71:23
    three sheets in wind, 71:12

typical American woman is not
    ⁓ woman, 257:29
Driver, William
    on flag, 88:4
Drum
    I hear great ⁓s pounding, 51:61
    muffled ⁓'s sad roll has beat
        soldier's last tattoo, 245:67
    now deeper roll maddening ⁓s,
        245:63
Drummer
    hears different ⁓, 120:28
Drunk
    ⁓ on books, 35:58
    ⁓ or sober, nothing in it—save
        Boston, 36:3
    every man had respect for himself
        would have got ⁓,—as was the
        custom of country, 71:55
    men as get ⁓ and abuse their
        wives do not deserve name of
        men, 71:14
Drunkard
    ⁓s as class proneness in brilliant
        and warm-blooded to fall into
        this vice, 71:38
    where have you disposed of their
        carcasses? those ⁓s and
        gluttons, 71:58
Drunken
    better sleep with sober cannibal
        than ⁓ Christian, 71:41
    no nation ⁓ where wine cheap,
        253:10
Drunkenness
    ⁓ is joy reserved for the gods,
        71:10
    ⁓ spoils health, dismounts mind,
        and unmans men, 71:46
    prohibition only drives ⁓ behind
        doors, 71:54
Dry
    how ⁓ I am, 71:4
    keep feet ⁓, 4:20
    let's get out of wet clothes into
        ⁓ martini, 71:9
D.T.'s
    ole ⁓ in dinner suit, 71:34
Du Bois, W.E.B.
    on civil rights, 50:10
    on liberty, 135:16, 135:17
Dubos, René
    on individuality, 120:5
Dubuque (Iowa)
    will not be edited for old lady
        from ⁓, 125:62
Duck
    Honey, I forgot to ⁓, 220:15
Duel
    whosoever committeth murder by
        ⁓ shall suffer death by
        hanging, 197:12

Education *(cont'd)*

idea of girl's ⁓ is whatever qualifies her for going to Europe, 74:39

I desire to see time when ⁓ shall become much more general, 74:66

[inadequate] political ⁓ of average American voter, 74:18

in field of public ⁓ doctrine of "separate but equal" has no place, 79:24

left over after forgotten everything learned, 74:1

makes straight-cut ditch of meandering brook, 74:94

making ⁓ in some sense compulsory, destiny of free republics of America settled, 74:68

most important subject we can be engaged in, 74:65

most uninformed mind with healthy body happier than wisest valetudinarian, 105:19

mother's heart is child's schoolroom, 85:2

musical ⁓ necessary for musical judgment, 160:24

neither justice nor freedom can be permanently maintained without popular ⁓, 74:45

newspapers are schoolmasters of common people, 125:5

no man is statesman who does not include ⁓ of the people in plans of administration, 74:72

no nation has ever borrowed largely for ⁓, 74:43

on diffusion of ⁓ rest preservation of free institutions, 74:100

opposed to state interference with parental rights in ⁓, 74:4

regret the trifling narrow ⁓ of females, 257:2

soap and ⁓ not as sudden as massacre, 74:96

to know right woman is liberal ⁓, 257:40

true ⁓ makes for inequality, 74:89

turgid style of Johnson, purple glare of Gibbon, and studied metaphors of Junius, 74:86

we need ⁓ in obvious more than investigation of obscure, 74:50

Educator

for ⁓ to scorn affiliation with cause is to forswear democratic responsibility, 74:20

observation, experience are prime ⁓s, 74:9

parents convinced that ⁓s know what is best for children, 74:30

Edwards, India

on America, 12:24

on elections, 75:7

on women's rights, 258:10

Edwards, Jonathan

on ancestry, 17:7

on animals, 19:6

on death, 63:18

on Heaven, 200:43

on Hell, 200:41, 200:42

on knowledge, 129:4

on music, 160:6

on nature, 161:15

on perception, 183:13

on power, 190:14

on religion, 200:40, 200:44, 200:45

on sin, 209:12, 209:13

on will, 47:5

on youth, 264:10

Edwards, Paul

on World War II, 261:3

Efficiency

cult of ⁓ profoundly anti-social, 73:18

Egg

can't unscramble scrambled ⁓s, 236:1

put all your ⁓s in one basket—and watch basket, 4:56, 256:38

unhatched ⁓ greatest challenge in life, 136:122

Wall Street lays ⁓, 73:38, 171:92

Egotism

religion is monumental chapter in history of human ⁓, 200:115

Ehrlichman, John

on Patrick L. Gray, 187:34

Eichmann, Adolph

Arendt, Hannah, on, 61:4

Eighties

my ⁓ are passionate, 7:68

Eighty

used to think main-spring broken by ⁓, 7:38

Einstein, Albert

on authority, 27:6

on earning living through science, 207:16

on humans as animals, 19:7

on individuality, 120:6, 120:7

on law, 134:30

on life, 136:22, 136:23

on nationalism, 180:15

on nuclear age, 174:6–9

on peace, 181:8

on personal independence, 118:3

on science, 207:12–15

on success, 224:10

on teaching, 74:31

on technology, 228:2

on truth, 237:15

on war, 245:17, 245:18

on wealth, 249:11

on youth, 264:11

Eisenhower, Dwight D.

campaign slogans, 41:29, 41:31

Eleanor Roosevelt on, 193:112

on Alaska, 10:4

on America, 12:25, 12:26

on American dissent, 15:8

on book banning, 35:17

on conduct, 53:4

on democracy, 66:21

on duty, 72:5

on freedom, 95:19, 95:20

on free press, 125:16

on Korean War, 130:2

on militarism, 152:2

on own presidency, 193:30

on peace, 181:9, 181:10

on politics, 187:35–38

on Richard M. Nixon, 193:31

on statesmen, 222:3

on vice presidency, 241:2

on Vietnam War, 243:9, 243:10

on war, 245:19–24

on Washington (D.C.), 247:3

on World War II, 261:4–6

on youth, 264:12

Elder

first a child, before an ⁓ of Jesus Christ, 133:16

Elderly

build orphanages next to homes for ⁓, 7:49

Elect

but then—we ⁓ed them, 187:146

everyone for more openness and an end to secrecy. Until ⁓ed, 101:83

let's re-re-re-⁓ Roosevelt, 41:27

never-ending audacity of ⁓ed persons, 66:104

we will ⁓ and ⁓, 75:12

Election

after unsuccessful ⁓ hurt too much to laugh, 137:49

as Maine goes, 142:2, 142:4

[direct primaries] accomplished confusion, 75:13

⁓ [campaigns] intolerable and disgraceful, 66:88

⁓ is both selection and rejection, 75:17

⁓ of senators by direct vote, 54:2

every four years, United States up for sale, 75:21

no bands play on ⁓ day, 75:22

difference between Whig and Tory of ~, 77:29

~ and United States are natural allies, 77:15

~ expects every American to do his duty, 77:1

~ is paradise of individuality, 77:38

extremes of opulence and of want are more constantly obvious in, 77:2

face [King William IV] which is probably largest uncivilized spot in ~, 77:20

France built its best colony on principle of exclusion, and failed: ~ reversed system and succeeded, 77:35

government divided into two parties, Ins and Outs, 77:25

governments of nations of shopkeepers must keep shop also, 77:12

New World's Sons, from ~'s breast we drew such milk as bids remember whence we came, 77:34

one successful country for last millennium is ~, 77:6

sea proved to be ring of marriage with all nations, 77:7

sun of her glory is fast descending, 77:22

English

American desires ~ admiration, 77:39

average ~ word is four letters and half, 132:55

Bostonians most servile imitators of ~, 36:30

commerce and corrupt government have rotted them to core, 77:27

conviction that whatever good there is in us [Americans] is wholly ~, 77:33

domesticity is taproot which enables ~ to branch wide and high, 77:8

~ are mentioned in Bible: Blessed are meek, for they shall inherit earth, 77:40

~ destined to be language of world, 132:2

~ history is aristocracy with doors open, 77:10

~ language is accretion and growth of every dialect, 132:60

~man shows no mercy to those below him in social scale, as he looks for none from those above him, 77:11

~man's strong point is vigorous insularity, 77:18

~man unfittest to argue another ~man into slavery, 14:20

~men! in blood and tongue our brothers, 77:43

~men not made of polishable substance, 77:17

~ of America not at all inferior to that of England, 132:36

[~] talk because they think sound more manageable than silence, 219:11

~ tourist's preconceived idea of us is thing he brings over with him and carries home intact, 77:4

every immigrant should be required to learn ~, 132:47

every one of these islanders is island himself, 77:9

from purest wells of ~ undefiled, 132:64

have everything in common with America except language, 132:65

if Americans did not speak ~ they would feel called on to create more high literature for themselves, 138:7

most important fact in modern history: North America speaks ~, 107:6

nothing equals my thankfulness when I meet an ~man who is not like every other, 77:31

one can get along by knowing two words of ~—swell and lousy, 108:2

selfish race, from all world disjoin'd, 77:14

serenity and repose well-known trait of ~ gentleman, 77:13

some subjects on which can be no argument, and to ~man this [loss of U.S.] is one, 77:37

takes great deal to produce ennui in ~man, 77:16

true character of ~ government most unprincipled at this day known, 77:26

when speak my native tongue, ~man can't understand me, 219:25

whin us free born Americans get through with ~ language, 132:10

Enjoy

Anglo-Saxon race do not know how to ~ ourselves, 103:14

do not ~ eating seldom have capacity for ~ment of any sort, 20:2

get what you want and ~ it, 11:20

never ~ed youth as I have old age, 7:66

sun gone in, I don't have to go out and ~ it, 250:16

to ~ bodily warmth, some small part must be cold, 183:35

Enlighten

~ people and tyranny will vanish, 238:15

Enough

had ~?, 41:28

Ensign

ay, tear her tattered ~ down, 88:5

Enterprise

most thriving when left free to individual ~, 73:26

private ~ backbone of economic well-being, 73:36

Environment

massively intervening in ~ without being aware of consequences, 188:7

must pay for every intrusion on natural ~, 188:6

Envy

greatest harm done by vast wealth is ~ and hatred, 29:9, 249:50

pain cause by good fortune of another, 179:2

Epicurus

Thomas Jefferson on, 184:17

Epitaph

~, inscription showing that virtues acquired by death have retroactive effect, 78:8

~ to be my story: I had lover's quarrel with world, 78:13

now he belongs to the ages, 137:47

rather be in Philadelphia, 182:9

Epitaphs, 78:1–21

Equal

all men and women are created ~, 258:27

all men born free and ~, 95:3

as man is ~ to the Church and ~ to the State, so he is ~ to every other man, 79:8

[authors of Declaration of Independence] did not intend to declare all men ~ in all respects, 79:17

believe Indian to be ~ to white man, 13:7

deal with men as ~s and like them for first time, 258:32

~ pay for ~ work, 258:5

~ right of all men to use of land as clear as their ~ right to breathe air, 79:13

Equal *(cont'd)*

~ rights of women just reached region of possibilities, 258:23

how ~ in their suffering lie groaning multitudes of earth, 79:25

in state where citizens are all practically ~, difficult to preserve their independence against aggressions of power, 79:22

ivry man is th' iv ivry other man befure th' law if he isn't careful, 79:7

minority possess ~ rights, 50:20

no longer be doubt that all men created free and ~, 210:41

no man has natural right to commit aggression on ~ rights of another, 50:21

provide women with economic opportunities ~ to men, 258:7

separate educational facilities are inherently un~, 79:24

struggle for ~ opportunity is struggle for America's soul, 79:14

talked long enough about ~ rights, 79:15

whilst rights are ~, in access to reason, rights in property are very un~, 79:9

Equality, 79:1–27

Americans so enamored of ~ they would rather be equal in slavery than unequal in freedom, 79:23

Death, only immortal who treats us all alike, 133:38

either grow up to advanced people, or pull advanced people down, 79:19

~ in society beats in~, 79:16

~ of condition in practice can only mean common misery, 79:3

great are blessings of ~; but what follies are committed in its name, 79:1

idea of ~ expands all generous souls, 79:21

I hate ~, 79:18

ivry man's as good as ivry other man, on'y th' other man don't know it, 79:6

little formula: "I'm as good as you be", 79:10

society that puts ~ . . . ahead of freedom will end up with neither, 95:27

very existence of government infers in~, 79:4

Equal rights. *See* Civil Rights; Rights; Women's Rights

Erikson, Erik
on nature, 161:35

Erikson, Kai
on war, 245:57

Err
~s, but ~s with integrity, 246:8

Erskine, John
on art, 26:20

Erudition
~, dust shaken out of book into empty skull, 74:12

~ not so attractive when turned loose upon defenseless public, 74:83

Ervin, Sam
on humor, 113:14, 113:15

on North Carolina, 172:5

on progress, 195:10

on religion, 200:69

Escape
we cannot ~ history, 51:38

Eskimo
~s are gentle people, 10:11

Espionage
Nathan Hale on, 14:43

Essayist
~, must take trousers off without showing his genitals, 262:91

Establishment
made up of little men, very frightened, 187:5

Estate
many would have been worse if ~ had been better, 249:26

Estuary
~ that enlarges and spreads, 7:79

Eternal
day of evil to ~ night, and night of just to ~ day, 67:9

every thing without exception has ~ soul, 117:20

Eternity
Divine Drama extends into ~, 117:14

time and ~ meet and blend, 7:75

world goes slowly, because it has ~ to go in, 234:44

Ethnic *(See also* Immigrants; *specific groups)*

New York City haven for oppressed, 171:43

"white ~", 15:17

Euclid
~ alone has looked on beauty bare, 31:29

Euphemism
resort to ~ denotes twinge in public-relations nerve, 243:32

Evans, Augusta
on money, 157:20

Evans, Bergen
Boston Toast, 37:3

Evans, Oliver
on New Orleans (La.), 169:2

on travel, 235:12

Evans, Rowland
on Ronald Reagan, 193:32

Eve. *See* Adam

Events
~ have controlled me, 137:30

Everett, Edward
on Abraham Lincoln, 137:12

on agriculture, 8:5

on character, 43:37

on education of blacks, 74:42

on George Washington, 246:5

Everybody
~ says it, and what ~ says must be true, 100:2

Evidence
cannot alter facts and ~, 126:1

some circumstantial ~ very strong, 237:84

Evil, 80:1–15

all ~, to crazy Ahab, personified in Moby-Dick, 80:10

chain reaction of ~ must be broken, 80:6

~ is challenge to our courage, 80:5

~ springs up, and flowers, and bears no seed, 80:8

first lesson of history is the good of ~, 80:4

how much pain have cost us ~s which never happened, 236:14

if men were basically ~, who would bother to improve world, 80:2

mistake supposing that spiritual ~ can be overcome by physical means, 80:3

most ~ arises because finite men pretend they are not so involved, 80:11

never label necessary ~ as good, 80:9

no ~ in atom, 174:16

no man justified in doing ~ on ground of expediency, 80:12

some men wish ~ and accomplish it but most men just let it happen, 80:1

those who corrupt public mind just as ~ as those who steal from public purse, 80:13

thousand hacking at branches of ~ to one striking at root, 80:14

torments of pain endured from ~s that never arrived, 236:8

Failure *(cont'd)*

living with sense of partial ⁓, 7:71

not ⁓, but low aim is crime, 11:16

we have raked the old ash heap of ⁓, 127:14

Fair

anything can happen at county agricultural ⁓, 8:21

meet me at ⁓, 212:27

Fair Deal

Harry Truman on, 101:134

Faith

⁓ is fine invention, 32:6

⁓ that right makes might, 72:23

in time and time has justified his ⁓, 137:13

man requires narrower [shelf] to spring his arch of ⁓ from, 200:159

not for all his ⁓ can see would I cowled churchman be, 200:50

only ⁓ wears well is that woven of conviction, 200:128

our ⁓ is ⁓ in someone else's ⁓, 32:10

religion not intelligence test, but ⁓, 200:91

through dark and stormy night ⁓ beholds feeble light, 200:183

'tis short sight to limit our ⁓, 207:17

Faithful

three ⁓ friends—old wife, old dog, ready money, 96:20

Fall

good to ⁓, battles lost in same spirit they are won, 83:8

greatest accomplishment is rising again after you ⁓, 83:6

if we ⁓, government stands ready with Bandaids, 83:1

probability that we may ⁓ ought not to deter from cause we believe just, 83:5

Falsehood

astonishing what force it requires for human to keep clear of ⁓s, 237:27

⁓s we spurn today truths of long ago, 237:95

some ⁓ mingles with all truth, 237:49

who speaks truth stabs ⁓ to heart, 237:53

Falwell, Jerry

on America, 12:34

on Christians in government, 101:41

on families, 85:7

on journalism, 125:18

on religious freedom, 201:5

Fame, 84:1–30

book written against ⁓ and learning has author's name on title-page, 84:9

⁓ comes only when deserved, for it is destiny, 84:22

⁓ in song, 224:6

⁓ is delightful, but as collateral does not rank high, 84:15

⁓ is fickle food, 84:4

⁓ is learning to understand what others want from you, 84:3

⁓ is scentless sunflower, 96:23

⁓ is what you have taken, 43:83

happiest of whom world says least, 84:18

how patient Nature smiles at ⁓, 84:13

idol today supplanted by successor tomorrow, 84:16

if cash comes with ⁓, come ⁓, 84:21

I trust good deal to common ⁓, 84:7

one of reasons people who achieve ⁓ don't find happiness is cut off from real people, 84:19

on ⁓'s eternal camping-ground, 245:67

outlined in ⁓'s illusive light, 84:27

pays too high price for ⁓ who sells his sinews to be wise, 84:10

problem of ⁓ is you get frozen in one frame, 84:25

what is ⁓? fitful tongue of leaping flame, 84:14

what is there which they call ⁓, 84:12

Familiar

be ⁓ with few, 4:27

Familiarity

⁓ in social ideas touchstone of acceptability, 42:9

Families

before nation collapses ⁓ must go down first, 85:7

⁓ mean audience to men. To women, mean more work, 85:1

Family, 85:1–21

average Georgian is good ⁓ man, 98:2

elevation of ⁓ life prime object of civilization, 85:6

⁓ of America, 15:6

father's treasure; brother's comfort; friend is both, 96:21

filial duty more effectually impressed by reading "King Lear" than by dry volumes of ethics, 72:20

one of nature's masterpieces, 85:15

total commitment to ⁓ and career possible, but fatiguing, 85:9

when educate woman educate whole ⁓, 257:56

would rather start ⁓ than finish one, 17:17

Famous

⁓, conspicuously miserable, 84:1

Fanatic

liberty in wild and freakish hands of ⁓s has once more proved effective helpmate of autocracy and tyranny, 135:48

Fancy

⁓ amuses; imagination expands and exalts, 183:23

trip into realms of ⁓, we see things that never were, 183:41

Far

people gone too ⁓ to retract, 14:24

Faraway

someday sun shine on me in some ⁓ place, 235:20

Farley, James A.

on Maine politics, 142:4

Farm

⁓ irregular patch of nettles, 8:14

how ya gonna keep 'em down on ⁓, 212:19

Mr. Beecher's ⁓ is not triumph, 8:17

rather be on his ⁓ than emperor of world, 193:133

Farmer

common fate of part-time ⁓s to be sneered at, 8:15

endless toil of ⁓'s wives, 8:7

⁓ endeavoring to solve problem of livelihood by formula more complicated than problem, 8:16

⁓ entitled to tariffs, 8:1

⁓s, founders of human civilization, 8:20

first ⁓ was first man, 8:4

glory of ⁓ is to create, 8:3

heap high ⁓'s wintry hoard, 8:22

no one hates job so heartily as ⁓, 8:13

on back burden of world, 8:12

what should American ⁓s be without soil, 8:2

Farragut, David G.

on Civil War, 51:17

Farrell, James T.

on literature, 138:20

Farrell, Thomas

on nuclear age, 174:10

Free *(cont'd)*

Boston opened more turnpikes to ⁓ thought, speech and deeds than any other city, 36:19

colonies are and ought to be ⁓, 14:8, 14:56

day country ceases to be ⁓ for irreligion will cease to be ⁓ for religion, 200:111

determined we will die ⁓ men, 14:75, 95:63

die to make men ⁓, 95:39

error of opinion tolerated where reason left ⁓ to combat it, 95:45

⁓ men cannot remain ⁓ and silent, 190:8

⁓ school is promoter which is to preserve us as ⁓ nation, 74:3

⁓ society is where safe to be unpopular, 95:73

⁓ soil, ⁓ speech, ⁓ labor, ⁓ men, 41:4

how rarely man who can be ⁓, even in thought, 95:79

hungry man is not ⁓ man, 95:72

if I want to be ⁓ from other man's dictation, I must have no other man under my control, 95:77

if nation expects to be ignorant and ⁓, it expects what never was, 74:60

if wish to be ⁓ must fight, 14:49

in ⁓ country duty of writers to pay no attention to duty, 138:64

in ⁓ country, ten men who care worth hundred who do not, 196:4

in ⁓ world, we must maintain opportunity for man to learn, 74:79

land of ⁓ only so long as it is home of brave, 38:4

man is man because ⁓ to operate within framework of his destiny, 112:35

men have got to make law ⁓, 134:101

merchants manage better, more left ⁓, 73:25

Nature and God, who has given to all men natural right to be ⁓, 95:60

no longer be doubt that all men created ⁓ and equal, 210:41

nor can we have thought half slave and half ⁓, 95:15

no such thing as ⁓ lunch, 73:9

not ⁓ thought for those who agree with us but for thought we hate, 95:34

not good to be Negro in land of ⁓, 34:15

Oh, Lord, I want to be ⁓, 95:2

only ⁓ peoples can hold their purpose and honor to common end, 95:84

personal wish that all men everywhere could be ⁓, 51:36

privacy essential to maintaining ⁓ society, 95:70

some books leave us ⁓ and some books make us ⁓, 35:20

thriving when left ⁓ to individual enterprise, 73:26

time near at hand [to] determine whether Americans are ⁓men or slaves, 14:81

to say man is ⁓ to choose to walk while only walk he can take will lead him over precipice is to strain words, 95:17

we are not ⁓; it was not intended we should be, 95:36

while there is soul in prison I am not ⁓, 61:14

you can only be ⁓ if I am ⁓, 135:14

your huddled masses yearning to breathe ⁓, 116:16

Freedom, 95:1–84 *(See also* Liberty; Religious Freedom; Rights)

absolute ⁓ of navigation upon seas, 162:18

academic ⁓ is way of saying leave management to people who know something about them, 74:54

American Revolution not fought to obtain ⁓ but to preserve liberties, 14:59

as long as men are free to ask, say, think, ⁓ can never be lost, 95:59

battle of ⁓ to be fought out on principle, 210:38

cabal is necessary effect of ⁓, 95:64

can be no friendship where no ⁓, 96:33

cannot choose ⁓ established on hierarchy of degrees of ⁓, 95:24

[capitalism] not sufficient condition for political ⁓, 39:33

cause of ⁓ identified with destinies of humanity, 95:49

defense of ⁓ grounded in appreciation of its value, 95:48

defense of ⁓ is everybody's business, 243:42

distinction between ⁓ and liberty not accurately known, 95:8

economic ⁓ is end in itself [and] indispensable means toward political ⁓, 95:25

every generation must wage new war for ⁓, 95:1

flags of ⁓ fly all over Europe, 261:31

⁓ all winged expands, 95:21

⁓ always purchased at great price, 95:47

⁓ breeds ⁓, 95:67

⁓, condition every nation supposes itself to enjoy in virtual monopoly, 95:8

⁓ exists only where people take care of government, 95:83

⁓ for thought we hate, 50:15

⁓ hunted round globe, 14:64, 95:61

⁓ in commons brings ruin to all, 188:9

⁓ is necessary, 47:6

⁓ is right to choose, 95:54

⁓ is right to dignity as man, 95:55

⁓ is tenable objective only for responsible individuals, 95:26

⁓ must be daily earned and refreshed, 95:19

⁓ needs all her poets, 95:53

⁓ not formula written out by some and used by others, 95:74

⁓ not ideal if means nothing more than ⁓ to stagnate, 95:76

⁓ not luxury, 95:14

⁓ of expression matrix of nearly every other form of ⁓, 95:13

⁓ of thought and private judgment direct their course to this happy country, 95:6

⁓ to do as one likes is denial of liberty, and leads straight to its overthrow, 135:30

fundamentals of democracy and would be nullified should ⁓ of press be successfully challenged, 95:68

history is realm in which human ⁓ and natural necessity curiously intermingled, 107:55

honor man willing to risk half his repute for ⁓ to think and risk t'other half for ⁓ to speak, 95:52

I am for ⁓ of religion, 201:11

if cherish ⁓, don't leave all up to BIG GOVERNMENT, 101:48

if our ⁓ means ease alone, may keep forms of free society, but its spirit will be dead, 95:75

if there is ⁓, folly will die of own poison, 95:82

inclined to confuse ⁓ and democracy, 66:28

let ⁓ ring, 12:93

look forward to world founded upon four essential ⁓s, 95:69

man possesses rational ⁓, 112:44

more instances of abridgment of ⁓ by gradual and silent encroachments than by violent usurpations, 95:56

necessary to preserve ⁓ for minority, to face majority down, 95:12

no finer purpose than preservation of ⁓, 95:66

no ⁓ on earth for those who deny ⁓ to others, 95:40

no such thing as ⁓ left had not been for America, 14:71

observe limits of human ⁓ even while exploit its creative possibilities, 95:58

people are our dependence for continued ⁓, 66:46

plenty of ⁓ in this country but not great deal of independence, 95:65

poverty curtails individual ⁓, 95:41

power in defense of ⁓ greater than in behalf of tyranny, 190:33

press liberty is essential to ⁓, 125:2

private property original source of ⁓, 95:50

proud of quill, which keeps germ of ⁓ in circulation, 262:87

revelation of thought takes men out of servitude into ⁓, 58:2

separation ensures government's ⁓ from religion and individual's ⁓ of religion, 201:19

shield of ⁓ and of worth, 125:57

society that puts equality . . . ahead of ⁓ will end up with neither, 95:27

so costly a sacrifice upon altar of ⁓, 51:42

three precious things: ⁓ of speech, ⁓ of conscience, and prudence never to practice either, 95:80

to be free you must afford ⁓ to your neighbor, and that is difficult, 95:18

to preserve his ⁓, Londoner will fight. So will citizen of Abilene, 95:20

to reap blessings of ⁓ must undergo fatigue of supporting it, 95:62

true ⁓ to share all chains our brothers wear, 95:51

two distinct orders of men—lovers of ⁓ and advocates of power, 95:31

what avail plough or sail, or land, or life, if ⁓ fail?, 95:22

what other liberty worth having, if have not ⁓ and peace in our minds, 95:78

when ⁓ from her mountain height unfurled her standard to the air, 88:3

when people talk of ⁓ of writing, speaking, or thinking, I cannot choose but laugh, 95:4

wherever snow falls usually civil ⁓, 50:11, 211:18

who deny ⁓ to others, deserve it not for themselves, 210:43

who ever walked behind anyone to ⁓?, 95:71

will not just respect us because we practice ⁓, will fear us because we do, 95:23

[women] not owned ⁓ long enough to know how it should be used, 258:19

Free enterprise
when I say liberty I do not simply mean "⁓", 135:63

Freeman, Douglas Southall
on Virginia, 244:7

Free press (See also Censorship)
consists in publishing truth from good motives, 135:29

difficult to have anywhere in world, 125:59

elimination of ⁓ is hardly way to eliminate hypocrisy, 125:67

embraces pamphlets and leaflets, 135:34

essential to freedom, 125:2

every man able to read, all is safe, 125:34

freedom of speech and ⁓ does not protect disturbances to public peace, 50:37

I du believe in gret Press's freedom, 125:40

legislature of United States shall pass no law touching, 135:59

most effectual [avenue of truth], 125:30

no government ought to be without censors, 125:26

one of great bulwarks of liberty, 125:43

only security is in ⁓, 125:37

suppression of press could not more deprive nation of its benefits, than is done by prostitution to falsehood, 125:31

to enjoy benefits, necessary to submit to inevitable evils, 125:71

will die even for newspapers that call me everything good deal less than gentleman, 125:16

Free Soil Party
campaign slogan, 41:4

Free speech
American freedom consists largely in talking nonsense, 95:37

does not protect disturbances to public peace, 50:37

fear of serious injury cannot alone justify suppression of ⁓, 95:11

first [of] four essential freedoms, 95:69

for First Amendment from first word to last, 95:9

⁓ does not live many hours after free industry and free commerce die, 95:35

⁓, free press, free soil, free men, 41:6

⁓ in Congress, 54:1

⁓ taken away, and dumb and silent we may be led, like sheep to slaughter, 95:81

granted to say things which displease, 95:30

it is not true, 95:38

jail more roomy than whole world if denied right to express myself, 95:29

justification to prevent error and discover truth, 95:16

limitations placed upon right of ⁓, 219:4

matrix of nearly every other form of freedom, 95:13

most stringent protection of ⁓ would not protect man falsely shouting fire and causing panic, 95:32

no wise laws nor enforcement unless expression of wisdom and folly, 95:82

risk t'other half [repute] for, 95:52

unconditional right to say what one pleases about public affairs, 95:10

utter with impunity that which he cannot publish with impunity, 125:11

Fritz
grits and ⌐, 41:39
Fritz, John
on own invention, 123:8
Frog
never see ⌐ so modest, for all he
was so gifted, 113:35
Frohman, Charles
last words, 133:20
Fromm, Erich
on power, 190:21
Frontier
wonderful how soon piano gets
into hut on ⌐, 62:4
Frost
⌐ is on the punkin and fodder's
in the shock, 28:16
tints of autumn blossoming under
spell of enchanter, ⌐,
28:17
Frost, Robert
on autumn, 28:13
on choice, 47:8
on duty, 72:12
on education, 74:44
on epitaphs, 78:13
on failure, 83:2
on home, 109:19
on love, 140:34, 140:35
on marriage, 145:32
on nature, 161:36
on New Hampshire, 166:4–6
on own books, 35:36
on personal independence, 118:8
on poetry, 186:8–10
on truth, 237:26
on winter, 254:4
on work, 259:27
on writing, 262:20
Fugitive
feel like ⌐ from th' law of
averages, 261:21
Fulbright, J. William
on America, 12:38
on change, 42:7
on democracy, 66:27, 66:28
on diplomacy, 68:18
on history, 107:28
on poverty, 189:18
on science, 207:20
on Senate, 54:22
Full
four more years of ⌐ dinner pail,
41:15
Fuller, Buckminster
on war, 245:30
Fuller, Margaret
on advice, 4:34
on genius, 97:13
on marriage, 145:33
on truth, 237:27
on women's rights, 258:14

Fun
indecency and ⌐ are old cronies,
149:4
love what you do and feel it
matters—how could anything
be more ⌐?, 259:29
Republicans have ⌐ but don't
want people to see it, 187:106
Function
form ever follows ⌐, 21:12
Funeral
⌐ eloquence rattles coffin-lid,
63:20
rejoice at birth and grieve at ⌐,
136:119
Funny
being ⌐ person does awful lot of
things to you, 113:8
Bismarck, North Dakota, ⌐
anywhere in United States,
113:16
everything is ⌐ as long as
happening to somebody else,
113:31
⌐ things they think of in
Congress, 54:50
hard to be ⌐ when you have to
be clean, 113:40
if nothing ⌐ in one house of
Congress, sure to be in other,
54:55
letters about my work, sometimes
⌐ in grotesque way, 113:1
never dare to write as ⌐ as I
can, 113:19
never saw anything ⌐ that
wasn't terrible, 113:17
Fury
every stroke our ⌐ strikes is sure
to hit ourselves, 18:12
Fusion
⌐ and fission revolutionized
foundation of human affairs,
174:17
Future
beauty is promise of ⌐, 31:25
best preparation for ⌐ is to live
as if there were none, 136:66
expect generations of ⌐ to be
superior, 191:6
⌐ no more uncertain than
present, 234:49
⌐ sits in judgment on past,
68:61
history will enable to judge of the
⌐, 107:36
I have seen ⌐; and it works,
204:27
like dreams of ⌐ better than
history of past, 107:38
no way of judging ⌐ but by past,
107:31

those dedicated to ⌐ not best
prophets, 191:1

Gabor, Zsa Zsa
on marriage, 145:34, 145:35
Gai
and i m toujours ⌐, 103:28
Galbraith, John Kenneth
on beauty, 31:23
on change, 42:8, 42:9
on diplomacy, 68:19
on drinking, 71:25
on economics, 73:10, 73:11
on government, 101:44
on humor, 113:18
on pollution, 188:8
on poverty, 189:19
on society, 211:21
on stock market crash (1929), 39:34
on wealth, 249:27
on writing, 262:21
Gallows
sheriff took Frankie to ⌐, 197:1
Game
"how you play ⌐" is for college
boys, 220:17
not how won or lost—but how
played ⌐, 93:14
Garagiola, Joe
on baseball, 30:18–22
Garbo, Greta
on herself, 159:12
Garcia
carry message to ⌐, 1:9
Gardening
commonest delight of race, 161:73
to plant seeds, and watch renewal
of life, 161:73
Gardner, Augustus P.
on World War I, 260:5
Garfield, James A.
on education, 74:45
on government, 101:45
on life, 136:51
on money, 157:32–34
on presidency, 193:36
on public opinion, 196:12
on revenge, 203:4
on war, 245:31
on White House, 193:37
Garland, Hamlin
on agriculture, 8:7, 8:8
on literature, 138:21, 138:22
on nature, 161:37
on own writing, 262:22, 262:23
Garland, Judy
on freedom, 95:28
on motion pictures, 159:13
Garner, John Nance
John L. Lewis on, 131:34
on vice presidency, 241:4

God *(cont'd)*
   cause of all things, 200:143
   don't believe in ~ because don't
     believe in Mother Goose,
     200:28
   duty of all to acknowledge
     providence of ~, 200:170
   easy for ~ to cast His enemies
     down to Hell, 200:41
   evidence for ~ in inner personal
     experiences, 200:116
   final proof of ~'s omnipotence,
     he need not exist to save us,
     200:30
   ~ builds his temple in the heart
     on ruins of churches, 200:60
   ~ cannot be for and against same
     thing at same time, 200:124
   ~ does not speak prose, 200:65
   ~ gave me my money, 249:47
   ~ give us men, 43:47
   ~ holds you over pit of Hell as
     spider over fire, 200:42
   ~ is, and all is well, 200:187
   ~ is just; and finally justice
     triumphs, 126:33
   ~ is love, 200:34
   ~ not finished with me yet,
     43:54
   ~ of the cannibals will be a
     cannibal, 200:61
   ~ will not look you over for
     medals, but for scars, 43:51,
     200:100
   Great Book best gift ~ given to
     man, 200:125
   hard to sneak look at ~'s cards,
     207:13
   honest ~ is noblest work of man,
     200:107
   I believe in one ~, 200:75
   I believe in one ~, and no more,
     200:140
   I did not know we had ever
     quarreled, 133:37
   if did not believe [in] future state,
     should believe in no ~, 200:7
   if he is ~, not absolute and
     infinite, 200:134
   I only know I cannot drift
     beyond His love and care,
     200:185
   John Doe of religion, 200:92
   knowing ~'s own time is best,
     200:183
   let ~ be magnified, 200:188
   looks odd to choke poor scamp
     for glory of ~, 200:127
   mills of ~ grind slowly, 86:8
   most acceptable service we render
     Him is doing good to His other
     children, 117:12

no half-way business in ~,
   200:129
often ~ has to shut door in our
   face, so can open door through
   which He wants us to go,
   200:130
one, on ~'s side, is majority, 143:7
one, with ~, always majority,
   194:8
sickness, sin and death do not
   originate in ~, 200:37
simplest person who worships ~,
   becomes ~, 200:56
thunder is voice of ~, 250:12
too many men of science, too few
   men of ~, 207:2
we never ask ~ to forgive
   anybody except where we
   haven't, 200:103
what hath ~ wrought, 123:14
when speak of ~, let it be
   seriously, 200:168
where ~ speaks to Jones in same
   tones he uses with Hadley and
   Dwight, 55:7
who tells us that with this sort of
   world ~ bids us to be
   content?, 200:78
Gods
   fear first created ~, 200:154
   ~ seem to have concentrated on
     him, 51:62
   if ~ think to speak outright to
     man, they will speak outright,
     200:132
   wonderful verse of the ~, 200:62
Goes
   rather there he ~ than here he
     lies, 60:1
Gogarty, Oliver St. John
   on America, 16:19
Going
   know I am ~ where Lucy is,
     133:23
Gold
   [Alaska] synonymous with ~,
     10:4
   crucify mankind upon cross of ~,
     157:8
   drop grain of blessed ~ into
     ground, 8:5
   ~ dollars as against balony
     dollars, 157:57
   how is ~ become dim, 17:7
   no cross of ~, 41:14
   rates of ~ outrival Trinity's
     chimes, 171:94
Goldberg, Isaac
   on diplomacy, 68:20
Golden
   biting hand that lays ~ egg, 99:8
   ~ age lies before us, 195:2

~ age never was present age,
   107:27
~ kisses over cheeks of meadow,
   90:1
~ moments fly, 1:13
~ rule best of current silver,
   53:22
lament for ~ age is only lament
   for ~ men, 107:66
Goldenrod
   trembles on arid stalk the hoar
     plume of ~, 28:18
Goldman, Emma
   on government, 101:47
   on revolution, 204:4, 204:5
   on women and labor, 131:20
Goldman, Eric
   on Lyndon B. Johnson, 193:38
Goldman, Peter
   on Congress, 54:23
Gold rush
   three thousand miles nearer to
     hell, 40:25
Goldwater, Barry M.
   campaign slogans, 41:35, 41:36
   on diplomacy, 68:21
   on government, 101:48
   on liberty, 135:26
   on religious freedom, 201:7
   on war, 245:32
Goldwynisms, 99:1-9
Golf
   ~ links lie so near the mill,
     131:7
   ~ matches won on first tee,
     220:1
   invites perfectionists, 220:12
Gompers, Samuel
   on free speech, 95:29, 95:30
   on labor rights, 131:21
Gone
   ~ to better land I know, 63:23
Good
   any ~ thing I can do, let me do
     it now, 53:1
   be ~ and you will be lonesome,
     53:23
   being too ~ is apt to be
     uninteresting, 43:90
   be not simply ~; be ~ for
     something, 4:50
   cynic never sees ~ quality, 43:11
   doing ~ is one of professions
     which are full, 44:19
   every human mind feels pleasure
     in doing ~ to another, 44:9
   every religion is ~ that teaches
     man to be ~, 200:138
   function of government is to
     make it easy to do ~, 101:18
   ~ and bad but names readily
     transferable, 183:16

~ for General Motors is ~ for
  the country, 39:68
~ world for purposes for which
  built, 184:3
hardly such thing to be found as
  old woman who is not ~
  woman, 257:25
if you can't be ~, be careful, 4:5
if you can't be ~, be sanitary,
  4:6
jest 'fore Christmas I'm as ~ as
  I kin be, 48:5
man as ~ as has to be, 144:13
many foxes grow grey, but few
  grow ~, 43:41
mass of men neither wise nor ~,
  112:29
measure of civilization is influence
  of ~ women, 257:23
none but ~ man is living man,
  136:89
my religion is to do ~, 200:137
nothing out of its place is ~,
  183:48
one thing people like that is ~
  for them: ~ night's sleep,
  105:16
power is first ~, 190:18
so much ~ in worst of us, 43:1,
  100:1
takes time to persuade men to do
  even what is for their own ~,
  135:44
time has been spent in doing ~,
  133:33
too much of ~ thing can be
  wonderful, 103:41
used to be a ~ hotel, 42:20
what one regards as ~, another
  may regard as harm, 190:19
when she was ~, very, very ~,
  264:29
you never had it so ~, 41:30
Goodbye
  ~ kid. Hurry back, 133:9
  ~ to flattery's fawning face,
  109:10
Goodman, Roy
  on New York City, 171:31
Goodness
  ~, armed with power, corrupted,
  190:34
  ~ had nothing to do with it,
  159:36
  ~ its own heaven, 209:10
  no odor so bad as from ~
  tainted, 43:87
Good night
  ~, dear heart, ~, ~, 78:21
Goodrich, Samuel
  on Connecticut, 55:4

Goose
  wild ~ more cosmopolite than
  we, 19:19
Goosestep
  natural gait is ~, 66:74
Gospel
  ~ songs are songs of hope,
  212:18
Gossip, 100:1–10
  all news is ~, 125:70
  ~ers, and ~ees, 100:9
  ~ is news running ahead of itself
  in red satin dress, 100:10
  ~ is only lack of worthy theme,
  100:6
  ~ is vice enjoyed vicariously,
  100:5
  historian, broad-gauge ~, 107:7
Goth
  scientific ~, destroying country as
  he goes, 51:58
Gotham
  renowned and ancient city of ~,
  171:54
Govern
  America stands for sovereignty of
  self-~ing people, 12:119
  best system to have one party and
  other party watch, 101:115
  have no ambition to ~ men,
  193:57
  it is to arraign Providence to
  suppose created beings
  incapable of ~ing themselves,
  101:20
  let the people think they ~ and
  they will be ~ed, 101:105
  man may be ~ed by reason and
  truth, 125:30
  mobs will never do to ~,
  101:5
  no man is good enough to ~
  another man without that
  other's consent, 101:85
  only Anglo-Saxons can ~
  themselves, 77:42
  only legitimate right to ~ is
  express grant of power from
  ~ed, 101:55
  people ~ed much by custom,
  196:32
  presumption of ~ing beyond
  grave most ridiculous and
  insolvent of all tyrannies,
  101:100
  under pretence of ~ing, have
  divided nations into two classes,
  wolves and sheep, 101:66
  when people become incapable of
  ~ing themselves, little
  consequence [where master]
  comes [from], 238:30

Government, 101:1–147
absorption of revenue by ~
  created economic problems,
  73:30
administration of ~ is firmest
  pillar of ~, 126:50
all free ~s managed by combined
  wisdom and folly of the people,
  101:45
all ~ is against liberty, 135:55
all ~ is dead weight that
  paralyzes free spirit, 101:47
all monarchical ~s are military,
  101:104
American ~ relies very little on
  officials, and arms them with
  little power of arbitrary
  interference, 101:13
Anglo-Saxon carries self-~ with
  him wherever he goes, 77:5
any ~ can for year spend little
  more than it earns, 64:14
autocratic ~, not self-~, has
  been prevailing, 101:29
be most on guard to protect
  liberty when ~'s purposes are
  beneficent, 135:9
born in possession of right of
  self-~, 12:99
burdens unnecessarily laid by
  their ~s, 101:11
cannot without disgrace be
  associated with it [American
  ~], 101:129
care of human life and happiness
  is only legitimate object of
  good ~, 101:76
Constitution most elastic
  compilation of rules of ~ ever
  written, 57:30
creating perfect system of ~,
  187:151
decide whether have ~ with
  newspapers, or newspapers
  without ~, 125:25
declaration that People are hostile
  to ~ made by themselves is
  insult, 66:2
despotic in its tendency as any
  absolute ~ that ever existed,
  101:16
duty of ~ to protect all religion,
  200:135
err in supposing that by
  multiplying representatives,
  strengthen barrier against ~ of
  few, 101:52
error alone which needs support
  of ~, 237:41
essence of free ~ consists in
  considering offices as public
  trusts, 101:15

Government *(cont'd)*

everybody knows that ~ never began anything, 101:108

every ~ degenerates when trusted to rulers of the people alone, 66:41

every ~ falls into wrong measures, 101:32

fanning of mass emotions greatest disservice to popular ~, 66:53

fault of ~ that remedy is worse than the evil, 134:100

fear is foundation of most ~s, 101:4

find little but damaged reputation in, 101:1

firm basis of ~ is justice, not pity, 101:146

first duty of ~ to protect citizen from assault, 61:28

for thirty years, Bible-believing Christians have been largely absent from ~, 101:41

forty years of experience in ~ is worth century of book-reading, 57:18

freedom exists only where people take care of ~, 95:83

free ~ is founded in jealousy and not in confidence, 101:70

[free man] regards ~ as means, 101:43

functionaries of every ~ have propensities to command at will their constituents, 101:78

function of ~ is to make it easy to do good and difficult to do wrong, 101:18

gives force to public opinion, 196:36

good ~ has for its objects protection of every person, 101:24

~ as filled with love as are American people, 12:14

~ by free consent of governed, 12:97

~ by guy who knows, 54:19

~ can suffer no rivals in field of coercion, 101:63

~ does little for respectable people except annoy them, 101:56

~ exists to protect rights which are ours from birth, 101:113

~ exists to protect us from each other, 101:114

~ founded upon intelligence of the people, 101:58

~ functions do not include support of the people, 101:27

~ has been fossil, 101:39

~ has come to be a trade, 187:40

~ has hardened into tyrannical monopoly, 101:33

~ instituted because passions of men not conform to dictates of reason, without constraint, 101:53

~ in well-constituted republic, requires no belief from man beyond what his reason authorizes, 101:101

~ is but necessary evil, 101:98

~ is contrivance of human wisdom to provide for human wants, 101:17

~ is for use of the people, and not the people for use of ~, 101:125

~ is trust, and officers are trustees, 101:22

~ is us, 101:120

~ neither subsists nor arises because good or useful, but because is inevitable, 101:124

~ not exact science, 101:12

~ of humans should elevate itself to higher order, 187:30

~ of naive, for naive, by naive, 12:81

~ of own choice, for which men will fight, 14:7

~ of Union is emphatically ~ of the people, 66:73, 101:96

~ of United States is lawyer's ~, 134:29

~ only creature of constitution, 57:27

~s can encourage private virtue, but cannot make us virtuous, 101:82

~s exist to protect rights of minorities, 101:109

~s mainly engaged in kicking people around, 190:44

~s of nations of shopkeepers must keep shop also, 77:12

~ strong enough to control men's minds, will have ~ strong enough to control everything, 101:28

~ strong enough to protect interests of the people, 101:119

~, to be safe and free, must consist of representatives having common interest and feeling with represented, 101:111

~ will not collapse if any of gentlemen seeking to be entrusted with its guidance should be left at home, 101:145

grand ideas of ~ depend on willingness of citizens and leaders to apply them, 101:117

great part of order which reigns among mankind is not effect of ~, 101:102

hand of the people has proved that ~ to be strongest of which every man feels himself a part, 101:74

happiness of people is sole end of ~ and consent is only foundation, 101:3

hereditary ~ is in its nature tyranny, 101:99

history only informs what bad ~ is, 107:37

I am against ~ by crony, 101:57

idea of national ~ involves in it indefinite supremacy over all persons and things, 101:95

idea of right of people to establish ~ presupposes duty to obey established ~, 101:138

I do not believe in ~ ownership of anything which with propriety can be left in private hands, 101:121

if cherish your freedom, don't leave it all up to BIG ~, 101:48

if ~ knew how, I should like to see it check, not multiply population, 101:40

if professors try to run ~, we shall end by having ~ run professors, 101:91

if representative system ultimately fail, popular ~s must be pronounced impossible, 101:140

in all that the people can individually do for themselves, ~ ought not to interfere, 101:84

influence over ~ must be shared among all the people, 101:65

in free ~, cannot restrain voice of multitude, 196:33

inherent right in the people to reform their ~ and right to resist unconstitutional laws without overturning the ~, 101:141

in rivers and bad ~s lightest things swim at top, 101:42

is the problem, 73:31

justice is end of ~, 126:35

legitimate powers of ~ extend to such acts only as are injurious to others, 101:64

less ~ the better, 101:35

liberty has never come from ~, 135:78

Grammar (cont'd)
    when thought takes breath away,
      lesson on ∼ impertinence,
      186:11
Grand Canyon
    is carven deep by master hand,
      52:5
Grandfather
    ∼'s hat fits Ben, 41:13
    to ∼'s house we go, 232:3
Grandmother
    now ∼'s cap I spy, 232:4
Grandparents
    reason ∼ and grandchildren get
      along, 85:12
Granite
    foothold tenon'd and mortis'd in
      ∼, 84:30
Grant, Ulysses S.
    Abraham Lincoln on, 51:40,
      51:41
    Henry Adams on, 81:1
    John Tyler, Jr., on, 51:58
    Mary Boykin Chestnut on, 51:10
    on Civil War, 51:19–22
    on duty, 72:13
    on English-U.S. relations, 77:15
    on labor, 131:22
    on law, 134:44
    on peace, 181:17
    on religion, 200:84
    on revolution, 204:6
    on the public, 196:13
    on war, 245:33
    Roscoe Conkling on, 193:24
    Walt Whitman on, 51:62
    William Tecumseh Sherman on,
      96:36
Grapes
    ∼ of wrath, 51:25
    ripe black ∼ ungathered, 28:5
    when trellised ∼ their flowers
      unmask, 221:4
Grapple
    let him rebuke who ne'er has
      known pure Platonic ∼,
      209:30
Grasp
    when seeming just within my ∼,
      11:13
Grass
    believe leaf of ∼ no less than
      journey-work of stars, 161:75
    child said, *What is the ∼?*,
      161:74
    climbs to soul in ∼ and flowers,
      161:58
    I am ∼; I cover all, 63:74
    not sprig of ∼ that shoots
      uninteresting to me, 161:47
    observing spear of summer ∼,
      58:12

Grasshopper
    all kings of earth, before God, are
      as ∼s, 190:14
    keeps ear so close to ground full
      of ∼s, 193:14
Gratification
    life no value but as it brings ∼s,
      211:28
Gratitude
    most painful thing to bear is ∼,
      179:1
Grau, Shirley Ann
    on appetite, 20:7
    on death, 63:27
    on government projects,
      101:49
Grave
    and ∼ not [life's] goal, 136:78
    are you ∼ of our day?, 16:25
    bitterest tears shed over ∼s are
      for words unsaid, 63:80
    ∼ but covered bridge, 63:55
    hearts beating funeral marches to
      ∼, 136:79
    mouldy as ∼, 7:73
    one day nearer ∼, Thurber,
      136:75
    private character canonized by ∼,
      43:80
    ∼stone of dead delight, 225:3
    we bargain for ∼s we lie in,
      63:59
    who can look down upon ∼ even
      of enemy, and not feel
      compunctious throb, 63:36
Gray
    hair as ∼ as was my sire's, 7:82
    pull out ∼ hair and seven will
      come, 7:1
    shoot, if must, this old ∼ head,
      88:9
    tremble at ∼ hair, 7:15
    will you love me when my hair
      all turned ∼?, 140:94
Gray, Francine du Plessix
    on Hawaii, 104:3, 104:4
Great
    baseball gives you every chance to
      be ∼, 30:21
    count him ∼ who inhabits higher
      sphere of thought, 102:15
    ∼ city is that which has ∼est
      men and women, 49:16, 102:42
    ∼est man in history was poorest,
      189:13
    ∼ man is he who in midst of
      crowd keeps independence of
      solitude, 102:10
    ∼ man is made of qualities that
      make ∼ occasions, 102:36
    ∼ men are rarely isolated
      mountainpeaks, 102:28

    ∼ men lifted upon shoulders of
      world conceive their ideas,
      102:25
    ∼ men not chosen President,
      192:6
    ∼ men serve us as insurrections
      do bad governments, 102:11
    ∼ minds [are interested] in
      commonplace, 102:32
    ∼ truths are portions of soul of
      man, 102:35
    he is ∼ who is what he is from
      nature, 102:16
    if be accounted ∼ by your
      contemporaries, be not too
      much ∼er, 102:1
    if companions noble, we should
      be ∼ also?, 102:5
    inwardly in secret to be ∼, 43:72
    lives of ∼ men all remind us,
      43:64
    necessities call out ∼ virtues,
      43:2
    never did nature and fortune
      combine more perfectly to
      make man ∼, 246:11
    never truly ∼ man that was not
      virtuous, 102:23
    no ∼ man ever modest, 137:15
    President can be only ∼ as
      American people are ∼, 102:38
    the ∼est man is he who choose
      the right, 102:3
    to be ∼ is to be misunderstood,
      102:9
    Washington and Natty Bumppo
      two only really ∼ men, 102:4
    when nature removes ∼ man, his
      class is extinguished, 102:17
    works of intellect are ∼ only by
      comparison, 102:14
    world's ∼ men have not been ∼
      scholars, 102:30
Great Britain. *See* British; England;
    English
Greatness, 102:1–42
    difficulty is nurse of ∼, 3:3
    essence of ∼ is perception that
      virtue is enough, 102:6
    ∼ may be present in lives whose
      range is small, 102:2
    ∼ not something written on
      campaign poster, 102:38
    his ∼ will shine whether they
      second him or not, 102:12
    if man seeks ∼, let him ask for
      truth, 102:37
    nothing is more simple than ∼,
      102:13
    people tired of ∼, 102:34
    what I must do, not what people
      think, 102:10

Great Society
 a woman I really loved—the ~,
  193:71
 ~ place where men more
  concerned with quality of goals,
  12:54
 Lyndon Johnson came into office
  seeking ~ and found instead
  ugly little war, 193:137
 man's first chance to build ~,
  67:6
Greece
 glory that was ~, 31:32, 107:58
Greed
 each generation wastes more of
  future with ~, 29:6
 ~ vs. ~ makes for lawsuits
  settled between lawyers,
  134:107
Greeks
 how those old ~ would have
  seized upon him, 51:62
Greeley, Horace
 campaign slogan, 41:10
 on education, 74:46
 on history, 107:29
 on labor conditions, 131:23
 on literature, 138:23
 on money, 157:36
 on perception, 183:25
 on politics, 187:51
 on work, 259:30
 on writing, 262:25
Green
 every ~ thing loves to die in
  bright colors, 28:2
Green, Thomas Jefferson
 Sam Houston on, 122:4
Green Bay Packers
 three important things: family,
  religion, and ~, 93:9
Greene, Albert Gordon
 on wine, 253:6
Greene, Amy
 on dress, 70:11
Greene, Nathanael
 on American Revolution, 14:41,
  14:42
Greenough, Horatio
 on architecture, 21:3
Gregory, Dick
 on America, 12:40
 on being Black American, 34:8
 on Chicago elections, 75:9
 on civil rights, 34:9
 on Constitution, 57:9
 on crime, 61:19
 on elections, 75:10
 on love, 140:37
 on nature, 161:39
 on peace, 181:18
 on politics, 187:52–54

on power, 190:22
on statesmen, 222:4, 224:5
on Vietnam War, 243:12
on youth, 264:19
Grief
 [beauty] leaves gift of ~, 31:30
 between ~ and nothing I will
  take ~, 213:5
 no man stated his ~s as lightly
  as he might, 6:2
Griffith, D.W.
 on California, 40:10
Grilling
 ~, broiling, barbecuing is art,
  92:2
Grimké, Angelina
 on slavery, 210:24
Griswold, Alfred Whitney
 on book banning, 35:37
Grits
 ~ and Fritz, 41:39
Grog-Shop
 horrible Light-House of Hell,
  71:11
Grose, Francis
 on Boston (Mass.), 36:17
Ground
 color of ~ was in him, 137:36
 ought to be under ~, inspiring
  cabbages, 122:11
 to own bit of ~, to plant seeds,
  and watch renewal of life,
  161:73
Groves
 ~ were God's first temples,
  161:10
Groves, Leslie R.
 on atomic bomb, 261:8, 261:9
Grow, Galusha A.
 on labor, 131:24
Growing
 all ~ is at same time dying,
  136:101
Guess, William Francis
 on Charleston (S.C.), 215:7
 on South Carolina, 215:6
Guest, Edgar
 on home, 109:20
 on success, 224:17
Guilt
 but Adam's ~ our souls hath
  spilt, 209:37
Guinan, Texas
 on success, 224:18
Guiteau, Charles Julius
 last words, 133:21
Guiterman, Arthur
 on amoeba, 81:11
 on New York City, 171:32
Gum (See also Chewing gum)
 can't fart and chew ~ at same
  time, 193:64

Gunther, John
 on Atlanta (Ga.), 98:4
 on Butte (Mont.), 158:2
 on Chicago (Ill.), 46:7, 46:8
 on Cleveland (Ohio), 175:5
 on Denver (Colo.), 52:3
 on Dust Bowl, 176:8
 on Idaho, 114:3, 114:4
 on Iowa, 124:2
 on Jews in Utah, 239:5
 on Midwest, 151:2
 on Montana, 158:3
 on Nevada, 164:3, 164:4
 on New England, 165:5
 on New Mexico, 168:6
 on Ohio, 175:4
 on Oklahoma, 176:5–7
 on Oregon, 178:4
 on politics, 187:55
 on Rhode Island, 205:4
 on Texas, 231:4
 on the West, 251:11
 on Vermont, 240:7
 on West Virginia, 252:5
 on Wyoming, 263:3–5
Guthrie, Tyrone
 on Metropolitan Opera,
  171:33
Guthrie, Woody
 on Detroit (Mich.), 150:4

Habersham
 out of hills of ~, 98:5
Habit
 grow up with good talk to form
  ~ of it, 59:18
 ~ coaxed downstairs step at time,
  42:21
 happiness is ~—cultivate it,
  103:19
 land of steady ~s, 55:2
 nothing so needs reforming as
  other people's ~s, 199:11
Had
 ~ enough?, 41:28
Hagen, Walter C.
 on advice, 4:35
Hague, Frank
 on civil rights, 50:12
 on law, 134:45
Hair
 hyacinth ~, classic face, 31:32
 pull out gray ~ and seven will
  come, 7:1
 tremble at gray ~, 7:15
 with ~ as gray as was my sire's,
  7:82
 woman ceases to alter her ~,
  passed crisis of her experience,
  257:7

secret motive of all men, 103:21
to achieve ∼ have clear
  conscience, or none at all,
  103:30
to fill hour—that is ∼, 103:9
tranquility and occupation give
  ∼, 103:24
uninformed mind with healthy
  body happier than wisest
  valetudinarian, 105:19
wealth must justify itself in ∼,
  249:51
wise grows it under his feet,
  103:32
Happy
  America is vast conspiracy to
    make you ∼, 12:104
  ∼ days are here again, 103:45
  ∼ woman is one who has no
    cares at all, 103:37
  I know I'm ∼, 133:7
  Puritanism—haunting fear that
    someone may be ∼, 103:29
  real life is ∼ because expecting it
    will be so, 103:33
  traveling makes men wiser but
    less ∼, 235:21
Hard
  strong men greet ∼ times, 3:6
Hardin, Garrett
  on civil rights, 50:13
  on pollution, 188:9
  on principle, 194:3
Harding, Florence Kling
  on husband's presidency, 193:41
Harding, Warren G.
  Alice Roosevelt Longworth on,
    193:83
  campaign slogan, 41:20
  E.E. Cummings on, 193:28
  Grover Cleveland on, 193:25
  Harry Daugherty on, 193:29
  on own presidency, 192:16
  on presidential nomination,
    193:42
  on World War I, 260:6
  Ralph Nader on, 193:88
  wife on, 193:41
Harlan, John Marshall
  on civil rights, 134:52
  on education, 74:47
Harlem
  invincible indescribable squalor of
    ∼, 171:7
  melting pot ∼ of honey and
    chocolate, 171:51
Harmony
  natural beauty consists of
    complicated ∼, 161:15
  velvet flute-note fell down
    pleasantly upon bosom of that
    ∼, 160:16

Harrington, Michael
  on change, 42:11
  on democracy, 66:34
  on economics, 73:18
  on genius, 97:14
  on government, 101:54
  on New York City, 171:35
  on nuclear age, 174:11
  on patriotism, 180:20
Harris, Charles K.
  song by, 212:16
Harris, Joel Chandler
  on drinking, 71:26
  on travel, 235:16
Harris, Sydney J.
  on New York City, 171:36
Harrison, Benjamin
  campaign slogan, 41:13
  higgledy-piggledy, ∼, 193:43
  John Hollander on, 193:43
  on Abraham Lincoln, 137:13
  on trusts, 39:35
Harrison, William Henry
  campaign slogans, 41:1, 41:2,
    41:13
  on government, 101:55
Hart, Lorenz
  on New York City, 171:37
Hart, Moss
  on New York City, 171:38
Harte, Bret
  on death, 63:28
  on labor, 131:25
  on luck, 141:5
  on sorrow, 213:6
  on theater, 233:14
  on youth, 264:20
Hartford (Conn.)
  "Camelot," said he, 55:9
Hartmann, Robert T.
  on presidency, 192:17, 192:18
Harvard
  enter to grow in wisdom, 74:32
  if white students choose to
    withdraw all income will be
    devoted to [black student's]
    education, 74:42
  it is with kind of joy I attack ∼,
    74:22
  studying literature at ∼, 138:6
  whale ship was my Yale College
    and my ∼, 74:77
Harvest
  rich ∼ in hungry land is
    impressive, 12:57
Has
  them as ∼, gits, 249:1
Haste
  marry'd in ∼ repent at leisure,
    145:25
  nothing more vulgar than ∼,
    53:7

Hat
  grandfather's ∼ fits Ben, 41:13
  my ∼ in ring, 187:130
Hatchet
  buried was bloody ∼, 181:25
Hate
  folks never understand folks they
    ∼, 76:6
  ∼ corrodes personality, 18:11
  my ∼s have always occupied my
    mind, 125:51
  not free thought for those who
    agree but for thought we ∼,
    95:34
  to be ∼d is to achieve distinction,
    140:5
  woman wronged can cherish ∼,
    257:85
Hatred
  doctrine of ∼ must be preached,
    140:23
  greatest harm done by vast wealth
    is envy and ∼, 29:9, 249:50
Have
  opposition between men who ∼
    and men who are, 249:38
Havemeyer, Henry O.
  on trusts, 39:36
Hawaii, 104:1–9
  eight beauty queens in row.
    That's what I like best about
    ∼, 104:5
  loveliest fleet of islands, 104:9
  no other land could so longingly
    haunt me, 104:8
  Pacific remain great solace, escape
    and nourishment, 104:4
  spiritual destiny of ∼ shaped by
    Calvinist paternalism, 104:3
  state motto, 104:1
Hawaiian
  future of ∼ race comes
    secondarily [to] plantation
    profits, 104:2
  ∼ people lovers of poetry and
    music, 104:7
Hawthorne, Nathaniel
  on affliction, 6:4
  on architecture, 21:4
  on art, 26:21
  on avarice, 29:5
  on death, 63:29, 63:30
  on England, 77:17
  on genius, 97:15, 97:16
  on greatness, 102:25, 102:26
  on happiness, 103:16
  on health, 105:14
  on heroism, 102:27
  on humankind, 112:20
  on justice, 126:18, 126:19
  on language, 132:21
  on life, 136:52, 136:53

Higginson, Thomas
Wentworth *(cont'd)*
    on greatness, 102:28
    on wealth, 249:33
Highbrow
    ⌐ is person educated beyond his
        intelligence, 74:74
Highway
    ⌐s always get beautiful near
        state capital, 101:49
Hill
    ⌐ and house should live together,
        21:13
    ⌐s rock-ribbed and ancient as
        sun, 63:8
    I loved those ⌐s, 55:4
Hill, Joe (Joseph Hillstrom)
    on labor, 131:27
Hillman, Sidney
    on politics, 187:59
Hinduism
    Ambrose Bierce on, 200:16
Hire
    we ⌐ man, not his history,
        228:4
Hiroshima
    American airplane dropped one
        bomb on ⌐, 261:32
Historian
    his function is to make known,
        107:71
    ⌐, broad-gauge gossip, 107:7
    ⌐s relate what they would have
        believed, 107:26
    ⌐ wants more documents than
        he can really use, 107:34
    no honest ⌐ can take part
        with—or against—forces he has
        to study, 107:1
    shoot all economists and elect
        ⌐s, 73:19
    study men, not ⌐s, 4:54
History, 107:1–75
    all ⌐ is modern ⌐, 107:64
    all ⌐ is one long story, 107:65
    Americans see ⌐ as straight line,
        15:14
    books are heart and core of ages
        past, 35:52
    can see my own vices without
        heat in distant persons, 107:16
    deeper knowledge produces
        insight, 107:61
    define ⌐ as past events of which
        we have knowledge, 107:70
    every generation writes ⌐ which
        corresponds with his view of
        world, 107:35
    failed world re-collecting withered
        forces to begin again, 107:20
    great results of ⌐ brought about
        by discreditable means, 107:22

half a continent has changed
    hands at scratch of pen, 107:57
⌐, account mostly false, of
    events mostly unimportant,
    107:8
⌐ condensed in catchwords of
    the people, 132:33
⌐ fades into fable, 107:33
⌐ instrument of those who make
    it, 107:28
⌐ is better guide than good
    intentions, 107:40
⌐ is bright and fiction dull with
    homely men who have charmed
    women, 107:30
⌐ is bunk, 107:24
⌐ is realm in which freedom and
    necessity curiously
    intermingled, 107:55
⌐ is torch to illuminate past, 107:9
⌐ is very chancy, 107:54
⌐ knows no resting places and
    no plateaus, 107:41
⌐ makes us understand moral
    arrogance of supposing that
    future will yield itself easily to
    us, 107:62
⌐ not cookbook offering
    pretested recipes, 107:42
⌐ of every country begins in
    heart of man or woman, 107:11
⌐ of oppressed people is hidden
    in lies of its conquerors, 107:46
⌐ of world is record of man in
    quest of daily bread and butter,
    107:72
⌐ only informs what bad
    government is, 107:37
⌐ outwits our certitudes, 107:60
⌐ perpetually tells of millions of
    people abandoned to caprice of
    maddest princes, 107:12
⌐ selects its heroes and its
    villains, 107:10
⌐ series of conspiracies, 107:23
⌐ supplies antidote to every
    generation's illusion that its
    own problems are uniquely
    oppressive, 107:63
⌐ teaches by analogy, not
    maxims, 107:42
⌐ teaches us to hope, 107:44
⌐ will enable to judge of the
    future, 107:36
human mind wrote ⌐, and must
    read it, 107:15
if ⌐ teaches anything it is can be
    no peace without equilibrium,
    107:43
if whole of ⌐ in one man,
    explained from individual
    experience, 107:15

illusion that times that were are
    better, 183:25
language is archives of ⌐, 132:15
legends and yarns and folktales
    are part of real ⌐, 107:5
less intention in ⌐ than we
    ascribe to it, 107:19
let ⌐ answer, 66:44
like dreams of future better than
    ⌐ of past, 107:38
men come and go; and that is all
    of ⌐, 107:53
men make ⌐ and not other way
    round, 107:68
morsel of genuine ⌐, thing so
    rare always valuable, 107:39
most important fact in modern
    ⌐: North America speaks
    English, 107:6
most memorable epoch in ⌐ of
    America, 14:9
Muse iv ⌐ . . . has long mim'ry
    but tis inaccrate, 107:13
[Nixon] deeper concern for his
    place in ⌐ than for people he
    governs, 193:19
no ⌐; only biography, 107:14
no inevitability in ⌐ except as
    men make it, 107:25
no man will read ⌐ aright, who
    thinks remote age has deeper
    sense than today, 107:17
no reason to repeat bad ⌐,
    107:56
only that survives of past ⌐
    which finds kindred in all
    hearts, 107:50
only thing new in world is ⌐
    you don't know, 107:69
page of ⌐ is worth volume of
    logic, 107:32
politics quarantines one from ⌐,
    187:95
public ⌐ is mask, richly colored,
    107:2
quarrel [conservatism and
    innovation] subject of civil ⌐,
    107:21
scenes shifted with swiftness on
    great stage of ⌐, 107:4
shallow village tale our so-called
    ⌐ is, 107:18
springs of American civilization
    lie revealed in clear light of ⌐,
    12:84
takes great deal of ⌐ to produce
    a little literature, 138:27
time is not come for impartial ⌐,
    107:45
ugly pages of American ⌐
    obscured and forgotten, 12:62
we cannot escape ⌐, 51:38

with unlocking of atom, mankind crossed watersheds of ~, 174:17

Hitch
  ~ your wagon to star, 11:5

Hoar, George Frisbie
  on American Revolution, 14:52

Hoboken
  Hell, Heaven or ~ by Christmas, 260:11

Hocking, William Ernest
  on punishment, 197:8

Hoe
  leans upon his ~ and on his back burden of world, 8:12

Hoffa, Jimmy
  on greatness, 102:29
  on labor, 131:28–30
  on penal system, 61:20

Hog
  Congressman is a ~, 54:3
  ~ Butcher for World, 46:15

Hogan, Frank J.
  on Constitution, 57:11

Hold
  can't ~ man down without staying down with him, 50:39

Holding company
  hand accomplice the goods while policeman searches you, 39:53

Holiday, Billie
  on her childhood, 264:21
  on recordings, 160:9
  on victory, 242:5

Holiness
  no other true excellence or beauty, 200:44

Holland, Josiah Gilbert
  on ambition, 11:7
  on art, 26:22
  on character, 43:47
  on home, 109:21, 109:22
  on law, 134:53
  on progress, 195:13
  on Walt Whitman, 262:36
  on women's drinking habits, 257:29

Hollander, John
  on Benjamin Harrison, 193:43

Hollings, Ernest
  on economics, 73:19

Hollywood, 108:1–20
  all ~ corrupts; and absolute ~ corrupts absolutely, 108:20
  anarchism of ~, 159:29
  as adjective, long been pejorative, 108:5
  "childish" is word which intelligentsia once branded ~, 108:9
  Communist plan for ~ was simple, 159:26

controlled by hoodlums of enormous wealth, 108:14

convictions of ~ made of boiled money, 159:14

going ~, 108:3

great place to live—if you're an orange, 108:1

~ always had streak of totalitarian, 108:10

~ is carnival where there are no concessions, 108:13

~'s kings and queens tossed money around, 108:11

~'s standard formula, 159:3

in ~, if didn't sing or dance, end up as after-dinner speaker, 108:15

know only one word of more than one syllable, 108:16

living in dream world, 108:18

mining town in lotus land, 108:6

place where inmates are in charge of asylum, 108:17

reduced to ~'s low, still rolling in luxury which destroyed Rome, 108:19

what I like about ~ is one can get along by knowing two words of English, 108:2

you can wake up and listen to birds coughing in trees, 108:7

Holmes, Fred L.
  on Wisconsin, 255:2

Holmes, John Haynes
  on evil, 80:5

Holmes, Oliver Wendell, Jr.
  on action, 1:7
  on age, 7:38, 7:39
  on belief, 32:9
  on business, 39:37
  on civil rights, 50:14, 50:15
  on duty, 72:14, 72:15
  on economics, 73:20
  on education, 74:50
  on free speech, 95:32, 95:33
  on free thought, 95:34
  on history, 107:32
  on individuality, 120:19
  on justice, 126:20
  on knowledge, 129:10
  on law, 134:55–63
  on life, 136:62–65
  on perception, 183:26
  on progress, 195:14
  on religious freedom, 201:8
  on science, 207:22
  on speech, 219:15
  on Supreme Court, 57:12, 57:13
  on taxation, 227:12, 227:13
  on Theodore Roosevelt, 193:44
  on time, 234:29
  on truth, 237:32

on war, 245:35
prediction, 191:2
you are in a war, Mr. President, 193:45

Holmes, Oliver Wendell, Sr.
  last words, 133:25
  on action, 1:6
  on affliction, 6:5
  on age, 7:32–37
  on America, 12:41–43
  on Americans, 15:16
  on ancestry, 17:11, 17:12
  on appetite, 20:8
  on architecture, 21:5
  on art, 26:23
  on beauty, 31:24, 31:25
  on books, 35:41, 35:42
  on Boston (Mass.), 36:18–22
  on character, 43:48, 43:49
  on Chicago (Ill.), 46:9
  on cities, 49:5
  on clergyman, 200:88
  on conversation, 59:20, 59:22
  on death, 63:32–34
  on dress, 70:12
  on drinking, 71:28–30
  on education, 74:48, 74:49
  on elections, 75:11
  on England, 77:19, 77:20
  on epitaphs, 78:15
  on experience, 82:10
  on fame, 84:13, 84:14
  on flag, 88:5
  on flowers, 90:6, 90:7
  on friends, 96:23
  on genius, 97:17
  on greatness, 102:30, 102:31
  on happiness, 103:18
  on heart, 106:7, 106:8
  on humor, 113:19
  on insanity, 121:5
  on kiss, 140:41
  on labor, 131:31
  on language, 132:22–26
  on lawyers, 134:54
  on life, 136:58–61
  on literary criticism, 262:38
  on love, 140:40, 140:42
  on majority rule, 143:3
  on marriage, 145:37–39
  on medicine, 148:10, 148:11
  on merriment, 149:6, 149:7
  on money, 157:39
  on music, 160:10, 160:11
  on nature, 161:41–43
  on New England, 165:6
  on oratory, 177:8
  on poet, 185:16, 185:17
  on professions, 259:33
  on puns, 113:20
  on religion, 200:89
  on reputation, 202:2

Hopkins, Harry L.
    on elections, 75:12
Hopkins, Johns
    on medical care, 148:12
Hopkinson, David
    on marriage, 145:40
Horack, H. Claude
    on Richard Nixon, 193:50
Horney, Karen
    on action, 1:8
Horrid
    when she was bad she was ~,
        264:29
Horse
    don't swap ~s, 41:9
    ~ does abominate camel, 19:13
    I'd ~whip you if had a horse,
        197:14
    never swap ~s crossing a stream,
        42:1
    not best to swap ~s while
        crossing river, 187:84
Horse race
    difference of opinion makes ~s,
        22:18
Horse Racing, 111:1–6
    gwine to run all night! gwine to
        run all day, 111:4
    ~ means loud clothes, 111:2
    losers walking around with money
        in pockets, 111:1
    lost few million here and there,
        111:3
    only man who makes money does
        so with broom and shovel,
        111:5
Hostility
    have no ~ towards men, 144:22
Hot
    highest civility never loved ~
        zones, 211:18
Hotel
    born in ~ room, died in ~
        room, 133:32
Hour
    fill my ~, ye gods, 136:41
    give me no changeless ~s, 234:8
    ~ to sing, to love and linger,
        136:87
    known as children's ~, 264:28
    this is ~ of lead, 63:16
    to fill the ~—that is happiness,
        103:9
House
    every ~ where love abides is
        surely home, 109:39
    every spirit makes its ~, 109:14
    happy is ~ that shelters friend,
        109:11
    honest ~ which has owner's
        honor built into its apartments,
        109:5

~ divided against itself cannot
    stand, 210:40
~, hollow edifice for man, rat,
    cockroach, 109:6
~ is castle which King cannot
    enter, 109:12
~ kept to display is impossible to
    all but few women, 109:15
~ of illusion, 233:26
~ should be *of* the hill, 21:13
swell ~ with all modern
    inconveniences, 195:33
wotta ~. Nothin' but rooms,
    33:6
Household
    ~ is school of power, 109:16
    many make ~, only one the
        home, 109:30
    O happy day, when new ~ finds
        place among homes of earth,
        109:27
House of Representatives
    duty of every member of ~ to
        act upon his conscience, 54:44
    gelatinous existence, 54:46
Housewives
    great vacationless class, 257:51
Housework
    ~ is inhumanly lonely, 109:29
Houston, Sam
    on Thomas Jefferson Green,
        122:4
Hovel
    ~, fruit of flower called Palace,
        109:7
Hovey, Richard
    on drinking, 71:32
    on failure, 83:3
    on love, 140:43
    on Spanish-American War, 218:8,
        218:9
    on spring, 221:5–8
    on travel, 235:17, 235:18
Howar, Barbara
    on Kissinger policies, 68:23
    on Washington (D.C.), 247:5
Howard, Anthony
    on journalism, 125:23
Howard, Joseph Kinsey
    on Butte (Mont.), 158:5
    on Montana, 158:4
Howe, Edgar Watson
    on advice, 4:36
    on age, 7:40, 7:41
    on ambition, 11:8
    on business, 39:38
    on common sense, 256:19
    on conduct, 53:12
    on duty, 72:16
    on enemies, 76:4
    on fear, 87:12
    on folly, 91:4

on freedom, 95:36
on free speech, 95:37, 95:38
on friends, 96:24
on government, 101:56
on health, 105:16
on hope, 110:4
on humankind, 112:22
on invention, 123:11
on law, 134:65
on love, 140:44–47
on majority rule, 143:4
on male-female relations, 257:36
on man, 144:12
on marriage, 145:41, 145:42
on money, 157:40
on music, 160:12
on parenthood, 85:11
on philosophy, 184:11
on poet, 185:18
on poetry, 186:12
on prejudice, 43:50
on punishment, 197:9
on raspberry pie, 92:10
on religion, 200:91
on reputation, 202:3
on revolution, 204:8
on success, 224:20
on wit, 113:21
on writers, 262:39
Howe, Julia Ward
    on Civil War, 51:25
    on freedom, 95:39
Howe, Louise Kapp
    on Americans, 15:17
Howe, Louis McHenry
    on politics, 187:61
Howells, William Dean
    on books, 35:43
    on Boston (Mass.), 36:23
    on humankind, 112:23
    on literary realism, 138:25
    on Mark Twain, 262:40
Hoyt, Charles H.
    on New York City, 171:49
Hub
    Boston called ~ of world, 36:36
    Boston State-house is ~ of solar
        system, 36:18
Hubbard, Elbert
    on action, 1:9
    on America, 12:44, 12:45
    on army, 25:11, 25:12
    on art, 26:24–26
    on baseball, 30:23
    on books, 35:44, 35:45
    on character, 43:51
    on culture, 62:5, 62:6
    on death, 63:35
    on divorce, 69:10, 69:11
    on drinking, 71:33
    on education, 74:51, 74:52
    on England, 77:21

Ideal *(cont'd)*

no force so democratic as force
of, 32:5

well if American people loved ⌢
somewhat more, 16:16

Identities

unique ⌢ of each of us, 120:24

Identity

television pollutes ⌢, 229:2

Idiot

in first place God made ⌢s; then
school boards, 74:98

Idleness

Adam cut us out of "blessing" of
⌢, 259:72

languid fingers of ⌢, 259:67

Idol

⌢ today pushes hero of yesterday
out of recollection, 84:16

Ignorance

admiration is daughter of ⌢, 2:4

fear always springs from ⌢, 87:6

⌢ is womb of monsters, 74:10

⌢ of law is no excuse, 134:74

⌢ once dispelled, impossible to
reestablish, 129:13

⌢ preferable to error, 237:42

learning, kind of ⌢ distinguishing
studious, 74:13

man's ⌢ is as much his private
property as family Bible, 74:49

man's ⌢ not only useful, but
beautiful, 129:16

negative knowledge, 129:15

preach crusade against ⌢, 74:58

science is topography of ⌢,
207:22

Ignorant

if nation expects to be ⌢ and
free, it expects what never was,
74:60

may be kept ⌢, cannot be made
⌢, 129:13

Reagan most ⌢ President since
Harding, 193:88

so ⌢ bought cow to ride on,
256:11

thankful that God created us all
⌢, 129:18

Ike

I like ⌢, 41:29

I still like ⌢, 41:31

Ill

blaming women for all ⌢s of
world, crowning blunder,
257:38

⌢-housed, ⌢-clad, ⌢-nourished,
189:41

Illegitimate

no ⌢ children—only ⌢ parents,
85:21

Illinois, 115:1–5

here my children have been born,
and one is buried, 115:5

⌢ is axis of nation, 115:2

⌢ U.S.A. in capsule, 115:3

state motto, 115:1

Illusion

house of ⌢, 233:26

⌢ that times that were are better,
183:25

life is loom, weaving ⌢, 136:76

Imagination

cowardice lack of ability to
suspend ⌢, 60:6

⌢ expands and exalts, 183:23

in ⌢, not perception, lies
substance of experience, 183:43

moment person forms theory, ⌢
sees only traits which favor
theory, 183:33

product of scientific ⌢ is new
vision of relations, 207:34

solitude is needful to ⌢, 58:7

Imitate

if you can't ⌢ him, don't copy
him, 33:3

Imitating

difference between ⌢ and
counterfeiting, 2:5

Imitator

man who succeeds in being
imitation, 120:21

Immigrant

an unenlightened person who
thinks one country better than
another, 116:6

every ⌢ should be required to
learn English, 132:47

he has embraced, the new
government he obeys, and the
new rank he holds, 116:9

Immigrants, 116:1–19 *(See also*
Ethnic; *specific groups)*

freedom of thought and private
judgment direct their course to
this happy country, 95:6

give us as many as come—we can
take it, 116:18

have become leaders of the
thought of the world, 116:15

I discovered that the ⌢ *were*
America, 116:14

room about her hearth for all
mankind, 12:74

they are ferried over the Atlantic
to ditch and to drudge and
then lie down prematurely to
make a spot of green grass on
the prairie, 116:13

we are a nation of ⌢, 116:17

we [Democratic Party] approve
all legitimate efforts to prevent

United States from being used
as dumping ground, 116:3

wide open and unguarded stand
our gates and through them
presses wild, motley throng,
116:5

Immigration

admitted right of a government to
prevent influx of elements
hostile to its internal peace may
not be questioned, 116:8

[European emigrants] will every
day become better acquainted
with the happiness we enjoy,
and seek means of transporting
themselves here, in spite of all
obstacles and laws, 116:10

every ship that comes to America
got its chart from Columbus,
116:12

foreign ⌢ should be fostered,
116:1

give me your tired, your poor,
your huddled masses, 116:16

no need of encouragment, while
taking place in a body, 116:19

we demand that ⌢ laws be
enforced and so extended to
exclude those who can neither
read nor write, 116:4

Immoral

things I really like either ⌢,
illegal, or fattening, 209:40

Immortal

beauty in flesh ⌢, 31:38

in wreck of noble lives something
⌢ still survives, 136:82

songs are ⌢, 212:13

soul of Man is ⌢, 117:12

universe leading nowhere unless
man is ⌢, 117:16

Immortality, 117:1–21 *(See also*
Heaven; Hell; Soul)

as soon hope to argue man into
good health as to argue him
into belief in ⌢, 117:4

better believers in ⌢ than we can
give grounds for, 117:11

blazing evidence of ⌢ is
dissatisfaction with other
solutions, 117:10

cannot conceive [God] could
make human merely to live and
die, 117:1

content with misery here in hope
of compensation hereafter,
200:85

departing leave behind us
Footprints on sands of time,
43:64

farther yet to Plato and preaching
⌢ of soul, 81:9

on time, 234:31
on travel, 235:21
on trouble, 236:14
on truth, 237:41–43
on tyranny, 238:11–16
on vice presidency, 241:6
on Virginia, 244:8, 244:9
on war, 245:43–47
on wine and whiskey, 253:10
on wisdom, 256:25, 256:26
on work, 259:41, 259:42
on writing, 138:30–32
own epitaph, 78:16
own philosophy, 184:17
whole world has become his
   pupil, 193:85
Woodrow Wilson on, 193:140
Jehovah
   has no superiority to Jupiter,
      200:160
Jesus
   as to ~, I have some doubts as to
      His divinity, 200:76
   ~ loves me, 200:167
   ~ overpowers sensual people,
      200:51
   nobody knows trouble I've seen
      but ~, 236:2
Jew
   ideals of America have been
      ideals of ~s for twenty
      centuries, 12:13
   ~ neither newcomer nor alien in
      this country, 15:48
   to be ~ is a destiny, 17:2
   Utah only place in world where
      ~s are Gentiles, 239:52
Jewett, Sarah Orne
   on conversation, 59:24
   on suffering, 213:10
Job
   any man who has ~ has chance,
      259:37
   no one hates ~ so heartily as
      farmer, 8:13
   recession when neighbor loses ~,
      73:32
Job (in Bible)
   ~ feels rod, yet blesses God,
      200:2
John Barleycorn
   ~ is everywhere, 71:40
John Brown
   ~'s body, 212:9
Johnson, Andrew
   epitaph, 78:2
   on Constitution, 57:22
   on democracy, 66:50
   on rebellion, 198:11
Johnson, Clifton
   on North Dakota, 173:6

Johnson, Gerald W.
   on freedom, 95:47
Johnson, James Weldon
   on being Black American, 34:11
   on blues, 160:15
   on death, 63:47
Johnson, John G.
   on business, 39:42
Johnson, Lady Bird
   on husband's presidency, 193:62
   on pain, 179:9
Johnson, Lyndon B.
   campaign slogan, 41:34
   Eric Goldman on, 193:38
   James Reston on, 193:110
   ~ told Nation Have no fear of
      escalation, 243:46
   Max Frankel on, 193:35
   mother on, 193:72
   on Abraham Lincoln, 137:20
   on America, 12:53, 12:55–57
   on Americans, 15:23
   on civil disorder, 50:22
   on education, 74:61
   on equality, 79:15
   on Gerald R. Ford, 193:63,
      193:64
   on Great Society, 12:54, 67:6
   on own intelligence, 193:70
   on own presidency, 193:65–69
   on peace, 181:21, 181:22
   on poverty, 189:28
   on slavery, 210:30
   regional qualities, 193:82
   Sam Rayburn on, 193:104
   Tom Wicker on, 193:136,
      193:137
   Vietnam War, 193:2, 193:71,
      243:11, 243:13, 243:15–18
   wife on, 193:62
Johnson, Philander
   on advice, 4:41, 4:42
   on weather, 250:7
Johnson, Rebekah Baines
   on son (Lyndon Johnson), 193:72
Johnson, Richard M.
   on religious freedom, 201:14
Johnson, Samuel
   on Americans, 16:20, 16:21
Johnson, "Tiny"
   on success, 224:28
Johnson, William
   on government, 101:80
Johnston, Alva
   on humor, 113:22
Johnston, Mary
   on contemplation, 58:4
Join
   if you can't lick 'em, ~ 'em, 22:2
Joke
   all ~s simply showcases of
      tellers' neuroses, 113:23

essence of all ~s seems to be
   honest halfness, 113:12
man takes whole universe for vast
   practical ~, 136:91
subtleties of American ~, 113:36
Jolson, Al
   ain't heard nothin' yet, 159:15
Jones, Frederick S.
   on New Haven (Conn.), 55:7
Jones, John Paul
   flag motto, 14:1
   on American Revolution, 14:54
Jones, Mary (Mother)
   on Senate, 54:30
Jones, Rufus Matthew
   on progress, 195:19
Jones, Tad
   on Yale football team, 93:5
Jones, Wesley Livsey
   on democracy, 66:51
Jong, Erica
   on solitude, 12:58
   on talent, 226:4
Jordan, Barbara
   on civil rights, 50:23
   on politics, 187:70
Joseph, Chief
   on American Indian, 13:8,
      13:9
   on war, 245:48
Journal
   editor of ~ does not possess same
      immunities he possesses as
      private citizen, 125:11
   not easy to write in ~ what
      interests us because to write it
      is not what interests us, 262:72
   so many public ~s, quality
      diminishes in inverse ratio to
      quantity, 125:12
Journalism, 125:1–79 (*See also*
   Free press; News; Newspaper;
   Press)
   assassins, 125:3
   discovered there was room at
      bottom, 125:64
   get facts first, and distort 'em as
      you please, 125:74
   highest ideals will save ~ from
      subservience, 125:55
   honest truth in my paper, and
      leave consequences to God,
      125:6
   information from which
      democracy drinks, 125:65
   institution that should fight for
      progress and reform, 125:54
   ~ consists in buying paper at two
      cents a pound and selling it at
      ten cents a pound, 125:13
   poor writers always with us—if
      we take daily paper, 262:41

Journalism *(cont'd)*

popular government, without popular information, but prologue to farce or tragedy, 125:42

president reigns for four years, and ⁓ governs for ever, 125:78

Tennesseean ⁓ too stirring for me, 230:7

to rule rightly [public] should be informed correctly, 125:22

typewriter is public trust, 125:66

world of daily—nay, almost hourly—⁓, 125:41

you furnish the pictures, and I'll furnish the war, 218:7

Journey

I ⁓ed fur, I ⁓ed fas', 235:16

Joy

have ⁓ or power, not both, 190:16

⁓ dwells beneath humble roof, 109:31

⁓, shipmate, ⁓, 63:91

no ⁓ in Mudville, 30:40

people need ⁓ as much as clothing, 103:15

religion without ⁓—is no religion, 200:146

to get full value of ⁓ you must have somebody to divide it with, 103:40

Judge

by being made ⁓s prejudices not diminished and intelligence not increased, 126:23

Constitution is what ⁓s say it is, 57:14

don't want to know what law is, want to know who ⁓ is, 134:25

I shall be subject to decision of no unwise ⁓ today, 126:51

⁓ a country by the minority, 66:26

⁓—a law student who marks his own examination-papers, 126:37

⁓ no representative of average man's common sense, 134:69

⁓ ourselves by what we feel capable while others ⁓ us by what we have done, 43:65

⁓s as honest as other men, and not more so, 57:20

⁓s training and aloofness prevent knowledge of needs of ordinary toiler, 126:41

Judgment

⁓ after lapse of time not equally true of decisions promptly taken, 66:6

lean award better than fat ⁓, 134:40

no nation fit to sit in ⁓ upon other, 68:69

one cool ⁓ worth thousand hasty counsels, 4:61

Judiciary

good ⁓ lends much to dignity of a state and happiness of the people, 101:59

Jug

little brown ⁓, 212:5

June

gives one leap from Aperl into ⁓, 221:14

⁓, month of leaves and roses, 90:13

knee-deep in ⁓, 225:5

skies put on old sophistries of ⁓, 28:11

what is so rare as day in ⁓?, 225:4

Jury

⁓ system puts ban upon intelligence and honesty, 126:47

⁓ too frequently has at least one member more ready to hang panel than to hang traitor, 126:31

mob law does not become due process by securing assent of terrorized ⁓, 126:20

lynch law little valid practiced by ⁓ as by mob, 134:62

Just

that which is ⁓ can harm no one, 126:12

true place for ⁓ man is prison, 126:46, 210:62

Justice, 126:1–55

all fair persons ought unite to effect change, 126:15

America owes debt of ⁓, 12:62

belief in ⁓ of cause, 14:79

blind she is, an' deef an' dumb an' has wooden leg, 126:6

can be no ⁓ without restraint, 107:43

communism is corruption of dream of ⁓, 126:43

community which establishes tolerable ⁓ is beneficiary, 126:39

due to accuser also, 126:2

exact ⁓ more merciful than pity, 126:34

firm basis of government is ⁓, not pity, 101:146

generosity is flower of ⁓, 126:18

God is just; and finally ⁓ triumphs, 126:33

hang him *anyhow*—try him afterwards, 126:48

hope of all who suffer, dread of all who wrong, 126:54

if in⁓ part of necessary friction of machine of government, let it go, 126:45

individual makes more noise than state, 126:25

in⁓ anywhere is threat to ⁓ everywhere, 126:29

in⁓ is relatively easy to bear; what stings is ⁓, 126:36

is instinct and innate, 126:28

judge weighs arguments, decides as he can, and hopes he has done ⁓, 126:8

⁓ application of [truth] to affairs, 238:18

⁓ at best is love correcting everything stands against love, 190:26

⁓ blind to racism, sexism, war, and poverty, 134:81

⁓ conquers everymore, 126:9

⁓ is always in jeopardy, 126:53

⁓ is always same, 126:24

⁓ is end of government, 126:35

⁓ is firmest pillar of government, 126:50

⁓ is instinct and innate, 126:28

⁓ is the great interest of man on earth, 126:52

⁓, system of revenge where State imitates criminal, 126:21

⁓ tolerable accommodation of conflicting interests of society, 126:17

love is more just than ⁓, 140:8

majority rule in all cases cannot be based on ⁓, 126:44

man endowed by nature with innate sense of ⁓, 43:58

man's capacity for ⁓ makes democracy possible, 126:38

man who murdered both parents, then pleaded for mercy, 126:32

moderation in pursuit of ⁓ is no virtue, 135:26

never could we hope to do such work for tolerance, for ⁓, 126:49

no such thing as ⁓—in or out of court, 126:5

one blasphemy, and that is in⁓, 126:22

one man's ⁓ is another's in⁓, 126:7, 183:18

patient confidence in ultimate ⁓ of the people, 126:30

peace based upon ⁓, 181:34

Kill *(cont'd)*
 to ~ in war not whit better than
  ordinary murder, 245:18
Kilmer, Joyce
 on tree, 161:48
 on World War I, 260:7
King
 all ~s of earth, before God, are
  as grasshoppers, 190:14
 home is kingdom and love is ~,
  109:9
 house is castle which ~ cannot
  enter, 109:12
 ~s and bears often worry their
  keepers, 19:9
 never strike ~ unless sure you
  shall kill him, 198:6
 no ~ not ready to make himself
  absolute, 238:12
King, Billie Jean
 on being top-ranked, 11:12
 on fame, 84:19
 on marriage, 257:49
 on sports, 220:23, 220:24
 on women's rights, 258:16
King, Clarence
 on California, 40:14
King, Martin Luther, Jr.
 last words, 133:28
 on advice, 4:44
 on America, 12:62
 on being Black American,
  34:12–14
 on civil rights, 43:59, 50:26–28
 on evil, 80:6
 on hate, 18:11
 on humankind, 112:35
 on justice, 126:29
 on man, 144:14
 on militarism, 152:9
 on nonviolence, 181:23
 on poverty, 189:29
 on power, 190:26
 on progress, 195:20
 on religious freedom, 201:17
 on riot, 198:12
 on Vietnam War, 243:25, 243:26
 on violence, 61:22
King, Martin Luther, Sr.
 on wealth, 249:39
King, Stoddard
 on World War I, 260:8
Kingdom
 she was child and I was child in
  ~ by sea, 140:78
Kinross, Lord
 on America, 16:23
Kipling, Rudyard
 on American army, 25:15
 on American eating habits, 92:12
 on Americans, 16:24
 on Black Americans, 34:15

 on Chicago (Ill.), 46:10
 on Denver (Colo.), 52:4
 on Mormons, 239:6
 on New England, 165:8
 on New York City, 171:59
 on Omaha (Neb.), 163:5
 on Portland (Ore.), 178:5, 178:6
 on San Francisco (Calif.), 206:5,
  206:6
 on Yellowstone National Park,
  263:6–8
Kirkpatrick, Jeane J.
 on culture, 62:7
 on freedom, 95:48
 on government, 101:81, 101:82
 on history, 107:40
 on power, 190:27
 on speech, 219:17
 on tyranny, 238:17
 on worldwide democracy,
  66:57–59
Kiss
 ~ has pleasant side, 140:15
 nobody wants to ~ when
  hungry, 140:20
 sound of ~ not loud, but echo
  lasts, 140:41
Kissinger, Henry
 Barbara Howar on, 68:23
 on admiration, 2:6
 on America, 12:63
 on civil rights, 50:29
 on diplomacy, 68:36–39
 on economics, 73:27
 on government, 101:83
 on history, 107:41–43
 on own character, 43:60
 on politics, 187:76, 187:77
 on power, 190:28, 190:29
 on revolution, 204:11, 204:12
 on Richard Nixon, 193:81
 on society, 211:30
 on statesman, 222:7, 222:8, 224:6
 on Vietnam War, 243:27
 on war, 245:52
Kitchen
 if can't stand heat, get out of ~,
  187:148
Kleptomaniac
 ~ is person who helps himself
  because he can't help himself,
  61:25
Knave
 ~ takes pleasure, and then suffers
  pains, 179:6
Knebel, Fletcher
 on New York City, 171:60,
  171:61
Knee
 ploughman on his legs is higher
  than gentleman on his ~s,
  43:43

Kneel
 where none ~, unless in their
  own way, 55:5
Knight, David
 on football, 93:6
Knight, Eric
 on Americans, 15:24
Knock
 not only do I ~ 'em out, I pick
  round, 220:4
Knott, James Proctor
 on Duluth (Minn.), 153:5, 153:6
Know
 all I ~ is what I see in the
  papers, 125:58
 better to ask questions than to ~
  all answers, 129:17
 better to ~ nothing than to ~
  what ain't so, 237:5
 don't ~ millionth of one percent
  about anything, 129:3
 first ~ where we are, better
  judge what to do, 129:12
 half world ~s how other half
  lives, 129:14
 hard enough to find way around
  Chinatown, 129:2
 how far un~n transcends what
  we ~, 63:58
 just ~ lines and don't bump into
  furniture, 233:27
 ~ing that we cannot ~, 129:77
 ~ enough who ~ how to learn,
  264:3
 ~ nothing but my Country, 41:8
 more you ~ more you think
  somebody owes you living,
  74:84
 only so much do I ~, as I have
  lived, 82:5
 to ~ is not less than to feel,
  129:10
 trouble with people is not that
  they don't ~ but ~ much that
  ain't so, 74:15
 who ~s most, ~s best how little
  he ~s, 256:25
 years teach much which days
  never ~, 82:6
 you shall not ~ too much, 129:6
Knowledge, 129:1–21
 amassed thought and experience,
  128:8
 great sun in firmament, 129:20
 ignorance is only absence of ~,
  129:13
 knowing that we cannot know,
  129:7
 ~ and timber shouldn't be much
  used till seasoned, 74:48
 ~ of God and ~ of ourselves
  most important, 129:4

leavened with magnanimity becomes wisdom, 256:31

obedience gateway through which ⏤ and love enter child, 74:92

positive ignorance, 129:15

proud of ⏤, blind with light, 129:9

to furnish means of acquiring ⏤ greatest benefit, 74:7

what it gains it never loses, 129:19

when man knows least and is most vain of his ⏤, 129:11

worse than useless, besides being ugly, 129:16

Knowles, John
on West Virginia, 252:6, 252:7

Know-Nothing Party
campaign slogans, 41:7, 41:8
Abraham Lincoln, on, 210:37, 210:37

Knox, Henry
on New York City, 171:62

Koch, Edward
on own writing, 262:44

Korea
attack upon ⏤ makes plain Communism passed beyond subversion, 130:11

I shall go to ⏤, 130:2

isn't just dust that is settling in ⏤, 130:6

issue in ⏤ is whether Communism or freedom shall prevail, 130:9

just left your fighting sons in ⏤, and they are splendid, 130:5

⏤ risked all against communism, 130:4

wasn't going to let attack on ⏤ go forward. Not while I was President, 130:12

Korean War, 130:1–15
authority of superiors not open to question, 25:22

[Chinese intervention] created new war, 130:3

fatal to enter any war without will to win, 130:8

fired him [MacArthur] because he wouldn't respect authority of President, 130:14

first line of defense for Western Europe, 130:7

gallant men will remain in my thoughts and prayers, 130:5

military goals, 25:23

moral courage in fighting army, 25:24

police action, a limited war, 130:13

settle for stalemate all that brought peace, 130:10

Western Europe would have gone into hands of Communists, 130:15

wrong war, wrong place, wrong time, wrong enemy, 130:1

Kossuth, Lajos
on freedom, 95:49

Krutch, Joseph Wood
on life, 136:73
on money, 157:46
on New England, 165:9

Kuhn, Maggie
on power, 190:30

Kuralt, Charles
on Americans, 15:25
on Arizona, 23:5, 23:6
on Great Salt Lake, 239:7
on Minnesota, 153:7, 153:8
on Nebraska, 163:6
on Tennessee, 230:5

Kush, Frank
on football, 93:7

Labor (*See also* Employment; Trade union; Wage; Work)
Adam won for us "curse" of ⏤, 259:72

aim of ⏤er should be to perform well, 259:69

all blessings fruits of ⏤, 131:55

American ⏤ capital of our workingmen, 259:8

American ⏤ force composed of rugged individualists, 131:28

at sixty, ⏤ ought to be over, 7:63

callous palms of ⏤er, 259:67

core of civil rights is equal opportunity for Negroes in ⏤ market, 50:41

denial of right to use of land denial of right of ⏤ to own produce, 131:16

direction of ⏤ toward production of greatest returns, 73:20

earth is given as common stock for man to ⏤ and live on, 8:10

few can be induced to ⏤ exclusively for posterity, 259:43

foundation of any right to property is man's ⏤, 131:24

fundamental principle that ⏤ entitled to all it creates, 131:46

if capital an' ⏤ ever git t'gether it's good night fer rest of us, 73:21

I like system which lets man quit when he wants, 131:36

in warm climate, no man will ⏤ for himself who can make another ⏤ for him, 210:28

⏤-baiting, poker-playing, whiskey-drinking, evil old man, 131:34

⏤ disgraces no man, 131:22

⏤ employer of capital, 131:14

⏤ foundation of all, 131:32

⏤ independent and proud, 131:58

⏤ing man be protected and cared for, 131:4

⏤in' man an' woman hev one glory an' one shame, 131:39

⏤ is curse of world, 259:31

⏤ means group selling its product, 131:31

⏤ of human not commodity of commerce, 131:21

⏤ of women in house enables men to produce more wealth, 131:19

⏤ prior to and independent of capital, 131:37

learn to ⏤ and to wait, 259:46

men who ⏤ cast the votes, 131:52

monopoly deprives ⏤ of its product, 73:40

no good thing without having first cost ⏤, 131:35

no goosestepping vigilantes will prevent onward march of ⏤, 131:33

no ⏤ leader can deliver vote, 131:49

poorly paid ⏤ inefficient ⏤, 131:17

process by which A acquires property for B, 259:4

property is fruit of ⏤, 73:28

prosecution of modern wars rests completely upon ⏤, 131:5

ruined by Chinese cheap ⏤, 131:25

should be organization of ⏤, 131:51

slave of the wheel of ⏤, 259:55

taste joy that springs from ⏤, 259:51

those who ⏤ in earth are chosen people of God, 8:9

to say picture shows great ⏤ is to say it is unfit for view, 26:58

unemployed ⏤ means human want, 131:57

whatever your ⏤ produces shall be yours, 73:16

when this dumb Terror shall rise to judge world, 131:41

while ⏤ builds sumptuous mansions . . . laborer lives in squalid lodging, 131:23

Labor Movement, 131:1–59

Laughter

always considered by theologians as crime, 149:8

comedy announces itself in pleasant spasms we call ⁓, 113:12

laffing is sensation ov pheeling good all over, 149:3

⁓ and tears are turn wheels of same sensibility, 149:7

⁓, best medicine, 149:2

⁓ is man's most distinctive emotional expression, 113:26

⁓ one of characteristics distinguishing man from animals, 113:5

Law, 134:1–114 (*See also* Legislation)

all citizens are equal before ⁓, 134:52

are ⁓s to be enforced simply because they are made?, 134:102

bad ⁓s should be repealed as soon as possible, in force religiously observed, 134:84

best measures seldom adopted from previous wisdom, 134:42

branch of science of transcendental nonsense, 134:24

break the ⁓, let your life be counter friction to stop the machine, 198:16

Connecticut in her blue-⁓s laying it down that ⁓s of God should be ⁓ of land, 55:6

contempt for ⁓ and consequences of ⁓breaking go from bottom to top of American society, 61:23

crystallization of habit and thought, 134:113

custom whereof memory runneth not back to contrary, 134:36

damn the ⁓!, 134:93

definition of liberty to be power of doing what ⁓ permits, 135:3

difficult to make material condition better by best ⁓s, 134:92

don't want to know what ⁓ is, want to know who judge is, 134:25

duty of citizen to observe ⁓ but let it known he is opposed to its violation, 134:27

each for all, all for each, 134:43

essential to ⁓ that it be attended with sanction, 134:47

every ⁓ and usage was man's expedient, 101:36

execution of ⁓s more important than making them, 134:75

general propositions do not decide cases, 134:58

good ⁓s teach men to trample bad ⁓s, 134:89

good men must not obey ⁓s too well, 101:37

government will cease if no remedy for violation of legal right, 134:87

great cases make bad ⁓, 134:56

higher ⁓ than Constitution, 57:33, 126:42

hundred years to make ⁓ and hundred years to get rid of it, 134:7

I am the ⁓, 134:45

if government becomes ⁓breaker it breeds contempt for ⁓, 61:8

if Indian breaks ⁓, punish him by ⁓, 13:9

if ⁓ upheld only by officials, all ⁓ is at end, 134:64

if man knows ⁓, people resort to him, 84:6

ignorance of ⁓ is no excuse, 134:74

inhabitants, during their generation, have right to declare the ⁓, 134:79

inherent right in the people to resist unconstitutional ⁓s without overturning government, 101:141

jokes those Birds [congressmen] make is ⁓, 54:50

just ⁓s make no distinction between rich and poor, 134:72

⁓ at end of nightstick, 134:111

⁓ cannot stand aside from social changes, 134:18

⁓ consists in forbidding men things they want to do, 134:63

⁓ expression and perfection of common sense, 134:22

⁓ favors those classes interested in evading it, 134:104

⁓ful, compatible with will of judge, 134:11

⁓ is deaf to clamors of populace, 134:4

⁓ is jealous mistress, 134:96

⁓ is only memorandum, 134:32

⁓ is what judge dispenses, 134:69

⁓ must be stable, but not stand still, 134:90

⁓ not end [but] means to serve what we think right, 134:17

⁓ not repealed continues in force, 134:88

⁓ retained on side of power, 134:28

⁓s are dead letter without true meaning, 134:48

⁓s are laughable, 134:35

⁓s are made for men of ordinary understanding, 134:80

⁓s are not masters but servants, 134:9

⁓, scheme for protecting parasite, 134:67

⁓s felt only when individual comes into conflict with them, 134:82

⁓s have no fixity, 134:3

⁓s instinct of self-preservation, 134:70

⁓s, like clocks, must be occasionally cleansed and set to right time, 134:8

⁓s like cobwebs catch small flies, 134:39

⁓s of self-preservation are of higher obligation, 134:78

⁓s that do not embody public opinion, 134:66

⁓s too gentle seldom obeyed, 134:41

⁓ whatever is boldly asserted and plausibly maintained, 134:20

⁓ will never make men free, 134:101

⁓ will preserve undeviating course, 134:4

lawyer only man in whom ignorance of ⁓ is not punished, 134:68

lean award better than fat judgment, 134:40

let man keep the ⁓, and his way will be strewn with satisfaction, 134:31

let the ⁓ take our course, 134:91

liberty achieved only by rule of ⁓, 135:38

liberty to do as he likes interfered with by ⁓s, 50:14

life of the ⁓ not logic, 134:55

little avail if ⁓s be so voluminous they cannot be read, 134:49

lovers of ⁓ and order observe the ⁓, 134:101

lynch ⁓ as little valid when practiced by jury as by mob, 134:62

may God twist my tripes if I string out obvious, 134:60

mob ⁓ does not become due process by securing assent of terrorized jury, 126:20

Law *(cont'd)*

more dangerous that guilty person be punished without forms of ~ than that he escape, 126:26

most certain stepping-stone in political line, 134:76

my agreement or disagreement has nothing to do with right of majority, 134:57

no bachelors of ~ should be allowed to come [to New World], 134:6

no grievance fit object of redress by mob, 134:85

no ~ so strong which little gladness may not transgress, 103:39

no man above the ~, 134:94

no man ever hanged for breaking spirit of ~, 134:23

no method to repeal bad ~s so effective as stringent execution, 134:44

no people shrewder than American in perceiving when ~ works ill, 134:19

not counsel any suit [unless] honestly debatable under ~ of land, 134:2

not desirable to cultivate respect for the ~, 134:99

no written ~ more binding than unwritten custom, 134:21

obedience to ~ not asked as favor, 134:94

one with ~ is majority, 134:26

only rogues feel restraint of ~, 134:53

opinion tends to become ~, 134:59

our defense is in ~ and order, 134:30

people lose respect for one bad ~, 134:105

people ruled by ~s in framing which they have no part, are slaves, 134:46

persecution feature of all religions established by ~, 200:136

prosecution conducted with little regard for English ~, 134:51

reign of ~ based upon consent, 134:114

rule of ~ is simple expression of sublime concept, 134:16

sheep are happier of themselves than under care of wolves, 134:73

sober second thought of the people shall be ~, 134:5

spirit of ~ keeps justice alive, 134:108

sword of ~ should never fall but on those whose guilt is apparent, 126:27

things have their ~s, as well as men, 134:33

unjust ~s exist: shall we be content to obey them?, 134:100

vice of democracies is to substitute public opinion for ~, 66:17

what do I care about the ~, 190:47

when President does it, means it is not illegal, 193:95

while there is doubt, time for ~ has not come, 134:61

white man does not abide by ~ in ghettos, 34:14

wholesale doctrine that there is common ~ in force in United States, 134:77

you of the ~ can talk till man in moon will allow it's cheese, 134:54

Lawrence, Amos
on Congress, 54:33

Lawrence, D.H.
on America, 16:25
on California, 40:15

Lawrence, Gertrude
on American men, 16:26

Lawrence, James
on naval duty, 162:10

Lawson, John
on North Carolina, 172:7

Lawsuit
nearly every ~ is insult to intelligence, 134:65

Lawyer
as peace-maker ~ has superior opportunity of being good, 134:86

Behold! a ~, an honest man, 134:38

good ~ throws himself on your part heartily, 134:37

government of United States is ~'s government, 134:29

if you would wax thin and savage, be ~, 259:33

[in colonial Pennsylvania] have no ~s, 182:3

In old days all you needed was handshake, 131:29

lawsuits settled between ~s, 134:107

~ only man in whom ignorance of law not punished, 134:68

~s do business together ought not to be expected, 54:28

~, skilled in circumvention of law, 134:12

~s live well, work hard, die poor, 134:110

never on cross-examination ask question you don't already know answer to, 134:83

next to confrontation between two ~s, jungle warfare is stately minuet, 134:106

prairie-~, master of us all, 137:33

tell me man is dishonest, I will answer he is no ~, 134:109

three Philadelphia ~s match for Devil, 134:1

unnecessary evil, 134:68

weary ~s with endless tongues, 134:112

why does hearse horse snicker hauling ~ away?, 134:95

young ~s attend courts because they have no business anywhere else, 134:71

Lay
~ him low, 25:7

Lazarus, Emma
on immigrants, 116:16
on Statue of Liberty, 171:64

Laziness
~ travels so slowly that poverty soon overtakes him, 189:17

life of leisure and life of ~, 136:49

Lazy
no ugly women, only ~ ones, 31:34

LBJ
all way with ~, 41:34

hey, hey ~, how many kids did you kill today?, 193:2

Leachman, Cloris
on age, 7:49

Leacock, Stephen
on Americans, 16:27

Lead
don't think you can ~ from position of vacillation, 193:90

hour of ~, 63:16

Leader *(See also* Statesman; Statesmanship)

being one with the people made possible for him to be ~ without being dictator, 193:101

has to lead or has no business in politics, 187:147

liberals! they're not ~s, 187:4

Leadership
get kind of ~ we demand and deserve, 66:56

man [who] enjoys power is essence of ~, 192:46

where no ~, society stands still, 107:68

expect to ~ to only a hundred, 7:17

great place to ~—if you're an orange, 108:1

half world knows how other half ~s, 129:14

how other half ~s, 189:39

how strange it seems to still ~ on, 7:82

I might have ~ out my life talking at street corners, 126:49

~ all you can; it's mistake not to, 136:71

~ enough befure thirty ye won't care to ~ afther fifty, 136:20

~ in people's hearts than only in their brains, 185:17

~ [so] that when die even undertaker will be sorry, 136:118

~ that you can look any man in eye and tell him to go to hell, 118:1

mass of men lead ~s of quiet desperation, 136:116

my god! what if you ~d here, 235:26

nothing meaner than anxiety to ~ on, 136:108

one ~d greatly whose record would bear full light of day, 136:4

so ~ that when thy summons comes to join caravan, 63:10

'tis fit man should ~ in pains, 136:90

to ~ in mankind is far more than to ~ in a name, 84:20

to ~ is to function, 136:65

want to love first, and ~ incidentally, 136:47

we ~ by desire to ~, 136:43

we ~ from one little space to another, 112:23

wish not so much to ~ long as to ~ well, 136:48

you might as well ~, 63:66

Living

cost of ~ going up, chance of ~ going down, 136:127

doubt if wisest man learned anything by ~, 82:15

fever called "~", 63:70, 179:11

getting ready to live but never ~ing, 136:26

know more about killing than ~, 112:5

~ and partly ~, 136:25

men who start with notion world owes them a ~, 259:62

next thing like ~ life over [is] putting it down in writing, 262:19

none but good man is ~ man, 136:89

one person's trash basket another's ~ space, 188:1

pity is for ~, envy for dead, 136:120

Livingston, Edward
John Randolph on, 122:8

Livingston, Robert
on Louisiana Purchase, 139:7

Lloyd, Henry Demarest
on corporations, 39:46
on language, 132:33

Loaf
I ~e and invite my soul, 58:12

Loans
inconsistent with neutrality, 260:1

Lockwood, Belva Ann
on militarism, 152:12

Locomotion
men who have reduced ~ to its simplest terms, 21:3

Locomotive
feel like ~ hitched to boy's express wagon, 193:23

Lodge, Henry Cabot
on Americans, 15:27
on George Washington/Abraham Lincoln, 246:14
on government, 101:92
on Walt Whitman, 262:47

Lodge, Henry Cabot, Jr.
on principle, 194:6

Lofland, John
on Delaware, 65:6

Log
~ cabin and hard cider, 41:2

Logan (Indian chief)
on charity, 44:10

Lombardi, Vince
on football, 93:8–11
on recovering from failure, 83:6
on sports, 220:25

London, Jack
on Alaska, 10:5, 10:6
on drinking, 71:39, 71:40
on fame, 84:21
on San Francisco (Calif.), 206:7

London, Meyer
on America, 12:72
on conscription, 152:13

Loneliness
surest sign of age is ~, 7:5

Lonely
housework is inhumanly ~, 109:29

Lonesome
be good and you will be ~, 53:23

leaves ~ place against sky, 137:38

Long
~ed for wayside well instead, 224:43
~est day must have its close, 67:9
~est wave quickly lost in the sea, 84:5

Long, Earl K.
campaign speech, 139:8

Long, Huey P.
on politics, 187:87–89
on success, 224:29
political statements, 139:8–10
Will Rogers on, 139:13

Long, Stephen H.
on Nebraska, 163:7

Longfellow, Henry Wadsworth
Charles Eliot Norton on, 138:45
on action, 1:12, 1:13
on adversity, 3:7–9
on affection, 5:5
on age, 7:50–55
on ambition, 11:14
on America, 12:73
on American Revolution, 14:58
on architecture, 21:6, 21:7
on art, 26:34–36
on autumn, 28:15
on beauty, 31:27
on books, 35:50, 35:51
on Boston (Mass.), 36:26
on change, 42:15
on character, 43:63–66
on Christmas, 48:6
on contemplation, 58:5
on conversation, 59:25
on death, 63:48–58
on dining, 20:9
on domesticity, 109:26–28
on evil, 80:7
on fame, 84:22
on fate, 86:8, 86:9
on friends, 96:31
on gifts, 44:11
on happiness, 103:25
on heart, 106:9–11
on history, 107:48, 107:49
on hope, 110:6–8
on humankind, 112:36
on immortality, 117:13
on justice, 126:33
on language, 132:34
on life, 136:78–84
on literary criticism, 138:37
on literature, 138:35, 138:36
on Louisiana (Evangeline), 139:11
on love, 140:57–61
on man, 144:16
on May, 212:12

in expressing ∼ we belong among underdeveloped countries, 140:9

in ∼ affair I wish to be hero, 140:45

irresistible desire to be irresistibly desired, 140:34

is there more than ∼ and Death?, 140:18

justice at best is ∼ correcting everything stands against ∼, 190:26

∼ alone can lend rapture in world, 140:14

∼ and grief and motherhood, 257:87

∼ and I had wit to win, 140:64

∼ conquers nothing, 140:63

∼d with ∼ that was more than ∼, 140:78

∼ 'em and leave 'em, 140:1

∼ endures when lovers ∼ many things together, 140:56

∼ goes to deserving, 140:50

∼ has never known law, 140:96

∼ him most for enemies he has made, 5:1

∼ is anterior to life, 140:19

∼ is more just than justice, 140:8

∼ keeps cold out, 140:58

∼ life as mixed up as dog's breakfast, 140:100

∼ means giving one's self to another fully, 140:80

∼ not for levity, 140:26

∼ scarce is ∼ that never knows forgiving, 140:97

∼s not wisely but two hundred well, 145:75

∼ that's wise will not say all, 140:81

∼ wakes anew this throbbing heart, 7:23

∼ will pay ten per cent to borrower and lender, 140:53

∼ without hope is agonizing death, 140:51

man remembers first ∼ with special tenderness, 140:66

man's natural endowment, 140:37

marriage without ∼, there will be ∼ without marriage, 145:24

moment ∼ becomes casual, it becomes commonplace, 140:4

more [to woman] than ambition is to man, 140:60

music is ∼ in search of word, 160:17

must have something I can put my arms around, 140:7

nicer to be in than automobile accident, 140:93

no joy like ∼ that has its will, 140:43

no more than wide blossom which wind assails, 140:69

none but ∼ to bid us laugh or weep, 140:17

no other thought than to ∼ and be ∼d by me, 140:78

nor any art we know of can conceal, 140:73

not ever having to say you're sorry, 140:88

nothing holier than first consciousness of ∼, 140:57

no true ∼ in world, 140:21

old story matrons tell with sharpened tongue, 140:40

only half illusion, 140:87

perceptual anesthesia, 140:65

power of ∼ never been tried, 140:30

pure ∼ without power, destroyed, 190:34

rather live with woman I ∼ in world full of trouble, 257:45

right place for ∼, 140:35

sometimes stronger than man's convictions, 140:89

sweet reverence, 140:38

talisman of human weal and woe, 140:90

Tarzan of Apes ∼s you, 140:13

third rail for Life's Empire State Express, 140:48

thou wast all that to me, ∼, 140:77

to be ∼d is demoralizing, 140:39

to be ∼d is fortunate, 140:5

to ∼ and be beloved; 'tis not to be improved, 140:31

true ∼ is humble, 140:62

unhappy in ∼, heart like fortress captured, sacked and abandoned, 140:54

want to ∼ first, and live incidentally, 136:47

were it not for ∼, 140:82

what I cannot ∼, I overlook, 140:72

when one voice could make heart bound, 140:25

where ∼ abides is surely home, 109:39

why am I crying after ∼?, 31:40

will you ∼ me in December as you do in May?, 140:94

women in ∼ less ashamed than men, 140:10

worms inclined to be in ∼, 140:2

Love, Edmund
on New York City, 171:69

no joy like

Lovecraft, H.P.
on Providence (R.I.), 205:6, 205:7

Lovely
loveliest of ∼ things, 161:11
what is ∼ never dies, 31:3

Lover
betrothed ∼ lost charm of his maiden in her acceptance of him, 140:28
Hell's afloat in ∼s' tears, 140:74
husband is what is left of ∼ after nerve extracted, 140:84
I am Last ∼, 63:94
I had ∼'s quarrel with world, 78:13
I'm good hater, but bad ∼, 140:99
in ∼'s eyes, 140:16
∼s are fools, 140:49
∼s should guard their strangeness, 140:29
scratch ∼, find foe, 140:75
tell me if ∼s are losers, 140:85
what ∼ has he not outloved?, 262:9

Loving
all things true and fair lay closely to my ∼ eye, 140:98
one thing man should do in private is his ∼, 140:44

Lowell, Amy
on art, 26:38
on books, 35:52, 35:53
on happiness, 103:27
on patterns, 90:8
on youth, 264:31

Lowell, James Russell
John Greenleaf Whittier on, 132:64
on action, 1:14
on adversity, 3:10, 43:70
on age, 7:56
on ambition, 11:16, 11:17
on America, 12:74, 12:75
on Americans, 15:28–30
on ancestry, 17:14
on army, 25:18
on authority, 27:8
on books, 35:54, 35:55
on bravery, 38:17
on business, 39:47
on character, 43:67–69, 43:71–73
on charity, 44:12–14
on compromise, 22:10
on contemplation, 58:6, 58:7
on death, 63:59
on democracy, 66:69, 66:70
on domesticity, 109:30
on Edgar Allan Poe, 262:55
on education, 74:68, 74:69

Man *(cont'd)*

chief occupation, extermination, 112:3

civilized ~ more experienced savage, 112:54

curious creature who possesses rational freedom, 112:44

difficult to make ~ miserable while he feels worthy, 144:15

every true ~ is cause, country, and age, 144:5

first farmer was first ~, 8:4

first-rate second-rate ~, 137:41

Heavenly Father invented ~ because disappointed in monkey, 81:17

honest God noblest work of ~, 200:107

I believe in patriotism and energy and initiative of average ~, 66:109

if ~ hasn't discovered something he will die for, he isn't fit to live, 144:14

I like ~, but not men, 112:13

in ~ is all beauty and worth he sees, 112:11

institution is lengthened shadow of one ~, 112:10

intellectual superiority, *moral* inferiority, 112:60

laughter is ~'s most distinctive emotional expression, 113:26

laughter one of characteristics distinguishing ~ from animals, 113:5

let no more be heard of confidence in ~, 57:17

lively faith in perfectibility of ~, 12:99

~ alone, a wonder; mankind, mob of unnecessary duplicates, 112:40

~ and his affairs—how little space they occupy, 112:56

~ as good as has to be, 144:13

~ both steel and velvet, 137:45

~ can marry and not change his life one iota, 145:71

~ cannot make principles; he can only discover them, 207:29

~ can paint, or make, or think nothing but ~, 144:8

~ drags ~ down, or ~ lifts ~ up, 112:61

~ has one interest—to be right, 112:27

~ is arch machine, 123:5

~ is daughter of horse leech, who constantly asks for more, 112:17

~ is golden impossibility, 144:6

~ is known by books he reads, 35:19

~ is ~ because free to operate within his destiny, 112:35

~ is not matter, 112:7

~ is soul informed by divine ideas, 112:2

~ is stumbling blindly through spiritual darkness, 112:5

~ is the great poet, language itself his work, 112:53

~ is timid and apologetic, 60:5

~ is unjust, but God is just, 126:33

~ never intended to become oyster, 1:21

~ ought to compare advantageously with river, oak, mountain, 144:9

~ passes away, name perishes, 112:26

~ rational animal, endowed by nature with rights, 43:58

~ sanctifies place, 112:24

~'s capacities never been measured, 82:16, 112:55

~'s conclusions reached by toil, 144:11

~ shaped in woman, 257:83

~'s role uncertain, undefined, perhaps unnecessary, 144:18

~ to hold against the world, 137:35

~ will prevail, because he has a soul, 112:14

meaning of ~'s life matches marvels of ~'s labor, 67:6

metal of ~ tested by presence of mind in untried emergencies, 43:69

modern ~ I sing, 112:64

more aggressive than other apes, 112:48

most ruthlessly ferocious of beasts, 112:28

must have bread and butter, also something to lift his heart, 217:4

natural ~ has difficult time getting along in world, 144:12

Nature cannot make ~ save on worn-out plan, 144:17

never lived ~ who wished he were woman, 257:36

no ~ above the law, 134:94

none but good ~ is living ~, 136:89

no one feels himself called to act for ~, 112:9

not made for defeat, 112:21

not most perfect being, 200:71

of all animals, ~ most brutal, 112:1

only animal that blushes, 112:58

only animal which devours own kind, 112:31

ordinary ~ is an anarchist, 57:35

pessimistic about ~'s future, 188:14

principal difference between ~ and dog, 19:20

reason is expression of ~ alone, 112:46

Republicans for ~ before dollar, 187:82

so frail a thing is ~, 136:1

sole sacred thing beneath heaven is ~, 112:65

spiritual being, 112:50

sum of his ancestors, 112:4

survives by adjusting his background to himself, 112:45

there is no indispensable ~, 101:145

vaster is ~ than his works, 112:34

very normal ~ but upon great scale, 137:59

what Bedlamite is ~, 112:32

when mean thing done, ~ did it, 112:25

who is Forgotten ~?, 196:28

whoso would be ~, must be nonconformist, 118:4

Manhattan

~ gentleman so delightfully small in his greatness, 171:42

my city, 171:106

My own ~, with spires, 171:106

O ~, offering me love, 171:105

served full term in hell right on ~ Island, 171:3

singing my own "~ Magnificat", 171:76

upper East Side of ~ is province of Let's Pretend, 171:91

wave of popular passion dashed to spray when hits hard rocks of ~, 171:77

we'll turn ~ into isle of joy, 171:37

Manhood

duty is essence of ~, 245:70

himself he bare at ~'s simple level, 43:71

Manifest

~ destiny, 251:12

Mankind

affections first for own country, then for all ~, 180:26

America proved it practicable to elevate mass of ~, 12:108

bulk of ~ schoolboys through life, 112:30

Marriage *(cont'd)*
    such as are in wish to get out, 145:23
    take hint when hint intended, 145:32
    their warfare is accomplished [epitaph], 78:3
    War between Men and Women, 145:72
    when man makes mistake in first ⁓, victim is second wife, 145:2
    who are happy in ⁓?, 145:59
Married
    alas, she ⁓ another, 145:74
    best part of ⁓ life is fights, 145:78
    I ⁓ beneath me, 145:7
    man incomplete until ⁓, 145:34
    most ⁓ man ever saw in my life, 145:75
    [Niagara Falls] one of earliest disappointments in American ⁓ life, 170:9
    well-⁓, man winged, 145:9
Marries
    widow who ⁓ second time doesn't deserve to be one, 145:50
Marry
    alas, that such Peach should ⁓ such Prune, 145:56
    ⁓'d at leisure, repent in haste, 145:25
    ⁓'d in haste repent at leisure, 145:25
    ⁓ing like buying something you've been admiring, 145:53
    more girl finds to regret she did not ⁓ you, more comfortable you will feel, 145:73
    some of us becoming men we wanted to ⁓, 257:69
    to ⁓ for love to invite tragedy, 145:18
    when girls of twenty with money ⁓ paupers, turned sixty, 140:52
    when two people ⁓ they become one person, the husband, 145:6
    women who ⁓ to get out of tiresome job are whores, 145:5
Marryat, Frederick
    on Americans, 16:29
    on language, 132:35
    on Philadelphia (Pa.), 182:12
Marsh, George Perkins
    on language, 132:36
Marshall, Catherine
    on religion, 200:130
Marshall, George C.
    on democracy, 66:72
    on Marshall Plan, 68:45

on peace, 181:27
on World War II, 261:20
Marshall, John
    Andrew Jackson on, 193:54
    on Constitution, 57:24–26
    on democracy, 66:73
    on government, 101:96
    on law, 134:96
    on states' rights, 223:19
    on taxation, 227:18
Marshall, Peter
    Senate prayer, 54:38
Marshall, Thomas Riley
    on Indiana, 119:5
    on vice presidency, 241:8, 241:9
Marshall Plan
    ⁓ one of America's greatest contributions to peace, 181:40
Marshalov, Boris
    on Congress, 54:39
Marshes
    publish yourselves to sky and offer to sea, 161:49
Martian
    that was no ⁓, it's Halloween, 229:8
Martin, Pepper
    on horse racing, 111:6
Martineau, Harriet
    on New England, 165:10
Martini
    let's get out of wet clothes into dry ⁓, 71:9
Martyr
    flame in which ⁓ passes more magnificent than royal apartment, 6:3
    many a ⁓ burned at stake while votes counted, 194:8
    no happiness so perfect as ⁓'s, 103:17
Marx, Groucho
    Irving Berlin on, 113:3
    on alimony, 69:13
    on conversation, 59:28
    on Hollywood, 108:11
    on humor examples, 113:24, 113:25
    on Maine, 142:5
    on marriage, 145:57
    on Midwest, 151:4
    on punishment, 197:14
    on society, 211:34
    on taxation, 227:19
    on women, 257:57
Marx, Karl
    Irving Berlin on, 113:3
Marxism
    opium of intellectuals, 187:159
Maryanna, Sister
    on New York City, 171:76

Maryland, 146:1–10
    Civil War neutrality, 51:2
    landscape raggedness of new kind, 146:2
    ⁓! My ⁓, 146:9
    religious freedom in, 201:1, 201:16
    state motto, 146:1
    summer in ⁓ delightful, 146:10
Mask
    man of many ⁓s, 193:118
Mason, Donald F.
    on submarine sinking, 162:8
Mason, George
    on free press, 125:43
Massachusetts, 147:1–12
    bards of ⁓ want to make New Hampshire people over, 166:7
    behold her, and judge for yourselves, 147:11
    constitution, 147:2
    first public love of my heart is Commonwealth of ⁓, 147:10
    have faith in ⁓, 147:3
    ⁓ is Italy upside down, 147:6
    no slave upon our land, 147:12
    religious freedom in, 201:2
    state motto, 147:1
Massa's
    ⁓ in de cold, cold ground, 63:22
Masses
    if make ⁓ prosperous, prosperity will find way up, 73:2
    leave this hypocritical prating about the ⁓, 196:10
    ⁓ of men exhibit their tyranny, 66:17
    religion which preach[es] down natural aspirations of the ⁓, 200:77
Master
    as I would not be slave, so I would not be ⁓, 66:64
    eye of ⁓ do more work than both his hands, 259:25
    measure of ⁓ is success in bringing all men round to his opinion years later, 102:19
    whoever employs is ⁓, 131:10
Masters, Edgar Lee
    on immortality, 117:15
    on life, 136:88
Mate
    for youth cannot ⁓ with age, 145:54
Mather, Cotton
    last words, 133:30
    on affliction, 6:7
    on argument, 22:12
    on charity, 44:15
    on Devil, 209:28
    on education, 74:73

on life, 136:89
on New England, 165:11
on thunder, 250:11
Mather, Increase
on animals, 19:13
on fear, 87:15
on religion, 200:131
on thunder, 250:12
Matthews, Brander
on education, 74:74
Maugham, W. Somerset
on Americans, 16:30
on Americans' conversation, 59:29
Mauldin, Bill
on World War II, 261:21,
261:22
May
word ⁓ is perfumed word,
212:12
Mayflower
Compact, 12:1
forefathers didn't come over on
⁓, but met boat, 17:20
Mayhew, Jonathan
on tyranny, 238:24
Mazo, Earl
on Richard Nixon, 193:87
Me
this is on ⁓, 78:19
Mead, Margaret
on choice, 47:12, 47:13
on cities, 49:7
on conduct, 53:18
on crime, 61:23
on education, 74:75, 74:76
on evil, 80:9
on families, 85:13
on gender differences, 112:39,
144:18
on humor, 113:26
on leisure, 58:8
on religious freedom, 201:20
on success, 224:31
on women's rights, 258:20,
258:21
Meaning
no poet, no artist has complete ⁓
alone, 26:9
Meaningless
man who regards life as ⁓,
136:23
Media
⁓ always have last word, 125:46
Medical
presumptuous band of ⁓ tyros
destroys more human life,
148:14
valuable therapy ⁓ profession has
cast out, 148:7
Medicine, 148:1–19
anatomists see no beautiful
woman, 31:41

if whole *materia medica* sunk to
bottom of sea, 148:10
laughter, best ⁓, 149:2
⁓, stone flung down Bowery,
148:1
nothing more strikingly betrays
credulity of mankind than ⁓,
148:18
one kind makes another necessary,
148:13
their ⁓ often worse than disease,
148:17
Mediocre
Nixon discovered laws of
vibration in all frozen
congelations of the ⁓, 193:86
Meditation
few men's courage proof against
protracted ⁓, 38:19
Meekness
turning other cheek is moral
jiu-jitsu, 43:61
Meet
⁓ me in St. Louis, Louis, 212:27
Melancholy
⁓ days of wailing winds and
naked woods, 28:4
Mellen, Grenville
on war, 245:63
Melody
crack voice of ⁓, 160:10
Melting pot
America is God's great ⁓, 16:60
Florida is ⁓, 89:6
individuals of all nations melted
into new race, 12:21
⁓ Harlem of honey and
chocolate, 171:51
not ⁓ but beautiful mosaic,
12:15
Melville, Herman
on Americans, 15:31, 15:32
on books, 35:56, 35:57
on bravery, 38:18, 38:19
on cowardice, 60:7
on death, 63:60
on drinking, 71:41
on evil, 80:10
on folly, 91:6
on genius, 97:23
on health, 105:20, 105:21
on humankind, 112:40
on insanity, 121:8, 121:9
on John Brown, 51:46
on life, 136:90–93
on marriage, 145:58
on merriment, 149:9
on money, 157:48
on Nantucket (Mass.), 147:8
on nature, 161:59
on own education, 74:77
on perception, 183:35

on religion, 200:132, 200:133
on spring, 221:15
on truth, 237:59
on youth, 264:33
Memorial
⁓s be in buildings for poor,
44:17
Memory
earth and water of existence,
140:16
gentlest ⁓ of world [Lincoln],
137:18
heart hath its own ⁓, 106:11
⁓ first [faculty] which suffers
decay from age, 7:46
⁓, tradition and myth frame our
response, 42:18
mixing ⁓ and desire, stirring dull
roots, 221:2
mystic chords of ⁓, 180:28
no man and no force can abolish
⁓, 35:64
no room in heart to hold ⁓ of
wrong, 137:11
two generations to kill off man
. . . first him, then his ⁓,
63:27
Men
all assemblages of ⁓ different
from ⁓ themselves, 144:21
all ⁓ would be tyrants if could,
258:2
attention American ⁓ shower on
women, 16:26
deal with ⁓ as equals and like
them for first time, 258:32
families mean support and
audience to ⁓, 85:1
few of our race can be said to be
finished ⁓, 144:10
God give us ⁓, 43:47
I have no hostility towards ⁓,
144:22
I like man, but not ⁓, 112:13
I'm no better than best of
fellow-⁓, 144:16
in America, geography sublime,
but ⁓ are not, 12:29
I only like two kinds of ⁓:
domestic and foreign, 144:24
let us treat ⁓ and women well,
112:12
mass of ⁓ neither wise nor good,
112:29
⁓ are like plants, 112:6
⁓ are not made like boxes, 144:4
⁓ are not philosophers, but
foolish children, 144:7
⁓ first, and subjects afterward,
120:25
⁓ in Congress represent *own*
point of view, 54:5

Men *(cont'd)*
  〜 judge by appearances, 70:10
  〜 seldom make passes at girls who wear glasses, 140:76
  〜 will become worms, 112:41
  〜 will not adopt measures for own good without coercive power, 101:136
  more I see of 〜, more I like dogs, 19:2
  multitudes of 〜 never false to their passions, 144:1
  nine hundred and ninety-nine 〜 of thousand are bastards, 136:19
  not 〜 in my life—it's life in my 〜, 144:23
  [of California] thriftless, proud, extravagant, and much given to gaming, 40:7
  only 〜 can make 〜, 112:39
  perfect friendship of two 〜 is deepest sentiment, 96:6
  seek to gratify desires with least exertion, 73:13
  single standard for 〜 and women, 45:2
  study 〜, not historians, 4:54
  ten 〜 who care worth hundred who do not, 196:4
  to poet all 〜 divine, 185:4
  when 〜 and women agree, it is only in their conclusions, 96:35
  will learn to speak better from women and children, 132:30
Mencken, H.L.
  on actors, 233:22
  on adultery, 145:61
  on advice, 4:47
  on age, 7:59
  on agriculture, 8:13
  on alimony, 69:14
  on America, 12:79
  on Americans, 15:33
  on artists' virtue, 26:39
  on Baltimore (Md.), 146:7, 146:8
  on beauty, 31:28
  on Black Americans, 34:24
  on business, 39:48
  on character, 43:76
  on democracy, 66:74–76
  on drinking, 71:42
  on duty, 72:25
  on fear, 87:16
  on happiness, 103:29
  on journalism, 125:44
  on justice, 126:36, 126:37
  on liberty, 135:55
  on life, 136:94
  on Los Angeles (Calif.), 40:18
  on love, 140:65, 140:66
  on marriage, 145:59, 145:60

  on New York City, 171:77, 171:78
  on Oregon, 178:7
  on patriotism, 180:31
  on poet, 185:27
  on poetry, 186:18, 186:19
  on politics, 187:97–99
  on poverty, 189:35
  on reading, 35:58
  on rebellion, 198:14
  on sense of humor, 113:27
  on teaching, 74:78
  on theater, 233:23
  on the public, 196:17, 196:18
  on time, 234:40
  on truth, 237:60, 237:61
  on war, 245:64, 245:65
  on wealth, 249:42
  on women, 257:58, 257:59
  on work, 259:56, 259:57
  own proposed epitaph, 78:18
Mend
  things have been 〜ed that were worse, 110:8
Menninger, Karl
  on life, 136:95
Menotti, Gian Carlo
  on love, 140:67
Mental
  need attack of 〜 disease to teach meaning of [fear], 121:6
Merchandise
  do not propose to make 〜 of American principles, 39:19
Merchant
  craft of 〜 is bringing thing from where it abounds to where it is costly, 39:27
  〜, one engaged in commercial pursuit, 39:7
  〜s love nobody, 39:40
  〜s manage better more they are left free, 73:25
  posthumous revenge of 〜 of Venice, 171:50
Mercy
  man who murdered both parents, and pleaded for 〜, 126:32
Merriment, 149:1–12
Merryman, Mildred Plew
  on Chicago (Ill.), 46:12
Message
  carry 〜 to Garcia, 1:9
Metaphysics
  explanation of thing by person who does not understand it, 184:12
Metropolitan Opera
  may still see Grandes Dames at 〜, 171:33
Mexican War
  true motive not distinctly avowed, 245:99

Mexico
  U.S. intervention in, 68:58
Meyer, Agnes
  on social change, 264:34
Miami (Fla.)
  〜 of unimaginable awfulness, 89:8
Michener, James A.
  on cities, 49:8
Michigan, 150:1–6
  bleak spine of upper peninsula of 〜, 150:3
  lake country of 〜, 150:6
  past, present and future tied up together, 150:2
  state motto, 150:1
Middle
  〜 of Nowhere, 235:26
  walks in 〜 of road gets hit from both sides, 68:57
Middle age
  〜d learned to have fun, 7:58
  〜d man concludes to build woodshed, 7:72
  〜 when every new person you meet reminds you of someone else, 7:60
Middle class
  〜es in America virtually the nation, 16:1
  tendency to crush out 〜, 211:39
Midnight
  came upon 〜 clear, 48:8
  〜 ride of Paul Revere, 14:58
  once upon a 〜 dreary, 58:9
Midwest, The, 151:1–6
  although many Peculiarities in their manners they appear friendly to Strangers, 151:5
  damn few good guys in 〜, 151:3
  〜 is marriage between New England puritanism and *rich* soil, 151:2
  strangers talked freely to one another, 151:6
Might
  〜 have been, 213:20
Milburn, John G.
  on business, 39:42
Militarism, 152:1–21
  great preserver of our ideals of hardihood, 152:3
  means conquest abroad and intimidation at home, 152:1
Military
  civilian control of 〜, 152:17
  I ask 〜 success, and I will risk dictatorship, 51:39
  looked [on] with suspicious eye, 196:32
  〜 force not so potent, 242:2
  〜 policy dependent on public opinion, 66:72

~ power will never awe
American to surrender his
liberty, 14:12

~ victory not what had been in
past, 130:10

must make ~ instruction part of
collegiate education, 152:7

nation that spends more on ~
than on social uplift
approaching spiritual death,
152:9

overgrown ~ establishments
hostile to republican liberty,
152:20

pride, arrogance, and lust of
conquest natural fruits of ~
preparation, 152:4

spirit of country adverse to large
~ force, 152:5

world's basic woes do not lend to
purely ~ solutions, 25:23

Military-industrial complex
guard against influence by ~,
152:2

Militia
dependence on ~ is resting upon
broken staff, 14:83

for people who are free,
well-organized, armed ~ best
security, 152:6

Mill
~s of God grind slowly, 86:8

Millay, Edna St. Vincent
on ancestry, 17:18
on beauty, 31:29
on death, 63:61, 63:62
on life, 136:96
on love, 140:68–70
on spring, 221:16
on travel, 235:25
on youth, 264:35

Miller, Alice Duer
on art, 26:40

Miller, Henry
on Alabama, 9:9
on America, 12:80
on artistic endeavor, 262:57
on classics, 138:41
on humankind, 112:41

Miller, Joaquin
on California, 40:19
on history, 107:53

Miller, Merle
on Vietnam War, 243:37

Miller, Vaughn
on prohibition, 71:43

Million
how many men fairly earn ~
dollars, 157:35

Millionaire
defend ~ [because] get defense
of society for hundreds to
protect his millions, 249:52

Mills, Ogden
on poverty, 189:36

Millstein, Gilbert
on New York City, 171:79

Milton, John
Augustine Birrell on, 138:5

Mind
Cambridge ladies have
comfortable ~s, 147:5

could never prove to ~ of most
ingenious mollusk that whale
possible, 183:22

dull saw that is routine ~, 80:1

health is condition of ~, 105:4

his ~ kept open house, 32:1

knowledge is amassed thought of
innumerable ~s, 128:8

man's foremost object to secure
peace of ~, 58:11

military victories are rarely victories
over ~s of men, 242:6

~ can never conceive state of
nothing, 183:13

~ can weave itself warmly in
cocoon of own thoughts, 58:6

~ is All-in-all, 200:36

~ maturing late, or rotted early?,
7:61

~ profits little by heavy reading,
35:39

~s so earnest and helpless, 170:7

~ which does work of world,
259:6

~ whose aspirations rise no
higher than roof is dwarfed,
257:68

most baseball players afflicted
with tobacco-chewing ~s, 30:9

music principal language of ~,
160:25

my ~ is as open as forty-acre
field, 43:17

mysterious form of matter, 183:5

nothing is sacred but integrity of
your ~, 43:21

only people who do not change
their ~s are in asylums and
cemeteries, 43:18

own ~ is own church, 200:141

presence of ~ in untried
emergencies that metal of man
is tested, 43:69

put in act invisible thought of his
~, 38:9

real problem in hearts and ~s,
174:6

sickness belief which must be
annihilated by divine ~, 105:6

tough ~ and tender heart, 4:44

traveled ~ is catholic ~, 235:3

uninformed ~ with healthy body
happier than wisest
valetudinarian, 105:19

unit and measure of things visible
and invisible, 112:2

what other liberty worth having,
if have not freedom and peace
in our ~s, 95:78

Mine
~ eyes have seen glory, 51:25

Minimum wage
~ dictated by law of nature,
131:43

Minneapolis (Minn.)
bones dug up and dragged
through streets of ~, 153:4

Minnesota, 153:1–8
glorious new Scandinavia, 153:3
state motto, 153:1
state seal should be ice cubes on
field of white, 153:8
to understand ~, respond to
youth, 153:2

Minnesotans
~ are just different, 153:7

Minorities
governments exist to protect
rights of ~, 101:109

Minority (See also Equality;
Majority; Rights)
debar [~] from equal
rights—mark failure of
constitutional system, 50:36

if man is ~ of one, we lock him
up, 120:19

judge country by the ~, 66:26

~ possess equal rights, 50:20

nation, in which ~ has no hope
of becoming majority, will
seem oppressive, 50:29

to preserve freedom for ~,
necessary to face majority
down, 95:12

Minow, Newton
on television, 229:3

Minute
so little ~s, make mighty ages of
eternity, 234:10

Miracle
beating four kings and ace with
four aces and king, 200:19

every inch of space is ~, 183:49

God's ~s found in nature,
32:13

~s are children of mendacity,
200:109

one ~ as easy to believe as
another, 32:3

word ~ gives false impression,
200:48

Miraculous
mark of wisdom to see ~ in
common, 256:2

Mire
men risen out of ~, 81:14

Mirth
 ~'s concussions rip outward case, 149:6

Miser
 nature laughs at ~, 248:29
 pay too much for your whistle, 29:4
 punishment of ~,—to pay drafts of heir in his tomb, 29:5

Miseries
 do not live to extenuate ~ of past, 136:100

Misery
 among blacks is ~ enough, 34:10
 if ~ loves company, ~ has company enough, 6:8
 if ~ of others leaves you indifferent, you cannot be called human being, 43:15
 playing politics at expense of human ~, 187:60

Misfortune (*See also* Adversity; Fortune)
 ~s hardest to bear never come, 236:17

Mishaps
 ~ are like knives that either serve or cut us, 43:70

Missile
 lone reckless hand upon switch of uninterceptible ~, 245:8

Missionaries
 sincere, self-deceived persons suffering from meddler's itch, 200:96

Mississippi, 154:1–3
 ~ begins in lobby of Memphis, Tennessee, hotel, 154:2
 ~ will drink wet and vote dry, 154:3
 state motto, 154:1

Mississippi River, 155:1–9
Missouri, 156:1–6
 be from ~; but forget it occasionally, 156:2
 I'm from ~, 156:6
 notorious ~ characters, 156:4
 state motto, 156:1

Missourian
 regional reactions to, 156:3

Mistake
 experience is name everyone gives his ~s, 82:11
 I have made many ~s, but I love my country, 133:40
 physician can bury ~s, 21:14

Mistress
 difference between wife and ~, 145:3
 law is jealous ~, 134:96

Misunderstood
 to be great is to be ~, 102:9

Mitchel, John
 on books, 35:59

Mitchell, Donald Grant
 on life, 136:97

Mitchell, Margaret
 E.B. White on, 262:89
 on avarice, 29:7
 on reputation, 202:5
 on the South, 214:4
 on trouble, 236:19

Mitford, Jessica
 on American word usage, 16:31
 on crime, 61:24

Mitford, Nancy
 on money, 157:49

Mizner, Wilson
 on Hollywood, 108:12, 108:13
 on life, 136:98
 on luck, 141:6
 on merriment, 149:10
 on success, 224:32
 on writing, 262:58

Mob
 a few men may make a ~, 126:40
 Baltimore known [as] ~town, 146:3
 course of ~s good practice for orators, 177:5
 I am the ~, 196:26
 lynch law as little valid when practiced by jury as when administered by ~, 134:62
 mankind ~ of unnecessary duplicates, 112:40
 ~ cannot be permanency, 196:9
 ~ law does not become due process by securing assent of terrorized jury, 126:20
 ~'s a monster, 126:11
 ~s will never do to govern states or command armies, 101:5
 neither intelligence or culture can prevent ~ acting as ~, 144:21
 no grievance fit object of redress by ~ rule, 134:85
 nose of ~ is its imagination, 196:23
 society of bodies bereaving themselves of reason, 196:8
 un-American that tends to government by ~, 101:123
 world made up of great ~, 112:22

Mobile (Ala.)
 city of intimacies, 9:7
 ~ stays in heart, 9:6
 not anybody working, 9:9

Moby-Dick
 all evil personified in, 80:10

Moderation
 I'm foe of ~, 43:6

Modern
 all ~ inconveniences, 195:33

Moderwell, Hiram K.
 on ragtime, 160:18

Modest
 no great man ever ~, 137:15
 rather be shut up in ~ cottage than occupy most splendid post, 11:10

Molasses
 ~ catches more flies, 4:3

Moment
 seize ~, 1:21

Monarchy
 absolute ~ is one in which sovereign does as he pleases so long as he pleases assassins, 101:10
 all governments are military, 101:104
 enemy to ~ before I came to Europe, 101:68
 ~ is merchantman which sails well, but sometimes will strike rock, 101:8
 ~ most expensive of all forms of government, 101:30

Mondale, Walter
 campaign slogan, 41:39

Money, 157:1–65
 all men in America make ~ their pursuit, 29:8
 all ~ is matter of belief, 157:56
 Americans want action for their ~, 157:51
 anyone who tries to understand ~ question goes crazy, 157:61
 as much ~ to be made out of wreckage of civilization as from upbuilding one, 29:7
 bank-note world, 157:37
 basic cure for poverty, 189:47
 can anybody remember when ~ not scarce?, 157:19
 convictions of Hollywood made of boiled ~, 159:14
 dally not with other Folks ~, 4:29
 dealers in ~ always dangerous class, 157:11
 divest visitor of so much ~ with so little enthusiasm, 171:61
 doing every thing for ~, 157:28
 don't take wooden nickels, 4:4
 everything to some and more than next to other poor souls, 157:20
 fellow says hain't the ~ but principle, it's th' ~, 157:41
 God gave me my ~, 249:47
 how cheerfully we consign ourselves to perdition, 157:48

Moon, William Least Heat
  on Missourian, 156:3
  on travel, 235:26
Moonlight
  ⁓'s fair tonight along the
    Wabash, 119:2
Moor
  I never saw ⁓, 183:12
Moore, Clement
  on Christmas, 48:7
  on laughter, 149:11
Moore, Grace
  on travel, 235:27
Moore, Marianne
  on Brooklyn, 171:80
  on marriage, 145:62
  on poet, 185:28
  on sense of humor, 113:28
Moral
  America died of delusion she had
    ⁓ leadership, 12:87
  continents and seas in ⁓ world,
    43:86
  dollar representative of ⁓ values,
    157:18
  easier to get spark out of stone
    than ⁓, 161:12
  learned not to doze off in
    presence of people who tell me
    they are more ⁓ than others,
    43:82
  ⁓ equivalent of war, 245:42
  ⁓ flabbiness born of worship of
    bitch-goddess SUCCESS,
    224:27
  ⁓ forces prevailed, 51:9
  ⁓ perfection in death, 194:3
  natural science outstripped ⁓
    science, 207:10
  [presidency] preeminently place of
    ⁓ leadership, 192:33
  so afraid of losing ⁓ sense, 194:9
  success of great ⁓ enterprise does
    not depend upon numbers,
    224:16
  time great legalizer, even in field
    of ⁓s, 234:40
Moralism
  much cant in American ⁓,
    12:38
Morality
  ⁓ is character and conduct
    required by community, 43:7
  ⁓ without religion, only kind of
    dead reckoning, 200:126
  never believed one code of ⁓ for
    public, and another for private
    man, 53:15
  reason and experience forbid us to
    expect national ⁓ can prevail
    in exclusion of religious
    principle, 200:175

More, Paul Elmer
  on religion, 200:134
Morgan, Henry
  on crime, 61:25
Morgan, J. P.
  Andrew Carnegie on, 39:14
  last words, 133:31
Morison, Samuel Eliot
  on American Revolution, 14:59
  on Declaration of Independence,
    14:60
  on history, 107:54
  on Navy, 162:9
Morley, Christopher
  on America, 12:81
  on argument, 22:13
  on domesticity, 109:31
  on humankind, 112:42
  on life, 136:99
  on marriage, 145:63
  on New York City, 171:81
  on philosophy, 184:21
  on poetry, 186:20
  on success, 224:33
  on time, 234:42
  on truth, 237:62, 237:63
Mormons
  our religion is simply the truth,
    200:190
  Rudyard Kipling on, 239:6
  will never be slain in cold blood
    for their beauty, 239:11
Morning
  cold, gray dawn of ⁓ after, 71:6
  'tis always ⁓ somewhere, 110:7
  what glorious ⁓, 14:14
Morris, George Pope
  on nature, 161:60
Morrow, Dwight W.
  on politics, 187:100
Morse, Samuel F.B.
  telegraph message, 123:12
Morton, Oliver P.
  on politics, 187:101
Moses
  go down, ⁓, 210:1
Moses, Grandma
  on painting, 26:41, 26:42
Moses, Robert
  on architecture, 21:8
Mother
  American children suffer too
    much ⁓, 85:17
  biological possibility and desires not
    same as biological need, 257:66
  hand that rocks cradle rules
    world, 257:76
  mighty ⁓ of mighty brood, 12:75
  ⁓ Knows Best, 85:8
  ⁓ of exiles, 171:64
  ⁓s great vacationless class,
    257:51

⁓'s heart is child's schoolroom,
    85:2
  tell ⁓ I died for my country,
    133:10
Motion Pictures, 159:1–36
  code, 159:1, 159:2
  leave them when you're looking
    good, 159:31
  only thing owe public is good
    performance, 159:6
  they'd give us pep-up pills, 159:13
  wouldn't pay $50,000 for any
    damn book, 159:33
  wouldn't want screen actor to be
    President, 193:132
Motive
  four great ⁓s hunger, love,
    vanity, and fear of superior
    powers, 245:88
Motto (See also under state names)
  national ⁓ has been root, hog, or
    die, 16:4
Moulton, Louise Chandler
  on death, 63:63
Mountain
  ⁓s are earth's undecaying
    monuments, 161:40
Mountaineers
  whether ⁓ always free, were
    almost always poor, 252:8
Mourn
  earth to chamber of ⁓ing turns,
    213:19
  I ⁓ no more my vanished years,
    264:44
Mouse-trap
  if man make better ⁓, world
    make path to his door, 84:8
Mouth
  heart of fool is in his ⁓, 106:6
  keep eyes open and ⁓ shut,
    4:48
Move
  have to ⁓ ahead, but not going
    to leave anyone behind,
    193:108
  reason man ⁓s slowly is because
    must ⁓ together, 195:27
Movie
  all Americans born between 1890
    and 1945 wanted to be ⁓
    stars, 159:32
  congressional bill titles like titles
    of Marx Brothers ⁓s, 54:63
  education only one thing that can
    kill ⁓s, 159:28
  good ⁓s make you care, 159:17
  most ⁓s nowadays are trash,
    159:24
  ⁓s doing so much of same thing
    few possibilities yet explored,
    159:16

Nash, Ogden *(cont'd)*
    on money, 157:50
    on orgy, 209:29
    on progress, 195:25
    on the Bronx, 171:82, 171:83
    on wealth, 249:43
Nashville (Tenn.)
    take of London fog 30 parts,
      230:4
Nathan, George Jean
    on art, 26:43, 26:44
    on love, 140:71
    on obscenity, 262:59
    on patriotism, 180:32
    on songs, 212:23
    on theater, 233:24, 233:25
    on the public, 196:19
Nathan, Robert
    on beauty, 31:30
Nation
    chief business of ⁓ is setting up
      heroes, 12:79
    contracts between ⁓ and
      individuals only binding on
      conscience of sovereign, 101:51
    general association of ⁓s must be
      formed, 68:70
    homes of ⁓ are bulwarks of
      safety, 109:22
    ⁓ guarantees nurture, education,
      and comfortable maintenance
      of every citizen from cradle to
      grave, 101:9
    ⁓ moving toward two societies,
      12:61
    ⁓ of shopkeepers, 77:3
    ⁓s are subjected to punishments,
      197:13
    ⁓s getting obsolete, 180:17
    ⁓s of shopkeepers must keep
      shop also, 77:12
    ⁓ so right it does not need to
      convince others by force, 94:8,
      181:50
    ⁓ too great to offend least,
      12:123
    never was art-loving ⁓, 26:57
    no calamity ⁓ can invite equals
      loss of ⁓al honor, 60:3
    no ⁓ fit to sit in judgment upon
      other ⁓, 68:69
    no ⁓ has monopoly of justice
      and capacity to enforce
      conceptions globally, 68:36
    no ⁓ ought to be without debt,
      64:13
    one ⁓, evermore, 12:43
    one ⁓ in foreign affairs, separate
      ones in domestic, 223:12
    rather be poor ⁓ that was free
      than rich ⁓ ceased to be in
      love with liberty, 135:79

Nation, Carry
    on own imprisonment, 197:15
National debt. *See* Debt
Nationalism
    ⁓ is infantile disease, 180:15
Natural
    every ⁓ action is graceful,
      161:17
    ⁓ beauty consists of complicated
      harmony, 161:15
    ⁓ man has difficult time getting
      along in world, 144:12
Nature, 161:1–83
    Amen! of ⁓ always a flower,
      90:6
    art can never match luxury and
      superfluity of ⁓, 161:67
    art is child of ⁓, 26:35
    art is difference [man] makes in
      ⁓, 26:20
    birds do not sing in caves, nor do
      doves cherish their innocence in
      dovecotes, 109:35
    bring not to field or stone fancies
      found in books, 161:31
    can never have enough of ⁓,
      161:69
    "control of ⁓" is phrase
      conceived in arrogance, 161:13
    devoted whole life to study of ⁓,
      161:2
    from pastures, pond, may see
      Christianity, 200:57
    full of mystery and fear, 161:42
    give us ⁓'s teaching, 161:81
    God's miracles found in ⁓, 32:13
    go forth and list to ⁓'s teachings,
      161:9
    great ⁓ made us men, 112:37
    harp at ⁓'s advent strung, 161:83
    I am integral with you, 161:77
    if plant cannot live according to
      its ⁓, it dies; and so a man,
      118:14
    I had rather be thy child and
      pupil, 161:72
    in Louisiana, live-oak is king, and
      magnolia queen, 139:5
    ⁓ abhors the old, 7:22
    ⁓ answered her purpose with
      curly, dimpled lunatic [child],
      264:15
    ⁓ cannot make man save on
      worn-out plan, 144:17
    ⁓ glories in death more than life,
      28:2
    ⁓ hates calculators, 161:28
    ⁓ hates monopolies and
      exceptions, 161:23
    ⁓ hides every wrinkle of her
      antiquity, 161:33
    ⁓ is autocratic, 161:35

    ⁓ is endless combination and
      repetition of very few laws,
      161:21
    ⁓ is full of freaks, 7:27
    ⁓ is full of genius, 161:70
    ⁓ is mutable cloud, 161:20
    ⁓ is neutral, 174:16
    ⁓ is no saint, 161:29
    ⁓ never blunders, 161:5
    ⁓ never rhymes her children,
      120:12
    ⁓ never wears mean appearance,
      161:16
    ⁓ not affected by finance, 161:39
    ⁓ pardons no errors, 161:34
    ⁓ profoundly imperturbable,
      161:43
    ⁓ punishes for most sins, 161:45
    ⁓'s dice always loaded, 161:18
    ⁓ seems dissipated hussy, 250:3
    ⁓ speaks in symbols and signs,
      161:82
    ⁓ tells every secret once, 161:30
    ⁓: Unseen Intelligence, 161:44
    ⁓ will bear closest inspection,
      161:65
    ⁓ will protect her own, 161:39
    no boon in ⁓, 131:55
    no fixtures in ⁓, 161:24
    not in ⁓ but in man is all beauty
      and worth he sees, 112:11
    regions yet untrod, 161:55
    religion puts affront upon ⁓,
      200:46
    serve ⁓ for bread, 185:8
    so ⁓ deals with us, and takes
      away our playthings, 63:58
    to him who in love of ⁓ holds
      communion with her visible
      forms, 161:8
    we make of ⁓'s giant powers
      slaves of human Art, 259:80
    what cannot defend itself shall
      not be defended, 161:32
    what ⁓ delivers is never stale,
      161:64
    what remains? ⁓ remains, 161:80
    word Miracle gives false
      impression, 200:48
Naval
    ⁓ force can never endanger our
      liberties, 162:5
    protection of ⁓ force
      indispensable, 162:16
    respect to neutral flag requires ⁓
      force, 162:17
Navigation
    absolute freedom of ⁓ upon seas,
      alike in peace and war, 162:18
Navy, 162:1–18
    believes in tradition of "Damn
      torpedoes", 162:12

Newport (R.I.)
  colony of rich, 205:3
  ~ was charming, but asked for
    no education and gave none,
    205:2
  placed there, by refinement in
    scheme of nature, 205:5
News
  all ~ is gossip, 125:70
  all ~ that's fit to print, 125:48
  literature is ~ that stays ~, 138:51
  sensational ~ sensationally
    written, 125:64
  when man bites dog, 125:14
  women, wampum, and
    wrongdoing always ~, 125:76
Newspaper (*See also* Free press;
  Journalism; Publish)
  advertisements contain only truths
    to be relied on in ~, 125:35
  all I know is what I see in the
    papers, 125:58
  all successful ~s querulous and
    bellicose, 125:44
  chimney to carry off noxious
    vapors, 125:29
  comforts th' afflicted, afflicts th'
    comfortable, 125:15
  consumption of ~s by
    Americans, 125:72
  decide whether have government
    without ~s, or ~s without
    government, 125:25
  determined never to put sentence
    into any ~, 125:28
  do not take single ~ and feel
    happier for it, 125:27
  editor might divide his ~ into
    Truths, Probabilities,
    Possibilities, Lies, 125:33
  government of men and morning
    ~s, 125:53
  hate to be defended in ~, 125:17
  I ain't no lady. I'm ~woman,
    125:63
  man who never looks into ~ is
    better informed than he who
    reads them, 125:32
  most important profession that of
    ~man, 125:61
  ~ as greatest organ of social life,
    125:7
  ~ private enterprise, owing
    nothing to public, 125:1
  ~s are schoolmasters of common
    people, 125:5
  nothing can now be believed
    which is seen in ~, 125:31
  reading ~ causes me to put in
    rest of day pleading for
    damnation of human race,
    125:73

to ~man human being is item
  with skin wrapped around it,
  125:4
vital measure of ~ is not size but
  spirit, 125:69
whole huge earth sent in
  brown-paper wrapper, 125:39
will die for freedom of ~s,
  125:16
Newton, Huey P.
  on humankind, 112:43
New York City, 171:1–112
  alien accent, 171:60
  all the reform we want, 171:52
  as Gotham, 171:54
  asked boldness to dream, 171:38
  ask, How much is he worth?,
    12:102
  as ~ went to sleep—if ~ ever
    did, 171:32
  attracts most talented, 171:69
  Bagdad-on-the-Subway, 171:40
  blackout's low rate of crime,
    171:57
  blazes like magnificent jewel,
    171:110
  [both] car, good manners useless
    in ~, 171:73
  Bow'ry, the Bow'ry, 171:49
  capital of memoranda, 171:103
  city of prose and fantasy, 171:100
  cloaca of all depravities, 171:56
  congestion in subway esteemed in
    night spots as intimacy, 171:96
  convenient to everything I can't
    afford, 171:9
  cruel, lovely, savage, 171:111
  don't get caught in wheels,
    171:13
  drives me crazy, 171:39
  energy in ~, 171:55
  engenders high expectations,
    171:18
  everybody wants to be Somebody,
    171:36
  expensiveness, 171:61
  Fiorello LaGuardia on being
    mayor of, 171:63
  food predictably commonplace,
    171:20
  for better or worse, this is real,
    171:6
  four hundred in ~ society,
    171:70
  full of people with feeling for
    tangential adventure, 171:25
  giant asparagus bed of
    skyscrapers, 171:10
  hardly day goes by innocent
    bystander ain't shot in ~,
    171:86
  has total depth, 171:66

haven for oppressed, 171:43
[hell] is ~, 171:28
humanity in microcosm, 171:71
hussy taken in sin again, 171:11
icing on pie called Christian
  Civilization, 171:78
ills of ~ cannot be solved by
  money, 171:75
I love ~, 171:58
inhabitants ascend right to
  heaven, 171:3
inhabitants brisk and lively,
  171:74
in ~ assumed we were best,
  171:35
little old ~, 171:45
Mammon chief temple in holy
  ~, 171:15
Moon of tides of men, 171:85
more one studied it, more
  grotesquely bad it grew, 171:59
nation's thyroid gland, 171:81
~ is beautiful catastrophe, 171:65
~ is different country, 171:27
~ is fullest expression of modern
  age, 171:100
~ is great stone desert, 171:112
~ is sucked orange, 171:26
~ is where I have to be, 171:4
~ is white plume saying way is
  up, 171:104
~ where every one is exile,
  171:30
nice place to visit, but wouldn't
  live there, 171:1
Noisyville-on-the-Subway, 171:46
no one should come to ~ to live
  unless he is lucky, 171:102
nothing ever gets old, 171:95
nothing to see and no way to see
  it, 171:98
nowhere is success pursued more
  ardently than in ~, 171:16
O Babylon! O Carthage! O ~,
  171:89
ocean on one side and New
  Jersey on other, 171:41
of right angles and tough,
  damaged people, 171:34
one big theater, 171:88
one can dine in ~, [but] one
  could not dwell there, 16:57
people are magnificent, 171:62
pneumatic noisemaker emblematic
  sound of ~, 171:97
posthumous revenge of Merchant
  of Venice, 171:50
present in ~ so powerful that
  past is lost, 171:19
prostitution only business that
  isn't leaving, 171:31
rises like Venice from sea, 171:99

Nonsense *(cont'd)*
    takes heap of sense to write good
    ~, 262:78
Nonviolence
    answer to crucial questions of our
    times, 181:23
Nonviolent
    ~ action way to supplement
    process of change, 50:27
Normal
    very ~ man upon great scale,
    137:59
Normalcy
    back to ~, 41:20
Norris, Frank
    on railroad monopoly, 39:50
    on truth, 237:65
Norris, Kathleen
    on South Dakota, 216:8
    on winter, 254:7
North Carolina, 172:1–9
    begins with brightness of sea,
    172:8
    Garden of Eden in ~, 172:5
    goodliest soil under cope of
    heaven, 172:6
    land of sky, 172:9
    last at Appomattox, 172:3
    richness of soil, 172:7
    state motto, 172:1
    Tar Heel born, bred, dead, 172:4
    vale of humility between two
    mountains of conceit, 172:2
North Dakota, 173:1–10
    doomed state, 173:2
    elbowroom, 173:4
    Fargo east-west middle of [U.S.],
    173:10
    farming unrivaled world over,
    173:6
    free-and-easy, non-eastern, 173:5
    high winds and tumbleweed,
    173:4
    Missouri River boundary between
    east and west, 173:9
    [Roosevelt, Theodore] never been
    President if not for ~, 173:7
    rural character, 173:3
    sad, slow wail of coyote, 173:4
    state motto, 173:1
    state without a millionaire,
    173:5
    work and pay for everything you
    get, 173:8
North Vietnam. *See* Vietnam
Norton, Charles Eliot
    on literature, 138:44
Norton, Eleanor Holmes
    on history, 107:56
    on marriage, 145:64
Norworth, Jack
    on baseball, 30:28, 30:29

Nothing
    mind can never conceive state of
    ~, 183:13
    most know how to say ~; few
    know when, 59:1
    ~ to look backward to and ~ to
    look forward to, 83:2
Notre Dame (University)
    don't want anybody going out to
    die for dear old ~, 93:16
Noun
    ~s and verbs are almost pure
    metal, 132:20
Nourishment
    squeezing from stone only ~ I
    get, 257:88
Novak, Robert
    on Ronald Reagan, 193:32
Novel
    between Bible and ~s there is
    gulf fixed, 35:16
    every ~ should have beginning,
    muddle, and end, 138:11
    every ~ suckled at breasts of
    older ~s, 138:40
    how far off from life ~ still us,
    138:19
    only reason for existence of ~ is
    attempt to represent life, 35:46
    use ~ for anything other than
    art, you pervert it, 138:46
Novelist
    teaching has ruined more ~s than
    drink, 262:82
November
    most disagreeable month in year,
    28:1
    [Philadelphia] City of Bleak ~
    Afternoons, 182:14
Nowhere
    Middle of ~, 235:26
Nuclear
    inventory of U.S. ~ warheads,
    sobering experience, 174:5
    lives under ~ sword of
    Damocles, 245:51
    ~ disaster could well engulf
    great and small, 245:50
    "~ exchange" sounds like mutual
    gift-giving, 174:12
    survivors inwardly and outwardly
    resemble the dead, 245:57
    took eighteen months to build
    first ~ power generator,
    174:20
    world of ~ giants and ethical
    infants, 174:4
Nuclear Age, 174:1–24
    harnessing of basic power of
    universe, 261:32
    in end beckons general
    annihilation, 174:9

    in loneliness of desert, would
    brew Apocalypse, 168:5
    mushroom of boiling dust, 174:21
    New Mexico birth to atomic
    bomb irony, 168:6
    one or two of those things
    [atomic bombs], and Japan will
    be finished, 261:8
    real problem in hearts and minds
    of men, 174:6
    roar which warned of doomsday,
    174:10
    Truman did not so much say
    "yes" as not say "no" [atomic
    bomb], 261:9
    world would not be same, 174:15
    worry what United States might
    do to other countries [atomic
    bomb], 261:30
Nullifiers
    if one drop of blood shed, I
    will hang the first one I can,
    223:10
Number
    tell me not, in mournful ~s,
    136:78
Nuts, 261:19
Nye, Edgar Wilson (Bill)
    on spring, 221:17

Oath
    ~, solemn appeal to Deity, made
    binding by penalty for perjury,
    134:15
Obedience
    child's first lesson be ~, 72:10
    ~ gateway through which
    knowledge and love enter child,
    74:92
Objector
    ~ against injustice hunches world
    along, 195:4
Obligation
    only ~ I have right to assume is
    to do what I think right, 72:29
Oblivion
    pastures of ~, 234:11
Obscenity
    no such thing as dirty theme,
    262:59
Observe
    you ~ a lot by watching, 33:2
Obsolete
    either man is ~ or war is, 245:30
Ochs, Adolph S.
    on *New York Times*, 125:48,
    125:49
O'Connell, William Cardinal
    on civil rights, 50:35
    on labor rights, 131:42,
    131:43

Penn, William *(cont'd)*
on drinking, 71:46
on friends, 96:32
on friendship, 96:33
on government, 101:105, 101:106
on oratory, 177:11
on pain, 179:10
on Pennsylvania, 182:13
on religion, 200:149, 200:150
on truth, 237:71
on wisdom, 256:28
Pennsylvania, 182:1–15
cradle of toleration and freedom
of religion, 182:11
[in colonial ～] no lawyers, 182:3
keystone of democratic arch,
182:2
～ mind not complex, 182:4
～, name king would give in
honor of my father, 182:13
～ produced but two great men,
182:10
state motto, 182:1
unsung, unpainted hills of ～,
182:6
Pension
～ list of republic a roll of honor,
101:26
People *(See also* Mob; Public)
all authority belongs to the ～,
27:7
all free governments managed by
combined wisdom and folly of
the ～, 101:45
all ～s of world are partners,
260:26
American Revolution real in
minds and hearts of ～, 14:11
average of the ～ immense, 15:51
basis of our political systems is
right of the ～ to make and
alter their constitutions,
101:138
biggest corporation must be held
to strict compliance with will
of ～, 39:56
cannot hope to succeed without
the ～, 137:29
can't fool all of the ～ all of the
time, 137:32
confidence in virtue of majority of
the ～, 101:60
Congress is the ～, 54:56
courts and cabinets, President and
advisers, derive their power
from the ～, 66:50
declaration that ～ are hostile to
government made by
themselves is insult, 66:2
democracy is government of all
the ～, by all the ～, for all
the ～, 66:78

democracy is self-government,
over all the ～, for all the ～,
by all the ～, 66:79
democracy is theory that common
～ know what they want and
deserve it, 66:75
do as ～ do, tribute to ～'s
majesty, 196:2
don't put no constrictions on da
～, 135:18
force not so potent and ～
intractable, 242:2
government does little for
respectable ～ except annoy
them, 101:56
government is for use of the ～,
and not the ～ for use of
government, 101:125
government of Union is
emphatically government of the
～, 66:73
great work of world done through
me, 196:26
handful of ～ clinging to
subcontinent, 10:7
hand of the ～ has proved that
government to be strongest of
which every man feels himself
a part, 101:74
happiness of the ～ is sole end of
government, consent of the ～
is only foundation, 101:3
his faith in the ～ never wavered,
78:2
I am the ～, 196:26
if happiness of the ～ can be
secured at expense of a little
tempest, it will be precious
purchase, 103:23
in all that the ～ can individually
do for themselves, government
ought not to interfere, 101:84
influence over government must be
shared among all the ～, 101:65
lead this great peaceful ～ into
war, 260:25
legislation is made by the ～ and
for the ～, 134:104
literature has never recognized the
～, 138:67
maintaining rights of ～ with
ultimate extinction of all
privileged classes, 66:11
men divided into those who fear
the ～ and those who identify
with the ～, 187:69
more than half the ～ are right
more than half of time, 66:102
national government possesses
those powers the people have
conferred, and no more,
101:142

no man ever saw the ～ of whom
he forms part, 101:147
no ～ ever lost liberties unless
first became corrupt, 135:37
no safe depository of ultimate
powers of society but ～, 66:47
on great occasions only, real voice
of the ～ can be known,
196:35
our government founded upon
intelligence of the ～, 101:58
～ are no keepers [of own
liberties] at all, 135:4
～ are only censors of their
governors, 135:41
～ are only safe depositories
[government's], 66:41
～ are our dependence for
continued freedom, 66:46
～ are turbulent; they seldom
judge right, 66:31
～ are wiser than wisest man,
66:6
～ governed much by custom,
196:32
～ have right to resist
unconstitutional laws without
overturning government,
101:141
～ have right to the truth, 237:65
～ not stupid enough to abandon
representative government,
54:19
[～] only sure reliance for
preservation of liberty, 66:40
～'s government made for the ～,
by the ～, and answerable to
the ～, 66:101
～ strong and well enough
informed to maintain control
over government, 101:119
policy to recommend, but none to
enforce against will of the ～,
196:13
politics the ～'s business, 187:140
power is inherent in the ～, 66:48
power under Constitution will
always be in the ～, 196:34
[President] last person to know
what the ～ really want,
193:36
prime enemy of the ～ is
government, 101:44
public officers are servants and
agents of the ～, 101:23
representative of the ～ sentinel
on watch-tower of liberty,
101:143
sovereign power of the ～,
12:95
this country belongs to the ～
who inhabit it, 204:16

though the ~ support
government the government
should not support the ~,
101:25

to be taken in very small doses,
196:11

tough, damaged ~, 171:34

truest expression of a ~ is in its
dances and music, 160:5

two kinds of ~ that really count,
112:15

voice of the ~, voice of humbug,
196:27

we, the ~, are boss and will get
leadership we demand and
deserve, 66:56

when ~ create own program, you
get action, 50:34

while the ~ should support
government, its functions do
not include support of the ~,
101:27

will of the ~ only legitimate
foundation of government,
101:71

wish to be settled, 42:6

worries of world are for the
common ~, 196:19

Peoria
will it play in ~?, 187:1

Pepper, Claude
on democracy, 66:80
on politics, 187:108

Perceive
we all ~ difference between
ourselves and inferiors, 183:11

Perception, 183:1–49
how can we speak of action of
mind, 183:19
in imagination, not in ~, lies
substance of experience, 183:43
never saw Moor, 183:12
~ of beauty is moral test, 183:46
world is all outside, 183:21

Perceptual
amnesia, 140:65

Perelman, S.J.
on Hollywood, 108:14
on Philadelphia (Pa.), 182:14
on would-be farmers, 8:14

Perfection
only ~ good enough for him,
138:43

Perjury
witnesses may commit ~, but
smoke cannot, 237:46

Perkins, Frances
on Franklin D. Roosevelt,
193:101
on public opinion, 196:20

Permissive
we are nothing if not ~, 262:81

Perrin, Noel
on Americans, 15:37
on cities, 49:10
on pigs, 19:17
on Vermont, 240:8
on would-be farmers, 8:15

Perry, George Sessions
on Detroit (Mich.), 150:5
on New Orleans (La.), 169:3,
169:4
on San Francisco (Calif.), 206:8
on Seattle (Wash.), 248:3, 248:4
on Wisconsin, 255:3

Perry, Oliver Hazard
on Battle of Lake Erie, 162:10,
162:11, 242:8

Persecution
feature of all religions established
by law, 200:136
not original feature in *any*
religion, 201:21

Pershing, John J.
on World War I, 260:11

Personal
nothing endures but ~ qualities,
43:94

Personality
hate corrodes ~, 18:11

Pessimism
~ is luxury of handful, 16:8

Pessimist
fears we live in best of possible
worlds, 183:10
~ breeds indifference to others,
43:81
~ic about man's future, 188:14
~ sees calamity in every
opportunity, 183:1
~ thinks all women are bad,
257:17

Pesticide
DDT one of safest ~s, 188:2

Peter Piper
~ picked a peck, 219:20

Petigru, James Louis
on epitaphs, 78:20
on South Carolina, 215:8

Petry, Ann
on literary criticism, 138:47

Phelps, Austin
on books, 35:61

Phelps, William Lyon
on war, 245:71

Philadelphia (Pa.)
ask, Who were his parents?,
12:102
City of Bleak November
Afternoons, 182:14
damnation seize them
[Philadelphians], 182:5
dreadfully provincial, 16:57

handsome city, but distractingly
regular, 182:7
on whole rather be in ~, 182:9
tell ~ ladies redcoats humbled
themselves, 14:90
they wash windows, doors, marble
steps, and pavements, 182:12
three ~ lawyers match for Devil,
134:1

Philanthropy
spirit of false ~, 44:8

Philippines
I came through and I shall
return, 261:16
I have returned, 261:17
I see old flagpole still stands,
261:18

Phillips, Wendell
on Abraham Lincoln, 137:41
on action, 1:16
on argument, 22:14
on Congress, 54:40
on Constitution, 57:28
on destiny, 67:7
on government, 101:107–109
on journalism, 125:53
on justice, 126:40
on labor rights, 131:45, 131:47
on law, 134:89
on liberty, 135:57, 135:58
on literature, 138:48
on majority rule, 143:7
on personal independence, 118:12
on Plymouth Rock, 147:9
on politics, 187:109, 187:110
on power, 190:36, 190:37
on presidency, 192:29
on progress, 195:26
on religion, 200:151
on revolution, 204:21, 204:22
on success, 224:35
on truth, 237:72

Philosopher
between laughing and weeping
~, no opposition, 184:22
knows less and less about more
and more, 184:1
man up in balloon, with family
and friends trying to haul him
down, 184:2
men are not ~s, but foolish
children, 144:7
no ~ who is ~ at all times,
184:8
to be ~ is not merely to have
subtle thoughts, 184:23

Philosophic
~ climate of our time forces own
clothing on us, 184:15
~ ideals altars to unknown gods,
184:14

Philosophies
  ~ unendurable not because men
    are cowards, 184:18
Philosophy, 184:1–23
  account mind gives to itself of
    constitution of world, 184:9
  dealing with problems not yet
    open to methods of science,
    184:6
  doctrines of Epicurus, everything
    rational in moral ~, 184:17
  every science begins as ~, 207:11
  highest conception of life, 184:13
  hundred pages is enough, 184:11
  many roads leading from nowhere
    to nothing, 184:4
  ~ drips gently from his tongue
    who hath three meals a day,
    184:21
  simple ~, scratch where it itches,
    184:20
Phobia
  hate to go to bed, hate to get up,
    hate to be alone, 136:6
  tell us your ~s and we will tell
    you what you are afraid of,
    87:1
Photograph
  things nobody would see if I
    didn't ~ them, 183:3
Photography
  Ansel Adams on, 31:2
Phraseology
  ~ of every nation has taint of
    drollery, 132:43
Physician
  best ~ that knows worthlessness
    of most medicines, 148:8
  good patient, having found good
    ~, sticks to him, 148:11
  need of ~ who shall minister to
    soul and body, 148:19
  ~ can bury mistakes, 21:14
  ~, one upon whom set hopes
    when ill, 148:2
  sun, my almighty ~, 105:17
Pianist
  please do not shoot ~, 52:2
Piano
  wonderful how soon ~ gets into
    hut on frontier, 62:4
Piatt, Donn
  on public opinion, 196:21
Picasso, Pablo
  Gertrude Stein on, 26:52
Picket
  ~'s off duty forever, 51:7
Pickett, George E.
  on Battle of Gettysburg, 51:48
  on Civil War, 51:47
Pickford, Mary
  on motion pictures, 159:23

Pickle
  look as if weaned on ~, 193:84
Picture
  one ~ in ten thousand ought to
    live, 26:21
  ~ about Russian secret
    police—GOP, 99:7
  to say ~ shows great labor is to
    say it is unfit for view, 26:58
Pie
  ~ in sky when you die, 131:27
  something in raspberry ~ that
    looks good to man, 92:10
Pierce, Franklin
  campaign slogan, 41:5
  James Bryce on, 193:11
Pierce, Ovid Williams
  on North Carolina, 172:8
Piety
  reverence for Supreme Being,
    based upon His supposed
    resemblance to man, 200:20
Pig
  ~s get bad press, 19:17
Pilgrim
  brave and high-souled ~s, 232:11
  come ~ and guest, 232:9
  is it not strange that descendants
    of ~ Fathers proved
    themselves intolerant, 201:18
  talk about their ~ blood, 17:14
  toast sturdy ~ band whose
    courage never ceased, 232:2
Pilot
  only entirely independent human
    being, 155:8
Pinckney, Charles
  on liberty, 135:59
Pine
  murmuring ~s and hemlocks
    stand like Druids, 161:52
  ~ mother of legends, 161:57
Pinkney, William
  on Declaration of Independence,
    118:13
  on language, 132:38
  on power, 190:38
Pioneers
  ~! O ~!, 15:50
  we are ~ of world, 15:32
Piracy
  ~ is commerce without its
    folly-swaddles, 39:8
Pitkin, Walter Boughton
  on the public, 196:22
Pitt, William
  on American Revolution, 14:73,
    14:74
Pittsburgh (Pa.)
  like Birmingham in England, 182:8
  six months' residence would
    justify suicide, 182:15

Pity
  exact justice is commonly more
    merciful than ~, 126:34
  firm basis of government is
    justice, not ~, 101:146
Plagiarism
  only "ism" she believes in is ~,
    262:62
  steal from one author it's ~;
    from many it's research,
    262:58
Plains
  at sea on ~ of Nebraska, 163:8
Plaintiff
  ~, court fool, 134:10
Plant
  ~s are young of world, 161:27
Plath, Sylvia
  on death, 63:67
Platte River
  Shallow River, 163:4
Play
  ~ed all his cards—if not more,
    193:44
  ~ it real pretty for me, 133:28
Playground
  ~ of America, 52:6
Pleasantville (N.Y.)
  I am suspicious of ~, 23:6
Please
  eat to ~ thyself, dress to ~
    others, 4:22
Pleasure
  do not bite at bait of ~, 4:38
  man richest whose ~s are
    cheapest, 249:57
Plenty
  never solve paradox of want in
    midst of ~ by doing away
    with ~, 189:36
Plimpton, George
  on swearing, 132:39
Plough
  ~ deep while sluggards sleep,
    259:24
Plumbing
  [Americans'] pride in, 16:30
Plumed knight
  Blaine marched down halls of
    Congress, 187:63
Plunkitt, George Washington
  on politics, 187:111
Plutocracy
  nothing to be said for government
    by ~, 101:122
  un-American that tends to
    government by ~, 101:123
Plymouth Rock
  corner-stone of nation, 147:7
  Kansas is child of ~, 127:15
  underlies all America: only crops
    out here, 147:9

man who pulls plow gets plunder
in ~, 187:89

modern ~ struggle not of men
but of forces, 187:7

most conservative persons, college
undergraduates, 264:47

mostly pill-taking, 187:116

my ~ are short and sweet, 137:21

my pollertics, bein of exceedin
accommodatin character,
187:153

no generalizations in ~ vested
selfishness cannot cut through,
187:55

not best to swap horses while
crossing river, 187:84

people astounded have no
slightest interest in ~, 187:36

playing ~ at expense of human
misery, 187:60

~ hold up torches of martyrdom,
187:68

~ is property, 187:72

~ is such torment, 187:67

~ quarantines one from history,
187:95

power ~ diplomatic name for
law of jungle, 190:13

requires sweat, work, combat, and
organization, 187:120

rules of war in ~, 187:88

science of exigencies, 187:107

science of ordered progress of
society, 187:161

science of who gets what, when,
why, 187:59

secret of Kennedy successes in ~
not money but planning,
187:73

similarities between football and
~, 187:105

skilled professional liars in
demand in ~ as in advertising,
187:143

straight and unadulterated venom,
187:35

takes lots of money to even get
beat, 187:123

television and, 229:4

the people's business, 187:140

to my princerples, I glory in
hevin' nothin' o' the sort,
187:90

to play game properly, know
every rule, 187:70

two kinds of promises in ~:
patronage and lies, 187:52

waving bloody shirt, 187:101

whenever man casts longing eye,
rottenness begins, 187:66

Wisconsin's ~ traditionally
uproar ~, 255:3

Polk, James K.
campaign slogan, 41:3
James Bryce on, 193:11
on presidency, 192:30
~ed you in '44, Pierce you in
'52, 41:5

Pollock, Channing
on happiness, 103:34

Polls
if do justice at ~ to our
conscience, do justice to nation,
75:18

Polluted
picnic on exquisitely packaged
food by ~ stream, 188:8

Pollution, 188:1-14

Ponder
while I ~ed weak and weary, 58:9

Poor
are they *my* ~, 44:5
for one ~ man hundred indigent,
189:15
God help rich; ~ can sleep with
windows shut, 189:42
greatest man in history was ~est,
189:13
happy be State whose ruler
heedeth more murmurs of ~,
189:46
have little, rich too much, 249:23
men always [whistle], 189:9
no disgrace t'be ~, 189:23
~ are ox-like, limp and
leaden-eyed, 189:30
~ no shame, but being ashamed
of it, is, 189:16
~ rich man! all he has is what
he has bought, 249:53
saloon is ~ man's club, 71:59
to appreciate beauty of country,
one has to go there ~, 235:27
town's ~ live most independent
lives, 189:44

Poorhouse
over hill to ~, 189:7
[spending more than earned]
means ~, 64:14
~ is vanishing from among us,
189:22

Pope
~ of Physics has moved, 207:27

Populace
where ~ rise against
never-ending audacity of elected
persons, 66:104

Popular
beware of over-great pleasure in
being ~, 4:34
free society is where safe to be
un~, 95:73

Popularity
~ is exhausting, 149:10

Population
if government knew how, I
should like to see it check, not
multiply ~, 101:40

Port
~, well worth the cruise, is near,
7:26

Porter, Cole
on wine and whiskey, 253:15

Porter, Sylvia
on money, 157:52

Portland (Ore.)
almost indistinguishable from ~,
Maine, 178:4
~ so busy it can't attend to own
sewage, 178:6
when man tells you it is
civilization, you object, 178:5

Portland (Wash.)
everybody in ~ is crazy about
~, 248:6

Positivism
denies knowledge of Real and
affirms ignorance of Apparent,
183:7

Possession
last breath—one ~ which
outvalues all others, 63:82

Posterity
think of your ~, 72:1

Pot
chicken in every ~, 41:24

Potomac
all quiet along ~, 51:6, 51:45

Potter, Henry Codman
on Presidents, 193:102

Pound, Ezra
Ernest Hemingway on, 185:15,
262:30
on America, 12:85
on architecture, 21:9
on art, 26:47
on genius, 97:27
on life, 136:102
on literature, 138:50, 138:51
on music, 160:22
on poetry, 186:24
on sin, 209:30
on winter, 254:8

Pound, Roscoe
on law, 134:90

Poverty, 189:1-49
all ov us dread but none ov us
pitty, 189:5
[Americans] not abject in their
~, 16:48
association of ~ with progress
great enigma, 189:20
basic cure for ~ is money,
189:47
cultivate ~ like garden herb,
189:45

Progress *(cont'd)*

slogan of ～ changing from full dinner pail to full garage, 195:15

social ～ makes well-being of all business of each, 195:12

society never advances, 211:10

step by step, see steady gain of man, 195:36

to follow whatever our fathers did would reject all ～, 195:22

took eighteen months to build first nuclear generator, 174:20

Progressive

insists on recognizing new facts, 187:160

Prohibition *(See also* Temperance)

～ law divided nation into three parts—wets, drys, and hypocrites, 71:50

～ law strikes blow at principles upon which government was founded, 71:37

～ only drives drunkenness behind doors, 71:54

Promise

two kinds of ～s in politics, 187:52

Pronounce

～ with the vulgar, 219:9

Proof

definition no ～, 132:38

Property

balance of power accompanies balance of ～, 190:4

by higher law, ～ will write every statute that respects ～, 134:34

cannot be secure in our ～ if others may take it away, 227:5

did any ～ class ever reform itself?, 210:55

everyone has ～ to defend, 16:42

foundation of any right to ～ is man's labor, 131:24

has no personal being, 50:28

labor process by which A acquires ～ for B, 259:4

no man acquires ～ without acquiring arithmetic also, 73:6

our liberty depends on almost equal diffusion of ～, 135:6

politics is ～, 187:72

positive good in world, 73:28

power *naturally* and *necessarily* follows ～, 190:49

private ～ original source of freedom [and] still main bulwark, 95:50

～ is fruit of labor, 73:28

～ owns them, 249:37

～ refers to rights granted by society, 50:13

right of possessor of ～ to be on equal footing with all fellow citizens, 249:10

rights in ～ are very unequal, 79:9

right to impart instruction substantial right of ～, 74:47

tax upon land values is most just and equal, 227:9

thing generally raised on city land is taxes, 227:25

those who hold and those without ～ have ever formed distinct interests in society, 211:33

universal suffrage could not long exist in community where great inequality of ～, 66:100

Prophet

dedicated to future not always best ～s, 191:1

poets are ～s whose prophesying never comes true, 185:18

～ has drunk more deeply of cup of bitterness, 200:112

Prosper

better some people ～ too much than no one ～ enough, 73:37

Prosperity

duty to see that wage worker, small producer, consumer, shall get fair share of business ～, 39:58

mass production means we must have mass ～, 39:61

～ of commercial nation regulated by ～ of rest, 73:29

surest breeder of insolence, 249:59

when you ascend hill of ～ may you not meet friend, 96:44

will leak through on those below, 73:2

Prosperous

to be ～ is not to be superior, 249:7

Prostitution

～ is only business that isn't leaving [New York City], 171:31

sin that's made quite a few people happier, 209:31

Protect

woman must be taught to ～ herself, 258:6

Protection

take back your ～, 73:3

Protestant churches

people think confessional unknown to ～, 200:89

Proud

look out how you use ～ words, 219:21

～er man is more he thinks he deserves, 43:10

to be ～ of virtue is to *poison* yourself with *antidote*, 43:42

too ～ to fight, 181:50

Proverb

God pity man or nation wise in ～s, 256:1

～s ready money of human experience, 82:14

treasures to dunces with good memories, 91:3

Providence

glory ascribed to manifest interposition of overruling ～, 200:171

go crazy if did not believe in ～, 200:189

～ has wild, rough, incalculable road to its end, 86:3

to trust in justice of cause without utmost exertions would be tempting ～, 200:169

ways of ～ are unscrutable, 200:176

Providence (R.I.)

～ is part of me—I *am* ～, 205:7

spires of ～ ascend against ancient skies, 205:6

Prudence

～ to give wisdom preference, 256:33

Psychiatrist

anybody who goes to see ～, 99:1

Psychotherapy

New York thing, 171:87

Public, The, 196:1–36 *(See also* Mob; People)

corruption that shocks in ～ affairs, 187:139

duties of all ～ officers plain and simple, 101:61

first mistake in ～ business, is going into it, 187:48

give ～ anything but never take away what have given, 196:22

no one ever went broke underestimating taste of American ～, 196:17

～ be damned, 196:30

～ bodies moved like the wind, 196:6

～ demands certainties, 196:18

～ is only critic whose opinion is worth anything, 138:57

～ man is private man, 193:117

～ office is dreadful burden, 101:75

～ office is ～ trust, 41:11

～ officers are servants and agents of the people, 101:23

～ questions come in third or

Quincy, Josiah
    on American Revolution,
        14:76
    on freedom, 95:63
    on government, 101:110
    on Massachusetts, 147:10
    on truth, 237:74
Quinn, Sally
    on Washington (D.C.), 247:7
Quotation
    every man is ⁓ from all his
        ancestors, 17:9
    I hate ⁓s. Tell me what you
        know, 117:9

Rabble
    will of majority is will of ⁓,
        135:11
Race
    baseball is game of ⁓, creed, and
        color, 30:22
    behavior determined not by ⁓
        but by ancestry and
        environment, 17:4
    conquering and unconquerable ⁓,
        56:7
    deplore suppressing artistic talent
        because of prejudice against ⁓,
        26:54
    no one has been barred on ⁓
        from fighting for America,
        50:25
    not to swift the ⁓, 224:40
    strong being is proof of the ⁓,
        43:95
Racism
    ⁓ crime so ghastly fight against
        it by any means necessary,
        34:23
    ⁓ new Calvinism, 50:4
Radical
    goes too far, 187:160
    man with feet firmly planted—in
        air, 187:127
    to be ⁓ is patriotic, 180:20
    women one group grows more ⁓
        with age, 257:72
Radicalism
    spirit of American ⁓ is
        destructive, 187:42
Radio
    chief pretender to throne of God
        is ⁓ itself, 229:9
    entire generation feeling inferior
        to just the *names* of guys on
        ⁓, 229:6
    "War of the Worlds" Martian
        invasion, 229:8
Raft
    get on ⁓ with Taft, 41:18

Rage
    to be black is to be in constant
        ⁓, 34:4
Ragtime
    Alexander's ⁓ Band, 212:8
    many native composer could save
        his soul, 160:18
Railroad
    Frank Norris on monopoly, 39:50
    I strenuously object to
        government ownership of ⁓s,
        101:121
    ⁓s not run for benefit of dear
        public, 39:67
Railway
    I sought trains; I found
        passengers, 235:30
    ⁓ aids traveling, 235:9
Rain
    April ⁓ of smiles and tears,
        264:44
    every ⁓drop had whole heaven
        within it, 250:8
    how beautiful is ⁓, 250:9
    into each life some ⁓ must fall,
        213:13
    old man in dry month, waiting
        for ⁓, 7:19
    ⁓eth drop and staineth slop,
        254:8
    when God sorts out weather and
        sends ⁓, 250:14
Rainbow
    nation is ⁓, 15:20
    ⁓ round my shoulder, 95:2
    who in ⁓ can draw line where
        violet ends and orange begins?,
        121:9
Rainier (Mt.)
    ⁓, from Puget Sound, is sight
        for gods, 248:2
Raleigh, Sir Walter
    James Russell Lowell on, 77:34
Rally
    we'll ⁓ round flag, boys, 88:8
Ramey, Estelle R.
    on gender differences, 144:20
    on women's rights, 258:22
Ramparts
    ⁓ of dead, 51:24
Rand, Ayn
    on humankind, 112:45
    on love, 140:79
Randall, James Ryder
    on Maryland, 146:9
Randolph, John
    invective, 122:8
    on character, 43:80
    on Constitution, 57:29
    on duty, 72:27
    on Edward Livingston, 122:8
    on elections, 75:15

    on equality, 79:18
    on freedom, 95:64
    on government, 101:111
    on journalism, 125:57
    on Martin Van Buren, 193:103
    on patriotism, 180:33
    on reform, 199:9
    on states' rights, 223:20
    on war, 245:72
    on wealth, 249:45
    Tristam Burges on, 122:2
Range
    home, home on the ⁓, 251:2
Rankin, Jeannette
    on war, 245:73, 245:74
Ransom, John Crowe
    on writing, 262:64
Rape
    can't commit ⁓ a little, 68:58
Raper, John W.
    on freedom, 95:65
Rascal
    turn ⁓s out!, 41:10
Rational
    man ⁓ animal, 43:58
Raven
    quoth ⁓, "Nevermore", 63:69
    there comes Poe, with his ⁓,
        262:55
Rayburn, Sam
    on Lyndon B. Johnson, 193:104
Reactionary
    doesn't go at all, 187:160
    somnambulist walking backward,
        187:127
Read
    books must be ⁓ as deliberately
        as written, 35:71
    dating new era in life from ⁓ing
        book, 35:72
    I ⁓ part of it all way through,
        99:3
    King George able to ⁓ that,
        14:44
    mind profits little by heavy ⁓ing,
        35:39
    no surer way to mis⁓ any
        document than to ⁓ it
        literally, 126:16
    people say life is thing, but I
        prefer ⁓ing, 35:66
    ⁓ best books first, 35:69
    ⁓ing, gymnast's struggle, 35:76
    ⁓ much, but not too many
        books, 35:35
    some who ⁓ too much, 35:58
    to be ⁓ after one's death cold
        comfort, 262:23
    when re⁓ classic you see more in
        you, 35:33
    where press is free, and every man
        able to ⁓, all is safe, 125:34

Roosevelt, Eleanor
  on death, 63:73
  on democracy and education,
    66:82
  on diplomacy, 68:54
  on Eisenhower-Nixon ticket,
    193:112
  on equality, 79:20
  on husband, 193:111
  on journalism, 125:59
  on peace, 181:31
  on politics, 187:125
  on United Nations, 68:53
Roosevelt, Franklin D.
  Alfred E. Smith on, 187:136,
    187:137
  campaign slogans, 41:26, 41:27
  Frances Perkins on, 193:101
  Harry S Truman on, 193:122
  Oliver Wendell Holmes, Jr., to,
    193:45
  on action, 1:17
  on Americans, 15:40
  on book banning, 35:64
  on bravery, 38:21
  on business and workers, 39:54
  on civil rights, 50:36
  on Constitution, 57:30, 57:31
  on democracy and economic
    security, 66:83, 66:84
  on destiny, 67:8
  on economics, 73:34–36
  on education, 74:85
  on fear, 87:20
  on freedom, 95:68, 95:69
  on Good Neighbor policy, 68:55
  on government, 101:118, 101:119
  on greatness, 102:41
  on labor, 131:50
  on liberty, 135:60
  on money, 157:53
  on national debt, 64:14, 64:15
  on Navy, 162:12
  on peace, 181:32
  on politics, 187:126, 187:127
  on poverty, 189:40, 189:41
  on power, 190:40
  on presidency, 192:33, 192:34
  on Prohibition repeal, 71:48
  on taxation, 227:21
  on Thanksgiving Day, 232:7
  on war, 245:77, 245:78
  on wealth, 249:48, 249:49
  on World War II, 261:26–29
  on youth, 264:39
  Westbrook Pegler on, 131:45
  wife on, 193:111
Roosevelt, Theodore
  bull moose statement, 193:113
  campaign slogan, 41:17
  Lincoln Steffens on, 193:117
  Mark Hanna on, 193:40

Oliver Wendell Holmes, Jr., on,
    193:44
  on action, 1:18–21
  on America, 12:88
  on Americans, 15:41–43
  on assassination potential, 193:114
  on business, 39:58, 39:59
  on Colorado, 52:6
  on corporations, 39:56, 39:57
  on democracy, 66:85, 66:86
  on diplomacy, 68:56
  on economics, 73:37
  on evil, 80:12
  on government, 101:120, 101:122,
    101:123
  on government ownership,
    101:121
  on journalism, 125:61
  on justice, 126:41
  on labor, 131:51
  on language, 132:46, 132:47
  on law, 134:92, 134:94
  on militarism, 152:16
  on monopolies, 39:55
  on muckraking, 125:60
  on Navy, 162:13–15
  on North Dakota, 173:7
  on own presidency, 192:36
  on pacifism, 180:35
  on Panama Canal, 134:93
  on patriotism, 180:36, 180:37
  on peace, 181:33, 181:34
  on politics, 187:128–131
  on presidency, 192:35, 192:37,
    192:38
  on prohibition, 71:49
  on religion, 200:152, 200:153
  on sex, 208:5
  on sports, 220:31
  on states' rights, 223:21
  on theft, 61:26
  on Thomas Paine, 200:152
  on war, 245:79–81
  on wealth, 29:9, 249:50
  on William Jennings Bryan, 177:12
  on wisdom, 256:29
  on work, 259:60, 259:61
  on World War I, 260:12–14
  Square Deal policy, 180:34
  William Allen White on,
    187:157, 193:134, 193:135
Rooster
  ~s lay eggs in Kansas, 127:4
Root, Elihu
  on labor, 131:52
Root, George Frederick
  on flag, 88:8
Roper, Jack
  on boxing, 220:32
Rose
  June, month of leaves and ~s,
    90:13

~ is a ~, 183:44
  ~ lives its little hour, 161:11
  white ~s please less than red,
    257:32
Rosen, Al
  on home run, 30:30
Rosewell, Rosey
  on home run, 30:31
Ross, Harold
  James Thurber on, 262:74
  Ogden Nash on, 138:43
  on *The New Yorker*, 125:62,
    138:52
Rossi, Alice
  on women's rights, 258:25
Rossner, Judith
  on bravery, 38:22
  on New Yorkers, 171:87
Rostow, Walt W.
  on life, 136:104
Rouge Bouquet
  in wood they call ~, new-made
    grave today, 260:7
Rough
  ~ land of earth, and stone and
    tree, 55:5
Roussel, Tom
  on football, 93:18
Rovere, Richard
  on politics, 187:132
Row
  ~ed to his objective with muffled
    oars, 193:103
Rowan, Carl T.
  on morality, 43:82
Rowland, Helen
  on love, 140:83
  on marriage, 140:84, 145:68
Royal, Darrell
  on football, 93:19
  on luck, 141:8
Royalist
  economic ~s complain, 73:35
Rubin, Jerry
  on fame, 84:25
  on life, 136:105
  on medicine, 148:17
  on New Yorkers, 171:88
  on power, 190:41
Rubinstein, Helena
  on beauty, 31:34
Ruckelshaus, Jill
  on argument, 22:15
  on men, 144:22
Rude
  no people so ~ as to be without
    politeness, 53:11
Ruffles
  ~ not mended will come in time
    to be lace, 70:9
Rug
  snug as bug in ~, 78:12

Sex *(cont'd)*

Indian neither more defective in
ardor, nor impotent than white,
13:5

in thousand of her not ⁓ appeal
enough to budge hermit, 257:89

liberated woman has ⁓ before
marriage and job after, 257:70

man cares most for, 208:6

poetry bill and coo of ⁓, 186:13

⁓ in America of feminine
mystique is strangely joyless,
208:3

⁓ roles and identity, 258:33

⁓ symbol becomes thing, 159:20

sexual revolution made ⁓
chaotically limitless, 208:1

turtle lives 'twixt plated decks
which practically conceal its ⁓,
19:16

woman's degradation man's idea
of his ⁓ual rights, 258:29

Seymour, Charles

on truth, 237:79

Shadow

as living ⁓s for moment seen on
eternal screen, 136:58

we are but ⁓s, 136:52

Shakespeare, William

could ⁓ give theory of ⁓, 138:14

give your rubbish to ⁓, he will
give it back in gold and stars,
97:10

injudicious in [Samuel] Johnson
to select ⁓ as one of principal
authorities, 262:83

not ten men in Boston equal to
⁓, 36:16

⁓, Madam, is obscene, 138:55

what sage has he not outseen?,
262:9

Shame

begun in anger ends in ⁓, 18:6

being poor no ⁓, but being
ashamed of it, is, 189:16

Shaw, George Bernard

on America, 16:35, 16:36

on Constitution, 57:34, 57:35

on dictators, 66:87

on elections, 66:88

on Hollywood, 159:29

Sheehy, Gail

on New York City, 171:91

Sheets

three ⁓ in wind, 71:12

Shell

leaving thine outgrown ⁓ by
life's unresting sea, 43:49

Shenandoah

gaunt shadow on your green, ⁓,
51:46

Oh, ⁓, I long to hear you, 212:4

Shepard, Alan

Tom Wolfe on, 217:13

Shepard, Jean

on radio, 229:6

Shepard, Odell

on Connecticut Yankee term,
55:8

Sheridan, Philip H.

on American Indians, 13:11

on Texas, 231:6

Thomas Buchanan Read on,
51:49

Sherman, John

on politics, 187:134

Sherman, William Tecumseh

on bravery, 38:24

on Civil War, 51:52–56

on friendship with Grant, 96:36

on presidency, 192:41, 192:42

on public opinion, 196:27

on war, 245:84–86

Sherwin, Louis

on Hollywood, 108:16

Shield

⁓ of freedom and of worth,
125:57

Shields, Ren

on summer, 225:6

Ship

don't give up ⁓, 162:10

never had as many ⁓s as nation
of such size needs, 162:13

O ⁓ of State, 12:73

sail, sail thy best, ⁓ of
Democracy, 12:116

⁓s that pass in night, 136:84

⁓ that is waiting for me, 63:28

whale ⁓ was my Yale College
and my Harvard, 74:77

when great gray ⁓s come in,
181:2

Shock

old to be amused rather than
⁓ed, 7:11

Shoot

nobody ⁓s at Santa Claus,
187:137

please do not ⁓ pianist, 52:2

⁓, if must, this old gray head,
88:9

Shopkeepers

governments of nations of ⁓
must keep shop also, 77:12

nation of ⁓, 77:3

Shot

⁓ heard round the world, 14:30

Show

I'm from Missouri, you've got to
⁓ me, 156:6

Shultz, George P.

on diplomacy, 68:57

on labor, 131:54

Sick

be not ⁓ too late, nor well too
soon, 105:12

⁓, civilized man six months
convalescing, ⁓ savage almost
half well again in day, 105:21

Sickness

⁓ is belief which must be
annihilated, 105:6

⁓, sin and death do not originate
in God, 200:37

Sidewalks

⁓ of New York, 171:17

Sights

have had enough of ⁓ and
shows, 235:31

Silence

observe moment of ⁓, like
deaf-mute who hit fingers with
hammer, 219:1

⁓ is still noise, 59:8

they think sound is more
manageable than ⁓, 219:11

white ⁓, 10:5

wisdom of ⁓, 234:6

Sill, Edward Rowland

on drinking, 71:51

Sills, Beverly

on happiness, 103:37

Silverman, Sime

on stock market crash, 73:38

on Wall Street, 171:92

Simcox, Carroll E.

on North Dakota, 173:8

Simple

are ⁓ answers, 193:106

⁓ man or ⁓ answer not enough,
193:9

to be ⁓ is to be great, 102:13

Simplicity

art of art is ⁓, 138:65

Simplify

life frittered away by detail . . .
⁓, 136:115

Sin, 209:1–41

biggest ⁓ is sitting on your ass,
209:25

can't take away that tendency to
⁓, ⁓, ⁓, 71:43

chose a ⁓ that's made people
happier, 209:31

depravities in New York, 171:56

duty of nations to confess their
⁓s, 209:27

every ⁓ result of collaboration,
209:5

fashions in ⁓ change, 209:18

he who never ⁓s can little boast,
209:39

highway of our virtue, 209:34

in Adam's Fall we ⁓ned all,
209:1

Smith, Hazel Brannon
    on journalism, 125:63
Smith, Langdon
    on evolution, 81:15
Smith, Lillian
    on education, 74:90
Smith, Liz
    on gossip, 100:10
Smith, Logan Pearsall
    on age, 7:70
    on ambition, 11:20
    on debt, 64:16
    on life, 136:111
    on reading, 35:66
    on weather, 250:16
    on writing, 262:67
Smith, Margaret Chase
    Senate membership, 54:4
Smith, Samuel Francis
    on America, 12:93
Smith, Sydney
    on America, 16:37
Smoke
    ~ and blood is mix of steel,
        39:60
    ~-filled room and decide
        nomination, 193:29
    witnesses may commit perjury,
        but ~ cannot, 237:46
SNAFU
    acronym, 25:1
Snivel
    I do not ~ that ~ that months
        are vacuums, 136:123
Snow
    announced by all trumpets of sky
        arrives ~, 254:2
    crossed and recrossed winged ~,
        254:10
    frolic architecture of ~, 254:3
    months of ~ make inhabitant of
        northern zones wiser and abler,
        250:2
    universe of sky and ~, 254:11
    wherever ~ falls there is civil
        freedom, 50:11, 211:18
Snow White
    used to be ~ but I drifted,
        45:7
Snug
    lies ~ as bug in rug, 78:12
Soap
    ~ and education not sudden as
        massacre, 74:96
Social
    America owes ~ prejudices to
        exaggerated religious opinions
        of sects establishing colonies,
        12:18
    children always chief victims of
        ~ chaos, 264:34

don't care to belong to any ~
    organization that will accept
    me as member, 211:34
for lifting everyone off ~
    bottom, 189:33
have to have ~ consciousness to
    take care of unfit, 211:35
nation that represses ~ problems
    with police power will become
    armed camp, 101:54
rioting leads to repression [not]
    ~ progress, 50:16
~ duties of gentleman are of
    high order, 211:5
~ virtue commonly virtue of pigs
    in litter, 211:40
Socialism
    degenerate capitalism of bankrupt
        capitalists, 187:97
    genuine object to get more money
        for its professors, 187:97
    ideal of ~ grand but cannot be
        manufactured, 211:22
    seems to be any government
        authority we do not like,
        101:127
    trend of Democracy is toward ~,
        187:3
Socialist Party
    campaign slogan, 41:22
Societies
    nation moving toward two ~,
        12:61
    ~ die from bottom to top,
        211:24

Society, 211:1–43
    Englishman shows no mercy to
        those below him as he looks for
        none from those above him,
        77:11
    every man under natural duty of
        contributing to necessities of
        ~, 50:21
    every ~ protects itself, 211:11
    every violation of truth stab at
        health of human ~, 237:17
    fine ~ is unprincipled decorum,
        211:16
    four hundred in New York ~,
        171:70
    genius does not seek high circles
        of ~, 97:29
    Grandes Dames at Metropolitan
        Opera, 171:33
    Great ~, 12:54
    high ~ for those who no longer
        have anything important to do,
        211:43
    in America everybody is, 15:46
    law of ~ is, each for all, 211:23
    mobile ~ [in New York City],
        171:18

mutual affection strongest link of
    new ~, 14:26
no man capable, without aid of
    ~, supplying own wants,
    211:36
of all cordials known, best is ~,
    211:20
ours is individualistic ~, 211:3
rational ~ informs mind,
    promotes health, 211:28
~ always diseased, and best most
    so, 211:41
~ frivolous, and shreds day into
    scraps, 211:14
~ in conspiracy against manhood
    of members, 211:9
~ in every state is blessing,
    101:98
~ is organism, not machine,
    211:22
~ like air, 211:38
~ loves what is conventional,
    211:12
~ never advances, 211:10
~ performs for itself almost
    everything ascribed to
    government, 101:103
~ that harpoons the conscience,
    211:4
~ wholesome for character,
    211:32
solitude impracticable, and ~
    fatal, 211:17
some things should never be
    mentioned in polite ~, 211:26
taxes, what we pay for civilized
    ~, 227:12
tendency to force ~ into only
    two classes, 211:39
those who hold and those without
    property have ever formed
    distinct interests in ~, 211:33
those who wallow in
    imperfections of ~ end up
    eroding restraints, 211:30
thoughts of best minds become
    last opinion of ~, 211:8
town that boasts inhabitants like
    me, 211:31
trailer park is Utopian ~, 211:42
without ~ men are never
    contented, 211:29
workers are saviors of ~, 131:11
worthless members of ~ think
    themselves most ill-used people,
    211:15
Soil
    precious ~, 8:2
Soldier
    as ~ prays for peace, must be
        prepared to cope with hardships
        of war, 245:101

Soldier *(cont'd)*

better to be ⁓'s widow than coward's wife, 25:6

faith which leads ⁓ to throw away his life to blindly accepted duty, 72:14

general of today should be ⁓ tomorrow, 25:13

glory lights ⁓'s tomb, 25:9

I am obliged to say, "This is the reason," and then he does it, 16:39

I should infallibly have been ⁓, 11:1

make every man ⁓, 152:8

man not raised to be ⁓ is not entitled to citizenship, 152:16

never have ⁓s been called upon to endure longer contact with vicious enemy, 261:6

old ⁓s never die, 25:19

O Lord our God, help to tear their ⁓s to bloody shreds, 245:95

show what good ⁓s, but also what good men, 25:28

⁓ applauded who refuses to serve in unjust war, 245:94

⁓, be strong, and hope for better things, 245:103

⁓ has hard life, 25:16

⁓ is slave, 25:12, 245:39

⁓'s last tattoo, 245:67

⁓s of America have killed more Americans than foreign foes, 25:11

when we assumed the ⁓, we did not lay aside the citizen, 25:27

Solitary

only ⁓ know full joys of friendship, 96:10

Solitude

great man in midst of crowd keeps independence of ⁓, 102:10

never found companion so companionable as ⁓, 96:41

⁓ as needful as society wholesome, 211:32

⁓ impracticable, and society fatal, 211:17

⁓ is needful to imagination, 58:7

⁓ is un-American, 12:58

Solvency

⁓ matter of temperament and not of income, 64:16

Song

deathless lust of ⁓, 212:10

glorious ⁓ of old, 48:8

good ⁓ ringing clear, 71:32

I breathed ⁓ into air, 96:31, 212:20

⁓ of mine is Song of Vine, 253:12

what is voice of ⁓, 212:17

Songs, 212:1–28

blues are ⁓ of despair, gospel ⁓ are ⁓ of hope, 212:18

care not who writes laws of country so long as I may listen to its ⁓, 212:23

⁓ are immortal, 212:13

⁓ have genealogies, 212:25

Sooners

origin of, 176:2

Sorrow, 213:1–20

being Negro means trying to smile when you want to cry, 34:12

every man has secret ⁓s, 213:12

every sufferer feels his secret ⁓ soothed, 160:7

lean ⁓ hardest to bear, 213:10

my ⁓, when she's here with me, 28:13

no such thing as old age; only ⁓, 7:76

O hearts that break and give no sign, 106:7

only in ⁓ bad weather masters us, 213:2

protest efforts to shield children and young people from death and ⁓, 264:4

sadness and longing resemble ⁓ as mist resembles rain, 213:14

⁓ for dead only ⁓ from which we refuse to be divorced, 213:8

⁓, great idealizer, 213:17

⁓ kept me from what I may accomplish yet, 213:15

when man has great ⁓, he should be indulged, 213:1

Sorry

I felt ⁓. John Wayne never felt ⁓, 243:4

Soul

art is stored honey of human ⁓, 26:6

belief consists in accepting affirmations of ⁓, 200:58

build thee more stately mansions, O my ⁓, 43:49

Cambridge ladies who live in furnished ⁓s, 147:5

can't weigh ⁓ with bar of pig iron, 131:21

every artist dips brush in own ⁓, 26:2

every thing has eternal ⁓, 117:20, 200:181

good for ⁓ work of ⁓, 259:64

great ⁓s are portions of eternity, 102:35

his ⁓ goes marching on, 212:9

in blind deep-buried roots of all men's ⁓s, 221:7

I pray thee Lord my ⁓ to keep, 200:1

large ⁓ will meet you as not having known you, 43:84

library is ⁓'s burial-ground, 35:6

Lord, help my poor ⁓, 133:34

lot worse to be ⁓-hungry than body-hungry, 74:5

love is open sesame to every human ⁓, 140:90

man is ⁓ informed by divine ideas, 112:2

man will prevail because he has a ⁓, 112:14

no necessity of ⁓ is free, 157:46

open ⁓ and open door, 12:74

rather see America save her ⁓ than her face, 243:49

⁓ is dead that slumbers, 136:78

theological problems are ⁓'s mumps, 200:54

this was prison which his ⁓ looked through, 63:32

times that try men's ⁓s, 14:66

to give up interest wrinkles ⁓, 7:57

Soule, John L.B.

on the West, 251:13

Sound

I ⁓ my barbaric yawp over roofs of world, 185:36

Sounds

all ⁓ of earth are like music, 160:8

South, The, 214:1–6

did not come to ⁓ with vindictiveness in heart, 193:136

Faulkner makes great differerence in what writer can and cannot do, 262:60

in ⁓ war is what A.D. is elsewhere, 214:5

O magnet-⁓!, 214:6

⁓, poor ⁓!, 133:13

throughout Old ⁓ "Connecticut Yankee" came to be pronounced "Damyank", 55:8

South Carolina, 215:1–9

aristocratic to degree which I cannot approve, 215:5

faults of state personal as wart on his nose, 215:3

have no secret envy of Virginians, 215:2

secession from Union, 51:1

state motto, 215:1

taught to be Ca-ro-li-ni-ans, 215:6

too small for republic and too large for lunatic asylum, 215:8

South Dakota, 216:1–9
always carry laughter in their throats, 216:5
Bad Lands like work of evil child, 216:9
Black Hills, region of fabulous wealth, 216:7
hard work legacy of generations who settled prairie, 216:2
looking for sign rest of world knew we existed, 216:3
nation's urban majority don't understand place like ⁓, 216:8
part of hell with fires burnt out, 216:6
⁓'s people grandest crop she grows, 216:4
state motto, 216:1
Southerner
⁓s are a mythological people, 214:1
⁓s can never resist a losing cause, 214:4
⁓ talks music, 219:26
Southey, Robert
on American character, 16:38
South Vietnam. *See* Vietnam
Souvenir
Americans fought for ⁓s, 260:16
Sovereign
contracts between nation and individuals only binding on conscience of ⁓, 101:51
gross error to confound exercise of ⁓ powers with ⁓ty itself, 101:14
majority held by constitutional checks is only true ⁓ of free people, 66:65
⁓s who seize whole body of people produce calamities of long duration, 66:38
word ⁓ty not in Constitution, 223:17
Soviet Union (*See also* Russia)
offered to trade apple for orchard, 68:33
people driven by fear of ⁓, 87:23
policy toward ⁓ must be long-term containment, 68:31
⁓ can choose either confrontation or cooperation, 68:9
Sow
were we directed from Washington when to ⁓ would soon want bread, 8:11
who ⁓s field is more than all, 8:23
Space
casting thin thread across ⁓, 217:3

every inch of ⁓ is miracle, 183:49
nothing to be conquered but pure ⁓, 235:9
passengers on little ⁓ship, 188:12
Space Exploration, 217:1–12
right stuff not bravery, 217:11
Spanish-American War, 218:1–13
God Almighty's war, 218:4
God takes care of drunken men, sailors, and the United States, 218:3
measures to secure full and final termination, 218:12
splendid little war, 218:6
Speak
before every free conscience in America is subpoenaed, please ⁓ up, 95:28
discover new side to intimate friend when hears him ⁓ in public, 96:37
hear no ill of friend, nor ⁓ any of enemy, 100:4
if man is fool, encourage him to advertise fact by ⁓ing, 219:33
man cannot ⁓ but judges himself, 177:4
nor ⁓ with double tongue, 4:15
⁓ clearly, if you ⁓ at all, 59:21
⁓ for yourself, John?, 219:19
⁓ little, do much, 219:10
⁓ softly and carry big stick, 68:56
teach child to hold tongue, he'll learn fast enough to ⁓, 4:21
think twice before you ⁓ and then say it to yourself, 59:23
use no hurtful deceit and ⁓ accordingly, 4:33
when I ⁓ my native tongue, Englishman can't understand me, 219:25
when you ⁓ to man, look on his eyes, 59:17
will learn to ⁓ better from women and children, 132:30
Speaker
in Hollywood, if didn't sing or dance, end up as after-dinner ⁓, 108:15
Speech, 219:1–33 (*See also* Free speech; Language; Oratory)
Edward Everett on brevity of Gettysburg Address, 137:12
ever "made light" of his remarks, more than he ever made of them, 122:9
flawless imperfection of New Yorker, 171:79
freedom of ⁓ in Congress, 54:1

function of ⁓ to free men from bondage of irrational fears, 95:11
good policy to leave few things unsaid, 237:34
learn how much he has lived through poverty or splendor of his ⁓, 132:11
man will be eloquent if you give him good wine, 253:3
music that can deepest reach is cordial ⁓, 59:14
no man ever made great ⁓ on mean subject, 177:3
poppycock gabblers in Congress, 54:61
sharp tongue only tool grows keener with constant use, 122:5
spartans, stoics, heroes, saints and gods use short and positive ⁓, 219:8
⁓es measured by hour, die with hour, 177:10
⁓ is twin of my vision, 219:29
well done is better than well said, 1:5
Yankee schoolmarms responsible for Eastern states nasal accent, 165:8
Spell
never ⁓ word wrong, 4:37
Spelling
bad ⁓ is generally best, conforming to sound, 132:19
simplified ⁓, like chastity, can carry it too far, 45:5
who cares about ⁓?, 138:5
Spencer, Herbert
on Pittsburgh (Pa.), 182:15
Spend
ask that Fortune send *little* more than I shall ⁓, 103:18
Sphinx
⁓ must solve own riddle, 107:15
Spider
everything belonging to ⁓ is admirable, 19:6
Spinster
old maids rush in where widows fear to tread, 145:49
Spire
bead with fire every ragged roof and ⁓, 46:12
city of ⁓s, 171:106, 171:107
fret with ⁓s western sky, 46:24
Spirit
dignity and beauty of man rests in human ⁓, 112:43
every ⁓ makes its house, 109:14
sporting ⁓ is ⁓ of Chicago, 46:20

Steinbeck, John _(cont'd)_
  on Oklahoma, 176:12
  on own writing, 262:70
  on San Francisco (Calif.), 206:9
  on Seattle (Wash.), 248:7
  on South Dakota, 216:9
  on Texas, 231:7
  on travel, 235:29
  on Wisconsin, 255:4
Steinberg, Saul
  on baseball, 30:32
Steinem, Gloria
  on childbirth, 257:73
  on families, 85:17
  on men, 258:32
  on men and women, 258:31
  on power, 190:43
  on revolution, 204:28
  on women, 257:69–72
  on women's rights, 258:33,
    258:34
Steiner, George
  on music, 160:25
Stengel, Casey
  on baseball, 30:33, 30:34,
    30:36–38
  on his retirement, 30:35
Step
  one small ⌐ for man, 217:2
  ⌐ by ⌐, see steady gain of man,
    195:36
Stephens, Alexander H.
  on Abraham Lincoln, 137:48
  on slavery, 210:56
Stephenson, Ralph
  on New York City, 171:95
Sterility
  wilful ⌐ sin for which penalty is
    national death, 208:5
Sterling, Andrew B.
  song by, 212:27
Steuben, Friedrich Wilhelm von
  on Americans, 16:39
Stevens, Thaddeus
  on American government, 12:95
  on Congress, 54:56
  on government, 101:126
Stevens, Wallace
  on beauty, 31:38
  on books, 35:67, 35:68
  on death, 63:77
  on history, 107:64
  on music, 160:26
  on poet, 185:31
  on poetry, 186:27
Stevenson, Adlai E.
  campaign slogans, 41:30, 41:32,
    41:33
  on advice, 4:49
  on age, 7:71
  on America, 12:96, 12:97
  on Americans, 15:47

  on democracy, 66:93
  on diplomacy, 68:59–62
  on elections, 75:17, 75:18
  on evil, 80:13
  on freedom, 95:72–76
  on journalism, 125:65, 125:66
  on justice, 126:43
  on nonconformity, 183:45
  on nuclear age, 174:16, 174:17
  on own and Lincoln's election
    defeat, 137:49
  on patriotism, 180:41
  on peace, 181:36, 181:37
  on politics, 187:140, 187:141
  on pollution, 188:12
  on power, 190:44
  on progress, 195:30
  on Richard Nixon, 193:118
  on socialism, 101:127
  on technology, 228:5
  on television, 229:7
  on truth, 237:80
  on tyranny, 238:27
  on wisdom, 256:31
  own belief, 32:16
Stevenson, Robert Louis
  on American nomenclature, 16:40
  on Nebraska, 163:8
  on Wyoming Black Hills, 263:9
Stewart, Potter
  on journalism, 125:67
Stick
  speak softly and carry big ⌐,
    68:56
Stimson, Henry L.
  on nuclear age, 174:18
  on sin, 209:32
Stink
  fish & visitors ⌐ in three days,
    235:14
  shines and ⌐s like rotten
    mackerel by moonlight, 122:8
Stockbridge, Frank Parker
  on Wisconsin, 255:5
Stockings
  ⌐ hung by chimney with care,
    48:7
Stock market
  autumn of 1929 was first occasion
    when men succeeded on large
    scale in swindling themselves,
    39:34
  October one of peculiarly
    dangerous months to speculate
    in ⌐, 39:65
Stoddard, Richard Henry
  on Abraham Lincoln, 137:50
Stolberg, Benjamin
  on death, 63:78
Stomach
  sentiments and emotions reside in
    ⌐, 106:1

  way to man's heart is through his
    ⌐, 140:32
  why so much trouble to keep ⌐
    full and quiet?, 20:7
Stone
  live by squeezing from a ⌐,
    257:88
  no sermons in ⌐s, 161:12
Stonewall
  Thomas Jackson's nickname, 51:5
  want you all to ⌐ it, cover-up or
    anything, 193:92
Stong, Phil
  on Iowa, 124:3, 124:4
Stood
  let that which ⌐ in front go
    behind, 42:23
Stop
  ⌐ and smell flowers, 4:35
Storm
  gigantic ⌐-wind of equinox,
    250:10
  in tumultuous privacy of ⌐,
    254:2
  they sicken of calm, who knew
    the ⌐, 250:13
Story, Joseph
  on journalism, 125:68
  on law, 134:96
  on politics, 187:142
Stowe, Harriet Beecher
  on beauty, 31:39
  on business, 39:62
  on death, 63:79, 63:80
  on destiny, 67:9
  on dress, 70:15
  on Kentuckians, 128:10
  on sin, 209:33
  on slavery, 210:57
  on superstition, 32:17
Straus, Oscar Solomon
  on Jews, 15:48
Stream
  mountain-⌐ that ends in mud is
    melancholy, 17:14
  ⌐ is brightest at its spring, 17:21
  ⌐ of consciousness, 183:29
Streisand, Barbra
  on success, 224:37
Strength
  ⌐en me by sympathizing with
    my ⌐, 3:2
Strife
  our ⌐ pertains to ourselves,
    51:37
Strike
  glad to see system under which
    laborers can ⌐, 131:36
  no right to ⌐ against public
    safety, 131:9
  nothing confers absolute right to
    ⌐, 131:6

if we start winning games we'll
have ∼, 93:12

in any other city [than
Hollywood] I'd rate as possibly
adequate night watchman,
108:8

knowing what you can *not* do,
226:1

most extraordinary collection of
∼ ever gathered at White
House, 193:78

never see frog so modest, for all
he was so gifted, 113:35

New York attracts most ∼ed,
171:69

please do not shoot pianist, 52:2

society does nominally estimate
men by their ∼s but knows
them by their characters, 43:85

∼ alone cannot make writer,
262:10

∼ finds its models, methods, and
ends in society, 97:7

took me fifteen years to discover I
had no ∼ for writing, 262:3

true ∼ delights the possessor
first, 226:2

Talk

bore ∼s when you wish him to
listen, 59:6

don't care how much man ∼s, if
he only says it in few words,
59:7

[English] ∼ because they think
sound more manageable than
silence, 219:11

everybody ∼s about weather,
250:20

form habit of good ∼, 59:18

hardly behooves any of us to ∼
about rest of us, 100:1

if we are to live together we have
to ∼, 68:54

more wit and insight dropped in
∼ than get into books, 219:7

Southerner ∼s music, 219:26

∼ing like playing on harp, 219:14

∼ing not better than not ∼ing
when do not know what going
to ∼ about, 68:48

∼ low, ∼ slow, and don't say
too much, 159:34

∼, to commit indiscretion
without temptation, 219:3

war ∼ by men who have been in
war always interesting, 59:32

when we ∼ about ourselves we
use Latin words, 219:2

you may ∼ of all subjects save
your maladies, 59:15

Talmadge, Constance

on motion pictures, 159:31

Tammany Hall

offices will be held by politicians,
187:27

∼ bears same relation to
penitentiary as Sunday-school to
church, 171:53

Taney, Roger Brooke

on slavery, 210:61

Taos (New Mexico)

at fiesta I saw ∼ man, 168:3

Tar heel

I'm ∼ born, bred, dead, 172:4

Tariff

farmer entitled to ∼, 8:1

mother of all trusts is ∼ law,
39:36

protects domestic producer against
greed of consumer, 227:3

Tarkenton, Fran

on football, 93:20

Tarkington, Booth

on drinking, 71:52

on science, 207:32

Tarzan

I am ∼. You are Jane,
140:13

Task

gilding of hard ∼, 8:8

hardest ∼ to think, 259:13

Taste

no one ever went broke
underestimating ∼ of
American public, 196:17

∼s like wrath to come,
253:2

world lacks ear of ∼, 212:17

Taught

not what you do for your
children but have ∼ them to
do for themselves, 74:63

Tavern

there is ∼ in town, 212:6

Tax

beggar is ∼ed for corner to die
in, 227:17

idleness and pride ∼ with heavier
hand than kings and
parliaments, 227:7

[no] foreign product enters
country un∼ed except answer
to prayer, 227:24

power to ∼ involves power to
destroy, 227:18

power to ∼ not power to destroy,
227:13

∼ing industry of fellow citizens
to accumulate treasures for
wars, 227:15

∼ upon land values is most just
and equal, 227:9

we will spend and spend, and ∼
and ∼, 75:12

Taxation, 227:1–27

driven by fear of income tax,
87:23

for law enforcement, 227:23

got so much ∼, 227:24

more moolah, quicker go in
higher bracket, 227:19

must not repress industry, 227:11

must not take what rightfully
belongs to individuals, 227:10

no right to put their hands into
my pocket, 227:27

purse of people real seat of
sensibility, 227:14

∼ without representation is
tyranny, 227:20

what a man honestly acquired
cannot be taken without his
consent, 227:2

Taxes

collecting more ∼ than necessary
is legalized robbery, 227:4

men least willing to pay ∼,
227:6

my compassion goes to millions
[who] pay exorbitant ∼,
227:21

no ∼ be imposed but with
people's consent, 227:1

nothing certain, except death and
∼, 227:8

paid in sweat of every man who
labors, 227:21

should be continued by annual or
biennial reenactments, 227:16

thing generally raised on city land
is ∼, 227:25

what we pay for civilized society,
227:12

Taylor, Bayard

on character, 43:83

Taylor, Bert Leston

on bores, 59:30

on poverty, 189:42

Taylor, Edward Thompson

last words, 133:36

Taylor, Maxwell B.

on military, 25:26

Taylor, Tom

on Abraham Lincoln, 137:51

Taylor, Zachary

on Kentucky, 128:11

Tea

Boston ∼ Party, 14:4

I smile, of course, and go on
drinking ∼, 264:13

Teach

natural that childhood should
inquire, and maturity ∼,
74:35

no ∼ing until pupil brought into
same state you are, 74:34

Teacher
> art of ~ to awaken joy in creative expression and knowledge, 74:31
> good ~ transcends accepted educational methods, 74:76
> I could be efficient pupil if it were possible to find efficient ~, 74:91
> parents right to say no ~ paid by their money shall rob children of faith, 74:17
> ~ affects eternity, 74:6
> ~'s life should have three periods, 74:80
> true ~ defends his pupils against his own personal influence, 74:8

Tear
> have come way that with ~s has been watered, 34:11
> Hell's afloat in lovers' ~s, 140:74
> no ~s in writer, no ~s in reader, 262:20
> so weary of toil and of ~s, 234:7
> wonder at idleness of ~s, 136:103

Teasdale, Sara
> on beauty, 31:40

Technological
> ~ powers increase, but side effects and hazards escalate, 188:13

Technology, 228:1–8
> America's ~ has turned in upon itself, 228:3
> great, growling engine of change——~, 228:6
> not yet learned to make sensible use of it, 228:2
> science and ~ revolutionize our lives, 42:18
> ~ and military systems threaten our survival, 228:1
> ~ feeds on itself, 228:7
> ~ throws daily another loop of fine wire around our souls, 228:5

Teeth
> Adam and Eve escaped ~ing, 6:9
> chaw terbacker to keep ~ white, 105:15

Telegraph
> attention, the universe, 123:12
> what hath God wrought, 123:14

Telephone
> ~, invention of devil, 123:3

Television
> chewing gum for the eyes, 229:10
> created aura of defeat [Vietnam], 243:50

> great journalistic tool for future, 229:1
> has more power than any of us know, 229:5
> nation glued to ~ screen isn't having good time, 229:7
> not so effective as in 1952, 229:4
> pollutes identity, 229:2
> vast wasteland, 229:3
> when ~ bad, nothing is worse, 229:3

Television & Radio, 229:1–10
Tell
> always ~ Yankee; but cannot ~ him much, 15:24

Teller, Edward
> on nuclear age, 174:19, 174:20

Temperament
> ~ is fate from whose jurisdiction its victims hardly escape, 43:3

Temperance (*See also* Prohibition)
> enactment of measures as will promote ~, 71:3
> father, dear father, come home with me now, 71:61
> great social and economic experiment, 71:31
> I prefer ~ hotels—although they sell worse liquor than any other kind, 71:56
> prohibition will work great injury to cause of ~, 71:37

Temptation
> not great ~s that ruin us, 209:6
> same name to woman's lack of ~ and man's lack of opportunity, 43:13
> should be judged but by ~s, 209:21
> surest protection against ~ is cowardice, 60:8

Ten Commandments
> public opinion nearly as strong as ~, 196:31
> sure in short space to be mumbling our ~, 200:55

Tender
> tough mind and ~ heart, 4:44

Tennessee, 230:1–7
> breakfast in east ~ is jug of good corn liquor, 230:5
> government ruined finest settlement of moonshiners in U.S.A., 230:6
> journalism too stirring for me, 230:7
> lives are unhurried, 230:2
> one place worth living in, and that's Middle ~, 230:3
> state motto, 230:1

Tennis
> five basic words in ~, 220:19
> ~ player is complete athlete, 220:29

Tent
> fold their ~s, like Arabs, 3:8
> strike the ~, 133:29

Terrible
> most ~ thing ever discovered, 174:22

Territory
> ~ is only part [of nation] which is of certain durability, 101:89

Terror
> thrilled me—filled me with fantastic ~s never felt before, 87:17
> what tale of ~, their turbulency tells, 87:18

Texas, 231:1–7
> a state of mind, 231:7
> could wear Rhode Island as watch fob, 231:5
> if man's from ~, he'll tell you, 231:4
> if owned ~ and Hell, would rent out ~ and live in Hell, 231:6
> John L. O'Sullivan on annexation of, 251:12
> Montana what small boy would think ~ like, 158:8
> Oklahoma most resembles, 176:5
> resolution for statehood, 231:3
> state motto, 231:1

Thackeray, William Makepeace
> on New Orleans (La.), 169:5

Thank
> ~ everybody for making this day necessary, 33:7

Thanksgiving, 232:1–11
> Abraham Lincoln Proclamation, 232:6
> Franklin D. Roosevelt Proclamation, 232:7
> from East and from West, come pilgrim and guest, 232:9
> George Washington Proclamation, 232:8
> heap high the board with plenteous cheer, 232:2
> hurrah for pumpkin pie, 232:4
> open up turkey's butt and fork out peas, 232:5
> to grandfather's house we go, 232:3
> who sighs for dainties far away?, 232:10
> with hearts of thankfulness keep ~, 232:11

Thayer, Ernest Lawrence
> Casey at the bat, 30:39, 30:40

Truth *(cont'd)*
~ is America's most potent
weapon, 237:64
~ is given eternal years of God,
237:75
~ is jewel which should not be
painted over, 237:78
"~ is mighty and will prevail"
most majestic compound
fracture of fact, 237:85
~ is one forever, absolute,
237:72
~ is tough, 237:31
~ law of annihilation to
everything unlike, 237:14
~ lies at end of circle, 237:37
~ most valuable thing we have,
237:89
~ must be suppressed, 237:12
~ never loses by [inquiry],
237:71
~ never yet fell dead in streets,
237:69
~ not diet but condiment, 237:62
~ only reached by expression of
free opinions, 135:76
~ passes through four distinct
stages, 237:35
~ silliest thing under sun, 237:59
~ sometimes poor competitor,
237:44
~ stands test of experience, 237:15
~ stood on one side and ease on
other, 237:70
~ stranger than Fiction because
Fiction obliged to stick to
possibilities, 237:91
~ stranger than fiction—to some
people, 237:90
~ summit of being, 237:18
~ survives, un~ perishes, 237:77
~ wears different face to
everybody, 237:56
we search world for ~, 200:186
when in doubt tell ~, 237:88
who dares to say he alone has
found ~?, 237:50
who finds a ~ lights torch,
237:38
who sees ~, let him proclaim it,
237:28
who speaks ~ stabs falsehood to
heart, 237:53
wit has ~ in it, 113:29
Try
above all, ~ something, 1:17
Tubman, Harriet
on liberty, 135:67
Tuchman, Barbara
on best-selling books, 138:56
on history, 107:70, 107:71
on honor, 183:47

Tucker, Benjamin R.
on economics, 73:40
on tyranny, 238:28
Tucker, Sophie
on women, 257:75
Tugwell, Rexford Guy
on contentment, 253:17
Tulsa (Okla.)
as sensitive as corduroy, 176:7
Tumult
cause of liberty, cause of too
much dignity to be sullied by
~, 14:27
Tune
why should Devil have all the
good ~s, 160:1
Turn
~ rascals out, 41:10
Turner, Frederick Jackson
on the West, 251:14
Turtle
clever of ~ to be so fertile, 19:16
Twain, Mark
epitaph for daughter, 78:21
Ernest Hemingway on, 138:24
humor example, 113:35
invective, 122:10, 122:11
last words, 133:38
Lincoln of our literature, 262:40
on advice, 4:56–58
on affliction, 6:9
on America, 12:100, 12:101
on American Indians, 13:15
on American regional differences,
12:102
on anger, 18:13
on ants, 19:21
on argument, 22:18
on Arkansas, 24:6
on art, 26:55
on avarice, 29:10
on Baton Rouge (La.) State
Capitol building, 139:14
on beauty, 31:41
on belief, 32:18–20
on Boston (Mass.), 36:34
on bravery, 38:27
on California, 40:26
on change, 42:20, 42:21
on chastity, 45:5
on Chicago (Ill.), 46:21, 46:22
on conduct, 53:23, 53:24
on Congress, 54:59, 54:60
on conversation, 59:32
on cowardice, 60:8
on crime, 61:27
on death, 63:81, 63:82
on dogs, 19:20
on domesticity, 109:37
on drinking, 71:54, 71:55
on duty, 72:30, 72:31
on education, 74:96–98

on England, 77:40
on evolution, 81:17
on experience, 82:17
on fame, 84:28
on families, 85:18
on folly, 91:9–11
on freedom, 95:80
on friends, 96:43, 96:44
on happiness, 103:40
on Hartford (Conn.), 55:9
on Hawaii, 104:8, 104:9
on health, 105:24
on Henry Ward Beecher, 8:17,
200:162
on humankind, 112:57–60
on humor, 113:36, 113:37
on ignorance, 129:18
on journalism, 125:73–75
on justice, 126:47, 126:48
on language, 132:53–55
on life, 136:118–120
on literary criticism, 138:57
on literature, 138:58–60
on luck, 141:9
on marriage, 145:73
on Mississippi River, 155:5–9
on Nevada, 164:5, 164:6
on New England, 165:13
on New Orleans (La.), 169:6
on own death, 63:83
on own writing, 262:79,
262:80
on peace of mind, 58:11
on poetry, 186:32
on politics, 187:149
on progress, 195:33
on reform, 199:10
on religion, 200:163, 200:164
on St. Louis (Mo.), 156:5
on Salt Lake City (Utah), 239:8,
239:9
on San Francisco (Calif.), 206:10,
206:11
on Satan, 80:15
on sex, 208:6
on slavery, 210:63–65
on speech, 219:25–27
on statesman, 222:11, 222:13
on statesmanship, 222:12
on stock market, 39:65
on success, 224:39
on taxation, 227:24
on Tennessee, 230:7
on the South, 214:5
on travel, 235:31–33
on truth, 237:85–92
on Wagner's music, 160:30
on war, 245:95
on Washington (D.C.), 247:9
on wealth, 249:59
on weather, 250:17–19
on whiskey, 253:18

on wisdom, 256:38

on work, 259:70–72

on writing, 262:77, 262:78

on youth, 264:41

Tweed, William Marcy (Boss)

on elections, 75:20

on power, 190:46

Twig

~ is so easily bended, 74:28

Twist

~ slowly, slowly, 187:34

Tyler, John

campaign slogans, 41:1, 41:2

Tyler, John, Jr.

on Ulysses S. Grant, 51:58

Type

Lincoln was not ~, 137:17

Typewriter

~ is public trust, 125:66

Tyrannical

"you work and toil and earn bread, and I'll eat it" is ~ principle, 238:18

Tyranny, 238:1–30

all hereditary government is in its nature ~, 101:99

all powers in same hands, definition of ~, 238:21

brings ignorance and brutality, 238:24

enlighten people and ~ will vanish, 238:15

eternal enmity to ~, 238:6

evils of ~ seen by him who resists it, 238:7

from extreme of anarchy to extreme of ~, 238:29

have sworn eternal hostility against every form of ~, 238:14

history of oppressed people is hidden in lies and myths of its conquerors, 107:46

masses of men exhibit their ~, 66:17

moment man says, "Give up your rights, here is money," there is ~, 238:4

normal pattern of government, 238:27

no ~ so despotic as that of public opinion, 196:21

no ~ so hateful as vulgar and anonymous ~, 238:26

power of pronouncing statute unconstitutional barrier against ~, 57:36

time to guard against ~ is before gotten hold, 238:11

~ and anarchy incompatible with freedom, 238:17

~, like hell, not easily conquered, 238:25

~ of Britain received repulse, 14:70

~ of legislatures, 54:26

ye that dare oppose ~ stand forth, 14:65

Tyrant

doctrines most fearful ~s to which men subject, 245:90

every ~ believed in freedom—for himself, 238:8

fear that reigns with ~, 238:19

how hard ~s die, 238:9

limits of ~s prescribed by endurance of those whom they oppress, 135:15

man capable of self-government, and only rendered otherwise by acts of ~s, 238:16

to ~s will give no quarter nor waste arguments, 238:5

~ can arrange that most trouble happens to other people, 238:23

~s take warning, 14:34

who endeavors to control mind by force is ~, 238:10

world of morons and natural ~s, 238:2

worst ~s those in our own breasts, 238:1

Udall, Stewart L.

on American Indians, 13:16

Ugliness

secret of ~ consists in being uninteresting, 31:14

Ugly

no ~ women, only lazy ones, 31:34

Unattained

how vast the ~, 83:10

Uncle Sam

done give myself to ~, 25:5

Uncommon

~ commoner, 137:7

Unconditional

~ and immediate surrender, 51:19

Understanding

enables one to know house from horse, 183:9

Undertaker

even ~ will be sorry, 136:118

Underwood, Oscar W.

on law, 134:105

Unemployed

~ purchasing power means ~ labor, 131:57

Union

[Civil War] not salvation of ~, rebirth of ~, 51:64

do not expect ~ to be dissolved, 210:40

extinguish resentments if expect harmony and ~, 51:44

federal ~; must be preserved, 180:24

government of ~ is emphatically government of the people, 66:73

hopes of long continuance of this ~ extinct, 223:1

if do not make common cause to save ship of ~, 51:32

if ~ is dissolved, I shall return to my native state, 51:27

indestructible ~, composed of indestructible States, 12:16

interests of state give way to interests of ~, 223:7

join ourselves to no party that does not keep step to music of the ~, 180:8

liberty and ~, one and inseparable, 135:70

no greater calamity than dissolution of ~, 51:26

not Nation, but ~, 223:5

paramount allegiance to whole ~, 223:6

paramount object is to save ~, 51:35

sail on, O ~, strong and great, 12:73

true friends of ~ would make federal not national ~, 223:8

true nationality of ~ fervid and tremendous Idea, 12:114

~ older than any of the States, 223:18

~ perfect, 14:29

~ preserved thus far by miracles, 57:26

~ restored as it was, but if we can't, I'm in favor of ~ as it wasn't, 51:59

~ shall be preserved, 12:48

was saved the ~ of these states, 137:57

what were states before ~?, 223:2

with Lincoln ~ rose to sublimity, 137:48

with mother country only on principles of liberty, 14:13

Unions. *See* Trade union

Union Square

George Washington sits his iron horse at corner of ~, 171:43

Unite

be ~d among yourselves and you will want nothing from rest of world, 118:2

United Nations
　Eleanor Roosevelt on, 68:53
United States
　~ has to move very fast to even
　　stand still, 12:60
Uniting
　by ~ we stand, 14:28
Unity
　mutual affection will preserve us
　　in ~, 14:26
Universe
　if anything in me of permanent
　　worth, ~ will know how to
　　preserve it, 117:3
　man takes this whole ~ for vast
　　practical joke, 136:91
　~ is all chemistry, 86:6
　~ is stairway leading nowhere,
　　117:16
　~ so aptly fitted to our
　　organization, 161:66
Universities
　~ largely gifts of very rich
　　handed back to middle class,
　　74:64
University
　best ~ is gauntlet of mob,
　　74:40
　if cannot state matter so that
　　intelligent twelve-year-old can
　　understand it, one should
　　remain within ~, 74:75
　last thing ~ should be concerned
　　with is being number one in
　　football or basketball, 74:25
　three major problems are sex for
　　students, athletics for alumni,
　　and parking for faculty, 74:62
　~ will not crusade for anything
　　except freedom of learning,
　　74:23
　use of ~ to make young
　　gentlemen unlike their fathers,
　　74:101
　who enters ~ walks on hallowed
　　ground, 74:24
University of Virginia
　Thomas Jefferson on, 200:120
Unknown
　how far ~ transcends what we
　　know, 63:58
Unrest
　fierce ~ seethes at core of all
　　existing things, 11:18
　~ of spirit is mark of life,
　　136:95
Unsaid
　good policy to leave a few things
　　~, 237:34
Up
　be nice to people on way ~,
　　224:32

Updike, John
　on America, 12:103, 12:104
　on life, 136:121
　on San Francisco (Calif.), 206:12
Utah, 239:1–12
　always had way of doing things
　　different, 239:2
　most staid and respectable of
　　states, 164:4
　only place in world where Jews
　　are Gentiles, 239:5
　splendid musicians there, 239:12
　state motto, 239:1
　water in ~ is precious, 239:3

Vacant
　no fireside but has one ~ chair,
　　63:51
Vacation
　mothers and housewives great
　　~less class, 257:51
Vail, Alfred
　telegraph message, 123:14
Valor
　dream not helm and harness sign
　　of ~ true, 181:49
　uncommon ~ was common
　　virtue, 261:23
Value
　dearness gives every thing ~,
　　238:25
　try to become man of ~, 224:10
　~ of thing is amount of laboring
　　its possession will save
　　possessor, 73:17
Van Buren, Abigail
　on advice, 4:59
　on character, 43:91
　on religion, 200:165
Van Buren, Martin
　campaign slogan, 41:4
　John Quincy Adams on, 193:6
　John Randolph on, 193:103
　on Andrew Jackson, 193:131
　on own presidency, 193:130
Vanderbilt, Amy
　on manners, 109:38
Vanderbilt, Cornelius
　on own business, 39:66
　on power, 190:47
Vanderbilt, William H.
　on politics, 187:150
　on railroads, 39:67
　on the public, 196:30
Vanderbilt, William K.
　on ambition, 11:22
　on wealth, 249:60
Vanderlip, Frank
　on money, 157:61
Vandiver, Willard D.
　on Missouri, 156:6

Van Doren, Mark
　on wit, 113:38
Van Dyke, Henry
　on America, 12:105
　on home, 109:39
　on religion, 200:166
　on success, 224:40
　on work, 259:73
Van Horne, Harriet
　on cooking, 92:13
Vanity
　only one ~: give advice better
　　than any other, 4:57
　wounded ~ knows when it is
　　mortally hurt, 43:53
Van Loon, Hendrik Willem
　on history, 107:72
　on progress, 195:34
Vanzetti, Bartolomeo
　on own death sentence, 126:49
Vaulting
　~ the sea, 171:22
Veblen, Thorstein
　on wealth, 249:61
Veeck, Bill
　on baseball, 30:41, 30:42
　on lawyers, 134:106, 134:107
　on sports, 220:33
Vegetarianism
　destiny of human race to leave off
　　eating animals, 195:32
Venus de Milo
　when archaeologists discover
　　missing arms of ~, 145:8
Verb
　nouns and ~s are almost pure
　　metal, 132:20
　~al contract isn't worth paper
　　written on, 99:6
Vermont, 240:1–11
　as Maine goes, so goes ~,
　　142:4
　bows to nothing, 240:7
　brave little state of ~, 240:6
　country unto itself, 240:3
　frost-clear, blue-nooned,
　　apple-ripening days, 240:5
　jewel state, small but precious,
　　240:4
　my heart is there with thee,
　　240:10
　no populous towns, seaports, or
　　large manufactories to collect
　　people together, 240:11
　no ~er ever left state unless
　　transportation was furnished in
　　advance, 240:9
　state motto, 240:1
　to specify each locality in ~
　　possessing attractions would
　　require description of each
　　town, 240:2

Wet
    keep your mouth ⁓, feet dry,
      4:20
    let's get out of ⁓ clothes into
      dry martini, 71:9
Whale
    all men live enveloped in ⁓-lines,
      136:92
    vulturism of earth from which
      not mightiest ⁓ is free, 161:59
    ⁓ ship was my Yale College and
      my Harvard, 74:77
Whalen, Grover A.
    on law, 134:111
Wharton, Edith
    on age, 7:76
    on duty, 72:33
    on women and culture, 257:80
Wheat
    first in freedom, first in ⁓,
      127:3
    wavin' ⁓ can sure smell sweet,
      176:9
Whig Party
    campaign slogans, 41:1, 41:2
Whipple, Edwin Percy
    on genius, 97:28
    on sin, 209:36
Whiskey
    advantages of ⁓ over dogs
      legion, 253:4
    aint gonna be no ⁓, 71:43
    [corn ⁓] smells like gangrene
      starting in mildewed silo, 253:2
    freely renounce treacherous joys
      of brandy, ⁓, rum and gin,
      71:5
    like it: reason I never use it,
      253:11
    like it too well to fool with it,
      253:9
    never delay kissing pretty girl or
      opening bottle of ⁓, 253:7
    tell me brand of ⁓ that Grant
      drinks, 51:40
    universal suffrage, furloughs and
      ⁓ have ruined us, 51:8
    ⁓ doesn't sustain life, but makes
      life sustainable, 71:15
    ⁓ is saving of Irishman, 253:18
    ⁓ nasty habit of running out, but
      so does dog, 253:4
    ⁓, which kills one-third of our
      citizens, 71:35
    wine only antidote to bane of ⁓,
      253:10
Whistle
    rich men never ⁓, 189:9
Whistler, James McNeill
    on argument, 22:20
    on art, 26:57–59
    on friends, 96:46

White
    Great ⁓ Way, 171:84
    ⁓ silence, 10:5
White, E.B.
    on agriculture, 8:21
    on book banning, 262:87, 262:88
    on civil rights, 50:40
    on democracy, 66:102
    on food, 92:14
    on Gertrude Stein, 262:92
    on Hollywood, 108:18, 108:19
    on journalism, 125:77
    on life, 136:122
    on lightning, 250:21
    on literature, 138:63, 138:64
    on love, 140:92
    on Maine, 142:9, 142:10
    on New York City, 171:102–104
    on own writing, 262:90
    on parenthood, 85:20
    on patriotism, 180:47–49
    on poetry, 186:33
    on pollution, 188:14
    on radio, 229:9
    on sadness, 213:18
    on sense of humor, 113:41
    on society, 211:42
    on women, 257:81
    on work, 259:77
    on writing, 262:86, 262:89,
      262:91
    on World War II, 261:33
White, Theodore H.
    on elections, 75:22
    on presidency, 192:45, 192:46
White, William Allen
    on England, 77:42
    on free speech, 95:82
    on Kansas, 127:13–15
    on liberty, 135:74
    on politics, 187:157
    on presidency, 192:47
    on Theodore Roosevelt, 193:134,
      193:135
White, William Lindsay
    on World War II, 261:34
White House
    another world, 192:9
    extraordinary collection of talent
      ever gathered at ⁓, 193:78
    forced to choose between
      penitentiary and ⁓, would say
      penitentiary, 192:41
    gone to ⁓, ha, ha, ha, 41:12
    in ⁓, can't help waking at 5
      A.M. and hearing old man
      calling, 193:127
    James Buchanan on leaving,
      193:13
    may none but honest and wise
      men ever rule under this roof,
      193:4

    nothing occupants can do will
      affect history of world for long,
      192:2
    one of those terrific, pummeling
      ⁓ days, 193:62
    planted four trees in ⁓ garden,
      193:18
    politician smelling ⁓ not much
      different from bull elk in rut,
      192:43
    President paid dear for his ⁓,
      192:12
    what is there in this place, 193:37
Whitman, Walt
    indulged in barbarous
      eccentricities, 262:47
    [*Leaves of Grass*] extraordinary
      wit and wisdom, 262:11
    on Abraham Lincoln, 137:53–57
    on age, 7:77–81
    on Alabama, 9:10
    on ambition, 11:24
    on America, 12:109, 12:110,
      12:112–116
    on American example of Liberty,
      12:111
    on Americans, 15:50, 15:51
    on animals, 19:24, 161:76
    on books, 35:76, 35:77
    on change, 42:23
    on character, 43:94, 43:95
    on charity, 44:20
    on cities, 49:16
    on Civil War, 51:61
    on contemplation, 58:12, 58:13
    on culture, 62:8, 62:9
    on death, 63:84–91
    on democracy, 66:103–106
    on drinking, 71:58
    on earth, 161:79
    on enemies, 76:9
    on failure, 83:8, 83:9
    on fame, 84:30
    on George Washington, 246:27
    on government, 101:144
    on greatness, 102:42
    on happiness, 103:42–44
    on history, 107:74, 107:75
    on human body, 105:25
    on humankind, 112:63, 112:64
    on immortality, 117:4, 117:20
    on individuality, 120:29–31
    on justice, 126:53
    on language, 132:59–61
    on liberty, 135:75
    on life, 136:123–125
    on lilacs, 90:11, 90:12
    on literature, 138:65–68
    on Manhattan, 171:105–107
    on militarism, 152:21
    on moon, 161:78
    on music, 160:31